CHILDREN

Fourteenth Edition

JOHN W. SANTROCK
University of Texas at Dallas

McGraw Hill Education

CHILDREN, FOURTEENTH EDITION

Published by McGraw-Hill Education, 2 Penn Plaza, New York, NY 10121. Copyright © 2019 by McGraw-Hill Education. All rights reserved. Printed in the United States of America. Previous editions © 2016, 2013, and 2010. No part of this publication may be reproduced or distributed in any form or by any means, or stored in a database or retrieval system, without the prior written consent of McGraw-Hill Education, including, but not limited to, in any network or other electronic storage or transmission, or broadcast for distance learning.

Some ancillaries, including electronic and print components, may not be available to customers outside the United States.

This book is printed on acid-free paper.

1 2 3 4 5 6 7 8 9 LWI 21 20 19 18

Bound:
ISBN 978-1-260-07393-5
MHID 1-260-07393-9

Looseleaf:
ISBN 978-1-260-15408-5
MHID 1-260-15408-4

Portfolio Manager: *Ryan Treat*
Lead Product Developer: *Dawn Groundwater*
Product Developer: *Vicki Malinee, Van Brien & Associates*
Digital Product Developer: *Sarah Colwell*
Senior Marketing Manager: *Ann Helgerson*
Content Project Managers: *Mary E. Powers, Jodi Banowetz*
Buyer: *Sandy Ludovissy*
Design: *Matt Backhaus*
Content Licensing Specialists: *Carrie Burger*
Cover Image: © *RichVintage/Getty Images*
Compositor: *Aptara®, Inc.*

All credits appearing on page are considered to be an extension of the copyright page.

Library of Congress Cataloging-in-Publication Data

Names: Santrock, John W., author.
Title: Children / John W. Santrock,
   University of Texas at Dallas.
Description: Fourteenth edition. | New York, NY : McGraw-Hill Education, [2019]
Identifiers: LCCN 2017039864| ISBN 9781260073935 (alk. paper) | ISBN
   1260073939 (alk. paper)
Subjects: LCSH: Child development. | Adolescence.
Classification: LCC HQ767.9 .S268 2019 | DDC 305.231—dc23 LC record available at https://lccn.loc.gov/2017039864

The Internet addresses listed in the text were accurate at the time of publication. The inclusion of a website does not indicate an endorsement by the authors or McGraw-Hill Education, and McGraw-Hill Education does not guarantee the accuracy of the information presented at these sites.

mheducation.com/highered

brief contents

contents

SECTION 1   THE NATURE OF CHILDREN'S DEVELOPMENT   2

©Ariel Skelley/Blend Images/Getty Images RF

SECTION 2   BEGINNINGS   44

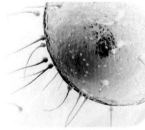

©MedicalRF.com/Getty Images RF

SECTION 3   INFANCY   119

©JGI/Jamie Grill/Blend Images/
Getty Images RF

SECTION 4 EARLY CHILDHOOD 219

©Ariel Skelley/age fotostock

©Ariel Skelley/Corbis

SECTION 6 ADOLESCENCE 415

©Comstock Images/Getty Images RF

CHAPTER 16
Socioemotional Development in Adolescence   473

about the author

John W. Santrock

John Santrock received his Ph.D. from the University of Minnesota in 1973. He taught at the University of Charleston and the University of Georgia before joining the Program in Psychology at the University of Texas at Dallas, where he currently teaches a number of undergraduate courses and has received the University's Effective Teaching Award.

John Santrock (back row middle) with the 2015 recipients of the Santrock Travel Scholarship Award in developmental psychology. Created by Dr. Santrock, this annual award provides undergraduate students with the opportunity to attend a professional meeting. As of 2017, 40 students have benefited from this award. A number of the students shown here attended the 2015 meeting of the Society for Research in Child Development.
Courtesy of Jessica Serna

John has been a member of the editorial boards of *Child Development* and *Developmental Psychology*. His research on father custody is widely cited and used in expert witness testimony to promote flexibility and alternative considerations in custody disputes. John also has authored these exceptional McGraw-Hill texts: *Life-Span Development* (16th edition), *Adolescence* (16th edition), *A Topical Approach to Life-Span Development* (9th edition), and *Educational Psychology* (6th edition).

For many years, John was involved in tennis as a player, teaching professional, and coach of professional tennis players. As an undergraduate, he was a member of the University of Miami (FL) tennis team that still holds the record for most consecutive wins (137) in any NCAA Division I sport. John has been married for four decades to his wife, Mary Jo, who is a Realtor. He has two daughters—Tracy and Jennifer—both of whom are Realtors after long careers in technology marketing and medical sales, respectively. He has one granddaughter, Jordan, age 25, who completed her master's degree from the Cox School of Business at SMU and currently works for Ernst & Young, and two grandsons—the Belluci brothers: Alex, age 12, and Luke, age 11. In the last two decades, John also has spent time painting expressionist art.

Jordan Bowles.
Courtesy of John Santrock.

Alex and Luke, the Bellucci brothers.
Courtesy of John Santrock.

Dedication:

With special appreciation to my grandchildren: Jordan, Alex, and Luke.

expert consultants

Children's development has become an enormous, complex field, and no single author, or even several authors, can possibly keep up with all of the rapidly changing content in the many periods and different areas of life-span development. To solve this problem, author John Santrock has sought the input of leading experts about content in a number of areas of children's development. These experts have provided detailed evaluations and recommendations in their area(s) of expertise.

The following individuals were among those who served as expert consultants for one or more of the previous editions of this text:

Urie Bronfenbrenner, *Cornell University*
Diana Baumrind, *University of California–Berkeley*
Tiffany Field, *University of Miami*
Scott Johnson, *University of California–Los Angeles*
Nel Noddings, *Stanford University*
Ross Thompson, *University of California–Davis*
Sandra Graham, *University of California–Los Angeles*
James Marcia, *Simon Fraser University*
John Bates, *Indiana University*
Florence Denmark, *Pace University*
Rosalind Charlesworth, *Weber State University*
David Sadker, *The American University–Washington DC*

Marilou Hyson, *University of Pennsylvania*
Algea Harrison-Hale, *Oakland University*
Campbell Leaper, *University of California-Santa Cruz*
Janet DiPietro, *Johns Hopkins University*
Allan Wigfield, *University of Maryland–College Park*
Barbara Pan, *Harvard University*
Peter Scales, *Search Institute*
Esther Leerkes, *University of North Carolina-Greensboro*
David Moore, *Pitzer College* and *Claremont Graduate University*
Elizabeth Gershoff, *University of Texas*
Susan Spieker, *University of Washington*

Following are the expert consultants for the fourteenth edition, who (like those of previous editions) literally represent a *Who's Who* in the field of child and adolescent development.

 James A. Graham Dr. Graham is a leading expert on diversity. He currently is a Professor of Psychology at The College of New Jersey (TCNJ). Dr. Graham received master's and doctoral degrees in developmental psychology from the University of Memphis. His research addresses the social-cognitive aspects of relationships between the group and dyadic levels across early, middle, and late childhood in community-based settings. Three interdependent dimensions of his research program examine (1) populations that are typically understudied, conceptually limited, and methodologically constrained; (2) children's development of empathy and prosocial behavior with peer groups and friends; and (3) developmental science in the context of community-engaged research partnerships. Currently, he is Coordinator of the Developmental Specialization in Psychology at TCNJ. For a decade, Dr. Graham taught graduate courses in psychology and education in Johannesburg, South Africa, through TCNJ's Graduate Summer Global Program. His co-authored book, *The African American Child: Development and Challenges*, is in its second edition, and he is co-author and co-editor of two other volumes. Dr. Graham has presented his work at a variety of international and national conferences and has published articles in professional journals such as *Social Development, Behavior Modification, Journal of College Student Development, Journal of Multicultural Counseling and Development*, and *American Journal of Evaluation*.

"Dr. Santrock seamlessly integrates the latest research on physical, cognitive, and socioemotional processes of children in an ever-evolving multicultural society. This book is an excellent resource for students in psychology and other social science fields. I am impressed with Dr. Santrock's sensitivity to the impact of culture, ethnicity and socioeconomic status on child and adolescent development. . . This text will help students learn to analyze, compare, and contrast alternative perspectives of children domestically and globally with the major principles and

theories of child development in cognitive, socioemotional, and social-contextual domains. This text will also help students to understand the latest research regarding societal values about ethnicity, socioeconomic, and gender issues in child development, and how they influence individual development as well as shape social policy." —**James A. Graham,** *The College of New Jersey*
Photo courtesy of James Graham

 Joan E. Grusec Dr. Grusec is one of the world's leading experts on parenting and children's socioemotional development. She obtained her Ph.D. from Stanford University and is currently a Professor Emerita in the Department of Psychology at the University of Toronto. Dr. Grusec was previously a professor at Wesleyan University and at the University of Waterloo. Her research focuses on socialization processes, with current studies focusing on the relationship between parenting in different domains of socialization (protection, mutual reciprocity, group participation, guided learning, and control) and internalization of prosocial values. Dr. Grusec is a Fellow of the Canadian and American Psychological Associations. She is past chair of the Examination Committee of the Association of State and Provincial Psychology Boards and has been an Associate Editor of *Developmental Psychology*. She has authored and edited several books, including *Social Development* (written with Hugh Lytton), *Handbook of Parenting and Internalization of Values* (edited with Leon Kuczynski), and *Handbook of Socialization* (two editions edited with Paul Hastings). Her work has been published in leading research journals including *Child Development, Developmental Psychology,* and *Social Development*.

"This is, of course, a very successful text. 'Socioemotional Development in Infancy' is a well-presented chapter. The exercises and the reference to previous material both in this and other chapters is an excellent feature. 'Socioemotional Development in Early Childhood,' again, is an impressive bringing together of a

great deal of research into a coherent package. 'Socioemotional Development in Middle and Late Childhood' is overall an engaging and informative chapter." —**Joan E. Grusec,** *University of Toronto*

Megan McClelland Dr. McClelland is a leading expert on young children's cognitive development. She is currently the Katherine E. Smith Professor of Healthy Children and Families in Human Development and Family Sciences at Oregon State University. Dr. McClelland also serves as Director of the Healthy Development in Early Childhood Research Core at the Hallie Ford Center for Healthy Children and Families. She obtained her Ph.D. from Loyola University–Chicago. Her research focuses on optimizing children's development, especially as it relates to children's self-regulation and school readiness. Dr. McClelland's investigations include links between self-regulation and academic achievement from early childhood to adulthood, recent advances in measuring self-regulation, and intervention efforts to improve these skills in young children. She has published more than 50 theoretical and empirical articles on the development of self-regulation with colleagues and collaborators around the world, including a new book on promoting self-regulation in the early childhood classroom. Dr. McClelland is currently conducting two federally funded projects to develop measures of self-regulation and an intervention to improve school readiness in young children.

"Strong developmental focus and coverage of relevant theories and concepts in cognitive development. I like the looking back and looking forward summaries and the Reach Your Learning Goals sections. I also think the Resources section is very useful." —**Megan McClelland,** *Oregon State University*

Virginia Marchman A leading expert on children's language development, Dr. Marchman is a Research Associate at the Stanford University Language Learning Laboratory. She obtained her Ph.D. at the University of California–Berkeley. Her main research areas are language development, language disorders, and early childhood development. Dr. Marchman's specific interests focus on individual differences in typically-developing and late-talking children, as well as lexical and grammatical development in monolingual and bilingual learners. Her studies have incorporated a variety of experimental methods as well as computational approaches and naturalistic observation. Dr. Marchman has worked extensively with the MacArthur-Bates Communicative Development Inventories (CDI), developing the CDI Scoring program and serving on the MacArthur-Bates CDI Advisory Board. She has been a consulting editor for *Journal of Speech, Language & Hearing Research* and *Child Development.* Dr. Marchman's most recent work involves the development of real-time spoken language understanding using the "looking-while-listening" task in typically-developing and at-risk children. Her current studies explore links between children's language processing skills, early learning environments, and individual differences in monolingual and bilingual English-Spanish learners from diverse backgrounds.

"This new edition of John Santrock's Children continues to offer a comprehensive, up-to-date but also nuanced overview of child development. The material is grounded in the traditional issues that are the core of our current understanding of development, but also offers students many opportunities to think about the open questions that remain. The format enables students from many different perspectives to relate easily to the material and to

make connections to their own personal and professional lives." —**Virginia Marchman,** *Stanford University*

Maureen Black Dr. Black is one of the world's leading experts on children's health and nutrition. She currently is the John A. Scholl and Mary Louise Scholl Endowed Professor in the Department of Pediatrics and the Department of Epidemiology and Public Health at the University of Maryland School of Medicine. She also is the founder/director of the Growth and Nutrition Clinic that provides services to children with inadequate growth and nutrition problems. Dr. Black obtained her Ph.D. from Emory University. Her major research focus in on evaluation of nutrition and caregiving intervention programs involving the health and development of young children. Dr. Black's intervention research not only targeted children from low-income communities in the United States but also in developing countries as well. Among her many awards are being a past president of two divisions in the American Psychological Association and induction into the Maryland Women's Hall of Fame.

"Very comprehensive coverage—I am impressed with the updated references! The inclusion of topics such as sleep and electronic device use will make the text very relevant and timely for students. Well done!" —**Maureen Black,** *University of Maryland*

Janet DiPietro One of the world's leading experts on prenatal development, Dr. DiPietro is Vice Dean for Research and Faculty as well as a Professor in the Bloomberg School of Public Health at Johns Hopkins University. She obtained her Ph.D. from the University of California–Berkeley. In her research, Dr. DiPietro uses digitized assessment methods to measure fetal neurobiological functioning to predict clinical and developmental outcomes in postnatal development. She also studies maternal factors, including substance exposure, maternal emotions, and physiological changes during pregnancy, as influences on prenatal development.

"Certainly, a tremendous effort went into this." —**Janet DiPietro,** *Johns Hopkins University*

Karen Adolph Dr. Karen Adolph is one of the world's leading experts on children's motor development. She currently is Professor of Psychology and Neural Science at New York University. Dr. Adolph obtained her Ph.D. at Emory University. She has conducted pioneering and leading-edge research on children's motor development. In her Infant Action Laboratory, she has created novel predicaments, including crawling over bridges, squeezing through openings, and reaching for targets with infants' bodies in motion. She observes infant behavior using computerized video recording and state-of-the-art technology, including motion-tracking and eye-tracking equipment. She recently was honored with the appointment of President of the International Congress of Infant Studies, has been awarded numerous research grants from such agencies as NICHD and NSF, and has served on the editorial boards of leading journals such as *Child Development, Developmental Psychology,* and *Developmental Science.* Dr. Adolph also has been given multiple teaching awards at New York University.

". . . readers can learn about the important debates with opposing viewpoints. Best of luck to John on this new edition!" —**Karen Adolph,** *New York University*

Connecting *Research* and *Results*

As a master teacher, John Santrock connects current research and real-world applications. Through an integrated, personalized digital learning program, students gain the insight they need to study smarter and improve performance.

McGraw-Hill Education Connect is a digital assignment and assessment platform that strengthens the link between faculty, students, and course work, helping everyone accomplish more in less time. Connect for Child Development includes assignable and assessable videos, quizzes, exercises, and interactivities, all associated with learning objectives. Interactive assignments and videos allow students to experience and apply their understanding of psychology to the world with fun and stimulating activities.

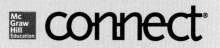

Real People, Real World, Real Life

At the higher end of Bloom's taxonomy (analyze, evaluate, create), the McGraw-Hill Education Milestones video series is an observational tool that allows students to experience life as it unfolds, from infancy to late adulthood. This ground-breaking, longitudinal video series tracks the development of real children as they progress through the early stages of physical, social, and emotional development in their first few weeks, months, and years of life. Assignable and assessable within Connect, Milestones also includes interviews with adolescents and adults to reflect development throughout the entire life span.

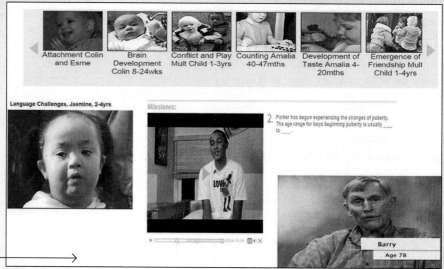

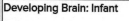

Developing Brain: Infant

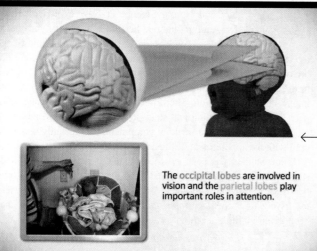

The occipital lobes are involved in vision and the parietal lobes play important roles in attention.

Inform and Engage on Psychological Concepts

At the lower end of Bloom's taxonomy, students are introduced to Concept Clips—the dynamic, colorful graphics and stimulating animations that break down some of psychology's most difficult concepts in a step-by-step manner, engaging students and aiding in retention. They are assignable and assessable in Connect or can be used as a jumping-off point in class. Now with audio narration, this edition also includes new Concept Clips on topics such as object permanence and conservation, as well as theories and theorists like Bandura's social cognitive theory, Vygotsky's sociocultural theory, Buss's evolutionary theory, and Kuhl's language development theory.

Better Data, Smarter Revision, Improved Results

Students helped inform the revision strategy of *Children*. McGraw-Hill Education's Smartbook is the first and only adaptive reading and learning experience! SmartBook helps students distinguish the concepts they know from the concepts they don't, while pinpointing the concepts they are about to forget. SmartBook continuously adapts to create a truly personalized learning path and offers students learning resources such as videos, Concept Clips, and slides to further reinforce difficult concepts. SmartBook's real-time reports help both students and instructors identify the concepts that require more attention, making study sessions and class time more efficient.

Informed by Students

Content revisions are informed by data collected anonymously through McGraw-Hill Education's SmartBook.

STEP 1. Over the course of three years, data points showing concepts that caused students the most difficulty were anonymously collected from Connect for Child Development's SmartBook®.

STEP 2. The data from LearnSmart was provided to the author in the form of a *Heat Map*, which graphically illustrates "hot spots" in the text that affect student learning (see image at right).

STEP 3. The author used the *Heat Map* data to refine the content and reinforce student comprehension in the new edition. Additional quiz questions and assignable activities were created for use in Connect to further support student success.

RESULT: Because the *Heat Map* gave the author empirically based feedback at the paragraph and even sentence level, he was able to develop the new edition using precise student data that pinpointed concepts that gave students the most difficulty.

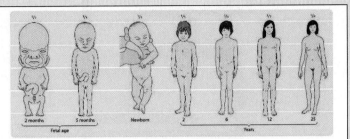

FIGURE 3.1

CHANGES IN PROPORTIONS OF THE HUMAN BODY DURING GROWTH. As individuals develop from infancy through adulthood, one of the most noticeable physical changes is that the head becomes smaller in relation to the rest of the body. The fractions listed refer to head size as a proportion of total body length at different ages.

Infancy The average North American newborn is 20 inches long and weighs 7½ pounds. Ninety-five percent of full-term newborns are 18 to 22 inches long and weigh between 5½ and 10 pounds.

In the first several days of life, most newborns lose 5 to 7 percent of their body weight. Once infants adjust to sucking, swallowing, and digesting, they grow rapidly, gaining an average of 5 to 6 ounces per week during the first month. Typically they have doubled their birth weight by the age of 4 months and have nearly tripled it by their first birthday. Infants grow about ¾ inch per month during the first year, increasing their birth length by about 40 percent by their first birthday.

Infants' rate of growth slows considerably in the second year of life (Burns & others, 2013). By 2 years of age, infants weigh approximately 26 to 32 pounds, having gained a quarter to half a pound per month during the second year; at age 2 they have reached about one fifth of their adult weight. The average 2-year-old is 32 to 35 inches tall, which is nearly one-half of adult height.

Early Childhood As the preschool child grows older, the percentage of increase in height and weight decreases with each additional year (Leifer, 2011). Girls are only slightly smaller and lighter than boys during these years. Both boys and girls slim down as the trunks of their bodies lengthen. Although their heads are still somewhat large for their bodies, by the end of the preschool years most children have lost their top-heavy look. Body fat also shows a slow, steady decline during the preschool years. Girls have more fatty tissue than boys; boys have more muscle tissue (McMahon & Stryjewski, 2012).

Growth patterns vary individually (Wilson & Hockenberry, 2012). Think back to your preschool years. This was probably the first time you noticed that some children were taller than you, some shorter; some were fatter, some thinner; some were stronger, some weaker. Much of the variation is due to heredity, but environmental experiences are also involved. A review of the height and weight of children around the world concluded that two important contributors to height differences are ethnic origin and nutrition (Meredith, 1978).

Why are some children unusually short? The culprits are genetic or congenital (present at birth) factors (being small for gestational age, or having fetal alcohol syndrome or certain other prenatal problems), growth hormone deficiency, a physical problem that develops in childhood, maternal smoking during pregnancy, or an emotional difficulty (Wit, Kiess, & Mullis, 2011).

Middle and Late Childhood The period of middle and late childhood involves slow, consistent growth. This is a period of calm before the rapid growth spurt of adolescence.

The bodies of 5-year-olds and 2-year-olds are different from one another. The 5-year-old not only is taller and heavier, but also has a longer trunk and legs than the 2-year-old. *What might be some other physical differences between 2- and 5-year-olds?*

Dev Psych - Life-Span Development - Santrock, 16e, PHYSICAL DEVELOPMENT IN INFANCY

Section Three

Page 107 / 616

1 Physical Growth and Development in Infancy

LG1 Discuss physical growth and development in infancy.

Patterns of Growth | Height and Weight | The Brain | Sleep | Nutrition

Chapter 4 Introduction

Infants' physical development in the first two years of life is extensive. Newborns' heads are quite large in comparison with the rest of their bodies. They have little strength in their necks and cannot hold their heads up, but they have some basic reflexes. In the span of 12 months, infants become capable of sitting anywhere, standing, stooping, climbing, and usually walking. During the second year, growth decelerates, but rapid increases in such activities as running and climbing take place. Let's now examine in greater detail the sequence of physical development in infancy.

1 Physical Growth and Development in Infancy

PATTERNS OF GROWTH

An extraordinary proportion of the total body is occupied by the head during prenatal development and early infancy (see **Figure 1**). The **cephalocaudal pattern** is the sequence in which the earliest growth always occurs at the top—the head—with physical growth and differentiation of features gradually working their way down from top to bottom (for example, shoulders, middle trunk, and so on). This same pattern occurs in the head area, because the top parts of the head—the eyes and brain—grow faster than the lower parts, such as the jaw.

2 Motor Development

Practice | ∠ Previous Highlight | < Previous Section | Next Section > | Next Highlight ∠ | A A

Powerful Reporting

Whether a class is face-to-face, hybrid, or entirely online, Connect for Child Development provides tools and analytics to reduce the amount of time instructors need to administer their courses. Easy-to-use course management tools allow instructors to spend less time administering and more time teaching, while easy-to-use reporting features allow students to monitor their progress and optimize their study time.

- The At-Risk Student Report provides instructors with one-click access to a dashboard that identifies students who are at risk of dropping out of the course due to low engagement levels.

- The Category Analysis Report details student performance relative to specific learning objectives and goals, including APA outcomes and levels of Bloom's taxonomy.

- Connect Insight is a one-of-a-kind visual analytics dashboard—now available for both instructors and students—that provides at-a-glance information regarding student performance.

- The LearnSmart Reports allow instructors and students to easily monitor progress and pinpoint areas of weakness, giving each student a personalized study plan to achieve success.

Online Instructor Resources

The resources listed here accompany *Children,* Fourteenth Edition. Please contact your McGraw-Hill representative for details concerning the availability of these and other valuable materials that can help you design and enhance your course.

Instructor's Manual   Broken down by chapter, this resource provides chapter outlines, suggested lecture topics, classroom activities and demonstrations, suggested student research projects, essay questions, and critical thinking questions.

Test Bank and Computerized Test Bank   This comprehensive Test Bank includes more than 1,500 multiple-choice and approximately 75 essay questions. Organized by chapter, the questions are designed to test factual, applied, and conceptual understanding. All test questions are available within TestGen™ software.

PowerPoint Slides   The PowerPoint presentations, now WCAG compliant, highlight the key points of the chapter and include supporting visuals. All of the slides can be modified to meet individual needs.

preface

Making Connections . . . From My Classroom to *Children* to You

Having taught two or more undergraduate courses in developmental psychology—child development, adolescence, and life-span development—every year across four decades, I'm always looking for ways to improve my course and *Children*. Just as McGraw-Hill looks to those who teach the child development course for input, each year I ask the students in my undergraduate developmental courses to tell me what they like about the course and the text, and what they think could be improved. What have my students told me about my course and text? Students said that highlighting connections among the different aspects of children's development would help them to better understand the concepts. As I thought about this, it became clear that a connections theme would provide a systematic, integrative approach to the course material. I used this theme to shape my goals for my course, which in turn influence the main goals of this text, as follows:

1. **Connecting with today's students** to help students learn about children's development more effectively;

2. **Connecting with research on children's development** to provide students with the best and most recent theory and research in the world today about each of the periods of children's development;

3. **Connecting development processes** to guide students in making developmental connections across different points in children's development;

4. **Connecting development to real life** to help students understand ways to apply content about child development to the real world and improve children's lives, and to motivate students to think deeply about their own personal journey through life and better understand who they were as children and how their experiences and development have influenced who they are today.

Connecting with Today's Students

In *Children,* I recognize that today's students are as different in some ways from the learners of the last generation as today's discipline of child development is different from the field 30 years ago. Students now learn in multiple modalities; rather than sitting down and reading traditional printed chapters in linear fashion from beginning to end, their work preferences tend to be more visual and more interactive, and their reading and study often occur in short bursts. For many students, a traditionally formatted printed textbook is no longer enough when they have instant, 24/7 access to news and information from around the globe. Two features that specifically support today's students are the adaptive ebook (*SmartBook*—see pages xv) and the learning goals system.

The Learning Goals System

My students often report that development courses are challenging because so much material is covered. To help today's students focus on the key ideas, the Learning Goals System I developed for *Children* provides extensive learning connections throughout the chapters. The learning system connects the chapter-opening

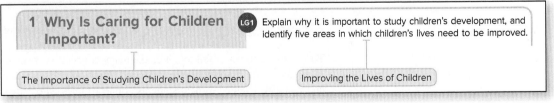

outline, learning goals for the chapter, mini-chapter maps that open each main section of the chapter, **Review, Connect, Reflect** questions at the end of each main section, and the chapter summary at the end of each chapter.

The learning system keeps the key ideas in front of the student from the beginning to the end of the chapter. The main headings of each chapter correspond to the learning goals, which are presented in the chapter-opening spread. Mini-chapter maps that link up with the learning goals are presented at the beginning of each major section in the chapter.

Then, at the end of each main section of a chapter, the learning goal is repeated in **Review, Connect, Reflect,** which prompts students to review the key topics in the section, to connect these topics to existing knowledge, and to relate what they have learned to their own personal journey through life. **Reach Your Learning Goals,** at the end of each chapter, guides students through the bulleted chapter review, connecting with the chapter outline/learning goals at the beginning of the chapter and the **Review, Connect, Reflect** material at the end of major chapter sections.

connecting with research

Caregivers' Emotional Expressiveness, Children's Emotion Regulation, and Behavior Problems in Head Start Children

A study by Dana McCoy and Cybele Raver (2011) explored links between caregivers' reports of their positive and negative emotional expressiveness, observations of young children's emotion regulation, and teachers' reports of the children's internalizing and externalizing behavior problems. The study focused on 97 children, most of whom were African American or Latino and whose mean age was 4 years and 3 months. The other participants in the study were the children's primary caregivers (90 mothers, 5 fathers, and 2 grandmothers).

To assess caregiver expressiveness, caregivers were asked to provide ratings on a scale from 1 (never/rarely) to 9 (very frequently) for 7 items that reflect caregiver expressiveness, such as "telling family members how happy you are" and "expressing anger at someone's carelessness." Children's emotion regulation was assessed with (a) the emotion regulation part of the PSRA (preschool self-regulation assessment) in which observers rated young children's behavior on 4 delay tasks, 3 executive function tasks, and 3

What did Dana McCoy and Cybele Raver discover about the importance of caregivers' emotions and children's emotion regulation in children's development?
©Najilah Feanny/Corbis

were linked to more internalizing behavior problems in the young Head Start children. Also, caregivers' reports of their positive emo-

Connecting with Research on Children's Development

Over the years, I have made every effort to include the most up-to-date research available. I continue this tradition in this edition by looking closely at specific areas of research, involving experts in related fields, and updating research throughout. **Connecting with Research** describes a study or program to illustrate how research in child development is conducted and how it influences our understanding of the discipline. Topics range from "How Can the Newborn's Perception Be Studied?" to "What Are Some Important Findings in the National Longitudinal Study of Child Care in the United States?" to "Caregivers' Emotional Expressiveness, Children's Emotion Regulation, and Behavior Problems in Head Start Children" to "Parenting and Children's Achievement: My Child Is My Report Card, Tiger Moms, and Tiger Babies Strike Back" to "Evaluation of a Family Program Designed to Reduce Drinking and Smoking in Young Adolescents."

The tradition of obtaining detailed, extensive input from a number of leading experts in different areas of child development also continues in this edition. Biographies and photographs of the leading experts in the field of child development appear on pages xii to xiii, and the chapter-by-chapter highlights of new research content are listed on pages xxi to xxxviii. Finally, the research discussions have been updated for each developmental period and topic. I expended every effort to make this edition of *Children* as contemporary and up-to-date as possible. To that end, there are more than 1,200 citations from 2016, 2017, and 2018 in this edition.

Connecting Developmental Processes

Too often we forget or fail to notice the many connections from one point in child development to another. I have substantially increased attention to these connections in the text narrative and included features to help students connect topics across the stages of child development.

Developmental Connections, which appear multiple times in each chapter, point readers to places where the topic is discussed in a previous, current, or subsequent chapter. This feature highlights links across topics of development *and* connections among biological, cognitive, and socioemotional processes. The key developmental processes are typically discussed in isolation from each other, so students often fail to see the connections among them. Included in *Developmental Connections* is a brief description of the backward or forward connection. For example, the developmental connection to the right appears in the margin next to the discussion of minimizing bias in research.

Furthermore, a Connect question is included in the self-reviews at the end of each section—**Review, Connect, Reflect**—so students can practice making connections among topics. For example:

- In "Cognitive Development in Infancy" and "Cognitive Development in Early Childhood," you read about the development of attention in infancy and early childhood. How might ADHD be linked to earlier attention difficulties?

Topical Connections: Looking Back and *Looking Forward* begin and conclude each chapter by placing the chapter's coverage in the larger context of development. The Looking Back section reminds the reader of what happened developmentally in previous periods of development.

developmental **connection**

Gender

Gender stereotyping continues to be extensive. Recent research indicates that girls and older children use a higher percentage of gender stereotypes than younger children and boys. Connect to "Socioemotional Development in Middle and Late Childhood."

Topical **Connections** *looking forward*

Next you will learn about the birth process and the transition from fetus to newborn, see how the newborn's health and responsiveness are assessed, read about low birth weight and preterm babies and find out about special ways to nurture these fragile newborns, and examine what happens during the postpartum period.

Connecting Development to Real Life

In addition to helping students make research and developmental connections, *Children* shows the important real-life connections to the concepts discussed in the text. In recent years, students in my development course have increasingly told me that they want more of this type of information. In this edition, real-life connections are explicitly made in the chapter-opening vignette as well as in *Caring Connections, Connecting with Diversity,* the *Milestones* video program, *Connecting with Careers, How Would You . . . ?* questions that pertain to five career areas, and *Reflect: Your Own Personal Journey of Life.*

Each chapter begins with a story designed to spark students' interest and motivate them to read the chapter. Among the chapter-opening stories are those involving the journey of pregnancy and the birth of "Mr. Littles," Reggio Emilia's children and their early childhood education program, children living in the South Bronx, and Jewel Cash and her amazing contributions to her community.

Caring Connections provides applied information about parenting, education, or health and well-being related to topics ranging from "From Waterbirth to Music Therapy" to "Parenting Strategies for Helping Overweight Children Lose Weight" to "Strategies for Increasing Children's Creative Thinking."

Children puts a strong emphasis on diversity. For a number of editions, this text has benefited from having one or more leading experts on diversity to ensure that it provides students with current, accurate, sensitive information related to diversity in children's development. The diversity expert for this edition of *Children* is James A. Graham.

Diversity is discussed in every chapter. *Connecting with Diversity* interludes also appear in every chapter, focusing on a diversity topic related to

caring connections

Parenting Strategies for Helping Overweight Children Lose Weight

Most parents with an overweight child want to help the child to lose weight but aren't sure of the best ways to accomplish this goal. Keep in mind the research we have discussed that indicates overweight children are likely to become overweight adolescents and adults, so it is important for parents to help their children attain a healthy weight and maintain it. Following are some recommended ways that parents can help their overweight children lose weight (DiLonardo, 2013; Matthiessen, 2013; Moninger, 2013):

- *Work on a healthy project together and involve the child in the decision-making process.* Get the child involved in an activity that can help him or her lose weight such as purchasing pedometers for all family members and developing goals for how many steps to take each day. By involving the child in making decisions about the family's health, the hope is that the child will begin to take responsibility for his or her own health.
- *Be a healthy model for your child.* In many aspects of life, what people do is more influential than what they say. So if parents are overweight and engaging in unhealthy behaviors such as eating unhealthy fast food and not exercising, then telling their overweight children to lose weight is unlikely to be effective.
- *Engage in physical activities with children.* Parents and children can engage in activities like bicycling, jogging, hiking, and swimming together. Parents might say something like, "Let's take a bike ride after dinner this evening. It would be fun and could help us both get in better shape."

What are positive strategies parents can adopt to help overweight children lose weight?
©vgajic/Getty Images RF

select the fruits and vegetables they are willing to eat. Let them choose which sport or type of exercise they would like to do.

- *Eat healthy family meals together on a regular basis.* Children who eat meals together with their family are less likely to be overweight.
- *Reduce screen time.* Children who spend large numbers of hours per day in screen time are more likely to be overweight

the material at that point in the chapter. Topics range from "The Increased Diversity of Adopted Children and Adoptive Parents" to "Cultural Variations in Guiding Infants' Motor Development" to "What Is the Best Way to Teach English Language Learners?" to "Cross-Cultural Comparisons of Secondary Schools."

The *Milestones* video program shows students what developmental concepts look like by letting them watch actual humans develop. Students are able to track several individuals starting from infancy and watch them achieve major developmental milestones, both physically and cognitively. (See page xiv for further details.)

Connecting with Careers profiles careers ranging from genetic counselor to toy designer to teacher of English Language Learners, all of which require a knowledge of children's development. The careers highlighted extend from the Careers Appendix immediately following "Introduction," which provides a comprehensive overview of careers to show students where knowledge of children's development could lead them.

How Would You . . . ? questions in the margins of each chapter highlight issues involving five main career areas of children's development: psychology, human development and family studies, education, health professions (such as nursing and pediatrics), and social work. The *How Would You . . . ?* questions ensure that this book orients students to concepts that are important to their understanding of children's development. I have asked instructors specializing in these fields to contribute *How Would You . . . ?* questions for each chapter. Strategically placed in the margin next to the relevant chapter content, these questions highlight essential ideas for students to take away from chapter content.

How Would You...?

If you were an **educator,** how would you work with low-socioeconomic-status families to increase parental involvement in their children's educational activities?

Finally, part of applying knowledge of children's development to the real world is understanding how it affects oneself. Accordingly, one of the goals of my child development course and this text is to motivate students to think deeply about their own journey of life. To encourage students to make personal connections to content in the text, I include a *Reflect: Your Own Personal Journey of Life* prompt in the end-of-section review. This question asks students to reflect on some aspect of the discussion in the section they have just read and connect it to their own life. For example, in relation to a discussion of the early-later experience issue in development, students are asked,

- Can you identify an early experience that you believe contributed in important ways to your development? Can you identify a recent or current (later) experience that you think had (is having) a strong influence on your development?

Content Revisions

A significant reason why *Children* has been successfully used by instructors for edition after edition is the painstaking effort and review that goes into making sure the text provides the latest research on all topic areas discussed in the classroom. This new edition is no exception, with more than 1,200 citations from 2016, 2017, and 2018.

Below is a sample of the many chapter-by-chapter changes that were made in this new edition of *Children*. Although every chapter has been extensively updated, three chapters ("Cognitive Development in Infancy," "Cognitive Development in Early Childhood," and "Socioemotional Development in Middle and Late Childhood") and the following content areas were especially targeted for revisions based on the results of the Heat Map data (discussed on page xv) and updated and expanded research: diversity and culture; genetics and epigenetics; neuroscience and the brain; identity issues, especially gender and transgender; health; and technology.

Chapter 1: Introduction

- Updated data on the dramatic increase in Latino and Asian American children in the United States, with recent projections from 2014 to 2060 (Colby & Ortman, 2015)
- Updated statistics on the recent increase in the percentage of U.S. children and adolescents under 18 years of age living in poverty, including data reported separately for African American and Latino families (DeNavas-Walt & Proctor, 2015; Proctor, Semega, & Kollar, 2016)
- Expanded content on the early-later experience issue regarding sensitive parenting to include the importance of positive close relationships later in childhood, in adolescence, and in adulthood (Antonucci & others, 2016)
- In the section on physiological methods, new discussion of recent advances in assessing genes, including specific genes linked to childhood obesity (Grigorenko & others, 2016; Moore, 2017)
- Updated and expanded coverage of the increased use of eye-tracking equipment to assess children's development (Loi & others, 2017; Meng, Uto, & Hashiva, 2017)
- New entries in Resources section: *Cambridge Handbook of International Prevention Science,* edited by Israelashvili and Romano (2017), provides up-to-date coverage of social policy and intervention in children's lives to improve their well-being and development in the United States and around the world. In *Encyclopedia of Lifespan Development* by Bornstein (2018), leading experts provide up-to-date discussions of many of the topics found in this edition.

Chapter 2: Biological Beginnings

- Revised and updated based on comments by leading experts Elena Grigorenko, David Moore, and Kirby Deater-Deckard
- Due to the increased emphasis on gene × environment interaction, the content on shared and non-shared environmental experiences has been deleted because it is now being given less attention.
- New description of recent research on how exercise, nutrition, and respiration can modify the expression of genes (Done & Traustadottir, 2016; Van Bussel & others, 2016)
- New coverage of the process of methylation, in which tiny atoms attach themselves to the outside of a gene. Researchers have found that exercise, diet, and tobacco use can change whether a gene is expressed or not through the methylation process (Butts, 2017; Chatterton & others, 2017; Godfrey & others, 2017).
- Updated and expanded discussion of genome-wide association studies, including research on suicide (Sokolowski, Wasserman, & Wasserman, 2016), autism (Connolly & others, 2017), attention deficit hyperactivity disorder (Naaijen & others, 2017), and glaucoma (Springelkamp & others, 2017)
- Expanded content about why recent improvements in next-generation sequencing have led to advances in analysis of genes and their links to various diseases (Bardak & others, 2017)
- Updated and expanded research on gene-gene interaction, including studies of immune system functioning (Heinonen & others, 2015), obesity (Bordoni & others, 2017), type 2 diabetes (Saxena, Srivastaya, & Banergee, 2017), cancer (Wu & others, 2017), and cardiovovascular disease (De & others, 2017)
- Inclusion of recent research in which a higher level of maternal responsivity to children with fragile X syndrome's adaptive behavior improved the children's communication skills (Warren & others, 2017)
- New content on how stem cell transplantation is being explored in the treatment of infants with sickle-cell anemia (Azar & Wong, 2017)
- Updated description of how research now supports the use of hydroxyurea therapy for infants with sickle cell anemia beginning at 9 months of age (Nevitt, Jones, & Howard, 2017; Yawn & John-Sawah, 2015)
- Description of a recent research review that concluded many aspects of the developing prenatal brain can be detected in the first trimester using ultrasound, which also can help to identify spina bifida early (Engels & others, 2016)
- Inclusion of information from a recent research review that concluded fetal MRI does not provide good results in the first trimester of pregnancy because of small fetal structures and movement artifacts (Wataganara & others, 2016). In this review, it also was argued that fetal MRI can especially be beneficial in assessing central nervous system abnormalities in the third trimester of pregnancy.
- New commentary that maternal blood screening can be used to detect congenital heart disease risk in the fetus (Sun & others, 2016)

- Inclusion of recent research that found ultrasound can accurately identify the sex of the fetus between 11 and 13 weeks of gestation (Manzanares & others, 2016)

- New content on fertility drugs being more likely to produce multiple births than in vitro fertilization (March of Dimes, 2017)

- New coverage of a recent national study in which low birthweight and preterm birth were significantly higher in infants conceived through assisted reproduction technology (Sunderam & others, 2017)

- Discussion of a recent study of 3- to 5-year-old children in which parents' secure attachment increased their adopted children's secure attachment, with mothers' secure attachment making a stronger contribution to their children's secure attachment than fathers' secure attachment (Barone, Lionetti, & Green, 2017)

- Description of a study of adoptees in emerging adulthood that found perceptions of secure parent-child attachment relationships, as well as sensitive and open communication about birth parent contact, were linked to greater satisfaction for adoptees (Farr, Grant-Marsney, & Grotevant, 2014)

- Coverage of a recent research review of internationally adopted adolescents in which a majority were well adjusted, but adoptees had a higher level of mental health problems than their non-adopted counterparts (Askeland & others, 2017)

- New commentary about the epigenetics of well-being (Szyf & Pluess, 2016)

- New entry in Resources: *The Developing Genome* by David Moore (2015) provides a superb overview of recent thinking and research on epigenetics.

Chapter 3: Prenatal Development

- Changes in the chapter based on feedback from leading expert consultant Janet DiPietro

- Updated data on the average length and weight of the fetus at different points in prenatal development, including revisions involving these data in Figure 10 in "Biological Beginnings"

- Coverage of a recent large-scale study in Brazil in which flour that was fortified with folic acid produced a significant reduction in neural tube defects (Santos & others, 2016)

- Description of a recent study in which higher maternal pre-pregnancy body mass was linked to a higher level of adiposity and inflammation in newborns (McCloskey & others, 2017)

- Discussion of a recent research review that concluded a combination of aerobic and resistance (muscle strength) exercise during pregnancy benefited maternal cardiorespiratory fitness (Perales & others, 2016)

- Inclusion of a recent meta-analysis that concluded regular aerobic exercise during pregnancy is associated with a decrease in preterm birth and a higher incidence of vaginal birth, as well as a lower level of caesarean delivery (Di Mascio & others, 2016)

- Coverage of a recent study that found women who exercised regularly during pregnancy were less likely to have high blood pressure and excessive weight gain (Barakat & others, 2016)

- Description of a recent study that revealed regular exercise by pregnant women was linked to more advanced development in the neonatal brain (Laborte-Lemoyne, Currier, & Ellenberg, 2017)

- Inclusion of recent research in which two weekly 70-minute yoga sessions reduced pregnant women's stress and enhanced their immune system functioning (Chen & others, 2017)

- Discussion of recent research that found isotretinoin (used to treat acne) is one of the most commonly prescribed drugs for adolescent girls seeking contraceptive advice, yet girls were not receiving adequate information about its harmful effects on offspring if they become pregnant (Eltonsy & others, 2016; Stancil & others, 2017)

- Coverage of recent research on negative outcomes for fetal alcohol spectrum disorders (FASD) that include lower executive function (Kingdon, Cardoso, & McGrath, 2016), as well as externalized and internalized behavior problems (Tsang & others, 2016), and a significantly lower life expectancy (Thanh & Johnsson, 2016)

- New description of the French Alcohol Society's (2016) recommendation that women should not consume any alcohol during pregnancy

- Inclusion of recent research indicating that maternal cigarette smoking during pregnancy was linked to increased risk of offspring smoking cigarettes at 16 years of age (De Genna & others, 2016)

- Description of recent research in which daughters whose mothers smoked during pregnancy were more likely to subsequently smoke during their own pregnancy (Ncube & Mueller, 2017)

- Coverage of recent research that found despite the plethora of negative outcomes for maternal smoking during pregnancy, 23 percent of pregnant adolescent and 15 percent of adult pregnant women reported using tobacco in the previous month (Oh & others, 2017)

- New content on the increasing use of e-cigarettes during pregnancy and research on pregnant women's misconceptions about e-cigarettes (Mark, 2015; Spindel & McEvoy, 2016)

- Coverage of recent research in which cocaine use during pregnancy was associated with impaired connectivity of the thalamus and prefrontal cortex in newborns (Salzwedel & others, 2016)

- Discussion of recent research indicating that cocaine use by pregnant women is linked to attention deficit hyperactivity disorder, oppositional defiant disorder, and posttraumatic stress disorder (PTSD) in offspring (Richardson & others, 2016), as well as self-regulation problems at age 12 (Minnes & others, 2016)

- Coverage of a recent meta-analysis that found marijuana use during pregnancy was associated with the following outcomes in offspring: low birth weight and an increased likelihood of being placed in a neonatal intensive care unit (Gunn & others, 2016)

- New research indicating that pregnant women have increased their use of marijuana in recent years (Brown & others, 2016)
- Description of recent research that found cardiac defects, pulmonary problems, and microencephaly were among the most common fetal and neonatal outcomes when pregnant women have rubella (Yazigi & others, 2017)
- Inclusion of two recent research reviews that concluded maternal obesity during pregnancy is associated with an increased likelihood of offspring becoming obese in childhood and adulthood (Pinto Pereira & others, 2016; Santangeli, Sattar, & Huda, 2015)
- New research indicating that offspring of mothers who have gestational diabetes are at increased risk for developing cardiovascular disease later in life (Amrithraj & others, 2017)
- Revised content stating that pregnant women are now being advised to increase their fish consumption, especially low-mercury-content fish such as salmon, shrimp, tilapia, and cod (American Pregnancy Association, 2016; Federal Drug Administration, 2016)
- Coverage of two recent studies that found very advanced maternal age (40 years and older) was linked to negative perinatal outcomes, including spontaneous abortion, preterm birth, stillbirth, and fetal growth restriction (Traisrisilp & Tongsong, 2015; Waldenstrom & others, 2015)
- Inclusion of recent research that revealed maternal prenatal stress and anxiety were linked to lower levels of infants' self-regulation (Korja & others, 2017)
- Description of a recent study in which taking antidepressants early in pregnancy was linked to increased risk of miscarriage (Almeida & others, 2016)
- Discussion of a recent study that found when fetuses were exposed to serotonin-based antidepressants, they were more likely to be born preterm (Podrebarac & others, 2017)
- Coverage of a recent study that revealed taking antidepressants in the second or third trimester was associated with increased risk of autism in children (Boukhris & others, 2016)
- Inclusion of a recent study that found intimate partner violence increased the mother's stress level during her pregnancy (Fonseca-Machado Mde & others, 2015)
- Description of recent research in which CenteringPregnancy participation was linked to reduced incidence of low birth weight and placement in a neonatal intensive care unit (Gareau & others, 2016)

Chapter 4: Birth

- Revisions based on feedback from leading expert Janet DiPietro
- Update on the percentage of U.S. births that take place in hospitals, at home, and in birthing centers and the percentage of babies born through cesarean delivery (Martin & others, 2017)

- New description of global cesarean delivery rates, with the Dominican Republic and Brazil having the highest rates (56 percent) and New Zealand and the Czech Republic having the lowest (26 percent) (McCullough, 2016). The World Health Organization recommends a cesarean rate of 10 percent or less.
- Discussion of a recent study that found waterbirth was associated with fewer negative outcomes for offspring (Bovjerg, Cheyney, & Everson, 2016)
- Discussion of a recent research review in which waterbirth neonates experienced fewer negative outcomes than non-waterbirth neonates (Bovbjerg, Cheyney, & Everson, 2016)
- Description of a recent research review that concluded waterbirth is associated with high levels of maternal satisfaction with pain relief and the experience of childbirth (Nutter & others, 2015)
- Inclusion of recent research indicating that both music therapy and Hoku point ice massage were effective in reducing labor pain (Dehcheshmeh & Rafiei, 2015)
- Discussion of a recent study in which acupuncture reduced labor pain 30 minutes after the intervention (Allameh, Tehrani, & Ghasemi, 2015)
- Revised and updated content on cesarean delivery to include two specific reasons for this intervention: failure to progress through labor and fetal distress
- Coverage of recent studies that have found low Apgar scores are linked to higher needs for long-term additional support needs in education and educational attainment (Tweed & others, 2016), risk of developmental vulnerability at five years of age (Razaz & others, 2016), and risk for developing ADHD (Hanc & others, 2016)
- Updated data on the recent decline in the percentage of births in the United States that are preterm, including ethnic variations (Martin & others, 2017)
- Coverage of a recent study that found especially in very preterm infants, the identical twin who was smaller (an index of prenatal environmental experience) than his/her co-twin was far more likely to have poorer working memory and a lower level of self-regulation at 8 years of age (Deater-Deckard, 2016). The most likely explanation of this outcome involves epigenetic influences.
- Description of a recent study that found kangaroo care significantly reduced the amount of crying and increased heart rate stability in preterm infants (Choudhary & others, 2016)
- Inclusion of recent research that revealed kangaroo care was effective in reducing neonatal pain (Johnston & others, 2017; Mooney-Leber & Brummelte, 2017)
- Coverage of a recent study in Great Britain in which the use of kangaroo care in neonatal units resulted in substantial cost savings mainly because of its reductions in diseases such as gastroenteritis and colitis (Lowson & others, 2015)
- Inclusion of a recent study in which massage therapy improved the scores of HIV-exposed infants on both physical and mental scales, as well as improving their hearing and speech (Perez & others, 2015)

- Updated data on the percentage of births in the United States that are preterm, low birth weight, and cesarean section (Hamilton, Martin, & Osterman, 2016)
- Inclusion of a longitudinal study in which the nurturing positive effects of kangaroo care with preterm and low birth weight infants at 1 year of age were still present 20 years later in a number of positive developmental outcomes (Charpak & others, 2017)
- Inclusion of information about a recent study in which kangaroo care and massage therapy were equally effective in improving body weight and reducing hospital stays for low birth weight infants (Rangey & Sheth, 2014)
- Description of recent research that found that women who had a history of depression were 20 times more likely to develop postpartum depression than women who had no history of depression (Silverman & others, 2017)
- Coverage of a recent study in which postpartum depression was associated with an increase in 4-month-olds' unintentional injuries (Yamaoka, Fujiwara, & Tamiva, 2016)
- Inclusion of recent research in which mothers' postpartum depression, but not generalized anxiety, was linked to their children's emotional negativity and behavior problems at 2 years of age (Prenoveau & others, 2017)
- Discussion of a recent study that found depressive symptoms in mothers and fathers were linked to impaired bonding with their infant in the postpartum period (Kerstis & others, 2016)

Chapter 5: Physical Development in Infancy

- Revisions based on feedback from leading expert Karen Adolph
- New discussion of how infant growth is often not smooth and continuous but rather is episodic, occurring in spurts (Adolph & Berger, 2015; Lampl & Schoen, 2017)
- New description indicating that neuronal connections number in the trillions (de Haan, 2015)
- Coverage of a recent study that found higher-quality mother-infant interaction predicted a higher level of frontal lobe functioning when assessed by EEG later in infancy (Bernier, Calkins, & Bell, 2016)
- New description of research done by Mark Johnson and his colleagues (Gliga & others, 2017; Johnson & others, 2015; Milovavlijeviz & others, 2017; Saez de Urabain, Nuthmann, & Johnson, 2017; Senju & others, 2016) on infant brain development, including their neuroconstructivist approach and studies of the development of the prefrontal cortex and its function, early identification of autism, face processing, and early social experiences
- New discussion of the recent increase in the use of functional near-infrared spectroscopy to assess infants' brain activity, a technique that is portable and allows researchers to monitor infants' brain activity while they are exploring the world around them (de Haan & Johnson, 2016; Emberson & others, 2017b). Also, new Figure 4 shows an infant in an experiment using near-infrared spectroscopy.

- Inclusion of a recent research review of 27 studies that confirmed pacifier use is associated with a lower incidence of SIDS (Alm & others, 2016)
- Description of a recent Swedish study that revealed bed sharing was more common in SIDS deaths (Mollborg & others, 2015)
- New commentary that after prone sleeping position, the two most critical factors in predicting SIDS are maternal smoking and bed sharing (Mitchell & Krous, 2015)
- Coverage of two recent studies that found sleep difficulties in infancy were linked to developmental problems in attention (Geva, Yaron, & Kuint, 2016; Sadeh & others, 2015)
- Inclusion of information about recent longitudinal studies that revealed when mothers participated prenatally and in early childhood in WIC programs, young children showed short-term cognitive benefits and longer-term reading and math benefits (Jackson, 2015)
- Updated data on the continuing increase in breast feeding by U.S. mothers (Centers for Disease Control and Prevention, 2016)
- Description of a recent Danish study that found breast feeding did not protect against allergic sensitization in early childhood and allergy-related diseases at 7 years of age (Jelding-Dannemand, Malby Schoos, & Bisgaard, 2015)
- Coverage of a recent large-scale study of more than 500,000 Scottish children found that those who were exclusively breast fed at 6 to 8 weeks were less likely to ever have been hospitalized through early childhood than their formula fed counterparts (Ajetunmobi & others, 2015)
- Inclusion of recent research that found breast feeding was associated with a small increase in intelligence in children (Kanazawa, 2015)
- New content on a key child undernutrition problem in developing countries: micronutrient deficiencies such as those involving iron, zinc, and iodine (Hwalla & others, 2017; Lazarus, 2017a, b; World Health Organization, 2017)
- New coverage of a recent study of infants' organization of exploratory behaviors in planning locomotion in challenging contexts (Kretch & Adolph, 2017)
- New discussion of how walking skills might produce a developmental cascade of changes in infancy, including increases in language skills (Adolph & Robinson, 2015; He, Walle, & Campo, 2015)
- Discussion of a recent study that examined a number of predictors of motor milestones in the first year (Flensborg-Madsen & Mortensen, 2017)
- Description of recent studies that indicated short-term training involving practice of reaching movements increased both preterm and full-term infants' reaching for and touching objects (Cunha & others, 2016; Guimaraes & Tudelia, 2015)
- Inclusion of recent research in which infants who were not yet engaging in reaching behavior were provided with reaching experiences at 3 months of age, and these infants

engaged in increased object exploration and attention focusing at 5.5 months (Libertus, Joh, & Needham, 2016)

- New coverage of a recent study that revealed 3-month-old infants who participated in active motor training using sticky mittens that allowed them to pick up toys engaged in more sophisticated object exploration at 5.5 months (Wiesen, Watkins, & Needham, 2016)
- Discussion of a study that found newborns' pain threshold was lower than that of adults (Goksan & others, 2015)
- Three new recommendations in Resources section: *Typical and Atypical Functional Brain Development* by Michelle de Haan and Mark Johnson (2016); *Healthy Sleep Habits, Happy Child* by Marc Weissbluth (2016); and *The Pediatrician's Guide to Feeding Babies and Toddlers* by Anthony Porto and Dina DiMaggio (2016)

Chapter 6: Cognitive Development in Infancy

- New coverage of a recent study of 5-month-olds that found their better performance on an A-not-B task was linked to how well they focused their attention on a different task, indicating that infants' attention may be involved in performance variations on the A-not-B task (Marcovitch & others, 2016)
- Expanded and updated criticism of the innate view of the emergence of infant morality, with an emphasis on the importance of infants' early interaction with others and later transformation through language and reflective thought (Carpendale & Hammond, 2016)
- Coverage of recent research that revealed problems in joint attention as early as 8 months of age were linked to a child being diagnosed with autism by 7 years of age (Veness & others, 2014)
- Inclusion of a recent study in which infants who initiated joint attention at 14 months of age had higher executive function at 18 months of age (Miller & Marcovitch, 2015)
- Coverage of a recent study in which hand-eye coordination involving connection of gaze with manual action on objects rather than gaze following alone predicted joint attention (Yu & Smith, 2017)
- Discussion of recent research by Patricia Bauer and her colleagues regarding when infantile amnesia begins to occur and why (Bauer, 2015; Bauer & Larkina, 2015; Pathman, Doydum, & Bauer, 2015). By 8 to 9 years of age, children's memory of events that occurred at 3 years of age began to significantly fade away (Bauer & Larkina, 2014).
- New coverage of a study that found early language skills at 24 months of age predicted IQ at 6 years of age and were linked to intellectual disability (predicted from 8 months) and giftedness (predicted from 12 months of age) (Peyre & others, 2017)
- Revisions and updates based on feedback from leading experts Roberta Golinkoff and Virginia Marchman
- New opening commentary about the nature of language learning and how it involves comprehending a sound system (or sign system for individuals who are deaf), the

world of objects, actions, and events, and how units such as words and grammar connect sound and world (Pace & others, 2016)

- Revised definition of infinite generativity to include comprehension as well as production
- Expanded description of how statistical regularity of information is involved in infant word learning (Pace & others, 2016)
- Description of recent research in which vocabulary development from 16 to 24 months of age was linked to vocabulary, phonological awareness, reading accuracy, and reading comprehension five years later (Duff & others, 2015)
- New content on the language of Korean children being more verb friendly than noun friendly (Waxman & others, 2013)
- New research on babbling onset predicting when infants would say their first words (McGillion & others, 2017)
- New commentary on why gestures such as pointing promote further advances in language development
- Inclusion of a recent study involving joint attention in which infants' eye-gaze behaviors during Spanish tutoring sessions at 9.5 to 10.5 months of age predicted the infants' second-language phonetic learning at 11 months of age, indicating a strong influence of social interaction at the earliest ages of learning a second language (Convoy & others, 2015)
- New discussion of Patricia Kuhl's (2015) findings that the periods when a baby's brain is most open to learning the sounds of a native language begin at age 6 months for vowels and age 9 months for consonants
- Expanded descriptions of the functions of child-directed speech, such as capturing infants' attention, maintaining social interaction between infants and caregivers, and providing infants with information about their native language through its contrast with speech directed to adults (Golinkoff & others, 2015)
- Coverage of recent research in which child-directed speech in a one-to-one social context for 11- to 14-month-olds was related to productive vocabulary at 2 years of age for Spanish-English bilingual infants for both languages and each language independently (Ramirez-Esparza, Garcia-Sierra, & Kuhl, 2017)
- New emphasis on the importance of social cues in infant language learning (Pace & others, 2016)
- New content on whether infants learn language effectively through television and videos
- Discussion of a recent study of toddlers in which frequent television exposure increased the risk of delayed language development (Lin & others, 2015)
- Coverage of a recent study that found Skype provides some improvement in children's language learning over television and videos (Roseberry, Hirsh-Pasek, & Golinkoff, 2014)
- Description of a recent study in which the quality of early foundational communication between parent and child at age 2 accounted for more variability in language outcomes

one year later than the amount of parent speech did (Hirsh-Pasek & others, 2015)

- Discussion of how joint engagement and relevant responsiveness by a social partner in infancy predict later growth in language, possibly because they improve the infant's mapping process that connects word and the world (Tamis-LeMonda & others, 2014)
- Coverage of a recent study in which both full term and pre-term infants who heard more caregiver talk based on all-day recordings at 16 months of age had better language skills at 18 months of age (Adams & others, 2017)
- Revised definitions of recasting, expanding, and labeling
- Expanded coverage of how parents can facilitate infants' and toddlers' language development

Chapter 7: Socioemotional Development in Infancy

- New introductory comments about the important role that cognitive processes, in addition to biological and experiential influences, play in children's emotional development, both in the moment and across childhood (Calkins, Perry, & Dollar, 2016)
- Coverage of recent research indicating that smiling and laughter at 7 months of age were associated with self-regulation at 7 years of age (Posner & others, 2014)
- Inclusion of a recent study in which mothers were more likely than fathers to use soothing techniques to reduce infant crying (Dayton & others, 2015)
- Coverage of a recent study that found depressed mothers rocked and touched their crying infants less than non-depressed mothers did (Esposito & others, 2017a)
- New description of a study in which young infants with a negative temperament used fewer emotion regulation strategies, while maternal sensitivity to infants was linked to more adaptive emotion regulation (Thomas & others, 2017)
- New discussion of describing temperament in terms of emotional reactivity and self-regulation (Bates & Pettit, 2015)
- New research that found positive affectivity, surgency, and self-regulation capacity assessed at 4 months of age was linked to school readiness at 4 years of age (Gartstein, Putnam, & Kliewer, 2016)
- Coverage of a recent study in which disinhibition in the toddler years was linked to career stability in middle adulthood (Blatney & others, 2015)
- Description of recent research that found an inhibited temperament at 2 to 3 years of age was related to social phobia related symptoms at 7 years of age (Lahat & others, 2014)
- Inclusion of recent findings indicating that an inhibited temperament in infants and young children is linked to the development of social anxiety disorder in adolescence and adulthood (Perez-Edgar & Guyer, 2014; Rapee, 2014)
- New description of how the use of positive parenting, which includes high levels of warmth and low levels of

harsh control, increases children's effortful control (Bates & Pettit, 2015)

- Two new research studies that linked a lower level of effortful control at 3 years of age with ADHD symptoms in the first grade (Willoughby, Gottfredson, & Stifter, 2017) and at 13 years of age (Einziger & others, 2017)
- Description of a recent study that revealed if parents had a childhood history of behavioral inhibition, their children who also had a high level of behavioral inhibition were at risk for developing anxiety disorders (Stumper & others, 2017)
- New coverage of recent research in which children who had a difficult temperament at 5 and 14 years were more likely to have mental health problems at 21 years of age (Kingsbury & others, 2017)
- New discussion of the recent interest in the *differential susceptibility* and *biological sensitivity to context* models emphasizing that certain characteristics—such as a difficult temperament—may render children more vulnerable to difficulty in adverse contexts but also make them more susceptible to optimal growth in very supportive conditions (Baptista & others, 2017; Belsky & others, 2015; Belsky & Pluess, 2016; Belsky & van IJzendoorn, 2017; Simpson & Belsky, 2016)
- New commentary about recent advances in infants' understanding of others (Rhodes & others, 2015), including research indicating that infants as young as 13 months of age seem to consider another's perspective when predicting their actions (Choi & Luo, 2015)
- Expanded and updated content on the increasing belief that babies are socially smarter than used to be thought, including information about research by Amanda Woodward and her colleagues (Krough-Jespersen & Woodward, 2016; Liberman, Woodward, & Kinzler, 2017; Shneidman & Woodward, 2016; Sodian & others, 2016) on how quickly infants understand and respond to others' meaningful intentions
- Inclusion of recent research in which infant attachment insecurity (especially insecure resistant attachment) and early childhood behavioral inhibition predicted adolescent social anxiety symptoms (Lewis-Morrarty & others, 2015)
- Inclusion of recent research conducted in Zambia, where siblings were substantially involved in caregiving activities, that revealed infants showed strong attachments to both their mothers and their sibling caregivers, with secure attachment being the most frequent attachment classification for both mother-infant and sibling-infant relationships (Mooya, Sichimba, & Bakermans-Kranenburg, 2016)
- Description of a recent study that did not find support for the view that genes influence mother-infant attachment (Leerkes & others, 2017b)
- Updated and expanded coverage of the neuroscience of attachment to include the role of the brain's neurotransmitter dopamine circuits that provide pleasure and reward when mothers care for their infants and are exposed to their infants' cues; these experiences and brain changes likely

promote mother-infant attachment and sensitive parenting (Feldman, 2017; Kim, Strathearn, & Swain, 2016; Sullivan & Wilson, 2018)

- Discussion of three recent studies on the transition to parenthood that found (1) men, especially men who were avoidantly attached, adapted more poorly to child care tasks (Fillo & others, 2015); (2) in dual-earner couples, after a child was born, women did more than 2 hours of additional work compared with 40 minutes more for men (Yavorsky & others, 2015); and (3) in comparison with married fathers, cohabiting fathers' personal dedication and relationship confidence decreased and their feelings of constraint increased across the transition to parenting (Kamp Dush & others, 2014)

- Expanded coverage of the types of behaviors infants and parents engage in when reciprocal socialization is occurring

- New commentary about how the expectations parents have for their toddlers' behavior are likely higher than the toddlers' ability to control their behavior and impulses based on what is known about the maturation of the prefrontal cortex

- Discussion of a recent study that found when adults used scaffolding, infants were twice as likely to engage in helping behavior (Dahl & others, 2017)

- Coverage of a recent study of disadvantaged families in which an intervention that involved improving early maternal scaffolding was linked to improvement in children's cognitive skills at 4 years of age (Obradovic & others, 2016)

- Description of a recent national poll that estimated there are 2 million stay-at-home dads in the United States, a significant increase from 1.6 million in 2004 and 1.1 million in 1989 (Livingston, 2014)

- Coverage of a recent study in which both paternal and maternal sensitivity assessed when the infant was 10 to 12 months old were linked to the child's cognitive development at 18 months of age and the child's language development at 36 months (Malmburg & others, 2016)

- Discussion of a recent study that found negative outcomes on cognitive development in infancy when fathers were more withdrawn and depressed and positive outcomes on cognitive development when fathers were more engaged and sensitive, as well as less controlling (Sethna & others, 2017)

- Added commentary that infants and toddlers are more likely to be found in family child care and informal care settings while older children are more likely to be in child care centers and preschool and early education programs

- Description of a recent Australian study in which higher-quality child care at 2 to 3 years of age was linked to children's better self-regulation of attention and emotion at 4 to 5 and 6 to 7 years of age (Gialamas & others, 2014)

- New entry in Resources, *Raising a Secure Child* by Kent Hoffman & others (2017), which provides valuable information and strategies for protecting and nurturing infants

Chapter 8: Physical Development in Early Childhood

- Description of a recent study that found positive effects of growth hormone treatment across five years for children born small for gestational age (Ross & others, 2015)

- Coverage of a recent research review that concluded an accurate assessment of growth hormone deficiency is difficult and that many children diagnosed with the deficiency re-test normal later in childhood (Murray, Dattani, & Clayton, 2016)

- Inclusion of recent research on how poverty is linked to maturational lags in children's frontal and temporal lobes, and these lags are associated with lower school readiness skills (Hair & others, 2015)

- Description of a recent study that revealed higher levels of maternal sensitivity in early childhood were related to higher total brain volume in children (Kok & others, 2015)

- Coverage of a recent study in which young children with higher cognitive ability showed increased myelination by 3 years of age (Deoni & others, 2016)

- Inclusion of recent research in which myelination in a number of brain areas was linked to young children's processing speed (Chevalier & others, 2015)

- Discussion of a recent study of 4-year-old girls that found a nine-week motor skill intervention improved the girls' ball skills (Veldman & others, 2017)

- Description of recent research indicating that higher motor skill proficiency in preschool was linked to engaging in a higher level of physical activity in adolescence (Venetsanou & Kambas, 2017)

- Inclusion of recent research that found children with a low level of motor competence had a lower motivation for sports participation and lower global self-worth than their counterparts who had a high level of motor competence (Bardid & others, 2017b)

- Coverage of a recent study of 36- to 42-month-old children in which consistent bedtime routine was linked to more nightly sleep and an increase in nightly sleep minutes across a six-month period (Staples, Bates, & Petersen, 2015)

- Inclusion of recent research in China that revealed preschool children who slept seven hours per day or less had worse school readiness profiles and that children who used electronic devices three hours per day or more had shortened sleep durations (Tso & others, 2015)

- Description of a recent study of 2- to 5-year-olds that revealed each additional hour of daily screen time was associated with a decrease in sleep time, less likelihood of sleeping 10 hours or more per night, and later bedtime (Xu & others, 2016)

- Discussion of a recent study that revealed 2½-year-old children's liking for fruits and vegetables was related to their eating more fruits and vegetables at 7 years of age (Fletcher & others, 2017)

- Updated data on the percentage of U.S. 2- to 5-year-old children who are obese (Ogden & others, 2016)

- Recent description by expert panels from Australia, Canada, the United Kingdom, and the United States that were remarkably similar in recommending that young children get an average of 15 or more minutes of physical activity per hour over a 12-hour period, or about 3 hours total per day (Pate & others, 2015)

- Coverage of recent research in which 60 minutes of physical activity per day in preschool academic contexts improved young children's early literacy (Kirk & Kirk, 2016)

- New discussion of a longitudinal study that revealed when young children were exposed to environmental tobacco smoke they were more likely to engage in antisocial behavior at 12 years of age (Pagani & others, 2017)

- New entry in Resources, *Early Childhood Development Coming of Age: Science through the Life Course* by Maureen Black and her colleagues (2017), which outlines the key features needed in early childhood programs to help at-risk children reach their potential

Chapter 9: Cognitive Development in Early Childhood

- Updates and revisions in this chapter based on feedback from leading expert Megan McClelland

- Inclusion of recent research showing the effectiveness of the Tools of the Mind approach in improving a number of cognitive processes and academic skills in young children (Blair & Raver, 2014)

- Discussion of recent research that found preschool sustained attention was linked to a greater likelihood of completing college by 25 years of age (McClelland & others, 2013)

- Inclusion of recent research that revealed myelination in a number of brain areas was linked to young children's information processing speed (Chevalier & others, 2015)

- Coverage of a recent study of young children that found executive function was associated with emergent literacy and vocabulary development (Becker & others, 2014)

- Description of recent research in which executive function at 3 years of age predicted theory of mind at 4 years of age, and executive function at 4 years of age predicted theory of mind at 5 years of age, but the reverse did not occur—theory of mind at earlier ages did not predict executive function at later ages (Marcovitch & others, 2015)

- New coverage of developmental changes in executive function in early childhood

- Description of recent research on executive function and school readiness (Willoughby & others, 2017)

- Inclusion of research in which secure attachment to mothers during the toddler years was linked to a higher level of executive function at 5 to 6 years of age (Bernier & others, 2015)

- Discussion of a recent observational study that found a higher level of control by fathers predicted a lower level of executive function in 3-year-olds (Meuwissen & Carlson, 2016)

- Coverage of recent research in which experiencing peer problems in early childhood was linked to lower executive function later in childhood (Holmes, Kim-Spoon, & Deater-Deckard, 2016)

- Expanded and updated coverage of factors that influence children's theory of mind development: prefrontal cortex functioning (Powers, Chavez, & Hetherington, 2016); various aspects of social interaction, including secure attachment and mental state talk, parental engagement in mind-mindedness (Hughes, Devine, & Wang, 2017); having older siblings and friends who engage in mental state talk, and living in a family with higher socioeconomic status (Devine & Hughes, 2017)

- New description of recent research indicating that children with an advanced theory of mind are more popular with their peers and have better social skills in peer relations (Peterson & others, 2016; Slaughter & others, 2014)

- Updated statistics on the increase in the estimated percentage of children who have autism spectrum disorders (Christensen & others, 2016)

- Coverage of a recent study in which theory of mind predicted the severity of autism in children (Hoogenhout & Malcolm-Smith, 2017)

- Revisions in the discussion of young children's language development based on feedback from leading experts Roberta Golinkoff and Virginia Marchman

- Update on the increase in publicly funded preschool programs that now occurs in 42 states plus the District of Columbia (National Institute for Early Education Research, 2016)

- Updated information about the dramatic increase in the number of Montessori schools in the United States and the estimated number worldwide (North American Montessori Teachers' Association, 2016)

- Inclusion of a recent study that found Latino children living in low-income communities who began the school year having at-risk pre-academic and behavioral skills benefited from a Montessori public pre-K program, ending the year scoring above national averages for school readiness (Ansari & Winsler, 2014)

- Description of a recent study that revealed neighborhood poverty was linked to lower levels of classroom quality in Head Start programs (McCoy & others, 2015)

- Description of two recent studies that confirmed the importance of improved parenting engagement and skills in the success of Head Start programs (Ansari & Gershoff, 2016; Roggman & others, 2016)

- New entry in *Connecting With Improving the Lives of Children*, "Engage children in activities that will improve their executive function", including a recommended resource for these activities: http://developingchild.harvard.edu/science/key-concepts/executive-function/

- New entry in *Connecting with Improving the Lives of Children:* "Monitor young children's ability to delay gratification"

- New entry in Resources, *Becoming Brilliant* by Roberta Golinkoff and Kathy Hirsh Pasek (2016), a terrific book in which two leading developmental psychologists make compelling arguments that education of children needs to place more emphasis on promoting collaboration, communication, critical thinking, creative innovations, and confidence

- New entry in Resources, *Executive Functions in Children's Everyday Lives* (edited by Maureen Hoskyn and her colleagues (2017), which explores many aspects of children's executive function, including the role of parental influence and the importance of executive function in school and academic achievement

- New entry in Resources, *Stop, Act, and Think: Integrating Self-Regulation in the Early Childhood Classroom* by Megan McClelland and Shauna Tominey (2015), which provides a wealth of strategies for improving young children's self-regulation, including the use of various games, songs, and puzzles

Chapter 10: Socioemotional Development in Early Childhood

- New coverage of links between perspective taking and young children's social relationships, including a recent study that found higher perspective taking in 2-year-olds predicted more stable mother-child security later in the preschool years (Meins, Bureau, & Ferryhough, 2017)

- Inclusion of recent research indicating that a broad capacity for self-evaluative emotion was present in the preschool years and was linked to young children's empathetic concern (Ross, 2017)

- Expanded coverage of the importance of emotion regulation in childhood and links between emotion regulation and executive function (Blair, 2016, 2017; Calkins & Perry, 2016; Griffin, Freund, & McCardle, 2015)

- Inclusion of two new key terms—empathy and sympathy—with their definitions (Eisenberg, Spinrad, & Valiente, 2016)

- Coverage of a recent study in which young children's sympathy predicted whether they would share (Ongley & Malti, 2014)

- New commentary about connections between different emotions and how they may influence development, including a recent study in which participants' guilt proneness combined with their empathy to predict an increase in prosocial behavior (Torstevelt, Sutterlin, & Lugo, 2016)

- Coverage of a recent study in Great Britain in which gender non-conforming boys were most at risk for peer rejection (Braun & Davidson, 2017)

- Inclusion of a recent research review of a large number of studies that found authoritarian parenting was associated with a higher level of externalizing problems (Pinquart, 2017)

- Discussion of a recent study that revealed children of authoritative parents engaged in more prosocial behavior than their counterparts whose parents used the other parenting styles discussed in the section (Carlo & others, 2017)

- Description of a recent research review in which authoritative parenting was the most effective parenting style in predicting which children and adolescents would be less likely to be overweight or obese later in their development (Sokol, Qin, & Puti, 2017)

- New commentary about how in many traditional cultures, fathers use an authoritarian style; in such cultures, children benefit more when mothers use an authoritative parenting style

- Inclusion of new information that physical punishment is outlawed in 41 countries (Committee on Rights of the Child, 2014)

- Coverage of a recent review that concluded there is widespread approval of corporal punishment by U.S. parents (Cocca, 2017)

- Discussion of a longitudinal study that found harsh physical punishment in childhood was linked to a higher incidence of intimate partner violence in adulthood (Afifi & others, 2017b)

- Description of a recent Japanese study in which occasional spanking at 3 years of age was associated with a higher level of behavioral problems at 5 years of age (Okunzo & others, 2017)

- Discussion of a recent meta-analysis that found when physical punishment was not abusive, it still was linked to detrimental child outcomes (Gershoff & Grogan-Kaylor, 2016)

- Discussion of a recent study in which experiencing parents' divorce, as well as child maltreatment, in childhood was linked to midlife suicidal ideation (Stansfield & others, 2017)

- Updated data on the number of U.S. children who were victims of child maltreatment in 2013 (U.S. Department of Health and Human Services, 2015)

- Inclusion of a recent study that revealed exposure to either physical or sexual abuse in childhood and adolescence was linked to an increase in 13- to 18-year-olds' suicidal ideation, plans, and attempts (Gomez & others, 2017)

- Coverage of a recent study that indicated a bidirectional association between a child's behavior (conduct problems, for example) and quality of sibling relationships (Pike & Oliver, 2017)

- Discussion of a recent study in which individuals who had experienced their parents' divorce were at greater lifetime risk of engaging in a suicide attempt (Alonzo & others, 2015)

- Inclusion of a 30-year longitudinal study that found offspring of parents who engaged in child maltreatment and neglect are at increased risk for engaging in child neglect and sexual maltreatment themselves (Widom, Czaja, & DuMont, 2015)

- Description of recent research on almost 3,000 adolescents that revealed a negative association of the father's, but not the mother's, unemployment on the adolescents' health (Bacikov-Sleskova, Benka, & Orosova, 2015)

- Coverage of recent research indicating that enriched work-family experiences were positively linked to better parenting quality, which in turn was associated with better child outcomes; by contrast, conflicting work-family experiences were related to poorer parenting quality, which in turn was linked to more negative child outcomes (Vieira & others, 2016)

- Inclusion of recent research in which children were more likely to have behavior problems if their post-divorce environment was less supportive and stimulating, their mother was less sensitive and more depressed, and if their household income was lower (Weaver & Schofield, 2015). Also in this study, a higher level of predivorce maternal sensitivity and child IQ served as protective factors in reducing child problems after the divorce.

- Coverage of a recent study that found interparental hostility was a stronger predictor of children's insecurity and externalizing problems than interparental disagreement and low levels of interparental cooperation (Davies & others, 2016)

- Inclusion of recent research in which maladaptive marital conflict when children were 2 years old was associated with an increase in internalizing problems eight years later due to an undermining of attachment security in girls, while negative emotional aftermath of conflict increased both boys' and girls' internalizing problems (Brock & Kochanska, 2016)

- Coverage of a longitudinal study that revealed parental divorce experienced prior to 7 years of age was linked to a lower level of the children's health through 50 years of age (Thomas & Hognas, 2015)

- Description of recent research on non-residential fathers in divorced families that found high father-child involvement and low interparental conflict were linked to positive child outcomes (Flam & others, 2016)

- Discussion of a recent study that found co-parenting following divorce was positively associated with better mental health and higher self-esteem and academic achievement (Lamela & Figueiredo, 2016)

- Updated data on the percentage of gay and lesbian parents who are raising children

- Inclusion of recent research that revealed no differences in the adjustment of school-aged children adopted in infancy by gay, lesbian, and heterosexual parents (Farr, 2017)

- Description of a recent study of lesbian and gay adoptive families in which 98 percent of the parents reported their children had adjusted well to school (Farr, Oakley, & Ollen, 2017)

- Update on the latest national survey of screen time indicating a dramatic shift to greater use of mobile devices by young children (Common Sense Media, 2013)

- Coverage of a recent study of preschool children in which each additional hour of screen time was linked to less nightly sleep, later bedtime, and reduced likelihood of sleeping 10 or more hours per night (Xu & others, 2016)

- Inclusion of a recent research review that concluded higher screen time was associated with a lower level of cognitive development in early childhood (Carson & others, 2015)

- Coverage of recent research on children in which higher viewing of TV violence, video game violence, and music video violence was independently associated with a higher level of physical aggression (Coker & others, 2015)

- Inclusion of recent research with 2- to 6-year-olds that indicated increased TV viewing on weekends was associated with a higher risk of being overweight or obese (Kondolot & others, 2017)

- New entry in Resources, *Parents and Digital Technologies* by Suzie Hayman and John Coleman, which provides excellent strategies parents can use to communicate more effectively with children about technology, as well as establish boundaries

Chapter 11: Physical Development in Middle and Late Childhood

- Description of a 14-year longitudinal study in which parental weight gain predicted children's weight change (Andriani, Liao, & Kuo, 2015)

- Coverage of a study that found both a larger waist circumference and a higher body mass index (BMI) combined to place children at higher risk for developing cardiovascular disease (de Koning & others, 2015)

- Discussion of a recent study of elementary school children that revealed 55 minutes or more of daily moderate-to-vigorous physical activity was associated with a lower incidence of obesity (Nemet, 2016)

- Description of a recent meta-analysis that found children who engage in regular physical activity have better cognitive inhibitory control (Jackson & others, 2016)

- Inclusion of recent research on 7- to 9-year-olds that found participating for approximately one year in organized leisure sports was linked to decreased cardiovascular risk (Hebert & others, 2017)

- Updated data on the percentage of 6- to 11-year-old U.S. children who are obese (Ogden & others, 2016)

- Inclusion of a recent Japanese study that revealed the highest incidence of overweight/obesity in children was linked to a family pattern of irregular mealtimes and high amounts of screen time for both parents (Watanabe & others, 2016)

- Discussion of a recent study in which children were less likely to be obese or overweight when they attended schools in states that had a strong policy implementation on healthy food and beverage (Datar & Nicosia, 2017)

- Coverage of a recent research review that concluded the elementary school programs that emphasized increased physical activity, decreased intake of sugar-sweetened beverages, and increased fruit intake were the most effective in reducing BMI measurements in children (Brown & others, 2016)

- Updated research on the Bogalusa Health Study, including these two studies: (1) body fatness and elevated blood pressure beginning in childhood were linked to premature death from coronary heart disease in adulthood (Berenson & others, 2016), and (2) secondhand smoke exposure in childhood was associated with increased carotid artery thickness in adulthood (Chen & others, 2015)

- Updated statistics on the percentage of U.S. children who have different types of disabilities and updated version of Figure 4 (National Center for Education Statistics, 2016)

- Updated statistics on the percentage of U.S. children who have ever been diagnosed with ADHD (Centers for Disease Control and Prevention, 2016)

- New research that revealed the dopamine transporter gene DAT 1 was involved in decreased cortical thickness in the prefrontal cortex of children with ADHD (Fernandez-Jaen & others, 2015)

- Description of a recent research review that found girls with ADHD had more problematic peer relations than typically developing girls in a number of areas (Kok & others, 2016)

- Coverage of a recent research review that concluded ADHD in childhood is linked to a number of long-term outcomes (Erksine & others, 2016)

- Discussion of a recent study that found childhood ADHD was associated with long-term underachievement in math and reading (Voigt & others, 2017)

- Coverage of a recent research review that concluded stimulant medications are effective in treating children with ADHD in the short term, but that long-term benefits of such medications are not clear (Rajeh & others, 2017)

- Inclusion of recent research in which a higher level of physical activity in adolescence was linked to a lower level of ADHD in emerging adulthood (Rommel & others, 2015)

- Description of a recent meta-analysis that concluded that short-term aerobic exercise is effective in reducing symptoms such as inattention, hyperactivity, and impulsivity (Cerillo-Urbina & others, 2015)

- Inclusion of a recent meta-analysis that concluded physical exercise is effective in reducing cognitive symptoms of ADHD in individuals 3 to 25 years of age (Tan, Pooley, & Speelman, 2016)

- Coverage of a recent meta-analysis in which exercise was associated with better executive function in children with ADHD (Vysniauske & others, 2017)

- Discussion of a recent meta-analysis in which mindfulness training significantly improved the attention of children with ADHD (Cairncross & Miller, 2016)

- Inclusion of new content on how 3-D printing and haptic devices provide important technology support for students with visual impairments (Pawluck & others, 2015)

- Updated data on the increasing percentage of children who are diagnosed with autism spectrum disorders (Christensen & others, 2016)

- Description of a recent study in which an 8-week yoga program improved the sustained attention of children with ADHD (Chou & Huang, 2017)

- Inclusion of a recent study that revealed a lower level of working memory was the executive function most strongly associated with autism spectrum disorders (Ziermans & others, 2017)

- New coverage of two recent surveys in which only a minority of parents reported that their child's autism spectrum disorder was identified prior to 3 years of age and that one-third to one-half of the cases were identified after 6 years of age (Sheldrick, Maye, & Carter, 2017)

- Update on the percentage of children with a disability who spend time in a regular classroom (*Condition of Education*, 2015).

- New entry in Resources, *Routledge Handbook of Talent Identification and Development in Sport* edited by Joseph Baker and others (2017), which provides extensive information and positive strategies for helping parents become more effective in raising children who are talented in sports; includes chapters on family influences and creating optimal sports environments

Chapter 12: Cognitive Development in Middle and Late Childhood

- Expanded and updated coverage of Alan Baddeley's important concept of working memory, including coverage of its link to improving many aspects of children's cognitive and academic development (Gerst & others, 2016; Peng & Fuchs, 2016)

- Description of recent research indicating that working memory develops slowly; for example, even by 8 years of age, children can hold in memory only half the items that adults can remember (Kharitonova, Winter, & Sheridan, 2015)

- Discussion of a recent study in which children's verbal working memory was linked to these aspects of both first and second language learners: morphology, syntax, and grammar (Verhagen & Leseman, 2016)

- Expansion of the activities that improve executive function to include scaffolding of self-regulation (Bodrova & Leong, 2015)

- Coverage of recent research in which mindfulness training improved children's attention and self-regulation (Poehlmann-Tynan & others, 2016), achievement (Singh & others, 2016), and coping strategies in stressful situations (Dariotis & others, 2016)

- Description of two recent studies that found mindfulness training reduced public school teachers' stress, improved their mood at school and at home, and produced better sleep (Crain, Schonert-Reichl, & Roeser, 2016; Taylor & others, 2016)

- Description of the most recent revision of the Wechsler Intelligence Scale for Children—V, and its increased number of subtests and composite scores (Canivez, Watkins, & Dombrowski, 2017)

- Description of a recent meta-analysis that revealed a correlation of +.54 between intelligence and school grades (Roth & others, 2015)

- Coverage of recent research that found a significant link between children's general intelligence and their self-control (Meldrum & others, 2017)

- Discussion of a recent two-year intervention study with families living in poverty in which maternal scaffolding and positive home stimulation improved young children's intellectual functioning (Obradovic & others, 2016)

- New content on stereotype threat in the section on cultural bias in intelligence tests (Pennington & others, 2016; Spencer, Logel, & Davies, 2016)

- Description of a recent study using Stanford Binet intelligence scales that found no differences between non-Latino White and African American preschool children when they were matched for age, gender, and level of parent education (Dale & others, 2014)

- Coverage of a recent analysis that concluded the underrepresentation of African Americans in STEM subjects and careers is linked to practitioners' expectations that they have less innate talent than non-Latino Whites (Leslie & others, 2015)

- Update on the percentage of U.S. students who are classified as gifted (National Association for Gifted Children, 2017)

- New description of how children who are gifted excel in various aspects of processing information (Ambrose & Sternberg, 2016a, b)

- Discussion of a recent study that revealed parents and teachers rated elementary school children who are not gifted as having more emotional and behavioral problems than children who are gifted (Eklund & others, 2015)

- New content on the importance of encouraging students to monitor their writing progress (Fidalgo, Harris, & Braaksma, 2016)

- Discussion of a recent strategy intervention with struggling second-grade writers and their teachers that provided positive results for a number of writing outcomes (Harris, Graham, & Atkins, 2015)

- Revised and updated content on bilingualism, including information about whether infants and young children benefit from learning two languages simultaneously (Bialystok, 2014, 2015)

- Coverage of a recent study of 6- to 10-year-old children that found early bilingual exposure was a key factor in bilingual children outperforming monolingual children on phonological awareness and word learning (Jasinsksa & Petitto, 2017)

- Discussion of research that documented bilingual children were better at theory of mind tasks than were monolingual children (Rubio-Fernandez, 2016)

- New description of the rate at which bilingual and monolingual children learn language(s) (Hoff, 2015) and inclusion of a recent study that found by 4 years of age children who continued to learn both Spanish and English had a total vocabulary growth that was greater than that of monolingual children (Hoff & others, 2014)

- Description of a recent study of minority low-SES youth that found their intrinsic motivation (but not their extrinsic motivation) predicted their intention to pursue a health-science-related career (Boekeloo & others, 2015)

- New coverage of contextual factors that influence students' interest and achievement motivation (Linnenbrink-Garcia & Patall, 2016)

- Revisions to the discussion of achievement based on feedback from leading expert Carol Dweck

- Inclusion of recent research that found students from lower-income families were less likely to have a growth mindset than were students from wealthier families but the achievement of students from lower-income families was more likely to be protected if they had a growth mindset (Claro, Paunesku, & Dweck, 2016)

- New coverage of a recent research review that concluded increases in family income for children in poverty were linked to increased achievement in middle school as well as higher educational attainment in adolescence and emerging adulthood (Duncan, Magnuson, & Votruba-Drzal, 2017)

- Updated data on U.S. students' math and science achievement in comparison with their counterparts in other countries (Desilver, 2017; PISA, 2015: TIMMS, 2015)

- Discussion of a recent study in China that found young adolescents with authoritative parents showed better adjustment than their counterparts with authoritarian parents (Zhang & others, 2017)

- New entry in Resources, *Motivation at School,* edited by Kathryn Wentzel and David Miele (2016), which explores many aspects of schools that influence students' achievement

Chapter 13: Socioemotional Development in Middle and Late Childhood

- New description of recent research studies indicating that children and adolescents who do not have good perspective-taking skills are more likely to have difficulty in peer relations and engage in more aggressive and oppositional behavior (Morosan & others, 2017; Nilsen & Basco, 2017; O'Kearney & others, 2017)

- Inclusion of a longitudinal study that revealed the quality of children's home environment (which involved assessment of parenting quality, cognitive stimulation, and the physical home environment) was linked to their self-esteem in early adulthood (Orth, 2017)

- Inclusion of recent research in which higher levels of self-control at 4 years of age were linked to improvements in math and reading achievement in the early elementary school years for children living predominantly in rural and low-income contexts (Blair & others, 2015)

- New description of an app that is effective in improving children's self-control: www.selfregulationstation.com/sr-ipad-app/

- New content on how during middle and late childhood, as part of their understanding of emotions, children can engage in "mental time travel," in which they anticipate and recall the cognitive and emotional aspects of events (Hjortsvang & Lagattuta, 2017; Kramer & Lagattuta, 2018; Lagattuta, 2014a, b)
- New section, "Social-Emotional Education Programs," that describes two increasingly implemented programs: (1) Second Step (Committee for Children, 2017) and (2) Collaborative for Academic, Social, and Emotional Learning (CASEL, 2017)
- New commentary on how children who have developed a number of coping techniques have the best chance of adapting and functioning competently in the face of disasters and traumas (Ungar, 2015)
- New section on Jonathan Haidt's (2013, 2017) criticism of Kohlberg's view of moral reasoning as always conscious and deliberate, and his lack of attention to the automatic, intuitive precursors of moral reasoning
- New section on criticism of Kohlberg's theory of moral development for not giving adequate attention to emotional influences (Gui, Gan, & Liu, 2016)
- Expanded and updated discussion of Darcia Narváez's view on how we need to make better progress in dealing with an increasing array of temptations and possible wrongdoings in a human social world in which complexity is accumulating over time (Christen, Narváez, & Gutzwiller, 2017)
- New commentary added about research indicating that young children's gender-typing is often rigid but becomes more flexible in middle and late childhood (Halim & others, 2016). Also, in some studies, girls' gender-typing becomes more flexible than boys' (Miller & others, 2009).
- New commentary about the multiple factors that may contribute to gender differences in academic achievement in areas such as reading and math (Wentzel & Miele, 2016)
- Inclusion of information from a meta-analysis in which females are better than males at recognizing nonverbal displays of emotion (Thompson & Voyer, 2014)
- Inclusion of recent research with eighth-grade students in 36 countries that revealed girls had more egalitarian attitudes about gender roles than did boys (Dotti Sani & Quaranta, 2017)
- New content on peer rejection being consistently linked to the development and maintenance of conduct problems (Chen, Drabick, & Burgers, 2015)
- Coverage of a recent study of young adolescents in which peer rejection predicted increases in aggressive and rule-breaking behavior (Janssens & others, 2017)
- Substantial expansion and updating of bullying and cyberbullying (Hall, 2017; Muijs, 2017; Zarate-Garza & others, 2017)
- Discussion of a recent analysis that concluded bullying can have long-term effects, including difficulty in establishing long-term relationships and difficulties at work (Wolke & Lereya, 2015)
- Description of a longitudinal study that revealed children who were bullied at 6 years of age were more likely to have excess weight gain when they were 12 to 13 years old (Sutin & others, 2016)
- Inclusion of a longitudinal study that revealed being a victim of bullying in childhood was linked to increased use of mental health services five decades later (Evans-Lacko & others, 2017)
- Description of recent longitudinal studies that indicated victims bullied in childhood and adolescence have higher rates of agoraphobia, depression, anxiety, panic disorder, and suicidality in their early to mid-twenties (Arseneault, 2017; Copeland & others, 2013)
- Coverage of recent research in which adolescents who were bullied in both a direct way and through cyberbullying had more behavioral problems and lower self-esteem than their counterparts who were bullied in only one of these ways (Wolke, Lee, & Guy, 2017)
- Description of a recent teacher intervention in elementary and secondary schools to decrease bullying that focused on increasing bullies' empathy and condemning their behavior; the intervention was effective in increasing the bullies' intent to stop bullying, but blaming the bully had no effect (Garandeau & others, 2016)
- New research review that found anti-bullying interventions that focused on the whole school, such as Olweus', were more effective than interventions involving classroom curricula or social skills training (Cantone & others, 2015)
- New content on the *Every Student Succeeds Act (ESSA)* that became U.S. law in December 2015 (Rothman, 2016). This law replaces *No Child Left Behind* and while not totally eliminating state standards for testing students, reduces their influence. Also, a 2017 update on ESSA with the Trump administration planning to go forward with ESSA but giving states much more flexibility in its implementation (Klein, 2017).
- Coverage of a recent intervention (City Connects program) with first-generation immigrant children attending high-poverty schools that was successful in improving the children's reading and math skills (Dearing & others, 2016)
- New entry in Resources; *The African American Child* (2nd ed.) by Yvette Harris and James Graham (2014), which provides valuable knowledge about African American children and their families in many different contexts
- New entry in Resources, *Cyberbullying and the Wild, Wild Web* by J.A. Hitchcock (2016), which provides excellent advice about preventing cyberbullying and what to do if it happens

Chapter 14: Physical Development in Adolescence

- Inclusion of a recent study of Chinese girls that confirmed childhood obesity contributed to an earlier onset of puberty (Zhai & others, 2015)

- Description of a recent study that revealed child sexual abuse was linked to earlier pubertal onset (Noll & others, 2017)

- Description of a recent research review that concluded there is insufficient quality research to confirm that changing testosterone levels in puberty are linked to adolescent males' mood and behavior (Duke, Glazer, & Steinbeck, 2014)

- Coverage of a recent Korean study in which early menarche was associated with risky sexual behavior in females (Cheong & others, 2015)

- Inclusion of a recent study that found early maturation predicted a stable higher level of depression for adolescent girls (Rudolph & others, 2014)

- New research indicating that early-maturing girls are at increased risk for physical and verbal abuse in dating (Chen, Rothman, & Jaffee, 2017)

- Discussion of a recent study that revealed early-maturing Chinese boys and girls engaged in delinquency more than their on-time or late-maturing counterparts (Chen & others, 2015)

- New summary of the influence of early and late maturation on adolescent development

- New discussion of neurotransmitter changes in adolescence, focusing especially on an increase in dopamine production (Monahan & others, 2016)

- Coverage of a longitudinal study that found 11- to 18-year-olds who lived in poverty conditions had diminished brain functioning at 25 years of age (Brody & others, 2017). However, those adolescents whose families participated in a supportive parenting intervention did not show this diminished brain functioning.

- New discussion of two recent studies of sexting, one indicating the frequency of sexting by high school students (Strassberg, Cann, & Velarde, 2017), the other documenting that for Latino adolescents, sexting is associated with engaging in oral, vaginal, and anal sex (Romo & others, 2017)

- Updated data on the occurrence of various sexual activities among adolescents according to age, gender, and ethnicity, including updates for Figures 5 and 6 (Kann & others, 2016a)

- New commentary that while the majority of sexual minority adolescents have competent and successful developmental paths through adolescence, a recent large-scale study revealed that sexual minority youth engage in a higher prevalence of health-risk factors than youth who are not part of a sexual minority group (Kann & others, 2016b)

- Updated data on the percentage of adolescent males and females who engage in oral sex (Child Trends, 2015)

- Description of a recent study that found early sexual debut was associated with a number of problems, including sexual risk taking, substance use, violent victimization, and suicidal thoughts and attempts in both sexual minority and heterosexual adolescents (Lowry & others, 2017)

- Discussion of a recent study of Korean girls in which early menarche was associated with earlier initiation of sexual intercourse (Kim & others, 2017)

- Description of a recent Swedish study of more than 3,000 adolescents indicating that sexual intercourse prior to age 14 was linked to a number of risky sexual behaviors at age 18 (Kastbom & others, 2015)

- Inclusion of recent research in which adolescents who in the eighth grade reported greater parental knowledge and more rules about dating were less likely to initiate sex between the eighth and tenth grades (Ethier & others, 2016)

- Discussion of a recent study of parenting practices that found the factor that best predicted a lower level of risky sexual behavior by adolescents was supportive parenting (Simons & others, 2016)

- New research indicating that adolescent males who play sports engage in more risky sexual behavior, while adolescent females who play sports engage in less risky sexual behavior (Lipowski & others, 2016)

- Updated data on the percentage of adolescents who use contraceptives when they have sexual intercourse (Kann & others, 2016)

- Important new section on the increasing number of medical organizations and experts who have recently recommended that adolescents use long-acting reversible contraception (LARC), which consists of intrauterine devices (IUDs) and contraceptive implants (Diedrich, Klein, & Peipert, 2017; Society for Adolescent Medicine, 2017)

- Updated data on the ongoing substantial decrease in adolescent pregnancy rates in the United States, especially among Latinas and African Americans (Martin, Hamilton, & Osterman, 2015)

- Inclusion of a recent cross-cultural study of adolescent pregnancy rates in 21 countries (Sedgh & others, 2015)

- Discussion of a recent study in which a higher level of education for adolescent mothers improved the achievement of their children through the eighth grade (Tang & others, 2016)

- Coverage of a recent study of long-term life outcomes for African American teen versus nonteen mothers and fathers in a number of areas (Assini-Meytim & Green, 2015)

- New research on factors linked to repeated adolescent pregnancy (Dee & others, 2017; Maravilla & others, 2017)

- Updated commentary on recent concerns about increased government funding of abstinence-only sexual education programs (Donovan, 2017)

- Updated data on the percentage of U.S. adolescents who are obese (Centers for Disease Control and Prevention, 2015)

- Description of a recent study in which participation in family meals during adolescence reduced the likelihood of becoming overweight or obese in adulthood (Berge & others, 2015)

- New research indicating that having an increase in Facebook friends across two years in adolescence was linked to an enhanced motivation to be thin (Tiggemann & Slater, 2017)

- Updated national data on adolescents' exercise patterns, including gender and ethnic variations (Kann & others, 2016)

- Updated data on significant gender differences in exercise during adolescence, with females exercising far less than males (YRBSS, 2016)

- Coverage of recent research indicating that a combination of regular exercise and a diet plan results in weight loss and enhanced executive function in adolescents (Xie & others, 2017)

- Inclusion of recent research in which an exercise program of 180 minutes per week improved the sleep patterns of obese adolescents (Mendelson & others, 2016)

- Discussion of a recent study in which a high-intensity exercise program decreased depressive symptoms and improved the moods of depressed adolescents (Carter & others, 2016)

- Description of a recent research review that identified memory as the cognitive factor that was most often improved by exercise in adolescence (Li & others, 2017)

- Coverage of a large-scale study of more than 270,000 adolescents from 1991–2012 that found adolescents have been decreasing the amount of sleep they get in recent years (Keyes & others, 2015)

- Description of recent Swedish studies of 16- to 19-year-olds in which shorter sleep duration was associated with a greater likelihood of school absences, and shorter sleep duration and sleep deficits were linked to having a lower grade point average (Hysing & others, 2015, 2016)

- Discussion of a recent experimental study in which restricting adolescents' sleep to five hours for five nights and then restoring it to ten hours for two nights negatively affected their sustained attention, especially in the early morning (Agostini & others, 2017)

- Inclusion of a recent national study of more than 10,000 13- to 18-year-olds that found a number of factors involving sleep timing and duration were associated with increased rates of anxiety, mood, substance abuse, and behavioral disorders (Zhang & others, 2017)

- Coverage of a longitudinal study of adolescents in which poor sleep patterns were linked to an increased likelihood of drinking alcohol and using marijuana four years later (Miller, Janssen, & Jackson, 2017)

- Discussion of a recent study that revealed early school start times were linked to a higher vehicle crash rate by adolescent drivers (Vorona & others, 2014)

- Inclusion of the recent recommendation by the American Academy of Pediatrics that schools institute start times from 8:30 to 9:30 a.m. to improve students' academic performance and quality of life (Adolescent Sleep Working Group, AAP, 2014)

- Updated coverage of the Monitoring the Future study's assessment of drug use by secondary school students, with 2016 data on U.S. eighth-, tenth-, and twelfth-graders (Johnston & others, 2017)

- New content on e-cigarette use by adolescents, which now surpasses traditional cigarette smoking among eighth-, tenth-, and twelfth-grade students (Johnston & others, 2017)

- Description of a longitudinal study in which earlier age at first use of alcohol was linked to increased risk of heavy alcohol use in early adulthood (Liang & Chikritzhs, 2015)

- New research that revealed early- and rapid-onset trajectories of alcohol, marijuana, and substance use were associated with substance use in early adulthood (Nelson, Van Ryzin, & Dishion, 2015)

- New website entry in Resources, http://kidshealth.org/en/parents/adolescence.html#, which provides excellent advice for parents, helping them understand, guide, and converse with teens about many topics, including puberty, sleep problems, body image, and drugs

Chapter 15: Cognitive Development in Adolescence

- New discussion of a recent meta-analysis that concluded greater use of social networking sites was linked to a higher level of narcissism (Gnambs & Appel, 2017)

- Revised discussion of information processing in adolescence based on recommendations by leading expert Valerie Reyna

- Coverage of a recent study that found adolescent binge drinkers had working memory deficits (Carbia & others, 2017)

- Discussion of a recent study in which adolescents took greater risks when they were with three same-aged peers than when they were alone (Silva, Chein, & Steinberg, 2016)

- Updated coverage of the fuzzy-trace theory dual-process model of adolescent decision making (Brust-Renck & others, 2017; Reyna & others, 2015; Reyna & Zayas, 2014)

- Inclusion of information about a recent experiment that showed encouraging gist-based thinking about risks (along with factual information) reduced self-reported risk taking up to one year after exposure to the curriculum (Reyna & Mills, 2014)

- Updated data on the goals of first-year college students in relation to the relative importance they assign to developing a meaningful philosophy of life versus becoming very well off financially (Eagan & others, 2016)

- Coverage of a recent study of young adolescent Chinese students that revealed engaging in more gratitude was associated with higher well-being at school (Ekema-Agbaw, McCutchen, & Geller, 2016)

- Description of a recent study that revealed adolescents who had a lower level of spirituality were more likely to engage in substance use (Debnam & others, 2016)

- Discussion of recent research on African American adolescent girls that found those who reported that religion was of low or moderate importance to them had an earlier sexual debut than did their counterparts who indicated that religion was extremely important to them (George Dalmida & others, 2017)

- New content on why the transition to high school may produce problems for students (Eccles & Roeser, 2015)

- Updated data on school dropouts, including the dramatic decrease in dropout rates for Latino adolescents in recent years (National Center for Education Statistics, 2016)

- Inclusion of new information on the Bill and Melinda Gates Foundation's (2011, 2016) funding of a new generation of digital courseware to improve students' learning

- Updates on the expansion of "I Have a Dream" programs to 28 states plus Washington, DC, and New Zealand ("I Have a Dream Foundation," 2017)

- Coverage of recent research in which immigrant adolescents who participated in extracurricular activities improved their academic achievement and increased their school engagement (Camacho & Fuligni, 2015)

- Discussion of a recent Australian study that found participation in extracurricular activities during the eighth grade was linked to a lower likelihood of binge drinking through the eleventh grade (Modecki, Barber, & Eccles, 2014)

Chapter 16: Socioemotional Development in Adolescence

- Revisions based on recommendations from leading expert Kate McLean

- New coverage of the narrative approach to identity, which involves having individuals tell their life stories and evaluate the extent to which the stories are meaningful and integrated (Adler & others, 2017; Maher, Winston, & Ur, 2017)

- Inclusion of a recent study that examined identity domains using both identity status and narrative approaches with the interpersonal domain (especially dating and friendship aspects) frequently mentioned (McLean & others, 2016). In the narrative approach, family stories were common.

- Coverage of two recent studies that found a strong and positive ethnic identity was linked to a lower incidence of substance abuse and psychiatric problems (Anglin & others, 2017; Grindal & Nieri, 2016)

- New discussion of recent longitudinal studies that revealed the ethnic identity of adolescents is influenced by positive and diverse friendships (Rivas-Drake & others, 2017; Santos & others, 2017)

- New main section on gender classification

- Changes in the discussion of gender based on feedback from leading expert Stephanie Budge

- New coverage of the gender classification category of transgender (Budge & others, 2017; Moradi & others, 2016; Savin-Williams, 2017)

- Inclusion of a recent research review that concluded transgender youth are more likely to have depression, suicide attempts, and eating disorders than their non-transgender peers (Connolly & others, 2016). This discussion also

highlights some of the reasons for the higher rate of these disorders in transgender individuals (Zucker, Lawrence, & Kreukels, 2016).

- Inclusion of recent research with fifth- to eighth-graders in which higher grades were associated with a higher level of parental monitoring (Top, Liew, & Luo, 2017)

- Description of recent research in which higher parental monitoring reduced negative peer influence on adolescent risk-taking (Wang & others, 2016)

- Coverage of a recent meta-analysis that found a higher level of parental monitoring and rule enforcement were linked to later initiation of sexual intercourse and increased use of condoms by adolescents (Dittus & others, 2016)

- New research on 10- to 18-year-olds in which lower disclosure to parents was linked to antisocial behavior (Chriss & others, 2015)

- Description of recent research that found snooping was a relatively infrequent parental monitoring technique (compared with solicitation and control) but was a better indicator of problems in adolescent and family functioning (Hawk, Becht, & Branje, 2016)

- Inclusion of a recent study that revealed from 16 to 20 years of age, adolescents perceived that they had increasing independence and a better relationship with their parents (Hadiwijaya & others, 2017)

- Coverage of a recent study that revealed insecure attachment to mothers was linked to becoming depressed and remaining depressed at 15 to 20 years of age (Agerup & others, 2015)

- Discussion of a recent study of Latino families that revealed a higher level of secure attachment with mothers during adolescence was linked to a lower level of heavy drug use (Gattamorta & others, 2017)

- New research of a longitudinal study that found a secure base of attachment knowledge in adolescence and emerging adulthood was predicted by observations of maternal sensitivity across childhood and adolescence (Waters, Ruiz, & Roisman, 2017)

- Coverage of recent research indicating that most adolescents have a fairly stable attachment style but that attachment stability increases in adulthood (Jones & others, 2017). Also in this study, family conflict and parental separation/divorce were likely candidates for undermining attachment stability.

- Description of a study in which high levels of parent-adolescent conflict were associated with lower levels of empathy across a six-year period (Van Lissa & others, 2015)

- Inclusion of a recent study that found higher levels of parent-adolescent conflict were linked to higher anxiety, depression, and aggression, and lower self-esteem (Smokowski & others, 2017)

- New research on Chinese American families that revealed parent-adolescent conflict was linked to a sense of alienation between parents and adolescents, which in turn was related to more depressive symptoms, delinquent behavior, and lower academic achievement (Hou, Kim, & Wang, 2016)

- Discussion of a recent study that found boys were more likely to be influenced by peer pressure involving sexual behavior than were girls (Widman & others, 2016)

- Coverage of a recent research review that concluded good peer relationships were an important factor in achieving a positive identity (Ragelienė, 2016)

- Description of recent research in which adolescents adapted their smoking and drinking behavior to reflect that of their best friends (Wang & others, 2016b)

- Inclusion of recent research on adolescent girls that found friends' dieting predicted whether adolescent girls would engage in dieting or extreme dieting (Balantekin, Birch, & Savage, 2017)

- Discussion of a recent study that found friendship quality was linked to the quality of romantic relationships in adolescence (Kochendorfer & Kerns, 2017)

- Inclusion of recent research in which having a supportive romantic relationship in adolescence was linked with positive outcomes for adolescents who had a negative relationship with their mother (Szwedo, Hessel, & Allen, 2017)

- Discussion of recent research that revealed mother-daughter conflict in Mexican American families was linked to an increase in daughters' romantic involvement (Tyrell & others, 2016)

- Description of a recent study comparing Asian, Latino, and non-Latino immigrant adolescents in which immigrant Asian adolescents had the highest level of depression, lowest self-esteem, and experienced the most discrimination (Lo & others, 2017)

- Inclusion of a recent research review in which a higher level of media multitasking was linked to lower levels of school achievement, executive function, and growth mindset in adolescents (Cain & others, 2016)

- Discussion of a recent study in which heavy media multitaskers were less likely to delay gratification and more likely to endorse intuitive, but wrong, answers on a cognitive reflection task (Schutten, Stokes, & Arnell, 2017)

- Coverage of recent research that found less screen time was linked to adolescents' better health-related quality of life (Wang & others, 2016a) and that a higher level of social media use was associated with a higher level of heavy drinking by adolescents (Brunborg, Andreas, & Kvaavik, 2017)

- Updated data on the percentage of adolescents who use social networking sites and engage in text messaging daily (Lenhart, 2015a, b)

- New content indicating that at 12 years of age, 5.2 percent of females and 2 percent of males had experienced first-onset depression (Breslau & others, 2017). Also in this study, the cumulative incidence of depression from 12 to 17 years of age was 36 percent for females and 14 percent for boys.

- Inclusion of a recent study that revealed adolescents who were isolated from their peers and whose caregivers emotionally neglected them were at significant risk for developing depression (Christ, Kwak, & Lu, 2017)

- Description of a recent meta-analysis in which adolescent females who were obese were more likely to have depression (Quek & others, 2017)

- Coverage of a recent study in which having friends who engage in delinquency is associated with early onset and more persistent delinquency (Evans, Simons, & Simons, 2016)

- Inclusion of a recent study of more than 10,000 children and adolescents revealing that a family environment characterized by poverty and child maltreatment was linked to entering the juvenile justice system in adolescence (Vidal & others, 2017)

- Inclusion of recent research in which having callous-unemotional traits predicts an increased risk of engaging in delinquency for adolescent males (Ray & others, 2017)

- New content on the link between low academic success and delinquency (Mercer & others, 2015) and the association of cognitive factors, such as low self-control, with delinquency (Fine & others, 2016)

- Discussion of a recent study that revealed family therapy improved juvenile court outcomes beyond what was achieved in non-family based treatment, especially in reducing criminal behavior and re-arrests (Dakof & others, 2015)

- New coverage of the roles of stress and loss in adolescent depression and inclusion of a recent study that found adolescents who became depressed were characterized by a sense of hopelessness (Weersing & others, 2016)

- Inclusion of recent research indicating that adolescents who were being treated in a suicide clinic experienced lower family cohesion than nonclinical adolescents and adolescents who were treated in a general psychiatric clinic (Jakobsen, Larson, & Horwood, 2017)

- New description of a recent study that found adolescent girls' greater experience of interpersonal dependent stress was linked to their higher level of rumination, which accounted for higher levels of depressive symptoms in girls compared with boys (Hamilton & others, 2015)

- Description of a recent study in which family therapy improved juvenile court outcomes beyond what was achieved in non-family-based treatment (Dakof & others, 2015)

- Inclusion of recent research that revealed positive parenting characteristics were associated with less depression in adolescents (Smokowski & others, 2015)

- New information from a research review that concluded SSRIs show clinical benefits for adolescents at risk for moderate and severe depression (Cousins & Goodyer, 2015)

- Updated data on the percentage of U.S. adolescents who seriously consider suicide each year (Kann & others, 2016)

- Discussion of recent research indicating that the most significant factor in a first suicide attempt during adolescence was major depressive episode, while for children it was child maltreatment (Peyre & others, 2017)

- Inclusion of recent research in which both depression and hopelessness were predictors of whether adolescents would repeat a suicide attempt across a six-month period (Consoli & others, 2015)

- Description of two recent studies that revealed maltreatment during childhood was linked with suicide attempts in adulthood (Park, 2017; Turner & others, 2017)

- Coverage of a recent study that found child maltreatment was linked to adolescent suicide attempts (Hadland & others, 2015)

- New research in which a lower level of school connectedness was associated with increased suicidal ideation in female and male adolescents, and with suicide attempts by female adolescents (Langille & others, 2015)

- New coverage of the most recent research on the Fast Track program in which one-third of its reduction in later crime outcomes in emerging adulthood was accounted for by improvements in social and self-regulation skills at 6 to 11 years of age (Sorensen, Dodge, and the Conduct Problems Prevention Research Group, 2016)

- New entry in Resources, *Age of Opportunity* by Laurence Steinberg (2014), which provides valuable information for parents, teachers, and other adults who work with adolescents

Acknowledgments

I very much appreciate the support and guidance provided to me by many people at McGraw-Hill. Ryan Treat, Portfolio Manager for Psychology, has provided excellent guidance, vision, and direction for this book. Vicki Malinee provided considerable expertise in coordinating many aspects of the editorial process for this text. Janet Tilden again did an outstanding job as the book's copy editor. Mary Powers did a terrific job in coordinating the book's production. Dawn Groundwater, Lead Product Developer, did excellent work on various aspects of the book's development, technology, and learning systems. Thanks also to Ann Helgerson for her extensive and outstanding work in marketing *Children*. And Jennifer Blankenship provided me with excellent choices of new photographs for this edition of the book.

I also want to thank my wife, Mary Jo, for her unwavering support of my writing and books over a number of decades. And special thanks to our children, Tracy and Jennifer, and more recently our granddaughter, Jordan, and grandsons, Alex and Luke, for providing many special moments that have helped to shape my thinking about how children and adolescents develop.

EXPERT CONSULTANTS

As I develop a new edition of this text, I consult with leading experts in their respective areas of child and adolescent development. Their invaluable feedback ensures that the latest research, understandings, and perspectives are presented throughout the text. Their willingness to devote their time and expertise to this endeavor is greatly appreciated. Coverage of the Expert Consultants who contributed to this edition, along with their biographies and commentary, can be found on pages xii–xiii.

REVIEWERS

I owe a special debt of gratitude to the reviewers who have provided detailed feedback on *Children* over the years.

John A. Addleman, *Messiah College;* **Linda Anderson,** *Northwestern Michigan College;* **Christine Anthis,** *Southern Connecticut State University;* **Harry H. Avis,** *Sierra College;* **Diana Baumrind,** *University of California–Berkeley;* **Lori A. Beasley,** *University of Central Oklahoma;* **Patricia J. Bence,** *Tompkins Cortland Community College;* **Michael Bergmire,** *Jefferson College;* **Belinda Blevins-Knabe,** *University of Arkansas–Little Rock;* **Albert Bramante,** *Union County College;* **Ruth Brinkman,** *St. Louis Community College, Florissant Valley;* **Eileen Donahue Brittain,** *City College of Harry S Truman;* **Urie Bronfenbrenner,** *Cornell University;* **Phyllis Bronstein,** *University of Vermont;* **Dan W. Brunworth,** *Kishwaukee College;* **Carole Burke-Braxton,** *Austin Community College;* **Jo Ann Burnside,** *Richard J. Daley College;* **Victoria Candelora,** *Brevard Community College;* **Alison S. Carson,** *Hofstra University;* **Rosalind Charlesworth,** *Weber State University;* **Nancy Coghill,** *University of Southwest Louisiana;* **Malinda**

Jo Colwell, *Texas Tech University;* **Jennifer Cousins,** *University of Houston;* **Dixie R. Crase,** *Memphis State University;* **Kathleen Crowley-Long,** *The College of Saint Rose;* **Florence Denmark,** *Pace University;* **Sheridan DeWolf,** *Grossmont Community College;* **Swen H. Digranes,** *Northeastern State University;* **Ruth Doyle,** *Casper College;* **Laura Duvall,** *Heartland Community College;* **Celina V. Echols,** *Southeastern Louisiana State University;* **Beverly Edmondson,** *Buena Vista University;* **Timothy P. Eicher,** *Dixie Community College;* **Sarah Erikson,** *University of New Mexico;* **Jennifer Fager,** *Western Michigan University;* **Karen Falcone,** *San Joaquin Delta College;* **JoAnn Farver,** *Oklahoma State University;* **Greta Fein,** *University of Maryland;* **Tiffany Field,** *University of Miami (FL);* **Johanna Filp,** *Sonoma State University;* **Kate Fogarty,** *University of Florida–Gainesville;* **Cheryl Fortner-Wood,** *Winthrop College;* **Dale Fryxell,** *Chaminade University;* **Janet Fuller,** *Mansfield University;* **Thomas Gerry,** *Columbia Greene Community College;* **Sam Givhan,** *Minnesota State University;* **Art Gonchar,** *University of La Verne;* **Sandra Graham,** *University of California–Los Angeles;* **Susan Hale,** *Holyoke Community College;* **Barbara Springer Hammons,** *Palomar College;* **Cory Anne Hansen,** *Arizona State University;* **Barbara H. Harkness,** *San Bernardino Valley College;* **Algea Harrison,** *Oakland University;* **Susan Heidrich,** *University of Wisconsin;* **Ashleigh Hillier,** *Ohio University;* **Alice S. Hoenig,** *Syracuse University;* **Sally Hoppstetter,** *Palo Alto College;* **Robert J. Ivy,** *George Mason University;* **Diane Carlson Jones,** *Texas A&M University;* **Ellen Junn,** *Indiana University;* **Marcia Karwas,** *California State University–Monterey;* **Melvyn B. King,** *State College of New York at Cortland;* **Kathleen Kleissler,** *Kutztown University;* **Dene G. Klinzing,** *University of Delaware;* **Claire B. Kopp,** *University of California–Los Angeles;* **Cally Beth Kostakis,** *Rockland Community College;* **Tara L. Kuther,** *Western Connecticut State University;* **Linda Lavine,** *State University of New York–Cortland;* **Sara Lawrence,** *California State University–Northridge;* **Hsin-Hui Lin,** *University of Houston–Victoria;* **Gloria Lopez,** *Sacramento City College;* **James E. Marcia,** *Simon Fraser University;* **Deborah N. Margolis,** *Boston College;* **Julie Ann McIntyre,** *Russell Sage College;* **Mary Ann McLaughlin,** *Clarion University;* **Chloe Merrill,** *Weber State College;* **Karla Miley,** *Black Hawk College;* **Jody Miller,** *Los Angeles Pierce College;* **Carrie L. Mori,** *Boise State University;* **Joyce Munsch,** *California State University–Northridge;* **Barbara J. Myers,** *Virginia Commonwealth University;* **Jeffrey Nagelbush,** *Ferris State University;* **Sonia Nieves,** *Broward Community College;* **Caroline Olko,** *Nassau Community College;* **Sandy Osborne,** *Montana State University;* **William H. Overman,** *University of North Carolina–Wilmington;* **Michelle Paludi,** *Michelle Paludi & Affiliates;* **Susan Peet,** *Bowling Green State University;* **Pete Peterson,** *Johnson County Community College;* **Joe Price,** *San Diego State University;* **Charles L. Reid,** *Essex County College;* **Barbara Reynolds,** *College of the Sequoias;* **Cynthia Rickert,** *Dominican College;* **Richard Riggle,** *Coe College;* **Lynne Rompelman,** *Concordia University–Wisconsin;* **James A. Rysberg,** *California State*

University–Chico; **Marcia Rysztak,** *Lansing Community College;* **David Sadker,** *The American University, Washington, DC;* **Peter C. Scales,** *Search Institute;* **Pamela Schuetze-Pizarro,** *Buffalo State College;* **Pamela A. Schulze,** *University of Akron;* **Diane Scott-Jones,** *University of Illinois;* **Clyde Shepherd,** *Keene State College;* **Carol S. Soule,** *Appalachian State University;* **Dorothy D. Sweeney,** *Bristol Community College;* **Anita Thomas,** *Northeastern Illinois University;* **Ross A. Thompson,** *University of Nebraska–Lincoln;* **Kourtney Vaillancourt,** *New Mexico State University;* **Naomi Wagner,** *San Jose State University;* **Richard L. Wagner,** *Mount Senario College;* **Patricia J. Wall,** *Northern Arizona University;* **Dorothy A. Wedge,** *Fairmont State College;* **Carla Graham Wells,** *Odessa College;* **Teion Wells,** *Florida State University;* **Becky G. West,** *Coahoma Community College;* **Alida Westman,** *Eastern Michigan University;* **Allan Wigfield,** *University of Maryland, College Park;* **Marilyn E. Willis,** *Indiana University of Pennsylvania;* **Mary E. Wilson,** *Northern Essex Community College;* **Susan D. Witt,** *University of Akron;* **Bonnie Wright,** *Gardner Webb University;* **Sarah Young,** *Longwood College;* **William H. Zachry,** *University of Tennessee–Martin*

If I had my child to raise over again

If I had my child to raise over again,

I'd finger paint more, and point the finger less.

I'd do less correcting, and more connecting.

I'd take my eyes off my watch, and watch with my eyes.

I would care to know less, and know to care more.

I'd take more hikes and fly more kites.

I'd stop playing serious, and seriously play.

I would run through more fields, and gaze at more stars.

I'd do more hugging, and less tugging.

I would be firm less often, and affirm much more.

I'd build self-esteem first, and the house later.

I'd teach less about the love of power,

And more about the power of love.

—DIANE LOOMANS

*In every child who is born, under no matter what circumstances,
and of no matter what parents, the potentiality of the human race
is born again.*

—JAMES AGEE
American Writer, 20th Century

©Ariel Skelley/Blend Images/Getty Images RF

The Nature of Children's Development

Examining the shape of childhood allows us to understand it better. Every childhood is distinct, the first chapter of a new biography in the world. This book is about children's development, its universal features, its individual variations, its nature at the beginning of the twenty-first century. *Children* is about the rhythm and meaning of children's lives, about turning mystery into understanding, and about weaving together a portrait of who each of us was, is, and will be. In Section 1 you will read "Introduction."

chapter 1

INTRODUCTION

chapter outline

① Why Is Caring for Children Important?

Learning Goal 1 Explain why it is important to study children's development, and identify five areas in which children's lives need to be improved.

The Importance of Studying Children's Development

Improving the Lives of Children

② What Characterizes Development?

Learning Goal 2 Discuss processes, periods, cohort effects, and issues in development.

Biological, Cognitive, and Socioemotional Processes

Periods of Development

Age and Cohort Effects

Issues in Development

③ How Is Child Development a Science?

Learning Goal 3 Summarize why research is important in child development, the main theories of child development, and research methods, designs, and challenges.

The Importance of Research

Theories of Child Development

Research Methods for Collecting Data

Research Designs

Research Challenges

©KidStock/Blend Images/age fotostock RF

Ted Kaczynski, the convicted Unabomber, traced his difficulties to growing up as a genius in a kid's body and not fitting in when he was a child.

©Seanna O'Sullivan

Ted Kaczynski, about age 14.
©WBBM-TV/AFP/Getty Images

What might be some reasons Alice Walker was able to overcome trauma in her childhood and develop in impressive ways?
©AP Images

Alice Walker, about age 8.
Courtesy of Alice Walker

Ted Kaczynski sprinted through high school, not bothering with his junior year and making only passing efforts at social contact. Off to Harvard at age 16, Kaczynski was a loner during his college years. One of his roommates at Harvard said that he avoided people by quickly shuffling by them and slamming the door behind him. After obtaining his Ph.D. in mathematics at the University of Michigan, Kaczynski became a professor at the University of California at Berkeley. His colleagues there remember him as hiding from social circumstances—no friends, no allies, no networking.

After several years at Berkeley, Kaczynski resigned and moved to a rural area of Montana where he lived as a hermit in a crude shack for 25 years. Town residents described him as a bearded eccentric. Kaczynski traced his own difficulties to growing up as a genius in a kid's body and sticking out like a sore thumb in his surroundings as a child. In 1996, he was arrested and charged as the notorious Unabomber, America's most wanted killer. Over the course of 17 years, Kaczynski had sent 16 mail bombs that left 23 people wounded or maimed and 3 people dead. In 1998, he pleaded guilty to the offenses and was sentenced to life in prison.

A decade before Kaczynski mailed his first bomb, Alice Walker spent her days battling racism in Mississippi. She had recently won her first writing fellowship, but rather than use the money to follow her dream of moving to Senegal, Africa, she put herself into the heart and heat of the civil rights movement. Walker had grown up knowing the brutal effects of poverty and racism. Born in 1944, she was the eighth child of Georgia sharecroppers who earned $300 a year. When Walker was 8, her brother accidentally shot her in the left eye with a BB gun. Because her parents had no car, it took them a week to get her to a hospital. By the time she received medical care, she was blind in that eye, and it had developed a disfiguring layer of scar tissue. Despite the counts against her, Walker overcame pain and anger and went on to win a Pulitzer Prize for her book *The Color Purple*. She became not only a novelist but also an essayist, a poet, a short-story writer, and a social activist.

What leads one individual, so full of promise, to commit brutal acts of violence and another to turn poverty and trauma into a rich literary harvest? If you have ever wondered why people turn out the way they do, you have asked yourself the central question we will explore.

preview

Why study children? Perhaps you are, or will be, a parent or teacher, and responsibility for children is, or will be, a part of your everyday life. The more you learn about children, the better you can guide them. Perhaps you hope to gain an understanding of your own history—as an infant, as a child, and as an adolescent. Perhaps you accidentally came across the course description and found it intriguing. Whatever your reasons, you will discover that the study of child development is provocative, intriguing, and informative. In this chapter, we explore why caring for children is so important, describe historical changes in the study of children's development, examine the nature of development, and outline how science helps us to understand it.

1 Why Is Caring for Children Important?

LG1 Explain why it is important to study children's development, and identify five areas in which children's lives need to be improved.

> The Importance of Studying Children's Development

> Improving the Lives of Children

Caring for children is an important theme of this text. To think about why caring for children is such an important theme, we will explore why it is beneficial to study children's development and identify some areas in which children's lives need to be improved.

Just what do we mean when we speak of an individual's development? **Development** is the pattern of change that begins at conception and continues throughout the life span. Most development involves growth, although it also includes decline.

THE IMPORTANCE OF STUDYING CHILDREN'S DEVELOPMENT

How might you benefit from examining children's development? Perhaps you are, or will be, a parent or teacher and you want to learn about children so that you can become a better parent or educator. Perhaps you hope to gain some insight about how your childhood experiences have shaped the person you are today. Or perhaps you think that the study of children's development might raise some provocative issues. Whatever your reasons for reading this book, you will discover that the study of children's development is fascinating and filled with information about who we are and how we came to be this way.

As we indicated earlier, most human development involves growth, but it also includes decline. For example, think about how your ability to speak and write your native language has grown since you were a young child. But your ability to achieve a high level of competence in learning to speak a new language has probably declined (Thomas & Johnson, 2008). In this book, we examine children's development from the point of conception through adolescence. You will see yourself as an infant, as a child, and as an adolescent—and be stimulated to think about how those years influenced you.

IMPROVING THE LIVES OF CHILDREN

If you were to pick up a newspaper or magazine in any U.S. town or city, you might see headlines like these: "Political Leanings May Be Written in the Genes," "Mother Accused of Tossing Children into Bay," "Gender Gap Widens," and "FDA Warns About ADHD Drug." Researchers are examining these and many other topics of contemporary concern. The roles that health and well-being, parenting, education, and sociocultural contexts play in children's development, as well as how social policy is related to these issues, are a special focus of this edition.

Health and Well-Being Does a pregnant woman endanger her fetus if she has a few beers a week? How does a poor diet affect a child's ability to learn? Are children getting less exercise today than in the past? What roles do parents and peers play in whether adolescents

---

We reach backward to our parents and forward to our children and through their children to a future we will never see, but about which we need to care.

—CARL JUNG
Swiss Psychoanalytic Theorist, 20th Century

Ah! What would the world be to us
If the children were no more?
We should dread the desert behind us
Worse than the dark before.

—HENRY WADSWORTH LONGFELLOW
American Poet, 19th Century

development The pattern of movement or change that begins at conception and continues through the human life span.

Luis Vargas, Clinical Child Psychologist

Luis Vargas conducts a child therapy session.
Courtesy of Luis Vargas

Luis Vargas is the director of the Clinical Child Psychology Internship Program and a professor in child and adolescent psychiatry at the University of New Mexico School of Medicine. Vargas obtained an undergraduate degree in psychology from Trinity University in Texas and a Ph.D. in clinical psychology at the University of Nebraska–Lincoln.

Vargas' work includes assessing and treating children, adolescents, and their families, especially when a child or adolescent has a serious mental disorder. He also trains mental health professionals to provide culturally responsive and developmentally appropriate mental health services. In addition, he is interested in cultural and assessment issues involving children, adolescents, and their families. He co-authored (with Joan Koss-Chioino, a medical anthropologist) *Working with Latino Youth: Culture, Context, and Development* (Koss-Chioino & Vargas, 1999).

Vargas' clinical work is heavily influenced by contextual and ecological theories of development (which we discuss later in this chapter). His first undergraduate course in human development, and subsequent courses in development, contributed to his decision to pursue a career in clinical child psychology.

For more information about the work of clinical child psychologists, see the Careers in Child Development Appendix.

---

abuse drugs? Throughout this text we discuss many questions like these regarding health and well-being. Investigating these questions, and exploring possible answers, is an important goal for just about everyone.

Health professionals today recognize the influence of lifestyles and psychological states on health and well-being (Blake, 2017; Hales, 2018; Insel & Roth, 2016; Rolfes, Pinna, & Whitney, 2018). In every chapter of this edition, issues of health and well-being are integrated into our discussion.

Clinical psychologists are among the health professionals who help people improve their well-being. In this chapter's *Connecting with Careers* profile, you can read about clinical psychologist Luis Vargas, who helps adolescents with problems. The Careers Appendix for this text describes the education and training required to become a clinical psychologist and to pursue other careers in child development.

Parenting Can two gay men raise a healthy family? Are children harmed if both parents work outside the home? Do adopted children fare as well as children raised by their biological parents? How damaging is divorce to children's development? We hear many questions like these related to pressures on the contemporary family (Cicchetti, 2017; Lockhart & others, 2017; Walsh, DeFlorio, & Burnham, 2017). We examine these questions and others that provide a context for understanding factors that influence parents' lives and how effectively they rear their children. How parents, as well as other adults, can make a positive difference in children's lives is a major theme of this edition.

You might become a parent someday or might already be one. You should take seriously the importance of rearing your children, because they are the future of our society. Good parenting takes considerable time. If you plan to become a parent, commit yourself day after day, week after week, month after month, and year after year to providing your children with a warm, supportive, safe, and stimulating environment that will make them feel secure and allow them to reach their full potential as human beings. The poster shown on this page, which states "Children learn to love when they are loved," reflects this theme.

Children learn to love when they are loved

©Robert Maust/Photo Agora

Understanding the nature of children's development can help you become a better parent (Carlo & others, 2017; Gershoff, Lee, & Durant, 2017; Nieto & Bode, 2018). Many parents learn parenting practices from their parents. Unfortunately, when parenting practices and child-care strategies are passed from one generation to the next, both desirable and undesirable ones are usually perpetuated. This book and your instructor's lectures in this course can help you become more knowledgeable about children's development and decide which practices in your own upbringing you should continue with your children and which you should abandon.

Education   There is widespread agreement that something needs to be done to improve the education of our nation's children (Borich, 2017; Bredekamp, 2017; Johnson & others, 2018; Morrison, 2018). A number of questions are involved in improving schools. For example, are they failing to teach children how to read and write and calculate adequately? Should there be more accountability in schools, with effectiveness of student learning and teaching assessed by formal tests? Should teachers have higher expectations for children? Should schooling involve less memorization and more attention to the development of children's ability to process information efficiently? In this text, we examine such questions about the state of education in the United States and consider recent research on solutions to educational problems.

Sociocultural Contexts and Diversity   Health and well-being, parenting, and education—like development itself—are all shaped by their sociocultural context (Cummings & others, 2017; Duncan, Magnuson, & Votruba-Drzal, 2017). The term **context** refers to the settings in which development occurs. These settings are influenced by historical, economic, social, and cultural factors (Masumoto & Juang, 2017). Four contexts to which we pay special attention in this text are culture, ethnicity, socioeconomic status, and gender.

Culture encompasses the behavior patterns, beliefs, and all other products of a specific group of people that are passed on from generation to generation. Culture results from the interaction of people over many years (Masumoto & Juang, 2017). A cultural group can be as large as the United States or as small as an isolated Appalachian town. Whatever its size, the group's culture influences the behavior of its members. **Cross-cultural studies** compare aspects of two or more cultures. The comparison provides information about the degree to which development is similar, or universal, across cultures, or is instead culture-specific (Chen & Liu, 2016; Vignoles & others, 2016).

Ethnicity (the word *ethnic* comes from the Greek word for "nation") is rooted in cultural heritage, nationality, race, religion, and language. African Americans, Latinos, Asian Americans, Native Americans, Polish Americans, and Italian Americans are a few examples of ethnic groups. Diversity exists within each ethnic group (Gollnick & Chinn, 2017; Gonzales & others, 2016; Nieto & Bode, 2018).

Relatively high rates of minority immigration have contributed to the growth in the proportion of ethnic minorities in the U.S. population (Cano & others, 2017; Chaudry & others, 2017). In 2014, 62 percent of children 18 years and younger were non-Latino White; by 2060, this figure is projected to decrease to 44 percent (Colby & Ortman, 2015). In 2014 in the United States, 17 percent were Latino but in 2060 that figure is projected to increase to 29 percent. Asian Americans are expected to be the fastest-growing ethnic group of children: In 2014, 5 percent were Asian American and that figure is expected to grow to 9 percent in 2060. The percent of African American children is anticipated to increase slightly from 2014 to 2060 (12.4 to 13 percent).

Contrary to stereotypes, not all African Americans live in low-income circumstances; not all Latinos are Catholics; not all Asian Americans are high school math whizzes. A special concern is the discrimination and prejudice experienced by ethnic minority children (Spencer & Swanson, 2016).

What are some questions that need to be answered when thinking about improving U.S. schools?
©iStockphoto RF

How Would You...?
If you were a **psychologist**, how would you explain the importance of examining sociocultural factors in developmental research?

context The settings, influenced by historical, economic, social, and cultural factors, in which development occurs.

culture The behavior patterns, beliefs, and all other products of a group that are passed on from generation to generation.

cross-cultural studies Comparisons of one culture with one or more other cultures. These comparisons provide information about the degree to which children's development is similar, or universal, across cultures, and the degree to which it is culture-specific.

ethnicity A characteristic based on cultural heritage, nationality, race, religion, and language.

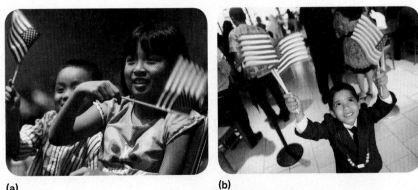

(a)   **(b)**

(*a*) These two Korean-born children on the day they became U.S. citizens represent the dramatic increase in the percentage of ethnic minority children in the United States.
(*b*) Inderjeet Poolust, 5, from India celebrates being one of 27 schoolchildren who recently became U.S. citizens at an induction ceremony in Queens, New York.
©Skip O'Rourke/Zuma Press Inc./Alamy; ©Debbie Egan-Chin/NY Daily News Archive/Getty Images

developmental **connection**

Socioeconomic Status

Growing up in poverty is linked to negative outcomes for children's language skill. Connect to "Cognitive Development in Infancy."

socioeconomic status (SES) An individual's position within society based on occupational, educational, and economic characteristics.

Ann Masten with a homeless family who is participating in her research on resilience. She and her colleagues have found that good parenting skills and good cognitive skills (especially attention and self-control) improve the likelihood that children in challenging circumstances will do better when they enter elementary school.
©Dawn Vilella Photography

Source	Characteristic
Individual	Good intellectual functioning
	Appealing, sociable, easygoing disposition
	Self-confidence, high self-esteem
	Talents
	Faith
Family	Close relationship to caring parent figure
	Authoritative parenting: warmth, structure, high expectations
	Socioeconomic advantages
	Connections to extended supportive family networks
Extrafamilial Context	Bonds to caring adults outside the family
	Connections to positive organizations
	Attending effective schools

FIGURE **1**

CHARACTERISTICS OF RESILIENT CHILDREN AND THEIR CONTEXTS

Socioeconomic status (SES) refers to a person's position within society based on occupational, educational, and economic characteristics. Socioeconomic status implies certain inequalities. Generally, members of a society have (1) occupations that vary in prestige, with some individuals having more access than others to higher-status occupations; (2) different levels of educational attainment, with some individuals having more access than others to better education; (3) different economic resources; and (4) different levels of power to influence a community's institutions. These differences in people's ability to control resources and to participate in society's rewards produce unequal opportunities (Orth, 2017; Yoshikawa & others, 2017).

Gender   Gender is another key dimension of children's development. **Gender** refers to the characteristics of people as males and females. Few aspects of our development are more central to our identity and social relationships than gender (Brannon, 2017; Helgeson, 2017). How you view yourself, your relationships with other people, your life, and your goals are shaped to a great extent by whether you are male or female and how your culture defines the proper roles of males and females.

Each of these dimensions of the sociocultural context—culture, ethnicity, SES, and gender—helps to mold how an individual develops through life, as discussions in later chapters demonstrate. We explore, for example, questions such as the following:

- Do infants around the world form attachments with their parents in the same way, or do these attachments differ from one culture to another?

- Does poverty influence the likelihood that young children will be provided with fewer educational opportunities than children growing up in more affluent families?

- Is there a parenting style that is universally effective, or does the effectiveness of different types of parenting depend on the ethnic group or culture?

- If adolescents from minority groups identify with their ethnic culture, is that likely to help or hinder their socioemotional development?

We discuss sociocultural contexts and diversity in each chapter. In addition, a *Connecting with Diversity* interlude appears in every chapter. See the first *Connecting with Diversity* interlude, which focuses on gender, families, and children's development around the world.

Resilience, Social Policy, and Children's Development   Some children develop confidence in their abilities despite negative stereotypes about their gender or their ethnic group. And some children triumph over poverty or other adversities. They show resilience. Think back to the chapter-opening story about Alice Walker. In spite of racism, poverty, her low socioeconomic status, and a disfiguring eye injury, she went on to become a successful author and champion for equality.

Are there certain characteristics that cause children like Alice Walker to be resilient? Are there other characteristics that influence children to behave like Ted Kaczynski, who despite his intelligence and education became a killer? After analyzing research on this topic, Ann Masten (2001, 2006, 2009, 2013, 2014a, b, 2015, 2016a, b, 2017; Masten & Cicchetti, 2016; Masten & Kalstabakken, 2017; Masten & others, 2015) concludes that a number of individual factors, such as good intellectual functioning, influence resiliency. In addition, as Figure 1 shows, the families and extrafamilial contexts of resilient children tend to show certain features. For example, resilient children are likely to have a close relationship to a caring parent figure and bonds to caring adults outside the family.

Should governments take action to improve the contexts of children's development and aid their resilience? **Social policy** is a government's course of action designed to promote the welfare of its citizens. The shape and

Gender, Families, and Children's Development

Around the world, the experiences of male and female children and adolescents continue to be quite different (Brown & Larson, 2002; UNICEF, 2017, 2018). Except in a few areas, such as Japan, the Philippines, and Western countries, males have far greater access to educational opportunities than females. In many countries, adolescent females have less freedom to pursue a variety of careers and engage in various leisure acts than males. Gender differences in sexual expression are widespread, especially in India, Southeast Asia, Latin America, and Arab countries—where there are far more restrictions on the sexual activity of adolescent females than of males. In certain areas around the world, these gender differences do appear to be narrowing over time. In some countries, educational and career opportunities for women are expanding, and in some parts of the world control over adolescent girls' romantic and sexual relationships is weakening. However, in many countries females still experience considerable discrimination, and much work is needed to bridge the gap between the rights of males and females.

In certain parts of the world, children grow up in closely knit families with extended-kin networks "that provide a web of connections and reinforce a traditional way of life" (Brown & Larson, 2002, p. 6). For example, in Arab countries, adolescents are required to adopt strict codes of conduct and loyalty. However, in Western countries such as the United States, children and adolescents are growing up in much larger numbers in divorced families and stepfamilies. Parenting in Western countries has become less authoritarian than it was in the past.

Doly Akter, age 17, lives in a slum in Dhaka, Bangladesh, where sewers overflow, garbage rots in the streets, and children are undernourished. Nearly two-thirds of young women in Bangladesh get married before they are 18. Doly organized a club supported by UNICEF in which girls go door-to-door to monitor the hygiene habits of households in their neighborhood. This has led to improved hygiene and health in the families. Also, her group has managed to stop several child marriages by meeting with parents and convincing them that it is not in their daughter's best interests. When talking with parents, they emphasize the importance of staying in school and how this will improve their daughter's future. Doly says that the girls in her UNICEF group are far more aware of their rights than their mothers ever were (UNICEF, 2007).
©Nasser Siddique/UNICEF Bangladesh

Some of the trends that are occurring in many countries around the world "include greater family mobility, migration to urban areas, family members working in distant cities or countries, smaller families, fewer extended-family households, and increases in mothers' employment" (Brown & Larson, 2002, p. 7). Unfortunately, many of these changes may reduce the ability of families to provide time and resources for children and adolescents.

---

scope of social policy related to children are tied to the political system. The values held by citizens and elected officials, the nation's economic strengths and weaknesses, and partisan politics all influence the policy agenda (McQueen, 2017; Ruck, Peterson-Badali, & Freeman, 2017; Sommer & others, 2016).

When concern about broad social issues is widespread, comprehensive social policies often result. Child labor laws were established in the early twentieth century not only to protect children but also to provide jobs for adults; federal child-care funding during World War II was justified by the need for women laborers in factories; and Head Start and other War on Poverty programs in the 1960s were implemented to decrease intergenerational poverty.

Out of concern that policy makers are doing too little to protect the well-being of children, researchers increasingly are undertaking studies that they hope will lead to wise and effective decision making about social policy (Gonzales & others, 2016; Israelashvili & Romano, 2017; McQueen, 2017; Wadsworth & others, 2016). Children who grow up in poverty represent a special concern (Duncan, Magnuson, & Votruba-Drzal, 2017; Mendoza & others, 2017). In 2014, 21.1 percent of U.S. children under 18 years of age were living in families with incomes below the poverty line, with African American and Latino families with children having especially high rates of poverty (more than 30 percent) (DeNavas-Walt & Proctor, 2015). In 2014, 12.7 percent of non-Latino White children were living in poverty. The poverty rate for U.S. children did drop 1.5 percent in 2015 to 19.7 percent (Proctor, Semega, & Kollar, 2016). The 19.7 percent figure represents an increase from 2001 (14.5 percent) but reflects a slight drop from a peak of 23 percent in 1993.

gender The characteristics of people as females or males.

social policy A government's course of action designed to promote the welfare of its citizens.

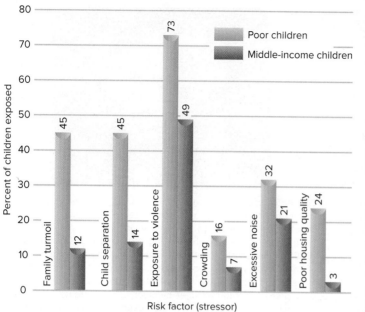

FIGURE **2**

EXPOSURE TO SIX STRESSORS AMONG POOR AND MIDDLE-INCOME CHILDREN. One study analyzed the exposure to six stressors among poor children and middle-income children (Evans & English, 2002). Poor children were much more likely to face each of these stressors.

Children are the legacy we leave for the time we will not live to see.

—**ARISTOTLE**

As indicated in Figure 2, one study found that a higher percentage of U.S. children in poor families than in middle-income families were exposed to family turmoil, separation from a parent, violence, crowding, excessive noise, and poor housing (Evans & English, 2002). One study also revealed that the more years children spent living in poverty, the higher their physiological indices of stress (Evans & Kim, 2007). The U.S. figure of 19.7 percent of children living in poverty is much higher than the rates in other industrialized nations. For example, Canada has a child poverty rate of 9 percent and Sweden has a rate of 2 percent.

In the United States, the national government, state governments, and city governments all play a role in influencing the well-being of children (Yoshikawa & others, 2016, 2017). When families fail or seriously endanger a child's well-being, governments often step in to help. At the national and state levels, policy makers have debated for decades whether helping poor parents ends up helping their children as well. Researchers are providing some answers by examining the effects of specific policies (Duncan, Magnuson, & Votruba-Drzal, 2017; Gonzales & others, 2016; Gottlieb & DeLoache, 2017).

For example, the Minnesota Family Investment Program (MFIP) was designed in the 1990s primarily to influence the behavior of adults—specifically, to move adults off the welfare rolls and into paid employment. A key element of the program was its guarantee that adults participating in the program would receive more income if they worked than if they did not. When the adults' income rose, how did that affect their children? A study of the effects of MFIP found that increases in the incomes of working poor parents were linked with benefits for their children (Gennetian & Miller, 2002). The children's achievement in school improved, and their behavior problems decreased.

There is increasing interest in developing two-generation educational interventions to improve the academic success of children living in poverty (Gardner, Brooks-Gunn, & Chase-Lansdale, 2016; Sommer & others, 2016). For example, a recent large-scale effort to help children escape from poverty is the *Ascend* two-generation educational intervention being conducted by the Aspen Institute (2013, 2017). The intervention emphasizes education (increasing postsecondary education for mothers and improving the quality of their children's early childhood education), economic support (housing, transportation, financial education, health insurance, and food assistance), and social capital (peer support including friends and neighbors; participation in community and faith-based organizations; school and work contacts).

Developmental psychologists and other researchers have examined the effects of many government policies. They are seeking ways to help families living in poverty improve their well-being, and they have offered many suggestions for improving government policies (Duncan, Magnuson, & Votruba-Drzal, 2017; McQueen, 2017; Yoshikawa & others, 2016, 2017).

Marian Wright Edelman, president of the Children's Defense Fund (shown here interacting with young children), has been a tireless advocate of children's rights and has been instrumental in calling attention to the needs of children. *What are some of these needs?*

Courtesy of the Children's Defense Fund and Marian Wright Edelman

Review *Connect* Reflect

LG1 Explain why it is important to study children's development, and identify five areas in which children's lives need to be improved.

Review

- Why is it important to study children's development?
- What are five aspects of children's development that need to be improved?

Connect

- How is the concept of resilience related to the story about Ted Kaczynski and Alice Walker?

Reflect *Your Own Personal Journey of Life*

- Imagine what your development as a child would have been like in a culture that offered fewer or distinctively different choices than your own. How might your development have been different if your family had been significantly richer or poorer than it was?

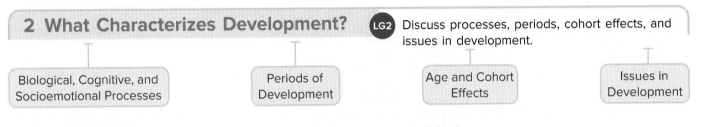

2 What Characterizes Development?

LG2 Discuss processes, periods, cohort effects, and issues in development.

| Biological, Cognitive, and Socioemotional Processes | Periods of Development | Age and Cohort Effects | Issues in Development |

Each of us develops in certain ways like all other individuals, like some other individuals, and like no other individuals. Most of the time, our attention is directed to a person's uniqueness, but psychologists who study development are drawn to our shared characteristics as well as what makes us unique. As humans, we all have traveled some common paths. each of us—Leonardo da Vinci, Joan of Arc, George Washington, Mother Teresa, Martin Luther King, Jr., and you—walked at about the age of 1, engaged in fantasy play as a young child, and became more independent as a youth. What shapes this common path of human development, and what are its milestones?

BIOLOGICAL, COGNITIVE, AND SOCIOEMOTIONAL PROCESSES

The pattern of human development is created by the interplay of several processes—biological, cognitive, and socioemotional. **Biological processes** produce changes in an individual's body. Genes inherited from parents, the development of the brain, height and weight gains, motor skills, and the hormonal changes of puberty all reflect the role of biological processes in development.

Cognitive processes refer to changes in an individual's thought, intelligence, and language. The tasks of watching a mobile swinging above a crib, putting together a two-word sentence, memorizing a poem, solving a math problem, and imagining what it would be like to be a movie star all involve cognitive processes.

Socioemotional processes involve changes in an individual's relationships with other people, changes in emotions, and changes in personality. An infant's smile in response to her mother's touch, a child's attack on a playmate, another's development of assertiveness, and an adolescent's joy at the senior prom all reflect socioemotional development.

Biological, cognitive, and socioemotional processes are inextricably intertwined (Diamond, 2013). Consider a baby smiling in response to a parent's touch. This response depends on biological processes (the physical nature of touch and responsiveness to it), cognitive processes (the ability to understand intentional acts), and socioemotional processes (the act of smiling often reflects a positive emotional feeling, and smiling helps to connect us in positive ways with other human beings). Nowhere is the connection across biological, cognitive, and socioemotional processes more obvious than in two rapidly emerging fields:

- *Developmental cognitive neuroscience,* which explores links between development, cognitive processes, and the brain (Bell & others, 2018; Crone, 2017; de Haan & Johnson, 2016)

biological processes Changes in an individual's body.

cognitive processes Changes in an individual's thought, intelligence, and language.

socioemotional processes Changes in an individual's relationships with other people, changes in emotions, and changes in personality.

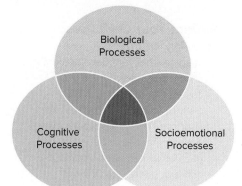

FIGURE **3**

CHANGES IN DEVELOPMENT ARE THE RESULT OF BIOLOGICAL, COGNITIVE, AND SOCIOEMOTIONAL PROCESSES. The processes interact as individuals develop.

- *Developmental social neuroscience,* which examines connections between socio-emotional processes, development, and the brain (Decety & Cowell, 2016; Silvers & others, 2017; Sullivan & Wilson, 2018)

In many instances, biological, cognitive, and socioemotional processes are bidirectional. For example, biological processes can influence cognitive processes and vice versa. Thus, although usually we will study the different processes of development (biological, cognitive, and socioemotional) in separate locations, keep in mind that we are talking about the development of an integrated human child with a mind and body that are interdependent (see Figure 3). In many places throughout the book we will call attention to these connections.

PERIODS OF DEVELOPMENT

For the purposes of organization and understanding, a child's development is commonly described in terms of periods, which are given approximate age ranges. The most widely used classification of developmental periods describes a child's development in terms of the following sequence: the prenatal period, infancy, early childhood, middle and late childhood, and adolescence.

The **prenatal period** is the time from conception to birth, roughly a nine-month period. During this amazing period, a single cell grows into an organism with a brain and behavioral capabilities.

Infancy is the developmental period that extends from birth to about 18 to 24 months of age. Infancy is a time of extreme dependence on adults. Many psychological activities are just beginning—the ability to speak, to coordinate sensations and physical actions, to think with symbols, and to imitate and learn from others.

Early childhood is the developmental period that extends from the end of infancy to about 5 or 6 years of age; sometimes this period is called the preschool years. During this time, young children learn to become more self-sufficient and to care for themselves; they develop school readiness skills (following instructions, identifying letters), and they spend many hours in play and with peers. First grade typically marks the end of this period.

Middle and late childhood is the developmental period that extends from about 6 to 11 years of age; sometimes this period is referred to as the elementary school years. Children master the fundamental skills of reading, writing, and arithmetic, and they are formally exposed to the larger world and its culture. Achievement becomes a more central theme of the child's world, and self-control increases.

Adolescence is the developmental period of transition from childhood to early adulthood, entered at approximately 10 to 12 years of age and ending at 18 to 22 years of age. Adolescence begins with rapid physical changes—dramatic gains in height and weight; changes in body contour; and the development of sexual characteristics such as enlargement of the breasts, development of pubic and facial hair, and deepening of the voice. The pursuit of independence and an identity are prominent features of this period of development. More and more time is spent outside the family. Thought becomes more abstract, idealistic, and logical.

Today, developmentalists do not suggest that change ends with adolescence (Cabeza, Nyberg, & Park, 2017; Fingerman & others, 2017). Instead, they describe development as a lifelong process. However, the purpose of this text is to describe the changes in development that take place from conception through adolescence. All of these periods of development are produced by the interplay of biological, cognitive, and socioemotional processes (see Figure 4).

AGE AND COHORT EFFECTS

A *cohort* is a group of people who are born at a similar point in history and share similar experiences such as living through the Vietnam War or growing up in the same city around the same time. These shared experiences may produce a range of differences among cohorts. For example, children and their parents who grew up during the Great Depression and World War II are likely to differ from their counterparts during the booming 1990s in their educational opportunities and economic status, how they were raised, their attitudes and experiences related to gender, and their exposure to technology. In research on development, **cohort effects** are due to a person's time of birth, era, or generation but not to actual age (Ganguli, 2017; Schaie, 2016).

prenatal period The time from conception to birth.

infancy The developmental period that extends from birth to 18 to 24 months of age.

early childhood The developmental period that extends from the end of infancy to about 5 to 6 years of age; sometimes called the preschool years.

middle and late childhood The developmental period that extends from about 6 to 11 years of age; sometimes called the elementary school years.

adolescence The developmental period of transition from childhood to early adulthood, entered at approximately 10 to 12 years of age and ending at 18 to 22 years of age.

cohort effects Effects due to a person's time of birth, era, or generation but not to actual age.

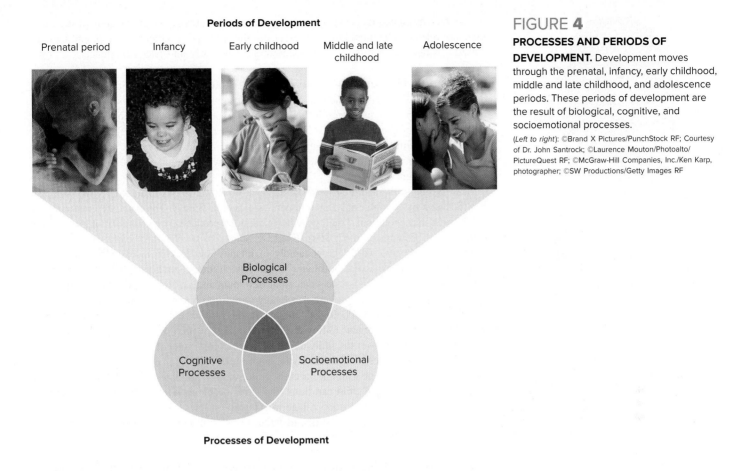

Periods of Development

Prenatal period   Infancy   Early childhood   Middle and late childhood   Adolescence

Biological Processes

Cognitive Processes   Socioemotional Processes

Processes of Development

FIGURE 4

PROCESSES AND PERIODS OF DEVELOPMENT. Development moves through the prenatal, infancy, early childhood, middle and late childhood, and adolescence periods. These periods of development are the result of biological, cognitive, and socioemotional processes.

(*Left to right*): ©Brand X Pictures/PunchStock RF; Courtesy of Dr. John Santrock; ©Laurence Mouton/Photoalto/ PictureQuest RF; ©McGraw-Hill Companies, Inc./Ken Karp, photographer; ©SW Productions/Getty Images RF

In recent years, generations have been given labels by the popular culture. The most recent label is **Millennials,** the generation born after 1980 that is the first to come of age and enter emerging adulthood in the new millennium. Thus, today's children and many of their parents are Millennials. Two characteristics of Millennials stand out: (1) their ethnic diversity, and (2) their connection to technology (Pew Research Center, 2010).

As their ethnic diversity has increased in comparison with prior generations, many Millennial adolescents and emerging adults are more tolerant and open-minded than their counterparts in older cohorts. One survey indicated that 60 percent of today's adolescents say their friends include someone from a different ethnic group (Teenage Research Unlimited, 2004).

Another major cohort change involving Millennials is the dramatic increase in their use of media and technology (Lever-Duffy & McDonald, 2018; Maloy & others, 2017). According to one analysis,

> They are history's first "always connected" generation. Steeped in digital technology and social media, they treat their multi-tasking hand-held gadgets almost like a body part—for better or worse. More than 8-in-10 say they sleep with a cell phone glowing by the bed, poised to disgorge texts, phone calls, e-mails, songs, news, videos, games, and wake-up jingles. But sometimes convenience yields to temptation. Nearly two-thirds admit to texting while driving. (Pew Research Center, 2010, p. 1)

We will have much more to say about technology in childhood and adolescence in the chapters entitled "Socioemotional Development in Early Childhood" and "Socioemotional Development in Adolescence."

Millennials The generation born after 1980, which is the first generation to come of age and enter emerging adulthood in the new millennium; members of this generation are characterized by their ethnic diversity and their connection to technology.

ISSUES IN DEVELOPMENT

Many questions about children's development remain unanswered. For example, what exactly drives the biological, cognitive, and socioemotional processes of development, and how do experiences during infancy influence middle childhood or adolescence? Despite all of the knowledge that researchers have acquired, debate continues about the relative importance of

©manaemedia/123RF

Continuity

Discontinuity

FIGURE 5

CONTINUITY AND DISCONTINUITY IN DEVELOPMENT. *Is our development like that of a seedling gradually growing into a giant oak? Or is it more like that of a caterpillar suddenly becoming a butterfly?*

How Would You...?

If you were an **educator,** how would you apply your understanding of the developmental influences of nature and nurture to create appropriate classroom strategies for students who display learning or behavioral problems?

nature-nurture issue The issue regarding whether development is primarily influenced by nature or nurture. The "nature" proponents claim that biological inheritance is the more important influence on development; the "nurture" proponents assert that environmental experiences are more important.

continuity-discontinuity issue The issue regarding whether development involves gradual, cumulative change (continuity) or distinct stages (discontinuity).

factors that influence the developmental processes and about how the periods of development are related. The most important issues in the study of children's development include nature and nurture, continuity and discontinuity, and early and later experience.

Nature and Nurture The **nature-nurture issue** involves the debate about whether development is primarily influenced by nature or by nurture. Nature refers to an organism's biological inheritance, nurture to its environmental experiences. Almost no one today argues that development can be explained by nature alone or by nurture alone. But some ("nature" proponents) claim that the more important influence on development is biological inheritance, and others ("nurture" proponents) claim that environmental experiences are the more important influence.

According to the nature proponents, just as a sunflower grows in an orderly way—unless it is defeated by an unfriendly environment—so does a person. The range of environments can be vast, but evolutionary and genetic foundations produce commonalities in growth and development (Freedman, 2017; Starr, Evers, & Starr, 2018). We walk before we talk, speak one word before two words, grow rapidly in infancy and less so in early childhood, and experience a rush of sexual hormones in puberty. Extreme environments—those that are psychologically barren or hostile—can stunt development, but nature proponents emphasize the influence of tendencies that are genetically wired into humans (Johnson, 2017).

By contrast, other psychologists emphasize the influence of nurture, or environmental experiences, on development (Almy & Cicchetti, 2018; Rubin & Barstead, 2018). Experiences run the gamut from the individual's biological environment (nutrition, medical care, drugs, and physical accidents) to the social environment (family, peers, schools, community, media, and culture). For example, a child's diet can affect how tall the child grows and even how effectively the child can think and solve problems. Despite their genetic wiring, a child born and raised in a poor village in Bangladesh and a child in the suburbs of Denver are likely to have different skills, different ways of thinking about the world, and different ways of relating to people.

Continuity and Discontinuity Think about your own development for a moment. Did you become the person you are gradually, like the seedling that slowly, cumulatively grows into a giant oak? Or did you experience sudden, distinct changes, like the caterpillar that changes into a butterfly (see Figure 5)?

The **continuity-discontinuity issue** focuses on the extent to which development involves gradual, cumulative change (continuity) or distinct stages (discontinuity). For the most part, developmentalists who emphasize nurture usually describe development as a gradual, continuous process, like the seedling's growth into an oak. Those who emphasize nature often describe development as a series of distinct stages, like the change from caterpillar to butterfly.

Consider continuity first. As the oak grows from seedling to giant oak, it becomes more oak—its development is continuous. Similarly, a child's first word, though seemingly an abrupt, discontinuous event, is actually the result of weeks and months of growth and practice. Puberty, another seemingly abrupt, discontinuous occurrence, is actually a gradual process occurring over several years.

Viewed in terms of discontinuity, each person is described as passing through a sequence of stages in which change is qualitatively rather than quantitatively different. As the caterpillar changes to a butterfly, it is not more caterpillar but an altogether different kind of organism—its development is discontinuous. Similarly, at some point a child moves from not being able to think abstractly about the world to being able to do so. This change is a qualitative, discontinuous change in development, not a quantitative, continuous change.

Early and Later Experience The **early-later experience issue** focuses on the degree to which early experiences (especially in infancy) or later experiences are the key determinants of the child's development. That is, if infants experience harmful circumstances, can those experiences be overcome by later, positive ones? Or are the early experiences so critical—possibly because they are the infant's first, prototypical experiences—that their influence cannot be overridden by a later, better environment? To those who emphasize early experiences, life is an unbroken trail on which a psychological quality can be traced back to its origin (Kagan, 1992, 2000). In contrast, to those who emphasize later experiences, development is like a river, continually ebbing and flowing.

The early-later experience issue has a long history and continues to be hotly debated among developmentalists (Roisman & Cicchetti, 2018). The ancient Greek philosopher Plato was sure that infants who were rocked frequently become better athletes. Nineteenth-century New England ministers told parents in Sunday afternoon sermons that the way they handled their infants would determine their children's later character. Some developmentalists argue that, unless infants experience warm, nurturing care during the first year or so of life, their development will never quite be optimal (Cassidy, 2016).

In contrast, later-experience advocates argue that children are malleable throughout development and that later sensitive caregiving is just as important as earlier sensitive caregiving (Fingerman & others, 2017; Padilla-Walker & Nelson, 2017). The later-experience advocates see children as malleable throughout development, with sensitive caregiving and positive close relationships playing important roles later in child development, adolescence, and adulthood just as they do in infancy (Antonucci & others, 2016). A number of experts on life-span development stress that too little attention has been given to later experiences in development (Allen & Tan, 2016). They accept that early experiences are important contributors to development but hold them to be no more important than later experiences. Jerome Kagan (2000, 2010, 2013) points out that even children who show the qualities of an inhibited temperament, which is linked to heredity, have the capacity to change their behavior. In his research, almost one-third of a group of children who had an inhibited temperament at 2 years of age were not unusually shy or fearful when they were 4 years of age (Kagan & Snidman, 1991).

People in Western cultures, especially those influenced by Freudian theory, have tended to support the idea that early experiences are more important than later experiences (Lamb & Sternberg, 1992). The majority of people in the world do not share this belief. For example, people in many Asian countries believe that experiences occurring after about 6 to 7 years of age are more important to development than are earlier experiences. This stance stems from the long-standing belief in Eastern cultures that children's reasoning skills begin to develop in important ways during middle childhood.

What is the nature of the early and later experience issue?
©JGI/Jamie Grill/Getty Images RF

Evaluating the Developmental Issues Most developmentalists recognize that it is unwise to take an extreme position on the issues of nature and nurture, continuity and discontinuity, and early and later experiences. Development is not all nature or all nurture; not all continuity or all discontinuity; and not all early or later experiences. Nature and nurture, continuity and discontinuity, and early and later experiences all play a part in development through the human life span. Along with this consensus, there is still spirited debate about how strongly development is influenced by each of these factors (Moore, 2017; Morrison, 2017). Are girls less likely to do well in math mostly because of inherited characteristics or because of society's expectations and because of how girls are raised? Can enriched experiences during adolescence remove deficits resulting from poverty, neglect, and poor schooling during childhood? The answers also have a bearing on social policy decisions about children and adolescents—and consequently on each of our lives.

developmental **connection**

Biological Processes

Can specific genes be linked to specific environmental experiences in influencing the child's development? Connect to "Biological Beginnings."

early-later experience issue The issue of the degree to which early experiences (especially infancy) or later experiences are the key determinants of the child's development.

Review Connect Reflect

LG2 Discuss processes, periods, cohort effects, and issues in development.

Review
- What are biological, cognitive, and socioemotional processes?
- What are the main periods of development?
- What are cohort effects?
- What are three important issues in development?

Connect
- Based on what you read earlier in the chapter, what do you think Ted Kaczynski would have to say about the early-later experience issue?

Reflect *Your Own Personal Journey of Life*
- Can you identify an early experience that you believe contributed in important ways to your development? Can you identify a recent or current (later) experience that you think had (is having) a strong influence on your development?

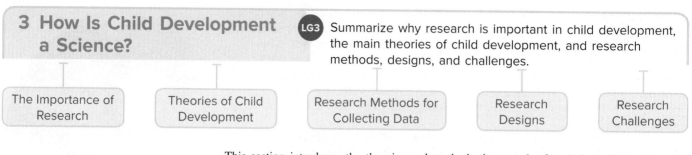

3 How Is Child Development a Science?

LG3 Summarize why research is important in child development, the main theories of child development, and research methods, designs, and challenges.

| The Importance of Research | Theories of Child Development | Research Methods for Collecting Data | Research Designs | Research Challenges |

This section introduces the theories and methods that are the foundation of the science of child development. We consider why research is important in understanding children's development and examine the main theories of children's development, as well as the main methods and research designs that researchers use. At the end of the section, we explore some of the ethical challenges researchers face and the biases they must guard against to protect the integrity of their results and respect the rights of the participants in their studies.

Science refines everyday thinking.

—**ALBERT EINSTEIN**
German-born American Physicist, 20th Century

scientific method An approach that can be used to obtain accurate information. It includes these steps: (1) conceptualize the problem, (2) collect data, (3) draw conclusions, and (4) revise research conclusions and theory.

theory An interrelated, coherent set of ideas that helps to explain and make predictions.

hypothesis A specific assumption or prediction that can be tested to determine its accuracy.

THE IMPORTANCE OF RESEARCH

Some individuals have difficulty thinking of child development as a science like physics, chemistry, and biology. Can a discipline that studies how parents nurture children, how peers interact, what are the developmental changes in children's thinking, and whether watching TV hour after hour is linked with being overweight be equated with disciplines that study the molecular structure of a compound and how gravity works? Is child development really a science? The answer is yes. Science is defined not by what it investigates, but by how it investigates. Whether you're studying photosynthesis, butterflies, Saturn's moons, or children's development, it is the way you study that makes the approach scientific or not.

Scientific research is objective, systematic, and testable. It reduces the likelihood that information will be based on personal beliefs, opinions, and feelings (Babbie, 2017; Smith & Davis, 2016). Scientific research is based on the **scientific method,** an approach that can be used to discover accurate information. It includes four steps: conceptualize the problem, collect data, analyze the data to reach conclusions, and revise research conclusions and theory.

The first step, *conceptualizing a problem,* involves identifying the problem. At a general level, this may not seem like a difficult task. However, researchers must go beyond a general description of the problem by isolating, analyzing, narrowing, and focusing more specifically on what they want to study. For example, a team of researchers decides to study ways to improve the achievement of children from impoverished backgrounds. Perhaps they choose to examine whether mentoring that involves sustained support, guidance, and concrete assistance can improve the children's academic performance. At this point, even more narrowing and focusing takes place. For instance, what specific strategies should the mentors use? How often will they see the children? How long will the mentoring program last? What aspects of the children's achievement will be assessed?

As part of the first step in formulating a problem to study, researchers often *draw on theories and develop a hypothesis.* A **theory** is an interrelated, coherent set of ideas that helps to explain and to make predictions. For example, a theory on mentoring might attempt to explain and predict why sustained support, guidance, and concrete experience make a difference in the lives of children from impoverished backgrounds. The theory might focus on children's opportunities to model the behavior and strategies of mentors, or it might focus on the effects of individual attention, which might be missing in the children's lives. A **hypothesis** is a specific testable assumption or prediction. A hypothesis is often written as an if-then statement. In our example, a sample hypothesis might be: If children from impoverished backgrounds are given individual attention by mentors, the children will spend more time studying and earn higher grades. Testing a hypothesis can inform researchers whether or not a theory may be accurate.

A high school senior mentors a kindergarten child as part of the Book Buddy mentoring program. *If a researcher wanted to study the effects of the mentoring program on children's academic achievement by following the scientific method, what steps would the researcher take in setting up the study?*

©Zuma Press Inc./Alamy

The second step in the scientific method is to *collect information (data)*. In the study of mentoring, the researchers might decide to conduct the mentoring program for six months. Their data might consist of classroom observations, teachers' ratings, and achievement tests given to the mentored children before the mentoring began and at the end of six months of mentoring.

Once data have been collected, child development researchers use *statistical procedures* to understand the meaning of the data. Then they try to *draw conclusions*. In this third step, statistics help to determine whether or not the researchers' observations are due to chance.

After data have been collected and analyzed, researchers compare their findings with those of other researchers on the same topic. The final step in the scientific method is *revising research conclusions and theory*.

How Would You...?

If you were a **health-care professional,** how would you apply the scientific method to examine developmental concerns such as adolescent pregnancy?

THEORIES OF CHILD DEVELOPMENT

A wide range of theories makes understanding children's development a challenging undertaking. Just when you think one theory has the most helpful explanation of children's development, another theory crops up and makes you rethink your earlier conclusion. To keep from getting frustrated, remember that child development is a complex, multifaceted topic. No single theory has been able to account for all aspects of child development. Each theory contributes an important piece to the child development puzzle. Although the theories sometimes disagree, much of their information is complementary rather than contradictory. Together they let us see the total landscape of development in all its richness.

We briefly explore five major theoretical perspectives on development: psychoanalytic, cognitive, behavioral and social cognitive, ethological, and ecological. As you will see, these theoretical approaches examine in varying degrees the three major processes involved in children's development: biological, cognitive, and socioemotional.

psychoanalytic theories Describe development as primarily unconscious and heavily colored by emotion. Behavior is merely a surface characteristic, and the symbolic workings of the mind have to be analyzed to understand behavior. Early experiences with parents are emphasized.

Psychoanalytic Theories   **Psychoanalytic theories** describe development as primarily unconscious (beyond awareness) and heavily colored by emotion. Psychoanalytic theorists emphasize that behavior is merely a surface characteristic and that a true understanding of development requires analyzing the symbolic meanings of behavior and the deep inner workings of the mind. Psychoanalytic theorists also stress that early experiences with parents extensively shape development. These characteristics are highlighted in the psychoanalytic theory of Sigmund Freud (1856–1939).

Freud's Theory   Freud (1917) proposed that personality has three structures: the id, the ego, and the superego. The *id* is the Freudian structure of personality that consists of instincts, which are an individual's reservoir of psychic energy. In Freud's view, the id is totally unconscious; it has no contact with reality. As children experience the demands and constraints of reality, a new structure of personality emerges—the *ego*. It deals with the demands of reality and is called the "executive branch" of personality because it uses reasoning to make decisions. The id and the ego have no morality—they do not take into account whether something is right or wrong. The *superego* is the Freudian structure of personality that is the moral branch of personality, the part that considers whether something is right or wrong. Think of the superego as what we often refer to as our "conscience."

As Freud listened to, probed, and analyzed his patients, he became convinced that their problems were the result of experiences early in life. He thought that as children grow up, their focus of pleasure and sexual impulses shifts from the mouth to the anus and eventually to the genitals. As a result, we go through five stages of psychosexual development: oral, anal, phallic, latency, and genital (see Figure 6). Our adult personality, Freud claimed, is

Sigmund Freud, the pioneering architect of psychoanalytic theory. *What are some characteristics of Freud's theory?*
©Bettmann/Getty Images

FIGURE 6

FREUDIAN STAGES. Sigmund Freud, the pioneering architect of psychoanalytic theory. *What are some characteristics of Freud's theory?*

Oral Stage	Anal Stage	Phallic Stage	Latency Stage	Genital Stage
Infant's pleasure centers on the mouth.	Child's pleasure focuses on the anus.	Child's pleasure focuses on the genitals.	Child represses sexual interest and develops social and intellectual skills.	A time of sexual reawakening; source of sexual pleasure becomes someone outside the family.
Birth to 1½ Years	**1½ to 3 Years**	**3 to 6 Years**	**6 Years to Puberty**	**Puberty Onward**

determined by the way we resolve conflicts between sources of pleasure at each stage and the demands of reality.

Freud's theory has been significantly revised by a number of psychoanalytic theorists. Many contemporary psychoanalytic theorists maintain that Freud overemphasized sexual instincts; they place more emphasis on cultural experiences as determinants of an individual's development. Unconscious thought remains a central theme, but most contemporary psychoanalysts stress that conscious thought plays a greater role than Freud envisioned. Next, we outline the ideas of an important revisionist of Freud's ideas—Erik Erikson.

Erikson's Psychosocial Theory   Erik Erikson (1902–1994) recognized Freud's contributions but argued that Freud misjudged some important dimensions of human development. For one thing, Erikson (1950, 1968) said we develop in psychosocial stages rather than in psychosexual stages, as Freud maintained. According to Freud, the primary motivation for human behavior is sexual in nature; according to Erikson, it is social and reflects a desire to affiliate with other people. According to Freud, our basic personality is shaped in the first five years of life; according to Erikson, developmental change occurs throughout the life span. Thus, in terms of the early versus later experience issue described earlier in this chapter, Freud argued that early experience is far more important than later experiences, whereas Erikson emphasized the importance of both early and later experiences.

In **Erikson's theory,** eight stages of development unfold as we go through life (see Figure 7). At each stage, a unique developmental task confronts individuals with a crisis that must be resolved. According to Erikson, this crisis is not a catastrophe but a turning point marked by both increased vulnerability and enhanced potential. The more successfully an individual resolves the crisis, the healthier his or her development will be.

Trust versus mistrust is Erikson's first psychosocial stage, which is experienced in the first year of life. Trust during infancy sets the stage for a lifelong expectation that the world will be a good and pleasant place to live.

After gaining trust in their caregivers, infants begin to discover that their behavior is their own. They start to assert their sense of independence, or autonomy. If infants are restrained too much or punished too harshly, they are likely to develop a sense of shame and doubt. This is Erikson's second stage of development, *autonomy versus shame and doubt,* which occurs in late infancy and toddlerhood (1 to 3 years of age).

Initiative versus guilt, Erikson's third stage of development, occurs during the preschool years. As preschool children encounter a widening social world, they face new challenges that require active, purposeful behavior. Children are asked to assume responsibility for their bodies, their behavior, their toys, and their pets—and they take initiative. Feelings of guilt may arise, though, if the child is irresponsible and is made to feel too anxious.

Industry versus inferiority is Erikson's fourth developmental stage, occurring approximately in the elementary school years. Children's initiative brings them in contact with a wealth of new experiences. As they move into middle and late childhood, they direct their energy toward mastering knowledge and intellectual skills. At no other time is the child more enthusiastic about learning than at the end of early childhood's period of expansive imagination. The danger is that the child can develop a sense of inferiority—feeling incompetent and unproductive.

During the adolescent years, individuals are faced with finding out who they are, what they are all about, and where they are going in life. This is Erikson's fifth developmental stage, *identity versus identity confusion.* Adolescents are confronted with many new roles and adult statuses—vocational and romantic, for example. If they explore roles in a healthy manner and arrive at a positive path to follow in life, then they achieve a positive identity. If parents push an identity on adolescents, and if adolescents do not adequately explore many roles and define a positive future path, then identity confusion reigns.

Intimacy versus isolation is Erikson's sixth developmental stage, which individuals experience during early adulthood. At this time, individuals face the developmental task of forming intimate relationships. Erikson describes intimacy as finding oneself yet losing

Erik Erikson with his wife, Joan, an artist. Erikson generated one of the most important developmental theories of the twentieth century. *Which stage of Erikson's theory are you in? Does Erikson's description of this stage characterize you?*
©Jon Erikson/The Image Works

Erikson's Stages	Developmental Period
Integrity versus despair	Late adulthood (60s onward)
Generativity versus stagnation	Middle adulthood (40s, 50s)
Intimacy versus isolation	Early adulthood (20s, 30s)
Identity versus identity confusion	Adolescence (10 to 20 years)
Industry versus inferiority	Middle and late childhood (elementary school years, 6 years to puberty)
Initiative versus guilt	Early childhood (preschool years, 3 to 5 years)
Autonomy versus shame and doubt	Infancy (1 to 3 years)
Trust versus mistrust	Infancy (first year)

FIGURE 7
ERIKSON'S EIGHT LIFE-SPAN STAGES

oneself in another. If the young adult forms healthy friendships and an intimate relationship with another, intimacy will be achieved; if not, isolation will result.

Generativity versus stagnation, Erikson's seventh developmental stage, occurs during middle adulthood. By generativity Erikson means primarily a concern for helping the younger generation to develop and lead useful lives. The feeling of having done nothing to help the next generation is stagnation.

Integrity versus despair is Erikson's eighth and final stage of development, which individuals experience in late adulthood. During this stage, a person reflects on the past. Through many different routes, the person may have developed a positive outlook in most or all of the previous stages of development. If so, the person's review of his or her life will reveal a life well spent, and the person will feel a sense of satisfaction—integrity will be achieved. If the person has resolved many of the earlier stages negatively, the retrospective glances likely will yield doubt or gloom—the despair Erikson described.

Each of Erikson's stages has a "positive" pole, such as trust, and a "negative" pole, such as mistrust. In the healthy solution to the crisis of each stage, the positive pole dominates, but Erikson maintained that some exposure or commitment to the negative side is sometimes inevitable. For example, learning to trust is an important outcome of Erikson's first stage, but you cannot trust all people under all circumstances and survive. We discuss Erikson's theory again in the chapters on socioemotional development. In the *Caring Connections* interlude, you can read about some effective strategies for improving the lives of children based on Erikson's view.

Evaluating the Psychoanalytic Theories The contributions of psychoanalytic theories include these ideas: (1) early experiences play an important part in development; (2) family relationships are a central aspect of development; (3) personality can be better understood if it is examined developmentally; (4) activities of the mind are not entirely conscious—unconscious aspects need to be considered; and (5) in Erikson's theory, changes take place in adulthood as well as in childhood.

Psychoanalytic theories have been criticized for several reasons. First, the main concepts of psychoanalytic theories are difficult to test scientifically. Second, much of the data used to support psychoanalytic theories come from individuals' reconstruction of the past, often the distant past, and are of unknown accuracy. Third, the sexual underpinnings of development

How Would You...?
If you were a **human development and family studies professional,** how would you apply psychoanalytic theory to advise the foster family of a newly placed child who has no reported history of abuse yet shows considerable violent behavior?

Erikson's theory Includes eight stages of human development. Each stage consists of a unique developmental task that confronts individuals with a crisis that must be resolved.

caring connections

Strategies for Parenting, Educating, and Interacting with Children Based on Erikson's Theory

Parents, child-care specialists, teachers, counselors, youth workers, and other adults can adopt positive strategies for interacting with children based on Erikson's theory. These strategies are described below.

1. ***Nurture infants and develop their trust, then encourage and monitor toddlers' autonomy.*** Because infants depend on others to meet their needs, it is critical for caregivers to consistently provide positive, attentive care for infants. Infants who experience consistently positive care feel safe and secure, sensing that people are reliable and loving, which leads them to develop trust in the world. Caregivers who neglect or abuse infants are likely to have infants who develop a sense of mistrust in their world. Having developed a sense of trust in their world, as infants move into the toddler years it is important that they are given the freedom to explore it. Toddlers whose caregivers are too restrictive or harsh are likely to develop shame and doubt, sensing that they can't adequately do things on their own. As toddlers gain more independence, caregivers need to monitor their exploration and curiosity because there are many things that can harm them, such as running into the street or touching a hot stove.

2. ***Encourage initiative in young children.*** Children should be given a great deal of freedom to explore their world. They should be allowed to choose some of the activities they engage in. If their requests for doing certain activities are reasonable, the requests should be honored. Children need to be provided with exciting materials that will stimulate their imagination. Young children at this stage love to play. It not only benefits their socioemotional development but also is an important medium for their cognitive growth. Criticism should be kept to a minimum so that children will not develop high levels of guilt and anxiety. Young children are going to make lots of mistakes and have lots of spills. They need good models far more than harsh critics. Structure their activities and environment for success rather than failure by giving them developmentally appropriate tasks. For example, young children get frustrated when they have to sit for long periods of time and do academic paper-and-pencil tasks.

3. ***Promote industry in elementary school children.*** It was Erikson's hope that teachers could provide an atmosphere in which children would become passionate about learning. In Erikson's

(continued)

(*continued*)

words, teachers should mildly but firmly coerce children into the adventure of finding out that they can learn to accomplish things that they themselves would never have thought they could do. In elementary school, children thirst to know. Most arrive at elementary school steeped in curiosity and motivated to master tasks. In Erikson's view, it is important for teachers to nourish this motivation for mastery and curiosity. Teachers need to challenge students but not overwhelm them; be firm in requiring students to be productive without being overly critical; and especially be tolerant of honest mistakes and make sure that every student has opportunities for many successes.

4. ***Stimulate identity exploration in adolescence.*** It is important to recognize that the adolescent's identity is multidimensional. Aspects include vocational goals; intellectual achievement; and

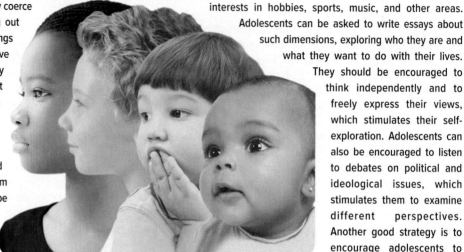

What are some applications of Erikson's theory for effective parenting?
(*right to left*): ©valeriebarry/Getty Images RF; ©Tomas Rodriguez/Corbis RF; ©Corbis RF; ©PunchStock/Image Source RF

interests in hobbies, sports, music, and other areas. Adolescents can be asked to write essays about such dimensions, exploring who they are and what they want to do with their lives. They should be encouraged to think independently and to freely express their views, which stimulates their self-exploration. Adolescents can also be encouraged to listen to debates on political and ideological issues, which stimulates them to examine different perspectives. Another good strategy is to encourage adolescents to talk with a school counselor about career options as well as other aspects of their identity. Teachers can have people from different careers come into the classroom and talk about their work with students regardless of grade level.

---

are given too much importance (especially in Freud's theory), and the unconscious mind is given too much credit for influencing development. In addition, psychoanalytic theories (especially Freud's theory) present an overly negative image of humans and are culture- and gender-biased, treating Western culture and males as the measure for evaluating everyone.

Cognitive Theories   Whereas psychoanalytic theories stress the importance of the unconscious, cognitive theories emphasize conscious thoughts. Three important cognitive theories are Piaget's cognitive developmental theory, Vygotsky's sociocultural cognitive theory, and information-processing theory.

Piaget's Cognitive Developmental Theory   **Piaget's theory** states that children actively construct their understanding of the world and go through four stages of cognitive development. Two processes underlie the four stages of development in Piaget's theory: organization and adaptation. To make sense of our world, we organize our experiences. For example, we separate important ideas from less important ideas, and we connect one idea to another. In addition to organizing our observations and experiences, we *adapt,* adjusting to new environmental demands (Miller, 2015).

Piaget (1896–1980) also proposed that we go through four stages in understanding the world (see Figure 8). Each stage is age-related and consists of a distinct way of thinking, a different way of understanding the world. Thus, according to Piaget (1954), the child's cognition is *qualitatively* different in one stage compared with another. What are Piaget's four stages of cognitive development like?

The *sensorimotor stage,* which lasts from birth to about 2 years of age, is the first Piagetian stage. In this stage, infants construct an understanding of the world by coordinating sensory experiences (such as seeing and hearing) with physical, motoric actions—hence the term *sensorimotor.*

The *preoperational stage,* which lasts from approximately 2 to 7 years of age, is Piaget's second stage. In this stage, children begin to go beyond simply connecting sensory information with physical action and represent the world with words, images, and drawings. However,

- - - - - - - - ➤

developmental **connection**

Cognitive Theory

We owe to Piaget the entire field of children's cognitive development, but a number of criticisms of his theory have been made. Connect to "Cognitive Development in Middle and Late Childhood."

◄ - - - - - - - - -

Piaget's theory States that children actively construct their understanding of the world and go through four stages of cognitive development.

Sensorimotor Stage	**Preoperational Stage**	**Concrete Operational Stage**	**Formal Operational Stage**
The infant constructs an understanding of the world by coordinating sensory experiences with physical actions. An infant progresses from reflexive, instinctual action at birth to the beginning of symbolic thought toward the end of the stage.	The child begins to represent the world with words and images. These words and images reflect increased symbolic thinking and go beyond the connection of sensory information and physical action.	The child can now reason logically about concrete events and classify objects into different sets.	The adolescent reasons in more abstract, idealistic, and logical ways.
Birth to 2 Years of Age	**2 to 7 Years of Age**	**7 to 11 Years of Age**	**11 Years of Age Through Adulthood**

FIGURE **8**

PIAGET'S FOUR STAGES OF COGNITIVE DEVELOPMENT.
(*Left to right*): ©Stockbyte/Getty Images RF; ©BananaStock/PunchStock RF; ©image100/Corbis RF; ©Purestock/Getty Images RF

according to Piaget, preschool children still lack the ability to perform what he calls operations, which are internalized mental actions that allow children to do mentally what they previously could only do physically. For example, if you imagine putting two sticks together to see whether they would be as long as another stick, without actually moving the sticks, you are performing a concrete operation.

The *concrete operational stage,* which lasts from approximately 7 to 11 years of age, is the third Piagetian stage. In this stage, children can perform operations that involve objects, and they can reason logically as long as reasoning can be applied to specific or concrete examples. For example, concrete operational thinkers understand that two rows of four nickels have the same number of nickels regardless of how far apart the nickels in the row are spaced. However, concrete operational thinkers cannot imagine the steps necessary to complete an algebraic equation, which is too abstract for thinking at this stage of development.

The *formal operational stage,* which appears between the ages of 11 and 15 and continues through adulthood, is Piaget's fourth and final stage. In this stage, individuals move beyond concrete experiences and think in abstract and more logical terms. As part of thinking more abstractly, adolescents develop images of ideal circumstances. They might think about what an ideal parent is like and compare their parents to this ideal standard. They begin to entertain possibilities for the future and are fascinated with what they can be. In solving problems, they become more systematic, developing hypotheses about why something is happening the way it is and then testing these hypotheses.

In sum, this brief introduction to Piaget's theory that children's cognitive development goes through four stages is provided here, along with other theories, to give you a broad understanding. Later in the text, when we study cognitive development in infancy, early childhood, middle and late childhood, and adolescence, we will return to Piaget and examine his theory in more depth.

Vygotsky's Sociocultural Cognitive Theory   Like Piaget, the Russian developmentalist Lev Vygotsky (1896–1934) said that children actively construct their knowledge. Unlike Piaget, Vygotsky (1962) did not propose that cognitive development occurs in stages, and he gave social interaction and culture far more important roles in cognitive development than

Jean Piaget, the famous Swiss developmental psychologist, changed the way we think about the development of children's minds. *What are some key ideas in Piaget's theory?*
©Yves de Braine/Black Star/Stock Photo

There is considerable interest today in Lev Vygotsky's sociocultural cognitive theory of child development. *What were Vygotsky's basic ideas about children's development?*
©A.R. Lauria/Dr. Michael Cole, Library of Human Cognition, UCSD

Piaget did. **Vygotsky's theory** is a sociocultural cognitive theory that emphasizes how culture and social interaction guide cognitive development.

Vygotsky portrayed the child's development as inseparable from social and cultural activities (Daniels, 2017; Gauvain, 2016). He argued that development of memory, attention, and reasoning involves learning to use the inventions of society, such as language, mathematical systems, and memory strategies. Thus in one culture, children might learn to count with the help of a computer; in another, they might learn by using beads. According to Vygotsky, children's social interaction with more-skilled adults and peers is indispensable to their cognitive development. Through this interaction, they learn to use the tools that will help them adapt and be successful in their culture. For example, if you regularly help a child learn how to read, you not only advance a child's reading skills but also communicate to the child that reading is an important activity in his or her culture.

Vygotsky's theory has stimulated considerable interest in the view that knowledge is situated and collaborative (Holzman, 2017). In this view, knowledge is not generated from within the individual but rather is constructed through interaction with other people and objects in the culture, such as books. This suggests that knowledge can best be advanced through interaction with others in cooperative activities.

Vygotsky's theory, like Piaget's, remained virtually unknown to American psychologists until the 1960s, but eventually both became influential among educators as well as psychologists. We will examine ideas about learning and teaching that are based on Vygotsky's theory when we study cognitive development in early childhood.

The Information-Processing Theory

Early computers may be the best candidates for the title of "founding fathers" of information-processing theory. Although many factors stimulated the growth of this theory, none was more important than the computer. Psychologists began to wonder whether the logical operations carried out by computers might tell us something about how the human mind works. They drew analogies between a computer's hardware and the brain and between computer software and cognition.

This line of thinking helped to generate **information-processing theory,** which emphasizes that individuals manipulate information, monitor it, and strategize about it. Unlike Piaget's theory, but like Vygotsky's theory, information-processing theory does not describe development as stage-like. Instead, according to this theory, individuals develop a gradually increasing capacity for processing information, which allows them to acquire increasingly complex knowledge and skills.

Robert Siegler (2006, 2011, 2013, 2016a, b, 2017), a leading expert on children's information-processing, states that thinking is information processing. In other words, when individuals perceive, encode, represent, store, and retrieve information, they are thinking. Siegler emphasizes that an important aspect of development is learning good strategies for processing information (Fazio, DeWolf, & Siegler, 2016; Siegler & Braithwaite, 2017). For example, becoming a better reader might involve learning to monitor the key themes of the material being read.

Siegler (2006, 2016a, b, 2017) also argues that the best way to understand how children learn is to observe them while they are learning. He emphasizes the importance of using the *microgenetic method* to obtain detailed information about processing mechanisms as they are occurring moment to moment. Siegler concludes that most research methods indirectly assess cognitive change, being more like snapshots than movies. The microgenetic method seeks to discover not just what children know but the cognitive processes involved in how they acquired the knowledge. A typical microgenetic study will be conducted across a number of trials assessed at various times over weeks or months (Miller, 2015). A number of microgenetic studies have focused on a specific aspect of academic learning, such as how children learn whole number arithmetic, fractions, and other areas of math (Siegler & others, 2015). Microgenetic studies also have been used to discover how children learn a particular issue in science or a key aspect of learning to read.

Evaluating the Cognitive Theories

The primary contributions of cognitive theories are that (1) they present a positive view of development, emphasizing conscious thinking; (2) they emphasize the individual's active construction of understanding (especially Piaget's and Vygotsky's theories); (3) Piaget's and Vygotsky's theories underscore the importance of examining developmental changes in children's thinking; and (4) information-processing theory offers detailed descriptions of cognitive processes.

There are several criticisms of cognitive theories. First, Piaget's stages are not as uniform as he theorized. Piaget also underestimated the cognitive skills of infants and overestimated the

Vygotsky's theory A sociocultural cognitive theory that emphasizes how culture and social interaction guide cognitive development.

information-processing theory Emphasizes that individuals manipulate information, monitor it, and strategize about it. Central to this theory are the processes of memory and thinking.

cognitive skills of adolescents. Second, the cognitive theories do not give adequate attention to individual variations in cognitive development. Third, information-processing theory does not provide an adequate description of developmental changes in cognition. In addition, psychoanalytic theorists argue that the cognitive theories do not give enough credit to unconscious thought.

Behavioral and Social Cognitive Theories   In the early twentieth century, as Freud was interpreting patients' unconscious minds through their early childhood experiences, Ivan Pavlov and John B. Watson were conducting detailed observations of behavior in controlled laboratory settings. Their work provided the foundations of *behaviorism,* which essentially holds that we can study scientifically only what can be directly observed and measured. Out of the behavioral tradition grew the belief that development is observable behavior that can be learned through experience with the environment (Maag, 2018; Spiegler, 2016). In terms of the continuity-discontinuity issue discussed earlier in this chapter, the behavioral and social cognitive theories emphasize continuity in development and argue that development does not occur in stage-like fashion. The three versions of the behavioral and social cognitive theories that we explore are Pavlov's classical conditioning, Skinner's operant conditioning, and Bandura's social cognitive theory.

Pavlov's Classical Conditioning   In the early 1900s, the Russian physiologist Ivan Pavlov (1927) knew that dogs innately salivate when they taste food. He became curious when he observed that dogs salivate to various sights and sounds before eating their food. For example, when an individual paired the ringing of a bell with the food, the bell ringing subsequently elicited salivation from the dogs when it was presented by itself. With this experiment, Pavlov discovered the principle of *classical conditioning,* in which a neutral stimulus (in our example, ringing a bell) acquires the ability to produce a response originally produced by another stimulus (in our example, food).

In the early twentieth century, John Watson demonstrated that classical conditioning occurs in humans. He showed an infant named Albert a white rat to see if he was afraid of it. He was not. As Albert played with the rat, a loud noise was sounded behind his head. As you might imagine, the noise caused little Albert to cry. After several pairings of the loud noise and the white rat, Albert began to cry at the sight of the rat even when the noise was not sounded (Watson & Rayner, 1920). Albert had been classically conditioned to fear the rat. Similarly, many of our fears may result from classical conditioning: Fear of the dentist may be learned from a painful experience, fear of driving from being in an automobile accident, fear of heights from falling off a high chair when we were infants, and fear of dogs from being bitten.

Skinner's Operant Conditioning   Classical conditioning may explain how we develop many involuntary responses such as fears, but B. F. Skinner argued that a second type of conditioning accounts for the development of other types of behavior. According to Skinner (1938), through *operant conditioning* the consequences of a behavior produce changes in the probability of the behavior's occurrence. A behavior followed by a rewarding stimulus is more likely to recur, whereas a behavior followed by a punishing stimulus is less likely to recur. For example, when a person smiles at a child after the child has done something, the child is more likely to engage in the activity than if the person gives the child a nasty look.

According to Skinner, such rewards and punishments shape development. For example, Skinner's approach argues that shy people learned to be shy as a result of experiences they had while growing up. It follows that modifications in an environment can help a shy person become more socially oriented. Also, for Skinner the key aspect of development is behavior, not thoughts and feelings. He emphasized that development consists of the pattern of behavioral changes that are brought about by rewards and punishments.

Bandura's Social Cognitive Theory   Some psychologists agree with the behaviorists' notion that development is learned and is influenced strongly by environmental interactions. However, unlike Skinner, they argue that cognition is also important in understanding development. **Social cognitive theory** holds that behavior, environment, and cognition are the key factors in development.

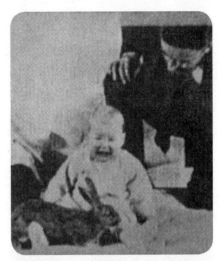

In 1920, John Watson and Rosalie Rayner conditioned 11-month-old Albert to fear a white rat by pairing the rat with a loud noise. When little Albert was subsequently presented with other stimuli similar to the white rat, such as the rabbit shown here with little Albert, he was afraid of them, too. This illustrates the principle of stimulus generalization in classical conditioning.
Courtesy of Dr. Benjamin Harris

social cognitive theory The view of psychologists who emphasize behavior, environment, and cognition as the key factors in development.

B. F. Skinner was a tinkerer who liked to make new gadgets. The younger of his two daughters, Deborah, was raised in Skinner's enclosed Air-Crib, which he invented because he wanted to control her environment completely. The Air-Crib was sound-proofed and temperature-controlled. Debbie, shown here as a child with her parents, is currently a successful artist, is married, and lives in London. *What do you think about Skinner's Air-Crib?*
©AP Images

Albert Bandura has been one of the leading architects of social cognitive theory. *What is the nature of his theory?*

Courtesy of Dr. Albert Bandura

developmental **connection**

Achievement

Bandura emphasizes that self-efficacy is a key person/cognitive factor in children's achievement. Connect to "Cognitive Development in Middle and Late Childhood."

ethology Stresses that behavior is strongly influenced by biology, is tied to evolution, and is characterized by critical or sensitive periods.

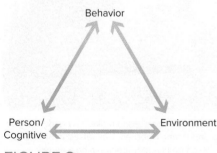

FIGURE 9

BANDURA'S SOCIAL COGNITIVE MODEL. The arrows illustrate how relations between behavior, person/cognition, and environment are reciprocal rather than unidirectional.

American psychologist Albert Bandura (1925–) is the leading architect of social cognitive theory. Bandura (2001, 2007, 2010a, 2012, 2015) emphasizes that cognitive processes have important links with the environment and behavior. His early research program focused heavily on *observational learning* (also called *imitation,* or *modeling*), which is learning that occurs through observing what others do. For example, a young boy might observe his father yelling in anger and treating other people with hostility; with his peers, the young boy later acts very aggressively, showing the same characteristics as his father's behavior. A girl might adopt the dominant and sarcastic style of her teacher, saying to her younger brother, "You are so slow. How can you do this work so slowly?" Social cognitive theorists stress that people acquire a wide range of behaviors, thoughts, and feelings through observing others' behavior and that these observations play important roles in children's development.

What is cognitive about observational learning, in Bandura's view? He proposes that people cognitively represent the behavior of others and then sometimes adopt this behavior themselves.

Bandura's (2001, 2007, 2010a, b, 2012, 2015) most recent model of learning and development includes three elements: behavior, the person/cognition, and the environment. An individual's confidence that he or she can control his or her success is an example of a person factor; strategies are an example of a cognitive factor. As shown in Figure 9, behavior, person/cognitive, and environmental factors operate interactively. Behavior can influence person factors and vice versa. Cognitive activities can influence the environment, the environment can change the person's cognition, and so on.

Evaluating the Behavioral and Social Cognitive Theories   Contributions of the behavioral and social cognitive theories include (1) their emphasis on the importance of scientific research; (2) their focus on environmental determinants of behavior; (3) the identification and explanation of observational learning (by Bandura); and (4) the inclusion of person/cognitive factors (in social cognitive theory).

Criticisms of the behavioral and social cognitive theories include the objections that they give (1) too little emphasis to cognition (in Pavlov's and Skinner's theories); (2) too much emphasis to environmental determinants; (3) inadequate attention to developmental changes; and (4) inadequate recognition to human spontaneity and creativity.

Behavioral and social cognitive theories emphasize the importance of environmental experiences in human development. Next we turn our attention to a theory that underscores the importance of the biological foundations of development—ethological theory.

Ethological Theory   American developmental psychologists began to pay attention to the biological bases of development thanks to the work of European zoologists who pioneered the field of ethology. **Ethology** stresses that behavior is strongly influenced by biology, is tied to evolution, and is characterized by critical or sensitive periods. These are specific time frames during which, according to ethologists, the presence or absence of certain experiences has a long-lasting influence on individuals.

European zoologist Konrad Lorenz (1903–1989) helped bring ethology to prominence. In his best-known experiment, Lorenz (1965) studied the behavior of greylag geese, which will follow their mother as soon as they hatch.

In a remarkable set of experiments, Lorenz separated the eggs laid by one goose into two groups. One group he returned to the goose to be hatched by her. The other group was hatched in an incubator. The goslings in the first group performed as predicted. They followed their mother as soon as they hatched. However, those in the second group, which saw Lorenz when they first hatched, followed him everywhere, as though he were their mother. Lorenz marked the goslings and then placed both groups under a box. Mother goose and "mother" Lorenz stood aside as the box lifted. Each group of goslings went directly to its "mother." Lorenz called this process *imprinting,* the rapid, innate learning within a limited critical period of time that involves attachment to the first moving object seen.

Ethological research and theory at first had little or nothing to say about the nature of social relationships across the human life span, and the theory stimulated few studies with humans. Ethologists' view that normal development requires that certain behaviors emerge during a critical period, a fixed time period very early in development, seemed to be overdrawn.

However, John Bowlby (1969, 1989) illustrated an important application of ethological theory to human development. Bowlby argued that attachment to a caregiver over the first year of life has important consequences throughout the life span. In his view, if this attach-

Konrad Lorenz, a pioneering student of animal behavior, is followed through the water by three imprinted greylag geese. Describe Lorenz's experiment with the geese. *Do you think his experiment would have the same results with human babies? Explain.*
©Nina Leen/Time Life Pictures/Getty Images

ment is positive and secure, the individual will likely develop positively in childhood and adulthood. If the attachment is negative and insecure, life-span development will likely not be optimal. Thus, in this view the first year of life is a sensitive period for the development of social relationships. In the chapter "Socioemotional Development in Infancy," we explore the concept of infant attachment in much greater detail.

Contributions of ethological theory include (1) an increased focus on the biological and evolutionary basis of development; (2) use of careful observations in naturalistic settings; and (3) an emphasis on sensitive periods of development.

Criticisms of ethological theory include the following: (1) the concepts of critical and sensitive periods are perhaps too rigid; (2) the emphasis on biological foundations is too strong; (3) cognition receives inadequate attention; and (4) the theory is better at generating research with animals than with humans.

Another theory that emphasizes the biological aspects of human development—evolutionary psychology—is presented in the chapter "Biological Beginnings," along with views on the role of heredity in development.

Ecological Theory Ethological theory stresses biological factors, whereas ecological theory emphasizes environmental factors. One ecological theory that has important implications for understanding children's development was created by Urie Bronfenbrenner (1917–2005).

Bronfenbrenner's ecological theory (1986, 2000; Bronfenbrenner & Morris, 2006) holds that development reflects the influence of several environmental systems. The theory identifies five environmental systems (see Figure 10):

- *Microsystem*—the setting in which the individual lives. These contexts include the person's family, peers, school, neighborhood, and work. It is in the microsystem that the most direct interactions with social agents take place—with parents, peers, and teachers, for example.
- *Mesosystem*—relations between microsystems or connections between contexts. Examples are the relation of family experiences to school experiences, school experiences to church experiences, and family experiences to peer experiences. For example, children whose parents have rejected them may have difficulty developing positive relations with teachers.
- *Exosystem*—links between a social setting in which the individual does not have an active role and the individual's immediate context. For example, a husband's or child's experience at home may be influenced by a mother's experiences at work. The mother might receive a promotion that requires more travel, which might increase conflict with the husband and change patterns of interaction with the child.
- *Macrosystem*—the culture in which individuals live. Remember from earlier in this chapter that *culture* refers to the behavior patterns, beliefs, and all other products of a group of people that are passed on from generation to generation. Remember also that cross-cultural studies—comparisons of one culture with one or more other cultures—provide information about the generality of development (Fung, 2011).
- *Chronosystem*—the patterning of environmental events and transitions over the life course, as well as sociohistorical circumstances (Schaie, 2013). For example, divorce

developmental **connection**
Attachment
Human babies go through a series of phases in developing an attachment to a caregiver. Connect to "Socioemotional Development in Infancy."

How Would You...?
If you were an **educator,** how might you explain a student's chronic failure to complete homework from the mesosystem level? From the exosystem level?

Bronfenbrenner's ecological theory An environmental systems theory that focuses on five environmental systems: microsystem, mesosystem, exosystem, macrosystem, and chronosystem.

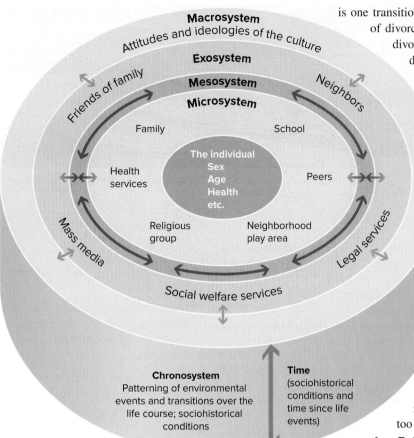

FIGURE **10**

BRONFENBRENNER'S ECOLOGICAL THEORY OF DEVELOPMENT. Bronfenbrenner's ecological theory consists of five environmental systems: microsystem, mesosytem, exosystem, macrosystem, and chronosystem.
Source: Simmons, J. "Bronfenbrenner's Ecological Theory of Development," in *Child Development in a Social Context*, Kopp, C. B., & Krakow, J. B., eds. New York: Addison-Wesley Longman, Inc., 1982, 648.

Urie Bronfenbrenner developed ecological theory, a perspective that is receiving increased attention. *What is the nature of ecological theory?*
©Cornell University Photography

is one transition. Researchers have found that the negative effects of divorce on children often peak in the first year after the divorce (Hetherington, 2006). By two years after the divorce, family interaction is less chaotic and more stable. As an example of sociohistorical circumstances, consider how the opportunities for women to pursue a career have increased during the last 30 years.

Bronfenbrenner (2000; Bronfenbrenner & Morris, 2006) has added biological influences to his theory and now describes it as a *bioecological* theory. Nonetheless, ecological, environmental contexts still predominate in Bronfenbrenner's theory.

Contributions of the theory include a systematic examination of macro and micro dimensions of environmental systems, and attention to connections between environmental systems. A further contribution of Bronfenbrenner's theory is its emphasis on a range of social contexts beyond the family, such as neighborhood, religious community, school, and workplace, as influences in children's development (Denault & Guay, 2017; Gauvain, 2016). Criticisms include giving inadequate attention to biological factors and placing too little emphasis on cognitive factors.

An Eclectic Theoretical Orientation The theories that we have discussed were developed at different points in the twentieth century, as Figure 11 shows. No single theory described in this chapter can explain entirely the rich complexity of children's development, but each has contributed to our understanding of development. Psychoanalytic theory best explains the unconscious mind. Erikson's theory best describes the changes that occur in adult development. Piaget's, Vygotsky's, and the information-processing views provide the most complete description of cognitive development. The behavioral and social cognitive and ecological theories have been the most adept at examining the environmental determinants of development. The ethological theories have highlighted biology's role and the importance of sensitive periods in development.

In short, although theories are helpful guides, relying on a single theory to explain development is probably a mistake. This book instead takes an **eclectic theoretical orientation,** which does not follow any one theoretical approach but rather selects from each theory whatever is considered its best features. In this way, you can view the study of development as it actually exists—with different theorists making different assumptions, stressing different empirical problems, and using different strategies to discover information. Figure 12 compares the main theoretical perspectives in terms of how they view important issues in children's development.

RESEARCH METHODS FOR COLLECTING DATA

If they follow an eclectic orientation, how do scholars and researchers determine that one feature of a theory is somehow better than another? The scientific method discussed earlier in this chapter provides the guide. Recall that the steps in the scientific method involve conceptualizing the problem, collecting data, drawing conclusions, and revising research conclusions and theories. Through scientific research, the features of theories can be tested and refined.

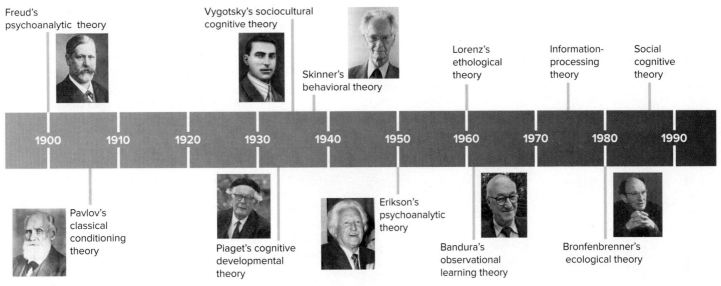

FIGURE 11

TIME LINE FOR MAJOR DEVELOPMENTAL THEORIES.

Source: Kopp, C. B., & Krakow, J. B., "Time Line for Major Developmental Theories," in *Child Development in a Social Context*, Kopp, C. B., & Krakow, J. B., eds., New York: Addison-Wesley Longman, Inc., 1982.

(Freud and Pavlov): ©Bettmann/Getty Images; *(Piaget):* ©Yves de Braine/Black Star/Stock Photo; *(Vygotsky):* ©A.R. Lauria/Dr. Michael Cole, Library of Human Cognition, UCSD; *(Skinner):* ©Harvard University Photo Services; *(Erikson):* ©Bettmann/Getty Images; *(Bandura):* Courtesy of Dr. Albert Bandura; *(Bronfenbrenner):* ©Cornell University Photography

Whether we are interested in studying attachment in infants, the cognitive skills of children, or the peer relations of adolescents, we can choose from several ways of collecting data. Here we outline the measures most often used, including their advantages and disadvantages, beginning with observation.

eclectic theoretical orientation An orientation that does not follow any one theoretical approach but rather selects from each theory whatever is considered the best in it.

Observation   Scientific observation requires an important set of skills (Leedy & Ormrod, 2016; Salkind, 2017). Unless we are trained observers and practice our skills regularly,

THEORY	ISSUES		
	Nature and nurture	**Early and later experience**	**Continuity and discontinuity**
Psychoanalytic	Freud's biological determinism interacting with early family experiences; Erikson's more balanced biological/cultural interaction perspective	Early experiences in the family very important influences	Emphasis on discontinuity between stages
Cognitive	Piaget's emphasis on interaction and adaptation; environment provides the setting for cognitive structures to develop. Vygotsky's theory involves interaction of nature and nurture with strong emphasis on culture. The information-processing approach has not addressed this issue extensively; mainly emphasizes biological/environment interaction.	Childhood experiences important influences	Discontinuity between stages in Piaget's theory; no stages in Vygotsky's theory or the information-processing approach
Behavioral and Social Cognitive	Environment viewed as the main influence on development	Experiences important at all points in development	Continuity with no stages
Ethological	Strong biological view	Early experience very important, which can contribute to change early in development; after early critical or sensitive period has passed, stability likely to occur	Discontinuity because of early critical or sensitive period; no stages
Ecological	Strong environmental view	Experiences involving the five environmental systems important at all points in development	No stages but little attention to the issue

FIGURE 12

A COMPARISON OF THEORIES AND ISSUES IN CHILD DEVELOPMENT

laboratory A controlled setting in which many of the complex factors of the "real world" are absent.

naturalistic observation Observing behavior in real-world settings.

What are some important strategies in conducting observational research with children?
©Philadelphia Inquirer/MCT/Landov Images

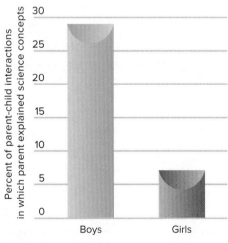

FIGURE **13**

PARENTS' EXPLANATIONS OF SCIENCE TO SONS AND DAUGHTERS AT A SCIENCE MUSEUM. In a naturalistic observation study at a children's science museum, parents were more than three times more likely to explain science to boys than to girls (Crowley & others, 2001). The gender difference occurred regardless of whether the father, the mother, or both parents were with the child, although the gender difference was greatest for fathers' science explanations to sons and daughters.

we might not know what to look for, we might not remember what we saw, we might not realize that what we are looking for is changing from one moment to the next, and we might not communicate our observations effectively.

For observations to be effective, they have to be systematic. We need to have some idea of what we are looking for. We have to know whom we are observing, when and where we will observe, how the observations will be made, and how they will be recorded.

Where should we make our observations? We have two choices: the laboratory and the everyday world.

When we observe scientifically, we often need to control certain factors that determine behavior but are not the focus of our inquiry (Leary, 2017; Stangor, 2015). For this reason, some research in children's development is conducted in a **laboratory,** a controlled setting with many of the complex factors of the "real world" removed. For example, suppose you want to observe how children react when they see other people act aggressively. If you observe children in their homes or schools, you have no control over how much aggression the children observe, what kind of aggression they see, which people they see acting aggressively, or how other people treat the children. In contrast, if you observe the children in a laboratory, you can control these and other factors and therefore have more confidence about how to interpret your observations.

Laboratory research does have some drawbacks, however. First, it is almost impossible to conduct research without the participants' knowing they are being studied. Second, the laboratory setting is unnatural and therefore can cause the participants to behave unnaturally. Third, people who are willing to come to a university laboratory may not fairly represent groups from diverse cultural backgrounds. Fourth, people who are unfamiliar with university settings and with the idea of "helping science" may be intimidated by the laboratory setting. In addition, some aspects of children's development are difficult, if not impossible, to examine in the laboratory. Last, laboratory studies of certain types of stress may even be unethical.

Naturalistic observation provides insights that we sometimes cannot achieve in the laboratory (Babbie, 2017). **Naturalistic observation** means observing behavior in real-world settings, making no effort to manipulate or control the situation. Life-span researchers conduct naturalistic observations at sporting events, child-care centers, work settings, malls, and other places people live in and frequent.

Naturalistic observation was used in one study that focused on conversations in a children's science museum (Crowley & others, 2001). Parents were more than three times more likely to engage boys than girls in explanatory talk while visiting exhibits at the science museum, suggesting a gender bias that encourages boys more than girls to be interested in science (see Figure 13). In another study, Mexican American parents who had completed high school used more explanations with their children when visiting a science museum than Mexican American parents who had not completed high school (Tenenbaum & others, 2002).

Survey and Interview Sometimes the best and quickest way to get information about people is to ask them for it. One technique is to *interview* them directly. A related method is the *survey* (sometimes referred to as a questionnaire), which is especially useful when information from many people is needed. A standard set of questions is used to obtain people's self-reported attitudes or beliefs about a specific topic. In a good survey, the questions are clear and unbiased, allowing respondents to answer unambiguously.

Surveys and interviews can be used to study a wide variety of topics ranging from religious beliefs to sexual habits to attitudes about gun control to beliefs about how to improve schools. Surveys and interviews today are conducted in person, over the telephone, and over the Internet.

One problem with surveys and interviews is the tendency of participants to answer questions in a way that they think is socially acceptable or desirable rather than telling what they truly think or feel. For example, on a survey or in an interview some individuals might say that they do not take drugs even though they do.

Standardized Test   A **standardized test** has uniform procedures for administration and scoring. Many standardized tests allow a person's performance to be compared with the performance of other individuals—thus they provide information about individual differences among people (Gregory, 2016; Kaplan & Saccuzzo, 2018). One example is the Stanford-Binet intelligence test, which is described in the chapter entitled "Cognitive Development in Middle and Late Childhood." Your score on the Stanford-Binet test tells you how your performance compares with that of thousands of other people who have taken the test.

Standardized tests also have three key weaknesses. First, they do not always predict behavior in nontest situations. Second, standardized tests are based on the belief that a person's behavior is consistent and stable, yet personality and intelligence—two primary targets of standardized testing—can vary with the situation. For example, individuals may perform poorly on a standardized intelligence test in an office setting but score much higher at home where they are less anxious. This criticism is especially relevant for members of minority groups, some of whom have been inaccurately classified as mentally retarded on the basis of their scores on intelligence tests. A third weakness of standardized tests is that many psychological tests developed in Western cultures might not be appropriate in other cultures. The experiences of people in differing cultures may lead them to interpret and respond to questions differently.

Case Study   A **case study** is an in-depth look at a single individual. Case studies are performed mainly by mental health professionals, when—for either practical or ethical reasons—the unique aspects of an individual's life cannot be duplicated and tested in other individuals. A case study provides information about one person's fears, hopes, fantasies, traumatic experiences, upbringing, family relationships, health, or anything that helps the psychologist understand the person's mind and behavior. In later chapters, we discuss vivid case studies, such as studies of Michael Rehbein, who had much of the left side of his brain removed at 7 years of age to end severe epileptic seizures.

Case histories provide dramatic, in-depth portrayals of people's lives, but we must be cautious about generalizing from this information (Yin, 2012). The subject of a case study is unique, with a genetic makeup and personal history that no one else shares. In addition, case studies involve judgments of unknown reliability. Psychologists who conduct case studies rarely check to see whether other psychologists agree with their observations.

Mahatma Gandhi was the spiritual leader of India in the middle of the twentieth century. Erik Erikson conducted an extensive case study of Gandhi's life to determine what contributed to his identity development. *What are some limitations of the case study approach?*
©Bettmann/Getty Images

Physiological Measures   Researchers are increasingly using physiological measures when they study children's development (Bell & others, 2018). Hormone levels are increasingly used in developmental research.

Cortisol is a hormone produced by the adrenal gland that is linked to the body's stress level and has been used in studies of temperament, emotional reactivity, and peer relations (Jacoby & others, 2016). Also, as puberty unfolds, the blood levels of certain hormones increase. To determine the nature of these hormonal changes, researchers analyze blood samples from adolescent volunteers (Ji & others, 2016).

Another physiological measure that is increasingly being used is neuroimaging, especially *functional magnetic resonance imaging* (fMRI), in which electromagnetic waves are used to construct images of a person's brain tissue and biochemical activity (Cabeza, Nyberg, & Park, 2017; Crone, 2017). Figure 14 compares the brain images of two adolescents—one a non-drinker and the other a heavy drinker—while they are engaged in a memory task. Electroencephaly (EEG) is a physiological measure that has been used for many decades to monitor overall electrical charges in the brain (Najjar & Brooker, 2017). Recent electroencephalograph research includes studies of infants' attention and memory (Bell & others, 2018; Lusby & others, 2017).

Heart rate has been used as an indicator of infants' and children's development of perception, attention, and memory (Kim, Yang, & Lee, 2015). Further, heart rate has been used as an index of different aspects of emotional development, such as inhibition, stress, and anxiety (Amole & others, 2017; Blood & others, 2015).

standardized test A test with uniform procedures for administration and scoring. Many standardized tests allow a person's performance to be compared with the performance of other individuals.

case study An in-depth look at a single individual.

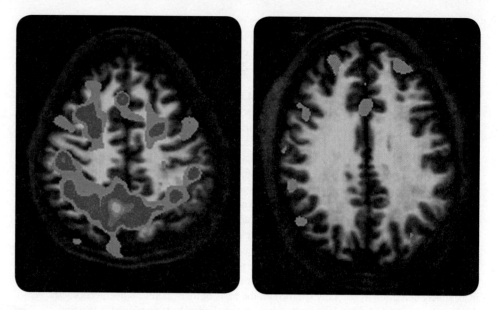

FIGURE 14

BRAIN IMAGING OF 15-YEAR-OLD ADOLESCENTS. The two brain images indicate how alcohol can influence the functioning of an adolescent's brain. Notice the pink and red coloring (which indicates effective brain functioning involving memory) in the brain of the 15-year-old non-drinker (*left*) while engaging in a memory task and the lack of those colors in the brain of the 15-year-old under the influence of alcohol (*right*).

©Dr. Susan Tapert, University of California, San Diego

Eye movement is increasingly being assessed to learn more about perceptual development and other developmental topics (Kretch & Adolph, 2017). Sophisticated eye-tracking equipment is especially being used to discover more detailed information about infants' perception (Boardman & Fletcher-Watson, 2017), attention (Meng, Uto, & Hashiya, 2017), autism (Finke, Wilkinson, & Hickerson, 2017), and preterm birth effects on language development (Loi & others, 2017).

Yet another dramatic change in physiological measures is the advancement in methods to assess the actual units of hereditary information—genes—in studies of biological influences on development (Grigorenko & others, 2016; Moore, 2017). For example, recent advances in assessing genes have revealed several specific genes that are linked to childhood obesity (Zandoná & others, 2017). We will have much more to say about these and other physiological measures in other chapters.

RESEARCH DESIGNS

Suppose you want to find out whether the children of permissive parents are more likely than other children to be rude and unruly. The data-collection method that researchers choose often depends on the goal of their research. The goal may be to describe a phenomenon, to describe relationships between phenomena, or to determine the causes or effects of a phenomenon.

Perhaps you decide that you need to observe both permissive and strict parents with their children and compare them. How would you do that? In addition to choosing a method for collecting data, you would need a research design (Leary, 2017). There are three main types of research designs: descriptive, correlational, and experimental.

Descriptive Research   All of the data-collection methods that we have discussed can be used in **descriptive research,** which aims to observe and record behavior. For example, a researcher might observe the extent to which people are altruistic or aggressive toward each other. By itself, descriptive research cannot prove what causes some phenomenon, but it can reveal important information about people's behavior.

Correlational Research   Correlational research goes beyond describing phenomena to provide information that will help us to predict how people will behave (Gravetter & Forzano, 2017). In **correlational research,** the goal is to describe the strength of the relationship between two or more events or characteristics. The more strongly the two events are correlated (or related or associated), the more effectively we can predict one event from the other (Aron, Aron, & Coups, 2017).

For example, to study whether children of permissive parents have less self-control than other children, you would need to carefully record observations of parents' permissiveness and their

descriptive research A research design that has the purpose of observing and recording behavior.

correlational research A research design whose goal is to describe the strength of the relationship between two or more events or characteristics.

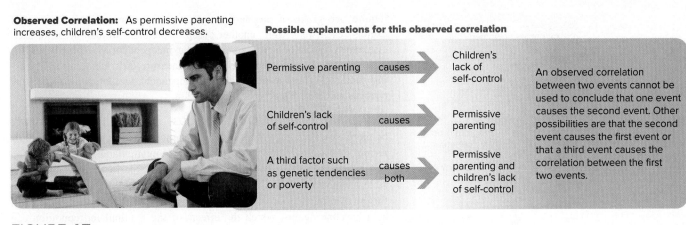

Observed Correlation: As permissive parenting increases, children's self-control decreases.

Possible explanations for this observed correlation

Permissive parenting — causes → Children's lack of self-control

Children's lack of self-control — causes → Permissive parenting

A third factor such as genetic tendencies or poverty — causes both → Permissive parenting and children's lack of self-control

An observed correlation between two events cannot be used to conclude that one event causes the second event. Other possibilities are that the second event causes the first event or that a third event causes the correlation between the first two events.

FIGURE **15**

POSSIBLE EXPLANATIONS OF CORRELATIONAL DATA

©Jupiterimages/Getty Images RF

children's self-control. The data could then be analyzed statistically to yield a numerical measure, called a **correlation coefficient,** a number based on a statistical analysis that is used to describe the degree of association between two variables. The correlation coefficient ranges from –1.00 to +1.00. A negative number means an inverse relation. For example, researchers often find a negative correlation between permissive parenting and children's self-control. By contrast, they often find a positive correlation between parental monitoring of children and children's self-control.

The higher the correlation coefficient (whether positive or negative), the stronger the association between the two variables. A correlation of 0 means that there is no association between the variables. A correlation of –2.40 is stronger than a correlation of +1.20 because we disregard whether the correlation is positive or negative in determining the strength of the correlation.

A caution is in order, however. Correlation does not equal causation (Howell, 2017). The correlational finding just mentioned does not mean that permissive parenting necessarily causes low self-control in children. It could mean that, but it also could mean that a child's lack of self-control caused the parents to simply throw up their arms in despair and give up trying to control the child. It also could mean that other factors, such as heredity or poverty, caused the correlation between permissive parenting and low self-control in children. Figure 15 illustrates these possible interpretations of correlational data.

Throughout this edition, you will read about numerous correlational research studies. Keep in mind how easy it is to assume causality when two events or characteristics merely are correlated (Jackson, 2017).

Experimental Research   To study causality, researchers turn to experimental research. An **experiment** is a carefully regulated procedure in which one or more factors believed to influence the behavior being studied are manipulated, while all other factors are held constant. If the behavior under study changes when a factor is manipulated, we say that the manipulated factor has caused the behavior to change (Kazdin, 2017). In other words, the experiment has demonstrated cause and effect. The cause is the factor that was manipulated. The effect is the behavior that changed because of the manipulation. Nonexperimental research methods (descriptive and correlational research) cannot establish cause and effect because they do not involve manipulating factors in a controlled way (Stangor, 2015).

Independent and Dependent Variables   Experiments include two types of changeable factors, or variables: independent and dependent. An *independent variable* is a manipulated, influential, experimental factor. It is a potential cause. The label *independent* is used because this variable can be manipulated independently of other factors to determine its effect. One experiment may include several independent variables.

A *dependent variable* is a factor that can change in an experiment, in response to changes in the independent variable. As researchers manipulate the independent variable, they measure the dependent variable for any resulting effect.

For example, suppose that you conducted a study to determine whether aerobic exercise by pregnant women changes the breathing and sleeping patterns of newborn babies. You might

correlation coefficient A number based on statistical analysis that is used to describe the degree of association between two variables.

experiment A carefully regulated procedure in which one or more of the factors believed to influence the behavior being studied are manipulated, while all other factors are held constant.

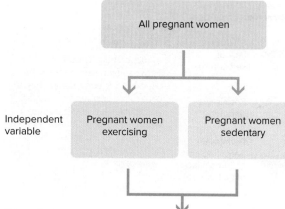

Independent variable

Dependent variable

FIGURE 16

PRINCIPLES OF EXPERIMENTAL RESEARCH. Imagine that you decide to conduct an experimental study of the effects of aerobic exercise by pregnant women on their newborns' breathing and sleeping patterns. You would randomly assign pregnant women to experimental and control groups. The experimental-group women would engage in aerobic exercise over a specified number of sessions and weeks. The control group would not. Then, when the infants are born, you would assess their breathing and sleeping patterns. If the breathing and sleeping patterns of newborns whose mothers were in the experimental group are different from those of the control group, you would conclude that aerobic exercise caused these effects.

cross-sectional approach A research strategy in which individuals of different ages are compared at one time.

longitudinal approach A research strategy in which the same individuals are studied over a period of time, usually several years or more.

require one group of pregnant women to engage in a certain amount of exercise each week while another group of pregnant women does not exercise; thus, the amount of exercise is the independent variable. When the infants are born, you would observe and measure their breathing and sleeping patterns. These patterns are the dependent variable, the factor that changes as the result of your manipulation.

Experimental and Control Groups Experiments can involve one or more experimental groups and one or more control groups. An *experimental group* is a group whose experience is manipulated. A *control group* is a comparison group that is as much like the experimental group as possible and that is treated in every way like the experimental group except for the manipulated factor (independent variable). The control group serves as a baseline against which the effects of the manipulated condition can be compared.

Random assignment is an important principle for deciding whether each participant will be placed in the experimental group or in the control group. Random assignment means that researchers assign participants to experimental and control groups by chance. It reduces the likelihood that the experiment's results will be due to any preexisting differences between groups (Gravetter & Forzano, 2017). In the example of the effects of aerobic exercise by pregnant women on the breathing and sleeping patterns of their newborns, you would randomly assign half of the pregnant women to engage in aerobic exercise over a period of weeks (the experimental group) and the other half to not exercise over the same number of weeks (the control group). Figure 16 illustrates the nature of experimental research.

Time Span of Research Researchers in child development have a special concern with studies that focus on the relation of age to some other variable. To do this, they can study different individuals of various ages and compare them, or they can study the same individuals as they age over time.

Cross-Sectional Approach The **cross-sectional approach** is a research strategy in which individuals of different ages are compared at one time. A typical cross-sectional study might include a group of 5-year-olds, 8-year-olds, and 11-year-olds. The groups can be compared with respect to a variety of dependent variables: IQ, memory, peer relations, attachment to parents, hormonal changes, and so on. All of these comparisons can be accomplished in a short time. In some studies, data are collected in a single day. Even in large-scale cross-sectional studies with hundreds of participants, data collection does not usually take longer than several months to complete.

The main advantage of the cross-sectional study is that researchers don't have to wait for children to grow older. Despite its efficiency, the cross-sectional approach has its drawbacks. It gives no information about how individual children change or about the stability of their characteristics. It can obscure the increases and decreases of development—the hills and valleys of growth and development.

Longitudinal Approach The **longitudinal approach** is a research strategy in which the same individuals are studied over a period of time, usually several years or more. For example, if a study of self-esteem were conducted longitudinally, the same children might be assessed three times—at 5, 8, and 11 years of age. Some longitudinal studies take place over shorter time frames, even just a year or so.

Longitudinal studies provide a wealth of information about important issues such as stability and change in development and the influence of early experience on later development, but they are not without their problems (Cicchetti & Toth, 2016). They are expensive and time-consuming. Also, the longer the study lasts, the more participants drop out. For example, children's families may move, get sick, lose interest, and so forth. Those who remain in the study may be dissimilar to those who drop out, biasing the results. Those individuals who remain in a longitudinal study over a number of years may be more compulsive and conformity-oriented or they might have more stable lives.

Earlier in the chapter we described *cohort effects,* which are effects due to a person's time of birth, era, or generation, but not to actual age. Cohort effects are important in research on children, adolescents, and their parents because they can powerfully affect the dependent measures in a study ostensibly concerned with age (Grondahl & others, 2017; Schaie, 2016). Cross-sectional studies can show how different cohorts respond, but they can confuse age changes and cohort effects. Longitudinal studies are effective in studying age changes but only within one cohort.

So far we have discussed many aspects of scientific research in child development. In the *Connecting with Research* interlude, you can read about the research journals in which the findings of research studies are published.

RESEARCH CHALLENGES

The scientific foundation of research in child development helps to minimize the effect of research bias and maximize the objectivity of the results. Still, subtle challenges remain for each researcher to resolve. One is to ensure that research is conducted in an ethical way; another is to recognize, and try to overcome, deeply buried personal biases related to gender and ethnicity.

Conducting Ethical Research   The explosion in technology has forced society to grapple with looming ethical questions that were unimaginable only a few decades ago. The same line of research that enables previously infertile couples to have children might someday let prospective parents "call up and order" the characteristics they prefer in their children or tip the balance of males and females in the world. As another example of an ethical dilemma, should embryos left over from procedures for increasing fertility be saved or discarded? Should people with inheritable fatal diseases (such as Huntington disease) be discouraged from having children?

Researchers also face ethical questions both new and old. They have a responsibility to anticipate the personal problems their research might cause and to at least inform the participants of the possible fallout. Safeguarding the rights of research participants is a challenge because the potential harm is not always obvious (Kazdin, 2017).

Ethics in research may affect you personally if you ever serve as a participant in a study. In that event, you need to know your rights as a participant and the responsibilities of researchers to ensure that these rights are safeguarded.

If you ever become a researcher in child development yourself, you will need an even deeper understanding of ethics. Even if you only carry out experimental projects in psychology courses, you must consider the rights of the participants in those projects.

Today, proposed research at colleges and universities must pass the scrutiny of a research ethics committee before the research can be initiated. In addition, the American Psychological Association (APA) has developed ethics guidelines for its members. The code of ethics instructs psychologists to protect their participants from mental and physical harm. The participants' best interests need to be kept foremost in the researcher's mind (Jackson, 2016). APA's guidelines address four important issues: informed consent, confidentiality, debriefing, and deception.

- *Informed consent.* All participants must know what their participation will involve and what risks might develop. For example, participants in a study on dating should be told beforehand that a questionnaire might stimulate thoughts about issues in their relationship that they have not considered. Participants also should be informed that in some instances a discussion of the issues might improve their relationship, but in others might worsen the relationship and even end it. Even after informed consent is given, participants must retain the right to withdraw from the study at any time and for any reason.
- *Confidentiality.* Researchers are responsible for keeping all of the data they gather on individuals completely confidential and, when possible, completely anonymous.
- *Debriefing.* After the study has been completed, participants should be informed of its purpose and the methods that were used. In most cases, the experimenter also can inform participants in a general manner beforehand about the purpose of the research without leading participants to behave in a way they think that the experimenter is expecting. When preliminary information about the study is likely to affect the results, participants can at least be debriefed after the study has been completed.
- *Deception.* This is an ethical issue that researchers debate extensively. In some circumstances, telling the participants beforehand what the research study is about

Why Are Research Journals Important in the Field of Child Development?

Regardless of whether you pursue a career in child development, psychology, or some related scientific field, you can benefit by learning about the journal process. As a student you might be required to look up original research in journals. As a parent, teacher, or nurse you might want to consult journals to obtain information that will help you understand and work more effectively with people. And as an inquiring person, you might look up information in journals after you have heard or read something that piqued your curiosity.

A journal publishes scholarly and academic information, usually in a specific domain—like physics, math, sociology, or our current interest, child development. Scholars in these fields publish most of their research in journals, which are the source of core information in virtually every academic discipline.

An increasing number of journals publish information about child development. Among the leading journals in child development are *Developmental Psychology, Child Development, Developmental Psychopathology, Pediatrics, Pediatric Nursing, Infant Behavior and Development, Journal of Research on Adolescence, Human Development,* and many others. Also, a number of journals that do not focus solely on development publish articles on various aspects of human development. These journals include *Journal of Educational Psychology, Sex Roles, Journal of Cross-Cultural Research, Journal of Marriage and the Family, Exceptional Children,* and *Journal of Consulting and Clinical Psychology.*

Every journal has a board of experts who evaluate articles submitted for publication. Each submitted paper is accepted or rejected on the basis of factors such as its contribution to the field, methodological excellence, and clarity of writing. Some of the most prestigious journals reject as many as 80 to 90 percent of the articles submitted.

Journal articles are usually written for other professionals in the specialized field of the journal's focus—therefore, they often contain technical language and terms specific to the discipline that are difficult for nonprofessionals to understand. Their organization often takes this course: abstract, introduction, method, results, discussion, and references.

The *abstract* is a brief summary that appears at the beginning of the article. The abstract lets readers quickly determine whether the article is relevant to their interests. The *introduction* introduces the problem or issue that is being studied. It includes a concise review of research relevant to the topic, theoretical ties, and one or more hypotheses to be tested. The *method* section consists of a clear description of the subjects evaluated in the study, the measures used, and the procedures that were followed. The method section should be sufficiently clear and detailed so that by reading it another researcher could repeat or replicate the study. The *results* section reports the analysis of the data collected. In most cases, the results section includes statistical analyses that are difficult for nonprofessionals to understand. The *discussion* section describes the author's conclusions, inferences, and interpretation of what was found. Statements are usually made about whether the hypotheses presented in the introduction were supported, limitations of the study, and suggestions for future research. The last part of the journal article, called *references,* includes bibliographic information for each source cited in the article. The references section is often a good resource for finding other articles relevant to a topic that interests you.

Research journals are the core of information in virtually every academic discipline. Those shown here are among the increasing number of research journals that publish information about child development. *What are the main parts of a research article that presents findings from original research?*

©McGraw Hill Companies/Mark Dierker, photographer

Where do you find journals such as those we have described? Your college or university library likely has some of them, and some public libraries also carry journals. Online resources such as PsycINFO and PubMed, which can facilitate the search for journal articles, are available to students on many campuses.

substantially alters the participants' behavior and invalidates the researcher's data. In all cases, however, the psychologist must ensure that the deception will not harm the participants and that the participants will be told the complete nature of the study (debriefed) as soon as possible after the study is completed.

Minimizing Bias Studies of children's development are most useful when they are conducted without bias or prejudice toward any specific group of people. Of special concern is bias based on gender and bias based on culture or ethnicity.

Gender Bias For most of its existence, our society has had a strong gender bias, a preconceived notion about the abilities of males and females that prevented individuals from pursuing their own interests and achieving their potential (Brannon, 2017; Helgeson, 2017). Gender bias also has had a less obvious effect within the field of child development. For example, it is not unusual for conclusions to be drawn about females' attitudes and behaviors from research conducted with males as the only participants.

Furthermore, when researchers find gender differences, their reports sometimes magnify those differences (Denmark & others, 1988). For example, a researcher might report that 74 percent of the boys in a study had high achievement expectations versus only 67 percent of the girls and go on to talk about the differences in some detail. In reality, this might be a rather small difference. It also might disappear if the study were repeated, or the study might have methodological problems that don't allow such strong interpretations.

Pam Reid, a leading researcher who has studied gender and ethnic bias in development, more recently has become a college president. To read about Pam's career, see the *Connecting with Careers* profile.

Cultural and Ethnic Bias In recent years, there has been a growing realization that research on children's development needs to include more children from diverse ethnic groups (Giuntella, 2017; Umana-Taylor & Douglass, 2017). Historically, children from ethnic minority groups (African American, Latino, Asian American, and Native American) were excluded from most research in the United States and simply thought of as variations from the norm or average. If minority children were included in samples and their scores didn't fit the norm, they were viewed as confounds or "noise" in data and discounted. Given the fact that children from diverse ethnic groups were excluded from research on child development for so long, we might reasonably conclude that children's real lives are perhaps more varied than research data have indicated in the past.

Researchers also have tended to overgeneralize about ethnic groups (Parrillo, 2014). **Ethnic gloss** is the use of an ethnic label such as African American or Latino in a superficial way that portrays an ethnic group as being more homogeneous than it really is (Trimble, 1988). For example, a researcher might describe a research sample like this:

developmental connection

Gender

Gender stereotyping continues to be extensive. Recent research indicates that girls and older children use a higher percentage of gender stereotypes than younger children and boys. Connect to "Socioemotional Development in Middle and Late Childhood."

ethnic gloss The use of an ethnic label such as African American or Latino in a superficial way that portrays an ethnic group as being more homogeneous than it really is.

connecting with careers

Pam Reid, Educational and Developmental Psychologist

When she was a child, Pam Reid liked to play with chemistry sets. Reid majored in chemistry during college and wanted to become a doctor. However, when some of her friends signed up for a psychology class as an elective, she also decided to take the course. She was intrigued by learning about how people think, behave, and develop—so much so that she changed her major to psychology. Reid went on to obtain her Ph.D. in psychology (American Psychological Association, 2003, p. 16).

For a number of years Reid was a professor of education and psychology at the University of Michigan, where she also was a research scientist at the Institute for Research on Women and Gender. Her main focus has been on how children and adolescents develop social skills, with a special interest in the development of African American girls (Reid & Zalk, 2001). In 2004, Reid became provost and executive vice-president at Roosevelt University in Chicago. In January 2008 she was appointed president of Saint Joseph College in Hartford, Connecticut.

Pam Reid (*center*) with students at Saint Joseph College in Hartford, Connecticut, where she is the president of the college.
Courtesy of Dr. Pam Reid

For more information about what professors, researchers, and educational psychologists do, see the Careers in Children's Development Appendix.

Look at these two photographs, one (*left*) of all non-Latino White boys, the other (*right*) of boys and girls from diverse ethnic backgrounds. Consider a topic in child development such as independence seeking, cultural values, parenting education, or health care. *If you were conducting research on this topic, might the results of the study be different depending on whether the participants in your study were the children in the photo on the left or the photo on the right?*

(*left*): ©Kevin Fleming/Corbis/Getty Images; (*right*): ©Ed Honowitz/The Image Bank/Getty Images

"The participants were 60 Latinos." A more complete description of the Latino group might be something like this: "The 60 Latino participants were Mexican Americans from low-income neighborhoods in the southwestern area of Los Angeles. Thirty-six were from homes in which Spanish is the dominant language spoken, 24 from homes in which English is the main language spoken. Thirty were born in the United States, 30 in Mexico. Twenty-eight described themselves as Mexican American, 14 as Mexican, 9 as American, 6 as Chicano, and 3 as Latino." Ethnic gloss can cause researchers to obtain samples of ethnic groups that are not representative of the group's diversity, which can lead to overgeneralization and stereotyping.

Research on ethnic minority children and their families has not been given adequate attention, especially in light of their significant rate of growth within the overall population. Until recently, ethnic minority families were combined in the category "minority," which masks important differences among ethnic groups as well as diversity within an ethnic group. At present and in the foreseeable future, the growth of minority families in the United States will be mainly due to the immigration of Latino and Asian families (Bas-Sarmiento & others, 2017; Lo & others, 2017). Researchers need to take into account their acculturation level and the generational status of both parents and adolescents (Umana-Taylor & Douglass, 2017). More attention needs to be given to biculturalism because many immigrant children and adolescents identify with two or more ethnic groups (Coard, 2017; Echevarria, Vogt, & Short, 2017; Nieto & Bode, 2018).

Review Connect Reflect

 LG3 Summarize why research is important in child development, the main theories of child development, and research methods, designs, and challenges.

Review
- Why is research on child development important?
- What are the main theories of child development?
- What are the main research methods for collecting data about children's development?
- What types of research designs do child development researchers use?
- What are some research challenges in studying children's development?

Connect
- Which of the research methods for collecting data would be appropriate or inappropriate for studying Erikson's stage of trust versus mistrust? Why?

Reflect *Your Own Personal Journey of Life*
- Imagine that you are conducting a research study on the sexual attitudes and behaviors of adolescents. What ethical safeguards should you use in conducting the study?

topical connections *looking forward*

You will continue to learn more about theory and research as we further explore the biological underpinnings of children's development. You will read about the evolutionary perspective and the genetic foundations of development. Challenges and choices people encounter when deciding to reproduce are covered, including the new reproductive choices made possible by advancing technology. Many aspects of adopting children also are examined. These topics set the stage for an introduction to the complex interaction of heredity and environment in children's development.

reach your **learning goals**

Introduction

1 Why Is Caring for Children Important?

LG1 Explain why it is important to study children's development, and identify five areas in which children's lives need to be improved.

The Importance of Studying Children's Development

Improving the Lives of Children

- Studying children's development is important because it will help you to better understand your own childhood and provide you with strategies for being a competent parent or educator.

- Health and well-being are important areas in which children's lives can be improved. Today, many children in the United States and around the world need improved health care. We now recognize the importance of lifestyles and psychological states in promoting health and well-being.

- Parenting is an important influence on children's development. One-parent families, working parents, and child care are among the family issues that influence children's well-being.

- Education can also contribute to children's health and well-being. There is widespread concern that the education of children needs to be more effective, and there are many views in contemporary education about ways to improve schools.

- Sociocultural contexts are important influences on children's development. Culture, ethnicity, socioeconomic status, and gender are four key aspects of sociocultural contexts.

- Social policy is a national government's course of action designed to influence the welfare of its citizens. Researchers increasingly are conducting studies that are related to social policy.

2 What Characterizes Development?

LG2 Discuss processes, periods, cohort effects, and issues in development.

Biological, Cognitive, and Socioemotional Processes

Periods of Development

Age and Cohort Effects

- Three key processes of development are biological, cognitive, and socioemotional. Biological processes (such as genetic inheritance) involve changes in an individual's physical nature. Cognitive processes (such as thinking) consist of changes in an individual's thought, intelligence, and language. Socioemotional processes (such as smiling) include changes in an individual's relationships with others, in emotions, and in personality.

- Childhood's five main developmental periods are (1) prenatal—conception to birth, (2) infancy—birth to 18 to 24 months, (3) early childhood—end of infancy to about 5 to 6 years of age, (4) middle and late childhood—about 6 to 11 years of age, and (5) adolescence—begins at about 10 to 12 and ends at about 18 to 22 years of age.

- Cohort effects are due to a person's time of birth, era, or generation but not to actual age. Two characteristics of today's children and many of their parents—the generation labeled Millennials—that stand out are (1) their ethnic diversity and (2) their connection to technology.

- The nature-nurture issue focuses on the extent to which development is mainly influenced by nature (biological inheritance) or nurture (environmental experience).

- Some developmentalists describe development as continuous (gradual, cumulative change), while others describe it as discontinuous (a sequence of abrupt stages).

- The early-later experience issue focuses on whether early experiences (especially in infancy) are more important in development than later experiences.

- Most developmentalists recognize that extreme positions on the nature-nurture, continuity-discontinuity, and early-later experience issues are not supported by research. Despite this consensus, they continue to debate the degree to which each factor influences children's development.

3 How Is Child Development a Science?

LG3 Summarize why research is important in child development, the main theories of child development, and research methods, designs, and challenges.

The Importance of Research

- When we base information on personal experience, we aren't always objective. Research provides a vehicle for evaluating the accuracy of information. Scientific research is objective, systematic, and testable. Scientific research is based on the scientific method, which includes these steps: conceptualize the problem, collect data, draw conclusions, and revise research conclusions and theory.

Theories of Child Development

- Psychoanalytic theories describe development as primarily unconscious and as heavily colored by emotion. The two main psychoanalytic theories in developmental psychology are Freud's and Erikson's. Freud proposed that individuals go through five psychosexual stages—oral, anal, phallic, latency, and genital. Erikson's theory emphasizes eight psychosocial stages of development.

- The three main cognitive theories are Piaget's cognitive developmental theory, Vygotsky's sociocultural cognitive theory, and information-processing theory. Cognitive theories emphasize conscious thoughts. In Piaget's theory, children go through four cognitive stages: sensorimotor, preoperational, concrete operational, and formal operational. Vygotsky's sociocultural cognitive theory emphasizes how culture and social interaction guide cognitive development. The information-processing theory emphasizes that individuals manipulate information, monitor it, and strategize about it.

- Three versions of the behavioral and social cognitive approach are Pavlov's classical conditioning, Skinner's operant conditioning, and Bandura's social cognitive theory.

- Ethology stresses that behavior is strongly influenced by biology, is tied to evolution, and is characterized by critical or sensitive periods.

- Ecological theory is Bronfenbrenner's environmental systems view of development. It consists of five environmental systems: microsystem, mesosystem, exosystem, macrosystem, and chronosystem. An eclectic theoretical orientation does not follow any one theoretical approach but rather selects from each theory whatever is considered the best aspects of it.

Research Methods for Collecting Data

- Research methods for collecting data about child development include observation (in a laboratory or a naturalistic setting), survey (questionnaire) or interview, standardized test, case study, and physiological measures.

Research Designs

- Descriptive research aims to observe and record behavior. In correlational research, the goal is to describe the strength of the relationship between two or more events or characteristics.

- Experimental research involves conducting an experiment, which can determine cause and effect. An independent variable is the manipulated, influential, experimental factor. A dependent variable is a factor that can change in an experiment, in response to changes in the independent variable.

- Experiments can involve one or more experimental groups and control groups. In random assignment, researchers assign participants to experimental and control groups by chance. When researchers decide about the time span of their research, they can conduct cross-sectional or longitudinal studies.

Research Challenges

- Researchers' ethical responsibilities include seeking participants' informed consent, ensuring their confidentiality, debriefing them about the purpose and potential personal consequences of participating, and avoiding unnecessary deception of participants.

- Researchers need to guard against gender, cultural, and ethnic bias in research. Every effort should be made to make research equitable for both females and males. Individuals from varied ethnic backgrounds need to be included as participants in child research, and overgeneralization about diverse members within a group must be avoided.

key terms

adolescence	cross-sectional approach	experiment	Piaget's theory
biological processes	culture	gender	prenatal period
Bronfenbrenner's ecological theory	descriptive research	hypothesis	psychoanalytic theories
case study	development	infancy	scientific method
cognitive processes	early childhood	information-processing theory	social cognitive theory
cohort effects	early-later experience issue	laboratory	social policy
context	eclectic theoretical orientation	longitudinal approach	socioeconomic status (SES)
continuity-discontinuity issue	Erikson's theory	middle and late childhood	socioemotional processes
correlational research	ethnic gloss	Millennials	standardized test
correlation coefficient	ethnicity	naturalistic observation	theory
cross-cultural studies	ethology	nature-nurture issue	Vygotsky's theory

key people

Albert Bandura	Erik Erikson	Ann Masten	Robert Siegler
John Bowlby	Sigmund Freud	Ivan Pavlov	B. F. Skinner
Urie Bronfenbrenner	Konrad Lorenz	Jean Piaget	Lev Vygotsky

connecting with improving the lives of children

STRATEGIES

Lessons for Life

Marian Wright Edelman is one of America's foremost crusaders in the quest for improving the lives of children. Here are some of the main strategies she advocates for improving not only children's lives but our own as well (Edelman, 1992, pp. xxi, 42, 60):

· *"Don't feel as if you are entitled to anything that you don't sweat and struggle for."* Take the initiative to create opportunities. Don't wait around for people to give you favors. A door never has to stay closed. Push on it until it opens.

· *"Don't be afraid of taking risks or of being criticized."* We all make mistakes. It is only through making mistakes that we learn how to do things right. "It doesn't matter how many times you fall down. What matters is how many times we get up." We need "more courageous shepherds and fewer sheep."

· *"Don't ever stop learning and improving your mind or you're going to get left behind."* College is a great investment, but don't think you can park your mind there and everything you need to know will somehow be magically poured into it. Be an active learner. Be curious and ask questions. Explore new horizons.

· *"Stand up for children."* According to Edelman, this is the most important mission in the world. Parenting and nurturing the next generation of children are our society's most important functions, and we need to take these responsibilities more seriously than we have in the past.

RESOURCES

Children's Defense Fund
www.childrensdefense.org

The Children's Defense Fund provides a strong and effective voice for children and adolescents who cannot vote, lobby, or speak for themselves. The Children's Defense Fund is especially interested in the needs of poor, minority, and handicapped children and adolescents. The fund provides information, technical assistance, and support to a network of state and local child and youth advocates. The Children's Defense Fund publishes a number of excellent books and pamphlets related to children's needs.

Cambridge Handbook of International Prevention Science (2017)
Moshe Israelashvili and John Romano, Editors
New York: Cambridge University Press

Provides up-to-date coverage of social policy and intervention in children's live to improve their well-being and development in the United States and countries around the world.

Encyclopedia of Lifespan Development (2018)
Marc Bornstein, Editor
Thousand Oaks, CA: SAGE

Leading experts provide up-to-date discussions of many topics in child development.

appendix

Careers in Children's Development

Each of us wants to find a rewarding career and enjoy the work we do. The field of child development offers an amazing breadth of career options that can provide extremely satisfying work.

If you decide to pursue a career in child development, what career options are available to you? There are many. Professors in colleges and universities teach courses in areas of child development, education, family development, nursing, and medicine. Teachers impart knowledge, understanding, and skills to children and adolescents. Counselors, clinical psychologists, nurses, and physicians help parents and children of different ages to cope more effectively with their lives and maintain their well-being. Various professionals work with families to improve the quality of family functioning.

Although an advanced degree is not absolutely necessary in some areas of child development, you usually can expand your opportunities (and income) considerably by obtaining a graduate degree. Many careers in child development pay reasonably well. For example, psychologists earn well above the median salary in the United States. Also, by working in the field of child development you can guide people in improving their lives, understand yourself and others better, possibly advance the state of knowledge in the field, and have an enjoyable time while you are doing these things.

If you are considering a career in child development, would you prefer to work with infants? Children? Adolescents? Parents? As you go through this term, try to spend some time with children of different ages. Observe their behavior. Talk with them about their lives. Think about whether you would like to work with children of this age in your life's work.

Another important aspect of exploring careers is talking with people who work in various jobs. For example, if you have some interest in becoming a school counselor, call a school, ask to speak with a counselor, and set up an appointment to discuss the counselor's career and work.

Something else that should benefit you is working in one or more jobs related to your career interests while you are in college. Many colleges and universities have internships or work experiences for students who major in fields such as child development. In some instances, these jobs earn course credit or pay; in others, they are strictly on a volunteer basis. Take advantage of these opportunities. They can provide you with valuable experiences to help

you decide if this is the right career for you—and they can help you get into graduate school, if you decide you want to go.

In the upcoming sections, we profile careers in four areas: education and research; clinical and counseling; medical, nursing, and physical development; and families and relationships. These are not the only career options in child development, but they should provide you with an idea of the range of opportunities available and information about some of the main career avenues you might pursue. In profiling these careers, we address the amount of education required, the nature of the training, and a description of the work.

Education and Research

Numerous career opportunities in child development involve education or research. These range from college professor to child-care director to school psychologist.

College/University Professor

Courses in child development are taught in many programs and schools within colleges and universities, including psychology, education, nursing, child and family studies, social work, and medicine. The work that college professors do includes teaching courses at either the undergraduate or graduate level (or both), conducting research in a specific area, advising students and/or directing their research, and serving on college or university committees. Some college instructors do not conduct research as part of their jobs but instead focus mainly on teaching. Research is most likely to be part of the job description at universities with master's and Ph.D. programs. A Ph.D. or master's degree almost always is required to teach in some area of child development in a college or university. Obtaining a doctoral degree usually takes four to six years of graduate work. A master's degree requires approximately two years of graduate work. The training involves taking graduate courses, learning to conduct research, and attending and presenting papers at professional meetings. Many graduate students work as teaching or research assistants for professors in an apprenticeship relationship that helps them to become competent teachers and researchers.

If you are interested in becoming a college or university professor, you might want to make an appointment with your instructor in this class on child development to learn more about his or her profession and work.

To read about the work of one college professor, see the Connecting with Careers profile about the career and work of Valerie Pang.

Researcher

Some individuals in the field of child development work in research positions. In most instances, they have either a master's or Ph.D. in some area of child development. The researchers might work at a university, in some cases in a university professor's research program, in a government agency such as the National Institute of Mental Health, or in private industry. Individuals who have full-time research positions in child development generate innovative research ideas, plan studies, and carry out the research by collecting data, analyzing the data, and then interpreting it. Then they will usually attempt to publish the research in a scientific journal. A researcher often works in a collaborative manner with other researchers on a project and may present the research at scientific meetings. One researcher might spend much of his or her time in a laboratory; another researcher might work primarily in the field, such as in schools, hospitals, and so on.

Elementary School Teacher

The work of an elementary or secondary school teacher involves teaching in one or more subject areas, preparing the curriculum, giving tests, assigning grades, monitoring students' progress, conducting parent-teacher conferences, and attending in-service workshops. Becoming an elementary or secondary school teacher requires a minimum of an undergraduate degree. The training involves taking a wide range of courses with a major or concentration in education, as well as completing a supervised practice-teaching internship.

Exceptional Children (Special Education) Teacher

A teacher of exceptional children spends concentrated time with individual children who have a disability or are gifted. Among the children a teacher of exceptional children might work with are children with learning disabilities, ADHD (attention deficit hyperactivity disorder), intellectual disabilities, or a physical disability such as cerebral palsy. Some of this work will usually be done outside of the student's regular classroom, and some of it will be carried out when the student is in the regular

Valerie Pang, Professor of Teacher Education

Valerie Pang is a professor of education at San Diego State University and formerly was an elementary school teacher. Like Dr. Pang, many professors of teacher education hold a doctoral degree and have experience in teaching at the elementary and/or secondary level.

Pang earned a doctorate at the University of Washington. She received a Multicultural Education Award from the National Association of Multicultural Education for her work on culture and equity. She also was given the Distinguished Scholar Award by the American Educational Research Association's Committee on the Role and Status of Minorities in Education.

Pang (2005) believes that competent teachers need to:

- Recognize the power and complexity of cultural influences on students
- Be sensitive to whether their expectations for students are culturally biased
- Evaluate whether they are doing a good job of seeing life from the perspective of students who come from different cultures

Valerie Ooka Pang is a professor in the School of Education of San Diego State University and formerly was an elementary school teacher. Valerie believes it is important for teachers to create a caring classroom that affirms all students.
Courtesy of Valerie Ooka Pang

---

classroom. A teacher of exceptional children works closely with the student's regular classroom teacher and parents to create the best educational program for the student. Becoming a teacher of exceptional children requires a minimum of an undergraduate degree. The training consists of taking a wide range of courses in education and a concentration of courses in educating children with disabilities or children who are gifted. Teachers of exceptional children often continue their education after obtaining their undergraduate degree and attain a master's degree.

To read about the work of one teacher of exceptional children, see the Connecting with Careers profile in "Physical Development in Middle and Late Childhood."

Early Childhood Educator

Early childhood educators work on college faculties and have a minimum of a master's degree in their field. In graduate school, they take courses in early childhood education and receive supervisory training in child-care or early childhood programs. Early childhood educators usually teach in community colleges that award an associate's degree in early childhood education.

Preschool/Kindergarten Teacher

Preschool teachers teach mainly 4-year-old children, and kindergarten teachers primarily teach 5-year-old children. They usually have an undergraduate degree in education, specializing in early childhood education. State certification to become a preschool or kindergarten teacher usually is required.

Family and Consumer Science Educator

Family and consumer science educators may specialize in early childhood education or instruct middle and high school students about such matters as nutrition, interpersonal relationships, sexuality, parenting, and human development. Hundreds of colleges and universities throughout the United States offer two- and four-year degree programs in family and consumer science. These programs usually include an internship requirement. Additional education courses may be needed to obtain a teaching certificate. Some family and consumer educators go on to graduate school for further training, which provides a background for possible jobs in college teaching or research.

To read about the work of one family and consumer science educator, see the Connecting with Careers profile in "Socioemotional Development in Middle and Late Childhood."

Educational Psychologist

An educational psychologist most often teaches in a college or university and conducts research in areas of educational psychology such as learning, motivation, classroom management, and assessment. Most educational psychologists have a doctorate in education, which takes four to six years of graduate work. They help to train students who will take various positions in education, including educational psychologist, school psychologist, and teacher.

To read about the work of one educational psychologist, see the Connecting with Careers profile in the "Introduction" chapter.

School Psychologist

School psychologists focus on improving the psychological and intellectual well-being of elementary and secondary school students. They may work in a centralized office in a school district or in one or more schools. They give psychological tests, interview students and their parents, consult with teachers, and may provide counseling to students and their families.

School psychologists usually have a master's or doctoral degree in school psychology. In graduate school, they take courses in counseling, assessment, learning, and other areas of education and psychology.

Clinical and Counseling

There are a wide variety of clinical and counseling jobs that are linked with child development.

These range from child clinical psychologist to adolescent drug counselor.

Clinical Psychologist

Clinical psychologists seek to help people with psychological problems. They work in a variety of settings, including colleges and universities, clinics, medical schools, and private practice. Some clinical psychologists only conduct psychotherapy; others do psychological assessment and psychotherapy; and some also do research. Clinical psychologists may specialize in a particular age group, such as children (child clinical psychologist).

Clinical psychologists have either a Ph.D. (which involves clinical and research training) or a Psy.D. degree (which involves only clinical training). This graduate training usually takes five to seven years and includes courses in clinical psychology and a one-year supervised internship in an accredited setting toward the end of the training. In most cases, they must pass a test to become licensed in a state and to call themselves clinical psychologists.

To read about the work of one clinical psychologist, see the Connecting with Careers profile in the "Introduction" chapter.

Psychiatrist

Like clinical psychologists, psychiatrists might specialize in working with children (child psychiatry) or adolescents (adolescent psychiatry). Psychiatrists might work in medical schools in teaching and research roles, in a medical clinic, or in private practice. In addition to administering drugs to help improve the lives of people with psychological problems, psychiatrists also may conduct psychotherapy. Psychiatrists obtain a medical degree and then do a residency in psychiatry. Medical school takes approximately four years, and the psychiatry residency takes another three to four years. Unlike psychologists (who do not go to medical school), in most states psychiatrists can administer drugs to clients.

To read about the work of one child psychiatrist, see the Connecting with Careers profile in "Socioemotional Development in Middle and Late Childhood."

Counseling Psychologist

Counseling psychologists work in the same settings as clinical psychologists and may do psychotherapy, teach, or conduct research. In many instances, however, counseling psychologists do not work with individuals who have a severe mental disorder. A counseling psychologist might specialize in working with children, adolescents, and/or families.

Counseling psychologists go through much of the same training as clinical psychologists, but in a graduate program in counseling rather than clinical psychology. Counseling psychologists have either a master's degree or a doctoral degree. They also must go through a licensing procedure. One type of master's degree in counseling leads to the designation of licensed professional counselor.

School Counselor

School counselors help to identify students' abilities and interests, guide students in developing academic plans, and explore career options with students. They may help students cope with adjustment problems. They may work with students individually, in small groups, or even in a classroom. They often consult with parents, teachers, and school administrators when trying to help students with their problems.

High school counselors advise students on choosing a major, fulfilling admissions requirements for college, taking entrance exams, applying for financial aid, and enrolling in appropriate vocational and technical training. Elementary school counselors are mainly involved in counseling students about social and personal problems. They may observe children in the classroom and at play as part of their work. School counselors usually have a master's degree in counseling.

To read about the work of one high school counselor, see the Connecting with Careers profile in "Cognitive Development in Adolescence."

Career Counselor

Career counselors help individuals to identify their best career options and guide them in applying for jobs. They may work in private industry or at a college or university. They usually interview individuals and give them vocational or psychological tests to target careers that fit their interests and abilities. Sometimes they help individuals to create résumés or conduct mock interviews to help them feel comfortable in a job interview. They may create and promote job fairs or other recruiting events to help individuals obtain jobs.

Social Worker

Social workers often are involved in helping people with social or economic problems. They may investigate, evaluate, and attempt to rectify reported cases of abuse, neglect, endangerment, or domestic disputes. They can intervene in families if necessary and provide counseling and referral services to individuals and families.

Social workers have a minimum of an undergraduate degree from a school of social work that includes course work in various areas of sociology and psychology. Some social workers also have a master's or doctoral degree. They often work for publicly funded agencies at the city, state, or national level, although increasingly they work in the private sector in areas such as drug rehabilitation and family counseling.

In some cases, social workers specialize in a certain area, as is true of a medical social worker who has a master's degree in social work (MSW). This involves graduate course work and supervised clinical experiences in medical settings. A medical social worker might coordinate a variety of support services provided to people with a severe or long-term disability. Family-care social workers often work with families who need support services.

Drug Counselor

Drug counselors provide counseling to individuals with drug abuse problems. They may work on an individual basis with a substance abuser or conduct group therapy sessions. They may work in private practice, with a state or federal government agency, with a company, or in a hospital setting. Some drug counselors specialize in working with adolescents or families. Most states provide a certification procedure for obtaining a license to practice drug counseling.

At a minimum, drug counselors go through an associate's or certificate program. Many have an undergraduate degree in substance-abuse counseling, and some have master's and doctoral degrees.

Medical, Nursing, and Physical Development

Careers in child development include a wide range of occupations in the medical and nursing areas, as well as jobs that pertain to improving some aspect of the child's physical development.

Obstetrician/Gynecologist

An obstetrician/gynecologist provides prenatal and postnatal health care and performs deliveries in maternity cases. The individual also treats diseases and injuries of the female reproductive system. Obstetricians may work in private practice, in a medical clinic, in a hospital, or in a medical school. Becoming an obstetrician/gynecologist requires a medical degree plus three to five years of residency in obstetrics/gynecology.

Pediatrician

A pediatrician monitors infants' and children's health, works to prevent disease or injury, helps children attain optimal health, and treats children with health problems. Pediatricians may work in private practice, in a medical clinic, in a hospital, or in a medical school. As medical doctors, they can administer drugs to children and may counsel parents and children on ways to improve the children's health. Many pediatricians on the faculty of medical schools also teach and conduct research on children's health and diseases. Pediatricians have attained a medical degree and completed a three- to five-year residency in pediatrics.

Neonatal Nurse

A neonatal nurse is involved in the delivery and care of the newborn infant. The neonatal nurse may work to improve the health and well-being of full-term infants or be involved in the delivery of care to premature and critically ill neonates.

A minimum of an undergraduate degree in nursing with a specialization in the newborn is required. This training involves course work in nursing and the biological sciences, as well as supervisory clinical experiences.

Nurse-Midwife

A nurse-midwife formulates and provides comprehensive care to selected maternity patients, cares for the expectant mother as she prepares to give birth and guides her through the birth process, and cares for the postpartum patient. The nurse-midwife also may provide care to the newborn, counsel parents on the infant's development and parenting, and provide guidance about health practices. Becoming a nurse-midwife generally requires an undergraduate degree from a school of nursing. A nurse-midwife most often works in a hospital setting.

Pediatric Nurse

Pediatric nurses have a degree in nursing that takes from two to five years to complete. Some also may obtain a master's or doctoral degree in pediatric nursing. Pediatric nurses take courses in biological sciences, nursing care, and pediatrics, usually in a school of nursing. They also undergo supervised clinical experiences in medical settings. They monitor infants' and children's health, work to prevent disease or injury, and help children attain optimal health. They may work in hospitals or schools of nursing, or with pediatricians in private practice or at a medical clinic.

To read about the work of one pediatric nurse practitioner, see the Connecting with Careers profile that describes the career of Barbara Deloian in "Physical Development in Early Childhood."

Audiologist

An audiologist has a minimum of an undergraduate degree in hearing science. This includes courses and supervisory training. Audiologists assess and identify the presence and severity of hearing loss, as well as problems in balance. Some audiologists also go on to obtain a master's and/or doctoral degree. They may work in a medical clinic, with a physician in private practice, in a hospital, or in a medical school.

Speech Therapist

Speech therapists are health-care professionals who are trained to identify, assess, and treat speech and language problems. They may work with physicians, psychologists, social workers, and other health-care professionals as a team to help individuals with physical or psychological problems that include speech and language disorders. Speech pathologists have a minimum of an undergraduate degree in speech and hearing science or communication disorders. They may work in private practice, in hospitals and medical schools, and in government agencies with individuals of any age. Some specialize in working with children or with a particular type of speech disorder.

Genetic Counselor

Genetic counselors work as members of a health-care team, providing information and support to families who have members with birth defects or genetic disorders and to families who may be at risk for a variety of inherited conditions. They identify families at risk and provide supportive counseling. They serve as educators and resource people for other health-care professionals and the public. Almost half of these individuals work in university medical centers, and another one-fourth work in private hospital settings.

Most genetic counselors enter the field after majoring in undergraduate disciplines such as biology, genetics, psychology, nursing, public health, and social work. They have specialized graduate degrees and experience in medical genetics and counseling.

Families and Relationships

A number of careers involve working with families and relationship problems. These range from being a child welfare worker to a marriage and family therapist.

Child Welfare Worker

A child welfare worker is employed by the child protective services unit of each state. The child welfare worker protects the child's rights, evaluates any maltreatment the child might experience, and may have the child removed from the home if necessary. A child social worker has a minimum of an undergraduate degree in social work.

Child Life Specialist

Child life specialists work with children and their families when the child needs to be hospitalized. They monitor the child patient's activities, seek to reduce the child's stress, help the child cope effectively, and assist the child in enjoying the hospital experience as much as possible. Child life specialists may provide parent education and develop individualized treatment plans based on an assessment of the child's development, temperament, medical plan, and available social supports.

Child life specialists have an undergraduate degree. As undergraduates, they take courses in child development and education and usually take additional courses in a child life program.

To read about the work of one child life specialist, see the Connecting with Careers profile in "Physical Development in Middle and Late Childhood."

Marriage and Family Therapist

Marriage and family therapists work on the principle that many individuals who have psychological problems benefit when psychotherapy is provided in the context of a marital or family relationship. Marriage and family therapists may provide marital therapy, couples therapy to individuals in a relationship who are not married, and family therapy to two or more members of a family.

Marriage and family therapists have a master's or doctoral degree. They go through a training program in graduate school similar to that of a clinical psychologist but with a focus on marital and family relationships. To practice marital and family therapy in most states, it is necessary to go through a licensing procedure.

To read about the work of one marriage and family specialist, see the Connecting with Careers profile in "Socioemotional Development in Early Childhood."

There are one hundred and ninety-three living species of monkeys and apes. One hundred and ninety-two of them are covered with hair. The exception is the naked ape, self-named Homo sapiens.

—DESMOND MORRIS
British Zoologist, 20th Century

Beginnings

The rhythm and meaning of life involve beginnings. Questions are raised about how, from so simple a beginning, endless forms develop, grow, and mature. What was this organism, what is this organism, and what will this organism be? In this section, you will read "Biological Beginnings," "Prenatal Development," and "Birth."

Chapter 2

BIOLOGICAL BEGINNINGS

chapter outline

① What Is the Evolutionary Perspective?

Learning Goal 1 Discuss the evolutionary perspective on development.

Natural Selection and Adaptive Behavior
Evolutionary Psychology

② What Are the Genetic Foundations of Development?

Learning Goal 2 Describe what genes are and how they influence human development.

The Collaborative Gene
Genes and Chromosomes
Genetic Principles
Chromosomal and Gene-Linked Abnormalities

③ What Are Some Reproductive Challenges and Choices?

Learning Goal 3 Identify some important reproductive challenges and choices.

Prenatal Diagnostic Tests
Infertility and Reproductive Technology
Adoption

④ How Do Heredity and Environment Interact? The Nature-Nurture Debate

Learning Goal 4 Characterize some of the ways that heredity and environment interact to produce individual differences in development.

Behavior Genetics
Heredity-Environment Correlations
The Epigenetic View and Gene × Environment (G × E) Interaction
Conclusions About Heredity-Environment Interaction

©Image Source/Getty Images RF

Jim Springer and Jim Lewis are identical twins. They were separated at 4 weeks of age and did not see each other again until they were 39 years old. Both worked as part-time deputy sheriffs, vacationed in Florida, drove Chevrolets, had dogs named Toy, and married and divorced women named Betty. One twin named his son James Allan, and the other named his son James Alan. Both liked math but not spelling, enjoyed carpentry and mechanical drawing, chewed their fingernails down to the nubs, had almost identical drinking and smoking habits, had hemorrhoids, put on 10 pounds at about the same point in development, first suffered headaches at the age of 18, and had similar sleep patterns.

Jim and Jim do have some differences. One wears his hair over his forehead, the other slicks it back and has sideburns. One expresses himself best orally; the other is more proficient in writing. But, for the most part, their profiles are remarkably similar.

Jim and Jim were part of the Minnesota Study of Twins Reared Apart, directed by Thomas Bouchard and his colleagues (Bouchard, 1995, 2008; Johnson & others, 2007). The study brings identical twins (identical genetically because they come from the same fertilized egg) and fraternal twins (who come from different fertilized eggs) from all over the world to Minneapolis to investigate their lives. There the twins complete personality and intelligence tests, and they provide detailed medical histories, including information about diet and smoking, exercise habits, chest X-rays, heart stress tests, and electroencephalograms (EEGs). The twins are asked more than 15,000 questions about their family and childhood, personal interests, vocational orientation, values, and aesthetic judgments.

Another pair of identical twins in the Minnesota study, Daphne and Barbara, are called the "giggle sisters" because, after being reunited, they were always making each other laugh. A thorough search of their adoptive families' histories revealed no gigglers. The giggle sisters ignored stress, avoided conflict and controversy whenever possible, and showed no interest in politics.

--topical connections *looking **back***

We have reviewed the historical background of child development, its growing importance as a field of study, and the way its researchers conduct their work. You studied the key processes and periods in child development and identified ways in which the science of child development can improve the lives of children. The forthcoming discussion of genetics and the previous coverage of theories (psychoanalytic, cognitive, behavioral and social cognitive, ethological, and ecological) in the "Introduction" chapter provide the background knowledge to help you examine one of development's major issues and debates—how strongly development is influenced by heredity (nature) and environment (nurture).

Two other identical twin sisters were separated at 6 weeks and reunited in their fifties. Both described hauntingly similar nightmares in which they had doorknobs and fishhooks in their mouths as they suffocated to death. The nightmares began during early adolescence and stopped within the past 10 to 12 years. Both women were bed wetters until about 12 or 13 years of age, and their educational and marital histories are remarkably similar.

When genetically identical twins who were separated as infants show such striking similarities in their tastes and habits and choices, can we conclude that their genes must have caused the development of those tastes and habits and choices? Other possible causes need to be considered. The twins shared not only the same genes but also some experiences. Some of the separated twins lived together for several months prior to their adoption; some of the twins had been reunited prior to testing (in some cases, many years earlier); adoption agencies often place twins in similar homes; and even strangers who spend several hours together and start comparing their lives are likely to come up with some coincidental similarities (Joseph, 2006). The Minnesota study of identical twins points to both the importance of the genetic basis of human development and the need for further research on genetic and environmental factors.

preview

The examples of Jim and Jim, the giggle sisters, and the identical twins who had the same nightmares stimulate us to think about our genetic heritage and the biological foundations of our existence. Organisms are not like billiard balls, moved by simple, external forces to predictable positions on life's pool table. Environmental experiences and biological foundations work together to make us who we are. Our exploration of life's biological beginnings focuses on evolution, genetic foundations, challenges and choices regarding reproduction, and the interaction of heredity and environment.

1 What Is the Evolutionary Perspective?

LG1 Discuss the evolutionary perspective on development.

Natural Selection and Adaptive Behavior

Evolutionary Psychology

As our earliest ancestors left the forest to feed in the savannahs and then to form hunting societies on the open plains, their minds and behaviors changed as humans gradually became the dominant species on Earth. How did this evolution come about?

NATURAL SELECTION AND ADAPTIVE BEHAVIOR

Natural selection is the evolutionary process by which those individuals of a species that are best adapted are the ones that survive and reproduce. To understand what this means, let's return to the middle of the nineteenth century, when the British naturalist Charles

How does the attachment of this Vietnamese baby to its mother reflect the evolutionary process of adaptive behavior?

©Frans Lemmens/age fotostock

Darwin was traveling around the world, observing many different species of animals in their natural surroundings. Darwin, who published his observations and thoughts in *On the Origin of Species* (1859), noted that most organisms reproduce at rates that would cause enormous increases in the population of most species and yet populations remain nearly constant. He reasoned that an intense, constant struggle for food, water, and resources must occur among the many young born in each generation, because many of the young do not survive. Those that do survive, and reproduce, pass on their characteristics to the next generation. Darwin observed that these survivors are better *adapted* to their world than are the nonsurvivors (Audesirk, Audesirk, & Byers, 2017; Johnson, 2017). The best-adapted individuals survive to leave the most offspring. Over the course of many generations, organisms with the characteristics needed for survival make up an increased percentage of the population. Over many, many generations, this could produce a gradual modification of the whole population. If environmental conditions change, however, other characteristics might become favored by natural selection, moving the species in a different direction (Starr, Evers, & Starr, 2018).

All organisms must adapt to particular places, climates, food sources, and ways of life (Simon, 2017). An eagle's claws are a physical adaptation that facilitates predation. *Adaptive behavior* is behavior that promotes an organism's survival in the natural habitat. For example, attachment between a caregiver and a baby ensures the infant's closeness to a caregiver for feeding and protection from danger, thus increasing the infant's chances of survival. Or consider pregnancy sickness, which is a tendency for women to become nauseated during pregnancy and avoid certain foods (Schmitt & Pilcher, 2004). Women with pregnancy sickness tend to avoid foods such as coffee that are higher in toxins that could harm the fetus. Thus, pregnancy sickness may be an evolution-based adaptation that enhances the offspring's ability to survive.

EVOLUTIONARY PSYCHOLOGY

Although Darwin introduced the theory of evolution by natural selection in 1859, his ideas have only recently become a popular framework for explaining behavior (Colmenares & Hernandez-Lloreda, 2017; Whiten, 2017). Psychology's newest approach, **evolutionary psychology,** emphasizes the importance of adaptation, reproduction, and "survival of the fittest" in shaping behavior. "Fit" in this sense refers to the ability to bear offspring that survive long enough to bear offspring of their own. In this view, natural selection favors behaviors that increase reproductive success: the ability to pass your genes to the next generation (Del Giudice & Ellis, 2016; Russell, Hertz, & McMillan, 2017).

David Buss (1995, 2008, 2012, 2015) has been especially influential in stimulating new interest in how evolution can explain human behavior. He argues that just as evolution shapes our physical features, such as body shape and height, it also pervasively influences our decision making, our degree of aggression, our fears, and our mating patterns. For example, assume that our ancestors were hunters and gatherers on the plains and that men did most of the hunting and women stayed close to home, gathering seeds and plants for food. If you have to travel some distance from your home in an effort to find and slay a fleeing animal, you need not only certain physical traits but also the ability to use certain types of spatial thinking. Men born with these traits would be more likely than men without them to survive, to bring home lots of food, and to be considered attractive mates—and thus to reproduce and pass on these characteristics to their children. In other words, if such assumptions were correct, these traits would provide a reproductive advantage for males and, over many generations, men with good spatial thinking skills might become more numerous in the population. Critics point out that this scenario might or might not have actually happened.

Evolutionary Developmental Psychology   Recently, interest has grown in using the concepts of evolutionary psychology to understand human development (Barbaro & others, 2017; Grinde, 2016; Lickliter, 2017). Following are some ideas proposed by evolutionary developmental psychologists (Bjorklund & Pellegrini, 2011).

evolutionary psychology Branch of psychology that emphasizes the importance of adaptation, reproduction, and "survival of the fittest" in shaping behavior.

An extended childhood period might have evolved because humans require time to develop a large brain and learn the complexity of human societies. Humans take longer to become reproductively mature than any other mammal (see Figure 1). During this extended childhood period, they develop a large brain and the experiences needed to become competent adults in a complex society.

Many evolved psychological mechanisms are domain-specific. That is, the mechanisms apply only to a specific aspect of a person's makeup. According to evolutionary psychology, information processing is one example. In this view, the mind is not a general-purpose device that can be applied equally to a vast array of problems. Instead, as our ancestors dealt with certain recurring problems such as hunting and finding shelter, specialized modules might have evolved that processed information related to those problems. For example, such specialized modules might include a module for physical knowledge about tracking animals, a module for mathematical knowledge for trading, and a module for language.

Evolved mechanisms are not always adaptive in contemporary society. Some behaviors that were adaptive for our prehistoric ancestors may not serve us well today. For example, the food-scarce environment of our ancestors likely led to humans' propensity to gorge when food is available and to crave high-caloric foods, a trait that might lead to an epidemic of obesity when food is plentiful.

Chimpanzee

FIGURE 1

THE BRAIN SIZES OF VARIOUS PRIMATES AND HUMANS IN RELATION TO THE LENGTH OF THE CHILDHOOD PERIOD. Compared with other primates, humans have both a larger brain and a longer childhood period. *What conclusions can you draw from the relationship indicated by this graph?*
Source: Bonner, J., "Brain Sizes of Various Primates and Humans," in *The Evolution of Culture in Animals*, Princeton, NJ: Princeton University Press, 1983.
©Getty Images RF

Evaluating Evolutionary Psychology   Although evolutionary psychology is getting increased attention, it remains just one theoretical approach among many and it has its critics (Hyde, 2014). Like the theories described earlier, it has limitations, weaknesses, and critics. Albert Bandura (1998), whose social cognitive theory was described earlier, acknowledges the important influence of evolution on human adaptation. However, he rejects what he calls "one-sided evolutionism," which sees social behavior as the product of evolved biology. An alternative is a *bidirectional view,* in which environmental and biological conditions influence each other. In this view, evolutionary pressures created changes in biological structures that allowed the use of tools, which enabled our ancestors to manipulate the environment, constructing new environmental conditions. In turn, environmental innovations produced new selection pressures that led to the evolution of specialized biological systems for consciousness, thought, and language.

In other words, evolution gave us bodily structures and biological potentialities; it does not dictate behavior. People have used their biological capacities to produce diverse cultures—aggressive and peaceful, egalitarian and autocratic. As American scientist Stephen Jay Gould (1981) concluded, in most domains of human functioning, biology allows a broad range of cultural possibilities.

The "big picture" idea of natural selection leading to the development of human traits and behaviors is difficult to refute or test because evolution occurs on a time scale that does not lend itself to empirical study. Thus, studying specific genes in humans and other species—and their links to traits and behaviors—may be the best approach for testing ideas that emerge from the evolutionary psychology perspective.

Children in all culture are interested in the tools that adults in their cultures use. For example, this young girl near the Angkor Temples in Cambodia is using a machete. *Might the young girl's behavior be biologically based or due to both biological and environmental influences?*
©Carol Adam/Getty Image

Review *Connect* Reflect

LG1 Discuss the evolutionary perspective on development.

Review

- How can natural selection and adaptive behavior be defined?
- What is evolutionary psychology? What are some basic ideas about human development proposed by evolutionary developmental psychologists? How can evolutionary psychology be evaluated?

Connect

- Earlier you learned about how different developmental processes interact. How was that principle reinforced by the information in this section?

Reflect *Your Own Personal Journey of Life*

- Which is more persuasive to you: the views of evolutionary psychologists or those of their critics? Why?

---

2 What Are the Genetic Foundations of Development?

LG2 Describe what genes are and how they influence human development.

| The Collaborative Gene | Genes and Chromosomes | Genetic Principles | Chromosomal and Gene-Linked Abnormalities |

Genetic influences on behavior evolved over time and across many species. Our many traits and characteristics that are genetically influenced have a long evolutionary history that is retained in our DNA. In other words, our DNA is not just inherited from our parents; it's also what we've inherited as a species from the species that came before us.

Let's take a closer look at DNA and its role in human development. How are characteristics that suit a species for survival transmitted from one generation to the next? Darwin did not know because genes and the principles of genetics had not yet been discovered. Each of us carries a "genetic code" that we inherited from our parents. Because a fertilized egg carries this human code, a fertilized human egg cannot grow into an egret, eagle, or elephant.

THE COLLABORATIVE GENE

Each of us began life as a single cell weighing about one twenty-millionth of an ounce! This tiny piece of matter housed our entire genetic code—information that helped us grow from that single cell to a person made of trillions of cells, each containing a replica of the original code. That code is carried by DNA, which includes our genes. What are genes and what do they do? For the answer, we need to look into our cells.

The nucleus of each human cell contains **chromosomes,** which are threadlike structures made up of deoxyribonucleic acid, or DNA. **DNA** is a complex molecule that has a double helix shape, like a spiral staircase, and contains genetic information. **Genes,** the units of hereditary information, are short segments of DNA, as you can see in Figure 2. They help cells to reproduce themselves and to assemble proteins. Proteins, in turn, are the building blocks of cells as well as the regulators that direct the body's processes (Goodenough & McGuire, 2017).

Each gene has its own location, its own designated place on a particular chromosome. Today, there is a great deal of enthusiasm about efforts to discover the specific locations of genes that are linked to certain functions and developmental outcomes (Sutphin & Korstanje, 2016). An important step in this direction was accomplished when the Human Genome Project completed a preliminary map of the human *genome*—the complete set of developmental information for creating proteins that initiate the making of a human organism (Johnson, 2017).

chromosomes Threadlike structures made up of deoxyribonucleic acid, or DNA.

DNA A complex molecule with a double helix shape; contains genetic information.

genes Units of hereditary information composed of DNA. Genes help cells to reproduce themselves and help manufacture the proteins that maintain life.

Among the major approaches to gene identification and discovery that are being used today are the genome-wide association method, linkage analysis, next-generation sequencing, and the 1,000 Genomes Project:

- Completion of the Human Genome Project has led to use of the *genome-wide association method* to identify genetic variations linked to a particular disease, such as obesity, cancer, or cardiovascular disease (Wang & others, 2016). To conduct a genome-wide association study, researchers obtain DNA from individuals who have the disease and those who don't have it. Then, each participant's complete set of DNA, or genome, is purified from the blood or other cells and scanned on machines to determine markers of genetic variation. If the genetic variations occur more frequently in people who have the disease, the variations point to the region in the human genome with the disease. Genome-wide association studies have recently been conducted for cancer (Shen & others, 2017); obesity (Amare & others, 2017); cardiovascular disease (Schick & others, 2016); depression (Knowles & others, 2016); suicide (Sokolowski, Wasserman, & Wasserman, 2016); autism (Connolly & others, 2017); attention deficit hyperactivity disorder (Naaijen & others, 2017); glaucoma (Springelkamp & others, 2017); and Alzheimer disease (Vanitallie, 2017).

- *Linkage analysis*, in which the goal is to discover the location of a gene (or genes) in relation to a marker gene (whose position is already known), is often used in the search for a disease-related gene (Cho & Suh, 2016). Genes transmitted to offspring tend to be in close proximity to each other so that the gene(s) involved in the disease are usually located near the marker gene. Gene linkage studies are now being conducted on a wide variety of disorders, including attention deficit hyperactivity disorder (Mastronardi & others, 2016; Sciberras & others, 2017); autism (Muller, Anacker, & Veenstra-VanderWeele, 2017); and depression (Mathias & others, 2016).

- *Next-generation sequencing* is a term used to describe the vast increase in genetic data generated at a much reduced cost and in a much shorter period of time. Next-generation sequencing has considerably increased knowledge about genetic influences on development in recent years (Au & others, 2016; Keller & others, 2016). Using recently developed next-generation sequencing, an entire human genome can be sequenced in one day. Prior to recent improvements, deciphering the human genome took over an entire decade! The new technology sequences millions of small DNA fragments (Bardak & others, 2017).

- The human genome varies between individuals in small but very important ways. Understanding these variations will require examination of the whole genomes of many individuals. A current project that began in 2008, the Thousand Genomes Project, is the most detailed study of human genetic variation to date. This project has the goal of determining the genomic sequences of at least 1,000 individuals from different ethnic groups around the world (Fukushima & others, 2015; Li & others, 2017). By compiling complete descriptions of the genetic variations of many people, studies of genetic variations in disease can be conducted in a more detailed manner.

One of the big surprises of the Human Genome Project was a report indicating that humans have only about 30,000 genes (U.S. Department of Energy, 2001). More recently, the number of human genes has been revised further downward to approximately 20,500 (Ensembl Human, 2008; Flicek & others, 2013). Further recent analysis proposes that humans may actually have fewer than 20,000 protein-producing genes (Ezkurdia & others, 2014). Scientists had thought that humans had as many as 100,000 or more genes. They had also believed that each gene programmed just one protein. In fact, humans appear to have far more proteins than they have genes, so there cannot be a one-to-one correspondence between genes and proteins (Commoner, 2002). Each gene is not translated, in automaton-like fashion, into one and only one protein. A gene does not act independently, as developmental psychologist David Moore (2001) emphasized by titling his book *The Dependent Gene*.

Rather than being a group of independent genes, the human genome consists of many genes that collaborate with each other and with nongenetic factors inside and outside the body (Moore, 2015, 2017). The collaboration operates at many points. For example, the cellular machinery mixes, matches, and links small pieces of DNA to reproduce the genes, and that machinery is influenced by what is going on around it.

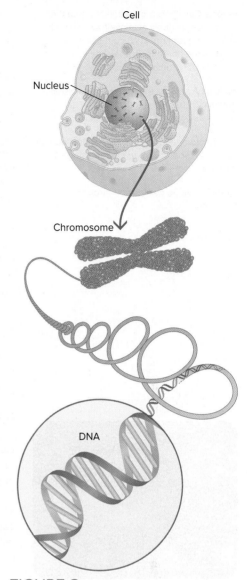

FIGURE 2

CELLS, CHROMOSOMES, DNA, AND GENES.
(*Top*) The body contains trillions of cells. Each cell contains a central structure, the nucleus. (*Middle*) Chromosomes are threadlike structures located in the nucleus of the cell. Chromosomes are composed of DNA. (*Bottom*) DNA has the structure of a spiral staircase. A gene is a segment of DNA.

How Would You...?
If you were a **psychologist,** how would you explain to an enthusiast of the Human Genome Project that genes don't provide an exact blueprint for how children's development will unfold?

mitosis Cellular reproduction in which the cell's nucleus duplicates itself with two new cells being formed, each containing the same DNA as the parent cell, arranged in the same 23 pairs of chromosomes.

meiosis A specialized form of cell division that occurs to form eggs and sperm (also known as *gametes*).

fertilization A stage in reproduction when an egg and a sperm fuse to create a single cell, called a zygote.

zygote A single cell formed through fertilization.

Whether a gene is turned "on"—that is, working to assemble proteins—is also a matter of collaboration. The activity of genes (genetic expression) is affected by their environment (Gottlieb, 2007; Moore, 2015, 2017). For example, hormones that circulate in the blood make their way into the cell where they can turn genes "on" and "off." And the flow of hormones can be affected by environmental conditions, such as light, day length, nutrition, and behavior. Numerous studies have shown that external events outside the original cell and the person, as well as events inside the cell, can excite or inhibit gene expression (Gottlieb, 2007).

Recent research has documented that factors such as stress, exercise, nutrition, respiration, radiation, temperature, and sleep can influence gene expression (Done & Traustadottir, 2016; Giles & others, 2016; Turecki & Meaney, 2016; Van Bussel & others, 2016). For example, one study revealed that an increase in the concentration of stress hormones such as cortisol produced a fivefold increase in DNA damage (Flint & others, 2007). Another study also found that exposure to radiation changed the rate of DNA synthesis in cells (Lee & others, 2011).

Scientists also have found that certain genes can be turned off or on as a result of exercise and diet through the process of *methylation*, in which tiny atoms attach themselves to the outside of a gene (Butts & others, 2017). This process makes the gene more or less capable of receiving and responding to biochemical signals from the body. Researchers also have found that diet and tobacco use may also affect gene behavior through the process of methylation (Chatterton & others, 2017; Godfrey & others, 2017).

GENES AND CHROMOSOMES

Genes are not only collaborative, they are enduring. How do the genes manage to get passed from generation to generation and end up in all of the trillion cells in the body? Three processes explain the heart of the story: mitosis, meiosis, and fertilization.

Mitosis, Meiosis, and Fertilization   All of the cells in your body, except the sperm and egg, have 46 chromosomes arranged in 23 pairs. These cells reproduce through a process called mitosis. During **mitosis,** the cell's nucleus—including the chromosomes—duplicates itself and the cell divides. Two new cells are formed, each containing the same DNA as the original cell, arranged in the same 23 pairs of chromosomes.

However, a different type of cell division—**meiosis**—forms eggs and sperm (which also are called *gametes*). During meiosis, a cell of the testes (in men) or ovaries (in women) duplicates its chromosomes but then divides *twice*, thus forming four cells, each of which has only half of the genetic material of the parent cell (Johnson, 2017). By the end of meiosis, each egg or sperm has 23 *unpaired* chromosomes.

During **fertilization,** an egg and a sperm fuse to create a single cell, called a **zygote** (see Figure 3). In the zygote, the 23 unpaired chromosomes from the egg and the 23 unpaired chromosomes from the sperm combine to form one set of 23 paired chromosomes—one chromosome of each pair having come from the mother's egg and the other from the father's sperm. In this manner, each parent contributes half of the offspring's genetic material.

Figure 4 shows 23 paired chromosomes of a male and a female. The members of each pair of chromosomes are both similar and different: Each chromosome in the pair contains

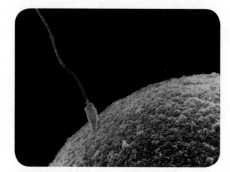

FIGURE 3

A SINGLE SPERM PENETRATING AN EGG AT THE POINT OF FERTILIZATION

©Don W. Fawcett/Science Source

FIGURE 4

THE GENETIC DIFFERENCE BETWEEN MALES AND FEMALES. Set (*a*) shows the chromosome structure of a male, and set (*b*) shows the chromosome structure of a female. The last pair of 23 pairs of chromosomes is in the bottom right box of each set. Notice that the Y chromosome of the male is smaller than the X chromosome of the female. To obtain this kind of chromosomal picture, a cell is removed from a person's body, usually from the inside of the mouth. The chromosomes are stained by chemical treatment, magnified extensively, and then photographed.

©CMSP/Custom Medical Stock Photo—All rights reserved.

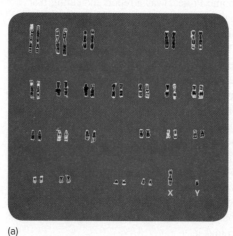

(a)

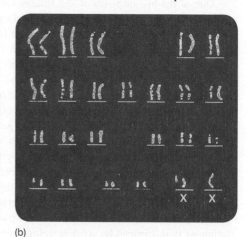

(b)

varying forms of the same genes, at the same location on the chromosome. A gene that influences hair color, for example, is located on both members of one pair of chromosomes, in the same location on each. However, one of those chromosomes might carry a gene associated with blond hair; the other chromosome in the pair might carry the gene associated with brown hair.

Do you notice any obvious differences between the chromosomes of the male and the chromosomes of the female in Figure 4? The difference lies in the 23rd pair. Ordinarily, in females this pair consists of two chromosomes called *X chromosomes;* in males the 23rd pair consists of an X and a *Y chromosome.* The presence of a Y chromosome is an important factor that makes an individual male rather than female.

Sources of Variability   Combining the genes of two parents in offspring increases genetic variability in the population, which is valuable for a species because it provides more characteristics for natural selection to operate on (Simon, 2017). In fact, the human genetic process creates several important sources of variability.

First, the chromosomes in the zygote are not exact copies of those in the mother's ovaries or the father's testes. During the formation of the sperm and egg in meiosis, the members of each pair of chromosomes are separated, but which chromosome in the pair goes to the gamete is a matter of chance. In addition, before the pairs separate, pieces of the two chromosomes in each pair are exchanged, creating a new combination of genes on each chromosome (Cho & Suh, 2016). Thus, when chromosomes from the mother's egg and the father's sperm are brought together in the zygote, the result is a truly unique combination of genes.

If each zygote is unique, how do identical twins like those discussed in the opening of the chapter exist? Identical twins (also called monozygotic twins) develop from a single zygote that splits into two genetically identical replicas, each of which becomes a person. *Fraternal twins* (called dizygotic twins) develop when two eggs are each fertilized by a different sperm, making them two zygotes that are genetically no more similar than ordinary siblings.

Another source of variability comes from DNA (Willey, Sherwood, & Woolverton, 2017). Chance, a mistake by cellular machinery, or damage from an environmental agent such as radiation may produce a *mutated gene,* which is a permanently altered segment of DNA (Cowan & Bunn, 2016).

Even when their genes are identical, however, people vary. The difference between genotypes and phenotypes helps us to understand this source of variability (Klug & others, 2017). All of a person's genetic material makes up his or her **genotype.** However, not all of the genetic material is apparent in our observed and measurable characteristics. A **phenotype** consists of observable characteristics. Phenotypes include physical characteristics (such as height, weight, and hair color) and psychological characteristics (such as personality and intelligence).

How does the process from genotype to phenotype work? It's very complex, but at a very basic level in a cell, DNA information is transcribed to RNA (ribonucleic acid), which in turn is translated into amino acids that will become proteins (Starr, Evers, & Starr, 2018). Once proteins have been assembled, they become capable of producing phenotype traits and characteristics. Also, environments interact with genotypes to produce phenotypes.

Thus, for each genotype, a range of phenotypes can be expressed, providing another source of variability (Freeman & others, 2017). An individual can inherit the genetic potential to grow very large, for example, but environmental influences involving good nutrition, among other things, will be essential to achieving that potential. The giggle sisters introduced in the chapter opening might have inherited the same genetic potential to be very tall, but if Daphne had grown up malnourished, she might have ended up noticeably shorter than Barbara. This principle is so widely applicable it has a name: heredity-environment interaction (or gene-environment interaction).

GENETIC PRINCIPLES

What determines how a genotype is expressed to create a particular phenotype? Much is unknown about the answer to this question (Moore, 2015, 2017). However, a number of genetic principles have been discovered, among them those of dominant-recessive genes, sex-linked genes, genetic imprinting, and polygenically determined characteristics.

Dominant-Recessive Genes Principle   In some cases, one gene of a pair always exerts its effects; it is *dominant,* overriding the potential influence of the other gene, called the *recessive* gene. This is the *dominant-recessive genes principle.* A recessive gene exerts its

genotype A person's genetic heritage; the actual genetic material.

phenotype The way an individual's genotype is expressed in observed and measurable characteristics.

FIGURE **5**

HOW BROWN-HAIRED PARENTS CAN HAVE A BLOND-HAIRED CHILD. In this example, both parents have brown hair, but each parent carries the recessive gene for blond hair. Therefore, the odds of their child having blond hair is one in four—the probability the child will receive a recessive gene (b) from each parent.

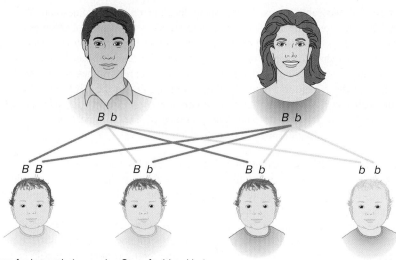

B = Gene for brown hair   *b* = Gene for blond hair

influence only if the two genes of a pair are both recessive. If you inherit a recessive gene for a trait from each of your parents, you will show the trait. If you inherit a recessive gene from only one parent, you may never know you carry the gene. Brown hair, farsightedness, and dimples rule over blond hair, nearsightedness, and freckles in the world of dominant-recessive genes.

Can two brown-haired parents have a blond-haired child? Yes, they can. Suppose that each parent has a dominant gene for brown hair and a recessive gene for blond hair. Because dominant genes override recessive genes, the parents have brown hair, but both are carriers of genes that contribute to blondness and pass on their recessive genes for producing blond hair. With no dominant gene to override them, the recessive genes can make the child's hair blond (see Figure 5).

Sex-Linked Genes   Most mutated genes are recessive. When a mutated gene is carried on the X chromosome, the result is called *X-linked inheritance*. The implications for males may be very different from those for females (Simon & others, 2016). Remember that males have only one X chromosome. Thus, if there is an absent or altered, disease-relevant gene on the X chromosome, males have no "backup" copy to counter the harmful gene and therefore may develop an X-linked disease. However, females have a second X chromosome, which is likely to be unchanged. As a result, they are not likely to have the X-linked disease. Thus, most individuals who have X-linked diseases are males. Females who have one abnormal copy of the gene on the X chromosome are known as "carriers," and they usually do not show any signs of the X-linked disease (Klug & others, 2017).

Genetic Imprinting   *Genetic imprinting* occurs when genes have differing effects depending on whether they are inherited from the mother or the father (Simon, 2017). A chemical process "silences" one member of the gene pair. For example, as a result of imprinting, only the maternally derived copy of a gene might be active, while the paternally derived copy of the same gene is silenced—or vice versa (John, 2017). Only a small percentage of human genes appears to undergo imprinting, but it is a normal and important aspect of development. When imprinting goes awry, development is disturbed, as in the case of Beckwith-Wiedemann syndrome, a growth disorder, and Wilms tumor, a type of cancer (Bachmann & others, 2017; Okun & others, 2014).

Polygenic Inheritance   Genetic transmission is usually more complex than the simple examples we have examined thus far (Moore, 2013, 2015). Few characteristics reflect the influence of only a single gene or pair of genes. Most are determined by the interaction of many different genes; they are said to be *polygenically determined* (Oreland & others, 2017; Zabaneh & others, 2017). Even simple characteristics such as height, for example, reflect the interaction of many genes, as well as the influence of the environment.

The term *gene-gene interaction* is increasingly used to describe studies that focus on the interdependence of two or more genes in influencing characteristics, behavior, diseases, and development (Lovely & others, 2017; Yi & others, 2017). For example, recent studies have documented gene-gene interaction in immune system functioning (Heinonen & others, 2015); asthma (Hua &

Down syndrome A form of intellectual disability that is caused by the presence of an extra copy of chromosome 21.

Name	Description	Treatment	Incidence
Down syndrome	An extra chromosome causes mild to severe intellectual disabilities and physical abnormalities.	Surgery, early intervention, infant stimulation, and special learning programs	1 in 1,900 births at age 20 1 in 300 births at age 35 1 in 30 births at age 45
Klinefelter syndrome (XXY)	An extra X chromosome causes physical abnormalities.	Hormone therapy can be effective	1 in 1,000 male births
Fragile X syndrome	An abnormality in the X chromosome can cause intellectual disabilities, learning disabilities, or short attention span.	Special education, speech and language therapy	More common in males than in females
Turner syndrome (XO)	A missing X chromosome in females can cause intellectual disabilities and sexual underdevelopment.	Hormone therapy in childhood and puberty	1 in 2,500 female births
XYY syndrome	An extra Y chromosome can cause above-average height.	No special treatment required	1 in 1,000 male births

FIGURE 6

SOME CHROMOSOMAL ABNORMALITIES. The treatments for these abnormalities do not necessarily erase the problem but may improve the individual's adaptive behavior and quality of life.

others, 2016); obesity (Bordoni & others, 2017); type 2 diabetes (Saxena, Srivastaya, & Banerjee, 2017); cancer (Wu & others, 2017); and cardiovascular disease (De & others, 2017).

CHROMOSOMAL AND GENE-LINKED ABNORMALITIES

Sometimes abnormalities characterize the genetic process. Some of these abnormalities involve whole chromosomes that do not separate properly during meiosis. Other abnormalities are produced by harmful genes.

Chromosomal Abnormalities   Occasionally when a gamete is formed, the sperm and ovum do not have their normal set of 23 chromosomes. The most notable examples involve Down syndrome and abnormalities of the sex chromosomes (see Figure 6).

Down Syndrome   **Down syndrome** is a chromosomally transmitted form of intellectual disability caused by the presence of an extra copy of chromosome 21 (Lewanda & others, 2016). It is not known why the extra chromosome is present, but the health of the male sperm or the female ovum may be involved. An individual with Down syndrome has a round face, a flattened skull, an extra fold of skin over the eyelids, a protruding tongue, short limbs, and motor and intellectual disabilities.

Down syndrome appears approximately once in every 700 live births. Women between the ages of 16 and 34 are less likely to give birth to a child with Down syndrome than are younger or older women. African American children are rarely born with Down syndrome.

These athletes, several of whom have Down syndrome, are participating in a Special Olympics competition. Notice the distinctive facial features of the individuals with Down syndrome, such as a round face and a flattened skull. *What causes Down syndrome?*
©James Shaffer/PhotoEdit

Sex-Linked Chromosomal Abnormalities   Recall that a newborn normally has either an X and a Y chromosome, or two X chromosomes. Human embryos must possess at least one X chromosome to be viable. The most common sex-linked chromosomal abnormalities involve the presence of an extra chromosome (either an X or Y) or the absence of one X chromosome in females.

Klinefelter syndrome is a chromosomal disorder in which males have an extra X chromosome, making them XXY instead of XY. Males with this disorder have undeveloped testes, and they usually have enlarged breasts and become tall (Lunenfeld & others, 2015). One study revealed significant impairment in language, academic, attentional, and motor abilities in boys with the

> **developmental connection**
>
> **Conditions, Diseases, and Disorders**
> Intellectual disabilities can be classified in several ways. Connect to "Cognitive Development in Middle and Late Childhood."

syndrome (Ross & others, 2012). Klinefelter syndrome occurs approximately once in every 1,000 live male births. Only 10 percent of individuals with Klinefelter syndrome are diagnosed before puberty, with the majority not identified until adulthood (Aksglaede & others, 2013).

Fragile X syndrome is a genetic disorder that results from an abnormality in the X chromosome, which becomes constricted and often breaks (Yudkin & others, 2014). The physical appearance of children with fragile X syndrome often appears normal, although these children typically have prominent ears, a long face, a high-arched palate, and soft skin. An intellectual difficulty frequently is an outcome, which may take the form of an intellectual disability, autism, a learning disability, or a short attention span (Hall & others, 2014; Thurman & others, 2017). One study revealed that boys with fragile X syndrome were characterized by cognitive deficits in inhibition, memory, and planning (Hooper & others, 2008). This disorder occurs more frequently in males than in females, possibly because the second X chromosome in females negates the effects of the abnormal X chromosome (Rocca & others, 2016). A recent study found that a higher level of maternal responsivity to the adaptive behavior of children with Fragile X syndrome had a positive effect on the children's communication skills (Warren & others, 2017).

Turner syndrome is a chromosomal disorder in females in which either an X chromosome is missing, making the person XO instead of XX, or part of one X chromosome is deleted (Murdock & others, 2017). Females with Turner syndrome are short in stature and have a webbed neck (Miguel-Neto & others, 2016). They might be infertile and have difficulty in mathematics, but their verbal ability often is quite good. Turner syndrome occurs in approximately 1 of every 2,500 live female births (Culen & others, 2017).

The **XYY syndrome** is a chromosomal disorder in which the male has an extra Y chromosome (Tartaglia & others, 2017). Early interest in this syndrome focused on the belief that the extra Y chromosome found in some males contributed to aggression and violence. However, researchers subsequently found that XYY males are no more likely to commit crimes than are normal XY males.

Gene-Linked Abnormalities   Abnormalities can be produced not only by an abnormal number of chromosomes but also by harmful genes. More than 7,000 such genetic disorders have been identified, although most of them are rare.

Phenylketonuria (PKU) is a genetic disorder in which the individual cannot properly metabolize phenylalanine, an amino acid. This condition results from a recessive gene and occurs about once in every 10,000 to 20,000 live births. Today, phenylketonuria is easily detected, and it is treated by a diet that prevents an excess accumulation of phenylalanine (Medford & others, 2017; Pinto & others, 2017). If phenylketonuria is left untreated, however, excess phenylalanine builds up in the child, producing intellectual disabilities and hyperactivity. Phenylketonuria accounts for approximately 1 percent of individuals who are institutionalized for intellectual disabilities, and it occurs primarily in non-Latino Whites.

The story of phenylketonuria has important implications for the nature-nurture issue. Although phenylketonuria is often described as a genetic disorder (nature), how or whether a gene's influence in phenylketonuria is played out depends on environmental influences because the disorder can be treated by an environmental manipulation (nurture). That is, the presence of a genetic defect *does not* inevitably lead to the development of the disorder *if* the individual develops in the right environment (one free of phenylalanine). This is one example of the important principle of heredity-environment interaction. Under one environmental condition (phenylalanine in the diet), intellectual disability results, but when other nutrients replace phenylalanine, intelligence develops in the normal range. The same genotype has different outcomes depending on the environment (in this case, the nutritional environment).

Sickle-cell anemia, which occurs most often in African Americans, is a genetic disorder that impairs the functioning of the body's red blood cells. More than 300,000 infants worldwide are born with sickle-cell anemia each year (Azar & Wong, 2017). Red blood cells carry oxygen to the body's other cells and are usually disk-shaped. In sickle-cell anemia, a recessive gene causes the red blood cell to become a hook-shaped "sickle" that cannot carry oxygen properly and dies quickly. As a result, the body's cells do not receive adequate oxygen, causing anemia and early death (Azar & Wong, 2017). About 1 in 400 African American babies is affected by sickle-cell anemia. One in 10 African Americans is a carrier, as is 1 in 20 Latin Americans. A National Institutes of Health (2008) panel concluded that the only FDA-approved drug (hydroxyurea) to treat sickle-cell anemia in adolescents and adults is not widely used. Stem cell transplantation is being explored as a possible treatment for sickle-cell anemia (Azar & Wong, 2017).

Klinefelter syndrome A chromosomal disorder in which males have an extra X chromosome, making them XXY instead of XY.

fragile X syndrome A genetic disorder involving an abnormality in the X chromosome, which becomes constricted and often breaks.

Turner syndrome A chromosomal disorder in females in which either an X chromosome is missing, making the person XO instead of XX, or the second X chromosome is partially deleted.

XYY syndrome A chromosomal disorder in which males have an extra Y chromosome.

phenylketonuria (PKU) A genetic disorder in which the individual cannot properly metabolize phenylalanine, an amino acid. PKU is now easily detected—but if left untreated, results in intellectual disability and hyperactivity.

sickle-cell anemia A genetic disorder that affects the red blood cells and occurs most often in people of African descent.

Name	Description	Treatment	Incidence
Cystic fibrosis	Glandular dysfunction that interferes with mucus production; breathing and digestion are hampered, resulting in a shortened life span.	Physical and oxygen therapy, synthetic enzymes, and antibiotics; most individuals live to middle age.	1 in 2,000 births
Diabetes	Body does not produce enough insulin, which causes abnormal metabolism of sugar.	Early onset can be fatal unless treated with insulin.	1 in 2,500 births
Hemophilia	Delayed blood clotting causes internal and external bleeding.	Blood transfusions/injections can reduce or prevent damage due to internal bleeding.	1 in 10,000 males
Huntington's disease	Central nervous system deteriorates, producing problems in muscle coordination and mental deterioration.	Does not usually appear until age 35 or older; death likely 10 to 20 years after symptoms appear.	1 in 20,000 births
Phenylketonuria (PKU)	Metabolic disorder that, left untreated, causes intellectual disability.	Special diet can result in average intelligence and normal life span.	1 in 10,000 to 1 in 20,000 births
Sickle-cell anemia	Blood disorder that limits the body's oxygen supply; it can cause joint swelling, as well as heart and kidney failure.	Penicillin, medication for pain, antibiotics, and blood transfusions.	1 in 400 African American children (lower among other groups)
Spina bifida	Neural tube disorder that causes brain and spine abnormalities.	Corrective surgery at birth, orthopedic devices, and physical/medical therapy.	2 in 1,000 births
Tay-Sachs disease	Deceleration of mental and physical development caused by an accumulation of lipids in the nervous system.	Medication and special diet are used, but death is likely by 5 years of age.	1 in 30 American Jews is a carrier.

FIGURE 7
SOME GENE-LINKED ABNORMALITIES

Recent research also supports the use of hydroxyurea therapy for infants with sickle-cell anemia beginning at 9 months of age (Nevitt, Jones, & Howard, 2017; Yawn & John-Sowah, 2015).

Other diseases that result from genetic abnormalities include cystic fibrosis, some forms of diabetes, hemophilia, spina bifida, Tay-Sachs disease, cardiovascular disease, and Alzheimer disease (Huang & others, 2017; Wang & others, 2017; Williams & others, 2016). Figure 7 provides further information about these diseases. Someday scientists may identify why these and other genetic abnormalities occur and discover how to cure them.

Dealing with Genetic Abnormalities   Every individual carries DNA variations that might predispose the person to serious physical diseases or mental disorders. But not all individuals who carry a genetic disorder develop the disorder. Other genes or developmental events sometimes compensate for genetic abnormalities (Klug & others, 2017; Moore, 2017). For example, recall the earlier example of phenylketonuria: Even though individuals might carry the genetic disorder associated with phenylketonuria, the phenotype does not develop when phenylalanine is replaced by other nutrients in their diet.

Thus, genes are not destiny, but genes that are missing, nonfunctional, or mutated can be associated with disorders (Russell, Hertz, & McMillan, 2017). Identifying such genetic flaws could enable doctors to predict an individual's risks, recommend healthy practices, and prescribe the safest and most effective drugs (Botkin, 2016). A decade or two from now, parents of a newborn baby may be able to leave the hospital with a full genome analysis of their offspring that reveals disease risks.

However, this knowledge might bring important costs as well as benefits. Who would have access to a person's genetic profile? An individual's ability to land and hold jobs or obtain insurance might be threatened if it is known that a person is considered at risk for some disease. For example, should an airline pilot or a neurosurgeon who is predisposed to develop a disorder that makes one's hands shake be required to leave that job early?

Genetic counselors, usually physicians or biologists who are well versed in the field of medical genetics, understand the kinds of problems just described, the odds of encountering them, and helpful strategies for offsetting some of their effects (Besser & Mounts, 2017; Stilwell, 2016). A research review found that many individuals who receive genetic counseling find it difficult to quantify risk and tend to overestimate risk (Sivell & others, 2008). To read about the career and work of a genetic counselor, see the *Connecting with Careers* profile.

Holly Ishmael, Genetic Counselor

Holly Ishmael is a genetic counselor at Children's Mercy Hospital in Kansas City. She obtained an undergraduate degree in psychology and then a master's degree in genetic counseling from Sarah Lawrence College.

Genetic counselors, like Ishmael, work as members of a health-care team, providing information and support to families with birth defects or genetic disorders. They identify families at risk by analyzing inheritance patterns and explore options with the family. Some genetic counselors, like Ishmael, become specialists in prenatal and pediatric genetics; others might specialize in cancer genetics or psychiatric genetic disorders.

Ishmael says, "Genetic counseling is a perfect combination for people who want to do something science-oriented, but need human contact and don't want to spend all of their time in a lab or have their nose in a book" (Rizzo, 1999, p. 3).

Genetic counselors have specialized graduate degrees in the areas of medical genetics and counseling. They enter graduate school with undergraduate backgrounds from a variety of disciplines, including biology, genetics, psychology, public health, and social work. There are approximately thirty graduate genetic counseling programs in the United States. If you are interested in this profession, you can obtain further information from the National Society of Genetic Counselors at www.nsgc.org.

Holly Ishmael (left) in a genetic counseling session.
Courtesy of Holly Ishmael Welsh

Review Connect Reflect

LG2 Describe what genes are and how they influence human development.

Review
- What are genes?
- How are genes passed on from one generation to another?
- What basic principles describe how genes interact?
- What are some chromosomal and gene-linked abnormalities?

Connect
- Explain how environment interacts with genes in gene-linked abnormalities.

Reflect *Your Own Personal Journey of Life*
- Would you want to be able to access a full genome analysis of yourself or your offspring? Why or why not?

3 What Are Some Reproductive Challenges and Choices?

LG3 Identify some important reproductive challenges and choices.

Prenatal Diagnostic Tests | Infertility and Reproductive Technology | Adoption

The facts and principles we have discussed regarding meiosis, genetics, and genetic abnormalities are a small part of the recent explosion of knowledge about human biology. This knowledge not only helps us understand human development but also opens up many new choices to prospective parents, choices that can also raise ethical questions.

PRENATAL DIAGNOSTIC TESTS

One choice open to prospective mothers is the extent to which they should undergo prenatal testing. A number of tests can indicate whether a fetus is developing normally; these include ultrasound sonography, fetal MRI, chorionic villus sampling, amniocentesis, and maternal blood screening. There has been a dramatic increase in research on the use of less invasive techniques, such as fetal MRI, which poses lower risks to the fetus than more invasive techniques such as chorionic villus sampling and amniocentesis.

Ultrasound Sonography   An ultrasound test is often conducted seven weeks into a pregnancy and at various times later in pregnancy. *Ultrasound sonography* is a prenatal medical procedure in which high-frequency sound waves are directed into the pregnant woman's abdomen (Gonçalves, 2016; Kitagawa & Pringle, 2017). The echo from the sounds is transformed into a visual representation of the fetus's inner structures. This technique can detect many structural abnormalities in the fetus, including microcephaly, a form of intellectual disability involving an abnormally small brain; it can also determine the number of fetuses (if a woman is carrying twins or triplets) and give clues to the baby's sex (Calvo-Garcia, 2016; Rink & Norton, 2016). A recent research review concluded that many aspects of the developing prenatal brain can be detected by ultrasound in the first trimester and that about 50 percent of spina bifida cases can be identified at this time, most of these being severe cases (Engels & others, 2016). Ultrasound involves virtually no risk to the woman or fetus.

A 6-month-old infant poses with the ultrasound sonography record taken four months into the baby's prenatal development. *What is ultrasound sonography?*
©Jacques Pavlovsky/Sygma/Corbis/Getty Images

Fetal MRI   The development of brain-imaging techniques has led to increasing use of *fetal MRI* to diagnose fetal malformations (Kang & others, 2017; Weistanner & others, 2017; You & others, 2016) (see Figure 8). MRI stands for magnetic resonance imaging, which uses a powerful magnet and radio images to generate detailed images of the body's organs and structure. Currently, ultrasound is still the first choice in fetal screening, but fetal MRI can provide more detailed images than ultrasound. In many instances, ultrasound will indicate a possible abnormality, and then fetal MRI will be used to obtain a clearer, more detailed image (Tee & others, 2016). Among the fetal malformations that fetal MRI may be able to detect better than ultrasound sonography are certain abnormalities of the central nervous system, chest, gastrointestinal tract, genital/urinary organs, and placenta (Milesi & others, 2014). In a recent research review, it was concluded that fetal MRI often does not provide good results in the first trimester of pregnancy because of small fetal structures and movement artifacts (Wataganara & others, 2016). Also, in this review, it was argued that fetal MRI can be especially beneficial in assessing central nervous system abnormalities in the third semester of pregnancy.

Chorionic Villus Sampling   At some point between 9.5 and 12.5 weeks of pregnancy, chorionic villus sampling may be used to detect genetic defects and chromosomal abnormalities such as the ones discussed in the previous section. Diagnosis takes approximately 10 days. *Chorionic villus sampling (CVS)* is a prenatal medical procedure in which a small sample of the placenta (the vascular organ that links the fetus to the mother's uterus) is removed (Monni & others, 2016). There is a small risk of limb deformity when CVS is used.

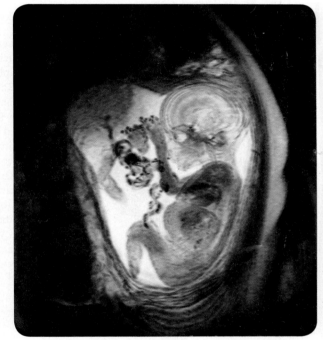

FIGURE **8**

A FETAL MRI, WHICH IS INCREASINGLY BEING USED IN PRENATAL DIAGNOSIS OF FETAL MALFORMATIONS
©Du Cane Medical Imagining Ltd./Science Source

Amniocentesis   Between the 14th and 20th weeks of pregnancy, amniocentesis may be performed. *Amniocentesis* is a prenatal medical procedure in which a sample of amniotic fluid is withdrawn by syringe and tested for chromosomal or metabolic disorders (Jung & others, 2017). The amniotic fluid is found within the amnion, a thin sac in which the embryo is suspended. Ultrasound sonography is often used during amniocentesis so that the syringe can be placed precisely. The later amniocentesis is performed, the better its diagnostic potential. The earlier it is performed, the more useful it is in deciding how to handle a pregnancy. It may take two weeks for enough cells to grow so that amniocentesis test results can be obtained. Amniocentesis brings a small risk of miscarriage—about 1 woman in every 200 to 300 miscarries after amniocentesis.

developmental **connection**

Biological Processes

Discover what the development of the fetus is like at the times when chorionic villus sampling and amniocentesis can be used. Connect to "Prenatal Development."

Maternal Blood Screening   During the 16th to 18th weeks of pregnancy, maternal blood screening may be performed. *Maternal blood screening* identifies pregnancies that have an elevated risk for birth defects such as spina bifida (a defect in the spinal cord) and Down syndrome, as well as congenital heart disease risk for children (Sun & others, 2016). The current blood test is called the *triple screen* because it measures three substances in the mother's blood. After an abnormal triple screen result, the next step is usually an ultrasound examination. If an ultrasound does not explain the abnormal triple screen results, amniocentesis is typically used.

Fetal Sex Determination   Chorionic villus sampling has often been used to determine the sex of the fetus at some point between 11 and 13 weeks of gestation. Also, in a recent study, ultrasound accurately identified the sex of the fetus between 11 and 13 weeks of gestation (Manzanares & others, 2016). Recently, however, some noninvasive techniques have been able to determine the sex of the fetus at an earlier point by assessing cell-free DNA in maternal plasma (Breveglieri & others, 2016; Koumbaris & others, 2016). A recent meta-analysis concluded that the baby's sex can be determined as early as seven weeks into pregnancy (Devaney & others, 2011). Being able to detect an offspring's sex and to identify various diseases and defects so early raises ethical concerns about couples' motivation to terminate a pregnancy (Browne, 2017).

INFERTILITY AND REPRODUCTIVE TECHNOLOGY

Recent advances in biological knowledge have also opened up many choices for infertile individuals (Liebermann, 2017; Silber, 2017; Zaca & Borini, 2017). Approximately 10 to 15 percent of couples in the United States experience infertility, which is defined as the inability to conceive a child after 12 months of regular intercourse without contraception. The cause of infertility can rest with the woman or the man. The woman may not be ovulating (releasing eggs to be fertilized), she may be producing abnormal ova, her fallopian tubes through which fertilized ova normally reach the womb may be blocked, or she may have a disease that prevents implantation of the embryo into the uterus. The man may produce too few sperm, his sperm may lack motility (the ability to move adequately), or he may have a blocked passageway (Xu & others, 2016).

In the United States, more than 2 million couples seek help for infertility every year. In some cases of infertility, surgery may correct the cause; in others, hormone-based drugs may improve the probability of having a child. Of the 2 million couples who seek help for infertility each year, about 40,000 try high-tech assisted reproduction. By far the most common technique used is *in vitro fertilization (IVF),* in which eggs and sperm are combined in a laboratory dish (Sunderam & others, 2017). If any eggs are successfully fertilized, one or more of the resulting embryos are transferred into the woman's uterus. A national U.S. study in 2004 by the Centers for Disease Control and Prevention found that the success rate of IVF depends on the mother's age (see Figure 9).

The creation of families by means of the new reproductive technologies raises important questions about the physical and psychological consequences for children (Sunderam & others, 2017). One result of fertility treatments is an increase in multiple births (Jones, 2007). Twenty-five to 30 percent of pregnancies achieved by fertility treatments—including in vitro fertilization—now result in multiple births. Fertility drugs are more likely to produce multiple births than in vitro fertilization (March of Dimes, 2017). Any multiple birth increases the likelihood that the babies will have life-threatening and costly problems, such as extremely low birth weight (March of Dimes, 2017). In a recent national study, low birth weight and preterm birth were significantly higher among infants conceived by assisted-reproduction technology (Sunderam & others, 2017).

Not nearly as many studies have examined the psychological outcomes of IVF as the physical outcomes. To read about a study that addresses these consequences, see the *Connecting with Research* interlude that follows.

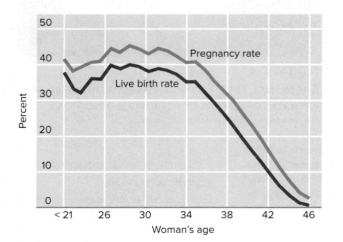

FIGURE 9

SUCCESS RATES OF IN VITRO FERTILIZATION VARY ACCORDING TO THE WOMAN'S AGE

Are There Developmental Outcomes in Adolescence of In Vitro Fertilization?

A longitudinal study examined 34 in vitro fertilization families, 49 adoptive families, and 38 families with a naturally conceived child (Golombok, MacCallum, & Goodman, 2001). Each type of family included a similar portion of boys and girls. Also, the age of the young adolescents did not differ according to family type (mean age of 11 years, 11 months).

Children's socioemotional development was assessed by (1) interviewing the mother and obtaining detailed descriptions of any problems the child might have; (2) administering a Strengths and Difficulties questionnaire to the child's mother and teacher; and (3) administering the Social Adjustment Inventory for Children and Adolescents, which examines functioning in school, peer relationships, and self-esteem.

No significant differences between the children from the in vitro fertilization, adoptive, and naturally conceiving families were found. The results from the Social Adjustment Inventory for Children and Adolescents are shown in Figure 10. Recent reviews by leading researchers conclude that the children and adolescents conceived through new reproductive technologies—such as in vitro fertilization— are as well adjusted as their counterparts conceived by natural means (Golombok, 2011a, b; Golombok & Tasker, 2010).

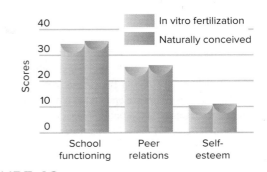

FIGURE 10

SOCIOEMOTIONAL FUNCTIONING OF CHILDREN CONCEIVED THROUGH IN VITRO FERTILIZATION OR NATURALLY CONCEIVED. This graph shows the results of a study that compared the socioemotional functioning of young adolescents who had either been conceived through in vitro fertilization (IVF) or naturally conceived (Golombok, MacCallum, & Goodman, 2001). For each type of family, the study included similar proportions of boys and girls and children of similar age (mean age of 11 years, 11 months). Although the means for the naturally conceived group were slightly higher, this is likely due to chance: There were no significant differences between the groups.

What additional types of studies do you think researchers might conduct to study possible developmental effects of new reproductive technologies? How long do you think the children in such studies should be followed?

ADOPTION

Although surgery and fertility drugs can sometimes resolve infertility problems, another choice is to adopt a child (Compton, 2016; Farr, 2017). Adoption is the social and legal process by which a parent-child relationship is established between persons unrelated at birth. As we see next in the *Connecting with Diversity* interlude, an increase in diversity has characterized the adoption of children in the United States in recent years.

How do adopted children fare after they are adopted? In a recent study of 3- to 5-year-olds, parents' secure attachment increased children's probability of having a secure attachment pattern, with mothers' secure attachment more strongly associated with children's secure attachment than was fathers' secure attachment (Barone, Lionetti, & Green, 2017). Also, a recent research review concluded that adopted children are at higher risk for externalizing (aggression and conduct problems, for example), internalizing (anxiety and depression, for example), and attention problems (ADHD, for example) (Grotevant & McDermott, 2014). In another recent research review of internationally adopted adolescents, although a majority were well adjusted, adoptees had a higher level of mental health problems than their non-adopted counterparts (Askeland & others, 2017). Indeed, a majority of adopted children and adolescents (including those adopted at older ages, transracially, and across national borders) adjust effectively, and their parents report considerable satisfaction with their decision to adopt (Brodzinsky & Pinderhughes, 2002; Castle & others, 2010; Compton, 2016).

Adopted children and adolescents fare much better than children and adolescents in long-term foster care or in an institutional environment (Bernard & Dozier, 2008). One study of infants in China revealed that their cognitive development improved 2 to 6 months following their adoption from foster homes and institutions (van den Dries & others, 2010).

The Increased Diversity of Adopted Children and Adoptive Parents

A number of changes have characterized adopted children and adoptive parents in the last three to four decades (Brodzinsky & Pinderhughes, 2002; Farr, 2017; Thomas, 2016). In the first half of the twentieth century, most children adopted in the United States were healthy, non-Latino White infants who were adopted at birth or soon after; however, in recent decades as abortion became legal and the use of contraception increased, fewer of these infants became available for adoption. Increasingly, U.S. couples adopted a much wider diversity of children—from other countries, from other ethnic groups, children with physical and/or mental problems, and children who had been neglected or abused (Compton, 2016; Pinderhughes, Zhang, & Agerbak, 2015).

Changes also have characterized adoptive parents in the last three to four decades (Brodzinsky & Pinderhughes, 2002). In the first half of the twentieth century, most adoptive parents were heterosexual couples from non-Latino White middle or upper socioeconomic status backgrounds who were married and did not have any type of disability. However, in recent decades, increased diversity has characterized adoptive parents. Many adoption agencies today have no income requirements for adoptive parents and now allow adults from a wide range of backgrounds to adopt children, including single adults, gay and lesbian adults, and older adults (Farr, 2017; Farr & others, 2016).

Further, many adoptions involve other family members (aunts/uncles/grandparents); currently, 30 percent of U.S. adoptions are made by relatives (Ledesma, 2012). And slightly more than 50 percent of U.S. adoptions occur through the foster care system; recently more than 100,000 children in the U.S. foster care system were waiting for someone to adopt them (Ledesma, 2012).

Three pathways to adoption are (1) domestic adoption from the public welfare system; (2) domestic infant adoption through private agencies and intermediaries; and (3) international adoption (Grotevant & McDermott, 2014). In the next decade, the mix of U.S. adoptions is likely to include fewer domestic infant and international adoptions and more adoptions via the child welfare system (Grotevant & McDermott, 2014).

An ongoing issue in adopting children is whether there should be any contact with the child's biological parents (Grant-Marsney, Grotevant, & Sayer, 2015). Open adoption involves sharing identifying information and having contact with the biological parents, while closed adoption does not include such sharing and contact. Most adoption agencies today offer birth parents and adoptive parents the opportunity to have either an open or a closed adoption. A longitudinal study found that when their adopted children reached adulthood, adoptive parents described open adoption positively and saw it as serving the child's best interests (Siegel, 2013). Another longitudinal study found that birth mothers, adoptive parents, and birth children who had contact were more satisfied with their arrangements than those who did not have contact (Grotevant & others, 2013). Also, in this study, contact was linked to more optimal adjustment for adolescents and emerging adults (Grotevant & others, 2013). Further, birth mothers who were more satisfied with their contact arrangements had less unresolved grief 12 to 20 years after placement. And in a study of adoptees in emerging adulthood, perceptions of secure parent-child attachment relationships, as well as sensitive and open communication about birth parent contact, were linked to greater satisfaction (Farr, Grant-Marsney, & Grotevant, 2014).

To read more about adoption, see the *Caring Connections* interlude that describes effective parenting strategies with adopted children.

Review Connect Reflect

LG3 Identify some important reproductive challenges and choices.

Review
- What are some common prenatal diagnostic tests?
- What are some techniques that help infertile people to have children?
- How does adoption affect children's development?

Connect
- Earlier you learned about different methods for collecting data. How would you characterize the methods used in prenatal diagnostic testing?

Reflect *Your Own Personal Journey of Life*
- If you were an adult who could not have children, would you want to adopt a child? Why or why not?

Parenting Adopted Children

Many of the keys to effectively parenting adopted children are no different from those for effectively parenting biological children: Be supportive and caring, be involved and monitor the child's behavior and whereabouts, be a good communicator, and help the child learn to develop self-control. However, parents of adopted children face some unique circumstances (Pace & others, 2015; Tan & others, 2017). They need to recognize the differences involved in adoptive family life, communicate about these differences, show respect for the birth family, and support the child's search for self and identity.

Following are some of the problems parents face when their adopted children are at different points in development and some recommendations for how to handle these problems (Brodzinsky & Pinderhughes, 2002, pp. 288–292):

- **Infancy.** Researchers have found few differences in the attachment that adopted and nonadopted infants form with their parents. However, attachment can become problematic if parents have unresolved fertility issues or the child does not meet the parents' expectations. Counselors can help prospective adoptive parents develop realistic expectations.
- **Early childhood.** Because many children begin to ask where they came from when they are about 4 to 6 years old, this is a natural time to begin to talk in simple ways to children about their adoption status (Warshak, 2008). Some parents (although not as many as in the past) decide not to tell their children about the adoption. This secrecy may create psychological risks for the child if he or she later finds out about the adoption.
- **Middle and late childhood.** During the elementary school years, children begin to show more interest in their origins and may ask questions related to where they came from, what their birth parents looked like, and why their birth parents chose not to raise them.

What are some strategies for parenting adopted children at different points in their development?
©Don Mason/Blend Images/Getty Images RF

As they grow older, children may develop mixed feelings about being adopted and question their adoptive parents' explanations. It is important for adoptive parents to recognize that this ambivalence is normal. Also, problems may arise from the desire of adoptive parents to make life too perfect for the adopted child and to present a perfect image of themselves to the child. The result too often is that adopted children feel that they cannot release any angry feelings or openly discuss problems.

- **Adolescence.** Adolescents are likely to develop more abstract and logical thinking, to focus their attention on their bodies, and to search for an identity. These characteristics provide the foundation for adopted adolescents to reflect on their adoption status in more complex ways, such as focusing on looking different from their adoptive parents. As they explore their identity, adopted adolescents may have difficulty incorporating their adoptive status into their identity in positive ways. It is important for adoptive parents to understand the complexity of the adopted adolescent's identity exploration and be patient with the adolescent's lengthy identity search.

4 How Do Heredity and Environment Interact? The Nature-Nurture Debate

LG4 Characterize some of the ways that heredity and environment interact to produce individual differences in development.

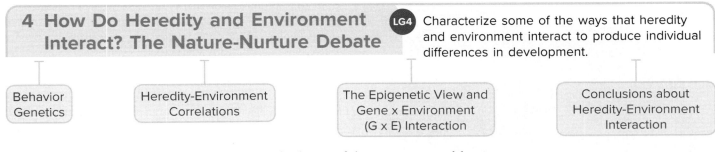

Behavior Genetics

Heredity-Environment Correlations

The Epigenetic View and Gene x Environment (G x E) Interaction

Conclusions about Heredity-Environment Interaction

In each section of this chapter so far, we have examined parts of the nature-nurture debate. We have seen how the environment exerts selective pressures on the characteristics of species over generations, examined how genes are passed from parents to children, and discussed how reproductive technologies and adoption influence the course of children's lives. But in all of these situations, heredity and environment interact to produce development. After all, Jim and Jim (and each of the other pairs of identical twins discussed in the opening of the chapter)

developmental **connection**

Nature and Nurture

The nature and nurture interaction is one of the main issues in the study of children's development. Connect to "Introduction."

have the same genotype, but they are not the same person; each is unique. What made them different? Whether we are studying how genes produce proteins, their influence on how tall a person is, or how PKU might affect an individual, we end up discussing heredity-environment interactions.

Is it possible to untangle the influence of heredity from that of environment and discover the role of each in producing individual differences in development? When heredity and environment interact, how does heredity influence the environment, and vice versa?

BEHAVIOR GENETICS

Behavior genetics is the field that seeks to discover the influence of heredity and environment on individual differences in human traits and development (Jaffee, 2016; Machalek & others, 2017). Note that behavior genetics does not determine the extent to which genetics or the environment affects an individual's traits. Instead, what behavior geneticists try to do is to figure out what is responsible for the differences among people—that is, to what extent do people differ because of differences in genes, environment, or a combination of these? To study the influence of heredity on behavior, behavior geneticists often use either twins or adoption situations.

In the most common **twin study,** the behavioral similarity of identical twins (who are genetically identical) is compared with the behavioral similarity of fraternal twins. Recall that although fraternal twins share the same womb, they are no more genetically alike than non-twin siblings. Thus, by comparing groups of identical and fraternal twins, behavior geneticists capitalize on the basic knowledge that identical twins are more similar genetically than are fraternal twins (Li & others, 2017; Rosenstrom & others, 2017; Segal, 2016). For example, one study revealed that conduct problems were more prevalent in identical twins than fraternal twins; the researchers concluded that the study demonstrated an important role for heredity in conduct problems (Scourfield & others, 2004).

What are some of the thoughts and feelings that children and youth have about being an identical twin? In college freshman Colin Kunzweiler's (2007) view,

> As a monozygotic individual, I am used to certain things. "Which one are you?" happens to be the most popular question I'm asked, which is almost always followed by "You're Colin. No, wait, you're Andy!"
>
> I have two names: one was given to me at birth, the other thrust on me in a random, haphazard way. . . . My twin brother and I are as different from each other as caramel sauce is from gravy. We have different personalities, we enjoy different kinds of music, and I am even taller than he is (by a quarter of an inch). We are different; separate; individual. I have always been taught that I should maintain my own individuality; that I should be my own person. But if people keep constantly mistaking me for my twin, how can I be my own person with my own identity?

"Am I an 'I' or 'We'?" was the title of an article written by Lynn Perlman (2008) about the struggle twins have in developing a sense of being an individual. Of course, triplets have the same issue, possibly even more strongly so. One set of triplets entered a beauty contest as one person and won the contest!

Perlman, an identical twin herself, is a psychologist who works with twins (her identical twin also is a psychologist). She says that how twins move from a sense of "we" to "I" is a critical task for them as children and sometimes even as adults. For non-twins, separating oneself from a primary caregiver—mother and/or father—is an important developmental task in childhood, adolescence, and emerging adulthood. When a child has a twin, the separation process is likely to be more difficult because of the constant comparisons with the twin. Because they are virtually identical in their physical appearance, identical twins are likely to have more problems distinguishing themselves from their twin than are fraternal twins.

behavior genetics The field that seeks to discover the influence of heredity and environment on individual differences in human traits and development.

twin study A study in which the behavioral similarity of identical twins is compared with the behavioral similarity of fraternal twins.

Twin studies compare identical twins with fraternal twins. Identical twins develop from a single fertilized egg that splits into two genetically identical organisms. Fraternal twins develop from separate eggs, making them genetically no more similar than nontwin siblings. *What is the nature of the twin study method?*

©68/Compassionate Eye Foundation/Corbis RF

The twin separation process often accelerates in adolescence when one twin is likely to mature earlier than the other (Pearlman, 2013). However, for some twins it may not occur until emerging adulthood when they may go to different colleges and/or live apart for the first time. And for some twins, even in adulthood twin separation can be emotionally painful. One 28-year-old identical twin female got a new boyfriend, but the new relationship caused a great deal of stress and conflict with her twin sister (Friedman, 2013).

In Lynn Perlman's (2008) view, helping twins develop their own identities needs to be done on a child-by-child basis, taking into account their preferences and what is in their best interests. She commented that most of the twins she has counseled consider having a twin a positive experience and while they also are usually strongly attached to each other, they are intensely motivated to be treated as unique individuals.

Certain issues complicate the interpretation of twin studies. For example, perhaps the environments of identical twins are more similar than the environments of fraternal twins. Adults might stress the similarities of identical twins more than those of fraternal twins, and identical twins might perceive themselves as a "set" and play together more than fraternal twins do. If so, the influence of the environment on the observed similarities between identical and fraternal twins might be very significant.

In an **adoption study,** investigators seek to discover whether the behavior and psychological characteristics of adopted children are more like those of their adoptive parents, who have provided a home environment, or more like those of their biological parents, who have contributed their DNA (Kendler & others, 2016). Another form of the adoption study compares adopted and biological siblings.

HEREDITY-ENVIRONMENT CORRELATIONS

The difficulties that researchers encounter when they interpret the results of twin studies and adoption studies reflect the complexities of heredity-environment interaction. Some of these interactions are *heredity-environment correlations,* which means that individuals' genes may be systematically related to the types of environments to which they are exposed (Klahr & Burt, 2014). In a sense, individuals "inherit," seek out, or "construct" environments that may be related or linked to genetic "propensities." Behavior geneticist Sandra Scarr (1993) described three ways that heredity and environment can be correlated (see Figure 11):

- **Passive genotype-environment correlations** occur because biological parents, who are genetically related to the child, provide a rearing environment for the child. For example, the parents might have a genetic predisposition to be intelligent and read skillfully. Because they read well and enjoy reading, they provide their children with books to read. The likely outcome is that their children, because of both their own inherited predispositions and their book-filled environment, will become skilled readers.

adoption study A study in which investigators seek to discover whether, in behavior and psychological characteristics, adopted children are more like their adoptive parents, who provided a home environment, or more like their biological parents, who contributed their heredity. Another form of the adoption study compares adopted and biological siblings.

passive genotype-environment correlations Correlations that exist when the biological parents, who are genetically related to the child, provide a rearing environment for the child.

Heredity-Environment Correlation	Description	Examples
Passive	Children inherit genetic tendencies from their parents, and parents also provide an environment that matches their own genetic tendencies.	Musically inclined parents usually have musically inclined children and they are likely to provide an environment rich in music for their children.
Evocative	The child's genetic tendencies elicit stimulation from the environment that supports a particular trait. Thus genes evoke environmental support.	A happy, outgoing child elicits smiles and friendly responses from others.
Active (niche-picking)	Children actively seek out "niches" in their environment that reflect their own interests and talents and are thus in accord with their genotype.	Libraries, sports fields, and a store with musical instruments are examples of environmental niches children might seek out if they have intellectual interests in books, talent in sports, or musical talents, respectively.

FIGURE 11

EXPLORING HEREDITY-ENVIRONMENT CORRELATIONS

- **Evocative genotype-environment correlations** occur because a child's genetically influenced characteristics elicit certain types of environments. For example, active, smiling children receive more social stimulation than passive, quiet children do. Cooperative, attentive children evoke more pleasant and instructional responses from the adults around them than uncooperative, distractible children do.
- **Active (niche-picking) genotype-environment correlations** occur when children seek out environments that they find compatible and stimulating. *Niche-picking* refers to finding a setting that is suited to one's genetically influenced abilities. Children select from their surrounding environment some aspect that they respond to, learn about, or ignore. Their active selections of environments are related to their particular genotype. For example, outgoing children tend to seek out social contexts in which to interact with people, whereas shy children don't. Children who are musically inclined are likely to select musical environments in which they can successfully perform their skills. How these "tendencies" come about will be discussed later in this chapter under the topic of the epigenetic view.

Scarr argues that the relative importance of the three genotype-environment correlations changes as children develop from infancy through adolescence. In infancy, much of the environment that children experience is provided by adults. Thus, passive genotype-environment correlations are more common in the lives of infants and young children than they are in the lives of older children and adolescents who can extend their experiences beyond the family's influence and create or and select their environments to a greater degree.

Notice that this analysis gives the preeminent role in development to heredity—the analysis describes how heredity may influence the types of environments that children experience. Critics argue that the concept of heredity-environment correlation gives heredity too much of a one-sided influence in determining development because it does not consider the role of prior environmental influences in shaping the correlation itself (Gottlieb, Wahlsten, & Lickliter, 2006). Before considering this criticism and exploring a different view of the heredity-environment linkage, let's take a closer look at how behavior geneticists analyze the environments involved in heredity.

THE EPIGENETIC VIEW AND GENE × ENVIRONMENT (G × E) INTERACTION

Critics argue that the concept of heredity-environment correlation gives heredity too much of a one-sided influence in determining development because it does not consider the role of prior environmental influences in shaping the correlation itself (Gottlieb, 2007). Consistent with this view, earlier in the chapter we discussed how genes are collaborative, not determining an individual's traits in an independent manner but rather in an interactive manner with the environment.

The Epigenetic View   In line with the concept of a collaborative gene, Gilbert Gottlieb (2007) emphasizes the **epigenetic view,** which states that development reflects an ongoing, bidirectional interchange between heredity and the environment. Figure 12 compares the heredity-environment correlation and epigenetic views of development.

Let's look at an example that reflects the epigenetic view. A baby inherits genes from both parents at conception. During prenatal development, toxins, nutrition, and stress can influence some genes to stop functioning while others become more active or less active (Pluess & others, 2011). During infancy, environmental experiences such as toxins, nutrition, stress, learning, and encouragement continue to modify the genetic activity and the activity of the nervous system that directly underlie behavior (Gottlieb, 2007). Heredity and environment operate together—or collaborate—to produce a person's well-being, intelligence, temperament, height, weight, skill in pitching a baseball, ability to read, and so on (Lickliter & Honeycutt, 2015; Moore, 2015; Szyf & Pluess, 2016).

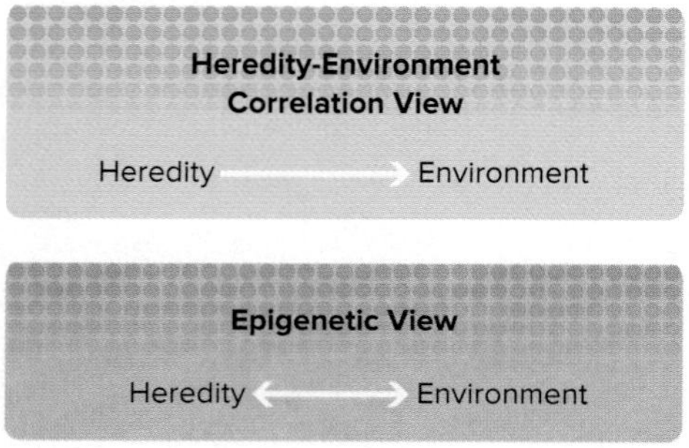

Gene × Environment (G × E) Interaction   An increasing number of studies are exploring how the interaction between heredity and environment influences development,

evocative genotype-environment correlations Correlations that exist when the child's genetically influenced characteristics elicit certain types of physical and social environments.

active (niche-picking) genotype-environment correlations Correlations that exist when children seek out environments they find compatible and stimulating. *Niche-picking* refers to finding a setting that is suited to one's genetically influenced abilities.

epigenetic view Emphasizes that development reflects an ongoing, bidirectional interchange between heredity and environment.

How Would You...?
If you were a **health-care professional,** how would you explain heredity-environment interaction to new parents who are upset about discovering that their child has a treatable genetic defect?

Heredity-Environment Correlation View

Heredity ⟶ Environment

Epigenetic View

Heredity ⟷ Environment

FIGURE 12
COMPARISON OF THE HEREDITY-ENVIRONMENT CORRELATION AND EPIGENETIC VIEWS

including interactions that involve specific DNA sequences (Bakusic & others, 2017; Grigorenko & others, 2016; Halldorsdottir & Binder, 2017; Hill & Roth, 2016). The epigenetic mechanisms involve the actual molecular modification of the DNA strand as a result of environmental inputs in ways that alter gene functioning (Moore, 2017; Philibert & Beach, 2016; Rozenblat & others, 2017).

One study found that individuals who have a short version of a gene labeled 5-HTTLPR (a gene involving the neurotransmitter serotonin) have an elevated risk of developing depression only if they *also* lead stressful lives (Caspi & others, 2003). Thus, the specific gene did not directly cause the development of depression; rather the gene interacted with a stressful environment in a way that allowed the researchers to predict whether individuals would develop depression. A recent meta-analysis indicated that the short version of 5-HTTLPR was linked with higher cortisol stress reactivity (Miller & others, 2013). Recent studies also have found support for the interaction between the 5-HTTLPR gene and stress levels in predicting depression in adolescents and older adults (Petersen & others, 2012; Zannas & others, 2012).

Other research involving interaction between genes and environmental experiences has focused on attachment, parenting, and supportive child-rearing environments (Hostinar, Cicchetti, & Rogosch, 2014). In one study, adults who experienced parental loss as young children were more likely to have unresolved attachment issues as adults only when they had the short version of the 5-HTTLPR gene (Caspers & others, 2009). The long version of the serotonin transporter gene apparently provided some protection and ability to cope better with parental loss. Other recent research has found that variations in dopamine-related genes interact with supportive or unsupportive rearing environments to influence children's development (Bakermans-Kranenburg & van IJzendoorn, 2011).

The type of research just described is referred to as studies of **gene × environment (G × E) interaction**—the interaction between a specific measured variation in DNA and a specific measured aspect of the environment (Naumova & others, 2016; Samek & others, 2017; Truzzi & others, 2017).

Although there is considerable enthusiasm about the concept of gene × environment interaction (G × E), a recent research review concluded that the area is plagued by difficulties in replicating results, inflated claims, and other weaknesses (Manuck & McCaffery, 2014). The science of G × E interaction is very young, and during the next several decades it will likely produce more precise findings.

CONCLUSIONS ABOUT HEREDITY-ENVIRONMENT INTERACTION

If a strong, fast, athletic girl wins a championship tennis match in her high school, is her success due to heredity or to environment? Of course, the answer is both.

The relative contributions of heredity and environment are not additive. That is, we can't say that such-and-such a percentage of nature and such-and-such a percentage of experience make us who we are. Nor is it accurate to say that full genetic expression happens once, around conception or birth, after which we carry our genetic legacy into the world to see how far it takes us. Genes produce proteins throughout the life span, in many different environments. Or they don't produce these proteins, depending in part on how harsh or nourishing those environments are.

The emerging view is that complex behaviors are influenced by genes in a way that gives people a propensity for a particular developmental trajectory (Rahmani & others, 2017; Zabaneh & others, 2017). However, the actual development requires more: an environment. And that environment is complex, just like the mixture of genes we inherit (Almy & Cicchetti, 2018; Carlo & others, 2017; Nikolaisen & Thorsen, 2017). Environmental influences range from the things we lump together under "nurture" (such as parenting, family dynamics, schooling, and neighborhood quality) to biological encounters (such as viruses, birth complications, and even biological events in cells).

In developmental psychologist David Moore's (2013, 2015, 2017) view, the biological systems that generate behaviors are extremely complex and too often these systems have been described in overly simplified ways that can be misleading. Thus, although genetic factors clearly contribute to behavior and psychological processes, they don't determine these

How Would You...? If you were a **human development and family studies professional,** how would you apply the epigenetic view to explain why one identical twin can develop alcoholism while the other twin does not?

gene × environment (G × E) interaction The interaction of a specific measured variation in the DNA and a specific measured aspect of the environment.

To what extent are this young girl's piano skills likely due to heredity, environment, or both? Explain.
©Francesco Romero/E+/Getty Images RF

phenotypes independently from the contexts in which they develop. From Moore's (2013, 2015, 2017) perspective, it is misleading to talk about "genes for" eye color, intelligence, personality, or other characteristics. Moore commented that in retrospect we should not have expected to be able to make the giant leap from DNA's molecules to a complete understanding of human behavior any more than we should anticipate being able to make the leap from understanding how sound waves move in a concert hall to a full-blown appreciation of a symphony's wondrous experience.

Consider for a moment the cluster of genes associated with diabetes. The child who carries this genetic mixture might experience a world of loving parents, nutritious meals, and regular medical intervention. Or the child's world might include parental neglect, a diet high in sugar, and little help from competent physicians. In which of these environments are the child's genes likely to result in diabetes?

If heredity and environment interact to determine the course of development, is that all there is to answering the question of what causes development? Are children completely at the mercy of their genes and environment as they develop? Children's genetic heritage and environmental experiences are pervasive influences on their development (Lickliter, 2017; Lockhart & others, 2017; Masten & Kalstabakken, 2017). But children's development is not only the outcome of their heredity and the environment they experience. Children also can author a unique developmental path by changing their environment. As one psychologist recently concluded:

> In reality, we are both the creatures and creators of our worlds. We are . . . the products of our genes and environments. Nevertheless . . . the stream of causation that shapes the future runs through our present choices. . . . Mind matters. . . . Our hopes, goals, and expectations influence our future. (Myers, 2010, p. 168)

Review Connect Reflect

LG4 Characterize some of the ways that heredity and environment interact to produce individual differences in development.

Review
- What is behavior genetics?
- What are three types of heredity-environment correlations?
- What is the epigenetic view of development? What characterizes gene x environment (G x E) interaction?
- What conclusions can be reached about heredity-environment interaction?

Connect
- Of passive, evocative, and active genotype-environment correlations, which is the best explanation for the similarities discovered between the twins (Jim and Jim, for example) discussed in the story that opened the chapter?

Reflect *Your Own Personal Journey of Life*
- Someone tells you that she has analyzed her genetic background and environmental experiences and reached the conclusion that environment definitely has had little influence on her intelligence. What would you say to this person about her ability to make this self-diagnosis?

topical connections *looking forward*

In the remaining chapters, you will continue to read about biological influences on development, especially in the chapters on prenatal development, birth, and physical development in infancy, early childhood, middle and late childhood, and adolescence, and also in the chapters on cognitive and socioemotional development. Next you will learn about the amazing developmental journey from conception to birth, including how expectant mothers can best promote their offspring's health and well-being during pregnancy.

Biological Beginnings

1 What Is the Evolutionary Perspective?

LG1 Discuss the evolutionary perspective on development.

- Natural Selection and Adaptive Behavior
- Evolutionary Psychology

- Natural selection is the process by which those individuals of a species that are best adapted survive and reproduce. Darwin proposed that natural selection fuels evolution. In evolutionary theory, adaptive behavior is behavior that promotes the organism's survival in a natural habitat.

- Evolutionary psychology holds that adaptation, reproduction, and "survival of the fittest" are important in shaping behavior. Ideas proposed by evolutionary developmental psychology include the view that we humans need an extended juvenile period to develop a large brain and learn the complexity of human social communities.

- Many evolved psychological mechanisms are domain-specific. Like other theoretical approaches to development, evolutionary psychology has limitations. Bandura rejects "one-sided evolutionism" and argues for a bidirectional link between biology and environment. Biology allows for a broad range of cultural possibilities.

2 What Are the Genetic Foundations of Development?

LG2 Describe what genes are and how they influence human development.

- The Collaborative Gene
- Genes and Chromosomes
- Genetic Principles
- Chromosomal and Gene-Linked Abnormalities

- Short segments of DNA constitute genes, the units of hereditary information that help cells to reproduce and manufacture proteins. Except in the sperm and egg, the nucleus of each human cell contains 46 chromosomes (arranged in 23 pairs), which are composed of DNA. Genes act collaboratively, not independently.

- Genes are passed on to new cells when chromosomes are duplicated during the processes of mitosis and meiosis, which are two ways in which new cells are formed. When an egg and a sperm unite in the fertilization process, the resulting zygote contains the genes from the chromosomes in the father's sperm and the mother's egg. Despite this transmission of genes from generation to generation, variability is created in several ways, including through the exchange of chromosomal segments during meiosis, through mutations, and through environmental influences.

- Genetic principles that describe how genes interact include those involving dominant-recessive genes, sex-linked genes, genetic imprinting, and polygenic inheritance.

- Chromosomal abnormalities produce Down syndrome, which is caused by the presence of an extra copy of chromosome 21. Other sex-linked conditions include Klinefelter syndrome, fragile X syndrome, Turner syndrome, and XYY syndrome. Gene-linked abnormalities involve harmful or absent genes. Gene-linked disorders include phenylketonuria (PKU) and sickle-cell anemia. Genetic counseling offers couples information about their risk of having a child with inherited abnormalities.

3 What Are Some Reproductive Challenges and Choices?

LG3 Identify some important reproductive challenges and choices.

- Prenatal Diagnostic Tests

- Amniocentesis, ultrasound sonography, fetal MRI, chorionic villus sampling, and maternal blood screening are used to determine whether a fetus is developing normally. There has been a dramatic increase in research on less invasive methods of diagnostic testing, such as fetal MRI.

- Approximately 10 to 15 percent of U.S. couples have infertility problems, some of which can be corrected through surgery or fertility drugs. An additional option is in vitro fertilization.

- Although adopted children and adolescents have more problems than their nonadopted counterparts, the vast majority of adopted children adapt effectively. When adoption occurs very early in development, the outcomes for the child are improved. Because of the dramatic changes that have occurred in adoption in recent decades, it is difficult to generalize about the average adopted child or average adoptive family.

4 How Do Heredity and Environment Interact? The Nature-Nurture Debate

LG4 Characterize some of the ways that heredity and environment interact to produce individual differences in development.

- Behavior genetics seeks to discover the influence of heredity and environment on individual differences in the traits and development of humans. Methods used by behavior geneticists include twin studies and adoption studies.

- In Scarr's view of heredity-environment correlations, heredity directs the types of environments that children experience. She describes three genotype-environment correlations: passive, evocative, and active (niche-picking). Scarr maintains that the relative importance of these three genotype-environment correlations changes as children develop.

- The epigenetic view emphasizes that development reflects an ongoing, bidirectional interchange between heredity and environment. Gene × environment interaction involves the interaction of a specific measured variation in the DNA and a specific measured aspect of the environment. An increasing number of G × E studies are being conducted.

- Behaviors are influenced by genes and environments in a way that gives people a propensity for a particular developmental trajectory. The actual development also requires both genes and an environment, and that environment is complex. The interaction of heredity and environment is extensive. Much remains to be discovered about the specific ways that heredity and environment interact to influence development.

key terms

active (niche-picking) genotype-environment correlations
adoption study
behavior genetics
chromosomes
DNA
Down syndrome

epigenetic view
evocative genotype-environment correlations
evolutionary psychology
fertilization
fragile X syndrome
gene × environment (G × E) interaction

genes
genotype
Klinefelter syndrome
meiosis
mitosis
passive genotype-environment correlations
phenotype

phenylketonuria (PKU)
sickle-cell anemia
Turner syndrome
twin study
XYY syndrome
zygote

key people

Albert Bandura
Thomas Bouchard

David Buss
Charles Darwin

Gilbert Gottlieb
Stephen Jay Gould

David Moore
Sandra Scarr

connecting with **improving the lives of children**

STRATEGIES

Preparing for Pregnancy

Even before a woman becomes pregnant, she can adopt some strategies that may make a difference in how healthy the pregnancy is and in her child's developmental outcomes:

- Become knowledgeable about prepregnancy planning and health-care providers. The kinds of health-care providers who are qualified to provide care for pregnant women include an obstetrician/gynecologist, a family practitioner, a nurse practitioner, and a certified nurse-midwife.

- Meet with a health professional before conception. A good strategy is for both potential parents to meet with a health professional prior to conception to assess their health and review personal and family histories. During this meeting, the health professional will discuss nutrition and other aspects of health that might affect the baby.

- Find a health-care provider who is competent. The health-care provider should (1) take time to do a thorough family history; (2) not be patronizing; (3) be knowledgeable and stay current on prenatal testing; (4) be honest about risks, benefits, and side effects of any tests or treatments; and (5) inspire trust.

RESOURCES

The Developing Genome: An Introduction to Behavioral Epigenetics (2015)
David Moore
New York: Oxford University Press

A superb overview of recent thinking and research on epigenetics, including many studies focused on gene × environment interaction studies.

American Fertility Association
www.theafa.org

The American Fertility Association provides information about infertility and possible solutions to it.

How Healthy Is Your Family Tree? (1995)
Carol Krause
New York: Simon & Schuster

In this book, you will learn how to create a family medical tree. Once you put together a family medical tree, a specialist or genetic counselor can help you interpret it.

National Down Syndrome Society
www.ndss.org

The National Down Syndrome Society (NDSS) provides resources and advocacy for individuals with Down syndrome and their families.

National Organization for Rare Disorders (NORD)
www.rarediseases.org

NORD supports awareness and education about rare birth defects and genetic disorders.

The Twins Foundation
www.twinsfoundation.com

For information about twins and multiple births, contact The Twins Foundation.

chapter 3

PRENATAL DEVELOPMENT

chapter **outline**

©Steve Allen/The Image Bank/Getty Images

Alex, also known as "Mr. Littles."
Courtesy of Dr. John Santrock

Diana and Roger married when he was 38 and she was 34. Both worked full-time and were excited when Diana became pregnant. Two months later, Diana began to have some unusual pains and bleeding. Just two months into her pregnancy she had lost the baby. Although most early miscarriages are the result of embryonic defects, Diana thought deeply about why she had been unable to carry the baby to full term and felt guilty that she might have done something "wrong."

Six months later, Diana became pregnant again. Because she was still worried about her prior loss, she made sure to follow every government recommendation such as getting enough folic acid, avoiding certain types of dairy products that might harbor bacteria, and letting someone else change their cat's litterbox to avoid toxoplasmosis. She and Roger read about pregnancy, prenatal development, and birth, and signed up for birth preparation classes. Each Friday night for eight weeks they practiced simulated contractions. They talked about what kind of parents they wanted to be and discussed what changes in their lives the baby would make. When they found out that their offspring was going to be a boy, they gave him a nickname: "Mr. Littles."

This time, Diana's pregnancy went well, and Alex, also known as Mr. Littles, was born. During the birth, however, Diana's heart rate dropped precipitously and she was given a stimulant to raise it. Apparently the stimulant also increased Alex's heart rate and breathing to a dangerous point, and he had to be placed in a neonatal intensive care unit (NICU).

Several times a day, Diana and Roger visited Alex in the NICU. A number of babies in the NICU who had a very low birth weight had been in intensive care for weeks, and some of these babies were not doing well. Fortunately, Alex was in better health. After several days in the NICU, his parents were permitted to take home a very healthy Alex.

topical connections   looking *back*

You have learned about the evolutionary perspective, genetic foundations of development, the reproductive challenges and choices parents today may face, and the nature-nurture debate. Now we will explore the remarkable course of prenatal development, including the phenomenal growth of the brain. Potential hazards to the offspring's and the mother's health also are covered.

preview

This chapter chronicles the truly amazing changes that take place from conception to birth. Imagine . . . at one time you were suspended in a sea of fluid in your mother's womb. In this chapter, you will explore the course of prenatal development, expectant parents' experiences, and some potential hazards to prenatal development.

1 What Is the Course of Prenatal Development?

LG1 Discuss the three periods of prenatal development.

| The Germinal Period | The Embryonic Period | The Fetal Period | The Brain |

> The history of man for nine months preceding his birth would probably be far more interesting and contain events of greater moment than all three score and ten years that follow it.
>
> —SAMUEL TAYLOR COLERIDGE
> *English Poet and Essayist, 19th Century*

germinal period The period of prenatal development that takes place in the first two weeks after conception. It includes the creation of the zygote, continued cell division, and the attachment of the zygote to the uterine wall.

blastocyst The inner mass of cells that develops during the germinal period. These cells later develop into the embryo.

trophoblast The outer layer of cells that develops in the germinal period. These cells later provide nutrition and support for the embryo.

embryonic period The period of prenatal development that occurs two to eight weeks after conception. During the embryonic period, the rate of cell differentiation intensifies, support systems for the cells form, and organs appear.

endoderm The inner layer of cells, which develops into digestive and respiratory systems.

mesoderm The middle layer of cells, which becomes the circulatory system, bones, muscles, excretory system, and reproductive system.

ectoderm The outermost layer of cells, which becomes the nervous system and brain, sensory receptors (ears, nose, and eyes, for example), and skin parts (hair and nails, for example).

Imagine how Alex ("Mr. Littles") came to be. Out of thousands of eggs and millions of sperm, one egg and one sperm united to produce him. Had the union of sperm and egg come a day or even an hour earlier or later, he would have been very different—maybe even of the opposite sex. Conception occurs when a single sperm cell from the male unites with an ovum (egg) in the female's fallopian tube in a process called fertilization. Over the next few months, the genetic code directs a series of changes in the fertilized egg, but many events and hazards will influence how that egg develops and becomes tiny Alex.

Typical prenatal development begins with fertilization and ends with birth, lasting 266 days (38 weeks) from conception. It can be divided into three periods: germinal, embryonic, and fetal.

THE GERMINAL PERIOD

The **germinal period** is the period of prenatal development that takes place in the first two weeks after conception. It includes the creation of the fertilized egg, called a *zygote,* cell division, and the attachment of the zygote to the uterine wall.

Rapid cell division by the zygote continues throughout the germinal period. (Recall that this cell division occurs through a process called *mitosis.*) By approximately one week after conception, the differentiation of these cells—their specialization for different tasks—has already begun. At this stage, the group of cells, now called the **blastocyst,** consists of an inner mass of cells that will eventually develop into the embryo and the **trophoblast,** an outer layer of cells that later provides nutrition and support for the embryo. *Implantation,* the attachment of the zygote to the uterine wall, takes place about 10 to 14 days after conception. Figure 1 illustrates some of the most significant developments during the germinal period.

THE EMBRYONIC PERIOD

The **embryonic period** is the period of prenatal development that occurs from two to eight weeks after conception. During the embryonic period, the rate of cell differentiation intensifies, support systems for cells form, and organs appear.

This period begins as the blastocyst attaches to the uterine wall. The mass of cells is now called an *embryo,* and three layers of cells form. The embryo's **endoderm** is the inner layer of cells, which will develop into the digestive and respiratory systems. The **mesoderm** is the middle layer, which will become the circulatory system, bones, muscles, excretory system, and reproductive system. The **ectoderm** is the outermost layer, which will become the nervous system and brain, sensory receptors (ears, nose, and eyes, for example), and skin parts (hair and nails, for example). Every body part eventually develops from these three layers. The endoderm primarily produces internal body parts, the mesoderm primarily produces parts that surround the internal areas, and the ectoderm primarily produces surface parts.

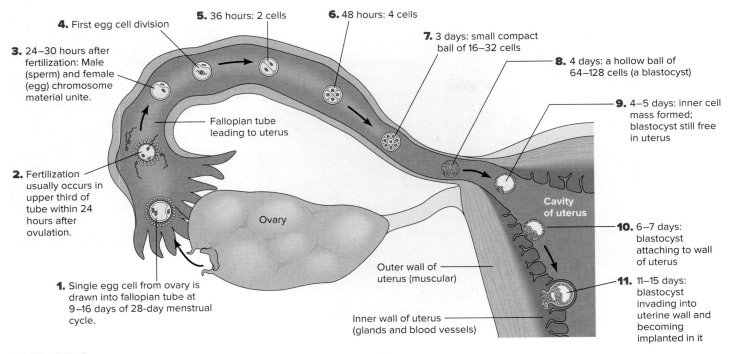

4. First egg cell division

5. 36 hours: 2 cells

6. 48 hours: 4 cells

7. 3 days: small compact ball of 16–32 cells

3. 24–30 hours after fertilization: Male (sperm) and female (egg) chromosome material unite.

8. 4 days: a hollow ball of 64–128 cells (a blastocyst)

Fallopian tube leading to uterus

9. 4–5 days: inner cell mass formed; blastocyst still free in uterus

2. Fertilization usually occurs in upper third of tube within 24 hours after ovulation.

Ovary

Cavity of uterus

10. 6–7 days: blastocyst attaching to wall of uterus

1. Single egg cell from ovary is drawn into fallopian tube at 9–16 days of 28-day menstrual cycle.

Outer wall of uterus (muscular)

Inner wall of uterus (glands and blood vessels)

11. 11–15 days: blastocyst invading into uterine wall and becoming implanted in it

FIGURE 1

SIGNIFICANT DEVELOPMENTS IN THE GERMINAL PERIOD. Just one week after conception, cells of the blastocyst have already begun specializing. The germinal period ends when the blastocyst attaches to the uterine wall. *Which of the steps shown in the drawing occur in the laboratory when IVF: (described in the "Biological Beginnings" chapter) is used?*

As the embryo's three layers form, life-support systems for the embryo develop rapidly. These life-support systems include the amnion, the umbilical cord (both of which develop from the fertilized egg, not the mother's body), and the placenta. The **amnion** is like a bag or an envelope and contains a clear fluid in which the developing embryo floats. The amniotic fluid provides an environment that is temperature and humidity controlled, as well as shockproof. The **umbilical cord** contains two arteries and one vein that connect the baby to the placenta. The **placenta** consists of a disk-shaped group of tissues in which small blood vessels from the mother and the offspring intertwine but do not join.

Figure 2 illustrates the placenta, the umbilical cord, and the blood flow in the expectant mother and developing organism. Very small molecules—oxygen, water, salt, food from the mother's blood, as well as carbon dioxide and digestive wastes from the offspring's blood—pass back and forth between the mother and embryo or fetus (Cuffe & others, 2017; Thornburg & others, 2016). Virtually any drug or chemical substance the pregnant woman ingests can cross the placenta to some degree, unless it is metabolized or altered during passage, or is too large (Pfeifer & Bunders, 2016). A recent study confirmed that ethanol crosses the human placenta and primarily reflects maternal alcohol use (Matlow & others, 2013). Another study revealed that cigarette smoke weakened and increased the oxidative stress of fetal membranes from which the placenta develops (Menon & others, 2011). Large molecules that cannot pass through the placental wall include red blood cells and harmful substances such as most bacteria, maternal wastes, and hormones. The complex mechanisms that govern the transfer of substances across the placental barrier are still not entirely understood (Huckle, 2017; Kohan-Ghadr & others, 2016; Lecarpentier & others, 2016; Vaughan & others, 2017).

By the time most women find out that they are pregnant, the major organs have begun to form. **Organogenesis** is the name given to the process of organ formation during the first two months of prenatal development. While the organs are being formed, they are especially vulnerable to environmental influences (Alby & others, 2016; Das & Red-Horse, 2016; Schittny, 2017; Zhu, 2016). In the third week after conception, the neural tube that eventually becomes the spinal cord forms. At about 21 days, eyes begin to appear, and at 24 days the

amnion The fetal life-support system, which consists of a thin bag or envelope that contains a clear fluid in which the developing embryo floats.

umbilical cord Contains two arteries and one vein, and connects the baby to the placenta.

placenta A disk-shaped group of tissues in which small blood vessels from the mother and the offspring intertwine but don't join.

organogenesis Process of organ formation that takes place during the first two months of prenatal development.

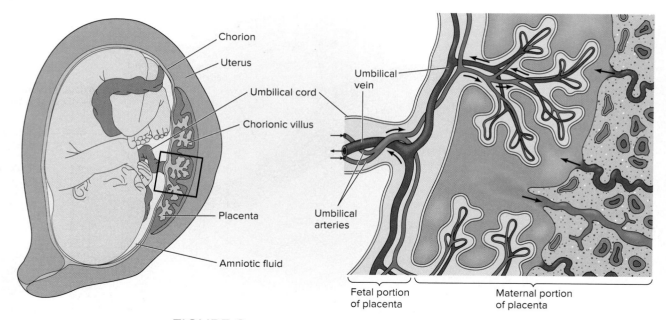

Chorion
Uterus
Umbilical cord
Chorionic villus
Placenta
Amniotic fluid

Umbilical vein
Umbilical arteries

Fetal portion of placenta
Maternal portion of placenta

FIGURE 2

THE PLACENTA AND THE UMBILICAL CORD. The area bound by the square in the left illustration is enlarged on the right. Arrows indicate uterine veins to the maternal circulation. The exchange of materials takes place across the layer separating the maternal and fetal blood supplies, so the bloods never come into contact. *What is known about how the placenta works and its importance?*

cells for the heart begin to differentiate. During the fourth week, the urogenital system becomes apparent, and arm and leg buds emerge. Four chambers of the heart take shape, and blood vessels appear. From the fifth to the eighth week, arms and legs differentiate further; at this time, the face starts to form but still is not very recognizable. The intestinal tract develops and the facial structures fuse. At eight weeks, the developing organism weighs about 1/30 ounce and is just over 1 inch long.

THE FETAL PERIOD

The **fetal period,** lasting about seven months, is the prenatal period between two months after conception and birth in typical pregnancies. Growth and development continue their dramatic course during this time.

Three months after conception (13 weeks), the fetus is about 3 inches long and weighs about four-fifths of an ounce. Its arms, legs, and head move randomly (or spontaneously), and its mouth opens and closes. The face, forehead, eyelids, nose, and chin are distinguishable, as are the upper arms, lower arms, hands, and lower limbs. In most cases, the genitals can be identified as male or female. By the end of the fourth month of pregnancy (17 weeks), the fetus has grown to about 5.5 inches in length and weighs about 5 ounces. At this time, a growth spurt occurs in the body's lower parts. For the first time, the mother can feel the fetus move.

By the end of the fifth month (22 weeks), the fetus is about 11 inches long and weighs close to a pound. Structures of the skin have formed—toenails and fingernails, for example. The fetus is more active, showing a preference for a particular position in the womb. By the end of the sixth month (26 weeks), the fetus is about 14 inches long and has gained another half pound to a pound. The eyes and eyelids are completely formed, and a fine layer of hair covers the head. A grasping reflex is present and irregular breathing movements occur.

As early as six months of pregnancy (about 24 to 25 weeks after conception), the fetus for the first time has a chance of surviving outside the womb—that is, it is *viable*. Infants born between 24 and 37 weeks of pregnancy usually need help breathing because their lungs are not yet fully mature. By the end of the seventh month, the fetus is about 16 inches long and weighs about 3 pounds.

How Would You...?
If you were a **human development and family studies professional,** how would you characterize the greatest risks at each period of prenatal development?

fetal period The prenatal period of development that begins two months after conception and lasts for seven months on average.

During the last two months of prenatal development, fatty tissues develop, and the functioning of various organ systems—heart and kidneys, for example—steps up. During the eighth and ninth months, the fetus grows longer and gains substantial weight—about another 4 pounds. At birth, the average American baby weighs 8 pounds and is about 20 inches long.

Figure 3 gives an overview of the main events during prenatal development. Notice that instead of describing development in terms of germinal, embryonic, and fetal periods, Figure 3 divides prenatal development into equal periods of three months, called *trimesters*. Remember that the three trimesters are not the same as the three prenatal periods we have discussed. The germinal and embryonic periods occur in the first trimester. The fetal period begins toward the end of the first trimester and continues through the second and third trimesters. Viability (the potential to survive outside the womb) occurs at the very end of the second trimester.

Prenatal Growth

First trimester (first 3 months)

Conception to 4 weeks
- Is less than 1/10 inch long
- Beginning development of spinal cord, nervous system, gastrointestinal system, heart, and lungs
- Amniotic sac envelops the preliminary tissues of entire body
- Is called a "zygote"

8 weeks
- Is about 0.6 inch long
- Face is forming with rudimentary eyes, ears, mouth, and tooth buds
- Arms and legs are moving
- Brain is forming
- Fetal heartbeat is detectable with ultrasound
- Is called an "embryo"

12 weeks
- Is about 2 inches long and weighs about 0.5 ounce
- Can move arms, legs, fingers, and toes
- Fingerprints are present
- Can smile, frown, suck, and swallow
- Sex is distinguishable
- Can urinate
- Is called a "fetus"

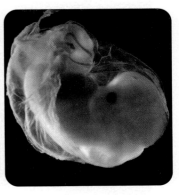

Second trimester (middle 3 months)

16 weeks
- Is about 5 inches long and weighs about 3.5 ounces
- Heartbeat is strong
- Skin is thin, transparent
- Downy hair (lanugo) covers body
- Fingernails and toenails are forming
- Has coordinated movements; is able to roll over in amniotic fluid

20 weeks
- Is about 6.5 inches long and weighs about 11 ounces
- Heartbeat is audible with ordinary stethoscope
- Sucks thumb
- Hiccups
- Hair, eyelashes, eyebrows are present

24 weeks
- Is about 12 inches long and weighs about 1.3 pounds
- Skin is wrinkled and covered with protective coating (vernix caseosa)
- Eyes are open
- Waste matter is collected in bowel
- Has strong grip

Third trimester (last 3 months)

28 weeks
- Is about 15 inches long and weighs about 2.3 pounds
- Is adding body fat
- Is very active
- Rudimentary breathing movements are present

32 weeks
- Is about 17 inches long and weighs about 4 pounds
- Has periods of sleep and wakefulness
- Responds to sounds
- May assume the birth position
- Bones of head are soft and flexible
- Iron is being stored in liver

36 to 38 weeks
- Is 19 to 20 inches long and weighs 6 to 8 pounds
- Skin is less wrinkled
- Vernix caseosa is thick
- Lanugo is mostly gone
- Is less active
- Is gaining immunities from mother

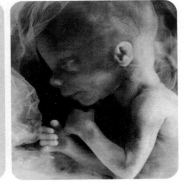

FIGURE 3

THE THREE TRIMESTERS OF PRENATAL DEVELOPMENT. Both the germinal and embryonic periods occur during the first trimester. The end of the first trimester as well as the second and third trimesters are part of the fetal period.

(*Top to bottom*): ©David Spears/PhotoTake, Inc.; ©Neil Bromhall/Science Source; ©Brand X Pictures/PunchStock RF

developmental connection

Brain Development

At birth, infants' brains weigh approximately 25 percent of what they will when adulthood is reached. Connect to "Physical Development in Infancy."

FIGURE 4

EARLY FORMATION OF THE NERVOUS SYSTEM. The photograph shows the primitive, tubular appearance of the nervous system at six weeks in the human embryo.

©Claude Edelmann/Science Source

Yelyi Nordone, 12, of New York City, recently cast her line out into the pond during Camp Spifida at Camp Victory, near Millville, Pennsylvania. Camp Spifida is a week-long residential camp for children with spina bifida.

©Bill Hughes/AP Images

THE BRAIN

One of the most remarkable aspects of the prenatal period is the development of the brain (Andescavage & others, 2017). By the time babies are born, they have approximately 100 billion **neurons,** or nerve cells, which handle information processing at the cellular level in the brain. During prenatal development, neurons gradually move to the right locations and start to become connected. The basic architecture of the human brain is assembled during the first two trimesters of prenatal development. In typical development, the third trimester of prenatal development and the first two years of postnatal life are characterized by increasing connectivity and functioning of neurons (Nelson, 2013).

Four important phases of the brain's development during the prenatal development involve (1) the neural tube, (2) neurogenesis, (3) neural migration, and (4) neural connectivity.

Neural Tube   As the human embryo develops inside its mother's womb, the nervous system begins forming as a long, hollow tube located on the embryo's back. This pear-shaped *neural tube,* which forms about 18 to 24 days after conception, develops out of the ectoderm. The tube closes at the top and bottom about 27 days after conception (Keunen, Counsell, & Benders, 2017). Figure 4 shows that the nervous system still has a tubular appearance six weeks after conception.

Two birth defects related to a failure of the neural tube to close are anencephaly and spina bifida. When *anencephaly* occurs (that is, when the head end of the neural tube fails to close), the highest regions of the brain fail to develop and the fetus dies in the womb, during childbirth, or shortly after birth (Steric & others, 2015). *Spina bifida,* an incomplete development of the spinal cord, results in varying degrees of paralysis of the lower limbs (Miller, 2017). Individuals with spina bifida usually need assistive devices such as crutches, braces, or wheelchairs. A strategy that can help to prevent neural tube defects is for pregnant women to take adequate amounts of the B vitamin folic acid, a topic covered later in this chapter (Bergman & others, 2016; Viswanathan & others, 2017). A recent large-scale study in Brazil found that when flour was fortified with folic acid it produced a significant reduction in neural tube defects (Santos & others, 2016). And both maternal diabetes and obesity place the fetus at risk for developing neural tube defects (McMahon & others, 2013; Yu, Wu, & Yang, 2016). Also, one study found that maternal exposure to secondhand tobacco smoke was linked to neural tube defects (Suarez & others, 2011). Further, a recent study revealed that a high level of maternal stress during pregnancy was associated with neural tube defects in offspring (Li & others, 2013).

Neurogenesis   In a normal pregnancy, once the neural tube has closed, a massive proliferation of new immature neurons begins to take place at about the fifth prenatal week and continues throughout the remainder of the prenatal period. The generation of new neurons is called **neurogenesis,** a process that continues through the remainder of the prenatal period although it is largely complete by the end of the fifth month after conception (Keunen, Cournsell, & Benders, 2017). At the peak of neurogenesis, it is estimated that as many as 200,000 neurons are being generated every minute.

Neural Migration   At approximately 6 to 24 weeks after conception, *neuronal migration* occurs (Keunen, Counsell, & Benders, 2017). This involves cells moving outward from their point of origin to their appropriate locations and creating the different levels, structures, and regions of the brain. Once a cell has migrated to its target destination, it must mature and develop a more complex structure (Higginbotham, Yokota, & Anton, 2011).

Neural Connectivity   At about 23 prenatal weeks, connections between neurons begin to occur, a process that continues postnatally (Miller, Huppi, & Mallard, 2016). We will have much more to consider about the structure of neurons, their connectivity, and the development of the infant brain in "Physical Development in Infancy."

Review Connect Reflect

LG1 Discuss the three periods of prenatal development.

Review

- How can the germinal period be characterized?
- What takes place during the embryonic period?
- How can the fetal period be described?
- How does the brain develop in the prenatal period?

Connect

- You have learned about the issue of continuity and discontinuity. Does thinking about prenatal development in terms of germinal, embryonic, and fetal periods reflect continuity or discontinuity? Explain.

Reflect *Your Own Personal Journey of Life*

- What is the most important thing you learned in the section on exploring prenatal development that you did not previously know?

2 What Are Some Important Strategies That Enhance the Expectant Mother's Health and Prenatal Care?

LG2 Summarize how nutrition, exercise, and prenatal care are important aspects of the expectant mother's pregnancy.

> The Expectant Mother's Nutrition and Weight Gain

> Exercise

> Prenatal Care

What can an expectant mother do to stay healthy and to improve her baby's chances of being born healthy? Some of the most important strategies she can adopt involve nutrition, exercise, and prenatal care.

THE EXPECTANT MOTHER'S NUTRITION AND WEIGHT GAIN

The mother's nutrition can have a strong influence on the development of the fetus. Here we discuss the mother's nutritional needs and optimal nutrition during pregnancy.

The best assurance of an adequate caloric intake during pregnancy is a satisfactory weight gain over time (Baugh & others, 2017). The optimal weight gain depends on the expectant mother's height, bone structure, and prepregnant nutritional state. However, a maternal weight gain of 25 to 35 pounds is associated with the best reproductive outcomes.

An increasing number of pregnant women gain more than this recommended amount (Poston & others, 2016). Maternal obesity adversely affects pregnancy outcomes through increased rates of hypertension, diabetes, respiratory complications, and infections in the mother (Baugh & others, 2017; Vernini & others, 2016). Also, pregnancies in obese women are characterized by higher rates of neural tube defects, preterm deliveries, and late-term fetal deaths (Poston & others, 2016). Recent studies have found that maternal overweight and obesity during pregnancy were associated with an increased risk of preterm birth, especially extremely preterm delivery (Baugh & others, 2017; Cnattingius & others, 2013). Further, research indicates that maternal obesity during pregnancy is linked to cardiovascular disease and type 2 diabetes in the adolescent and adult offspring of these mothers (Galliano & Bellver, 2013; Kominiarek & Chauhan, 2016).

Management of obesity including weight loss and increased exercise prior to pregnancy is likely to benefit the mother and the baby (Poston & others, 2016). For example, a recent study found that higher maternal pre-pregnancy body mass was linked to a higher incidence of adiposity (body fat) and inflammation in newborns (McCloskey & others, 2017). For pregnant women who are obese, limiting gestational weight gain to 11 to 20 pounds is likely to improve outcomes for the mother and the child (Simmons, 2011). We further discuss obesity as a potential hazard to prenatal development later in the chapter.

How much do you know about prenatal development and maintaining a healthy pregnancy? How much weight gain on average should occur during pregnancy?
©Tony Metaxas/Asia Images/Corbis

neurons The term for nerve cells, which handle information processing at the cellular level.

neurogenesis The formation of new neurons.

The pattern of weight gain is also important. The ideal pattern of weight gain during pregnancy is 2 to 4.4 pounds during the first trimester, followed by an average gain of 1 pound per week during the last two trimesters. In the second trimester, most of the weight gain is due to increased blood volume; the enlargement of breasts, uterus, and associated tissue and fluid; and storage of maternal fat. In the third trimester, weight gain mainly involves the fetus, placenta, and amniotic fluid. A 25-pound weight gain during pregnancy is generally distributed in this way: 11 pounds: fetus, placenta, and amniotic fluid; 5 pounds: maternal fat stores; 4 pounds: increased blood volume; 3 pounds: tissue fluid; and 2 pounds: uterus and breasts.

During the second and third trimesters, inadequate gains of less than 2.2 pounds per month or excessive gains of more than 6.6 pounds per month should be evaluated and the need for nutritional counseling considered. Inadequate maternal weight gain has been associated with low birth weight of offspring. Sudden sharp increases in weight of 3 to 5 pounds in a week may result from fluid retention and may require evaluation.

The recommended daily allowance (RDA) for all nutrients increases during pregnancy. The expectant mother should eat three meals a day, with nutritious snacks of fruits, cheese, milk, or other foods between meals if desired. More frequent, smaller meals also are recommended. Water is an essential nutrient. Four to six 8-ounce glasses of water and a total of 8 to 10 cups (64 to 80 ounces) of total fluid should be consumed daily. The need for protein, iron, vitamin D, folacin, calcium, phosphorus, and magnesium increases by 50 percent or more. Recommended increases for other nutrients range from 15 to 40 percent (see Figure 5). Researchers have found that women who take a multivitamin prior to pregnancy may be at a reduced risk for delivering a preterm infant (Vahratian & others, 2004).

What are some guidelines for expectant mothers' eating patterns?
©Vladimir Pcholkin/Getty Images RF

EXERCISE

How much and what type of exercise is best during pregnancy depend to some degree on the course of the pregnancy, the expectant mother's fitness, and her customary activity level. Normal participation in exercise can continue throughout an uncomplicated pregnancy. In general, a skilled sportswoman is no longer discouraged from participating in sports she participated in prior to her pregnancy. However, pregnancy is not the appropriate time to begin strenuous activity.

A research review indicated that only about 40 percent of pregnant women exercise (Field, 2012). In this review, exercise during pregnancy increased infant birth weight to within the normal range but only if exercise was decreased in late pregnancy.

Because of the increased emphasis on physical fitness in our society, more women routinely jog as part of a physical fitness program prior to pregnancy. There are few concerns about continuing to jog during the

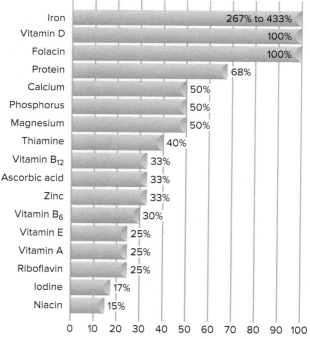

Nutrient	Percent above RDA
Iron	267% to 433%
Vitamin D	100%
Folacin	100%
Protein	68%
Calcium	50%
Phosphorus	50%
Magnesium	50%
Thiamine	40%
Vitamin B₁₂	33%
Ascorbic acid	33%
Zinc	33%
Vitamin B₆	30%
Vitamin E	25%
Vitamin A	25%
Riboflavin	25%
Iodine	17%
Niacin	15%

Percent above RDA for nonpregnant female (23 to 40)

FIGURE 5

RECOMMENDED NUTRIENT INCREASES FOR EXPECTANT MOTHERS

How might a woman's exercise in pregnancy benefit her and her offspring?
©Tracy Frankel/The Image Bank/Getty Images

early part of pregnancy, but in the latter part of pregnancy there is some concern about the jarring effect of jogging on the breasts and abdomen. As pregnancy progresses, low-impact activities such as walking, swimming, water aerobics, and bicycling are safer and provide fitness as well as greater comfort, eliminating the bouncing associated with jogging (Hazeldean, 2014). Exercise increasingly is recommended as part of a comprehensive pre-natal care program (Owe & others, 2016). An increasing number of studies are finding that exercise either benefits the mother's health and has positive neonatal outcomes or that there are no differences in outcomes (Baker & others, 2017; Barakat & others, 2017; Harrison & others, 2016; Huang & others, 2017; Moyer, Reoyo, & May, 2016). Exercise during preg-nancy helps prevent constipation, conditions the body, reduces the likelihood of excessive weight gain, lowers the risk of developing hypertension, and is associated with a more positive mental state, including a reduced level of depression (Bacchi & others, 2017; Magro-Malosso & others, 2017). The following positive outcomes of exercise for pregnant women have been revealed by recent studies and research reviews:

- A recent research review indicated that engaging in a combination of aerobic and resistance exercise during pregnancy has positive benefits for maternal cardiorespira-tory fitness (Perales & others, 2016).

- A recent meta-analysis concluded that aerobic exercise for 35 to 90 minutes 3 to 4 times a week during pregnancy was not associated with a decrease in preterm birth and was linked to a higher incidence of vaginal birth, as well as a lower occurrence of caesarean delivery (Di Mascio & others, 2016).

- Women who exercised regularly during pregnancy were less likely to have high blood pressure and excessive weight gain (Barakat & others, 2016).

- At 22 weeks gestation, prenatally depressed pregnant women were randomly assigned to participate in (1) a 20-minute group session of tai chi/yoga each week for 12 weeks, or (2) a wait list control group (Field & others, 2013). At the end of the treatment period, the exercise group had less depression, lower anxiety levels, less sleep distur-bance, and fewer bodily complaints.

- Two weekly 70-minute yoga sessions reduced pregnant women's stress and enhanced their immune system functioning (Chen & others, 2017).

- Moderate exercise throughout pregnancy did not increase the risk of preterm delivery (Tinloy & others, 2014).

- Regular exercise by pregnant women was linked to more advanced development of the neonatal brain (Laborte-Lemoyne, Currier, & Ellenberg, 2017).

To read about some guidelines for exercise during pregnancy, see the *Caring Connections* interlude.

PRENATAL CARE

Although prenatal care varies enormously, it usually involves a defined schedule of visits for medical care, which typically includes screening for manageable conditions and treatable diseases that can affect the baby or the mother (Jarris & others, 2017; Kroll-Desrosiers & others, 2016; Sheeder & Weber Yorga, 2017). In addition to medical care, prenatal programs often include comprehensive educational, social, and nutritional services (Craswell, Kearney, & Reed, 2016).

The education provided in prenatal care varies during the course of pregnancy. Those in the early stages of pregnancy as well as couples who are anticipating a pregnancy may par-ticipate in early prenatal classes. In addition to providing information on dangers to the fetus, early prenatal classes often discuss the development of the embryo and the fetus; sexuality during pregnancy; choices about the birth setting and care providers; nutrition, rest, and exercise; common discomforts of pregnancy and relief measures; psychological changes in the expectant mother and her partner; and factors that increase the risk of preterm labor and possible symptoms of preterm labor. Early classes also may include information about the advantages and disadvantages of breast feeding and bottle feeding. (Fifty to eighty percent of expectant mothers decide how they will feed their infant prior to the sixth month of preg-nancy.) During the second or third trimester of pregnancy, prenatal classes focus on preparing for the birth, infant care and feeding, choices about birth, and postpartum self-care.

Partners or friends take classes with prospective mothers in many prenatal care programs. *What characterizes the content of prenatal care programs?*

©Roger Tully/The Image Bank/Getty Images

caring connections

Exercise Guidelines for Expectant Mothers

Exercise is just as important during pregnancy as it is before or after pregnancy. The following guidelines for exercise are recommended for expectant mothers by the American College of Obstetricians and Gynecologists (2008, pp. 1–4):

- *Adapting to changes in the woman's body.* Some of the changes in the woman's body during pregnancy require adaptations in exercise. Joints and ligaments become more mobile during pregnancy. Avoiding jerky, bouncy, or high-impact motions can reduce the risk of injuring joints and ligaments. During pregnancy women carry extra weight, and the pregnant woman's center of gravity shifts, placing stress on joints and muscles, especially in the pelvis and lower back. Thus, maintaining balance while exercising during pregnancy is sometimes difficult and requires attention. The extra weight pregnant women carry makes their bodies work harder, so it is important not to exercise too strenuously.

- *Getting started.* Before starting an exercise program, pregnant women should talk with their doctor to ensure that they don't have an obstetric or health condition that might limit their activity. Women with the following conditions will be advised by their doctor not to exercise during pregnancy: risk factors for preterm labor, vaginal bleeding, and premature rupture of membranes.

- *Choosing safe exercises.* Most types of exercise are safe during pregnancy, but some types involve positions and movements that may be uncomfortable, tiring, or harmful. For example, after

What are some recommended guidelines for exercise during pregnancy?
©Stockbyte/Getty Images RF

the first trimester of pregnancy, women should not do exercises that require them to lie flat on their backs. Some sports are safe during pregnancy, even for beginners. Walking is a good exercise for anyone, swimming is excellent because it works so many muscles, cycling provides a good aerobic workout (because balance is affected by pregnancy, a stationary bicycle is recommended in later pregnancy); aerobic exercise is effective in keeping the heart and lungs strong; and strength training can tone muscles and help prevent some common aches and pains during pregnancy. Women who were runners or played racquet sports before becoming pregnant should talk with their doctor about taking certain precautions if they plan to continue these activities during pregnancy. The following activities should be avoided during pregnancy: downhill snow skiing, contact sports, and scuba diving.

- *Establishing a routine.* Exercise is most practical during the first 24 weeks of pregnancy; during the last three months many exercises that were easy earlier in pregnancy are often difficult. It is important to begin each exercise session with a 5- to 10-minute warm-up and end each session with a 5- to 10-minute cool-down. During the warm-up and cool-down periods, stretching exercises should be done. Pregnant women should not exercise to the point of exhaustion. If pregnant women experience any of the following problems, they should stop exercising and call their doctor: vaginal bleeding, dizziness or feeling faint, increased shortness of breath, chest pain, headache, muscle weakness, calf pain or swelling, uterine contractions, decreased fetal movement, or fluid leaking from the vagina.

How Would You...?
If you were a **human development and family studies professional,** how would you justify the need for prenatal education classes for couples expecting a child?

Does prenatal care matter? Information about pregnancy, labor, delivery, and caring for the newborn can be especially valuable for first-time mothers (Yeo, Crandell, & Jones-Vessey, 2016). Prenatal care is also very important for women in poverty because it links them with other social services (Cohen & others, 2016; Mazul, Salm Ward, & Ngui, 2017). The legacy of prenatal care continues after the birth because women who experience this type of care are more likely to get preventive care for their infants.

Research contrasting the experiences of mothers who had prenatal care and those who did not supports the importance of prenatal care (X. Liu & others, 2017; McDonald & others, 2015). One study found that U.S. women who had no prenatal care were far more likely than their counterparts who received prenatal care to have infants who had low birth weight, increased mortality, and a number of other physical problems (Herbst & others, 2003). A recent study also found that inadequate prenatal care was associated with very low birth weight (Xaverius & others, 2016). In other studies, low birth weight and preterm deliveries were common among U.S. mothers who received no prenatal care, and the absence of prenatal

Rachel Thompson, Obstetrician/ Gynecologist

Rachel Thompson is the senior member of Houston Women's Care Associates, one of Houston's most popular obstetrics/gynecology (OB/GYN) practices. Thompson's medical degree is from Baylor College of Medicine, where she also completed her internship and residency.

In addition to her clinical practice, Thompson is a clinical instructor in the Department of Obstetrics and Gynecology at Baylor College of Medicine. Thompson says that one of the unique features of their health-care group is that the staff comprises only women who are full-time practitioners.

Rachel Thompson (*right*), talks with one of her patients at Houston Women's Care Associates.

Courtesy of Dr. Rachel Thompson

care increased the risk for preterm birth almost threefold in both non-Latino White and African American women (Stringer & others, 2005).

Inadequate prenatal care may help explain a disturbing fact: Rates of infant mortality and low birth weight indicate that many other nations have healthier babies than the United States (Goldenberg & Culhane, 2007). In many countries that have a lower percentage of low birth weight infants than the United States, mothers receive either free or very low cost prenatal and postnatal care, and can receive paid maternity leave from work that ranges from 9 to 40 weeks. In Norway and the Netherlands, prenatal care is coordinated among a general practitioner, an obstetrician, and a midwife. To read about the work and career of a U.S. obstetrician/gynecologist, see the *Connecting with Careers* profile.

Why do some U.S. women receive inadequate prenatal care? The reasons may be linked to the health-care system, to provider practices, and to their own individual and social characteristics (Chandra-Mouli, Camacho, & Michaud, 2013; Handler & others, 2012). Women who do not want to be pregnant, who have negative attitudes about being pregnant, or who unintentionally become pregnant are more likely to delay prenatal care or to miss appointments. As we noted earlier, adolescent girls are less likely than adult women to obtain prenatal care.

Usage of prenatal care in the United States has been improving. From 1990 to 2004, the use of timely prenatal care increased among women from a variety of ethnic backgrounds in the United States, although non-Latino White women were still more likely to obtain prenatal care than African American and Latino women (Martin & others, 2005) (see Figure 6). The United States needs more comprehensive medical and educational services to improve the quality of prenatal care and to reduce the number of low birth weight and preterm infants (Burger, 2010).

An innovative program that is rapidly expanding in the United States and other countries is CenteringPregnancy (Benediktsson & others, 2013; Chae & others, 2017; Hale & others, 2014; Heberlein & others, 2016; R. Liu & others, 2017). This relationship-centered program provides complete prenatal care in a group setting. CenteringPregnancy replaces traditional 15-minute physician visits with 90-minute peer group support sessions and self-examination led by a physician or certified nurse-midwife. Groups of up to 10 women (and often their partners) meet regularly beginning at 12 to 16 weeks of pregnancy. The sessions emphasize empowering women to play an active role in experiencing a positive pregnancy. In a recent study with adolescent mothers, CenteringPregnancy was successful in getting

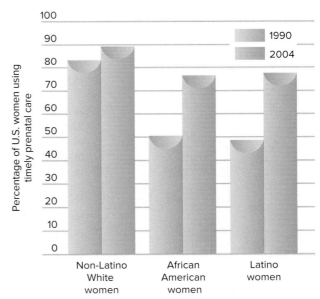

FIGURE 6

PERCENTAGE OF U.S. WOMEN USING TIMELY PRENATAL CARE: 1990 TO 2004. From 1990 to 2004, the use of timely prenatal care increased by 7 percent (to 89.1) for non-Latino White women, by 25 percent (to 76.5) for African American women, and by 28 percent (to 77.4) for Latino women in the United States.

The increasingly popular CenteringPregnancy program alters routine prenatal care by bringing women out of exam rooms and into relationship-oriented groups.
©Stephen Maturen

participants to attend meetings, have appropriate weight gain, increase the use of highly effective contraceptive methods postpartum, and increase breast feeding (Trotman & others, 2015). Research has revealed that CenteringPregnancy group prenatal care is associated with a reduction in preterm birth (Novick & others, 2013), as well as reduced rates of low birth weight and placement in a neonatal intensive care unit (Crockett & others, 2017; Gareau & others, 2016).

Some prenatal programs for parents focus on home visitation (Meghea & others, 2015; Yun & others, 2014; Williams & others, 2017). A research review concluded that prenatal home visits were linked to improved use of prenatal care, although there was less evidence that they improve newborns' birth weight (Issel & others, 2011). However, a recent study found that home visiting services reduced the risk of low birth weight (Shah & Austin, 2014).

Research evaluations indicate that one of the most successful home visitation programs is the Nurse-Family Partnership created by David Olds and his colleagues (2004, 2007, 2014). The Nurse-Family Partnership involves home visits by trained nurses beginning in the second or third trimester of prenatal development. The extensive program consists of approximately 50 home visits from the prenatal period through 2 years of age. The home visits focus on the mother's health, access to health care, parenting, and improvement of the mother's life by providing her with guidance in education, work, and relationships. Research revealed that the Nurse-Family Partnership has numerous positive outcomes including fewer pregnancies, better work circumstances, and stability in relationship partners for the mother and improved academic success and social development for the child (Olds & others, 2004, 2007, 2014).

Cultures around the world have differing views of pregnancy. In the *Connecting with Diversity* interlude, we explore some of these beliefs.

Some cultures treat pregnancy simply as a natural occurrence; others see it as a medical condition (Walsh, 2006). How expectant mothers behave during pregnancy may depend in part on the prevalence of traditional home-care remedies and folk beliefs, the importance of indigenous healers, and the influence of health-care professionals in their culture. In various cultures women may consult herbalists and/or faith healers during pregnancy (Mbonye, Neema, & Magnussen, 2006).

Health-care workers should assess whether a woman's beliefs or practices pose a threat to her or the fetus. If a health risk is posed, health-care professionals should consider a culturally sensitive way to handle the problem (Kenner, Sugrue, & Finkelman, 2007).

Cultural Beliefs About Pregnancy

All cultures have beliefs and practices that surround life's major events, and one such event is pregnancy. When a woman who has immigrated to the United States becomes pregnant, the beliefs and practices of her native culture may be as important as, or more important than, those of the mainstream U.S. culture that now surrounds her. The conflict between cultural traditions and Western medicine may pose a risk for the pregnancy and a challenge for the health-care professional who wishes to give proper care while respecting the woman's values.

The American Public Health Association (2006) has identified a variety of cultural beliefs and practices that are observed among various immigrant groups, such as the following:

- *Food cravings.* Latin American, Asian, and some African cultures believe that it is important for a pregnant woman's food cravings to be satisfied because they are thought to be the cravings of the baby. If cravings are left unsatisfied, the baby might take on certain unpleasant personality and/or physical traits, perhaps characteristic of the food (Taylor, Ko, & Pan, 1999). As an example, in African cultures women often eat soil, chalk, or clay during pregnancy; this is believed to satisfy the baby's hunger as well as affirming soil as a symbol of female fertility (American Public Health Association, 2006).
- *"Hot-cold" theory of illness.* Many cultures in Latin America, Asia, and Africa characterize foods, medications, and illnesses as "hot" or "cold"; this has nothing to do with temperature or spiciness, but with traditional definitions and categories. Most of these cultures view pregnancy as a "hot" condition, although the Chinese view it as "cold" (Taylor, Ko, & Pan, 1999). As a result, a woman may resist taking a prescribed medication because of concern that it could create too much "heat" and cause a miscarriage. In Indian culture, iron-rich foods are also considered unacceptably "hot" for pregnant women (DeSantis, 1998).

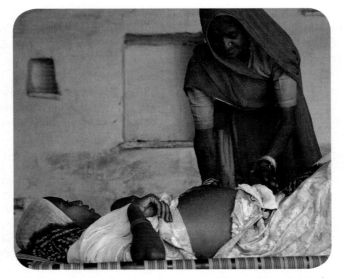

In India, a midwife checks on the size, position, and heartbeat of a fetus. Midwives deliver babies in many cultures around the world. *What are some cultural variations in prenatal care?*
©Viviane Moos/Corbis/Getty Images

- *Extended family.* In many immigrant cultures, the extended family is a vital support system, and health-care decisions are made that prioritize the needs of the family over those of the individual. Western health-care providers need to be sensitive to this dynamic, which runs counter to today's practices of protecting patient confidentiality and autonomy.
- *Stoicism.* In many Asian cultures, stoicism is valued, as suffering is seen as part of life (Uba, 1992). Physicians are also viewed with great respect. As a result, a pregnant Asian woman may behave submissively and avoid voicing complaints to her health-care provider, but may privately refrain from following the provider's advice (Assanand & others, 1990).

Review Connect Reflect

 LG2 Summarize how nutrition, exercise, and prenatal care are important aspects of the expectant mother's pregnancy.

Review

- What are some recommendations for the expectant mother's nutrition and weight gain?
- What role does exercise play in the mother's health during pregnancy?
- What are some important aspects of prenatal care?

Connect

- How would nutrition and exercise be incorporated into an ideal prenatal care program?

Reflect *Your Own Personal Journey of Life*

- What are some beliefs about pregnancy and prenatal development in your culture?

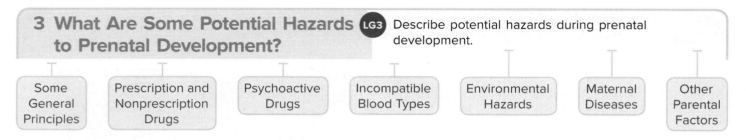

3 What Are Some Potential Hazards to Prenatal Development?

LG3 Describe potential hazards during prenatal development.

Some General Principles | Prescription and Nonprescription Drugs | Psychoactive Drugs | Incompatible Blood Types | Environmental Hazards | Maternal Diseases | Other Parental Factors

For Alex, the baby discussed at the opening of this chapter, the course of prenatal development went smoothly. His mother's womb protected him as he developed. Despite this protection, however, the environment can affect the embryo or fetus in many well-documented ways.

SOME GENERAL PRINCIPLES

A **teratogen** is any agent that can potentially cause a physical birth defect. (The word comes from the Greek word *tera,* meaning "monster.") The field of study that investigates the causes of birth defects is called *teratology* (Cassina & others, 2017; Kaushik & others, 2016). Some exposures to teratogens do not cause physical birth defects but can alter the developing brain and influence cognitive and behavioral functioning, in which case the field of study is called *behavioral teratology*.

Teratogens include drugs, incompatible blood types, environmental pollutants, infectious diseases, nutritional deficiencies, maternal stress, advanced maternal and paternal age, and environmental pollutants. In fact, thousands of babies are born each year with physical deformities or intellectual disabilities as a result of events that occurred in the mother's life as early as one or two months before conception. As we further discuss teratogens, you will see that factors related to the father also can influence prenatal development.

So many teratogens exist that practically every fetus is exposed to at least some of them. For this reason, it is difficult to determine which teratogen causes which problem. In addition, it may take a long time for the effects of a teratogen to show up. Only about half of all potential effects appear at birth.

The time of exposure, dose, and genetic susceptibility to a particular teratogen influence both the severity of the damage to an embryo or fetus and the type of defect:

- *Time of Exposure.* Teratogens do more damage when they occur at some points in development than at others. Damage during the germinal period may even prevent implantation. In general, the embryonic period is more vulnerable than the fetal period (Ortigosa & others, 2012).

- *Dose.* The dose effect is rather obvious—the greater the dose of an agent, such as a drug, the greater the effect.

- *Genetic Susceptibility.* The type or severity of abnormalities caused by a teratogen is linked to the genotype of the pregnant woman and the genotype of the embryo or fetus (Charlet & others, 2012; Lin & others, 2017). For example, how a mother metabolizes a particular drug can influence the degree to which the drug effects are transmitted to the embryo or fetus. Differences in placental membranes and placental transport also affect exposure. The extent to which an embryo or fetus is vulnerable to a teratogen may also depend on its genotype (Middleton & others, 2017). Also, for unknown reasons, male fetuses are far more likely to be affected by teratogens than are female fetuses (DiPietro, 2008).

Figure 7 summarizes additional information about the effects of time of exposure to a teratogen. The probability of a structural defect is greatest early in the embryonic period, when organs are being formed (Holmes, 2011). Each body structure has its own critical period of formation. Recall that a *critical period* is a fixed time period very early in development during which certain experiences or events can have a long-lasting effect on development. The critical period for the nervous system (week 3) is earlier than that for arms and legs (weeks 4 and 5).

After organogenesis is complete, teratogens can no longer cause anatomical defects. Instead, exposure during the fetal period is more likely to stunt growth or to create problems in the way organs function. This is especially true for the developing fetal brain, which continues to develop connections throughout pregnancy. To examine some key teratogens and their effects, let's begin with drugs.

teratogen Any agent that can potentially cause a physical birth defect. The field of study that investigates the causes of birth defects is called *teratology*.

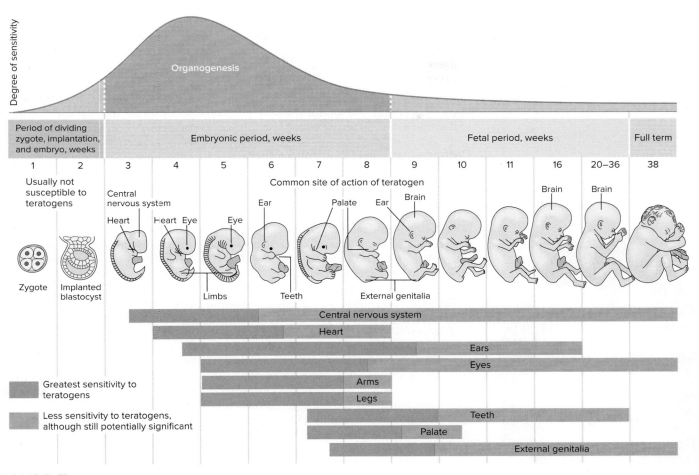

FIGURE **7**

TERATOGENS AND THE TIMING OF THEIR EFFECTS ON PRENATAL DEVELOPMENT. The danger of structural defects caused by teratogens is greatest early in embryonic development. The period of organogenesis (red color) lasts for about six weeks. Later assaults by teratogens (blue color) mainly occur in the fetal period and instead of causing structural damage are more likely to stunt growth or cause problems with organ function.

PRESCRIPTION AND NONPRESCRIPTION DRUGS

Many U.S. women are given prescriptions for drugs while they are pregnant—especially antibiotics, analgesics, and asthma medications. Prescription as well as nonprescription drugs, however, may have effects on the embryo or fetus that the women never imagined.

The damage that drugs can do was tragically highlighted in 1961, when many pregnant women took a popular sedative, thalidomide, to alleviate their morning sickness. In adults, the effects of thalidomide are typically not damaging; in embryos, however, they are devastating. Not all infants were affected in the same way. If the mother took thalidomide on day 26 (probably before she knew she was pregnant), an arm might not grow. If she took the drug two days later, the arm might not grow past the elbow. The thalidomide tragedy shocked the medical community and parents and taught a valuable lesson: Taking the wrong drug at the wrong time is enough to physically handicap the offspring for life (Holmes, 2011).

Prescription drugs that can function as teratogens include antibiotics, such as streptomycin and tetracycline; some antidepressants; certain hormones such as progestin and synthetic estrogen; and isotretinoin (often prescribed for acne) (Brown & others, 2017; Gonzalez-Echavarri & others, 2015). In a recent study, isotretinoin was the fourth most common drug given to female adolescents who were seeking contraception advice from a physician (Stancil & others, 2017). However, physicians did not give the adolescent girls adequate information about the negative effects of isotretinoin on offspring if the girls become pregnant. In a recent review of teratogens that should never be taken during the first trimester of pregnancy, isotreninoin was on the prohibited list (Eltonsy & others, 2016). Nonprescription drugs that can be harmful include diet pills and high doses of aspirin.

PSYCHOACTIVE DRUGS

Psychoactive drugs are drugs that act on the nervous system to alter states of consciousness, modify perceptions, and change moods. Examples include caffeine, alcohol, and nicotine, as well as illicit drugs such as cocaine, methamphetamine, marijuana, and heroin.

Caffeine   People often consume caffeine when they drink coffee, tea, or cola, or when they eat chocolate. Somewhat mixed results have been found for the extent to which maternal caffeine intake influences an offspring's development (Adams, Keisberg, & Safranek, 2016; Chen & others, 2016; De Medeiros & others, 2017). However, a large-scale study of almost 60,000 women revealed that maternal caffeine intake was linked to lower birth weight and babies being born small for gestational age (Sengpiel & others, 2013). Also, researchers have not yet studied the effects of prenatal consumption of energy drinks that typically have extremely high levels of caffeine. The U.S. Food and Drug Administration recommends that pregnant women either not consume caffeine or consume it only sparingly.

Fetal alcohol spectrum disorders (FASD) are characterized by a number of physical abnormalities and learning problems. Notice the wide-set eyes, flat cheekbones, and thin upper lip in this child with FASD.

Streissguth, AP., Landesman-Dwyer S., Martin, JC., & Smith, DW. (1980). Teratogenic effects of alcohol in humans and laboratory animals. *Science*, 209, 353–361

How Would You...?

If you were a **social worker,** how would you counsel a woman who continues to drink alcohol in the early weeks of pregnancy because she believes alcohol can't harm the baby until it has developed further?

fetal alcohol spectrum disorders (FASD) A cluster of abnormalities and problems that appears in the offspring of mothers who drink alcohol heavily during pregnancy.

Alcohol   Heavy drinking by pregnant women can have devastating consequences for their offspring (Jacobson & others, 2017). **Fetal alcohol spectrum disorders (FASD)** are a cluster of abnormalities and problems that appear in the offspring of mothers who drink alcohol heavily during pregnancy (Cook & others, 2016; Del Campo & Jones, 2017). The abnormalities include facial deformities and defects of the limbs, face, and heart (Coles & others, 2016; Pei & others, 2017; Petrenko & Alto, 2017). Some children with FASD have these bodily malformations, but others don't. Most children with FASD are characterized by neurocognitive difficulties and learning problems, and many are below average in intelligence or have an intellectual disability (Khoury & Milligan, 2017). A recent study revealed that children with FASD have deficiencies in the brain pathways involved in working memory (Diwadkar & others, 2013). Also, in a recent study in the United Kingdom, the life expectancy of individuals with FASD was only 34 years of age, about 42 percent of the average life expectancy in the general population (Thanh & Jonsson, 2016). In this study, the most common causes of death among individuals with FASD were suicide (15 percent), accidents (14 percent), and poisoning by illegal drugs or alcohol (7 percent).

Although women who drink heavily during pregnancy are at a higher risk of having a child with FASD, not all pregnant heavy drinkers have children with FASD. A recent research review concluded that FASD is linked to a lower level of executive function in children, especially in planning (Kingdon, Cardoso, & McGrath, 2016). And in a recent study, FASD was associated with both externalized and internalized behavior problems in childhood (Tsang & others, 2016).

What are some guidelines for alcohol use during pregnancy? Even drinking just one or two servings of beer or wine or one serving of hard liquor a few days a week may have negative effects on the fetus, although it is generally agreed that this level of alcohol use will not cause fetal alcohol spectrum disorders (Valenzuela & others, 2012). The U.S. Surgeon General recommends that no alcohol be consumed during pregnancy, as does the French Alcohol Society (Rolland & others, 2016).

Despite such recommendations, a recent large-scale U.S. study found that 11.5 percent of adolescent and 8.7 percent of adult pregnant women reported using alcohol in the previous month (Oh & others, 2017). However, in Great Britain, the National Institutes of Care and Health Excellence have concluded that one to two drinks not more than twice a week are safe during pregnancy (O'Keeffe, Greene, & Kearney, 2014). A recent study of more than 7,000 7-year-olds found that children born to mothers who were light drinkers during pregnancy (up to two drinks per week) did not show more developmental problems than children born to non-drinking mothers (Kelly & others, 2013).

Nonetheless, some research suggests that it may not be wise to consume alcohol at the time of conception. One study revealed that intakes of alcohol by both men and women during the week of conception increased the risk of early pregnancy loss (Henriksen & others, 2004).

Nicotine   Cigarette smoking by pregnant women also can adversely influence prenatal development, birth, and postnatal development. Preterm births and low birth weights, fetal and neonatal deaths, and respiratory problems and sudden infant death syndrome (SIDS, also known as crib death) are more common among the offspring of mothers who smoked during pregnancy (Zhang & others, 2017). Prenatal smoking has been implicated in up to 25 percent of low birth weight cases (Brown & Graves, 2013). One study also linked heavy smoking during pregnancy to nicotine withdrawal symptoms in newborns (Godding & others, 2004).

Maternal smoking during pregnancy has been identified as a risk factor for the development of attention deficit hyperactivity disorder in offspring (Pohlabein & others, 2017; Weissenberger & others, 2017). And in a recent study, maternal cigarette smoking during pregnancy was linked to higher rates of cigarette smoking among offspring at 16 years of age (De Genna & others, 2016). Further, a recent study revealed that daughters whose mothers smoked during their pregnancy were more likely to subsequently smoke during their own pregnancy (Ncube & Mueller, 2017). Also, a meta-analysis indicated that maternal smoking during pregnancy was linked to a modest increase in risk for childhood non-Hodgkins lymphoma (Antonopoulos & others, 2011). Also, a recent study found that maternal smoking during pregnancy was associated with increased risk of asthma and wheezing in adolescence (Hollams & others, 2014). Despite the plethora of negative outcomes for maternal smoking during pregnancy, a recent large-scale U.S. study revealed that 23 percent of adolescent and 15 percent of adult pregnant women reported using tobacco in the previous month (Oh & others, 2017).

Smoking by pregnant women is not the only source of prenatal risk posed by tobacco use (Patel & others, 2017; Vardavas & others, 2016). Maternal exposure to environmental tobacco smoke, or secondhand smoke, has been linked to an increased risk of low birth weight in offspring (Salama & others, 2014) and to diminished ovarian functioning in female offspring (Kilic & others, 2012). And in one study, environmental tobacco smoke was associated with 114 deregulations of gene expression, especially those involving immune functioning, in the fetal cells of offspring (Votavova & others, 2012). Another recent study found that environmental tobacco smoke during prenatal development increased the risk of stillbirth (Varner & others, 2014). And a recent study found that simultaneous exposure to environmental tobacco smoke and alcohol during pregnancy increased the offspring's risk of having ADHD (Han & others, 2015).

A final point about nicotine use during pregnancy involves the recent dramatic increase in the use of e-cigarettes (Spindel & McEvoy, 2016; Wagner, Camerota, & Propper, 2017; Wigginton, Gartner, & Rowlands, 2017). A recent study found widespread misconceptions about e-cigarettes among pregnant women (Mark & others, 2015). The most common reasons pregnant women gave for using e-cigarettes were the perceptions that they are less harmful than regular cigarettes (74 percent) and that they promote smoking cessation (72 percent).

Intervention programs designed to help pregnant women stop smoking can reduce some of smoking's negative effects, especially by raising birth weights (Murin, Rafii, & Bilello, 2011). One study revealed that women who quit smoking during pregnancy had offspring with higher birth weights than their counterparts who continued smoking (Jaddoe & others, 2008). To read further about the negative outcomes of smoking during pregnancy, see the *Connecting with Research* interlude.

Cocaine Does cocaine use during pregnancy harm the developing embryo and fetus? One research study found that cocaine quickly crossed the placenta to reach the fetus (De Giovanni & Marchetti, 2012). The most consistent finding is that cocaine exposure during prenatal development is associated with reduced birth weight, length, and head circumference (Gouin & others, 2011). Also, in other studies, prenatal cocaine exposure has been linked to impaired connectivity of the thalamus and prefrontal cortex in newborns (Salzwedel & others, 2016); lower arousal, less effective self-regulation, higher excitability, and lower quality of reflexes at 1 month of age (Ackerman, Riggins, & Black, 2010; Lester & others, 2002); self-regulation problems at age 12 (Minnes & others, 2016); impaired motor development in the second year of life (Richardson & others, 2011); slower growth rate through 10 years of age (Richardson, Goldschmidt, & Larkby, 2008); elevated blood pressure at 9 years of age (Shankaran & others, 2010); impaired language development and information processing (Beeghly & others, 2006; Buckingham-Howes & others, 2013; Lewis & others, 2007); attention deficit hyperactivity disorder (Richardson & others, 2016); learning disabilities at age 7 (Morrow & others, 2006); increased likelihood of being in a special education program that involves support services (Levine & others, 2008); increased behavioral problems, especially externalizing problems such as high rates of aggression and delinquency (Minnes & others, 2010; Richardson & others, 2011, 2016); and posttraumatic stress disorder (PTSD) (Richardson & others, 2016).

What are some links between expectant mothers' drinking and cigarette smoking and outcomes for their offspring?
©Monkey Business Images Ltd/Photolibrary RF

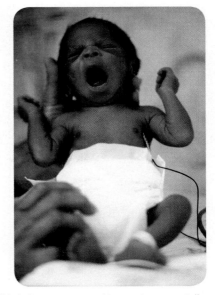

This baby was exposed to cocaine prenatally. *What are some of the possible effects on development of being exposed to cocaine prenatally?*
©Chuck Nacke/Alamy

Is Expectant Mothers' Cigarette Smoking Related to Cigarette Smoking by Their Adolescent Offspring?

Nicotine and other substances in cigarette smoke cross the placental barrier and pass from the expectant mother to the fetus, stimulating the fetal brain as early as the first trimester of pregnancy (Menon & others, 2011). Researchers are exploring the possibility that this prenatal exposure of the brain to cigarette smoke may predispose individuals to be more vulnerable to addiction in adolescence.

One study explored whether expectant mothers' cigarette smoking and marijuana use were linked to an increased risk for substance use in adolescence by their offspring (Porath & Fried, 2005). One hundred fifty-two 16- to 21-year-olds were asked to complete a drug history questionnaire that included their past and current cigarette smoking. A urine sample was also obtained from the participants and analyzed for the presence of drugs. The adolescent participants' mothers had been asked about the extent of their cigarette smoking during their pregnancy as part of the Ottawa Prenatal Prospective Study.

The results indicated that adolescent offspring of mothers who reported having smoked cigarettes during pregnancy were more than twice as likely to have initiated smoking during adolescence than their counterparts whose mothers reported not smoking during their pregnancy. These findings indicate that cigarette smoking by expectant mothers is a risk factor for later cigarette smoking by their adolescent offspring. Such results add to the strength of the evidence that supports drug use prevention and cessation among expectant mothers.

How do you think health-care professionals might use this type of evidence to counsel expectant mothers about cigarette smoking during pregnancy? Should the government include this evidence as part of its antismoking campaign?

Some researchers argue that these findings should be interpreted cautiously. Why? Because other factors in the lives of pregnant women who use cocaine (such as poverty, malnutrition, and other substance abuse) often cannot be ruled out as possible contributors to the problems found in their children (Hurt & others, 2005; Messiah & others, 2011). For example, cocaine users are more likely than nonusers to smoke cigarettes, use marijuana, drink alcohol, and take amphetamines.

Despite these cautions, the weight of research evidence indicates that children born to mothers who use cocaine are likely to have neurological and cognitive deficits (Cain, Bornick, & Whiteman, 2013; Field, 2007; Martin & others, 2016; Mayer & Zhang, 2009; Richardson & others, 2011, 2016; Scott-Goodwin, Puerto, & Moreno, 2016). Cocaine should never be used by pregnant women.

Methamphetamine Methamphetamine, like cocaine, speeds up an individual's nervous system. Babies born to mothers who use methamphetamine, or "meth," during pregnancy are at risk for a number of problems, including high infant mortality, low birth weight, and developmental and behavioral problems (Dinger & others, 2017; Parrott & others, 2014). One study revealed that meth exposure during prenatal development was linked to decreased arousal, increased stress, and poor movement quality in newborns (Smith & others, 2008). Another study found that prenatal exposure to meth was linked to less brain activation in a number of areas, especially the frontal lobes, in 7- to 15-year-olds (Roussotte & others, 2011). Another recent study revealed that prenatal meth exposure was associated with smaller head circumference, increased likelihood of admission to a neonatal intensive care unit, and higher rates of referral to child protective services (Shah & others, 2012). And a recent study discovered that prenatal methamphetamine exposure was associated with risk for developing ADHD in 5-year-old children (Kiblawi & others, 2013).

Marijuana An increasing number of studies find that marijuana use by pregnant women also has negative outcomes for their offspring (Huizink & Mulder, 2006; Volkow, Compton, & Wargo, 2017; Williams & Ross, 2007). In a recent meta-analysis, marijuana use during pregnancy was linked to offsprings' low birth weight and greater likelihood of being placed in a neonatal intensive care unit (Gunn & others, 2016). Also, a research review concluded that marijuana use by pregnant women is related to deficits in memory and information processing in their offspring (Kalant, 2004). For example, in a longitudinal study, prenatal marijuana exposure was related to learning and memory difficulties at age 11 (Richardson & others,

2002). Other studies have linked prenatal marijuana exposure to lower intelligence in children (Goldschmidt & others, 2008) and to depressive symptoms at 10 years of age (Gray & others, 2005). Further, research results have found connections between prenatal exposure to marijuana and marijuana use at 14 years of age (Day, Goldschmidt, & Thomas, 2006). And a recent study discovered that marijuana use by pregnant women was associated with stillbirth (Varner & others, 2014). In sum, marijuana use is not recommended for pregnant women.

Despite the widespread evidence of negative outcomes, a recent survey found that marijuana use by pregnant women increased from 2.4 percent in 2002 to 3.85 percent in 2014 (Brown & others, 2016). And there is considerable concern that marijuana use by pregnant women may increase further given the increasing number of states that have legalized marijuana (Chasnoff, 2017; Wang, 2017).

Heroin It is well documented that infants whose mothers are addicted to heroin show several behavioral difficulties at birth (Lindsay & Burnett, 2013). These difficulties include withdrawal symptoms such as tremors, irritability, abnormal crying, disturbed sleep, and impaired motor control. Many infants still show behavioral problems at their first birthday, and attention deficits may appear later in development. The most common treatment for heroin addiction, methadone, is associated with very severe withdrawal symptoms in newborns (Blandthorn, Forster, & Love, 2011). One study revealed that in comparison with late methadone treatment (less than six months prior to birth), continuous methadone treatment during pregnancy was linked to improved neonatal outcomes (Burns & others, 2007).

INCOMPATIBLE BLOOD TYPES

Incompatibility between the mother's and father's blood types poses another risk to prenatal development. Blood types are created by differences in the surface structure of red blood cells. One type of difference in the surface of red blood cells creates the familiar blood groups—A, B, O, and AB. A second difference creates what is called Rh-positive and Rh-negative blood. If a surface marker, called the Rh factor, is present in an individual's red blood cells, the person is said to be Rh-positive; if the Rh marker is not present, the person is said to be Rh-negative. If a pregnant woman is Rh-negative and her partner is Rh-positive, the fetus may be Rh-positive. If the fetus' blood is Rh-positive and the mother's is Rh-negative, the mother's immune system may produce antibodies that will attack the fetus. Such an assault can result in any number of problems, including miscarriage or stillbirth, anemia, jaundice, heart defects, brain damage, or death soon after birth (Li & others, 2010).

Generally, the first Rh-positive baby of an Rh-negative mother is not at risk, but with each subsequent pregnancy the risk increases. A vaccine (RhoGAM) may be given to the mother within three days of the first child's birth to prevent her body from making antibodies that will attack any future Rh-positive fetuses in subsequent pregnancies. Also, babies affected by Rh incompatibility can be given blood transfusions before or immediately after birth (Fasano, 2017; Goodnough & others, 2011).

ENVIRONMENTAL HAZARDS

Many aspects of our modern industrial world can endanger the embryo or fetus. Some specific hazards to the embryo or fetus that are worth a closer look include radiation, toxic wastes, and other chemical pollutants (Dursun & others, 2016; Sreetharan & others, 2017; Yang, Ren, & Tang, 2017).

Radiation can cause a gene mutation (an abrupt, permanent change in DNA). Chromosomal abnormalities are elevated among the offspring of fathers exposed to high levels of radiation in their occupations (Schrag & Dixon, 1985). X-ray radiation also can affect the developing embryo or fetus, especially during the first several weeks after conception when women do not yet know they are pregnant. Possible effects include microencephaly (an abnormally small brain), intellectual disabilities, and leukemia. Women and their physicians should weigh the risk of an X-ray when an actual or potential pregnancy is involved (Menias & others, 2007; Rajaraman & others, 2011). However, a routine diagnostic X-ray of a body area other than the abdomen, with the woman's abdomen protected by a lead apron, is generally considered safe (Brent, 2009, 2011).

Environmental pollutants and toxic wastes are also sources of danger to unborn children. Among the dangerous pollutants are carbon monoxide, mercury, and lead, as well as certain

An explosion at the Chernobyl nuclear power plant in the Ukraine produced radioactive contamination that spread to surrounding areas. Thousands of infants were born with health problems and deformities as a result of the nuclear contamination, including this boy whose arm did not form. *Other than radioactive contamination, what are some types of environmental hazards to prenatal development?*
©Sergey Guneev/RIA Novosti

fertilizers and pesticides (Lin & others, 2013; Wang & others, 2017). Exposure to lead can come from lead-based paint that flakes off the walls of a home or from leaded gasoline emitted by cars on a nearby busy highway. Early exposure to lead can affect children's mental development (Canfield & Jusko, 2008). For example, a study revealed that a moderately high maternal lead level in the first trimester of pregnancy was linked to lower scores on an index of mental development in infancy (Hu & others, 2007).

MATERNAL DISEASES

Maternal diseases and infections can produce defects in offspring by crossing the placental barrier, or they can cause damage during birth (Cuffe & others, 2017). Rubella (German measles) is one disease that can cause prenatal defects. The greatest damage occurs if a mother contracts rubella in the third or fourth week of pregnancy, although infection during the second month is also damaging (Kobayashi & others, 2005). A recent study found that cardiac defects, pulmonary problems, and microcephaly (a condition in which the baby's head is significantly smaller and less developed than normal) were among the most common fetal and neonatal outcomes when pregnant women have rubella (Yazigi & others, 2017). Elaborate preventive efforts ensure that rubella will never again have such disastrous effects. A vaccine that prevents German measles is now routinely administered to children, and women who plan to have children should have a blood test before they become pregnant to determine whether they are immune to the disease (Reef & others, 2011).

Syphilis (a sexually transmitted infection) is more damaging later in prenatal development—four months or more after conception. Rather than affecting organogenesis, as rubella does, syphilis damages organs after they have formed. Damage includes eye lesions, which can cause blindness, and skin lesions (Qin & others, 2014). When syphilis is present at birth, problems can develop in the central nervous system and gastrointestinal tract (Braccio, Sharland, & Ladhari, 2016). Penicillin is the only known treatment for syphilis during pregnancy (Moline & Smith, 2016).

Another infection that has received widespread attention recently is genital herpes. Newborns contract this virus when they are delivered through the birth canal of a mother with genital herpes (Sampath, Maduro, & Schillinger, 2017). About one-third of babies delivered through an infected birth canal die; another one-fourth become brain damaged. If an active case of genital herpes is detected in a pregnant woman close to her delivery date, a cesarean section can be performed (delivery of the infant through an incision in the mother's abdomen) to keep the virus from infecting the newborn (Patel & others, 2011).

AIDS is a sexually transmitted infection that is caused by the human immunodeficiency virus (HIV), which destroys the body's immune system. A mother can infect her offspring with HIV/AIDS in three ways: (1) during gestation across the placenta, (2) during delivery through contact with maternal blood or fluids, and (3) postpartum (after birth) through breast feeding. The transmission of AIDS through breast feeding is especially a problem in many developing countries (UNICEF, 2017). Babies born to HIV-infected mothers can be (1) infected and symptomatic (show HIV symptoms), (2) infected but asymptomatic (not show HIV symptoms), or (3) not infected at all. An infant who is infected and asymptomatic may still develop HIV symptoms until 15 months of age.

In the early 1990s, before preventive treatments were available, 1,000 to 2,000 infants were born with HIV infection each year in the United States. Since then, transmission of HIV from mothers to fetuses has been reduced dramatically (Anderson & Cu-Uvin, 2009; Taylor & others, 2017). Only about one-third as many cases of newborns with HIV appear today as in the early 1990s. This decline is due to the increase in counseling and voluntary testing of pregnant women for HIV and to the administration of zidovudine (AZT) to infected women during pregnancy and to the infant after birth. In many poor countries, however, treatment with AZT is limited, and HIV infection of infants remains a major problem.

The more widespread disease of diabetes, characterized by high levels of sugar in the blood, also affects offspring (Haertle & others, 2017). A research review indicated that newborns with physical defects are more likely to have diabetic mothers than newborns without such defects (Eriksson, 2009). Moreover, women who have gestational diabetes (a condition in which women without previously diagnosed diabetes develop high blood glucose levels during pregnancy) may deliver very large infants (weighing 10 pounds or more), and the infants themselves are at risk for diabetes (Alberico & others, 2014) and cardiovascular disease (Amrithraj & others, 2017).

developmental **connection**

Conditions, Diseases, and Disorders
The highest incidence of HIV/AIDS is in sub-Saharan Africa, where as many as 30 percent of mothers have HIV; many are unaware that they are infected with the virus. Connect to "Physical Development in Infancy," "Physical Development in Early Childhood," and "Physical Development in Adolescence."

OTHER PARENTAL FACTORS

So far we have discussed drugs, environmental hazards, maternal diseases, and incompatible blood types that can harm the embryo or fetus. Here we explore other characteristics of the mother and father that can affect prenatal and child development, including nutrition, age, and emotional states and stress.

Maternal Diet and Nutrition A developing embryo or fetus depends completely on its mother for nutrition, which comes from the mother's blood. The nutritional status of the embryo or fetus is determined by the mother's total caloric intake and by her intake of proteins, vitamins, and minerals. Children born to malnourished mothers are more likely than other children to be malformed.

Being overweight before and during pregnancy can also put the embryo or fetus at risk, and an increasing number of pregnant women in the United States are overweight (Baugh & others, 2017; Poston & others, 2016). Maternal obesity adversely affects pregnancy outcomes through elevated rates of hypertension, diabetes, respiratory complications, and infections in the mother (Cheng & others, 2017). A recent research review concluded that pregestational diabetes increases the risk of fetal heart disease (Pauliks, 2015). Recent research studies have found that maternal obesity is linked to an increase in stillbirth (Gardosi & others, 2013) and increased likelihood that the newborn will be placed in a neonatal intensive care unit (Minsart & others, 2013). Further, two recent research reviews concluded that maternal obesity during pregnancy is associated with an increased likelihood of offspring being obese in childhood and adulthood (Pinto Pereira & others, 2016; Santangeli, Sattar, & Huda, 2015). Management of obesity that includes weight loss and increased exercise prior to pregnancy is likely to benefit the mother and the baby (Hanson & others, 2017; Ingul & others, 2016).

One aspect of maternal nutrition that is important for normal prenatal development is folic acid, a B-complex vitamin. As we indicated earlier in the chapter, a lack of folic acid during prenatal development is linked with neural tube defects such as spina bifida in offspring (Atta & others, 2016; Viswanathan & others, 2017). A study of more than 34,000 pregnant women revealed that taking folic acid either alone or as part of a multivitamin for at least one year prior to conceiving was linked with a 70 percent lower risk of delivering between 20 to 28 weeks and a 50 percent lower risk of delivering between 28 and 32 weeks (Bukowski & others, 2008). The U.S. Public Health Service recommends that pregnant women consume a minimum of 400 micrograms of folic acid per day (about twice the amount the average woman gets in one day). Orange juice and spinach are examples of foods rich in folic acid.

Fish is often recommended as part of a healthy diet and in general fish consumption during pregnancy has positive benefits for children's development (Golding & others, 2016; Julvez & others, 2016). The U.S. Food and Drug Administration (FDA) (2017) recommends that pregnant women increase their consumption of fish because it contains vital nutrients such as omega-3 fatty acids, protein, vitamins, and minerals such as iron.

However, pollution has made some kinds of fish a risky choice for pregnant women. Some fish contain high levels of mercury, which is released into the air both naturally and by industrial processes (Wells & others, 2011). Mercury that falls into the water can accumulate in large fish, such as shark, swordfish, king mackerel, and some species of large tuna (American Pregnancy Association, 2017; Mayo Clinic, 2017). Researchers have found that prenatal mercury exposure is linked to adverse outcomes, including miscarriage, preterm birth, and lower intelligence (Xue & others, 2007).

Recently, the American Pregnancy Association (2017) revised its conclusions about fish consumption during pregnancy but continued to recommend avoiding fish with a high mercury content, such as tilefish from the Gulf of Mexico, swordfish, shark, and king mackerel.

Because the fetus depends entirely on its mother for nutrition, it is important for the pregnant woman to have good nutritional habits. In Kenya, this government clinic provides pregnant women with information about how their diet can influence the health of their fetus and offspring. *What might the information about diet be like?*
©Delphine Bousquet/AFP/Getty Images

developmental connection

Conditions, Diseases, and Disorders
What are some key factors that influence whether individuals will become overweight or obese? Connect to "Physical Development in Early Childhood," "Physical Development in Middle and Late Childhood," and "Physical Development in Adolescence."

©George Peters/E+/Getty Images RF

developmental **connection**

Parenting

Adolescent pregnancy creates negative developmental trajectories for both mothers and their offspring. Connect to "Physical Development in Adolescence."

What are some of the risks for infants born to adolescent mothers?

©Barbara Penoyar/Getty Images RF

How Would You...?

If you were a **health-care professional,** how would you advise a couple in their late thirties or early forties who are considering having a baby?

How Would You...?

If you were a **health-care professional,** how would you advise an expectant mother who is experiencing extreme psychological stress?

The association and the FDA now recommend that pregnant women increase their consumption of fish that have a low mercury content, such as salmon, shrimp, tilapia, and cod.

Maternal Age   When possible harmful effects on the fetus and infant are considered, two maternal ages are of special interest: adolescents and women 35 years of age and older (Gockley & others, 2016; Kawakita & others, 2016). One study revealed that the rate of stillbirth was elevated for adolescent girls and for women 35 years and older (Bateman & Simpson, 2006).

The mortality rate of infants born to adolescent mothers is double that of infants born to mothers in their twenties. Although this high rate probably reflects the immaturity of the mother's reproductive system, other factors such as poor nutrition, lack of prenatal care, and low socioeconomic status may also play a role (Smithbattle, 2007). Adequate prenatal care decreases the probability that a child born to an adolescent girl will have physical problems. However, adolescents are the least likely age group to obtain prenatal health care from clinics and health services.

Maternal age is also linked to the risk that a child will have Down syndrome (Ghosh & others, 2010; Jaruratanasirikul & others, 2017). An individual with *Down syndrome* has distinctive facial characteristics, short limbs, and impaired development of motor and mental abilities. Advanced maternal age confers a much greater risk of having a baby with Down syndrome. When the mother reaches 40 years of age, the probability is slightly more than 1 in 100 that a baby born to her will have Down syndrome, and by age 50 it is almost 1 in 10.

When mothers are 35 years and older, risks also increase for low birth weight, for preterm delivery, and for fetal death (Mbugua Gitau & others, 2009). One study found that low birth weight delivery increased by 11 percent and preterm delivery increased by 14 percent in women 35 years and older (Tough & others, 2002). In another study, fetal death was low for women 30 to 34 years of age but increased progressively for women 35 to 44 years of age (Canterino & others, 2004). Also, a recent Norwegian study found that maternal age of 30 years or older was linked to the same level of increased risk for fetal deaths as 25- to 29-year-old pregnant women who were overweight/obese or were smokers (Waldenstrom & others, 2014). Also, in two recent studies, very advanced maternal age (40 years and older) was linked to adverse perinatal outcomes, including spontaneous abortion, preterm birth, stillbirth, and fetal growth restriction (Traisrisilp & Tongsong, 2015; Waldenstrom & others, 2015).

We still have much to learn about the role of the mother's age in pregnancy and childbirth (Montana, 2007). As women remain active, exercise regularly, and are careful about their nutrition, their reproductive systems may remain healthier at older ages than was thought possible in the past. For example, in one study, two-thirds of the pregnancies of women 45 years and older in Australia were free of complications (Callaway, Lust, & McIntyre, 2005).

Emotional States and Stress   When a pregnant woman experiences intense fears, anxieties, and other emotions or negative mood states, physiological changes occur that may affect her fetus.

High maternal anxiety and stress during pregnancy can have long-term consequences for the offspring (Bauer, Knapp, & Parsonage, 2016; Dalke, Wentzel, & Kim, 2016; Isgut & others, 2017; Pinto & others, 2017). A recent study found that high levels of depression, anxiety, and stress during pregnancy were linked to internalizing problems in adolescence (Betts & others, 2014). A research review indicated that pregnant women with high levels of stress are at increased risk for having a child with emotional or cognitive problems, attention deficit hyperactivity disorder (ADHD), and language delay (Taige & others, 2007). Maternal emotions and stress also can influence the fetus indirectly by increasing the likelihood that the mother will engage in unhealthy behaviors such as taking drugs and receiving inadequate prenatal care. Further, a recent research review concluded that regardless of the form of maternal prenatal stress or anxiety and the prenatal trimester in which the stress or anxiety occurred, during their first two years of life the offspring displayed lower levels of self-regulation (Korja & others, 2017).

Might maternal depression also have an adverse effect on birth outcomes? Research indicates that maternal depression during pregnancy is linked to preterm birth as well as low birth weight in full-term offspring (Chang & others, 2014; Dunkel Schetter, 2011; Fatima, Srivastav, & Mondal, 2017; Mparmpakas & others, 2013). Another study revealed that maternal depression during pregnancy was related to increased risk for depression in 18-year-olds (Pearson & others, 2013). Also, a recent study found that taking antidepressants early in pregnancy was linked to an increased risk of miscarriage (Almeida & others, 2016). In another study, when fetuses were exposed to serotonin-based antidepressants, they were more likely to be born preterm (Podrebarac & others, 2017). Further, a recent study revealed that taking antidepressants in the second or third trimester of pregnancy was linked to an increased risk of autism spectrum disorders in children (Boukhris & others, 2016).

Positive emotional states also appear to make a difference to the fetus. Pregnant women who are optimistic thinkers have less adverse outcomes than pregnant women who are pessimistic thinkers (Loebel & Yali, 1999). Optimists are more likely to believe that they have control over the outcomes of their pregnancies.

Paternal Factors So far, we have discussed how characteristics of the mother—such as drug use, disease, diet and nutrition, age, and emotional states—can influence prenatal development and the development of the child. Might there also be some paternal risk factors? Indeed, there are several (Pedersen & others, 2014). Men's exposure to lead, radiation, certain pesticides, and petrochemicals may cause abnormalities in sperm that lead to miscarriage or to diseases such as childhood cancer (Cordier, 2008; Fear & others, 2007). Also, it has been speculated that when fathers take cocaine, it may attach itself to sperm and cause birth defects, but the evidence for this effect is not yet strong. In one study, long-term use of cocaine by men was related to low sperm count, low motility, and a higher number of abnormally formed sperm (Bracken & others, 1990). Cocaine-related infertility appears to be reversible if users stop taking the drug for at least one year.

The father's smoking during the mother's pregnancy also can cause problems for the offspring (Agricola & others, 2016). In one investigation, the newborns of fathers who smoked around their wives during the pregnancy were 4 ounces lighter at birth for each pack of cigarettes smoked per day than were the newborns whose fathers had not smoked while their wives were pregnant (Rubin & others, 1986). In a study in China, the longer the fathers smoked, the higher the risk that their children would develop cancer (Ji & others, 1997). In yet another study, heavy paternal smoking was associated with the risk of early pregnancy loss (Venners & others, 2004). All of these negative effects may be related to maternal exposure to secondhand smoke. And in a recent study, paternal smoking around the time of the child's conception was linked to an increased risk of the child developing leukemia (Milne & others, 2012). Also, a recent research review concluded that there is an increased risk of spontaneous abortion, autism, and schizophrenic disorders when the father is 40 years of age or older at the time of conception (Reproductive Endocrinology and Infertility Committee & others, 2011). And a recent research study revealed that children born to fathers who were 40 years of age or older had increased risk of developing autism because of an increase in random gene mutations in the older fathers (Kong & others, 2012). However, the age of the offspring's mother was not linked to development of autism in children.

There are also risks to offspring in some circumstances when both the mother and father are older (Dunson, Baird, & Colombo, 2004). In one study, the risk of an adverse pregnancy outcome such as miscarriage rose considerably when the woman was 35 years of age or older and the man was 40 years of age or older (de la Rocheborchard & Thonneau, 2002).

The father may contribute to positive outcomes for the fetus by providing support to the mother and having a positive attitude toward the pregnancy. Earlier you read about how maternal stress and depression have negative developmental outcomes for offspring. Fathers can play an important role in helping to reduce stress and depression in the mothers by contributing to a positive marital relationship, not engaging in spousal abuse, sharing more in household tasks, and participating in childbirth classes. A recent study found that intimate partner violence increased the mother's stress level (Fonseca-Machado Mde & others, 2015).

Much of our discussion in this chapter has focused on what can go wrong with prenatal development. Prospective parents should take steps to avoid the hazards to fetal development that we have described. But it is important to keep in mind that most of the time, prenatal development does not go awry and development occurs along the positive path that we described at the beginning of the chapter.

In a study conducted in China, the longer fathers smoked the greater the risk that their children would develop cancer (Ji & others, 1997). *What are some other paternal factors that can influence the development of the fetus and the child?*

©David Butow/Corbis/Getty Images

Review Connect Reflect

LG3 Describe potential hazards during prenatal development.

Review

- What is teratology? What are some general principles regarding teratogens?
- Which prescription and nonprescription drugs can influence prenatal development?
- How do different psychoactive drugs affect prenatal development?
- How do incompatible blood types influence prenatal development?
- What are some environmental hazards that can influence prenatal development?
- Which maternal diseases can affect prenatal development?
- What other parental factors can affect prenatal development?

Connect

- Earlier you read about chromosomal and gene-linked abnormalities that can affect prenatal development. How are the symptoms of the related conditions or risks similar to or different from those caused by teratogens or other hazards?

Reflect *Your Own Personal Journey of Life*

- If you are a woman, imagine that you have just found out you are pregnant. What health-enhancing strategies will you follow during the prenatal period? If you are a man, imagine you are the partner of a woman who has just learned that she is pregnant. What can you do to increase the likelihood that the prenatal period will go smoothly?

┌-Topical **Connections** *looking forward*

Next you will learn about the birth process and the transition from fetus to newborn, see how the newborn's health and responsiveness are assessed, read about low birth weight and preterm babies and find out about special ways to nurture these fragile newborns, and examine what happens during the postpartum period.

reach your **learning goals**

Prenatal Development

1 What Is the Course of Prenatal Development?

LG1 Discuss the three periods of prenatal development.

- The Germinal Period
- The Embryonic Period
- The Fetal Period
- The Brain

- The germinal period lasts from conception until about two weeks later. It includes the creation of a fertilized egg, which is called a zygote, and cell division. The period ends when the zygote attaches to the uterine wall in a process called implantation.

- The embryonic period lasts from about two to eight weeks after conception. The embryo differentiates into three layers of cells (endoderm, mesoderm, and ectoderm), life-support systems develop, and organ systems form (organogenesis).

- The fetal period lasts from about two months after conception until nine months, or when the infant is born. Growth and development continue their dramatic course, and organ systems mature to the point at which life can be sustained outside the womb.

- The growth of the brain during prenatal development is nothing short of remarkable. By the time babies are born, they have approximately 100 billion neurons, or nerve cells. Neurogenesis is the term that means the formation of new neurons.

- Development of the nervous system begins with the formation of a neural tube at 18 to 24 days after conception. Proliferation and neuronal migration are two processes that characterize brain development in the prenatal period. The basic architecture of the brain is formed in the first two trimesters of prenatal development.

2 What Are Some Important Strategies That Enhance the Expectant Mother's Health and Prenatal Care?

LG2 Summarize how nutrition, exercise, and prenatal care are important aspects of the expectant mother's pregnancy.

The Expectant Mother's Nutrition and Weight Gain

Exercise

Prenatal Care

- The best assurance of adequate caloric intake during pregnancy is a satisfactory weight gain over time. Maternal weight gain that averages 25 to 35 pounds is often linked with the best reproductive outcomes. The RDA for all nutrients increases during pregnancy, and the need for such nutrients as vitamin D, folacin, and iron increases by more than 50 percent.
- If the expectant mother's health allows, exercise can benefit her well-being during pregnancy and may reduce the risk of a preterm birth. How much and what type of exercise are appropriate depends to some extent on the course of pregnancy, the expectant mother's fitness, and her customary activity level.
- Prenatal care varies extensively but usually involves medical care services with a defined schedule of visits and often includes educational, social, and nutritional services. Much needs to be done to improve prenatal care in the United States, especially for low-income families.

3 What Are Some Potential Hazards to Prenatal Development?

LG3 Describe potential hazards during prenatal development.

Some General Principles

Prescription and Nonprescription Drugs

Psychoactive Drugs

- Teratology is the field that investigates the causes of birth defects. Any agent that can potentially cause birth defects is called a teratogen. The time of exposure, dose, and genetic susceptibility influence the severity of the damage to an unborn child and the type of defect that occurs.
- Prescription drugs that can harm a developing fetus include antibiotics, some antidepressants, and certain hormones. Nonprescription drugs that can be harmful include diet pills and aspirin.
- Legal psychoactive drugs that are potentially harmful to prenatal development include alcohol, nicotine, and caffeine. Fetal alcohol spectrum disorders (FASD) consist of a cluster of abnormalities that appear in offspring of mothers who drink heavily during pregnancy. Even when pregnant women drink moderately, negative effects on their offspring have been found. Cigarette smoking by pregnant women can have serious adverse effects on prenatal and child development (such as low birth weight and SIDS).
- Illegal psychoactive drugs that are potentially harmful to offspring include methamphetamine, which can produce high infant mortality, low birth weight, and developmental problems; marijuana, which can result in a child's impaired information processing; cocaine, which is associated with reduced birth weight, length, and head circumference; and heroin, which produces behavioral problems at birth and may result in attention deficits later in development.

Incompatible Blood Types

- Incompatibility of the mother's and the father's blood types can also be harmful to the fetus. A woman is at risk when she has a negative Rh factor and her partner has a positive Rh factor. If the fetus is Rh-positive and the mother is Rh-negative, the mother's immune system may attack the fetus, resulting in problems such as miscarriage or brain damage.

Environmental Hazards

- Environmental hazards include radiation, environmental pollutants, and toxic wastes.

Maternal Diseases

- Syphilis, rubella (German measles), genital herpes, and AIDS are infectious diseases that can harm the fetus.

Other Parental Factors

- Other parental factors that affect prenatal development include maternal diet and nutrition, age, emotional states and stress, and paternal factors. A developing fetus depends entirely on its mother for nutrition. One nutrient that is especially important very early in development is folic acid. A potential hazard to prenatal development occurs when the mother consumes fish with a high mercury content. Maternal age can negatively affect the offspring's development if the mother is an adolescent or over 35. High stress in the mother is linked with less than optimal prenatal and birth outcomes. Paternal factors that can adversely affect prenatal development include exposure to lead, radiation, certain pesticides, and petrochemicals, as well as smoking.

key **terms**

amnion	fetal alcohol spectrum disorders	neurogenesis	trophoblast
blastocyst	(FASD)	neurons	umbilical cord
ectoderm	fetal period	organogenesis	
embryonic period	germinal period	placenta	
endoderm	mesoderm	teratogen	

key **people**

David Olds

connecting with **improving the lives of children**

STRATEGIES

Maximizing Positive Prenatal Outcomes

What are some strategies during pregnancy that are likely to maximize positive outcomes for prenatal development?

- *Eat nutritious foods and monitor weight gain.* The recommended daily allowances for all nutrients increase during pregnancy. A pregnant woman should eat three balanced meals a day and nutritious snacks between meals if desired. Weight gains that average 25 to 35 pounds are associated with the best reproductive outcomes.
- *Engage in safe exercise.* How much and what type of exercise is best during pregnancy depends to some degree on the course of the pregnancy, the expectant mother's fitness, and her customary activity level. Normal participation in exercise can continue throughout an uncomplicated pregnancy. It is important to remember not to overdo exercise. Exercising for shorter intervals and decreasing the intensity of exercise as pregnancy proceeds are good strategies. Pregnant women should always consult a physician before starting an exercise program.
- *Don't drink alcohol or take other potentially harmful drugs.* An important strategy for pregnancy is to totally abstain from alcohol and other drugs such as nicotine and cocaine. In this chapter, we considered the harmful effects that these drugs can have on the developing fetus. Fathers also need to be aware of potentially harmful effects of their behavior on prenatal development.
- *Have a support system of family and friends.* The pregnant woman benefits from a support system of family members and friends. A positive relationship with a spouse helps keep stress levels down, as does a close relationship with one or more friends.
- *Reduce stress and stay calm.* Try to maintain an even, calm emotional state during pregnancy. High stress levels can harm the fetus. Pregnant women who are feeling a lot of anxiety can reduce their anxiety level through a relaxation or stress management program.
- *Stay away from environmental hazards.* We saw in this chapter that some environmental hazards, such as pollutants and toxic wastes, can harm prenatal development. Be aware of these hazards and avoid them.
- *Get excellent prenatal care.* The quality of prenatal care varies extensively. The education the mother receives about pregnancy, labor and delivery, and care of the newborn can be valuable, especially for first-time mothers.
- *Read a good book for expectant mothers.* An excellent one is *What to Expect When You're Expecting,* which is described under Resources.

RESOURCES

March of Dimes
www.marchofdimes.com

The March of Dimes organization strives to promote healthy pregnancy. Their Web site includes extensive information about many aspects of pregnancy and prenatal development.

National Center for Education in Maternal and Child Health (NCEMCH)
www.ncemch.org

NCEMCH answers questions about pregnancy and childbirth, high-risk infants, and maternal and child health programs. It also publishes free maternal and child health publications.

Pregnancy.org
www.pregnancy.org

This extensive Web site provides up-to-date information about pregnancy and prenatal development.

What to Expect When You're Expecting (5th ed., 2016)
Heidi Murkoff and Sharon Mazel
New York: Workman

This highly popular book on pregnancy and prenatal development provides detailed month-by-month descriptions of pregnancy and prenatal growth.

Prenatal Care Tips

Pregnant women can call this toll-free number provided by the federal government for prenatal care advice and referral to local health-care providers: 800–311–2229.

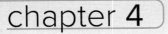

BIRTH

chapter **outline**

Tanner Roberts was born in a suite at St. Joseph's Medical Center in Burbank, California (Warrick, 1992).

Let's examine what took place in the hours leading up to his birth. It is day 266 of his mother Cindy's pregnancy. She is in the frozen-food aisle of a convenience store and feels a sharp pain, starting in the small of her back and reaching around her middle, which causes her to gasp. For weeks, painless Braxton Hicks spasms (named for the gynecologist who discovered them) have been flexing her uterine muscles. But these practice contractions were not nearly as intense and painful as the one she just experienced. After six hours of irregular spasms, her uterus settles into a more predictable rhythm.

At 3 a.m., Cindy and her husband Tom are wide awake. They time Cindy's contractions with a stopwatch. The contractions are now only six minutes apart. It's time to call the hospital. A short time later, Tom and Cindy arrive at the hospital's labor-delivery suite. A nurse puts a webbed belt and fetal monitor around Cindy's middle to measure her labor. The monitor picks up the fetal heart rate. With each contraction of the uterine wall, Tanner's heartbeat jumps from its resting state of about 140 beats to 160 to 170 beats per minute. When the cervix is dilated to more than 4 centimeters, or almost half open, Cindy receives her first medication. As Demerol begins to drip into her veins, the pain of her contractions is less intense. Tanner's heart rate dips to 130 and then 120.

Contractions are now coming every three to four minutes, each one lasting about 25 seconds. The Demerol does not completely obliterate Cindy's pain. She hugs her husband as the nurse urges her to "Relax those muscles. Breathe deep. Relax. You're almost there."

Each contraction briefly cuts off Tanner's source of oxygen, his mother's blood. However, in the minutes of rest between contractions, Cindy's deep breathing helps rush fresh blood to the baby's heart and brain.

At 8 a.m., Cindy's cervix is almost completely dilated and the obstetrician arrives. Using a tool made for the purpose, he reaches into the birth canal and tears the membranes of the amniotic sac, and about half a liter of clear fluid flows out. Contractions are now coming every two minutes, and each one is lasting a full minute.

By 9 a.m., the labor suite has been transformed into a delivery room. Tanner's body is compressed by his mother's contractions and pushes. As he nears his entrance into the world, the compressions help press the fluid from his lungs in preparation for his first breath. Squeezed tightly in the birth canal, the top of Tanner's head emerges. His face is puffy and scrunched. Although he is fiercely squinting because of the sudden light, Tanner's eyes are open. Tiny bubbles of clear mucus are on his lips. Before any more of his body emerges, the nurse cradles Tanner's head and suctions his nose and mouth. Tanner takes his first breath, a large gasp followed by whimpering, and then a loud cry. Tanner's body is wet but only slightly bloody as the doctor lifts him onto his mother's abdomen.

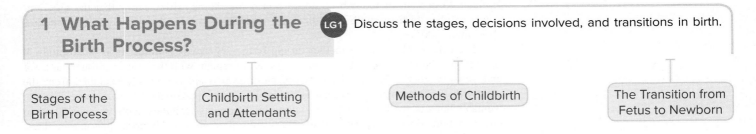

topical connections *looking back*

You have read about prenatal development and the strategies expectant mothers can use to enhance their health and their offspring's health. You also learned about some potential hazards that can occur during prenatal development. And you read about the remarkable prenatal development of the brain, which contains approximately 100 billion neurons when birth takes place. This chapter takes you through the birth process and its immediate aftermath—the postpartum period.

The umbilical cord, still connecting Tanner with his mother, slows and stops pulsating. The obstetrician cuts it, severing Tanner's connection to his mother's womb. Now Tanner's blood flows not to his mother's body for nourishment—but to his own lungs, intestines, and other organs.

Warrick, P. "The Fantastic Voyage of Tanner Roberts," Los Angeles Times, 1992, E1, E12, and E13. Copyright ©1992 Los Angeles Times. All rights reserved. Used with permission.

preview

As the story of Tanner Roberts' birth reveals, many changes take place during the birth of a baby. In this chapter, we explore what happens during the birth process, describe measures of neonatal health and responsiveness, discuss the development of preterm and low birth weight infants, and identify characteristics of the postpartum period.

1 What Happens During the Birth Process?

LG1 Discuss the stages, decisions involved, and transitions in birth.

| Stages of the Birth Process | Childbirth Setting and Attendants | Methods of Childbirth | The Transition from Fetus to Newborn |

Nature writes the basic script for how birth occurs, but parents make important choices about conditions surrounding birth. What is the sequence of physical steps when a child is born?

STAGES OF THE BIRTH PROCESS

The birth process occurs in three stages. The first stage is the longest of the three. Uterine contractions are 15 to 20 minutes apart at the beginning and last up to a minute apiece. These contractions cause the woman's cervix to stretch and open. As the first stage progresses, the contractions come closer together, appearing every two to five minutes. Their intensity increases. By the end of the first birth stage, contractions dilate the cervix to an opening of about 4 inches, so that the baby can move from the uterus to the birth canal. For a woman having her first child, the first stage lasts an average of 12 to 14 hours; for subsequent children, this stage may be shorter.

The second birth stage begins when the baby's head starts to move through the cervix and the birth canal. It terminates when the baby completely emerges from the mother's body. With each contraction, the mother bears down hard to push the baby out of her body. By the time the baby's head is out of the mother's body, the contractions come almost every minute and last for about a minute. This stage typically lasts approximately 45 minutes to an hour.

> There was a star danced, and under that I was born.
>
> —**WILLIAM SHAKESPEARE**
> *English Playwright, 17th Century*

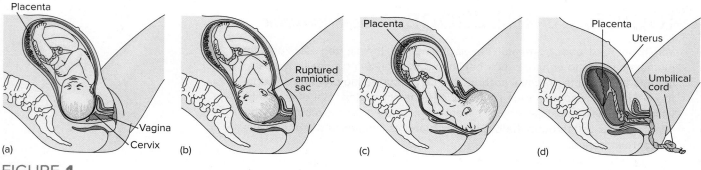

FIGURE 1

THE STAGES OF BIRTH. (*a*) First stage: cervix is dilating; (*b*) late first stage (transition stage): cervix is fully dilated and the amniotic sac has ruptured, releasing amniotic fluid; (*c*) second stage: birth of the infant; (*d*) third stage: delivery of the placenta (afterbirth).

Afterbirth is the third stage, at which time the placenta, umbilical cord, and other membranes are detached and expelled. This final stage is the shortest of the three birth stages, lasting only minutes (see Figure 1).

CHILDBIRTH SETTING AND ATTENDANTS

In 2015 in the United States, 98.5 percent of births took place in hospitals (Martin & others, 2017). Of the 1.5 percent of births occurring outside of a hospital, 63 percent took place in homes and almost 31 percent in free-standing birthing centers. The percentage of U.S. births at home is the highest since reporting of this context began in 1989. An increase in home births has occurred mainly among non-Latino White women, especially those who are older and married. For these non-Latino White women, two-thirds of their home births are attended by a midwife.

Some women with good medical histories and low risk for problems may choose a delivery at home or in a free-standing birth center, which is usually staffed by nurse-midwives. Births at home are far more common in many other countries—for example, in Holland 35 percent of the babies are born at home. Some critics worry that the U.S. tendency to view birth through a medical lens may lead to unnecessary medical procedures (Hausman, 2005).

The people who assist a mother during birth vary across cultures. In U.S. hospitals, it has become the norm for fathers or birth coaches to remain with the mother throughout labor and delivery. In the East African Nigoni culture, men are completely excluded from the childbirth process. When a woman is ready to give birth, female relatives move into the woman's hut and the husband leaves, taking his belongings (clothes, tools, weapons, and so on) with him. He is not permitted to return until after the baby is born. In some cultures, childbirth is an open, community affair. For example, in the Pukapukan culture in the Pacific Islands, women give birth in a shelter that is open for villagers to observe.

Midwives A *midwife* is a trained health practitioner who helps women during their labor, delivery, and afterbirth of their baby (Christensen & Overgaard, 2017; Faucher, 2017). Midwives also may give women information about reproductive health and annual gynecological examinations (Reed, Rowe, & Barnes, 2016). They may refer women to general practitioners or obstetricians if a pregnant woman needs medical care beyond a midwife's expertise and skill.

Midwifery is practiced in most countries throughout the world (Miyake & others, 2017; ten Hoope-Bender & others, 2016). In Holland, more than 40 percent of babies are delivered by midwives rather than by doctors. However, in the United States, recently only 8 percent of all hospital births were attended by a midwife (Martin & others, 2017). Nonetheless, the 8 percent figure represents a substantial increase from less than 1 percent in 1975.

Compared with physicians, certified nurse-midwives generally spend more time with patients during prenatal visits, place more emphasis on patient counseling and education, provide more emotional support, and are more likely to stay with the patient during the entire labor and delivery process, which may explain the higher rate of positive outcomes for babies delivered by certified nurse-midwives than for those delivered by doctors (Davis, 2005).

afterbirth The third stage of birth, when the placenta, umbilical cord, and other membranes are detached and expelled from the uterus.

Doulas   In many countries, a doula attends a childbearing woman. *Doula* is a Greek word that means "a woman who helps." A **doula** is a caregiver who provides continuous physical, emotional, and educational support for the mother before, during, and after childbirth. Doulas remain with the mother throughout labor, assessing and responding to her needs. Researchers have found positive effects when a doula is present at the birth of a child (Wilson & others, 2017; Zielinski, Brody, & Low, 2016). A recent study found that doula-assisted mothers were four times less likely to have a low birth weight baby and two times less likely to experience a birth complication involving themselves or their baby (Gruber, Cupito, & Dobson, 2013). Another recent study also revealed that for Medicaid recipients the odds of having a cesarean delivery were 41 percent lower for doula-supported births in the United States (Kozhimmanil & others, 2013). Thus, increasing doula-supported births could substantially lower the cost of a birth by reducing cesarean rates.

In the United States, most doulas work as independent providers hired by the expectant mother. Doulas typically function as part of a "birthing team," serving as an adjunct to the midwife or the hospital's obstetric staff (Dundek, 2006). Managed care organizations are increasingly offering doula support as a part of regular obstetric care.

METHODS OF CHILDBIRTH

U.S. hospitals often allow the mother and her obstetrician to choose from a range of options available for delivering a baby. Key choices involve the use of medication, whether to use any of a number of nonmedicated techniques to reduce pain, and when to resort to a cesarean delivery.

Medication   Three basic kinds of drugs are used for labor: analgesics, anesthesia, and oxytocics. **Analgesics** are used to relieve pain. Analgesics include tranquilizers, barbiturates, and narcotics (such as Demerol).

Anesthesia is used in late first-stage labor and during expulsion of the baby to block sensation in an area of the body or to block consciousness. There is a trend toward not using general anesthesia, which blocks consciousness, in normal births because general anesthesia can be transmitted through the placenta to the fetus (Edwards & Jackson, 2017). An *epidural block* is regional anesthesia that numbs the woman's body from the waist down. Even this drug, thought to be relatively safe, has come under recent criticism because it is associated with fever, extended labor, and increased risk for cesarean delivery (Birnbach & Ranasinghe, 2008). A research review concluded that epidural analgesia provides effective pain relief but at the cost of increasing the likelihood of having to use instruments during vaginal birth (Jones & others, 2012). Researchers are continuing to explore safer drug mixtures for use at lower doses to improve the effectiveness and safety of epidural anesthesia (Eisharkawy, Sonny, & Chin, 2017; Kobayashi & others, 2017).

Oxytocin is a hormone that promotes uterine contractions; a synthetic form called Pitocin™ is widely used to decrease the first stage of labor. The relative benefits and risks of administering synthetic forms of oxytocin during childbirth continue to be debated (Carlson, Corwin, & Lowe, 2017; Shiner, Many, & Maslovitz, 2016).

Predicting how a drug will affect an individual woman and her fetus is difficult (Ansari & others, 2016). A particular drug might have only a minimal effect on one fetus yet have a much stronger effect on another. The drug's dosage also is a factor (Rankin, 2017). Stronger doses of tranquilizers and narcotics given to decrease the mother's pain potentially have a more negative effect on the fetus than mild doses. It is important for the mother to assess her level of pain and have a voice in deciding whether she should receive medication.

Natural and Prepared Childbirth   For a brief time not long ago, the idea of avoiding all medication during childbirth gained favor in the United States. Instead, many women chose to reduce the pain of childbirth through techniques known as natural childbirth, and a method called prepared childbirth became popular. Today, at least some medication is used in the typical childbirth, but elements of natural childbirth and prepared childbirth remain popular (London & others, 2017).

Natural childbirth is a method that aims to reduce the mother's pain by decreasing her fear through education about childbirth and by teaching her to use breathing methods and relaxation techniques during delivery (Bacon & Tomich, 2017). This approach was developed in 1914 by English obstetrician Grantly Dick-Read. Dick-Read believed that the doctor's

> We must respect this instant of birth, this fragile moment. The baby is between two worlds, on a threshold.
>
> —**FREDERICK LEBOYER**
> *French Obstetrician, 20th Century*

doula A caregiver who provides continuous physical, emotional, and educational support to the mother before, during, and after childbirth.

analgesics Drugs used to alleviate pain, such as tranquilizers, barbiturates, and narcotics.

anesthesia Drugs used in late first-stage labor and during expulsion of the baby to block sensation in an area of the body or to block consciousness.

oxytocin A hormone that is sometimes administered during labor to stimulate contractions.

natural childbirth Method developed in 1914 by English obstetrician Grantly Dick-Read that attempts to reduce the mother's pain by decreasing her fear through education about childbirth and breathing methods and relaxation techniques during delivery.

An instructor conducting a Lamaze class.
What characterizes the Lamaze method?
©Purestock/Getty Images RF

prepared childbirth Developed by French obstetrician Ferdinand Lamaze, this childbirth method is similar to natural childbirth but teaches a special breathing technique to control pushing in the final stages of labor and also provides a more detailed anatomy and physiology course.

relationship with the mother plays an important role in reducing her perception of pain and that the doctor should be present, providing reassurance, during her active labor prior to delivery. One type of natural childbirth that is used today is the *Bradley Method,* which involves husbands as coaches, relaxation for easier birth, and prenatal nutrition and exercise.

French obstetrician Ferdinand Lamaze developed a method similar to natural childbirth that is known as **prepared childbirth,** or the Lamaze method. It includes a special breathing technique to control pushing in the final stages of labor, as well as more detailed education about anatomy and physiology than Dick-Read's approach provides. The Lamaze method has become very popular in the United States (Podgurski, 2016). The pregnant woman's partner usually serves as a coach who attends childbirth classes with her and encourages her to use specific breathing and relaxation techniques during delivery.

Many other prepared childbirth techniques have been developed (Bindler & others, 2017; Smith, 2017). They usually include elements of Dick-Read's natural childbirth or Lamaze's method, plus one or more other components. For instance, the Bradley method emphasizes the father's role as a labor coach. Virtually all of the prepared childbirth methods emphasize education, relaxation and breathing exercises, and support.

In sum, proponents of current natural and prepared childbirth methods believe that when information and support are provided, women know how to give birth. To read about one nurse whose research focuses on fatigue during childbearing and breathing exercises during labor, see the *Connecting with Careers* profile. And to read about the increased variety of techniques now being used to reduce stress and control pain during labor, see the *Caring Connections* interlude.

Cesarean Delivery   In a **cesarean delivery,** the baby is removed from the mother's uterus through an incision made in her abdomen. Cesarean deliveries also are performed if the baby is lying crosswise in the uterus, if the baby's head is too large to pass through the mother's pelvis, if the baby develops complications, or if the mother is bleeding vaginally.

Because of increased rates of respiratory complications, elective cesarean delivery is not recommended prior to 39 weeks of gestation unless there is an indication of fetal lung maturity (Greene, 2009). The benefits and risks of cesarean deliveries continue to be debated in the United States and around the world (Kupari & others, 2016; Ladewig, London, & Davidson, 2017). Some critics believe that too many babies are delivered by cesarean section in the United States (Blakey, 2011). The World Health Organization states that a country's cesarean rate should be 10 percent or less. The U.S. cesarean birth rate in 2015 was 32 percent, the lowest rate since 2007 (Martin &

connecting with careers

Linda Pugh, Perinatal Nurse

Perinatal nurses work with childbearing women to support health and growth during the childbearing experience. Linda Pugh (Ph.D., R.N.C.) is a perinatal nurse on the faculty at the Johns Hopkins University School of Nursing. She is certified as an inpatient obstetric nurse and specializes in the care of women during labor and delivery. Pugh teaches nursing to both undergraduate and graduate students. In addition to educating professional nurses and conducting research, Pugh consults with hospitals and organizations about women's health issues.

Pugh's research interests include nursing interventions with low-income breast-feeding women, ways to prevent and ameliorate fatigue during childbearing, and the effectiveness of breathing exercises during labor.

Linda Pugh (*right*) with a new mother and baby.
Courtesy of Dr. Linda Pugh

caring connections

From Waterbirth to Music Therapy

The effort to reduce stress and control pain during labor has recently led to an increase in the use of some older and some newer non-medicated techniques (Bindler & others, 2017; Henderson & others, 2014; Simkin & Bolding, 2004). These include waterbirth, massage, acupuncture, hypnosis, and music therapy.

Waterbirth

Waterbirth involves giving birth in a tub of warm water. Some women go through labor in the water and get out for delivery, while others remain in the water during the delivery. The rationale for waterbirth is that the baby has been in an amniotic sac for many months and that delivery in a similar environment is likely to be less stressful for the baby and the mother (Taylor & others, 2016). Mothers get into the warm water when contractions become closer together and more intense. Getting into the water too soon can cause labor to slow or stop. An increasing number of studies are either showing no differences in neonatal and maternal outcomes for waterbirth and non-waterbirth deliveries or positive outcomes (Davies & others, 2015; Taylor & others, 2016). For example, a recent large-scale study of more than 16,000 waterbirth and non-waterbirth deliveries found fewer negative outcomes for the waterbirth newborns (Bovjerg, Cheyney, & Everson, 2016). Further, a recent research review concluded that waterbirth is associated with high levels of maternal satisfaction and reduced use of drugs for pain relief during childbirth (Nutter & others, 2014). Waterbirth has been practiced more often in European countries such as Switzerland and Sweden than in the United States in recent decades, but it is increasingly being included in U.S. birth plans.

Massage

Massage is increasingly used to assist mothers prior to and during delivery (Frawley & others, 2016). Researchers have found that massage can reduce pain and anxiety during labor (Chang, Chen, & Huang, 2006; Jones & others, 2012). One study revealed that massage therapy reduced pain in pregnant women and alleviated prenatal depression in both parents and improved their relationship (Field, Diego, & Hernandez-Reif, 2008). A recent variation in traditional massage that is being used to relieve labor pain is Hoku point ice massage (Dehcheshmeh & Rafiel, 2015).

What characterizes the use of waterbirth in delivering a baby?
©Eddie Lawrence/Science Source

Acupuncture

Acupuncture, the insertion of very fine needles into specific locations in the body, is used as a standard procedure to reduce the pain of childbirth in China, although only recently has it been used in the United States for this purpose (Jo & Lee, 2017). Recent research indicates that acupuncture can have positive effects on labor and delivery (Smith, Armour, & Ee, 2016). For example, in a recent study acupuncture was successful in reducing labor pain 30 minutes after the intervention (Allameh, Tehrani, & Ghasemi, 2015).

Hypnosis

Hypnosis, the induction of a psychological state of altered attention and awareness in which the individual is unusually responsive to suggestions, is increasingly being used during childbirth (Madden & others, 2016; McAllister & others, 2017). Some studies have indicated positive effects of hypnosis for reducing pain during childbirth (Abbasi & others, 2011).

Music Therapy

Music therapy during childbirth, in which music is played to reduce stress and manage pain, is increasingly used (Hunter, 2009; Liu, Chang, & Chen, 2010). Few research studies have been conducted to determine its effectiveness, although a recent study found that both music therapy and Hoku point ice massage were effective in relieving labor pain (Dehcheshmeh & Rafiel, 2015).

---

others, 2017). The highest cesarean rates are in the Dominican Republic and Brazil (56 percent); the lowest in New Zealand and the Czech Republic (26 percent) (McCulloch, 2016).

What are some of the specific reasons that physicians perform cesarean deliveries? One of the most common reasons is failure to progress through labor (hindered by epidurals, for example) and fetal distress. Another reason for cesarean delivery involves the baby's positioning in the uterus. Normally the baby's head comes through the vagina first. But if the baby is in a **breech position,** the baby's buttocks would be the first part to emerge from the vagina. In 1 of every 25 deliveries, the baby's head is still in the uterus when the rest of the body is out. Breech births can cause respiratory problems.

cesarean delivery Delivery in which the baby is removed from the mother's uterus through an incision made in her abdomen. This also is sometimes referred to as a cesarean section.

breech position Position of the baby within the uterus that causes the buttocks to be the first part to emerge from the vagina.

THE TRANSITION FROM FETUS TO NEWBORN

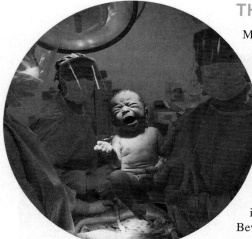

What characterizes the transition from fetus to newborn?
©ERproductions Ltd/Blend Images LLC RF

Much of our discussion of birth so far has focused on the mother. Being born also involves considerable stress for the baby. During each contraction, when the placenta and umbilical cord are compressed as the uterine muscles draw together, the supply of oxygen to the fetus decreases. If the delivery takes too long, the baby can develop *anoxia*, a condition in which the fetus or newborn receives an insufficient supply of oxygen. Anoxia can cause brain damage (London & others, 2017).

The baby has considerable capacity to withstand the stress of birth. Large quantities of adrenaline and noradrenaline, hormones that protect the fetus in the event of oxygen deficiency, are secreted in stressful circumstances. These hormones increase the heart's pumping activity, speed up heart rate, channel blood flow to the brain, and raise the blood-sugar level. Never again in life will such large amounts of these hormones be secreted. This circumstance underscores how stressful it is to be born and also how well prepared and adapted the fetus is for birth (Van Beveren, 2011).

At the time of birth, the baby is covered with a protective skin grease called *vernix caseosa*. This substance, which consists of fatty secretions and dead cells, is thought to help protect the baby's skin against heat loss before and during birth.

Immediately after birth, the umbilical cord is cut and the baby is on its own. Before birth, oxygen came from the mother via the umbilical cord, but now the baby is self-sufficient and can breathe on its own. Now 25 million little air sacs in the lungs must be filled with air. These first breaths may be the hardest ones an individual takes.

Review Connect Reflect

LG1 Discuss the stages, decisions involved, and transitions in birth.

Review

- What are the three stages involved in the birth process?
- What characterizes the childbirth setting and attendants?
- What are the main methods of childbirth?
- What is the fetus/newborn transition like?

Connect

- How might prenatal care be linked to the difficulty of the birth process?

Reflect *Your Own Personal Journey of Life*

- If you are a female who would like to have a baby, which birth strategy would you prefer? Why? If you are male, how involved would you want to be in helping your partner through the birth of your baby? Explain.

2 What Are Some Measures of Neonatal Health and Responsiveness?

 LG2 Describe three measures of neonatal health and responsiveness.

Apgar Scale A widely used method to assess the newborn's chances of survival and determine whether medical attention is needed.

Almost immediately after birth, after the baby and mother have been introduced, a newborn is taken to be weighed, cleaned up, and tested for signs of problems that might require urgent attention. The **Apgar Scale** is widely used to assess the newborn's chances of survival and determine whether medical attention is needed. The Apgar Scale is used one and five minutes after birth and evaluates infants' heart rate, respiratory effort, muscle tone, body color, and reflex irritability. An obstetrician or a nurse does the evaluation and gives the newborn a score, or reading, of 0, 1, or 2 on each of these five health signs (see Figure 2). A total score of 7 to 10 indicates that the newborn's condition is good; lower scores may indicate an emergency that requires medical attention.

The Apgar Scale is especially good at assessing the newborn's ability to respond to the stress of delivery and the demands of a new environment (Ladewig, London, & Davidson, 2017). It also identifies high-risk infants who need resuscitation. One study revealed that in comparison with children who have high Apgar scores (9 to 10), the risk of developing

Score	0	1	2
Heart rate	Absent	Slow—less than 100 beats per minute	Fast—100–140 beats per minute
Respiratory effort	No breathing for more than one minute	Irregular and slow	Good breathing with normal crying
Muscle tone	Limp and flaccid	Weak, inactive, but some flexion of extremities	Strong, active motion
Body color	Blue and pale	Body pink, but extremities blue	Entire body pink
Reflex irritability	No response	Grimace	Coughing, sneezing, and crying

FIGURE 2

THE APGAR SCALE. A newborn's score on the Apgar Scale indicates whether the baby has urgent medical problems. *What are some trends in the Apgar scores of U.S. babies?*

Art: *Source:* Apgar, V. "The Apgar Scale," A Proposal for a New Method of Evaluation of the Newborn Infant, from Anesthesia and Analgesia, vol 32. New York: Lippincott, Williams & Wilkins, 1953.

Photo: ©Jonathan Nourok/Stone/Getty Images

attention deficit hyperactivity disorder (ADHD) in childhood was 75 percent higher for newborns with low Apgar scores (1 to 4) and 63 percent higher for those with Apgar scores of 5 or 6 (Li & others, 2011). Recent studies have found that low Apgar scores are associated with long-term additional support needs in education and educational attainment (Tweed & others, 2016), risk of developmental vulnerability at 5 years of age (Razaz & others, 2016), and risk for developing ADHD (Hanc & others, 2016).

For a more thorough assessment of the newborn, however, the Brazelton Neonatal Behavioral Assessment Scale or the Neonatal Intensive Care Unit Network Neurobehavioral Scale may be used. The **Brazelton Neonatal Behavioral Assessment Scale (NBAS)** is typically performed within 24 to 36 hours after birth. It is also used as a sensitive index of neurological competence, behavior, and emotion up to one month after birth for typical infants and in many studies as a measure of infant development (Braithwaite & others, 2017; Zhang & others, 2017). The NBAS assesses the newborn's neurological development, reflexes, and reactions to people and objects. Sixteen reflexes, such as sneezing, blinking, and rooting, are assessed, along with reactions to circumstances, such as the infant's reaction to a rattle (Craciunoiu & Holsti, 2017).

A very low NBAS score can indicate brain damage, or stress to the brain that may heal in time. If an infant merely seems sluggish, parents are encouraged to give the infant attention and become more sensitive to the infant's needs. Parents are shown how the newborn can respond to people and how to stimulate such responses. These communications with parents can improve their interaction skills with both high-risk infants and healthy, responsive infants (Girling, 2006).

An "offspring" of the NBAS, the **Neonatal Intensive Care Unit Network Neurobehavioral Scale (NNNS)** provides a more comprehensive analysis of the newborn's behavior, neurological and stress responses, and regulatory capacities (Aubuchon-Endsley & others, 2017; Lester & others, 2011; Spittle & others, 2017). Whereas the NBAS was developed to assess normal, healthy, full-term infants, the NNNS was developed by T. Berry Brazelton, along with Barry Lester and Edward Tronick, to assess the "at-risk" infant. It is especially useful for evaluating preterm infants (although it may not be appropriate for those younger than 30 weeks' gestational age) and substance-exposed infants (Lester & others, 2011).

developmental **connection**

Physical Development

What are some individual differences in the reflex of sucking in young infants? Connect to "Physical Development in Infancy."

Brazelton Neonatal Behavioral Assessment Scale (NBAS) A test performed within 24 to 36 hours after birth to assess newborns' neurological development, reflexes, and reactions to people.

Neonatal Intensive Care Unit Network Neurobehavioral Scale (NNNS) An "offspring" of the NBAS, the NNNS provides a more comprehensive analysis of the newborn's behavior, neurological and stress responses, and regulatory capacities.

3 How Do Low Birth Weight and Preterm Infants Develop?

LG3 Characterize the development of low birth weight and preterm infants.

| Preterm and Small for Date Infants | Consequences of Preterm Birth and Low Birth Weight | Nurturing Preterm Infants |

---

developmental connection

Nutrition

One study revealed that taking folic acid either alone or as part of a multivitamin for one year prior to conceiving was linked to a substantial reduction in preterm birth (Bukowski & others, 2008). Connect to "Prenatal Development."

How Would You...?

If you were a **social worker**, how would you advise couples living in poverty who are considering having a child about ways to reduce the risk of having a low birth weight child?

low birth weight infants Babies that weigh less than 5½ pounds at birth.

preterm infants Babies born three weeks or more before the pregnancy has reached its full term.

small for date (small for gestational age) infants Babies whose birth weight is below normal when the length of pregnancy is considered.

Various conditions that pose threats for newborns have been given different labels. We next examine these conditions and discuss interventions for improving outcomes of preterm infants.

PRETERM AND SMALL FOR DATE INFANTS

Three related conditions pose threats to many newborns: having a low birth weight, being preterm, and being small for date. **Low birth weight infants** weigh less than 5½ pounds at birth. *Very low birth weight* newborns weigh less than 3½ pounds, and *extremely low birth weight* newborns weigh less than 2 pounds. **Preterm infants** are those born three weeks or more before the pregnancy has reached its full term—in other words, before the completion of 37 weeks of gestation (the time between fertilization and birth). **Small for date (small for gestational age) infants** are those whose birth weight is below normal when the length of the pregnancy is considered. They weigh less than 90 percent of what all babies of the same gestational age weigh. Small for date infants may be preterm or full term. One study found that small for date infants had more than a fourfold risk of death (Regev & others, 2003).

In 2015, 11.3 percent of U.S. infants were born preterm—a significant increase since the 1980s (Martin & others, 2017). The increase in preterm birth is likely due to such factors as the increasing number of births to women 35 years of age or older, increasing rates of multiple births, increased management of maternal and fetal conditions (for example, inducing labor preterm if medical technology indicates that it will increase the likelihood of survival), increased maternal substance abuse (tobacco, alcohol), and increased stress (Goldenberg & Culhane, 2007). Ethnic variations characterize preterm birth (Raglan & others, 2016; Sorbye, Wanigaratne, & Urgula, 2016). In 2015, the likelihood of being born preterm in the United States was 8.9 percent for non-Latino White infants, down from 11.4 percent in 2011 (Martin & others, 2017). The preterm birth rate was 13.4 percent for African American infants (down from 16.7 percent in 2011) and 9.1 for Latino infants, down from 11.6 percent in 2011 (Martin & others, 2017).

Recently, there has been considerable interest in the role that progestin might play in reducing preterm births (Awwad & others, 2015). A recent meta-analysis found that among women with preterm birth and a singleton pregnancy, progestin treatment reduced subsequent preterm birth by 22 percent and neonatal death by 42 percent (Likis & others, 2012). However, progestin did not prevent preterm birth and neonatal death in multiple gestations. Also, a recent study discovered that progestin treatment was associated with a decrease in preterm birth for women with a history of one or more spontaneous births (Markham & others, 2014).

See the *Connecting with Diversity* interlude to learn how the incidence and causes of low birth weight vary across countries.

Incidence and Causes of Low Birth Weight Around the World

Most, but not all, preterm babies are also low birth weight babies. The incidence of low birth weight varies considerably from country to country. In some countries, such as India and Sudan, where poverty is rampant and the health and nutrition of mothers are poor, the percentage of low birth weight babies reaches as high as 31 percent (see Figure 3). In the United States, there has been an increase in low birth weight infants in the last two decades, and the U.S. low birth weight rate of 8.1 percent in 2015 is considerably higher than that of many other developed countries (Martin & others, 2017). For example, only 4 percent of the infants born in Sweden, Finland, Norway, and Korea are low birth weight, and only 5 percent of those born in New Zealand, Australia, and France are low birth weight.

The causes of low birth weight also vary. In the developing world, low birth weight stems mainly from the mother's poor health and nutrition (Bird & others, 2017; Katz & others, 2013). For example, diarrhea and malaria, which are common in developing countries, can impair fetal growth if the mother becomes affected while she is pregnant. In developed countries, cigarette smoking during pregnancy is the leading cause of low birth weight (Fertig, 2010; Pereira & others, 2017). In both developed and developing countries, adolescents who give birth when their bodies have not fully matured are at risk for having low birth weight babies (Kirbas, Gulerman, & Daglar, 2016). In the United States, the increase in the number of low birth weight infants is due to such factors as the use of drugs, poor nutrition, multiple births, reproductive technologies, and improved technology and prenatal care, resulting in a higher survival rate of high-risk babies (Chen & others, 2007).

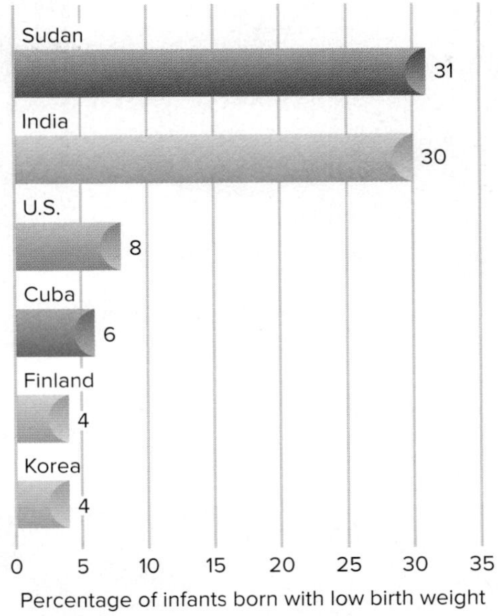

FIGURE 3

PERCENTAGE OF INFANTS BORN WITH LOW BIRTH WEIGHT IN SELECTED COUNTRIES

Nonetheless, poverty still is a major factor in preterm birth in the United States (Huynh & others, 2017; Wallace & others, 2016). Women living in poverty are more likely to be obese, have diabetes and hypertension, smoke cigarettes and use illicit drugs, and they are less likely to have regular prenatal care (Nagahawatte & Goldenberg, 2008).

CONSEQUENCES OF PRETERM BIRTH AND LOW BIRTH WEIGHT

Although most preterm and low birth weight infants are healthy, as a group they have more health and developmental problems than normal birth weight infants (London & others, 2017). For preterm birth, the terms *extremely preterm* and *very preterm* are increasingly used (Kato & others, 2016). *Extremely preterm infants* are those born at less than 28 weeks gestation, and *very preterm infants* are those born between 28 and 33 weeks of gestational age. Figure 4 shows the results of a Norwegian study indicating that the earlier preterm infants are born, the more likely they are to eventually drop out of school (Swamy, Ostbye, & Skjaerven, 2008).

The number and severity of these problems increase when infants are born very early and as their birth weight decreases (Tchamo, Prista, & Leandro, 2016). Survival rates for infants who are born very early and very small have risen, but with this improved survival rate have come increased rates of severe brain damage (Linsell & others, 2017; McNicholas & others, 2014). One study revealed that very preterm, low birth weight infants had abnormal axon development in their brains and impaired cognitive development at 9 years of age (Iwata & others, 2012). Low birth weight children are more likely than their normal birth weight counterparts to develop a learning disability, attention deficit hyperactivity disorder, autism spectrum disorders, or breathing problems such as asthma (Brinksma & others, 2017; Leung & others, 2016; Maramara, He, & Ming, 2014; Ng & others, 2017; Schieve & others, 2016). Approximately 50 percent of all low birth weight children are enrolled in special education programs.

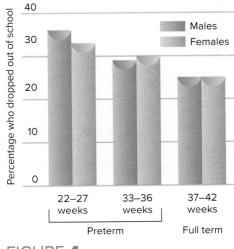

FIGURE 4

PERCENTAGE OF PRETERM AND FULL-TERM BIRTH INFANTS WHO DROPPED OUT OF SCHOOL

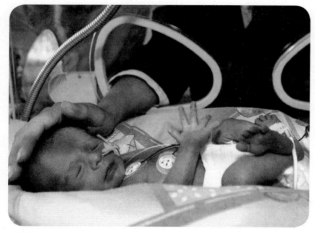

A "kilogram kid," weighing less than 2.3 pounds at birth. *What are some long-term outcomes for weighing so little at birth?*
©Diether Endlicher/AP Images

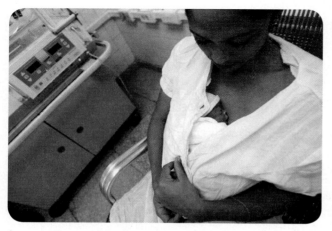

A new mother practicing kangaroo care. *What is kangaroo care?*
©Claudia Daut/Reuters/Alamy

How Would You...?

If you were a **health-care professional,** how would you advise hospital administrators about implementing kangaroo care or massage therapy in the neonatal intensive care unit?

- - - - - - - - - - →

developmental **connection**

Attachment

A classic study of infant monkeys with cloth and wire surrogate mothers demonstrated the important role that touch plays in infant attachment. Connect to "Socioemotional Development in Infancy."

← - - - - - - - - - -

kangaroo care A way of holding a preterm infant so that there is skin-to-skin contact.

A recent study examined the possible influence of genetic and prenatal environmental factors on whether an infant would be born preterm (Deater-Deckard, 2016). In this study, especially in very preterm infants, the identical twin who was smaller (an index of prenatal environmental experience) than his or her co-twin was far more likely to have poorer working memory and a lower level of effortful control at 8 years of age. This study documents how the prenatal environment can be a powerful influence on development, even when genetic influences are controlled (indexed by the twins' identical genetic makeup). Further, the most likely explanation of the outcomes in this study involves epigenetic factors.

NURTURING PRETERM INFANTS

An important strategy when considering how to treat low birth weight and preterm births is to reduce the risk of low birth weight before it occurs. Some effects of being born low in birth weight can be reduced or even reversed. Intensive enrichment programs that provide medical and educational services for both the parents and children can improve short-term outcomes for low birth weight children (Nearing & others, 2012).

At present, federal laws mandate that services for school-aged children must be expanded to include family-based care for infants born with severe disabilities. The availability of services for moderately low birth weight children who do not have severe physical problems varies, but most states do not provide these services.

Two increasingly used interventions in the neonatal intensive care unit (NICU) are kangaroo care and massage therapy. **Kangaroo care** involves skin-to-skin contact, in which the baby, wearing only a diaper, is held upright against the parent's bare chest, much as a baby kangaroo is carried by its mother (Hendricks-Munoz & Mayers, 2014; Stockwell, 2017). Kangaroo care is typically practiced for two to three hours per day, skin-to-skin over an extended time in early infancy.

Why use kangaroo care with preterm infants? Preterm infants often have difficulty coordinating their breathing and heart rate, and the close physical contact with the parent provided by kangaroo care can help to stabilize the preterm infant's heartbeat, temperature, and breathing (Boundy & others, 2017; Cho & others, 2016; Furman, 2017). Preterm and low birth weight infants who experience kangaroo care also gain more weight than their counterparts who are not given this care (Evereklian & Posmontier, 2017; Faye & others, 2016). Recent research also revealed that kangaroo care decreased pain in newborns (Johnston & others, 2017; Mooney-Leber & Brummelte, 2017). One study revealed that kangaroo care led to better physical development in low birth weight infants (Bera & others, 2014). Further, a recent study found that kangaroo care significantly reduced the amount of crying and improved the stability of heart rates in preterm infants (Choudhary & others, 2016). Also, a recent study in the United Kingdom found that the use of kangaroo care in neonatal units resulted in substantial cost savings mainly because of reduced rates of diseases such as gastroenteritis and colitis (Lowson & others, 2015). And in a longitudinal study, the nurturing positive effects of kangaroo care with preterm and low birth weight infants that were initially found for intelligence and home environment at 1 year of age were still positive 20 years later in emerging adults' reduced school absenteeism, reduced hyperactivity, lower aggressiveness, and higher levels of social skills (Charpak & others, 2017).

A recent U.S. survey found that mothers had a much more positive view of kangaroo care than did neonatal intensive care nurses and that the mothers were more likely to think it should be provided daily (Hendricks-Munoz & others, 2013). There is concern that kangaroo care is not used more often in neonatal intensive care units (Kymre, 2014; Smith & others, 2017). Increasingly, kangaroo care is recommended as standard practice for all newborns (Rodgers, 2013).

Many preterm infants experience less touch than full-term infants because they are isolated in temperature-controlled incubators. A recent study found that both kangaroo care and massage therapy were equally effective in improving body weight and reducing length of hospital stay for low birth weight infants (Rangey & Sheth, 2014). The research of Tiffany Field has led to a surge of interest in the role that massage might play in improving developmental outcomes for preterm infants. To read about Field's research, see the *Connecting with Research* interlude.

How Does Massage Therapy Benefit the Health and Well-Being of Babies?

Throughout history and in many cultures, caregivers have massaged infants. In Africa and Asia, infants are routinely massaged by parents or other family members for several months after birth. In the United States, interest in using touch and massage to improve the growth, health, and well-being of infants has been stimulated by the research of Tiffany Field (2001, 2007; Diego, Field, & Hernandez-Reif, 2008, 2014), director of the Touch Research Institute at the University of Miami School of Medicine.

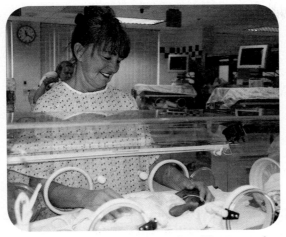

Tiffany Field massages a newborn infant. *What types of infants benefit from massage therapy?*
Courtesy of Dr. Tiffany Field

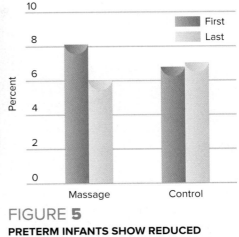
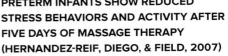

FIGURE 5

PRETERM INFANTS SHOW REDUCED STRESS BEHAVIORS AND ACTIVITY AFTER FIVE DAYS OF MASSAGE THERAPY (HERNANDEZ-REIF, DIEGO, & FIELD, 2007)

In one study, preterm infants in a neonatal intensive care unit (NICU) were randomly assigned to a massage therapy group or a control group. For five consecutive days, the preterm infants in the massage group were given three 15-minute moderate-pressure massages (Hernandez-Reif, Diego, & Field, 2007). Behavioral observations of the following stress behaviors were made on the first and last days of the study: crying, grimacing, yawning, sneezing, jerky arm and leg movements, startles, and finger flaring. The various stress behaviors were summarized in a composite stress behavior index. As indicated in Figure 5, massage had a stress-reducing effect on the preterm infants, which is especially important because they encounter numerous stressors while they are hospitalized.

In another study, Field and her colleagues (2004) tested a more cost-effective massage strategy. They taught mothers how to massage their full-term infants rather than having health-care professionals do the massage. Beginning from day one of the newborn's life to the end of the first month, once a day before bedtime the mothers massaged the babies using either light or moderate pressure. Infants who were massaged with moderate pressure gained more weight, performed better on the orientation scale of the Brazelton, were less excitable and less depressed, and were less agitated during sleep.

Field (2016) has demonstrated the benefits of massage therapy for infants who face a variety of problems. For example, preterm infants exposed to cocaine in utero who received massage therapy gained weight and improved their scores on developmental tests (Wheeden & others, 1993). In other research, massage therapy improved the scores of HIV-exposed infants on both physical and mental scales, while also improving their hearing and speech development (Perez & others, 2015). Another study investigated 1- to 3-month-old infants born to depressed adolescent mothers (Field & others, 1996). The infants of depressed mothers who received massage therapy had lower stress—as well as improved emotionality, sociability, and soothability—compared with nonmassaged infants of depressed mothers.

In a research review of massage therapy with preterm infants, Field and her colleagues (2004) concluded that the most consistent findings involve two positive results: (1) increased weight gain, and (2) discharge from the hospital three to six days earlier. A recent study revealed that the mechanisms responsible for increased weight gain as a result of massage therapy were stimulation of the vagus nerve (one of 12 cranial nerves leading to the brain), which in turn promoted the release of insulin (a food absorption hormone) (Field, Diego, & Hernandez-Reif, 2010). Another recent study found that both massage therapy (moderate-pressure stroking) and exercise (flexion and extension of the limbs) led to weight gain in preterm infants (Diego, Field, & Hernandez-Reif, 2014). In this study, massage was linked to increased vagal activity while exercise was associated with increased calorie consumption.

In light of Field's findings, do you think expectant parents should routinely be taught how to massage their infants, even when prenatal development and birth have gone smoothly? Why or why not?

Review Connect Reflect

LG3 Characterize the development of low birth weight and preterm infants.

Review

- What is a low birth weight infant? How can preterm and small for date infants be distinguished?
- What are the long-term outcomes for low birth weight infants?
- What is known about the roles of kangaroo care and massage therapy with preterm infants?

Connect

- What are some different types of learning disabilities?

Reflect *Your Own Personal Journey of Life*

- Imagine that you are the parent of a newborn. Would you rather have your newborn experience kangaroo care or massage therapy?

4 What Happens During the Postpartum Period?

LG4 Explain the physical and psychological aspects of the postpartum period.

Physical Adjustments

Emotional and Psychological Adjustments

Bonding

postpartum period The period after childbirth when the mother adjusts, both physically and psychologically, to the process of childbearing. This period lasts for about six weeks, or until her body has completed its adjustment and has returned to a near-prepregnant state.

The weeks after childbirth present challenges for many new parents and their offspring. This is the **postpartum period,** the period after childbirth or delivery that lasts for about six weeks or until the mother's body has completed its adjustment and has returned to a nearly prepregnant state. It is a time when the woman adjusts, both physically and psychologically, to the process of childbearing.

The postpartum period involves a great deal of adjustment and adaptation. The baby has to be cared for. The mother has to recover from childbirth, to learn how to take care of the baby, and to learn to feel good about herself as a mother. The father needs to learn how to take care of his recovering partner, to learn how to take care of the baby, and to learn how to feel good about himself as a father. Many health professionals believe that the best way to meet these challenges is with a family-centered approach that uses the family's resources to support an early and smooth adjustment to the newborn by all family members. The adjustments needed are physical, emotional, and psychological.

PHYSICAL ADJUSTMENTS

A woman's body makes numerous physical adjustments in the first days and weeks after childbirth (Durham & Chapman, 2014; Neiterman & Fox, 2017). She may have a great deal of energy or feel exhausted and let down. Most new mothers feel tired and need rest. Though these changes are normal, the fatigue can undermine the new mother's sense of well-being and confidence in her ability to cope with a new baby and a new family life (Doering, Sims, & Miller, 2017; Mon & others, 2017).

A concern is the loss of sleep that the primary caregiver experiences in the postpartum period (McBean, Kinsey, & Montgomery-Downs, 2016). One analysis indicated that the primary caregiver loses as much as 700 hours of sleep in the first year following the baby's birth (Maas, 2008). In the 2007 Sleep in America Survey, a substantial percentage of women reported loss of sleep during pregnancy and in the postpartum period (National Sleep Foundation, 2007) (see Figure 6). The loss of sleep can contribute to stress, relationship conflict, and impaired decision making (Thomas & Spieker, 2016). A recent study, though, found that postpartum depression was linked to poor sleep quality (such

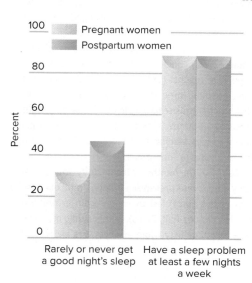

FIGURE 6

SLEEP DEPRIVATION IN PREGNANT AND POSTPARTUM WOMEN

as disrupted, fragmented sleep) rather than to lesser amounts of sleep (Park, Meltzer-Brody, & Stickgold, 2013).

After delivery, a mother's body undergoes sudden and dramatic changes in hormone production. When the placenta is delivered, estrogen and progesterone levels drop steeply and remain low until the ovaries start producing hormones again. **Involution** is the process by which the uterus returns to its prepregnant size five or six weeks after birth. Immediately following birth, the uterus weighs 2 to 3 pounds. By the end of five or six weeks, the uterus weighs 2 to 3½ ounces. Nursing the baby helps contract the uterus at a rapid rate.

If a woman has regularly engaged in conditioning exercises during pregnancy, exercise will help her recover her former body contour and strength. With a caregiver's approval, the new mother can begin some exercises as soon as one hour after delivery. One study found that women who maintained or increased their exercise from prepregnancy to postpartum had better well-being than women who engaged in no exercise or decreased their exercise from prepregnancy to postpartum (Blum, Beaudoin, & Caton-Lemos, 2005).

Relaxation techniques are also helpful during the postpartum period. Five minutes of slow breathing on a stressful day during the postpartum period can relax and refresh the new mother, and this will indirectly benefit the new baby.

EMOTIONAL AND PSYCHOLOGICAL ADJUSTMENTS

Emotional fluctuations are common for mothers in the postpartum period. For some women, emotional fluctuations decrease within several weeks after the delivery, but other women experience more long-lasting emotional swings (Pawluski, Lonstein, & Fleming, 2017).

As shown in Figure 7, about 70 percent of new mothers in the United States have what are called "baby blues." About two to three days after birth, they begin to feel depressed, anxious, and upset. These feelings may come and go for several weeks after the birth, often peaking about three to five days after birth.

Postpartum depression involves a major depressive episode that typically occurs about four weeks after delivery. In other words, women with postpartum depression have such strong feelings of sadness, anxiety, or despair that for at least a two-week period they have trouble coping with their daily tasks. Without treatment, postpartum depression may become worse and last for many months (Di Florio & others, 2014; O'Hara & McCabe, 2013). And many women with postpartum depression don't seek help. For example, one study found that 15 percent of the women reported postpartum depression symptoms but less than half sought help (McGarry & others, 2009). Estimates indicate that 10 to 14 percent of new mothers experience postpartum depression.

A recent research review concluded that the following are risk factors for developing postpartum depression: a history of depression, depression and anxiety during pregnancy, neuroticism, low self-esteem, postpartum blues, a poor marital relationship, and a low level of social support (O'Hara & McCabe, 2013). Also, in this research review, a number of perinatal-related stressors such as perinatal complications, infant health and temperament, and type of delivery (emergency cesarean section, for example) were found to be potential risk factors for postpartum depression. A subset of women are likely to develop postpartum depression in the context of hormonal changes associated with late pregnancy and childbirth (O'Hara & McCabe, 2013). Further, a recent study found that depression during pregnancy, a history of physical abuse, migrant status, and postpartum physical complications were major risk factors for postpartum depression (Gaillard & others, 2014). And another recent study revealed that women who had a history of depression were 20 times more likely to develop postpartum depression than women who had no history of depression (Silverman & others, 2017).

Several antidepressant drugs have been proposed as possibly effective in treating postpartum depression and appear to be safe for breast-feeding women (Logsdon, Wisner, & Hanusa, 2009). However, a recent research review concluded that there is no evidence that these drugs are more effective in treating postpartum depression than a placebo (O'Hara & McCabe, 2013). Psychotherapy, especially cognitive therapy, has been documented as a more effective treatment of postpartum depression for many women

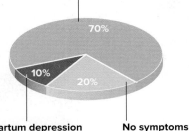

Postpartum blues
Symptoms appear 2 to 3 days after delivery and usually subside within 1 to 2 weeks.

70%

10% 20%

Postpartum depression
Symptoms linger for weeks or months and interfere with daily functioning.

No symptoms

FIGURE 7

POSTPARTUM BLUES AND POSTPARTUM DEPRESSION AMONG U.S. WOMEN. Some health professionals refer to the postpartum period as the "fourth trimester." Though the time span of the postpartum period does not necessarily cover three months, the term "fourth trimester" suggests continuity and the importance of the first several months after birth for the mother. *Source:* American College of Obstetricians and Gynecologists, Postpartum Depresssion, 2002.

involution The process by which the uterus returns to its prepregnant size.

postpartum depression Involves a major depressive episode characterized by strong feelings of sadness, anxiety, or despair in new mothers, making it difficult for them to carry out daily tasks.

(Bevan, Wittkowski, & Wells, 2013; Dennis, 2017). In addition, engaging in regular exercise may help reduce postpartum depression (Daley, Macarthur, & Winter, 2007; Ko & others, 2013).

A mother's postpartum depression can affect the way she interacts with her infant (Brummelte & Galea, 2016). A research review concluded that the interaction difficulties of depressed mothers and their infants occur across cultures and socioeconomic status groups, and encompass less sensitivity of the mothers and less responsiveness on the part of infants (Field, 2010). In a recent study, postpartum depression was associated with an increase in 4-month-old infants' unintentional injuries (Yamaoka, Fujiwara, & Tamiya, 2016). Further, a recent study revealed that mothers' postpartum depression, but not generalized anxiety, were linked to their children's emotional negativity and behavior problems at 2 years of age (Prenoveau & others, 2017). Several caregiving activities also are compromised, including feeding, sleep routines, and safety practices.

How is postpartum depression linked to children's development? Research indicates that children's physical health and cognitive development are affected (O'Hara & McCabe, 2013). Studies link postpartum depression to a lower level of cardiovascular functioning in children (Gump & others, 2009) and higher rates of gastrointestinal and respiratory infections (Ban & others, 2010). In terms of cognitive development, children whose mothers have postpartum depression are more likely to have a lower level of intelligence and poorer language development (Brand & Brennan, 2009).

To read about an individual who specializes in helping women adjust during the postpartum period, see the *Connecting with Careers* profile.

Fathers also undergo considerable adjustment in the postpartum period, even when they work away from home all day (Gutierrez-Galve & others, 2015; Paulson & others, 2016). When the mother develops postpartum depression, many fathers also experience depressed feelings (Gawlik & others, 2014; Sundstrom Poromaa & others, 2017). Many fathers feel that the baby comes first and gets all of the mother's attention; some feel that they have been replaced by the baby. A recent study found 5 percent of fathers had depressive symptoms in the first two weeks following delivery (Anding & others, 2016).

The father's support and caring can play a role in whether the mother develops postpartum depression (Darwom & others, 2017; Flanagan & others, 2015). One study revealed that a higher level of support by fathers was related to a lower incidence of postpartum depression in women (Smith &

The postpartum period is a time of considerable adjustment and adaptation for both the mother and the father. Fathers can provide an important support system for mothers, especially in helping mothers care for young infants. *What kinds of tasks might the father of a newborn do to support the mother?*
©Howard Grey/Getty Images RF

connecting with careers

Diane Sanford, Clinical Psychologist and Postpartum Expert

Diane Sanford has a doctorate in clinical psychology, and for many years she had a private practice that focused on marital and family relationships. But after she began collaborating with a psychiatrist whose clients included women with postpartum depression, Dr. Sanford, along with a women's health nurse, founded Women's Healthcare Partnership in St. Louis, Missouri, which specializes in women's adjustment during the postpartum period. Subsequently, they added a marriage and family relationships counselor and a social worker to their staff, and then later hired nurse educators, a dietician, and a fitness expert as consultants (Source: Clay, 2001).

Diane Sanford is a leading expert on postpartum depression.
Courtesy of Dr. Diane Sanford

Howard, 2008). Also, a recent study found that depressive symptoms in both the mother and father were associated with impaired bonding with their infant during the postpartum period (Kerstis & others, 2016).

Some fathers develop postpartum depression, and it can be detrimental to the child's development (Schumacher, Zubaran, & White, 2008). A recent study revealed that paternal postpartum depression (independent of maternal postpartum depression) was linked to psychological disorders in their children seven years later (Ramchandani & others, 2008).

To help the father adjust, parents should set aside some special time to spend together. The father's postpartum reaction also likely will be improved if he has taken childbirth classes with the mother and is an active participant in caring for the baby.

BONDING

A special component of the parent-infant relationship is **bonding,** the formation of a connection, especially a physical bond involving touch, between parents and the newborn in the period shortly after birth. Sometimes hospitals seem determined to deter bonding. Drugs given to the mother to make her delivery less painful can make the mother drowsy, interfering with her ability to respond to and stimulate the newborn. Mothers and newborns are often separated shortly after delivery, and preterm infants are isolated from their mothers even more than are full-term infants.

Do these practices do any harm? Some physicians believe that during the period shortly after birth, the parents and newborn need to form an emotional attachment as a foundation for optimal development in years to come (Kennell, 2006). Is there evidence that close contact between mothers in the first several days after birth is critical for optimal development later in life? Although some research supports this bonding hypothesis (Klaus & Kennell, 1976), a body of research challenges the significance of the first few days of life as a critical period (Bakeman & Brown, 1980; Rode & others, 1981). Indeed, the extreme form of the bonding hypothesis—the idea that the newborn must have close contact with the mother in the first few days of life to develop optimally— simply is not true.

Nonetheless, the weakness of the bonding hypothesis should not be used as an excuse to keep motivated mothers from interacting with their newborns. Such contact brings pleasure to many mothers. In some mother-infant pairs—including preterm infants, adolescent mothers, and mothers from disadvantaged circumstances—early close contact may establish a climate for improved interaction after the mother and infant leave the hospital.

Many hospitals now offer a rooming-in arrangement, in which the baby remains in the mother's room most of the time during its hospital stay. However, if parents choose not to use this rooming-in arrangement, the weight of the research suggests that this decision will not harm the infant emotionally (Lamb, 1994).

---- ➤

developmental **connection**

Theories

Lorenz demonstrated the importance of bonding in greylag geese, but the first few days of life are unlikely to be a critical period for bonding in human infants. Connect to "Introduction."

A mother bonds with her infant moments after it is born. *How critical is bonding for the development of social competence later in childhood?*

©Kaz Mori/The Image Bank/Getty Images

bonding A close connection, especially a physical bond, between parents and their newborn in the period shortly after birth.

Review Connect Reflect

 Explain the physical and psychological aspects of the postpartum period.

Review

- What does the postpartum period involve? What physical adjustments does the woman's body make during this period?
- What emotional and psychological adjustments characterize the postpartum period?
- Is bonding critical for optimal development?

Connect

- How can exercise help pregnant women before delivery and women with postpartum depression?

Reflect *Your Own Personal Journey of Life*

- If you are a female who plans to have children, what can you do to adjust effectively in the postpartum period? If you were the partner of a new mother, what could you do to help during the postpartum period?

topical connections *looking forward*

You will explore the physical, cognitive, and socioemotional development of infants, including key theoretical, research, and applied aspects of the first 18 to 24 months of life. You will learn about the remarkable and complex physical development of infants' motor skills, such as learning to sit and walk; read about the early development of infants' cognitive skills, such as the ability to form concepts; and examine infants' surprisingly sophisticated socioemotional development, as reflected in their motivation to share and perceive others' actions as intentionally motivated.

Next, you will follow the dramatic physical development of the infant through the first months of life, tracing how motor skills are acquired and how perception and the senses develop during a period of remarkable physical growth and change.

reach your **learning goals**

Birth

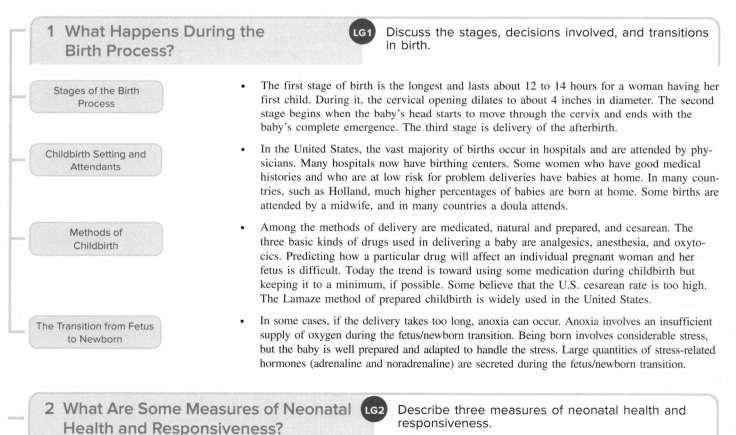

1 What Happens During the Birth Process?

LG1 Discuss the stages, decisions involved, and transitions in birth.

Stages of the Birth Process

Childbirth Setting and Attendants

Methods of Childbirth

The Transition from Fetus to Newborn

- The first stage of birth is the longest and lasts about 12 to 14 hours for a woman having her first child. During it, the cervical opening dilates to about 4 inches in diameter. The second stage begins when the baby's head starts to move through the cervix and ends with the baby's complete emergence. The third stage is delivery of the afterbirth.

- In the United States, the vast majority of births occur in hospitals and are attended by physicians. Many hospitals now have birthing centers. Some women who have good medical histories and who are at low risk for problem deliveries have babies at home. In many countries, such as Holland, much higher percentages of babies are born at home. Some births are attended by a midwife, and in many countries a doula attends.

- Among the methods of delivery are medicated, natural and prepared, and cesarean. The three basic kinds of drugs used in delivering a baby are analgesics, anesthesia, and oxytocics. Predicting how a particular drug will affect an individual pregnant woman and her fetus is difficult. Today the trend is toward using some medication during childbirth but keeping it to a minimum, if possible. Some believe that the U.S. cesarean rate is too high. The Lamaze method of prepared childbirth is widely used in the United States.

- In some cases, if the delivery takes too long, anoxia can occur. Anoxia involves an insufficient supply of oxygen during the fetus/newborn transition. Being born involves considerable stress, but the baby is well prepared and adapted to handle the stress. Large quantities of stress-related hormones (adrenaline and noradrenaline) are secreted during the fetus/newborn transition.

2 What Are Some Measures of Neonatal Health and Responsiveness?

LG2 Describe three measures of neonatal health and responsiveness.

- For many years, the Apgar Scale has been used to assess the newborn's health. It is used one and five minutes after birth and assesses heart rate, respiratory effort, muscle tone, body color, and reflex irritability.

- The Brazelton Neonatal Behavioral Assessment Scale (NBAS) is performed within 24 to 36 hours after birth to evaluate the newborn's neurological development, reflexes, and reactions to people.
- Recently, the Neonatal Intensive Care Unit Network Neurobehavioral Scale (NNNS) was constructed; it provides a more comprehensive analysis of the newborn's behavior, neurological and stress responses, and regulatory capacities.

3 How Do Low Birth Weight and Preterm Infants Develop?

 LG3 Characterize the development of low birth weight and preterm infants.

- Preterm and Small for Date Infants
- Consequences of Preterm Birth and Low Birth Weight
- Nurturing Preterm Infants

- Low birth weight infants weigh less than 5½ pounds at birth. Low birth weight babies may be preterm (born three weeks or more before the pregnancy has reached full term) or small for date (also called small for gestational age, which refers to infants whose birth weight is below normal when the length of pregnancy is considered). Small for date infants may be preterm or full term.
- Although most low birth weight babies are normal and healthy, as a group they have more health and developmental problems than full-term babies do. The number and severity of the problems increase when infants are born very early and at very low birth weight.
- Kangaroo care, a way of holding a preterm infant so that there is skin-to-skin contact, has positive effects on preterm infants. Massage therapy is increasingly being used with preterm infants and has positive outcomes.

4 What Happens During the Postpartum Period?

LG4 Explain the physical and psychological aspects of the postpartum period.

- Physical Adjustments
- Emotional and Psychological Adjustments
- Bonding

- The postpartum period is the period after childbirth or delivery. It is a time when the woman adjusts, both physically and psychologically, to the process of childbearing. It lasts for about six weeks, or until the body has completed its adjustment. Physical adjustments include fatigue, involution, hormonal changes that include a dramatic drop in estrogen and progesterone, and exercises to recover former body contour and strength.
- Emotional fluctuations are common among mothers during the postpartum period. These fluctuations may be due to hormonal changes, fatigue, inexperience or lack of confidence in caring for a newborn, or the extensive demands involved in caring for a newborn. For some, these emotional fluctuations are minimal and disappear within a few weeks, but for others they can be more long-lasting. Postpartum depression involves such strong feelings of sadness, anxiety, or despair that new mothers have difficulty carrying out daily tasks. Postpartum depression affects approximately 10 percent of new mothers.
- The father also goes through a postpartum adjustment. He may feel that the baby now receives all of his wife's attention. Being an active participant in caring for the baby helps ease the father's postpartum reaction. Both parents need to set aside special time to spend together.
- Bonding refers to the formation of a connection between parents and the newborn shortly after birth. Bonding has not been found to be critical in the development of a competent infant or child, although it may stimulate positive interaction in some mother-infant pairs.

key terms

afterbirth
analgesics
anesthesia
Apgar Scale
bonding
Brazelton Neonatal Behavioral
    Assessment Scale (NBAS)

breech position
cesarean delivery
doula
involution
kangaroo care
low birth
    weight infants

natural childbirth
Neonatal Intensive Care Unit
    Network Neurobehavioral
    Scale (NNNS)
oxytocin
postpartum
    depression

postpartum period
prepared
    childbirth
preterm infants
small for date
    (small for gestational
    age) infants

key people

T. Berry Brazelton
Grantly Dick-Read

Tiffany Field
Ferdinand Lamaze

Barry Lester

Edward Tronick

connecting with improving the lives of children

STRATEGIES

Preparing for Childbirth

Here are some birth strategies that may benefit the baby and the mother:

· *Take a childbirth class.* These classes provide information about the childbirth experience.

· *Become knowledgeable about different childbirth techniques.* We considered a number of different childbirth techniques in this chapter, including Lamaze and use of doulas. Obtain more detailed information about such techniques by reading an informative book, such as *YOU: Having a Baby* by Michael Rosen and Mehmet Oz (New York: Free Press, 2011) and *Be Prepared: A Practical Handbook for New Dads* by Gary Greenberg and Jeannie Hayden (New York: Simon & Schuster, 2004).

· *Use positive intervention with at-risk infants.* Massage can improve the developmental outcome of at-risk infants. Intensive enrichment programs that include medical, educational, psychological, occupational, and physical domains can benefit low birth weight infants. Intervention with low birth weight infants should involve an individualized plan.

· *Involve the family in the birth process.* If they are motivated to participate, the husband, partner, and siblings can benefit from being involved in the birth process. A mother, sister, or friend can also provide support.

· *Know about the adaptation required in the postpartum period.* The postpartum period involves considerable adaptation and adjustment by the mother and the father. The mother's adjustment is both physical and emotional. Exercise and relaxation techniques can benefit mothers during the postpartum period. So can an understanding, supportive husband.

RESOURCES

Lamaze International
www.lamaze.com

Lamaze provides information about the Lamaze method and taking or teaching Lamaze classes.

***The Doula Book* (2002)**
Marshall Klaus, John Kennell, and Phyllis Klaus
New York: Perseus Books

Learn more about how valuable a doula can be in the childbirth process.

Birth: Issues in Perinatal Care
This multidisciplinary journal on perinatal care is written for health professionals and contains articles on research and clinical practice, review articles, and commentary.

International Cesarean Awareness Network
www.ican-online.org
This organization provides extensive information and advice about cesarean birth.

Postpartum Support International (PSI)
www.postpartum.net
PSI provides information about postpartum depression.

section three

Babies are such a nice way to start people.

—Don Herold
American Writer, 20th Century

Infancy

As newborns, we were not empty-headed organisms. We had some basic competencies. We slept a lot, and occasionally we smiled, although the meaning of our first smiles was not entirely clear. We ate and we grew. We crawled and then we walked, a journey of a thousand miles beginning with a single step. Sometimes we conformed; sometimes others conformed to us. Our development was a continuous creation of more complex forms. Our helpless kind demanded meeting the eyes of love. We juggled the necessity of curbing our will with becoming what we could will freely. Section 3 contains three chapters: "Physical Development in Infancy," "Cognitive Development in Infancy," and "Socioemotional Development in Infancy."

chapter 5

PHYSICAL DEVELOPMENT IN INFANCY

chapter outline

Latonya is a newborn baby in Ghana. During her first days of life, she has been kept apart from her mother and bottle fed. Manufacturers of infant formula provide the hospital where she was born with free or subsidized milk powder. Her mother has been persuaded to bottle feed rather than breast feed her. When her mother bottle feeds Latonya, she overdilutes the milk formula with unclean water. Latonya's feeding bottles have not been sterilized. Latonya becomes very sick. She dies before her first birthday.

Ramona was born in a Nigerian hospital with a "baby-friendly" program. In this program, babies are not separated from their mothers when they are born, and the mothers are encouraged to breast feed them. The mothers are told of the perils that bottle feeding can bring because of unsafe water and unsterilized bottles. They also are informed about the advantages of breast milk, which include its nutritious and hygienic qualities, its ability to immunize babies against common illnesses, and its role in reducing the mother's risk of breast and ovarian cancer. Ramona's mother is breast feeding her. At 1 year of age, Ramona is very healthy.

For many years, maternity units in hospitals favored bottle feeding and did not give mothers adequate information about the benefits of breast feeding. In recent years, the World Health Organization and UNICEF have tried to reverse the trend toward bottle feeding of infants in many impoverished countries. They instituted a baby-friendly program in many of these countries. They also persuaded the International Association of Infant Formula Manufacturers to stop marketing their baby formulas to hospitals in countries where the government supports the baby-friendly initiatives. For the hospitals themselves, costs actually were reduced as infant formula, feeding bottles, and separate nurseries became unnecessary. For example, baby-friendly Jose Fabella Memorial Hospital in the Philippines reported saving 8 percent of its annual budget. Still, there are many places in the world where the baby-friendly initiatives have not been implemented (UNICEF, 2004).

The advantages of breast feeding in impoverished countries are substantial (UNICEF, 2017; Williams & others, 2016). However, these advantages must be balanced against the risk of passing HIV to the baby through breast milk if the mother has the virus; the majority of mothers don't know their HIV status (Coovadia & Moodley, 2016; Mnyani & others, 2017; Wojcicki, 2017). In some areas of Africa, more than 30 percent of mothers have the HIV virus.

(Top) An HIV-infected mother breast feeding her baby in Nairobi, Africa. *(Bottom)* A Rwandan mother bottle feeding her baby. *What are some concerns about breast versus bottle feeding in impoverished countries?*

(Top) ©Wendy Stone/Corbis/Getty Images; *(bottom)* ©Dave Bartruff/Corbis/Getty Images

topical connections *looking **back***

You have read about the transformation from fetus to newborn, and the baby's remarkable capacity to withstand the stress of the birth process. You learned how preterm and low birth weight babies can be nurtured in their first days and weeks of life, and how new mothers adjust—physically and psychologically—during the postpartum period. In this chapter, you will read about many aspects of the infant's physical development, including breathtaking advances in the development of the brain, motor skills, and perception.

preview

It is very important for infants to get a healthy start. When they do, their first two years of life are likely to be a time of amazing development. In this chapter, we focus on the biological domain and the infant's physical development, exploring physical growth, motor development, and sensory and perceptual development.

1 How Do Infants Grow and Develop Physically?

LG1 Discuss physical growth and development in infancy.

Patterns of Growth | Height and Weight | The Brain | Sleep | Nutrition | Health

> A baby is the most complicated object made by unskilled labor.
>
> —**ANONYMOUS**

PATTERNS OF GROWTH

An extraordinary proportion of the total body is occupied by the head during prenatal development and early infancy (see Figure 1). The **cephalocaudal pattern** is the sequence in which the earliest growth always occurs at the top—the head—with physical growth and differentiation of features gradually working their way down from top to bottom (for example,

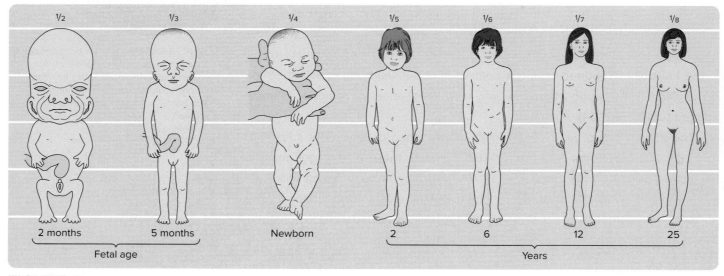

| 1/2 | 1/3 | 1/4 | 1/5 | 1/6 | 1/7 | 1/8 |

| 2 months | 5 months | Newborn | 2 | 6 | 12 | 25 |

Fetal age | Years

FIGURE 1

CHANGES IN PROPORTIONS OF THE HUMAN BODY DURING GROWTH. As individuals develop from infancy through adulthood, one of the most noticeable physical changes is that the head becomes smaller in relation to the rest of the body. The fractions listed refer to head size as a proportion of total body length at different ages.

shoulders, middle trunk, and so on). This same pattern occurs in the head area, because the top parts of the head—the eyes and brain—grow faster than the lower parts, such as the jaw.

Sensory and motor development generally proceed according to the cephalocaudal principle (London & others, 2017). For example, infants see objects before they can control their torso, and they can use their hands long before they can crawl or walk. However, development does not follow a rigid blueprint. One study found that infants reached for toys with their feet prior to reaching with their hands (Galloway & Thelen, 2004). On average, infants first touched the toy with their feet when they were 12 weeks old and with their hands when they were 16 weeks old.

Growth also follows the **proximodistal pattern,** the sequence in which growth starts at the center of the body and moves toward the extremities. For example, infants control the muscles of their trunk and arms before they control their hands and fingers, and they use their whole hands before they can control several fingers.

HEIGHT AND WEIGHT

The average North American newborn is 20 inches long and weighs 7½ pounds. Ninety-five percent of full-term newborns are 18 to 22 inches long and weigh between 5½ and 10 pounds.

In the first several days of life, most newborns lose 5 to 7 percent of their body weight before they adjust to feeding by sucking, swallowing, and digesting. Then they grow rapidly, gaining an average of 5 to 6 ounces per week during the first month. They have doubled their birth weight by the age of 4 months and have nearly tripled it by their first birthday. Infants grow about 1 inch per month during the first year, reaching approximately 1½ times their birth length by their first birthday.

Growth slows considerably in the second year of life (Bindler & others, 2017). By 2 years of age, infants weigh approximately 26 to 32 pounds, having gained a quarter to half a pound per month during the second year; now they have reached about one-fifth of their adult weight. At 2 years of age, the average infant is 32 to 35 inches in height, which is nearly half of their adult height.

An important point about growth is that it often is not smooth and continuous but rather is *episodic*, occurring in spurts (Adolph & Berger, 2015). In infancy, growth spurts may occur in a single day and alternate with long time frames characterized by little or no growth for days and weeks (Lampl & Johnson, 2011; Lampl & Schoen, 2017). In two analyses, in a single day, infants grew 0.7 inch in length (Lampl, 1993) and their head circumference increased 0.3 inch (Caino & others, 2010).

THE BRAIN

We described the amazing growth of the brain from conception to birth in "Prenatal Development." By the time it is born, the infant that began as a single cell is estimated to have a brain that contains approximately 100 billion nerve cells, or neurons. Extensive brain development continues after birth, through infancy and later (Crone, 2017; de Haan & Johnson, 2016; Sullivan & Wilson, 2018).

Because the brain is still developing so rapidly in infancy, the infant's head should be protected from falls or other injuries and the baby should never be shaken. *Shaken baby syndrome,* which includes brain swelling and hemorrhaging, affects hundreds of babies in the United States each year (Bartschat & others, 2016; Hellgren & others, 2017). A recent analysis found that fathers most often were the perpetrators of shaken baby syndrome, followed by child-care providers and boyfriends of the victims' mothers (National Center on Shaken Baby Syndrome, 2012).

Researchers have been successful in using the electroencephalogram (EEG), a measure of the brain's electrical activity, to learn about the brain's development in infancy (Hari & Puce, 2017; Perry & others, 2016) (see Figure 2). For example, a recent study found that higher-quality mother-infant interaction early in infancy predicted higher-quality frontal lobe functioning that was assessed with EEG later in infancy (Bernier, Calkins, & Bell, 2016).

Recently Patricia Kuhl and her colleagues at the Institute for Learning and Brain Sciences at the University of Washington have been using magnetoencephalography, or MEG, brain-imaging machines to assess infants' brain activity. MEG maps brain activity by recording magnetic fields produced by electrical currents and is being used with infants to assess perceptual and cognitive activities such as vision, hearing, and language (see Figure 3).

cephalocaudal pattern The sequence in which the earliest growth always occurs at the top—the head—with physical growth and feature differentiation gradually working from top to bottom.

proximodistal pattern The sequence in which growth starts at the center of the body and moves toward the extremities.

How Would You...?
If you were a **health-care professional,** how would you talk with parents about shaken baby syndrome?

FIGURE 2

MEASURING THE ACTIVITY OF AN INFANT'S BRAIN WITH AN ELECTROENCEPHALOGRAM (EEG). By attaching up to 128 electrodes to a baby's scalp to measure the brain's activity, Charles Nelson and his colleagues (2006) have found that newborns produce distinctive brain waves that reveal they can distinguish their mother's voice from another woman's, even while they are asleep. *Why is it so difficult to measure infants' brain activity?*
Courtesy of Vanessa Vogel Farley

FIGURE 3

MEASURING THE ACTIVITY OF AN INFANT'S BRAIN WITH MAGNETOEN-CEPHALOGRAPHY (MEG). This baby's brain activity is being assessed with a MEG brain-imaging device while the baby is listening to spoken words in a study at the Institute of Learning and Brain Sciences at the University of Washington. The infant sits under the machine and when he or she experiences a word, touch, sight, or emotion, the neurons working together in the infant's brain generate magnetic fields and MEG pinpoints the location of the fields in the brain.

©Dr. Patricia Kuhl, Institute for Learning and Brain Sciences, University of Washington

FIGURE 4

FUNCTIONAL NEAR-INFRARED SPECTROSCOPY (fNIRS). This brain-imaging technique is increasingly being used to examine the brain activity of infants. fNIRS is non-invasive and can assess infants as they move and explore their environment.

©Oli Scarff/Getty Images

developmental **connection**

Brain Development

How does the brain change from conception to birth? Connect to "Prenatal Development."

forebrain The region of the brain that is farthest from the spinal cord and includes the cerebral cortex and several structures beneath it.

cerebral cortex Tissue that covers the forebrain like a wrinkled cap and includes two halves, or hemispheres.

Researchers also are increasingly using functional near-infrared spectroscopy (fNIRS), which uses very low levels of near-infrared light to monitor changes in blood oxygen, to study infants' brain activity (de Haan & Johnson, 2016; Emberson, 2017; Emberson & others, 2017b; Kashou & others, 2017) (see Figure 4). Unlike fMRI, which uses magnetic fields or electrical activity, fNIRS is portable and allows the infants to be assessed as they explore the world around them.

The following researchers and many others are uncovering new information about the brain's development in infancy:

- Martha Ann Bell and her colleagues (Bell, 2015; Bell & Cuevas, 2012, 2014, 2015; Bell & others, 2018; Bell, Ross, & Patton, 2017; Li & others, 2017; Lusby & others, 2017; Perry & others, 2016; Smith & others, 2016) are studying brain-behavior links, emotion regulation, and the integration of cognition and emotion.

- Charles Nelson and his colleagues (Bick & Nelson, 2017; Bick & others, 2017; Finch & others, 2017; McLaughlin, Sheridan, & Nelson, 2017; Nelson, 2007, 2013a, b; Nelson, Fox, & Zeanah, 2014; Righi & others, 2014; Vanderwert & others, 2016; Varcin & others, 2016) are exploring various aspects of memory development, face recognition and facial emotion, and the role of experience in influencing the course of brain development.

- Mark Johnson and his colleagues (Anzures & others, 2016; Gliga & others, 2017; Johnson, Jones, & Gliga, 2015; Johnson, Senju, & Tomalski, 2015; Johnson & others, 2015; Milosavlijevic & others, 2017; Saez de Urabain, Nuthmann, & Johnson, 2017; Senju & others, 2016) are examining neuroconstructivist links between the brain, cognitive and perceptual processes, and environmental influences; their research focuses on the development of the prefrontal cortex and its function, early identification of autism, face processing, and early social experiences.

- John Richards and his colleagues (Emberson & others, 2017a; Lloyd-Fox & others, 2015; Richards, 2009, 2010, 2013; Richards & others, 2015; Richards, Reynolds, & Courage, 2010; Xie & Richards, 2016, 2017) are examining sustained attention, perception of TV programs, and eye movements.

The Brain's Development At birth, the newborn's brain is about 25 percent of its adult weight. By the second birthday, the brain is about 75 percent of its adult weight. However, the brain's areas do not mature uniformly.

Mapping the Brain Scientists analyze and categorize areas of the brain in numerous ways. We are most concerned with the portion farthest from the spinal cord, known as the **forebrain,** which includes the cerebral cortex and several structures beneath it. The **cerebral cortex** covers the forebrain like a wrinkled cap. It has two halves, or hemispheres (see Figure 5). Based on ridges and valleys in the cortex, scientists distinguish four main areas, called lobes, in each hemisphere. Although the lobes usually work together, each has a somewhat different primary function (see Figure 6):

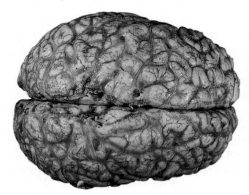

FIGURE 5

THE HUMAN BRAIN'S HEMISPHERES. The two hemispheres of the human brain are clearly seen in this photograph. It is a myth that the left hemisphere is the exclusive location of language and logical thinking or that the right hemisphere is the exclusive location of emotion and creative thinking.

©A.Glauberman/Science Source

- *Frontal lobes* are involved in voluntary movement, thinking, personality, emotion, memory, sustained attention, and intentionality or purpose.

- *Occipital lobes* function in vision.

- *Temporal lobes* have an active role in hearing, language processing, and memory.

- *Parietal lobes* play important roles in registering spatial location, maintaining attention, and administering motor control.

To some extent, the type of information handled by neurons depends on whether they are in the left or right hemisphere of the cortex (McAvoy & others, 2016). Speech and grammar, for example, depend on activity in the left hemisphere in most people; humor and the use of metaphors depend on activity in the right hemisphere (Holler-Wallscheid & others, 2017). This specialization of function in one hemisphere of the cerebral cortex or the other is called **lateralization.** However, most neuroscientists agree that complex functions such as reading or performing music involve both hemispheres. Labeling people as "left-brained" because they are logical thinkers and "right-brained" because they are creative thinkers does not correspond to the way the brain's hemispheres work (Stroobant, Buijus, & Vingerhoets, 2009). Complex thinking in normal people is the outcome of communication between both hemispheres of the brain (Nora & others, 2017; Ries, Dronkers, & Knight, 2016).

At birth, the hemispheres of the cerebral cortex already have started to specialize: Newborns show greater electrical brain activity in the left hemisphere than the right hemisphere when they are listening to speech sounds (Hahn, 1987). How do the areas of the brain in the newborn and the infant differ from those in an adult, and why do the differences matter? Important differences have been documented at both cellular and structural levels.

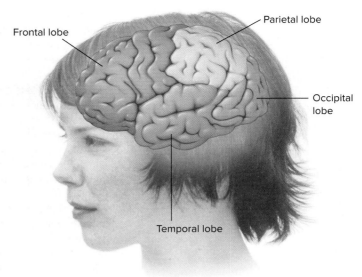

FIGURE 6

THE BRAIN'S FOUR LOBES. Shown here are the locations of the brain's four lobes: frontal, occipital, temporal, and parietal.

lateralization Specialization of function in one hemisphere of the cerebral cortex or the other.

Changes in Neurons Within the brain, the type of nerve cells called neurons send electrical and chemical signals, communicating with each other. As we discussed in "Prenatal Development," a *neuron* is a nerve cell that handles information processing (see Figure 7). Extending from the neuron's cell body are two types of fibers known as axons and dendrites. Generally, the axon carries signals away from the cell body and dendrites carry signals toward it. A *myelin sheath,* which is a layer of fat cells, encases many axons (see Figure 7). The myelin sheath insulates axons and helps electrical signals travel faster down the axon (Cercignani & others, 2017). Myelination also is involved in providing energy to neurons and in facilitating communication between them (Kiray & others, 2016; Tomassy, Dershowitz, & Arlotta, 2016). At the end of the axon are terminal buttons that release chemicals called *neurotransmitters* into synapses, which are tiny gaps between neurons' fibers. Chemical interactions in synapses connect axons and dendrites, allowing information to pass from neuron to neuron (Beart, 2016).

Think of the synapse as a river that blocks a road. A delivery truck arrives at one bank of the river, crosses by ferry, and continues its journey to market. Similarly, a message in the brain is "ferried" across the synapse by a neurotransmitter, which pours out information contained in chemicals when it reaches the other side of the river.

How complex are these neural connections? In a recent analysis, it was estimated that each of the billions of neurons is connected to as many as 1,000 other neurons, producing neural networks with trillions of connections (de Haan, 2015).

Neurons change in two very significant ways during the first years of life. First, *myelination,* the process of encasing axons with fat cells, begins prenatally and continues after birth, even into adolescence and emerging adulthood (Juraska & Willing, 2017; Monahan & others, 2016). Second, connectivity among neurons increases, creating new neural pathways. New dendrites grow, connections among dendrites increase, and synaptic connections between axons and dendrites proliferate. Whereas myelination speeds up neural transmissions, the expansion of dendritic connections facilitates the spreading of neural pathways in infant development.

Researchers have discovered an intriguing aspect of synaptic connections: Nearly twice as many of these connections are made as will ever be used (Huttenlocher & Dabholkar, 1997).

FIGURE 7

THE NEURON. (*a*) The dendrites of the cell body receive information from other neurons, muscles, or glands through the axon. (*b*) Axons transmit information away from the cell body. (*c*) A myelin sheath covers most axons and speeds information transmission. (*d*) As the axon ends, it branches out into terminal buttons.

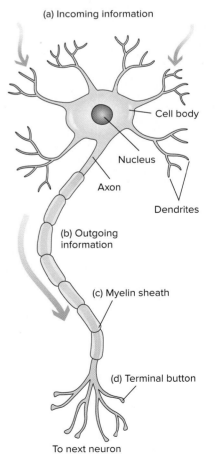

(a) Incoming information

Cell body

Nucleus

Axon

Dendrites

(b) Outgoing information

(c) Myelin sheath

(d) Terminal button

To next neuron

The connections that are used grow stronger and survive, while the unused ones are replaced by other pathways or disappear (Gould, 2017; Selemon, 2016). In the language of neuroscience, these connections are "pruned." For example, the more a baby engages in physical activity or uses language, the more those pathways will be strengthened.

Changes in Regions of the Brain   Figure 8 vividly illustrates the dramatic growth and later pruning of synapses in the visual, auditory, and prefrontal cortex (Huttenlocher & Dabholkar, 1997). Notice that "blooming and pruning" vary considerably by brain region. In the prefrontal cortex, the area of the brain where higher-level thinking and self-regulation occur, the peak of overproduction occurs at just over 3 years of age; it is not until middle to late adolescence that the adult density of synapses is achieved. Both heredity and environment are thought to influence the timing and course of synaptic overproduction and subsequent retraction.

Meanwhile, the pace of myelination also varies in different areas of the brain (Croteau-Chonka & others, 2016; Gogtay & Thompson, 2010). Myelination for visual pathways occurs rapidly after birth and is completed in the first six months. Auditory myelination is not completed until 4 or 5 years of age.

In general, some areas of the brain, such as the primary motor areas, develop earlier than others, such as the primary sensory areas. The frontal lobes are immature in the newborn. However, as neurons in the frontal lobes become myelinated and interconnected during the first year of life, infants develop an ability to regulate their physiological states, such as sleep, and gain more control over their reflexes. Cognitive skills that require deliberate thinking do not emerge until later in the first year (Bell, Ross, & Patton, 2017). Indeed, the prefrontal region of the frontal lobe has the most prolonged development of any brain region, with changes detectable at least into adolescence and emerging adulthood (Juraska & Willing, 2017).

Early Experience and the Brain   Children who grow up in a deprived environment may have depressed brain activity (Bick & others, 2017; Gao & others, 2016; McLaughlin,

developmental **connection**

Brain Development

Changes in the prefrontal cortex in adolescents have important implications for their development. Connect to "Physical Development in Adolescence."

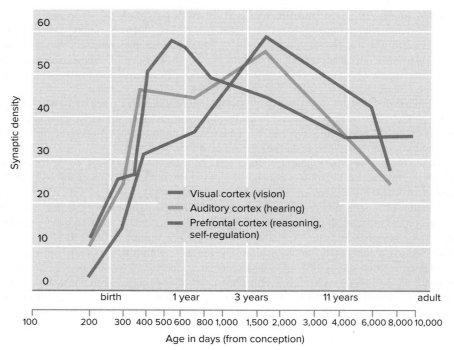

FIGURE **8**

SYNAPTIC DENSITY IN THE HUMAN BRAIN FROM INFANCY TO ADULTHOOD. The graph shows the dramatic increase and then pruning in synaptic density for three regions of the brain: visual cortex, auditory cortex, and prefrontal cortex. Synaptic density is believed to be an important indication of the extent of connectivity between neurons.

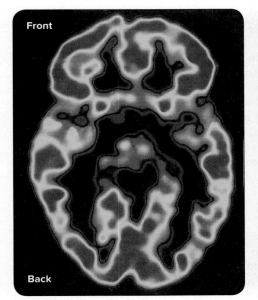
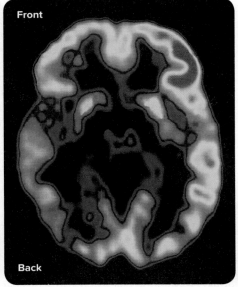

(a)

(b)

FIGURE 9

EARLY DEPRIVATION AND BRAIN ACTIVITY. These two photographs are PET (positron emission tomography) scans—which use radioactive tracers to image and analyze blood flow and metabolic activity in the body's organs. These scans show the brains of (a) a typically developing child and (b) an institutionalized Romanian orphan who experienced substantial deprivation since birth. In PET scans, the highest to lowest brain activity is reflected in the colors of red, yellow, green, blue, and black, respectively. As can be seen, red and yellow show up to a much greater degree in the PET scan of the typically developing child than in that of the deprived Romanian orphan.

Courtesy of Dr. Harry T. Chugani, Children's Hospital of Michigan

developmental **connection**

Nature and Nurture

In the epigenetic view, development is an ongoing, bidirectional interchange between heredity and environment. Connect to "Biological Beginnings."

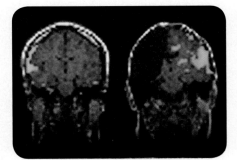

(a)

(b)

FIGURE 10

PLASTICITY IN THE BRAIN'S HEMISPHERES. (a) Michael Rehbein at 14 years of age. (b) Michael's right hemisphere has reorganized to take over the language functions normally carried out by corresponding areas in the left hemisphere of an intact brain (shown at left). However, the right hemisphere is not as efficient as the left, and more areas of the brain are recruited to process speech.

Courtesy of The Rehbein Family

Sheridan, & Nelson, 2017; Nelson, Fox, & Zeanah, 2014). As shown in Figure 9, a child who grew up in the unresponsive and unstimulating environment of a Romanian orphanage showed considerably depressed brain activity compared with a child who grew up in a normal environment.

Are the effects of deprived environments reversible? There is reason to think that at least for some individuals the answer is yes (Bick & Nelson, 2017; de Haan & Johnson, 2016; McLaughlin, Sheridan, & Nelson, 2017; Sharma, Classen, & Cohen, 2013). The brain demonstrates both flexibility and resilience. Consider 14-year-old Michael Rehbein. At age 7, he began to experience uncontrollable seizures—as many as 400 a day. Doctors said the only solution was to remove the left hemisphere of his brain where the seizures were occurring. Recovery was slow, but his right hemisphere began to reorganize and take over functions that normally occur in the brain's left hemisphere, including speech (see Figure 10).

Neuroscientists believe that what wires the brain—or rewires it, in the case of Michael Rehbein—is repeated experience. Each time a baby tries to touch an attractive object or gazes intently at a face, tiny bursts of electricity shoot through the brain, knitting together neurons into circuits. The results are some of the behavioral milestones we discuss in this chapter.

The Neuroconstructivist View Not long ago, scientists thought that our genes determined how our brains were "wired" and that the brain cells responsible for processing information just maturationally unfolded with little or no input from environmental experiences. Whatever brain your heredity dealt you, you were essentially stuck with. This view, however, turned out to be wrong. Instead, it has become clear that the brain has plasticity and its development depends on context (Bick & Nelson, 2017; D'Souza & Karmiloff-Smith, 2017; Ismail, Fatemi, & Johnston, 2017; Villeda, 2017).

The infant's brain depends on experiences to determine how connections are made (Bick & others, 2017; Vogels, 2017). Before birth, it appears that genes mainly direct basic wiring patterns. Neurons grow and travel to distant places awaiting further instructions (Shenoda, 2017). After birth, the inflowing stream of sights, sounds, smells, touches, language, and eye contact help shape the brain's neural connections.

In the increasingly popular **neuroconstructivist view,** (a) biological processes (genes, for example) and environmental experiences (enriched or impoverished, for example) influence the brain's development; (b) the brain has plasticity and is influenced by contexts; and (c) development of the brain is closely linked with the child's cognitive development. These factors constrain or advance the construction of cognitive skills (Crone, 2017; D'Souza & Karmiloff-Smith, 2017; Goldberg, 2017; Westermann, Thomas, & Karmiloff-Smith, 2011). The neuroconstructivist view emphasizes the importance of interactions between experience and gene expression in the brain's development, in much the same way that the epigenetic view proposes (Moore, 2017; Ismael, Fatemi, & Johnston, 2017; Westermann, 2016).

SLEEP

developmental **connection**

Sleep

What are some sleep problems that can develop in childhood and adolescence? Connect to "Physical Development in Early Childhood" and "Physical Development in Adolescence."

neuroconstructivist view In this view, biological processes and environmental conditions influence the brain's development; the brain has plasticity and is context dependent; and brain development is closely linked with cognitive development.

When we were infants, sleep consumed more of our time than it does now (Lushington & others, 2014). Newborns sleep 16 to 17 hours a day, although some sleep more and others less—the range is from a low of about 10 hours to a high of about 21 hours per day. A research review concluded that infants 0 to 2 years of age slept an average of 12.8 hours out of the 24, within a range of 9.7 to 15.9 hours (Galland & others, 2012). One study revealed that by 6 months of age the majority of infants slept through the night, awakening their mothers only once or twice a week (Weinraub & others, 2012).

Although total sleep remains somewhat consistent for young infants, their sleep during the day does not always follow a rhythmic pattern. An infant might change from sleeping for long bouts of 7 or 8 hours to three or four shorter sessions only several hours in duration. By about 1 month of age, most infants have begun to sleep longer at night. By 6 months of age, they usually have moved closer to adult-like sleep patterns, spending their longest span of sleep at night and their longest span of waking during the day (Sadeh, 2008).

The most common infant sleep-related problem reported by parents is nighttime waking (Hospital for Sick Children & others, 2010). Surveys indicate that 20 to 30 percent of infants have difficulty going to sleep and staying asleep at night (Sadeh, 2008). One study revealed that maternal depression during pregnancy, early introduction of solid foods, infant TV viewing, and child-care attendance were related to shorter duration of infant sleep (Nevarez & others, 2010). And a recent study found that nighttime wakings at 1 year of age predicted lower sleep efficiency at 4 years of age (Tikotzky & Shaashua, 2012).

REM Sleep In REM sleep, the eyes flutter beneath closed lids; in non-REM sleep, this type of eye movement does not occur and sleep is quieter (Sankupellay & others, 2011). Figure 11 shows developmental changes in the average number of total hours spent in REM and non-REM sleep. By the time they reach adulthood, individuals spend about one-fifth of their night in REM sleep, and REM sleep usually appears about one hour after non-REM sleep. However, about half of an infant's sleep is REM sleep, and infants often begin their sleep cycle with REM sleep rather than non-REM sleep (Sadeh, 2008). A much greater amount of time is taken up by REM sleep in infancy than at any other point in the life span (Funk & others, 2016). By the time infants reach 3 months of age, the percentage of time they spend in REM sleep falls to about 40 percent, and REM sleep no longer begins their sleep cycle.

Why do infants spend so much time in REM sleep? Researchers are not certain. The large amount of REM sleep may provide infants with added self-stimulation, since they spend less time awake than do older children. REM sleep also might promote the brain's development in infancy (Graven, 2006).

When adults are awakened during REM sleep, they frequently report that they have been dreaming, but when they are awakened during non-REM sleep they are much less likely to report they have been dreaming (Cartwright & others, 2006). Since infants spend more time than adults in REM sleep, can we conclude that they dream a lot? We don't know whether infants dream or not, because they don't have any way of reporting dreams.

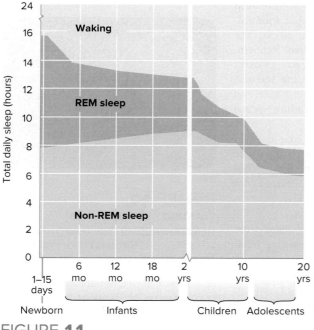

FIGURE 11

DEVELOPMENTAL CHANGES IN REM AND NON-REM SLEEP

Shared Sleeping   Some child experts stress that there are benefits to shared sleeping (as when an infant sleeps in the same bed with its mother). They state that it can promote breast feeding, lets the mother respond more quickly to the baby's cries, and allows her to detect breathing pauses in the baby that might be dangerous (Pelayo & others, 2006). Sharing a bed with a mother is common practice in many countries, such as Guatemala and China, whereas in others, such as the United States and Great Britain, most newborns sleep in a crib, either in the same room as the parents or in a separate room.

Shared sleeping remains a controversial issue (Burnham, 2014). Some experts recommend shared sleeping and others argue against it, although recently the recommendation trend in the United States has been to avoid infant-parent bed sharing, especially before the infant is 6 months of age (Byard, 2012a, b; Hoffend & Sperhake, 2014; Weber & others, 2012). The American Academy of Pediatrics Task Force on Infant Positioning and SIDS (AAPT-FIPS) (2000) recommends against shared sleeping. Its members argue that in some instances bed sharing might lead to sudden infant death syndrome (SIDS), as could be the case if a sleeping mother rolls over on her baby. Recent studies have found that bed sharing is linked with a greater incidence of SIDS, especially when parents smoke (Byard, 2012a, b; Senter & others, 2010). And a study of 2-month-old infants revealed that they had more sleep problems such as disordered breathing when they shared a bed with parents (Kelmanson, 2010).

SIDS   **Sudden infant death syndrome (SIDS)** is a condition that occurs when infants stop breathing, usually during the night, and die suddenly without an apparent cause. SIDS remains the most frequent cause of infant death in the United States, with nearly 3,000 infant deaths attributed to it annually (Heron, 2016). Risk of SIDS is highest at 2 to 4 months of age, decreasing considerably after 6 months of age (NICHD, 2017).

Since 1992, the American Academy of Pediatrics (AAP) has recommended that infants be placed to sleep on their backs to reduce the risk of SIDS, and the frequency of prone sleeping (on their stomachs) among U.S. infants has dropped dramatically (AAPTFIPS, 2000). Researchers have found that SIDS does indeed decrease when infants sleep on their backs rather than their stomachs or sides (Carlin & Moon, 2017; Moon, Hauck, & Colson, 2016; Siren, 2017). Among the reasons given for prone sleeping being a high-risk factor for SIDS are that it impairs the infant's arousal from sleep and restricts the infant's ability to swallow effectively (Franco & others, 2010).

In addition to sleeping in a prone position, researchers have found that the following are risk factors for SIDS:

- SIDS occurs more often in infants with abnormal brain stem functioning involving the neurotransmitter serotonin (Rognum & others, 2014; Rubens & Sarnat, 2013).
- Heart arrhythmias are estimated to occur in as many as 15 percent of SIDS cases, and recent studies found that gene mutations were linked to the occurrence of these arrhythmias (Brion & others, 2012; Sarquella-Brugada & others, 2016).
- Six percent of infants with sleep apnea, a temporary cessation of breathing in which the airway is completely blocked, usually for 10 seconds or longer, die of SIDS (Ednick & others, 2010).
- Breast feeding is linked to a lower incidence of SIDS (Byard, 2013).
- Low birth weight infants are 5 to 10 times more likely to die of SIDS than are their normal-weight counterparts (Horne & others, 2002).
- SIDS is more likely to occur in infants who do not use a pacifier when they go to sleep than in those who do use a pacifier (Carlin & Moon, 2017; Walsh & others, 2014). A recent research review of 27 studies confirmed that pacifier use is linked to a lower incidence of SIDS (Alm & others, 2016).
- Infants whose siblings have died of SIDS are two to four times as likely to die of it (Lenoir, Mallet, & Calenda, 2000).
- African American and Eskimo infants are four to six times as likely as all others to die of SIDS (Ige & Shelton, 2004; Kitsantas & Gaffney, 2010; Moon, Hauck, & Colson, 2017).
- SIDS is more common in lower socioeconomic groups (Hogan, 2014).
- Breast feeding is linked to a lower incidence of SIDS (Carlin & Moon, 2017).
- SIDS is more common in infants who are passively exposed to cigarette smoke (Jarosinska & others, 2014).

Is this a good sleep position for infants? Why or why not?
©Picture Partners/age fotostock

How Would You...?
If you were a **health-care professional,** how would you advise parents about preventing SIDS?

sudden infant death syndrome (SIDS) A condition that occurs when an infant stops breathing, usually during the night, and suddenly dies without an apparent cause.

- SIDS is more common when infants and parents share the same bed (Carlin & Moon, 2017; Senter & others, 2010). A recent Swedish study confirmed that bed sharing was more common in SIDS cases than in other types of infant deaths (Mollborg & others, 2015).
- SIDS is more common if infants sleep in soft bedding (Carlin & Moon, 2017; McGarvey & others, 2006).
- SIDS is less common when infants sleep in a bedroom with a fan. One study revealed that sleeping in a bedroom with a fan lowers the risk of SIDS by 70 percent (Coleman-Phox, Odouli, & Li, 2008).

In a recent analysis, it was concluded that after prone sleeping, the two factors that best predict SIDS are (1) maternal smoking, and (2) bed sharing (Mitchell & Krous, 2015). Also, one concern about the "back to sleep movement" of ensuring that young infants sleep on their back rather than their stomach is a decline in prone skills. To prevent this decline, many mothers provide their young infants with "tummy time" by periodically placing them on their stomachs when they are awake.

Sleep and Cognitive Development   Might infant sleep be linked to children's cognitive development? One study revealed that infants who did most of their sleeping at night (rather than during the daytime) engaged in a higher level of executive function at age 4 (Bernier & others, 2013). Another study revealed that a lower quality of sleep at 1 year of age was linked to lower attention regulation and more behavior problems at 3 to 4 years of age (Sadeh & others, 2015). And in another recent study, infants with poorer sleep patterns showed more distractibility during an attention task (Geva, Yaron, & Kuint, 2016). The link between infant sleep and children's cognitive functioning likely occurs because of sleep's role in brain maturation and memory consolidation, which may improve daytime alertness and learning.

NUTRITION

From birth to 1 year of age, human infants nearly triple their weight and increase their length by 50 percent. What do they need to sustain this growth, and what characterizes their eating behavior?

Nutritional Needs and Eating Behavior   Individual differences among infants in terms of their nutrient reserves, body composition, growth rates, and activity patterns make defining actual nutrient needs difficult (Rolfes & Pinna, 2018; Schiff, 2017). However, because parents need guidelines, nutritionists recommend that infants consume approximately 50 calories per day for each pound they weigh—more than twice an adult's requirement per pound.

A number of developmental changes involving eating characterize the infant's first year (Black & Hurley, 2007). As infants' motor skills improve, they change from using suck-and-swallow movements with breast milk or formula to chew-and-swallow movements with semisolid and then more complex foods. As their fine motor control improves in the first year, they transition from being fed by others toward self-feeding. "By the end of the first year of life, children can sit independently, can chew and swallow a range of textures, are learning to feed themselves, and are making the transition to the family diet and meal patterns" (Black & Hurley, 2007, p. 1). At this point, infants need to have a diet that includes a variety of foods—especially fruits and vegetables.

Caregivers play very important roles in infants' early development of eating patterns (Brown, 2017; Harrison, Brodribb, & Hepworth, 2017). Caregivers who are not sensitive to developmental changes in infants' nutritional needs, neglectful caregivers, and conditions of poverty can contribute to the development of eating problems in infants (Perez-Escamilla & Moran, 2017). One study found that low maternal sensitivity when infants were 15 and 24 months of age was linked to a higher risk of obesity in adolescence (Anderson & others, 2012).

A national study of more than 3,000 randomly selected 4- to 24-month-olds documented that many U.S. parents aren't feeding their babies enough fruits and vegetables but are feeding

developmental **connection**

Nutrition

Children's eating behavior is strongly influenced by their caregivers' behavior. Connect to "Physical Development in Early Childhood."

them too much junk food (Fox & others, 2004). Up to one-third of the babies ate no vegetables and fruit but frequently ate French fries, and almost half of the 7- to 8-month-old babies were fed desserts, sweets, or sweetened drinks. By 15 months, French fries were the most common vegetable the babies ate. Such poor dietary patterns early in development can result in more infants being overweight (Blake, 2017).

Breast Versus Bottle Feeding

For the first four to six months of life, human milk or an alternative formula is the baby's source of nutrients and energy. For years, debate has focused on whether breast feeding is better for the infant than bottle feeding. The growing consensus is that breast feeding is better for the baby's health (DeBruyne & Pinna, 2017; Schiff, 2017).

Since the 1970s, breast feeding by U.S. mothers has soared (see Figure 12). In 2016, 81 percent of U.S. mothers breast fed their newborns, and 52 percent breast fed their 6-month-olds (Centers for Disease Control and Prevention, 2016). The American Academy of Pediatrics Section on Breastfeeding (2012) reconfirmed its recommendation of exclusive breast feeding in the first six months followed by continued breast feeding as complementary foods are introduced, with further breast feeding for one year or longer as mutually desired by the mother and infant.

What are some of the benefits of breast feeding? The following conclusions reflect the current state of research.

Evaluation of Benefits for the Child

- *Gastrointestinal infections.* Breast-fed infants have fewer gastrointestinal infections (Le Doare & Kampmann, 2014).
- *Lower respiratory tract infections.* Breast-fed infants have fewer lower respiratory tract infections (Prameela, 2011).
- *Allergies.* A research review by the American Academy of Pediatrics indicated that there is no evidence that breast feeding reduces the risk of allergies in children (Greer & others, 2008). A recent Danish study also found that breast feeding did not protect against allergic sensitization in early childhood and allergy-related diseases at 7 years of age (Jelding-Dannemand, Malby Schoos, & Bisgaard, 2015).
- *Asthma.* The recent research review by the American Academy of Pediatrics concluded that exclusive breast feeding for three months protects against wheezing in babies, but whether it prevents asthma in older children is unclear (Greer & others, 2008).
- *Otitis media.* Breast-fed infants are less likely to develop this middle ear infection (Pelton & Leibovitz, 2009).
- *Overweight and obesity.* Consistent evidence indicates that breast-fed infants are less likely to become overweight or obese in childhood, adolescence, and adulthood (Carling & others, 2015; Rossiter & others, 2015).
- *Diabetes.* Breast-fed infants are less likely to develop type 1 diabetes in childhood (Ping & Hagopian, 2006) and type 2 diabetes in adulthood (Villegas & others, 2008).
- *SIDS.* Breast-fed infants are less likely to experience SIDS (Wennergen & others, 2015).

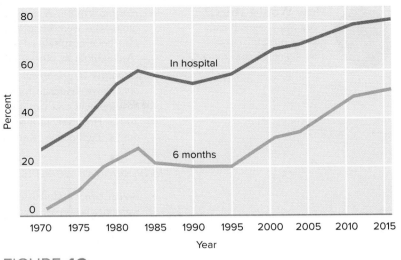

FIGURE 12

TRENDS IN BREAST FEEDING IN THE UNITED STATES: 1970–2016. Human milk or an alternative formula is a baby's source of nutrients for the first four to six months. The growing consensus is that breast feeding is better for the baby's health, although controversy still swirls about the issue of breast feeding versus bottle feeding. *Why is breast feeding strongly recommended by pediatricians?*

Human milk or an alternative formula is a baby's source of nutrients for the first four to six months. The growing consensus is that breast feeding is better for the baby's health, although controversy still swirls about the issue of breast feeding versus bottle feeding. *Why is breast feeding strongly recommended by pediatricians?*
©Blend Images/Getty Images RF

How Would You...?

If you were a **health-care professional,** how would you advise mothers about whether to breast feed or bottle feed their infants?

- *Hospitalization.* A recent study of more than 500,000 Scottish children found that those who were breast fed exclusively at 6 to 8 weeks of age were less likely to have ever been hospitalized through early childhood than their formula-fed counterparts (Ajetunmobi & others, 2015).
- *Cognitive development and cardiovascular health.* In a large-scale research review, no conclusive evidence for benefits of breast feeding was found for children's cognitive development and cardiovascular system (Agency for Healthcare Research and Quality, 2007). However, in a recent study, breast feeding did result in a small increase in children's intelligence (Kanazawa, 2015).

Evaluation of Benefits for the Mother

- *Breast cancer.* Consistent evidence indicates a lower incidence of breast cancer in women who breast feed their infants (Akbari & others, 2011).
- *Ovarian cancer.* Evidence also reveals a reduction in ovarian cancer in women who breast feed their infants (Stuebe & Schwarz, 2010).
- *Type 2 diabetes.* Some evidence suggests a small reduction in type 2 diabetes in women who breast feed their infants (Jager & others, 2014).
- *Weight loss, bone health, and mental health.* In a large-scale research review, no conclusive evidence could be found for maternal benefits of breast feeding on return to prepregnancy weight, osteoporosis, and postpartum depression (Agency for Healthcare Research and Quality, 2007; Ip & others, 2009).

Which women are least likely to breast feed? They include mothers who work full-time outside the home, mothers under age 25, mothers without a high school education, African American mothers, and mothers in low-income circumstances (Colen & Ramey, 2014; Merewood & others, 2007). In one study of low-income mothers in Georgia, interventions (such as counseling focused on the benefits of breast feeding and the free loan of a breast pump) increased the incidence of breast feeding (Ahluwalia & others, 2000). Increasingly, mothers who return to work in the infant's first year of life use a breast pump to extract breast milk that can be stored for later feeding of the infant when the mother is not present.

The American Academy of Pediatrics Section on Breastfeeding (2012) strongly endorses breast feeding throughout the first year of life. Are there circumstances when mothers should not breast feed? Yes. A mother should not breast feed (1) when the mother is infected with HIV or some other infectious disease that can be transmitted through her milk, (2) if she has active tuberculosis, or (3) if she is taking any drug that may not be safe for the infant (Brown & others, 2017; Schultz, Kostic, & Kharasch, 2017; Williams & others, 2016).

Some women cannot breast feed their infants because of physical difficulties; others feel guilty if they terminate breast feeding early. Mothers may also worry that they are depriving their infants of important emotional and psychological benefits if they bottle feed rather than breast feed. Some researchers have found, however, that there are no psychological differences between breast-fed and bottle-fed infants (Ferguson, Harwood, & Shannon, 1987; Young, 1990).

A further issue in interpreting the benefits of breast feeding was underscored in a large-scale research review (Ip & others, 2009). While highlighting a number of breast feeding benefits for children and mothers, the report issued a caution about breast feeding research: None of the findings imply causality. Breast versus bottle feeding studies are correlational, not experimental, and women who breast feed are wealthier, older, more educated, and likely more health-conscious than their bottle-feeding counterparts—characteristics that could explain why breast-fed children are healthier.

developmental **connection**

Research Methods

How does a correlational study differ from an experimental study? Connect to "Introduction."

Malnutrition in Infancy   Many infants around the world are malnourished (UNICEF, 2017). Early weaning of infants from breast milk to inadequate sources of nutrients, such as unsuitable and unsanitary cow's milk formula, can cause protein deficiency and malnutrition in infants. However, as we saw in the chapter-opening story, a concern in developing countries is the increasing number of women who are HIV-positive and the fear that they will transmit this virus to their offspring (Mnyani & others, 2017; Williams & others, 2016). Breast feeding is more optimal for mothers and infants in developing countries, except for mothers who have or are suspected of having HIV/AIDS.

A special concern in many developing countries is child undernutrition involving inadequate intake of micronutrients. This problem has sometimes been called the "hidden hunger" when it occurs in individuals who get adequate calories but the micronutrient content of their diet is inadequate. According to the World Health Organization (WHO) (2017), iron deficiency is the most significant micronutrient deficiency in developing countries. More than 30 percent of the world's population is anemic, in many cases because of iron deficiency. Other micronutrient deficiencies include vitamin A (the leading cause of preventable blindness in children), zinc (can increase susceptibility to pneumonia and malaria), and iodine (can cause brain damage) (Hwalla & others, 2017; Lazarus, 2017a, b).

Two life-threatening conditions that can result from malnutrition are marasmus and kwashiorkor. **Marasmus** is caused by a severe protein-calorie deficiency and results in a wasting away of body tissues in the infant's first year. The infant becomes grossly underweight and his or her muscles atrophy. **Kwashiorkor,** caused by severe protein deficiency, usually appears between 1 and 3 years of age. Children with kwashiorkor sometimes appear to be well fed even though they are not because the disease can cause the child's abdomen and feet to swell with water (Ahrens & others, 2008). Kwashiorkor causes a child's vital organs to collect the nutrients that are present and deprive other parts of the body of them. The child's hair becomes thin, brittle, and colorless, and the child's behavior often becomes listless.

Even if not fatal, severe and lengthy malnutrition is detrimental to physical, cognitive, and social development (UNICEF, 2017; Wardlaw, Smith, & Collene, 2018). One study found that Asian Indian children who had a history of chronic malnutrition performed more poorly on tests of attention and memory than their counterparts who were not malnourished (Kar, Rao, & Chandramouli, 2008). And a longitudinal study revealed that Barbadians who had experienced moderate to severe protein/energy malnutrition during infancy had persisting attention deficits when they were 40 years old (Galler & others, 2012).

Researchers also have found that interventions can benefit individuals who have experienced malnutrition in infancy. For example, in one study standard nutritional care combined with a psychosocial intervention (group meetings with mothers and play sessions with infants, as well as six months of home visits) reduced the negative effects of malnutrition on severely malnourished Bangladeshi 6- to 24-month-olds' cognitive development (Najar & others, 2008). To read further about providing nutritional supplements to improve infants' and young children's nutrition, see the *Caring Connections* interlude.

Adequate early nutrition is an important aspect of healthy development (Rolfes & Pinna, 2018; Schiff, 2017). In addition to sound nutrition, children need a nurturing, supportive environment (Blake, 2017). One individual who has stood out as an advocate of caring for children is T. Berry Brazelton, who is featured in the *Connecting with Careers* profile.

HEALTH

Among the most important measures used to promote infant health are immunization and accident prevention. Immunization has greatly improved children's health.

Immunization   One of the most dramatic advances in infant health has been the decline of infectious disease over the last five decades because of widespread immunization for preventable diseases. Although many available immunizations can be given at any age, the recommended schedule is to begin in infancy. The recommended ages for various immunizations are presented in Figure 13.

Accident Prevention   Accidents are a major cause of death in infancy and childhood, especially from 6 to 12 months of age (Cameron & others, 2017). Infants need to be closely monitored as they acquire increased locomotor and manipulative skills along

marasmus A wasting away of body tissues in the infant's first year, caused by severe protein-calorie deficiency.

kwashiorkor A condition caused by a severe deficiency in protein in which the child's abdomen and feet become swollen with water; usually appears between 1 and 3 years of age.

Age	Immunization
Birth	Hepatitis B
2 months	Diphtheria, tetanus, pertussis Polio Influenza Pneumococcal
4 months	Hepatitis B Diphtheria, tetanus, pertussis Polio Influenza Pneumococcal
6 months	Diphtheria, tetanus, pertussis Influenza Pneumococcal
1 year	Influenza Pneumococcal
15 months	Measles, mumps, rubella Influenza Varicella
18 months	Hepatitis B Diphtheria, tetanus, pertussis Polio
4 to 6 years	Diphtheria, tetanus, pertussis Polio Measles, mumps, rubella
11 to 12 years	Measles, mumps, rubella
14 to 16 years	Tetanus, diphtheria

FIGURE 13

RECOMMENDED IMMUNIZATION SCHEDULE FOR INFANTS AND CHILDREN

Improving the Nutrition of Infants and Young Children Living in Low-Income Families

Poor nutrition is a special concern in the lives of infants in low-income families in the United States. To address this problem, the WIC (Women, Infants, and Children) program provides federal grants to states for healthy supplemental foods, health-care referrals, and nutrition education for women from low-income families beginning in pregnancy, and to infants and young children up to 5 years of age who are at nutritional risk (Chang, Brown, & Nitzke, 2017; Kennedy & Guthrie, 2016). WIC serves approximately 7,500,000 participants in the United States.

Positive influences on infants' and young children's nutrition and health have been found for participants in WIC (Gross & others, 2017; Martinez-Brockman & others, 2017). A recent study revealed that a WIC program that introduced peer counseling services for pregnant women increased breast feeding initiation by 27 percent (Olson & others, 2010). Another study found that entry in the first trimester of pregnancy to the WIC program in Rhode Island reduced maternal cigarette smoking (Brodsky, Viner-Brown, & Handler, 2009). And a multiple-year literacy intervention with Spanish-speaking families in the WIC program in Los Angeles increased literacy resources and activities at home, which in turn led to a higher level of school readiness in children (Whaley & others, 2011). Also, in recent longitudinal studies, when mothers participated prenatally and in early childhood in WIC programs, young

Participants in the WIC program. *What are some of the changes that were implemented in the WIC program recently?*
©D. Blume/The Image Works

children showed short-term cognitive benefits and longer-term reading and math benefits (Jackson, 2015).

How Would You...?
If you were a **human development and family studies professional**, how would you discuss infant safety concerns with parents?

with a strong desire to explore their environment (Bindler & others, 2017; London & others, 2017). Aspiration of foreign objects, suffocation, falls, poisoning, burns, and motor vehicle accidents are among the most common accidents in infancy (Shimony-Kanat & Benbenishty, 2017). All infants, newborns included, should be secured in special infant car seats in the backseat of a car rather than being held on an adult's lap or placed on the seat of the car.

T. Berry Brazelton, Pediatrician

T. Berry Brazelton is America's best-known pediatrician as a result of his numerous books, television appearances, and newspaper and magazine articles about parenting and children's health. He takes a family-centered approach to child development issues and communicates with parents in easy-to-understand ways.

Dr. Brazelton founded the Child Development Unit at Boston Children's Hospital and created the Brazelton Neonatal Behavioral Assessment Scale, a widely used measure of the newborn's health and well-being. He also has conducted a number of research studies on infants and children and has been president of the Society for Research in Child Development, a leading research organization.

T. Berry Brazelton, pediatrician, with a young child.
Courtesy of Brazelton Touchpoints Center

2 How Do Infants Develop Motor Skills?   **LG2** Describe infants' motor development.

The Dynamic Systems View   Reflexes   Gross Motor Skills   Fine Motor Skills

As a newborn, Ramona, whom we met in the chapter-opening story, could suck, fling her arms wide, and tightly grip a finger placed in her tiny hand. Within just two years, she would be toddling around on her own, opening doors and jars as she explored her little world. Are her accomplishments inevitable? How do infants develop their motor skills, and which skills do they develop at various ages?

THE DYNAMIC SYSTEMS VIEW

Developmentalist Arnold Gesell (1934) thought his painstaking observations had revealed how people develop their motor skills. He had discovered that infants and children develop rolling, sitting, standing, and other motor skills in a fixed order and within specific time frames. These observations, said Gesell, show that motor development comes about through the unfolding of a genetic plan, or maturation.

Later studies, however, demonstrated that the sequence of developmental milestones is not as fixed as Gesell indicated and not due as much to heredity as Gesell argued (Adolph, 2018; Adolph & Robinson, 2013, 2015; Cole, Robinson, & Adolph, 2016; Karasik, Tamis-LeMonda, & Adolph, 2016). Beginning in the 1980s, the study of motor development experienced a renaissance as psychologists developed new insights about *how* motor skills develop (Adolph, 2018; Adolph & Berger, 2015; Kretch & Adolph, 2017). One increasingly influential perspective is dynamic systems theory, proposed by Esther Thelen (Thelen & Smith, 1998, 2006).

According to **dynamic systems theory,** infants assemble motor skills for perceiving and acting (Thelen & Smith, 2006). To develop motor skills, infants must perceive something in the environment that motivates them to act and use their perceptions to fine-tune their movements. Motor skills represent solutions to the infant's goals (Keen, 2011).

How is a motor skill developed, according to this theory? When infants are motivated to do something, they might create a new motor behavior. The new behavior is the result of many converging factors: the development of the nervous system, the body's physical properties and its possibilities for movement, the goal the child is motivated to reach, and the environmental support for the skill (Adolph, 2018; Corbetta, 2009; D'Souza & others, 2017; von Hofsten, 2008). For example, babies learn to walk only when the maturation of the nervous system allows them to control certain leg muscles, when they want to move, when their legs have grown strong enough to support their weight, and when they have sufficient balance control to support their body on one leg.

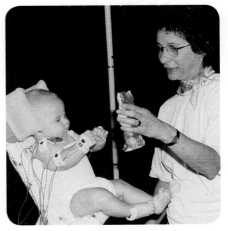

Esther Thelen conducts an experiment to discover how infants learn to control their arms to reach and grasp for objects. A computer device is used to monitor the infant's arm movements and to track muscle patterns. Thelen's research is conducted from a dynamic systems perspective. *What is the nature of this perspective?*
Courtesy of Dr. David Thelen

dynamic systems theory The perspective on motor development that seeks to explain how motor skills are assembled for perceiving and acting.

How might dynamic systems theory explain the development of this infant's walking skills?
©Harry Bartlett/The Image Bank/Getty Images

reflexes Built-in reactions to stimuli that govern the newborn's movements, which are automatic and beyond the newborn's control.

rooting reflex A newborn's built-in reaction that occurs when the infant's cheek is stroked or the side of the mouth is touched. In response, the infant turns its head toward the side that was touched in an apparent effort to find something to suck.

sucking reflex A newborn's built-in reaction to automatically suck an object placed in the mouth. The sucking reflex enables the infant to get nourishment before he or she has associated a nipple with food and also serves as a self-soothing or self-regulating mechanism.

Mastering a motor skill requires the infant's active efforts to coordinate several components of the skill. Infants explore and select possible solutions to the demands of a new task; they assemble adaptive patterns by modifying their current movement patterns (Adolph, 2018). The first step occurs when the infant is motivated by a new challenge—such as the desire to cross a room—and gets into the "ballpark" of the task demands by taking a couple of stumbling steps. Then, the infant "tunes" these movements to make them smoother and more effective. The tuning is achieved through repeated cycles of action and perception of the consequences of that action. According to the dynamic systems view, even universal milestones, such as crawling, reaching, and walking, are learned through this process of adaptation: Infants modulate their movement patterns to fit a new task by exploring and selecting possible configurations (Cole, Robinson, & Adolph, 2016; Comalli, Persand, & Adolph, 2017; D'Souza & others, 2017).

To see how dynamic systems theory explains motor behavior, imagine that you offer a new toy to a baby named Gabriel (Thelen & others, 1993). There is no exact program that can tell Gabriel ahead of time how to move his arm and hand and fingers to grasp the toy. Gabriel must adapt to his goal—grasping the toy—and the context. From his sitting position, he must make split-second adjustments to extend his arm, holding his body steady so that his arm and torso don't plow into the toy. Muscles in his arm and shoulder contract and stretch in a host of combinations, exerting a variety of forces. He improvises a way to reach out with one arm and wrap his fingers around the toy.

Thus, according to dynamic systems theory, motor development is not a passive process in which genes dictate the unfolding of a sequence of skills over time. Rather, the infant actively puts together a skill to achieve a goal within the constraints set by the infant's body and environment. Nature and nurture, the infant and the environment, are all working together as part of an ever-changing system.

As we examine the course of motor development, we will see how dynamic systems theory applies to some specific skills. First, though, let's examine how motor development begins with reflexes.

REFLEXES

Newborns are not completely helpless. Among other things, they have some basic reflexes. For example, newborns hold their breath and contract their throat to keep water out. **Reflexes** allow infants to respond adaptively to their environment before they have had the opportunity to learn.

The rooting and sucking reflexes are important examples. Both have survival value for newborn mammals, who must find a mother's breast to obtain nourishment. The **rooting reflex** occurs when the infant's cheek is stroked or the side of the mouth is touched. In response, the infant turns its head toward the side that was touched in an apparent effort to find something to suck. The **sucking reflex** occurs when newborns suck an object placed in their mouth. This reflex enables newborns to get nourishment before they have associated a nipple with food; it also serves as a self-soothing or self-regulating mechanism.

Another example is the **Moro reflex,** which occurs in response to a sudden, intense noise or movement. Figure 14 describes the Moro reflex along with other infant reflexes. When startled, newborns will arch their back, throw back their head, and fling out their arms and legs. Then they rapidly close their arms and legs. The Moro reflex is believed to be a way of grabbing for support while falling; it would have had survival value for our primate ancestors.

Some reflexes—coughing, sneezing, blinking, shivering, and yawning, for example—persist throughout life. They are as important for the adult as they are for the infant. Other reflexes, though, disappear several months following birth, as the infant's brain matures and voluntary control over many behaviors develops. The rooting and Moro reflexes, for example, tend to disappear when the infant is 3 to 4 months old.

The movements involved in some reflexes eventually become incorporated into more complex, voluntary actions. One important example is the **grasping reflex,** which occurs when something touches the infant's palms (see Figure 14). The infant responds by grasping tightly. By the end of the third month, the grasping reflex diminishes, and the infant shows a more voluntary grasp. As its motor development becomes smoother, the infant will grasp objects, carefully manipulate them, and explore their qualities.

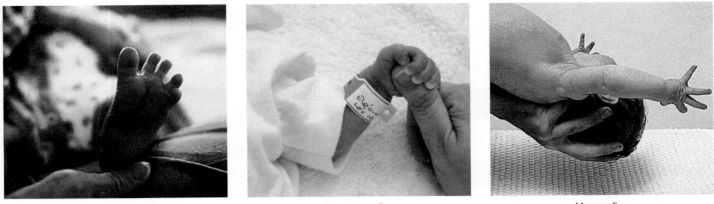

| | Babinski reflex | Grasping reflex | Moro reflex |

Reflex	Stimulation	Infant's Response	Developmental Pattern
Blinking	Flash of light, puff of air	Closes both eyes	Permanent
Babinski	Sole of foot stroked	Fans out toes, twists foot in	Disappears after 9 months to 1 year
Grasping	Palms touched	Grasps tightly	Weakens after 3 months, disappears after 1 year
Moro (startle)	Sudden stimulation, such as hearing loud noise or being dropped	Startles, arches back, throws head back, flings out arms and legs and then rapidly closes them to center of body	Disappears after 3 to 4 months
Rooting	Cheek stroked or side of mouth touched	Turns head, opens mouth, begins sucking	Disappears after 3 to 4 months
Stepping	Infant held above surface and feet lowered to touch surface	Moves feet as if to walk	Disappears after 3 to 4 months
Sucking	Object touching mouth	Sucks automatically	Disappears after 3 to 4 months
Swimming	Infant put face down in water	Makes coordinated swimming movements	Disappears after 6 to 7 months
Tonic neck	Infant placed on back	Forms fists with both hands and usually turns head to the right (sometimes called the "fencer's pose" because the infant looks like it is assuming a fencer's position)	Disappears after 2 months

FIGURE 14

INFANT REFLEXES. This chart describes some of the infant's reflexes.

(Left to right): ©Elizabeth Crews/The Image Works; ©BSIP SA/Alamy; ©Petit Format/Science Source

Individual differences in reflexive behavior are apparent soon after birth. For example, the sucking capabilities of newborns vary considerably. Some newborns are efficient at forcefully sucking and obtaining milk; others are not as adept and get tired before they are full. Most infants take several weeks to establish a sucking style that is coordinated with the way the mother is holding the infant, the way milk is coming out of the bottle or breast, and the infant's temperament (Blass, 2008).

The old view of reflexes was that they were exclusively genetic, built-in mechanisms that governed the infant's movements. The new perspective on infant reflexes says that they are not entirely automatic or completely beyond the infant's control. For example, infants can control such movements as alternating their legs to make a mobile jiggle or changing their sucking rate to listen to a recording (Adolph & Robinson, 2015).

GROSS MOTOR SKILLS

Ask any parents about their baby, and sooner or later you are likely to hear about one or more advances in motor skills, such as "Cassandra just learned to crawl," "Jesse is finally

Moro reflex A neonatal startle response that occurs in reaction to a sudden, intense noise or movement. When startled, newborns arch their back, throw their head back, and fling out their arms and legs. Then they rapidly close their arms and legs, bringing them close to the center of the body.

grasping reflex A neonatal reflex that occurs when something touches the infant's palms. The infant responds by grasping tightly.

gross motor skills Motor skills that involve large-muscle activities, such as walking.

sitting alone," or "Angela took her first step last week." Parents proudly announce such milestones as their children transform themselves from babies unable to lift their heads to toddlers who grab things off the grocery store shelf, chase a cat, and participate actively in the family's social life (Thelen, 2000). These milestones are examples of **gross motor skills,** skills that involve large-muscle activities, such as moving one's arms and walking.

The Development of Posture How do gross motor skills develop? As a foundation, these skills require postural control (Adolph & Robinson, 2015). For example, to track moving objects, you must be able to control your head in order to stabilize your gaze; before you can walk, you must be able to balance on one leg.

Posture is more than just holding still and straight. Posture is a dynamic process that is linked with sensory information in the skin, joints, and muscles, which tell us where we are in space; in vestibular organs in the inner ear that regulate balance and equilibrium; and in vision and hearing (Thelen & Smith, 2006).

Newborn infants cannot voluntarily control their posture. Within a few weeks, though, they can hold their heads erect, and soon they can lift their heads while prone. By 2 months of age, babies can sit while supported on a lap or an infant seat, but they cannot sit independently until they are 6 or 7 months of age. Standing also develops gradually during the first year of life. By about 8 to 9 months of age, infants usually learn to pull themselves up and hold onto a chair, and they often can stand alone by about 10 to 12 months of age.

Learning to Walk Locomotion and postural control are closely linked, especially in walking upright (Adolph & Robinson, 2013, 2015; Kretch & Adolph, 2017). To walk upright, the baby must be able both to balance on one leg as the other is swung forward and to shift weight from one leg to the other.

Even young infants can make the alternating leg movements that are needed for walking. The neural pathways that control leg alternation are in place from a very early age, even at birth or before. Indeed, researchers have found that alternating leg movements occur during the fetal period and at birth (Adolph & Robinson, 2015).

If infants can produce forward stepping movements so early, why does it take them so long to learn to walk? The key skills in learning to walk appear to be stabilizing balance on one leg long enough to swing the other forward and shifting the weight without falling. This is a difficult biomechanical problem to solve, and it takes infants about a year to do it.

In learning to locomote, infants discover what kinds of places and surfaces are safe for locomotion (Adolph, 2018; Karasik, Tamis-LeMonda, & Adolph, 2016). Karen Adolph (1997) investigated how experienced and inexperienced crawling infants and walking infants go down steep slopes (see Figure 15). Newly crawling infants, who averaged about 8½ months in age, rather indiscriminately went down the steep slopes, often falling in the process (with an experimenter next to the slope to catch them). After weeks of practice, the crawling babies became more adept at judging which slopes were too steep to crawl down and which ones they could navigate safely. New walkers also could not judge the safety of the slopes, but experienced walkers accurately matched their skills with the steepness of the slopes. They rarely fell downhill, either refusing to go down the steep slopes or going down backward in a cautious manner. Experienced walkers perceptually assessed the situation—looking, swaying, touching, and thinking before they moved down the slope. With experience, both the crawlers and the walkers learned to avoid the risky slopes where they would fall, integrating perceptual information with the development of a new motor behavior. In this research, we again see the importance of perceptual-motor coupling in the development of motor skills. Thus, practice is very important in the development of new motor skills (Adolph & Robinson, 2013, 2015). In a recent study, Adolph and her colleagues (2012) observed 12- to 19-month-olds during free play. Locomotor experience was extensive, with the infants averaging 2,368 steps and 17 falls per hour.

A recent study explored how infants plan and guide their locomotion in the challenging context of navigating a series of bridges varying in width (Kretch & Adolph, 2017). Infants' visual exploration (direction of their gaze) was assessed using a head-mounted eye-tracking device, and their locomotor actions were captured using video. The 14-month-olds engaged in visual exploration from a distance as an initial assessment before they crossed almost every bridge. The visual information led to modifications in their gait when approaching narrow bridges, and they used haptic (touch) information at the edge of the bridges. As they gained

Newly crawling infant

Experienced walker

FIGURE 15

THE ROLE OF EXPERIENCE IN CRAWLING AND WALKING INFANTS' JUDGMENTS OF WHETHER TO GO DOWN A SLOPE. Karen Adolph (1997) found that locomotor experience rather than age was the primary predictor of adaptive responding on slopes of varying steepness. Newly crawling and walking infants could not judge the safety of the various slopes. With experience, they learned to avoid slopes where they would fall. When expert crawlers began to walk, they again made mistakes and fell, even though they had judged the same slope accurately when crawling. Adolph referred to this as the *specificity of learning* because it does not transfer across crawling and walking.
©Dr. Karen Adolph, New York University

more walking experience, their exploratory behaviors became more efficient and they became more adept at deciding which bridges were safe to walk across.

Might the development of walking be linked to advances in other aspects of development? Walking experience leads to being able to gain contact with objects that were previously out of reach and to initiate interaction with parents and other adults, thereby promoting language development (Adolph & Robinson, 2015; He, Walle, & Campos, 2015). Thus, walking skills can produce a cascade of changes in the infant's development.

The First Year: Motor Development Milestones and Variations   Figure 16 summarizes important accomplishments in gross motor skills during the first year, culminating in the ability to walk easily. The timing of these milestones, especially the later ones, may vary by as much as two to four months, and experiences can modify the onset of these accomplishments. For example, in the early 1990s, pediatricians began recommending that parents place their babies on their backs when they sleep. Following that instruction, babies who back-sleep began crawling later, typically several weeks later than babies who sleep prone (Davis & others, 1998). Also, some infants do not follow the standard sequence of motor accomplishments (Eaton, 2008). For example, many American infants never crawl on their belly or on their hands and knees. They may discover an idiosyncratic form of locomotion before walking, such as rolling, or they might never locomote until they can stand upright (Adolph & Robinson, 2013, 2015). In Jamaica, approximately one-fourth of babies skip crawling (Hopkins, 1991).

According to Karen Adolph and Sarah Berger (2005), the early view that growth and motor development simply reflect the age-related output of maturation is, at best, incomplete. Rather, infants develop new skills with the guidance of their caregivers in a real-world environment of objects, surfaces, and planes.

How Would You...?
If you were a **psychologist**, how would you advise parents who are concerned that their infant is one or two months behind the average gross motor milestones?

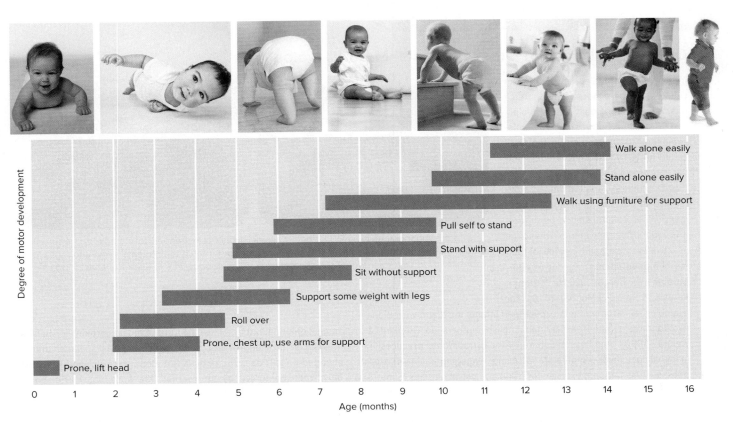

FIGURE 16

MILESTONES IN GROSS MOTOR DEVELOPMENT. The horizontal red bars indicate the range in which most infants reach various milestones in gross motor development.

(Photo credit left to right) ©Barbara Penoyar/Getty Images RF; ©Evan Kafka/Getty Images; ©Image Source/Alamy RF; ©Victoria Blackie/Getty Images RF; ©Digital Vision RF; ©Fotosearch/Getty Images RF; ©Corbis/PictureQuest RF; ©Monika Wisniewska/123RF

A recent study found a number of factors that are linked to motor development in the first year of life (Flensborg-Madsen & Mortensen, 2017). Twelve developmental milestones were assessed, including grasping, rolling, sitting, and crawling; standing and walking; and overall mean of milestones. A larger size at birth (such as birth weight, birth length, and head circumference) was the aspect of pregnancy and delivery that showed the strongest link to reaching motor milestones earlier. Maternal smoking in the last trimester of prenatal development was associated with reaching the motor milestones later. Also, increase in size (weight, length, and head circumference) in the first year were related to reaching the motor milestones earlier. Breast feeding also was linked to reaching the milestones earlier.

Development in the Second Year   The motor accomplishments of the first year bring increasing independence, allowing infants to explore their environment more extensively and to initiate interaction with others more readily. In the second year of life, toddlers become more motorically skilled and mobile. Motor activity during the second year is vital to the child's competent development and few restrictions, except for safety, should be placed on their adventures.

By 13 to 18 months, toddlers can pull a toy attached to a string and use their hands and legs to climb up a number of steps. By 18 to 24 months, toddlers can walk quickly or run stiffly for a short distance, balance on their feet in a squatting position while playing with objects on the floor, walk backward without losing their balance, stand and kick a ball without falling, stand and throw a ball, and jump in place.

Can parents give their babies a head start on becoming physically fit and physically talented through structured exercise classes? Most infancy experts recommend against structured exercise classes for babies. But there are other ways of guiding infants' motor development. Caregivers in some cultures do handle babies vigorously, and this practice might advance motor development, as we discuss in the *Connecting with Diversity* interlude.

> A baby is an angel whose wings decrease as his legs increase.
>
> —**MARK TWAIN**
> *American Writer, 19th Century*

connecting with diversity

Cultural Variations in Guiding Infants' Motor Development

In many African, Indian, and Caribbean cultures, mothers massage and stretch their infants during daily baths (Adolph, 2018; Adolph, Karasik, & Tamis-LeMonda, 2010). Mothers in the Gusii culture of Kenya also encourage vigorous movement in their babies.

Do cultural variations make a difference in the infant's motor development? When cultural standards suggest it is a good idea for infants to engage in active exercise, some aspects of their motor development occur earlier (Adolph & Berger, 2015; Adolph, Karasik, & Tamis-LeMonda, 2010). For example, Jamaican mothers expect their infants to sit and walk alone two to three months earlier than English mothers do (Hopkins & Westra, 1990). And in sub-Saharan Africa, traditional practices in many villages involve mothers and siblings engaging babies in exercises, such as frequent exercise for trunk and pelvic muscles (Super & Harkness, 2010).

Many forms of restricted movement—such as Chinese sandbags, orphanage restrictions, and failure of caregivers to encourage movement in Budapest—have been found to produce substantial delays in motor development (Adolph, Karasik, &

(Left) In the Algonquin culture in Quebec, Canada, babies are strapped to a cradle board for much of their infancy. *(Right)* In Jamaica, mothers massage and stretch their infants' arms and legs. *To what extent do cultural variations in the activity infants engage in influence the time at which they reach motor milestones?*
(Left) ©Michael Greenlar/The Image Works; *(right)* ©Pippa Hetherington/ Earthstock/Newscom

Tamis-LeMonda, 2010). In some rural Chinese provinces, babies are placed in a bag of fine sand, which acts as a diaper and is changed once a day. The baby is left alone, face up, and is visited only when being fed by the mother (Xie & Young, 1999). Some studies of swaddling show small effects on creating delays in motor development, but other studies show no delays. Cultures that do swaddle infants usually do so early in the infant's development when the infant is not yet mobile; as the infant becomes more mobile, swaddling decreases.

FINE MOTOR SKILLS

Whereas gross motor skills involve large muscle activity, **fine motor skills** involve finely tuned movements. Grasping a toy, using a spoon, buttoning a shirt, or accomplishing anything that requires finger dexterity demonstrates fine motor skills. Infants have hardly any control over fine motor skills at birth, but newborns do have many components of what will become finely coordinated arm, hand, and finger movements.

The onset of reaching and grasping marks a significant achievement in infants' ability to interact with their surroundings. During the first two years of life, infants refine how they reach and grasp (Dosso, Herrera, & Boudreau, 2017; Libertus & others, 2013, 2016; Sacrey & others, 2014). Initially, infants reach by moving their shoulders and elbows crudely, swinging their arms toward an object. Later, when infants reach for an object they move their wrists, rotate their hands, and coordinate their thumb and forefinger. Infants do not have to see their own hands in order to reach for an object (Clifton & others, 1993). Cues from muscles, tendons, and joints, not sight of the limb, guide reaching by 4-month-old infants.

Infants refine their ability to grasp objects by developing two types of grasps. Initially, infants grip with the whole hand, which is called the *palmer grasp*. Later, toward the end of the first year, infants also grasp small objects with their thumb and forefinger, which is called the *pincer grip*. Their grasping system is very flexible. They vary their grip on an object depending on its size, shape, and texture, as well as the size of their own hands relative to the object's size. Infants grip small objects with their thumb and forefinger (and sometimes their middle finger too), whereas they grip large objects with all of the fingers of one hand or both hands.

Perceptual-motor coupling is necessary for the infant to coordinate grasping (Keen, 2005). Which perceptual system the infant is most likely to use in coordinating grasping varies with age. Four-month-old infants rely greatly on touch to determine how they will grip an object; 8-month-olds are more likely to use vision as a guide (Newell & others, 1989). This developmental change is efficient because vision lets infants preshape their hands as they reach for an object.

Especially when they can manage a pincer grip, infants delight in picking up small objects. Many develop the pincer grip and begin to crawl at about the same time, and infants at this stage of development pick up virtually everything in sight, especially small items on the floor, and put the objects in their mouth. Thus, parents need to be vigilant in regularly monitoring what objects are within the infant's reach (Keen, 2005).

Rachel Keen (2011; Keen, Lee, & Adolph, 2014) emphasizes that tool use is an excellent context for studying problem solving in infants because tool use provides information about how infants plan to reach a goal. Researchers in this area have studied infants' intentional actions that range from picking up a spoon in different orientations to retrieving rakes placed inside tubes (Libertus & others, 2016). A recent study explored motor origins of tool use by assessing developmental changes in banging movements in 6- to 15-month-olds (Kahrs, Jung, & Lockman, 2013). In this study, younger infants were inefficient and variable when banging an object but by 1 year of age infants showed consistent straight up-and-down hand movements that resulted in precise aiming and consistent levels of force.

Experience plays a role in reaching and grasping (Smitsman & Corbetta, 2010). In a recent study, 3-month-olds who were not yet engaging in reaching behavior were provided with reaching experiences. These experiences were linked to increased object exploration and attention focusing skills at 15 months of age (Libertus, Joh, & Needham, 2016). Recent research studies have also found that short-term training involving practice of reaching movements increased both preterm and full-term infants' reaching for and touching objects (Cunha & others, 2016; Guimaraes & Tudellia, 2015).

Amy Needham and her colleagues have used "sticky mittens" to enhance young infants' active grasping and manipulation of objects. In one study, 3-month-old infants participated in play sessions wearing sticky mittens—"mittens with palms that stuck to the edges of toys and allowed the infants to pick up the toys" (Needham, Barrett, & Peterman, 2002, p. 279) (see Figure 17).

A young girl using a pincer grip to pick up puzzle pieces.
©Newstockimages/SuperStock RF

fine motor skills Motor skills that involve finely tuned movements, such as finger dexterity.

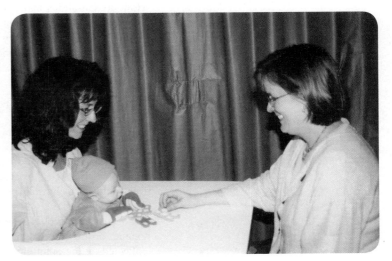

FIGURE 17

INFANTS' USE OF "STICKY MITTENS" TO EXPLORE OBJECTS. Amy Needham (on the right in this photo) and her colleagues (2002) found that "sticky mittens" enhanced young infants' object exploration skills.

Courtesy of Dr. Amy Needham

Infants who participated in sessions with the mittens grasped and manipulated objects earlier in their development than a control group of infants who did not receive the "mitten" experience. The infants with sticky mittens looked at the objects longer, swatted at them more during visual contact, and were more likely to mouth the objects. In a recent study, 3-month-old infants participated in active motor training using sticky mittens that allowed them to pick up toys, and these infants engaged in more sophisticated object exploration at 5.5 months of age (Wiesen, Watkins, & Needham, 2016).

Review Connect Reflect

LG2 Describe infants' motor development.

Review

- What is dynamic systems theory?
- What are some reflexes that infants have?
- How do gross motor skills develop in infancy?
- How do fine motor skills develop in infancy?

Connect

- What are the differences between the grasping reflex present at birth and the fine motor grasping skills an infant develops between 4 and 12 months of age?

Reflect *Your Own Personal Journey of Life*

- Think of a motor skill that you perform. How would dynamic systems theory explain your motor skill performance?

3 How Can Infants' Sensory and Perceptual Development Be Characterized?

LG3 Explain sensory and perceptual development in infancy.

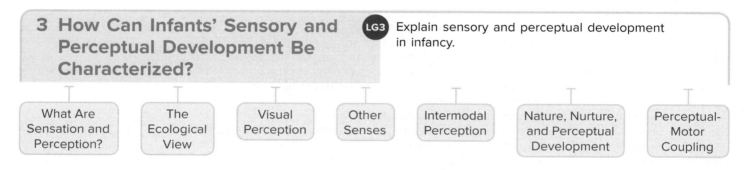

| What Are Sensation and Perception? | The Ecological View | Visual Perception | Other Senses | Intermodal Perception | Nature, Nurture, and Perceptual Development | Perceptual-Motor Coupling |

How do sensations and perceptions develop? Can newborns see? If so, what can they perceive? What about the other senses—hearing, smell, taste, and touch? What are they like in newborns, and how do they develop? Can infants put together information from two modalities, such as sight and sound? These are among the intriguing questions that we will explore in this section.

WHAT ARE SENSATION AND PERCEPTION?

How does a newborn know that her mother's skin is soft rather than rough? How does a 5-year-old know what color his hair is? How does a 10-year-old know that a firecracker is louder than a cat's meow? Infants and children "know" these things because of information that comes through the senses. Without vision, hearing, touch, taste, smell, and other senses, we would be isolated from the world; we would live in dark silence, a tasteless, colorless, feelingless void.

Sensation occurs when information interacts with sensory *receptors*—the eyes, ears, tongue, nostrils, and skin. The sensation of hearing occurs when waves of pulsating air are collected by the outer ear and conducted through the bones of the inner ear and the *cochlea*, where mechanical vibrations are converted into electrical impulses. Then the electrical impulses move to the *auditory nerve*, which transmits them to the brain. The sensation of vision occurs as rays of light contact the eyes and become focused on the *retina*, where light is converted into electrical impulses. Then the electrical impulses are transmitted by the *optic nerve* to the visual centers of the brain.

sensation The product of the interaction between information and the sensory receptors—the eyes, ears, tongue, nostrils, and skin.

Perception is the interpretation of what is sensed. The air waves that contact the ears might be interpreted as noise or as musical sounds, for example. The physical energy transmitted to the retina of the eye might be interpreted as a particular color, pattern, or shape, depending on how it is perceived.

THE ECOLOGICAL VIEW

In recent decades, much of the research on perceptual development in infancy has been guided by the ecological view of Eleanor and James J. Gibson (E. Gibson, 1969, 1989, 2001; J. Gibson, 1966, 1979). They argue that we do not have to take bits and pieces of data from sensations and build up representations of the world in our minds. Instead, our perceptual system can select from the rich information that the environment itself provides.

According to the Gibsons' **ecological view,** we directly perceive information that exists in the world around us. Perception brings us into contact with the environment in order to interact with and adapt to it (Kretch & Adolph, 2017). Perception is designed for action. Perception gives people such information as when to duck, when to turn their bodies as they move through a narrow passageway, and when to put up their hands to catch something (Franchak & Adolph, 2014; Kretch & Adolph, 2017).

In the Gibsons' view, all objects and surfaces have **affordances,** which are opportunities for interaction offered by objects that fit within our capabilities to perform activities. A pot may afford you something to cook with, and it may afford a toddler something to bang. Adults immediately know when a chair is appropriate for sitting, when a surface is safe for walking, or when an object is within reach. We directly and accurately perceive these affordances by sensing information from the environment—the light or sound reflecting from the surfaces of the world—and from our own bodies through muscle receptors, joint receptors, and skin receptors.

An important developmental question is "What affordances can infants or children detect and use?" (Ishak, Franchak, & Adolph, 2014). In one study, for example, when babies who could walk were faced with a squishy waterbed, they stopped and explored it, then chose to crawl rather than walk across it (Gibson & others, 1987). They combined perception and action to adapt to the demands of the task.

Studying the infant's perception has not been an easy task. What do you think some of the research challenges might be? The *Connecting with Research* interlude describes some of the ingenious ways researchers study the infant's perception.

VISUAL PERCEPTION

What do newborns see? How does visual perception develop in infancy?

Visual Acuity and Human Faces   Psychologist William James (1890/1950) called the newborn's perceptual world a "blooming, buzzing confusion." More than a century later, we can safely say that he was wrong (Bremner & others, 2017; Singarajah & others, 2017; Weatherhead & White, 2017). Even the newborn perceives a world with some order. That world, however, is far different from the one perceived by the toddler or the adult.

Just how well can infants see? At birth, the nerves and muscles and lens of the eye are still developing. As a result, newborns cannot see small things that are far away. Estimates of the newborn's visual acuity varies from 20/240 to 20/640 on the well-known Snellen chart used for eye examinations, which means that a newborn can see at 20 feet what a normal adult can see at 240 to 640 feet. In other words, an object 20 feet away is only as clear to the newborn as it would be if it were 640 feet away from an adult with normal vision (20/20). By 6 months of age, though, *on average* vision is 20/40 (Aslin & Lathrop, 2008).

Faces are possibly the most important visual stimuli in children's social environment, and it is important that they extract key information from others' faces (Jakobsen, Umstead, & Simpson, 2016; Sugden & Moulson, 2017). Infants show an interest in human faces soon after birth (Johnson & Hannon, 2015; Lee & others, 2013). Research shows that infants only a few hours old prefer to look at faces rather than other objects and to look at attractive faces more than at unattractive ones (Lee & others, 2013).

How would you use the Gibsons' ecological theory of perception and the concept of affordance to explain the role that perception is playing in this baby's activity?
©Ryan KC Wong/Getty Images RF

perception The interpretation of what is sensed.

ecological view The view that perception functions to bring organisms in contact with the environment and to increase adaptation.

affordances Opportunities for interaction offered by objects that fit within our capabilities to perform functional activities.

visual preference method A method used to determine whether infants can distinguish one stimulus from another by measuring the length of time they attend to different stimuli.

habituation Decreased responsiveness to a stimulus after repeated presentations of the stimulus.

dishabituation Recovery of a habituated response after a change in stimulation.

How Can the Newborn's Perception Be Studied?

After years of work, scientists have developed research methods and tools sophisticated enough to examine the subtle abilities of infants and to interpret their complex actions (Bendersky & Sullivan, 2007).

Visual Preference Method

Robert Fantz (1963) was a pioneer in this effort. Fantz made an important discovery that advanced the ability of researchers to investigate infants' visual perception: Infants look at different things for different lengths of time. Fantz placed infants in a "looking chamber," which had two visual displays on the ceiling above the infant's head. An experimenter viewed the infant's eyes by looking through a peephole. If the infant was fixating on one of the displays, the experimenter could see the display's reflection in the infant's eyes. This arrangement allowed the experimenter to determine how long the infant looked at each display. Fantz (1963) found that infants only 2 days old look longer at patterned stimuli, such as faces and concentric circles, than at red, white, or yellow discs. Infants 2 to 3 weeks old preferred to look at patterns—a face, a piece of printed matter, or a bull's-eye—longer than at red, yellow, or white discs (see Figure 18). Fantz's research method—studying whether infants can distinguish one stimulus from another by measuring the length of time they attend to different stimuli—is referred to as the **visual preference method**.

Habituation and Dishabituation

Another way that researchers have studied infant perception is to present a stimulus (such as a sight or a sound) a number of times. If there is a decrease in the infant's response to the stimulus after several presentations, it indicates that the infant is no longer interested in looking at the stimulus. If the researcher now presents a new stimulus, the infant's response will recover—indicating the infant could discriminate between the old and new stimulus (Baker, Pettigrew, & Poulin-Dubois, 2014; Gerson & Woodward, 2014).

Habituation is the name given to decreased responsiveness to a stimulus after repeated presentations of the stimulus. **Dishabituation** is the recovery of a habituated response after a change in stimulation. Newborn infants can habituate to repeated sights, sounds, smells, or touches (Rovee-Collier, 2004). Among the measures researchers use in habituation studies are sucking behavior (sucking stops when the young infant attends to a novel object), heart and respiration rates, and the length of time the infant looks at an object. Figure 19 shows the results of one study of habituation and dishabituation with newborns (Slater, Morison, & Somers, 1988).

High-Amplitude Sucking

To assess an infant's attention to sound, researchers often use a method called high-amplitude sucking. In this method, infants are given a nonnutritive nipple to suck, and the nipple is connected to "a sound generating system. Each suck causes a noise to be generated and the infant learns quickly that sucking brings about this noise. At first, babies suck frequently, so the noise occurs often. Then, gradually, they lose interest in hearing repetitions of the same noise and begin to suck less frequently. At this point, the experimenter changes the sound that is being generated. If the babies renew vigorous sucking, we infer that they have discriminated the sound change and are sucking more because they want to hear the interesting new sound" (Menn & Stoel-Gammon, 2009, p. 67).

The Orienting Response and Tracking

A technique that can be used to determine whether an infant can see or hear is the orienting response, which involves turning one's head toward a sight or sound. However, the most important recent advance in measuring infant perception is the development of sophisticated eye-tracking

(continued)

FIGURE 18

FANTZ'S EXPERIMENT ON INFANTS' VISUAL PERCEPTION. *(a)* Infants 2 to 3 weeks old preferred to look at some stimuli more than others. In Fantz's experiment, infants preferred to look at patterns rather than at color or brightness. For example, they looked longer at a face, a piece of printed matter, or a bull's-eye than at red, yellow, or white discs. *(b)* Fantz used a "looking chamber" to study infants' perception of stimuli.

©David Linton, Courtesy of the Linton Family

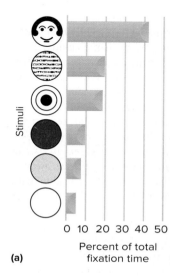

(a)

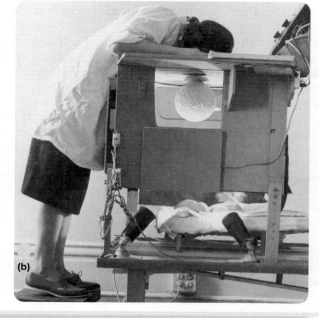

(b)

(*continued*)

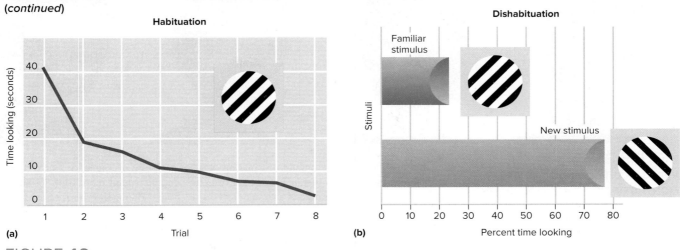

FIGURE **19**

HABITUATION AND DISHABITUATION. In the first part of one study (*a*), 7-hour-old newborns were shown a stimulus. As indicated, the newborns looked at it an average of 41 seconds when it was first presented to them (Slater, Morison, & Somers, 1988). Over seven more presentations of the stimulus, they looked at it less and less. In the second part of the study (*b*), infants were presented with both the familiar stimulus to which they had just become habituated and a new stimulus (which was rotated 90 degrees). The newborns looked at the new stimulus three times as much as the familiar stimulus.

equipment (Kretch & Adolph, 2017; Kretch, Franchak, & Adolph, 2014). Figure 20 shows an infant wearing an eye-tracking headgear in a recent study on visually guided motor behavior and social interaction. Most studies of infant development use remote optics eye trackers that have a camera that is not attached to the infant's head.

One of the main reasons that infant perception researchers are so enthusiastic about the recent availability of sophisticated eye-tracking equipment is that looking time is among the most important measures of infant perceptual and cognitive development (Aslin, 2012). The new eye-tracking equipment allows for much greater precision than human observation in assessing various aspects of infant looking and gaze (Boardman & Fletcher-Watson, 2017; Franchak & others, 2016). Among the areas of infant perception in which eye-tracking equipment is being used are attention (Jia & others, 2017; Meng, Uto, & Hashiya, 2017), memory (Kingo & Krojgaard, 2015), and face processing (Jakobsen, Umstead, & Simpson, 2016). Eye-tracking equipment also is improving our understanding of atypically developing infants, such as those who have autism or were born preterm (Finke, Wilkinson, & Hickerson, 2017; Liberati & others, 2017; Loi & others, 2017).

FIGURE **20**

AN INFANT WEARING EYE-TRACKING HEADGEAR. Using the ultralight, wireless, head-mounted eye-tracking equipment shown here, researchers can record where infants look while the infants freely locomote.

Courtesy of Dr. Karen Adolph, New York University

A recent eye-tracking study shed light on the effectiveness of TV programs and DVDs that claim to educate infants (Kirkorian, Anderson, & Keen, 2012). In this study, 1-year-olds, 4-year-olds, and adults watched Sesame Street and the eye-tracking equipment recorded precisely what they looked at on the screen. The 1-year-olds were far less likely to consistently look at the same part of the screen as their older counterparts, suggesting that the 1-year-olds showed little understanding of the Sesame Street video but instead were more likely to be attracted by what was salient than by what was relevant.

Equipment

Technology can facilitate the use of most methods for investigating the infant's perceptual abilities. Videotape equipment allows researchers to investigate elusive behaviors. High-speed computers make it possible to perform complex data analysis in minutes. Other equipment records respiration, heart rate, body movement, visual fixation, and sucking behavior, which provide clues to what the infant is perceiving.

What other applications of computer technology, such as motion-capture or three-dimensional modeling, do you think might some-day be useful in studying children's perception?

FIGURE 21

VISUAL ACUITY DURING THE FIRST MONTHS OF LIFE. The four photographs represent a computer estimation of what a picture of a face looks like to a 1-month-old, 2-month-old, 3-month-old, and 1-year-old (which approximates that of an adult).
©Kevin Peterson/Getty Images/Simulation by Vischeck RF

Figure 21 shows a computer estimation of what a picture of a face looks like to an infant at different ages from a distance of about 6 inches. Infants spend more time looking at their mother's face than a stranger's face as early as 12 hours after being born (Bushnell, 2003). By 3 months of age, infants match voices to faces, distinguish between male and female faces, and discriminate between faces of their own ethnic group and those of other ethnic groups (Gaither, Pauker, & Johnson, 2012; Kelly & others, 2007, 2009; Lee & others, 2013).

Experience has an important role in face processing in infancy and later in development. One aspect of this experience involves the concept of *perceptual narrowing*, in which infants are more likely to pay attention to faces to which they have been exposed than to faces to which they have not been exposed (Lee & others, 2013). Also, as we discussed in the *Connecting with Research* interlude, young infants can perceive certain patterns. With the help of his "looking chamber," Robert Fantz (1963) revealed that even 2- to 3-week-old infants prefer to look at patterned displays rather than nonpatterned displays. For example, they prefer to look at a normal human face rather than one with scrambled features, and prefer to look at a bull's-eye target or black and white stripes rather than a plain circle.

Color Vision The infant's color vision also improves over time (Aslin & Lathrop, 2008; Atkinson & Braddick, 2013). By 8 weeks, and possibly as early as 4 weeks, infants can discriminate some colors (Kelly, Borchert, & Teller, 1997). By 4 months of age, they have color preferences that mirror those of adults in some cases, preferring saturated colors such as royal blue over pale blue, for example (Bornstein, 1975). One study involving viewing of blue, yellow, red, and green hues by 4- to 5-month-old infants revealed that they looked longest at reddish hues and shortest at greenish hues (Franklin & others, 2010). In part, the changes in vision described here reflect maturation. Experience, however, is also necessary for color vision to develop normally (Sugita, 2004).

Perceptual Constancy Some perceptual accomplishments are especially intriguing because they indicate that the infant's perception goes beyond the information provided by the senses (Bremner & others, 2017; Johnson, 2013; Slater & others, 2011). This is the case in perceptual constancy, in which sensory stimulation is changing but perception of the physical world remains constant. If infants did not develop perceptual constancy, each time they saw an object at a different distance or in a different orientation, they would perceive it as a different object. Thus, the development of perceptual constancy allows infants to perceive their world as stable. Two types of perceptual constancy are size constancy and shape constancy.

Size constancy is the recognition that an object remains the same even though the retinal image of the object changes as you move toward or away from the object. The farther away from us an object is, the smaller its image is on our eyes. Thus, the size of an object on the retina is not sufficient to tell us its actual size. For example, you perceive a bicycle standing right in front of you as smaller than the car parked across the street, even though the bicycle casts a larger image on your eyes than the car does. When you move away from the bicycle, you do not perceive it to be shrinking even though its image on your retinas shrinks; you perceive its size to be constant.

But what about babies? Do they have size constancy? Researchers have found that babies as young as 3 months of age show size constancy (Bower, 1966; Day & McKenzie, 1973). However, at 3 months of age, a baby's ability is not full-blown. It continues to develop until 10 or 11 years of age (Kellman & Banks, 1998).

size constancy The recognition that an object remains the same even though the retinal image of the object changes as you move toward or away from the object.

shape constancy The recognition that an object's shape remains the same even though its orientation to us changes.

FIGURE 22

INFANTS' PREDICTIVE TRACKING OF A BRIEFLY OCCLUDED MOVING BALL. The top panel shows the visual scene that infants experienced. At the beginning of each event, a multicolored ball bounced up and down with an accompanying bounding sound, and then rolled across the floor until it disappeared behind the partition. Parts a, b, and c show the three stimulus events that the 5- to 9-month-old infants experienced: (a) *Gradual occlusion*—the ball gradually disappears behind the right side of the occluding partition located in the center of the display. (b) *Abrupt occlusion*—the ball abruptly disappears when it reaches the location of the white circle and then abruptly reappears 2 seconds later at the location of the second white circle on the other side of the occluding partition. (c) *Implosion*—the rolling ball quickly decreases in size as it approaches the occluding partition and rapidly increases in size as it reappears on the other side of the occluding partition.

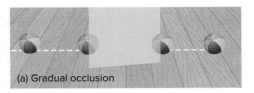

(a) Gradual occlusion

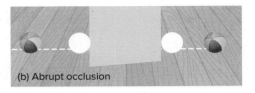

(b) Abrupt occlusion

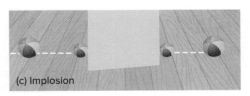

(c) Implosion

Shape constancy is the recognition that an object remains the same shape even though its orientation to us changes. Look around the room you are in right now. You likely see objects of varying shapes, such as tables and chairs. If you get up and walk around the room, you will see these objects from different sides and angles. Even though your retinal image of the objects changes as you walk and look, you will still perceive the objects as the same shape.

Do babies have shape constancy? As with size constancy, researchers have found that babies as young as 3 months of age have shape constancy (Bower, 1966; Day & McKenzie, 1973). Three-month-old infants, however, do not have shape constancy for irregularly shaped objects such as tilted planes (Cook & Birch, 1984).

Perception of Occluded Objects

Once again, look around the context where you are now. You likely see that some objects are partly occluded by other objects that are in front of them—possibly a desk behind a chair, some books behind a computer, or a car parked behind a tree. Do infants perceive an object as complete when it is partly occluded by an object in front of it?

In the first two months of postnatal development, infants don't perceive occluded objects as complete, instead perceiving only what is visible (Johnson, 2013; Johnson & Hannon, 2015). Beginning at about 2 months of age, infants develop the ability to perceive occluded objects as whole (Slater, Field, & Hernandez-Reif, 2007). How does perceptual completion develop? In Scott Johnson's (2010, 2011, 2013) research, learning, experience, and self-directed exploration via eye movements play key roles in the development of perceptual completion in young infants.

Many of the objects in the world that are occluded appear and disappear behind closer objects, as when you are walking down the street and see cars appear and disappear behind buildings as they move or you move. Can infants predictively track briefly occluded moving objects? They develop the ability to track briefly occluded moving objects at about 3 to 5 months of age (Bertenthal, 2008). A study explored 5- to 9-month-old infants' ability to track moving objects that disappeared gradually behind an occluded partition, disappeared abruptly, or imploded (shrank quickly in size) (see Figure 22) (Bertenthal, Longo, & Kenny, 2007). In this study, the infants were more likely to accurately predict the reappearance of the moving object when it had disappeared gradually rather than when it had disappeared abruptly or imploded.

Depth Perception

Might infants even perceive depth? To investigate this question, Eleanor Gibson and Richard Walk (1960) constructed a miniature cliff with a drop-off covered by glass in their laboratory. They placed infants on the edge of this visual cliff and had their mothers coax them to crawl onto the glass (see Figure 23). Most infants would not crawl out on the glass, choosing instead to remain on the opaque side, an indication that they could perceive depth. However, critics point out that the visual cliff likely is a better test of social referencing and fear of heights than depth perception.

In a recent research review, Karen Adolph and her colleagues (Adolph, Kretch, & LoBue, 2014) described how for

FIGURE 23

EXAMINING INFANTS' DEPTH PERCEPTION ON THE VISUAL CLIFF. Eleanor Gibson and Richard Walk (1960) found that most infants would not crawl out on the glass, which, according to Gibson and Walk, indicated that they had depth perception. However, critics point out that the visual cliff is a better indication of the infant's social referencing and fear of heights than of the infant's perception of depth.
©Mark Richards/PhotoEdit

many decades it was believed that crawling infants would not cross the clear glass indicating a dangerous drop-off because they have a fear of heights. However, Adolph and her colleagues concluded that there is no research support for the view that infants have a fear of heights. Rather, research indicates that infants either crawl or walk across the glass precipice or don't do so because of their perception of the affordances it does or does not provide. Research indicates that infants' exploration of the affordances increases on more challenging cliffs (deeper ones, for example) through such behaviors as patting the glass with their hands (Ueno & others, 2011).

Although researchers do not know precisely how early in life infants perceive depth, we do know that infants develop the ability to use binocular cues about depth by approximately 3 to 4 months of age. Thus, Adolph and her colleagues (2014) argue that the reason the visual cliff is not a great test of depth perception is that it requires infants to locomote, and infants have depth perception long before they can crawl.

OTHER SENSES

Other sensory systems besides vision also develop during infancy. We explore development in hearing, touch and pain, smell, and taste.

Hearing   During the last two months of pregnancy, as the fetus nestles in its mother's womb, it can hear sounds such as the mother's voice, music, and so on (Kisilevsky & others, 2009). Two psychologists wanted to find out if a fetus that heard Dr. Seuss' classic story *The Cat in the Hat* while still in the mother's womb would prefer hearing the story after birth (DeCasper & Spence, 1986). During the last months of pregnancy, 16 women read *The Cat in the Hat* to their fetuses. Then, shortly after the infants were born, the mothers read either *The Cat in the Hat* or a story with a different rhyme and pace, *The King, the Mice and the Cheese* (which had not been read aloud during prenatal development). The infants sucked on a nipple in a different way when the mothers read the two stories, suggesting that the infants recognized the pattern and tone of *The Cat in the Hat* (see Figure 24). This study illustrates not only that a fetus can hear but also that it has a remarkable ability to learn even before birth. A recent fMRI study confirmed that the fetus can hear at 33 to 34 weeks into the prenatal period by assessing fetal brain response to auditory stimuli (Jardri & others, 2012).

What kind of changes in hearing take place during infancy? They involve perception of a sound's loudness, pitch, and localization:

- *Loudness.* Immediately after birth, infants cannot hear soft sounds quite as well as adults can; a stimulus must be louder to be heard by a newborn than by an adult (Trehub & others, 1991). For example, an adult can hear a whisper from about 4 to 5 feet away, but a newborn requires that sounds be closer to a normal conversational level to be heard at that distance. By 3 months of age, infants' perception of sounds improves, although some aspects of loudness perception do not reach adult levels until 5 to 10 years of age (Trainor & He, 2013).

FIGURE 24

HEARING IN THE WOMB. *(a)* Pregnant mothers read *The Cat in the Hat* to their fetuses during the last few months of pregnancy. *(b)* When they were born, the babies preferred listening to a recording of their mothers reading *The Cat in the Hat*, as evidenced by their sucking on a nipple that produced this recording, rather than another story, *The King, the Mice and the Cheese.*

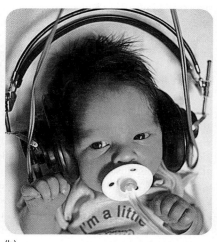

(a)   (b)

- *Pitch.* Infants are also less sensitive to the pitch of a sound than adults are. Pitch is the perception of the frequency of a sound. A soprano voice sounds high-pitched, a bass voice low-pitched. Infants are less sensitive to low-pitched sounds and are more likely to hear high-pitched sounds (Aslin, Jusczyk, & Pisoni, 1998). A recent study revealed that by 7 months of age, infants can process simultaneous pitches when they hear voices but they are more likely to encode the higher-pitched voice (Marie & Trainor, 2013). By 2 years of age, infants have considerably improved their ability to distinguish sounds with different pitches.

- *Localization.* Even newborns can determine the general location from which a sound is coming—but by 6 months of age, they are more proficient at localizing sounds or detecting their origins. Their ability to localize sounds continues to improve during the second year (Burnham & Mattock, 2010).

Although young infants can process variations in sound loudness, pitch, and localization, these aspects of hearing continue to improve through the childhood years (Trainor & He, 2013).

Touch and Pain   Do newborns respond to touch? Can they feel pain? Newborns do respond to touch. A touch to the cheek produces a turning of the head; a touch to the lips produces sucking movements.

Newborns can also feel pain (Bellieni & others, 2016; Witt & others, 2016). If and when you have a son and consider whether he should be circumcised, the issue of an infant's pain perception probably will become important to you. If circumcision is performed, it is usually done about the third day after birth. Will your young son experience pain if he is circumcised when he is 3 days old? An investigation by Megan Gunnar and her colleagues (1987) found that newborn infant males cried intensely during circumcision. The circumcised infants also display amazing resiliency. Within several minutes after the surgery, they can nurse and interact in a normal manner with their mothers. And, if allowed to, the newly circumcised newborn drifts into a deep sleep, which seems to serve as a coping mechanism.

For many years, doctors performed operations on newborns without anesthesia. This practice was accepted because of the dangers of anesthesia and because of the supposition that newborns do not feel pain. As researchers demonstrated that newborns can feel pain, the practice of operating on newborns without anesthesia is being challenged. Anesthesia now is used in some circumcisions (Taddio, 2008).

A recent neuroimaging study revealed that the pain threshold in newborns occurs at a lower level of stimulation than for adults, confirming newborns' heightened pain sensitivity that has been found in earlier behavioral studies (Goksan & others, 2015). And in a recent study, kangaroo care was effective in reducing neonatal pain, especially indicated by the significantly lower level of crying when the care was instituted after the newborn's blood had been drawn by a heel stick (Seo, Lee, & Ahn, 2016).

Smell   Newborns can differentiate odors (Doty & Shah, 2008). The expressions on their faces seem to indicate that they like the way vanilla and strawberry smell but do not like the way rotten eggs and fish smell (Steiner, 1979). In one investigation, 6-day-old infants who were breast fed showed a clear preference for smelling their mother's used breast pad rather than a clean breast pad (MacFarlane, 1975). However, when they were 2 days old, they did not show this preference, an indication that they require several days of experience to recognize this odor.

Taste   Sensitivity to taste is present even before birth (Doty & Shah, 2008). Human newborns learn tastes prenatally through the amniotic fluid and in breast milk after birth (Beauchamp & Mennella, 2009; Mennella, 2009). In one study, even at only 2 hours of age, babies made different facial expressions when they tasted sweet, sour, and bitter solutions (Rosenstein & Oster, 1988). At about 4 months of age, infants begin to prefer salty tastes, which as newborns they had found to be aversive (Doty & Shah, 2008).

INTERMODAL PERCEPTION

Imagine yourself playing basketball or tennis. You are experiencing many visual inputs: the ball coming and going, other players moving around, and so on. However, you are experiencing many auditory inputs as well: the sound of the ball bouncing or being hit, the grunts

What is intermodal perception? Which two senses is this infant using to integrate information about the blocks?
©Kaori Ando/Cultura/Getty Images RF

and groans of the players, and so on. There is good correspondence between much of the visual and auditory information: When you see the ball bounce, you hear a bouncing sound; when a player stretches to hit a ball, you hear a groan. When you look at and listen to what is going on, you do not experience just the sounds or just the sights; you put all these things together. You experience a unitary episode. This is **intermodal perception,** which involves integrating information from two or more sensory modalities, such as vision and hearing (Bremner & others, 2012). Most perception is intermodal (Bahrick, 2010; Kirkham & others, 2012).

Early, exploratory forms of intermodal perception exist even in newborns (Bahrick & Hollich, 2008; Sann & Streri, 2007). For example, newborns turn their eyes and their head toward the sound of a voice or rattle when the sound is maintained for several seconds (Clifton & others, 1981), but the newborn can localize a sound and look at an object only in a crude way (Bechtold, Bushnell, & Salapatek, 1979). These early forms of intermodal perception become sharpened with experience during the first year of life (Hollich, Newman, & Jusczyk, 2005). In one study, infants as young as 3½ months old looked more at their mother when they also heard her voice and longer at their father when they also heard his voice (Spelke & Owsley, 1979). Thus, even young infants can coordinate visual-auditory information involving people.

Can young infants put vision and sound together as precisely as adults do? In the first six months, infants have difficulty connecting sensory input from different modes, but in the second half of the first year they show an increased ability to make this connection mentally.

Thus, babies are born into the world with some innate abilities to perceive relations among sensory modalities, but their intermodal abilities improve considerably through experience (Bahrick, 2010). As with all aspects of development, in perceptual development, nature and nurture interact and cooperate (Maurer, 2016; Slater & others, 2011).

NATURE, NURTURE, AND PERCEPTUAL DEVELOPMENT

Now that we have discussed many aspects of perceptual development, let's explore one of developmental psychology's key issues as it relates to perceptual development: the nature-nurture issue. There has been a long-standing interest in how strongly infants' perception is influenced by nature or nurture (Aslin, 2009; Bremner & others, 2017; Johnson & Hannon, 2015; Maurer, 2016; Slater & others, 2011). In the field of perceptual development, nature proponents are referred to as *nativists* and those who emphasize learning and experience are called *empiricists.*

In the nativist view, the ability to perceive the world in a competent, organized way is inborn or innate. A completely nativist view of perceptual development no longer is accepted in developmental psychology.

The Gibsons argued that a key question in infant perception is what information is available in the environment and how infants learn to generate, differentiate, and discriminate the information—certainly not a nativist view. The Gibsons' ecological view also is quite different from Piaget's constructivist view. According to Piaget, much of perceptual development in infancy must await the development of a sequence of cognitive stages for infants to construct more complex perceptual tasks. Thus, in Piaget's view, the ability to perceive size and shape constancy, a three-dimensional world, intermodal perception, and so on develops later in infancy than the Gibsons envision.

What roles do nature and nurture play in the infant's perceptual development?
©lostinbids/Getty Images RF

intermodal perception The ability to relate and integrate information from two or more sensory modalities, such as vision and hearing.

The longitudinal research of Daphne Maurer and her colleagues (Lewis & Maurer, 2005, 2009; Maurer, 2016; Maurer & Lewis, 2013; Maurer & others, 1999) has focused on infants born with cataracts—a thickening of the lens of the eye that causes vision to become cloudy, opaque, and distorted and thus severely restricts infants' ability to experience their visual world. Studying infants whose cataracts were removed at different points in development, they discovered that those whose cataracts were removed and new lenses placed in their eyes in the first several months after birth showed a normal pattern of visual development. However, the longer the delay in removing the cataracts, the more their visual development was impaired. In their research, Maurer and her colleagues (2007) have found that experiencing patterned visual input early in infancy is important for holistic and detailed face processing after infancy. Maurer's research program illustrates how deprivation and experience influence visual development, and it identifies an early sensitive period in which visual input is necessary for normal visual development (Maurer & Lewis, 2013).

Today, it is clear that just as an extreme nativist position on perceptual development is unwarranted, an extreme empiricist position also is unwarranted. Much of very early perception develops from innate (nature) foundations, and the basic foundation of many perceptual abilities can be detected in newborns (Bornstein, Arterberry, & Mash, 2015). However, as infants develop, environmental experiences (nurture) refine or calibrate many perceptual functions, and they may be the driving force behind some functions. The accumulation of experience with and knowledge about their perceptual world contributes to infants' ability to process coherent perceptions of people and things (Bremner & others, 2017; Johnson & Hannon, 2015; Slater & others, 2011).

Thus, a full portrait of perceptual development includes the influence of nature, nurture, and a developing sensitivity to information (Bornstein, Arterberry, & Mash, 2015).

PERCEPTUAL-MOTOR COUPLING

As we come to the end of this chapter, we return to the important theme of perceptual-motor coupling. The distinction between perceiving and doing has been a time-honored tradition in psychology. However, a number of experts on perceptual and motor development question whether this distinction makes sense (Adolph & Robinson, 2013, 2015; Slater & others, 2010, 2011; Thelen & Smith, 2006). The main thrust of research in Esther Thelen's dynamic systems approach is to explore how people assemble motor behaviors for perceiving and acting. The main theme of the ecological approach of Eleanor and James J. Gibson is to discover how perception guides action. Action can guide perception, and perception can guide action. Only by moving one's eyes, head, hands, and arms and by moving from one location to another can an individual fully experience his or her environment and learn how to adapt to it. Perception and action are coupled.

How are perception and action coupled in infants' development?
©Olivier Renck/Aurora/Getty Images

Babies, for example, continually coordinate their movements with perceptual information to learn how to maintain balance, reach for objects in space, and move across various surfaces and terrains (Kretch & Adolph, 2017; Slater & others, 2010, 2011; Thelen & Smith, 2006). They are motivated to move by what they perceive. Consider the sight of an attractive toy across the room. In this situation, infants must perceive the current state of their bodies and learn how to use their limbs to reach the toy. Although their movements at first are awkward and uncoordinated, babies soon learn to select patterns of movement that are appropriate for reaching their goals.

Equally important is the other part of the perception-action coupling. That is, action educates perception (Adolph, 2018). For example, watching an object while exploring it manually helps infants to discriminate its texture, size, and hardness. Locomoting in the environment teaches babies about how objects and people look from different perspectives, or whether surfaces will support their weight. Individuals perceive in order to move and move in order to perceive. Perceptual and motor development do not occur in isolation from each other but instead are coupled.

How do infants develop new perceptual-motor couplings? Recall from our discussion earlier in this chapter that in the traditional view of Gesell, infants' perceptual-motor development is prescribed by a genetic plan to follow a fixed and sequential progression of stages in development. The genetic determination view has been replaced by the dynamic systems view that infants learn new perceptual-motor couplings by assembling skills for perceiving and acting. New perceptual-motor coupling is not passively accomplished; rather, the infant actively develops a skill to achieve a goal within the constraints set by the infant's body and the environment (Kretch & Adolph, 2017).

Review
- What are sensation and perception?
- What is the ecological view of perception?
- How does visual perception develop in infancy?
- How do hearing, touch and pain, smell, and taste develop in infancy?
- What is intermodal perception?
- What is the nativist view of perception? What is the empiricist view?
- How is perceptual-motor development coupled?

Connect
- How might the development of vision and hearing contribute to infants' gross motor development?

Reflect *Your Own Personal Journey of Life*
- How much sensory stimulation would you provide for your baby? A little? A lot? Could you overstimulate your baby? Explain.

---

topical connections *looking forward*

In the next chapter, you will read about the remarkable cognitive changes that characterize infant development and how early infants process information about their world. Advances in infants' cognitive development—together with the development of the brain and perceptual-motor advances that were discussed in this chapter—allow infants to adapt more effectively to their world.

---

reach your **learning goals**

Physical Development in Infancy

1 How Do Infants Grow and Develop Physically?

LG1 Discuss physical growth and development in infancy.

Patterns of Growth

- The cephalocaudal pattern is the sequence in which growth proceeds from top to bottom. The proximodistal pattern is the sequence in which growth starts at the center of the body and moves toward the extremities.

Height and Weight

- The average North American newborn is 20 inches long and weighs 7½ pounds. Infants grow about 1 inch per month in the first year and nearly triple their weight by their first birthday. The rate of growth slows in the second year.

The Brain

- One of the most dramatic changes in the brain in the first two years of life is dendritic spreading, which increases the connections between neurons. Myelination, which speeds the conduction of nerve impulses, continues through infancy and even into adolescence.

- The cerebral cortex has two hemispheres (left and right). Lateralization refers to specialization of function in one hemisphere or the other.

- Early experiences play an important role in brain development. Neural connections are formed early in an infant's life.

- The neuroconstructivist view is an increasingly popular view of the brain's development. Before birth, genes mainly direct neurons to different locations. After birth, the inflowing stream of sights, sounds, smells, touches, language, and eye contact helps shape the brain's neural connections, as does stimulation from caregivers and others.

Sleep

- Newborns usually sleep about 18 hours a day. By 6 months of age, many American infants approach adultlike sleeping patterns. REM sleep—during which dreaming occurs—is present more in early infancy than in childhood and adulthood.

- Sleeping arrangements for infants vary across cultures. In America, infants are more likely to sleep alone than in many other cultures. Some experts believe shared sleeping can lead to sudden infant death syndrome (SIDS), a condition that occurs when a sleeping infant suddenly stops breathing and dies without an apparent cause. Better sleep in infancy is linked to better cognitive and language functioning in early childhood.

Nutrition

- A number of developmental changes characterize infants' nutritional needs and eating behavior in infancy. Caregivers play important roles in infants' development of healthy eating patterns.

- The growing consensus is that in most instances breast feeding is superior to bottle feeding for both the infant and the mother, although the correlational nature of studies must be considered. Severe infant malnutrition is still prevalent in many parts of the world. A special concern in impoverished countries is early weaning from breast milk and the misuse and hygiene problems associated with bottle feeding in these countries.

Health

- Widespread immunization of infants has led to a significant decline in infectious diseases. Accidents are a major cause of death in infancy. These accidents include the aspiration of foreign objects, suffocation, falls, and automobile accidents.

2 How Do Infants Develop Motor Skills? **LG2** Describe infants' motor development.

The Dynamic Systems View

- Thelen's dynamic systems theory seeks to explain how motor skills are assembled for perceiving and acting. Perception and action are coupled. According to this theory, motor skills are the result of many converging factors, such as the development of the nervous system, the body's physical properties and its movement possibilities, the goal the child is motivated to reach, and environmental support for the skill. In the dynamic systems view, motor development is far more complex than the result of a genetic blueprint.

Reflexes

- Reflexes—built-in reactions to stimuli—govern the newborn's behavior. They include the sucking, rooting, and Moro reflexes. The rooting and Moro reflexes disappear after three to four months. Permanent reflexes include coughing and blinking. For infants, sucking is an especially important reflex because it provides a means of obtaining nutrition.

Gross Motor Skills

- Gross motor skills involve large-muscle activities. Key skills developed during infancy include control of posture and walking. Although infants usually learn to walk by their first birthday, the neural pathways that allow walking begin to form earlier. The time at which infants reach milestones in the development of gross motor skills may vary by as much as two to four months, especially for milestones in late infancy.

Fine Motor Skills

- Fine motor skills involve finely tuned movements. The onset of reaching and grasping marks a significant accomplishment, and this becomes more refined during the first two years of life.

3 How Can Infants' Sensory and Perceptual Development Be Characterized? **LG3** Explain sensory and perceptual development in infancy.

What Are Sensation and Perception?

- Sensation occurs when information interacts with sensory receptors. Perception is the interpretation of sensation.

The Ecological View

- Created by the Gibsons, the ecological view states that we directly perceive information that exists in the world around us. Perception brings people in contact with the environment to interact with and adapt to it. Affordances provide opportunities for interaction offered by objects that fit within our capabilities to perform activities.

Visual Perception	• Researchers have developed a number of methods to assess the infant's perception, including the visual preference method (which Fantz used to determine young infants' interest in looking at patterned over nonpatterned displays), habituation and dishabituation, and tracking.
	• The infant's visual acuity increases dramatically in the first year of life. Infants' color vision improves as they develop. Young infants systematically scan human faces. By 3 months of age, infants show size and shape constancy. At approximately 2 months of age, infants develop the ability to perceive occluded objects as complete. In Gibson and Walk's classic study, infants as young as 6 months of age had depth perception.
Other Senses	• The fetus can hear several weeks prior to birth. Immediately after birth, newborns can hear, but their sensory threshold is higher than that of adults. Developmental changes in the perception of loudness, pitch, and localization of sound occur during infancy. Newborns can respond to touch and feel pain. Newborns can differentiate odors, and sensitivity to taste may be present before birth.
Intermodal Perception	• Early, exploratory forms of intermodal perception—the ability to relate and integrate information from two or more sensory modalities—are present in newborns and become sharper over the first year of life.
Nature, Nurture, and Perceptual Development	• In perception, nature advocates are referred to as nativists and nurture proponents are called empiricists. The Gibsons' ecological view that has guided much of perceptual development research leans toward a nativist approach but still allows for developmental changes in distinctive features. Piaget's constructivist view leans toward an empiricist approach, emphasizing that many perceptual accomplishments must await the development of cognitive stages in infancy.
	• A strong empiricist approach is unwarranted. A full account of perceptual development includes the roles of nature, nurture, and the developing sensitivity to information.
Perceptual-Motor Coupling	• Perception and action are often not isolated but rather are coupled. Individuals perceive in order to move and move in order to perceive.

key **terms**

affordances	forebrain	marasmus	sensation
cephalocaudal pattern	grasping reflex	Moro reflex	shape constancy
cerebral cortex	gross motor skills	neuroconstructivist view	size constancy
dishabituation	habituation	perception	sucking reflex
dynamic systems theory	intermodal perception	proximodistal pattern	sudden infant death syndrome
ecological view	kwashiorkor	reflexes	(SIDS)
fine motor skills	lateralization	rooting reflex	visual preference method

key **people**

Karen Adolph	Eleanor Gibson	Rachel Keen	Charles Nelson
Martha Ann Bell	James J. Gibson	Patricia Kuhl	John Richards
T. Berry Brazelton	William James	Daphne Maurer	Esther Thelen
Robert Fantz	Mark Johnson	Amy Needham	Richard Walk

connecting with improving the lives of children

STRATEGIES

Supporting the Infant's Physical Development

What are some good strategies for helping the infant develop in physically competent ways?

- Be flexible about the infant's sleep patterns. Don't try to put the infant on a rigid sleep schedule. By about 4 months of age, most infants have moved closer to adultlike sleep patterns.

- Provide the infant with good nutrition. Make sure the infant has adequate energy and nutrient intake. Provide this in a loving and supportive environment. Don't put an infant on a diet. Weaning should be gradual, not abrupt.

- Breast feed the infant, if possible. Breast feeding provides more ideal nutrition than bottle feeding. If work prevents the mother from breast feeding the infant while she is away from home, she should consider "pumping."

- Give the infant extensive opportunities to explore safe environments. Infants don't need exercise classes, but they should be provided with many opportunities to actively explore safe environments. Infants should not be restricted to small, confined environments for any length of time.

- Don't push the infant's physical development or get uptight about physical norms. In American culture, we tend to want our child to grow faster than other children. Remember that there is wide individual variation in normal physical development. Just because an infant is not at the top of a physical chart doesn't mean parents should start pushing the infant's physical skills. Infants develop at different paces. Respect and nurture the infant's individuality.

RESOURCES

Typical and Atypical Functional Brain Development

Michelle de Haan and Mark Johnson
In D. Cicchetti (Ed.), *Development and Psychopathology* (3rd ed., 2016)
New York: Oxford University Press

Leading experts discuss many aspects of the infant's developing brain, including normal and abnormal development.

Healthy Sleep Habits, Happy Child (4th ed., 2016)

Dr. Marc Weissbluth
New York: Ballantine

A leading pediatrician describes how parents can help their infants develop better sleep habits.

The Pediatrician's Guide to Feeding Babies and Toddlers (2016)

Anthony Porto and Dina DiMaggio
New York: The Speed Press

Good recommendations are provided for parents to guide them in making good decisions about what and how to feed their infants and toddlers.

chapter 6

COGNITIVE DEVELOPMENT IN INFANCY

chapter outline

Jean Piaget, the famous Swiss psychologist, was a meticulous observer of his three children: Laurent, Lucienne, and Jacqueline. His books on cognitive development are filled with these observations. Here are a few of Piaget's observations of his children in infancy (Piaget, 1952):

- At 21 days of age, "Laurent found his thumb after three attempts: prolonged sucking begins each time. But, once he has been placed on his back, he does not know how to coordinate the movement of the arms with that of the mouth and his hands draw back even when his lips are seeking them" (p. 27).
- "During the third month, thumb sucking becomes less important to Laurent because of new visual and auditory interests. But, when he cries, his thumb goes to the rescue."
- Toward the end of Lucienne's fourth month, while she is lying in her crib, Piaget hangs a doll above her feet. Lucienne thrusts her feet at the doll and makes it move. "Afterward, she looks at her motionless foot for a second, then recommences. There is no visual control of her foot, for the movements are the same when Lucienne only looks at the doll or when I place the doll over her head. On the other hand, the tactile control of the foot is apparent: after the first shakes, Lucienne makes slow foot movements as though to grasp and explore" (p. 159).
- At 11 months, "Jacqueline is seated and shakes a little bell. She then pauses abruptly in order to delicately place the bell in front of her right foot; then she kicks hard. Unable to recapture it, she grasps a ball which she then places at the same spot in order to give it another kick" (p. 225).
- At 1 year, 2 months, "Jacqueline holds in her hands an object which is new to her: a round, flat box which she turns all over, shakes, [and] rubs against the bassinet. . . . She lets it go and tries to pick it up. But she only succeeds in touching it with her index finger, without grasping it. She nevertheless makes an attempt and presses on the edge. The box then tilts up and falls again" (p. 273). Jacqueline shows an interest in this result and studies the fallen box.

topical connections   *looking **back***

Impressive advances occur in the development of the brain during infancy. Engaging in various physical, cognitive, and socioemotional activities strengthens the baby's neural connections. Motor and perceptual development also are key aspects of the infant's development. An important part of this development is the coupling of perceptions and actions. The nature-nurture issue continues to be debated in relation to the infant's perceptual development. In this chapter, you will build on your understanding of the infant's brain, motor, and perceptual development by further examining how infants develop their competencies, focusing on how advances in their cognitive development help them adapt to their world, and how the nature-nurture issue applies to the infant's cognitive and language development.

For Piaget, these observations reflect important changes in the infant's cognitive development. Piaget believed that infants go through a series of substages as they rapidly gain new skills during their first two years.

preview

Piaget's descriptions of infants are just the starting point for our exploration of cognitive development. Excitement and enthusiasm about the study of infant cognition have been fueled by an interest in what newborns and infants know, by continued fascination about innate and learned factors in the infant's cognitive development, and by controversies about whether infants construct their knowledge (Piaget's view) or know their world more directly. In this chapter, you will study not only Piaget's theory of infant development but also the development of learning, remembering, and conceptualizing by infants; individual differences in cognitive capabilities; and language development.

1 What Is Piaget's Theory of Infant Development?

LG1 Summarize and evaluate Piaget's theory of infant development.

Cognitive Processes — The Sensorimotor Stage — Evaluating Piaget's Sensorimotor Stage

We are born capable of learning.

—**JEAN-JACQUES ROUSSEAU**
Swiss-born French Philosopher, 18th Century

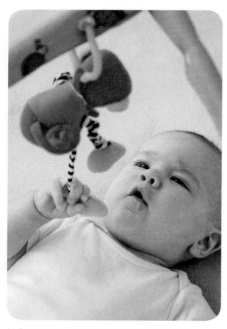

In Piaget's view, what is a scheme? What schemes might this young infant be displaying?
©Maya KovachevaPhotography/GettyImages RF

schemes In Piaget's theory, actions or mental representations that organize knowledge.

Poet Nora Perry once asked, "Who knows the thoughts of a child?" As much as anyone, Piaget knew. Through careful observations of his own three children—Laurent, Lucienne, and Jacqueline—and observations of and interviews with other children, Piaget changed perceptions of the way children think about the world.

Piaget's theory is a general, unifying story of how biology and experience sculpt cognitive development. Piaget thought that just as our physical bodies have structures that enable us to adapt to the world, we build mental structures that help us to adapt to the world. Adaptation involves adjusting to new environmental demands. Piaget stressed that children actively construct their own cognitive worlds; information is not just poured into their minds from the environment. He sought to discover how children at different points in their development think about the world and how systematic changes in their thinking occur.

COGNITIVE PROCESSES

What processes do children use as they construct their knowledge of the world? Piaget developed several concepts to answer this question; especially important are schemes, assimilation, accommodation, organization, equilibrium, and equilibration.

Schemes As the infant or child seeks to construct an understanding of the world, said Piaget (1954), the developing brain creates **schemes.** These are actions or mental representations that organize knowledge. In Piaget's theory, behavioral schemes (physical activities) characterize infancy and mental schemes (cognitive activities) develop in childhood (Lamb, Bornstein, & Teti, 2002). A baby's schemes are structured by simple actions that can be performed on objects, such as sucking, looking, and grasping. Older children have schemes that include strategies and plans for solving problems. For example, in the descriptions at the opening of this chapter, Laurent displayed a scheme for sucking; Jacqueline displayed a scheme for investigating when she examined the box. By the time we have reached adulthood, we have constructed an enormous number of diverse schemes, ranging from driving a car to balancing a budget to understanding the concept of fairness.

Assimilation and Accommodation To explain how children use and adapt their schemes, Piaget offered two concepts: assimilation and accommodation. **Assimilation** occurs when children use their existing schemes to deal with new information or experiences.

Accommodation occurs when children adjust their schemes to take new information and experiences into account.

Think about a toddler who has learned the word *car* to identify the family's car. The toddler might call all moving vehicles on roads "cars," including motorcycles and trucks; the child has assimilated these objects to his or her existing scheme. But the child soon learns that motorcycles and trucks are not cars and fine-tunes the category to exclude motorcycles and trucks, thus accommodating the scheme.

Assimilation and accommodation operate even in very young infants. Newborns reflexively suck everything that touches their lips; they assimilate all sorts of objects into their sucking scheme. By sucking different objects, they learn about their taste, texture, shape, and so on. After several months of experience, though, they construct their understanding of the world differently. Some objects, such as fingers and the mother's breast, can be sucked, and others, such as fuzzy blankets, should not be sucked. In other words, they accommodate their sucking scheme.

Organization   To make sense of their world, said Piaget, children cognitively organize their experiences. **Organization** in Piaget's theory is the grouping of isolated behaviors and thoughts into a higher-order system. Continual refinement of this organization is an inherent part of development. A boy who has only a vague idea about how to use a hammer may also have a vague idea about how to use other tools. After learning how to use each one, he relates these uses, organizing his knowledge.

Equilibration and Stages of Development   Assimilation and accommodation always take the child to a higher ground, according to Piaget. In trying to understand the world, the child inevitably experiences cognitive conflict, or *disequilibrium*. That is, the child is constantly faced with counterexamples to his or her existing schemes and with inconsistencies. For example, if a child believes that pouring water from a short and wide container into a tall and narrow container changes the amount of water, then the child might be puzzled by where the "extra" water came from and whether there is actually more water to drink. The puzzle creates disequilibrium; for Piaget, an internal search for equilibrium creates motivation for change. The child assimilates and accommodates, adjusting old schemes, developing new schemes, and organizing and reorganizing the old and new schemes. Eventually, the organization is fundamentally different from the old organization; it is a new way of thinking.

In short, according to Piaget, children constantly assimilate and accommodate as they seek *equilibrium*. There is considerable movement between states of cognitive equilibrium and disequilibrium as assimilation and accommodation work in concert to produce cognitive change. **Equilibration** is the name Piaget gave to this mechanism by which children shift from one stage of thought to the next.

The result of these processes, according to Piaget, is that individuals go through four stages of development. A different way of understanding the world makes each stage more advanced than the one before it. Cognition is *qualitatively* different in one stage compared with another. In other words, the way children reason at one stage is different from the way they reason at another stage. In this chapter, our focus is on Piaget's stage of infant cognitive development. In later chapters, when we study cognitive development in early, middle, and late childhood, and in adolescence, we explore the last three Piagetian stages.

THE SENSORIMOTOR STAGE

The **sensorimotor stage** lasts from birth to about 2 years of age. In this stage, infants construct an understanding of the world by coordinating sensory experiences (such as seeing and hearing) with physical, motoric actions—hence the term "sensorimotor." At the beginning of this stage, newborns have little more than reflexes with which to work. At the end of the sensorimotor stage, 2-year-olds can produce complex sensorimotor patterns and use primitive symbols. We first summarize Piaget's descriptions of how infants develop. Later we consider criticisms of his view.

Substages   Piaget divided the sensorimotor stage into six substages: (1) simple reflexes; (2) first habits and primary circular reactions; (3) secondary circular reactions; (4) coordination

developmental **connection**

Cognitive Theory
Recall the main characteristics of Piaget's four stages of cognitive development. Connect to "Introduction."

assimilation Piagetian concept involving incorporation of new information into existing schemes.

accommodation Piagetian concept of adjusting schemes to fit new information and experiences.

organization Piaget's concept of grouping isolated behaviors and thoughts into a higher-order system, a more smoothly functioning cognitive system.

equilibration A mechanism that Piaget proposed to explain how children shift from one stage of thought to the next.

sensorimotor stage The first of Piaget's stages, which lasts from birth to about 2 years of age, in which infants construct an understanding of the world by coordinating sensory experiences with motoric actions.

Substage	Age	Description	Example
1 Simple reflexes	Birth to 1 month	Coordination of sensation and action through reflexive behaviors.	Rooting, sucking, and grasping reflexes; newborns suck reflexively when their lips are touched.
2 First habits and primary circular reactions	1 to 4 months	Coordination of sensation and two types of schemes: habits (reflex) and primary circular reactions (reproduction of an event that initially occurred by chance). Main focus is still on the infant's body.	Repeating a body sensation first experienced by chance (sucking thumb, for example); then infants might accommodate actions by sucking their thumb differently from how they suck on a nipple.
3 Secondary circular reactions	4 to 8 months	Infants become more object-oriented, moving beyond self-preoccupation; repeat actions that bring interesting or pleasurable results.	An infant coos to make a person stay near; as the person starts to leave, the infant coos again.
4 Coordination of secondary circular reactions	8 to 12 months	Coordination of vision and touch—hand-eye coordination; coordination of schemes and intentionality.	Infant manipulates a stick in order to bring an attractive toy within reach.
5 Tertiary circular reactions, novelty, and curiosity	12 to 18 months	Infants become intrigued by the many properties of objects and by the many things they can make happen to objects; they experiment with new behavior.	A block can be made to fall, spin, hit another object, and slide across the ground.
6 Internalization of schemes	18 to 24 months	Infants develop the ability to use primitive symbols and form enduring mental representations.	An infant who has never thrown a temper tantrum before sees a playmate throw a tantrum; the infant retains a memory of the event, then throws one himself the next day.

FIGURE 1

PIAGET'S SIX SUBSTAGES OF SENSORIMOTOR DEVELOPMENT

of secondary circular reactions; (5) tertiary circular reactions, novelty, and curiosity; and (6) internalization of schemes (see Figure 1).

Simple reflexes, the first sensorimotor substage, correspond to the first month after birth. In this substage, sensation and action are coordinated primarily through reflexive behaviors such as rooting and sucking. Soon the infant produces behaviors that resemble reflexes in the absence of the usual stimulus for the reflex. For example, a newborn will suck a nipple or bottle only when it is placed directly in the baby's mouth or touched to the lips. Even in the first month of life, the infant is initiating action and actively structuring experiences.

First habits and primary circular reactions is the second sensorimotor substage, which develops between 1 and 4 months of age. In this substage, the infant coordinates sensation and two types of schemes: habits and primary circular reactions. A habit is a scheme based on a reflex that has become completely separated from its eliciting stimulus. For example, infants in substage 1 suck when bottles are put to their lips or when they see a bottle. Infants in substage 2 might suck even when no bottle is present. A circular reaction is a repetitive action.

A **primary circular reaction** is a scheme based on the attempt to reproduce an event that initially occurred by chance. For example, suppose an infant accidentally sucks his fingers when they are placed near his mouth. Later, he searches for his fingers to suck them again, but the fingers do not cooperate because the infant cannot coordinate visual and manual actions.

Habits and circular reactions are stereotyped—that is, the infant repeats them the same way each time. During this substage, the infant's own body remains the infant's center of attention. There is no outward pull by environmental events.

Secondary circular reactions is the third sensorimotor substage, which develops between 4 and 8 months of age. In this substage, the infant becomes more object-oriented, moving beyond preoccupation with the self. The infant's schemes are not intentional or goal-directed, but they are repeated because of their consequences. By chance, an infant might shake a rattle. The infant repeats this action for the sake of its fascination. This is a *secondary circular reaction:* an action repeated because of its consequences. The infant also imitates some simple actions, such as the baby talk or burbling of adults, and some physical gestures. However, the baby imitates only actions that he or she is already able to produce.

Coordination of secondary circular reactions is Piaget's fourth sensorimotor substage, which develops between 8 and 12 months of age. To progress into this substage, the infant must coordinate vision and touch, eye and hand. Actions become more outwardly directed. Significant changes during this substage involve the coordination of schemes and intentionality.

This 7-month-old is in Piaget's substage of secondary circular reactions. *What might the infant do to suggest he is in this substage?*
©Johnny Valley/Getty Images RF

simple reflexes Piaget's first sensorimotor substage, which corresponds to the first month after birth. In this substage, sensation and action are coordinated primarily through reflexive behaviors.

first habits and primary circular reactions Piaget's second sensorimotor substage, which develops between 1 and 4 months of age. In this substage, the infant coordinates sensation and two types of schemes: habits and primary circular reactions.

primary circular reaction A scheme based on the attempt to reproduce an event that initially occurred by chance.

Infants readily combine and recombine previously learned schemes in a coordinated way. They might look at an object and grasp it simultaneously, or they might visually inspect a toy, such as a rattle, and finger it simultaneously, exploring it tactilely. Actions are even more outwardly directed than before. Related to this coordination is the second achievement—the presence of intentionality. For example, infants might manipulate a stick in order to bring a desired toy within reach or they might knock over one block to reach and play with another one. Similarly, when 11-month-old Jacqueline, as described in the chapter opening, placed the ball in front of her and kicked it, she was demonstrating intentionality.

Tertiary circular reactions, novelty, and curiosity is Piaget's fifth sensorimotor substage, which develops between 12 and 18 months of age. In this substage, infants become intrigued by the many properties of objects and by the many things that they can make happen to objects. A block can be made to fall, spin, hit another object, and slide across the ground. *Tertiary circular reactions* are schemes in which the infant purposely explores new possibilities with objects, continually doing new things to them and exploring the results. Piaget says that this stage marks the starting point for human curiosity and interest in novelty.

Internalization of schemes is Piaget's sixth and final sensorimotor substage, which develops between 18 and 24 months of age. In this substage, the infant develops the ability to use primitive symbols. For Piaget, a symbol is an internalized sensory image or word that represents an event. Primitive symbols permit the infant to think about concrete events without directly acting them out or perceiving them. Moreover, symbols allow the infant to manipulate and transform the represented events in simple ways. In a favorite Piagetian example, Piaget's young daughter saw a matchbox being opened and closed. Later, she mimicked the event by opening and closing her mouth. This was an obvious expression of her image of the event.

Object Permanence

Imagine how chaotic and unpredictable your life would be if you could not distinguish between yourself and your world. This is what the life of a newborn must be like, according to Piaget. There is no differentiation between the self and world; objects have no separate, permanent existence.

By the end of the sensorimotor period, objects are both separate from the self and permanent. **Object permanence** is the understanding that objects continue to exist even when they cannot be seen, heard, or touched. Acquiring the sense of object permanence is one of the infant's most important accomplishments, according to Piaget.

How could anyone know whether an infant had developed a sense of object permanence? The principal way that object permanence is studied is by watching an infant's reaction when an interesting object disappears (see Figure 2). If infants search for the object, it is assumed that they believe it continues to exist.

Object permanence is just one of the basic concepts about the physical world developed by babies. To Piaget, children, even infants, are much like little scientists, examining the world to see how it works. How do adult scientists try to discover what these "baby scientists" are finding out about the world? The *Connecting with Research* interlude describes some of the ways.

This 17-month-old is in Piaget's stage of tertiary circular reactions. *What might the infant do to suggest that she is in this stage?*
©Corbis/PunchStock RF

developmental **connection**

Cognitive Processes

What are some changes in symbolic thought in young children? Connect to "Cognitive Development in Early Childhood."

secondary circular reactions Piaget's third sensorimotor substage, which develops between 4 and 8 months of age. In this substage, the infant becomes more object-oriented, moving beyond preoccupation with the self.

coordination of secondary circular reactions Piaget's fourth sensorimotor substage, which develops between 8 and 12 months of age. Actions become more outwardly directed, and infants coordinate schemes and act with intentionality.

tertiary circular reactions, novelty, and curiosity Piaget's fifth sensorimotor substage, which develops between 12 and 18 months of age. In this substage, infants become intrigued by the many properties of objects and by the many things that they can make happen to objects.

internalization of schemes Piaget's sixth and final sensorimotor substage, which develops between 18 and 24 months of age. In this substage, the infant develops the ability to use primitive symbols.

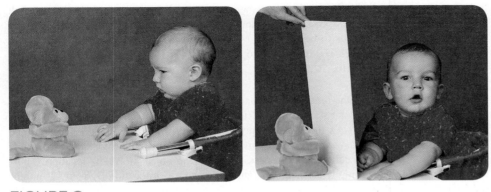

FIGURE 2

OBJECT PERMANENCE. Piaget argued that object permanence is one of infancy's landmark cognitive accomplishments. For this 5-month-old boy, "out-of-sight" is literally out of mind. The infant looks at the toy monkey (*left*), but, when his view of the toy is blocked (*right*), he does not search for it. Several months later, he will search for the hidden toy monkey, an action reflecting the presence of object permanence.
©Doug Goodman/Science Source

How Do Researchers Study Infants' Understanding of Object Permanence and Causality?

Two accomplishments of infants that Piaget examined were the development of object permanence and the child's understanding of causality. Let's examine two research studies that address these topics.

In both studies, Renée Baillargeon and her colleagues used a research method that involves violation of expectations. In this method, infants see an event happen as it normally would. Then the event is changed, often in a way that creates a physically impossible event. Infants look longer at the changed event, indicating that they are surprised by it. In other words, the infant's reaction is interpreted to indicate that the infant had certain expectations about the world that were violated.

In one study focused on object permanence, researchers showed infants a toy car that moved down an inclined track, disappeared behind a screen, and then reemerged at the other end, still on the track (Baillargeon & DeVos, 1991). After this sequence was repeated several times, something different occurred: A toy mouse was placed behind the tracks but was hidden by the screen while the car rolled by. This was the "possible" event. Then, the researchers created an "impossible event": The toy mouse was placed on the tracks but was secretly removed after the screen was lowered so that the car seemed to go through the mouse. In this study, infants as young as 3½ months of age looked longer at the impossible event than at the possible event, an indication that they were surprised by it. Their surprise suggested that they remembered not only the existence of the toy mouse (object permanence) but also its location.

Another study focused on the infant's understanding of causality (Kotovsky & Baillargeon, 1994). In this research, a cylinder rolls down a ramp and hits a toy bug at the bottom of the ramp. By 5½ and 6½ months of age, after infants have seen how far the bug will be pushed by a medium-sized cylinder, their reactions indicate that they understand that the bug will roll farther if it is hit by a large cylinder than if it is hit by a small cylinder. Thus, by the middle of the first year of life, these infants understand that the size of a moving object determines how far it will move a stationary object that it collides with.

In Baillargeon's (2008, 2014; Baillargeon & others, 2012; Luo & Baillargeon, 2010) view, infants have a preadapted, innate bias called the principle of persistence that explains their assumption that objects don't change their properties—including how solid they are, their location, their color, and their form—unless some external factor (a person who moves the object, for example) obviously intervenes. Shortly, we revisit the extent to which nature and nurture are at work in the changes that take place in the infant's cognitive development.

The research findings discussed in this interlude and other research indicate that infants develop object permanence and causal reasoning much earlier than Piaget proposed (Baillargeon & others, 2011). Indeed, as you will see in the next section, a major theme of infant cognitive development today is that infants are more cognitively competent than Piaget envisioned.

How does the discovery of infants' early cognitive competence affect our understanding of Piaget's research on infant development?

Infants know that objects are substantial and permanent at an earlier age than Piaget envisioned.

—**Renée Baillargeon**
Contemporary Psychologist, University of Illinois

object permanence Piagetian term for understanding that objects continue to exist, even when they cannot directly be seen, heard, or touched.

A-not-B error This occurs when infants make the mistake of selecting the familiar hiding place (A) rather than the new hiding place (B) of an object as they progress into substage 4 in Piaget's sensorimotor stage.

EVALUATING PIAGET'S SENSORIMOTOR STAGE

Piaget opened up a new way of looking at infants with his view that their main task is to coordinate their sensory impressions with their motor activity. However, the infant's cognitive world is not as neatly packaged as Piaget portrayed it, and some of Piaget's explanations of the causes of change are debated. In the past several decades, sophisticated experimental techniques have been devised to study infants, and there have been a large number of research studies on infant development. Much of the new research suggests that Piaget's view of sensorimotor development needs to be modified (Adolph, 2018; Baillargeon, 2016; Bremner & others, 2017; Carpendale & Hammond, 2016; Needham, 2016; Spelke, 2016a, b; Van de Vandervoort & Hamlin, 2016, 2018).

The A-not-B Error   One modification concerns Piaget's claim that certain processes are crucial in transitions from one stage to the next. The data do not always support his explanations. For example, in Piaget's theory, an important feature in the progression into substage 4, *coordination of secondary circular reactions*, is an infant's inclination to search for a hidden object in a familiar location rather than to look for the object in a new location. Thus, if a toy is hidden twice, initially at location A and subsequently at location B, 8- to 12-month-old infants search correctly at location A initially. But when the toy is subsequently hidden at location B, they make the mistake of continuing to search for it at location A. **A-not-B error** is the term used to describe this common mistake. Older infants are less likely to make the A-not-B error because their concept of object permanence is more complete.

Researchers have found, however, that the A-not-B error does not show up consistently (Sophian, 1985). The evidence indicates that A-not-B errors are sensitive to the delay between hiding the object at B and the infant's attempt to find it (Diamond, 1985). Thus, the A-not-B error might be due to a failure in memory. And A-not-B performance may be linked to attention as well. For example, in a recent study, 5-month-olds' more focused attention on a separate task involving a puppet was linked to better performance on an A-not-B task that involved locating an object after it was hidden from view (Marcovitch & others, 2016). Another explanation is that infants tend to repeat a previous motor behavior (Clearfield & others, 2006; Smith, 1999).

Perceptual Development and Expectation   A number of theorists, such as Eleanor Gibson (2001) and Elizabeth Spelke (2011, 2013), maintain that infants' perceptual abilities are highly developed very early in life. Spelke argues that young infants interpret the world as having predictable occurrences. For example, earlier we discussed research that demonstrated the presence of intermodal perception—the ability to coordinate information from two or more sensory modalities, such as vision and hearing—by 3½ months of age, much earlier than Piaget would have predicted (Spelke & Owsley, 1979).

Research also suggests that infants develop the ability to understand how the world works at a very early age (Baillargeon, 2014, 2016; Spelke, 2016a, b).What kinds of expectations do infants form? Are we born expecting the world to obey basic physical laws, such as gravity? If not, when do we learn how the world works? Experiments by Elizabeth Spelke and her colleagues (Dillon & others, 2015; Spelke, 1991, 2000, 2003, 2016a, b; Spelke, Bernier, & Snedeker, 2013; Spelke & Hespos, 2001) have addressed these questions. She placed babies before a puppet stage and showed them a series of actions that are unexpected if you know how the physical world works—for example, one ball seemed to roll through a solid barrier, another seemed to leap between two platforms, and a third appeared to hang in midair (Spelke, 1979). Spelke measured and compared the babies' looking times for unexpected and expected actions. She concluded that, by 4 months of age, even though infants do not yet have the ability to talk about objects, move around objects, manipulate objects, or even see objects with high resolution, they expect objects to be solid and continuous. However, at 4 months of age, infants do not expect an object to obey gravitational constraints (Spelke & others, 1992). Similarly, research by Renée Baillargeon (1995, 2004, 2014) documents that infants as young as 3 to 4 months expect objects to be *substantial* (in the sense that other objects cannot move through them) and *permanent* (in the sense that objects continue to exist when they are hidden).

In sum, researchers such as Baillargeon and Spelke conclude that infants see objects as bounded, unitary, solid, and separate from their background, possibly at birth or shortly thereafter, but definitely by 3 to 4 months of age, much earlier than Piaget envisioned. Young infants still have much to learn about objects, but the world appears both stable and orderly to them.

By 6 to 8 months, infants have learned to perceive gravity and support—that an object hanging on the end of a table should fall, that ball bearings will travel farther when rolled down a longer rather than a shorter ramp, and that cup handles will not fall when attached to a cup (Slater, Field, & Hernandez-Reif, 2007). As infants develop, their experiences and actions on objects help them to understand physical laws (Johnson & Hannon, 2015).

The Nature-Nurture Issue   In considering the big issue of whether nature or nurture plays the more important role in infant development, Elizabeth Spelke (Spelke, 2000, 2003, 2011, 2013, 2016a, b) comes down clearly on the side of nature. Spelke endorses a **core knowledge approach,** which states that infants are born with domain-specific innate knowledge systems. Among these domain-specific knowledge systems are those involving space, number sense, object permanence, and language (which we discuss later in this chapter). Strongly influenced by evolution, the core knowledge domains are theorized to be prewired to allow infants to make sense of their world (Coubart & others, 2014). After all, Spelke concludes, how could infants possibly grasp the complex world in which they live if they didn't come into the world equipped with core sets of knowledge? In this approach, the innate core knowledge domains form a foundation around which more mature cognitive functioning and learning develop. The core knowledge approach argues that Piaget greatly underestimated the cognitive abilities of infants, especially young infants (Huang & Spelke, 2015; Spelke, 2016a, b).

Recently, researchers also have explored whether preverbal infants might have a built-in, innate sense of morality (Steckler & Hamlin, 2016; Van de Vandervoort & Hamlin, 2016, 2018). In this research, infants as young as 4 months of age are more likely to make visually

developmental **connection**

Perception

Eleanor Gibson was a pioneer in crafting the ecological view of development. Connect to "Physical Development in Infancy."

developmental **connection**

Nature and Nurture

The nature-nurture issue is also important in understanding perceptual development. Connect to "Physical Development in Infancy."

core knowledge approach View that infants are born with domain-specific innate knowledge systems.

What revisions in Piaget's theory of sensorimotor development do contemporary researchers recommend? What characterizes the nature-nurture controversy in infant cognitive development?

©baobao ou/Flickr/Getty Images RF

guided reaches toward a puppet who has acted as a helper (such as helping someone get up a hill, assisting in opening a box, or giving a ball back) rather than toward a puppet who has acted as a hinderer to others' efforts to achieve such goals (Hamlin, 2013, 2014). And recently, the view that the emergence of morality in infancy is innate was described as problematic (Carpendale & Hammond, 2016). Instead it was argued that morality may emerge through infants' early interaction with others and later transformation through language and reflective thought.

In criticizing the core knowledge approach, British developmental psychologist Mark Johnson (2008) says that the infants Spelke assesses in her research already have accumulated hundreds, and in some cases even thousands, of hours of experience in grasping what the world is about, which gives considerable room for the environment's role in the development of infant cognition (Highfield, 2008). According to Johnson (2008), infants likely come into the world with "soft biases to perceive and attend to different aspects of the environment, and to learn about the world in particular ways." A major criticism is that nativists completely neglect the infant's social immersion in the world and instead focus only on what happens inside the infant's head, apart from the environment (Nelson, 2013).

Although debate about the cause and course of infant cognitive development continues, most developmentalists today agree that Piaget underestimated the early cognitive accomplishments of infants and that both nature and nurture are involved in infants' cognitive development (Bell & others, 2018; Bremner & others, 2017; Gomez, 2017).

Conclusions   In sum, many researchers conclude that Piaget wasn't specific enough about how infants learn about their world and that infants, especially young infants, are more competent than Piaget thought (Baillargeon, 2016; Needham, 2016; Spelke, 2016a, b; Van de Vandervoort & Hamlin, 2016, 2018; Xie & Richards, 2017). As researchers have examined the specific ways that infants learn, the field of infant cognition has become very specialized. There are many researchers working on different questions, with no general theory emerging that can connect all of the different findings (Nelson, 1999). Their theories often are local theories, focused on specific research questions, rather than grand theories like Piaget's (Kuhn, 1998).

Among the unifying themes in the study of infant cognition are seeking to understand more precisely how developmental changes in cognition take place, to answer questions about the relative importance of nature and nurture, and to examine the brain's role in cognitive development. As they seek to assess more precisely the contributions of nature and nurture to infant development, researchers face the difficult task of determining whether the course of acquiring information, which is very rapid in some domains, is better accounted for by an innate set of biases (that is, core knowledge), or by the extensive input of environmental experiences to which the infant is exposed (Aslin, 2009). Also, recall that exploring connections between brain, cognition, and development is the focus of the recently emerging field of *developmental cognitive neuroscience* (Bell & others, 2018; de Haan & Johnson, 2016; Gliga & others, 2017; Saez de Urabain & others, 2017).

Review *Connect* Reflect

LG1 Summarize and evaluate Piaget's theory of infant development.

Review

- What cognitive processes are important in Piaget's theory?
- What are some characteristics of Piaget's stage of sensorimotor development?
- What are some contributions and criticisms of Piaget's sensorimotor stage?

Connect

- You just read that by the age of 6 to 8 months infants have learned to perceive gravity and support. What physical development occurring around this same time period might contribute to the infant's understanding of these concepts?

Reflect *Your Own Personal Journey of Life*

- What are some implications of Piaget's theory of infant development for parenting?

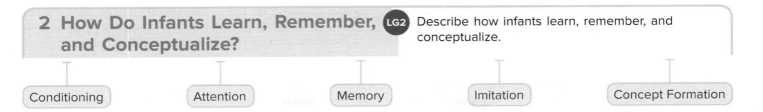

2 How Do Infants Learn, Remember, and Conceptualize? **LG2** Describe how infants learn, remember, and conceptualize.

Conditioning Attention Memory Imitation Concept Formation

When Piaget hung a doll above 4-month-old Lucienne's feet, as described at the beginning of the chapter, would she remember the doll? If Piaget had rewarded her for moving the doll with her foot, would the reward have affected Lucienne's behavior? If he had shown her how to shake the doll's hand, could she have imitated him? If he had shown her a different doll, could she have formed the concept of a "doll"?

Questions like these might be examined by researchers taking behavioral and social cognitive or information processing approaches. In contrast with Piaget's theory, these approaches do not describe infant development in terms of stages. Instead, they document gradual changes in the infant's ability to understand and process information about the world. In this section, we explore what researchers using these approaches can tell us about how infants learn, remember, and conceptualize.

CONDITIONING

Earlier, we described Pavlov's classical conditioning (in which, as a result of pairing, a new stimulus comes to elicit a response previously given to another stimulus) and Skinner's operant conditioning (in which the consequences of a behavior produce changes in the probability of the behavior's occurrence). Infants can learn through both types of conditioning. For example, if an infant's behavior is followed by a rewarding stimulus, the behavior is likely to recur.

Operant conditioning has been especially helpful to researchers in their efforts to determine what infants perceive (Rovee-Collier & Barr, 2010; Rovee-Collier & Cuevas, 2009). For example, infants will suck faster on a nipple when the sucking behavior is followed by a visual display, music, or a human voice (Rovee-Collier, 2008).

Carolyn Rovee-Collier (1987) also demonstrated how infants can retain information from the experience of being conditioned. She placed a 2½-month-old baby in a crib under an elaborate mobile (see Figure 3). She then tied one end of a ribbon to the baby's ankle and the other end to the mobile. Subsequently, she observed that the baby kicked and made the mobile move. The movement of the mobile was the reinforcing stimulus (which increased the baby's kicking behavior) in this experiment. Weeks later, the baby was returned to the crib, but its foot was not tied to the mobile. The baby kicked, which suggests it had retained the information that if it kicked a leg, the mobile would move.

ATTENTION

Attention, the focusing of mental resources on select information, improves cognitive processing on many tasks (Benitez & others, 2017; Reynolds & Romano, 2016; Salley & Colombo, 2016; Salley & others, 2016; Wu & Scerif, 2018; Yu & Smith, 2016, 2017). At any one time, though, people can pay attention to only a limited amount of information. Even newborns can detect a contour and fix their attention on it. Older infants scan patterns more thoroughly. By 4 months, infants can selectively attend to an object. A recent study examined 7- and 8-month-old infants' visual attention to sequences of events that varied in complexity (Kidd, Piantadosi, & Aslin, 2012). The infants tended to look away from events that were overly simple or complex, preferring instead to attend to events of intermediate complexity. Also, in recent research, 5-month-olds whose attention involved more efficient speed of processing information (called "short lookers") engaged in a higher level of executive function (higher-level cognitive functioning, such as being cognitively flexible and having better inhibitory control) during the preschool years than their counterparts who were less efficient in attending to information (referred to as "long lookers") (Cuevas & Bell, 2014).

Attention in the first year of life is dominated by an *orienting/investigative process* (Colombo & Salley, 2015). This process involves directing attention to potentially important

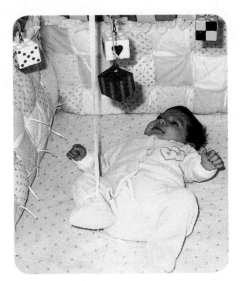

FIGURE 3

CONDITIONING AND MEMORY IN INFANTS. In Rovee-Collier's experiment, operant conditioning was used to demonstrate that infants as young as 2½ months of age can retain information from the experience of being conditioned. *What did infants recall in Rovee-Collier's experiment?*
©Dr. Carolyn Rovee-Collier

attention The focusing of mental resources on select information.

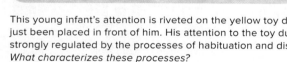

developmental connection

Attention

In early childhood, children make significant advances in sustained attention. Connect to "Cognitive Development in Early Childhood."

locations in the environment (that is, *where*) and recognizing objects and their features (such as color and form) (that is, *what*) (Richards, 2011). Orienting attention to an object or event involves the parietal lobes in the cerebral cortex (Ellison & others, 2014).

From 3 to 9 months of age, infants can deploy their attention more flexibly and quickly. Another important type of attention is *sustained attention,* also referred to as *focused attention* (Richards, 2011). New stimuli typically elicit an orienting response followed by sustained attention. It is sustained attention that allows infants to learn about and remember characteristics of a stimulus as it becomes familiar. Researchers have found that infants as young as 3 months of age can engage in 5 to 10 seconds of sustained attention. From this age through the second year, the length of sustained attention increases (Courage & Richards, 2008).

Habituation and Dishabituation   Closely linked with attention are the processes of habituation and dishabituation. If you say the same word or show the same toy to a baby several times in a row, the baby usually pays less attention to it each time. This is *habituation*—decreased responsiveness to a stimulus after repeated presentations of the stimulus. *Dishabituation* is the increase in responsiveness after a change in stimulation. Some of the measures that researchers use to study whether habituation is occurring include sucking behavior (sucking stops when an infant attends to a novel object), heart rates, and the length of time the infant looks at an object.

Infants' attention is strongly governed by novelty and habituation (Snyder & Torrence, 2008). When an object becomes familiar, attention becomes shorter, making infants more vulnerable to distraction.

This young infant's attention is riveted on the yellow toy duck that has just been placed in front of him. His attention to the toy duck will be strongly regulated by the processes of habituation and dishabituation. *What characterizes these processes?*

©Sporrer/Rupp/GettyImages RF

Researchers study habituation to determine the extent to which infants can see, hear, smell, taste, and experience touch (Colombo & Mitchell, 2009). Studies of habituation can also indicate whether infants recognize something they have previously experienced. Habituation provides a measure of an infant's maturity and well-being. Infants who have brain damage do not habituate well.

Knowing about habituation and dishabituation can help parents interact effectively with infants. Infants respond to changes in stimulation. Wise parents sense when an infant shows an interest and realize that they may have to repeat something many times for the infant to process information. But if the stimulation is repeated often, the infant stops responding to the parent. In parent-infant interaction, it is important for parents to do novel things and to repeat them often until the infant stops responding. The parent stops or changes behaviors when the infant redirects his or her attention (Rosenblith, 1992).

Joint Attention   Another aspect of attention that is an important part of infant development is **joint attention,** in which individuals focus on the same object or event. Joint attention requires (1) an ability to track another's behavior, such as following someone's gaze; (2) one person directing another's attention; and (3) reciprocal interaction. Early in infancy, joint attention usually involves a caregiver pointing or using words to direct an infant's attention. Emerging forms of joint attention occur at about 7 to 8 months, but it is not until toward the end of the first year that joint attention skills are frequently observed (Heimann & others, 2006). In a study conducted by Rechele Brooks and Andrew Meltzoff (2005), at 10 to 11 months of age infants first began engaging in "gaze following," looking where another person has just looked (see Figure 4). And by their first birthday, infants have begun to direct adults' attention to objects that capture their interest (Heimann & others, 2006). Also, a recent study found that problems in joint attention as early as 8 months of age were linked to a child being diagnosed with autism by 7 years of age (Veness & others, 2014). Also, another recent study involving the use of eye-tracking equipment with 11- to 24-month-olds revealed that infants' hand-eye coordination involving the connection of gaze with manual actions on objects rather than gaze following alone predicted joint attention (Yu & Smith, 2017).

Joint attention plays important roles in many aspects of infant development and considerably increases infants' ability to learn from other people (Brooks & Meltzoff, 2014; Salley & Colombo, 2016; Salley & others, 2016). Nowhere is this more apparent than in

joint attention Occurs when individuals focus on the same object or event and are able to track each other's behavior; one individual directs another's attention, and reciprocal interaction is present.

memory A central feature of cognitive development, involving the retention of information over time.

(a)

(b)

FIGURE 4

GAZE FOLLOWING IN INFANCY. Researcher Rechele Brooks shifts her eyes from the infant to a toy in the foreground (*a*). The infant then follows her eye movement to the toy (*b*). Brooks and colleague Andrew Meltzoff (2005) found that infants begin to engage in this kind of behavior called "gaze following" at 10 to 11 months of age. *Why might gaze following be an important accomplishment for an infant?*
©2005 University of Washington, Institute for Learning & Brain Sciences

observations of interchanges between caregivers and infants while the infants are learning language (Tomasello, 2011). When caregivers and infants frequently engage in joint attention, infants say their first word earlier and develop a larger vocabulary (Beuker & others, 2013; Mastin & Vogt, 2017). Later in this chapter in our discussion of language, we further discuss joint attention as an early predictor of language development in older infants and toddlers (Tomasello, 2011).

Joint attention skills in infancy also are associated with the development of self-regulation later in childhood. For example, one study revealed that responding to joint attention at 12 months of age was linked to self-regulation skills at 3 years of age that involved delaying gratification for an attractive object (Van Hecke & others, 2012). And in other research, infants who initiated joint attention at 14 months of age had higher executive function at 18 months of age (Miller & Marcovitch, 2015).

MEMORY

Memory involves retaining information over time. Attention plays an important role in memory as part of a process called *encoding,* which is the process by which information gets into memory. What can infants remember, and when?

Some researchers such as Rovee-Collier (2008) have concluded that infants as young as 2 to 6 months of age can remember some experiences through 1½ to 2 years of age. However, critics such as Jean Mandler (2004), a leading expert on infant cognition, argue that the infants in Rovee-Collier's experiments are displaying only implicit memory. **Implicit memory** refers to memory without conscious recollection—memories of skills and routine procedures that are performed automatically. In contrast, **explicit memory** refers to the conscious memory of facts and experiences.

When people think about memory, they are usually referring to explicit memory. Most researchers find that babies do not show explicit memory until the second half of the first year (Bauer, 2013; Bauer & Fivush, 2014; Bauer & Larkina, 2016; Bauer & others, 2003; Mandler & McDonough, 1993). Then explicit memory improves substantially during the second year of life (Bauer, 2013; Bauer & Fivush, 2014; Carver & Bauer, 2001; Lukowski & Bauer, 2014). In a longitudinal study, infants were assessed several times during their second year (Bauer & others, 2000). Older infants showed more accurate memory and required fewer prompts to demonstrate their memory than younger infants. Figure 5 summarizes how long infants of different ages can remember information (Bauer, 2009a, b). As indicated in Figure 5, researchers have documented that 6-month-olds can remember

FIGURE 5

AGE-RELATED CHANGES IN THE LENGTH OF TIME OVER WHICH MEMORY OCCURS

From *Learning and the Infant Mind* edited by Amanda Woodward and Amy Needham (2008), p. 12, Table 1. ©2005 by Amanda Woodward and Amy Needham. By permission of Oxford University Press, Inc.

A mother and her infant daughter engaging in joint attention. *What about this photograph tells you that joint attention is occurring? Why is joint attention an important aspect of infant development?*
©Ocean/Corbis RF

How Would You...?
If you were a **human development and family studies professional,** what strategies would you recommend to help parents improve an infant's development of attention?

implicit memory Memory without conscious recollection; involves skills and routine procedures that are automatically performed.

explicit memory Conscious memory of facts and experiences.

Age Group	Length of Delay
6-month-olds	24 hours
9-month-olds	1 month
10–11-month-olds	3 months
13–14-month-olds	4–6 months
20-month-olds	12 months

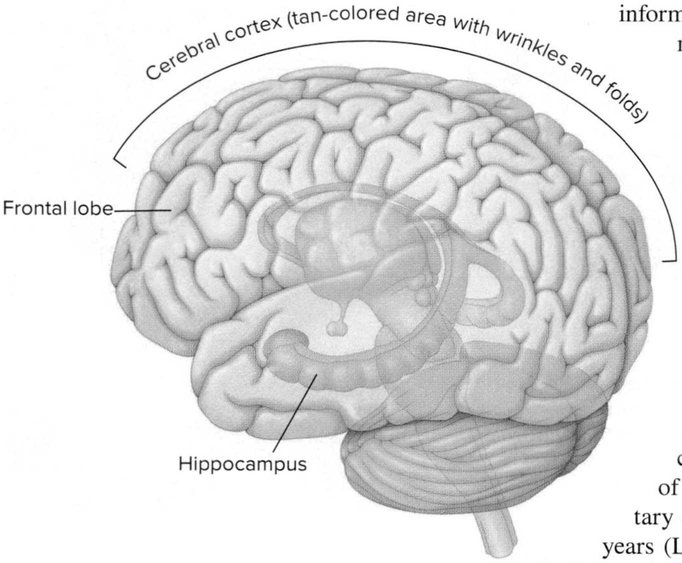

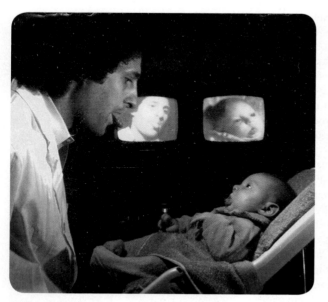

Cerebral cortex (tan-colored area with wrinkles and folds)

Frontal lobe

Hippocampus

FIGURE 6

KEY BRAIN STRUCTURES INVOLVED IN EXPLICIT MEMORY DEVELOPMENT IN INFANCY

deferred imitation Imitation that occurs after a delay of hours or days.

information for 24 hours, but by 20 months of age infants can remember information they encountered 12 months earlier (Bauer, Larkina, & Deocampo, 2011).

What changes in the brain are linked to infants' memory development? From about 6 to 12 months of age, the maturation of the hippocampus and the surrounding cerebral cortex, especially the frontal lobes, makes the emergence of explicit memory possible (Morasch & Bell, 2009; Nelson, 2013) (see Figure 6). Explicit memory continues to improve in the second year as these brain structures further mature and connections between them increase. Less is known about the areas of the brain involved in implicit memory in infancy.

Let's examine another aspect of memory. Do you remember your third birthday party? Probably not. Most adults can remember little if anything from the first three years of their life (Riggins, 2012). This is called *infantile,* or *childhood, amnesia.* The few reported adult memories of life at age 2 or 3 are at best very sketchy (Newcombe, 2008). Elementary school children also do not remember much from their early childhood years (Lie & Newcombe, 1999).

What is the cause of infantile amnesia? One reason older children and adults have difficulty recalling events from their infant and early childhood years is that during these early years the prefrontal lobes of the brain are immature; this area of the brain is believed to play an important role in storing memories of events (Boyer & Diamond, 1992).

Patricia Bauer and her colleagues (Bauer & Larkina, 2014, 2016; Pathman, Doydum, & Bauer, 2013) have been recently studying when infantile amnesia begins to occur. In one study, children's memory for events that occurred at 3 years of age was periodically assessed through age 9 (Bauer & Larkina, 2014). By 8 to 9 years of age, children's memory of events that occurred at 3 years of age began to significantly fade away. In Bauer's (2015) view, the processes that account for these developmental changes are early, gradual development of the ability to form, retain, and later retrieve memories of personally relevant past events followed by an accelerated rate of forgetting in childhood.

In sum, most of young infants' conscious memories appear to be rather fragile and short-lived, although their implicit memory of perceptual-motor actions can be substantial (Bauer, Larkina, & Deocampo, 2011; Mandler, 2004). By the end of the second year, long-term memory is more substantial and reliable (Lukowski & Bauer, 2014).

IMITATION

Can infants imitate someone else's emotional expressions? If an adult smiles, will the baby follow with a smile? If an adult protrudes her lower lip, wrinkles her forehead, and frowns, will the baby show a sad face?

Infant development researcher Andrew Meltzoff (2004, 2007, 2011; Meltzoff & Moore, 1999; Meltzoff & Williamson, 2013) has conducted numerous studies of infants' imitative abilities. He sees infants' imitative abilities as biologically based, because infants can imitate a facial expression within the first few days after birth. He also emphasizes that the infant's imitative abilities do not resemble a hardwired response but rather involve flexibility and adaptability. In Meltzoff's observations of infants across the first 72 hours of life, the infants gradually displayed more complete imitation of an adult's facial expression, such as protruding the tongue or opening the mouth wide (see Figure 7).

Meltzoff (2007, 2011; Meltzoff & Williamson, 2013; Meltzoff, Williamson, & Marshall, 2013) concludes that infants don't blindly imitate everything they see and often make creative errors. He also argues that beginning at birth there is an interplay between learning by observing and learning by doing (Piaget emphasized learning by doing).

FIGURE 7

INFANT IMITATION. Infant development researcher Andrew Meltzoff protrudes his tongue in an attempt to get the infant to imitate his behavior. *How do Meltzoff's findings about imitation compare with Piaget's descriptions of infants' abilities?*
©Dr. Andrew Meltzoff

Not all experts on infant development accept Meltzoff's conclusions that newborns are capable of imitation. Some say that these babies were engaging in little more than automatic responses to a stimulus.

Meltzoff (2005, 2011) also has studied **deferred imitation,** which occurs after a time delay of hours or days. Piaget held that deferred imitation doesn't occur until about 18 months of age. Meltzoff's research suggested that it occurs much earlier. In one study, Meltzoff (1988) demonstrated that 9-month-old infants could imitate actions—such as pushing a recessed button in a box, which produced a beeping sound—that they had seen performed 24 hours earlier. Also, in a recent study, engagement in deferred imitation at 9 months of age was a strong predictor of more extensive production of communicative gestures at 14 months of age (Heimann & others, 2006). Two of the most common infant gestures are (1) extending the arm to show the caregiver something the infant is holding, and (2) pointing with the arm and index finger extended at some interesting object or event.

CONCEPT FORMATION

Along with attention, memory, and imitation, concepts are key aspects of infants' cognitive development (Gelman, 2013; Quinn, 2016; Rakison & Lawson, 2013). **Concepts** are cognitive groupings of similar objects, events, people, or ideas. Without concepts, you would see each object and event as unique; you would not be able to make any generalizations.

Do infants have concepts? Yes, they do, although we do not know just how early concept formation begins (Mandler, 2009; Quinn, 2016; Quinn & others, 2013). Using habituation experiments like those described earlier in the chapter, some researchers have found that infants as young as 3 to 4 months of age can group together objects with similar appearances, such as animals (Quinn, 2016; Rakison & Lawson, 2013). This research capitalizes on the knowledge that infants are more likely to look at a novel object than a familiar object.

Jean Mandler (2004, 2010) argues that these early categorizations are best described as *perceptual categorization*. That is, the categorizations are based on similar perceptual features of objects, such as size, color, and movement, as well as parts of objects, such as legs for animals. Mandler (2004) concludes that it is not until about 7 to 9 months of age that infants form *conceptual* categories rather than just making perceptual discriminations between different categories. In one study of 9- to 11-month-olds, infants classified birds as animals and airplanes as vehicles even though the objects were perceptually similar—airplanes and birds with their wings spread (Mandler & McDonough, 1993) (see Figure 8).

In addition to infants categorizing items on the basis of external, perceptual features such as shape, color, and parts, they also may categorize items on the basis of prototypes, or averages, that they extract from the structural regularities of items (Rakison & Lawson, 2013).

Further advances in categorization occur in the second year of life (Rakison & Lawson, 2013). Many infants' "first concepts are broad and global in nature, such as 'animal' or 'indoor thing.' Gradually, over the first two years these broad concepts become more differentiated into concepts such as 'land animal,' then 'dog,' or to 'furniture,' then 'chair'" (Mandler, 2009, p. 1). Also in the second year, infants often categorize objects on the basis of their shape (Landau, Smith, & Jones, 1998).

Learning to put things into the correct categories—what makes something one kind of thing rather than another kind of thing, such as what makes a bird a bird, or a fish a fish—is an important aspect of cognitive development. As infant development researcher Alison Gopnik (2010, p. 159) recently pointed out, "If you can sort the world into the right categories—put things in the right boxes—then you've got a big advance on understanding the world."

Do some very young children develop an intense, passionate interest in a particular category of objects or activities? A study

> Infants are creating concepts and organizing their world into conceptual domains that will form the backbone of their thought throughout life.
>
> —JEAN MANDLER
> *Contemporary Psychologist, University of California–San Diego*

How Would You...?
If you were an **educator,** how would you talk with parents about the importance of their infant developing concepts?

concepts Cognitive groupings of similar objects, events, people, or ideas.

FIGURE 8

CATEGORIZATION IN 9- TO 11-MONTH-OLDS. These are the stimuli used in the study that indicated 9- to 11-month-old infants categorize perceptually similar objects as different (birds and planes) (Mandler & McDonough, 1993).

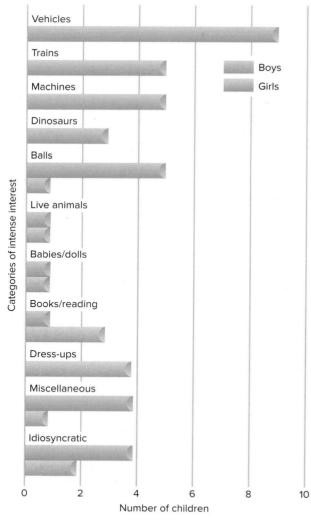

FIGURE **9**

CATEGORIZATION OF BOYS' AND GIRLS' INTENSE INTERESTS

of 11-month-old to 6-year-old children confirmed that they do (DeLoache, Simcock, & Macari, 2007). A striking finding was the large gender difference in categories, with an intense interest in particular categories stronger among boys than among girls. Categorization of boys' intense interests focused on vehicles, trains, machines, dinosaurs, and balls; girls' intense interests were more likely to involve dress-ups and books/reading (see Figure 9). When your author's grandson Alex was 18 to 24 months old, he already had developed an intense, passionate interest in the category of vehicles. He categorized vehicles into such subcategories as cars, trucks, earthmoving equipment, and buses. In addition to common classifications of cars into police cars, jeeps, taxis, and such, and trucks into fire trucks, dump trucks, and the like, his categorical knowledge of earthmoving equipment included bulldozers and excavators, and he categorized buses into school buses, London buses, and funky Malta buses (retro buses on the island of Malta). Later, at 2 to 3 years of age, Alex developed an intense, passionate interest in categorizing dinosaurs.

In sum, the infant's advances in processing information—through attention, memory, imitation, and concept formation—is much richer, more gradual, and less stage-like and occurs earlier than was envisioned by earlier

theorists, such as Piaget (Bell & others, 2018; Bremner & others, 2017; Gomez, 2017; Xie & Richards, 2017). As leading infant researcher Jean Mandler (2004) concluded, "The human infant shows a remarkable degree of learning power and complexity in what is being learned and in the way it is represented" (p. 304).

The author's grandson Alex at 2 years of age showing his intense, passionate interest in the category of vehicles while playing with a London taxi and a funky Malta bus.
Courtesy of Dr. John Santrock

Review *Connect* Reflect

LG2 Describe how infants learn, remember, and conceptualize.

Review

- How do infants learn through conditioning?
- What is attention? What characterizes attention in infants?
- What is memory?
- To what extent can infants remember?
- How is imitation involved in infant learning?
- When do infants develop concepts, and how does concept formation change during infancy?

Connect

- In this section, you learned that explicit memory develops in the

second year as the hippocampus and frontal lobes mature and connections between them increase. What did you learn in the text associated with Figure 6 in the chapter "Physical Development in Infancy" that might also contribute to improvements in a cognitive process like memory during this same time frame?

Reflect *Your Own Personal Journey of Life*

- If a friend told you that she remembers being abused by her parents when she was 2 years old, would you believe her? Explain your answer.

3 How Are Individual Differences in Infancy Assessed, and Do These Assessments Predict Intelligence?

LG3 Discuss infant assessment measures and the prediction of intelligence.

Measures of Infant Development

Predicting Intelligence

So far in this chapter, we have discussed how the cognitive development of infants generally progresses. We have emphasized what is typical of the largest number of infants or the average infant, but the results obtained for most infants do not apply to all infants. It is advantageous to know whether an infant is developing at a slow, normal, or advanced pace during the course of infancy. If an infant advances at an especially slow rate, then some form of enrichment may be necessary. If an infant develops at an advanced pace, parents may be advised to provide toys that stimulate cognitive growth in slightly older infants. How is an infant's cognitive development assessed?

MEASURES OF INFANT DEVELOPMENT

Individual differences in infant cognitive development have been studied primarily through the use of developmental scales or infant intelligence tests. For example, the Brazelton Neonatal Behavioral Assessment Scale (NBAS) and the Neonatal Intensive Care Unit Network Neurobehavioral Scale (NNNS) are used to evaluate newborns. To read about the work of one infant assessment specialist, see the *Connecting with Careers* profile.

The most important early contributor to the testing of infants was Arnold Gesell (1934a, b). He developed a measure that helped to sort out potentially normal babies from abnormal ones. This was especially useful to adoption agencies, which had large numbers of babies

connecting with careers

Toosje Thyssen Van Beveren, Infant Assessment Specialist

Toosje Thyssen Van Beveren is a developmental psychologist at the University of Texas Medical Center in Dallas and a senior lecturer at the University of Texas at Dallas. She has a master's degree in child clinical psychology and a Ph.D. in human development. Recently, Van Beveren has been involved in a 12-week program called New Connections, a comprehensive intervention for young children who were affected by substance abuse prenatally and for their caregivers.

In the New Connections program, Van Beveren assesses infants' developmental status and progress. She might refer the infants to a speech, physical, or occupational therapist and monitor the infants' services and progress. Van Beveren trains the program staff and encourages them to use the exercises she recommends. She also discusses the child's problems with the primary caregivers, suggests activities, and assists them in enrolling infants in appropriate programs.

During her graduate work at the University of Texas at Dallas, Van Beveren was author John Santrock's teaching assistant in his undergraduate course on life-span development for four years. As a teaching assistant, she attended classes, graded exams, counseled

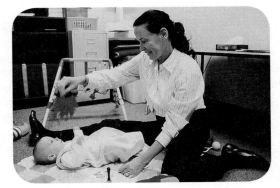

Toosje Thyssen Van Beveren conducts an infant assessment.
Courtesy of Dr. John Santrock

students, and occasionally gave lectures. Currently, Van Beveren is a senior lecturer in the psychology department at UT–Dallas, teaching an undergraduate course in child development and a graduate course in infant development. In Van Beveren's words, "My days are busy and full. My work with infants is often challenging. There are some disappointments, but mostly the work is enormously gratifying."

Items in the Bayley-III Scales of Infant Development.
©Amy Kiley Photography

awaiting placement. Gesell's examination was used widely for many years and still is frequently employed by pediatricians to distinguish between normal and abnormal infants. The current version of the Gesell test has four categories of behavior: motor, language, adaptive, and personal-social. The **developmental quotient (DQ)** combines subscores in these categories to provide an overall score.

The widely used **Bayley Scales of Infant Development** were developed by Nancy Bayley (1969) in order to assess infant behavior and predict later development. The current version, the Bayley Scales of Infant and Toddler Development—Third Edition (Bayley-III), has five scales: cognitive, language, motor, socio-emotional, and adaptive (Bayley, 2005). The first three scales are administered directly to the infant, and the latter two are questionnaires given to the caregiver. The Bayley-III also is more appropriate for use in clinical settings than the two previous editions (Lennon & others, 2008).

How should a 6-month-old perform on the Bayley cognitive scale? The 6-month-old infant should be able to vocalize pleasure and displeasure, persistently search for objects that are just out of immediate reach, and approach a mirror that is placed in front of the infant by the examiner. By 12 months of age, the infant should be able to inhibit behavior when commanded to do so, imitate words the examiner says (such as *Mama*), and respond to simple requests (such as "Take a drink").

The explosion of interest in infant development has produced many new measures, especially tasks that evaluate the ways infants process information (Rose, Feldman, & Wallace, 1992). The Fagan Test of Infant Intelligence is increasingly being used (Fagan, 1992). This test focuses on the infant's ability to process information in such ways as encoding the attributes of objects, detecting similarities and differences between objects, forming mental representations, and retrieving these representations. For example, it estimates babies' intelligence by comparing the amount of time they look at a new object with the amount of time they spend looking at a familiar object.

PREDICTING INTELLIGENCE

The infant-testing movement grew out of the tradition of IQ testing. However, IQ tests of older children pay more attention to verbal ability. Tests for infants contain far more items related to perceptual-motor development and include measures of social interaction.

A longitudinal study examined the intelligence of 200 children from 12 months (using the Bayley scales) to 4 years (using the Stanford-Binet test) of age (Blaga & others, 2009). The results indicated considerable stability from late infancy through the preschool years. However, overall scores on tests such as the Gesell and the Bayley scales in infancy do not correlate highly with IQ scores obtained later in childhood. This is not surprising, because the components tested in infancy are not the same as the components assessed by IQ tests later in childhood.

Unlike the Gesell and Bayley scales, the Fagan test is correlated with measures of intelligence in older children. In fact, evidence is accumulating that measures of habituation and dishabituation are linked to intelligence in childhood and adolescence (Fagan, Holland, & Wheeler, 2007; Kavsek, 2004). One study revealed that habituation at 3 or 6 months of age was linked to verbal skills and intelligence assessed at 32 months of age (Domsch, Lohaus, & Thomas, 2009). And a longitudinal study revealed that four information-processing domains (attention, processing speed, memory, and representational competence) assessed in infancy and early childhood were linked to general intelligence scores on the Wechsler Intelligence Scale for Children–III assessed at 11 years of age (Rose & others, 2012).

Also, a longitudinal study found that developmental milestones at 24 months of age were strongly linked to IQ at 5 to 6 years of age, but milestones at 4, 8, and 12 months were only slightly associated with IQ at 5 to 6 years (Peyre & others, 2017). Of the four developmental milestones (language, gross motor skills, fine motor skills, and socialization), early language skills were the best predictor of IQ. Further, early language skills were linked to which children had an IQ lower than 70 (intellectual disability) (predicted from 8 months of age) or higher than 130 (gifted) (predicted from 12 months of age) at 5 to 6 years of age.

- - - - - - →
developmental **connection**

Intelligence

The two most widely used tests of intelligence in older children, adolescents, and adults are the Stanford-Binet tests and the Wechsler scales. Connect to "Cognitive Development in Middle and Late Childhood."

← - - - - - - -

developmental quotient (DQ) An overall score that combines subscores in motor, language, adaptive, and personal-social domains in the Gesell assessment of infants.

Bayley Scales of Infant Development Scales developed by Nancy Bayley that are widely used in assessing infant development. The current version, the Bayley Scales of Infant and Toddler Development—Third Edition (Bayley-III), has five components: a cognitive scale, a language scale, a motor scale, a socio-emotional scale, and an adaptive scale.

language A form of communication, whether spoken, written, or signed, that is based on a system of symbols.

It is important not to go too far and think that connections between cognitive development in early infancy and later cognitive development are so strong that no discontinuity takes place. Some important changes in cognitive development occur after infancy—changes that we describe in later chapters.

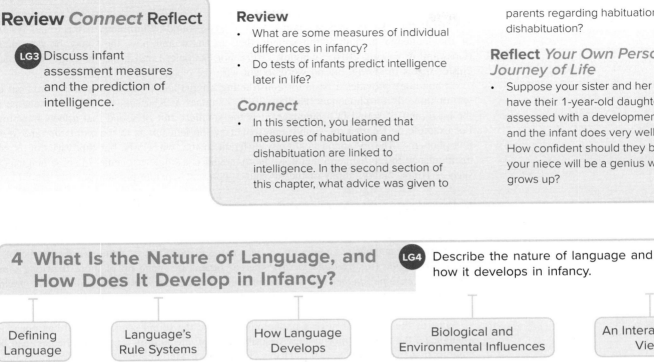

Review Connect Reflect

LG3 Discuss infant assessment measures and the prediction of intelligence.

Review
- What are some measures of individual differences in infancy?
- Do tests of infants predict intelligence later in life?

Connect
- In this section, you learned that measures of habituation and dishabituation are linked to intelligence. In the second section of this chapter, what advice was given to parents regarding habituation and dishabituation?

Reflect *Your Own Personal Journey of Life*
- Suppose your sister and her husband have their 1-year-old daughter assessed with a developmental scale, and the infant does very well on it. How confident should they be that your niece will be a genius when she grows up?

---

4 What Is the Nature of Language, and How Does It Develop in Infancy?

LG4 Describe the nature of language and how it develops in infancy.

| Defining Language | Language's Rule Systems | How Language Develops | Biological and Environmental Influences | An Interactionist View |

In 1799, a nude boy was observed running through the woods in France. The boy was captured when he was 11 years old. He was called the Wild Boy of Aveyron and was believed to have lived in the woods alone for six years (Lane, 1976). When found, he made no effort to communicate. He never learned to communicate effectively. A modern-day wild child named Genie was discovered in Los Angeles in 1970. Sadly, despite intensive intervention, Genie has never acquired more than a primitive form of language. Both cases—the Wild Boy of Aveyron and Genie—raise questions about the biological and environmental determinants of language, topics that we also examine later in the chapter. First, though, we need to define language.

DEFINING LANGUAGE

Language is a form of communication—whether spoken, written, or signed—that is based on a system of symbols. Language consists of the words used by a community and the rules for varying and combining them.

Think how important language is in our everyday lives. We need language to speak with others, listen to others, read, and write. Our language enables us to describe past events in detail and to plan for the future. Language lets us pass down information from one generation to the next and create a rich cultural heritage. Language learning involves comprehending a sound system (or sign system for individuals who are deaf), the world of objects, actions, and events, and how units such as words and grammar connect sound and world (Pace & others, 2016; van der Hulst, 2017; Wilcox & Occhino, 2017).

All human languages have some common characteristics (Clark, 2017; Waxman & others, 2014). These include infinite generativity and organizational rules. **Infinite generativity** is the ability to produce and comprehend an endless number of meaningful sentences using a finite set of words and rules. Rules describe the way language works. Let's explore what these rules involve.

Language allows us to communicate with others. *What are some important characteristics of language?*
©Vanessa Davies/Dorling Kindersley/Getty Images

infinite generativity The ability to produce an endless number of meaningful sentences using a finite set of words and rules.

LANGUAGE'S RULE SYSTEMS

When nineteenth-century American writer Ralph Waldo Emerson said, "The world was built in order and the atoms march in tune," he must have had language in mind. Language is highly ordered and organized. The organization involves five systems of rules: phonology, morphology, syntax, semantics, and pragmatics.

Phonology Every language is made up of basic sounds. **Phonology** is the sound system of the language, including the sounds that are used and how they may be combined (Goswami & Bryant, 2016; Swingley, 2017). For example, English has the initial consonant cluster *spr* as in *spring,* but no words begin with the cluster *rsp.*

Phonology provides a basis for constructing a large and expandable set of words out of two or three dozen phonemes (Nathan, 2017; Zamuner & Kharlamov, 2017). A phoneme is the basic unit of sound in a language; it is the smallest unit of sound that affects meaning. For example, in English the sound represented by the letter *p,* as in the words *pot* and *spot,* is a phoneme. The /p/ sound is slightly different in the two words, but this variation is not distinguished in English, and therefore the /p/ sound is a single phoneme. In some languages, such as Hindi, the variations of the /p/ sound represent separate phonemes.

Morphology **Morphology** refers to the units of meaning involved in word formation. A *morpheme* is a minimal unit of meaning; it is a word or a part of a word that cannot be broken into smaller meaningful parts (Lems, Miller, & Soro, 2017; Payne, 2017). Every word in the English language is made up of one or more morphemes. Some words consist of a single morpheme (for example, *help*), whereas others are made up of more than one morpheme (for example, *helper* has two morphemes, *help* and *er,* with the morpheme *-er* meaning "one who," in this case "one who helps"). Thus, not all morphemes are words by themselves; for example, *pre-, -tion,* and *-ing* are morphemes.

Just as the rules that govern phonology describe the sound sequences that can occur in a language, the rules of morphology describe the way meaningful units (morphemes) can be combined in words (Beck, 2017; Deevy, Leonard, & Marchman, 2017). Morphemes have many jobs in grammar, such as marking tense (for example, *she walks* versus *she walked*) and number (*she walks* versus *they walk*).

Syntax **Syntax** involves the way words are combined to form acceptable phrases and sentences (Langacker, 2017; Narrog, 2017). If someone says to you, "Bob slugged Tom" or "Bob was slugged by Tom," you know who did the slugging and who was slugged in each case because you have a syntactic understanding of these sentence structures. You also understand that the sentence "You didn't stay, did you?" is a grammatical sentence but that "You didn't stay, didn't you?" is unacceptable and ambiguous.

If you learn another language, English syntax will not get you very far. For example, in English an adjective usually precedes a noun (as in *blue sky*), whereas in Spanish the adjective usually follows the noun (*cielo azul*). Despite the differences in their syntactic structures, however, syntactic systems in all of the world's languages have some common ground (Hoffman, 2017; Koeneman & Zeijstra, 2017). For example, no language we know of permits sentences like the following one:

The mouse the cat the farmer chased killed ate the cheese.

It appears that language users cannot process subjects and objects arranged in too complex a fashion in a sentence.

Semantics **Semantics** refers to the meaning of words and sentences (McKeown & others, 2017). Every word has a set of semantic features, which are required attributes related to meaning. *Girl* and *woman,* for example, share many semantic features but differ semantically in regard to age.

Words have semantic restrictions on how they can be used in sentences (Taylor, 2017). The sentence *The bicycle talked the boy into buying a candy bar* is syntactically correct but semantically incorrect. The sentence violates our semantic knowledge that bicycles don't talk.

phonology The sound system of the language, including the sounds that are used and how they may be combined.

morphology Units of meaning involved in word formation.

syntax The ways words are combined to form acceptable phrases and sentences.

semantics The meaning of words and sentences.

pragmatics The appropriate use of language in different contexts.

Rule System	Description	Examples
Phonology	The sound system of a language. A phoneme is the smallest sound unit in a language.	The word *chat* has three phonemes or sounds: /ch/ /ã/ /t/. An example of a phonological rule in the English language is that while the phoneme /r/ can follow the phonemes /t/ or /d/ in an English consonant cluster (such as *track* or *drab*), the phoneme /l/ cannot follow these letters.
Morphology	The system of meaningful units involved in word formation.	The smallest sound units that have a meaning are called morphemes, or meaning units. The word *girl* is one morpheme, or meaning unit; it cannot be broken down any further and still have meaning. When the suffix *s* is added, the word becomes *girls* and has two morphemes because the *s* changed the meaning of the word, indicating that there is more than one girl.
Syntax	The system that involves the way words are combined to form acceptable phrases and sentences.	Word order is very important in determining meaning in the English language. For example, the sentence "Sebastian pushed the bike" has a different meaning than "The bike pushed Sebastian."
Semantics	The system that involves the meaning of words and sentences.	Vocabulary involves knowing the meaning of individual words. For example, semantics includes knowing the meaning of such words as *orange*, *transportation*, and *intelligent*.
Pragmatics	The system of using appropriate conversation and knowledge of how to effectively use language in context.	An example is using polite language in appropriate situations, such as being mannerly when talking with one's teacher. Taking turns in a conversation involves pragmatics.

Pragmatics   A final set of language rules involves **pragmatics,** the appropriate use of language in different contexts. Pragmatics covers a lot of territory (Clark, 2014, 2017; Wilce, 2017). When you take turns speaking in a discussion or use a question to convey a command ("Why is it so noisy in here? What is this, Grand Central Station?"), you are demonstrating knowledge of pragmatics. You also apply the pragmatics of English when you use polite language in appropriate situations (for example, when talking to your teacher) or tell stories that are interesting, jokes that are funny, and lies that convince. In each of these cases, you are demonstrating that you understand the rules of your culture for adjusting language to suit the context.

At this point, we have discussed five important rule systems involved in language. An overview of these rule systems is presented in Figure 10.

HOW LANGUAGE DEVELOPS

According to an ancient historian, in the thirteenth century Emperor Frederick II of Germany had a cruel idea. He wanted to know what language children would speak if no one talked to them. He selected several newborns and threatened their caregivers with death if they ever talked to the infants. Frederick never found out what language the children spoke because they all died. Today, we are still curious about infants' development of language, although our experiments and observations are, to say the least, far more humane than the evil Frederick's.

Whatever language they learn, infants all over the world follow a similar path in language development. What are some key milestones in this development?

Recognizing Language Sounds   Long before they begin to learn words, infants can make fine distinctions among the sounds of the language (Masapollo, Polka, & Menard, 2016). In Patricia Kuhl's (1993, 2000, 2007, 2009, 2011, 2015) research, phonemes from languages all over the world are piped through a speaker for infants to hear (see Figure 11). A box with a toy bear in it is placed where the infant can see it. A string of identical syllables is played, and then the syllables are changed (for example, *ba ba ba ba* and then *pa pa pa pa*). If the infant turns its head when the syllables change, the box lights up and the bear dances and drums, and the infant is rewarded for noticing the change.

Kuhl's (2007, 2009, 2011, 2013) research has demonstrated that from birth up to about 6 months of age, infants are "citizens of the world": they recognize when sounds change most of the time, no matter what language the syllables come from. But over the next six months, infants get even better at perceiving the changes in sounds from their "own" language, the one their parents speak, and they gradually lose the ability to recognize differences that are not important in their own language. Recently, Kuhl (2015) found that the developmental stage when a baby's brain is most open to learning the sounds of a native language begins at 6 months for vowels and at 9 months for consonants.

FIGURE **10**

THE RULE SYSTEMS OF LANGUAGE

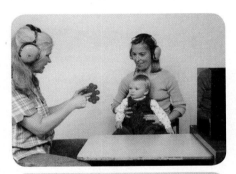

FIGURE **11**

FROM UNIVERSAL LINGUIST TO LANGUAGE-SPECIFIC LISTENER. In Patricia Kuhl's research laboratory, babies listen to recorded voices that repeat syllables. When the sounds of the syllables change, the babies quickly learn to look at the bear. Using this technique, Kuhl has demonstrated that babies are universal linguists until about 6 months of age, but in the next six months become language-specific listeners. *Does Kuhl's research give support to the view that either "nature" or "nurture" is the source of language acquisition?*

©Dr. Patricia Kuhl, Institute for Learning and Brain Science, University of Washington

Long before infants speak recognizable words, they communicate by producing a number of vocalizations and gestures. *At approximately what ages do infants begin to produce different types of vocalizations and gestures?*
©Don Hammond/Design Pics RF

Also, in the second half of the first year, infants begin to segment the continuous stream of speech they encounter into words (Estes & Lew-Williams, 2015; Ota & Skarabela, 2017; Polka & others, 2017; Werker & Gervain, 2013). Initially, they likely rely on statistical information such as the co-occurrence patterns of phonemes and syllables, which allows them to extract potential word forms. For example, discovering that the sequence *br* occurs more often at the beginning of words while *nt* is more common at the end of words helps infants detect word boundaries. And as infants extract an increasing number of potential word forms from the speech stream they hear, they begin to associate these with concrete, perceptually available objects in their world (Zamuner, Fais, & Werker, 2014). For example, infants might detect that the spoken word "monkey" has a reliable statistical regularity of occurring in the visual presence of an observed monkey but not in the presence of other animals, such as bears (Pace & others, 2016).

Babbling and Other Vocalizations

Long before infants speak recognizable words, they produce a number of vocalizations. The functions of these early vocalizations are to practice making sounds, to communicate, and to attract attention (Ramsdell & others, 2012). Babies' sounds go through this sequence during the first year:

- *Crying.* Babies cry even at birth. Crying can signal distress, but different types of cries signal different things.
- *Cooing.* Babies first coo at about 1 to 2 months. These gurgling sounds are made in the back of the throat and usually express pleasure during interaction with the caregiver.
- *Babbling.* In the middle of the first year babies babble—that is, they produce strings of consonant-vowel combinations, such as *ba ba ba ba.* In a recent study, babbling onset predicted when infants would say their first words (McGillion & others, 2017a).

Gestures

Infants start using gestures, such as showing and pointing, at about 8 to 12 months of age. They may wave bye-bye, nod to mean "yes," show an empty cup to ask for more milk, and point to a dog to draw attention to it. Some early gestures are symbolic, as when an infant smacks her lips to indicate food/drink. Pointing is considered by language experts to be an important index of the social aspects of language, and it follows a specific developmental sequence: from pointing without checking on adult gaze to pointing while looking back and forth between an object and the adult (Cooperrider & Goldin-Meadow, 2017; Goldin-Meadow, 2014a, b, 2015, 2017a, b).

Lack of pointing is a significant indicator of problems in the infant's communication system (Brentari & Goldin-Meadow, 2017; Cochet & Byrne, 2016; Walle, 2016). For example, failure to engage in pointing characterizes many autistic children. The ability to use the pointing gesture effectively improves in the second year of life as advances in other aspects of language communication occur (Colonnesi & others, 2011).

One study found that in families of high socioeconomic status (SES), parents were more likely to use gestures when communicating with their 14-month-old infants (Rowe & Goldin-Meadow, 2009). Further, the infants' use of gestures at 14 months of age in high-SES families was linked to a larger vocabulary at 54 months of age.

Why might gestures such as pointing promote further language development? An infant's gestures advance their language development since caregivers often talk to them about what they are pointing to. Also, babies' first words often are for things they have previously pointed to.

First Words

Babies understand their first words earlier than they speak them (Harris, Golinkoff, & Hirsh-Pasek, 2012; Pace & others, 2016). As early as 5 months of age, infants recognize their name when someone says it. And as early as 6 months, they recognize "Mommy" and "Daddy." On average, infants understand about 50 words at about 13 months, but they can't say this many words until about 18 months (Menyuk, Liebergott, & Schultz, 1995). Thus, in infancy *receptive vocabulary* (words the child understands) considerably exceeds *spoken vocabulary* (words the child uses). One study revealed that 6-month-olds understand words that refer to body parts, such as "hand" and "feet," even though they cannot yet speak these words (Tincoff & Jusczyk, 2012).

A child's first words include those that name important people (*dada*), familiar animals (*kitty*), vehicles (*car*), toys (*ball*), food (*milk*), body parts (*eye*), clothes (*hat*), household items (*clock*), and greeting terms (*bye*). These were the first words of babies 50 years ago. They are the first words of babies today. Children often express various intentions with their single words, so that "cookie" might mean, "That's a cookie" or "I want a cookie."

The infant's spoken vocabulary rapidly increases once the first word is spoken (Fenson & others, 2007). The average 18-month-old can speak about 50 words, but the average 2-year-old can speak about 200 words. This rapid increase in vocabulary that begins at approximately 18 months is called the *vocabulary spurt* (Bloom, Lifter, & Broughton, 1985).

Like the timing of a child's first word, the timing of the vocabulary spurt varies (Lieven, 2008). Figure 12 shows the range for these two language milestones in 14 children. On average, these children said their first word at 13 months and had a vocabulary spurt at 19 months. However, the ages for the first word of individual children varied from 10 to 17 months and for their vocabulary spurt from 13 to 25 months.

The spurt actually involves the increase in the rate at which words are learned. That is, early on, a few words are learned every few days, then later on, a few words are learned each day, and eventually many words each day.

Does early vocabulary development predict later language development? A recent study found that infant vocabulary development at 16 to 24 months of age was linked to vocabulary, phonological awareness, reading accuracy, and reading comprehension five years later (Duff, Tomblin, & Catts, 2015).

Cross-linguistic differences occur in word learning (Waxman & others, 2013). Children who are learning Mandarin Chinese, Korean, and Japanese acquire more verbs earlier in their development than do children learning English. This cross-linguistic difference reflects the greater use of verbs in the language input to children in these Asian languages. Indeed, the language of Korean children is often described as verb friendly and the language of English as noun friendly (Waxman & others, 2013).

Children sometimes overextend or underextend the meanings of the words they use (Woodward & Markman, 1998). *Overextension* is the tendency to apply a word to objects that are inappropriate for the word's meaning by going beyond the set of referents an adult would use. For example, children at first may say "*dada*" not only for "father" but also for other men, strangers, or boys. Another example of overextension is calling any animal with four legs a "dog." With time, overextensions decrease and eventually disappear. *Underextension* is the tendency to apply a word too narrowly; it occurs when children fail to use a word to name a relevant event or object. For example, a child might use the word *boy* to describe a 5-year-old neighbor but not apply the word to a male infant or to a 9-year-old male.

Two-Word Utterances By the time children are 18 to 24 months of age, most of their communication consists of two-word utterances (Tomasello, 2011). To convey meaning with just two words, the child relies heavily on gesture, tone, and context. The wealth of meaning children can communicate with a two-word utterance includes the following (Slobin, 1972):

- Identification: "See doggie."
- Location: "Book there."
- Repetition: "More milk."
- Negation: "Not wolf."
- Possession: "My candy."
- Attribution: "Big car."
- Agent-action: "Mama walk."
- Action-direct object: "Hit you."
- Action-indirect object: "Give Papa."
- Action-instrument: "Cut knife."
- Question: "Where ball?"

What characterizes the infant's early word learning?
©Niki Mareschal/Photographer's Choice/Getty Images

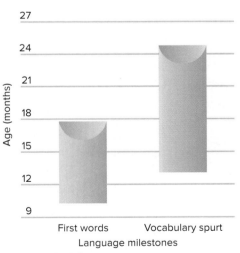

FIGURE **12**

VARIATION IN LANGUAGE MILESTONES.
What are some possible explanations for variations in the timing of these milestones?
Source: Bloom, L. "Variation in Language Milestones," in Handbook of Child Psychology, 5e, New York: Wiley, 1998, 309–370.

Around the world, most young children learn to speak in two-word utterances at about 18 to 24 months of age. *What are some examples of these two-word utterances?*

©McPhoto/age fotostock

Typical Age	Language Milestones
Birth	Crying
2 to 4 months	Cooing begins
5 months	Understands first word
6 months	Babbling begins
7 to 11 months	Change from universal linguist to language-specific listener
8 to 12 months	Uses gestures, such as showing and pointing Comprehension of words appears
13 months	First word spoken
18 months	Vocabulary spurt starts
18 to 24 months	Uses two-word utterances Rapid expansion of understanding of words

FIGURE 13

SOME LANGUAGE MILESTONES IN INFANCY.
Despite great variations in the language input received by infants, around the world they follow a similar path in learning to speak.

These examples are from children whose first language is English, German, Russian, Finnish, Turkish, or Samoan.

Notice that the two-word utterances omit many parts of speech and are remarkably succinct. In fact, in every language, a child's first combinations of words have this economical quality; they are telegraphic. **Telegraphic speech** is the use of content words without grammatical markers such as articles, auxiliary verbs, and other connectives. Telegraphic speech is not limited to two words. "Mommy give ice cream" and "Mommy give Tommy ice cream" also are examples of telegraphic speech.

BIOLOGICAL AND ENVIRONMENTAL INFLUENCES

We have discussed a number of language milestones in infancy; Figure 13 summarizes the approximate time at which infants typically reach these milestones. But what makes this amazing development possible? Everyone who uses language in some way "knows" its rules and has the ability to create an infinite number of words and sentences. Where does this knowledge come from? Is it the product of biology? Is language learned and influenced by experiences?

Biological Influences   The ability to speak and understand language requires a certain vocal apparatus as well as a nervous system with certain capabilities. The nervous system and vocal apparatus of humanity's predecessors changed over hundreds of thousands or millions of years. With advances in the nervous system and vocal structures, *Homo sapiens* went beyond the grunting and shrieking of other animals to develop speech (Lieberman, 2016). Although estimates vary, many experts believe that humans acquired language about 100,000 years ago, which in evolutionary time represents a very recent acquisition. It gave humans an enormous edge over other animals and increased the chances of human survival (McMurray, 2016).

Some language scholars view the remarkable similarities in how children acquire language all over the world as strong evidence that language has a biological basis. There is evidence that particular regions of the brain are predisposed to be used for language (Coulson, 2017; Schutze, 2017). Two regions involved in language were first discovered in studies of brain-damaged individuals: **Broca's area,** an area in the left frontal lobe of the brain involved in producing words (Zhang & others, 2017), and **Wernicke's area,** a region of the brain's left hemisphere involved in language comprehension (Bruckner & Kammer, 2017) (see Figure 14). Damage to either of these areas produces types of **aphasia,** which is a loss or impairment of language processing. Individuals with damage to Broca's area have difficulty producing words correctly; individuals with damage to Wernicke's area have poor comprehension and often produce incomprehensible speech.

Linguist Noam Chomsky (1957) proposed that humans are biologically prewired to learn language at a certain time and in a certain way. He said that children are born into the world with a **language acquisition device (LAD),** a biological endowment that enables the child to detect certain features and rules of language, including phonology, syntax, and semantics (McGilvray, 2017). Children are prepared by nature with the ability to detect the sounds of language, for example, and to follow rules such as how to form plurals and ask questions.

Chomsky's LAD is a theoretical construct, not a physical part of the brain. Is there evidence for the existence of a LAD? Supporters of the LAD concept cite the uniformity of language milestones across languages and cultures, evidence that children create language even in the absence of well-formed input, and biological substrates of language. But, as we will see, critics argue that even if infants have something like a LAD, it cannot explain the whole story of language acquisition.

Environmental Influences   Decades ago, behaviorists opposed Chomsky's hypothesis and argued that language represents nothing more than chains of responses acquired through reinforcement (Skinner, 1957). A baby happens to babble "Ma-ma"; Mama rewards the baby with hugs and smiles; the baby says "Mama" more and more. Bit by bit, said the behaviorists, the baby's language is built up. According to behaviorists, language is a complex learned skill, much like playing the piano or dancing.

There are several problems with the behaviorist view of language learning. First, it does not explain how people create novel sentences—sentences that people have never heard or spoken before. Second, children learn the syntax of their native language even if they are not reinforced for doing so. Social psychologist and psycholinguist Roger Brown (1973) spent long hours observing parents and their young children. He found that parents did not directly or explicitly reward or correct the syntax of most children's utterances. That is, parents did not say "good," "correct," "right," "wrong," and so on. Also, parents did not offer direct corrections such as "You should say two shoes, not two shoe." However, as we will see shortly, many parents do expand on their young children's grammatically incorrect utterances and recast many of those that have grammatical errors.

The behavioral view is no longer considered a viable explanation of how children acquire language (Pace, Hirsh-Pasek, & Golinkoff, 2016). But a great deal of research describes ways in which children's environmental experiences influence their language skills (Vallotton & others, 2017; Yazejian & others, 2017). Many language experts argue that a child's experiences, the particular language to be learned, and the context in which learning takes place can strongly influence language acquisition (Clark, 2017; Marchman & others, 2017; Wilce, 2017).

Language is not learned in a social vacuum. Most children are bathed in language from a very early age (Kuhl, 2009, 2011, 2013, 2015). The Wild Boy of Aveyron who never learned to communicate effectively had lived in social isolation for years.

Thus, social cues play an important role in infant language learning (McGillion & others, 2017b; Pace & others, 2016). Joint engagement and relevant responsiveness by a social partner predict better growth in language later in development, possibly because they improve the infant's mapping process between words and the world (Tamis-LeMonda, Kurchirko, & Song, 2014).

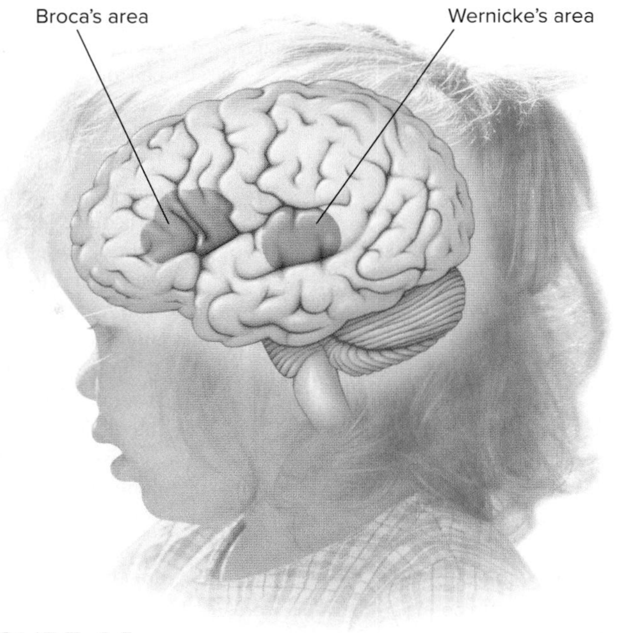

The support and involvement of caregivers and teachers greatly facilitate a child's language learning (Pace & others, 2016; Vallotton & others, 2017). In a recent study, the quality of early foundational communication between parent and child at age 2 accounted for more variability in language outcomes one year later than the amount of parent speech did (Hirsh-Pasek & others, 2015). In another study, both full-term and preterm infants who heard more caregiver talk based on all-day recordings at 16 months of age had better language skills (receptive and expressive language, language comprehension) at 18 months of age (Adams & others, 2017). And in yet another study, when mothers immediately smiled and touched their 8-month-old infants after they babbled, the infants subsequently made more complex speechlike sounds than when mothers responded to their infants in a random manner (Goldstein, King, & West, 2003) (see Figure 15).

Given that social interaction is a critical component for infants to learn language effectively, might they also be able to learn language effectively through television and videos? Researchers have found that infants and young children cannot effectively learn language (phonology or words) from television or videos (Kuhl, 2007; Roseberry & others, 2009; Zosh & others, 2017). A recent study of toddlers found that frequent viewing of television increased the risk of delayed language development (Lin & others, 2015). Thus, just hearing language is not enough, even when infants seemingly are fully engaged in the experience. However, a recent study revealed that Skype provides some improvement in child language learning over videos and TV (Roseberry, Hirsh-Pasek, & Golinkoff, 2014), and older children can use information from television in their language development.

FIGURE 15

SOCIAL INTERACTION AND BABBLING. One study focused on two groups of mothers and their 8-month-old infants (Goldstein, King, & West, 2003). One group of mothers was instructed to smile and touch their infants immediately after the babies cooed and babbled; the other group was also told to smile and touch their infants but in a random manner, unconnected to sounds the infants made. The infants whose mothers immediately responded in positive ways to their babbling subsequently made more complex, speechlike sounds, such as "da" and "gu." The research setting for this study, which underscores how important caregivers are in the early development of language, is shown here.
Courtesy of Dr. Michael H. Goldstein, Cornell University

Broca's area   Wernicke's area

FIGURE 14

BROCA'S AREA AND WERNICKE'S AREA. Broca's area is located in the frontal lobe of the brain's left hemisphere, and it is involved in the control of speech. Wernicke's area is a portion of the left hemisphere's temporal lobe that is involved in understanding language. *How does the role of these areas of the brain relate to lateralization?*

telegraphic speech The use of content words without grammatical markers such as articles, auxiliary verbs, and other connectives.

Broca's area An area in the brain's left frontal lobe that is involved in speech production.

Wernicke's area An area of the brain's left hemisphere that is involved in language comprehension.

aphasia A loss or impairment of language processing caused by brain damage in Broca's area or Wernicke's area.

language acquisition device (LAD) Chomsky's term describing a biological endowment that enables the child to detect the features and rules of language, including phonology, syntax, and semantics.

Michael Tomasello (2003, 2006, 2011, 2014; Tomasello & Vaish, 2013) stresses that young children are intensely interested in their social world and that early in their development they can understand the intentions of other people. He emphasizes that children learn language in specific interactive contexts. For example, when a toddler and a father are jointly focused on a book, the father might say, "See the birdie." In this case, even a toddler understands that the father intends to name something and knows to look in the direction of the pointing. Through this kind of joint attention, early in their development children are able to use their social skills to acquire language (Carpenter, 2011; Tomasello, 2014). For example, one study revealed that joint visual attention behavior at 10 to 11 months of age (before children spoke their first words) was linked to vocabulary growth at 14, 18, and 24 months of age (Brooks & Meltzoff, 2008). Another study revealed that joint attention at 12 and 18 months predicted language skills at 24 months of age (Mundy & others, 2007). Also, in a recent study involving joint attention, infants' eye-gaze behaviors during Spanish tutoring sessions at 9.5 to 10.5 months of age predicted their second-language phonetic learning at 11 months of age, indicating a strong influence of social interaction at the earliest ages of learning a second language (Conboy & others, 2015).

In particular, researchers have found that the child's vocabulary development is linked to the family's socioeconomic status and the type of talk that parents direct to their children (Pan & Uccelli, 2009). To read about these links, see the *Connecting with Diversity* interlude that follows.

One intriguing component of the young child's linguistic environment is **child-directed speech** (also referred to as *parentese*), which is language spoken in a higher pitch, slower tempo, and exaggerated intonation than normal, with simple words and sentences (Broesch & Bryant, 2017; Hayashi & Mazuka, 2017; Kuhl, 2015). It is hard to use child-directed speech

child-directed speech Language spoken in a higher pitch than normal, with simple words and sentences.

connecting with diversity

Language Environment, Poverty, and Language Development

What characteristics of a family make a difference to a child's language development? Socioeconomic status has been linked with how much parents talk to their children and with young children's vocabulary (Leffel & Suskind, 2013; McGillion & others, 2017b). Betty Hart and Todd Risley (1995) observed the language environments of children whose parents were professionals and children whose parents were on welfare. Compared with the professional parents, the parents on welfare talked much less to their young children, talked less about past events, and provided less elaboration. The children of the professional parents had a much larger vocabulary at 36 months of age than the children of the welfare parents. A recent study also found that at 18 to 24 months of age, infants in low-SES families already had a smaller vocabulary and less efficient language processing than their infant counterparts in middle-SES families (Fernald, Marchman, & Weisleder, 2013).

Other research has linked how much mothers speak to their infants with the size of the infants' vocabularies. For example, in one study by Janellen Huttenlocher and her colleagues (1991), infants whose mothers spoke more often to them had markedly larger vocabularies. By the second birthday, vocabulary differences were substantial. However, a study of 1- to 3-year-old children living in low-income families found that the sheer amount of maternal talk was not the best predictor of a child's vocabulary growth (Pan & others, 2005). Rather, it was maternal language and literacy skills, and mothers' use of diverse vocabulary, that best predicted children's vocabulary development. Also, mothers who frequently used pointing gestures had children with a larger vocabulary. Pointing usually occurs in concert with speech and it may enhance the meaning of mothers' verbal input to their children.

One study revealed that maternal sensitivity (responding warmly to the child's bids and anticipating her child's emotional needs, for example), regardless of socioeconomic status and ethnicity, was positively linked with growth in young children's receptive and expressive language development from 18 to 36 months of age (Pungello & others, 2009). In this study, negative intrusive parenting (physically restraining the child or dominating interaction with the child with unnecessary verbal direction, for example) was related to slower growth of receptive language.

These research studies and others (NICHD Early Child Care Research Network, 2005; Perkins, Finegood, & Swain, 2013) demonstrate the important effect that early speech input and poverty can have on the development of a child's language skills. Children in low-income families are more likely to have less educated parents, have inadequate nutrition, live in low-income communities, and attend substandard schools than children in middle- and high-income families (Snow, Burns, & Griffin, 1998). However, living in a low-income family should not be used as the sole identifier in predicting whether children will have difficulties in language development, such as a low vocabulary and reading problems. If children growing up in low-income families experience effective instruction and support, they can develop effective language skills (Hirsh-Pasek & Golinkoff, 2014; Perkins, Finegood, & Swain, 2013).

How can parents in low-income families improve their infants' language development?

when not in the presence of a baby. As soon as we start talking to a baby, though, most of us shift into child-directed speech. Much of this is automatic and something most parents are not aware they are doing. Child-directed speech serves the important functions of capturing the infant's attention, maintaining communication and social interaction between infants and caregivers, and providing infants with information about their native language by heightening differences between speech directed to children and adults (Golinkoff & others, 2015). Even 4-year-olds speak in simpler ways to 2-year-olds than to their 4-year-old friends.

Child-directed speech has the important function of capturing the infant's attention and maintaining communication (Ratner, 2013). A recent study found that child-directed speech in a one-to-one social context at 11 to 14 months of age was linked to greater word production at 2 years of age than standard speech and speech in a group setting (Ramirez-Esparza, Garcia-Sierra, & Kuhl, 2014). In recent research, child-directed speech in a one-to-one social context for 11 to 14 years of age was also related to productive vocabulary at 2 years of age for Spanish-English bilingual infants across languages and in each individual language (Ramirez-Esparza, Garcia-Sierra, & Kuhl, 2017). Yet another recent study of low-SES Spanish-speaking families revealed that infants who experienced more child-directed speech were better at processing words in real time and had larger vocabularies at 2 years of age (Weisleder & Fernald, 2013).

Adults often use strategies other than child-directed speech to enhance the child's acquisition of language, including recasting, expanding, and labeling:

- *Recasting* occurs when an adult rephrases something the child has said that might lack the appropriate morphology or contain some other error. The adult restates the child's immature utterance in the form of a fully grammatical sentence. For example, when a 2-year-old says, "Dog bark," the adult may respond by saying, "Oh, you heard the dog barking!" The adult sentence acknowledges that the child was heard and then adds the morphology (/ing/) and the article (the) that the child's utterance lacked.

- *Expanding* involves adding information to a child's incomplete utterance. For example, a child says, "Doggie eat," and the parent replies, "Yes, the dog is eating his food out of his special dish."

- *Labeling* is naming objects that children seem interested in. Young children are forever being asked to identify the names of objects. Roger Brown (1958) called this "the original word game." Children want more than the names of objects, though; they often want information about the object as well.

Parents use these strategies naturally and in meaningful conversations. Parents do not need to use a particular method to teach their children to talk, even for children who are slow in learning language. Children usually benefit when parents follow the child's lead, talking about things the child is interested in at the moment, and when parents provide information in ways that children can process effectively (Pan, 2008). If children are not ready to take in some information, they are likely to tell you (perhaps by turning away). Thus, giving the child more information is not always better.

Infants, toddlers, and young children benefit when adults read books to and with them (shared reading) (Chaco & others, 2017; Marjanovic-Umek, Fekonja-Peklaj, & Socan, 2017; Wesseling, Charistmann, & Lachmann, 2017). In one study, a majority of U.S. mothers in low-income families reported that they were reading to their infants and toddlers with some regularity (Raikes & others, 2006). In this study, non-Latino White, more highly educated mothers who were parenting a firstborn child were more likely to read books to their infants and toddlers than were African American and Latino mothers who were parenting later-born children. Reading daily to children at 14 to 24 months of age was positively related to the children's language and cognitive development at 36 months of age.

Remember that encouragement of language development, not drill and practice, is the key. Language development is not a simple matter of imitation and reinforcement. To read further about ways that parents can facilitate children's language development, see the applications in the *Caring Connections* interlude.

What is shared reading and how might it benefit infants and toddlers?
©Elyse Lewin/Brand X Pictures/Getty Images RF

AN INTERACTIONIST VIEW

If language acquisition depended only on biology, then the Wild Boy of Aveyron and Genie (discussed earlier in the chapter) should have talked without difficulty. A child's experiences

How Parents Can Facilitate Infants' and Toddlers' Language Development

Linguist Naomi Baron (1992) in *Growing Up with Language,* developmental psychologists Roberta Golinkoff and Kathy Hirsh-Pasek (2000) in *How Babies Talk,* and more recently Ellen Galinsky (2010) in *Mind in the Making,* provided ideas to help parents facilitate their infants' and toddlers' language development. Their suggestions are summarized below:

- *Be an active conversational partner.* Talk to your baby from the time it is born. Initiate conversation with the baby. If the baby is in a day-long child-care program, ensure that the baby receives adequate language stimulation from adults.

- *Talk in a slowed-down pace and don't worry about how you sound to other adults when you talk to your baby.* Talking in a slowed-down pace will help your baby detect words in the sea of sounds they experience. Babies enjoy and attend to the high-pitched sound of child-directed speech.

- *Narrate your daily activities to the baby as you do them.* For example, talk about how you will put the baby in a high chair for lunch and ask what she would like to eat, and so on.

- *Use parent-look and parent-gesture, and name what you are looking at.* When you want your child to pay attention to something, look at it and point to it. Then name it—for example, by saying "Look, Alex, there's an airplane."

- *When you talk with infants and toddlers, be simple, concrete, and repetitive.* Don't try to talk to them in abstract,

It is a good idea for parents to begin talking to their babies at the start. The best language teaching occurs when the talking is begun before infants become capable of their first intelligible speech. *What are some other guidelines for parents to follow in helping their infants and toddlers develop their language skills?*
©John Carter/Science Source

high-level ways or think you have to say something new or different all of the time. Using familiar words often will help them remember the words.

- *Play games.* Use word games like peek-a-boo and pat-a-cake to help infants learn words.

- *Remember to listen.* Since toddlers' speech is often slow and laborious, parents are often tempted to supply words and thoughts for them. Be patient and let toddlers express themselves, no matter how painstaking the process is or how great a hurry you are in.

- *Expand and elaborate language abilities and horizons with infants and toddlers.* Ask questions that encourage answers other than "Yes" and "No." Actively repeat, expand, and recast the utterances. Your toddler might say, "Dada." You could follow with "Where's Dada?," and then you might continue, "Let's go find him."

- *Adjust to your child's idiosyncrasies instead of working against them.* Many toddlers have difficulty pronouncing words and making themselves understood. Whenever possible, make toddlers feel that they are being understood.

- *Resist making normative comparisons.* Be aware of the ages at which your child reaches specific milestones (such as the first word, first 50 words), but do not measure this development rigidly against that of other children. Such comparisons can bring about unnecessary anxiety.

influence language acquisition. But we have seen that language does have strong biological foundations. No matter how much you converse with a dog, it won't learn to talk. In contrast, children are biologically prepared to learn language. Children all over the world acquire language milestones at about the same time and in about the same order. However, there are cultural variations in the type of support given to children's language development. For example, caregivers in the Kaluli culture prompt young children to use a loud voice and particular morphemes that direct the speech act performed (calling out) and to refer to names, kinship relations, and places where there has been a shared past experience that indicates a closeness to the person being addressed (Ochs & Schieffelin, 2008; Schieffelin, 2005).

Environmental influences are also very important in developing competence in language. Children whose parents provide them with a rich verbal environment show many positive benefits (Marchman & others, 2017; Vallotton & others, 2017). Parents who pay attention to what their children are trying to say, expand their children's utterances, read to them, and label things in the environment, are providing valuable benefits for them (Yazejian & others, 2017).

An interactionist view emphasizes that both biology and experience contribute to language development. How much of the language is biologically determined and how much depends on interaction with others is a subject of debate among linguists and psychologists (Adams & others, 2017; McGillion & others, 2017b). However, all agree that both biological capacity and relevant experience are necessary (Green & others, 2017; Peterson & others, 2017; Warren & others, 2017).

LG4 Describe the nature of language and how it develops in infancy.

Review
- What is language?
- What are language's rule systems?
- How does language develop in infancy?
- What are some biological and environmental influences on language?
- To what extent do biological and environmental influences interact to produce language development?

Connect
- The more years children spend living in poverty, the more their physiological indices of stress are elevated. In this chapter, you learned about the role of SES in children's language acquisition and vocabulary building. How might these factors influence children's performance when they go to school?

Reflect *Your Own Personal Journey of Life*
- Would it be a good idea for you as a parent to hold large flash cards of words in front of your baby for several hours each day to help the baby learn language and improve the baby's intelligence? Why or why not? What do you think Piaget would say about this activity?

topical connections *looking forward*

Advances in infants' cognitive development are linked to their socioemotional development. For example, you will learn about the infant's developing social orientation and understanding, which involve perceiving people as engaging in intentional and goal-directed behavior, joint attention, and cooperation. Also in "Socioemotional Development in Infancy" you will study many aspects of the infant's emotional development, temperament, attachment, and child care. And in "Cognitive Development in Early Childhood" you will read about two major theorists—Piaget and Vygotsky—and their views of how young children's thinking advances. You will see how young children become more capable of sustaining their attention; learn about the astonishing rate at which preschool children's vocabulary expands; and explore variations in early childhood education.

reach your **learning goals**

Cognitive Development in Infancy

1 What Is Piaget's Theory of Infant Development?

LG1 Summarize and evaluate Piaget's theory of infant development.

Cognitive Processes

- In Piaget's theory, children construct their own cognitive worlds, building mental structures to adapt to their world.

- Schemes are actions or mental representations that organize knowledge. Behavioral schemes (physical activities) characterize infancy, whereas mental schemes (cognitive activities) develop in childhood. Assimilation occurs when children incorporate new information into existing schemes; accommodation refers to children's adjustment of their schemes in the face of new information.

- Through organization, children group isolated behaviors into a higher-order, more smoothly functioning cognitive system.

The Sensorimotor Stage

- Equilibration is a mechanism Piaget proposed to explain how children shift from one stage of thought to the next. As children experience cognitive conflict in trying to understand the world, they use assimilation and accommodation to attain equilibrium. The result is a new stage of thought. According to Piaget, there are four qualitatively different stages of thought.

- In sensorimotor thought, the first of Piaget's four stages, the infant organizes and coordinates sensory experiences with physical movements. The stage lasts from birth to about 2 years of age.

- The sensorimotor stage has six substages: simple reflexes; first habits and primary circular reactions; secondary circular reactions; coordination of secondary circular reactions; tertiary circular reactions, novelty, and curiosity; and internalization of schemes. One key accomplishment of this stage is object permanence, the ability to understand that objects continue to exist even though the infant is no longer observing them. Another aspect involves infants' understanding of cause and effect.

Evaluating Piaget's Sensorimotor Stage

- Piaget opened up a whole new way of looking at infant development in terms of coordinating sensory input with motoric actions. In the past decades, revisions of Piaget's view have been proposed based on research. For example, researchers have found that a stable and differentiated perceptual world is established earlier than Piaget envisioned, and infants begin to develop concepts as well. The nature-nurture issue in regard to infant cognitive development continues to be debated. Spelke endorses a core knowledge approach, which states that infants are born with domain-specific innate knowledge systems. Critics argue that Spelke has not given adequate attention to the influence of early experiences on infants' cognitive development.

2 How Do Infants Learn, Remember, and Conceptualize?

LG2 Describe how infants learn, remember, and conceptualize.

Conditioning

- Both classical and operant conditioning occur in infants. Operant conditioning techniques have especially been useful to researchers in demonstrating infants' perception and retention of information about perceptual-motor actions.

Attention

- Attention is the focusing of mental resources on select information, and in infancy attention is closely linked with habituation. In the first year, much of attention is of the orienting/investigative type, but sustained attention also becomes important.

- Habituation is the repeated presentation of the same stimulus, causing reduced attention to the stimulus. If a different stimulus is presented and the infant pays increased attention to it, dishabituation is occurring. Joint attention plays an important role in infant development, especially in the infant's acquisition of language.

Memory

- Memory is the retention of information over time. Infants as young as 2 to 6 months of age can retain information about some experiences. However, many experts argue that what we commonly think of as memory (consciously remembering the past, or explicit memory) does not occur until the second half of the first year of life. By the end of the second year, explicit memory continues to improve.

- The hippocampus and frontal lobes of the brain are involved in development of explicit memory in infancy.

- The phenomenon of not being able to remember events that occurred before the age of 2 or 3—known as infantile, or childhood, amnesia—may be due to the immaturity of the prefrontal lobes of the brain at that age.

Imitation

- Meltzoff has shown that newborns can match their behaviors (such as protruding their tongue) to a model. His research also shows that deferred imitation occurs as early as 9 months of age.

Concept Formation

- Concepts are cognitive groupings of similar objects, events, people, or ideas. Mandler argues that it is not until about 7 to 9 months of age that infants form conceptual categories, although we do not know precisely when concept formation begins. Infants' first concepts are broad. Over the first two years of life, these broad concepts gradually become more differentiated. Many infants and young children develop an intense interest in a particular category (or categories) of objects.

3 How Are Individual Differences in Infancy Assessed, and Do These Assessments Predict Intelligence?

 LG3 Discuss infant assessment measures and the prediction of intelligence.

Measures of Infant Development

- Developmental scales for infants grew out of the tradition of IQ testing of older children. These scales are less verbal than IQ tests. Gesell's test is still widely used by pediatricians to distinguish between normal and abnormal infants; it provides a developmental quotient (DQ). The Bayley scales, developed by Nancy Bayley, continue to be widely used today to assess infant development. The current version, the Bayley-III, consists of cognitive, language, motor, socioemotional, and adaptive scales. Increasingly used, the Fagan Test of Infant Intelligence assesses how effectively the infant processes information.

Predicting Intelligence

- Global scores on the Gesell and Bayley scales are not good predictors of childhood intelligence. However, measures of information processing such as speed of habituation and degree of dishabituation do correlate with intelligence later in childhood. There is both continuity and discontinuity between infant cognitive development and cognitive development later in childhood.

4 What Is the Nature of Language, and How Does It Develop in Infancy?

LG4 Describe the nature of language and how it develops in infancy.

Defining Language

- Language is a form of communication, whether spoken, written, or signed, that is based on a system of symbols. Language consists of all the words used by a community and the rules for varying and combining them. It is marked by infinite generativity.

Language's Rule Systems

- Phonology is the sound system of the language, including the sounds that are used and how they may be combined. Morphology refers to the units of meaning involved in word formation. Syntax is the way words are combined to form acceptable phrases and sentences. Semantics involves the meaning of words and sentences. Pragmatics is the appropriate use of language in different contexts.

How Language Develops

- Among the milestones in infant language development are crying (birth), cooing (1 to 2 months), babbling (6 months), making the transition from universal linguist to language-specific listener (7 to 11 months), using gestures (8 to 12 months), comprehending words (8 to 12 months), speaking of first word (13 months), vocabulary spurt (18 months), rapid expansion of understanding words (18 to 24 months), and two-word utterances (18 to 24 months).

Biological and Environmental Influences

- In evolution, language clearly gave humans an enormous advantage over other animals and increased their chance of survival. Broca's area and Wernicke's area are important locations for language processing in the brain's left hemisphere. Chomsky argues that children are born with the ability to detect basic features and rules of language. In other words, they are biologically prepared to learn language with a prewired language acquisition device (LAD). The behaviorists' view—that children acquire language as a result of reinforcement—has not been supported.

- Adults help children acquire language through child-directed speech, recasting, expanding, and labeling. Environmental influences are demonstrated by differences in the language development of children as a consequence of being exposed to different language environments in the home. Parents should talk extensively with an infant, especially about what the baby is attending to.

An Interactionist View

- Today, most language researchers believe that children everywhere are born with special social and linguistic capacities that make language acquisition possible. How much of the language is biologically determined and how much depends on interaction with others is a subject of debate among linguists and psychologists. However, all agree that both biological capacity and relevant experience are necessary.

key terms

A-not-B error	core knowledge approach	language	secondary circular
accommodation	deferred imitation	language acquisition	reactions
aphasia	developmental	device (LAD)	semantics
assimilation	quotient (DQ)	memory	sensorimotor stage
attention	equilibration	morphology	simple reflexes
Bayley Scales of Infant	explicit memory	object permanence	syntax
Development	first habits and primary	organization	telegraphic
Broca's area	circular reactions	phonology	speech
child-directed speech	implicit memory	pragmatics	tertiary circular
concepts	infinite generativity	primary circular	reactions, novelty,
coordination of secondary	internalization of schemes	reaction	and curiosity
circular reactions	joint attention	schemes	Wernicke's area

key people

Renée Baillargeon	Arnold Gesell	Patricia Kuhl	Todd Risley
Naomi Baron	Eleanor Gibson	Jean Mandler	Carolyn
Nancy Bayley	Roberta Golinkoff	Andrew Meltzoff	Rovee-Collier
Roger Brown	Betty Hart	Kathy Hirsh-Pasek	Elizabeth Spelke
Noam Chomsky	Janellen Huttenlocher	Jean Piaget	Michael Tomasello

connecting with improving the lives of children

STRATEGIES

Nourishing the Infant's Cognitive Development

What are some good strategies for helping infants develop in cognitively competent ways?

- *Provide the infant with many play opportunities in a rich and varied environment.* Give the infant extensive opportunities to experience objects of different sizes, shapes, textures, and colors. Recognize that play with objects stimulates the infant's cognitive development.

- *Actively communicate with the infant.* Don't let the infant spend long bouts of waking hours in social isolation. Infants need caregivers who actively communicate with them. This active communication with adults is necessary for the infant's competent cognitive development.

- *Don't try to accelerate the infant's cognitive development.* Most experts stress that infants cognitively benefit when they learn concepts naturally. The experts emphasize that restricting infants to a passive role and showing them flash cards to accelerate their cognitive development are not good strategies.

RESOURCES

Mind in the Making (2010)
Ellen Galinsky
New York: HarperCollins

A must-read book for parents of infants and young children. Galinsky interviewed a number of leading experts in children's development and distilled their thoughts in easy-to-read fashion. The book provides abundant examples of how to improve infants' attention, communication, cognitive skills, and learning.

Growing Up with Language (1992)
Naomi Baron
Reading, MA: Addison-Wesley

Baron focuses on three representative children and their families. She explores how children put their first words together, struggle to understand meaning, and use language as a creative tool. She shows parents how they play a key role in their child's language development.

How Babies Talk (2000)
Roberta Golinkoff and Kathy Hirsh-Pasek
New York: Plume

Targeted to parents, this book by leading experts details the fascinating world of infant language. Included are activities parents can use with their infants and indicators of delayed language that can alert parents to possible language problems.

The Development of Language (7th ed., 2009)
Jean Berko Gleason and Nan Ratner
Boston: Allyn & Bacon

A number of leading experts provide up-to-date discussion of many aspects of language development, including the acquisition of language skills, language rule systems, and communication in infancy.

chapter 7

SOCIOEMOTIONAL DEVELOPMENT IN INFANCY

chapter **outline**

An increasing number of fathers are staying home to care for their children (Dette-Hagenmeyer, Erzinger, & Reichle, 2016). And researchers are finding positive outcomes when fathers are positively engaged with their infants (Alexander & others, 2017; Sethna & others, 2017). Consider 17-month-old Darius. On weekdays, Darius' father, a writer, cares for him during the day while his mother works full-time as a landscape architect. Darius' father is doing a great job of caring for him. He keeps Darius nearby while he is writing and spends lots of time talking to him and playing with him. From their interactions, it is clear that they genuinely enjoy each other.

Last month, Darius began spending one day a week at a child-care center. His parents carefully selected the center after observing a number of centers and interviewing teachers and center directors. His parents placed him in the center one day a week so Darius could get some experience with peers and his father could have time off from caregiving.

Darius' father looks to the future and imagines the Little League games Darius will play in and the many other activities he can enjoy with Darius. Remembering how little time his own father spent with him, he is dedicated to making sure that Darius has an involved, nurturing experience with his father.

When Darius' mother comes home in the evening, she spends considerable time with him. Darius shows a positive attachment to both his mother and his father.

Many fathers are spending more time with their infants today than in the past.
©Rick Gomez/Corbis/Getty Images

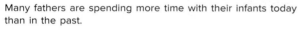

topical connections *looking **back***

"Cognitive Development in Infancy" described the development of cognitive abilities in infancy, including the ability to learn, remember, and conceptualize, as well as to understand and acquire language. Up to this point, what you have read about socioemotional development has mainly focused on topics such as the social situations and emotions of parents before and after the arrival of their infants, including parents' feelings of joy, anticipation, anxiety, and stress during pregnancy; how a mother's optimism may lead to less adverse outcomes for her fetus; and parents' emotional and psychological adjustments during the postpartum period. In this chapter, you will study many intriguing aspects of infants' socioemotional development.

preview

In "Physical Development in Infancy" and "Cognitive Development in Infancy" you read about how the infant perceives, learns, and remembers. Infants also are socioemotional beings, capable of displaying emotions and initiating social interaction with people close to them. The main topics that we will explore are emotional understanding and attachment, and the social contexts of the family and child care.

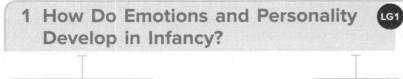

1 How Do Emotions and Personality Develop in Infancy?

LG1 Discuss emotional and personality development in infancy.

Emotional Development   Temperament   Personality Development

Anyone who has been around infants for even a brief time detects that they are emotional beings. Not only do infants express emotions, but they also vary in their temperament. Some are shy and others are outgoing, for example. In this section, we explore these and other aspects of emotional and personality development in infants.

EMOTIONAL DEVELOPMENT

Imagine your life without emotion. Emotion is the color and music of life, as well as the tie that binds people together. How do psychologists define and classify emotions, and why are they important to development? How do emotions develop during the first two years of life?

What Are Emotions? For our purposes, we will define **emotion** as feeling, or affect, that occurs when a person is in a state or an interaction that is important to him or her, especially in relation to his or her well-being. Particularly in infancy, emotions play important roles in (1) communication with others, and (2) behavioral organization. Through emotions, infants communicate important aspects of their lives such as joy, sadness, interest, and fear (Witherington & others, 2010). In terms of behavioral organization, emotions influence infants' social responses and adaptive behavior as they interact with others in their world (Roos & others, 2017).

One of the most common ways to classify emotions is as positive or negative (Parsons & others, 2017; Planalp & others, 2017; Shuman & Scherer, 2014). Positive emotions include enthusiasm, joy, and love. Negative emotions include anxiety, anger, guilt, and sadness. Although emotion consists of more than communication, in infancy the communication aspect is at the forefront of emotion (Witherington & others, 2010).

Biological, Cognitive, and Environmental Influences Emotions are influenced by biological foundations, cognitive processes, and a person's experiences (Causadias, Telzer, & Lee, 2017). Biology's importance to emotion also is apparent in the changes in a baby's emotional capacities (Martin & others, 2017; Miller & others, 2017; Thompson & Goodvin, 2016). Certain regions of the brain that develop early in life (such as the brain stem, hippocampus, and amygdala) play a role in distress, excitement, and rage, and even infants display these emotions (Frenkel & Fox, 2015; Santiago, Aoki, & Sullivan, 2017). But, as we discuss later in the chapter, infants only gradually develop the ability to regulate their emotions, and this ability seems to be tied to the gradual maturation of frontal regions of the cerebral cortex that can exert control over other areas of the brain (Bell & others, 2018; Calkins, Perry, & Dollar, 2016; Lusby & others, 2017).

Cognitive processes, both in immediate "in the moment" contexts, and across childhood development, influence infants' and children's emotional development (Jiang & others, 2017; Perry & others, 2016). Attention toward or away from an experience can influence infants' and children's emotional responses. For example, children who can distract themselves from

Blossoms are scattered by the wind
And the wind cares nothing, but
The blossoms of the heart,
No wind can touch.

—**YOSHIDA KENKO**
Buddhist Monk, 14th century

---

developmental connection

Brain Development

The maturation of the amygdala and prefrontal cortex may be linked to adolescent risk taking. Connect to "Physical Development in Adolescence."

---

emotion Feeling, or affect, that occurs when a person is in a state or interaction that is important to him or her. Emotion can be characterized as positive (enthusiasm, joy, love, for example) or negative (anxiety, guilt, or sadness, for example).

How do Japanese mothers handle their infants' and children's emotional development differently from non-Latino White mothers?

©Zen Sekizawa/The Image Bank/Getty Images

Joy   *Sadness*

Fear   *Surprise*

FIGURE 1

EXPRESSION OF DIFFERENT EMOTIONS IN INFANTS

(*Top left*) ©Kozak_O_O/Shutterstock RF; (*top right*) ©McGraw Hill Companies/Jill Braaten, Photographer; (*bottom left*) ©David Sacks/Getty Images; (*bottom right*) ©EyeWire/Getty Images RF

a stressful encounter show a lower level of negative affect in the context and less anxiety over time (Crockenberg & Leerkes, 2006). Also, as children become older, they develop cognitive strategies for controlling their emotions and become more adept at modulating their emotional arousal (Kaunhoven & Dorjee, 2017).

Biological evolution has endowed human beings to be *emotional,* but embeddedness in relationships and culture provides diversity in emotional experiences (Bedford & others, 2017; Norona & Baker, 2017; Ostlund & others, 2017; Thompson, 2016). Emotional development and coping with stress are influenced by whether caregivers have maltreated or neglected children and whether or not children's caregivers are depressed (Doyle & Cicchetti, 2018; Granat & others, 2017). When infants become stressed, they show better biological recovery from the stressors when their caregivers engage in sensitive caregiving with them (Thompson & Goodvin, 2016).

Social relationships, in turn, provide the setting for the development of a rich variety of emotions (Thompson, 2016). When toddlers hear their parents quarreling, they often react with distress and inhibit their play. Well-functioning families make each other laugh and may develop a light mood to defuse conflicts.

Cultural influences are linked to variations in emotional expression (Cole, 2016; Qu & Telzer, 2017). For example, researchers have found that East Asian infants display less frequent and less positive and negative emotions than non-Latino White infants (Cole & Tan, 2007). Throughout childhood, East Asian parents encourage their children to be emotionally reserved rather than emotionally expressive (Cole, 2016). Further, Japanese parents try to prevent children from experiencing negative emotions, whereas non-Latino White mothers more frequently respond after their children become distressed and then help them cope (Rothbaum & Trommsdorff, 2007).

Early Emotions   A leading expert on infant emotional development, Michael Lewis (2010, 2015, 2016) distinguishes between primary emotions and self-conscious emotions. **Primary emotions** are emotions that are present in humans and other animals; these emotions appear in the first six months of the human infant's development. Primary emotions include surprise, interest, joy, anger, sadness, fear, and disgust (see Figure 1 for infants' facial expressions of some of these early emotions). In Lewis' classification, **self-conscious emotions** require self-awareness that involves consciousness and a sense of "me." Self-conscious emotions include jealousy, empathy, embarrassment, pride, shame, and guilt—most of these occurring for the first time at some point in the second half of the first year or during the second year.

Researchers such as Joseph Campos (2005) and Michael Lewis (2015, 2016) debate about how early in the infant and toddler years various emotions first appear and in what sequence. As an indication of the controversy regarding when certain emotions first are displayed by infants, consider jealousy. Some researchers argue that jealousy does not emerge until approximately 18 months of age (Lewis, 2007), whereas others assert that it is displayed much earlier (Hart & Behrens, 2013).

Consider the results of two research studies. First, 9-month-old infants engaged in more approach-style, jealousy-related behaviors when their mothers gave attention to a social rival (a lifelike doll) than to a non-social rival (a book) (Mize & others, 2014). Further, in this study, the infants showed EEG activity during the social-rival condition that is associated with jealousy. In a second study, 6-month-old infants observed their mothers in situations similar to the first study: either giving attention to a lifelike baby doll (hugging or gently rocking it, for example) or to a book (Hart & Carrington, 2002). When mothers directed their attention to the doll, the infants were more likely to display negative emotions, such as anger and sadness, which may have indicated their jealousy (see Figure 2). On the other hand, their expressions of anger and sadness may have reflected frustration in not being able to have the novel doll to play with.

Debate about the onset of an emotion such as jealousy illustrates the complexity and difficulty of indexing early emotions. That said, some experts on infant socioemotional development, such as Jerome Kagan (2010), conclude that the structural immaturity of the infant brain makes it unlikely that emotions requiring thought—such as guilt, pride, despair, shame, empathy, and jealousy—can be experienced in the first year. Thus, both Kagan (2010) and Campos (2009) argue that so-called "self-conscious" emotions don't occur until after the first year, which increasingly reflects the view of most developmental psychologists. Thus, in regard to the photograph in Figure 2, it is unlikely that the 6-month-old infant is experiencing jealousy.

Emotional Expression and Social Relationships

Emotional expressions are involved in infants' first relationships. The ability of infants to communicate emotions permits coordinated interactions with their caregivers and the beginning of an emotional bond between them (Thompson, 2015, 2016). Not only do parents change their emotional expressions in response to infants' emotional expressions, but infants also modify their emotional expressions in response to their parents' emotional expressions. In other words, these interactions are mutually regulated. Because of this coordination, the interactions are described as reciprocal, or synchronous, when all is going well. Sensitive, responsive parents help their infants grow emotionally, whether the infants respond in distressed or happy ways (Bedford & others, 2017; Norona & Baker, 2017; Thompson, 2015, 2016). A recent study revealed that parents' elicitation of talk about emotion with toddlers was associated with the toddlers' sharing and helping behaviors (Brownell & others, 2013).

A recent study also documented how babies pick up on their mothers' stress (Waters, West, & Mendes, 2014). In this study, mothers were separated from their babies to give a 5-minute speech, with half of the mothers receiving a positive evaluation, the other half a negative evaluation. Mothers who received negative feedback reported an increase in negative emotion and cardiac stress, while those who were given positive feedback reported an increase in positive emotion. The babies quickly detected their mothers' stress, as reflected in an increased heart rate when reunited with them. And the greater the mother's stress response, the more her baby's heart rate increased.

Cries and smiles are two emotional expressions that infants display when interacting with parents. These are babies' first forms of emotional communication.

Crying Crying is the most important mechanism newborns have for communicating with their world. The first cry verifies that the baby's lungs have filled with air. Cries also may provide information about the health of the newborn's central nervous system. Newborns even tend to respond with cries and negative facial expressions when they hear other newborns cry (Dondi, Simion, & Caltran, 1999). However, a recent study revealed that newborns of depressed mothers showed less vocal distress when another infant cried, reflecting emotional and physiological dysregulation (Jones, 2012).

Babies have at least three types of cries:

- **Basic cry.** A rhythmic pattern that usually consists of a cry, followed by a briefer silence, then a shorter inspiratory whistle that is somewhat higher in pitch than the main cry, then another brief rest before the next cry. Some infancy experts stress that hunger is one of the conditions that incite the basic cry.

- **Anger cry.** A variation of the basic cry in which more excess air is forced through the vocal cords. The anger cry has a loud, harsh sound to it, almost like shouting.

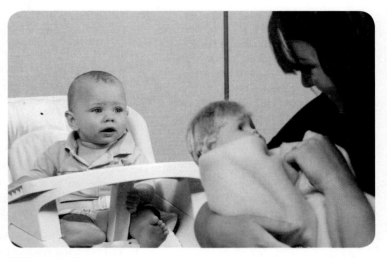

FIGURE 2

IS THIS THE EARLY EXPRESSION OF JEALOUSY? in the study by Hart and Carrington (2002), the researchers concluded that the 6-month-old infants who observed their mothers giving attention to a baby doll displayed negative emotions—such as anger and sadness—which may indicate the early appearance of jealousy. However, experts on emotional development, such as Joseph Campos (2009) and Jerome Kagan (2010), argue that it is unlikely emotions such as jealousy appear in the first year. *Why do they conclude that it is unlikely jealousy occurs in the first year?*
©Kenny Braun/Braun Photography

What are some different types of cries?
©Andy Cox/The Image Bank/Getty Images

primary emotions Emotions that are present in humans and other animals, and emerge early in life; examples are joy, anger, sadness, fear, and disgust.

self-conscious emotions Emotions that require self-awareness, especially consciousness and a sense of "me"; examples include jealousy, empathy, and embarrassment.

basic cry A rhythmic pattern usually consisting of a cry, a briefer silence, a shorter inspiratory whistle that is higher pitched than the main cry, and then a brief rest before the next cry.

anger cry A cry similar to the basic cry, with more excess air forced through the vocal cords.

How Would You...?

If you were a **human development and family studies professional,** how would you respond to the parents of a 13-month-old baby who are concerned because their son has suddenly started crying every morning when they drop him off at child care—despite the fact that he has been going to the same child-care center for over six months?

He who binds to himself a joy.
Does the winged life destroy;
But he who kisses the joy as
it flies
Lives in eternity's sun rise.

—**WILLIAM BLAKE**
English Poet, 19th Century

pain cry A sudden appearance of a long, initial loud cry without preliminary moaning, followed by breath holding.

reflexive smile A smile that does not occur in response to external stimuli. It happens during the month after birth, usually during sleep.

social smile A smile in response to an external stimulus, which, early in development, typically is a face.

stranger anxiety An infant's fear and wariness of strangers; it tends to appear in the second half of the first year of life.

separation protest An infant's distressed reaction when the caregiver leaves.

- **Pain cry.** A sudden long, initial loud cry followed by breath holding; no preliminary moaning is present. The pain cry is triggered by a high-intensity stimulus.

Most adults can determine whether an infant's cries signify anger or pain (Zeskind, 2007). Parents can interpret the cries of their own baby better than those of another baby.

Smiling   Smiling is critical as a means of developing a new social skill and is a key social signal (Dau & others, 2017; Martin & Messinger, 2018). Two types of smiling can be distinguished in infants:

- **Reflexive smile.** A smile that does not occur in response to external stimuli and appears during the first month after birth, usually during sleep.
- **Social smile.** A smile that occurs in response to an external stimulus, typically a face in the case of the young infant. Social smiling occurs as early as 4 to 6 weeks of age in response to a caregiver's voice.

The infant's social smile can have a powerful impact on caregivers (Martin & Messinger, 2018). Following weeks of endless demands, fatigue, and little reinforcement, an infant starts smiling at them and all of the caregivers' efforts are rewarded. Recent research found that smiling and laughter at 7 months of age were associated with self-regulation at 7 years of age (Posner & others, 2014). A recent study found that higher maternal effortful control and positive emotionality predicted more initial infant smiling and laughter, while a higher level of parenting stress predicted a lower trajectory of infant smiling and laughter (Bridgett & others, 2013).

Fear   One of a baby's earliest emotions is fear, which typically first appears at about 6 months of age and peaks at about 18 months. However, abused and neglected infants can show fear as early as 3 months (Witherington & others, 2010). Researchers have found that infant fear is linked to guilt, empathy, and low aggression at 6 to 7 years of age (Rothbart, 2011).

The most frequent expression of an infant's fear involves **stranger anxiety,** in which an infant shows a fear and wariness of strangers. Stranger anxiety usually emerges gradually. It first appears at about 6 months of age in the form of wary reactions. By age 9 months, the fear of strangers is often more intense, reaching a peak toward the end of the first year of life (Scher & Harel, 2008).

Not all infants show distress when they encounter a stranger. Besides individual variations, whether an infant shows stranger anxiety also depends on the social context and the characteristics of the stranger (Kagan, 2008).

Infants show less stranger anxiety when they are in familiar settings. It appears that when infants feel secure, they are less likely to show stranger anxiety.

In addition to stranger anxiety, infants experience fear of being separated from their caregivers. The result is **separation protest**—crying when the caregiver leaves. Separation protest is initially displayed by infants at approximately 7 to 8 months and peaks at about 15 months (Kagan, 2008). One study revealed that separation protest peaked at about 13 to 15 months in four different cultures (Kagan, Kearsley, & Zelazo, 1978). The percentage of infants who engaged in separation protest varied across cultures, but the infants reached a peak of protest at about the same age—just before the middle of the second year of life.

Emotion Regulation and Coping   During the first year of life, the infant gradually develops an ability to inhibit, or minimize, the intensity and duration of emotional reactions (Calkins & Perry, 2016). From early in infancy, babies put their thumbs in their mouths to soothe themselves. But at first, infants mainly depend on caregivers to help them soothe their emotions, as when a caregiver rocks an infant to sleep, sings lullabies to the infant, gently strokes the infant, and so on. In a recent study, young infants with a negative temperament used fewer emotion regulation strategies while maternal sensitivity to infants was lined to more adaptive emotion regulation (Thomas & others, 2017).

Later in infancy, when they become aroused, infants sometimes redirect their attention or distract themselves in order to reduce their arousal. By 2 years of age, toddlers can use language to define their feeling states and the context that is upsetting them (Kopp, 2008). A toddler might say, "Feel bad. Dog scare." This type of communication may allow caregivers to help the child regulate emotions.

Contexts can influence emotion regulation (Groh & others, 2015; Thompson, 2016). Infants are often affected by fatigue, hunger, time of day, which people are around them, and where they are. Infants must learn to adapt to different contexts that require emotion regulation. Further, new demands appear as the infant becomes older and parents modify their expectations. For example, a parent may take it in stride if a 6-month-old infant screams in a grocery store but may react very differently if a 2-year-old starts screaming.

To soothe or not to soothe—should a crying baby be given attention and soothed, or does this attention spoil the infant? Many years ago, the behaviorist John Watson (1928) argued that parents spend too much time responding to infant crying. As a consequence, he said, parents reward crying and increase its incidence. Some researchers, such as Jacob Gewirtz, have found that a caregiver's quick, soothing response to crying increased crying (Gewirtz, 1977). However, infancy experts Mary Ainsworth (1979) and John Bowlby (1989) stress that you can't respond too much to infant crying in the first year of life. They argue that a quick, comforting response to the infant's cries is an important ingredient in the development of a strong bond between the infant and caregiver. In one of Ainsworth's studies, infants whose mothers responded quickly when they cried at 3 months of age cried less later in the first year of life (Bell & Ainsworth, 1972). Further, a recent study revealed that depressed mothers rocked and touched their crying infants less than non-depressed mothers (Esposito & others, 2017a).

Controversy still characterizes the question of whether or how parents should respond to an infant's cries. Some developmentalists argue that an infant cannot be spoiled in the first year of life, a view suggesting that parents should soothe a crying infant. This reaction should help infants develop a sense of trust and secure attachment to the caregiver. One study revealed that mothers' negative emotional reactions (anger and anxiety) to crying increased the risk of subsequent attachment insecurity (Leerkes, Parade, & Gudmundson, 2011). Another study found that problems in infant soothability at 6 months of age were linked to insecure attachment at 12 months of age (Mills-Koonce, Propper, & Barnett, 2012). And a recent study found that mothers were more likely than fathers to use a soothing technique to reduce infant crying (Dayton & others, 2015).

TEMPERAMENT

Do you get upset a lot? Does it take much to get you angry, or to make you laugh? Even at birth, babies seem to have different emotional styles. One infant is cheerful and happy much of the time; another baby seems to cry constantly. These tendencies reflect **temperament,** which involves individual differences in behavioral styles, emotions, and characteristic ways of responding. With regard to its link to emotion, temperament refers to individual differences in how quickly the emotion is shown, how strong it is, how long it lasts, and how quickly it fades away (Campos, 2009).

Another way of describing temperament is in terms of predispositions toward emotional reactivity and self-regulation (Bates & Pettit, 2015). *Reactivity* involves variations in the speed and intensity with which an individual responds to situations with positive or negative emotions. *Self-regulation* involves variations in the extent or effectiveness of an individual's control over emotion.

Describing and Classifying Temperament

How would you describe your temperament or the temperament of a friend? Researchers have described and classified the temperaments of individuals in different ways (Abulizi & others, 2017; Gartstein, Putnam, & Kliewer, 2016; Janssen & others, 2017; Stifter & Dollar, 2016). Here we examine three of those ways.

Chess and Thomas' Classification Psychiatrists Stella Chess and Alexander Thomas (Chess & Thomas, 1977; Thomas & Chess, 1991) identified three basic types, or clusters, of temperament:

- An **easy child** is generally in a positive mood, quickly establishes regular routines in infancy, and adapts readily to new experiences.
- A **difficult child** reacts negatively and cries frequently, engages in irregular daily routines, and is slow to accept change.
- A **slow-to-warm-up child** has a low activity level, is somewhat negative, and displays a low intensity of mood.

How Would You...?
If you were a **social worker,** how would you advise a parent who is frustrated with her 18-month-old child because she tends to whine and cry excessively in comparison with her 3-year-old sibling?

temperament An individual's behavioral style and characteristic way of emotionally responding.

easy child A child who is generally in a positive mood, who quickly establishes regular routines in infancy, and who adapts easily to new experiences.

difficult child A child who tends to react negatively and cry frequently, who engages in irregular daily routines, and who is slow to accept new experiences.

slow-to-warm-up child A child who has a low activity level, is somewhat negative, and displays a low intensity of mood.

In their longitudinal investigation, Chess and Thomas found that 40 percent of the children they studied could be classified as easy, 10 percent as difficult, and 15 percent as slow to warm up. Notice that 35 percent did not fit any of the three patterns. Researchers have found that these three basic clusters of temperament are moderately stable across the childhood years. A recent study revealed that young children with a difficult temperament showed more problems when they experienced low-quality child care and fewer problems when they experienced high-quality child care than did young children with an easy temperament (Pluess & Belsky, 2009).

Kagan's Behavioral Inhibition Another way of classifying temperament focuses on the differences between a shy, subdued, timid child and a sociable, extraverted, bold child (Asendorph, 2008). Jerome Kagan (2002, 2008, 2010, 2013) regards shyness with strangers (peers or adults) as one feature of a broad temperament category called *inhibition to the unfamiliar.* Beginning at about 7 to 9 months, inhibited children react to many aspects of unfamiliarity with initial avoidance, distress, or subdued affect. In Kagan's research, inhibition shows some continuity from infancy through early childhood, although a substantial number of infants who are classified as inhibited become less so by 7 years of age. In recent research, having an inhibited temperament at 2 to 3 years of age was related to having social phobia symptoms at 7 years of age (Lahat & others, 2014). And recent findings also indicate that infants and young children who have an inhibited temperament are at risk for developing social anxiety disorder in adolescence and adulthood (Perez-Edgar & Guyer, 2014; Rapee, 2014).

Rothbart and Bates' Classification New classifications of temperament continue to be forged. Mary Rothbart and John Bates (2006) argue that three broad dimensions best represent what researchers have found to characterize the structure of temperament: extraversion/surgency, negative affectivity, and effortful control (self-regulation):

- *Extraversion/surgency* includes "positive anticipation, impulsivity, activity level, and sensation seeking" (Rothbart, 2004, p. 495). Kagan's uninhibited children fit into this category.
- *Negative affectivity* includes "fear, frustration, sadness, and discomfort" (Rothbart, 2004, p. 495). These children are easily distressed; they may fret and cry often. Kagan's inhibited children fit this category. In a recent study, positive affectivity and surgency at 4 months of age was linked to school readiness at 4 years of age (Gartstein, Putnam, & Kliewer, 2016).
- *Effortful control* (self-regulation) includes "attentional focusing and shifting, inhibitory control, perceptual

What are some ways that developmentalists have classified infants' temperaments? Which classification makes the most sense to you, based on your observations of infants?
©Tom Merton/Getty Images RF

sensitivity, and low-intensity pleasure" (Rothbart, 2004, p. 495). Infants who are high on effortful control show an ability to keep their arousal from getting too high and have strategies for soothing themselves. By contrast, children low on effortful control are often unable to control their arousal; they become easily agitated and intensely emotional. A recent study found that young children higher in effortful control were more likely to wait longer to express anger and were more likely to use a self-regulatory strategy, distraction (Tan, Armstrong, & Cole, 2013). Another recent study revealed that self-regulation capacity at 4 months of age was linked to school readiness at 4 years of age (Gartstein, Putnam, & Kliewer, 2016). In two recent studies, effortful control was linked to attention deficit hyperactivity disorder (ADHD). In the first study, a lower level of children's temperament regulation at 3 years of age predicted the presence of ADHD symptoms in the first grade (Willoughby, Gottfredson, & Stifter, 2016). In the second study, children with a lower level of effort control at 3 years of age were more likely to have ADHD symptoms at 13 years of age (Einziger & others, 2017).

The description of temperament categories so far reflects the development of normative capabilities of children, not individual differences in children. The development of these capabilities, such as effortful control, allows individual differences to emerge (Bates, 2008, 2012a, b). For example, although maturation of the brain's prefrontal lobes must occur for any child's attention to improve and the child to achieve effortful control, some children develop effortful control but others do not. And it is these individual differences in children that are at the heart of what temperament is (Bates, 2008, 2012a, b).

Biological Foundations and Experience   How does a child acquire a certain temperament? Kagan (2002, 2008, 2010, 2013) argues that children inherit a physiology that biases them to have a particular type of temperament. However, through experience they may learn to modify their temperament to some degree (Goodvin, Winer, & Thompson, 2015). For example, children may inherit a physiology that biases them to be fearful and inhibited, but they learn to reduce their fear and inhibition to some degree.

Physiological characteristics have been linked with different temperaments (Clauss, Avery, & Blackford, 2015; Mize & Jones, 2012). In particular, an inhibited temperament is associated with a unique physiological pattern that includes high and stable heart rate, high level of the hormone cortisol, and high activity in the right frontal lobe of the brain (Kagan, 2008). This pattern may be tied to the excitability of the amygdala, a structure of the brain that plays an important role in fear and inhibition. And the development of effortful control is linked to advances in the brain's frontal lobes (Bates, 2008, 2012a, b).

What is heredity's role in the biological foundations of temperament? Twin and adoption studies suggest that heredity has a moderate influence on differences in temperament within a group of people (Buss & Goldsmith, 2007). Too often, though, the biological foundations

developmental **connection**

Nature and Nurture

Twin and adoption studies have been used in the effort to sort out hereditary and environmental influences on development. Connect to "Biological Beginnings."

of temperament are interpreted as meaning that temperament cannot develop or change. However, important self-regulatory dimensions of temperament such as adaptability, soothability, and persistence look very different in a 1-year-old and a 5-year-old (Thompson, 2015). These temperament dimensions develop and change with the growth of the neurobiological foundations of self-regulation (Calkins & Perry, 2016).

Developmental Links   Is temperament in childhood linked with adjustment in adulthood? In one study, children who had an easy temperament at 3 to 5 years of age were likely to be well adjusted as young adults (Chess & Thomas, 1977). In contrast, many children who had a difficult temperament at 3 to 5 years of age were not well adjusted as young adults. Also, other researchers have found that boys with a difficult temperament in childhood are less likely as adults to continue their formal education, whereas girls with a difficult temperament in childhood are more likely to experience marital conflict as adults (Wachs, 2000). And in a longitudinal study, children who had a difficult temperament at 5 and 14 years of age were more likely to have mental health problems at 21 years of age (Kingsbury & others, 2017).

Inhibition is another temperament characteristic that has been studied extensively (Kagan, 2008, 2010, 2013). Research indicates that individuals with an inhibited temperament in childhood are less likely as adults to be assertive or to experience social support, and more likely to delay entering a stable job track (Asendorph, 2008). In the Uppsala (Sweden) Longitudinal Study, shyness/inhibition in infancy/childhood was linked to social anxiety at 21 years of age (Bohlin & Hagekull, 2009). Also, a recent study found that disinhibition in the toddler years was linked to career stability in middle adulthood (Blatny & others, 2015). And in another study, if parents had a childhood history of behavioral inhibition, their children who had a high level of behavioral inhibition were at risk for developing anxiety disorders (Stumper & others, 2017).

In sum, these studies reveal some continuity between certain aspects of temperament in childhood and adjustment in early adulthood (Janssen & others, 2017; Kingsbury & others, 2017; Rothbart, 2011; Shiner & DeYoung, 2013). However, keep in mind that these connections between childhood temperament and adult adjustment are based on only a small number of studies; more research is needed to verify these linkages.

Developmental Contexts   What accounts for the continuities and discontinuities between a child's temperament and an adult's personality? Physiological and heredity factors likely are involved in continuity (Clauss, Avery, & Blackford, 2015). Links between temperament in childhood and personality in adulthood also might vary, depending on the contexts in individuals' experience (Wachs & Bates, 2011).

The reaction to an infant's temperament may depend, in part, on culture (Chen, Fu, & Zhao, 2015; Chen & Schmidt, 2015). For example, behavioral inhibition is more highly valued in China than in North America, and researchers have found that Chinese infants are more inhibited than Canadian infants (Chen & others, 1998). The cultural differences in temperament were linked to parental attitudes and behaviors. Canadian mothers of inhibited 2-year-olds were less accepting of their infants' inhibited temperament, whereas Chinese mothers were more accepting. Also, a recent study revealed that U.S. infants showed more temperamental fearfulness while Finnish infants engaged in more positive affect, such as effortful control (Gaias & others, 2012).

In short, many aspects of a child's environment can encourage or discourage the persistence of temperament characteristics (Bates, 2012a, b; Shiner & DeYoung, 2013). For example, a recent study found that fathers' internalizing problems (anxiety and depression, for example) were linked to a higher level of negative affectivity in 6-month-olds (Potapova, Gartstein, & Bridgett, 2014). One useful way of thinking about these relationships applies the concept of goodness of fit, which we examine next.

Goodness of Fit   **Goodness of fit** refers to the match between a child's temperament and the environmental demands the child must cope with. Suppose Jason is an active toddler who is made to sit still for long periods of time and Jack is a slow-to-warm-up toddler who is abruptly pushed into new situations on a regular basis. Both Jason and Jack face a lack of fit between their temperament and environmental demands. Lack of fit can produce adjustment problems (Rothbart, 2011).

goodness of fit Refers to the match between a child's temperament and the environmental demands with which the child must cope.

developmental **connection**

Culture

Cross-cultural studies seek to determine culture-universal and culture-specific aspects of development. Connect to "Introduction."

An infant's temperament can vary across cultures. *What do parents need to know about a child's temperament?*
©Alan Oddie/PhotoEdit

Some temperament characteristics pose more parenting challenges than others, at least in modern Western societies (Goodvin, Winer, & Thompson, 2015; Rothbart, 2011). When children are prone to distress, as exhibited by frequent crying and irritability, their parents may eventually respond by ignoring the child's distress or trying to force the child to "behave." In one research study, though, extra support and training for mothers of distress-prone infants improved the quality of mother-infant interaction (van den Boom, 1989). The training led the mothers to alter their demands on the child, improving the fit between the child and the environment. Researchers also have found that decreases in infants' negative emotionality are linked to higher levels of parental sensitivity, involvement, and responsivity (Bates, 2012a, b; Penela & others, 2012). Other findings support the use of positive parenting, including high levels of warmth and low levels of harsh control, to increase children's effortful control (Bates & Pettit, 2015).

A final comment about temperament is that recently the *differential susceptibility model* and the *biological sensitivity to context model* have been proposed and studied (Baptista & others, 2017; Belsky & others, 2015; Belsky & Pluess, 2016; Belsky & van IJzendoorn, 2017; Simpson & Belsky, 2016). These models emphasize that certain characteristics—such as a difficult temperament—that render children more vulnerable to difficulty in adverse contexts can also make them more likely to experience optimal growth in very supportive conditions. These models may help us see "negative" temperament characteristics in a new light.

To read further about some positive strategies for parenting that take into account the child's temperament, see the *Caring Connections* interlude.

How Would You...?

If you were a **social worker**, how would you apply information about an infant's temperament to maximize the goodness of fit in a clinical setting?

caring connections

Parenting and the Child's Temperament

What are the implications of temperamental variations for parenting? Although answers to this question necessarily are speculative, the following conclusions regarding the best parenting strategies to use in relation to children's temperament were reached by temperament experts Ann Sanson and Mary Rothbart (1995):

- *Attention to and respect for individuality.* One implication is that it is difficult to generate general prescriptions for "good" parenting. A goal might be accomplished in one way with one child and in another way with another child, depending on the child's temperament. Parents need to be sensitive and flexible in responding to the infant's signals and needs. Researchers have found that decreases in infants' negative emotionality are related to higher levels of parental sensitivity, involvement, and responsiveness (Wachs & Bates, 2011).
- *Structuring the child's environment.* Crowded, noisy environments can pose greater problems for some children (such as "difficult" children) than others (such as "easygoing" children). We might also expect that a fearful, withdrawing child would benefit from slower entry into new contexts.
- *The "difficult child" and packaged parenting programs.* Programs for parents often focus on dealing with children who have

What are some good strategies for parents to adopt when responding to their infant's temperament?

©Ariel Skelley/Blend Images RF

"difficult" temperaments. In some cases, "difficult child" refers to Thomas and Chess' description of a child who reacts negatively, cries frequently, engages in irregular daily routines, and is slow to accept change. In others, the concept might be used to describe a child who is irritable, displays anger frequently, does not follow directions well, or shows some other negative characteristic. Acknowledging that some children are harder than others to parent is often helpful, and advice on how to handle specific difficult characteristics can be useful. However, whether a specific characteristic is difficult depends on its fit with the environment. To label a child "difficult" has the danger of becoming a self-fulfilling prophecy. If a child is identified as "difficult," people may treat the child in a way that actually elicits "difficult" behavior.

Too often, we pigeonhole children into categories without examining the context (Bates, 2012a, b; Rothbart, 2011). Nonetheless, caregivers need to take children's temperament into account. Research does not yet allow for many highly specific recommendations, but, in general, caregivers should (1) be sensitive to the individual characteristics of the child, (2) be flexible in responding to these characteristics, and (3) avoid applying negative labels to the child.

PERSONALITY DEVELOPMENT

Emotions and temperament represent key aspects of personality—the enduring personal characteristics of individuals. Let's now examine characteristics that often are thought of as central to personality development during infancy: trust and the development of self and independence.

Trust   According to Erik Erikson (1968), the first year of life is characterized by the trust versus mistrust stage of development. Following a life of regularity, warmth, and protection in the mother's womb, the infant faces a world that is less secure. Erikson proposed that infants learn trust when they are cared for in a consistent, warm manner. If the infant is not well fed and kept warm on a consistent basis, a sense of mistrust is likely to develop.

Trust versus mistrust is not resolved once and for all in the first year of life. It arises again at each successive stage of development, a pathway that can have positive or negative outcomes. For example, children who leave infancy with a sense of trust can still have their sense of mistrust activated at a later stage, perhaps if their parents are separated or divorced under conflictual circumstances.

The Developing Sense of Self   Real or imagined, the sense of self is a strong motivating force in life. When does the individual begin to sense a separate existence from others?

Studying the self in infancy is difficult mainly because infants cannot tell us how they experience themselves. Infants cannot verbally express their views of the self. They also cannot understand complex instructions from researchers.

One ingenious strategy to test infants' visual self-recognition is the use of a mirror technique, in which an infant's mother first puts a dot of rouge on the infant's nose. Then an observer watches to see how often the infant touches its nose. Next, the infant is placed in front of a mirror, and observers detect whether nose touching increases. Why does this matter? The idea is that increased nose touching indicates that the infant recognizes the self in the mirror and is trying to touch or rub off the rouge because the rouge violates the infant's view of the self. Increased touching indicates that the infant realizes that it is the self in the mirror but that something is not right since the real self does not have a dot of rouge on it.

Figure 3 displays the results of two investigations that used the mirror technique. The researchers found that before they were 1 year old, infants did not recognize themselves in the mirror (Amsterdam, 1968; Lewis & Brooks-Gunn, 1979). Signs of self-recognition began to appear among some infants when they were 15 to 18 months old. By the time they were 2 years old, most children recognized themselves in the mirror. In sum, infants begin to develop a self-understanding called self-recognition at approximately 18 months of age (Hart & Karmel, 1996; Lewis, 2005).

developmental **connection**

Personality

Erikson proposed that individuals go through eight stages in the course of human development. Connect to "Introduction."

FIGURE 3

THE DEVELOPMENT OF SELF-RECOGNITION IN INFANCY. The graph shows the findings of two studies in which infants less than 1 year of age did not recognize themselves in the mirror. A slight increase in the percentage of infant self-recognition occurred around 15 to 18 months of age. By 2 years of age, a majority of children recognized themselves. *Why do researchers study whether infants recognize themselves in a mirror?*
©Digital Vision/Getty Images RF

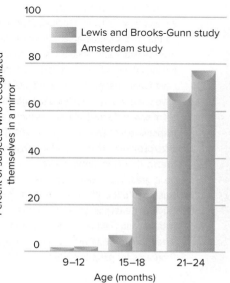

Late in the second year and early in the third year, toddlers show other emerging forms of self-awareness that reflect a sense of "me" (Goodvin, Winer, & Thompson, 2015). For example, they refer to themselves by saying "Me big"; they label internal experiences such as emotions; they monitor themselves as when a toddler says, "Do it myself"; and they say that things are theirs (Bullock & Lutkenhaus, 1990; Fasig, 2000). One study revealed that it is not until the second year that infants develop a conscious awareness of their own bodies (Brownell & others, 2009). This developmental change in body awareness marks the beginning of children's representation of their own three-dimensional body shape and appearance, providing an early step in the development of their self-image and identity (Brownell, 2011).

Also, researchers recently have found that the capacity to understand others may begin to develop during infancy (Carpendale & Lewis, 2015; Rhodes & others, 2015). Research indicates that as early as 13 months of age, infants seem to consider another's perspective when predicting their actions (Choi & Luo, 2015).

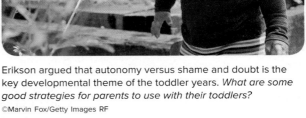

Erikson argued that autonomy versus shame and doubt is the key developmental theme of the toddler years. *What are some good strategies for parents to use with their toddlers?*
©Marvin Fox/Getty Images RF

Independence   Not only does the infant develop a sense of self in the second year of life, but independence also becomes a more central theme in the infant's life (Mangelsdorf & Wong, 2008). The theories of Margaret Mahler and Erik Erikson have important implications for both self-development and independence. Mahler (1979) argues that the child goes through a separation and then an individuation process. *Separation* involves the infant's movement away from the mother. *Individuation* involves the development of self.

Erikson (1968), like Mahler, stressed that independence is an important issue in the second year of life. Erikson describes the second stage of development as the stage of autonomy versus shame and doubt. Autonomy builds as the infant's mental and motor abilities develop. At this point in development, not only can infants walk, but they can also climb, open and close, drop, push and pull, and hold and let go. Infants feel pride in these new accomplishments and want to do everything themselves, whether the activity is flushing a toilet, pulling the wrapping off a package, or deciding what to eat. It is important for parents to recognize the motivation of toddlers to do what they are capable of doing at their own pace. Then they can learn to control their muscles and their impulses themselves. But when caregivers are impatient and do for toddlers what they are capable of doing themselves, shame and doubt develop. Every parent has rushed a child from time to time. It is only when parents consistently overprotect toddlers or criticize accidents (wetting, soiling, spilling, or breaking, for example) that children develop an excessive sense of shame and doubt about their ability to control themselves and their world. As we discuss in later chapters, Erikson argued that the stage of autonomy versus shame and doubt has important implications for the individual's future development.

How Would You...?
If you were a **human development and family studies professional,** how would you work with a parent who shows signs of being overly protective or critical to the point of impairing the toddler's independence?

developmental connection

Personality

Two key points in development when there is a strong push for independence are the second year of life and early adolescence. Connect to "Socioemotional Development in Adolescence."

Review Connect Reflect

LG1 Discuss emotional and personality development in infancy.

Review

- What is the nature of an infant's emotions, and how do they change?
- What is temperament, and how does it develop in infancy?
- What are some important aspects of personality in infancy, and how do they develop?

Connect

- Earlier in this section, you read that the early development of the hippocampus in infants plays a role in their emotions.

The hippocampus is also connected to another key cognitive process. What is that process?

Reflect *Your Own Personal Journey of Life*

- How would you describe your temperament? Does it fit one of Chess and Thomas' three styles—easy, slow to warm up, or difficult? If you have siblings, is your temperament similar to or different from theirs?

2 How Do Social Orientation/Understanding and Attachment Develop in Infancy?

LG2 Describe the development of social orientation/understanding and attachment in infancy.

| Social Orientation/ Understanding | Attachment and Its Development | Individual Differences in Attachment | Developmental Social Neuroscience and Attachment |

developmental connection

Biological, Cognitive, and Socioemotional Processes

Discussing biological, cognitive, and socioemotional processes together reminds us of an important aspect of development: These processes are intricately intertwined. Connect to "Introduction."

So far, we have discussed how emotions and emotional competence change as children develop. We have also examined the role of emotional style; in effect, we have seen how emotions set the tone of our experiences in life. But emotions also write the lyrics because they are at the core of our relationships with others.

SOCIAL ORIENTATION/UNDERSTANDING

In Ross Thompson's view (2006, 2015, 2016), infants are socioemotional beings who show a strong interest in the social world and are motivated to orient to it and understand it. In other chapters, we described many of the biological and cognitive foundations that contribute to the infant's development of social orientation and understanding. We call attention to relevant biological and cognitive factors as we explore social orientation; locomotion; intention, goal-directed behavior, and cooperation; and social referencing.

Social Orientation From early in their development, infants are captivated by the social world. Young infants stare intently at faces and are attuned to the sounds of human voices, especially those of their caregivers (Jakobsen, Umstead, & Simpson, 2016; Singarajah & others, 2017; Sugden & Moulson, 2017). Later, they become adept at interpreting the meaning of facial expressions (Weatherhead & White, 2017). *Face-to-face play* often begins to characterize caregiver-infant interactions when the infant is about 2 to 3 months of age. The focused social interaction of face-to-face play may include vocalizations, touch, and gestures (Beebe & others, 2016). Such play is part of many mothers' efforts to create a positive emotional state in their infants (Laible, Thompson, & Froimson, 2015).

In part because of such positive social interchanges between caregivers and infants, by 2 to 3 months of age infants respond to people differently from the way they do to objects, showing more positive emotion toward people than inanimate objects such as puppets (Legerstee, 1997). At this age, most infants expect people to react positively when the infants initiate a behavior, such as a smile or a vocalization. This finding has been discovered by use of a method called the *still-face paradigm*, in which the caregiver alternates between engaging in face-to-face interaction with the infant and remaining still and unresponsive (Busuito & Moore, 2017). As early as 2 to 3 months of age, infants show more withdrawal, negative emotions, and self-directed behavior when their caregivers are still and unresponsive (Adamson & Frick, 2003). The frequency of face-to-face play decreases after 7 months of age as infants become more mobile (Thompson, 2006).

Infants also learn about the social world through contexts other than face-to-face play with a caregiver (Swingler & others, 2017; Thompson, 2015, 2016). Even though infants as young as 6 months of age show an interest in each other, their interaction with peers increases considerably in the last half of the second year. As increasing numbers of U.S. infants experience child care outside the home, they are spending more time in social play with peers (Lamb & Lewis, 2015). Later in the chapter, we further discuss child care.

A mother and her baby engage in face-to-face play. *At what age does face-to-face play usually begin, and when does it typically start decreasing in frequency?*

©Britt Erlanson/Getty Images

Locomotion Recall from earlier in the chapter how important independence is for infants, especially in the second year of life. As infants develop the ability to crawl, walk, and run, they are able to explore and expand their social world. These newly developed self-produced locomotor skills allow the infant to independently initiate social interchanges on a more frequent basis. Remember that the development of these gross motor skills reflects a number of factors, including the development of the nervous system, the goal the infant is motivated to reach, and environmental support for the skill (Adolph, 2018; Kretch & Adolph, 2017).

The infant's and toddler's push for independence also is likely paced by the development of locomotion skills (Campos, 2009). Locomotion is also important for its motivational implications. Once infants have the ability to move in goal-directed pursuits, the reward from these pursuits leads to further efforts to explore and develop skills.

Intention, Goal-Directed Behavior, and Cooperation Perceiving people as engaging in intentional and goal-directed behavior is an important social cognitive accomplishment, and this initially occurs toward the end of the first year (Thompson, 2015). Joint attention and gaze following help the infant to understand that other people have intentions (Hoehl & Striano, 2015; Yu & Smith, 2017). *Joint attention* occurs when the caregiver and infant focus on the same object or event. By their first birthday, infants have begun to direct the caregiver's attention to objects that capture their interest (Marsh & Legerstee, 2017).

Amanda Woodward and her colleagues (Krogh-Jespersen, Liberman, & Woodward, 2015; Krogh-Jespersen & Woodward, 2016; Liberman, Woodward, & Kinzler, 2017; Shneidman & Woodward, 2016; Shneidman & others, 2016; Sodian & others, 2016) argue that infants' ability to understand and respond to others' meaningful intentions is a critical cognitive foundation for effectively engaging in the social world. They especially emphasize that an important aspect of this ability is the capacity to grasp social knowledge quickly in order to make an appropriate social response. Although processing speed is an important contributor to social engagement, other factors are involved such as infants' motivation to interact with someone, the infant's social interactive history with the individual, the interactive partner's social membership, and culturally specific aspects of interaction (Howard & others, 2015; Krogh-Jespersen & Woodward, 2016; Liberman, Woodward, & Kinzler, 2017).

Cooperating with others also is a key aspect of effectively engaging with others in the social world. Can infants engage in cooperation with others? One study involved presenting 1- and 2-year-olds with a simple cooperative task that consisted of pulling a lever to get an attractive toy (Brownell, Ramani, & Zerwas, 2006) (see Figure 4). Any coordinated actions of the 1-year-olds appeared to be more coincidental than cooperative, whereas the 2-year-olds' behavior was more likely to be characterized as active cooperation to reach a goal. In this study, the infants also were assessed using two social understanding tasks, observation of children's behavior in a joint attention task, and the parents' perceptions of the language the children use about the self and others (Brownell, Ramani, & Zerwas, 2006). Those with more advanced social understanding were more likely to cooperate. To cooperate, the children had to connect their own intentions with the peer's intentions and put this understanding to use in interacting with the peer to reach a goal.

Social Referencing Another important social cognitive accomplishment in infancy is developing the ability to "read" the emotions of other people (Carbajal-Valenzuela & others, 2017). **Social referencing** is the term used to describe "reading" emotional cues in others to help determine how to act in a specific situation. The development of social referencing helps infants to interpret ambiguous situations more accurately, as when they encounter a stranger and need to know whether or not to fear the person (Stenberg, 2017). By the end of the first year, a mother's facial expression—either smiling or fearful—influences whether an infant will explore an unfamiliar environment.

Infants become better at social referencing in the second year of life (Witherington & others, 2010). At this age, they tend to "check" with their mother before they act; they look at her to see if she is happy, angry, or fearful.

Infants' Social Sophistication and Insight In sum, researchers are discovering that infants are more socially sophisticated and insightful at younger ages than was previously envisioned (Thompson, 2015, 2016). Such sophistication and insight are reflected in infants' perceptions of others' actions as intentionally motivated and goal-directed and their motivation to share and participate in that intentionality by their first birthday. More advanced social cognitive skills of infants could be expected to influence their understanding and awareness of **attachment** to a caregiver.

--→

developmental connection

Theories
The dynamic systems view is increasingly used to explain how infants develop. Connect to "Physical Development in Infancy."

←--

social referencing "Reading" emotional cues in others to help determine how to act in a particular situation.

attachment A close emotional bond between two people.

FIGURE **4**

THE COOPERATION TASK. The cooperation task consisted of two handles on a box, atop which was an animated musical toy, surreptitiously activated by remote control when both handles were pulled. The handles were placed far enough apart that one child could not pull both handles. The experimenter demonstrated the task, saying, "Watch! If you pull the handles, the doggie will sing" (Brownell, Ramani, & Zerwas, 2006).
Courtesy of Celia A. Brownell, University of Pittsburgh

ATTACHMENT AND ITS DEVELOPMENT

There is no shortage of theories about why infants become attached to a caregiver. Three theorists—Freud, Erikson, and Bowlby—proposed influential views.

Freud noted that infants become attached to the person or object that provides oral satisfaction. For most infants, this is the mother, since she is most likely to feed the infant. Is feeding as important as Freud thought? A classic study by Harry Harlow (1958) revealed that the answer is no (see Figure 5).

Harlow removed infant monkeys from their mothers at birth; for six months they were reared by surrogate (substitute) "mothers." One surrogate mother was made of wire, the other of cloth. Half of the infant monkeys were fed by the wire mother, half by the cloth mother. Periodically, the amount of time the infant monkeys spent with either the wire or the cloth mother was computed. Regardless of which mother fed them, the infant monkeys spent far more time with the cloth mother. Even if the wire mother but not the cloth mother provided nourishment, the infant monkeys spent more time with the cloth mother. And when Harlow frightened the monkeys, those "raised" by the cloth mother ran to the mother and clung to it; those raised by the wire mother did not. Whether the mother provided comfort seemed to determine whether the monkeys associated the mother with security. This study clearly demonstrated that feeding is not the crucial element in the attachment process and that contact comfort is important.

Physical comfort also plays a role in Erik Erikson's (1968) view of the infant's development. Recall Erikson's proposal that the first year of life represents the stage of trust versus mistrust. Physical comfort and sensitive care, according to Erikson (1968), are key to establishing a basic trust in infants. The infant's sense of trust, in turn, is the foundation for attachment and sets the stage for a lifelong expectation that the world will be a good and pleasant place to be.

The ethological perspective of British psychiatrist John Bowlby (1969, 1989) also stresses the importance of attachment in the first year of life and the responsiveness of the caregiver. Bowlby stresses that infants and their primary caregivers are biologically predisposed to form attachments to each other. He argues that the newborn is biologically equipped to elicit attachment behavior. The baby cries, clings, coos, and smiles. Later, the infant crawls, walks, and follows the mother. The immediate result is to keep the primary caregiver nearby; the long-term effect is to increase the infant's chances of survival.

Attachment does not emerge suddenly but rather develops in a series of phases, moving from a baby's general preference for human beings to a partnership with primary

FIGURE 5

CONTACT TIME WITH WIRE AND CLOTH SURROGATE MOTHERS. Regardless of whether the infant monkeys were fed by a wire or a cloth mother, they overwhelmingly preferred to spend contact time with the cloth mother. *How do these results compare with what Freud's theory and Erikson's theory would predict about human infants?*

©Martin Rogers/Getty Images

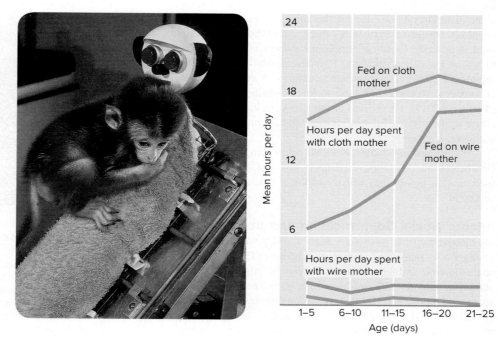

caregivers. Following are four such phases based on Bowlby's conceptualization of attachment (Schaffer, 1996):

- *Phase 1: From birth to 2 months.* Infants instinctively direct their attachment to human figures. Strangers, siblings, and parents are equally likely to elicit smiling or crying from the infant.
- *Phase 2: From 2 to 7 months.* Attachment becomes focused on one figure, usually the primary caregiver, as the baby gradually learns to distinguish familiar from unfamiliar people.
- *Phase 3: From 7 to 24 months.* Specific attachments develop. With increased locomotor skills, babies actively seek contact with regular caregivers, such as the mother or father.
- *Phase 4: From 24 months on.* Children become aware of others' feelings, goals, and plans and begin to take these into account in forming their own actions.

Researchers' recent findings that infants are more socially sophisticated and insightful than was previously envisioned suggests that some of the characteristics of Bowlby's phase 4, such as understanding the goals and intentions of the attachment figure, appear to be developing in phase 3 as attachment security is taking shape.

Bowlby argued that infants develop an *internal working model* of attachment, a simple mental model of the caregiver, their relationship, and the self as deserving of nurturant care. The infant's internal working model of attachment with the caregiver influences the infant's and later, the child's, subsequent responses to other people (Cassidy, 2016). The internal model of attachment also has played a pivotal role in the discovery of links between attachment and subsequent emotional understanding and self-perception (Bretherton & Munholland, 2016; Hoffman & others, 2017; Thompson, 2015, 2016).

In sum, attachment emerges from the social cognitive advances that allow infants to develop expectations for the caregiver's behavior and to determine the affective quality of their relationship (Challacombe & others, 2017; Leerkes & others, 2017a; Lopez-Maestro & others, 2017; Thompson, 2015, 2016). These social cognitive advances include recognizing the caregiver's face, voice, and other features, as well as developing an internal working model of expecting the caregiver to provide pleasure in social interaction and relief from distress.

INDIVIDUAL DIFFERENCES IN ATTACHMENT

Although attachment to a caregiver intensifies midway through the first year, isn't it likely that the quality of babies' attachment experiences varies? Mary Ainsworth (1979) thought so. Ainsworth created the **Strange Situation,** an observational measure of infant attachment in which the infant experiences a series of introductions, separations, and reunions with the caregiver and an adult stranger in a prescribed order. In using the Strange Situation, researchers hope that their observations will provide information about the infant's motivation to be near the caregiver and the degree to which the caregiver's presence provides the infant with security and confidence (Brownell & others, 2015).

Based on how babies respond in the Strange Situation, they are described as being securely attached or insecurely attached (in one of three ways) to the caregiver:

- **Securely attached babies** use the caregiver as a secure base from which to explore the environment. When in the presence of their caregiver, securely attached infants explore the room and examine toys that have been placed in it. When the caregiver departs, securely attached infants might protest mildly, and when the caregiver returns these infants reestablish positive interaction with her, perhaps by smiling or climbing on her lap. Subsequently, they often resume playing with the toys in the room.
- **Insecure avoidant babies** show insecurity by avoiding the mother. In the Strange Situation, these babies engage in little interaction with the caregiver, are not distressed when she leaves the room, usually do not reestablish contact on her return, and may even turn their back on her. If contact is established, the infant usually leans away or looks away.
- **Insecure resistant babies** often cling to the caregiver and then resist her by fighting against the closeness, perhaps by kicking or pushing away. In the Strange Situation,

Strange Situation An observational measure of infant attachment that requires the infant to move through a series of introductions, separations, and reunions with the caregiver and an adult stranger in a prescribed order.

securely attached babies Babies that use the caregiver as a secure base from which to explore their environment.

insecure avoidant babies Babies that show insecurity by avoiding the caregiver.

insecure resistant babies Babies that often cling to the caregiver, then resist her by fighting against the closeness, perhaps by kicking or pushing away.

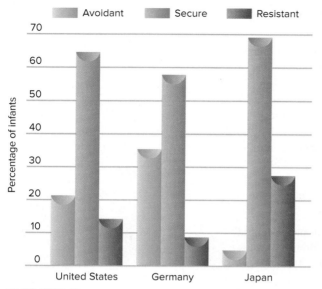

FIGURE **6**

CROSS-CULTURAL COMPARISON OF ATTACHMENT. In one study, infant attachment in three countries—the United States, Germany, and Japan—was measured in the Ainsworth Strange Situation (van IJzendoorn & Kroonenberg, 1988). The dominant attachment pattern in all three countries was secure attachment. However, German infants were more avoidant and Japanese infants were less avoidant and more resistant than U.S. infants. *What are some explanations for differences in how German, Japanese, and American infants respond to the Strange Situation?*

How Would You...?
If you were a **psychologist**, how would you identify an insecurely attached infant? How would you encourage a parent to strengthen the attachment bond?

insecure disorganized babies Babies that show insecurity by being disorganized and disoriented.

What is the nature of secure and insecure attachment? How are caregiving styles related to attachment classification?
©Corbis/age fotostock RF

these babies often cling anxiously to the caregiver and don't explore the playroom. When the caregiver leaves, they often cry loudly and push away if she tries to comfort them on her return.

- **Insecure disorganized babies** are disorganized and disoriented. In the Strange Situation, these babies might appear dazed, confused, and fearful. To be classified as disorganized, babies must show strong patterns of avoidance and resistance or display certain specified behaviors, such as extreme fearfulness around the caregiver.

Evaluating the Strange Situation Does the Strange Situation capture important differences among infants? As a measure of attachment, it may be culturally biased (Gernhardt, Keller, & Rubeling, 2016; Otto & Keller, 2013). For example, German and Japanese babies often show different patterns of attachment from those of American infants. As illustrated in Figure 6, German infants are more likely to show an avoidant attachment pattern and Japanese infants are less likely to display this pattern than U.S. infants (van IJzendoorn & Kroonenberg, 1988). The avoidant pattern in German babies likely occurs because their caregivers encourage them to be independent (Grossmann & others, 1985). Also as shown in Figure 6, Japanese babies are more likely than American babies to be categorized as resistant. This may have more to do with the Strange Situation as a measure of attachment than with attachment insecurity itself. Japanese mothers rarely allow anyone unfamiliar with their babies to care for them. Thus, the Strange Situation might create considerably more stress for Japanese infants than for American infants, who are more accustomed to separation from their mothers (Miyake, Chen, & Campos, 1985). Even though there are cultural variations in attachment classification, the most frequent classification in every culture studied so far is secure attachment (Mooya, Sichimba, & Bakermans-Kranenburg, 2016; van IJzendoorn & Kroonenberg, 1988).

Some critics stress that behavior in the Strange Situation—like other laboratory assessments—might not indicate what infants would do in a natural environment. But researchers have found that infants' behaviors in the Strange Situation are closely related to how they behave at home in response to separation and reunion with their mothers (Pederson & Moran, 1996). Thus, many infant researchers stress that the Strange Situation continues to show merit as a measure of infant attachment.

Caregiving Styles and Attachment Is the style of caregiving linked with the quality of the infant's attachment? Securely attached babies have caregivers who are sensitive to their signals and are consistently available to respond to their infants' needs (Hoffman & others, 2017; Pasco-Fearon & Belsky, 2016). These caregivers often let their babies have an active part in determining the onset and pacing of interaction in the first year of life. A recent study revealed that maternal sensitivity in responding was linked to infant attachment security (Finger & others, 2009). Another study found that maternal sensitivity in parenting was linked with secure attachment in infants in two different cultures: the United States and Colombia (Posada & others, 2002). Although maternal sensitivity is linked to the development of secure attachment in infancy, it is important to note that the connection is not especially strong (Campos, 2009).

How do the caregivers of insecurely attached babies interact with them? Caregivers of avoidant babies tend to be unavailable or rejecting (Posada & Kaloustian, 2010). They often don't respond to their babies' signals and have little physical contact with them. When they do interact with their babies, they may behave in an angry and irritable way. Caregivers of resistant babies tend to be inconsistent; sometimes they respond to their babies' needs, and sometimes they don't. In general, they tend not to be very affectionate with their babies and show little synchrony when interacting with them. Caregivers of disorganized babies often neglect or physically abuse them (Cicchetti, 2017). In some cases, these caregivers are depressed. In sum, caregivers' interactions with infants influence whether infants are securely or insecurely attached to the caregivers (Sroufe, 2016).

Interpreting Differences in Attachment   Do individual differences in attachment matter? Ainsworth notes that secure attachment in the first year of life provides an important foundation for psychological development later in life. The securely attached infant moves freely away from the mother but keeps track of where she is through periodic glances. The securely attached infant responds positively to being picked up by others and, when put back down, freely moves away to play. An insecurely attached infant, by contrast, avoids the mother or is ambivalent toward her, fears strangers, and is upset by minor, everyday separations.

If early attachment to a caregiver is important, it should influence a child's social behavior later in development. For some children, early attachments seem to foreshadow later functioning (Cassidy, 2016; Sroufe, 2016). In the extensive longitudinal study conducted by Alan Sroufe and his colleagues (2005, 2016; Sroufe, Coffino, & Carlson, 2010), early secure attachment (assessed by the Strange Situation at 12 and 18 months) was linked with positive emotional health, high self-esteem, self-confidence, and socially competent interaction with peers, teachers, camp counselors, and romantic partners through adolescence. Another study found that attachment security at 24 and 36 months was linked to the child's enhanced social problem-solving at 54 months (Raikes & Thompson, 2009). Also, a recent meta-analysis found that secure attachment in infancy was linked to social competence with peers in childhood (Groh & others, 2014). Further, a recent study revealed that infant attachment insecurity (especially insecure resistant attachment) and early childhood behavioral inhibition predicted adolescent social anxiety symptoms (Lewis-Morrarty & others, 2015). And a meta-analysis revealed that disorganized attachment was more strongly linked to externalizing problems (aggression and hostility, for example) than were avoidant and resistant attachment (Fearon & others, 2010).

Few studies have assessed infants' attachment security to the mother and the father separately. However, a recent study revealed that infants who were insecurely attached to their mother and father ("double-insecure") at 15 months of age had more externalizing problems (out-of-control behavior, for example) in the elementary school years than their counterparts who were securely attached to at least one parent (Kochanska & Kim, 2013).

An important issue regarding attachment is whether infancy is a critical or sensitive period for development. Many, but not all, research studies reveal the power of infant attachment to predict subsequent development (Hudson & others, 2016; Lamb & Lewis, 2015; Roisman & others, 2017; Thompson, 2015, 2016). In one longitudinal study, attachment classification in infancy did not predict attachment classification at 18 years of age (Lewis, Feiring, & Rosenthal, 2000). In this study, the best predictor of an insecure attachment classification at 18 was the occurrence of parental divorce in the intervening years. Consistently positive caregiving over a number of years is likely an important factor in connecting early attachment with the child's functioning later in development. Indeed, researchers have found that early secure attachment and subsequent experiences, especially maternal care and life stresses, are linked with children's later behavior and adjustment (Roisman & Cicchetti, 2018; Thompson, 2015, 2016). For example, a longitudinal study revealed that changes in attachment security/insecurity from infancy to adulthood were linked to stresses and supports in socioemotional contexts (Van Ryzin, Carlson, & Sroufe, 2011). These results suggest that attachment continuity may be a reflection of stable social contexts as much as early working models. The study just described (Van Ryzin, Carlson, & Sroufe, 2011) reflects an increasingly accepted view of the development of attachment and its influence on development. That is, it is important to recognize that attachment security in infancy does not always by itself produce long-term positive outcomes, but rather is linked to later outcomes through connections with the way children and adolescents subsequently experience various social contexts as they develop.

The Van Ryzin, Carlson, and Sroufe (2011) study reflects a **developmental cascade model,** which involves connections across domains over time that influence developmental pathways and outcomes (Almy & Cicchetti, 2018; Groh & others, 2015; Masten & Kalstabakken, 2017). Developmental cascades can include connections between a wide range of biological, cognitive, and socioemotional processes (attachment, for example), and also can involve social contexts such as families peers, schools, and culture. Further, links can produce positive or negative outcomes at different points in development, such as infancy, early childhood, middle and late childhood, adolescence, and adulthood.

A recent meta-analysis supported the views just described (Pinquart, Feubner, & Ahnert, 2013). In this analysis of 127 research reports, the following conclusions were reached: (1) moderate stability of attachment security occurred from early infancy to adulthood; (2) no significant stability occurred for time intervals of more than 15 years; (3) attachment stability

How Would You...?
If you were a **health-care professional,** how would you use an infant's attachment style and/or a parent's caregiving style to determine whether an infant might be at risk for neglect or abuse?

developmental cascade model Involves connections across domains over time that influence developmental pathways and outcomes.

developmental connection

Nature and Nurture

What is involved in gene-environment (G × E) interaction? Connect to "Biological Beginnings."

was greater when the time span was less than 2 years than when it was more than 5 years; and (4) securely attached children at risk were less likely to maintain attachment security while insecurely attached children at risk were likely to continue to be insecurely attached.

In addition to challenging whether secure attachment in infancy serves as a critical or sensitive period, some developmentalists argue that the secure attachment concept does not adequately consider certain biological factors in development, such as genes and temperament (Bakermans-Kranenburg & van IJzendoorn, 2016; Belsky & van IJzendoorn, 2017; Esposito & others, 2017b; Kim & others, 2017; Vaughn & Bost, 2016). Jerome Kagan (2000), for example, emphasizes that infants are highly resilient and adaptive; he argues that they are evolutionarily equipped to stay on a positive developmental course, even in the face of wide variations in parenting. Kagan and others stress that genetic characteristics and temperament play more important roles in a child's social competence than the attachment theorists, such as Bowlby and Ainsworth, are willing to acknowledge (Bakermans-Kranenburg & van IJzendoorn, 2011, 2016; Belsky & van IJzendoorn, 2017; Esposito & others, 2017b). For example, if some infants inherit a low tolerance for stress, this characteristic, rather than an insecure attachment bond, may be responsible for an inability to get along with peers. A recent study found links between disorganized attachment in infancy, a specific gene, and level of maternal responsiveness. In this study, a disorganized attachment style developed in infancy only when infants had the short version of the serotonin transporter gene—5-HTTLPR (Spangler & others, 2009). Infants were not characterized by this attachment style when they had the long version of the gene (Spangler & others 2009). Further, this gene-environment interaction occurred only when mothers showed a low level of responsiveness toward their infants. However, some researchers have not found support for genetic influences on infant-mother attachment (Leerkes & others, 2017b) or for gene-environment interactions related to infant attachment (Fraley & others, 2013).

Another criticism of attachment theory is that it ignores the diversity of socializing agents and contexts that exists in an infant's world. A culture's value system can influence the nature of attachment (van IJzendoorn & Sagi-Schwartz, 2009). Mothers' expectations for infants to be independent are high in northern Germany, whereas Japanese mothers are more strongly motivated to keep their infants close to them (Grossmann & others, 1985; Rothbaum & others, 2000). Not surprisingly, northern German infants tend to show less distress than Japanese infants when separated from their mother. Also, in some cultures, infants show attachments to many people. Among the Hausa (who live in Nigeria), both grandmothers and siblings provide a significant amount of care for infants (Harkness & Super, 1995). Infants in agricultural societies tend to form attachments to older siblings, who are assigned a major responsibility for younger siblings' care. In a recent study in Zambia where siblings were substantially involved in caregiving activities, infants showed strong attachments to both their mothers and their sibling caregivers (Mooya, Sichimba, & Bakermans-Kranenburg, 2016). In this study, secure attachment was the most frequent attachment classification for both mother-infant and sibling-infant relationships.

Despite such criticisms, there is ample evidence that security of attachment is important in development (Cassidy, 2016; Hoffman & others, 2017; Sroufe, 2016; Thompson, 2015, 2016). Secure attachment in infancy reflects a positive parent-infant relationship and provides a foundation that supports healthy socioemotional development in the years that follow.

Thus, researchers recognize the importance of competent, nurturant caregivers in an infant's development (Almy & Cicchetti, 2018). At issue, though, is whether or not secure attachment, especially to a single caregiver, is critical (Thompson, 2015, 2016).

In the Hausa culture, siblings and grandmothers provide a significant amount of care for infants. *How might these variations in care affect attachment?*

©Penny Tweedie/The Image Bank/Getty Images

DEVELOPMENTAL SOCIAL NEUROSCIENCE AND ATTACHMENT

In "Introduction" you read about the emerging field of *developmental social neuroscience,* which examines connections between socioemotional processes, development, and the brain (Esposito & others, 2017b; Silvers & others, 2017; Steinberg & others, 2017; Sullivan & Wilson, 2018). Attachment is one of the main areas in which theory and research on developmental social neuroscience has focused. These connections between attachment and the brain involve the neuroanatomy of the brain, neurotransmitters, and hormones.

Theory and research on the role of the brain's regions in mother-infant attachment is just emerging (Coan, 2016; Esposito & others, 2017b; Feldman, 2017; Sullivan & Wilson, 2018).

One theoretical view proposed that the prefrontal cortex probably plays an important role in maternal attachment behavior, as do the subcortical (areas of the brain lower than the cortex) regions of the amygdala (which is strongly involved in emotion) and the hypothalamus (Gonzalez, Atkinson, & Fleming, 2009). An ongoing fMRI longitudinal study is exploring the possibility that different attachment patterns can be distinguished by different patterns of brain activity (Kim, Strathearn, & Swain, 2016; Strathearn, 2007).

Research on the role of hormones and neurotransmitters in attachment has emphasized the importance of the neuropeptide hormone *oxytocin* and the neurotransmitter *dopamine* in the formation of the maternal-infant bond (Feldman, 2017; Kim, Strathearn, & Swain, 2016). Oxytocin, a mammalian hormone that also acts as a neurotransmitter in the brain, is released during breast feeding and by contact and warmth (Erlich & others, 2016; Polan & Hofer, 2016). Oxytocin is especially thought to be a likely candidate in the formation of infant-mother attachment (Feldman, 2017; Kohlhoff & others, 2017). A research review found strong links between levels or patterns of oxytocin and aspects of mother-infant attachment (Galbally & others, 2011).

It is well known that oxytocin release is stimulated by birth and lactation in mothers, but might it also be released in fathers? Oxytocin is secreted in males, and one research study found that at both 6 weeks and 6 months after birth, when fathers engaged in more stimulation contact with babies, encouraged their exploration, and directed their attention to objects, the fathers' oxytocin levels increased (Gordon & others, 2010). In this study, mothers' behaviors that increased their oxytocin levels involved more affectionate parenting, such as gazing at their babies, expressing positive affect toward them, and touching them. A recent study also found that fathers with lower testosterone levels engaged in more optimal parenting with their infants (Weisman, Zagoory-Sharon, & Feldman, 2014). Also in this study, when fathers were administered oxytocin, their parenting behavior improved, as evidenced in increased positive affect, social gaze, touch, and vocal synchrony when interacting with their infants.

In mothers, the experience of pleasure and reward is reflected in the brain's dopamine circuits when mothers care for their infant and are exposed to their infants' cues, such as eye contact, smiling, and so on (Feldman, 2017; Kim, Strathearn, & Swain, 2016). These experiences and brain changes likely promote mother-infant attachment and sensitive parenting. Also, the influence of oxytocin on dopamine in the mother's nucleus accumbens (a collection of neurons in the forebrain that are involved in pleasure) likely is important in motivating the mother's approach to the baby (de Haan & Gunnar, 2009). Figure 7 shows the regions of the brain we have described that are likely to play important roles in infant-mother attachment.

In sum, it is likely that a number of brain regions, neurotransmitters, and hormones are involved in the development of infant-mother attachment (Feldman, 2017; Sullivan & Wilson, 2018). Key candidates for influencing this attachment are connections between the prefrontal cortex, amygdala, and hypothalamus; the neuropeptides oxytocin and vasopressin; and the activity of the neurotransmitter dopamine in the nucleus accumbens.

developmental **connection**

Brain Development

Connections are increasingly being made between brain development and socioemotional processes. Connect to "Introduction" and "Physical Development in Adolescence."

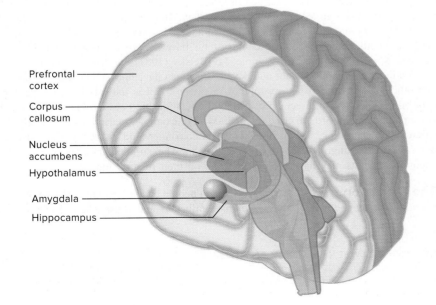

FIGURE **7**

REGIONS OF THE BRAIN PROPOSED AS LIKELY IMPORTANT IN INFANT-MOTHER ATTACHMENT.

Note: This illustration shows the brain's left hemisphere. The corpus callosum is the large bundle of axons that connect the brain's two hemispheres.

Prefrontal cortex

Corpus callosum

Nucleus accumbens

Hypothalamus

Amygdala

Hippocampus

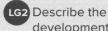

Review *Connect* Reflect

LG2 Describe the development of social orientation/understanding and attachment in infancy.

Review

- How do social orientation/understanding develop in infancy?
- What is attachment, and how is it conceptualized?
- What are some individual variations in attachment? How are caregiving styles related to attachment? What are some criticisms of attachment theory?
- What characterizes the study of developmental social neuroscience and attachment?

Connect

- How might the infant's temperament be related to the way in which

attachment is classified? Look at the temperament categories we described in the first main section of this chapter and reflect on how these might be more likely to show up in infants in some attachment categories than in others.

Reflect *Your Own Personal Journey of Life*

- Imagine that you are the parent of an infant. What could you do to improve the likelihood that your baby will form a secure attachment with you?

---

3 How Do Social Contexts Influence Socioemotional Development in Infancy?

LG3 Explain how social contexts influence the infant's development.

The Family   Child Care

Now that we have explored the infant's emotional and personality development and attachment, let's examine the social contexts in which these occur. We begin by studying a number of aspects of the family and then turn to a social context in which infants increasingly spend time—child care.

THE FAMILY

The family can be thought of as a constellation of subsystems—a complex whole made up of interrelated, interacting parts—defined in terms of generation, gender, and role. Each family member participates in several subsystems (Chen, Hughes, & Austin, 2017). The father and child represent one subsystem, the mother and father another, the mother-father-child represent yet another, and so on. These subsystems have reciprocal influences on each other (Nomaguchi & others, 2017). For example, Jay Belsky (1981) emphasizes that marital relations, parenting, and infant behavior and development can have both direct and indirect effects on each other (see Figure 8). An example of a direct effect is the influence of the parents' behavior on the child. An indirect effect is how the relationship between the spouses mediates the way a parent acts toward the child (Hsu, 2004). For example, marital conflict might reduce the efficiency of parenting, in which case marital conflict would indirectly affect the child's behavior (Cummings, Koss, & Cheung, 2015). The simple fact that two people are becoming parents may have profound effects on their relationship.

The Transition to Parenthood   When people become parents through pregnancy, adoption, or stepparenting, they face disequilibrium and must adapt. Parents want to

Marital relationship

Child behavior and development

Parenting

FIGURE **8**

INTERACTION BETWEEN CHILDREN AND THEIR PARENTS: DIRECT AND INDIRECT EFFECTS
Illustration Source: Belsky, J., "Early Human Experiences: A Family Perspective," in Developmental Psychology, Vol. 59, Washington, DC: American Psychological Association, 1981, 147–156.
Photo: ©Katrina Wittkamp/Photodisc/Getty Images RF

develop a strong attachment with their infant, but they also want to maintain strong attachments to their spouse and friends, and possibly continue their careers. Parents ask themselves how the presence of this new being will change their lives. A baby places new restrictions on partners; no longer will they be able to rush out to a movie on a moment's notice, and money may not be readily available for vacations and other luxuries. Dual-career parents ask, "Will it harm the baby to place her in child care? Will we be able to find responsible baby-sitters?"

In a longitudinal investigation of couples from late pregnancy until 3½ years after the baby was born, couples enjoyed more positive marital relations before the baby was born than after (Cowan & Cowan, 2000; Cowan & others, 2005). Still, almost one-third showed an increase in marital satisfaction. Some couples said that the baby had both brought them closer together and moved them farther apart; being parents enhanced their sense of themselves and gave them a new, more stable identity as a couple. Babies opened men up to a concern with intimate relationships, and the demands of juggling work and family roles stimulated women to manage family tasks more efficiently and pay attention to their own personal growth.

Other studies have explored the transition to parenthood (Ferriby & others, 2015). A recent study indicated that women and less avoidantly attached new parents adapted better to the introduction of child care tasks better than most men, especially men who were avoidantly attached (Fillo & others, 2015). In another study, mothers experienced unmet expectations in the transition to parenting, with fathers doing less than their partners had anticipated (Biehle & Mickelson, 2012). Also, in a recent study of dual-earner couples, a gender division of labor across the transition to parenthood occurred (Yavorsky & others, 2015). In this study, a gender gap was not present prior to the transition to parenthood, but after a child was born, women did more than 2 hours of additional work per day compared with an additional 40 minutes for men. And in another recent study, in comparison with married fathers, cohabiting fathers' personal dedication and relationship confidence decreased and their feelings of constraint increased across the transition to parenting (Kamp Dush & others, 2014).

The Bringing Home Baby project is a workshop for new parents that emphasizes strengthening the couple's relationship, understanding and becoming acquainted with the baby, resolving conflict, and developing parenting skills (Gottman, 2014). Evaluations of the project revealed that parents who participated improved their ability to work together as parents, fathers were more involved with their baby and sensitive to the baby's behavior, mothers had a lower incidence of postpartum depression symptoms, and their babies showed better overall development compared with families in a control group (Gottman, Shapiro, & Parthemer, 2004; Shapiro & Gottman, 2005).

Reciprocal Socialization   Socialization between parents and children is not a one-way process. Parents do socialize children, but socialization in families is reciprocal (Klein & others, 2017; Nishamura, Kanakogi, & Myowa-Yamakoshi, 2016). **Reciprocal socialization** is socialization that is bidirectional; children socialize parents just as parents socialize children. These reciprocal interchanges and mutual influence processes are sometimes referred to as *transactional* (Sameroff, 2009).

For example, the interaction of mothers and their infants is sometimes symbolized as a dance in which successive actions of the partners are closely coordinated. This coordinated dance can assume the form of synchrony—that is, each person's behavior depends on the partner's previous behavior. Or the interaction can be reciprocal in a precise sense—in which the actions of the partners can be matched, as when one partner imitates the other or when there is mutual smiling.

An important example of early synchronized interaction is mutual gaze or eye contact. In one study, the mother and infant engaged in a variety of behaviors while they looked at each other; by contrast, when they looked away from each other, the rate of such behaviors dropped considerably (Stern & others, 1977). In another study, synchrony in parent-child relationships was positively related to children's social competence (Harrist, 1993). The types of behaviors involved in reciprocal socialization in infancy are temporally connected, mutually contingent behaviors such as one partner imitating the sound of another or the mother responding with a vocalization to the baby's arm movements. The types of behaviors involved in reciprocal socialization in infancy are temporally connected, mutually contingent behaviors such as one partner imitating the sound of another or the mother responding with a vocalization to the baby's arm movements.

Another example of synchronization occurs in **scaffolding,** which means adjusting the level of guidance to fit the child's performance (Erickson & others, 2013; Melzi, Schick, &

What characterizes the transition to parenting?
©Chris Ryan/OJO Images/Getty Images RF

We never know the love of our parents until we have become parents.

—**HENRY WARD BEECHER**
American Writer, 19th Century

developmental **connection**

Cognitive Theory
A version of scaffolding is an important aspect of Lev Vygotsky's sociocultural cognitive theory. Connect to "Physical and Cognitive Development in Early Childhood."

reciprocal socialization Socialization that is bidirectional; children socialize parents, just as parents socialize children.

scaffolding Adjusting the level of guidance to fit the child's performance.

How Would You...?

If you were an **educator,** how would you explain the value of games and the role of scaffolding in the development of infants and toddlers?

Caregivers often play games such as peek-a-boo and pat-a-cake. *How is scaffolding involved in these games?*

(*Top*) ©BrandXPictures/PunchStock RF; (*bottom*) ©Stephanie Rausser/The Image Bank/Getty Images

- - - - - - - - ▶

developmental **connection**

Parenting

Psychologists give a number of reasons why harsh physical punishment can be harmful to children's development. Connect to "Socioemotional Development in Early Childhood."

◀ - - - - - - - -

Kennedy, 2011). The parent responds to the child's behavior with scaffolding, which in turn affects the child's behavior. For example, in the game peek-a-boo, parents initially cover their babies, then remove the covering, and finally register "surprise" at the babies' reappearance. As infants become more skilled at peek-a-boo, infants gradually do some of the covering and uncovering. Parents try to time their actions in such a way that the infant takes turns with the parent. In addition to peek-a-boo, pat-a-cake and "so-big" are other caregiver games that exemplify scaffolding and turn-taking sequences.

Scaffolding can be used to support children's efforts at any age. A recent study found that when adults used explicit scaffolding (encouragement and praise) with 13- and 14-month-old infants they were twice as likely to engage in helping behavior as were their counterparts who did not receive the scaffolding (Dahl & others, 2017). Also, a study of Hmong families living in the United States revealed that maternal scaffolding, especially in the form of cognitive support of young children's problem solving the summer before kindergarten, predicted the children's reasoning skills in kindergarten (Stright, Herr, & Neitzel, 2009). And another study of disadvantaged families revealed that an intervention designed to enhance maternal scaffolding with infants was linked to improved cognitive skills when the children were 4 years old (Obradovic & others, 2016).

Increasingly, genetic and epigenetic factors are being studied to discover not only parental influences on children but also children's influence on parents (Bakermans-Kranenburg & van IJzendoorn, 2016; Baptista & others, 2017; Belsky & Pluess, 2016; Lomanowska & others, 2017). Recall that the *epigenetic view* emphasizes that development is the result of an ongoing, bidirectional interchange between heredity and the environment (Moore, 2015, 2017). For example, harsh, hostile parenting is associated with negative outcomes for children, such as being defiant and oppositional (Deater-Deckard, 2013; Thompson & others, 2017). This likely reflects bidirectional influences rather than a unidirectional parenting effect. That is, the parents' harsh, hostile parenting and the children's defiant, oppositional behavior may mutually influence each other. In this bidirectional influence, the parents' and children's behavior may have genetic linkages as well as experiential connections.

Managing and Guiding Infants' Behavior   In addition to sensitive parenting that involves warmth and caring and can result in secure attachment to parents, other important aspects of parenting infants involve managing and guiding their behavior in an attempt to reduce or eliminate undesirable behaviors (Holden, Vittrup, & Rosen, 2011). This management process includes (1) being proactive and childproofing the environment so infants won't encounter potentially dangerous objects or situations, and (2) using corrective methods when infants engage in undesirable behaviors such as excessive fussing and crying, throwing objects, and so on.

One study assessed discipline and corrective methods that parents had used by the time infants were 12 and 24 months old (Vittrup, Holden, & Buck, 2006) (see Figure 9). Notice in Figure 9 that the main corrective method parents used by the time infants were 12 months old was diverting the infants' attention, followed by reasoning, ignoring, and negotiating. Also note in Figure 9 that more than one-third of parents had yelled at their infant, about one-fifth had slapped the infant's hands or threatened the infant, and approximately one-sixth had spanked the infant by his or her first birthday.

As infants move into the second year of life and become more mobile and capable of exploring a wider range of environments, parental management of the toddler's behavior often triggers even more corrective feedback and discipline (Holden, Vittrup, & Rosen, 2011). As indicated in Figure 9, in the study just described, parental yelling increased from 36 percent at 1 year of age to 81 percent at 2 years of age, slapping the infant's hands increased from 21 percent at 1 year to 31 percent at age 2, and spanking increased from 14 percent at 1 year to 45 percent at age 2 (Vittrup, Holden, & Buck, 2006).

An important aspect of understanding why parents might increase their disciplinary corrective feedback in the second year involves their expectations for their toddlers' behavior. A national poll of parents who had children 3 years of age and younger found that parents have stricter expectations for their toddlers' ability to control their behavior than is warranted based on the maturation of the prefrontal cortex (Newton & Thompson, 2010). Thus, some of parents' corrective feedback likely arises because parents anticipate that toddlers and young children should be exercising greater self-control over their emotions and impulses than they are capable of achieving.

A special concern is that such corrective disciplinary tactics not become abusive. Too often what starts out as mild to moderately intense discipline on the part of parents can move into highly intense anger. In "Socioemotional Development in Early Childhood," you will read more extensively about the use of punishment with children and the occurrence of child abuse.

Mothers and Fathers as Caregivers

Much of our discussion of attachment has focused on mothers as caregivers. Do mothers and fathers differ in their caregiving roles? In general, mothers on average still spend considerably more time in caregiving with infants and children than do fathers (Blakemore, Berenbaum, & Liben, 2009; Lamb & Lewis, 2015). Mothers especially are more likely to engage in a managerial role with their children, coordinating their activities, making sure their health-care needs are met, and so on (Clarke-Stewart & Parke, 2014).

However, an increasing number of U.S. fathers stay home full-time with their children (Dette-Hagenmeyer, Erzinger, & Reichle, 2016). The number of stay-at-home dads in the United States was estimated to be two million in 2012 (Livingston, 2014). This figure represents a significant increase from 1.6 million in 2004 and 1.1 million in 1989. A large portion of the full-time fathers have career-focused wives who provide the main family income. One study revealed that the stay-at-home fathers were as satisfied with their marriage as traditional parents, although they indicated that they missed their daily life in the workplace (Rochlen & others, 2008). In this study, the stay-at-home fathers reported that they tended to be ostracized when they took their children to playgrounds and often were excluded from parent groups.

Can fathers take care of infants as competently as mothers can? Observations of fathers and their infants suggest that fathers have the ability to care for their infants as sensitively and responsively as mothers do (Lamb & Lewis, 2015). Consider the Aka pygmy culture in Africa where fathers spend as much time interacting with their infants as do their mothers (Hewlett, 2000; Hewlett & MacFarlan, 2010). Also, a recent study found that infants who showed a higher level of externalizing, disruptive problems at 1 year of age had fathers who displayed a low level of engagement with them as early as the third month of life (Ramchandani & others, 2013). Another recent study revealed that fathers with a college-level education engaged in more stimulating physical activities with their infants than less-educated fathers did and that fathers in a conflictual couple relationship participated in less caregiving and physical play with their infants (Cabrera, Hofferth, & Chae, 2011). And in a recent study, when fathers of 3-month-old infants were withdrawn and depressed, the children had a lower level of cognitive development at 24 months of age (Sethna & others, 2017). Also in this study, when fathers of 3-month-old infants were more engaged and sensitive, as well as less controlling, the children showed a higher level of cognitive development at 24 months.

Remember, however, that although fathers can be active, nurturant, involved caregivers with their infants as Aka pygmy fathers do, in many cultures men have not chosen to follow this pattern (Parke & Clarke-Stewart, 2011). Also, if fathers have mental health problems, they may interact less effectively with their infants than fathers without such problems. One study revealed that depressed fathers focused more on their own needs than on their infants' needs and that they directed more negative and critical speech toward infants (Sethna, Murray, & Ramchandani, 2012). And a recent study revealed that both fathers' and mothers' sensitivity, as assessed when infants were 10 to 12 months old, were linked to children's cognitive development at 18 months and language development at 36 months (Malmberg & others, 2016).

Do fathers behave differently toward infants than mothers do? Maternal interactions usually center on child-care activities—feeding, changing diapers, bathing. Paternal interactions

Method	12 Months	24 Months
Spank with hand	14	45
Slap infant's hand	21	31
Yell in anger	36	81
Threaten	19	63
Withdraw privileges	18	52
Time-out	12	60
Reason	85	100
Divert attention	100	100
Negotiate	50	90
Ignore	64	90

FIGURE 9

PARENTS' METHODS FOR MANAGING AND CORRECTING INFANTS' UNDESIRABLE BEHAVIORS. Shown here are the percentages of parents who had used various corrective methods by the time infants were 12 and 24 months old.
Source: Vittrup, B., Holden, G.W., & Buck, M. "Attitudes Predict the Use of Physical Punishment: A Prospective Study of the Emergence of Disciplinary Practices," Pediatrics, 117, 2006, 2055–2064.

An Aka pygmy father with his infant son. In the Aka culture, fathers were observed to be holding or nearby their infants 47 percent of the time.
©Nick Greaves/Almay

are more likely to include play (Lamb & Lewis, 2015; Parke & Clarke-Stewart, 2011). Fathers tend to engage in more rough-and-tumble play than mothers do. They bounce infants, throw them up in the air, tickle them, and so on. Mothers do play with infants, but their play is less physical and arousing than that of fathers.

CHILD CARE

Many U.S. children today experience multiple caregivers. Most do not have a parent staying home to care for them; instead, the children have some type of care provided by others—"child care." Many parents worry that time spent in child care will reduce their infants' emotional attachment to them, slow down the infants' cognitive development, fail to teach them how to control anger, and allow them to be unduly influenced by their peers. How extensive is the use of child care? Are the worries of these parents justified?

Parental Leave   Today far more young children are in child care than at any other time in history. About 2 million children in the United States currently receive formal, licensed child care, and uncounted millions of children are cared for by unlicensed baby-sitters. To read about child-care policies in different countries, see the *Connecting with Diversity* interlude.

Variations in Child Care   Because the United States does not have a policy of paid leave for child care, child care in the United States has become a major national concern (Belsky, 2009, Lamb, 2013). Many factors influence the effects of child care, including the age of the child, the type of child care, and the quality of the program.

Types of child care vary extensively (Burchinal & others, 2015; Hasbrouck & Pianta, 2016; Shivers & Farago, 2016). Child care is provided in large centers with elaborate facilities and in private homes. Some child-care centers are commercial operations; others are nonprofit centers run by churches, civic groups, and employers. Some child-care providers are professionals; others are mothers who want to earn extra money. Infants and toddlers are more likely to be found in family child care and informal care settings, while older children are more likely to be in child care centers and preschool and early education programs. Figure 10 presents the primary care arrangements for children under 5 years of age with employed mothers (Clarke-Stewart & Miner, 2008).

How do most fathers and mothers interact differently with infants?
©Polka Dot Images/Photolibrary RF

We have all the knowledge necessary to provide absolutely first-rate child care in the United States. What is missing is the commitment and the will.

—EDWARD ZIGLER
Contemporary Developmental Psychologist, Yale University

connecting with diversity

Child-Care Policies Around the World

Child-care policies around the world vary in eligibility criteria, leave duration, benefit level, and the extent to which parents take advantage of the policies (Tolani & Brooks-Gunn, 2008). Europe has led the way in creating new standards of parental leave: The European Union (EU) mandated a paid 14-week maternity leave in 1992. In most European countries today, working parents on leave receive from 70 to 100 percent of the worker's prior wage, and paid leave averages about 16 weeks (Tolani & Brooks-Gunn, 2008). The United States currently allows workers up to 12 weeks of unpaid leave to care for a newborn.

Most countries restrict eligibility for benefits to women employed for a minimum time prior to childbirth (Tolani & Brooks-Gunn, 2008). In Denmark, even unemployed mothers are eligible for extended parental leave related to childbirth. In Sweden, parents can take an 18-month job-protected parental leave with benefits that can be shared by parents and applied to full-time or part-time work.

How are child-care policies in many European countries, such as Sweden, different from those in the United States?
©Matilda Lindeblad/Johner Images/Getty Images

In the United States, approximately 15 percent of children 5 years of age and younger attend more than one child-care arrangement. A recent study of 2- and 3-year-olds revealed that an increase in the number of child-care arrangements the children experienced was linked to an increase in behavioral problems and a decrease in prosocial behavior (Morrissey, 2009).

Child-care quality makes a difference (Howes, 2016; Sanders & Guerra, 2016; Vu, 2016). A recent Australian study revealed that higher-quality child care that included positive child-caregiver relationships at 2 to 3 years of age was linked to children's better self-regulation of attention and emotion at 4 to 5 and 6 to 7 years of age (Gialamas & others, 2014).

What constitutes a high-quality child-care program for infants? In high-quality child care (Clarke-Stewart & Miner, 2008, p. 273):

> . . . caregivers encourage the children to be actively engaged in a variety of activities, have frequent, positive interactions that include smiling, touching, holding, and speaking at the child's eye level, respond properly to the child's questions or requests, and encourage children to talk about their experiences, feelings, and ideas.

High-quality child care also involves providing children with a safe environment, access to age-appropriate toys and participation in age-appropriate activities, and a low caregiver-to-child ratio that allows caregivers to spend considerable time with children on an individual basis. Quality of child care matters in children's development and according to UNICEF, the United States meets or exceeds only 3 of 10 child care quality benchmarks. An analysis of U.S. child care studies found that a greater quantity of child care was a strong predictor of socioemotional problems (Jacob, 2009). However, a recent study in Norway (a country that meets or exceeds 8 of 10 UNICEF benchmarks) revealed that high quantity of child care there was not linked to children's externalizing problems (Zachrisson & others, 2013). To read about one individual who provides quality child care to individuals from impoverished backgrounds in the United States, see the *Connecting with Careers* profile. What do U.S. studies of child care tell us about its outcomes? In the *Connecting with Research* interlude, you can find out about one ongoing research project.

What are some strategies parents can follow in regard to child care? Child-care expert Kathleen McCartney (2003, p. 4) offered this advice:

- *Recognize that the quality of your parenting is a key factor in your child's development.*
- *Make decisions that will improve the likelihood you will be good parents.* "For some this will mean working full-time"—for personal fulfillment, income, or both. "For others, this will mean working part-time or not working outside the home."

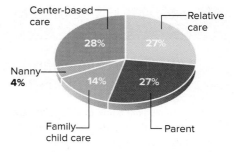

FIGURE 10

PRIMARY CARE ARRANGEMENTS IN THE UNITED STATES FOR CHILDREN UNDER 5 YEARS OF AGE WITH EMPLOYED MOTHERS

How Would You...?
If you were a **psychologist,** what factors would you encourage parents to consider in deciding whether to place their infant in child care so that both parents can return to work?

connecting with careers

Wanda Mitchell, Child-Care Director

Wanda Mitchell is the Center Director of the Hattie Daniels Day Care Center in Wilson, North Carolina. Her responsibilities include directing the operation of the center, which involves creating and maintaining an environment in which young children can learn effectively, and ensuring that the center meets state licensing requirements. Wanda obtained her undergraduate degree from North Carolina A & T University, majoring in child development. Prior to her current position, she had been an education coordinator for Project Head Start and an instructor at Wilson Technical Community College. Describing her work, Wanda says, "I really enjoy working in my field. This is my passion. After graduating from college, my goal was to advance in my field."

Wanda Mitchell, child-care director, works with some of the children at her center.
Courtesy of Wanda Mitchell

What Are Some Important Findings in the National Longitudinal Study of Child Care in the United States?

A longitudinal study of U.S. child care was initiated by the National Institute of Child Health and Human Development (NICHD) in 1991. Data were collected on a diverse sample of almost 1,400 children and their families at ten locations across the United States over a period of seven years. Researchers used multiple methods (trained observers, interviews, questionnaires, and testing), and measured many facets of children's development, including physical health, cognitive development, and socioemotional development. Following are some of the results of what is now referred to as the NICHD Study of Early Child Care and Youth Development, or NICHD SECCYD (NICHD Early Child Care Network, 2001, 2002, 2003, 2004, 2005 a, b, 2006, 2010).

What are some important findings from the national longitudinal study of child care conducted by the National Institute of Child Health and Human Development?
©Reena Rose Sibayan/The Jersey Journal/Landov Images

- *Patterns of use.* Many families placed their infants in child care very soon after the child's birth, and there was considerable instability in the child-care arrangements. By 4 months of age, nearly three-fourths of the infants had entered some form of nonparental child care. Almost half of the infants were cared for by a relative when they first entered care; only 12 percent were enrolled in child-care centers. Low-income families were more likely than more affluent families to use child care, but infants from low-income families who were in child care averaged as many hours as other income groups. In the preschool years, mothers who were single, those with more education, and families with higher incomes used more hours of center-based care than other families did. Minority families and mothers with less education used more hours of care by relatives.

- *Quality of care.* Evaluations of quality of care were based on characteristics such as group size, child–adult ratio, physical environment, caregiver characteristics (such as formal education, specialized training, and child-care experience), and caregiver behavior (such as sensitivity to children). An alarming conclusion is that a majority of the child care in the first three years of life was of unacceptably low quality. Positive caregiving by non-parents in child-care settings was infrequent—only 12 percent of the children studied experienced positive nonparental child care (such as positive talk and language stimulation)! Further, infants from low-income families experienced lower quality of child care than infants from higher-income families. When quality of caregivers' care was high, children performed better on cognitive and language tasks, were more cooperative with their mothers during play, showed more positive and skilled interaction with peers, and had fewer behavior problems. Caregiver training and good child–staff ratios were linked with higher cognitive and social competence when children were 54 months of age. One study revealed that higher-quality child care from birth to 4½ years of age was linked to higher cognitive-academic achievement at 15 years of age (Vandell & others, 2010). In this study, early higher-quality care also was related to youth reports of less externalizing behavior (lower rates of delinquency, for example). In a recent study, high-quality infant-toddler child care was linked to better memory skills at the end of the preschool years (Li & others, 2013).

- *Amount of child care.* In general, when children spent 30 hours or more per week in child care, their development was less than optimal (Ramey, 2005). In a recent study, more time spent in early nonrelative child care was related to higher levels of risk taking and impulsivity at 15 years of age (Vandell & others, 2010).

- *Family and parenting influences.* The influence of families and parenting was not weakened by extensive child care. Parents played a significant role in helping children to regulate their emotions. Especially important parenting influences were being sensitive to children's needs, being involved with children, and cognitively stimulating them. Indeed, parental sensitivity has been the most consistent predictor of a secure attachment, with child-care experiences being relevant in many cases only when mothers engage in insensitive parenting (Friedman, Melhuish, & Hill, 2010). An important point about the extensive NICHD research is that findings show that family factors are considerably stronger and more consistent predictors of a wide variety of child outcomes than are child-care experiences (such as quality, quantity, type). The worst outcomes for children occur when both home and child-care settings are of poor quality. For example, a recent study involving the NICHD SECCYD data revealed that worse socioemotional outcomes (more problem behavior, low level of prosocial behavior) for children occurred when they experienced both home and child-care environments that conferred risk (Watamura & others, 2011).

What do these research findings suggest about what the U.S. child-care system is doing well? What could be improved about the system? If you were a researcher involved in this study, what other questions would you want to explore?

- *Monitor your child's development.* "Parents should observe for themselves whether their children seem to be having behavior problems." They need to talk with their child-care providers and their pediatrician about their child's behavior.
- *Take some time to find the best child care.* Observe different child-care facilities and be certain that you like what you see. "Quality child care costs money, and not all parents can afford the child care they want. However, state subsidies, and other programs like Head Start, are available for families in need."

Review Connect Reflect

LG3 Explain how social contexts influence the infant's development.

Review
- What are some important family processes in infant development?
- How does child care influence infant development?

Connect
- Earlier, you learned about a fine motor skills experiment involving 3-month-olds and grasping. What concept in the last section of this chapter relates to the use of "sticky mittens"?

Reflect *Your Own Personal Journey of Life*
- Imagine that a friend of yours is getting ready to put her baby in child care. What advice would you give to her? Do you think she should stay home with the baby? Why or why not? What type of child care would you recommend?

topical connections *looking forward*

You will study socioemotional development in early childhood. Babies no more, young children make considerable progress in the development of their self, their emotions, and their social interactions. In early childhood, they show increased self-understanding and understanding of others, as well as ability to regulate their emotions. In early childhood, relationships and interactions with parents and peers expand children's knowledge of and connections with their social world. Additionally, play becomes not only something they enjoy doing on a daily basis but also a wonderful context for advancing both their socioemotional and cognitive development. Many of the advances in young children's socioemotional development become possible because of the remarkable changes in their brain and cognitive development.

reach your learning goals

Socioemotional Development in Infancy

| 1 How Do Emotions and Personality Develop in Infancy? | **LG1** Discuss emotional and personality development in infancy. |

Emotional Development

- Emotion is feeling, or affect, that occurs when people are in a state or an interaction that is important to them. Emotion can be classified as either positive (for example, joy) or negative (for example, anger).

- Psychologists hold that emotions, especially facial expressions of emotions, have a biological foundation. Biological evolution endowed humans to be emotional.

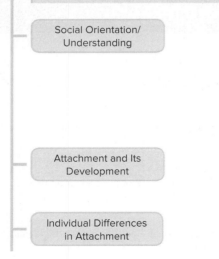

- Cognitive processes also play important roles in emotional development. And embeddedness in culture and relationships provides diversity in emotional experiences.

- Emotions play key roles in parent-child relationships. Infants display a number of emotions early in their development, although researchers debate the onset and sequence of these emotions. Lewis distinguishes between primary emotions and self-conscious emotions.

- Crying is the most important mechanism newborns have for communicating with their world. Babies have at least three types of cries—basic, anger, and pain cries. Controversy swirls about whether babies should be soothed when they cry, although increasingly experts recommend immediately responding in a caring way during the first year.

- Social smiling occurs as early as 2 months of age and then increases considerably from 2 to 6 months.

- Two fears that infants develop are stranger anxiety and separation from a caregiver (which is reflected in separation protest). As infants develop, it is important for them to engage in emotion regulation.

Temperament

- Temperament is an individual's behavioral style and characteristic way of emotionally responding. Chess and Thomas classified infants as (1) easy, (2) difficult, or (3) slow to warm up. Kagan proposed that inhibition to the unfamiliar is an important temperament category. Rothbart and Bates' view of temperament emphasizes this classification: (1) extraversion/surgency, (2) negative affectivity, and (3) effortful control (self-regulation).

- Physiological characteristics are associated with different temperaments. Children inherit a physiology that biases them to have a particular type of temperament, but through experience they learn to modify their temperament style to some degree.

- Goodness of fit refers to the match between a child's temperament and the environmental demands the child must cope with. Goodness of fit can be an important aspect of a child's adjustment. Although research evidence is sketchy at this point in time, some general recommendations are that caregivers should (1) be sensitive to the individual characteristics of the child, (2) be flexible in responding to these characteristics, and (3) avoid negative labeling of the child.

Personality Development

- Erikson argued that an infant's first year is characterized by the stage of trust versus mistrust. Some infants develop signs of self-recognition at about 15 to 18 months of age.

- Independence becomes a central theme in the second year of life. Mahler argues that the infant separates himself or herself from the mother and then develops individuation. Erikson stressed that the second year of life is characterized by the stage of autonomy versus shame and doubt.

2 How Do Social Orientation/ Understanding and Attachment Develop in Infancy?

LG2 Describe the development of social orientation/ understanding and attachment in infancy.

Social Orientation/ Understanding

- Infants show a strong interest in the social world and are motivated to understand it. Infants orient to the social world early in their development. Face-to-face play with a caregiver begins to occur at 2 to 3 months of age. Newly developed self-produced locomotion skills significantly expand infants' ability to initiate social interchanges and explore their social world more independently.

- Perceiving people as engaging in intentional and goal-directed behavior is an important social cognitive accomplishment, and this initially occurs toward the end of the first year. Social referencing increases during the second year of life.

Attachment and Its Development

- Attachment is a close emotional bond between two people. In infancy, contact comfort and trust are important in the development of attachment. Bowlby's ethological theory stresses that the caregiver and the infant are biologically predisposed to form an attachment. Attachment develops in four phases during infancy.

Individual Differences in Attachment

- Securely attached babies use the caregiver, usually the mother, as a secure base from which to explore the environment. Three types of insecure attachment are avoidant, resistant, and disorganized. Ainsworth created the Strange Situation, an observational measure of attachment.

Ainsworth argues that secure attachment in the first year of life provides an important foundation for psychological development later in life. Caregivers of secure babies are sensitive to the babies' signals and are consistently available to meet their needs. Caregivers of avoidant babies tend to be unavailable or rejecting. Caregivers of resistant babies tend to be inconsistently available to their babies and usually are not very affectionate. Caregivers of disorganized babies often neglect or physically abuse their babies.

- The strength of the link between early attachment and later development has varied somewhat across studies. Some critics argue that attachment theorists have not given adequate attention to genetics and temperament. Other critics stress that not enough attention has been given to the diversity of social agents and contexts. Cultural variations in attachment have been found, but in all cultures studied to date, secure attachment is the most common classification.

Developmental Social Neuroscience and Attachment

- Increased interest is being directed toward the role of the brain in the development of attachment. The hormone oxytocin is a key candidate for influencing the development of maternal-infant attachment.

3 How Do Social Contexts Influence Socioemotional Development in Infancy?

LG3 Explain how social contexts influence the infant's development.

The Family

- The transition to parenthood requires considerable adaptation and adjustment on the part of parents. Children socialize parents, just as parents socialize children. Mutual regulation and scaffolding are important aspects of reciprocal socialization. Belsky's model points out that marital relations, parenting, and infant behavior and development can have direct and indirect effects on each other. An important parental task involves managing and correcting infants' undesirable behaviors. The mother's primary role when interacting with the infant is caregiving; the father's is playful interaction.

Child Care

- More U.S. children are in child care now than at any earlier point in history. The quality of child care is uneven, and child care remains a controversial topic. Quality child care can be achieved and seems to have few adverse effects on children. In the NICHD child-care study, infants from low-income families were more likely to receive the lowest quality of care. Also, higher quality of child care was linked with fewer child problems.

key terms

anger cry	goodness of fit	primary emotions	separation protest
attachment	insecure avoidant	reciprocal socialization	slow-to-warm-up child
basic cry	babies	reflexive smile	social referencing
developmental cascade model	insecure disorganized	scaffolding	social smile
difficult child	babies	securely attached	Strange Situation
easy child	insecure resistant babies	babies	stranger anxiety
emotion	pain cry	self-conscious emotions	temperament

key people

Mary Ainsworth	Stella Chess	Michael Lewis	Ross Thompson
John Bates	Erik Erikson	Margaret Mahler	John Watson
Jay Belsky	Jacob Gewirtz	Kathleen McCartney	Amanda Woodward
John Bowlby	Harry Harlow	Mary Rothbart	
Joseph Campos	Jerome Kagan	Alexander Thomas	

connecting with **improving the lives of children**

STRATEGIES

Nurturing the Infant's Socioemotional Development

What are the best ways to help an infant develop socioemotional competencies?

- *Develop a secure attachment with the infant.* Infants need the warmth and support of one or more caregivers. The caregiver(s) should be sensitive to the infant's signals and respond in a nurturing way.
- *Be sure that both the mother and the father nurture the infant.* Infants develop best when both the mother and the father provide warm, nurturant support. Fathers need to seriously evaluate their responsibility in rearing a competent infant.
- *Select competent child care.* If the infant will be placed in child care, spend time evaluating different options. Be sure the infant–caregiver ratio is low. Also assess whether the adults enjoy and are knowledgeable about interacting with infants. Confirm that the facility is safe and provides stimulating activities.
- *Understand and respect the infant's temperament.* Be sensitive to the characteristics of each child. It may be necessary to provide extra support for distress-prone infants, for example. Avoid negative labeling of the infant.
- *Adapt to developmental changes in the infant.* An 18-month-old toddler is very different from a 6-month-old infant. Be knowledgeable about how infants develop, and adapt to the changing infant. Let toddlers explore a wider but safe environment.
- *Be physically and mentally healthy.* Infants' socioemotional development benefits when their caregivers are physically and mentally healthy. For example, a depressed parent may not respond sensitively to the infant's signals.
- *Read a good book on infant development.* Any of T. Berry Brazelton's books is a good start. One is *Touchpoints*.

RESOURCES

The Happiest Baby on the Block (2002)

Harvey Karp
New York: Bantam

An outstanding book on ways to calm a crying baby.

Touchpoints: Birth to Three (2006)

T. Berry Brazelton and Joshua Sparrow
Cambridge, MA: Da Capo Press

Covering the period from birth through age 3, Brazelton and Sparrow focus on the concerns and questions parents have about the child's feelings, behavior, and development.

Raising a Secure Child (2017)

Kent Hoffman and others
New York: Guilford Press

An excellent book for parents that provides valuable information and strategies for protecting and nurturing infants.

Infant and Toddler Development and Responsive Parenting (3rd ed., 2013)

Donna Wittmer and Sandy Peterson
Upper Saddle River, NJ: Pearson

This excellent book provides families and teachers with valuable strategies for developing positive relationships with infants and toddlers.

You are troubled at seeing him spend his early years doing nothing. What! Is it nothing to be happy? Is it nothing to skip, to play, to run about all day long? Never in his life will he be so busy as now.

—Jean-Jacques Rousseau
Swiss-born French Philosopher, 18th Century

Early Childhood

In early childhood, our greatest untold poem was being only 4 years old. We skipped and ran and played all the sun long, never in our lives so busy, busy being something we had not quite grasped yet. Who knew our thoughts, which we worked up into small mythologies all our own? Our thoughts and images and drawings took wings. The blossoms of our heart, no wind could touch. Our small world widened as we discovered new refuges and new people. When we said, "I," we meant something totally unique, not to be confused with any other. Section 4 consists of three chapters: "Physical Development in Early Childhood," "Cognitive Development in Early Childhood," and "Socioemotional Development in Early Childhood."

chapter 8

PHYSICAL DEVELOPMENT IN EARLY CHILDHOOD

chapter **outline**

① How Does a Young Child's Body and Brain Grow and Change?

Learning Goal 1 Discuss growth and change in the young child's body and brain.

Height and Weight

The Brain

② How Do Young Children's Motor Skills Develop?

Learning Goal 2 Describe changes in motor development in early childhood.

Gross and Fine Motor Skills

Perceptual Development

Young Children's Artistic Drawings

③ What Are Some Important Aspects of Young Children's Health?

Learning Goal 3 Characterize the health of young children.

Sleep and Sleep Problems

Nutrition

Exercise

Health, Safety, and Illness

Teresa Amabile remembers that when she was in kindergarten, she rushed in every day, excited and enthusiastic about getting to the easel and painting with bright colors and big brushes. Children in Teresa's class had free access to a clay table with all kinds of art materials on it. Teresa remembers going home every day and telling her mother she wanted to draw and paint. Teresa's kindergarten experience, unfortunately, was the high point of her enthusiasm for art classes in school.

A description of Teresa's further childhood experiences with art and creativity follows (Goleman, Kaufman, & Ray, 1993, p. 60):

> The next year she entered a strict, traditional school, and things began to change. As she tells it, "Instead of having free access to art materials every day, art became just another subject, something you had for an hour and a half every Friday afternoon." Week after week, all through elementary school, it was the same art class. And a very restricted, even demoralizing one at that.

The children were not given any help in developing their skills. Also, the teacher graded the children on the art they produced, adding evaluation pressure to the situation. Teresa was aware at that time that her motivation for doing art-work was being completely destroyed. In her words, "I no longer wanted to go home at the end of the day and take out my art materials and draw or paint."

In spite of the negative instruction imposed upon her in art classes, Teresa Amabile continued her education and eventually obtained a Ph.D. in psychology. In part because of her positive experiences in kindergarten, she became one of the leading researchers on creativity. Her hope is that more schools will not crush children's enthusiasm for creativity, the way hers did. So many young children, like Teresa, are excited about exploring and creating, but by the time they reach the third or fourth grade, many don't like school, let alone have any sense of pleasure in their own creativity.

topical connections   looking back

Physical growth in infancy is dramatic. Even though physical growth in early childhood slows, it is not difficult to distinguish young children from infants when you look at them. Most young children lose their "baby fat," and their legs and trunks become longer. In addition to what you can see with the naked eye, much development also continues below the surface in the brain. In infancy, myelination of axons in the brain paved the way for development of such functions as full visual capacity. Continued myelination in early child-hood provides children with much better hand-eye coordination.

preview

As twentieth-century Welsh poet Dylan Thomas artfully observed, young children do "run all the sun long." And as their physical development advances, young children's small worlds widen. We begin this chapter by examining how young children's bodies grow and change. Then we discuss the development of young children's motor skills and conclude by exploring important aspects of their health.

---

1 How Does a Young Child's Body and Brain Grow and Change? **LG1** Discuss growth and change in the young child's body and brain.

Height and Weight   The Brain

> The greatest poem ever known
> Is one all poets have
> outgrown;
> The poetry, innate and
> untold,
> Of being only four years old.
>
> —**CHRISTOPHER MORLEY**
> *American Novelist, 20th Century*

growth hormone deficiency The absence or deficiency of growth hormone produced by the pituitary gland to stimulate the body to grow.

The bodies of 5-year-olds and 2-year-olds are different. Notice that the 5-year-old not only is taller and weighs more, but also has a longer trunk and legs than the 2-year-old. *Can you think of some other physical differences between 2- and 5-year-olds?*
©Michael Hitoshi/Getty Images RF

In this section, we examine the height and weight changes for boys and girls in early childhood along with individual growth patterns. In addition, we look at how the brain and nervous system continue to develop, and how young children's cognitive abilities expand.

HEIGHT AND WEIGHT

Remember from "Physical Development in Infancy" that the infant's growth in the first year is rapid. During the infant's second year, the growth rate begins to slow down, and the growth rate continues to slow in early childhood. If it did not, we would be a species of giants. The average child grows 2½ inches in height and gains between 5 and 7 pounds a year during early childhood. As the preschool child grows older, the percentage of increase in height and weight decreases with each additional year (McMahon & Stryjewski, 2012). Figure 1 shows the average height and weight of children as they age from 2 to 6 years (Centers for Disease Control and Prevention, 2000). Girls are only slightly smaller and lighter than boys during these years, a difference that continues until puberty. During the preschool years, both boys and girls slim down as the trunks of their bodies lengthen. Although their heads are still somewhat large for their bodies, by the end of the preschool years most children have lost their top-heavy look. Body fat also shows a slow, steady decline during the preschool years. The chubby baby often looks much leaner by the end of early childhood. Girls have more fatty tissue than boys, and boys have more muscle tissue.

Growth patterns vary individually (Hockenberry, Wilson, & Rodgers, 2017; Kliegman & others, 2016). Think back to your elementary school years. This was probably the first time you noticed that some children were taller than you, some shorter; some were stronger, some weaker. Much of the variation is due to heredity, but environmental experiences are involved to some extent. A review of the height and weight of children around the world concluded that the two most important contributors to height differences are ethnic origin and nutrition (Meredith, 1978). Urban, middle-socioeconomic-status, and firstborn children were taller than rural, lower-socioeconomic-status, and later-born children. The children whose mothers smoked during pregnancy were half an inch shorter than the children whose mothers did not smoke during pregnancy. In the United States, African American children are taller than non-Latino White children.

Why are some children unusually short? The primary contributing influences are congenital factors (genetic or prenatal problems), growth hormone deficiency, a physical problem that develops in childhood, maternal smoking during pregnancy, or an emotional difficulty (Hay & others, 2017; Krebs & others, 2016). Chronically sick children are shorter than their rarely sick counterparts. Children who have been physically abused or neglected may not secrete adequate growth hormone, the lack of which can restrict their physical growth. **Growth hormone deficiency** is the absence or deficiency of growth hormone produced by the pituitary gland to stimulate the body to grow. Growth hormone deficiency may occur during infancy or later in childhood (Grimberg & Allen, 2017; Krebs & others, 2016).

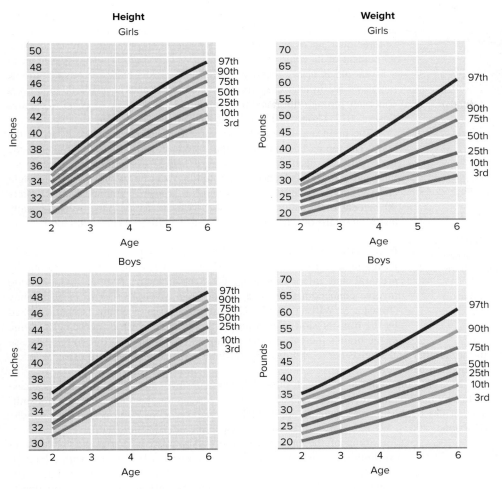

FIGURE **1**

HEIGHT AND WEIGHT CHANGES FROM 2 THROUGH 6 YEARS OF AGE. These graphs show the percentiles of height and weight for boys and girls from 2 through 6 years of age in the United States.

As many as 10,000 to 15,000 U.S. children may have growth hormone deficiency (Stanford University Medical Center, 2017). Without treatment, most children with growth hormone deficiency will not reach a height of five feet. Treatment involves regular injections of growth hormone and usually lasts several years (Pawlikowska-Haddal, 2013). Some children receive injections daily, others several times a week. Twice as many boys as girls are treated with growth hormone (Lee & Howell, 2006).

A recent study of children born small for gestational age or short in stature revealed that five years of growth hormone treatment in childhood was linked to an increase to close to average height (Ross & others, 2015). Also, a recent review concluded that accurate assessment of growth hormone deficiency is difficult and that many children diagnosed with growth hormone deficiency re-test normal later in childhood (Murray, Dattani, & Clayton, 2016).

There has been a significant upsurge in treating very short children with growth hormone therapy (Grimberg & Allen, 2017; Reinehr & others, 2014). Some medical experts have expressed concern that many young children who are being treated with growth hormone therapy are merely short but don't have a growth hormone deficiency. In such cases, parents often perceive that there is a handicap in being short, especially for boys.

Few studies have been conducted on the psychological and social outcomes of having very short stature in childhood. One study did reveal that growth hormone treatment of children very short in stature was linked to an increase in height as well as improvements in self-esteem and mood (Chaplin & others, 2011).

THE BRAIN

One of the most important physical developments during early childhood is the continuing development of the brain and nervous system (Bell & Cuevas, 2015; Bell, Ross, & Patton, 2018).

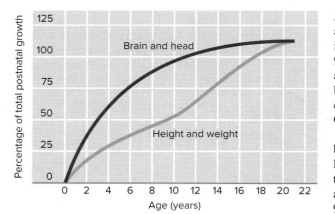

FIGURE 2

GROWTH CURVES FOR THE HEAD AND BRAIN AND FOR HEIGHT AND WEIGHT. The more rapid growth of the brain and head can easily be seen. Height and weight advance more gradually over the first two decades of life.

Source: Damon, Albert, *Human Biology and Ecology,* New York: W. W. Norton & Company, 1977, Figure 10.6

myelination The process in which the nerve cells are covered and insulated with a layer of fat cells, which increases the speed at which information travels through the nervous system.

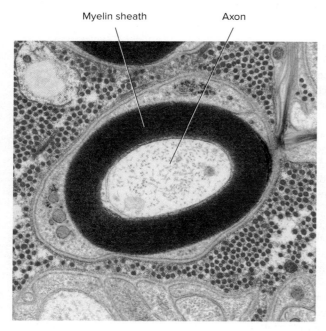

FIGURE 3

A MYELINATED NERVE FIBER. The myelin sheath, shown in brown, encases the axon (white). This image was produced by an electron microscope that magnified the nerve fiber 12,000 times. *What role does myelination play in the brain's development and children's cognition?*

©Steve Gschmeissner/Science Source

Although the brain continues to grow in early childhood, it does not grow as rapidly as in infancy. By the time children reach 3 years of age, the brain is three-quarters of its adult size. By age 6, the brain has reached about 95 percent of its adult volume (Lenroot & Giedd, 2006). Thus, the brain of a 5-year-old is nearly the size it will be when the child reaches adulthood, but as we see in later chapters, the development that occurs inside the brain continues through the remaining childhood and adolescent years (Cohen & Casey, 2017; Crone, 2017; Steinberg & others, 2017).

The brain and the head grow more rapidly than any other part of the body. The top parts of the head, the eyes, and the brain grow faster than the lower portions, such as the jaw. Figure 2 reveals how the growth curve for the head and brain advances more rapidly than the growth curve for height and weight. At 5 years of age, when the brain has attained approximately 90 percent of its adult weight, the 5-year-old's total body weight is only about one-third of what it will be when the child reaches adulthood.

Neuronal Changes In "Prenatal Development" and "Physical Development in Infancy," we discussed the brain's development during the prenatal and infancy periods. Changes in neurons in early childhood involve connections between neurons and myelination, just as in infancy (Juraska & Willing, 2017). Communication in the brain is characterized by the transmission of information between neurons, or nerve cells. Some of the brain's increase in size during early childhood is due to the increase in the number and size of nerve endings and receptors, which allows more effective communication to occur.

Neurons communicate with each other through *neurotransmitters* (chemical substances) that carry information across gaps (called *synapses*) between the neurons. One neurotransmitter that has been shown to increase substantially in the 3-to-6-year age period is *dopamine* (Diamond, 2001). We return to a discussion of dopamine later in this section.

Some of the brain's increase in size also is due to the increase in **myelination,** in which nerve cells are covered and insulated with a layer of fat cells (see Figure 3). This has the effect of increasing the speed and efficiency of information traveling through the nervous system. Myelination is important in the development of a number of abilities in children and adolescents (Cercignani & others, 2017). For example, myelination in the areas of the brain related to hand-eye coordination is not complete until about 4 years of age. One fMRI study of children (mean age: 4 years) found that children with developmental delays of motor and cognitive milestones had significantly reduced levels of myelination (Pujol & others, 2004). Myelination in the areas of the brain related to focusing attention is not complete until the end of middle childhood or later.

Structural Changes Until recently, scientists lacked adequate technology to detect sensitive changes and view detailed maps of the developing human brain. However, sophisticated brain-scanning techniques, such as magnetic resonance imaging (MRI), now allow us to better detect these changes (de Haan & Johnson, 2016). With high-resolution MRI, scientists have evolved spatially complex, four-dimensional growth pattern maps of the developing brain, allowing the brain to be monitored with greater sensitivity than ever before. Using these techniques, scientists have discovered that children's brains undergo dramatic anatomical changes between the ages of 3 and 15 (Thompson & others, 2000). By repeatedly obtaining brain scans of the same children for up to four years, they found that the children's brains experience rapid, distinct spurts of growth. The amount of brain material in some areas can nearly double within as little as a year, followed by a drastic loss of tissue as unneeded cells are purged and the brain continues to reorganize itself. The scientists found that the overall size of the brain did not show dramatic growth in the 3-to-15-year age range. However, what did dramatically change were local patterns within the brain.

Researchers have found that in children from 3 to 6 years of age, the most rapid growth takes place in the frontal lobe areas involved in planning and organizing new actions and in maintaining attention to tasks. They have discovered that from age 6 through puberty, the most rapid growth takes place in the temporal and parietal lobes, especially areas that play major roles in language and spatial relations.

Recently, researchers have found that contextual factors such as poverty and parenting quality are linked to the development of the brain (Black & others, 2017; Johnson, Riis, & Noble, 2016; Lomanowska & others, 2017). In one study of children, children from the poorest homes had significant maturational lags in their frontal and temporal lobes at 4 years of age, and these lags were associated with lower school readiness skills (Hair & others, 2015). In another study, higher levels of maternal sensitivity in early childhood were associated with higher total brain volume (Kok & others, 2015).

The Brain and Cognitive Development   The substantial increases in memory and rapid learning that characterize infants and young children are related to cell loss, myelination, and synaptic growth. In a recent study, young children with higher cognitive ability showed increased myelination by 3 years of age (Deoni & others, 2016). Neuroscientists have found that the density of synapses peaks at 4 years of age (Moulson & Nelson, 2008). Some leading cognitive scientists argue that the true episodic memory (memory for the when and where of life's happenings, such as remembering what one had for breakfast this morning) and self-awareness do not develop until about this time (4 years of age) (Craik, 2006). However, recall that some infant development researchers conclude that episodic memory and self-awareness emerge during infancy (Bauer & Leventon, 2015). These aspects of the brain's maturation, combined with opportunities to experience a widening world, contribute to children's emerging cognitive abilities (Bell, Ross, & Patton, 2018). Consider a child who is learning to read and is asked by a teacher to read aloud to the class. Input from the child's eyes is transmitted to the child's brain, then passed through many brain systems, which translate (process) the patterns of black and white into codes for letters, words, and associations. The output occurs in the form of messages to the child's lips and tongue. The child's own gift of speech is possible because brain systems are organized in ways that permit language processing.

The brain is organized according to many neural circuits, which are neural networks composed of many neurons with certain functions (Blankenship & others, 2016; Colunga & Sims, 2017; Marusak & others, 2017). One specific neural circuit is thought to have an important function in the development of attention and working memory (a type of short-term memory that is used like a mental workbench in performing many cognitive tasks) (Krimer & Goldman-Rakic, 2001). This neural circuit involves the *prefrontal cortex,* and the neurotransmitter dopamine may be a key aspect of information transmission in the prefrontal cortex and this neural circuit (Diamond, 2001) (see Figure 4). The maturation of the prefrontal cortex is important in the development of a number of cognitive and socioemotional skills, including attention, memory, and self-regulation (de Haan & Johnson, 2016).

In sum, scientists are beginning to chart connections between children's cognitive development in areas such as attention and memory, brain regions such as the prefrontal cortex, and the transmission of information at the level of the neuron such as the neurotransmitter dopamine (Bell, Ross, & Patton, 2018; Steinberg & others, 2017). As advancements in technology allow scientists to "look inside" the brain to observe its activity, we will likely see an increased precision in our understanding of the brain's functioning in various aspects of cognitive development (Blankenship & others, 2017; Rosenberg & others, 2016).

developmental connection
Brain Development
In middle and late childhood, cortical thickening occurs in the frontal lobes, which may be linked to improvements in language abilities such as reading. Connect to "Physical Development in Middle and Late Childhood."

Prefrontal cortex

Side view

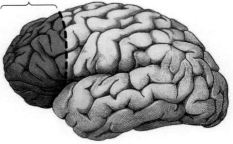

Frontal view

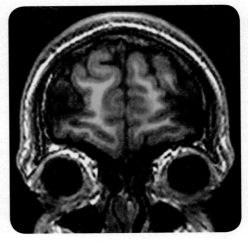

FIGURE 4

THE PREFRONTAL CORTEX. The prefrontal cortex, the highest level in the brain, shows extensive development from 3 to 6 years of age and continues to grow through the remainder of childhood and adolescence. The prefrontal cortex plays important roles in attention, memory, and self-regulation. The image on the top shows a side view of the location of the prefrontal cortex. The image on the bottom (frontal view) is a composite of more than 100 fMRI images of the prefrontal cortex that were taken to assess individuals' speed of processing information under different conditions.

Courtesy of Dr. Sam Gilbert, Institute of Cognitive Neuroscience, UK

Review Connect Reflect

LG1 Discuss growth and change in the young child's body and brain.

Review
- What changes in height and weight characterize early childhood?
- How does the brain change in young children?

Connect
- How do changes in the brain in early childhood represent advances over the child's brain at the end of infancy?

Reflect *Your Own Personal Journey of Life*
- Think back to when you were a young child. How would you characterize your body growth? Was your growth about the same as that of most children your age or was it different?

2 How Do Young Children's Motor Skills Develop?

LG2 Describe changes in motor development in early childhood.

Gross and Fine Motor Skills   Perceptual Development   Young Children's Artistic Drawings

Running as fast as you can, falling down, getting right back up and running just as fast as you can . . . building towers with blocks . . . scribbling, scribbling, and scribbling some more . . . cutting paper with scissors . . . During your preschool years, you probably developed the ability to perform all of these activities.

GROSS AND FINE MOTOR SKILLS

Considerable progress is made in both gross and fine motor skills during early childhood (Maddison & others, 2016). Young children develop a sense of mastery through increased proficiency in gross motor skills such as walking and running (Ball, Bindler, & Cowen, 2014). Improvement in fine motor skills—such as being able to turn the pages of a book, one at a time—also contributes to the child's sense of mastery in the second year. First, let's explore changes in gross motor skills.

Gross Motor Skills   The preschool child no longer has to make an effort simply to stay upright and to move around. As children move their legs with more confidence and carry themselves more purposefully, moving around in the environment becomes more automatic.

At 3 years of age, children enjoy simple movements, such as hopping, jumping, and running back and forth, just for the sheer delight of performing these activities. They take considerable pride in showing how they can run across a room and jump all of 6 inches. The run-and-jump will win no Olympic gold medals, but for the 3-year-old the activity is a source of considerable pride in accomplishment.

At 4 years of age, children are still enjoying the same kinds of activities, but they have become more adventurous. They scramble over low jungle gyms as they display their athletic prowess. Although they have been able to climb stairs with one foot on each step for some time, they are just beginning to be able to come down the same way. They still often revert to putting two feet on each step.

At 5 years of age, children are even more adventuresome than they were at 4. It is not unusual for self-assured 5-year-olds to perform hair-raising stunts on practically any climbing object. Five-year-olds run hard and enjoy races with each other and their parents. A summary of development in gross motor skills during early childhood is shown in Figure 5.

You probably have arrived at one important conclusion about preschool children: They are very, very active. Indeed, 3-year-old children have the highest activity level of any age in the entire human life span. They fidget when they watch television. They fidget when they sit at the dinner table. Even when they sleep, they move around quite a bit.

developmental connection

Physical Development

Participation in sports can have positive or negative outcomes for children. Connect to "Physical Development in Middle and Late Childhood."

37 to 48 Months	49 to 60 Months	61 to 72 Months
Throws ball underhanded (4 feet)	Bounces and catches ball	Throws ball (44 feet, boys; 25 feet, girls)
Pedals tricycle 10 feet	Runs 10 feet and stops	Carries a 16-pound object
Catches large ball	Pushes/pulls a wagon/doll buggy	Kicks rolling ball
Completes forward somersault (aided)	Kicks 10-inch ball toward target	Skips alternating feet
Jumps to floor from 12 inches	Carries 12-pound object	Roller skates
Hops three hops with both feet	Catches ball	Skips rope
Steps on footprint pattern	Bounces ball under control	Rolls ball to hit object
Catches bounced ball	Hops on one foot four hops	Rides bike with training wheels

FIGURE 5

THE DEVELOPMENT OF GROSS MOTOR SKILLS IN EARLY CHILDHOOD.
Note: The skills are listed in the approximate order of difficulty within each age period.

Designing and implementing a developmentally appropriate movement curriculum (one that's appropriate for the child's age and the child individually) facilitates the development of children's gross motor skills (Bardid & others, 2017). To read further about supporting young children's motor development, see the *Caring Connections* interlude.

There can be long-term negative effects for children who fail to develop basic motor skills (Barnett, Salmon, & Hesketh, 2016). These children will not be as able to join in group games or participate in sports during their school years and in adulthood. However, the positive development of motor skills has benefits besides participation in games and sports. Engaging in motor skills fulfills young children's needs and desires for movement, and exercise builds muscles, strengthens the heart, and enhances aerobic capacity. In a recent study, children with a low level of motor competence had a lower motivation for sports participation

caring connections

Supporting Young Children's Motor Development

If you observe young children, you will see that they spend a great deal of time engaging in motor activities such as running, jumping, throwing, and catching. These activities can form the basis of advanced, sports-related skills. For children to progress to effective, coordinated, and controlled motor performance, interaction with and instruction from supportive adults can be beneficial (Henniger, 2017; Morrison, 2017, 2018).

How can early childhood educators support young children's motor development? When planning physical instruction for young children, it is important to keep in mind that their attention span is rather short, so instruction should be brief and to the point. Young children need to practice skills in order to learn them, so instruction should be followed with ample time for practice (Morrison, 2017, 2018). A recent study of 4-year-old girls found that a nine-week motor skill intervention improved the girls' ball skills (Veldman & others, 2017).

Young children practicing their motor skills in an early childhood education program.
©PeopleImages/Getty Images RF

Fitness is an important dimension of people's lives, and it is beneficial to develop a positive attitude toward exercise early in life. Preschoolers need vigorous activities for short periods of time. They can be encouraged to rest or change to a quieter activity as needed.

Movement, even within the classroom, can improve a child's stamina. Such movement activities might be as basic as practicing locomotor skills or as complex as navigating an obstacle course. A number of locomotor skills (such as walking, running, jumping, sliding, skipping, and leaping) can be practiced forward and backward. And it is important to keep practice fun, allowing children to enjoy movement for the sheer pleasure of it (Bredekamp, 2017).

What are some effective strategies for supporting young children's motor development?

and lower global self-worth than their counterparts with a high level of motor competence (Bardid & others, 2017b).

Another recent study found that higher motor proficiency in preschool was linked to engaging in a higher level of physical activity in adolescence (Venetsanou & Kambas, 2017).

Fine Motor Skills   At 3 years of age, children show a more mature ability to place and handle things than they did when they were infants. Although for some time they have had the ability to pick up the tiniest objects between their thumb and forefinger, they are still somewhat clumsy at it. Three-year-olds can build surprisingly high block towers, each block placed with intense concentration but often not in a completely straight line. When 3-year-olds play with a simple jigsaw puzzle, they are rather rough in placing the pieces. Even when they recognize the location a piece fits into, they are not very precise in positioning the piece. They often try to force the piece in the location or pat it vigorously.

By 4 years of age, children's fine motor coordination has improved substantially and is more precise. Sometimes 4-year-old children have trouble building high towers with blocks because in their efforts to place each of the blocks perfectly, they may upset those already stacked. By age 5, children's fine motor coordination has improved. Hand, arm, and body all move together under better command of the eye. Mere towers no longer interest the 5-year-old, who now wants to build a house or a church, complete with steeple, although adults may still need to be told what each finished project is meant to be. A summary of the development of fine motor skills in early childhood is shown in Figure 6.

How do developmentalists measure children's motor development? The **Denver Developmental Screening Test II** is a simple, inexpensive, fast method of diagnosing developmental delays in children from birth through 6 years of age. The test is individually administered and includes separate assessments of gross and fine motor skills, as well as language and personal-social ability (Comuk-Balci & others, 2016; Ribeiro & others, 2017; Rubio-Codina & others, 2016). Among the gross motor skills this test measures are the child's ability to sit, walk, long jump, pedal a tricycle, throw a ball overhand, catch a bounced ball, hop on one foot, and balance on one foot (Yilmaz & others, 2017). Fine motor skills measured by the test include the child's ability to stack cubes, reach for objects, and draw a person.

PERCEPTUAL DEVELOPMENT

Changes in children's perceptual development continue in childhood (Bremner & Spence, 2017; Gomez-Moya, Diaz, & Fernandez-Ruiz, 2016). Children become increasingly efficient at detecting the boundaries between colors (such as red and orange) at 3 to 4 years of age (Gibson, 1969). When children are about 4 or 5 years old, their eye muscles usually are developed enough that they can move their eyes efficiently across a series of letters. Many preschool children are farsighted, unable to see close up as well as they can see far away. By the time they enter the first grade, though, most children can focus their eyes and sustain their attention effectively on close-up objects.

Denver Developmental Screening Test II A test used to diagnose developmental delay in children from birth to 6 years of age; includes separate assessments of gross and fine motor skills, language, and personal-social ability.

37 to 48 Months	49 to 60 Months	61 to 72 Months
Approximates a circle in drawing	Strings and laces shoelace	Folds paper into halves and quarters
Cuts paper	Cuts following a line	Traces around hand
Pastes using pointer finger	Strings 10 beads	Draws rectangle, circle, square, and triangle
Builds three-block bridge	Copies figure X	Cuts interior piece from paper
Builds eight-block tower	Opens and places clothespins (one-handed)	Uses crayons appropriately
Draws 0 and +	Builds a five-block bridge	Makes clay object with two small parts
Dresses and undresses doll	Pours from various containers	Reproduces letters
Pours from pitcher without spilling	Prints first name	Copies two short words

FIGURE 6

THE DEVELOPMENT OF FINE MOTOR SKILLS IN EARLY CHILDHOOD.

Note: The skills are listed in the approximate order of difficulty within each age period.

What are the signs of vision problems in children? They include rubbing the eyes, blinking or squinting excessively, appearing irritable when playing games that require good distance vision, shutting or covering one eye, and tilting the head or thrusting it forward when looking at something. A child who shows any of these behaviors should be examined by an ophthalmologist.

After infancy, children's visual expectations about the physical world continue to develop. In one study, 2- to 4½-year-old children were given a task in which the goal was to find a ball that had been dropped through an opaque tube (Hood, 1995). As shown in Figure 7, if the ball is dropped into the tube at the top left, it will land in the box at the bottom right. However, in this task, most of the 2-year-olds, and even some of the 4-year-olds, persisted in searching in the box immediately beneath the dropping point. For them, gravity ruled and they had failed to perceive the end location of the curved tube.

In one study 3-year-olds were presented with the same task shown in Figure 7 (Joh, Jaswal, & Keen, 2011). In the group that was told to imagine the various paths the ball might take, the young children were more accurate in predicting where the ball would land. In another recent study, 3-year-olds improved their performance on the ball-dropping task shown in Figure 7 when they were instructed to follow the tube with their eyes to the bottom (Bascandziev & Harris, 2011). Thus, in these two studies, 3-year-olds were able to overcome the gravity bias and their impulsive tendencies when they were given verbal instructions from a knowledgeable adult (Keen, 2011).

How do children learn to deal with situations like that in Figure 7, and how do they come to understand other laws of the physical world? These questions are addressed by studies of cognitive development, which we discuss in more detail later.

YOUNG CHILDREN'S ARTISTIC DRAWINGS

In the story that opened the chapter, you read about Teresa Amabile's artistic skills and interest during kindergarten. The story revealed how these skills were restricted once she went to elementary school. Indeed, many young children show a special interest in drawing, just as Teresa did (Bullard, 2014).

The unintended irregularities of children's drawings suggest spontaneity, freedom, and directness (Golomb, 2008). They may use lavish colors that come close, but perhaps won't match the reality of their subjects. Form and clarity give way to bold lines flowing freely on the page. It is not the end product that matters so much, but the joy of creating, the fun of mixing colors, experimenting with different mediums, and getting messy in the process.

Young children often use the same formula for drawing different things. Though modified in small ways, one basic form can cover a range of objects. When children begin to draw animals, they portray them in the same way they portray humans: standing upright with a smiling face, two legs, and outstretched arms. Pointed ears may be a clue to adults about the nature of the particular beast. As children become more sophisticated, their drawing of a cat will look more catlike to an adult. It may be resting on all four paws, tail in the air, with fur standing on end.

Not all children embrace art with equal enthusiasm, and the same child may want to draw one day but have no interest in it the next day. For most children, however, art is an important vehicle for conveying feelings and ideas that are not easily expressed in words (Kostelnik & others, 2014). Drawing and constructing also provide children with a hands-on opportunity to use their problem-solving skills to develop creative ways to represent scale, space, and motion (Moravcik, Nolte, & Feeney, 2013). Parents can provide a context for artistic exploration by giving children a work space where they are not overly concerned about messiness or damage. They can make supplies available, have a bulletin board display space for the child's art, and support and encourage the child's art activity. When viewing children's art, many parents take special delight in hearing about the creative process. Questions such as "Can you tell me about this?" and "What were you thinking about when you made this?" encourage children and help parents to see the world through their children's eyes.

Developmental Changes and Stages   The development of fine motor skills in the preschool years allows children to become budding artists. There are dramatic changes in how children depict what they see. Art provides unique insights into children's perceptual worlds— what they are attending to, how space and distance are viewed, how they experience patterns

FIGURE 7

VISUAL EXPECTATIONS ABOUT THE PHYSICAL WORLD. When young children see the ball dropped into the tube, many of them will search for it immediately below the dropping point.

Courtesy of Dr. Bruce Hood

placement stage Kellogg's term for 2- to 3-year-olds' drawings that are drawn on a page in placement patterns.

shape stage Kellogg's term for 3-year-olds' drawings consisting of diagrams in different shapes.

design stage Kellogg's term for 3- to 4-year-olds' drawings that mix two basic shapes into more complex designs.

pictorial stage Kellogg's term for 4- to 5-year-olds' drawings depicting objects that adults can recognize.

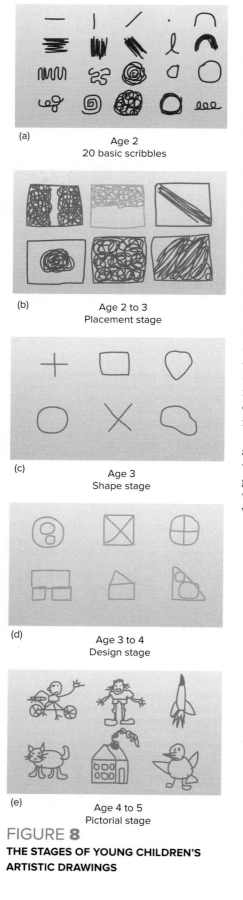

(a)
Age 2
20 basic scribbles

(b)
Age 2 to 3
Placement stage

(c)
Age 3
Shape stage

(d)
Age 3 to 4
Design stage

(e)
Age 4 to 5
Pictorial stage

FIGURE **8**

THE STAGES OF YOUNG CHILDREN'S ARTISTIC DRAWINGS

and forms (Bullard, 2014). Rhoda Kellogg is a creative teacher of preschool children who has observed and guided young children's artistic efforts for many decades. She has assembled an impressive array of tens of thousands of drawings produced by more than 2,000 preschool children. Adults who are unfamiliar with young children's art often view the productions of this age group as meaningless scribbles. However, Kellogg (1970) documented that young children's artistic productions are orderly, meaningful, and structured.

By their second birthday, children can scribble. Scribbles represent the earliest form of drawing. Every form of graphic art, no matter how complex, contains the lines found in children's artwork, which Kellogg calls the 20 basic scribbles. These include vertical, horizontal, diagonal, circular, curving, waving or zigzag lines, and dots. As young children progress from scribbling to picture making, they go through four distinguishable stages: placement, shape, design, and pictorial (see Figure 8).

Following young children's scribbles (Figure 8a) is the **placement stage,** Kellogg's term for 2- to 3-year-olds' drawings, drawn on a page in placement patterns. One example of these patterns is the spaced border pattern shown in Figure 8b. The **shape stage** is Kellogg's term for 3-year-olds' drawings consisting of diagrams in different shapes (see Figure 8c). Young children draw six basic shapes: circles, squares or rectangles, triangles, crosses, Xs, and forms. The **design stage** is Kellogg's term for 3- to 4-year-olds' drawings in which young children mix two basic shapes into a more complex design (see Figure 8d). This stage occurs rather quickly after the shape stage. The **pictorial stage** is Kellogg's term for 4- to 5-year-olds' drawings that consist of objects that adults can recognize (see Figure 8e).

Child Art in Context   Claire Golomb (2002, 2008, 2011, 2016) has studied and conducted research on children's art for a number of decades. Golomb especially criticizes views of young children's art that describe it as primitive and a reflection of conceptual immaturity. She argues that children, like all novices, tend to use forms economically, and their comments indicate that their simplified version works. Rather than seeing children's art as reflections of their conceptual immaturity, Golomb (2011, 2016) focuses on the inventive problem solving that goes into creating these drawings.

Golomb (2011, 2016) maintains that developmental changes in the way children draw are not strictly age-related but also depend on talent, motivation, familial support, and cultural values. Thus, her view contrasts with Kellogg's universal stage approach in which all children go through the same sequence in developing art skills, which we just discussed. In Golomb's view, children's art flourishes in sociocultural contexts where tools are made available and where this activity is valued.

At which of Kellogg's stages of children's art is this young girl's drawing?
©13/Katy McDonnell/Ocean/Corbis RF

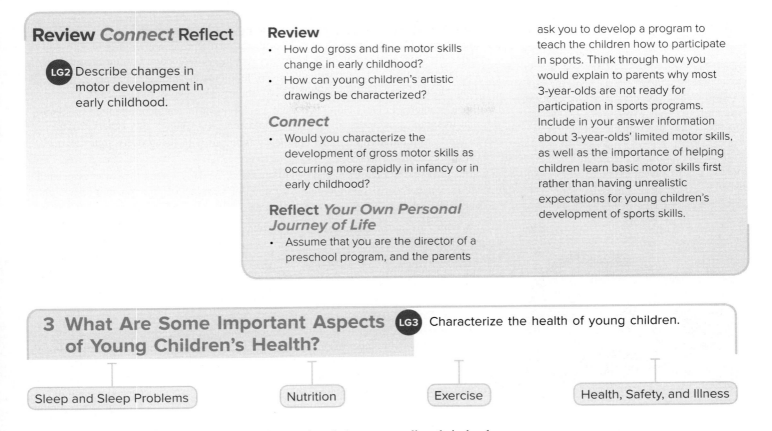

Review Connect Reflect

LG2 Describe changes in motor development in early childhood.

Review
- How do gross and fine motor skills change in early childhood?
- How can young children's artistic drawings be characterized?

Connect
- Would you characterize the development of gross motor skills as occurring more rapidly in infancy or in early childhood?

Reflect *Your Own Personal Journey of Life*
- Assume that you are the director of a preschool program, and the parents ask you to develop a program to teach the children how to participate in sports. Think through how you would explain to parents why most 3-year-olds are not ready for participation in sports programs. Include in your answer information about 3-year-olds' limited motor skills, as well as the importance of helping children learn basic motor skills first rather than having unrealistic expectations for young children's development of sports skills.

3 What Are Some Important Aspects of Young Children's Health?

LG3 Characterize the health of young children.

Sleep and Sleep Problems	Nutrition	Exercise	Health, Safety, and Illness

So far, we have discussed young children's body growth and change, as well as their development of motor skills. In this section, we explore another aspect of young children's physical development—health. To learn more about young children's health, we focus on how it is affected by sleep, nutrition, exercise, safety practices, and illnesses.

SLEEP AND SLEEP PROBLEMS

A good night's sleep is an important aspect of a child's development (Conway, Modrek, & Gorroochurn, 2017; El-Sheikh & Buckhalt, 2015; El-Sheikh & Sadeh, 2015; Kouros & El-Sheikh, 2017; Paul & Pinto, 2017). Experts recommend that young children get 11 to 13 hours of a sleep each night (National Sleep Foundation, 2017). Most young children sleep through the night and have one daytime nap.

Not only is the amount of sleep children get important, but so is uninterrupted sleep (Owens & Mindell, 2011). However, it sometimes is difficult to get young children to go to sleep as they drag out their bedtime routine. One study found that bedtime resistance was associated with conduct problems or hyperactivity in children (Carvalho Bos & others, 2009).

Mona El-Sheikh (2013) recommends adjusting the following aspects of the child's environment to improve the child's sleep: making sure that the bedroom is cool, dark, and comfortable; maintaining consistent bedtimes and wake times; and building positive family relationships. Also, helping the child slow down before bedtime often contributes to less resistance in going to bed. Reading the child a story, playing quietly with the child in the bath, and letting the child sit on the caregiver's lap while listening to music are quieting activities.

Children can experience a number of sleep problems (Caldwell & Redeker, 2015; El-Sheikh, Hinnant, & Philbrook, 2017; Palermo, 2014). One estimate indicates that more than 40 percent of children experience a sleep problem at some point in their development (Boyle & Cropley, 2004). The following research studies indicate links between children's sleep and their developmental outcomes:

- Children 36 to 42 months old who had a consistent bedtime routine got more nightly sleep and an increase in nightly sleep minutes across a six-month period (Staples, Bates, & Petersen, 2015).

How Would You...?
If you were a **human development and family studies professional,** how would you advise parents of a young child who is resisting going to bed at night?

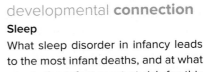

developmental **connection**

Sleep

What sleep disorder in infancy leads to the most infant deaths, and at what age is the infant most at risk for this disorder? Connect to "Physical Development in Infancy."

- In a Chinese study, preschool children who slept seven hours per night or less had a worse school readiness profile (including language/cognitive deficits and emotional immaturity) (Tso & others, 2016). Also in this study, preschool children who used electronic devices three or more hours per day had shortened sleep durations.
- Preschool children who had a longer sleep duration were more likely have better peer acceptance, social skills, and receptive vocabulary (Vaughn & others, 2015).
- Sleep problems in early childhood were a subsequent indicator of attention problems that in some cases persisted into early adolescence (O'Callaghan & others, 2010).
- A short sleep duration in young children was linked with being overweight (Hart, Cairns, & Jelalian, 2011).
- In 2- to 5-year-old children, each additional hour of daily screen time was associated with a decrease in sleep time, less likelihood of sleeping 10 hours or more per night, and later bedtime (Xu & others, 2016).

Let's now explore four specific sleep problems in children: nightmares, night terrors, sleepwalking, and sleep talking. **Nightmares** are frightening dreams that awaken the sleeper, more often toward the morning than just after the child has gone to bed at night (Ivanenko & Larson, 2013). Caregivers should not worry about young children having occasional nightmares because almost every child has them. If children have nightmares persistently, it may indicate that they are feeling too much stress during their waking hours (Akinsanya, Marwaha, & Tampi, 2017; Owens & Mindell, 2011).

Night terrors are characterized by a sudden arousal from sleep and an intense fear, usually accompanied by a number of physiological reactions, such as rapid heart rate and breathing, loud screams, heavy perspiration, and physical movement (Sasayama, Washizuka, & Honda, 2017). In most instances, the child has little or no memory of what happened during the night terror. Night terrors are less common than nightmares and occur more often in deep sleep than do nightmares. Many children who experience night terrors return to sleep rather quickly after the night terror. Children usually outgrow night terrors.

Somnambulism (sleepwalking) occurs during the deepest stage of sleep. Approximately 15 percent of children sleepwalk at least once, and from 1 to 5 percent do it regularly. Most children outgrow the problem without professional intervention.

Sleep talkers are soundly asleep as they speak, although occasionally they make fairly coherent statements for a brief period of time. Most of the time, though, you can't understand what children are saying during sleep talking. There is nothing abnormal about sleep talking, and there is no reason to try to stop it from occurring.

NUTRITION

Four-year-old Bobby is on a steady diet of double cheeseburgers, French fries, and chocolate milk shakes. Between meals, he gobbles up candy bars and marshmallows. He hates green vegetables. Bobby, a preschooler, already has developed poor nutritional habits. What are a preschool child's energy needs? What is a preschooler's eating behavior like?

Energy Needs Feeding and eating habits are important aspects of development during early childhood (Blake, 2017; Sorte, Daeschel, & Amador, 2017; Wardlaw, Smith, & Collene, 2018). What children eat affects their skeletal growth, body shape, and susceptibility to disease. The preschool child requires up to 1,800 calories per day. Figure 9 shows the increasing energy

What characterizes young children's sleep? What are some sleep problems in childhood?
©Dennis Welsh/The Image Bank/Getty Images

nightmares Frightening dreams that awaken the sleeper.

night terrors Incidents characterized by sudden arousal from sleep, intense fear, and usually physiological reactions such as rapid heart rate and breathing, loud screams, heavy perspiration, and physical movement.

somnambulism Sleepwalking; occurs in the deepest stage of sleep.

FIGURE 9

RECOMMENDED ENERGY INTAKES FOR CHILDREN AGES 1 THROUGH 10

Age	Weight (lb)	Height (in)	Energy needs (calories)	Calorie ranges
1 to 3	29	35	1,300	900 to 1,800
4 to 6	44	44	1,700	1,300 to 2,300
7 to 10	62	52	2,400	1,650 to 3,300

needs of children as they move from infancy through the childhood years. Energy needs of individual children of the same age, sex, and size vary. However, an increasing number of children have an energy intake that exceeds what they need (Blake, 2017). A recommendation by the World Health Organization is that on average for children 7 years of age and younger, boys should have an 18 percent, and girls a 20 percent, reduction in energy intake (Butte, 2006).

Diet, Eating Behavior, and Parental Feeding Styles A national study found that from the late 1970s through the late 1990s, several dietary shifts took place in U.S. children: greater away-from-home consumption; large increases in total energy from salty snacks, soft drinks, and pizza; and large decreases in energy from low- and medium-fat milk and medium- and high-fat beef and pork (Nielsen, Siega-Riz, & Popkin, 2002). These dietary changes occurred for children as young as 2 years of age through the adult years.

A national study revealed that 45 percent of children's meals exceed recommendations for saturated and trans fat, which can raise cholesterol levels and increase the risk of heart disease (Center for Science in the Public Interest, 2008). In addition, this study found that one-third of children's daily caloric intake comes from restaurants, twice the percentage consumed away from home in the 1980s. Nearly all of the available children's meals at KFC, Taco Bell, Sonic, Jack in the Box, and Chick-fil-A were too high in calories. A recent study of 2- and 3-year-olds found that French fries and other fried potatoes were the vegetable they were most likely to consume (Fox & others, 2010).

Young children's eating behavior is strongly influenced by their caregivers' behavior (Black & Hurley, 2017; Brown, 2017; Sorte, Daeschel, & Amador, 2017). Young children's eating behavior improves when caregivers eat with children on a predictable schedule, model eating healthy food, make mealtimes pleasant occasions, and engage in certain feeding styles. Distractions from television, family arguments, and competing activities should be minimized so children can focus on eating. A sensitive/responsive caregiver feeding style, in which the caregiver is nurturant, provides clear information about what is expected, and responds appropriately to children's cues, is recommended (Black & others, 2017). Forceful and restrictive caregiver behaviors are not recommended. For example, a restrictive feeding style is linked to children being overweight (Black & Hurley, 2017; Holland & others, 2014; Tylka, Lumeng, & Eneli, 2015).

Another problem is that many parents do not recognize that their children are overweight. One study of parents with 2- to 17-year-old children found that few parents of overweight children perceived their children to be too heavy or were worried about their children's weight (Eckstein & others, 2006).

What are some positive strategies parents can adopt regarding their young children's eating behavior?
©pixelfit/Getty Images RF

Fat and Sugar Consumption Although some health-conscious parents may be providing too little fat in their infants' and children's diets, other parents are raising their children on diets in which the percentage of fat is far too high (Blake, 2017). Too many young children already have developed a pattern of not eating enough fruits and vegetables, a pattern that can have negative consequences later in development. For example, a recent study revealed that 2½-year-old children's liking for fruits and vegetables was related to their eating more fruits and vegetables at 7 years of age (Fletcher & others, 2017).

Our changing lifestyles, in which we often eat on the run and pick up fast-food meals, contribute to the increased fat levels in children's diets. Most fast-food meals are high in protein, especially meat and dairy products. But the average American child does not need to be concerned about getting enough protein. What must be of concern is the vast number of young children who are being raised on fast foods that are not only high in protein but also high in fat. Eating habits become ingrained very early in life; unfortunately, it is during the preschool years that many people get their first taste of fast food. The American Heart Association recommends that the daily limit for calories from fat should be approximately 35 percent.

The concern surrounding food choices not only involves excessive fat in children's diets but also excessive sugar (Pawellek & others, 2017). Consider Robert, age 3, who loves chocolate. His mother lets him have three chocolate candy bars a day. He also drinks an average of four cans of caffeinated cola a day, and he eats sugar-coated cereal each morning at breakfast. The average American child consumes almost 2 pounds of sugar per week. One study found that children from low-income families were likely to consume more sugar than their counterparts from higher-income families (Kranz & Siega-Riz, 2002).

How does sugar consumption influence the health and behavior of young children? The association of sugar consumption with children's health problems—dental cavities and obesity, for example—has been widely documented (Zalewski & others, 2017).

In sum, although there is individual variation in appropriate nutrition for children, their diets should be well balanced and should include fats, carbohydrates, protein, vitamins, and minerals (Wardlaw, Smith, & Collene, 2018). An occasional candy bar does not hurt, but a steady diet of hamburgers, French fries, milk shakes, and candy bars should be avoided.

"Fussy Eaters," Sweets, and Snacks Many young children get labeled as "fussy" or "difficult eaters" when they are only trying to exercise the same rights to personal taste and appetite that adults take for granted (Dovey & others, 2008). Caregivers should allow for the child's developing tastes in food. However, when young children eat too many sweets—candy bars, cola, and sweetened cereals, for example—they can spoil their appetite and then not want to eat more nutritious foods at mealtime. Thus, caregivers need to be firm in limiting the amount of sweets young children eat.

Overweight Young Children Being overweight has become a serious health problem in early childhood (Blake, 2017; Perry & others, 2017; Ward & others, 2017). The Centers for Disease Control and Prevention (2017) has established categories for obesity, overweight, and at risk for being overweight. These categories are determined by body mass index (BMI), which is computed by a formula that takes into account height and weight. Children and adolescents whose BMI is at or above the 97th percentile are classified as obese; those whose BMI is at or above the 95th percentile are overweight; and those whose BMI is at or above the 85th percentile are at risk of becoming overweight.

The percentages of young children who are overweight or at risk of being overweight in the United States have increased dramatically in recent decades, but in the last several years there are indications that fewer preschool children are obese. In 2009–2010, 12.1 percent of U.S. 2- to 5-year-olds were classified as obese, compared with 5 percent in 1976–1980 and 10.4 percent in 2007–2008 (Ogden & others, 2016). However, in 2013–2014, a substantial drop in the obesity rate of 2- to 5-year-old children occurred in comparison with their counterparts in 2003–2004 (Ogden & others, 2016). In 2013–2014, 9.4 percent of 2- to 5-year-olds were obese compared with 14 percent in 2004. It is not clear why this drop occurred, but possible causes include families buying lower-calorie foods and the influence of the Special Supplementation Program for Women, Infants, and Children that subsidizes food for women in low-income families and emphasizes consuming less fruit juice, cheese, and eggs and more whole fruits and vegetables.

What are some trends in the eating habits and weight of young children?
©Lilian Perez/age fotostock

The risk that overweight children will continue to be overweight when they are older was supported in a recent U.S. study of nearly 8,000 children (Cunningham, Kramer, & Narayan, 2014). In this study, overweight 5-year-olds were four times more likely to be obese by 14 years of age than their 5-year-old counterparts who began kindergarten at a normal weight. Also, in the recent study described earlier in which obesity was reduced in preschool children, the preschoolers who were obese were five times more likely to be overweight or obese as adults (Ogden & others, 2014).

One comparison of 34 countries revealed that the United States had the second-highest rate of childhood obesity (Janssen & others, 2005). Childhood obesity contributes to a number of health problems in young children. For example, physicians are now seeing type 2 (adult-onset) diabetes (a condition directly linked with obesity and a low level of fitness) and hypertension in children as young as 5 years of age (Chaturvedi & others, 2014; Riley & Bluhm, 2012).

Being overweight also is linked to young children's psychological makeup. In one study, the correlation between weight status and self-esteem in 5-year-old girls was examined (Davison & Birth, 2001). The girls who were overweight had lower body self-esteem than those who were not overweight. Thus, as early as 5 years of age, being overweight is linked with lower self-esteem.

Prevention of obesity in children includes helping children and parents see food as a way to satisfy hunger and nutritional needs, not as proof of love or as a reward for good behavior

developmental **connection**

Nutrition

A number of intervention programs have been conducted in an effort to help overweight and obese children to lose weight. Connect to "Physical Development in Middle and Late Childhood."

(Sorte, Daeschel, & Amador, 2017). Snack foods should be low in fat, simple sugars, and salt, as well as high in fiber. Routine physical activity should be a daily occurrence (Powers & Dodd, 2017; Wuest & Fisette, 2015). A research review concluded that a higher level of screen time (watching TV, using a computer) at 4 to 6 years of age was linked to a lower activity level and being overweight from preschool through adolescence (te Velde & others, 2012). A recent intervention study with children attending Head Start programs found that getting parents involved in activities such as nutrition counseling, becoming more aware of their child's weight status, and developing healthy lifestyles was effective in lowering children's rates of obesity, increasing children's physical activity, reducing children's TV viewing, and improving children's eating habits (Davison & others, 2013). Other researchers also are finding that interventions with parents can reduce children's overweight and obesity (Byrne & others, 2017; Foster & others, 2016). A recent research review concluded that family-based interventions were often effective in helping obese children lose weight (Kothandan, 2014).

What are some effective strategies for preventing childhood obesity?
©Larry Williams/Corbis/Getty Images

Malnutrition in Young Children from Low-Income Families   Malnutrition continues to be a major threat to millions during the childhood years (Black & others, 2013, 2017; Blake, 2017). Malnutrition and starvation are a daily fact of life for children in many developing countries that have high rates of poverty (UNICEF, 2017). One study revealed that two food-assisted maternal and child health programs (both of which emphasized food provision, communication about behavior change, and preventive health services) helped to reduce the impact of economic hardship on stunting of children's growth in Haiti (Donnegan & others, 2010).

A common nutritional problem in early childhood is iron deficiency anemia, which results in chronic fatigue (Lundblad & others, 2017). This problem results from the failure to eat adequate amounts of quality meats and dark green vegetables. Young children from low-income families are most likely to develop iron deficiency anemia (Petry & others, 2017).

Some researchers argue that malnutrition is directly linked to cognitive deficits because of negative effects on brain development (Nyaradi & others, 2013). However, an increasing number of researchers conclude that the links between child undernutrition, physical growth, and cognitive development are more complex. For example, nutritional influences can be viewed in the context of socioemotional factors that often coincide with undernutrition. Thus, children who vary considerably from the norm in physical growth also differ on other biological and socioemotional factors that might influence cognitive development. For example, children who are underfed often are also less supervised, less stimulated, and less educated than children who are well nourished. As we discussed earlier, poverty is an especially strong risk factor that interacts with children's nutritional status to affect physical and cognitive development (Black & others, 2013, 2017).

Malnutrition may be linked to other aspects of development in addition to cognitive deficits. One longitudinal study found that U.S. children who were malnourished at 3 years of age showed more aggressive and hyperactive behavior at age 8, had more externalizing problems at age 11, and evidenced more excessive motor behavior at age 17 (Liu & others, 2004).

EXERCISE

Because of their activity level and the development of large muscles, especially in the arms and legs, preschool children need daily exercise (Innella & others, 2016; Lintu & others, 2017; Powers & Dodd, 2017). Recently, four expert panels from Australia, Canada, the United Kingdom, and the United States issued physical activity guidelines for young children that were quite similar (Pate & others, 2015). The guidelines recommend that young children get 15 or more minutes of physical activity per hour over a 12-hour period, or about 3 hours per day total. These guidelines reflect an increase from earlier guidelines established in 2002.

Too often, though, preschool children are not getting enough exercise (Dowda & others, 2017). In one study, observations of 3- to 5-year-old children during outdoor play at preschools revealed that the preschool children were mainly sedentary even when participating in outdoor play (Brown & others, 2009). In this study, throughout the day the preschoolers were sedentary 89 percent of the time, engaged in light activity 8 percent of the time, and participated in moderate to vigorous physical activity only 3 percent of the time. In another study, preschool children's physical activity was enhanced by family members' engaging in sports together and by parents' perception that it was safe for their children to play outside (Beets & Foley, 2008). And a recent research review of 17 studies concluded that exercise

developmental **connection**

Health

As boys and girls reach and progress through adolescence, they exercise less. Connect to "Physical Development in Adolescence."

How much physical activity should preschool children engage in per day?
©RubberBall Productions/Getty Images RF

was an effective strategy for reducing body fat in overweight and obese children (Kelley & Kelley, 2013). Further, in a recent study, 60 minutes of physical activity per day in preschool academic contexts improved early literacy (Kirk & Kirk, 2016).

In sum, the child's life should be centered around activities, not meals (Powers & Dodd, 2017; Wuest & Fisette, 2015). Just how important are these activities in young children's lives? See the *Connecting with Research* interlude for insight from one research study.

connecting with research

Physical Activity in Young Children Attending Preschools

One study examined the activity levels of 281 3- to 5-year-olds in nine preschools (Pate & others, 2004). The preschool children wore accelerometers, a small activity monitor, for four to five hours a day. Height and weight assessments of the children were made to calculate their BMI.

Guidelines recommend that preschool children engage in two hours of physical activity per day, divided into one hour of structured activity and one hour of unstructured free play (National Association for Sport and Physical Education, 2002). In this study, the young children participated in an average of 7.7 minutes per hour of moderate to vigorous activity, usually in a block of time when they were outside. Over the course of eight hours of a preschool day, these children would get approximately one hour of moderate and vigorous physical activity—only about 50 percent of the amount recommended. The researchers concluded that young children are unlikely to engage in another hour per day of moderate and vigorous physical activity outside their eight hours spent in preschool and thus are not getting adequate opportunities for physical activity.

Gender and age differences characterized the preschool children's physical activity. Boys were more likely to engage in moderate or vigorous physical activity than girls were. Four- and 5-year-old children were more likely to be sedentary than 3-year-old children.

The young children's physical activity levels also varied according to the particular preschool they attended. The extent to which they participated in moderate and vigorous physical activity ranged from

What are some guidelines for preschool children's exercise?
©skynesher/Getty Images RF

4.4 to 10.2 minutes per hour across the nine preschools. Thus, the policies and practices of particular preschools influence the extent to which children engage in physical activity. The researchers concluded that young children need more vigorous play and organized activities.

Can you think of any other ways in which researchers could test and confirm the findings of this study?

HEALTH, SAFETY, AND ILLNESS

In the effort to make a child's world safer, one of the main strategies is to prevent childhood injuries. And in considering young children's health, it important to examine the contexts in which they live.

Preventing Childhood Injuries Young children's active and exploratory nature, coupled with unawareness of danger in many instances, often puts them in situations in which they are at risk for injuries. Most of young children's cuts, bumps, and bruises are minor, but some accidental injuries can produce serious injuries or even death (Taylor & others, 2017).

In the United States, motor vehicle accidents are the leading cause of death in young children, followed by cancer and cardiovascular disease (National Vital Statistics Reports, 2004) (see Figure 10). In addition to motor vehicle accidents, other accidental deaths in children involve drowning, falls, burns, and poisoning (Alnababtah, Khan, & Ashford, 2016; Emond & others, 2017).

Notice in Figure 10 that the seventh leading cause of death in young children in the United States involves firearms. In one cross-cultural comparison, the rate of firearm-related death among children under 15 years of age in 26 industrialized countries was the highest in the United States (American Academy of Pediatrics, 2001). Among those industrialized countries with no firearm-related deaths in children were Japan, Singapore, and the Netherlands. Many of young children's injuries can be prevented (Sorte, Daeschel, & Amador, 2017). Among the preventive measures are regularly restraining children in automobiles, reducing access to firearms, and making homes and playgrounds safer (Li, Alonge, & Hyder, 2016; Naranjo, 2017; Saunders & others, 2017).

Influences on children's safety include the acquisition and practice of individual skills and safety behaviors, family and home influences, school and peer influences, and the community's actions. Notice that these influences reflect Bronfenbrenner's ecological model of development. Ecological contexts can influence children's safety, security, and injury prevention (Sleet & Mercy, 2003). We will have more to say about contextual influences on young children's health shortly.

Reducing access to firearms is a wise strategy (Dodington & others, 2017; Kalesan & others, 2017). In 12 states that passed laws requiring that firearms be made inaccessible to children, unintentional shooting deaths of children fell by almost 25 percent. In one study, many parents in homes with firearms reported that their children never handled the firearms, but interviews with their children contradicted the parents' perceptions (Baxley & Miller, 2006).

Deaths of young children due to automobile accidents have declined considerably in the United States since the invention of the seat belt. All U.S. states and the District of Columbia have laws that require young children to be restrained in the back seats of cars, either in specially designed seats or by seat belts. In many instances, when young children are killed today in automobile accidents, they are unrestrained. Although many parents today use car seats or "booster seats" for their children, most don't install the seats properly. If the seat is not installed correctly, children are at risk for serious injury or death in automobile accidents (Ludvigsson & others, 2017). Nearly all local police departments will assist parents in installing their children's car seats safely. This service is provided free of charge.

Most fatal non-vehicle-related deaths in young children occur in or around the home. Young children have drowned in bathtubs and swimming pools, been burned in fires and explosions, experienced falls from heights, and drunk or eaten poisonous substances.

Playgrounds also can be a source of children's injuries (Macpherson & others, 2010). One of the major problems is that playground equipment is often not constructed over impact-absorbing surfaces such as wood chips or sand.

Contexts of Young Children's Health Among the contexts affecting young children's health are poverty and ethnicity, home and child care, environmental tobacco smoke, and exposure to lead. In addition to discussing these issues, we will discuss the state of illness and health in the world's children.

How Would You...?
If you were a **health-care professional,** what changes would you advise parents of young children to make in order to improve the safety of their home?

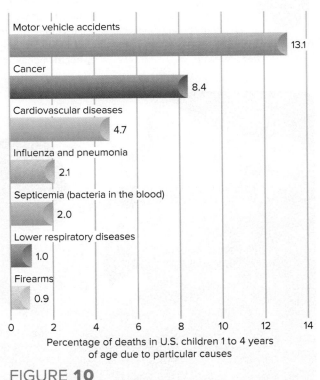

FIGURE **10**

MAIN CAUSES OF DEATH IN CHILDREN 1 THROUGH 4 YEARS OF AGE. These figures show the percentages of deaths in U.S. children 1 to 4 years of age due to particular causes in 2002 (National Vital Statistics Reports, 2004).

Poverty and Ethnicity   Low income is linked with poor health in young children (Hughes & others, 2017; Lin & Seo, 2017). Many health problems of young children in poverty begin before birth when their mothers receive little or no health care, which can produce a low birth weight child and other complications that may continue to affect the child years later (Sadovsky & others, 2016). Children living in poverty may experience unsanitary conditions, live in crowded housing, and be inadequately supervised (Doob, 2013; Pelissari & Diaz-Quijano, 2017). Children in poverty are more likely to be exposed to lead poisoning than children growing up in higher socioeconomic conditions (Morrissey-Ross, 2000). The families of many children in poverty do not have adequate medical insurance, and thus the children often receive less adequate medical care than do children living in higher socioeconomic conditions (Black & others, 2017).

Ethnicity is also linked to children's health (Black & others, 2017). For example, one study found that even when socioeconomic status was controlled, Latino, African American, and Asian American children were less likely to have had a usual health-care source, health professional, doctor visit, and dental visit in the past year (Shi & Stevens, 2005). Another study revealed that children whose parents had limited English proficiency were three times more likely to have fair or poor health status than their English-proficient counterparts (Flores, Abreu, & Tomany-Korman, 2005).

Safety at Home and in Child Care   Caregivers—whether they are parents at home or teachers and supervisors in child care—play an important role in protecting the health of young children (Sorte, Daeschel, & Amador, 2017). For example, by controlling the speed of the vehicles they drive, by decreasing or eliminating their drinking—especially before driving—and by not smoking around children, caregivers enhance the likelihood that children will be healthy (Tinsley, 2003).

Young children may lack the intellectual skills—including reading ability—to discriminate between safe and unsafe household substances. And they may lack the impulse control to keep from running out into a busy street while chasing a ball. In these and many other situations, competent adult supervision and monitoring of young children are important to prevent injuries. In communicating with young children, caregivers need to make sure that the information they give to children is cognitively simple. And an important strategy is that parents guide children in learning how to control and regulate their own health behavior.

How Would You...?

If you were a **health-care professional,** how would you talk with parents about the impact of secondhand smoke on children's health in order to encourage parents to stop smoking?

Parents also should invest effort in finding a competent health-care provider for their children. This "includes consulting sources of information and asking questions likely to provide useful information about practice characteristics that may affect the parent-doctor relationship. Parents, for example, might seek information concerning a physician's willingness to answer questions and involve parents in decision making or at least to outline options. Parents might also inquire about the physician's style of practice and philosophies about treatment, behavior management, nutrition, and other general health maintenance practices" (Hickson & Clayton, 2002, p. 456). To read about Barbara Deloian, a pediatric nurse who promotes positive parent-child experiences and helps create positive links between families and the health-care system, see the *Connecting with Careers* profile that follows.

Environmental Tobacco Smoke   Estimates indicate that approximately 22 percent of children and adolescents in the United States are exposed to tobacco smoke in the home. An increasing number of studies reach the conclusion that children are at risk for health problems when they live in homes in which a parent smokes (Miyahara & others, 2017; Pugmire, Sweeting, & Moore, 2017). In one study, if the mother smoked, her children were twice as likely to develop respiratory problems (Etzel, 1988). In another study, young

What are some negative outcomes for children when they experience environmental tobacco smoke?
©Image Source/Getty Images RF

Barbara Deloian, Pediatric Nurse

Barbara Deloian is a pediatric nurse in Denver, Colorado. She practices nursing in the Pediatric Oral Feeding Clinic and is involved in research as part of an irritable infant study for the Children's Hospital in Denver. She is on the faculty of nursing at the Colorado Health Sciences Center. Deloian previously worked in San Diego where she was coordinator of the Child Health Program for the County of San Diego.

Deloian's research interests focus on children with special health-care needs, especially high-risk infants and children, and promoting positive parent-child experiences. She is a former president of the National Association of Pediatric Nurse Associates and Practitioners.

For more information about what pediatric nurses do, see the Careers in Children's Development appendix.

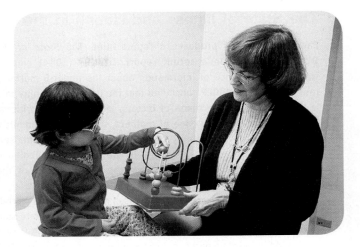

Barbara Deloian conducts a pediatric evaluation.
Courtesy of Dr. Barbara Deloian

children whose fathers smoked at home were more likely to have upper respiratory tract infections than those whose fathers did not smoke at home (Shiva & others, 2004). Children exposed to tobacco smoke in the home are more likely to develop wheezing symptoms and asthma than children in nonsmoking homes (Merianos, Dixon, & Mahabee-Gittens, 2017; Vo & others, 2017). Also, a recent study revealed that maternal cigarette smoking and alcohol consumption when children were 5 years of age were linked to children subsequently engaging in early onset of smoking in adolescence (Hayatbakhsh & others, 2013). And a recent study found that young children who were exposed to environmental tobacco smoke were more likely to engage in antisocial behavior when they were 12 years old (Pagani & others, 2017).

Exposure to Lead   There are special concerns about lead poisoning in young children (Hanna-Attisha & Kuehn, 2016). Approximately 3 million children under 6 years of age are estimated to be at risk for lead poisoning, which might harm their development (Ahamed & others, 2005). As we mentioned earlier, children in poverty are at greater risk for lead poisoning than children living in higher socioeconomic conditions (Blackowicz & others, 2017). Lead can get into children's bloodstreams through ingesting food or water that is contaminated by lead, putting lead-contaminated fingers in their mouths, or inhaling dust from lead-based paint. The negative effects of high lead levels in children's blood include lower intelligence, lower achievement, attention deficit hyperactivity disorder, and elevated blood pressure (Abelsohn & Sanborn, 2010; Bellinger, 2008; Blackowicz & others, 2017). One study found that 5-year-old children exposed to lead performed more poorly on tests of memory and problem solving (Canfield, Gendle, & Cory-Slechta, 2004). Because of such negative outcomes, the Centers for Disease Control and Prevention recommends that children be screened for the presence of lead contamination in their blood.

To read further about children's illness and health, see the *Connecting with Diversity* interlude.

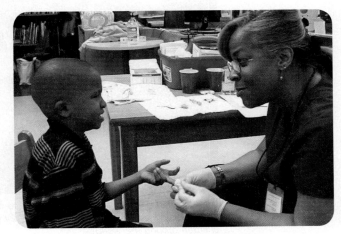

What are some negative effects of high levels of lead in children's blood?
©Mike Householder/AP Images

The State of Illness and Health in the World's Children

Each year UNICEF produces a report titled *The State of the World's Children*. In a recent report, UNICEF (2014) emphasized the importance of information about the under-5 mortality rate of a nation. UNICEF concluded that the under-5 mortality rate is the result of a wide range of factors, including the nutritional health and health knowledge of mothers, the level of immunization, dehydration, availability of maternal and child health services, income and food availability in the family, availability of clean water and safe sanitation, and the overall safety of the child's environment.

UNICEF periodically reports rankings of nations' under-5 mortality rates. In 2012, 40 nations had a lower under-5 mortality rate than the United States, with Luxembourg and Iceland having the lowest rates and Sierra Leone and Angola having the highest rates (UNICEF, 2014). The relatively high under-5 mortality rate of the United States compared with other developed nations is due to such factors as poverty and inadequate health care. The devastating effects on the health of young children occur in countries where poverty rates are high (UNICEF, 2014). The poor are the majority in nearly one of every five nations in the world. They often experience lives of hunger, malnutrition, illness, inadequate access to health care, unsafe water, and a lack of protection from harm (Black & others, 2013, 2017; UNICEF, 2017).

A leading cause of childhood death in impoverished countries is dehydration caused by diarrhea. In 1980, diarrhea was responsible for over 4.6 million childhood deaths. Oral rehydration therapy (ORT) was introduced in 1979 and quickly became the foundation for controlling diarrheal diseases. ORT now is given to the majority of children in impoverished countries suffering with diarrhea, which has decreased the number of deaths due to dehydration caused by diarrhea.

Acute respiratory infections, such as pneumonia, also have killed many children under the age of 5. Many of these children's lives could have been saved with antibiotics administered by a community health worker. Undernutrition also is a contributing factor to many deaths of children under the age of 5 in impoverished countries (Amuna & Zotor, 2008).

In recent decades, there has been a dramatic increase in the number of young children who have died because of HIV/AIDS transmitted to them by their parents (UNICEF, 2014, 2017). Deaths in young children due to HIV/AIDS especially occur in countries with high rates of poverty and low levels of education (Tomlinson & others, 2016). For example, the uneducated are four times more likely to believe that there is no way to avoid AIDS and three times more likely to be unaware that the virus can be transmitted from mother to child (UNICEF, 2012).

Many of the deaths of young children around the world can be prevented by a reduction in poverty and improvements in nutrition, sanitation, education, and health services (Black & others, 2013, 2017; Lu, Black, & Richter, 2016; UNICEF, 2017).

Many children in impoverished countries die before reaching the age of 5 from dehydration and malnutrition brought about by diarrhea. *What are some of the other main causes of death in young children around the world?*
©Kent Page/AP Images

Review

- What is the nature of sleep and sleep problems in young children?
- What are young children's energy needs? What characterizes young children's eating behavior?
- What are some important aspects of exercise in the lives of young children?
- How can the nature of children's injuries be summarized? How do contexts influence children's health?

Connect

- In this section, you learned that experts recommend that young children get 11 to 13 hours of sleep a night during early childhood. How does that compare with what you learned about sleep requirements in infancy?

Reflect *Your Own Personal Journey of Life*

- If you become a parent of a young child, what precautions will you take to improve your child's health?

---

topical connections *looking forward*

Next, you will explore the fascinating world of young children's cognitive development, their remarkable advances in language development, and the role of education in their development. Later, you will read about the continuing changes in children's physical development in middle and late childhood. Their motor skills become smoother and more coordinated during the elementary school years. And the development of their brain—especially in the prefrontal cortex—provides the foundation for a number of cognitive and language advances, including the use of strategies and reading skills.

---

reach your **learning goals**

Physical Development in Early Childhood

1 How Does a Young Child's Body and Brain Grow and Change?

LG1 Discuss growth and change in the young child's body and brain.

Height and Weight

The Brain

- The average child grows 2½ inches in height and gains between 5 and 7 pounds a year during early childhood. Growth patterns vary individually, though. Some children are unusually short because of congenital factors, growth hormone deficiency, a physical problem that develops during childhood, maternal smoking during pregnancy, or an emotional difficulty.

- By age 6, the brain has reached about 95 percent of its adult volume. Some of the brain's growth is due to increases in the number and size of nerve endings and receptors. One neurotransmitter that increases in concentration from 3 to 6 years of age is dopamine.

- Researchers have found that changes in local patterns in the brain occur from 3 to 15 years of age. From 3 to 6 years of age, the most rapid growth occurs in the frontal lobes. From age 6 through puberty, the most substantial growth takes place in the temporal and parietal lobes.

- Increasing brain maturation contributes to changes in cognitive abilities. One such link involves the prefrontal cortex, dopamine, and improved attention and working memory.

2 How Do Young Children's Motor Skills Develop?

 LG2 Describe changes in motor development in early childhood.

Gross and Fine Motor Skills

- Gross motor skills increase dramatically in early childhood. Children become increasingly adventuresome as their gross motor skills improve. It is important for early childhood educators to design and implement developmentally appropriate activities for young children's gross motor skills. Three types of these activities are fundamental movement, daily fitness, and perceptual-motor. Fine motor skills also improve substantially during early childhood.

- The Denver Developmental Screening Test II is a simple, inexpensive method of diagnosing developmental delay and includes separate assessments of gross and fine motor skills.

Perceptual Development

- Among the changes in young children's perceptual development are better detection of color boundaries and increased focusing of their eyes.

Young Children's Artistic Drawings

- The development of fine motor skills allows young children to become budding artists. Scribbling begins at 2 years of age, followed by four stages of drawing, culminating in the pictorial stage at 4 to 5 years of age.

- Golomb argues that it is important to explore the sociocultural contexts of children's art and that factors such as talent, motivation, familial support, and cultural values influence the development of children's art.

3 What Are Some Important Aspects of Young Children's Health?

LG3 Characterize the health of young children.

Sleep and Sleep Problems

- Young children should get 11 to 13 hours of sleep each night. Most young children sleep through the night and have one daytime nap. Helping the young child slow down before bedtime often leads to less resistance in going to bed. Among the sleep problems that can develop in young children are nightmares, night terrors, somnambulism (sleepwalking), and sleep talking.

Nutrition

- Energy needs increase as children go through the early childhood years. The preschool child requires up to 1,800 calories daily. National assessments indicate that a large majority of young children in the United States do not have a healthy diet and that their eating habits have worsened over the last two decades. Too many parents are rearing young children on diets that are high in fat and sugar. Children's diets should contain well-balanced proportions of fats, carbohydrates, protein, vitamins, and minerals. A special concern is malnutrition in young children from low-income families.

Exercise

- Exercise should be a daily occurrence for young children. Guidelines recommend that they get two hours of exercise per day. The young child's life should be centered around activities rather than meals.

Health, Safety, and Illness

- In the United States, motor vehicle accidents are the leading cause of deaths among young children. Firearm deaths are especially high among young children in the United States in comparison with other countries. Among the strategies for preventing childhood injuries are restraining children in automobiles, preventing access to firearms, and making the home and playground safer.

- Among the contexts involved in children's health are poverty and ethnicity, home and child care, environmental tobacco smoke, and exposure to lead. The most devastating effects on the health of young children occur in countries with high poverty rates. Among the problems that low-income families face in these countries are hunger, malnutrition, illness, inadequate access to health care, unsafe water, and a lack of protection from harm.

- In recent decades, the trend in children's illness and health has been toward prevention as vaccines have been developed to reduce the occurrence of diseases in children. Parents play an important role in protecting young children's health. They influence their children's health by the way they behave in regard to children's illness symptoms. Parents can use a number of positive strategies in coping with the stress of having a chronically ill child. Parents need to invest effort in selecting a competent health-care provider for their children.

key **terms**

Denver Developmental Screening Test II	growth hormone deficiency	night terrors nightmares	placement stage shape stage
design stage	myelination	pictorial stage	somnambulism

key **people**

Teresa Amabile	Mona El-Sheikh	Claire Golomb	Rhoda Kellogg

connecting with **improving the lives of children**

STRATEGIES

Supporting Young Children's Physical Development

What are some good strategies for supporting young children's physical development?

· *Give young children plenty of opportunities to be active and explore their world.* Young children are extremely active and should not be constrained for long periods of time. Competent teachers plan daily fitness activities for young children. Preschool-aged children are too young for organized sports.

· *Make sure that young children's motor activities are fun and appropriate for their age.* Young children should enjoy the motor activities they participate in. Also, don't try to push young children into activities more appropriate for older children. For example, don't try to train a 3-year-old to ride a bicycle or enroll a 4-year-old in tennis lessons.

· *Give young children ample opportunities to engage in art.* Don't constrain young children's drawing. Let them freely create their artwork.

· *Provide young children with good nutrition.* Know how many calories preschool children need to meet their energy requirements, which are greater than in infancy. Too many young children are raised on fast foods. Monitor the amount of fat and sugar in young children's diets. Nutritious midmorning and midafternoon snacks are recommended, in addition to breakfast, lunch, and dinner. Make sure that young children get adequate iron, vitamins, and protein.

· *Make sure that young children have regular medical checkups.* These are especially important for children living in impoverished conditions, who are less likely to get such checkups.

· *Be a positive health role model for young children.* When you have young children as passengers, control the speed of the vehicle you are driving. Don't smoke in their presence. Eat healthy foods. Just by being in your presence, young children will imitate many of your behaviors.

· *Make sure children play in safe places.* Walk through the areas where children play and check for any potential hazards.

RESOURCES

Early Childhood Development Coming of Age: Science Through the Life Course (2017)

Maureen Black and her colleagues
Lancet (2017), 389 (10074), 77–90.
Leading expert Maureen Black outlines the key features needed in early childhood programs that will especially benefit at-risk children and help them reach their potential.

The Creation of Imaginary Worlds: The Role of Art, Magic, and Dreams in Child Development (2016)

Claire Golomb
London: Jessica Kinsgley Publishers
A leading expert analyzes the rich imaginary worlds of children with a special emphasis on children's art and how they express themselves through art.

American Academy of Pediatrics

www.aap.org
This Web site provides extensive information about strategies for improving children's health.

How Children Learn to Be Healthy (2003)

Barbara Tinsley
New York: Cambridge University Press
A leading expert explores the ways in which health behavior develops in children, especially focusing on the roles of parents, schools, and the media in influencing children's health.

The State of the World's Children 2017

UNICEF
Geneva, Switzerland: UNICEF
Each year, UNICEF publishes *The State of the World's Children,* which has a special focus on children's health. Enter the title of the book on a search engine and you will be able to access the entire book at no charge.

chapter 9

COGNITIVE DEVELOPMENT IN EARLY CHILDHOOD

chapter outline

©Ariel Skelley/Blend Images/Getty Images RF

The Reggio Emilia approach is an educational program for young children that was developed in the northern Italian city of Reggio Emilia. Children of single parents and children with disabilities have priority in admission; other children are admitted according to a scale of needs. Parents pay on a sliding scale based on income.

The children are encouraged to learn by investigating and exploring topics that interest them (Bredekamp, 2017). A wide range of stimulating media and materials is available for children to use as they learn music, movement, drawing, painting, sculpting, collages, puppets and disguises, and photography, for example (Bond, 2015).

A Reggio Emilia classroom in which young children explore topics that interest them.
©Ruby Washington/The New York Times/Redux Pictures

In this program, children often explore topics in a group, which fosters a sense of community, respect for diversity, and a collaborative approach to problem solving (Hyson, Copple, & Jones, 2006). Two co-teachers are present to serve as guides for children. The Reggio Emilia teachers consider a project to be an adventure, which can start from an adult's suggestion, from a child's idea, or from an event such as a snowfall or another unexpected happening. Every project is based on what the children say and do. The teachers allow children enough time to plan and craft a project.

At the core of the Reggio Emilia approach is the image of children who are competent and have rights, especially the right to outstanding care and education. Parent participation is considered essential, and cooperation is a major theme in the schools. Many early childhood education experts believe the Reggio Emilia approach provides a supportive, stimulating context in which children are motivated to explore their world in a competent and confident manner (Morrison, 2017).

-topical connections *looking **back***

In "Physical Development in Early Childhood" you learned how a young child's body and brain grow and change. In "Cognitive Development in Infancy" a special emphasis was the increasing consensus that infants' cognitive development is more advanced than Piaget envisioned. You learned that infants make amazing progress in their attentional, memory, concept formation, and language skills. In this chapter, you will discover that these information-processing skills continue to show remarkable advances in early childhood.

preview

Children make a number of significant cognitive advances in early childhood. In the opening section, we explore the cognitive changes described by three major theories of cognitive development. Then we examine the dramatic changes in young children's language, and we conclude by discussing a wide range of topics involving early childhood education.

1 What Are Three Views of the Cognitive Changes That Occur in Early Childhood?

LG1 Describe three views of the cognitive changes that occur in early childhood.

Piaget's Preoperational Stage   Vygotsky's Theory   Information Processing

The cognitive world of the preschool child is creative, free, and fanciful. Preschool children's imaginations work overtime, and their mental grasp of the world improves. Our coverage of cognitive development in early childhood focuses on three theories: Piaget's, Vygotsky's, and information processing.

PIAGET'S PREOPERATIONAL STAGE

Recall that during Jean Piaget's first stage of development, the sensorimotor stage, the infant progresses in the ability to organize and coordinate sensations and perceptions with physical movements and actions. The **preoperational stage,** which lasts from approximately 2 to 7 years of age, is the second Piagetian stage. In this stage, children begin to represent the world with words, images, and drawings. They form stable concepts and begin to reason. At the same time, the young child's cognitive world is dominated by egocentrism and magical beliefs.

Because Piaget called this stage "preoperational," it might sound like an unimportant waiting period. Not so. However, the label *preoperational* emphasizes that the child does not yet perform **operations,** which are reversible mental actions that allow children to do mentally what before they could do only physically. Mentally adding and subtracting numbers are examples of operations. *Preoperational thought* is the beginning of the ability to reconstruct in thought what has been established in behavior. The preoperational stage can be divided into two substages: the symbolic function substage and the intuitive thought substage.

The Symbolic Function Substage   The **symbolic function substage** is the first substage of preoperational thought, occurring roughly between the ages of 2 and 4. In this substage, the young child gains the ability to mentally represent an object that is not present. This ability vastly expands the child's mental world (Callaghan, 2013; DeLoache, 2011; Lillard & Kavanaugh, 2014). Young children use scribble designs to represent people, houses, cars, clouds, and so on; they begin to use language and engage in pretend play. However, although young children make distinct progress during this substage, their thought still has important limitations, two of which are egocentrism and animism.

Egocentrism is the inability to distinguish between one's own perspective and someone else's perspective. Piaget and Barbel Inhelder (1969) initially studied young children's egocentrism by devising the three mountains task (see Figure 1). The child walks around the model of the mountains and becomes familiar with what the mountains look like from different perspectives and can see that there are different objects on the mountains. The child is then seated on one side of the table on which the mountains are placed. The experimenter moves a doll to different locations around the table, at each location asking the child to select from a series of photos the one photo that most accurately reflects the view that the doll is seeing. Children in the preoperational stage often pick their own view rather than the doll's view. Preschool children frequently show the ability to take another's perspective on some tasks but not others.

---→

developmental connection

Cognitive Development

Object permanence is an important accomplishment during the sensorimotor stage. Connect to "Cognitive Development in Infancy."

←---

preoperational stage Piaget's second stage, lasting from 2 to 7 years of age, when children begin to represent the world with words, images, and drawings. In this stage, they also form stable concepts and begin to reason. At the same time, their cognitive world is dominated by egocentrism and magical beliefs.

operations In Piaget's theory, reversible mental actions that allow children to do mentally what they formerly did physically.

symbolic function substage Piaget's first substage of preoperational thought, in which the child gains the ability to mentally represent an object that is not present (occurs roughly between 2 and 4 years of age).

egocentrism Piaget's concept that describes the inability to distinguish between one's own perspective and someone else's perspective.

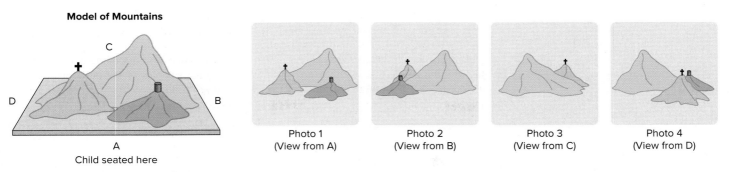

Model of Mountains

C

D   B

A
Child seated here

| Photo 1 (View from A) | Photo 2 (View from B) | Photo 3 (View from C) | Photo 4 (View from D) |

FIGURE **1**

THE THREE MOUNTAINS TASK. The mountain model on the far left shows the child's perspective from view A, where he or she is sitting. The four squares represent photos showing the mountains from four different viewpoints of the model—A, B, C, and D. The experimenter asks the child to identify the photo in which the mountains look as they would from position B. To identify the photo correctly, the child has to take the perspective of a person sitting at spot B. Invariably, a child who thinks in a preoperational way cannot perform this task. When asked what a view of the mountains looks like from position B, the child selects Photo 1, taken from location A (the child's own view at the time) instead of Photo 2, the correct view.

Animism, another limitation of preoperational thought, is the belief that inanimate objects have lifelike qualities and are capable of action. A young child might show animism by saying, "That tree pushed the leaf off, and it fell down" or "The sidewalk made me mad; it made me fall down." A young child who uses animism fails to distinguish the appropriate occasions for using human and nonhuman perspectives (Opfer & Gelman, 2011).

Possibly because young children are not very concerned about reality, their drawings are fanciful and inventive. Suns might be blue, skies green, and cars shown floating on clouds in their symbolic, imaginative world. One 3½-year-old looked at a scribble he had just drawn and described it as a pelican kissing a seal (see Figure 2a). The symbolism is simple but strong, like abstractions found in some modern art. Twentieth-century Spanish artist Pablo Picasso commented, "I used to draw like Raphael but it has taken me a lifetime to draw like young children." During the elementary school years, a child's drawings become more realistic, neat, and precise (see Figure 2b). Suns are orange, skies are blue, and cars travel on roads (Winner, 1986).

The Intuitive Thought Substage

The **intuitive thought substage** is the second substage of preoperational thought, occurring between approximately 4 and 7 years of age. During this substage, children begin to use primitive reasoning and want to know the answers to all sorts of questions. Consider 4-year-old Tommy, who is at the beginning of the intuitive thought substage. Although he is starting to develop his own ideas about the world he lives in, his ideas are still simple, and he is not very good at thinking things out. He has difficulty understanding events that he knows are taking place but that he cannot see. His fantasized thoughts bear little resemblance to reality. He cannot yet answer the question "What if?" in any reliable way. For example, he has only a vague idea of what would happen if a car were

animism The belief that inanimate objects have lifelike qualities and are capable of action.

intuitive thought substage Piaget's second substage of preoperational thought, in which children begin to use primitive reasoning and want to know the answers to all sorts of questions (occurs between about 4 and 7 years of age).

FIGURE **2**

THE SYMBOLIC DRAWING OF YOUNG CHILDREN. (*a*) A 3½-year-old's symbolic drawing. Halfway into his drawing, the 3½-year-old artist said it was a "pelican kissing a seal." (*b*) This 11-year-old's drawing is neater and more realistic but also less inventive.

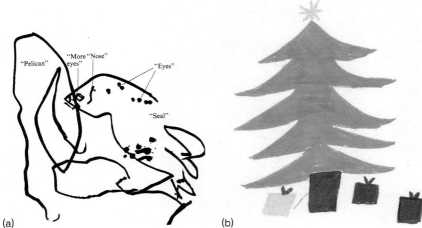

"Pelican"   "More eyes"   "Nose"   "Eyes"

"Seal"

(a)   (b)

to hit him. He also has difficulty negotiating traffic because he cannot do the mental calculations necessary to estimate whether an approaching car will hit him when he crosses the road.

By the age of 5, children have just about exhausted the adults around them with "why" questions. The child's questions signal the emergence of interest in reasoning and in figuring out why things are the way they are. Following are some samples of the questions children ask during the questioning period of 4 to 6 years of age (Elkind, 1976):

> What makes you grow up?
>
> Who was the mother when everybody was a baby?
>
> Why do leaves fall?
>
> Why does the sun shine?

Piaget called this substage *intuitive* because young children seem so sure about their knowledge and understanding yet are unaware of how they know what they know. That is, they know something but know it without the use of rational thinking.

Centration and the Limits of Preoperational Thought   One limitation of preoperational thought is **centration,** a centering of attention on one characteristic to the exclusion of all others. Centration is most clearly evidenced in young children's lack of **conservation,** the awareness that altering an object's or a substance's appearance does not change its basic properties. For example, to adults, it is obvious that a certain amount of liquid will have the same volume, regardless of a container's shape. But this is not at all obvious to young children. Instead, they are struck by the height of the liquid in the container; they focus on that characteristic to the exclusion of others.

The situation that Piaget devised to study conservation is his most famous task. In the conservation task, children are presented with two identical beakers, each filled to the same level with liquid (see Figure 3). They are asked if these beakers have the same amount of liquid, and they usually say yes. Next, the liquid from one beaker is poured into a third beaker, which is taller and thinner than the first two. Then, the children are asked if the amount of liquid in the tall, thin beaker is equal to that which remains in one of the original beakers. Children who are less than 7 or 8 years old usually say no and justify their answers in terms of the differing height or width of the beakers. Older children usually answer yes and justify their answers appropriately ("If you poured the water back, the amount would still be the same").

In Piaget's theory, failing the conservation-of-liquid task is a sign that children are at the preoperational stage of cognitive development. The failure demonstrates not only centration but also an inability to mentally reverse actions. For example, in the conservation-of-matter example shown in Figure 4, preoperational children say that the longer shape has more clay because they assume that "longer is more." Preoperational children cannot mentally reverse

centration The focusing of attention on one characteristic to the exclusion of all others.

conservation The concept that an object's or substance's basic properties stay the same even if its appearance has been altered.

FIGURE **3**

PIAGET'S CONSERVATION TASK. The beaker task is a well-known Piagetian task to determine whether a child can think operationally—that is, can mentally reverse actions and show conservation of the substance. (*a*) Two identical beakers are presented to the child. Then the experimenter pours the liquid from B into C, which is taller and thinner than A or B. (*b*) The child is asked if these beakers (A and C) have the same amount of liquid. The preoperational child says "no." When asked to point to the beaker that has more liquid, the preoperational child points to the tall, thin beaker.

©Tony Freeman/PhotoEdit

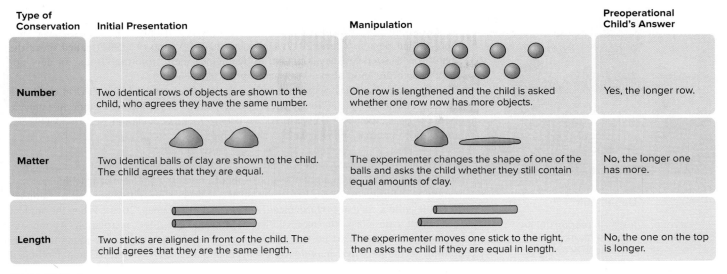

Type of Conservation	Initial Presentation	Manipulation	Preoperational Child's Answer
Number	Two identical rows of objects are shown to the child, who agrees they have the same number.	One row is lengthened and the child is asked whether one row now has more objects.	Yes, the longer row.
Matter	Two identical balls of clay are shown to the child. The child agrees that they are equal.	The experimenter changes the shape of one of the balls and asks the child whether they still contain equal amounts of clay.	No, the longer one has more.
Length	Two sticks are aligned in front of the child. The child agrees that they are the same length.	The experimenter moves one stick to the right, then asks the child if they are equal in length.	No, the one on the top is longer.

FIGURE 4

SOME DIMENSIONS OF CONSERVATION: NUMBER, MATTER, AND LENGTH. *What characteristics of preoperational thought do children demonstrate when they fail these conservation tasks?*

the clay-rolling process to see that the amount of clay is the same in both the shorter ball shape and the longer stick shape. A recent fMRI brain imaging study of conservation of number revealed that advances in a network in the parietal and frontal lobes were linked to 9- and 10-year-olds' conservation success compared with non-conserving 5- and 6-year-olds (Houde & others, 2011).

Some developmentalists disagree with Piaget's estimate of when children's conservation skills emerge (Byrnes, 2008). For example, Rochel Gelman (1969) showed that when the child's attention to relevant aspects of the conservation task is improved, the child is more likely to conserve. Gelman has also demonstrated that attentional training on one dimension, such as number, improves the preschool child's performance on another dimension, such as mass. Thus, Gelman argues that conservation appears earlier than Piaget thought and that attention is especially important in explaining conservation.

VYGOTSKY'S THEORY

Piaget's theory is a major developmental theory. Another developmental theory that focuses on children's cognition is Lev Vygotsky's theory. Like Piaget, Vygotsky (1896–1934) emphasized that children actively construct their knowledge and understanding. In Piaget's theory, children develop ways of thinking and understanding by their actions and interactions with the physical world. In Vygotsky's theory, children are more often described as social creatures than in Piaget's theory (Moura da Costa & Tuleski, 2017; Yasnitsky & Van der Veer, 2016; Yu & Hu, 2017). They develop their ways of thinking and understanding primarily through social interaction (Clara, 2017; Roth, 2016). Their cognitive development depends on the tools provided by society, and their minds are shaped by the cultural context in which they live (Daniels, 2017; Yasnitsky & Van der Veer, 2016). Let's take a closer look at Vygotsky's ideas about how children learn and his view of the role of language in cognitive development.

The Zone of Proximal Development Vygotsky's (1962) belief in the impact of social influences, especially instruction, on children's cognitive development is reflected in his concept of the zone of proximal development. **Zone of proximal development (ZPD)** is Vygotsky's term for the range of tasks that are too difficult for the child to master alone but that can be learned with guidance and assistance of adults or more-skilled children. Thus, the lower limit of the ZPD is the level of skill reached by the child working independently. The upper limit is the level of additional responsibility the child can accept with the assistance

How Would You...?

If you were an **educator,** how would you apply Vygotsky's concept of the zone of proximal development and the concept of scaffolding to help a young child complete a puzzle?

zone of proximal development (ZPD)
Vygotsky's term for the range of tasks that are too difficult for children to achieve alone but can be achieved with the guidance and assistance of adults or more-skilled children.

Upper limit

Level of additional responsibility
child can accept with assistance
of an able instructor

**Zone of proximal
development (ZPD)**

Lower limit

Level of problem solving
reached on these tasks by
child working alone

FIGURE 5

**VYGOTSKY'S ZONE OF PROXIMAL
DEVELOPMENT.** Vygotsky's zone of
proximal development has a lower limit and
an upper limit. Tasks in the ZPD are too
difficult for the child to perform alone. They
require assistance from an adult or a
more-skilled child. As children experience the
verbal instruction or demonstration, they
organize the information in their existing
mental structures so that they can eventually
perform the skill or task alone.

©Ariel Skelley/Blend Images RF

developmental **connection**

Parenting

Scaffolding also is an important strategy for parents to adopt in interacting
with their infants. Connect to "Socioemotional Development in Infancy."

scaffolding In regard to cognitive development,
Vygotsky used this term to describe the
changing level of support provided over the
course of a teaching session, with the more-
skilled person adjusting guidance to fit the
child's current performance level.

of an able instructor (see Figure 5). The ZPD captures the child's cognitive skills that are in the process of maturing and can be accomplished only with the assistance of a more-skilled person (Clara, 2017; Holzman, 2016). Vygotsky (1962) called these the "buds" or "flowers" of development, to distinguish them from the "fruits" of development, which the child already can accomplish independently.

What are some factors that can influence the effectiveness of the ZPD in children's learning and development? Researchers have found that the following factors can enhance the ZPD's effectiveness (Gauvain, 2013): better emotion regulation, secure attachment, absence of maternal depression, and child compliance.

Scaffolding   Closely linked to the idea of the ZPD is the concept of scaffolding. **Scaffolding** means changing the level of support. Over the course of a teaching session, a more-skilled person (a teacher or an advanced peer) adjusts the amount of guidance to fit the child's current performance (Daniels, 2017; Holzman, 2016). When the student is learning a new task, the more-skilled person may use direct instruction. As the student's competence increases, the person gives less guidance. One study found that scaffolding techniques that heightened engagement, directed exploration, and facilitated "sense-making," such as guided play, improved 4- to 5-year-old children's acquisition of geometric knowledge (Fisher & others, 2013).

Language and Thought   According to Vygotsky, children use speech not only for social communication but also to help in solving problems. Vygotsky (1962) further argued that young children use language to plan, guide, and monitor their behavior. This use of language for self-regulation is called *private speech*. For Piaget, private speech is egocentric and immature—but for Vygotsky, it is an important tool of thought during the early childhood years (Alderson-Day & Fernyhough, 2014; Lantolf, 2017).

Vygotsky said that language and thought initially develop independently of each other and then merge. He emphasized that all mental functions have external, or social, origins. Children must use language to communicate with others before they can focus inward on their own thoughts. Children also must communicate externally and use language for a long period of time before they can make the transition from external to internal speech. This transition period occurs between 3 and 7 years of age and involves talking to oneself. After a while, the self-talk becomes second nature to children, and they can act without verbalizing. At this point, children have internalized their egocentric speech in the form of *inner speech,* which becomes their thoughts.

Vygotsky maintained that children who use a lot of private speech are more socially competent than those who don't. He argued that private speech represents an early transition in becoming more socially communicative. For Vygotsky, when young children talk to themselves, they are using language to govern their behavior and guide themselves. For example, a child working on a puzzle might say to herself, "Which pieces should I put together first? I'll try those green ones first. Now I need some blue ones. No, that blue one doesn't fit there. I'll try it over here."

Researchers have found support for Vygotsky's view that private speech plays a positive role in children's development (Winsler, Carlton, & Barry, 2000). Researchers have found that children use private speech more when tasks are difficult, after they have made an error, and when they are not sure how to proceed (Berk, 1994). They also have discovered that children who use private speech are more attentive and improve their performance more than children who do not use private speech (Berk & Spuhl, 1995).

Teaching Strategies   Vygotsky's theory has been embraced by many teachers and has been successfully applied to education (Adams, 2015; Clara, 2017; Gauvain & Perez, 2015; Holzman, 2016). Here are some ways Vygotsky's theory can be incorporated in classrooms:

- *Assess the child's ZPD.* Like Piaget, Vygotsky did not hold that formal, standardized tests are the best way to assess children's learning. Rather, Vygotsky argued that assessment should focus on determining the child's zone of proximal development. The skilled helper presents the child with tasks of varying difficulty to determine the best level at which to begin instruction.

- *Use the child's ZPD in teaching.* Teaching should begin toward the zone's upper limit, so that the child can reach the goal with help and move to a higher level of skill and knowledge. Offer just enough assistance. You might ask, "What can I do to help you?" Or simply observe the child's intentions and attempts and provide support when needed. When the child hesitates, offer encouragement. And encourage the child to practice the skill. You may watch and appreciate the child's practice or offer support when the child forgets what to do.

- *Use more-skilled peers as teachers.* Remember that it is not just adults who are important in helping children learn. Children also benefit from the support and guidance of more-skilled children.

- Monitor and encourage children's use of private speech. Be aware of the developmental change from externally talking to oneself when solving a problem during the preschool years to privately talking to oneself in the early elementary school years. In the elementary school years, encourage children to internalize and self-regulate their talk to themselves.

- *Place instruction in a meaningful context.* Educators today are moving away from abstract presentations of material and instead are providing students with opportunities to experience learning in real-world settings. For example, instead of just memorizing math formulas, students work on math problems with real-world implications.

- *Transform the classroom with Vygotskian ideas.* What does a Vygotskian classroom look like? The Kamehameha Elementary Education Program (KEEP) is based on Vygotsky's theory (Tharp, 1994). The ZPD is the key element of instruction in this program. Children might read a story and then interpret its meaning. Many of the learning activities take place in small groups. All children spend at least 20 minutes each morning in a setting called "Center One." In this context, scaffolding is used to improve children's literacy skills. The instructor asks questions, responds to students' queries, and builds on the ideas that students generate. Thousands of children from low-income families have attended KEEP public schools—in Hawaii, on an Arizona Navajo reservation, and in Los Angeles. Compared with a control group of non-KEEP children, the KEEP children participated more actively in classroom discussion, were more attentive in class, and had higher reading achievement (Tharp & Gallimore, 1988).

The *Caring Connections* interlude further explores the implications of Vygotsky's theory for children's education.

Lev Vygotsky (1896–1934), shown here with his daughter, reasoned that children's cognitive development is advanced through social interaction with more-skilled individuals embedded in a sociocultural backdrop. *How is Vygotsky's theory different from Piaget's?*
Courtesy of James V. Wertsch, Washington University

Evaluating Vygotsky's Theory   Even though their theories were proposed at about the same time, most of the world learned about Vygotsky's theory later than they learned about Piaget's theory, so Vygotsky's theory has not yet been evaluated as thoroughly. Vygotsky's view of the importance of sociocultural influences on children's development fits with the current belief that it is important to evaluate the contextual factors in learning (Gauvain, 2013, 2016).

We already have compared certain aspects of Vygotsky's and Piaget's theories, such as Vygotsky's emphasis on the importance of inner speech in development and Piaget's view that such speech is immature. Although both theories are constructivist, Vygotsky's is a **social constructivist approach,** which emphasizes the social contexts of learning and the construction of knowledge through social interaction (Clara, 2017; Muller Mirza, 2016; Yasnitsky & Van Der Veer, 2016; Yu & Hu, 2017).

In moving from Piaget to Vygotsky, the conceptual shift is from the individual to collaboration, social interaction, and sociocultural activity (Gauvain, 2016). The endpoint of cognitive development for Piaget is formal operational thought. For Vygotsky, the endpoint can differ depending on which skills are considered to be the most important in a particular culture (Clara, 2017). For Piaget, children construct knowledge by transforming, organizing, and reorganizing previous knowledge. For Vygotsky, children construct knowledge through social interaction (Daniels, 2017; Yasnitsky & Van Der Veer, 2016). The implication of Piaget's theory for teaching is that children need support to explore their world and discover knowledge. The main implication of Vygotsky's theory for teaching is that students need many opportunities to learn with the teacher and more-skilled peers. In both Piaget's and Vygotsky's theories, teachers serve as facilitators and guides, rather than as directors and molders of learning. Figure 7 compares Vygotsky's and Piaget's theories.

Criticisms of Vygotsky's theory also have surfaced (Karpov, 2006). Some critics point out that Vygotsky was not specific enough about age-related changes (Goncu & Gauvain, 2011). Another criticism claims that Vygotsky did not adequately describe how changes in socioemotional capabilities contribute to cognitive development. Yet another criticism is that he overemphasized the role of language in thinking. Also, his emphasis on collaboration and

social constructivist approach An approach that emphasizes the social contexts of learning and the fact that knowledge is mutually built and constructed; Vygotsky's theory is a social constructivist approach.

Tools of the Mind

Tools of the Mind is an early childhood education curriculum that emphasizes children's development of self-regulation and the cognitive foundations of literacy (Hyson, Copple, & Jones, 2006). The curriculum was created by Elena Bodrova and Deborah Leong (2007, 2015) and has been implemented in more than 200 classrooms. Most of the children in the Tools of the Mind programs are at risk because of their living circumstances, which in many instances involve poverty and other difficult conditions such as being homeless and having parents with drug problems.

Tools of the Mind is grounded in Vygotsky's (1962) theory, with special attention given to cultural tools and self-regulation, the zone of proximal development, scaffolding, private speech, shared activity, and the importance of play. In a Tools of the Mind classroom, dramatic play has a central role. Teachers guide children in creating themes that are based on the children's interests, such as treasure hunt, store, hospital, and restaurant. Teachers also incorporate field trips, visitor presentations, videos, and books in the development of children's play. They help children develop a play plan, which increases the maturity of their play. Play plans describe what the children expect to do in the play period, including the imaginary context, roles, and props to be used. The play plans increase the quality of their play and self-regulation.

Scaffolding writing is another important theme in the Tools of the Mind classroom. Teachers guide children in planning their own message by drawing a line to stand for each word the child says. Children then repeat the message, pointing to each line as they say the word. Then, the child writes on the lines, trying to represent each word with some letters or symbols. Figure 6 shows how the scaffolding writing process improved a 5-year-old child's writing over the course of two months.

Research assessments of children's writing in Tools of the Mind classrooms revealed more advanced writing skills than those of children in other early childhood programs (Bodrova & Leong, 2007, 2015) (see Figure 6). For example, children in these classrooms write more complex messages, use more words, spell more accurately, show better letter recognition, and have a better understanding of the concept of a sentence.

The effectiveness of the Tools of the Mind approach was examined in 29 schools, 79 classrooms, and 759 schools (Blair & Raver, 2014). Positive effects of the Tools of the Mind program were found for the cognitive processes of executive function (improved self-regulation, for example) and attention control. Further, the Tools of the Mind program improved children's reading, vocabulary, and mathematics at the end of kindergarten and into the first grade. The most significant improvements occurred in students living in high-poverty areas.

(a) Five-year-old Aaron's independent journal writing prior to using the scaffolding writing technique.

(b) Aaron's journal two months after using the scaffolding writing technique.

FIGURE 6

WRITING PROGRESS OF A 5-YEAR-OLD BOY OVER TWO MONTHS USING THE SCAFFOLDING WRITING PROCESS IN TOOLS OF THE MIND.

Leong, Deborah J., & Bodrova, Elena. "Tools of the Mind." Copyright ©2007 by Deborah J. Leong and Elena Bodrova. All rights reserved. Used with permission.

	Vygotsky	Piaget
Sociocultural Context	Strong emphasis	Little emphasis
Constructivism	Social constructivist	Cognitive constructivist
Stages	No general stages of development proposed	Strong emphasis on stages (sensorimotor, preoperational, concrete operational, and formal operational)
Key Processes	Zone of proximal development, language, dialogue, tools of the culture	Schema, assimilation, accommodation, operations, conservation, classification
Role of Language	A major role; language plays a powerful role in shaping thought	Language has a minimal role; cognition primarily directs language
View on Education	Education plays a central role, helping children learn the tools of the culture	Education merely refines the child's cognitive skills that have already emerged
Teaching Implications	Teacher is a facilitator and guide, not a director; establish many opportunities for children to learn with the teacher and more-skilled peers	Also views teacher as a facilitator and guide, not a director; provide support for children to explore their world and discover knowledge

FIGURE 7

COMPARISON OF VYGOTSKY'S AND PIAGET'S THEORIES

(*Left*) ©A.R. Lauria/Dr. Michael Cole, Library of Human Cognition, UCSD; (*right*) ©Bettmann/Getty Images

guidance has potential pitfalls. Might facilitators be too helpful in some cases, as when a parent becomes too overbearing and controlling? Further, some children might become lazy and expect help when they could have done something on their own.

INFORMATION PROCESSING

Piaget's and Vygotsky's theories provided important ideas about how young children think and how their thinking changes. More recently, the information-processing approach has generated research that illuminates how children process information during the preschool years (Siegler, 2016a, b; Siegler & Braithwaite, 2017). What are the limitations and advances in young children's ability to pay attention to the environment, to remember, to develop strategies and solve problems, and to understand their own mental processes and those of others?

Attention   Recall that attention was defined as the focusing of mental resources on select information. The child's ability to pay attention improves significantly during the preschool years (Rothbart & Posner, 2015; Wu & Scerif, 2017). Toddlers wander around, shift attention from one activity to another, and seem to spend little time focused on any one object or event. By comparison, the preschool child might be observed watching television for a half hour. One study videotaped young children in their homes (Anderson & others, 1985). In 99 families who were observed for 4,672 hours, visual attention to television dramatically increased during the preschool years. However, a recent research study revealed that television watching and video game playing were both linked to attention problems in children (Swing & others, 2010).

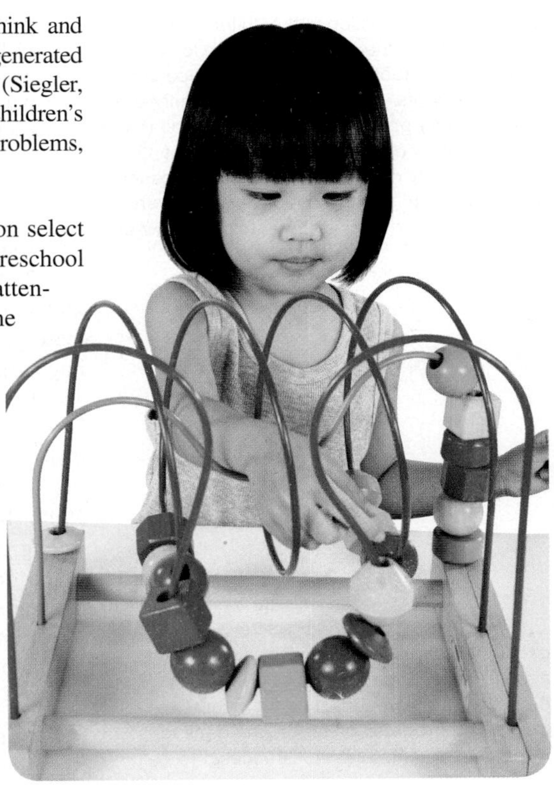

Young children especially make advances in two aspects of attention—executive attention and sustained attention (Rothbart & Posner, 2015). **Executive attention** involves planning actions, allocating attention to goals, detecting and compensating for errors, monitoring progress on tasks, and dealing with novel or difficult circumstances. **Sustained attention** is focused and extended engagement with an object, task, event, or other aspect of the environment. Sustained attention also is referred to as *vigilance* (Benitez & others, 2017). One study found a considerable increase from 2½ to 3½ years of age in the ability to sustain attention and then regain attention after being distracted (Danis & others, 2008). In this study, children showed more consistent control of their attention after 4½ years of age. Research indicates that although older children and adolescents show increases in vigilance, it is during the preschool years that individuals show the greatest increase in

What are some advances in children's attention in early childhood?

©kiankhoon/Getty Images RF

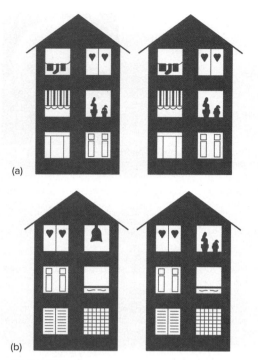

(a)

(b)

FIGURE 8

THE PLANFULNESS OF ATTENTION. In one study, children were given pairs of houses to examine, like the ones shown here (Vurpillot, 1968). For three pairs of houses, what was in the windows was identical (*a*). For the other three pairs, the windows had different items in them (*b*). By filming the reflection in the children's eyes, it could be determined what they were looking at, how long they looked, and the sequence of their eye movements. Children under 6 examined only a fragmentary portion of each display and made their judgment on the basis of insufficient information. By contrast, older children scanned the windows in more detailed ways and were more accurate in their judgments of which were identical.

executive attention Involves planning actions, allocating attention to goals, detecting and compensating for errors, monitoring progress on tasks, and dealing with novel or difficult circumstances.

sustained attention Focused and extended engagement with an object, task, event, or other aspect of the environment.

vigilance (Rothbart & Posner, 2015). A recent study found that preschoolers' sustained attention was linked to a greater likelihood of completing college by 25 years of age (McClelland & others, 2013).

Mary Rothbart and Maria Gartstein (2008, p. 332) recently described why advances in executive and sustained attention are so important in early childhood:

> The development of the . . . executive attention system supports the rapid increases in effortful control in the toddler and preschool years. Increases in attention are due, in part, to advances in comprehension and language development. As children are better able to understand their environment, this increased appreciation of their surroundings helps them to sustain attention for longer periods of time.

In at least two ways, however, the preschool child's control of attention is still deficient:

- *Salient versus relevant dimensions.* Preschool children are likely to pay attention to stimuli that stand out, or are salient, even when those stimuli are not relevant to solving a problem or performing a task. For example, if a flashy, attractive clown presents the directions for solving a problem, preschool children are likely to pay more attention to the clown than to the directions. After the age of 6 or 7, children attend more efficiently to the dimensions of the task that are relevant, such as the directions for solving a problem. This change reflects a shift to cognitive control of attention, so that children behave less impulsively and reflect more.

- *Planfulness.* Although in general young children's planning improves as part of advances in executive attention, when experimenters ask children to judge whether two complex pictures are the same, preschool children tend to use a haphazard comparison strategy, not examining all of the details before making a judgment. By comparison, elementary-school-age children are more likely to systematically compare the details across the pictures, one detail at a time (Vurpillot, 1968) (see Figure 8).

In Central European countries, such as Hungary, kindergarten children participate in exercises designed to improve their attention (Mills & Mills, 2000; Posner & Rothbart, 2007). For example, in one eye-contact exercise, the teacher sits in the center of a circle of children, and each child is required to catch the teacher's eye before being permitted to leave the group. In other exercises created to improve attention, teachers have children participate in stop-go activities during which they have to listen for a specific signal, such as a drumbeat or an exact number of rhythmic beats, before stopping the activity.

Computer exercises also recently have been developed to improve children's attention (Rothbart & Posner, 2015). For example, one study revealed that five days of computer exercises that involved learning how to use a joystick, working memory, and the resolution of conflict improved the attention of 4- to 6-year-old children (Rueda, Posner, & Rothbart, 2005). In one of the computer games, young children have to move a joystick to keep a cat on the grass and out of the mud, and in another they help a cat find a duck in a pond. Although these games are not commercially available, further information about computer exercises for improving children's attention can be found at www.teach-the-brain.org/learn/attention/index.

Preschool children's ability to control and sustain their attention is related to school readiness (Rothbart & Posner, 2015). For example, a study of more than 1,000 children revealed that their ability to sustain their attention at 54 months of age was linked to their school readiness (which included achievement and language skills) (NICHD Early Child Care Research Network, 2005). In another study, children whose parents and teachers rated them higher on a scale of having attention problems at 54 months of age had a lower level of social skills in peer relations in the first and third grades than did their counterparts who were rated lower on the attention problems scale at 54 months of age (NICHD Early Child Care Research Network, 2009). And in yet another study, the ability to focus attention better at age 5 was linked to a higher level of school achievement at age 9 (Razza, Martin, & Brooks-Gunn, 2012).

Memory *Memory*—the retention of information over time—is a central process in children's cognitive development. During infancy, memories are often fragile and, for the most part, short-lived—except for the memory of perceptual-motor actions, which can be substantial (Bauer & Larkina, 2016). In the chapter on "Cognitive Development in Infancy," we noted that in discussing an individual's capacity to remember, it is important to distinguish *implicit memory* from *explicit memory.* Implicit memory refers to memory without conscious recollection, while explicit memory refers to the conscious recollection of facts and experiences.

Explicit memory itself comes in many forms (Radvansky, 2017). One distinction occurs between relatively permanent retention, or *long-term memory,* and *short-term memory.*

Short-Term Memory   In **short-term memory,** individuals retain information for up to 30 seconds if there is no rehearsal of the information. By using rehearsal (repeating information after it has been presented), we can keep information in short-term memory for a much longer period. One method of assessing short-term memory is the memory-span task. You hear a short list of stimuli—usually digits—presented at a rapid pace (one per second, for example). Then you are asked to repeat the digits.

Research with the memory-span task suggests that short-term memory increases during early childhood (Schneider, 2011). For example, in one investigation, memory span increased from about 2 digits in 2- to 3-year-old children to about 5 digits in 7-year-old children, yet between 7 and 13 years of age memory span increased only by 1½ digits (Dempster, 1981) (see Figure 9). Keep in mind, though, that memory span varies from one individual to another.

Why does memory span change with age? Rehearsal of information is important; older children rehearse the digits more than younger children do. Speed and efficiency of processing information are important, too, especially the speed with which memorized items can be identified (Schneider, 2011). The speed-of-processing explanation highlights a key point in the information-processing perspective: The speed with which a child processes information is an important aspect of the child's cognitive abilities, and there is abundant evidence that the speed with which many cognitive tasks are completed improves dramatically across the childhood years (Rose, Feldman, & Jankowski, 2015). A recent study found that myelination (the process by which the sheath that encases axons helps electrical signals travel faster down the axon) in a number of brain areas was linked to young children's processing speed (Chevalier & others, 2015).

How Accurate Are Young Children's Long-Term Memories?   In contrast with short-term memory, *long-term memory* is relatively permanent type of memory that stores huge amounts of information for a long time. Sometimes the long-term memories of preschoolers may seem erratic, but young children can remember a great deal of information if they are given appropriate cues and prompts. One area in which children's long-term memory is being examined extensively relates to whether young children should be allowed to testify in court (Andrews & Lamb, 2017; Bruck & Ceci, 2012; Melinder & others, 2016). This is especially important if a child is the sole witness to abuse, a crime, and so forth (Lamb & others, 2015). Several factors can influence the accuracy of a young child's memory (Bruck & Ceci, 1999):

- *There are age differences in children's susceptibility to suggestion.* Preschoolers are the most suggestible age group in comparison with older children and adults (Andrews & Lamb, 2017; Ceci, Papierno, & Kulkofsky, 2007). For example, preschool children are more susceptible to retaining misleading or incorrect post-event information (Ghetti & Alexander, 2004). Despite these age differences, there is still concern about the accuracy of older children's recollections when they are subjected to suggestive interviews (Brown & Lamb, 2015).

- *There are individual differences in susceptibility.* Some preschoolers are highly resistant to interviewers' suggestions, whereas others immediately succumb to the slightest suggestion (Ceci, Hritz, & Royer, 2016). A research review concluded that suggestibility is linked to low self-concept, low support from parents, and mothers' insecure attachment in romantic relationships (Bruck & Melnyk, 2004).

- *Interviewing techniques can produce substantial distortions in children's reports about highly salient events.* Children are suggestible not just regarding peripheral details but also about the central aspects of an event (Bruck & Ceci, 2012). Nonetheless, young children are capable of recalling much that is relevant about an event (Lamb & others, 2015). When children do accurately recall an event, the interviewer often has a neutral tone, there is limited use of misleading questions, and there is an absence of any motivation for the child to make a false report (Andrews & Lamb, 2017).

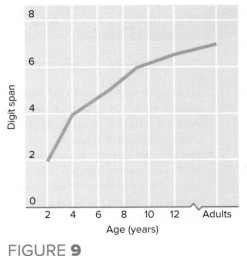

FIGURE 9

DEVELOPMENTAL CHANGES IN MEMORY SPAN. In one study, from 2 years of age to 7 years of age children's memory span increased about 2 digits to 5 digits (Dempster, 1981). By 12 years of age, memory span had increased on average only another 1½ digits, to 6½ digits. *What factors might contribute to the increase in memory span during childhood?*

short-term memory The memory component in which individuals retain information for up to 30 seconds, assuming there is no rehearsal.

Can Parents Suggest False Events to Children?

As described in Bruck and Ceci (1999, pp. 429–430), a study by Deborah Poole and D. Stephen Lindsay revealed how parents can subtly influence their young children's memories of events. Preschool children participated in four activities (such as lifting cans with pulleys) with "Mr. Science" in a university laboratory (Poole & Lindsay, 1995). Four months later, the children's parents were mailed a storybook with a description of their child's visit to see **Mr. Science**. The storybook described two of the activities in which the child had participated, but it also described two in which the child had not participated. Each description ended with this fabrication of what happened when it was time to leave the laboratory: "Mr. Science wiped (child's name) hands and face with a wet-wipe. The cloth got close to (child's name) mouth and tasted real yucky."

Parents read the descriptions to their children three times. Later, the children told the experimenter that they had participated in the activities that actually had only been mentioned in the descriptions read by their parents. For example, when asked whether **Mr. Science** had

put anything yucky in their mouth, more than half of the young children said that he had. Subsequently, when asked whether **Mr. Science** put something in their mouth or their parent just read this to them in a story, 71 percent of the young children said that it really happened.

This study shows how subtle suggestions can influence children's inaccurate reporting of nonevents. If such inaccurate reports are pursued in follow-up questioning by an interviewer who suspected that something sexual occurred, the result could be a sexual interpretation. This study also revealed the difficulty preschool children have in identifying the source of a suggestion (called *source-monitoring errors*). Children in this study confused their parent's reading the suggestion to them with their experience of the suggestion.

How might researchers expand on this study to test the influence of other adults on children's memories? Do you think any ethical issues would arise in such research?

Can false memories be induced in children? See the *Connecting with Research* interlude to read about a study that addresses this question.

In sum, whether a young child's eyewitness testimony is accurate or not may depend on a number of factors such as the type, number, and intensity of the suggestive techniques the child has experienced (Andrews & Lamb, 2017; Lamb & others, 2015). It appears that the reliability of young children's reports has as much to do with the skills and motivation of the interviewer as with any natural limitations on young children's memory (Ceci, Hritz, & Royer, 2016).

Autobiographical Memory   Another aspect of long-term memory that has been extensively studied in children's development is autobiographical memory (Pathman & St. Jacques, 2014; Valentino & others, 2014). *Autobiographical memory* involves memory of significant events and experiences in one's life. You are engaging in autobiographical memory when you answer questions such as: Who was your first grade teacher and what was s/he like? What is the most traumatic event that happened to you as a child?

During the preschool years, young children's memories increasingly take on more autobiographical characteristics (Bauer, 2013; Bauer & Fivush, 2014; Bauer & Larkina, 2016). In some areas, such as remembering a story, a movie, a song, or an interesting event or experience, young children have been shown to have reasonably good memories. From 3 to 5 years of age, they (1) increasingly remember events as occurring at a specific time and location, such as "on my birthday at Chuck E. Cheese's last year" and (2) include more elements that are rich in detail in their narratives (Bauer, 2013). In one study, children went from using four descriptive items per event at 3½ years of age to 12 such items at 6 years of age (Fivush & Haden, 1997).

Executive Function   Recently, increasing interest has been directed toward the development of children's **executive function,** an umbrella-like concept that consists of a number of higher-level cognitive processes linked to the development of the brain's prefrontal cortex (Bardikoff & Sabbagh, 2017; Knapp & Morton, 2017; McClelland & others, 2017; Perone, Almy & Zelazo, 2017). Executive function involves managing one's thoughts to engage in goal-directed behavior and exercise self-control (Hoskyn, Iarocci, & Young, 2017; McClelland & Tominey, 2015; Muller & others, 2017). Earlier in this chapter, we described the recent interest in *executive attention,* which comes under the umbrella of executive function.

executive function An umbrella-like concept that consists of a number of higher-level cognitive processes linked to the development of the brain's prefrontal cortex. Executive function involves managing one's thoughts to engage in goal-directed behavior and exercise self-control.

In early childhood, executive function especially involves developmental advances in cognitive inhibition (such as inhibiting a strong tendency that is incorrect), cognitive flexibility (such as shifting attention to another item or topic), goal-setting (such as sharing a toy or mastering a skill like catching a ball), and delay of gratification (waiting longer to get a more attractive reward, for example) (Cassidy, 2016; Groppe & Elsner, 2017; Moriguchi, Chevalier, & Zelazo, 2016; Semenov & Zelazo, 2017). During early childhood, the relatively stimulus-driven toddler is transformed into a child capable of flexible, goal-directed problem solving that characterizes executive function (Zelazo & Muller, 2011). Walter Mischel and his colleagues (Berman & others, 2013; Mischel, Cantor, & Feldman, 1996; Mischel & Moore, 1980; Mischel & others, 2011; Schlam & others, 2013) have conducted a number of studies of delay of gratification with young children. One way they assess delay of gratification is to place a young child alone in a room with an alluring cookie that is within their reach. The children are told that they can either ring a bell at any time and eat the cookie or wait until the experimenter returns and then get two cookies. When young children waited for the experimenter to return, what did they do to help them wait? They engaged in a number of strategies to distract their attention from the cookies, including singing songs, picking their noses, or doing something else to keep from looking at the cookies. Mischel and his colleagues labeled these strategies "cool thoughts" (that is, doing non-cookie-related thoughts and activities), whereas they labeled what young children were doing when they looked at the cookie as engaging in "hot thoughts." The young children who engaged in cool thoughts were more likely to eat the cookie later or wait until the experimenter returned to the room. In one study using the delay of gratification task just described, longer delay of gratification at 4 years of age was linked to a lower body mass index (BMI) three decades later (Schlam & others, 2013).

How did Walter Mischel and his colleagues study young children's delay of gratification? In their research, what later developmental outcomes were linked to the preschoolers' ability to delay gratification?
©Amy Kiley Photography

Stephanie Carlson and her colleagues (2010, 2011; Carlson, Claxton, & Moses, 2015; Carlson & White, 2013; Carlson, White, & Davis-Unger, 2014; Prager, Sera, & Carlson, 2016; White & Carlson, 2016; White & others, 2017) also have conducted a number of research studies on young children's executive function. In one study, Carlson and her colleagues (2005) gave young children a task called Less Is More, in which they are shown two trays of candy—one with five pieces, the other with two—and told that the tray they pick will be given to a stuffed animal seated at the table. Three-year-olds consistently selected the tray with the five pieces of candy, thus giving away more candy than they kept for themselves. However, 4-year-olds were far more likely to choose the tray with only two pieces of candy, keeping five pieces for themselves, and thus inhibiting their impulsiveness far better than the 3-year-olds did. In another study, young children were read either *Planet Opposite*—a fantasy book in which everything is turned upside down—or *Fun Town*—a reality-oriented fiction book (Carlson & White, 2011). After being read one of the books, the young children completed the Less Is More task. Sixty percent of the 3-year-olds who heard the *Planet Opposite* story chose the five pieces of candy compared with only 20 percent of their counterparts who heard the more straightforward story. The results indicated that learning about a topsy-turvy imaginary world likely helped the young children become more flexible in their thinking.

Researcher Stephanie Carlson administers the Less Is More task to a 4-year-old boy. *What were the results of Carlson's research?*
©Dawn Villella Photography

Researchers have found that advances in executive function during the preschool years are linked with math skills, language development, and school readiness (Blair, 2017; Hoskyn, Iarocci, & Young, 2017; Muller & others, 2017; Schmitt & others, 2017). A recent study revealed that executive function skills predicted mathematical gains in kindergarten (Fuhs & others, 2014). Another recent study of young children also revealed that executive function was associated with emergent literacy and vocabulary development (Becker & others, 2014). And a recent study found that young children who showed delayed development of executive function had a lower level of school readiness (Willoughby & others, 2017).

A longitudinal study of an important dimension of executive function—inhibitory control—found that 3- to 11-year-old children who had better inhibitory control (were more able to wait their turn, not as easily distracted, more persistent, and less impulsive) were more likely as adolescents to still be in school, less likely to engage in risk-taking behavior, and less likely to be taking drugs (Moffitt & others, 2011). Thirty years after they were initially assessed, the individuals with better inhibitory control had better physical and mental health (they were less likely to be overweight, for example), had better earnings in their career, were more law-abiding, and were happier (Moffitt, 2012; Moffitt & others, 2011).

What are some predictors of young children's executive function? Parenting practices are linked to children's development of executive function (Bernier & others, 2017; Carlson, Zelazo, & Faja, 2013; Cuevas & others, 2014; Diaz & McClelland, 2017; Monn & others,

Helen Hadani, Developmental Psychologist, Toy Designer, and Children's Museum Director

Helen Hadani obtained a Ph.D. from Stanford University in developmental psychology. As a graduate student at Stanford, she worked part-time for Hasbro Toys testing software and other computer products for young children. Her first job after graduate school was with Zowie Intertainment, which was subsequently bought by LEGO. In her work as a toy designer there, Helen conducted experiments and led focus groups at different stages of a toy's development, in addition to studying the age-effectiveness of the toy. In Helen's words, "Even in a toy's most primitive stage of development . . . you see children's creativity in responding to challenges, their satisfaction when a problem is solved or simply their delight in having fun" (Schlegel, 2000, p. 50).

More recently, Helen began working for the Bay Area Discovery Museum's Center for Childhood Creativity (CCC) in Sausalito, California, an education-focused think tank that pioneers new research, thought-leadership, and teacher training programs that advance creative thinking in children. Helen is currently the Associate Director of Research for the CCC.

Helen Hadani, a developmental psychologist whose career path has involved improving children's cognitive developmental opportunities.
Courtesy of Helen Hadani

2017). For example, several studies have linked greater use of verbal scaffolding by parents (providing age-appropriate support during cognitive tasks) to children's more advanced executive function (Bernier, Carlson, & Whipple, 2010; Hammond & others, 2012). A recent study revealed that secure attachment to mothers during the toddler years was linked to a higher level of executive function at 5 to 6 years of age (Bernier & others, 2015). Another recent observational study found that a higher level of control by fathers was linked to 3-year-olds' lower executive function (Meuwissen & Carlson, 2015). And a recent study revealed that experiencing peer problems (such as victimization and rejection) beginning in early childhood is linked to lower executive function later in childhood (Holmes, Kim-Spoon, & Deater-Deckard, 2016). Also in this study, better executive function reduced the likelihood of experiencing peer problems later in childhood.

Other predictors of better executive function in children that researchers have found include higher socioeconomic status (Duncan, McClelland, & Acock, 2017; Obradovic, 2010); some aspects of language, including vocabulary size, verbal labeling, and bilingualism (Bell, Wolfe, & Adkins, 2007; Bialystok, 2010; Muller & others, 2008); imagination (generating novel ideas, for example) (Carlson & White, 2013); cultural background (Asian children, especially urban Chinese and Korean children, show better executive function than U.S. children do) (Lan & others, 2011; Sabbagh & others, 2006); and fewer sleep problems (Friedman & others, 2009).

Some developmental psychologists use their training in areas such as cognitive development to pursue careers in applied areas. To read about the work of Helen Hadani, an individual who has followed this path, see the *Connecting with Careers* profile.

The Child's Theory of Mind   Even young children are curious about the nature of the human mind (Birch & others, 2017; Devine & Hughes, 2017; Hughes & Devine, 2015; Lane & others, 2016; Sodian & others, 2016; Wellman, 2011, 2015). They have a **theory of mind,** which refers to awareness of one's own mental processes and the mental processes of others. Studies of theory of mind view the child as "a thinker who is trying to explain, predict, and understand people's thoughts, feelings, and utterances" (Harris, 2006, p. 847). Researchers are increasingly discovering that children's theory of mind is linked to cognitive processes (Birch & others, 2017; Wellman, 2011, 2015). For example, one study found that theory of mind competence at age 3 is related to a higher level of metamemory at age 5 (Lockl & Schneider, 2007).

theory of mind A concept that refers to awareness of one's own mental processes and the mental processes of others.

Developmental Changes Although some experts question whether infants have a theory of mind (Rakoczy, 2012), the consensus is that some changes occur quite early in development, as we see next (Scott & Baillargeon, 2017). From 18 months to 3 years of age, children begin to understand three mental states:

- *Perceptions*. By 2 years of age, children recognize that another person will see what's in front of her own eyes instead of what's in front of the child's eyes (Lempers, Flavell, & Flavell, 1977), and by 3 years of age, they realize that looking leads to knowing what's inside a container (Pratt & Bryant, 1990).

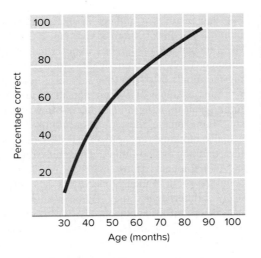

- *Emotions*. The child can distinguish between positive (for example, happy) and negative (for example, sad) emotions. A child might say, "Tommy feels bad."

- *Desires*. All humans have some sort of desires. But when do children begin to recognize that someone else's desires may be different from their own? Toddlers recognize that if people want something, they will try to get it. For instance, a child might say, "I want my mommy."

Two- to three-year-olds understand that desires are related to actions and to simple emotions. For example, they understand that people will search for what they want and that if they obtain it, they are likely to feel happy, but if they don't get it they will keep searching for it and are likely to feel sad or angry (Wellman & Woolley, 1990). Children also refer to desires earlier and more frequently than they refer to cognitive states such as thinking and knowing (Bartsch & Wellman, 1995).

One of the landmark developments in understanding others' desires is recognizing that someone else may have desires that differ from one's own (Wellman, 2011, 2015). Eighteen-month-olds understand that their own food preferences may not match the preferences of others—they will give an adult the food to which she says "Yummy!" even if the food is something that the infants detest (Repacholi & Gopnik, 1997). As they get older, they can verbalize that they themselves do not like something but an adult might (Flavell & others, 1992).

Between the ages of 3 and 5, children come to understand that the mind can represent objects and events accurately or inaccurately (Rhodes & Brandone, 2014; Tompkins & others, 2017). The realization that people can have *false beliefs*—beliefs that are not true—develops in a majority of children by the time they are 5 years old (Wellman, Cross, & Watson, 2001) (see Figure 10). This point is often described as a pivotal one in understanding the mind—recognizing that beliefs are not just mapped directly into the mind from the surrounding world, but also that different people can have different, and sometimes incorrect, beliefs (Liu & others, 2008). In a classic false-belief task, young children were shown a Band-Aids box and asked what was inside (Jenkins & Astington, 1996). To the children's surprise, the box actually contained pencils. When asked what a child who had never seen the box would think was inside, 3-year-olds typically responded, "Pencils." However, the 4- and 5-year-olds, grinning in anticipation of the false beliefs of other children who had not seen what was inside the box, were more likely to say "Band-Aids."

In a similar task, children are told a story about Sally and Anne: Sally places a toy in a basket and then leaves the room (see Figure 11). In her absence, Anne takes the toy from the basket and places it in a box. Children are asked where Sally will look for the toy when she returns. The major finding is that 3-year-olds tend to fail false-belief tasks, saying that Sally will look in the box (even though Sally could not know that the toy has been moved to this new location). Four-year-olds and older children tend to pass the task, correctly saying that Sally will have a "false belief"—she will think the object is in the basket, even though that belief is now false. The conclusion from these studies is that children younger than 4 years old do not understand that it is possible to have a false belief.

However, there are reasons to question the focus on this one supposedly pivotal moment in the development of a theory of mind. For example, the false-belief task is a complicated

FIGURE 10

DEVELOPMENTAL CHANGES IN FALSE-BELIEF PERFORMANCE. False-belief performance—the child's understanding that a person may have a false belief that contradicts reality—dramatically increases from 2½ years of age through the middle of the elementary school years. In a summary of the results of many studies, 2½-year-olds gave incorrect responses about 80 percent of the time (Wellman, Cross, & Watson, 2001). At 3 years, 8 months, they were correct about 50 percent of the time, and after that, they gave increasingly correct responses.

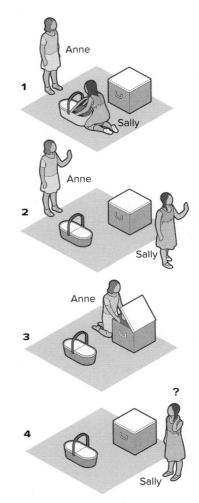

FIGURE 11

THE SALLY AND ANNE FALSE-BELIEF TASK. In the false-belief task, the skit above in which Sally has a basket and Anne has a box is shown to children. Sally places a toy in her basket and then leaves. While Sally is gone and can't watch, Anne removes the toy from Sally's basket and places it in her box. Sally then comes back and the children are asked where they think Sally will look for her toy. Children are said to "pass" the false-belief task if they understand that Sally will look in her basket first before realizing the toy isn't there.

FIGURE 12
AMBIGUOUS LINE DRAWING

one that involves a number of factors such as the characters in the story and all of their individual actions (Bloom & German, 2000). Children also have to disregard their own knowledge in making predictions about what others would think, which is difficult for young children (Birch & Bloom, 2003). Another important issue is that there is more to understanding the minds of others than this false-belief task would indicate.

One example of a limitation in 3- to 5-year-olds' understanding the mind is how they think about thinking. Preschoolers often underestimate when mental activity is likely occurring. For example, they sometimes think that a person who is sitting quietly or reading is not actually thinking very much (Flavell, Green, & Flavell, 1995). Their understanding of their own thinking is also limited. One study revealed that even 5-year-olds have difficulty reporting their thoughts (Flavell, Green, & Flavell, 1995). Children were asked to think quietly about the room in their home where they kept their toothbrushes. Shortly after this direction, many children denied they had been thinking at all and failed to mention either a toothbrush or a bathroom. In another study, when 5-year-olds were asked to try to have no thoughts at all for about 20 seconds, they reported that they were successful at doing this (Flavell, Green, & Flavell, 2000). By contrast, most of the 8-year-olds said they engaged in mental activity during the 20 seconds and reported specific thoughts.

It is only beyond the preschool years—at approximately 5 to 7 years of age—that children have a deepening appreciation of the mind itself rather than just an understanding of mental states. For example, they begin to recognize that people's behaviors do not necessarily reflect their thoughts and feelings (Flavell, Green, & Flavell, 1993). Not until middle and late childhood do children see the mind as an active constructor of knowledge or a processing center (Flavell, Green, & Flavell, 1998) and move from understanding that beliefs can be false to realizing that the same event can be open to multiple interpretations (Carpendale & Chandler, 1996). For example, in one study, children saw an ambiguous line drawing (for example, a drawing that could be seen as either a duck or a rabbit); one puppet told the child she believed the drawing was a duck while another puppet told the child he believed the drawing was a rabbit (see Figure 12). Before the age of 7, children said that there was one right answer, and it was not okay for the two puppets to have different opinions.

Although most research on children's theory of mind focuses on children around or before their preschool years, at 7 years of age and beyond there are important developments in the ability to understand the beliefs and thoughts of others. While it is important to understand that people may have different interpretations of the same thing, it is also important to recognize that some interpretations and beliefs may still be evaluated on the basis of the merits of arguments and evidence (Kuhn, Cheney, & Weinstock, 2000). In early adolescence, children begin to understand that people can have ambivalent feelings (Harter, 2006). They start to recognize that the same person can feel both happy and sad about the same event. They also engage in more recursive thinking: thinking about what other people are thinking about.

Individual Differences   As in other developmental research, there are individual differences in the ages when children reach certain milestones in their theory of mind (Birch & others, 2017; Devine & Hughes, 2017; Wellman, 2011, 2015). For example, executive function also is connected to theory of mind development (Benson & Sabbagh, 2017; Devine & others, 2016). In one executive function task, children are asked to say the word *night* when they see a picture of a sun, and the word *day* when they see a picture of a moon and stars. To do this correctly, children have to engage in inhibitory control by suppressing the most realistic responses (saying the word *day* when seeing a picture of a sun, for example).

Children who perform better at such executive function tasks show a better understanding of theory of mind (Astington & Hughes, 2013; Benson & Sabbagh, 2017). In recent research, executive function at 3 years of age predicted theory of mind at 4 years of age, and likewise executive function at 4 years of age predicted theory of mind at 5 years of age (Marcovitch & others, 2015). In this research, the reverse did not occur—that is, theory of mind at earlier ages did not predict executive function at later ages.

Young children's symbolic skills also contribute to the development of theory of mind. One study found that young children's symbolic understanding provided a foundation for their theory of mind and also for language, pretend play, and representational understanding (Lillard & Kavanaugh, 2014).

Language development also likely plays a prominent role in the increasingly reflective nature of theory of mind as children go through the early childhood and middle and late childhood years (Meins & others, 2013). Researchers have found that differences in children's language skills predict performance on theory of mind tasks (Hughes & Devine, 2015).

Among other factors that influence children's development of theory of mind are advances in prefrontal cortex functioning (Powers, Chavez, & Heatherton, 2016), engaging in make-believe play (Kavanaugh, 2006), and various aspects of social interaction (Devine & Hughes, 2017). Among the social interaction factors that advance children's theory of mind are being securely attached to parents who engage children in mental state talk ("That's a good thought you have" or "Can you tell what he's thinking?") (Devine & Hughes, 2017; Laranjo & others, 2010); having older siblings and friends who engage in mental state talk (Hughes & others, 2010), and living in a family of higher socioeconomic status (Devine & Hughes, 2017). A recent study found that parental engagement in mind-mindedness (viewing children as mental agents by making mind-related comments to them) advanced preschool children's theory of mind (Hughes, Devine, & Wang, 2017). Also, recent research indicates that children who have an advanced theory of mind are more popular with their peers and have better social skills in peer relations (Peterson & others, 2016; Slaughter & others, 2014).

A young boy with autism. *What are some characteristics of autistic children? What are some deficits in autistic children's theory of mind?*
©Robin Nelson/PhotoEdit

Theory of Mind and Autism   Another individual difference in understanding the mind involves autism (Fletcher-Watson & others, 2014; Leung & others, 2016). In 2016, approximately 1 in 68 children were estimated to have some type of autism (Christensen & others, 2016). Autism can usually be diagnosed by the age of 3 years and sometimes earlier. Children with autism show a number of behaviors different from those exhibited by other children their age, including theory of mind, social interaction, and communication, as well as repetitive behaviors or interests (Mazza & others, 2017; von dem Hagen & Bright, 2017). A recent study found that theory of mind predicted the severity of autism in children (Hoogenhout & Malcolm-Smith, 2017). However, children with autism might have difficulty understanding others' beliefs and emotions not solely due to theory of mind deficits but to other aspects of cognition such as problems in focusing attention, eye gaze, face recognition, memory, executive function, language impairment, or some general intellectual impairment (Mukherjee, 2017; Mutreja, Craig, & O'Boyle, 2016; Oberwelland & others, 2017; Wang & others, 2017).

Children and adults with autism have difficulty in social interactions, often described as deficits in theory of mind (Broekhof & others, 2015; Luiselli, 2014). These deficits are generally greater than deficits in children the same mental age with an intellectual disability (O'Reilly & others, 2014). Researchers have found that autistic children have difficulty developing a theory of mind, especially in understanding others' beliefs and emotions (Williams & Happe, 2010). Although children with autism tend to do poorly when reasoning about false-belief tasks and task sequencing (Peterson, 2005; Peterson, Wellman, & Slaughter, 2012), they can perform much better on reasoning tasks that require an understanding of physical causality.

---

developmental **connection**

Disorders

The current consensus is that autism is a brain dysfunction involving abnormalities in brain structure and neurotransmitters, and that genetic factors play an important role in its occurrence. Connect to "Physical Development in Middle and Late Childhood."

developmental **connection**

Disorders

Boys are four times more likely to be autistic than girls are. Connect to "Physical Development in Middle and Late Childhood."

Review **Connect** Reflect

LG1 Describe three views of the cognitive changes that occur in early childhood.

Review
- What characterizes Piaget's stage of preoperational thought?
- What does Vygotsky's theory suggest about how preschool children construct knowledge?
- What are some important ways in which information processing changes during early childhood? What characterizes children's theory of mind?

Connect
- What are some differences between the attention of young children and the attention of infants?

Reflect *Your Own Personal Journey of Life*
- If you were the parent of a 4-year-old child, would you try to train the child to develop conservation skills? Explain.

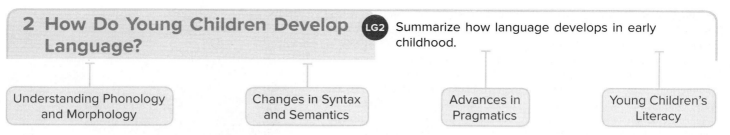

| Understanding Phonology and Morphology | Changes in Syntax and Semantics | Advances in Pragmatics | Young Children's Literacy |

Toddlers move rather quickly from producing two-word utterances to creating three-, four-, and five-word combinations. Between 2 and 3 years of age, they begin the transition from saying simple sentences that express a single proposition to saying complex sentences.

As young children learn the special features of their own language, there are extensive regularities in how they acquire that particular language (Clark, 2017; Litz, Snyder, & Pater, 2017). For example, all children learn the prepositions *on* and *in* before other prepositions. Children learning other languages, such as Russian or Chinese, also acquire the particular features of those languages in a consistent order.

However, some children develop language problems, including speech and hearing problems. To read about the work of one individual who helps children who have speech/language and hearing problems, see *Connecting with Careers*.

UNDERSTANDING PHONOLOGY AND MORPHOLOGY

During the preschool years, most children gradually become more sensitive to the sounds of spoken words and become increasingly capable of producing all the sounds of their language (Bailey, Osipova, & Kelly, 2016; Goad, 2017). By the time children are 3 years of age, they can produce all the vowel sounds and most of the consonant sounds (Stoel-Gammon & Sosa, 2010). They can also recognize sounds before they can produce them. For example, they might recognize the words "merry-go-round" before they are able to say them.

Young children can even produce complex consonant clusters such as *str-* and *mpt-*. They notice rhymes, enjoy poems, make up silly names for things by substituting one sound for

connecting with careers

Sharla Peltier, Speech Pathologist

A speech pathologist is a health professional who works with individuals who have a communication disorder. Sharla Peltier is a speech pathologist in Manitoulin, Ontario, Canada. Peltier works with Native American children in the First Nations Schools. She conducts screening for speech/language and hearing problems and assesses infants as young as 6 months of age as well as school-aged children. She works closely with community health nurses to identify hearing problems.

Diagnosing problems is only about half of what Peltier does in her work. She especially enjoys treating speech/language and hearing problems. She conducts parent training sessions to help parents understand and help with their children's language problems. As part of this training, she guides parents in improving their communication skills with their children.

For more information about what speech therapists do, see the Careers in Children's Development appendix.

Speech therapist Sharla Peltier helps a young child improve his language and communication skills.
Courtesy of Sharla Peltier

another (such as *bubblegum, bubblebum, bubbleyum*), and clap along with each syllable in a phrase.

By the time children move beyond two-word utterances, they demonstrate a knowledge of morphology rules (Clark, 2017; Snyder, 2017). Children begin using the plural and possessive forms of nouns (such as *dogs* and *dog's*). They put appropriate endings on verbs (such as *-s* when the subject is third-person singular and *-ed* for the past tense). They use prepositions (such as *in* and *on*), articles (such as *a* and *the*), and various forms of the verb *to be* (such as "I *was* going to the store"). Some of the best evidence for changes in children's use of morphological rules occurs in their overgeneralization of the rules, as when a preschool child says "foots" instead of "feet," or "goed" instead of "went."

In a classic experiment that was designed to study children's knowledge of morphological rules, such as how to make a plural, Jean Berko (1958) presented preschool children and first-grade children with cards such as the one shown in Figure 13. Children were asked to look at the card while the experimenter read aloud the words on the card. Then the children were asked to supply the missing word. This task might sound easy, but Berko was interested in the children's ability to apply the appropriate morphological rule—in this case, to say "wugs" with the *z* sound that indicates the plural.

Although the children's answers were not perfect, they were much better than what could have been achieved by chance. What makes Berko's study impressive is that most of the words were made up for the experiment. Thus, the children could not have based their responses on remembering past instances of hearing the words. The fact that they could make the plurals or past tenses of words they had never heard before was proof that they knew the morphological rules.

CHANGES IN SYNTAX AND SEMANTICS

Preschool children also learn and apply rules of syntax (Clark, 2017; de Villiers & de Villiers, 2013; Sugisaki, 2017). They show a growing mastery of complex rules for how words should be ordered (Fletcher & Frizelle, 2017; Kyratzis, 2017).

Consider *wh-* questions, such as "Where is Daddy going?" or "What is that boy doing?" To ask these questions properly, the child must know two important differences between *wh-* questions and affirmative statements (for instance, "Daddy is going to work" and "That boy is waiting for the school bus"). First, a *wh-* word must be added at the beginning of the sentence. Second, the auxiliary verb must be inverted—that is, exchanged with the subject of the sentence. Young children learn quite early where to put the *wh-* word, but they take much longer to learn the auxiliary-inversion rule. Thus, preschool children might ask, "Where Daddy is going?" and "What that boy is doing?"

Gains in semantics also characterize early childhood (McGregor, 2017; van Hout, 2017). Vocabulary development is dramatic (Bailey, Osipova, & Kelly, 2016; Parrish-Morris, Golinkoff, & Hirsh-Pasek, 2013; Thornton, 2016). Some experts have concluded that between 18 months and 6 years of age, young children learn approximately one new word every waking hour (Gelman & Kalish, 2006)! By the time they enter first grade, it is estimated that children know about 14,000 words (Clark, 1993).

Why can children learn so many new words so quickly? One possibility is **fast mapping,** which involves children's ability to make an initial connection between a word and its referent after only limited exposure to the word (Bailey, Osipova, & Kelly, 2016; Brady & Goodman, 2014; Woodward, Markman, & Fitzsimmons, 1994). Researchers have found that exposure to words on multiple occasions over several days results in more successful word learning than the same number of exposures in a single day (Childers & Tomasello, 2002). Recent research using eye-tracking devices found that even 15-month-old infants fast map words (Puccini & Liszkowski, 2012). Also, fast mapping promotes a deeper understanding of word meaning, as in where the word can apply and its nuances.

What are some important aspects of how word learning optimally occurs? Following are six key principles in young children's vocabulary development (Harris, Golinkoff, & Hirsh-Pasek, 2011):

This is a wug.

Now there is another one.
There are two of them.
There are two _____.

FIGURE **13**

STIMULI IN BERKO'S STUDY OF YOUNG CHILDREN'S UNDERSTANDING OF MORPHOLOGICAL RULES. In Jean Berko's (1958) study, young children were presented with cards, such as this one with a "wug" on it. Then the children were asked to supply the missing word; in supplying the missing word, they had to say it correctly, too. "Wugs" is the correct response here.

Gleason, Jean Berko, "The Child's Learning of English Morphology," *Word*, Vol. 14, 1958, p. 154. Copyright ©1958 by Jean Berko Gleason. All rights reserved. Used with permission.

What are some strategies parents can adopt to increase their young children's vocabulary development?

©Thanasis Zovoilis/Getty Images RF

developmental **connection**

Language Development

The average 2-year-old can speak about 200 words. Connect to "Cognitive Development in Infancy."

fast mapping A process that helps to explain how young children learn the connection between a word and its referent so quickly.

1. *Children learn the words they hear most often.* They learn the words that they encounter during interactions with parents, teachers, siblings, peers, and also from books. They especially benefit from encountering words that they do not know.

2. *Children learn words for things and events that interest them.* Parents and teachers can direct young children to experience words in contexts that interest the children; playful peer interactions are especially helpful in this regard.

3. *Children learn words best in responsive and interactive contexts rather than passive contexts.* Children who participate in turn-taking opportunities, joint focusing experiences, and positive, sensitive socializing contexts with adults encounter the scaffolding necessary for optimal word learning. They learn words less effectively when they are passive learners.

4. *Children learn words best in contexts that are meaningful.* Young children learn new words more effectively when new words are encountered in integrated contexts rather than as isolated facts.

5. *Children learn words best when they access clear information about word meaning.* Children whose parents and teachers are sensitive to words the children might not understand and provide support and elaboration with hints about word meaning learn words better than they do if parents and teachers quickly state a new word and don't monitor whether children understand its meaning.

6. *Children learn words best when grammar and vocabulary are considered.* Children who experience a large number of words and diversity in verbal stimulation develop a richer vocabulary and better understanding of grammar. In many cases, vocabulary and grammar development are connected.

ADVANCES IN PRAGMATICS

Changes in pragmatics also characterize young children's language development (Fujiki & Brinton, 2017; Waxman, 2013). A 6-year-old is simply a much better conversationalist than a 2-year-old is. What are some of the improvements in pragmatics during the preschool years?

Young children begin to engage in extended discourse (Bryant, 2012). For example, they learn culturally specific rules of conversation and politeness, and become sensitive to the need to adapt their speech in different settings. Their developing linguistic skills and increasing ability to take the perspective of others contribute to their generation of more competent narratives.

As children get older, they become increasingly able to talk about things that are not here (Grandma's house, for example) and not now (what happened to them yesterday or might happen tomorrow, for example). A preschool child can tell you what she wants for lunch tomorrow, something that would not have been possible at the two-word stage of language development.

Around 4 to 5 years of age, children learn to change their speech style to suit the situation. For example, even 4-year-old children speak to a 2-year-old differently from the way they would talk to a same-aged peer; they use shorter sentences with the 2-year-old. They also speak to an adult differently from a same-aged peer, using more polite and formal language with the adult (Shatz & Gelman, 1973).

Peers also can play an important role in aspects of language other than pragmatics. A recent study of more than 1,800 4-year-olds revealed that peers' expressive language abilities (transmitting language to others) were positively linked with young children's expressive and receptive (what a child hears and reads) language development (Mashburn & others, 2009).

YOUNG CHILDREN'S LITERACY

The concern about the ability of U.S. children to read and write has led to a careful examination of preschool and kindergarten children's experiences, with the hope that a positive orientation toward reading and writing can be fostered early in life (Temple & others, 2018; Tompkins, 2017). The most obvious literacy necessity is knowing a language. Children will not be able to comprehend the text they read if they don't understand the words and sentence structures. Parents and teachers need to provide young children with a supportive environment in which to develop literacy skills (Vukelich & others, 2016). Children should be active participants and be immersed in a wide range of interesting listening, talking, writing, and reading experiences (Tompkins, 2016). One study revealed that children whose mothers had more education had more advanced emergent literacy skills than children whose mothers had less education (Korat, 2009). Another recent study found that literacy experiences (such as how often the child was read to), the quality of the mother's engagement with her child (such as attempts to cognitively stimulate the child), and provision of learning materials (such as age-appropriate learning materials and books) were important home literacy experiences in low-income families that were linked to the children's language development in positive ways (Rodriguez & others, 2009).

Catherine Snow, a leading expert on children's language development, thinks that mealtimes are an excellent context for promoting young children's literacy. Snow and her colleague Diane Beals (Snow & Beals, 2006) described some of the ways that mealtimes can improve young children's literacy: mealtime conversations often include information about current events and what is going on in the world; they provide an opportunity for everyday problems to be aired and solutions to be discussed; and they provide a context for learning about being polite and having good manners.

Snow (2010) emphasizes that parents can promote literacy skills in young children at mealtime by using extended discourse, which involves talking about a topic that goes beyond a sentence or two and extends to several conversational turns. While engaging in such extended discourse, parents often use words young children haven't heard before or don't understand, which provides opportunities to expand children's vocabularies. In describing parents' use of sophisticated vocabulary in such mealtime contexts, Snow (2010, p. 128) commented:

What are some strategies for increasing young children's literacy?
©Deepak Budhraja/Asia Images/Corbis

> In these dinner table conversations, of course, there's always a lot of talk about "Eat your peas" and "Keep your elbows off the table" and "Pass the noodles," but in some of the families, in addition, there's wonderfully interesting conversation about what proposals the governor just suggested for a new budget, or how the construction of the expressway is going to influence the neighborhood. And these conversations are full of wonderful words like *budget* and *governor* and *proposal* and *neighborhood*—words that children might not use and probably won't understand fully. We found that families that used words like that in their dinner table conversations had children with much larger vocabularies two years later.

So far, our discussion of early literacy has focused on U.S. children. Researchers have found that the extent to which phonological awareness is linked to learning to read effectively varies across language to some extent (McBride-Chang, 2004). For example, one study of second-grade students from Beijing, Hong Kong, Korea, and the United States revealed that phonological awareness may be more important for early reading development in English and Korean than in Chinese (McBride-Chang & others, 2005). Further, rates of dyslexia (severe reading disability) differ across countries and are linked to the spelling and phonetic rules that characterize the language (McBride-Chang & others, 2008). English is one of the more difficult languages because of its irregular spellings and pronunciations. In countries where English is spoken, the rate of dyslexia is higher than in countries where the alphabet script is more phonetically pronounced.

How might mealtimes provide a context for improving young children's literacy?
©Ronnie Kaufman/Corbis

What are some strategies for using books effectively with preschool children? Ellen Galinsky (2010) suggested these strategies:

- *Use books to initiate conversation with young children.* Ask them to put themselves in the book characters' places and imagine what they might be thinking or feeling.
- *Use what and why questions.* Ask young children what they think is going to happen next in a story and then to see if it occurs.
- *Encourage children to ask questions about stories.*
- *Choose some books that play with language.* Creative books on the alphabet, including those with rhymes, often interest young children.

The advances in language that take place in early childhood lay the foundation for later development during the elementary school years, as we will see in "Cognitive Development in Middle and Late Childhood."

Review

- How do phonology and morphology change during early childhood?
- What characterizes young children's understanding of syntax and semantics in early childhood?
- What advances in pragmatics occur in early childhood?
- What are some effective ways to guide young children's literacy?

Connect

- In this section, you learned that children can sometimes overgeneralize the rules for morphology. How is this different from or similar to the concept of overextension as it relates to infants' speech?

Reflect *Your Own Personal Journey of Life*

- As a parent, what would you do to improve the likelihood that your child would enter first grade with excellent literacy skills?

---

3 What Are Some Important Features of Young Children's Education?

LG3 Evaluate different approaches to early childhood education.

| Variations in Early Childhood Education | Educating Young Children Who Are Disadvantaged | Controversies in Early Childhood Education |

To the teachers at a Reggio Emilia program (described in the chapter opening), preschool children are active learners, exploring the world with their peers, constructing their knowledge of the world in collaboration with their community, aided but not directed by the teachers. In many ways, the Reggio Emilia approach applies ideas consistent with the views of Piaget and Vygotsky discussed in this chapter. Do educators' beliefs make a difference to the children they teach? How do other early education programs treat children, and how do the children fare? Our exploration of early childhood education focuses on variations in programs, education for children who are disadvantaged, and some controversies in early childhood education.

VARIATIONS IN EARLY CHILDHOOD EDUCATION

Attending preschool is rapidly becoming the norm for U.S. children (Follari, 2015). Forty-two states plus the District of Columbia have publicly funded preschool programs for 3- and 4-year-old children (National Institute for Early Education Research, 2016). Many other 3- and 4-year-old children attend private preschool programs.

There are many variations in the ways young children are educated (Bredekamp, 2017; Feeney, Moravcik, & Nolte, 2016; Henniger, 2017; Morrison, 2017, 2018). The foundation of early childhood education has been the child-centered kindergarten.

The Child-Centered Kindergarten Nurturing is a key aspect of the **child-centered kindergarten,** which emphasizes the education of the whole child and concern for his or her physical, cognitive, and socioemotional development (Gordon & Browne, 2017). Instruction is organized around the child's needs, interests, and learning styles. Emphasis is on the process of learning, rather than what is learned (Bredekamp, 2017; Gestwicki, 2017). The child-centered kindergarten honors three principles: each child follows a unique developmental pattern; young children learn best through firsthand experiences with people and materials; and play is extremely important to the child's total development. *Experimenting, exploring, discovering, trying out, restructuring, speaking,* and *listening* are frequent activities in excellent kindergarten programs. Such programs are closely attuned to the developmental status of 4- and 5-year-old children.

child-centered kindergarten Education that involves the whole child by considering the child's physical, cognitive, and socioemotional development and addressing the child's needs, interests, and learning styles.

The Montessori Approach   Montessori schools are patterned after the educational philosophy of Maria Montessori (1870–1952), an Italian physician-turned-educator who crafted a revolutionary approach to young children's education at the beginning of the twentieth century. Her work began in Rome with a group of children with an intellectual disability. She was successful in teaching them to read, write, and pass examinations designed for normal children. Some time later, she turned her attention to poor children from the slums of Rome and had similar success in teaching them. Her approach has since been adopted extensively in private nursery schools in the United States. The number of Montessori schools in the United States has expanded dramatically in recent years, from one school in 1959 to 355 schools in 1970 to approximately 4,500 in 2016 with estimates of Montessori schools worldwide at approximately 20,000 in 2016 (North American Montessori Teachers' Association, 2016).

Larry Page and Sergey Brin, founders of the highly successful Internet search engine, Google, said that their early years at Montessori schools were a major factor in their success (International Montessori Council, 2006). During an interview with Barbara Walters, they said they learned how to be self-directed and self-starters at Montessori (ABC News, 2005). The Montessori experiences encouraged them to think for themselves and allowed them the freedom to develop their own interests.
©James Leynse/Corbis

The **Montessori approach** is a philosophy of education in which children are given considerable freedom and spontaneity in choosing activities. They are allowed to move from one activity to another as they desire. The teacher acts as a facilitator rather than a director. The teacher shows the child how to perform intellectual activities, demonstrates interesting ways to explore curriculum materials, and offers help when the child requests it (Murray, 2011). Montessori teachers encourage children to make decisions from an early age, which helps them to engage in self-regulated problem solving and learn to manage their time effectively (Hyson, Copple, & Jones, 2006; Rambusch, 2010). One study found that children in classic Montessori programs, compared with children in supplemented Montessori and conventional programs, showed greater school-year gains in executive function, math, vocabulary, and social problem-solving (Lillard, 2012). In another study, researchers found that Latino children in low-income communities who began the school year having at-risk pre-academic and behavioral skills benefitted from a Montessori public school pre-K program, ending the year scoring above national averages for school readiness (Ansari & Winsler, 2014).

Some developmentalists favor the Montessori approach, but others believe that it neglects children's social development (Chattin-McNichols, 1992). For example, while Montessori fosters independence and the development of cognitive skills, it deemphasizes verbal interaction between the teacher and child and peer interaction. Montessori's critics also argue that it restricts imaginative play and that its heavy reliance on self-corrective materials may not adequately allow for creativity and for a variety of learning styles (Goffin & Wilson, 2001).

Developmentally Appropriate and Inappropriate Education   Many educators and psychologists conclude that preschool and young elementary school children learn best through active, hands-on teaching methods such as games and dramatic play. They know that children develop at varying rates and believe that schools need to allow for these individual differences (Morrison, 2017, 2018). They also argue that schools should focus on facilitating children's socioemotional development as well as their cognitive development. Educators refer to this type of schooling as **developmentally appropriate practice (DAP),** which is based on knowledge of the typical development of children within a particular age span (age appropriateness), as well as on the uniqueness of the individual child (individual appropriateness). DAP emphasizes the importance of creating settings that encourage children to be active learners and reflect children's interests and capabilities (Beaver, Wyatt, & Jackman, 2018; Gestwicki, 2017). Desired outcomes for DAP include thinking critically, working cooperatively, solving problems, developing self-regulatory skills, and enjoying learning. The emphasis in DAP is on the process of learning rather than on its content (Bredekamp, 2017).

Do developmentally appropriate educational practices improve young children's development? Some researchers have found that young children in developmentally appropriate classrooms are likely to feel less stress, be more motivated, be more socially skilled, have better work habits, be more creative, have better language skills, and demonstrate better math

Montessori approach An educational philosophy in which children are given considerable freedom and spontaneity in choosing activities and specially designed curriculum materials.

developmentally appropriate practice (DAP) Education that focuses on the typical developmental patterns of children (age appropriateness) as well as the uniqueness of each child (individual appropriateness). Such practice contrasts with *developmentally inappropriate practice,* which ignores the concrete, hands-on approach to learning. For example, direct teaching largely through abstract paper-and-pencil activities presented to large groups of young children is believed to be developmentally inappropriate.

What are some differences in developmentally appropriate and inappropriate practice?

©Blend Images/Getty Images RF

How Would You...?

If you were an **educator,** how would you design a developmentally appropriate lesson to teach kindergarten children the concept of gravity?

How Would You...?

If you were a **health-care professional,** how would you explain the importance of including health services as part of an effective Head Start program?

Project Head Start Compensatory education designed to provide children from low-income families the opportunity to acquire skills and experiences that are important for school success.

skills than children in developmentally inappropriate classrooms (Hart & others, 2003). However, not all studies find DAP to have significant positive effects (Hyson, Copple, & Jones, 2006). Among the reasons that it is difficult to generalize from the research findings on developmentally appropriate education is that individual programs often vary, and developmentally appropriate education is an evolving concept. Recent changes in the concept have given more attention to how strongly academic skills should be emphasized and how they should be taught.

EDUCATING YOUNG CHILDREN WHO ARE DISADVANTAGED

For many years, U.S. children from low-income families did not receive any education before they entered the first grade. Often, they began first grade several steps behind their classmates in their readiness to learn. In the summer of 1965, the federal government began an effort to break the cycle of poverty and inadequate education for young children in the United States through **Project Head Start.** It is a compensatory program designed to provide children from low-income families the opportunity to acquire the skills and experiences important for success in school. After almost half a century, Head Start continues to be the largest federally funded program for U.S. children, with almost 1 million U.S. children enrolled annually (Hustedt, Friedman, & Barnett, 2012; Miller, Farkas, & Duncan, 2016; Zigler & Styfco, 2010). In 2007, 3 percent of Head Start children were 5 years old, 51 percent were 4 years old, 36 percent were 3 years old, and 10 percent were under 3 years of age (Administration for Children and Families, 2008).

Early Head Start was established in 1995 to serve children from birth to 3 years of age. In 2007, half of all new funds appropriated for Head Start programs were used for the expansion of Early Head Start (Burgette & others, 2017). Researchers have found positive effects for Early Head Start (Hoffman & Ewen, 2007). One study revealed that Early Head Start had a protective effect on risks young children might experience in relation to parenting stress, language development, and self-control (Ayoub, Vallotton, & Mastergeorge, 2011).

Head Start programs are not all created equal (McCoy & others, 2016). One estimate is that 40 percent of the 1,400 Head Start programs are of questionable quality (Zigler & Styfco, 1994). More attention needs to be given to developing Head Start programs that are of consistently high quality. One individual who is strongly motivated to make Head Start a valuable learning experience for young children from disadvantaged backgrounds is Yolanda Garcia. To read about her work, see the *Connecting with Careers* profile.

Mixed results have been found for Head Start. Some evaluations support the positive influence of quality early childhood programs on both the cognitive and social worlds of disadvantaged young children (Bierman & others, 2014; Phillips & Lowenstein, 2011). A recent study found that one year of Head Start was linked to higher performance in early math, early reading, and receptive vocabulary (Miller, Farkas, & Duncan, 2016).

Also, a national evaluation of Head Start revealed that the program had a positive influence on the language and cognitive development of 3- and 4-year-olds (Puma & others, 2010). However, by the end of the first grade, there were few lasting outcomes. One exception was a larger vocabulary for those who went to Head Start as 4-year-olds and better oral comprehension for those who went to Head Start as 3-year-olds. Also, two recent studies found that improved parenting engagement and skills were linked to the success of children in Head Start programs (Ansari & Gershoff, 2016; Roggman & others, 2016).

Positive outcomes for Early Head Start have been found. In an experimental study of low-income families, data were collected when the children were 1, 2, and 3 years old in Early Head Start, and also at 5 years of age (2 years after leaving Early Head Start) (Love & others, 2013). In this study, positive outcomes for the Early Head Start children (compared with a control group who did not receive the Early Head Start experience) occurred at 2, 3, and 5 years of age. At 2 and 3 years of age, Early Head Start children showed higher levels of cognition, language, attention, and health, as well as fewer behavior problems than other children from low-income families; at age 5, the Early Head Start children had better

Yolanda Garcia, Head Start Director and College Dean

Yolanda Garcia is the Director of WestEd's E3 Institute–Excellence in Early Education, a project for the Center for Child and Family Studies. She previously directed the Children's Services Department, Santa Clara County Office of Education. Her training includes two master's degrees, one in public policy and child welfare from the University of Chicago and another in education administration from San Jose State University.

Garcia has served on many national advisory committees that have resulted in improvements in the staffing of Head Start programs. Most notably, she served on the Head Start Quality Committee that recommended the development of Early Head Start and revised performance standards for Head Start programs.

After earning her master's degrees, Yolanda went on to obtain a doctorate from the University of San Francisco in 2011 in Leadership

Yolanda Garcia, director of Children's Services/Head Start, works with a Head Start child in Santa Clara, California.
Courtesy of Yolanda Garcia

and Organizational Development. Currently, she is Dean of Child Development and Teacher Education for the Sonoma County College District in northern California.

attention and approaches to learning as well as fewer behavior problems, but they did not differ from control group children in early school achievement. Also, another study revealed that Early Head Start had a protective effect on risks young children might experience in regard to parenting stress, language development, and self-control (Ayoub, Vallotton, & Mastergeorge, 2011).

One high-quality early childhood education program (although not a Head Start program) was the Perry Preschool program in Ypsilanti, Michigan, a two-year preschool program that included weekly home visits from program personnel. In analyses of the long-term effects of the program, adults who had been in the Perry Preschool program were compared with a control group of adults from the same background who had not received the enriched early childhood education (Schweinhart & others, 2005; Weikart, 1993). Those who had been in the Perry Preschool program had fewer teen pregnancies and better high school graduation rates, and at age 40 they were more likely to be employed, own a home, and have a savings account, and they also had fewer arrests.

CONTROVERSIES IN EARLY CHILDHOOD EDUCATION

Three controversies in early childhood education involve (1) the curriculum, (2) universal preschool education, and (3) school readiness.

What Should the Curriculum Emphasize in Early Childhood Education? Regarding the curriculum controversy, on one side are those who advocate a child-centered, constructivist approach much like that emphasized by the NAEYC along the lines of developmentally appropriate practice (Bredekamp, 2017; Feeney, Moravcik, and Nolte, 2016; Gordon & Browne, 2017; Morrison, 2017, 2018). On the other side are those who advocate an academic, direct instruction approach.

In practice, many high-quality early childhood education programs include both academic and constructivist approaches. Many education experts such as Lilian Katz (1999), though, worry about academic approaches that place too much pressure on young children to achieve and don't provide any opportunities to actively construct knowledge. Competent early childhood programs also should focus on both cognitive development and socioemotional development, not exclusively on cognitive development (Bredekamp, 2017; Gestwicki, 2017; NAEYC, 2009).

What is the curriculum controversy in early childhood education? Should all children be provided with preschool education?
©Ronnie Kaufman/Corbis/Getty Images

Should All Children Be Provided with Preschool Education? Another early childhood education controversy focuses on whether preschool education should be instituted for all U.S. 4-year-old children. Edward Zigler and his colleagues (2006) have argued that the United States should have universal preschool education. They emphasize that quality preschools prepare children for school readiness and later academic success. Zigler and his colleagues (2006) cite research that shows quality preschool programs increase the likelihood that once children go to elementary and secondary school they will not repeat a grade or drop out of school. They also point to analyses indicating that universal preschool would bring cost savings on the order of billions of dollars because of a diminished need for remedial services (Karoly & Bigelow, 2005).

Critics of universal preschool education argue that the gains attributed to preschool and kindergarten education are often overstated. They especially stress that research has not proven that nondisadvantaged children benefit academically from attending a preschool. Thus, the critics say it is more important to improve preschool education for young children who are disadvantaged than to fund preschool education for all 4-year-old children. Some critics, especially homeschooling advocates, emphasize that young children should be educated by their parents, not by schools. Thus, controversy continues to surround proposals for universal preschool education.

What Is Required for School Readiness? Educational reform has prompted considerable concern about children's readiness to enter kindergarten and first grade (Johnson, Martin, & Brooks-Gunn, 2013; Pressler & others, 2016; Scharf, 2016). National studies suggest that 40 percent of children who finish kindergarten are not ready for first grade (Kauffman Early Education Exchange, 2002).

Craig and Sharon Ramey (1999, 2004) reviewed scientific research on school readiness and concluded that the following six caregiver activities are necessary in the infant and early childhood years to ensure that children will be ready for elementary school (Ramey & Ramey, 1999, p. 145):

1. Encourage exploration.
2. Mentor in basic skills.

A child's attention is an important aspect of school entry readiness.
©Russ Rohde/age fotostock RF

3. Celebrate developmental advances.
4. Research and extend new skills.
5. Protect from inappropriate disapproval, teasing, and punishment.
6. Guide and limit behavior.

A longitudinal study using six data sets examined various factors that might be linked to school readiness and assessed the extent to which they predicted later achievement in reading and math (Duncan & others, 2007). Across all six data sets, the strongest predictors of later achievement were school-entry-level math, reading, and attention skills. However, school-entry-level socioemotional behaviors, such as degrees of internalizing and externalizing problems and social skills, showed little connection to later academic achievement.

In some developed countries, such as Japan, as well as in many developing countries, the goals of early childhood education are quite different from those of American programs. To read about the differences, see the *Connecting with Diversity* interlude.

connecting with diversity

Early Childhood Education in Japan and Developing Countries

As in the United States, there is diversity in Japanese early childhood education. Some Japanese kindergartens have specific aims, such as providing early musical training or practicing Montessori strategies. In large cities, some kindergartens are attached to universities that have elementary and secondary schools. In most Japanese preschools, however, little emphasis is put on academic instruction.

In one study, 300 Japanese and 210 American preschool teachers, child development specialists, and parents were asked about various aspects of early childhood education (Tobin, Wu, & Davidson, 1989). Only 2 percent of the Japanese respondents mentioned "to give children a good start academically" as one of their top three reasons for a society to have preschools. In contrast, over half the American respondents chose this as one of their top three choices. Japanese preschools do not teach reading, writing, and mathematics but rather skills like persistence, concentration, and the ability to function as a member of a group. The vast majority of young Japanese children are taught to read at home by their parents.

In the comparison of Japanese and American parents, more than 60 percent of the Japanese parents said that the purpose of preschool is to give children experience being a member of the group, compared with only 20 percent of the U.S. parents (Tobin,

Wu, & Davidson, 1989) (see Figure 14). Lessons in living and working together grow naturally out of the Japanese culture. In many Japanese kindergartens, children wear the same uniforms, including caps, in specific colors to indicate the classrooms to which they belong. They have identical sets of equipment, kept in identical drawers and shelves. This system is not intended to turn the young children into robots, as some Americans have surmised, but to impress on them that other people, just like themselves, have needs and desires that are equally important (Hendry, 1995).

Japan is a highly advanced industrialized country. What about developing countries—how do they compare to the United States in educating young children? The wide range of programs and emphasis on the education of the whole child—physically, cognitively, and socioemotionally—that characterizes U.S. early childhood education does not exist in many developing countries (Roopnarine & Metingdogan, 2006). Economic pressures and parents' belief that education should be academically rigorous have produced teacher-centered rather than child-centered early childhood education programs in most developing countries. Among the countries in which this type of early childhood education has been observed are Jamaica, China,

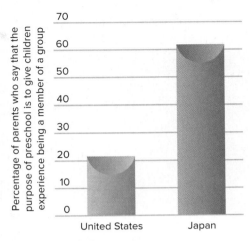

FIGURE 14

COMPARISON OF JAPANESE AND U.S. PARENTS' VIEWS ON THE PURPOSE OF PRESCHOOL

Thailand, Kenya, and Turkey. In these countries, young children are usually given few choices and are educated in highly structured settings. Emphasis is on learning academic skills through rote memorization and recitation (Lin, Johnson, & Johnson, 2003). Programs in Mexico, Singapore, Korea, and Hong Kong have been observed to be closer to those in the United States in their emphasis on curriculum flexibility and play-based methods (Cisneros-Cohernour, Moreno, & Cisneros, 2000).

What characterizes early childhood education in Japan?
©Andreas Meichsner/laif/Redux

What characterizes kindergarten in many developing countries like Jamaica (shown here)?
©Nik Wheeler/Corbis

LG3 Evaluate different approaches to early childhood education.

Review
- What are some variations in early childhood education?
- What are the main efforts to educate young children who are disadvantaged?
- What are four controversies about early childhood education?

Connect
- Earlier in the chapter, you read about Piaget's and Vygotsky's cognitive

theories. Which side of the curriculum controversy in early childhood education—child-centered, constructivist, or direct instruction—would be supported by Piaget's and Vygotsky's theories? Why?

Reflect *Your Own Personal Journey of Life*
- What type of early childhood education program would you want your child to attend?

┌topical **connections** *looking forward*┐

In the next chapter, you will read about the many advances in the socioemotional development of young children. The cognitive advances we discussed in this chapter, combined with the socioemotional experiences young children have in interacting with others, pave the way for social cognitive advances in understanding the self and others. In "Physical Development in Middle and Late Childhood" and "Cognitive Development in Middle and Late Childhood," you will read about further changes in children's physical and cognitive development. In terms of physical development, the development of the brain—especially the prefrontal cortex—provides the foundation for a number of cognitive advances, including the development of strategies and reading skills.

---

reach your **learning goals**

Cognitive Development in Early Childhood

1 What Are Three Views of the Cognitive Changes That Occur in Early Childhood?

LG1 Describe three views of the cognitive changes that occur in early childhood.

Piaget's Preoperational Stage

- According to Piaget, in the preoperational stage, which lasts from about 2 to 7 years of age, children cannot yet perform operations, which are reversible mental actions, but they begin to represent the world with words, images, and drawings, to form stable concepts, and to reason.

- During the symbolic function substage, which occurs between 2 and 4 years of age, children begin to mentally represent an object that is not present; their thought is limited by egocentrism and animism.

- During the intuitive thought substage, which stretches from about 4 to 7 years of age, children begin to reason and to bombard adults with questions. Thought at this substage is called intuitive because children seem so sure about their knowledge yet are unaware of how they know what they know. Centration and a lack of conservation also characterize the preoperational stage.

Vygotsky's Theory

- Vygotsky's theory represents a social constructivist approach to development. According to Vygotsky, children construct knowledge through social interaction, and they use language not only to communicate with others but also to plan, guide, and monitor their own behavior and to help them solve problems. His theory suggests that adults should access and use the child's zone of proximal development (ZPD), which is the range of tasks that are too difficult for children to master alone but that can be learned with the guidance and assistance of adults or more-skilled children.

- Vygotsky's theory also suggests that adults and peers should teach through scaffolding, which involves changing the level of support over the course of a teaching session, with the more-skilled person adjusting guidance to fit the student's current performance level.

Information Processing

- The child's ability to attend to stimuli dramatically improves during early childhood. Advances in executive attention and sustained attention are especially important in early childhood, but the young child still attends to the salient rather than the relevant features of a task. Significant improvement in short-term memory occurs during early childhood. With good prompts, young children's long-term memories can be accurate, although young children can be led into developing false memories. During the preschool years, children's memories take on more autobiographical characteristics.

- Advances in executive function, an umbrella-like concept that consists of a number of higher-level cognitive processes linked to the development of the prefrontal cortex, occur in early childhood. Executive function involves managing one's thoughts to engage in goal-directed behavior and to exercise self-control.

- Theory of mind is the awareness of one's own mental processes and the mental processes of others. Children begin to understand mental states involving perceptions, desires, and emotions from 18 months to 3 years of age; by 5 years of age a majority realize that people can have false beliefs. It is only beyond the preschool years that children have a deepening appreciation of the mind itself rather than just an understanding of mental states. Autistic children have difficulty developing a theory of mind.

2 How Do Young Children Develop Language?

LG2 Summarize how language develops in early childhood.

Understanding Phonology and Morphology

Changes in Syntax and Semantics

Advances in Pragmatics

Young Children's Literacy

- Young children increase their grasp of language's rule systems. In terms of phonology, most young children become more sensitive to the sounds of spoken language. Berko's classic experiment demonstrated that young children understand morphological rules.

- Preschool children learn and apply rules of syntax involving how words should be ordered. In terms of semantics, vocabulary development increases dramatically during early childhood.

- Young children's conversational skills improve, they increase their sensitivity to the needs of others in conversation, and they learn to change their speech style to suit the situation.

- There has been increased interest in young children's literacy. Young children need to develop positive images of reading and writing skills through a supportive environment. Children should be active participants in their education and be immersed in a wide range of interesting and enjoyable listening, talking, writing, and reading experiences.

3 What Are Some Important Features of Young Children's Education?

LG3 Evaluate different approaches to early childhood education.

Variations in Early Childhood Education

- The child-centered kindergarten emphasizes the education of the whole child, with particular attention to individual variation, the process of learning, and the importance of play in development. The Montessori approach allows children to choose from a range of activities while teachers serve as facilitators. Developmentally appropriate practice focuses on the typical patterns of children (age appropriateness) and the uniqueness of each child (individual appropriateness). Such practice contrasts with developmentally inappropriate practice, which ignores the concrete, hands-on approach to learning.

- The U.S. government has tried to break the poverty cycle with programs such as Head Start. Model programs have been shown to have positive effects on children who live in poverty.

- Controversy surrounds early childhood education curricula. On the one side are the child-centered, constructivist advocates; on the other are those who advocate a direct instruction, academic approach. Another controversy involves whether universal preschool education should be provided for all U.S. 4-year-olds. A third controversy focuses on school readiness, in which skills in math, reading, and attention are especially important in predicting later academic achievement.

key **terms**

animism	egocentrism	operations	sustained attention
centration	executive attention	preoperational stage	symbolic function substage
child-centered kindergarten	executive function	Project Head Start	theory of mind
conservation	fast mapping	scaffolding	zone of proximal development
developmentally appropriate practice (DAP)	intuitive thought substage	short-term memory	(ZPD)
	Montessori approach	social constructivist approach	

key **people**

Jean Berko	Maria Gartstein	Deborah Leong	Mary Rothbart
Elena Bodrova	Rochel Gelman	Maria Montessori	Catherine Snow
Stephanie Carlson	Barbel Inhelder	Jean Piaget	Lev Vygotsky

connecting with **improving the lives of children**

STRATEGIES

Nourish the Young Child's Cognitive Development

What are some good strategies for helping young children develop their cognitive competencies?

- *Provide opportunities for the young child's development of symbolic thought.* Give the child ample opportunities to scribble and draw. Provide the child with opportunities to engage in make-believe play. Don't criticize the young child's art and play. Let the child's imagination flourish.

- *Engage children in activities that will improve their executive function.* A good resource for such activities is: http://developingchild. harvard.edu/science/key-concepts/executive-function/

- *Monitor young children's ability to delay gratification.* Delay of gratification is a key element of many aspects of children's competence. Create exercises and activities for young children to practice their delay of gratification.

- *Encourage exploration.* Let the child select many of the activities he or she wants to explore. Don't have the child do rigid paper-and-pencil exercises that involve rote learning. The young child should not be spending lots of time passively sitting, watching, and listening.

- *Be an active language partner with the young child.* Encourage the young child to speak in entire sentences instead of using single words. Be a good listener. Ask the child lots of questions. Don't spend time correcting the child's grammar; simply model correct grammar yourself when you talk with the child. Don't correct the young child's writing. Spend time selecting age-appropriate books for the young child. Read books with the young child.

- *Become sensitive to the child's zone of proximal development.* Monitor the child's level of cognitive functioning. Know what tasks the child can competently perform alone and those that are too difficult, even with your help. Guide and assist the child in the proper performance of skills and use of tools in the child's zone of proximal development. Warmly support the young child's practice of these skills.

- *Evaluate the quality of the child's early childhood education program.* Make sure the early childhood program the child attends involves developmentally appropriate education. The program should be age appropriate and individual appropriate for the child. It should not be a high-intensity, academic-at-all-costs program. Don't pressure the child to achieve at this age.

RESOURCES

Becoming Brilliant (2016)
Roberta Golinkoff and Kathy Hirsh-Pasek
Washington, DC: American Psychological Association

Becoming Brilliant is a terrific book by two leading developmental psychologists that provides up-to-date recommendations for how children should be educated. They emphasize that too often schools give attention only to content and not enough to other key processes that will help children succeed in life: collaboration, communication, critical thinking, creative innovation, and confidence.

Stop, Act, Think: Integrating Self-Regulation in the Early Childhood Classroom (2015)
Megan McClelland and Shauna Tominey
New York: Taylor & Frances

This excellent book provides many exercises and activities, including games, puzzles, and songs, that teachers and parents can use to improve young children's self-regulation skills, especially those involving executive function.

National Association for the Education of Young Children (NAEYC)
800-424-2460
www.naeyc.com

NAEYC is an important professional organization that advocates for young children and has developed guidelines for a number of dimensions of early childhood education. It publishes the excellent journal *Young Children*.

Mind in the Making (2010)
Ellen Galinsky
New York: HarperCollins

An excellent book for parents who want to guide their children's cognitive development in a positive direction. Drawing upon interviews with leading experts in children's cognitive development, Galinsky describes seven essential skills that children need.

Executive Functions in Children's Everyday Lives (2017)
Edited by Maureen Hoskyn and her colleagues

An up-to-date exploration of many aspects of children's executive function, including chapters on the supportive role parents can play as well as how important executive function is to children's schooling and academic achievement.

chapter 10

SOCIOEMOTIONAL DEVELOPMENT IN EARLY CHILDHOOD

chapter **outline**

©Fotosearch/PhotoLibrary RF

Like many children, Sarah Newland loves animals. During a trip to the zoo at age 4, Sarah learned about an animal that was a member of an endangered species, and she became motivated to help. With her mother's guidance, she baked lots of cakes and cookies, then sold them on the sidewalk outside her home. She was excited about making $35 from the cake and cookie sales, and she mailed the money to the World Wildlife Fund. Several weeks later, Sarah received a letter thanking her for the donation and requesting more money. Sarah was devastated because she thought she had taken care of the animal problem. Her mother consoled her and explained that the endangered animal problem and many others are so big that it takes continued help from many people to solve them. Her mother's guidance when Sarah was a young child must have worked because by the end of elementary school, Sarah had begun helping out at a child-care center and working with her mother to provide meals to the homeless.

As Sarah's mother did, sensitive parents can make a difference in encouraging young children's sense of morality. Just as parents support and guide their children to become good readers, musicians, or athletes, they also play key roles in young children's socioemotional development (*Source:* Kantrowitz, 1991).

topical connections *looking **back***

In "Socioemotional Development in Infancy" you learned that infants' socio-emotional development reflects considerable progress as their caregivers (especially their parents) socialize them, and they develop more sophisticated ways of initiating social interactions with others. Development of a secure attachment is a key aspect of infancy, and the development of autonomy in the second year of life also signals an important accomplishment. As children move through infancy, it is important for caregivers to guide them in regulating their emotions. Temperament also is a central characteristic of the infant's profile, and some temperament styles are more adaptive than others. The use of child-care providers has become increasingly common in recent years, and the quality of this care varies considerably. Parents continue to play key roles in children's development in the early childhood period, but peers begin to play more important roles as well.

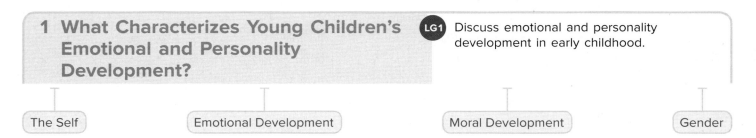

preview

In early childhood, children's emotional lives and personalities develop in significant ways as their small worlds widen. In addition to the continuing influence of family relationships, peers take on a more significant role in children's development and play fills the days of many young children's lives.

1 What Characterizes Young Children's Emotional and Personality Development?

LG1 Discuss emotional and personality development in early childhood.

[The Self]   [Emotional Development]   [Moral Development]   [Gender]

When I say "I," I mean
something absolutely unique
and not to be confused with
any other.

—UGO BETTI

Italian Playwright, 20th Century

*What characterizes young children's
self-understanding?*

©Kevin Dodge/Corbis/Getty Images

self-understanding The child's cognitive
representation of self; the substance and
content of the child's self-conceptions.

Many changes characterize young children's socioemotional development in early childhood. Their developing minds and social experiences produce remarkable advances in the development of their self-understanding, emotional maturity, moral understanding, and gender awareness.

THE SELF

During the second year of life, children make considerable progress in self-recognition. In the early childhood years, young children develop in many ways that enable them to enhance their self-understanding.

Initiative Versus Guilt   In "Introduction" you read about Erik Erikson's (1968) eight developmental stages that are encountered during certain time periods in the human life span. Erikson's first stage, trust versus mistrust, describes what he considers to be the main developmental task of infancy. Erikson's psychosocial stage associated with early childhood is *initiative versus guilt.* By now, children have become convinced that they are persons of their own; during early childhood they begin to discover what kind of person they will become. They identify intensely with their parents, who most of the time appear to them to be powerful and beautiful, although often unreasonable, disagreeable, and sometimes even dangerous. During early childhood, children use their perceptual, motor, cognitive, and language skills to make things happen. They have a surplus of energy that permits them to forget failures quickly and to approach new areas that seem desirable—even if dangerous—with undiminished zest and an increased sense of direction. On their own *initiative,* then, children at this stage exuberantly move out into a wider social world.

The great governor of initiative is *guilt.* Young children's initiative and enthusiasm may bring them not only rewards but also guilt, which lowers self-esteem.

Self-Understanding and Understanding Others   Recent research studies have revealed that young children are more psychologically aware—of themselves and others—than used to be thought (Thompson, 2015). This increased psychological awareness reflects young children's expanding psychological sophistication.

Self-Understanding   In Erikson's portrait of early childhood, the young child clearly has begun to develop **self-understanding,** which is the representation of self, the substance and content of self-conceptions (Harter, 2006, 2012). Though not the whole of personal identity, self-understanding provides its rational underpinnings.

Early self-understanding involves self-recognition. In early childhood, young children think that the self can be described by material characteristics such as size, shape, and color. They distinguish themselves from others through many physical and material attributes. Says 4-year-old Sandra, "I'm different from Jennifer because I have brown hair and she has blond hair." Says 4-year-old Ralph, "I am different from Hank because I am taller and I am different from my sister because I have a bicycle." Physical activities are also a central component of the self in early childhood (Keller, Ford, & Meacham, 1978). For example, preschool children often describe themselves in terms of activities such as play. In sum, during early childhood, children often provide self-descriptions that involve body attributes, material possessions, and physical activities.

Although young children mainly describe themselves in terms of concrete, observable features and action tendencies, at about 4 to 5 years of age, as they hear others use psychological trait and emotion terms, they begin to include these in their own self-descriptions (Thompson, 2006). Thus, in a self-description, a 4-year-old might say, "I'm not scared. I'm always happy."

Many young children's self-descriptions are typically unrealistically positive, as reflected in the comment of the 4-year-old above who says he is always happy, which he is not (Harter, 2006, 2012, 2016). This optimism occurs because they don't yet distinguish between their desired competence and their actual competence, tend to confuse ability and effort (thinking that differences in ability can be changed as easily as can differences in effort), don't engage in spontaneous social comparison of their abilities with those of others, and tend to compare their present abilities with what they could do at an earlier age (which usually makes them look quite good). Perhaps as adults we should all be so optimistic about our abilities!

However, as in virtually all areas of human development, there are individual variations in young children's self-conceptions. In addition, there is increasing evidence that some children are vulnerable to negative self-attributions (Harter, 2016). For example, one study revealed that insecurely attached preschool children whose mothers reported a high level of parenting stress and depressive symptoms had a lower self-concept than other young children in more positive family circumstances (Goodvin & others, 2008). This research indicates that young children's generally optimistic self-ascriptions do not buffer them from adverse, stressful family conditions.

Understanding Others   Children also make advances in their understanding of others in early childhood (Harter, 2012, 2016; Landrum, Pflaum & Mills, 2017; Mills & Elashi, 2014; Thompson, 2015). Young children's theory of mind includes understanding that other people have emotions and desires (Birch & others, 2017; Devine & Hughes, 2017; Wellman, 2015). And, at about 4 to 5 years of age, children not only start describing themselves in terms of psychological traits but they also begin to perceive others in terms of psychological traits. Thus, a 4-year-old might say, "My teacher is nice."

To understand others, it is necessary to take their perspective. **Perspective taking** is the social cognitive process involved in assuming the perspective of others and understanding their thoughts and feelings. Executive function is at work in perspective taking (Galinsky, 2010). Among the executive functions called on when young children engage in perspective taking are cognition inhibition (controlling one's own thoughts to consider the perspectives of others) and cognitive flexibility (seeing situations in different ways).

Perspective taking in young children also is linked to the quality of their social relationships. A recent study found that higher perspective-taking ability in 2-year-olds predicted more stable mother-child attachment later in the preschool years (Meins, Bureau, & Ferryhough, 2017).

One type of understanding that children need to develop is an awareness that people don't always give accurate reports of their beliefs (Mills & Elashi, 2014). Researchers have found that even 4-year-olds understand that people may make statements that aren't true to obtain what they want or to avoid trouble (Lee & others, 2002). For example, one study revealed that 4- and 5-year-olds were increasingly skeptical of another child's claim to be sick when the children were informed that the child was motivated to avoid having to go to camp (Gee & Heyman, 2007). Also, a recent study compared preschool children's trust in an expert's comments (Landrum, Mills, & Johnston, 2013). In this study, in one condition, 5-year-olds trusted the expert's claim more than did 3-year-olds. However, in other conditions, preschoolers tended to trust a nice non-expert more than a mean expert, indicating that young children often are likely to believe someone who is nice to them even if that person is not an expert.

Another important aspect of understanding others involves understanding joint commitments. As children approach their third birthday, their

perspective taking The social cognitive process involved in assuming the perspective of others and understanding their thoughts and feelings.

Young children are more psychologically aware of themselves and others than used to be thought. Some children are better than others at understanding people's feelings and desires—and, to some degree, these individual differences are influenced by conversations caregivers have with young children about feelings and desires.

©Don Hammond/Design Pics/Corbis RF

collaborative interactions with others increasingly involve obligations to the partner (Tomasello & Hamann, 2012). One study revealed that 3-year-olds, but not 2-year-olds, recognized when an adult is committed and when they themselves are committed to joint activity that involves obligation to a partner (Grafenhain & others, 2009).

Individual differences characterize young children's social understanding (Birch & others, 2017; Mills & Elashi, 2014). Some young children are better than others at understanding what people are feeling and what they desire, for example. To some degree, these individual differences are linked to conversations caregivers have with young children about other people's feelings and desires, and children's opportunities to observe others talking about people's feelings and desires. For example, a mother might say to a 3-year-old, "Next time, you should think about Raphael's feelings before you hit him."

In recent research studies, young children's ability to understand their own and others' emotions preceded advances in their theory of mind (Nelson & others, 2013; O'Brien & others, 2011). These studies indicated that a better basic understanding of emotions in early childhood enabled them to develop a more advanced understanding of others' perspectives.

Both the extensive theory of mind research and the recent research on young children's social understanding underscore that young children are not as egocentric as Piaget envisioned (Birch & others, 2017; Decety, Meidenbauer, & Cowell, 2017; Thompson, 2012). Piaget's concept of egocentrism has become so ingrained in people's thinking about young children that too often the current research on social awareness in infancy and early childhood has been overlooked. Research increasingly shows that young children are more socially sensitive and perceptive than was previously envisioned, suggesting that parents and teachers can help them to better understand and interact in the social world by how they interact with them (Thompson, 2015, 2016). If young children are seeking to better understand various mental and emotional states (intentions, goals, feelings, desires) that they know underlie people's actions, then talking with them about these internal states can improve young children's understanding of them (Thompson, 2015, 2016).

However, there is ongoing debate about whether young children are socially sensitive or basically egocentric. Ross Thompson (2012) comes down on the side of viewing young children as socially sensitive, while Susan Harter (2012, 2016) argues that there is still evidence to support the conclusion that young children are essentially egocentric.

Whichever side is taken in this debate, it is important to underscore that social interactions and relationships with others contribute significantly to young children's development of the self and understanding of others. In Thompson's (2013, p. 113) view, "When caregivers exuberantly applaud their child's accomplishments, focus their young child's attention on the consequences of misbehavior, acknowledge shared intentions, work to repair affective mismatches, or talk with their child about emotions, they act as *relational catalysts*, fostering the child's socioemotional growth and helping to refine the child's representations of who they are (and) what other people are like."

developmental **connection**

Cognitive Theory

In Piaget's view, young children are egocentric in that they don't distinguish between their perspective and someone else's. Connect to "Cognitive Development in Early Childhood."

EMOTIONAL DEVELOPMENT

The young child's growing awareness of self is linked to the ability to feel an expanding range of emotions. Young children, like adults, experience many emotions during the course of a day. Their emotional development in early childhood allows them to try to make sense of other people's emotional reactions and to begin to control their own emotions (Rogers & others, 2016; Thompson, 2015).

Expressing Emotions Recall that even young infants experience emotions such as joy and fear, but to experience *self-conscious emotions,* children must be able to refer to themselves and be aware of themselves as distinct from others (Lewis, 2010, 2014, 2015, 2016). Pride, shame, embarrassment, and guilt are examples of self-conscious emotions. Self-conscious emotions do not appear to develop until self-awareness appears around 18 months of age. In a recent study, a broad capacity for self-evaluative emotion was present in the preschool years and was linked to young children's empathetic concern (Ross, 2017). In this study, young children's moral pride, pride in response to achievement, and resilience to shame were linked to a greater tendency to engage in spontaneous helping.

During the early childhood years, emotions such as pride and guilt become more common and they are especially influenced by parents' responses to children's behavior. For example, a young child may experience shame when a parent says, "You should feel bad about biting your sister." One study revealed that young children's emotional expression was linked to their parents' own expressive behavior (Nelson & others, 2012). In this study, mothers who expressed a high incidence of positive emotions and a low incidence of negative emotions at home had children who were observed to use more positive emotion words during mother-child interactions than did the children of mothers who expressed few positive emotions at home.

Understanding Emotions   Among the most important changes in emotional development in early childhood is an increased understanding of emotion (Calkins & Perry, 2016; Cole, 2016; Denham, Bassett, & Wyatt, 2015; Goodvin, Winer, & Thompson, 2015; Kuhnert & others, 2017; O'Kearney & others, 2107). During early childhood, young children increasingly understand that certain situations are likely to evoke particular emotions, facial expressions indicate specific emotions, emotions affect behavior, and emotions can be used to influence others' emotions (Cole & others, 2009). In one study, young children's emotional understanding was linked to how extensively they engaged in prosocial behavior (Ensor, Spencer, & Hughes, 2010). Also, in a recent study of 5- to 7-year-olds, understanding others' emotions was linked to the children's emotion regulation (Hudson & Jacques, 2014).

Between 2 and 4 years of age, children considerably increase the number of terms they use to describe emotions. During this time, they are also learning about the causes and consequences of feelings (Denham, Bassett, & Wyatt, 2015).

When they are 4 to 5 years of age, children show an increased ability to reflect on emotions. They also begin to understand that the same event can elicit different feelings in different people. Moreover, they show a growing awareness that they need to manage their emotions to meet social standards.

A young child expressing the emotion of shame, which occurs when a child evaluates his or her actions as not living up to standards. A child experiencing shame wishes to hide or disappear. *Why is shame called a self-conscious emotion?*
©James Woodson/Digital Vision/Getty Images RF

Regulating Emotions   Many researchers consider the growth of emotion regulation in children as fundamental to the development of social competence (Blair, 2016, 2017; Calkins & Perry, 2016; Eisenberg, Spinrad, & Valiente, 2016). Emotion regulation can be conceptualized as an important component of self-regulation or of executive function. Recall that executive function is increasingly thought to be a key concept in describing the young child's higher-level cognitive functioning (Griffin, Freund, & McCardle, 2015). Cybele Raver and her colleagues (Blair, 2016, 2017; Blair & Raver, 2012, 2015; Blair, Raver, & Finegood, 2016; McCoy & Raver, 2011; Raver & others, 2011, 2012, 2013; Zhai, Raver, & Jones, 2012) are using interventions, such as increasing caregiver emotional expressiveness, to improve young children's emotion regulation and reduce behavior problems in Head Start families. To read in greater detail about one of Cybele Raver's recent studies, see *Connecting with Research.*

Emotion-Coaching and Emotion-Dismissing Parents   Parents can play an important role in helping young children regulate their emotions (Cole, 2016; Loop & others, 2017; Norona & Baker, 2017). Depending on how they talk with their children about emotion, parents can be described as taking an *emotion-coaching* or an *emotion-dismissing* approach (Gottman, 2017). The distinction between these approaches is most evident in the way the parent deals with the child's negative emotions (anger, frustration, sadness, and so on). *Emotion-coaching parents* monitor their children's emotions, view their children's negative emotions as opportunities for teaching, assist them in labeling emotions, and coach them in how to deal effectively with emotions. In contrast, *emotion-dismissing parents* view their role as to deny, ignore, or change negative emotions. One study found that mothers tended to be more sensitive and supportive of their young children's negative emotions than were fathers (Nelson & others, 2009).

Researchers have observed that emotion-coaching parents interact with their children in a less rejecting manner, use more scaffolding and praise, and are more nurturant than are emotion-dismissing parents (Gottman & DeClaire, 1997). Moreover, the children of emotion-coaching parents are better at soothing themselves when they get upset, more effective in regulating their negative affect, focus their attention better, and have fewer behavior problems than the children of

What are some differences in emotion-coaching (shown here) and emotion-dismissing parents?
©LWA-Dann Tardif/Corbis/Getty Images

Caregivers' Emotional Expressiveness, Children's Emotion Regulation, and Behavior Problems in Head Start Children

A study by Dana McCoy and Cybele Raver (2011) explored links between caregivers' reports of their positive and negative emotional expressiveness, observations of young children's emotion regulation, and teachers' reports of the children's internalizing and externalizing behavior problems. The study focused on 97 children, most of whom were African American or Latino and whose mean age was 4 years and 3 months. The other participants in the study were the children's primary caregivers (90 mothers, 5 fathers, and 2 grandmothers).

To assess caregiver expressiveness, caregivers were asked to provide ratings on a scale from 1 (never/rarely) to 9 (very frequently) for 7 items that reflect caregiver expressiveness, such as "telling family members how happy you are" and "expressing anger at someone's carelessness." Children's emotion regulation was assessed with (a) the emotion regulation part of the PSRA (preschool self-regulation assessment) in which observers rated young children's behavior on 4 delay tasks, 3 executive function tasks, and 3 compliance tasks; (b) an assessment report on children's emotion and emotion regulation; and (c) observations of the children's real-time emotion regulation related to positive emotion (expressions of happiness, for example) and negative emotion (expressions of anger or irritability, for example). Children's internalizing and externalizing behavior problems were rated by their teachers, who reported the extent to which the children had shown such behavioral problems in the last 3 months.

The researchers found that a higher level of caregiver negativity and a lower level of children's emotion regulation independently

What did Dana McCoy and Cybele Raver discover about the importance of caregivers' emotions and children's emotion regulation in children's development?
©Najilah Feanny/Corbis

were linked to more internalizing behavior problems in the young Head Start children. Also, caregivers' reports of their positive emotional expressiveness were associated with a lower level of young children's externalizing behavior problems. The findings demonstrate the importance of family emotional climate and young children's emotion regulation in the development of young children.

The study you just read about was correlational in nature. If you were interested in conducting an experimental study of the effects of caregivers' emotional expressiveness and children's emotion regulation on children's problem behaviors, how would you conduct the study differently?

emotion-dismissing parents (Gottman, 2017). Recent studies found that fathers' emotion coaching was related to children's social competence (Baker, Fenning, & Crnic, 2011) and that mothers' emotion coaching was linked to less oppositional behavior by their children (Dunsmore, Booker, & Ollendick, 2013).

Knowledge of their children's emotional world can help parents guide their children's emotional development and teach them how to cope effectively with problems. One study found that mothers' knowledge about what distresses and comforts their children predicts the children's coping, empathy, and prosocial behavior (Vinik, Almas, & Grusec, 2011).

Regulation of Emotion and Peer Relations Emotions play a strong role in determining the success of a child's peer relationships (Denham, Bassett, & Wyatt, 2015). Moody and emotionally negative children are more likely to experience rejection by their peers, whereas emotionally positive children are more popular. One study revealed that 4-year-olds recognized and generated strategies for controlling their anger more than did 3-year-olds (Cole & others, 2009). Also, a recent study found that children who regulated their frustration and distress at an earlier age during preschool (3 years) had a more rapid decline in externalizing problem behavior when interacting with peers across the early childhood period (3 to 5 years of age) (Perry & others, 2013). Emotion regulation at ages 4 and 5 did not reduce problem behavior to the extent that it did at 3 years of age, suggesting that earlier emotion regulation puts children on a more adaptive trajectory in interacting with peers.

MORAL DEVELOPMENT

Moral development involves the development of thoughts, feelings, and behaviors regarding rules and conventions about what people should do in their interactions with other people. Major developmental theories have focused on different aspects of moral development (Annas, Narváez, & Snow, 2016; Gray & Graham, 2018; Hoover & others, 2018; Killen & Dahl, 2018; Narváez, 2017a, b, 2018; Turiel & Gingo, 2017).

Moral Feelings Feelings of anxiety and guilt are central to the account of moral development provided by Sigmund Freud's psychoanalytic theory. According to Freud, to reduce anxiety, avoid punishment, and maintain parental affection, children identify with parents, internalizing their standards of right and wrong, and thus form the *superego,* the moral element of personality. The superego consists of two main components: the ego ideal and the conscience. The *ego ideal* rewards the child by conveying a sense of pride and personal value when the child acts according to ideal standards approved by the parents. The **conscience** punishes the child for behaviors disapproved by the parents, making the child feel guilty and worthless.

Freud's ideas are not backed by research, but guilt certainly can motivate moral behavior. Freud's claims regarding the formation of the ego ideal and conscience cannot be verified. However, researchers can examine the extent to which children feel guilty when they misbehave. Grazyna Kochanska and her colleagues (Kochanska & Aksan, 2007; Kochanska & Kim, 2012, 2013; Kochanska, Koenig, & others, 2010; Kochanska & others, 2002, 2005, 2008) have conducted a number of studies that explore children's conscience development. Reflecting the presence of a conscience in young children, Kochanska and her colleagues have found that young children are aware of right and wrong, have the capacity to show empathy toward others, experience guilt, indicate discomfort following a transgression, and are sensitive to violating rules.

A major focus of interest regarding young children's conscience involves children's relationships with their caregivers (Kim & others, 2014; Kochanska & Kim, 2012, 2013). Especially important in this regard is the emergence of young children's willingness to embrace the values of their parents, an orientation that flows from a positive, close relationship (Kochanska & Aksan, 2007). For example, children who are securely attached are more likely to internalize their parents' values and rules (Kim & Kochanska, 2017; Kochanska & Kim, 2012).

Other emotions, however, also contribute to the child's moral development, including positive feelings. One important example is *empathy,* which is responding to another person's feelings with an emotion that echoes the other's feelings (Denham, Bassett, & Wyatt, 2011).

Infants have the capacity for some purely empathic responses, but empathy often requires the ability to discern another's inner psychological states, or what is called *perspective taking,* which we discussed earlier in our coverage of self-development. Learning how to identify a wide range of emotional states in others and to anticipate what kinds of action will improve another person's emotional state help to advance children's moral development (Thompson & Newton, 2010).

Today, many child developmentalists believe that both positive feelings—such as empathy, sympathy, admiration, and self-esteem—and negative feelings—such as anger, outrage, shame, and guilt—contribute to children's moral development (Eisenberg, Spinrad, & Valiente, 2016; Ross, 2017). When strongly experienced, these emotions influence children to act in accord with standards of right and wrong.

Empathy is an affective response to another's feelings in which the onlooker's emotional response is similar to the other's feelings (Eisenberg, Spinrad, & Valiente, 2016; Ross, 2017). To empathize is not just to sympathize; it is to put oneself in another's place emotionally. **Sympathy** is an emotional response to another person in which the observer feels sad or concerned about the other person's well-being (Eisenberg, Spinrad, & Valiente, 2016). Feeling sympathy often motivates moral behavior. For example, a recent study indeed found that young children's sympathy predicted whether they would share their possessions with others (Ongley & Malti, 2014).

Emotions such as empathy, shame, guilt, and anxiety over other people's violations of standards are present early in development and undergo developmental change throughout childhood and beyond (Damon, 1988). Also, connections between these emotions can occur

developmental connection

Theories

Freud theorized that individuals go through five psychosexual stages. Connect to "Introduction."

What types of positive emotions are associated with young children's moral development?
©Stockbyte/Getty Images RF

moral development Development that involves thoughts, feelings, and behaviors regarding rules and conventions about what people should do in their interactions with other people.

conscience An internal regulator of standards of right and wrong that involves an integration of moral thought, feeling, and behavior.

empathy An affective response to another's feelings with an emotional response that is similar to the other's feelings.

sympathy An emotional response to another person in which the observer feels sad or concerned about the individual's well-being.

and the connections may influence children's development. For example, in a recent study, participants' guilt proneness combined with their empathy predicted an increase in prosocial behavior (Torstveit, Sutterlin, & Lugo, 2016).

Emotions such as empathy, shame, guilt, and anxiety over other people's violations of standards are present early in development and undergo developmental change throughout childhood and beyond (Damon, 1988). These emotions provide a natural base for children's acquisition of moral values, motivating them to pay close attention to moral events. However, moral emotions do not operate in a vacuum to build a child's moral awareness, and they are not sufficient in themselves to generate moral responses. They do not give the "substance" of moral regulation—the rules, values, and standards of behavior that children need to understand and act on. Moral emotions are inextricably interwoven with the cognitive and social aspects of children's development (Narváez, 2010).

How is this child's moral thinking likely to be different about stealing a cookie depending on whether he is in Piaget's heteronomous or autonomous stage?
©Fuse/Getty Images RF

Moral Reasoning   Interest in how children think about moral issues was stimulated by Jean Piaget (1932), who extensively observed and interviewed children from the ages of 4 through 12. Piaget watched children play marbles to learn how they thought about and used the game's rules. He also asked children about ethical issues—theft, lies, punishment, and justice, for example. Piaget concluded that children go through two distinct stages in how they think about morality.

- From 4 to 7 years of age, children display **heteronomous morality,** the first stage of moral development in Piaget's theory. Children think of justice and rules as unchangeable properties of the world, removed from the control of people.
- From 7 to 10 years of age, children are in a transition, showing some features of the first stage of moral reasoning and some features of the second stage, autonomous morality.
- From about 10 years of age and older, children show **autonomous morality.** They become aware that rules and laws are created by people, and, in judging an action, they consider the actor's intentions as well as the consequences.

developmental **connection**

Cognitive Theory

Lawrence Kohlberg's theory, like Piaget's, emphasizes that peers play a much stronger role in the development of moral thinking than parents do. Connect to "Socioemotional Development in Early Childhood."

heteronomous morality The first stage of moral development in Piaget's theory, occurring from approximately 4 to 7 years of age. Justice and rules are conceived of as unchangeable properties of the world, removed from the control of people.

autonomous morality The second stage of moral development in Piaget's theory, displayed by older children (about 10 years of age and older). The child becomes aware that rules and laws are created by people and that, in judging an action, one should consider the actor's intentions as well as the consequences.

immanent justice The expectation that, if a rule is broken, punishment will be meted out immediately.

Because young children are heteronomous moralists, they judge the rightness or goodness of behavior by considering its consequences, not the intentions of the actor. For example, to the heteronomous moralist, breaking twelve cups accidentally is worse than breaking one cup intentionally. As children develop into moral autonomists, intentions become more important than consequences.

The heteronomous thinker also believes that rules are unchangeable and are handed down by all-powerful authorities. When Piaget suggested to young children that they use new rules in a game of marbles, they resisted. By contrast, older children—moral autonomists—accept change and recognize that rules are merely convenient conventions, subject to change.

The heteronomous thinker also believes in **immanent justice,** the concept that if a rule is broken, punishment will be meted out immediately. The young child believes that a violation is connected automatically to its punishment. Thus, young children often look around worriedly after doing something wrong, expecting inevitable punishment. Immanent justice also implies that if something unfortunate happens to someone, the person must have transgressed earlier. Older children are moral autonomists—that is, they recognize that punishment occurs only if someone witnesses the wrongdoing and that, even then, punishment is not inevitable.

How do these changes in moral reasoning occur? Piaget argued that as children develop, they become more sophisticated in thinking about social matters, especially about the possibilities and conditions of cooperation. Piaget emphasized that this social understanding comes about through the mutual give-and-take of peer relations. In the peer group, where others have power and status similar to the child's, plans are negotiated and coordinated, and disagreements are reasoned about and eventually settled. Parent-child relations, in which parents have power and children do not, are less likely to advance moral reasoning, because rules are often handed down in an authoritarian way.

Earlier in this chapter we discussed Ross Thompson's view that young children are not as egocentric as Piaget envisioned. Thompson (2012) further elaborated on this view, arguing that recent research indicates that young children often show a non-egocentric awareness of others' goals, feelings, and desires and how such internal states are influenced by the actions of others. These ties between advances in moral understanding and theory of mind indicate that young children possess cognitive resources that allow them to be aware of others' intentions and know when someone violates a moral prohibition.

However, because of limitations in their self-control skills, social understanding, and cognitive flexibility, young children's moral advancements often are inconsistent and vary across situations. They still have a long way to go before they have the capacity for developing a consistent moral character and making ethical judgments.

Moral Behavior   The behavioral and social cognitive theory of child development focuses on moral behavior rather than on moral reasoning. It holds that the processes of reinforcement, punishment, and imitation explain the development of moral behavior. When children are rewarded for behavior that is consistent with laws and social conventions, they are likely to repeat that behavior. When models who behave morally are provided, children are likely to adopt their actions. And, when children are punished for immoral behavior, those behaviors are likely to be reduced or eliminated. However, because punishment may have adverse side effects, as we discuss later in this chapter, it needs to be used judiciously and cautiously.

If a 4-year-old boy has been rewarded by his mother for telling the truth when he breaks a glass at home, does that mean he is likely to tell the truth to his preschool teacher when he knocks over a vase and breaks it? Not necessarily; the situation influences behavior. More than half a century ago, a comprehensive study of thousands of children in many situations—at home, at school, and at church, for example—found that the totally honest child was virtually nonexistent; so was the child who cheated in all situations (Hartshorne & May, 1928–1930). Behavioral and social cognitive researchers emphasize that what children do in one situation is often only weakly related to what they do in other situations. A child might cheat in class but not in a game; a child might steal a piece of candy when alone but not steal it when others are present.

And when provided with models who behave morally, individuals are likely to adopt their actions. In a recent study, 2-year-olds watched a video of an adult engaging in prosocial behavior in response to another person's distress (Williamson, Donohue, & Tully, 2013). Children who saw the prosocial video were more likely to imitate the prosocial behavior in response to their own parents' distress than were children who had not seen the video.

Social cognitive theorists also believe that the ability to resist temptation is closely tied to the development of self-control (Mischel, 2004). To achieve this self-control, children must learn to delay gratification. According to social cognitive theorists, cognitive factors are important in the child's development of self-control (Bandura, 2010a, b, 2015).

Parenting and Young Children's Moral Development   Young children's relationship with their parents is an important aspect of moral development (Eisenberg, Spinrad, & Valiente, 2016; Kim & Kochanska, 2017; Thompson & Newton, 2010, 2013). Especially important in this regard is the emergence of young children's willingness to embrace the values of their parents, which flows from a positive, close relationship. For example, children who are securely attached are more likely to internalize their parents' values and rules (Thompson & Newton, 2010).

In Ross Thompson's (2006) view, young children are moral apprentices, striving to understand what is moral. They can be assisted in this quest by the "sensitive guidance of adult mentors in the home who provide lessons about morality in everyday experiences" (Thompson, Meyer, & McGinley, 2006, p. 290). An important parenting strategy is to proactively avert potential misbehavior by children before it takes place (Thompson, Meyer, & McGinley, 2006). With younger children, being proactive means using diversion, such as distracting their attention or moving them to alternative activities. With older children, being proactive may involve talking with them about values that the parents deem important. Transmitting these values can help older children and adolescents to resist the temptations that inevitably emerge in contexts such as peer relations and media exposure beyond the scope of direct parental monitoring.

┌ ─ ─ ─ ─ ─ ─ ─ ─ ─ →
developmental **connection**

Social Cognitive Theory

What are the main themes of Bandura's social cognitive theory? Connect to "Introduction."
← ─ ─ ─ ─ ─ ─ ─ ─ ─ ┘

What are some aspects of relationships between parents and children that contribute to children's moral development?

©Tanya Constantine/Blend Images/Getty Images RF

GENDER

Gender refers to the characteristics of people as males and females. **Gender identity** involves a sense of one's own gender, including knowledge, understanding, and acceptance of being male or female (Brannon, 2017; Martin & others, 2017). One aspect of gender identity involves knowing whether you are a girl or boy, which most children can do by about 2½ years of age (Blakemore, Berenbaum, & Liben, 2009). **Gender roles** are sets of expectations that prescribe how females or males should think, act, and feel. During the preschool years, most children increasingly act in ways that match their culture's gender roles. **Gender typing** refers to acquisition of a traditional masculine or feminine role. For example, fighting is more characteristic of a traditional masculine role and crying is more characteristic of a traditional feminine role (Helgeson, 2017). One study revealed that sex-typed behavior (boys playing with cars and girls with jewelry, for example) increased during the preschool years, and children engaging in the most sex-typed behavior during the preschool years were still doing so at 8 years of age (Golombok & others, 2008).

How is gender influenced by biology? By children's social experiences? By cognitive factors?

Biological Influences   Biology clearly plays a role in gender development. Among the possible biological influences are chromosomes, hormones, and evolution (Antfolk, 2017; Buss, 2015; Hines, 2015; Johnson, 2017).

Chromosomes and Hormones   Biologists have learned a great deal about how sex differences develop. Recall that humans normally have 46 chromosomes arranged in pairs (see "Biological Beginnings"). The 23rd pair consists of a combination of X and Y chromosomes, usually two X chromosomes in a female and an X and a Y in a male. In the first few weeks of gestation, however, female and male embryos look alike.

Males start to differ from females when genes on the Y chromosome in the male embryo trigger the development of testes rather than ovaries; the testes secrete copious amounts of the class of hormones known as androgens, which lead to the development of male sex organs. Low levels of androgens in the female embryo allow the normal development of female sex organs.

Thus, hormones play a key role in the development of sex differences (Hines, 2015; Li, Kung, & Hines, 2017). The two main classes of sex hormones are estrogens and androgens, which are secreted by the *gonads* (ovaries in females, testes in males). *Estrogens,* such as estradiol, influence the development of female physical sex characteristics. *Androgens,* such as testosterone, promote the development of male physical sex characteristics. Sex hormones also can influence children's socioemotional development. One study revealed that higher fetal testosterone level measured from amniotic fluid was linked to increased male-typical play in 6- to 10-year-old boys and girls (Auyeung & others, 2009).

The Evolutionary Psychology View   How might physical differences between the sexes give rise to psychological differences between males and females? Evolutionary psychology offers one answer. According to evolutionary psychology, adaptation during human evolution produced psychological differences between males and females (Antfolk, 2017; Buss, 2012, 2015). Because of their differing roles in reproduction, males and females faced differing pressures when the human species was evolving (Johnson, 2017). In particular, because having multiple sexual liaisons improves the likelihood that males will pass on their genes, natural selection favored males who adopted short-term mating strategies. These are strategies that allow a male to win the competition with other males for sexual access to females. Therefore, say evolutionary psychologists, males evolved dispositions that favor violence, competition, and risk taking.

In contrast, according to evolutionary psychologists, females' contributions to the gene pool were improved when they secured resources that ensured that their offspring would survive; this outcome was promoted by obtaining long-term mates who could provide their offspring with resources and protection (Buss, 2015). As a consequence, natural selection favored females who devoted effort to parenting and chose successful, ambitious mates who could provide their offspring with resources and protection.

Critics of evolutionary psychology argue that its hypotheses are backed by speculations about prehistory, not evidence, and that in any event people are not locked into behavior that was adaptive in the evolutionary past. Critics also claim that the evolutionary view pays little attention to cultural and individual variations in gender differences (Hyde & DeLamater, 2017).

gender identity The sense of one's own gender, including knowledge, understanding, and acceptance of being male or female.

gender role A set of expectations that prescribes how females or males should think, act, and feel.

gender typing Acquisition of a traditional masculine or feminine role.

Social Influences Many social scientists do not locate the cause of psychological gender differences in biological dispositions. Rather, they argue that these differences are due to social experiences. Explanations for how gender differences come about through experience include both social and cognitive theories (Liben, 2017; Martin & others, 2017).

Social Theories of Gender Three main social theories of gender have been proposed—social role theory, psychoanalytic theory, and social cognitive theory. Alice Eagly (2001, 2010, 2012) proposed **social role theory,** which states that gender differences result from the contrasting roles of women and men. In most cultures around the world, women have less power and status than men, and they control fewer resources (Helgeson, 2017). Compared with men, women perform more domestic work, spend fewer hours in paid employment, receive lower pay, and are more thinly represented in the highest levels of organizations. In Eagly's view, as women adapted to roles with less power and less status in society, they showed more cooperative, less dominant profiles than men. Thus, the social hierarchy and division of labor are important causes of gender differences in power, assertiveness, and nurture (Eagly & Wood, 2016).

The **psychoanalytic theory of gender** stems from Freud's view that the preschool child develops a sexual attraction to the opposite-sex parent. This is the process known as the Oedipus complex (for boys) or Electra complex (for girls). At 5 or 6 years of age, the child renounces this attraction because of anxious feelings. Subsequently, the child identifies with the same-sex parent, unconsciously adopting the same-sex parent's characteristics. However, developmentalists have observed that gender development does not proceed as Freud proposed (Blakemore, Berenbaum, & Liben, 2009). Children become gender-typed much earlier than 5 or 6 years of age, and they become masculine or feminine even when the same-sex parent is not present in the family.

The social cognitive approach provides an alternative explanation of how children develop gender-typed behavior. According to the **social cognitive theory of gender,** children's gender development occurs through observing and imitating what other people say and do, and through being rewarded and punished for gender-appropriate and gender-inappropriate behavior (Bussey & Bandura, 1999). From birth onward, males and females are treated differently. When infants and toddlers show gender differences, adults tend to reward them. Parents often use rewards and punishments to teach their daughters to be feminine ("Karen, you are being a good girl when you play gently with your doll") and their sons to be masculine ("Keith, a boy as big as you is not supposed to cry"). Parents, however, are only one of many sources through which children learn gender roles (Helgeson, 2017; Leaper, 2015; Liben, 2017; Lord & others, 2017). Culture, schools, peers, the media, and other family members also provide gender-role models. For example, children also learn about gender from observing adults in the neighborhood and engaging in screen time. As children get older, peers become increasingly important. Let's take a closer look at the influence of parents and peers.

Parental Influences Parents, by action and by example, influence their children's gender development (Brannon, 2017; Endendijk & others, 2017; Helgeson, 2017; Leaper & Farkas, 2015; Liben, 2017). Both mothers and fathers are psychologically important to their children's gender development (Tenenbaum & May, 2014). Cultures around the world, however, tend to give mothers and fathers different roles (Chen & Liu, 2016). A research review provided these conclusions (Bronstein, 2006):

- *Mothers' socialization strategies.* In many cultures mothers socialize their daughters to be more obedient and responsible than their sons. They also place more restrictions on daughters' autonomy.

- *Fathers' socialization strategies.* Fathers show more attention to sons than to daughters, engage in more activities with sons, and put forth more effort to promote sons' intellectual development.

Thus, despite increased awareness in the United States and other Western nations of the negative outcomes of gender stereotyping, many parents continue to foster behaviors and perceptions that reflect traditional gender-role norms (Bronstein, 2006).

Peer Influences Parents provide the earliest discrimination of gender roles, but before long, peers join the process of responding to and modeling masculine and feminine behavior (Andrews & others, 2016; Martin, Fabes, & Hanish, 2018; Zosuls & others, 2016). In fact, peers become so important to gender development that the playground has been called "gender school" (Luria & Herzog, 1985).

First imagine that this is a photograph of a baby girl. *What expectations would you have of her?* Then imagine that this is a photograph of a baby boy. *What expectations would you have of him?*
©Kwame Zikomo/Purestock/SuperStock RF

How Would You...?
If you were a **human development and family studies professional,** how would you describe the ways in which parents influence their children's notions of gender roles?

social role theory A theory that gender differences arise from the contrasting roles of men and women.

psychoanalytic theory of gender A theory deriving from Freud's view that the preschool child develops a sexual attraction to the opposite-sex parent, by approximately 5 or 6 years of age renounces this attraction because of anxious feelings, and subsequently identifies with the same-sex parent, unconsciously adopting the same-sex parent's characteristics.

social cognitive theory of gender A theory that emphasizes that children's gender development occurs through the observation and imitation of gender behavior and through the rewards and punishments children experience for gender-appropriate and gender-inappropriate behavior.

What role does gender play in children's peer relations?
(*Left*) ©altrendo images/Getty Images; (*right*) ©Cindy Charles/PhotoEdit

Peers extensively reward and punish gender behavior (Leaper, 2015). For example, when children play in ways that the culture says are sex-appropriate, their peers tend to reward them. But peers often reject children who act in a manner that is considered more characteristic of the other gender (Andrews & others, 2016; Matlin, 2012). A little girl who brings a doll to the park may find herself surrounded by new friends; a little boy who does the same thing might be jeered at. However, there is greater pressure for boys to conform to a traditional male role than for girls to conform to a traditional female role (Fagot, Rodgers, & Leinbach, 2000). For example, a preschool girl who wants to wear boys' clothing receives considerably more approval than a boy who wants to wear a dress. The very term "tomboy" implies broad social acceptance of girls' adopting traditional male behaviors. In a recent study of 9- to 10-year-olds in Great Britain, gender-nonconforming boys were most at risk for peer rejection (Braun & Davidson, 2017). In this study, gender-nonconforming girls were preferred more than gender-conforming girls, with children most often citing masculine activities as the reason for this choice.

Gender molds important aspects of peer relations (Liben, 2017). It influences the composition of children's groups, the size of groups, and interactions within a group (Maccoby, 1998, 2002):

- *Gender composition of children's groups.* Around the age of 3, children already show a preference to spend time with same-sex playmates. From 4 to 12 years of age, this preference for playing in same-sex groups increases, and during the elementary school years children spend a large majority of their free time with children of their own sex (see Figure 1).
- *Group size.* From about 5 years of age onward, boys are more likely to congregate in larger clusters than girls are. Boys are also more likely to participate in organized group games than girls are.
- *Interaction in same-sex groups.* Boys are more likely than girls to engage in rough-and-tumble play, competition, conflict, ego displays, risk taking, and dominance seeking. By contrast, girls are more likely to engage in "collaborative discourse," in which they talk and act in a more reciprocal manner. A recent study of preschool children (average age: 4 years) found that children selected playmates of the same sex who engaged in similar levels of gender-typed activities (Martin & others, 2013). In selecting a playmate, sex of the playmate was found to be more important than activity.

Cognitive Influences One influential cognitive theory is **gender schema theory,** which states that gender typing emerges as children gradually develop gender schemas of what is gender-appropriate and gender-inappropriate in their culture (Halim & others, 2016; Martin & Cook, 2017; Miller & others, 2013). A schema is a cognitive structure, a network of associations that guide an individual's perceptions. A gender schema organizes the world in terms of female and male. Children and adolescents are internally motivated to perceive the world and to act in accordance with their developing schemas. Bit by bit, children and adolescents pick up what is gender-appropriate and gender-inappropriate in their culture, developing gender schemas that shape how they perceive the world and what they remember (Conry-Murray, Kim, & Turiel, 2012). Children and adolescents are motivated to act in ways that conform to these gender schemas.

gender schema theory The theory that gender typing emerges as children gradually develop gender schemas of what is considered gender-appropriate and gender-inappropriate in their culture.

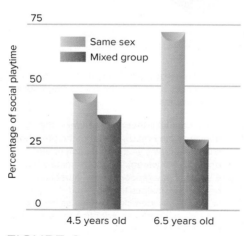

FIGURE **1**

DEVELOPMENTAL CHANGES IN PERCENTAGE OF TIME SPENT IN SAME-SEX AND MIXED-GROUP SETTINGS. Observations of children show that they are more likely to play in same-sex than mixed-sex groups. This tendency increases between 4 and 6 years of age.

Review Connect Reflect

LG1 Discuss emotional and personality development in early childhood.

Review

- What changes in the self occur during early childhood?
- What changes take place in emotional development in early childhood?
- What are some key aspects of moral development in young children?
- How does gender develop in young children?

Connect

- In the previous section, you read about the influence of parents on children's gender development. How does this compare with what you have learned about parents' influence on temperament?

Reflect *Your Own Personal Journey of Life*

- Imagine you are the parent of a 4-year-old. What strategies would you use to increase your child's understanding of others?

2 What Roles Do Families Play in Young Children's Development?

LG2 Explain how families can influence young children's development.

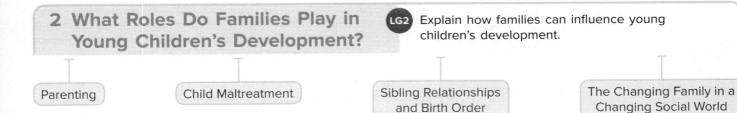

- Parenting
- Child Maltreatment
- Sibling Relationships and Birth Order
- The Changing Family in a Changing Social World

Attachment to a caregiver is a key social relationship during infancy. Social and emotional development is also shaped by other relationships and by temperament, contexts, and social experiences in the early childhood years and later. In this section, we discuss social relationships of early childhood beyond attachment.

PARENTING

Some recent media accounts portray many parents as unhappy, feeling little joy in caring for their children. However, recent research found that parents were more satisfied with their lives than were nonparents, felt relatively better on a daily basis than did nonparents, and had more positive feelings related to caring for their children than to other daily activities (Nelson & others, 2013). Also, a recent research review concluded that parents are unhappy when they experience more negative emotions, financial problems, sleep problems, and troubled marriages (Nelson, Kushley, & Lyubomirsky, 2014). This review concluded that parents were happy when they experienced meaning in life, satisfaction of basic needs, more positive emotions, and positive social roles.

Good parenting takes time and effort (Bornstein, 2016; Serrano-Villar, Huang, & Calzada, 2017). You can't do it with a minute here and a minute there, such as playing Mozart CDs and reading one-minute bedtime stories to children (Gleason & others, 2017). Of course, it's not just the quantity of time parents spend with children that is important for children's development—the quality of the parenting is clearly influential as well (Grusec, 2017; Holden & others, 2017; Kerig, 2016; Orth, 2017; Stifter & Dollar, 2016). For example, a recent study found that maternal scaffolding, sensitivity, and support for autonomy were linked to better executive function in preschool children (Blair, Raver, & Berry, 2014).

Baumrind's Parenting Styles Diana Baumrind (1971, 2012) holds that parents should be neither punitive nor aloof. Rather, they should develop rules for their children and be affectionate with them. She has described four types of parenting styles:

- **Authoritarian parenting** is a restrictive, punitive style in which parents exhort the child to follow their directions and respect their work and effort. The authoritarian parent places firm limits and controls on the child and allows little verbal exchange.

> Parenting is a very important profession, but no test of fitness for it is ever imposed in the interest of children.
>
> —**GEORGE BERNARD SHAW**
> *Irish Playwright, 20th Century*

> We never know the love of our parents until we have become parents.
>
> —**HENRY WARD BEECHER**
> *American Clergyman, 19th Century*

authoritarian parenting A restrictive, punitive parenting style in which parents exhort the child to follow their directions and to respect their work and effort. The authoritarian parent places firm limits and controls on the child and allows little verbal exchange. Authoritarian parenting is associated with children's social incompetence.

	Accepting, responsive	Rejecting, unresponsive
Demanding, controlling	Authoritative	Authoritarian
Undemanding, uncontrolling	Indulgent	Neglectful

FIGURE 2

CLASSIFICATION OF PARENTING STYLES. The four types of parenting styles (authoritative, authoritarian, indulgent, and neglectful) involve the dimensions of acceptance and responsiveness, on the one hand, and demand and control on the other. For example, authoritative parenting involves being both accepting/responsive and demanding/controlling.

©Paul Barton/Corbis/Getty Images

How Would You...?

If you were a **psychologist,** how would you use the research on parenting styles to design a parent education class that teaches effective skills for interacting with young children?

authoritative parenting A parenting style in which parents encourage their children to be independent but still place limits and controls on their actions. Extensive verbal give-and-take is allowed, and parents are warm and nurturant toward the child. Authoritative parenting is associated with children's social competence.

neglectful parenting A style of parenting in which the parent is very uninvolved in the child's life; it is associated with children's social incompetence, especially a lack of self-control.

indulgent parenting A style of parenting in which parents are highly involved with their children but place few demands or controls on them. Indulgent parenting is associated with children's social incompetence, especially a lack of self-control.

For example, an authoritarian parent might say, "You will do it my way or else." Authoritarian parents also might spank the child frequently, enforce rules rigidly but not explain them, and show rage toward the child. Children of authoritarian parents are often unhappy, fearful, and anxious about comparing themselves with others; fail to initiate activity; and have weak communication skills. Also, a recent research review of a large number of studies concluded that authoritarian parenting is linked to a higher level of externalizing problems (acting out, high levels of aggression, for example) (Pinquart, 2017).

- **Authoritative parenting** encourages children to be independent but still places limits and controls on their actions. Extensive verbal give-and-take is allowed, and parents are warm and nurturant toward the child. An authoritative parent might put his arm around the child in a comforting way and say, "You know you should not have done that. Let's talk about how you can handle the situation better next time." Authoritative parents show pleasure and support in response to children's constructive behavior. They also expect mature, independent, and age-appropriate behavior by children. Children whose parents are authoritative are often cheerful, self-controlled and self-reliant, and achievement-oriented; they tend to maintain friendly relations with peers, cooperate with adults, and cope well with stress. In a recent study, children of authoritative parents engaged in more prosocial behavior than their counterparts whose parents used the other parenting styles described in this section (Carlo & others, 2017). Also, in a recent research review, the authoritative parenting style was most effective in predicting which children and adolescents would be less likely to be overweight or obese later in their development (Sokol, Qin, & Puti, 2017).

- **Neglectful parenting** is a style in which the parent is uninvolved in the child's life. Children whose parents are neglectful develop the sense that other aspects of their parents' lives are more important than they are. These children tend to be socially incompetent. Many have poor self-control and don't handle independence well. They frequently have low self-esteem, are immature, and may be alienated from the family. In adolescence, they may show patterns of truancy and delinquency. In the recent research review of studies described under authoritarian parenting, the review also found that neglectful parenting was associated with a higher level of externalizing problems.

- **Indulgent parenting** is a style in which parents are highly involved with their children but place few demands or controls on them. Such parents let their children do what they want. The result is that the children never learn to control their own behavior and always expect to get their way. Some parents deliberately rear their children in this way because they believe the combination of warm involvement and few restraints will produce a creative, confident child. However, children whose parents are indulgent rarely learn respect for others and tend to have difficulty controlling their behavior. They might be domineering, egocentric, noncompliant, and have difficulties in peer relations.

These four classifications of parenting involve combinations of acceptance and responsiveness on the one hand and demand and control on the other (Maccoby & Martin, 1983). How these dimensions combine to produce authoritarian, authoritative, neglectful, and indulgent parenting is shown in Figure 2. Especially for non-Latino White children, authoritative parenting is linked with more positive child outcomes than the other three parenting styles (Bornstein & Zlotnik, 2008).

Parenting Styles in Context   Do the benefits of authoritative parenting transcend the boundaries of ethnicity, socioeconomic status (SES), and household composition? Although occasional exceptions have been found, evidence linking authoritative parenting with competence on the part of the child occurs in research across a wide range of ethnic groups, social strata, cultures, and family structures (Steinberg, 2014).

Other research with ethnic groups suggests that some aspects of the authoritarian style may be associated with positive child outcomes (Clarke-Stewart & Parke, 2014). For example, Asian American parents exert considerable control over their children's lives. However, Ruth Chao (2005, 2007) argues that the style of parenting used by many Asian American parents, which she calls *training parents,* is distinct from the domineering control of the authoritarian style. In recent research on Chinese American adolescents and their parents, parental control was endorsed, as were the Confucian parental goals of perseverance, working hard in school, obedience, and being sensitive to parents' wishes (Russell, Crockett, & Chao, 2010).

An emphasis on requiring respect and obedience is also associated with the authoritarian style, but in Latino child rearing this focus may be positive rather than punitive. Rather than suppressing the child's development, it may encourage the development of an identity that is embedded in the family (Dixon, Graber, & Brooks-Gunn, 2008). Furthermore, many Latino families have several generations living together and helping each other (Zinn & Wells, 2000). In these circumstances, emphasizing respect and obedience by children may be part of maintaining a harmonious home and may be important in shaping the child's identity (Umana-Taylor & Updegraff, 2013; Umana-Taylor & others, 2013).

Further Thoughts on Parenting Styles   Several caveats about parenting styles are in order. First, the parenting styles do not capture the important themes of reciprocal socialization and synchrony. Keep in mind that children socialize parents, just as parents socialize children (Bush & Peterson, 2013; Klein & others, 2017). Second, many parents use a combination of techniques rather than a single technique, although one technique may be dominant. Although consistent parenting is usually recommended, the wise parent may sense the importance of being more permissive in certain situations, more authoritarian in others, and more authoritative in yet other circumstances. In addition, parenting styles often are talked about as if both parents have the same style, although this may not be the case. Finally, some critics argue that the concept of parenting style is too broad and that more research needs to be conducted to "unpack" parenting styles by studying various components that compose the styles (Maccoby, 2007). For example, is parental monitoring more important than warmth in predicting child and adolescent outcomes?

Further, much of the parenting style research has involved mothers, not fathers. In many families, mothers will use one style, fathers another style. Especially in traditional cultures, fathers have an authoritarian style and mothers a more permissive, indulgent style. It has often been said that it is beneficial for parents to engage in a consistent parenting style; however, if fathers are authoritarian and aren't willing to change, children benefit when mothers use an authoritative style.

Punishment   Use of corporal (physical) punishment is legal in every state in the United States. A national survey of U.S. parents with 3- and 4-year-old children found that 26 percent of parents reported spanking their children frequently, and 67 percent reported yelling at their children frequently (Regalado & others, 2004). A recent study of more than 11,000 U.S. parents indicated that 80 percent of the parents reported spanking their children by the time they reached kindergarten (Gershoff & others, 2012). Another recent research review concluded that there is widespread approval of corporal punishment by U.S. parents (Chiocca, 2017). A cross-cultural comparison found that individuals in the United States and Canada were among those with the most favorable attitudes toward corporal punishment and were most likely to remember it being used by their parents (see Figure 3) (Curran & others, 2001). Physical punishment is outlawed in 41 countries, with a number of countries increasing the ban on physical punishment mainly to promote children's rights to protection from abuse and exploitation (Committee on the Rights of the Child, 2014).

What are some reasons for avoiding spanking or similar punishments? They include the following:

- When adults punish a child by yelling, screaming, or spanking, they are presenting children with out-of-control models for handling stressful situations. Children may imitate this behavior.

How Would You...?
If you were a **human development and family studies professional,** how would you characterize the parenting style that prevails within your own family?

According to Ruth Chao, what type of parenting style do many Asian American parents use?
©Blend Images/SuperStock RF

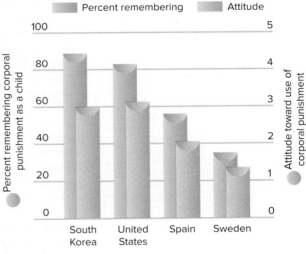

| ▇ Percent remembering | ▇ Attitude |

FIGURE 3

CORPORAL PUNISHMENT IN DIFFERENT COUNTRIES.
A 5-point scale was used to assess attitudes toward corporal punishment, with scores closer to 1 indicating an attitude against its use and scores closer to 5 suggesting an attitude favoring its use. *Why are studies of corporal punishment correlational studies, and how does that affect their usefulness?*

- Punishment can instill fear, rage, or avoidance. For example, spanking the child may cause the child to avoid being near the parent and to fear the parent.
- Punishment tells children what not to do rather than what to do. Children should be given constructive feedback, such as "Why don't you try this?"
- Parents might unintentionally become so angry when they are punishing the child that they become abusive.

Most child psychologists recommend handling misbehavior by reasoning with the child, especially explaining the consequences of the child's actions for others. *Time out,* in which the child is removed from a setting that offers positive reinforcement, can also be effective.

Debate about the effects of punishment on children's development continues (Deater-Deckard, 2013; Ferguson, 2013; Gershoff, 2013; Gershoff & Grogan-Kaylor, 2016; Gershoff, Lee, & Durrant, 2017; Grusec & others, 2013; Holden & others, 2017; Knox, 2010; Laible, Thompson, & Froimson, 2015). Several recent longitudinal studies also have found that physical punishment of young children is associated with higher levels of aggression later in childhood and adolescence (Berlin & others, 2009; Gershoff & others, 2012; Lansford & others, 2014; Taylor & others, 2010). In one longitudinal study, harsh physical punishment in childhood was linked to a higher incidence of intimate partner violence in adulthood (Afifi & others, 2017b).

However, a meta-analysis that focused on longitudinal studies revealed that the negative outcomes of punishment on children's internalizing and externalizing problems were minimal (Ferguson, 2013). A research review of 26 studies concluded that only severe or predominant use of spanking, not mild spanking, compared unfavorably with alternative discipline practices (Larzelere & Kuhn, 2005). Nonetheless, in a recent meta-analysis, when physical punishment was not abusive it still was linked to detrimental child outcomes (Gershoff & Grogan-Kaylor, 2016). And in a recent Japanese study, occasional spanking at 3 years of age was associated with a higher level of behavioral problems at 5 years of age (Okuzono & others, 2017).

In addition to considering whether physical punishment is mild or out-of-control, another factor in evaluating effects on children's development involves cultural contexts. Recently researchers have found that in countries such as Kenya in which physical punishment is considered normal and necessary for handling children's transgressions, the effects of physical punishment are less harmful than in countries such as Thailand where physical punishment is perceived as more harmful to children's development (Lansford & others, 2005, 2012).

Thus, in the view of some experts, it is still difficult to determine whether the effects of physical punishment are harmful to children's development, although such a view might be distasteful to some individuals (Ferguson, 2013; Grusec & others, 2013). Also, as with other research on parenting, research on punishment is correlational in nature, making it difficult to discover causal factors. Further, consider the concept of reciprocal socialization, which emphasizes bidirectional child and parent influences. Researchers have found links between children's early behavioral problems and parents' greater use of physical punishment over time (Laible, Thompson, & Froimson, 2015; Sheehan & Watson, 2008). Nonetheless, a large majority of leading experts on parenting conclude that physical punishment has harmful effects on children and should not be used (Afifi & others, 2017a; Gershoff, Lee, & Durrant, 2017; Holden & others, 2017).

In a recent research review, Elizabeth Gershoff (2013) concluded that the defenders of spanking have not produced any evidence that spanking produces positive outcomes for children and that negative outcomes of spanking have been replicated in many studies. Also, it is clear that when physical punishment involves abuse, it can be very harmful to children's development, as discussed later in this chapter (Almy & Cicchetti, 2018; Cicchetti, 2017; Cicchetti & Toth, 2016, 2017).

Coparenting The relationship between marital conflict and the use of punishment highlights the importance of *coparenting,* which is the support that parents provide one another in jointly raising a child. Poor coordination between parents, undermining of the other parent, lack of cooperation and warmth, and disconnection by one parent are conditions that place children at risk for problems (Galdiolo & Roskam, 2016; Parent & others, 2016; Pruett & others, 2017; Reader, Teti, & Cleveland, 2017). One study revealed that coparenting predicted young children's effortful control above and beyond maternal and paternal parenting (Karreman & others, 2008). Another study indicated that greater father involvement in a child's play was linked to an increase in coparenting one year later (Jia & Schoppe-Sullivan, 2011).

How Would You...?
If you were a **human development and family studies professional,** how would you advise parents about why they should or should not spank their children? Also, what alternatives to spanking would you recommend?

Darla Botkin, Marriage and Family Therapist

Darla Botkin is a marriage and family therapist who teaches, conducts research, and engages in marriage and family therapy. She is on the faculty of the University of Kentucky. Botkin obtained a bachelor's degree in elementary education with a concentration in special education and then went on to receive a master's degree in early childhood education. She spent the next six years working with children and their families in a variety of settings, including child care, elementary school, and Head Start. These experiences led Botkin to recognize the interdependence of the developmental settings that children and their parents experience (such as home, school, and work). She returned to graduate school and obtained a Ph.D. in family studies from the University of Tennessee. She then became a faculty member in the Family Studies program at the University of Kentucky. Completing further coursework and clinical training in marriage and family therapy, she became certified as a marriage and family therapist.

Botkin's current interests include working with young children in family therapy, exploring gender and ethnic issues in family therapy, and understanding the role of spirituality in family wellness.

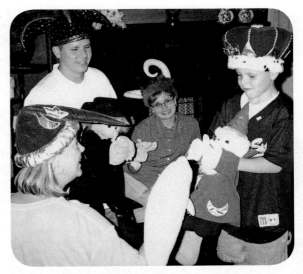

Darla Botkin (*left*) conducts a family therapy session.
Courtesy of Dr. Darla Botkin

For more information about what marriage and family therapists do, see the Careers in Children's Development appendix.

Parents who do not spend enough time with their children or who have problems in child rearing can benefit from counseling and therapy. To read about the work of marriage and family counselor Darla Botkin, see the *Connecting with Careers* profile.

CHILD MALTREATMENT

Unfortunately, punishment sometimes leads to the abuse of infants and children (Cicchetti, 2017; Doyle & Cicchetti, 2018). In 2013, 679,000 U.S. children were found to be victims of child abuse at least once during that year (U.S. Department of Health and Human Services, 2015). Eighty-one percent of these children were abused by a parent or parents. Laws in many states now require physicians and teachers to report suspected cases of child abuse, yet many cases go unreported, especially those involving battered infants.

Whereas the public and many professionals use the term *child abuse* to refer to both abuse and neglect, developmentalists increasingly use the term *child maltreatment* (Almy & Cicchetti, 2018; Cicchetti, 2017; Cicchetti & Toth, 2016, 2017; Doyle & Cicchetti, 2018). This term does not have quite the emotional impact of the term *abuse* and acknowledges that maltreatment includes diverse conditions.

> Child maltreatment involves grossly inadequate and destructive aspects of parenting.
>
> **—DANTE CICCHETTI**
> *Contemporary Developmental Psychologist, University of Minnesota*

Types of Child Maltreatment The four main types of child maltreatment are physical abuse, child neglect, sexual abuse, and emotional abuse (National Clearinghouse on Child Abuse and Neglect, 2017):

- *Physical abuse* is characterized by the infliction of physical injury as a result of punching, beating, kicking, biting, burning, shaking, or otherwise physically harming a child. The parent or other person may not have intended to hurt the child; the injury may have resulted from excessive physical punishment (Lo & others, 2017; Villodas & others, 2016).
- *Child neglect* is characterized by failure to provide for the child's basic needs. Neglect can be physical (abandonment, for example), educational (allowing chronic truancy, for example), or emotional (marked inattention to the child's needs, for example) (Naughton &

others, 2017). Child neglect is by far the most common form of child maltreatment. In every country where relevant data have been collected, neglect occurs up to three times more often than abuse (O'Hara & others, 2017).

- *Sexual abuse* includes fondling a child's genitals, intercourse, incest, rape, sodomy, exhibitionism, and commercial exploitation through prostitution or the production of pornographic materials (Daigneault & others, 2017; Mathews, Lee, & Norman, 2016).
- *Emotional abuse (psychological/verbal abuse/mental injury)* includes acts or omissions by parents or other caregivers that have caused, or could cause, serious behavioral, cognitive, or emotional problems (Hagborg, Tidefors, & Fahlke, 2017).

Although any of these forms of child maltreatment may be found separately, they often occur in combination. Emotional abuse is almost always present when other forms are identified.

How Would You...?

If you were a **health-care professional**, how would you work with parents during infant and child checkups to prevent child maltreatment?

The Context of Abuse

No single factor causes child maltreatment (Cicchetti & Toth, 2017). A combination of factors, including the culture, family, and developmental characteristics of the child, likely contributes to child maltreatment.

The extensive violence that takes place in American culture is reflected in the occurrence of violence in the family (Durrant, 2008). A regular diet of violence appears on television screens, and parents often resort to power assertion as a disciplinary technique. In China, where physical punishment is rarely used to discipline children, the incidence of child abuse is reportedly very low.

The family itself is obviously a key part of the context of abuse (Almy & Cicchetti, 2018; McCarroll & others, 2017). Among the family and family-associated characteristics that may contribute to child maltreatment are parenting stress, substance abuse, social isolation, single parenting, and socioeconomic difficulties (especially poverty) (Cicchetti & Toth, 2017). The interactions of all family members need to be considered, regardless of who performs the violent acts against the child. For example, even though the father may be the one who physically abuses the child, the behavior of the mother, the child, and siblings also should be evaluated. A mother who conveniently goes shopping whenever the father is angry with the child, or siblings who tease the child for "deserving" a beating, may contribute to the abuse.

Were parents who abuse children abused by their own parents? A 30-year longitudinal study found that offspring of parents who had engaged in child maltreatment and neglect are at risk for engaging in child neglect and sexual maltreatment themselves (Widom, Czaja, & DuMont, 2015). About one-third of parents who were abused themselves when they were young go on to abuse their own children (Doyle & Cicchetti, 2018). Thus, some, but not a majority, of parents are involved in an intergenerational transmission of abuse. Mothers who break out of the intergenerational transmission of abuse often report having had at least one warm, caring adult in their background; having a close, positive marital relationship; and having received therapy (Egeland, Jacobvitz, & Sroufe, 1988).

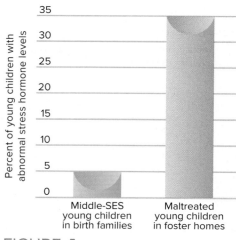

Eight-year-old Donnique Hein lovingly holds her younger sister, 6-month-old Maria Paschel, after a meal at Laura's Home, a crisis shelter run by the City Mission in a suburb of Cleveland, Ohio.
©Joshua Gunter/The Plain Dealer/Landov Images

Developmental Consequences of Abuse

Among the consequences of child maltreatment in childhood and adolescence are poor emotion regulation, attachment problems, problems in peer relations, difficulty in adapting to school, and other psychological problems such as depression, suicide, and delinquency (Doyle & Cicchetti, 2018). As shown in Figure 4, maltreated young children in foster care were more likely to show abnormally high levels of stress hormones than were middle-SES young children living with their birth family (Gunnar & others, 2006). In this study, the abnormal stress hormone levels were mainly present in the foster children who experienced neglect, best described as "institutional neglect" (Fisher, 2005). Adolescents who experienced abuse or neglect as children are more likely than adolescents who were not maltreated as children to engage in violent romantic relationships, delinquency, sexual risk taking, and substance abuse (Wekerle & others, 2009). And one study revealed that a significant increase in suicide attempts before age 18 occurred with repeated child maltreatment (Jonson-Reid, Kohl, & Drake, 2012). Further, a recent study found that exposure to physical or sexual abuse in childhood and adolescence was linked to an increase in 13- to 18-year-olds' suicidal ideation, plans, and attempts (Gomez & others, 2017).

FIGURE 4

ABNORMAL STRESS HORMONE LEVELS IN YOUNG CHILDREN IN DIFFERENT TYPES OF REARING CONDITIONS

Figure 4 bar chart: Percent of young children with abnormal stress hormone levels (y-axis, 0 to 35). Middle-SES young children in birth families: approximately 3. Maltreated young children in foster homes: approximately 32.

Later, during the adult years, individuals who were maltreated as children are more likely to experience physical, emotional, and sexual problems (Lacelle & others, 2012). A 30-year longitudinal study found that middle-aged adults who had experienced child maltreatment had increased risk for diabetes, lung disease, malnutrition, and vision problems (Widom, Czaja, & DuMont, 2012). Another study revealed that child maltreatment was linked to depression in adulthood and to unfavorable outcomes for treatment of depression (Nanni, Uher, & Danese, 2012). A recent study revealed that young adults who had experienced child maltreatment, especially physical abuse, at any age were more likely to be depressed and to engage in suicidal ideation as adults (Dunn & others, 2013). Further, adults who had been maltreated as children often have difficulty establishing and maintaining healthy intimate relationships (Dozier, Stovall-McClough, & Albus, 2009). As adults, maltreated children are also at higher risk for violent behavior toward other adults—especially dating partners and marital partners (Miller-Perrin, Perrin, & Kocur, 2009). One study also found that children who had been maltreated were at increased risk for financial and employment-related difficulties (Zielinski, 2009).

An important strategy for reducing the incidence of these lifelong emotional and physical problems is to prevent child maltreatment (Almy & Cicchetti, 2018; Weiler & Taussig, 2017). In one study of maltreating mothers and their 1-year-olds, two treatments were effective in reducing child maltreatment: (1) home visitation that emphasized improved parenting, coping with stress, and increased support for the mother; and (2) psychotherapy that focused on improving maternal-infant attachment (Cicchetti, Toth, & Rogosch, 2005).

SIBLING RELATIONSHIPS AND BIRTH ORDER

How do developmentalists characterize sibling relationships? How extensively does birth order influence behavior?

Sibling Relationships   Approximately 80 percent of American children have one or more siblings—that is, sisters and brothers (Dunn, 2007, 2015; Fouts & Bader, 2017). In a recent study, a bidirectional association between a child's behavior and sibling relationship quality was found (Pike & Oliver, 2017). In this study, a child's behavior (prosocial behavior, presence of conduct problems, for example) at 4 years of age predicted sibling relationship quality at 7 years of age, and sibling relationship quality (degree of conflict, for example) at 4 years of age predicted child behavior at 7 years of age as well (Pike & Oliver, 2017). It would be expected that improvement in sibling relationship quality or an individual child's behavior would have positive developmental outcomes.

If you grew up with siblings, you probably have abundant memories of aggressive, hostile interchanges. Siblings in the presence of each other when they are 2 to 4 years of age, on average, have a conflict once every 10 minutes and then the conflicts go down somewhat from 5 to 7 years of age (Kramer, 2006).

What do parents do when they encounter siblings having a verbal or physical confrontation? One study revealed that they do one of three things: (1) intervene and try to help them resolve the conflict, (2) admonish or threaten them, or (3) do nothing at all (Kramer & Perozynski, 1999). Of interest is that in families with two siblings 2 to 5 years of age, the most frequent parental reaction is to do nothing at all.

Laurie Kramer (2006), who conducted a number of research studies on siblings, said that not intervening and letting sibling conflict escalate are not good strategies. She developed a program titled "More Fun with Sisters and Brothers," which teaches 4- to 8-year-old siblings social skills for developing positive interactions (Kramer & Radey, 1997). Among the social skills taught in the program are how to appropriately initiate play, how to accept and refuse invitations to play, how to take another's perspective, how to deal with angry feelings, and how to manage conflict. A study of 5- to 10-year-old siblings and their parents found that training parents to mediate sibling disputes increased children's understanding of conflicts and reduced sibling conflict (Smith & Ross, 2007).

However, conflict is only one of the many dimensions of sibling relations (Fouts & Bader, 2017; McHale, Updegraff, & Whiteman, 2013). Sibling relations also include helping, sharing, teaching, fighting, and playing—and siblings can act as emotional supports, rivals, and communication partners.

What characterizes children's sibling relationships?
©RubberBall Productions/Getty Images RF

Do parents usually favor one sibling over others—and if so, does it make a difference in an adolescent's development? One study of 384 sibling pairs revealed that 65 percent of their mothers and 70 percent of their fathers showed favoritism toward one sibling (Shebloski, Conger, & Widaman, 2005). When favoritism of one sibling occurred, it was linked to lower self-esteem and sadness in the less-favored sibling. Indeed, equality and fairness are major concerns of siblings' relationships with each other and how they are treated by their parents (Aldercotte, White, & Hughes, 2016; Campione-Barr, Greer, & Kruse, 2013).

Judy Dunn (2007, 2015), a leading expert on sibling relationships, described three important characteristics of sibling relationships:

- *Emotional quality of the relationship.* Both intensive positive and negative emotions are often expressed by siblings toward each other. Many children have mixed feelings toward their siblings.
- *Familiarity and intimacy of the relationship.* Siblings typically know each other very well and this intimacy suggests that they can either provide support or tease and undermine each other, depending on the situation.
- *Variation in sibling relationships.* Some siblings describe their relationships more positively than others. Thus, there is considerable variation in sibling relationships. Above we saw that many siblings have mixed feelings about each other, but some children mainly describe their sibling in warm, affectionate ways, whereas others primarily talk about how irritating and mean a sibling is.

Birth Order Whether a child has older or younger siblings has been linked to development of certain personality characteristics. For example, a recent review concluded that "firstborns are the most intelligent, achieving, and conscientious, while later-borns are the most rebellious, liberal, and agreeable" (Paulhus, 2008, p. 210). Compared with later-born children, firstborn children have also been described as more adult-oriented, helpful, conforming, and self-controlled. However, when such birth order differences are reported, they often are small.

What might account for even small differences related to birth order? Proposed explanations usually point to variations in interactions with parents and siblings associated with being in a particular position in the family. This is especially true in the case of the firstborn child (Teti, 2001). The oldest child is the only one who does not have to share parental love and affection with other siblings—until another sibling comes along. An infant requires more attention than an older child; thus, the firstborn sibling receives less attention after the newborn arrives. Does this result in conflict between parents and the firstborn? In one research study, mothers became more negative, coercive, and restraining and played less with the firstborn following the birth of a second child (Dunn & Kendrick, 1982).

What is the only child like? The popular conception is that the only child is a "spoiled brat," with such undesirable characteristics as dependency, lack of self-control, and self-centered behavior. But researchers present a more positive portrayal of the only child. Only children often are achievement-oriented and display a desirable personality, especially in comparison with later-borns and children from large families (Falbo & Poston, 1993).

So far, our discussion suggests that birth order might be a strong predictor of behavior. However, an increasing number of family researchers stress that when all of the factors that influence behavior are considered, birth order itself shows limited ability to predict behavior. Think about some of the other important factors in children's lives that influence their behavior beyond birth order. They include heredity, models of competency or incompetency that parents present to children on a daily basis, peer influences, school influences, socioeconomic factors, sociohistorical factors, and cultural variations. When someone says firstborns are always like this but last-borns are always like that, the person is making overly simplistic statements that do not adequately take into account the complexity of influences on a child's development.

A one-child policy has been in place for a number of decades in China. However, in 2016, the Chinese government began allowing two children per family without a financial penalty. *In general, though, what have researchers found the only child to be like?*
©Image Source/Getty Images RF

THE CHANGING FAMILY IN A CHANGING SOCIAL WORLD

Beyond variations in the number of siblings, the families that children experience differ in many important ways (Hoffman & others, 2017; Morrill, Hawrilenko, & Cordova, 2016; Parke, 2017; Patterson & others, 2018; Yu, Cheah, & Calvin, 2016). The number of children

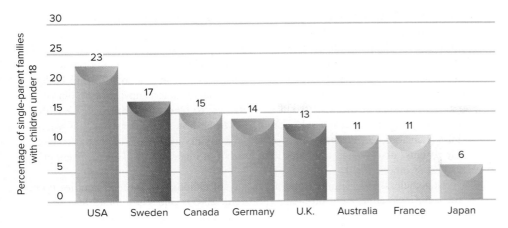

FIGURE **5**

SINGLE-PARENT FAMILIES IN DIFFERENT COUNTRIES

growing up in single-parent families is staggering. As shown in Figure 5, the United States has one of the highest percentages of single-parent families in the world. Among two-parent families, there are those in which both parents work, those in which divorced parents have remarried, or those with gay or lesbian parents. Differences in culture and SES also influence families. How do these variations in families affect children?

Working Parents   More than one of every two U.S. mothers with a child under the age of 5 is in the labor force; more than two of every three with a child from 6 to 17 years of age is. Maternal employment is a part of modern life, but its effects are still being debated.

Most research on parental work has focused on young children and the mother's employment (Brooks-Gunn, Han, & Waldfogel, 2010). However, the effects of working parents involve the father as well as the mother when such matters as work schedules and work-family stress are considered (Clarke-Stewart & Parke, 2014). Recent research indicates that the nature of a parent's work has a stronger influence on children's development than whether the parent works outside the home (O'Brien & others, 2014). For example, a recent study of almost 3,000 adolescents found a negative association of the father's, but not the mother's, unemployment on the adolescents' health (Bacikova-Sleskova, Benka, & Orosova, 2015). Also, a recent study of dual-earner couples found that work-family enrichment experiences had positive outcomes on parenting quality, which in turn was linked to positive child outcomes. By contrast, work-family conflict experiences were associated with poorer parenting quality, which in turn was related to negative child outcomes (Vieira & others, 2016).

Work can produce positive and negative effects on parenting (O'Brien & others, 2014). Ann Crouter (2006) described how parents bring their experiences at work into their homes. She concluded that parents who have poor working conditions, such as long hours, overtime work, stressful work, and lack of autonomy at work, are likely to be more irritable at home and engage in less effective parenting than their counterparts who have better work conditions. A consistent finding is that children (especially girls) of working mothers engage in less gender stereotyping and have more egalitarian views of gender (Goldberg & Lucas-Thompson, 2008).

Children in Divorced Families   Divorce rates changed dramatically in the United States and many countries around the world in the late twentieth century (Braver & Lamb, 2013). The U.S. divorce rate increased rapidly in the 1960s and 1970s but has declined since the 1980s. However, the divorce rate in the United States is still much higher than that of most other countries.

It is estimated that 40 percent of children born to married parents in the United States will experience their parents' divorce (Hetherington & Stanley-Hagan, 2002). Let's examine some important questions about children in divorced families:

- *Are children better adjusted in intact, never-divorced families than in divorced families?* Most researchers agree that children from divorced families show poorer adjustment than their counterparts in nondivorced families (Amato & Anthony, 2014;

How does work affect parenting?
©Eric Audras/PictureQuest RF

developmental connection

Social Contexts

Research consistently shows that family factors are considerably better at predicting children's developmental outcomes than are child-care experiences. Connect to "Socioemotional Development in Infancy."

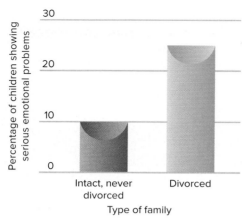

FIGURE 6

DIVORCE AND CHILDREN'S EMOTIONAL PROBLEMS. In Hetherington's research, 25 percent of children from divorced families showed serious emotional problems compared with only 10 percent of children from intact, never-divorced families. However, keep in mind that a substantial majority (75 percent) of the children from divorced families did not show serious emotional problems.

Arkes, 2015; Hetherington, 2006; Lansford, 2012, 2013; Wallerstein, 2008) (see Figure 6). Those who have experienced multiple divorces are at greater risk. Children in divorced families are more likely than children in nondivorced families to have academic problems, to show externalized problems (such as acting out and delinquency) and internalized problems (such as anxiety and depression), to be less socially responsible, to have less competent intimate relationships, to drop out of school, to become sexually active at an early age, to take drugs, to associate with antisocial peers, to have low self-esteem, and to be less securely attached as young adults (Lansford, 2009, 2013). In a recent study, individuals who had experienced their parents' divorce had a greater lifetime risk of engaging in a suicide attempt (Alonzo & others, 2014).

Nonetheless, keep in mind that a majority of children in divorced families do not have significant adjustment problems (Lansford, 2009). One study found that 20 years after their parents had divorced when they were children, approximately 80 percent of adults concluded that their parents' decision to divorce had been a wise one (Ahrons, 2004). A recent study, though, concluded that parental divorce was linked to an increased number of cohabiting/marital partnerships and negative partner relationships from 16 to 30 years of age (Fergusson, McLeod, & Horwood, 2014). An important point is that the outcomes just described for the life event of parental divorce were explained by a variety of other factors and social contexts—parental history of illicit drug use, experience of childhood sexual abuse, lower SES status at the child's birth, and parental history of criminality.

- *Should parents stay together for the sake of the children?* Whether parents should stay in an unhappy or conflictual marriage for the sake of their children is one of the most commonly asked questions about divorce (Deutsch & Pruett, 2009; Hetherington, 2006; Ziol-Guest, 2009; Morrison, Fife, & Hertlein, 2017). If the stresses and disruptions in family relationships associated with an unhappy marriage are reduced by the move to a divorced, single-parent family, divorce can be advantageous. However, if the diminished resources and increased risks associated with divorce also are accompanied by inept parenting and sustained or increased conflict, not only between the divorced couple but also among the parents, children, and siblings, the best choice for the children would be for an unhappy marriage to be retained (Hetherington & Stanley-Hagan, 2002). It is difficult to determine how these "ifs" will play out when parents either remain together in an acrimonious marriage or become divorced.

Note that marital conflict may have negative consequences for children in the context of marriage or divorce (Davies & others, 2016a, b; El-Sheikh & others, 2013; Jouriles, McDonald, & Kouros, 2016). A longitudinal study revealed that conflict in nondivorced families was associated with emotional problems in children (Amato, 2006). Indeed, many of the problems that children from divorced homes experience begin during the predivorce period, a time when parents are often in active conflict with each other. Thus, when children from divorced homes show problems, the problems may be due not only to the divorce, but also to the marital conflict that led to it.

E. Mark Cummings and his colleagues (Cummings & Davies, 2010; Cummings, El-Sheikh, & Kouros, 2009; Cummings & Merrilees, 2009; Cummings & Miller, 2015; Cummings & others, 2017; Cummings & Valentino, 2015; Cummings & others, 2012; Davies, Martin, & Sturge-Apple, 2016; Koss & others, 2011, 2013, 2014; McCoy & others, 2013; Miller-Graff, Cummings, & Bergman, 2016) have proposed *emotional security theory,* which has its roots in attachment theory and states that children appraise marital conflict in terms of their sense of security and safety in the family. These researchers make a distinction between marital conflict that is negative for children (such as hostile emotional displays and destructive conflict tactics) and marital conflict that can be positive for children (such as marital disagreement that involves a calm discussion of each person's perspective and working together to reach a solution). In a recent study, Cummings and his colleagues (2012) found that parental conflict when children were in kindergarten was linked to emotional insecurity later in childhood, which in turn was associated with a lower level of adolescent adjustment, including a higher incidence of depression and anxiety. In another recent study, interparental hostility was a stronger predictor of children's insecurity and externalizing problems than interparental disengagement and low levels of interparental cooperation (Davies & others, 2016a, b). Also in a recent study, maladaptive marital conflict (destructive strategies, severity of arguments) when children were 2 years old was associated with increased internalizing problems 8 years later due to an undermining of attachment security for girls, while negative emotional aftermath of conflict (unresolved, lingering tension) increased both boys' and girls' internalizing problems (Brock & Kochanska, 2016).

- *How much do family processes matter in divorced families?* In divorced families, family processes matter a great deal (Demby, 2016; Hetherington, 2006; Lansford, 2009, 2012, 2013; Luecken & others, 2016; Parke, 2013; Warshak, 2014). When the divorced parents have a harmonious relationship and use authoritative parenting, the adjustment of adolescents is improved (Hetherington, 2006). When the divorced parents can agree on child-rearing strategies and can maintain a cordial relationship with each other, frequent visits by the noncustodial parent usually benefit the child (Fabricius & others, 2010). Following a divorce, father involvement with children drops off more than mother involvement, especially for fathers of girls. Also, a recent study involving divorced families revealed that an intervention focused on improving the mother-child relationship was linked to improvements in relationship quality that increased children's coping skills over the short term (6 months) and long term (6 years) (Velez & others, 2011). And a longitudinal study revealed that parental divorce experienced before age 7 was linked to a lower level of the children's health through 50 years of age (Thomas & Hognas, 2015). Further, a recent study of noncustodial fathers in divorced families indicated that high father-child involvement and low interparental conflict were linked to positive child outcomes (Flam & others, 2016). Also, a recent research review concluded that coparenting (coparental support, cooperation, and agreement) following divorce was associated with positive child outcomes such as reduced anxiety and depression, as well as higher levels of self-esteem and academic performance (Lamela & Figueiredo, 2016).

What concerns are involved in whether parents should stay together for the sake of the children or become divorced?
©Image Source/PunchStock RF

- *What factors influence an individual child's vulnerability to negative consequences from living in a divorced family?* Among the factors involved in the child's risk and vulnerability are the child's adjustment prior to the divorce, as well as the child's personality, temperament, and custody situation (Hetherington, 2006). Children whose parents later divorce show poorer adjustment before the breakup (Amato & Booth, 1996). Children who are socially mature and responsible, who show few behavioral problems, and who have an easy temperament are better able to cope with their parents' divorce. Children with a difficult temperament often have problems coping with their parents' divorce (Hetherington, 2006). Joint custody works best for children when the parents can get along with each other (Clarke-Stewart & Parke, 2014).

    Earlier studies reported gender differences in response to divorce, with divorce being more negative for girls than for boys in mother-custody families. However, more recent studies have shown that gender differences are less pronounced and consistent than was previously believed (Parke, 2013). Some of the inconsistency may be due to the increase in father custody, joint custody, and involvement of noncustodial fathers, especially in their sons' lives.

As marriage has become a more optional, less permanent institution in contemporary America, children and adolescents are encountering stresses and adaptive challenges associated with their parents' marital transitions.

—E. MAVIS HETHERINGTON
Contemporary Psychologist, University of Virginia

- *What role does socioeconomic status play in the lives of children in divorced families?* Custodial mothers experience the loss of about one-fourth to one-half of their predivorce income, in comparison with a loss of only one-tenth by custodial fathers (Emery, 1994). This income loss for divorced mothers is accompanied by increased workloads, high rates of job instability, and residential moves to less desirable neighborhoods with inferior schools (Braver & Lamb, 2013).

In sum, many factors are involved in determining how divorce influences a child's development. To read about some strategies for helping children cope with their parents' divorce, see the *Caring Connections* interlude.

How Would You...?
If you were a **human development and family studies professional,** how would you apply the guidelines on communicating about divorce to help parents discuss the death of a family member with their children?

Communicating with Children About Divorce

Ellen Galinsky and Judy David (1988) developed a number of guidelines for communicating with children about divorce:

- **Explain the separation.** As soon as daily activities in the home make it obvious that one parent is leaving, tell the children. If possible, both parents should be present when children are told about the separation to come. The reasons for the separation are very difficult for young children to understand. No matter what parents tell children, children can find reasons to argue against the separation. It is extremely important for parents to tell the children who will take care of them and to describe the specific arrangements for seeing the other parent.

- **Explain that the separation is not the child's fault.** Young children often believe their parents' separation or divorce is their own fault. Therefore, it is important to tell children that they are not the cause of the separation. Parents need to repeat this message a number of times.

- **Explain that it may take time to feel better.** Tell young children that it's normal not to feel good about what is happening and that many other children feel this way when their parents become separated. It is also okay for divorced parents to share some of their emotions with children by saying something like "I'm having a hard time since the separation just like you, but I know it's going to get better after a while." Such statements are best kept brief and should not criticize the other parent.

- **Keep the door open for further discussion.** Tell your children to come to you any time they want to talk about the separation. It is healthy for children to express their pent-up emotions in discussions with their parents and to learn that the parents are willing to listen to their feelings and fears.

- **Provide as much continuity as possible.** The less children's worlds are disrupted by the separation, the easier their transition to a single-parent family will be. This means maintaining the rules already in place as much as possible. Children need parents who care enough not only to give them warmth and nurturance but also to set reasonable limits.

- **Provide support for your children and yourself.** Parents are as important to children after a divorce or separation as they were before the divorce or separation. Divorced parents need to provide children with as much support as possible. Parents function best when other people are available to give them support as adults and as parents. Divorced parents can find people who provide practical help and with whom they can talk about their problems. For example, many individuals going through a divorce report that they benefit enormously from having a support system of friends with whom they can discuss their situation.

Gay and Lesbian Parents   Data indicate that approximately 20 percent of same-sex couples in the United States are raising children under the age of 18 (Gates, 2013). An important aspect of gay and lesbian families with children is the sexual identity of parents at the time of a child's birth or adoption (Farr, 2017; Oakley, Farr, & Scherer, 2017; Patterson, 2013, 2014; Patterson & D'Augelli, 2013; Patterson & Farr, 2014; Patterson, Farr, & Hastings, 2015; Sumontha, Farr, & Patterson, 2016). The largest group of children with gay and lesbian parents are likely those who were born in the context of heterosexual relationships, with one or both parents only later identifying themselves as gay or lesbian. Gay and lesbian parents may be single or have same-gender partners. In addition, gays and lesbians are increasingly choosing parenthood through donor insemination or adoption. Researchers have found that the children conceived through new reproductive technologies—such as in vitro fertilization—are as well adjusted as their counterparts conceived by natural means (Golombok, 2011a, b; Golombok & Tasker, 2010).

Earlier in the chapter, we described the positive outcomes of coparenting for children. A recent study compared the incidence of coparenting in adoptive heterosexual, lesbian, and gay couples with preschool-aged children (Farr & Patterson, 2013). Both self-reports and observations found that lesbian and gay couples shared child care more than heterosexual couples, with lesbian couples being more supportive than gay couples. Further, a recent study revealed more positive parenting in adoptive gay father families and fewer child externalizing problems in these families than in heterosexual families (Golombok & others, 2014).

Another issue focuses on custody arrangements for children. Many gays and lesbians have lost custody of their children to heterosexual spouses following divorce. For this reason, many gay fathers and lesbian mothers are noncustodial parents.

Researchers have found few differences between children growing up with gay fathers or lesbian mothers and those who are raised by heterosexual parents (Patterson, 2013, 2014).

What are the research findings regarding the development and psychological well-being of children raised by gay and lesbian couples?
©2009 JupiterImages Corporation RF

For example, children growing up in gay or lesbian families are just as popular with their peers, and there are no differences in the adjustment and mental health of children living in these families as compared with children in heterosexual families (Hyde & DeLamater, 2017). For example, in a recent study, the adjustment of school-aged children adopted during infancy by gay, lesbian, and heterosexual parents showed no differences (Farr, 2017). Rather, children's behavior patterns and family functioning were predicted by earlier child adjustment issues and parental stress. In another recent study of lesbian and gay adoptive parents, 98 percent of the adoptive parents reported that their children had adjusted well to school (Farr, Oakley, & Ollen, 2017). Also, the overwhelming majority of children growing up in a gay or lesbian family have a heterosexual orientation (Golombok & Tasker, 2010).

Cultural, Ethnic, and Socioeconomic Variations   Parenting can be influenced by culture, ethnicity, and socioeconomic status. Recall from Bronfenbrenner's ecological theory (discussed in the "Introduction" chapter) that a number of social contexts influence the child's development. In Bronfenbrenner's theory, culture, ethnicity, and socioeconomic status are classified as part of the macrosystem because they represent broader, societal contexts.

Cross-Cultural Studies   Different cultures often give different answers to such basic questions as what the father's role in the family should be, what support systems are available to families, and how children should be disciplined (Gaskins, 2016). There are important cross-cultural variations in parenting (Matsumoto & Juang, 2017; Mistry & Dutta, 2015; Suh & others, 2017). In some cultures (such as Arab countries), authoritarian parenting is widespread.

Cultural change, brought about by such factors as increasingly frequent international travel, the Internet and electronic communications, and economic globalization, affects families in many countries around the world. There are trends toward greater family mobility, migration to urban areas, separation as some family members work in cities or countries far from home, smaller families, fewer extended-family households, and increases in maternal employment (Brown & Larson, 2002). These trends can change the resources that are available to children. For example, when several generations no longer live near each other, children may lose support and guidance from grandparents, aunts, and uncles. On the positive side, smaller families may produce more openness and communication between parents and children.

Ethnicity   Families within different ethnic groups in the United States differ in their typical size, structure, composition, reliance on kinship networks, and levels of income and education (Gollnick & Chinn, 2017; Gonzales & others, 2016; Nieto & Bode, 2018). Large and extended families are more common among minority groups than among the non-Latino White majority. For example, 19 percent of Latino families have three or more children, compared with 14 percent of African American and 10 percent of non-Latino White families. African American and Latino children interact more with grandparents, aunts, uncles, cousins, and more-distant relatives than do non-Latino White children.

Single-parent families are more common among African Americans and Latinos than among non-Latino White Americans (Doob, 2013). In comparison with two-parent households, single parents often have more limited resources of time, money, and energy (Evans, Li, & Sepanski Whipple, 2013). Ethnic minority parents also tend to be less educated and are more likely to live in low-income circumstances than their non-Latino White counterparts. Still, many impoverished ethnic minority families manage to find ways to raise competent children (Hurst, 2013).

A major change in families in the last several decades has been the dramatic increase in the immigration of Latino and Asian families into the United States (Bas-Sarmiento & others, 2017; Giuntella, 2017; Koppelman, 2017; Umana-Taylor & Douglass, 2017). Immigrant families often experience stressors uncommon to or less prominent among long-time residents, such as language barriers, dislocations and separations from support networks, the dual struggle to preserve identity and to acculturate, health, and changes in SES status (Cano & others, 2017; Chaudry & others, 2017; Wang & Palacios, 2017).

Further, an increasing number of children are growing up in transnational families, who move back and forth between the United States and another country, such as Mexico or China (Dreby, 2010; Mazzucato & Schans, 2011). In some cases, these children are left behind in their home country or in other cases (especially in China), they are sent back to China to be raised by grandparents during their early childhood years. Such children might benefit from economic remittances but suffer emotionally from prolonged separation from their parents.

Immigration and Ethnic Minority Parenting

Recent research indicates that many members of families that have recently immigrated to the United States adopt a bicultural orientation, selecting characteristics of the U.S. culture that help them to survive and advance, while still retaining aspects of their culture of origin (Moro, 2014). Immigration also involves cultural brokering, which has increasingly occurred in the United States as children and adolescents serve as mediators (cultural and linguistic) for their immigrant parents (Buriel, 2011; Villanueva & Buriel, 2010).

In adopting characteristics of the U.S. culture, Latino families are

How is acculturation involved in ethnic minority parenting?
©Spencer Grant/PhotoEdit

increasingly embracing the importance of education (Cooper, 2011). Although their school dropout rates have remained higher than for other ethnic groups, toward the end of the first decade of the twenty-first century they declined considerably (National Center for Education Statistics, 2016). In addition to adopting aspects of American culture, immigrants often retain positive aspects of their culture of origin. Parenting in many ethnic minority families emphasizes issues associated with promoting children's ethnic pride, knowledge of their ethnic group, and awareness of discrimination (Umana-Taylor & Douglass, 2017).

How might socioeconomic status and poverty be linked to parenting and young children's development?

©Jens Kalaene/picture-alliance/dpa/AP Images

How Would You...?

If you were an **educator**, how would you work with low-socioeconomic-status families to increase parental involvement in their children's educational activities?

Of course, individual families vary, and how ethnic minority families deal with stress depends on many factors (Yoshikawa & others, 2016). Whether the parents are native-born or immigrants, how long the family has been in this country, and their socioeconomic status and national origin all make a difference (Berry, 2015). The characteristics of the family's social context also influence its adaptation. What are the attitudes toward the family's ethnic group within its neighborhood or city? Can the family's children attend good schools? Are there community groups that welcome people from the family's ethnic group? Do members of the family's ethnic group form community groups of their own? To read further about ethnic minority parenting, see the *Connecting with Diversity* interlude.

Socioeconomic Status   Low-income families have less access to resources than higher-income families do (Wadsworth & others, 2016; Yoshikawa & others, 2017). The differential in access to resources includes nutrition, health care, protection from danger, and enriching educational and socialization opportunities, such as tutoring and lessons in various activities.

Persistent and long-standing poverty can have especially damaging effects on children (Chaudry & others, 2017; Coley & others, 2017). One study revealed that the more years children spent in poverty, the higher were their physiological indices of stress (Evans & Kim, 2007). Also, a recent study found that persistent economic hardship as well as very early poverty was linked to lower cognitive functioning in children at 5 years of age (Schoon & others, 2012). And in another recent study, poverty-related adversity in family and school contexts in early childhood was linked to less effective executive function in second and third grades (Raver & others, 2013).

In the United States and most Western cultures, differences have been found in child rearing among different SES groups (Hoff, Laursen, & Tardif, 2002, p. 246):

- "Lower-SES parents (1) are more concerned that their children conform to society's expectations, (2) create a home atmosphere in which it is clear that parents have authority over children," (3) use physical punishment more in disciplining their children, and (4) are more directive and less conversational with their children.

- "Higher-SES parents (1) are more concerned with developing children's initiative" and delay of gratification, (2) "create a home atmosphere in which children are more nearly equal participants and in which rules are discussed as opposed to being laid down" in an authoritarian manner, (3) are less likely to use physical punishment, and (4) "are less directive and more conversational" with their children.

Parents in different socioeconomic groups also tend to think differently about education (Doob, 2013). Middle- and upper-income parents more often think of education as something that should be mutually encouraged by parents and teachers. By contrast, low-income parents are more likely to view education as the teacher's job. Thus, increased school-family linkages can especially benefit students from low-income families.

Review Connect Reflect

LG2 Explain how families can influence young children's development.

Review

- What aspects of parenting are linked with young children's development?
- What are the types and consequences of child maltreatment?
- How are sibling relationships and birth order related to young children's development?
- How is children's development affected by having two wage-earning parents, having divorced parents, or being part of a particular cultural, ethnic, and socioeconomic group?

Connect

- Fathers are most often the perpetrators of shaken baby syndrome. Given what you learned in this section, which family interactions would a researcher or marriage and family therapist likely explore in cases of child maltreatment?

Reflect Your Own Personal Journey of Life

- Which style or styles of parenting did your mother and father use in rearing you? What effects do you think their parenting styles have had on your development?

3 How Are Peer Relations, Play, and Media/Screen Time Involved in Young Children's Development?

LG3 Describe the roles of peers, play, and media/screen time in young children's development.

| Peer Relations | Play | Media/Screen Time |

The family is an important social context for children's development. However, children's development also is strongly influenced by what goes on in other social contexts, such as in peer groups, at play, or while watching television.

PEER RELATIONS

As children grow older, they spend an increasing amount of time with their peers—children of about the same age or maturity level.

What are the functions of a child's peer group? One of its most important functions is to provide a source of information and comparison about the world outside the family. Children receive feedback about their abilities from their peer group. Children evaluate what they do in terms of whether it is better than, as good as, or worse than what other children do. It is hard to make these judgments at home because siblings are usually older or younger.

Good peer relations can be necessary for normal socioemotional development (Bukowski, Laursen, & Rubin, 2018; Prinstein & Giletta, 2016; Schneider, 2016). Special concerns focus on children who are withdrawn or aggressive. Withdrawn children who are rejected by peers or are victimized and feel lonely are at risk for depression. Children who are aggressive with their peers are at risk of developing

Why are peer relations so important in children's development?
©Michelle Del Guercio/Science Source

developmental **connections**

Peers

Children's peer relations have been classified in terms of five peer statuses. Connect to "Socioemotional Development in Middle and Late Childhood."

a number of problems, including delinquency and dropping out of school (Nesi & others, 2017; Rubin & Barstead, 2018; Rubin & others, 2016).

Developmental Changes   Recall from our discussion of gender that by about the age of 3, children already prefer to spend time with same-sex rather than opposite-sex playmates, and this preference increases in early childhood. During these same years, the frequency of peer interaction, both positive and negative, picks up considerably (Cillessen & Bellmore, 2011). Many preschool children spend considerable time in peer interaction conversing with playmates about such matters as "negotiating roles and rules in play, arguing, and agreeing" (Rubin, Bukowski, & Parker, 2006). And during early childhood, children's interactions with peers become more coordinated and involve longer turns and sequences.

Friends   In early childhood, children distinguish between friends and nonfriends (Howes, 2009). For most young children, a friend is someone to play with. Young preschool children are more likely than older children to have friends who are of different gender and ethnicity (Howes, 2009).

The Connected Worlds of Parent-Child and Peer Relations   Parents may influence their children's peer relations in many ways, both direct and indirect (Caruthers, Van Ryzin, & Dishion, 2014; Tilton-Weaver & others, 2013). Parents affect their children's peer relations through their interactions with their children, how they manage their children's lives, and the opportunities they provide their children (Brown & Bakken, 2011). For example, a recent study found that when mothers coached their preschool daughters about the negative aspects of peer conflicts involving relational aggression (harming someone by manipulating a relationship), the daughters engaged in lower rates of relational aggression (Werner & others, 2014).

Basic lifestyle decisions by parents—their choices of neighborhoods, churches, schools, and their own friends—largely determine the pool from which their children select possible friends. These choices in turn affect which children their children meet, their purpose in interacting, and eventually which children become their friends.

Researchers also have found that children's peer relations are linked to attachment security and parents' marital quality (Pallini & others, 2014). Early attachments to caregivers provide a connection to children's peer relations not only by creating a secure base from which children can explore social relationships beyond the family but also by conveying a working model of relationships (Hartup, 2009).

Do these results indicate that children's peer relations always are wedded to parent-child relationships? Although parent-child relationships influence children's subsequent peer relations, children also learn other modes of relating through their relationships with peers. For example, rough-and-tumble play occurs mainly with other children, not in parent-child interaction. In times of stress, children often turn to parents rather than peers for support. In parent-child relationships, children learn how to relate to authority figures. With their peers, children are likely to interact on a much more equal basis and to learn a mode of relating based on mutual influence.

PLAY

An extensive amount of peer interaction during childhood involves play, but social play is only one type of play. *Play* is a pleasurable activity that is engaged in for its own sake, and its functions and forms vary.

Play's Functions   Play is essential to the young child's health (Quinn, 2017). Theorists have focused on different aspects of play and highlighted a long list of functions (Clark, 2015, 2016; Henricks, 2015a, b).

According to Freud and Erikson, play helps the child master anxieties and conflicts (Demanchick, 2015). Because tensions are relieved in play, the child can cope more effectively with life's problems. Play permits the child to work off excess physical energy and to release pent-up tensions. Therapists use *play therapy* both to allow the child to work off frustrations and to analyze the child's conflicts and ways of coping with them (Clark, 2015, 2016). Children may feel less threatened and be more likely to express their true feelings in the context of play (Yanof, 2013).

©Margo Harrison/123RF

Play also is an important context for cognitive development. Piaget (1962) maintained that play advances children's cognitive development. At the same time, he said that children's cognitive development constrains the way they play. Play permits children to practice their competencies and acquired skills in a relaxed, pleasurable way. Piaget thought that cognitive structures need to be exercised, and play provides the perfect setting for this exercise (DeLisi, 2015). For example, children who have just learned to add or multiply begin to play with numbers in different ways as they perfect these operations, laughing as they do so.

Lev Vygotsky (1962) also considered play to be an excellent setting for cognitive development. He was especially interested in the symbolic and make-believe aspects of play, as when a child substitutes a stick for a horse and rides the stick as if it were a horse. For young children, the imaginary situation is real. Parents should encourage such imaginary play, because it advances the child's cognitive development, especially creative thought.

Daniel Berlyne (1960) described play as exciting and pleasurable in itself because it satisfies our exploratory drive. This drive involves curiosity and a desire for information about something new or unusual. Play is a means whereby children can safely explore and seek out new information. Play encourages exploratory behavior by offering children the possibilities of novelty, complexity, uncertainty, surprise, and incongruity.

More recently, play has been described as an important context for the development of language and communication skills (Taggart, Eisen, & Lillard, 2017). Language and communication skills may be enhanced through discussions and negotiations regarding roles and rules in play as young children practice various words and phrases. These types of social interactions during play can benefit young children's literacy skills (Bredekamp, 2017). And, as we saw in "Cognitive Development in Early Childhood," play is a central focus of the child-centered kindergarten and is thought to be an essential aspect of early childhood education (Henniger, 2018; Morrison, 2017, 2018).

Types of Play   The contemporary perspective on play emphasizes both the cognitive and the social aspects of play (Akhutina & Romanova, 2017; Bergen, 2015; Loizou, 2017; Sim & Xu, 2017; Zosh, Hirsh-Pasek, & Golinkoff, 2015). Among the most widely studied types of children's play today are sensorimotor and practice play, pretense/symbolic play, social play, constructive play, and games (Bergen, 1988).

Sensorimotor and Practice Play   **Sensorimotor play** is behavior by infants to derive pleasure from exercising their sensorimotor schemes. The development of sensorimotor play follows Piaget's description of sensorimotor thought. Infants initially engage in exploratory and playful visual and motor transactions in the second quarter of the first year of life. For example, at 9 months of age, infants begin to select novel objects for exploration and play, especially responsive objects such as toys that make noise or bounce. At 12 months of age, infants enjoy making things work and exploring cause and effect.

Practice play involves the repetition of behavior when new skills are being learned or when physical or mental mastery and coordination of skills are required for games or sports. Sensorimotor play, which often involves practice play, is primarily confined to infancy, whereas practice play can be engaged in throughout life. During the preschool years, children often engage in practice play. Although practice play declines in the elementary school years, practice play activities such as running, jumping, sliding, twirling, and throwing balls or other objects are frequently observed on the playgrounds at elementary schools.

Pretense/Symbolic Play   **Pretense/symbolic play** occurs when the child transforms aspects of the physical environment into symbols. Between 9 and 30 months of age, children increase their use of objects in symbolic play. They learn to transform objects—substituting them for other objects and acting toward them as if they were these other objects (Edmiston, 2017; Hakkarainen, Bredikyte, & Safarov, 2017; Taggart, Eisen, & Lillard, 2018). For example, a preschool child treats a table as if it were a car and says, "I'm fixing the car," as he grabs a leg of the table.

Many experts on play consider the preschool years the "golden age" of symbolic/pretense play that is dramatic or sociodramatic in nature (Fein, 1986). This type of make-believe play often appears at about 18 months of age and reaches a peak at 4 to 5 years of age, then gradually declines.

Some child psychologists conclude that pretend play is an important aspect of young children's development and often reflects advances in their cognitive development, especially as an indication of symbolic understanding (Kang & others, 2016). For example, Catherine Garvey

Let us play, for it is yet day
And we cannot go to sleep;
Besides, in the sky the little
birds fly
And the hills are all covered
with sheep.

—**WILLIAM BLAKE**
English Poet, 19th Century

developmental connection

Cognitive Theory
Vygotsky emphasized the importance of culture and social interaction in children's cognitive development. Connect to "Cognitive Development in Early Childhood."

A preschool "superhero" at play.
©Dann Tardif/LWA/Corbis

sensorimotor play Behavior engaged in by infants to derive pleasure from exercising their existing sensorimotor schemas.

practice play Play that involves repetition of behavior when new skills are being learned or when physical or mental mastery and coordination of skills are required for games or sports.

pretense/symbolic play Play in which the child transforms aspects of the physical environment into symbols.

And that park grew up with me; that small world widened as I learned its secrets and boundaries, as I discovered new refuges in its woods and jungles: hidden homes and lairs for the multitudes of imagination, for cowboys and Indians. . . . I used to dawdle on half holidays along the bent and Devon-facing seashore, hoping for gold watches or the skull of a sheep or a message in a bottle to be washed up with the tide.

—**DYLAN THOMAS**
Welsh Poet, 20th Century

How Would You...?
If you were an **educator,** how would you integrate play in the learning process?

social play Play that involves social interactions with peers.

constructive play Play that combines sensorimotor/practice play with symbolic representation. Constructive play occurs when children engage in self-regulated creation or construction of a product or a solution.

games Activities engaged in for pleasure that include rules and often competition with one or more individuals.

(2000) and Angeline Lillard (2006; Taggart, Eisen, & Lillard, 2018) emphasize that hidden in young children's pretend play narratives are remarkable capacities for role-taking, balancing of social roles, metacognition (thinking about thinking), testing of the reality-pretense distinction, and numerous nonegocentric capacities that reveal the remarkable cognitive skills of young children.

Social Play **Social play** involves interaction with peers. Social play increases dramatically during the preschool years. For many children, social play is the main context for social interactions with peers (Solovieva & Quintanar, 2017).

Constructive Play **Constructive play** combines sensorimotor/practice play with symbolic representation. Constructive play occurs when children engage in the self-regulated creation of a product or a solution. Constructive play increases in the preschool years as symbolic play increases and sensorimotor play decreases. Constructive play is also a frequent form of play in the elementary school years, both inside and outside the classroom.

Games **Games** are activities that are engaged in for pleasure and that have rules. Often they involve competition. Preschool children may begin to participate in social games that involve simple rules of reciprocity and turn-taking. However, games take on a much more important role in the lives of elementary school children. After age 12, playground and neighborhood games decline in popularity (Bergen, 1988).

In sum, play ranges from an infant's simple exercise of a new sensorimotor skill to a preschool child's riding a tricycle to an older child's participation in organized games. Note that children's play can involve a combination of the play categories we have discussed. For example, social play can be sensorimotor (rough-and-tumble), symbolic, or constructive.

Trends in Play Kathy Hirsh-Pasek, Roberta Golinkoff, and Dorothy Singer (Hirsh-Pasek & others, 2009; Singer, Golinkoff, & Hirsh-Pasek, 2006) are concerned about the limited amount of time for free play that young children have today, reporting that it has declined considerably in recent decades. They especially are worried about young children's playtime being restricted at home and school so they can spend more time on academic subjects. They also point out that many schools have eliminated recess. And it is not just the decline in free play time that bothers them. They underscore that learning in playful contexts captivates children's minds in ways that enhance their cognitive and socioemotional development—Singer, Golinkoff, and Hirsh-Pasek's (2006) first book on play was titled *Play = Learning*. Among the cognitive benefits of play they described are these skills: creative, abstract thinking; imagination; attention, concentration, and persistence; problem-solving; social cognition, empathy, and perspective taking; language; and mastering new concepts. Among the socioemotional experiences and development they believe play promotes are enjoyment, relaxation, and self-expression; cooperation, sharing, and turn-taking; anxiety reduction; and self-confidence. With so many positive cognitive and socioemotional outcomes of play, clearly it is important that we find more time for play in young children's lives (Robson, 2017).

MEDIA/SCREEN TIME

If the amount of time spent in an activity is any indication of its importance, there is no doubt that media/screen time plays important roles in children's and adolescents' lives (Lever-Duffy & McDonald, 2018; Maloy & others, 2017; Roblyer, 2016). Few developments in society in the second half of the twentieth century had a greater impact on children than television. Television continues to have a strong influence on children's development, but children's use of other media and information/communication devices has led to the use of the term *screen time,* which includes how much time individuals spend watching television or DVDs, playing video games, and using computers or hand-held electronic devices such as smartphones (Gebremariam & others, 2017; Goh & others, 2016; Li & others, 2017; Straker & Howie, 2016). In a recent national survey, there was a dramatic increase in young children's use of mobile devices in just two years from 2011 to 2013 (Common Sense Media, 2013). In this survey, playing games was the most common activity on mobile devices, followed by using apps, watching videos, and watching TV or movies.

What are some of the benefits of play for children, according to Hirsh-Pasek and her colleagues?
©Temple University, photo by Joseph V. Labolito

Despite the move to mobile devices, television is still the elephant in young children's media life, with 2- to 4-year-old children watching TV approximately 2 to 4 hours per day (Common Sense Media, 2013; Rideout, 2011). In the recent U.S. national survey, 50 percent of children's screen time was spent in front of TV sets (Common Sense Media, 2013). Compared with their counterparts in other developed countries, children in the United States watch television for considerably longer periods (see Figure 7). The American Academy of Pediatrics (2016) recommends that 2- to 5-year-olds watch no more than one hour of TV a day. The Academy also recommends that TV viewing by this age group should consist of high-quality programs, such as *Sesame Street* and other PBS shows for young children.

A recent study revealed that 12 percent of 2- to 4-year-old U.S. children use computers every day and 22 percent of 5- to 8-year-olds use computers daily (Common Sense Media, 2011). A recent recommendation stated that for children 2 to 4 years of age, screen time should be limited to no more than 1 hour per day (Tremblay & others, 2012). Many children spend more time with various screen media than they do interacting with their parents and peers.

How does screen time influence children's development?
©Luca Cappelli/E+/Getty Images RF

Among other concerns about young children having so much screen time are decreased time spent in play, less time interacting with peers, lower levels of physical activity, increased risk of overweight and obesity, poor sleep habits, and higher rates of aggression. One research review concluded that a higher level of screen time at 4 to 6 years of age was linked to increased obesity and lower physical activity from preschool through adolescence (te Velde & others, 2012). Also, a recent study of preschool children found that each additional hour of screen time was linked to less nightly sleep, later bedtime, and less likelihood of sleeping 10 or more hours per night (Xu & others, 2016).

Learning from media is difficult for infants and toddlers, and they learn much more easily from direct experiences with people. At about 3 years of age, children can learn from media with educational material if the media use effective strategies such as repeating concepts a number of times, use images and sounds that capture young children's attention, and use children's rather than adults' voices. However, the vast majority of media that young children experience is geared toward entertainment rather than education.

The American Academy of Pediatrics (2001) recommends that children under 2 years of age not watch television because doing so is likely to reduce the amount of time spent in direct interactions with parents. One study found that the more hours of TV viewed per day by 1- and 3-year-olds,

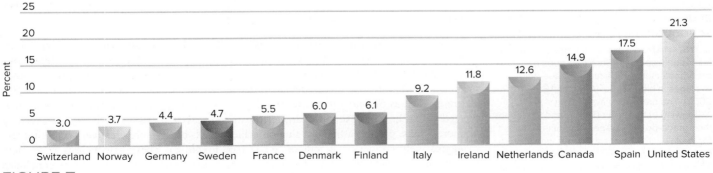

FIGURE 7

PERCENTAGE OF 9-YEAR-OLD CHILDREN WHO REPORT WATCHING MORE THAN FIVE HOURS OF TELEVISION PER WEEKDAY

the more likely they were to have attention problems at 7 years of age (Christakis & others, 2004), and a recent study also revealed that daily TV exposure at 18 months was linked to increased inattention/hyperactivity at 30 months of age (Cheng & others, 2010). A study of 2- to 48-month-olds indicated that each hour of audible TV was linked to a reduction in child vocalizations (Christakis & others, 2009), and another study revealed that 8- to 16-month-olds who viewed baby DVDs/videos had poor language development (Zimmerman, Christakis, & Meltzoff, 2007).

Television can have a negative influence on children by making them passive learners, distracting them from doing homework, teaching them stereotypes, providing them with violent models of aggression, presenting them with unrealistic views of the world, and increasing sleep problems (Calvert, 2015). In one study, sleep problems were more common in 3- to 5-year-old children who (1) watched TV after 7 p.m. and (2) watched TV shows with violence (Garrison, Liekweg, & Christakis, 2011). Further, researchers have found that a high level of TV viewing is linked to a greater incidence of obesity in children and adolescents. For example, a recent study of 2- to 6-year-olds indicated that increased TV viewing time on weekends was associated with a higher risk of being overweight or obese (Kondolot & others, 2017).

However, television also can have a positive influence on children's development by presenting motivating educational programs, increasing their information about the world beyond their immediate environment, and providing models of prosocial behavior (Wilson, 2008). A recent meta-analysis of studies conducted in 15 countries found that watching *Sesame Street* had the following positive outcomes for children: (1) developing cognitive skills (literacy and numeracy, for example); (2) learning about the world (health and safety knowledge, for example); and (3) increasing social reasoning and encouraging tolerant and accepting attitudes toward out-groups (Mares & Pan, 2013).

Effects of Television on Children's Aggression

The extent to which children are exposed to violence and aggression on television raises special concern (Calvert, 2015). For example, some cartoon shows average more than 25 violent acts per hour. Researchers have found links between watching television violence as a child and acting aggressively years later (Prot & others, 2015).

In addition to television violence, there is increased concern about children who play violent video games, especially those that are highly realistic. Children can become so deeply immersed in some electronic games that they experience an altered state of consciousness in which rational thought is suspended and arousing aggressive scripts are learned (Roberts, Henriksen, & Foehr, 2004). Research reviews have concluded that playing violent video games is linked to aggression in both males and females (Gentile, 2011; Holtz & Appel, 2011). For example, in a recent study of children, greater exposure to TV violence, video game violence, and music video violence was independently associated with higher levels of physical aggression (Coker & others, 2015).

Effects of Television on Children's Prosocial Behavior

Television also can teach children that it is better to behave in positive, prosocial ways than in negative, antisocial ways (Maloy & others, 2017; Prot & others, 2015; Truglio & Kotler, 2014). In an early study, Aimee Leifer (1973) selected episodes from the television show *Sesame Street* that reflected positive social interchanges in which children were taught how to use their social skills. For example, in one interchange, two men were fighting over the amount of space available to them; they gradually began to cooperate and to share the space. Children who watched these episodes copied these behaviors, and in later social situations they applied the prosocial lessons they had learned.

Television, Achievement, and Cognitive Development

Watching television has been linked with lower school achievement (Comstock & Scharrer, 2006). However, some types of television—such as educational programming for young children—may enhance achievement. For example, in one longitudinal study, viewing educational programs such as *Sesame Street* and *Mr. Rogers' Neighborhood* as preschoolers was associated with a host of desirable characteristics in adolescence: getting higher grades, reading more books, placing a higher value on achievement, being more creative, and acting less aggressively (Anderson & others, 2001) (see Figure 8). These associations were more consistent for boys than girls. On a less positive note, a recent research review concluded that higher levels of screen time (mostly involving TV viewing) were associated with lower levels of cognitive development in early childhood (Carson & others, 2015).

How Would You...?

If you were a **human development and family studies professional,** how would you talk with parents about strategies for improving television viewing by their children?

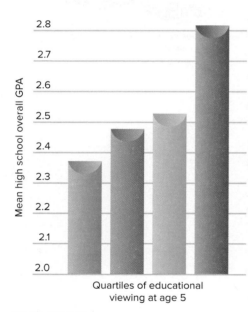

Mean high school overall GPA (y-axis: 2.0, 2.1, 2.2, 2.3, 2.4, 2.5, 2.6, 2.7, 2.8)

Quartiles of educational viewing at age 5

FIGURE 8

EDUCATIONAL TV VIEWING AND HIGH SCHOOL GRADE-POINT AVERAGE FOR BOYS. When boys watched more educational television (especially *Sesame Street*) as preschoolers, they had higher grade-point averages in high school (Anderson & others, 2001). The graph displays the boys' early TV-viewing patterns in quartiles and the means of their grade-point averages. The bar on the left is for the lowest 25 percent of boys who viewed educational TV programs, the next bar the next 25 percent, and so on, with the bar on the right for the 25 percent of the boys who watched the most educational TV shows as preschoolers.

Review *Connect* Reflect

LG3 Describe the roles of peers, play, and media/ screen time in young children's development.

Review
- How do peers affect young children's development?
- What are some theories about the purposes of various types of play?
- How do media and screen time influence children's development?

Connect
- Earlier in the chapter, you read about Laurie Kramer's program for teaching siblings social skills to reduce sibling conflict. Would her recommendations also apply to reducing conflict in peer relations? Explain.

Reflect *Your Own Personal Journey of Life*
- What guidelines would you adopt for your own children's screen time/ media use?

topical connections *looking forward*

This chapter brings your exploration of early childhood to a close. In the next chapter you will begin to study middle and late childhood, especially the physical, brain, and motor skill changes that occur during this period of development. The middle and late childhood years also produce further changes in children's socioemotional development, which you will study in "Socioemotional Development in Middle and Late Childhood." Development of self-understanding and understanding others becomes more sophisticated, emotional understanding improves, and moral reasoning advances. Children in this age group spend less time with parents, but parents still play very important roles in children's lives, especially in guiding their academic achievement and managing their opportunities. Peer status and friendship become more important in children's peer relations, and school takes on a stronger academic focus.

reach your **learning goals**

Socioemotional Development in Early Childhood

1 What Characterizes Young Children's Emotional and Personality Development?

LG1 Discuss emotional and personality development in early childhood.

The Self

- In Erikson's theory, early childhood is a period when development involves resolving the conflict of initiative versus guilt. The toddler's rudimentary self-understanding develops into the preschooler's representation of the self in terms of body attributes, material possessions, and physical activities. At about 4 to 5 years of age, children also begin to use traitlike self-descriptions. Young children display more sophisticated self-understanding and understanding of others than was previously thought.

Emotional Development

- Young children's range of emotions expands during early childhood as they increasingly experience self-conscious emotions such as pride, shame, and guilt. Between 2 and 4 years of age, children use an increasing number of terms to describe emotion and learn more about the causes and consequences of feelings. At 4 to 5 years of age, children show an increased ability to reflect on emotions and to understand that a single event can elicit different emotions in different people. They also show a growing awareness of the need to manage emotions to meet social standards.

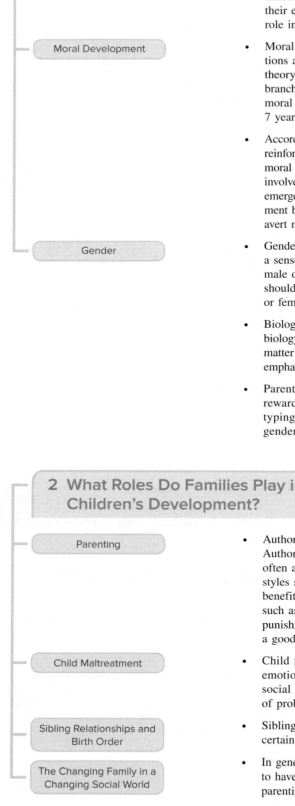

Moral Development

- Emotion-coaching parents have children who engage in more effective self-regulation of their emotions than do emotion-dismissing parents. Emotion regulation plays an important role in successful peer relations.

- Moral development involves thoughts, feelings, and behaviors regarding rules and regulations about what people should do in their interactions with others. Freud's psychoanalytic theory emphasizes the importance of feelings in the development of the superego, the moral branch of personality. Positive emotions, such as empathy, also contribute to the child's moral development. Piaget analyzed moral reasoning and concluded that children from 4 to 7 years of age display heteronomous morality, judging behavior by its consequences.

- According to behavioral and social cognitive theorists, moral behavior develops as a result of reinforcement, punishment, and imitation, and there is considerable situational variability in moral behavior. Conscience refers to an internal regulation of standards of right and wrong that involves an integration of moral thought, feeling, and behavior. Young children's conscience emerges out of relationships with parents. Parents influence young children's moral development by developing quality parent-child relationships, by being proactive in helping children avert misbehavior, and by engaging children in conversational dialogue about moral issues.

Gender

- Gender refers to the characteristics of people as males or females. Gender identity involves a sense of one's own gender, including knowledge, understanding, and acceptance of being male or female. A gender role is a set of expectations that prescribes how females or males should think, act, and feel. Gender typing refers to the acquisition of a traditional masculine or feminine role.

- Biological influences on gender development include chromosomes and hormones. However, biology is not the sole determinant of gender development; children's socialization experiences matter a great deal. Social role theory, psychoanalytic theory, and social cognitive theory emphasize various aspects of social experiences in the development of gender characteristics.

- Parents influence children's gender development, and peers are especially adept at rewarding gender-appropriate behavior. Gender schema theory emphasizes that gender typing emerges as children develop schemas of their culture's gender-appropriate and gender-inappropriate behaviors.

2 What Roles Do Families Play in Young Children's Development?

 Explain how families can influence young children's development.

Parenting

- Authoritarian, authoritative, neglectful, and indulgent are four main parenting styles. Authoritative parenting is the most widely used style around the world and is the style most often associated with children's social competence. However, ethnic variations in parenting styles suggest that in Asian American families, some aspects of authoritarian control may benefit children. Some criticisms of the categorization of parenting styles have been made such as its failure to capture the themes of reciprocal socialization and synchrony. Physical punishment is widely used by U.S. parents, but there are a number of reasons why it is not a good choice. Coparenting has positive effects on children's development.

Child Maltreatment

- Child maltreatment may take the form of physical abuse, child neglect, sexual abuse, and emotional abuse. Child maltreatment places the child at risk for academic, emotional, and social problems. Adults who suffered child maltreatment are also vulnerable to a range of problems.

Sibling Relationships and Birth Order

- Siblings interact with each other in positive and negative ways. Birth order is related in certain ways to child characteristics, but by itself it is not a good predictor of behavior.

The Changing Family in a Changing Social World

- In general, having both parents employed full-time outside the home has not been shown to have negative effects on children. However, the nature of parents' work can affect their parenting quality.

- Divorce can have negative effects on children's adjustment, but so can an acrimonious relationship between parents who stay together for their children's sake. If divorced parents develop a harmonious relationship and practice authoritative parenting, children's adjustment improves.

- Researchers have found few differences between children growing up in gay or lesbian families and children growing up in heterosexual families.

- Cultures vary on a number of issues regarding families. African American and Latino children are more likely than White American children to live in single-parent families and larger families and to have extended-family connections.

- Low-income families have less access to resources than higher-income families. Lower-SES parents create a home atmosphere that involves more authority and physical punishment with children than higher-SES parents. Higher-SES parents are more concerned about developing children's initiative and delay of gratification.

3 How Are Peer Relations, Play, and Media/Screen Time Involved in Young Children's Development?

LG3 Describe the roles of peers, play, and media/screen time in young children's development.

Peer Relations

Play

Media/Screen Time

- Peers are powerful socialization agents. Peers provide a source of information and comparison about the world outside the family.

- Play's functions include affiliation with peers, tension release, advances in cognitive development, exploration, and provision of a safe haven. The contemporary perspective on play emphasizes both the cognitive and the social aspects of play. Among the most widely studied types of children's play are sensorimotor play, practice play, pretense/symbolic play, social play, constructive play, and games.

- There is substantial concern about the increase in media/screen time in young children. Extensive media/screen time in young children is linked to a number of negative developmental outcomes. Television can have both negative developmental influences (such as turning children into passive learners and presenting them with aggressive models) and positive influences (such as providing models of prosocial behavior). TV violence is not the only cause of children's aggression, but it can induce aggression. Prosocial behavior on TV can teach children positive behavior. High levels of overall TV viewing are linked to lower achievement in school, but watching educational TV programs in early childhood is linked to higher academic achievement.

key terms

authoritarian parenting	gender identity	moral development	self-understanding
authoritative parenting	gender role	neglectful parenting	sensorimotor play
autonomous morality	gender schema theory	perspective taking	social cognitive
conscience	gender typing	practice play	theory of gender
constructive play	heteronomous morality	pretense/symbolic play	social play
empathy	immanent justice	psychoanalytic theory	social role theory
games	indulgent parenting	of gender	sympathy

key people

Diana Baumrind	Erik Erikson	Kathy Hirsh-Pasek	Cybele Raver
Daniel Berlyne	Sigmund Freud	Grazyna Kochanska	Dorothy Singer
Ruth Chao	Catherine Garvey	Lawrence Kohlberg	Ross Thompson
Ann Crouter	Elizabeth Gershoff	Laurie Kramer	Lev Vygotsky
E. Mark Cummings	Roberta Golinkoff	Angeline Lillard	
Judy Dunn	Susan Harter	Jean Piaget	

connecting with **improving the lives of children**

STRATEGIES

Guiding Young Children's Socioemotional Development

How can young children's socioemotional skills be nourished? These strategies can help:

- *Look for opportunities to help children with their emotions.* Parents, teachers, and other adults can help children understand and handle their emotions in socially acceptable ways.

- *Present positive moral models for the child and use emotional situations to promote moral development.* Children benefit when they are around people who engage in prosocial rather than antisocial behavior. Encourage children to show empathy and learn to deal with their emotions.

- *Be an authoritative parent.* Children's self-control and social competence benefit when both parents are authoritative—that is, when they are neither punitive and overcontrolling nor permissive or neglectful. Authoritative parents are nurturant, engage the child in verbal give-and-take, monitor the child, and use nonpunitive control.

- *Adapt to the child's developmental changes.* Parents should use less physical manipulation and more reasoning or withholding of special privileges in disciplining a 5-year-old in comparison with strategies used for disciplining a 2-year-old.

- *Communicate effectively with children in a divorced family.* Good strategies are to explain the separation and say it is not the child's fault, assure the child that it may take time to feel better, keep the door open for further discussion, provide as much continuity as possible, and supply a support system for the child.

- *Provide the child with opportunities for peer interaction.* Children learn a great deal from the mutual give-and-take of peer relations. Make sure the child gets considerable time to play with peers rather than watching TV or attending an academic early childhood program for the entire day.

- *Provide the child with many opportunities for play.* Positive play experiences can greatly support the young child's socioemotional development.

- *Monitor the child's media/screen time.* Keep exposure to TV violence to a minimum with no more than one hour of screen time per day. Develop a set of guidelines for the child's media/screen time, especially emphasizing quality TV programs such as *Sesame Street.*

RESOURCES

Societal Contexts of Child Development (2014)
Elizabeth Gershoff, Rashmita Mistry, and Danielle Crosby (Eds.)
New York: Oxford University Press

Leading experts describe many aspects of social contexts that influence children's development and have implications for improving children's lives.

The Future of Families (2013)
Ross Parke
New York: Wiley

One of the world's leading experts on children's socioemotional development, Ross Parke, explores the wide diversity in family forms that increasingly characterize children's lives, including fathers as single parents, same-gender parents, new reproductive technologies, and immigrant families.

The Emotional Development of Young Children (2004)
Marylou Hyson
New York: Teachers College Press

An excellent book by a leading expert on early childhood that provides a good overview of young children's emotional development and offers many applications to children's experiences in preschool and kindergarten.

For Better or For Worse: Divorce Reconsidered (2002)
E. Mavis Hetherington and John Kelly
New York: W. W. Norton

E. Mavis Hetherington, a leading researcher, provides excellent descriptions of how divorce affects children and parents.

Gender Development (2009)
Judith Blakemore, Sheri Berenbaum, and Lynn Liben
Clifton, NJ: Psychology Press

Many facets of children's gender development are covered by leading experts.

Parents and Digital Technologies (2016)
Suzie Hayman and John Coleman
New York: Oxford University Press

An excellent book with recommendations to help parents develop effective strategies for communicating with children about technology, as well as set boundaries and establish rules.

Every forward step we take we leave some phantom of ourselves behind.

—**JOHN LANCASTER SPALDING**
American Educator, 19th Century

©Ariel Skelley/Corbis

Middle and Late Childhood

In middle and late childhood, children are on a different plane, belonging to a generation and feeling all their own. It is the wisdom of the human life span that at no time are children more ready to learn than during the period of expansive imagination at the end of early childhood. Children develop a sense of wanting to make things—and not just to make them, but to make them well and even perfectly. They seek to know and to understand. They are remarkable for their intelligence and for their curiosity. Their parents continue to be important influences in their lives, but their growth also is shaped by peers and friends. They don't think much about the future or about the past, but they enjoy the present moment. Section 5 consists of three chapters: "Physical Development in Middle and Late Childhood," "Cognitive Development in Middle and Late Childhood," and "Socioemotional Development in Middle and Late Childhood."

chapter 11

PHYSICAL DEVELOPMENT IN MIDDLE AND LATE CHILDHOOD

chapter outline

(1) What Changes Take Place in Body Growth, the Brain, and Motor Development?

Learning Goal 1 Discuss changes in body growth, the brain, and motor development in middle and late childhood.

Skeletal and Muscular Systems
The Brain
Motor Development

(2) What Are the Central Issues in Children's Health?

Learning Goal 2 Characterize children's health in middle and late childhood.

Nutrition
Exercise and Sports

Overweight Children
Diseases
Accidents and Injuries

(3) What Are the Prevalent Disabilities in Children?

Learning Goal 3 Summarize information about children with disabilities.

Who Are Children with Disabilities?
The Range of Disabilities
Educational Issues

©SolStock/Getty Images RF

The following comments are by Angie, an elementary-school-age girl:

When I was eight years old, I weighed 125 pounds. My clothes were the size that large teenage girls wear. I hated my body and my classmates teased me all the time. I was so overweight and out of shape that when I took a P.E. class my face would get red and I had trouble breathing. I was jealous of the kids who played sports and weren't overweight like I was.

I'm nine years old now and I've lost 30 pounds. I'm much happier and proud of myself. How did I lose the weight? My mom said she had finally decided enough was enough. She took me to a pediatrician who specializes in helping children lose weight and keep it off. The pediatrician counseled my mom about my eating and exercise habits, then had us join a group that he had created for overweight children and their parents. My mom and I go to the group once a week and we've now been participating in the program for six months. I no longer eat fast-food meals and my mom is cooking more healthy meals. Now that I've lost weight, exercise is not as hard for me and I don't get teased by the kids at school. My mom's pretty happy too because she's lost 15 pounds herself since we've been in the counseling program.

Not all overweight children are as successful as Angie at reducing their weight. Indeed, being overweight in childhood has become a major national concern in the United States. Later in the chapter, we explore in detail being overweight in childhood, including its causes and outcomes.

topical connections _looking **back**_

In the last chapter you concluded your study of early childhood by looking at socioemotional development in young children, the accompanying moral development that takes place, and children's growing sense of self and gender. You became familiar with the role of family, siblings, peers, play, and the media in early childhood. You learned that children grow more slowly in early childhood than in infancy, but they still grow an average of 2½ inches and 5 to 7 pounds a year. In early childhood, the most rapid growth in the brain occurs in the prefrontal cortex.

preview

Considerable progress in children's physical development continues to take place in the middle and late childhood years. Children grow taller, heavier, and stronger. They become more adept at using their physical skills. We begin the chapter by exploring the changes that characterize body growth and motor skills, then examine the central issues in children's health, and conclude by discussing children with disabilities and their education.

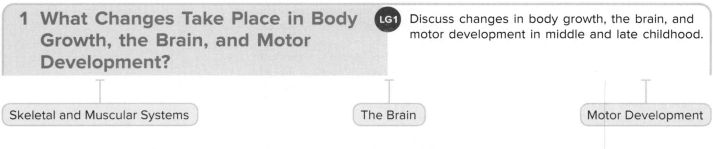

1 What Changes Take Place in Body Growth, the Brain, and Motor Development?

LG1 Discuss changes in body growth, the brain, and motor development in middle and late childhood.

Skeletal and Muscular Systems   The Brain   Motor Development

The period of middle and late childhood involves slow, consistent growth. This is a period of calm before the rapid growth spurt of adolescence (Hockenberry, Wilson, & Rodgers, 2017). Among the important aspects of body growth and proportion in this developmental period are those involving skeletal and muscular systems, the brain, and motor development.

What characterizes physical growth during middle and late childhood?
©Chris Windsor/Digital Vision/Getty Images RF

SKELETAL AND MUSCULAR SYSTEMS

During the elementary school years, children grow an average of 2 to 3 inches a year until, at the age of 11, the average girl is 4 feet, 9 inches tall, and the average boy is 4 feet, 7¾ inches tall. During the middle and late childhood years, children gain about 5 to 7 pounds a year. The weight increase is due mainly to increases in the size of the skeletal and muscular systems, as well as the size of some body organs (Hockenberry, Wilson, & Rogers, 2017). Muscle mass and strength gradually increase as "baby fat" decreases. The loose movements and knock-knees of early childhood give way to improved muscle tone. The increase in muscular strength is due both to heredity and to exercise. Children also double their strength capabilities during these years. Because of their greater number of muscle cells, boys are usually stronger than girls. A summary of the changes in height and weight in middle and late childhood appears in Figure 1.

Proportional changes are among the most pronounced physical changes in middle and late childhood (Kliegman & others, 2016, 2017). Head circumference, waist circumference, and leg length decrease in relation to body height. A less noticeable physical change is that bones continue to ossify (harden) during middle and late childhood.

THE BRAIN

The development of brain-imaging techniques, such as magnetic resonance imaging (MRI), has led to increased research on changes in the brain during middle and late childhood and on how these brain

	HEIGHT (INCHES)					
Age	Female Percentiles			Male Percentiles		
	25th	50th	75th	25th	50th	75th
6	43.75	45.00	46.50	44.25	45.75	47.00
7	46.00	47.50	49.00	46.25	48.00	49.25
8	48.00	49.75	51.50	48.50	50.00	51.50
9	50.25	53.00	53.75	50.50	52.00	53.50
10	52.50	54.50	56.25	52.50	54.25	55.75
11	55.00	57.00	58.75	54.50	55.75	57.25

	WEIGHT (POUNDS)					
6	39.25	43.00	47.25	42.00	45.50	49.50
7	43.50	48.50	53.25	46.25	50.25	55.00
8	49.00	54.75	61.50	51.00	55.75	61.50
9	55.75	62.75	71.50	56.00	62.00	69.25
10	63.25	71.75	82.75	62.00	69.25	78.50
11	71.75	81.25	94.25	69.00	77.75	89.00

FIGURE 1

CHANGES IN HEIGHT AND WEIGHT IN MIDDLE AND LATE CHILDHOOD.
Note: The percentile tells how the child compares with other children of the same age. The 50th percentile tells us that half of the children of a particular age are taller (heavier) or shorter (lighter). The 25th percentile tells us that 25 percent of the children of that age are shorter (lighter) and 75 percent are taller (heavier).

changes are linked to improvements in cognitive development (de Haan & Johnson, 2016). One such change involves increased myelination, which improves the speed of processing information and communication in the higher regions of the brain, such as the cerebral cortex. The increase in myelination during middle and late childhood is linked to more effective processing of information on cognitive tasks (Wendelken & others, 2016). Recall from our discussion in "Physical Development in Early Childhood" that myelination is the process of encasing axons with fat cells.

Total brain volume stabilizes by the end of late childhood, but significant changes in various structures and regions of the brain continue to occur. In particular, the brain pathways and circuitry involving the prefrontal cortex, the highest level in the brain, continue to increase (Denes, 2016). These advances in the prefrontal cortex are linked to children's improved attention, reasoning, and cognitive control (Carlson, Zelazo, & Faja, 2013). (See Figure 6 for the location of the prefrontal cortex in the brain.)

Leading developmental cognitive neuroscientist Mark Johnson and his colleagues (2009) have proposed that the prefrontal cortex likely orchestrates the functions of many other brain regions during development. As part of this neural leadership and organizational role, the prefrontal cortex may provide an advantage to neural networks and connections that include the prefrontal cortex. According to these researchers, the prefrontal cortex coordinates the best neural connections for solving a problem at hand.

Changes also occur in the thickness of the cerebral cortex (cortical thickness) in middle and late childhood. One study used brain scans to assess cortical thickness in 5- to 11-year-old children (Sowell & others, 2004). Cortical thickening across a two-year time period was observed in the temporal and frontal lobe areas that function in language, which may account for improvements in language abilities such as reading.

As children develop, activation of some brain areas increases, while that of others decreases (Denes, 2016). One shift in activation that occurs as children develop is from diffuse, larger areas to more focal, smaller areas. This shift is characterized by synaptic pruning, in which areas of the brain not being used lose synaptic connections and those being used show increased connections. In one study, researchers found less diffusion and more focal activation in the prefrontal cortex from 7 to 30 years of age (Durston & others, 2006). The activation change was linked to advances in executive function, especially in cognitive control, which involves flexible and effective control in a number of areas. These areas include focusing attention, reducing interfering thoughts, inhibiting motor actions, and being flexible in switching between competing choices (Blair, 2017).

developmental **connection**

Brain Development

Synaptic pruning is an important aspect of the brain's development, and the pruning varies by region across children's development. Connect to "Physical Development in Infancy."

Age	Motor skills
6	Children can skip. Children can throw with proper weight shift and step. Girls and boys can vertically jump 7 inches. Girls can do a standing long jump of 33 inches, boys 36 inches. Children can cut and paste. Children enjoy making simple figures in clay.
7	Children can balance on one foot without looking. Children can walk 2-inch-wide balance beams. Children can hop and jump accurately into small squares. Children can participate in jumping jack exercise. Girls can throw a ball 25 feet, boys 45 feet. Girls can vertically jump 8 inches, boys 9 inches. Girls can do a standing long jump of 41 inches, boys 43 inches.
8	Children can engage in alternate rhythmic hopping in different patterns. Girls can throw a ball 34 feet, boys 59 feet. Girls can vertically jump 9 inches, boys 10 inches. Girls can perform a standing long jump of 50 inches, boys 55 inches. Children's grip strength increases. Children can use common tools, such as a hammer.
9	Girls can throw a ball 41 feet, boys 71 feet. Girls can vertically jump 10 inches, boys 11 inches. Girls can perform a standing long jump of 53 inches, boys 57 inches. Children's perceptual-motor coordination becomes smoother.
10	Children can judge and intercept pathways of small balls thrown from a distance. Girls can throw a small ball 49 feet, boys 94 feet. Girls can vertically jump 10 inches, boys 11 inches.

FIGURE 2

CHANGES IN MOTOR SKILLS DURING MIDDLE AND LATE CHILDHOOD

MOTOR DEVELOPMENT

During middle and late childhood, children's motor development becomes much smoother and more coordinated than it was in early childhood (Hockenberry, Wilson, & Rodgers, 2017). For example, only one child in a thousand can hit a tennis ball over the net at the age of 3, yet by the age of 10 or 11 most children can learn to play the sport. Running, climbing, skipping rope, swimming, bicycle riding, and skating are just a few of the many physical skills elementary school children can master. And, when mastered, these skills are a source of great pleasure and accomplishment for children. In gross motor skills involving large muscle activity, boys usually outperform girls.

As children move through the elementary school years, they gain greater control over their bodies and can sit for longer periods of time. However, elementary school children are far from being physically mature, and they need to be active. Elementary school children become more fatigued by long periods of sitting than by running, jumping, or bicycling. Physical action is essential for children to refine their developing skills, such as batting a ball, skipping rope, or balancing on a beam. An important principle of practice for elementary school children, therefore, is that they should be physically active whenever possible.

Increased myelination of the nervous system is reflected in the improvement of fine motor skills during middle and late childhood. Children use their hands more adroitly as tools. Six-year-olds can hammer, paste, tie shoes, and fasten clothes. By 7 years of age, children's hands have become steadier. At this age, children prefer a pencil to a crayon for printing, reversal of letters is less common, and printing becomes smaller. At 8 to 10 years of age, children can use their hands independently with more ease and precision. Fine motor coordination develops to the point at which children use cursive writing rather than printing. Letter size becomes smaller and more even. At 10 to 12 years of age, children begin to show manipulative skills similar to the abilities of adults. They can now master the complex, intricate, and rapid movements needed to produce fine-quality crafts or to play a difficult piece on a musical instrument. Girls usually outperform boys in fine motor skills. A summary of changes in motor skills in middle and late childhood appears in Figure 2. Note that some children perform these skills earlier or later than other children.

Review Connect Reflect

LG1 Discuss changes in body growth, the brain, and motor development in middle and late childhood.

Review
- How do skeletal and muscular systems change in middle and late childhood?
- What characterizes changes in the brain during middle and late childhood?
- How do children's gross and fine motor skills change in middle and late childhood?

Connect
- In this section, you learned about advances in the prefrontal cortex. Earlier, you read about the prefrontal cortex's role in executive function.

What executive function skills were described as important in early childhood cognitive development?

Reflect *Your Own Personal Journey of Life*
- Look again at Figure 2. On which of the motor skills were you especially competent? On which skills were you less competent? Do you think your motor skills as a child were primarily influenced by your heredity or your environment? Explain.

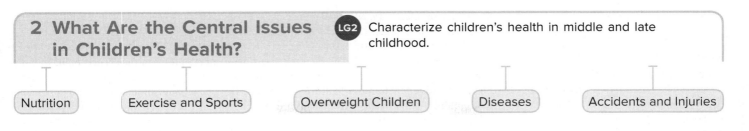

2 What Are the Central Issues in Children's Health?

LG2 Characterize children's health in middle and late childhood.

Nutrition Exercise and Sports Overweight Children Diseases Accidents and Injuries

Although we have become a health-conscious nation, many children as well as adults do not practice good health habits. Too much junk food and too much couch-potato behavior describe the habits of far too many children. We begin our exploration of children's health with nutrition and exercise, then turn to a number of health problems that can emerge during this period of development.

NUTRITION

During middle and late childhood, children's average body weight doubles. Children exert considerable energy as they engage in many different motor activities. To support their growth and active lives, children need to consume more food than they did in early childhood. From 1 to 3 years of age, infants and toddlers should consume about 1,300 calories per day. At 4 to 6 years of age, young children should take in around 1,700 calories per day. From 7 to 10 years of age, children should consume about 2,400 calories per day; however, depending on the child's size, the range of recommended calories for 7- to 10-year-olds is 1,650 to 3,300 per day.

Within these calorie ranges, it is important to impress on children the value of a balanced diet to promote their growth (Sorte, Daeschel, & Amador, 2017). Children usually eat as their families eat, so the quality of their diet often depends largely on their family's pattern of eating (Showell & others, 2013). Most children acquire a taste for an increasing variety of food in middle and late childhood. However, with the increased availability of fast-food restaurants and media inducements, too many children fill up on food that has "empty calories" that do not promote effective growth. Many of these empty-calorie foods have a high content of sugar, starch, and excess fat.

Both parents and teachers can help children learn to eat better (Finnane & others, 2017). For example, they can help children learn about the Food Guide Pyramid and what a healthy diet entails (Byrd-Bredbenner & others, 2014).

Children should begin their day by eating a healthy breakfast. According to nutritionists, breakfast should make up about one-fourth of the day's calories. A nutritious breakfast helps children have more energy and be more alert in the morning hours of school.

EXERCISE AND SPORTS

How much exercise do children get? What are children's sports like? These topics and more are explored in the following section of this chapter.

Exercise American children and adolescents are not getting enough exercise (Gomez-Bruton & others, 2017; Nemet, 2016; Pan & others, 2017; Powers & Dodd, 2017). Increasing children's exercise levels has positive outcomes (Dumuid & others, 2017; Wuest & Fisette, 2015).

An increasing number of studies document the importance of exercise in children's physical development (Dowda & others, 2017; Lintu & others, 2016; Pan & others, 2017). A recent study of more than 6,000 elementary school children revealed that 55 minutes or more of moderate-to-vigorous physical activity daily was associated with a lower incidence of obesity (Nemet, 2016). Further, a recent research review concluded that exercise programs consisting of three weekly sessions lasting longer than 60 minutes were effective in lowering both systolic and diastolic blood pressure (Garcia-Hermoso, Saavedra, & Escalante, 2013).

A research review concluded that aerobic exercise also increasingly is linked to children's cognitive skills (Best, 2010). Researchers have found that aerobic exercise benefits children's attention, memory, effortful and goal-directed thinking

> We are underexercised as a nation. We look instead of play. We ride instead of walk. Our existence deprives us of the minimum of physical activity essential for healthy living.
>
> **—JOHN F. KENNEDY**
> *American President, 20th Century*

What are some good strategies for increasing children's exercise?

©FatCamera/Getty Images RF

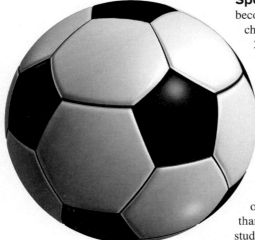

developmental connection

Exercise

Guidelines recommend that pre-school children engage in two hours of physical activity per day. Connect to "Physical Development in Early Childhood."

and behavior, creativity, and academic success (Davis & Cooper, 2011; Davis & others, 2007, 2011; Hillman & others, 2009; Jackson & others, 2016; Krafft & others, 2014; Pan & others, 2017; Tomporowski, 2016). In a recent fMRI study of physically unfit 8- to 11-year-old overweight children, a daily instructor-led aerobic exercise program that lasted eight months was effective in improving the efficiency or flexible modulation of neural circuits that support better cognitive functioning (Krafft & others, 2014). Further, a recent meta-analysis concluded that children who engage in regular physical activity have better cognitive inhibitory control (Jackson & others, 2016).

Parents play important roles in children's exercise (Aires & others, 2016; de Heer & others, 2017; Kesten & others, 2015; Lo & others, 2017). Growing up with parents who regularly exercise provides positive models of exercise for children. One study revealed that mothers were more likely than fathers to limit boys' and girls' sedentary behavior (Edwardson & Gorely, 2010).

Some of the blame for inactivity in middle and late childhood also falls on the nation's schools, many of which fail to provide daily physical education classes (Lumpkin, 2014). Many children's school weeks do not include adequate physical education classes, and the majority of children do not exercise vigorously even when they are in such classes (Kovar & others, 2007). A recent study found that school-based physical activity was successful in improving children's fitness and lowering their levels of body fat (Kriemler & others, 2010).

Screen time also is linked with low activity levels and obesity in children (Biddle, Garcia Bengoechea, & Wiesner, 2017; Dumuid & others, 2017; Shang & others, 2015; Tanaka & others, 2017; Xu & others, 2016). A related concern is the dramatic increase in computer use by children. A longitudinal study found that a higher incidence of TV viewing in childhood and adolescence was linked with being overweight, being less physically fit, and having higher cholesterol levels at 26 years of age (Hancox, Milne, & Poulton, 2004).

©Photodisc/Getty Images RF

Sports Despite the growing concern about lack of exercise, more and more children become involved in sports every year. Both in public schools and in community agencies, children's sports programs have changed the shape of many children's lives (Baker & others, 2017; Davids & Mayo, 2017).

Participation in sports can have both positive and negative consequences for children. Participation can provide exercise, opportunities to learn how to compete, enhanced self-esteem, persistence, and a setting for developing peer relations and friendships. A recent study found that 8-year-old children who continued to participate in sports over the next 24 months were rated by their parents as having a higher health-related quality of life than children who did not participate in sports (Vella & others, 2014). In this study, the positive effects of sports participation were stronger for girls than boys. Further, recent research indicates that participating in sports reduces the likelihood that children will become obese (Basterfield & others, 2015). One study revealed that 10- to 12-year-old girls who participated in more than 3 hours per week of extracurricular sports activities were 59 percent less likely to be overweight or obese than their nonparticipating counterparts (Antonogeorgos & others, 2011). Also, a recent study of 7- to 9-year-olds found that participating in organized leisure-time sports for approximately one year was linked to decreased cardiovascular risk (Hebert & others, 2017).

However, sports also can bring pressure to achieve and win, physical injuries, a distraction from academic work, and unrealistic expectations for success as an athlete (Conant-Norville, 2016; Kerr & Stirling, 2017; LaPrade & others, 2016; Lemez & Rongen, 2017; Pelka & Kellman, 2017).

Injuries are a special concern when children participate in sports (Cheron, Le Scanff, & Leboeuf-Yde, 2016; Sheu, Chen, & Hedegaard, 2016). A recent study found differences in the type of sports injuries that occur among children and adolescents (Stracciolini & others, 2013). Five- to 12-year-old children were more likely to sustain injuries that were traumatic in nature and more often in the upper extremities, whereas 13- to 17-year-olds were more likely to be treated for chest, hip/pelvis, and spine injuries, as well as overuse injuries. Another recent study revealed that for 6- to 18-year-olds, 39 percent of life-threatening injuries were sport-related, with nearly one-fourth of pediatric spinal fractures being sport-related (Meehan & Mannix, 2013). There also is increasing concern about the occurrence of concussions in youth football (Macdonald & Hauber, 2016).

In the *Caring Connections* interlude, you can read about some positive strategies for parents to follow regarding their children's sports participation.

How Would You...?

If you were a **human development and family studies professional**, what advice would you offer to parents who want to make their children's participation in sports enjoyable?

Parents, Coaches, and Children's Sports

Most sports psychologists stress that it is important for parents to show an interest in their children's sports participation. Most children want their parents to watch them perform in sports. Many children whose parents do not come to watch them play in sporting events feel that their parents do not adequately support them. However, some children become extremely nervous when their parents watch

What are some of the potential positive and negative aspects of children's participation in sports? What are some guidelines that can benefit parents and coaches of children in sports?
©SW Productions/Getty Images RF

them perform, or they get embarrassed when their parents cheer too loudly or make a fuss. If children request that their parents not watch them perform, parents should respect their children's wishes (Schreiber, 1990).

Parents should compliment their children for their sports performance, and if they don't become overinvolved, they can help their children build their physical skills and emotional maturity—discussing with them how to deal with a difficult coach, how to cope with a tough loss, and how to put in perspective a poorly played game (Knight, 2017).

The following guidelines provided by the Women's Sports Foundation (2001) in its booklet *The 10 Commandments for Parents and Coaches in Youth Sports* can benefit both parents and coaches of children who participate in sports:

The Do's

- Make sports fun; the more children enjoy sports, the more they will want to play.
- Remember that it is okay for children to make mistakes; it means they are trying.
- Allow children to ask questions about the sport and discuss the sport in a calm, supportive manner.
- Show respect for the child's sports participation.
- Be positive and convince the child that he or she is making a good effort.
- Be a positive role model for the child in sports.

The Don'ts

- Yell or scream at the child.
- Condemn the child for poor play or continue to bring up failures long after they happen.
- Point out the child's errors in front of others.
- Expect the child to learn something immediately.
- Expect the child to become a pro.
- Ridicule or make fun of the child.
- Compare the child to siblings or to more talented children.
- Make sports all work and no fun.

Now let's turn our attention to additional children's health issues. For most children, middle and late childhood is a time of excellent health. Disease and death are less prevalent in this period than in other periods of childhood and adolescence. However, some children do have health problems, such as obesity, cancer, diabetes, cardiovascular disease, asthma, and injuries due to accidents.

OVERWEIGHT CHILDREN

Being overweight is an increasingly prevalent health problem in the United States and elsewhere (Blake, 2017; Schiff, 2016). Recall that being overweight is defined in terms of body mass index (BMI), which is computed by a formula that takes into account height and weight. Also, children at or above the 95th percentile of BMI are included in the overweight category,

developmental **connection**

Nutrition and Weight

In one international comparison of 34 countries, the United States had the second highest rate of childhood obesity. Connect to "Physical Development in Early Childhood."

©Jules Frazier/Getty Images RF

whereas children at or above the 85th percentile are described as at risk for being overweight (Centers for Disease Control and Prevention, 2017). Over the last three decades, the percentage of U.S. children who are at risk for being overweight has increased dramatically. Recently there has been a decrease in the percentage of 2- to 5-year-old children who are obese, which dropped from 12.1 percent in 2009–2010 to 9.4 percent in 2013–2014 (Ogden & others, 2016). In 2013-2014, 17.4 percent of 6- to 11-year-old U.S. children were classified as obese, which is essentially unchanged from 2009–2010 (Ogden & others, 2016).

It is not just in the United States that children are becoming more overweight (Y.X. Zhang & others, 2016). For example, a study found that general and abdominal obesity in Chinese children increased significantly from 1993 to 2009 (Liang & others, 2012). Further, a recent study revealed that overweight and obese Chinese children had a greater risk of having high blood pressure than children who were not overweight (Dong & others, 2013).

Note that in the United States, girls are more likely than boys to be overweight, and this gender difference occurs in many countries (Sweeting, 2008). In a large-scale U.S. study, African American and Latino children were more likely to be overweight or obese than non-Latino White children (Benson, Baer, & Kaelber, 2009).

Researchers have found that being overweight as a child is a risk factor for being obese as an adult (Janssen & others, 2005; Thompson, Manore, & Vaughan, 2017). For example, a longitudinal study revealed that girls who were overweight in childhood were 11 to 30 times more likely to be obese in adulthood than girls who were not overweight in childhood (Thompson & others, 2007). In another study, researchers found that children with high body mass index and waist circumference are at risk for metabolic syndrome (a constellation of factors including obesity, high blood pressure, and type 2 diabetes that places individuals at risk for developing cardiovascular disease) in adulthood (Sun & others, 2008).

What Factors Are Linked with Being Overweight in Childhood?
Heredity and environmental contexts are related to being overweight in childhood (Thompson, Manore, & Vaughan, 2017). Recent genetic analysis indicates that heredity is an important factor in children becoming overweight (Donatelle, 2017). Overweight parents tend to have overweight children (Vergara-Castaneda & others, 2010). For example, one study found that the greatest risk factor for being overweight at 9 years of age was having a parent who is overweight (Agras & others, 2004). Also, in a 14-year longitudinal study, parental weight change predicted children's weight change (Andriani, Liao, & Kuo, 2015). And one study revealed that having two overweight/obese parents significantly increased the likelihood of a child being overweight/obese (Xu & others, 2011). Characteristics such as body type, height, body fat composition, and metabolism are inherited from parents (Blake, 2017). Environmental factors that influence whether children become overweight include availability of food (especially food high in fat content), use of energy-saving devices, levels of physical activity, parents' eating habits and monitoring of children's eating habits, the context in which a child eats, and screen time (Nguyen & others, 2016; Parkes & others, 2016; Ren & others, 2017). A recent study revealed that screen time increased the risk of obesity in 9-year-old children with both high and low levels of overall physical activity (Lane, Harrison, & Murphy, 2014). A recent behavior modification study of overweight and obese children made watching TV contingent on their engagement in exercise (Goldfield, 2012). The intervention markedly increased their exercise and reduced their TV viewing time.

Consequences of Being Overweight in Childhood
The increasing percentage of overweight children in recent decades is cause for great concern because being overweight raises the risk for many medical and psychological problems (Powers & Dodd, 2017; Song & others, 2017; Sorte, Daeschel, & Amador, 2017). Diabetes, hypertension (high blood pressure), and elevated blood cholesterol levels are common in children who are overweight (Levy & others, 2017; Martin-Espinosa & others, 2017; Riano-Galan & others, 2017).

Once considered rare, hypertension in children has become increasingly common in overweight children (Tanrikulu,

What are some concerns about overweight children?
©Image Source/PunchStock RF

Agirbasli, & Berenson, 2017). A recent Chinese study revealed that high blood pressure in 23 percent of boys and 15 percent of girls was linked to being overweight or obese (Dong & others, 2015). In a recent study, a larger waist circumference and a higher body mass index (BMI) combined to place children at higher risk for cardiovascular disease (de Koning & others, 2015). Social and psychological consequences of being overweight in childhood include low self-esteem, depression, and some exclusion of obese children from peer groups (Rankin & others, 2016). In one study, obese children were perceived as less attractive, more tired, and more socially withdrawn than non-obese peers (Zeller, Reiter-Purtill, & Ramey, 2008). And in one study, overweight children reported being teased more by their peers and family members than did normal-weight children (McCormack & others, 2011).

Treatment of Children Who Are Overweight   Many experts recommend a program that involves a combination of diet, exercise, and behavior modification to help children lose weight. Exercise is an extremely important component of a successful weight-loss program for overweight children (Fairclough & others, 2017). Exercise increases the child's lean body mass, which increases the child's resting metabolic rate. These changes result in more calories being burned in the resting state.

Children's activity levels are influenced by their motivation to engage in energetic activities, as well as by caregivers who model an active lifestyle and are motivated to provide children with opportunities to be active (Morgan & others, 2017). In a typical behavior modification program, children are taught to monitor their own behavior, keeping a food diary while attempting to lose weight. The diary should record not only the type and amount of food eaten but also when, with whom, and where it was eaten. That is, do children eat in front of the TV, by themselves, or at times when they are angry or depressed? A food diary identifies behaviors that need to be changed.

How Would You...?

If you were a **health-care professional,** how would you use your knowledge of risk factors for being overweight to design a workshop to help parents and children learn about healthy lifestyle choices?

Parents play an important role in preventing children from becoming overweight (Davis & others, 2016; Morgan & others, 2017). They can encourage healthy eating habits in children by "increasing the number of family meals eaten together, making healthful foods available, and reducing the availability of sugar-sweetened beverages and sodas" (Lindsay & others, 2006, p. 173). They also can help reduce the likelihood their children will become overweight by reducing children's screen time, getting children involved in sports and other physical activities, and being healthy, physically active models themselves (Ren & others, 2017). As we learned in Angie's story at the beginning of the chapter, a combination of behavior modification techniques, parental involvement, and a structured program can effectively help overweight children. Intervention programs that emphasize getting parents to engage in more healthful lifestyles themselves, as well as to feed their children nutrient-dense food and get them to exercise more, can produce weight reduction in overweight and obese children (Muthuri & others, 2016). For example, a recent study found that a combination of a child-centered activity program and a parent-centered dietary modification program were successful in helping overweight children lose pounds over a two-year period (Collins & others, 2011). And in a recent Japanese study, the family pattern that was linked to the highest overweight/obesity in children was a combination of irregular mealtimes and the most screen time for both parents (Watanabe & others, 2016).

What can parents do to prevent their children from being overweight or obese?
©Corbis RF

To read further about helping overweight children lose weight, see *Caring Connections.*

Some intervention programs with overweight children are conducted through schools and often focus on teaching children and parents about selecting a healthy diet, exercising more, and reducing screen activity (time spent watching TV, playing video games, texting, and so on) (Bustos & others, 2016; Harris & others, 2016). A promising strategy is to provide students with more nutritious foods to eat at school. Some states now have laws that require more healthful foods to be sold in vending machines at schools. In a recent study, children were less likely to be overweight or obese if they attended schools in states that had a strong policy implementation on healthy foods and beverages (Datar & Nicosia, 2017). And a recent research review concluded that elementary school programs emphasizing increased physical activity, decreased intake of sugar-sweetened beverages, and increased fruit intake were the most effective in reducing BMI in children (Brown & others, 2016).

Parenting Strategies for Helping Overweight Children Lose Weight

Most parents with an overweight child want to help the child to lose weight but aren't sure of the best ways to accomplish this goal. Keep in mind the research we have discussed that indicates overweight children are likely to become overweight adolescents and adults, so it is important for parents to help their children attain a healthy weight and maintain it. Following are some recommended ways that parents can help their overweight children lose weight (DiLonardo, 2013; Matthiessen, 2013; Moninger, 2013):

- *Work on a healthy project together and involve the child in the decision-making process.* Get the child involved in an activity that can help him or her lose weight such as purchasing pedometers for all family members and developing goals for how many steps to take each day. By involving the child in making decisions about the family's health, the hope is that the child will begin to take responsibility for his or her own health.
- *Be a healthy model for your child. In many aspects of life, what people do is more influential than what they say.* So if parents are overweight and engaging in unhealthy behaviors such as eating unhealthy fast food and not exercising, then telling their overweight children to lose weight is unlikely to be effective.
- *Engage in physical activities with children.* Parents and children can engage in activities like bicycling, jogging, hiking, and swimming together. Parents might say something like, "Let's take a bike ride after dinner this evening. It would be fun and could help us both get in better shape."
- *Give children choices in what they want to do to lose weight.* Take them to the grocery store with you and let them

What are positive strategies parents can adopt to help overweight children lose weight?
©vgajic/Getty Images RF

select the fruits and vegetables they are willing to eat. Let them choose which sport or type of exercise they would like to do.
- *Eat healthy family meals together on a regular basis.* Children who eat meals together with their family are less likely to be overweight.
- *Reduce screen time.* Children who spend large numbers of hours per day in screen time are more likely to be overweight than their counterparts whose screen time takes up a smaller part of their day.

DISEASES

Four childhood diseases that can be especially harmful to children's development are cancer, diabetes, cardiovascular disease, and asthma.

Cancer Cancer is the second leading cause of death (after accidents) in U.S. children 5 to 14 years of age. One in every 330 children in the United States develops cancer before the age of 19. The incidence of cancer in children has risen slightly in recent years (National Cancer Institute, 2017).

Cancers in children mainly attack the white blood cells (leukemia), brain, bone, lymph system, muscles, kidneys, and nervous system. All are characterized by an uncontrolled proliferation of abnormal cells (Marcoux & others, 2017). As indicated in Figure 3, the most common cancer in children is leukemia, a cancer in which bone marrow manufactures an abundance of abnormal white blood cells, which crowd out normal cells, making the child susceptible to bruising and infection (Shago, 2017).

When cancer strikes children, it behaves differently from the way it attacks adults. Children frequently have a more advanced stage of cancer when they are first diagnosed. When cancer is first diagnosed in adults, it has spread to distant parts of the body in only about 20 percent of the cases; however, that figure rises to 80 percent in children. Most cancers in adults result from lifestyle factors, such as smoking, diet, occupation, and exposure to other cancer-causing agents. By contrast, little is known about the causes of childhood cancers. Researchers are searching for possible genetic links to childhood cancers (Shago, 2017; Shiba & others, 2016).

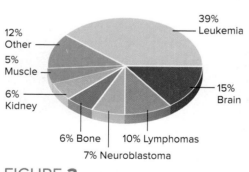

12% Other
5% Muscle
6% Kidney
39% Leukemia
15% Brain
6% Bone
10% Lymphomas
7% Neuroblastoma

FIGURE 3

TYPES OF CANCER IN CHILDREN. Cancers in children have a different profile from adult cancers, which attack mainly the lungs, colon, breast, prostate, and pancreas.

Because of advancements in cancer treatment, children with cancer are surviving longer (National Cancer Institute, 2017). Approximately 80 percent of children with acute lymphoblastic leukemia are cured with current chemotherapy treatment.

Diabetes   Diabetes is one of the most common chronic diseases in children and adolescents. Rates of diabetes in children have increased in the United States and other countries (National Center for Health Statistics, 2017c). In type 1 diabetes, the body produces little or no insulin (the hormone that regulates the body's blood sugar level) (Mitchell, 2017). **Type 1 diabetes** is an autoimmune disease in which the body's immune system destroys insulin-producing cells. In **type 2 diabetes,** the most common type of diabetes, the body is able to produce insulin, but the amount may be insufficient or the body's cells may be unable to use it. Risk factors for type 2 diabetes include being overweight and/or physically inactive, having relatives with this disease, or belonging to certain ethnic groups (Ehehalt & others, 2017; Evans, 2017). A recent study found that an 8-week exercise program improved the insulin resistant profile of obese children (McCormack & others, 2014). Native Americans, African Americans, Latinos, and Asian Americans are at greater risk than non-Latino White Americans for developing diabetes (Hasson & others, 2013).

Cardiovascular Disease   Cardiovascular disease is uncommon in children. Nonetheless, environmental experiences and behavior in the childhood years can sow the seeds for cardiovascular disease in adulthood (Schaefer & others, 2017). Many elementary-school-aged children already possess one or more of the risk factors for cardiovascular disease, such as hypertension and obesity (Badeli & others, 2016; Zoller & others, 2017). One study revealed that high blood pressure goes undiagnosed in 75 percent of children with the disease (Hansen, Gunn, & Kaelber, 2007). Another study found that high blood pressure was most likely to be present in Latino children (25 percent) and least characteristic of Asian American children (14 percent) (Sorof & others, 2004). Yet another study revealed that more than 2 hours of TV viewing per day was associated with higher blood pressure in children (Stamatakis & others, 2013).

How might research studies help us improve children's cardiovascular health? The Bogalusa Heart Study discussed in the *Connecting with Research* interlude seeks to answer this question.

Asthma   **Asthma** is a chronic lung disease that involves episodes of airflow obstruction (Rutman & others, 2016). Symptoms of an asthma attack include shortness of breath, wheezing, or tightness in the chest. The incidence of asthma has risen steadily in recent decades, possibly because of increased air pollution (Ding & others, 2017). Asthma is the most common chronic disease in U.S. children, being present in 8.6 percent of them (National Center for Health Statistics, 2017a). Asthma is the primary reason for absences from school, and it is responsible for a number of pediatric admissions to emergency rooms and hospitals (Rutman & others, 2016). Children with asthma account for more than 600,000 emergency room visits per year in the United States (Rutman & others, 2016).

The exact causes of asthma are not known, but it is believed that the disease results from hypersensitivity to environmental substances that triggers an allergic reaction (Altug & others, 2013). A research review concluded that the following are asthma risk factors: being male, having one or both parents with asthma, and/or having allergy sensitivity, stress early in life, infections, obesity, and exposure to environmental tobacco smoke, indoor allergens, and outdoor pollutants (Feleszko & others, 2006). There is increasing concern about children's exposure to secondhand smoke as a contributor to asthma (Puranik & others, 2017). A recent study found that secondhand smoke more than doubled the odds of hospitalization for children with asthma (Jin, Seiber, & Ferketich, 2013).

Corticosteroids, which generally are inhaled, are the most effective anti-inflammatory drugs for treating asthmatic children (Morton & others, 2017). Often, parents have kept asthmatic children from exercising because they feared that exercise might provoke an asthma attack. However, today it is believed that children with asthma should be encouraged to exercise, provided their asthma is under control, and participation should be evaluated on an

type 1 diabetes An autoimmune disease in which the body's immune system destroys insulin-producing cells.

type 2 diabetes The most common type of diabetes, in which the body is able to produce insulin, but the amount may be insufficient or the body's cells may be unable to use it.

asthma A chronic lung disease that involves episodes of airflow obstruction.

What are some concerns about children's cardiovascular health and obesity?
©Felicia Martinez Photography/PhotoEdit

What are some of the risk factors for developing asthma during childhood?
©Ian Boddy/Science Photo Library/Alamy RF

Heart Smart

The Bogalusa Heart Study, also called Heart Smart, is a large-scale investigation designed to improve children's cardiovascular health. It involves an ongoing evaluation of 8,000 boys and girls in Bogalusa, Louisiana (Berenson, 2005; Berenson & Bogalusa Heart Study Group, 2012; Berenson & others, 2016; Chen & others, 2015; Harville & others, 2017; Tanrikulu, Agirbasli, & Berenson, 2017; T. Zhang & others, 2016). Heart Smart intervention takes place in schools. Since 95 percent of children and adolescents aged 5 to 18 are in school, school is an efficient context in which to educate individuals about health. Special attention is given to teachers, who serve as role models. Teachers who value the role of health in life and who engage in health-enhancing behavior present children and adolescents with positive models for health. Teacher in-service education is conducted by an interdisciplinary team of specialists, including physicians, psychologists, nutritionists, physical educators, and exercise physiologists. The school's staff is introduced to information about heart health, the nature of cardiovascular disease, and risk factors for heart disease. Coping behavior, exercise behavior, and eating behavior are discussed with the staff, and a Heart Smart curriculum is explained.

The Heart Smart curriculum for grade 5 includes strategies for improving cardiovascular health, eating behavior, and exercise. The physical education component of Heart Smart involves two to four class periods each week devoted to a "Superkids-Superfit" exercise program. The physical education instructor teaches skills required by the school system plus aerobic activities aimed at cardiovascular conditioning, including jogging, racewalking, interval workouts, rope skipping, circuit training, aerobic dance, and games. Classes begin and end with five minutes of walking and stretching.

The school lunch program serves as an intervention site, where sodium, fat, and sugar levels are decreased. Children and adolescents are given reasons why they should eat healthy foods, such as a tuna sandwich, and why they should not eat unhealthy foods, such as a hot dog with chili. The school lunch program includes a salad bar where children and adolescents can serve themselves. The amount and type of snack foods sold on the school premises are monitored.

High-risk children—those with elevated blood pressure, cholesterol, and high weight—are identified as part of Heart Smart. A multidisciplinary team of physicians, nutritionists, nurses, and behavioral counselors works with the high-risk boys and girls and their parents through group-oriented activities and individual-based family counseling. High-risk boys and girls and their parents receive diet, exercise, and relaxation prescriptions in an intensive 12-session program, followed by long-term monthly evaluations.

Extensive assessment is a part of this ongoing program. Short-term and long-term changes in children's knowledge about cardiovascular disease and changes in their behavior are assessed.

Following are some results from the Bogalusa Heart Study:

- More than half of the children exceeded the recommended intake of salt, fat, cholesterol, and sugar (Nicklas & others, 1995).
- Consumption of sweetened beverages, sweets (desserts, candy), and total consumption of low-quality food were associated with being overweight in childhood (Nicklas & others, 2003).
- High levels of body fat and elevated blood pressure beginning in childhood were linked to premature death from coronary heart disease in adulthood (Berenson & others, 2016).
- Higher body mass index (BMI) in childhood was linked to the likelihood of developing metabolic syndrome (a cluster of characteristics that include excessive fat around the abdomen, high blood pressure, and diabetes) in adulthood (Freedman & others, 2005).
- Secondhand smoke exposure in childhood was associated with increased carotid artery thickness in adulthood (Chen & others, 2015).

How do you think parents, siblings, and peers might influence children's health behavior such as exercise habits and food choices?

individual basis (Minic & Sovtic, 2017). A recent research review concluded that physical activity is a possible protective factor against asthma development (Eijkemans & others, 2012). Some asthmatic children lose their symptoms in adolescence and adulthood (Vonk & others, 2004).

One individual who helps children cope with their health-care experiences is child life specialist Sharon McLeod. To read about her work, see the *Connecting with Careers* profile.

ACCIDENTS AND INJURIES

Injuries are the leading cause of death during middle and late childhood. The most common cause of severe injury and death during this period is motor vehicle accidents, either as a pedestrian or as a passenger (National Center for Health Statistics, 2017b). For this reason, safety advocates recommend the use of safety-belt restraints and child booster seats in vehicles because they can greatly reduce the severity of motor vehicle injuries (Hafner & others, 2017). For example, a recent study found that child booster seats reduced the risk for serious injury by 45 percent for 4- to 8-year-old children (Sauber-Schatz & others, 2014).

connecting with careers

Sharon McLeod, Child Life Specialist

Sharon McLeod is a child life specialist who is clinical director of the Child Life and Recreational Therapy Department at the Children's Hospital Medical Center in Cincinnati.

Under McLeod's direction, the goals of the Child Life Department are to promote children's optimal growth and development, reduce the stress of health-care experiences, and provide support to child patients and their families. These goals are accomplished through therapeutic play and developmentally appropriate activities, educating and psychologically preparing children for medical procedures, and serving as a resource for parents and other professionals regarding developmental and health-care issues.

McLeod says that knowledge of human growth and development provides the foundation for her profession of child life specialist. She says her best times as a student were when she conducted fieldwork, had an internship, and received hands-on experience applying theories and concepts she learned in her courses.

Sharon McLeod, child life specialist, works with a child at Children's Hospital Medical Center in Cincinnati.
Courtesy of Sharon McLeod

For more information about what child life specialists do, see the Careers in Children's Development appendix.

Other serious injuries in this age group involve bicycles, skateboards, roller skates, and other sports equipment.

Most accidents occur in or near the child's home or school. The most effective prevention strategy is to educate the child about proper use of equipment and the hazards of risk-taking behaviors (Souza & others, 2017). Safety helmets, protective eye and mouth shields, and protective padding are recommended for children who engage in active sports.

Caregivers play a key role in preventing childhood injuries (Thornton & others, 2017). A study that was conducted in four developing countries (Ethiopia, Peru, Vietnam, and India) revealed that depression in caregivers was consistently linked to children's risk of all types of injury assessed (burns, serious falls, broken bones, and near-fatal injury) (Howe, Huttly, & Abramsky, 2006).

How Would You...?
If you were a **health-care professional,** how would you work with school-age children to reduce their chances of injury due to accidents?

Review Connect Reflect

 LG2 Characterize children's health in middle and late childhood.

Review
- What are key aspects of children's nutrition in middle and late childhood?
- What roles do exercise and sports play in children's development?
- What are the consequences of being overweight in childhood?
- Which four diseases are especially harmful to children?
- What is the most common cause of severe injury and death in childhood?

Connect
- What are some positive and negative parental feeding patterns that are likely to play a role in children's eating patterns in middle and late childhood?

Reflect *Your Own Personal Journey of Life*
- How good were your eating habits as a child? How much did you exercise in middle and late childhood? Are your eating and exercise habits today similar to or different from your eating and exercise habits as a child? Why are they similar or different?

Who Are Children with Disabilities? | The Range of Disabilities | Educational Issues

In the previous section of this chapter, our discussion of children's health focused on nutrition and exercise. In addition, we discussed some of the most common health problems, including obesity, cancer, diabetes, cardiovascular disease, and asthma. In this section, we turn our attention to children with disabilities and the issues involved in their education.

WHO ARE CHILDREN WITH DISABILITIES?

Of all children in the United States, 12.9 percent from 3 to 21 years of age received special education or related services in 2012–2013, an increase of 3 percent since 1980–1981 (Condition of Education, 2016). Figure 4 shows the five largest groups of students with a disability who were served by federal programs during the 2012–2013 school year (National Center for Education Statistics, 2016). As indicated in Figure 4, students with a learning disability were by far the largest group of students with a disability to be given special education, followed by children with speech or language impairments, autism, intellectual disabilities, and emotional disturbance. Note that the U.S. Department of Education includes both students with a learning disability and students with ADHD in the category of learning disability.

Educators now prefer to speak of "children with disabilities" rather than "handicapped children" in order to focus on the person rather than the disability (Heward, Alber-Morgan, & Konrad, 2017). The term "handicapping conditions" is still used to describe impediments imposed by society that restrict the learning and functioning of individuals with a disability. For example, in the case of children who use a wheelchair and do not have access to a bathroom, transportation, and so on, this is referred to as a handicap situation.

THE RANGE OF DISABILITIES

In this section, we examine learning disabilities, attention deficit hyperactivity disorder, speech disorders, sensory disorders, physical disorders, emotional and behavioral disorders, and autism. Later, we will study intellectual disabilities.

Learning Disabilities   Bobby's second-grade teacher complains that his spelling is awful. Eight-year-old Tim says reading is really hard for him, and often the words don't make much sense. Alishavv has good oral language skills but has considerable difficulty in computing correct answers to arithmetic problems. Each of these students has a learning disability.

Characteristics and Identification   The U.S. government created a definition of learning disabilities in 1997 and then reauthorized the definition with a few minor changes in 2004. Following is a description of the government's definition of what determines whether a child should be classified as having a learning disability. A child with a **learning disability** has difficulty in learning that involves understanding or using spoken or written language, and the difficulty can appear in listening, thinking, reading, writing, or spelling. A learning disability also may involve difficulty in doing mathematics. To be classified as a learning disability, the learning problem is not primarily the result of visual, hearing, or motor disabilities; intellectual disabilities; emotional disorders; or environmental, cultural, or economic disadvantage (Friend, 2018; Turnbull & others, 2016).

About three times as many boys as girls are classified as having a learning disability. Among the explanations for this gender difference are a greater biological vulnerability among boys and referral bias (that is, boys are more likely to be referred by teachers for treatment because of their behavior) (Liederman, Kantrowitz, & Flannery, 2005).

Most learning disabilities are lifelong. Compared with children without a learning disability, children with a learning disability are more likely to show poor academic performance, high dropout rates, and poor employment and postsecondary education records (Berninger & O'Malley, 2011). Children with a learning disability who are taught in the regular classroom

---

learning disability Disability in which a child has difficulty in learning that involves understanding or using spoken or written language, and the difficulty can appear in listening, thinking, reading, writing, or spelling. A learning disability also may involve difficulty in doing mathematics. To be classified as a learning disability, the learning problem is not primarily the result of visual, hearing, or motor disabilities; intellectual disabilities; emotional disorders; or environmental, cultural, or economic disadvantage.

Disability	Percentage of All Children in Public Schools
Learning disabilities	4.6
Speech or hearing impairments	2.7
Autism	1.0
Intellectual disabilities	0.9
Emotional disturbance	0.7

FIGURE 4

U.S. CHILDREN WITH A DISABILITY WHO RECEIVE SPECIAL EDUCATION SERVICES. Figures are for the 2012–2013 school year and represent the five categories with the highest numbers and percentages of children. Both learning disability and attention deficit hyperactivity disorder are combined in the learning disabilities category (Condition of Education, 2016).

without extensive support rarely achieve even the level of competence attained by children who are low-achieving and do not have a disability (Hocutt, 1996). Still, despite the problems they encounter, many children with a learning disability grow up to lead normal lives and engage in productive work. For example, actress Whoopi Goldberg and investment company owner Charles Schwab have learning disabilities.

Diagnosing whether a child has a learning disability is often a difficult task. Because federal guidelines are just that—guidelines—it is up to each state, or in some cases each school system within a state, to determine how to define and implement diagnosis of learning disabilities. The same child might be diagnosed as having a learning disability in one school system and receive services but not be diagnosed and not receive services in another school system. In such cases, parents sometimes will move to a new location to obtain or to avoid the diagnosis.

Initial identification of a possible learning disability usually is made by the classroom teacher. If a learning disability is suspected, the teacher calls on specialists. An interdisciplinary team of professionals is best suited to determine whether a student has a learning disability. Individual psychological evaluations (of intelligence) and educational assessments (such as current level of achievement) are required (Hallahan, Kauffman, & Pullen, 2015). In addition, tests of visual-motor skills, language, and memory may be used.

How Would You…?

If you were an **educator,** how would you explain the nature of learning disabilities to a parent whose child had recently been diagnosed with a learning disability?

Reading, Writing, and Math Difficulties   The most common academic areas in which children with a learning disability have problems are reading, writing, and math (Dohla & Heim, 2016). A problem with reading affects approximately 80 percent of children with a learning disability (Shaywitz, Gruen, & Shaywitz, 2007). Such children have difficulty with phonological skills, which involve being able to understand how sounds and letters match up to make words, and also can have problems in comprehension. **Dyslexia** is a category reserved for individuals with a severe impairment in their ability to read and spell (Shaywitz & Shaywitz, 2017).

Dysgraphia is a learning disability that involves difficulty in handwriting (Hook & Haynes, 2017). Children with dysgraphia may write very slowly, their writing products may be virtually illegible, and they may make numerous spelling errors because of their inability to match up sounds and letters.

Dyscalculia, also known as developmental arithmetic disorder, is a learning disability that involves difficulty in math computation (Stein & others, 2018; Kucian & von Aster, 2015). It is estimated to characterize 2 to 6 percent of U.S. elementary school children (National Center for Learning Disabilities, 2006). A child may have both a reading and a math disability, and there are cognitive deficits that characterize both types of disabilities, such as poor working memory (Siegel, 2003).

dyslexia A category of learning disabilities involving a severe impairment in the ability to read and spell.

dysgraphia A learning disability that involves difficulty in handwriting.

dyscalculia Also known as developmental arithmetic disorder; a learning disability that involves difficulty in math computation.

Causes and Intervention Strategies   The precise causes of learning disabilities have not yet been determined (Heward, Alber-Morgan, & Konrad, 2017). However, some possible causes have been proposed. Learning disabilities tend to run in families, with higher rates among children having one parent with a disability such as dyslexia or dyscalculia.

Researchers currently are exploring the role of genetics in learning disabilities (Mehta, Gruen, & Zhang, 2017). Also, some learning disabilities are likely to be caused by problems during prenatal development or delivery. For example, a number of studies have found that learning disabilities are more prevalent in low birth weight and preterm infants (Taylor & others, 2016).

Researchers also use brain-imaging techniques, such as magnetic resonance imaging and event-related potentials, to examine any regions of the brain that might be involved in learning disabilities (Richards & others, 2017; Shaywitz, Morris, & Shaywitz, 2008; Shaywitz & Shaywitz, 2017) (see Figure 5). This research indicates that it is unlikely learning disabilities stem from disorders in a single, specific brain location. More likely, learning disabilities are due to problems integrating information from multiple brain regions or to subtle defects in brain structure and function.

Many interventions have focused on improving the child's reading ability (Cunningham, 2017; Cunningham & Allington, 2016; Temple & others, 2018). Intensive instruction over a period of time by a competent teacher can help many children (Thompson & others, 2017). For example, a brain-imaging study involved 15 children with severe reading difficulties who had

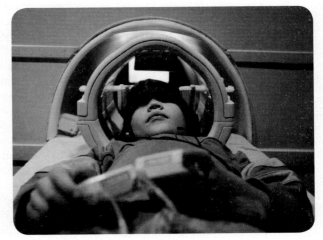

FIGURE **5**

BRAIN SCANS AND LEARNING DISABILITIES. An increasing number of studies are using MRI brain scans to examine the brain pathways involved in learning disabilities. Shown here is 9-year-old Patrick Price, who has dyslexia. Patrick is going through an MRI scanner disguised by drapes to look like a child-friendly castle. Inside the scanner, children must lie virtually motionless as words and symbols flash on a screen, and they are asked to identify them by clicking different buttons.
©Manuel Balce Ceneta/AP Images

not shown adequate progress in response to reading instruction in the first grade and were given eight weeks of intensive instruction in phonological decoding skills followed by eight weeks of intensive instruction in word recognition skills (Simos & others, 2007). The intervention led to significant improvement in a majority of the children's reading skills as well as changes in brain regions involved in reading.

Attention Deficit Hyperactivity Disorder   Seven-year-old Matthew has attention deficit hyperactivity disorder, and the outward signs are fairly typical. He has trouble attending to the teacher's instructions and is easily distracted. He can't sit still for more than a few minutes at a time, and his handwriting is messy. His mother describes him as very fidgety.

Characteristics   **Attention deficit hyperactivity disorder (ADHD)** is a disability in which children consistently show one or more of the following characteristics over a period of time: (1) inattention, (2) hyperactivity, and (3) impulsivity. For an ADHD diagnosis, onset of these characteristics early in childhood is required, and the characteristics must be debilitating for the child.

Inattentive children have difficulty focusing on any one thing and may get bored with a task after only a few minutes. One study found that problems in sustaining attention were the most common type of attention problem in children with ADHD (Tsal, Shalev, & Mevorach, 2005). Hyperactive children show high levels of physical activity, almost always seeming to be in motion. Impulsive children have difficulty curbing their reactions and don't do a good job of thinking before they act. Depending on the characteristics that children with ADHD display, they can be diagnosed as having (1) ADHD with predominantly inattention, (2) ADHD with predominantly hyperactivity/impulsivity, or (3) ADHD with both inattention and hyperactivity/impulsivity.

Many children with ADHD show impulsive behavior. *How would you handle this situation if you were a teacher and noticed this happening in your classroom?*
©Nicole Hill/Rubberball/Getty Images RF

Diagnosis and Developmental Status   The number of children diagnosed and treated for ADHD has increased substantially, by some estimates doubling in the 1990s (Stein, 2004). The Centers for Disease Control and Prevention (2016) estimates that ADHD has continued to increase in 4- to 17-year-old children, going from 8 percent in 2003 to 9.5 percent in 2007 and to 11 percent in 2016. Approximately 13.2 percent of U.S. boys and 5.6 of U.S. girls have ever been diagnosed with ADHD. The disorder occurs as much as four to nine times more often in boys than in girls. There is controversy about the increased diagnosis of ADHD, however (Watson & others, 2014). Some experts attribute the increase mainly to heightened awareness of the disorder. Others are concerned that many children are being diagnosed without undergoing extensive professional evaluation based on input from multiple sources.

One study examined the possible misdiagnosis of ADHD (Bruchmiller, Margraf, & Schneider, 2012). In this study, child psychologists, psychiatrists, and social workers were given vignettes of children with ADHD (some vignettes matched the diagnostic criteria for the disorder, while others did not). Whether each child was male or female varied. The researchers assessed whether the mental health professionals gave a diagnosis of ADHD to the child described in the vignette. The professionals overdiagnosed ADHD almost 20 percent of the time, and regardless of the symptoms described, boys were twice as likely as girls to be given a diagnosis of ADHD.

Although signs of ADHD are often present during the preschool years, children with ADHD are not usually classified until the elementary school years (Zentall, 2006). The increased academic and social demands of formal schooling, as well as stricter standards for behavioral control, often illuminate the problems of the child with ADHD. Elementary school teachers typically report that this type of child has difficulty in working independently, completing seatwork, and organizing work. Restlessness and distractibility also are often noted. These problems are more likely to be observed in repetitive or difficult tasks, or tasks the child perceives to be boring (such as completing worksheets or doing homework).

Experts previously thought that most children "grow out" of ADHD. However, recent evidence suggests that as many as 70 percent of adolescents (Sibley & others, 2012) and 66 percent of adults (Buitelaar, Karr, & Asherton, 2010) who were diagnosed as children continue to experience ADHD symptoms.

Causes and Treatment   Definitive causes of ADHD have not been found. However, a number of causes have been proposed (Lewis, Wheeler, & Carter, 2017). Some children likely inherit a tendency to develop ADHD from their parents (Gallo & Posner, 2016; Walton & others, 2017). Other children likely develop ADHD because of damage to their brain during prenatal or

How Would You...?
If you were a **health-care professional,** how would you respond to the following remarks by a parent? "I do not believe that ADHD is a real disorder. Children are supposed to be active."

attention deficit hyperactivity disorder (ADHD) A disability in which children consistently show one or more of the following characteristics: (1) inattention, (2) hyperactivity, and (3) impulsivity.

postnatal development (Bos & others, 2017; Cecil, Walton, & Barker, 2016). Among early possible contributors to ADHD are cigarette and alcohol exposure, as well as a high level of maternal stress during prenatal development and low birth weight (Scheinost & others, 2017).

As with learning disabilities, the development of brain-imaging techniques is leading to a better understanding of the brain's role in ADHD (Gold & others, 2016; Wyciszkiewicz, Pawlak, & Krawlec, 2017). One study revealed that peak thickness of the cerebral cortex occurred three years later (10.5 years) in children with ADHD than in children without ADHD (peak at 7.5 years) (Shaw & others, 2007). The delay was more prominent in the prefrontal regions of the brain that are especially important in attention and planning (see Figure 6). A study also found delayed development of the brain's frontal lobes in children with ADHD, linked to delayed or decreased myelination (Nagel & others, 2011). Researchers are exploring the roles that various neurotransmitters, such as serotonin and dopamine, might play in ADHD (Auerbach & others, 2017; Baptista & others, 2017). A recent study found that the dopamine transporter gene DAT 1 was involved in decreased cortical thickness in the prefrontal cortex of children with ADHD (Fernandez-Jaen & others, 2015).

The delays in brain development just described are in areas linked to executive function (Weyandt & others, 2017). A focus of increasing interest in studies of children with ADHD is their difficulty on tasks involving executive function, such as behavioral inhibition when necessary, use of working memory, and effective planning (Craig & others, 2016; van Lieshout & others, 2017; Toplak, West, & Stanovich, 2017; Wu & others, 2017). Researchers also have found deficits in theory of mind in children with ADHD (Mary & others, 2016).

Adjustment and optimal development also are difficult for children who have ADHD, so it is important that the diagnosis be accurate (Hechtman & others, 2016; Peasgood & others, 2016). Children diagnosed with ADHD have an increased risk of problematic peer relations, school dropout, adolescent pregnancy, substance use problems, and antisocial behavior. For example, a recent research review concluded that in comparison with typically developing girls, girls with ADHD had more problems in friendship, peer interaction, social skills, and peer victimization (Kok & others, 2016). Also, a recent research review concluded that ADHD in childhood was linked to the following long-term outcomes: failure to complete high school, other mental and substance use disorders, criminal activity, and unemployment (Erskine & others, 2016). Also, a recent study found that childhood ADHD was associated with long-term underachievement in math and reading (Voigt & others, 2017).

Stimulant medication such as Ritalin (methylphenidate) or Adderall (amphetamine and dextroamphetamine) is effective in improving the attention of many children with ADHD, but it usually does not improve their attention to the same level as children who do not have ADHD (Brams, Mao, & Doyle, 2009). A recent research review also concluded that stimulant medications are effective in treating ADHD during the short term but that longer-term benefits of stimulant medications are not clear (Rajeh & others, 2017). A meta-analysis concluded that behavior management treatments are effective in reducing the symptoms of ADHD (Fabiano & others, 2009). Researchers have often found that a combination of medication (such as Ritalin) and behavior management may improve the behavior of children with ADHD better than medication alone or behavior management alone, although this does not happen in all cases (Centers for Disease Control and Prevention, 2016).

The sheer number of ADHD diagnoses has prompted speculation that psychiatrists, parents, and teachers might be labeling normal childhood behavior as psychopathology (Mash & Wolfe, 2016). One reason for concern about overdiagnosing ADHD is that the form of treatment in well over 80 percent of cases is psychoactive drugs, including stimulants such as Ritalin and Adderall (Garfield & others, 2012). Further, there is increasing concern that children who are given stimulant drugs such as Ritalin or Adderall are at risk for developing substance abuse problems in adolescence and adulthood, although research results so far have been mixed (Brook & others, 2014; Erskine & others, 2016; McCabe & others, 2017; Molina & others, 2013, 2014; Nogueira & others, 2014).

Recently, researchers have been exploring the possibility that neurofeedback might improve the attention of children with ADHD (Alegria & others, 2017; Jiang, Abiri, & Zhao, 2017; Mohagheghi & others, 2017; Van Doren & others, 2017). *Neurofeedback* trains individuals to become more aware of their physiological responses so that they can attain better control over their brain's prefrontal cortex, where executive control primarily occurs. Individuals with ADHD have higher levels of electroencephalogram (EEG) abnormalities, such as lower beta waves that involve attention and memory, and lower sensorimotor rhythms (which involve control

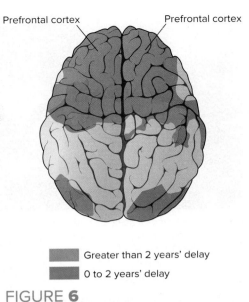

Prefrontal cortex   Prefrontal cortex

☐ Greater than 2 years' delay
☐ 0 to 2 years' delay

FIGURE 6

REGIONS OF THE BRAIN IN WHICH CHILDREN WITH ADHD HAD A DELAYED PEAK IN THE THICKNESS OF THE CEREBRAL CORTEX.
Note: The greatest delays occurred in the prefrontal cortex.

developmental connections

Cognitive Processes

Working memory is a "mental workbench" that includes a central executive function whereby individuals monitor and control information. Connect to "Cognitive Development in Middle and Late Childhood."

How is neurofeedback being used to reduce ADHD symptoms in children?
©Jerilee Bennett/KRT/Newscom

developmental connections

Cognitive Processes

Mindfulness training is being used to improve students' executive function. Connect to "Cognitive Development in Middle and Late Childhood."

of movements). Neurofeedback produces audiovisual profiles of brain waves so that individuals can learn how to achieve normal EEG functioning. In a recent study, 7- to 14-year-olds with ADHD were randomly assigned either to take Ritalin or to undergo 40 sessions of a neurofeedback treatment (Meisel & others, 2013). Both groups showed a lower level of ADHD symptoms six months after the treatment, but only the neurofeedback group performed better academically.

Recently, mindfulness training also has been given to children and adolescents with ADHD (Edel & others, 2017). A recent meta-analysis concluded that mindfulness training significantly improved the attention of children with ADHD (Cairncross & Miller, 2017). Also, in one study, 11- to 15-year-old adolescents with ADHD received eight weeks of mindfulness training (van de Weijer-Bergsma & others, 2012). Immediately after and eight weeks following the training, the adolescents' attention improved and they engaged in fewer behavioral problems, although at 16 weeks post-training the effects had waned.

Exercise also is being investigated as a possible treatment for children with ADHD (Den Heijer & others, 2017; Grassman & others, 2017; Pan & others, 2017). A recent study found that a single 20-minute bout of moderately intense aerobic exercise improved the neurocognitive function and inhibitory control of children with ADHD (Pontifex & others, 2013). Another recent study revealed that higher levels of physical activity in adolescence were linked with a lower incidence of ADHD in emerging adulthood (Rommel & others, 2015). Further, a recent study confirmed that an 8-week yoga program was effective in improving the sustained attention of children with ADHD (Chou & Huang, 2017). Also, a recent meta-analysis concluded that physical exercise is effective in reducing cognitive symptoms of ADHD in individuals 3 to 25 years of age (Tan, Pooley & Speelman, 2016). A second recent meta-analysis concluded that short-term aerobic exercise is effective in reducing symptoms such as inattention, hyperactivity, and impulsivity (Cerrillo-Urbina & others, 2015). And another recent meta-analysis indicated that exercise is associated with better executive function in children with ADHD (Vysniauske & others, 2017).

Among the reasons given as to why exercise might reduce ADHD symptoms in children are (1) better allocation of attention resources, (2) positive influence on prefrontal cortex functioning, and (3) exercise-induced dopamine release (Chang & others, 2012).

Despite the encouraging recent studies of the use of neurofeedback, mindfulness training, and exercise to improve the attention of children with ADHD, it has not been determined whether these non-drug therapies are as effective as stimulant drugs and/or whether they benefit children as add-ons to stimulant drugs to provide a combination treatment (Den Heijer & others, 2017).

Speech Disorders Speech disorders include articulation disorders, voice disorders, and fluency disorders. **Articulation disorders** are problems in pronouncing sounds correctly (Bernthal, Bankson, & Flipsen, 2017). A child's articulation at 6 to 7 years is still not always error-free, but it should be by age 8. A child with an articulation problem may find communication with peers and the teacher difficult or embarrassing. As a result, the child may avoid asking questions, participating in discussions, or talking with peers. Articulation problems can usually be improved or resolved with speech therapy, although it may take months or years.

Voice disorders are reflected in speech that is hoarse, harsh, too loud, too high-pitched, or too low-pitched. Children with a cleft palate often have a voice disorder that makes their speech difficult to understand. If a student speaks in a way that is consistently difficult to understand, the child should be referred to a speech therapist (Bernthal, Bankson, & Flipsen, 2017).

Fluency disorders often involve what is commonly called "stuttering." Stuttering occurs when a child's speech has a spasmodic hesitation, prolongation, or repetition (Howell, 2013). The anxiety many children feel because they stutter can make their stuttering worse. Speech therapy is recommended.

Sensory Disorders Sensory disorders include visual and hearing impairments. Sometimes these impairments are described as part of a larger category called "communication disorders" that also encompasses speech and language disorders.

Visual Impairments Some children may have mild vision problems that have not been corrected. If children frequently squint, hold books close to their face when they read, rub their eyes often, say that things look blurred, or mention that words move about on the page, they should be referred to appropriate professionals to have their vision checked. In many cases, corrective lenses will solve the child's vision problem. However, a small proportion of

articulation disorders Problems in pronouncing sounds correctly.

voice disorders Disorders reflected in speech that is hoarse, harsh, too loud, too high-pitched, or too low-pitched.

fluency disorders Various disorders that involve what is commonly called "stuttering."

children (about 1 in 1,000) have more serious visual problems and are classified as visually impaired. This category includes children with low vision and blind children.

Children with **low vision** have visual acuity of between 20/70 and 20/2000 (on the Snellen scale, in which 20/20 is normal) with corrective lenses. Children with low vision can read with the aid of large-print books or a magnifying glass. Children who are **educationally blind** cannot use their vision in learning and must use their hearing and touch to learn. Approximately 1 in every 3,000 children is educationally blind. Almost half of these children were born blind, and another one-third lost their vision during the first year of life. Many children who are educationally blind have normal intelligence and function very well academically with appropriate supports and learning aids. 3-D printing provides an important technology support for students with visual impairments. Also, haptic devices (involving the sense of touch) have been found to increase the learning and exploration of students with a visual impairment (Nam & others, 2012).

An important task when working with a visually impaired child is to determine the modality (such as touch or hearing) through which the child learns best. Preferential seating in the front of the classroom is also helpful.

Hearing Impairments   A hearing impairment can make learning difficult for children. Children who are born deaf or experience a significant hearing loss in the first several years of life may not develop normal speech and language (Waldman & Cleary, 2017). Some children in middle and late childhood have hearing impairments that have not yet been detected. If children turn one ear toward the speaker, frequently ask to have something repeated, don't follow directions, or frequently complain of earaches, colds, and allergies, their hearing needs to be evaluated by a specialist, such as an audiologist (Patterson & Wright, 1990).

Many hearing-impaired children receive supplementary instruction beyond that of the regular classroom (Hall, 2014). Educational approaches for children with hearing impairments fall into two categories: oral and manual (Hoskin & Herman, 2001):

- **Oral approaches** include using lip reading, speech reading (relying on visual cues to teach reading), and use of whatever hearing the child has.
- **Manual approaches** involve sign language and finger spelling. Sign language is a system of hand movements that symbolize words. Finger spelling consists of "spelling out" each word by placing the hand in different positions.

A total communication approach that includes both oral and manual approaches is increasingly being used with children who are hearing impaired (Hallahan, Kauffman, & Pullen, 2015).

Today many hearing-impaired children are educated in the regular classroom. With appropriate accommodations such as preferential seating and the assistance of hearing aids, cochlear implants, and other amplification devices, hearing-impaired children can be educated effectively (Hall, 2014).

Physical Disorders   Physical disorders in middle and late childhood include orthopedic impairments such as cerebral palsy. Many children with physical disorders require special education as well as related services. The related services may include transportation, physical therapy, school health services, and psychological services.

Orthopedic impairments involve restricted movement or lack of control over movement due to muscle, bone, or joint problems. The severity of problems ranges widely. Orthopedic impairments can be caused by prenatal or perinatal problems, or they can result from diseases or accidents during the childhood years. With the help of adaptive devices and medical technology, many children with orthopedic impairments function well in the classroom (Hallahan, Kauffman, & Pullen, 2015; Lewis, Wheeler, & Carter, 2017).

Cerebral palsy is a disorder that involves a lack of muscular coordination, shaking, and unclear speech. The most common cause of cerebral palsy is lack of oxygen at birth (O'Callaghan & others, 2013). In the most common type of cerebral palsy, which is called spastic, children's muscles are stiff and difficult to move. The rigid muscles often pull the limbs into contorted positions. In a less common type, ataxia, children's muscles are rigid one moment and floppy the next moment, making movements clumsy and jerky.

Computers especially help children with cerebral palsy learn. If they have the coordination to use the keyboard, they can do their written work on the computer. A pen with a light can be added to a computer and used by the child as a pointer. Children with cerebral palsy sometimes have unclear speech. For these children, speech and voice synthesizers, communication boards, and page turners can improve their communication.

low vision Visual acuity between 20/70 and 20/2000.

educationally blind Unable to use one's vision in learning and needing to use hearing and touch to learn.

oral approaches Educational approaches to help hearing-impaired children, including lip reading, speech reading, and use of whatever hearing the child has.

manual approaches Educational approaches to help hearing-impaired children, including sign language and finger spelling.

orthopedic impairments Restrictions in movement abilities due to muscle, bone, or joint problems.

cerebral palsy A disorder that involves a lack of muscular coordination, shaking, and unclear speech.

Special input devices can help students with physical disabilities use computers more effectively. Many students with physical disabilities such as cerebral palsy cannot use a conventional keyboard and mouse but can use alternative keyboards effectively.
©Wendy Maeda/The Boston Globe/Getty Images

emotional and behavioral disorders Serious, persistent problems that involve relationships, aggression, depression, fears associated with personal or school matters, as well as other inappropriate socioemotional characteristics.

autism spectrum disorders (ASDs) Also called pervasive developmental disorders, this category ranges from the severe disorder labeled autistic disorder to the milder disorder called Asperger syndrome. Children with these disorders are characterized by problems with social interaction, verbal and nonverbal communication, and repetitive behaviors.

What characterizes autism spectrum disorders?
©Rob Crandall/Alamy

Emotional and Behavioral Disorders Most children have minor emotional difficulties at some point during their school years. A small percentage have problems so serious and persistent that they are classified as having an emotional or a behavioral disorder (Mash & Wolfe, 2016). **Emotional and behavioral disorders** consist of serious, persistent problems that involve relationships, aggression, depression, fears associated with personal or school matters, as well as other inappropriate socioemotional characteristics (Lewis, Asbury, & Plomin, 2017; Weersing & others, 2017). Approximately 8 percent of children who have a disability and require an individualized education plan fall into this classification. Boys are three times as likely as girls to have these disorders.

Autism Spectrum Disorders **Autism spectrum disorders (ASD),** also called pervasive developmental disorder, range from the severe disorder labeled autistic disorder to the milder disorder called Asperger syndrome. Autism spectrum disorders are characterized by problems in social interaction, problems in verbal and nonverbal communication, and repetitive behaviors (Boutot, 2017; Gerenser & Lopez, 2017). Children with these disorders may also show atypical responses to sensory experiences (National Institute of Mental Health, 2017). Intellectual disability is present in some children with autism, while others show average or above-average intelligence (Bernier & Dawson, 2016). Autism spectrum disorders can often be detected in children as early as 1 to 3 years of age.

Recent estimates of autism spectrum disorders indicate that they are increasing in occurrence or are increasingly being detected and labeled. They were once thought to affect only 1 in 2,500 individuals. However, in 2008 it was estimated that 1 in 88 children had an autism spectrum disorder (Centers for Disease Control & Prevention, 2012). And in the most recent survey, the estimated percentage of 8-year-old children with autism spectrum disorders had increased to 1 in 68 (Christensen & others, 2016). In the recent surveys, autism spectrum disorders were identified five times more often in boys than in girls, and 8 percent of individuals aged 3 to 21 with these disorders were receiving special education services (Centers for Disease Control and Prevention, 2017).

Also, in two recent surveys, only a minority of parents reported that their child's autistic spectrum disorder was identified prior to 3 years of age and that one-third to one-half of the cases were identified after 6 years of age (Sheldrick, Maye, & Carter, 2017). However, researchers are conducting studies that seek to find earlier determinants of autism spectrum disorders (Reiersen, 2017).

Autistic disorder is a severe developmental autism spectrum disorder that has its onset in the first three years of life and includes deficiencies in social relationships, abnormalities in communication, and restricted, repetitive, and stereotyped patterns of behavior. Estimates indicate that approximately 2 to 5 of every 10,000 young children in the United States have autistic disorder. Boys are about four times more likely to have autistic disorder than girls.

Asperger syndrome is a relatively mild autism spectrum disorder in which the child has relatively good verbal language skills, milder nonverbal language problems, and a restricted range of interests and relationships (Boutot, 2017). Children with Asperger syndrome often engage in obsessive, repetitive routines and are preoccupied with a particular subject. For example, a child may be obsessed with baseball scores or specific videos on YouTube.

Children with autism show some deficits in cognitive processing of information. For example, a recent study found that a lower level of working memory was the executive function most strongly associated with autism spectrum disorders (Ziermans & others, 2017). Children with these disorders may also show atypical responses to sensory experiences (National Institute of Mental Health, 2017). Intellectual disability is present in some children with autism; others show average or above-average intelligence (Volkmar & others, 2014). Autism spectrum disorders often can be detected in children as young as 1 to 3 years of age.

In 2013, the American Psychiatric Association proposed that in the new DSM-V psychiatric classification of disorders, autistic disorder, Asperger syndrome, and several other autistic variations ought to be consolidated in the overarching category of autism spectrum disorder (Autism Research Institute, 2013). Distinctions are made in terms of the severity of problems based on amount of support needed due to challenges involving social communication, restricted interests, and repetitive behaviors. Critics of this proposal argue that the umbrella category proposed for autism spectrum disorder masks the heterogeneity that characterizes the subgroups of autism (Lai & others, 2013).

What causes autism spectrum disorders? The current consensus is that autism is a brain dysfunction characterized by abnormalities in brain structure and neurotransmitters (Ecker, 2017; Khundrakpam & others, 2017). Recent interest has focused on a lack of connectivity between brain regions as a key factor in autism (Green & others, 2017; Li, Karmath, & Xu, 2017; Nair & others, 2017).

Genetic factors likely play a role in the development of autism spectrum disorders (Wang & others, 2017; Yuan & others, 2017). One study revealed that mutations—missing or duplicated pieces of DNA on chromosome 16—can raise a child's risk of developing autism 100-fold (Weiss & others, 2008). There is no evidence that family socialization causes autism (Rutter & Schopler, 1987).

As mentioned previously, boys are five times as likely to have an autism spectrum disorder as girls are (Centers for Disease Control and Prevention, 2017). Expanding on autism's male linkage, Simon Baron-Cohen and his colleagues (2008, 2011; Lai & others, 2017; Murray & others, 2017) recently have argued that autism reflects an extreme male brain, especially indicative of males' less effective ability to show empathy and read facial expressions and gestures in comparison with girls. In an attempt to improve these skills in 4- to 8-year-old autistic boys, Baron-Cohen and his colleagues (2007) produced a number of animations on a DVD that place faces with different emotions on toy train and tractor characters in a boy's bedroom. After watching the animations 15 minutes every weekday for one month, the autistic children's ability to recognize emotions on real faces in a different context equaled that of children without autism. A research review concluded that when these behavior modifications are intensely provided and used early in the autistic child's life, they are more effective than if they are introduced later (Howlin, Magiati, & Charman, 2009).

Many children with autism benefit from a well-structured classroom, individualized teaching, and small-group instruction (Simmons, Lanter, & Lyons, 2014). As with children who have an intellectual disability, behavior modification techniques are sometimes effective in helping autistic children learn (Alberto & Troutman, 2017; Zirpoli, 2016).

EDUCATIONAL ISSUES

The legal requirement that schools serve all children with a disability is fairly recent. Beginning in the mid-1960s and into the mid-1970s, legislators, the federal courts, and the U.S. Congress laid down special educational rights for children with disabilities. Prior to that time, most children with a disability were either refused enrollment or inadequately served by schools. In 1975, **Public Law 94-142,** the Education for All Handicapped Children Act, required that all students with disabilities be given a free, appropriate public education and be provided the funding to help implement this education.

In 1990, Public Law 94-142 was recast as the **Individuals with Disabilities Education Act (IDEA).** IDEA was amended in 1997 and then reauthorized in 2004 and renamed the Individuals with Disabilities Education Improvement Act. IDEA spells out broad mandates for providing services to all children with disabilities (Cook & Richardson-Gibbs, 2018; Heward, Alber-Morgan, & Konrad, 2017). These include evaluation and eligibility determination, appropriate education and an individualized education plan (IEP), and education in the least restrictive environment (LRE) (Hallahan, Kauffman, & Pullen, 2015; Lewis, Wheeler, & Carter, 2017).

A major aspect of the 2004 reauthorization of IDEA involved aligning it with the government's No Child Left Behind (NCLB) legislation, which was designed to improve the educational achievement of all students, including those with disabilities. Both IDEA and NCLB mandate that most students with disabilities be included in general assessments of educational progress. This alignment includes requiring most students with disabilities "to take standard tests of academic achievement and to achieve at a level equal to that of students without disabilities. Whether this expectation is reasonable is an open question" (Hallahan & Kauffman, 2006, pp. 28–29). Alternate assessments for students with disabilities and funding to help states improve instruction, assessment, and accountability for educating students with disabilities are included in the 2004 reauthorization of IDEA.

developmental **connections**

Disabilities

Autistic children have difficulty in developing a theory of mind, especially in understanding others' beliefs and emotions. Connect to "Cognitive Development in Early Childhood."

autistic disorder A severe autism spectrum disorder that has its onset in the first three years of life and includes deficiencies in social relationships, abnormalities in communication, and restricted, repetitive, and stereotyped patterns of behavior.

Asperger syndrome A relatively mild autism spectrum disorder in which the child has relatively good verbal language skills, milder nonverbal language problems, and a restricted range of interests and relationships.

Public Law 94-142 The Education for All Handicapped Children Act, created in 1975, which requires that all children with disabilities be given a free, appropriate public education and which provides the funding to help with the costs of implementing this education.

Individuals with Disabilities Education Act (IDEA) The IDEA spells out broad mandates for providing services to all children with disabilities (IDEA is a renaming of Public Law 94-142); these include evaluation and eligibility determination, appropriate education and an individualized education plan (IEP), and education in the least restrictive environment (LRE).

Increasingly, children with disabilities are being taught in the regular classroom, as is this child with an intellectual disability.
©E.D. Torial/Alamy RF

Evaluation and Eligibility Determination   Children who are thought to have a disability are evaluated to determine their eligibility for services under IDEA. Schools are prohibited from planning special education programs in advance and offering them on a space-available basis.

Children must be evaluated before a school can begin providing special services (Heward, Alber-Morgan, & Konrad, 2017). Parents should be involved in the evaluation process. Reevaluation is required at least every three years (sometimes every year), when requested by parents, or when conditions suggest that a reevaluation is needed. A parent who disagrees with the school's evaluation can obtain an independent evaluation, which the school is required to consider in providing special education services. If the evaluation finds that the child has a disability and requires special services, the school must provide them to the child.

The IDEA has many specific provisions involving the parents of a child with a disability. These include requirements that schools send notices to parents of proposed actions, of attendance at meetings regarding the child's placement or individualized education plan, and of the right to appeal school decisions to an impartial evaluator.

Appropriate Education and the Individualized Education Plan (IEP)   The IDEA requires that students with disabilities have an **individualized education plan (IEP),** a written statement that spells out a program tailored specifically for the student with a disability. In general, the IEP should be (1) related to the child's learning capacity, (2) specially constructed to meet the child's individual needs and not merely a copy of what is offered to other children, and (3) designed to provide educational benefits.

Under IDEA, the child with a disability must be educated in the **least restrictive environment (LRE),** a setting as similar as possible to the one in which children who do not have a disability are educated. And schools must make an effort to educate children with a disability in the regular classroom. The term **inclusion** means educating a child with special educational needs full-time in the regular classroom (Mastropieri & Scruggs, 2018; Turnbull & others, 2016). In a recent school year (2014), 61 percent of U.S. students with a disability spent more than 80 percent of their school day in a general classroom (compared with only 33 percent in 1990) (Condition of Education, 2015).

Not long ago, it was considered appropriate to educate children with disabilities outside the regular classroom. However, today, schools must make every effort to provide inclusion for children with disabilities (Hallahan, Kauffman, & Pullen, 2015). These efforts can be very costly financially and very time consuming in terms of faculty effort.

The principle of least restrictive environment compels schools to examine possible modifications of the regular classroom before moving the child with a disability to a more restrictive placement. Also, regular classroom teachers often need specialized training to help some children with a disability, and state educational agencies are required to provide such training.

Many of the legal changes regarding children with disabilities have been extremely positive. Compared with several decades ago, far more children today are receiving competent, specialized services. For many children, inclusion in the regular classroom, with modifications or supplemental services, is appropriate (Turnbull & others, 2016). However, some leading experts on special education argue that the effort to use inclusion to educate children with disabilities has become too extreme in some cases. For example, James Kauffman and his colleagues (Kauffman & Hallahan, 2005; Kauffman, McGee, & Brigham, 2004) state that inclusion too often has meant making accommodations in the regular classroom that do not always benefit children with disabilities. They advocate a more individualized approach that does not always involve full inclusion but provides options such as special education outside the regular classroom. Kauffman and his colleagues (2004, p. 620) acknowledge that children with disabilities "*do* need the services of specially trained professionals to achieve their full potential. They *do* sometimes need altered curricula or adaptations to make their learning possible." However, "we sell students with disabilities short when we pretend that they are not different from typical students. We make the same error when we pretend that they must not be expected to put forth extra effort if they are to learn to do some things— or learn to do something in a different way." As is true of general education, an important aspect of special education should be to challenge students with disabilities "to become all they can be."

One concern about special education involves disproportionate representation of students from minority backgrounds in special education programs and classes (Jarquin & others, 2011). The *Connecting with Diversity* interlude addresses this issue.

individualized education plan (IEP) A written statement that spells out a program tailored to a child with a disability. The plan should be (1) related to the child's learning capacity, (2) specially constructed to meet the child's individual needs and not merely a copy of what is offered to other children, and (3) designed to provide educational benefits.

least restrictive environment (LRE) The concept that a child with a disability must be educated in a setting that is as similar as possible to the one in which children who do not have a disability are educated.

inclusion Educating a child with special educational needs full-time in the regular classroom.

Disproportionate Representation of Minority Students in Special Education

The U.S. Office of Education (2000) has three concerns about the over-representation of minority students in special education programs and classes:

- Students may be unserved or receive services that do not meet their needs.
- Students may be misclassified or inappropriately labeled.
- Placement in special education classes may be a form of discrimination.

African American students are overrepresented in special education—15 percent of the U.S. student population is African American, but 20 percent of special education students are African American. In some disabilities, the discrepancies are even greater. For example, African American students represent 32 percent of the students in programs for mild intellectual disability, 29 percent in programs for moderate intellectual disability, and 24 percent in programs for serious emotional disturbance.

However, it is not just a simple matter of overrepresentation of certain minority groups in special education. Latino children may be underidentified in the categories of intellectual disability and emotional disturbance.

More appropriate inclusion of minority students in special education is a complex problem and requires the creation of a successful school experience for all students. Recommendations for reducing disproportionate representation in special education include the following (Burnette, 1998):

- Reviewing school practices to identify and address factors that might contribute to having school difficulties
- Forming policy-making groups that include community members and promote partnerships with service agencies and cultural organizations
- Helping families get social, medical, mental health, and other support services
- Training more teachers from minority backgrounds and providing all teachers with more extensive course work and training in educating children with disabilities and in understanding diversity issues

---

Review *Connect* Reflect

LG3 Summarize information about children with disabilities.

Review

- Who are children with disabilities?
- What are some characteristics of the range of children's disabilities?
- What are some important issues in the education of children with disabilities?

Connect

- Earlier, you learned about the development of attention in infancy and early childhood. How might ADHD be linked to attention difficulties during infancy and early childhood?

Reflect *Your Own Personal Journey of Life*

- Think back to your own schooling and how students with learning disabilities were or were not diagnosed. Were you aware of such individuals in your classes? Were they given special attention by teachers and/or specialists? You may know one or more individuals with a learning disability. Interview them about their school experiences. Ask them what they think could have been done better to help them with their disability.

---

topical connections *looking forward*

This chapter introduced you to the physical and brain changes of middle and late childhood. In "Physical Development in Adolescence," you will read about how the slow physical growth of middle and late childhood gives way to the dramatic changes of puberty in early adolescence. Significant changes also occur in the adolescent's brain, and such changes may be linked to an increase in risk taking and sensation seeking. In "Cognitive Development in Middle and Late Childhood," you will explore developmental changes in children's cognition in middle and late childhood, including Piaget's theory and a number of changes in children's information processing. You'll also read about some important processes that influence children's achievement and changes in language development in older children, including reading skills.

reach your **learning goals**

Physical Development in Middle and Late Childhood

1 What Changes Take Place in Body Growth, the Brain, and Motor Development?

LG1 Discuss changes in body growth, the brain, and motor development in middle and late childhood.

Skeletal and Muscular Systems

- The period of middle and late childhood involves slow, consistent growth. During this period, children grow an average of 2 to 3 inches a year. Muscle mass and strength gradually increase. Among the most pronounced changes are decreases in head circumference, waist circumference, and leg length in relation to body height.

The Brain

- Changes in the brain continue to occur in middle and late childhood, and these changes, such as increased myelination, are linked to improvements in cognitive functioning. In particular, there is an increase in pathways involving the prefrontal cortex—changes that are related to improved attention, reasoning, and cognitive control. During middle and late childhood, less diffusion and more focal activation occur in the prefrontal cortex, changes that are associated with an increase in cognitive control.

Motor Development

- During middle and late childhood, motor development becomes much smoother and more coordinated. Children gain greater control over their bodies and can sit and attend for longer periods of time. However, their lives should be filled with physical activity.

- Gross motor skills are expanded during this period, and children refine such skills as hitting a tennis ball, skipping rope, or balancing on a beam. Increased myelination of the nervous system is reflected in improved fine motor skills, such as more legible handwriting and the ability to play a difficult piece on a musical instrument. Boys are usually better at gross motor skills, girls at fine motor skills.

2 What Are the Central Issues in Children's Health?

LG2 Characterize children's health in middle and late childhood.

Nutrition

- During middle and late childhood, weight doubles and considerable energy is expended in motor activities. To support their growth, children need to consume more calories than they did when they were younger. A balanced diet is important. A special concern is that too many children fill up on "empty-calorie" foods that are high in sugar, starch, and excess fat and low in nutrients. A nutritious breakfast promotes higher energy and better alertness in school.

Exercise and Sports

- Every indication suggests that children in the United States are not getting enough exercise. Television viewing, parents who are poor role models for exercise, and inadequate physical education classes in schools are among the culprits. Children's participation in sports can have both positive and negative consequences.

Overweight Children

- Although the increase of child obesity in the United States has begun to level off, over the last four decades the percentage of U.S. children who are overweight has tripled. An increasing number of children in many countries, such as mainland China and Australia, are overweight.

- Being overweight in middle and late childhood substantially increases the risk of being overweight in adolescence and adulthood. Factors linked with being overweight in childhood include heredity and environmental contexts. Being overweight in childhood is related to a number of problems. Diet, exercise, and behavior modification are recommended for helping children to lose weight.

Diseases

- Cancer is the second leading cause of death in children (after accidents). Childhood cancers have a different profile from that of adult cancers. Diabetes is also a common disease in childhood. Cardiovascular disease is uncommon in children, but the precursors to adult cardiovascular disease are often already apparent in children. Asthma is the most common chronic disease in U.S. children.

- The most common cause of severe injury and death in childhood is motor vehicle accidents.

3 What Are the Prevalent Disabilities in Children?

LG3 Summarize information about children with disabilities.

Who Are Children with Disabilities?

- Approximately 14 percent of children from 3 to 21 years of age in the United States receive special education or related services. Students with a learning disability are by far the largest group of students with a disability who receive special education. Substantial percentages also include children with speech or language impairments, intellectual disabilities, and emotional disturbance.

- The term "children with disabilities" is now recommended rather than "handicapped children." The newer terminology is intended to focus more on the child than on the disability.

The Range of Disabilities

- Children's disabilities cover a wide range and include learning disabilities, ADHD, speech disorders, sensory disorders, physical disorders, emotional and behavioral disorders, and autism spectrum disorders.

- A child with a learning disability has difficulty in learning that involves understanding or using spoken or written language, and the difficulty can appear in listening, thinking, reading, writing, and spelling. A learning disability also may involve difficulty in doing mathematics. To be classified as a learning disability, the learning problem is not primarily the result of visual, hearing, or motor disabilities; intellectual disabilities; emotional disorders; or due to environmental, cultural, or economic disadvantage. Diagnosing whether a child has a learning disability is difficult. About three times as many boys as girls have a learning disability.

- The most common academic problem for children with a learning disability is difficulty reading. Dyslexia is a severe impairment in the ability to read and spell. Dysgraphia is a learning disability that involves difficulty in handwriting. Dyscalculia is a learning disability that involves difficulties in math computation. Controversy surrounds the "learning disability" category. Many interventions targeted for learning disabilities focus on improving the child's reading ability and include such strategies as improving decoding skills.

- Attention deficit hyperactivity disorder (ADHD) is a disability in which children consistently show problems in one or more of the following areas: inattention, hyperactivity, and impulsivity. For an ADHD diagnosis, the characteristics must appear early in childhood and be debilitating for the child. Although signs of ADHD may be present in early childhood, diagnosis of ADHD often doesn't occur until the elementary school years. Many experts recommend a combination of academic, behavioral, and medical interventions to help students with ADHD learn and adapt.

- Speech disorders include articulation disorders, voice disorders, and fluency disorders. Sensory disorders include visual and hearing impairments. Physical disorders that children may have include orthopedic impairments and cerebral palsy. Emotional and behavioral disorders consist of serious, persistent problems that involve relationships, aggression, depression, fears associated with personal or school matters, as well as other inappropriate socioemotional characteristics.

- Autistic disorder is a severe developmental autism spectrum disorder with an onset in the first three years of life, and it involves abnormalities in social relationships and communication. It also is characterized by repetitive behaviors. The current consensus is that autism spectrum disorders involve an organic brain dysfunction. Autism spectrum disorders (ASDs) range from autistic disorder to the milder Asperger syndrome.

Educational Issues

- Beginning in the 1960s and 1970s, the educational rights of children with disabilities were laid down. In 1975, Public Law 94-142 required school systems to provide all children with a free, appropriate public education. In 1990, Public Law 94-142 was renamed and called the Individuals with Disabilities Education Act (IDEA). Children who are thought to have a disability are evaluated to determine their eligibility for services. An individualized education plan (IEP) is a written plan that spells out a program tailored to the needs of a child with a disability. The concept of a least restrictive environment (LRE) is contained in the IDEA. The term *inclusion* means educating children with disabilities full-time in the general classroom. The trend is toward greater use of inclusion.

key **terms**

articulation disorders	cerebral palsy	inclusion	manual approaches
Asperger syndrome	dyscalculia	individualized education plan (IEP)	oral approaches
asthma	dysgraphia	Individuals with Disabilities	orthopedic impairments
attention deficit hyperactivity	dyslexia	Education Act (IDEA)	Public Law 94-142
disorder (ADHD)	educationally blind	learning disability	type 1 diabetes
autism spectrum disorders (ASDs)	emotional and behavioral disorders	least restrictive environment (LRE)	type 2 diabetes
autistic disorder	fluency disorders	low vision	voice disorders

key **people**

Simon Baron-Cohen   Mark Johnson   James Kauffman

connecting with **improving the lives of children**

STRATEGIES

Nurturing Children's Physical Development and Health

What are some good strategies for supporting children's physical development and health in the middle and late childhood years?

· *Elementary school children should be physically active whenever possible.* Goals should especially include reducing screen time and increasing participation in activities such as swimming, skating, and bicycling.

· *Parents should monitor children's eating behavior.* Children need more calories now than they did when they were younger. However, a special concern is the increasing number of obese children. Children who are overweight need to have a medical checkup, to revise their diet, and to participate in a regular exercise program.

· *Elementary schools need to develop more and better physical education programs.* Only about one of every three elementary school children participates in a physical education program daily. Many of those who do aren't exercising much during the program.

· *Parents need to engage in physical activities that they can enjoy together with their children.* Suggested activities include running, bicycling, hiking, and swimming.

· *Parents should try to make their children's experiences in sports positive ones.* They should stress the benefits of sports rather than displaying a win-at-all-costs philosophy.

· *Parents should help children avoid accidents and injuries.* They should educate their children about the hazards of risk-taking behaviors and improper use of equipment.

RESOURCES

Routledge Handbook of Talent Identification and Development in Sport (2017)

Edited by Joseph Baker and his colleagues
New York: Routledge.

Extensive information and strategies that can help parents become more effective in raising children who are talented in sports in positive ways.

Children's HeartLink

www.childrensheartlink.org

This organization provides treatment for needy children with heart disease and support for rheumatic fever prevention programs. It also supports the education of foreign medical professionals and provides technical advice and medical equipment and supplies.

The Council for Exceptional Children (CEC)

www.cec.sped.org

The CEC maintains an information center on the education of children and adolescents with disabilities and publishes materials on a wide variety of topics.

Learning Disabilities Association of America (LDA)

www.ldaamerica.org

The LDA provides education and support for parents of children with learning disabilities, interested professionals, and others. More than 500 chapters are in operation nationwide, offering information services, pamphlets, and book recommendations.

Autism Spectrum Disorders (2nd ed.) (2017)

E. Amanda Boutot
Upper Saddle River, NJ: Pearson

This book on various aspects of autism spectrum disorders describes research and practical approaches for improving the lives of autistic children.

Exceptional Learners (13th ed.) (2015)

Daniel Hallahan, James Kauffman, and Paige Pullen
Upper Saddle River, NJ: Pearson.

This excellent book by leading experts provides a very up-to-date examination of many child disabilities, including learning disabilities, ADHD, and autism, as well as effective strategies for teaching children who have these conditions.

chapter 12

COGNITIVE DEVELOPMENT IN MIDDLE AND LATE CHILDHOOD

chapter **outline**

① What Is Piaget's Theory of Cognitive Development in Middle and Late Childhood?

Learning Goal 1 Discuss Piaget's stage of concrete operational thought and apply Piaget's theory to education.

Concrete Operational Thought
Evaluating Piaget's Concrete Operational Stage
Applications to Education

② What Is the Nature of Children's Information Processing?

Learning Goal 2 Describe changes in information processing in middle and late childhood.

Memory
Thinking
Metacognition

③ How Can Children's Intelligence Be Described?

Learning Goal 3 Characterize children's intelligence

Intelligence and Its Assessment
Types of Intelligence
Interpreting Differences in IQ Scores
Extremes of Intelligence

④ What Changes in Language Development Occur in Middle and Late Childhood?

Learning Goal 4 Summarize language development in middle and late childhood.

Vocabulary, Grammar, and Metalinguistic Awareness
Reading and Writing
Dual-Language and Second-Language Learning

⑤ What Characterizes Children's Achievement?

Learning Goal 5 Explain the development of achievement in children.

Extrinsic and Intrinsic Motivation
Sustained Attention, Effort, and Task Persistence
Mastery Motivation and Mindset
Self-Efficacy
Goal Setting, Planning, and Self-Regulation
Social Relationships and Contexts

©Simon Jarratt/Corbis

Marva Collins, challenging a child to achieve.
©Elizabeth Flores/Milwaukee Journal Sentinel

On the first day of school, Chicago teacher Marva Collins tells her students, many of whom are repeating the second grade,

"I know most of you can't spell your name. You don't know the alphabet, you don't know how to read. . . . I promise you that you will. None of you has ever failed. School may have failed you. Well, goodbye to failure, children. Welcome to success. You will read hard books in here and understand what you read. You will write every day. . . . But you must help me to help you. If you don't give anything, don't expect anything. Success is not coming to you, you must come to it." (Dweck, 2006, pp. 188–189)

Her second-grade students usually have to start with the lowest level of reader available, but by the end of the school year most of the students are reading at the fifth-grade level.

Collins takes inner-city children living in low-income, often poverty-level, circumstances, and challenges them to be all they can be. She won't accept failure by her students and teaches students to be responsible for their behavior every day of their lives. Collins tells students that being excellent at something is not a one-time thing but a habit, that determination and persistence are what move the world, and that thinking others will make you successful is a sure way to fail.

-topical connections *looking **back***

You have studied the physical changes that characterize development in middle and late childhood, including the substantial advances in the development of the brain. Early childhood is a period in which young children increasingly engage in symbolic thought. Young children's information-processing skills also improve considerably—executive and sustained attention advance, short-term memory gets better, and their understanding of the human mind makes considerable progress. Young children also increase their knowledge of language's rule systems, and their literacy benefits from active participation in a wide range of language experiences. Most young children attend an early childhood education program, and there are many variations in these programs. In this chapter, you will study a number of advances in children's cognitive development during the elementary school years.

preview

We just saw that challenging children to succeed after they have been taught to fail is an important theme of Marva Collins' teaching. Later in the chapter, we explore many aspects of achievement. First, we will examine three main aspects of cognitive changes—the concrete operational stage of Piaget's cognitive developmental theory, information processing, and intelligence—that characterize middle and late childhood. Then we will look at language changes and explore children's achievement.

1 What Is Piaget's Theory of Cognitive Development in Middle and Late Childhood?

LG1 Discuss Piaget's stage of concrete operational thought and apply Piaget's theory to education.

- Concrete Operational Thought
- Evaluating Piaget's Concrete Operational Stage
- Applications to Education

According to Jean Piaget (1952), the preschool child's thought is preoperational. Preschool children can form stable concepts, and they have begun to reason, but their thinking is flawed by egocentrism and magical belief systems. However, Piaget may have underestimated the cognitive skills of preschool children. Some researchers argue that under the right conditions, young children may display abilities that are characteristic of Piaget's next stage of cognitive development, the stage of concrete operational thought (Gelman, 1969). Here we cover the characteristics of concrete operational thought, an evaluation of Piaget's portrait of this stage, and applications of Piaget's ideas to education.

developmental connection

Cognitive Processes

Centration, a centering of attention on one characteristic to the exclusion of others, is present in young children's lack of conservation. Connect to "Cognitive Development in Early Childhood."

CONCRETE OPERATIONAL THOUGHT

Piaget proposed that the *concrete operational stage* lasts from approximately 7 to 11 years of age. In this stage, children can perform concrete operations, and they can reason logically as long as they can apply their reasoning to specific or concrete examples. Remember that *operations* are mental actions that are reversible, and *concrete operations* are operations that are applied to real, concrete objects.

The conservation tasks described in "Cognitive Development in Early Childhood" indicate whether children are capable of concrete operations. For example, recall that in one task involving conservation of matter, the child is presented with two identical balls of clay. The experimenter rolls one ball into a long, thin shape; the other remains in its original ball shape. The child is then asked if there is more clay in the ball or in the long, thin piece of clay. By the time children reach the age of 7 or 8, most answer that the amount of clay is the same. To answer this problem correctly, children have to imagine rolling the elongated clay back into a ball. This type of imagination involves a reversible mental action applied to a real, concrete object. Concrete operations allow the child to consider several characteristics rather than to focus on a single property of an object. In the clay example, the preoperational child is likely to focus on height or width. The concrete operational child coordinates information about both dimensions.

What other abilities are characteristic of children who have reached the concrete operational stage? One important skill is the ability to classify or divide things into different sets or subsets and to consider their interrelationships. Consider the family tree of four generations that is shown in Figure 1 (Furth & Wachs, 1975). This family tree suggests that the grandfather (A) has three children (B, C, and D), each of whom has two children (E through J), and that one of these children (J) has three children (K, L, and M). A child who comprehends the classification system can move up and down a level, across a level, and up and down and across within the system. The concrete operational child understands that person J can at the same time be father, brother, and grandson, for example.

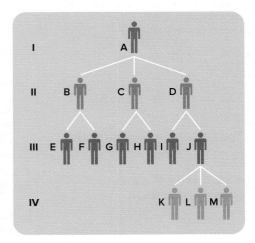

FIGURE 1

CLASSIFICATION: AN IMPORTANT ABILITY IN CONCRETE OPERATIONAL THOUGHT. A family tree of four generations (*I to IV*): The preoperational child has trouble classifying the members of the four generations; the concrete operational child can classify the members vertically, horizontally, and obliquely (up and down and across). For example, the concrete operational child understands that a family member can be a son, a brother, and a father, all at the same time.

Children who have reached the concrete operational stage are also capable of **seriation,** which is the ability to order stimuli along a quantitative dimension (such as length). To see if students can serialize, a teacher might haphazardly place eight sticks of different lengths on a table. The teacher then asks the students to order the sticks by length. Many young children end up with two or three small groups of "big" sticks or "little" sticks, rather than a correct ordering of all eight sticks. Another mistaken strategy they use is to evenly line up the tops of the sticks but ignore the bottoms. The concrete operational thinker simultaneously understands that each stick must be longer than the one that precedes it and shorter than the one that follows it.

Another aspect of reasoning about the relations between classes is **transitivity,** which is the ability to logically combine relations to understand certain conclusions. In this case, consider three sticks (A, B, and C) of differing lengths. A is the longest, B is intermediate in length, and C is the shortest. Does the child understand that if A is longer than B and B is longer than C, then A is longer than C? In Piaget's theory, concrete operational thinkers do; preoperational thinkers do not.

EVALUATING PIAGET'S CONCRETE OPERATIONAL STAGE

Has Piaget's portrait of the concrete operational child stood the test of research? According to Piaget, various aspects of a stage should emerge at the same time. In fact, however, some concrete operational abilities do not appear in synchrony. For example, children do not learn to conserve at the same time they learn to cross-classify.

Furthermore, education and culture exert stronger influences on children's development than Piaget maintained (Bredekamp, 2017; Morrison, 2017, 2018). Some preoperational children can be trained to reason at a concrete operational stage. And the age at which children acquire conservation skills is related to how much practice their culture provides in these skills. Among Wolof children in the West African nation of Senegal, for example, only 50 percent of the 10- to 13-year-olds understood the principle of conservation (Greenfield, 1966). Comparable studies among cultures in central Australia, New Guinea (an island north of Australia), the Amazon jungle region of Brazil, and rural Sardinia (an island off the coast of Italy) yielded similar results (Dasen, 1977).

Thus, although Piaget was a giant in the field of developmental psychology, his conclusions about the concrete operational stage have been challenged. Later, after we examine the final stage in his theory of cognitive development, we will evaluate Piaget's contributions and discuss the criticisms of his theory.

Neo-Piagetians argue that Piaget got some things right but that his theory needs considerable revision. They place greater emphasis on how children use attention, memory, and strategies to process information (Case & Mueller, 2001; Morra & others, 2007). According to neo-Piagetians, a more accurate portrayal of children's thinking requires attention to children's strategies, the speed at which children process information, the particular task involved, and the division of problems into smaller, more precise steps. These are issues addressed by the information-processing approach, and we discuss some of them later in this chapter.

Another alternative to concrete operational thought comes from Lev Vygotsky. Vygotsky, like Piaget, held that children construct their knowledge of the world. But Vygotsky did not propose stages of cognitive development, and he emphasized the importance of social interaction, the social contexts of learning, and the young child's use of language to plan, guide, and monitor behavior (Clara, 2017; Daniels, 2017; Holzman, 2016).

APPLICATIONS TO EDUCATION

Although Piaget was not an educator, he provided a sound conceptual framework for viewing learning and education. Following are some ideas in Piaget's theory that can be applied to teaching children (Elkind, 1976; Heuwinkel, 1996):

1. *Take a constructivist approach.* Piaget emphasized that children learn best when they are active and seek solutions for themselves. Piaget opposed teaching methods

An outstanding teacher and education in the logic of science and mathematics are important cultural experiences that promote the development of operational thought. *Might Piaget have underestimated the roles of culture and schooling in children's cognitive development?*
©Majority World/Getty Images

The thirst to know and understand . . .
These are the goods in life's rich hand.

—Sir William Watson
British Poet, 20th Century

seriation The concrete operation that involves ordering stimuli along a quantitative dimension (such as length).

transitivity The ability to logically combine relations to understand certain conclusions.

neo-Piagetians Developmentalists who have elaborated on Piaget's theory, giving more emphasis to information processing, strategies, and precise cognitive steps.

that treat children as passive receptacles. The educational impli-cation of Piaget's view is that, in all subjects, students learn best by making discoveries, reflecting on them, and discussing them, rather than by blindly imitating the teacher or doing things by rote.

2. *Facilitate rather than direct learning.* Effective teachers design situations that allow students to learn by doing. These situations promote students' thinking and discovery. Teachers listen, watch, and question students, to help them gain better understanding.

3. *Consider the child's knowledge and level of thinking.* Students do not come to class with empty minds. They have concepts of space, time, quantity, and causality. These ideas differ from the ideas of adults. Teachers need to interpret what a student is saying and respond in a way that is not too far from the student's level. Also, Piaget suggested that it is important to examine children's mistakes in thinking, not just what they get correct, to help guide them to a higher level of understanding.

4. *Promote the student's intellectual health.* When Piaget came to lecture in the United States, he was asked, "What can I do to get my child to a higher cognitive stage sooner?" He was asked this question so often here compared with other countries that he called it the American question. For Piaget, children's learning should occur naturally. Children should not be pushed and pressured into achieving too much too early in their development, before they are maturationally ready. Some parents spend long hours every day holding up large flash cards with words on them to improve their baby's vocabulary. In the Piagetian view, this is not the best way for infants to learn. It places too much emphasis on speeding up intellectual development, involves passive learning, and will not lead to positive outcomes.

5. *Turn the classroom into a setting of exploration and discovery.* What do actual classrooms look like when the teachers adopt Piaget's views? Several first- and second-grade math classrooms provide some good examples (Kamii, 1985, 1989). The teachers emphasize students' own exploration and discovery. The classrooms are less structured than what we think of as a typical classroom. Workbooks and predetermined assignments are not used. Rather, the teachers observe the students' interests and natural participation in activities to determine what the course of learning will be. For example, a math lesson might be constructed around counting the day's lunch money or dividing supplies among students. Games are often used in the classroom to stimulate mathematical thinking.

What are some educational strategies that can be derived from Piaget's theory?
©John Lund/Mark Romanelli/Blend Images/Getty Images RF

Review Connect Reflect

LG1 Discuss Piaget's stage of concrete operational thought and apply Piaget's theory to education.

Review
- How can concrete operational thought be characterized?
- How can Piaget's concrete operational stage be evaluated?
- How can Piaget's theory be applied to education?

Connect
- How is the application of Piaget's theory to children's education similar to or different from the application of Vygotsky's theory to their education?

Reflect *Your Own Personal Journey of Life*
- Imagine that you are an elementary school teacher. Based on Piaget's theory, in what important ways is your thinking likely to differ from that of the children in your classroom? What adjustments in thinking might you need to make when you communicate with the children?

2 What Is the Nature of Children's Information Processing?

LG2 Describe changes in information processing in middle and late childhood.

Memory | Thinking | Metacognition

long-term memory A relatively permanent type of memory that holds huge amounts of information for a long period of time.

working memory A mental "workbench" where individuals manipulate and assemble information when making decisions, solving problems, and comprehending written and spoken language.

During middle and late childhood, most children dramatically improve their ability to sustain and control attention. They pay more attention to task-relevant stimuli such as teacher instructions than to salient stimuli such as the colors in the teacher's attire. Other changes in information processing during middle and late childhood involve memory, thinking, and metacognition (Casey & others, 2016; Sala & Gobet, 2017; Swanson, 2016). In the following pages, we examine each of these areas.

MEMORY

Short-term memory increases considerably during early childhood but after the age of 7 does not show as great an increase. **Long-term memory,** a relatively permanent and unlimited type of memory, increases with age during middle and late childhood. In part, improvements in memory reflect children's increased knowledge and their increased use of strategies to retain information (Bjorklund, 2012).

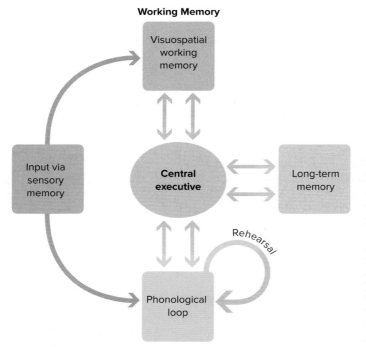

Working Memory

Visuospatial working memory

Input via sensory memory

Central executive

Long-term memory

Rehearsal

Phonological loop

FIGURE 2

WORKING MEMORY. In Baddeley's working memory model, working memory is like a mental workbench where a great deal of information processing is carried out. Working memory consists of three main components: the phonological loop and visuospatial working memory serve as assistants, helping the central executive do its work. Input from sensory memory goes to the phonological loop, where information about speech is stored and rehearsal takes place, and visuospatial working memory, where visual and spatial information, including imagery, are stored. Working memory is a limited-capacity system, and information is stored there for only a brief time. Working memory interacts with long-term memory, using information from long-term memory in its work and transmitting information to long-term memory for longer storage.

Working Memory Short-term memory is like a passive storehouse with shelves to store information until it is moved to long-term memory. Alan Baddeley (2007, 2010a, b, 2012, 2013, 2015) defines **working memory** as a kind of mental "workbench" where individuals manipulate and assemble information when they make decisions, solve problems, and comprehend written and spoken language (see Figure 2). Working memory is described as more active and powerful in modifying information than short-term memory.

Note in Figure 2 that a key component of working memory is the *central executive*, which supervises and controls the flow of information. The central executive focuses on selective attention and inhibition, planning and decision making, and trouble shooting. Recall that *executive function* is an umbrella-like concept that comprises a number of higher-level cognitive processes. One of those cognitive processes is working memory, especially its central executive dimension.

Working memory develops slowly. Even by 8 years of age, children can only hold in memory half the items that adults can remember (Kharitonova, Winter, & Sheridan, 2015). Working memory is linked to many aspects of children's development (Gerst & others, 2017; Nouwens, Groen, & Verhoeven, 2017; Sala & Gobet, 2017; Swanson, 2017). For example, children who have better working memory are more advanced in language comprehension, math skills, and problem solving than their counterparts with less effective working memory (Fuchs & others, 2016; Ogino & others, 2017; Peng & Fuchs, 2016; Tsubomi & Watanabe, 2017). In a recent study, children's verbal working memory was linked to these aspects of both first and second language learners: morphology, syntax, and grammar (Verhagen & Leseman, 2016).

Knowledge and Expertise Much of the research on the role of knowledge in memory has compared experts and novices (Ericsson, 2017; Ericsson & others, 2006; Ericsson & others, 2016; Varga & others, 2018). *Experts* have acquired extensive knowledge about a particular content area; this knowledge influences what they notice and how they organize, represent, and interpret information.

These skills in turn affect their ability to remember, reason, and solve problems. When individuals have expertise about a particular subject, their memory also tends to be good regarding material related to that subject (Staszewski, 2013).

For example, one study found that 10- and 11-year-olds who were experienced chess players ("experts") were able to remember more information about the location of chess pieces than college students who were not chess players ("novices") (Chi, 1978) (see Figure 3). In contrast, when the college students were presented with other stimuli, they were able to remember them better than the children were. Thus, the children's expertise in chess gave them superior memories, but only for items involving chess.

There are developmental changes in expertise. Older children usually have more expertise about a subject than younger children do, which can contribute to their better memory for the subject.

©Tetra Images/Alamy RF

FIGURE 3

THE ROLE OF EXPERTISE IN MEMORY. Notice that when 10- to 11-year-old children and college students were asked to remember a string of random numbers that had been presented to them, the college students fared better. However, the 10- to 11-year-olds who had experience playing chess "experts" had better memory for the location of chess pieces on a chess board than the college students with no chess experience ("novices") (Chi, 1978).

Strategies If we know anything at all about long-term memory, it is that long-term memory depends on the learning activities individuals engage in when learning and remembering information (Miller, McCulloch, & Jarrold, 2015). A key learning activity involves the use of **strategies,** which consist of deliberate mental activities to improve the processing of information. For example, organizing is a strategy that older children, adolescents, and adults use to remember information more effectively. Strategies do not occur automatically; they require effort and work. Strategies, which are also called *control processes,* are under the learner's conscious control and can be used to improve memory. Two important strategies are creating mental images and elaborating on information (Murray, 2007).

Elaboration is an important strategy that involves engaging in more extensive processing of information. When individuals engage in elaboration, their memory benefits (Schneider, 2011). Thinking of examples, especially those related to yourself, is a good way to elaborate information. Thinking about personal associations with information makes the information more meaningful and helps children to remember it. For example, if the word *win* is on a list of words a child is asked to remember, the child might think of the last time he won a bicycle race with a friend.

Fuzzy Trace Theory Might something other than knowledge and strategies be responsible for improvement in memory during the elementary school years? Charles Brainerd and Valerie Reyna (1993, 2014; Reyna, 2004; Reyna & Brainerd, 1995) argue that *fuzzy traces* account for much of this improvement. Their **fuzzy trace theory** states that memory is best understood by considering two types of memory representations: (1) verbatim memory trace and (2) gist. The *verbatim memory trace* consists of the precise details of the information, whereas *gist* refers to the central idea of the information. When gist is used, fuzzy traces are built up. Although individuals of all ages extract gist, young children tend to store and retrieve verbatim traces. At some point during the early elementary school years, children begin to use gist more and, according to the theory, its use contributes to the improved memory and reasoning of older children because fuzzy traces are more enduring and less likely to be forgotten than verbatim traces.

Autobiographical Memory Recall that *autobiographical memory* involves memory of significant events and experiences in one's life. You are engaging in autobiographical memory when you answer questions such as: Who was your first grade teacher and what was s/he like? What is the most traumatic event that happened to you as a child? As children go through middle and late childhood, and through adolescence, their autobiographical narratives broaden and become more elaborated (Bauer, 2013; Bauer & Fivush, 2014; Bauer, Hattenschwiler, & Larkina, 2016; DeMarie & Lopez, 2014; Pathman & St. Jacques, 2014). Researchers have found that children develop more detailed, coherent, and evaluative autobiographical memories when their mothers reminisce with them in elaborated and evaluative ways (Fivush, 2010).

Culture influences children's autobiographical memories. American children, especially American girls, describe autobiographical narratives that are longer, more detailed, more specific, and more personal than narratives by children from China and Korea (Bauer, 2013). The pattern is consistent with their conversations about past events. American mothers and their

strategies Deliberate mental activities designed to improve the processing of information.

elaboration An important strategy that involves engaging in more extensive processing of information.

fuzzy trace theory A theory stating that memory is best understood by considering two types of memory representations: (1) verbatim memory trace and (2) gist. In this theory, older children's better memory is attributed to the fuzzy traces created by extracting the gist of information.

children are more elaborative and more focused on themes related to being independent, while Korean mothers and their children less often engage in detailed conversations about the past. Possibly the more elaborated content of American children's narratives contributes to the earlier first memories researchers have found in American adults (Han, Leichtman, & Wang, 1998).

Improving Children's Memory   Some strategies adults can adopt when guiding children to remember information more effectively over the long term include assisting them to organize information, elaborate the information, and develop images of the information. Another good strategy is to encourage children to understand the material that needs to be remembered rather than rotely memorizing it. Two additional strategies adults can use to guide children's retention of memory were recently proposed:

- *Repeat with variation on the instructional information and link early and often.* These are memory development research expert Patricia Bauer's (2009) recommendations to improve children's consolidation and reconsolidation of the information they are learning. Variations on a lesson theme increase the number of associations in memory storage, and linking expands the network of associations in memory storage; both strategies expand the routes for retrieving information from storage.
- *Embed memory-relevant language when instructing children.* Teachers vary considerably in how much they use memory-relevant language that encourages students to remember information. In recent research that involved extensive observations of a number of first-grade teachers in the classroom, Peter Ornstein and his colleagues (Ornstein, Grammer, & Coffman, 2010; Ornstein, Coffman, & Grammer, 2007; Ornstein & others, 2010) found that in the time segments observed, the teachers rarely used strategy suggestions or metacognitive (thinking about thinking) questions. In this research, when lower-achieving students were placed in classrooms in which teachers were categorized as "high-mnemonic teachers" who frequently embedded memory-relevant information in their teaching, their achievement increased (Ornstein, Coffman, & Grammer, 2007).

Keep in mind that it is important not to view memory in terms of how children add something to it but rather to underscore how children actively construct their memory (Bauer, Hattenschwiler, & Larkina, 2016).

THINKING

Four important aspects of thinking are executive function and being able to think critically, creatively, and scientifically.

Executive Function   There has been a surge of interest in studying children's *executive function,* an umbrella-like concept that encompasses a number of higher-level cognitive processes linked to the development of the brain's prefrontal cortex. Executive function involves managing one's thoughts to engage in goal-directed behavior and exercise self-control (Bardikoff & Sabbagh, 2017; Cassidy, 2016; Groppe & Elsner, 2017; Knapp & Morton, 2017; Moriguchi, Chevalier, & Zelazo, 2016; Muller & others, 2017).

How might executive function change in the middle and late childhood years and be linked to children's success in school? Adele Diamond and Kathleen Lee (2011) recently highlighted the following dimensions of executive function that they conclude are the most important for 4- to 11-year-old children's cognitive development and school success:

- *Self-control/inhibition.* Children need to develop self-control that will allow them to concentrate and persist on learning tasks, to inhibit their tendencies to repeat incorrect responses, and to resist the impulse to do something now that they later would regret.
- *Working memory.* Children need an effective working memory to efficiently process the masses of information they will encounter as they go through school and beyond.
- *Flexibility.* Children need to be flexible in their thinking to consider different strategies and perspectives.

A number of diverse activities have been found to increase children's executive function, including computerized training that uses games to improve working memory (CogMed,

©Anthony Harvel/Getty Images RF

2013), aerobic exercise (Hillman & others, 2014; Kvalo & others, 2017), scaffolding of self-regulation (Bodrova & Leong, 2015), mindfulness (Gallant, 2016), and some types of school curricula (the Montessori curriculum, for example) (Diamond, 2013; Diamond & Lee, 2011).

Ann Masten and her colleagues (Herbers & others, 2011, 2014; Labella, Narayan, & Masten, 2016; Masten, 2013, 2014a, b; Masten & Labella, 2016; Masten & others, 2008, 2015; Monn & others, 2017) have found that executive function and parenting skills are linked to homeless children's success in school. Masten believes that executive function and good parenting skills are related. In her words, "When we see kids with good executive function, we often see adults around them that are good self-regulators. Parents model, they support, and they scaffold these skills" (Masten, 2012, p. 11).

developmental connection

Education

A criticism of the No Child Left Behind legislation is that it does not give adequate attention to critical thinking skills. Connect to "Socioemotional Development in Middle and Late Childhood."

Critical Thinking   Currently, there is considerable interest in critical thinking among psychologists and educators (Bonney & Sternberg, 2017). **Critical thinking** involves thinking reflectively and productively, as well as evaluating evidence. In this edition, the "Connect" and "Reflect" questions at the end of each section challenge you to think critically about a topic or an issue related to the discussion.

Jacqueline and Martin Brooks (2001) lament that few schools really teach students to think critically and to develop a deep understanding of concepts. Deep understanding occurs when students are stimulated to rethink previously held ideas. In Brooks and Brooks' view, schools spend too much time getting students to give a single correct answer in an imitative way, rather than encouraging them to expand their thinking by coming up with new ideas and rethinking earlier conclusions. They observe that too often teachers ask students to recite, define, describe, state, and list, rather than to analyze, infer, connect, synthesize, criticize, create, evaluate, think, and rethink. Many successful students complete their assignments, do well on tests, and get good grades, yet they don't ever learn to think critically and deeply. They think superficially, staying on the surface of problems rather than stretching their minds and becoming deeply engaged in meaningful thinking.

According to Ellen Langer (2005), **mindfulness**—being alert, mentally present, and cognitively flexible while going through life's everyday activities and tasks—is an important aspect of thinking critically. Mindful children and adults maintain an active awareness of the circumstances in their life and are motivated to find the best solutions to tasks. Mindful individuals create new ideas, are open to new information, and are able to use multiple perspectives. By contrast, mindless individuals are entrapped in old ideas, engage in automatic behavior, and operate from a single perspective.

Recently, Robert Roeser and his colleagues (Roeser & Eccles, 2015; Roeser & others, 2014; Roeser & Zelazo, 2012) have emphasized that mindfulness is an important mental process that children can engage in to improve a number of cognitive and socioemotional skills, such as executive function, focused attention, emotion regulation, and empathy. It has been proposed that mindfulness training could be implemented in schools through practices such as using age-appropriate activities that increase children's reflection on moment-to-moment experiences, resulting in improved self-regulation (Zelazo & Lyons, 2012).

In addition to mindfulness, activities such as yoga, meditation, and tai chi have been recently suggested as candidates for improving children's cognitive and socioemotional development. Together these activities are being grouped under the topic of *contemplative science,* a cross-disciplinary term that involves the study of how various types of mental and physical training might enhance children's development (Roeser & Zelazo, 2012). For example, a training program in mindfulness and caring for others was effective in improving the cognitive control of fourth- and fifth-graders (Schonert-Reichl & others, 2015). In other recent research, mindfulness training has been found to improve children's attention and self-regulation (Poehlmann-Tynan & others, 2016), achievement (Singh & others, 2016), and coping strategies in stressful situations (Dariotis & others, 2016). Also, in two recent studies, mindfulness-based interventions reduced public school teachers' stress, produced a better mood at school and at home, and resulted in better sleep (Crain, Schonert-Reichl, & Roeser, 2017; Taylor & others, 2016).

How might mindfulness training be implemented in schools?
©Ariel Skelley/Blend Images/Getty Images RF

Creative Thinking   Cognitively competent children think not only critically, but also creatively. **Creative thinking** is the ability to think in novel and unusual ways and to come up with unique solutions to problems. Thus, intelligence and creativity are not the same thing (Sternberg, 2018g, h; Sternberg & Kaufman, 2018b; Sternberg & Sternberg, 2017). This difference was recognized by J. P. Guilford (1967), who distinguished between **convergent thinking,**

critical thinking The ability to think reflectively and productively, as well as to evaluate the evidence.

mindfulness Being alert, mentally present, and cognitively flexible while going through life's everyday activities and tasks.

creative thinking The ability to think in novel and unusual ways and to come up with unique solutions to problems.

convergent thinking Thinking that produces one correct answer and is characteristic of the kind of thinking tested by standardized intelligence tests.

which produces one correct answer and characterizes the kind of thinking that is required on conventional tests of intelligence, and **divergent thinking,** which produces many different answers to the same question and characterizes creativity. For example, a typical item on a conventional intelligence test is "How many quarters will you get in return for 60 dimes?" In contrast, the following question has many possible answers: "What image comes to mind when you hear the phrase 'sitting alone in a dark room' or 'some unique uses for a paper clip'?"

A special concern is that creative thinking appears to be declining in U.S. children. A study of approximately 300,000 U.S. children and adults found that creativity scores rose until 1990, but since then have been steadily declining (Kim, 2010). Among the likely causes of the creativity decline are the number of hours U.S. children spend watching TV and playing video games instead of engaging in creative activities, as well as the lack of emphasis on creative thinking skills in schools (Beghetto & Kaufman, 2017; Sternberg & Kaufman, 2018b; Renzulli, 2017). Some countries, though, are placing increasing emphasis on creative thinking in schools. For example, historically, creative thinking has typically been discouraged in Chinese schools. However, Chinese educators are now encouraging teachers to spend more classroom time on creative activities (Plucker, 2010).

An important goal is to help children become more creative (Sternberg, 2017c). The *Caring Connections* interlude recommends some ways to accomplish this goal.

Scientific Thinking   Like scientists, children ask fundamental questions about reality and seek answers to problems that seem utterly trivial or unanswerable to other people (such as "Why is the sky blue?"). Do children generate hypotheses, perform experiments, and reach conclusions about their data in ways resembling those of scientists?

Scientific reasoning often is aimed at identifying causal relations. Like scientists, children place a great deal of emphasis on causal mechanisms. Their understanding of how events are caused weighs more heavily in their causal inferences than even such strong influences as whether the cause happened immediately before the effect.

There also are important differences between the reasoning of children and the reasoning of scientists (Kuhn, 2011, 2013). Children are more influenced by happenstance events than by an overall pattern (Kuhn, 2011, 2013). Often, children maintain their old theories regardless of the evidence (Kuhn, Schauble, & Garcia-Mila, 1992).

Children might go through mental gymnastics trying to reconcile seemingly contradictory new information with their existing beliefs. For example, after learning about the solar system, children sometimes conclude that there are two earths, the seemingly flat world in which they live and the round ball floating in space that their teacher described.

Children also have difficulty designing experiments that can distinguish among alternative causes. Instead, they tend to bias the experiments in favor of whatever hypothesis they began with. Sometimes they see the results as supporting their original hypothesis even when the results directly contradict it. Thus, although there are important similarities between children and scientists in their basic curiosity and in the kinds of questions they ask, there are also important differences in the degree to which they can separate theory and evidence and in their ability to design conclusive experiments (Lehrer & Schauble, 2006).

Too often, the skills scientists use, such as careful observation, graphing, self-regulatory thinking, and knowing when and how to apply one's knowledge to solve problems, are not routinely taught in schools. Children have many concepts that are incompatible with science and reality. Good teachers perceive and understand a child's underlying scientific concepts, then use the concepts as a scaffold for learning (Contant & others, 2018). Effective science teaching helps children distinguish between fruitful errors and misconceptions, and detect plainly wrong ideas that need to be replaced by more accurate conceptions (Contant & others, 2018).

It is important for teachers to initially scaffold students' science learning, extensively monitor their progress, and ensure that they are learning science content (DeRosa & Abruscato, 2015). Thus, in pursuing science investigations, students need to learn inquiry skills and science content (Lehrer & Schauble, 2006).

METACOGNITION

One expert in children's thinking, Deanna Kuhn (1999), argues that to help students become better thinkers, schools should pay more attention to helping students develop skills that entail knowing about their own (and others') knowing. In other words, schools should do more to

How Would You...?
If you were a **psychologist,** how would you talk with teachers and parents about ways to improve children's creative thinking?

developmental connection

Cognitive Processes

Theory of mind—awareness of one's own mind and the mental processes of others—involves metacognition. Connect to "Cognitive Development in Early Childhood."

divergent thinking Thinking that produces many different answers to the same question and is characteristic of creativity.

brainstorming A technique in which individuals are encouraged to come up with creative ideas in a group, play off each other's ideas, and say practically whatever comes to mind.

Strategies for Increasing Children's Creative Thinking

Strategies for increasing children's creative thinking include the following:

- **Encourage brainstorming.** **Brainstorming** is a technique in which people are encouraged to come up with creative ideas in a group, play off each other's ideas, and say practically whatever comes to mind that seems relevant to a particular issue. Participants are usually told to hold off from criticizing others' ideas at least until the end of the brainstorming session.

- **Provide environments that stimulate creativity.** Some environments nourish creativity, while others inhibit it (Baer, 2016; Skiba & others, 2017). Parents and teachers who encourage creativity often rely on children's natural curiosity. They provide exercises and activities that stimulate children to find insightful solutions to problems, rather than ask a lot of questions that require rote answers (Gotlieb & others, 2017). Teachers also encourage creativity by taking students on field trips to locations where creativity is valued. Howard Gardner (1993) emphasizes that science, discovery, and children's museums offer rich opportunities to stimulate creativity.

What are some good strategies for guiding children in thinking more creatively?
©Colorblind/Cardinal/Corbis RF

- **Don't overcontrol students.** Teresa Amabile (1993) says that telling children exactly how to do things leaves them feeling that originality is a mistake and exploration is a waste of time. If, instead of dictating which activities they should engage in, you let children select activities that match their interests and you support their inclinations, you will be less likely to destroy their natural curiosity (Hennessey, 2011, 2017).

- **Encourage internal motivation.** Excessive use of prizes, such as gold stars, money, or toys, can stifle creativity by undermining the intrinsic pleasure students derive from creative activities. Creative children's motivation is the satisfaction generated by the work itself.

Competition for prizes and formal evaluations often undermine intrinsic motivation and creativity (Hennessey & Amabile, 2010). However, this strategy should not rule out material rewards altogether.

- **Build children's confidence.** To expand children's creativity, encourage children to believe in their own ability to create something innovative and worthwhile. Building children's confidence in their creative skills aligns with Bandura's (2012) concept of self-efficacy, the belief that one can master a situation and produce positive outcomes.

- **Guide children to be persistent and delay gratification.** Most highly successful creative products take years to develop, and creative individuals often work on ideas and projects for months and years without being rewarded for their efforts (Sternberg & Kaufman, 2018b). Children don't become experts at sports, music, or art overnight. It usually takes many years of working at something to become an expert at it; and it takes time for a creative thinker to produce a unique, worthwhile product (Sternberg, 2017c).

- **Encourage children to take intellectual risks.** Creative individuals take intellectual risks and seek to discover or invent something never before discovered or invented (Sternberg & Kaufman, 2018b). They risk spending extensive time on an idea or project that may not work. Creative people are not afraid of failing or getting something wrong.

- **Introduce children to creative people.** Teachers can invite creative people to their classrooms and ask them to describe what helps them become creative or to demonstrate their creative skills. A writer, poet, musician, scientist, or another creative individual can bring their props and productions to the class, turning it into a theater for stimulating students' creativity.

---

develop **metacognition,** which is cognition about cognition, or knowing about knowing (Flavell, 2004; Fitzgerald, Arvaneh, & Dockree, 2017; Norman, 2017). Metacognition can take many forms, including thinking about and knowing when and where to use particular strategies for learning or solving problems (Allen & others, 2017; Fergus & Bardeen, 2017). Conceptualization of metacognition consists of several dimensions of executive function, such as planning (deciding how much time to spend focusing on a task, for example), self-regulation (modifying strategies as work on a task progresses, for example) (McCormick, Dimmitt, & Sullivan, 2013), or a child's confidence in eyewitness judgments (Buratti, Allwood, & Johansson, 2014).

A number of early developmental studies classified as "metacognitive" focused on *metamemory,* or knowledge about memory. This includes general knowledge about memory,

How Would You...?

If you were an **educator,** how would you advise teachers and parents regarding ways to improve children's metacognitive skills?

metacognition Cognition about cognition, or knowing about knowing.

Cognitive developmentalist John Flavell is a pioneer in providing insights about children's thinking. Among his many contributions are establishing the field of metacognition and conducting numerous studies in this area, including metamemory and theory of mind studies.
Courtesy of Dr. John Flavell

What are some developmental changes in metacognition?
©Sigrid Olsson/PhotoAlto/Getty Images RF

such as knowing that recognition tests are easier than recall tests. It also encompasses knowledge about one's own memory, such as a student's ability to monitor whether she has studied enough for a test that is coming up next week.

Young children do have some general knowledge about memory (Lukowski & Bauer, 2014). By 5 or 6 years of age, children usually already know that familiar items are easier to learn than unfamiliar ones, that short lists are easier to remember than long ones, that recognition is easier than recall, and that forgetting is more likely to occur over time (Lyon & Flavell, 1993). However, in other ways young children's metamemory is limited. They don't understand that related items are easier to remember than unrelated ones and that remembering the gist of a story is easier than remembering information verbatim (Kreutzer, Leonard, & Flavell, 1975). By the fifth grade, however, students understand that gist recall is easier than verbatim recall.

Young children also have only limited knowledge about their own memory. They have an inflated opinion of their memory abilities. For example, in one study a majority of young children predicted that they would be able to recall all 10 items on a list of 10 items. When tested for this, none of the young children managed this feat (Flavell, Friedrichs, & Hoyt, 1970). As they move through the elementary school years, children give more realistic evaluations of their memory skills (Bjorklund, 2012; Schneider, 2011).

In addition to metamemory, metacognition includes knowledge about strategies. Strategies have been the focus of a number of microgenetic investigations (Siegler, 2016a, b). A number of microgenetic studies have focused on a specific aspect of academic learning, such as how children learn whole number arithmetic, fractions, and other areas of math (Kuhn, 2013). Using the microgenetic approach, researchers have shown that developing effective strategies doesn't occur abruptly but rather gradually. This research has found considerable variability in children's use of strategies, even revealing that they may use an incorrect strategy in solving a math problem for which they had used a correct strategy several trials earlier (Siegler & Braithwaite, 2017).

In the view of Michael Pressley (2003), the key to education is helping students learn a rich repertoire of strategies that result in solutions to problems. Good thinkers routinely use strategies and effective planning to solve problems. Good thinkers also know when and where to use strategies. Understanding when and where to use strategies often results from monitoring the learning situation (Pressley & McCormick, 2007).

Pressley and his colleagues (Pressley & others, 2001, 2003, 2004; Pressley, Mohan, Fingeret, & others, 2007; Pressley, Mohan, Raphael, & Fingeret, 2007) have spent considerable time in recent years observing strategy instruction by teachers and strategy use by students in elementary and secondary school classrooms. They conclude that strategy instruction tends to be far less complete and intense than what students need in order to learn how to use strategies effectively. They argue that education ought to be restructured so that students are provided with more opportunities to become competent strategic learners.

Review Connect Reflect

LG2 Describe changes in information processing in middle and late childhood.

Review

- What characterizes children's memory in middle and late childhood?
- What is involved in thinking critically, thinking creatively, and thinking scientifically?
- What is metacognition?

Connect

- In discussing memory, thinking, and metacognition, the topic of recommended educational strategies came up. Compare these recommendations in this main section with those you have already learned.

Reflect *Your Own Personal Journey of Life*

- When you were in elementary school, did classroom instruction prepare you adequately for critical thinking tasks? If you were a parent of an 8-year-old, what would you do to guide your child to think more critically and creatively?

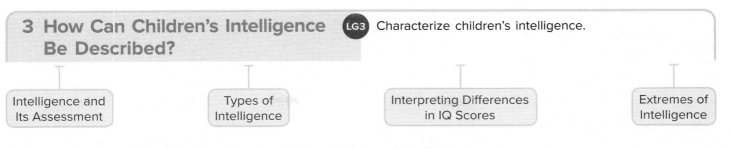

Intelligence and Its Assessment | Types of Intelligence | Interpreting Differences in IQ Scores | Extremes of Intelligence

Twentieth-century English novelist Aldous Huxley said that children are remarkable for their curiosity and intelligence. What did Huxley mean when he used the word *intelligence*? How can intelligence be assessed?

INTELLIGENCE AND ITS ASSESSMENT

Just what is meant by the concept of "intelligence"? Some experts describe intelligence as problem-solving skills. Others describe it as the ability to adapt to and learn from life's everyday experiences. Combining these ideas, we can arrive at a definition of **intelligence** as problem-solving skills and the ability to learn from and adapt to life's everyday experiences.

Interest in intelligence has often focused on individual differences and assessment. **Individual differences** are the stable, consistent ways in which people are different from each other (Sackett & others, 2017). We can talk about individual differences in personality or any other domain, but it is in the domain of intelligence that the most attention has been directed at individual differences (Estrada & others, 2017; Giofre & others, 2017). For example, an intelligence test purports to inform us about whether a student can reason better than others who have taken the test (Jaarsveld & Lachmann, 2017). Let's go back in history and see what the first intelligence test was like.

The Binet Tests   In 1904, the French Ministry of Education asked psychologist Alfred Binet to devise a method of identifying children who were unable to learn in school. School officials wanted to reduce crowding by placing students who did not benefit from regular classroom teaching in special schools. Binet and his student Theophile Simon developed an intelligence test to meet this request. The test, called the 1905 Scale, consisted of 30 questions on topics ranging from the ability to touch one's ear to the ability to draw designs from memory and define abstract concepts.

Binet developed the concept of **mental age (MA),** an individual's level of mental development relative to that of others. Not much later, in 1912, William Stern created the concept of **intelligence quotient (IQ),** a person's mental age (MA) divided by chronological age (CA), multiplied by 100. That is: $IQ = MA/CA \times 100$. If mental age is the same as chronological age, then the person's IQ is 100. If mental age is above chronological age, then IQ is more than 100. If mental age is below chronological age, then IQ is less than 100.

The Binet test has been revised many times to incorporate advances in the understanding of intelligence and intelligence tests. These revisions are called the *Stanford–Binet tests* (the revisions have been done at Stanford University). By administering the test to large numbers of people of different ages (from preschool through late adulthood) from different backgrounds, researchers have found that scores on the Stanford–Binet approximate a normal distribution (see Figure 4). A **normal distribution** is symmetrical, with a majority of the scores falling in the middle of the possible range of scores and few scores appearing toward the extremes of the range.

The Wechsler Scales   Another set of tests widely used to assess students' intelligence is called the Wechsler scales. Developed by psychologist David Wechsler, they include the Wechsler Preschool and Primary Scale of Intelligence—Fourth Edition (WPPSI-IV) to test children from 2 years 6 months to 7 years 3 months of age; the Wechsler Intelligence Scale for Children—Fifth Edition (WISC-V) for children and adolescents 6 to 16 years of age; and the Wechsler Adult Intelligence Scale—Fourth Edition (WAIS-IV).

The WISC-V now not only provides an overall IQ score but also yields five composite scores (Verbal Comprehension, Working Memory, Processing Speed, Fluid Reasoning, and

intelligence Problem-solving skills and the ability to learn from and adapt to the experiences of everyday life.

individual differences The stable, consistent ways in which people differ from each other.

mental age (MA) Binet's measure of an individual's level of mental development, compared with that of others.

intelligence quotient (IQ) A person's mental age divided by chronological age, multiplied by 100.

normal distribution A symmetrical distribution with most scores falling in the middle of the possible range of scores and few scores appearing toward the extremes of the range.

FIGURE 4

THE NORMAL CURVE AND STANFORD-BINET IQ SCORES. The distribution of IQ scores approximates a normal curve. Most of the population falls in the middle range of scores. Notice that extremely high and extremely low scores are very rare. Slightly more than two-thirds of the scores fall between 85 and 115. Only about 1 in 50 individuals has an IQ higher than 130, and only about 1 in 50 individuals has an IQ lower than 70.

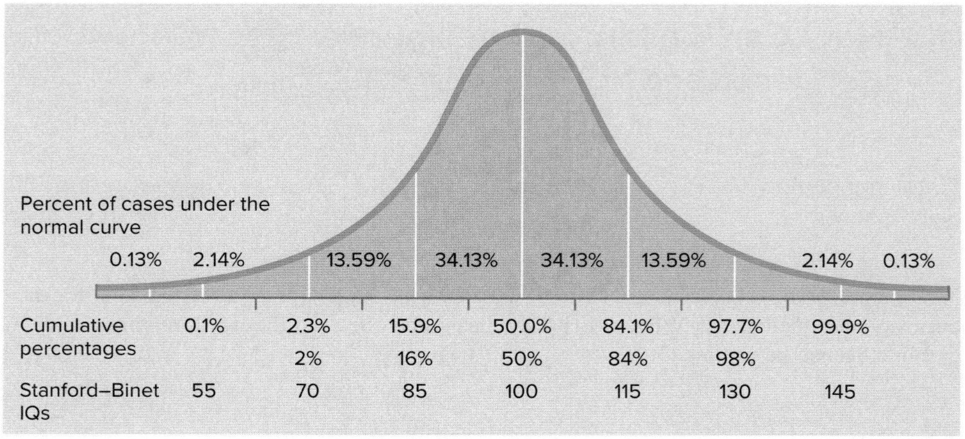

Percent of cases under the normal curve								
	0.13%	2.14%	13.59%	34.13%	34.13%	13.59%	2.14%	0.13%
Cumulative percentages	0.1%	2.3%	15.9%	50.0%	84.1%	97.7%	99.9%	
		2%	16%	50%	84%	98%		
Stanford–Binet IQs	55	70	85	100	115	130	145	

triarchic theory of intelligence Sternberg's theory that intelligence consists of analytical intelligence, creative intelligence, and practical intelligence.

Visual Spatial) (Canivez, Watkins, & Dombowski, 2017). These allow the examiner to quickly see whether the individual is strong or weak in different areas of intelligence. The Wechsler also include 16 verbal and nonverbal subscales. Three of the Wechsler subscales are shown in Figure 5.

TYPES OF INTELLIGENCE

Is it more appropriate to think of a child's intelligence as a general ability or as a number of specific abilities? Robert Sternberg and Howard Gardner have proposed influential theories oriented to this second viewpoint.

Sternberg's Triarchic Theory Robert J. Sternberg (1986, 2004, 2010, 2011, 2012, 2013, 2014a, b, 2015, 2016a, b, 2017a, b, 2018a, b, c, d) developed the **triarchic theory of intelligence,** which states that intelligence comes in three forms:

- *Analytical intelligence,* referring to the ability to analyze, judge, evaluate, compare, and contrast
- *Creative intelligence,* consisting of the ability to create, design, invent, originate, and imagine
- *Practical intelligence,* involving the ability to use, apply, implement, and put ideas into practice

Sternberg (2017a, b, 2018a, b, c, d) says that children with different triarchic patterns "look different" in school. Students with high analytical intelligence tend to be favored in conventional schooling. They often do well under direct instruction, in which the teacher lectures and gives students objective tests. They often are considered to be "smart" students who get good grades, show up in high-level tracks, do well on traditional tests of intelligence and the SAT, and later get admitted to competitive colleges.

In contrast, children who are high in creative intelligence often are not on the top rung of their class. Many teachers have specific expectations about how assignments should be done, and creatively intelligent students may not conform to those expectations. Instead of giving conformist answers, they give unique answers, for which they might get reprimanded or marked down. No teacher wants to discourage creativity, but Sternberg stresses that too often a teacher's desire to increase students' knowledge suppresses creative thinking.

Like children high in creative intelligence, children who are high in practical intelligence often do not relate well to the demands of school. However, many of these children do well outside the classroom's walls. They may have excellent social skills and good common sense. As adults, some

Verbal Subscales

Similarities

A child must think logically and abstractly to answer a number of questions about how things might be similar.

Example: "In what way are a lion and a tiger alike?"

Comprehension

This subscale is designed to measure an individual's judgment and common sense.

Example: "What is the advantage of keeping money in a bank?"

Nonverbal Subscales

Block Design

A child must assemble a set of multicolored blocks to match designs that the examiner shows.
Visual-motor coordination, perceptual organization, and the ability to visualize spatially are assessed.

Example: "Use the four blocks on the left to make the pattern on the right."

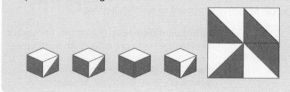

FIGURE 5

SAMPLE SUBSCALES OF THE WECHSLER INTELLIGENCE SCALE FOR CHILDREN—FIFTH EDITION (WISC-V). The WISC now includes 16 subscales. Three of the subscales are shown here. Simulated items are similar to those found in the Wechsler Intelligence Scale for Children, Fifth Edition.
Source: Wechsler Intelligence Scale for Children, Fifth Edition (WISC-V), Upper Saddle River, NJ: Pearson Education, Inc., 2014.

become successful managers, entrepreneurs, or politicians in spite of having undistinguished school records.

Recently, Sternberg (2016c, 2018e) has applied his triarchic theory of intelligence to the concept of *wisdom*. In his view, academic intelligence is a necessary but in many cases insufficient requirement for wisdom (Sternberg & Hagen, 2018). Practical knowledge about the realities of life also is needed for wisdom. For Sternberg, balance between self-interest, the interests of others, and contexts produces a common good. Thus, wise individuals don't just look out for themselves—they also need to consider others' needs and perspectives, as well as the particular context involved. Sternberg assesses people's wisdom by presenting problems requiring solutions that highlight various intrapersonal, interpersonal, and contextual interests. He also emphasizes that such aspects of wisdom should be taught in schools (Sternberg & Hagen, 2018).

Gardner's Eight Frames of Mind   Howard Gardner (1983, 1993, 2002, 2016) suggests that there are eight types of intelligence, or "frames of mind." These are described here, with examples of the types of occupations in which they function as strengths (Campbell, Campbell, & Dickinson, 2004):

- *Verbal:* the ability to think in words and use language to express meaning (occupations: authors, journalists, speakers)
- *Mathematical:* the ability to carry out mathematical operations (occupations: scientists, engineers, accountants)
- *Spatial:* the ability to think three-dimensionally (occupations: architects, artists, sailors)
- *Bodily-kinesthetic:* the ability to manipulate objects and be physically adept (occupations: surgeons, craftspeople, dancers, athletes)
- *Musical:* a sensitivity to pitch, melody, rhythm, and tone (occupations: composers, musicians, sensitive listeners)
- *Interpersonal:* the ability to understand and interact effectively with others (occupations: successful teachers, mental health professionals)
- *Intrapersonal:* the ability to understand oneself (occupations: theologians, psychologists)
- *Naturalist:* the ability to observe patterns in nature and understand natural and human-made systems (occupations: farmers, botanists, ecologists, landscapers)

According to Gardner, everyone has all of these intelligences to varying degrees. As a result, we prefer to learn and process information in different ways. People learn best when they can do so in a way that uses their stronger intelligences.

Evaluating the Multiple-Intelligence Approaches   Sternberg's and Gardner's approaches have much to offer. They have stimulated teachers to think more broadly about what makes up children's competencies (Sternberg, 2017a, b, 2018a, b, c). And they have motivated educators to develop programs that instruct students in multiple domains. These approaches have also contributed to interest in assessing intelligence and classroom learning in innovative ways, such as by evaluating student portfolios.

Still, doubts about multiple-intelligence approaches persist. A number of psychologists think that the multiple-intelligence views have taken the concept of specific intelligences too far (Jensen, 2008). Some argue that a research base to support the three intelligences of Sternberg or the eight intelligences of Gardner has not yet emerged. A number of psychologists continue to support the concept of general intelligence (Burkhart, Schubiger, & van Schaik, 2017; Hagmann-von Arx, Lemola, & Grob, 2017; Hilger & others, 2017; Holding & others, 2017). One expert on intelligence, Nathan Brody (2007), observes that people who excel at one type of intellectual task are likely to excel in others. Thus, individuals who do well at memorizing lists of digits are also likely to be good at solving verbal problems and spatial layout problems. If musical skill reflects a distinct type of intelligence, ask other critics, why not label the skills of outstanding chess players, prizefighters, painters, and poets as types of intelligence?

Advocates of the concept of general intelligence point to its success in predicting school and job success. For example, scores on tests of general intelligence are substantially correlated with school grades and achievement test performance, both at the time of the test and years later (Cucina & others, 2016; Strenze, 2007). A recent meta-analysis of 240 independent samples and more than 100,000 individuals found a correlation of +.54 between intelligence

Robert J. Sternberg developed the triarchic theory of intelligence.
Courtesy of Dr. Robert Sternberg

Howard Gardner, here working with a young child, developed the view that intelligence comes in the forms of these eight kinds of skills: verbal, mathematical, spatial, bodily-kinesthetic, musical, intrapersonal, interpersonal, and naturalist.
Courtesy of Dr. Howard Gardner and Jay Gardner

How Would You...?
If you were a **psychologist,** how would you use Gardner's theory of multiple intelligences to respond to a child who is distressed to receive a below-average score on a traditional intelligence test?

and school grades (Roth & others, 2015). Also, a recent study found a significant link between children's general intelligence and their self-control (Meldrum & others, 2017).

The argument between those who support the concept of general intelligence and those who advocate the multiple-intelligences view is ongoing (Gardner, 2016; Trzaskowski & others, 2014). Sternberg (2017a, b, 2018b, c) actually accepts that there is a general intelligence for the kinds of analytical tasks that traditional IQ tests assess, but he thinks that the range of tasks those tests measure is far too narrow (Sternberg, 2018a, b, c).

INTERPRETING DIFFERENCES IN IQ SCORES

The IQ scores that result from tests such as the Stanford–Binet and Wechsler scales provide information about children's mental abilities. However, the significance of performance on an intelligence test is debated (Sternberg, 2017a, b, 2018a, b, c).

An area of considerable debate in the study of intelligence centers on the extent to which intelligence is influenced by genetics (nature) versus the extent to which it is influenced by environment (nurture) (Davies & others, 2016; Eilertsen & others, 2016; Weber, Dekhtyar, & Herlitz, 2017). It is difficult to tease apart these influences, but psychologists keep trying to unravel them.

Genetic Influences Have scientists been able to pinpoint specific genes that are linked to intelligence? A research review concluded that there may be more than 1,000 genes that affect intelligence, each possibly having a small influence on an individual's intelligence (Davies & others, 2011). Some scientists argue that there is a strong genetic component to intelligence (Rimfeld & others, 2017; Zabaneh & others, 2017).

One strategy for examining the role of heredity in intelligence is to compare the IQs of identical and fraternal twins. Recall that identical twins have exactly the same genetic makeup but fraternal twins do not. If intelligence is genetically determined, say some investigators, the IQs of identical twins should be more similar than the intelligence of fraternal twins. A research review of many studies found that the difference in the average correlation of intelligence between identical and fraternal twins was +.15, a relatively low correlation (Grigorenko, 2000) (see Figure 6).

Today, most researchers agree that genetics and environment interact to influence intelligence. For most people, this means that modifications in environment can change their IQ scores considerably. Although genetic endowment may always influence a person's intellectual ability, the environmental influences and opportunities we provide children and adults do make a difference (Grigorenko & others, 2016).

Environmental Influences Although genetic endowment influences a child's intellectual ability, the environmental experiences of children do make a difference (Grigorenko & others, 2016; Sternberg 2017a, 2018a). In one study, researchers went into homes and observed how extensively parents from welfare and middle-income professional families talked and communicated with their young children (Hart & Risley, 1995). They found that the middle-income professional parents were much more likely to communicate with their young children than the welfare parents were. How much the parents communicated with their children in the first three years of their lives was correlated with the children's Stanford–Binet IQ scores at age 3. The more parents communicated with their children, the higher the children's IQs were. And a recent research analysis by Richard Nisbett and his colleagues (2012) supported the importance of environmental influences on intelligence: A 12- to 18-point increase in IQ was found when children are adopted from low-income families into middle- and upper-income families. And another recent study revealed that children with more highly educated (especially college-educated) mothers and/or children born into higher-income families showed higher scores on math achievement tests than children who had less-educated mothers and came from lower-income families (Ang, Rodgers, & Wanstrom, 2010).

Schooling also influences intelligence (Gustafsson, 2007; Love & others, 2013). The biggest effects have been found when large groups of children have been deprived of formal education for an extended period, resulting in lower intelligence (Ceci & Gilstrap, 2000). Another possible effect of education can be seen in rapidly increasing IQ test scores around the world (Flynn, 1999, 2007, 2011, 2013). IQ scores have been increasing so quickly that a high percentage of people regarded as having average intelligence at the

developmental **connection**

Nature and Nurture

The epigenetic view emphasizes that development is an ongoing, bidirectional interchange between heredity and environment. Connect to "Biological Beginnings."

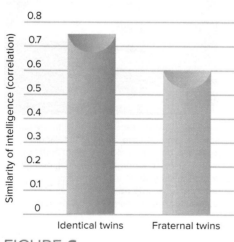

FIGURE 6

CORRELATION BETWEEN INTELLIGENCE TEST SCORES AND TWIN STATUS. The graph represents a summary of research findings that have compared the intelligence test scores of identical and fraternal twins. An approximate .15 difference has been found, with a higher correlation for identical twins (.75) and a lower correlation for fraternal twins (.60).

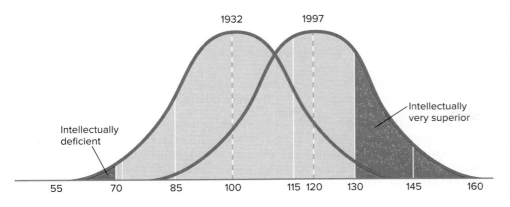

FIGURE 7

INCREASING IQ SCORES FROM 1932 TO 1997. As measured by the Stanford–Binet intelligence test, American children seem to be getting smarter. Scores of a group tested in 1932 fell along a bell-shaped curve with half below 100 and half above. Studies show that if children took that same test today, half would score above 120 on the 1932 scale. Very few of them would score in the "intellectually deficient" end, on the left side, and about one-fourth would rank in the "very superior" range.

Ulric Neisser, "The Increase in IQ Scores from 1932 to 1997." Copyright by The Estate of Ulric Neisser. All rights reserved. Used with permission.

turn of the century would be considered below average in intelligence today (see Figure 7). If a representative sample of people today took the Stanford–Binet test version used in 1932, about 25 percent would be defined as having very superior intelligence, a label usually accorded to less than 3 percent of the population. Because the increase has taken place within a relatively short time, it can't be due to heredity, but rather may be due to increasing levels of education attained by a much greater percentage of the world's population, or to other environmental factors such as the explosion of information to which people are exposed (Laciga & Cigler, 2017; Shenk, 2017; Weber, Dekhtyar, & Herlitz, 2017). This worldwide increase in intelligence test scores over a short time frame is called the *Flynn effect* after the researcher who discovered it—James Flynn (1999, 2007, 2011, 2013).

Researchers are increasingly concerned about improving the early environment of children who are at risk for impoverished intelligence (Black & others, 2017; Morris & others, 2017; Wadsworth & others, 2016). For various reasons, many low-income parents have difficulty providing an intellectually stimulating environment for their children. Programs that educate parents to be more sensitive caregivers and better teachers, as well as support services such as quality child-care programs, can make a difference in a child's intellectual development (Bredekamp, 2017; Morrison, 2017, 2018). In a recent two-year intervention study with families living in poverty, maternal scaffolding and positive home stimulation improved young children's intellectual functioning (Obradovic & others, 2016).

In a study at the University of North Carolina at Chapel Hill conducted by Craig Ramey and his associates (Campbell, 2007; Campbell & others, 2012; Ramey & Campbell, 1984; Ramey & Ramey, 1998), 111 young children from low-income, poorly educated families were assigned randomly to either an intervention group, which received full-time, year-round child care along with medical and social work services, or a control group, which received medical and social benefits but no child care. The child-care program included gamelike learning activities aimed at improving language, motor, social, and cognitive skills.

The success of the program in improving IQ was evident by the time the children were 3 years of age. At that age, the experimental group showed normal IQs averaging 101, a 17-point advantage over the control group. Recent follow-up results suggest that the effects are long-lasting. More than a decade later, at 15, children from the intervention group still maintained an IQ advantage of 5 points over the control-group children (97.7 to 92.6) (Campbell, 2007; Campbell & others, 2001; Ramey, Ramey, & Lanzi, 2001). They also did better on standardized tests of reading and math, and were less likely to be held back a year in school. Also, the greatest IQ gains were made by the children whose mothers had especially low IQs—below 70. At age 15, these children showed a 10-point IQ advantage over a group of children whose mothers' IQs were below 70 but who had not experienced the child-care intervention. In a recent analysis of participants in the intervention project, at age 30 the children who experienced the early intervention had attained more years of education but the intervention did not lead to any benefits involving social adjustment and criminal activity (Campbell & others, 2012).

Revisiting the Nature-Nurture Issue   In sum, there is a consensus among psychologists that both heredity and environment influence intelligence (Sternberg, 2017a, 2018a). This consensus reflects the nature-nurture issue. Recall that the nature-nurture issue focuses on the extent to which development is influenced by nature (heredity) and nurture (environment). Although psychologists agree that intelligence is the product of both nature and nurture, there is still disagreement about how strongly each factor influences intelligence (Grigorenko & others, 2016; Rimfeld & others, 2017; Sternberg, 2018a, b; Zabaneh & others, 2017).

Culture and Intelligence   Do cultures define intelligence differently? Are there ethnic variations in children's intelligence? What are some cautions in interpreting IQ scores?

Culture and Culture-Fair Tests   Cultures vary in the way they describe what it means to be intelligent (Zhang & Sternberg, 2012; Sternberg, 2018f). People in Western cultures tend to view intelligence in terms of reasoning and thinking skills, whereas people in Eastern cultures see intelligence as a way for members of a community to successfully engage in social roles (Nisbett, 2003).

Culture-fair tests are tests of intelligence that are intended to be free of cultural bias. Two types of culture-fair tests have been devised. The first includes items that are familiar to children from all socioeconomic and ethnic backgrounds, or items that at least are familiar to the children taking the test. For example, a child might be asked how a bird and a dog are different, on the assumption that all children have been exposed to birds and dogs. The second type of culture-fair test has no verbal questions.

Why is it so hard to create culture-fair tests? Most tests tend to reflect what the dominant culture thinks is important (Greenfield, Suzuki, & Rothstein-Fisch, 2006). Time limits on tests will bias the test against groups not concerned with time. If languages differ, the same words might have different meanings for different language groups. Even pictures can produce bias because some cultures have less experience with drawings and photographs than others (Anastasi & Urbina, 1997). Within the same culture, different subgroups could have different attitudes, values, and motivation, and these could affect their performance on intelligence tests. Items that ask why buildings should be made of brick are biased against children who have little or no experience with brick houses. Questions about railroads, furnaces, snow, distances between cities, and so on can be biased against groups who have less experience than others with these contexts. Recall, too, that cultures define intelligence differently. Because of such difficulties in creating culture-fair tests, Robert Sternberg (2018f) concludes that there are no culture-fair tests, only *culture-reduced tests.*

Ethnic Variations   On average, African American schoolchildren in the United States score 10 to 15 points lower on standardized intelligence tests than White American schoolchildren do (Brody, 2000). Children from Latino families also score lower than White children do. These are average scores, however, and there is significant overlap in the distribution of scores. About 15 to 25 percent of African American schoolchildren score higher than half of White schoolchildren do, and many White schoolchildren score lower than most African American schoolchildren.

As African Americans have gained social, economic, and educational opportunities, the gap between African Americans and non-Latino Whites on standardized intelligence tests has begun to narrow (Ogbu & Stern, 2001). A research review concluded that the IQ gap between African Americans and non-Latino Whites has been reduced considerably in recent years (Nisbett & others, 2012). This gap especially narrows in college, where African American and non-Latino White students often experience more similar environments than during the elementary and high school years (Myerson & others, 1998). Further, a recent study using the Stanford–Binet Intelligence Scales found no differences in overall intellectual ability between non-Latino White and African American preschool children when the children were matched on age, gender, and parental education level (Dale & others, 2014). Nonetheless, a recent analysis concluded that the underrepresentation of African Americans in STEM (science, technology, engineering, and math) subjects and careers is linked to practitioners' expectations that they have less innate talent than non-Latino Whites (Leslie & others, 2015).

One potential influence on intelligence test performance is **stereotype threat**, the anxiety that one's behavior might confirm a negative stereotype about one's group (Grand, 2017; Pennington & others, 2016; Spencer, Logel, & Davies, 2016; Steele & Aronson, 2004; von Hippel, Kalokerinos, & Zacher, 2017). For example, when African Americans take an intelligence test, they may experience anxiety about confirming the old stereotype that Blacks are "intellectually inferior." Some studies have confirmed the existence of stereotype threat (Wasserberg, 2014). Also, African American students do more poorly on standardized tests if they perceive that they are being evaluated. If they think the test doesn't count, they perform as well as White

culture-fair tests Tests of intelligence that are designed to be free of cultural bias.

stereotype threat Anxiety that one's behavior might confirm a negative stereotype about one's group.

students (Aronson, 2002). However, some critics argue that the extent to which stereotype threat explains the testing gap has been exaggerated (Sackett, Borneman, & Connelly, 2009).

Using Intelligence Tests   Psychological tests are tools. Like all tools, their effectiveness depends on the knowledge, skill, and integrity of the user. A hammer can be used to build a beautiful kitchen cabinet, or it can be used as a weapon of assault. Like a hammer, psychological tests can be used for positive purposes, or they can be badly abused. Here are some cautions about IQ that can help you avoid the pitfalls of using information about a child's intelligence test score in negative ways:

- *Avoid stereotyping and preconceived expectations.* A special concern is that the scores on an IQ test easily can lead to stereotypes and preconceived expectations about students. Sweeping generalizations are too often made on the basis of an IQ score. An IQ test should always be considered a measure of current performance. It is not a measure of fixed potential. Maturational changes and enriched environmental experiences can advance a student's intelligence.
- *Know that IQ is not a sole indicator of competence.* Another concern about IQ tests occurs when they are used as the main or sole assessment of competence. A high IQ is not the ultimate human value. As we have seen in this chapter, it is important to consider students' intellectual competence not only in areas such as verbal skills but also in their creative and practical skills.
- *Use caution in interpreting an overall IQ score.* In evaluating a child's intelligence, it is wiser to think of intelligence as consisting of a number of domains. Keep in mind the different types of intelligence described by Sternberg and Gardner. By considering the different domains of intelligence, you will find that every child has areas of strength.

How Would You...?
If you were a **social worker**, how would you explain the role and purpose of intelligence test scores to a parent whose child is preparing to take a standardized intelligence test?

developmental **connection**

Conditions, Diseases, and Disorders
Down syndrome is caused by the presence of an extra copy of chromosome 21. Connect to "Biological Beginnings."

EXTREMES OF INTELLIGENCE

Intelligence tests have been used to discover indications of intellectual disability or intellectual giftedness, the extremes of intelligence. At times, intelligence tests have been misused for this purpose. Keeping in mind the theme that an intelligence test should not be used as the sole indicator of intellectual disability or giftedness, we will explore the nature of these intellectual extremes.

Intellectual Disability   The most distinctive feature of intellectual disability (formerly called mental retardation) is inadequate intellectual functioning. Long before formal tests were developed to assess intelligence, individuals with an intellectual disability were identified by a lack of age-appropriate skills in learning and caring for themselves. Once intelligence tests were developed, they were used to identify the degree of intellectual disability. But of two individuals with an intellectual disability who have the same low IQ, one might be married, employed, and involved in the community and the other might require constant supervision in an institution. Such differences in social competence led psychologists to include deficits in adaptive behavior in their definition of intellectual disability.

Intellectual disability is a condition of limited mental ability in which the individual (1) has a low IQ, usually below 70 on a traditional intelligence test; (2) has difficulty adapting to the demands of everyday life; and (3) first exhibits these characteristics by age 18 (Heward, Alber-Morgan, & Konrad, 2017; Hodapp & others, 2011). The age limit is included in the definition of intellectual disability because, for example, we don't usually think of a college student who suffers massive brain damage in a car accident, resulting in an IQ of 60, as having an "intellectual disability." The low IQ and low adaptiveness should be evident in childhood, not after normal functioning is interrupted by damage of some form. About 5 million Americans fit this definition of intellectual disability.

Some cases of intellectual disability have an organic cause. **Organic intellectual disability** describes a genetic disorder or a lower level of intellectual functioning caused by brain damage. Down syndrome is one form of organic intellectual disability, and it occurs when an extra chromosome is present. Other causes of organic intellectual disability include fragile X syndrome, an abnormality in the X chromosome that was discussed in "Biological Beginnings"; prenatal malformation; metabolic disorders; and diseases that affect the brain. Most people who suffer from organic intellectual disability have IQs between 0 and 50.

What causes a child to develop Down syndrome? In which major classification of intellectual disability does the condition fall?
©Stockbyte/Veer RF

intellectual disability A condition of limited mental ability in which an individual has a low IQ, usually below 70 on a traditional test of intelligence, and has difficulty adapting to the demands of everyday life.

organic intellectual disability Involves physical causes such as a genetic disorder or brain damage.

At 2 years of age, art prodigy Alexandra Nechita (shown here as an adolescent) colored in coloring books for hours and also took up pen and ink. She had no interest in dolls or friends. By age 5 she was using watercolors. Once she started school, she would paint as soon as she got home. At the age of 8, she saw the first public exhibit of her work. Since then, working quickly and impulsively on canvases as large as 5 feet by 9 feet, she has completed hundreds of paintings, some of which sell for close to $100,000 apiece. As an adult, she continues to paint today—relentlessly and passionately. It is, she says, what she loves to do. *What are some characteristics of children who are gifted?*

©Koichi Kamoshida/Newsmakers/Getty Images

cultural-familial intellectual disability
Condition in which there is no evidence of organic brain damage but the individual's IQ generally is between 50 and 70.

gifted Having above-average intelligence (an IQ of 130 or higher) and/or superior talent for something.

When no evidence of organic brain damage can be found, cases are labeled **cultural-familial intellectual disability.** Individuals with this type of disability have IQs between 55 and 70. Psychologists suspect that this type of disability often results from growing up in a below-average intellectual environment. Children with this type of disability can be identified in schools, where they often fail, need tangible rewards (candy rather than praise), and are highly sensitive to what others expect of them. However, as adults, they are usually not noticeably different from others, perhaps because adult settings don't tax their cognitive skills as sorely. It may also be that they increase their intelligence as they move toward adulthood.

Giftedness There have always been people whose abilities and accomplishments outshine those of others—the whiz kid in class, the star athlete, the natural musician. People who are **gifted** have above-average intelligence (an IQ of 130 or higher) and/or superior talent for something. When it comes to programs for the gifted, most school systems select children who have intellectual superiority and academic aptitude, whereas children who are talented in the visual and performing arts (arts, drama, dance), athletics, or have other special aptitudes tend to be overlooked (Sternberg, 2017c, d; Sternberg & Kaufman, 2018a).

Characteristics Estimates vary but indicate that approximately 6 to 10 percent of U.S. students are classified as gifted (National Association for Gifted Children, 2017). This percentage is likely conservative because it focuses more on children who are gifted intellectually and academically, often failing to include those who are gifted in creative thinking or the visual and performing arts (Ford, 2012).

Despite speculation that giftedness is linked with having a mental disorder, no relation between giftedness and mental disorder has been found. Similarly, the idea that gifted children are maladjusted is a myth, as Lewis Terman (1925) found when he conducted an extensive study of 1,500 children whose Stanford–Binet IQs averaged 150. The children in Terman's study were socially well adjusted, and many went on to become successful doctors, lawyers, professors, and scientists. Studies support the conclusion that gifted people tend to be more mature than others, have fewer emotional problems, and grow up in a positive family climate (Davidson, 2000). For example, a recent study revealed that parents and teachers identified elementary school children who are not gifted as having more emotional and behavioral risks than children who are gifted (Eklund & others, 2015). In this study, when children who are gifted did have problems, they were more likely to be internalized problems, such as anxiety and depression, than externalized problems, such as acting out and high levels of aggression.

Ellen Winner (1996) described three criteria that characterize gifted children, whether in art, music, or academic domains:

1. *Precocity.* Gifted children are precocious. They begin to master an area earlier than their peers. Learning in their domain is more effortless for them than for ordinary children. In most instances, these gifted children are precocious because they have an inborn high ability in a particular domain or domains.

2. *Marching to their own drummer.* Gifted children learn in qualitatively different ways from ordinary children. One way that they march to a different drummer is that they need minimal help, or scaffolding, from adults to learn. In many instances, they resist any kind of explicit instruction. They often make discoveries on their own and solve problems in unique ways.

3. *A passion to master.* Gifted children are driven to understand the domain in which they have high ability. They display an intense, obsessive interest and an ability to focus. They motivate themselves, says Winner, and do not need to be "pushed" by their parents.

A fourth area in which children who are gifted excel involves *information-processing skills.* Researchers have found that children who are gifted learn at a faster pace, process information more rapidly, are better at reasoning, use superior strategies, and monitor their understanding better than their nongifted counterparts (Ambrose & Sternberg, 2016a, b).

To read about one individual who is making a difference in programs for children who are gifted, see the *Connecting with Careers* profile.

Nature-Nurture Issue Is giftedness a product of heredity or environment? Likely both (Ambrose & Sternberg, 2016a, b; Duggan & Friedman, 2014; Johnson & Bouchard, 2014). Individuals who are gifted recall that they had signs of high ability in a particular area at a

Sterling Jones, Supervisor of Gifted and Talented Education

Sterling Jones is program supervisor for gifted and talented children in the Detroit Public School System. Jones has been working for more than three decades with children who are gifted. He believes that students' mastery of skills mainly depends on the amount of time devoted to instruction and the length of time allowed for learning. Thus, he believes that many basic strategies for challenging children who are gifted to develop their skills can be applied to a wider range of students than was once believed. He has rewritten several pamphlets for use by teachers and parents, including *How to Help Your Child Succeed* and *Gifted and Talented Education for Everyone.*

Jones has undergraduate and graduate degrees from Wayne State University and taught English for a number of years before becoming involved in the program for gifted children. He also has written materials on African Americans, such as *Voices from the Black Experience,* that are used in the Detroit schools.

Sterling Jones with some of the children in the gifted program in the Detroit Public School System.
Courtesy of Helen Dove-Jones

To read more about what teachers of children who are exceptional do, see the Careers in Children's Development appendix.

---

very young age, prior to or at the beginning of formal training (Howe & others, 1995). This suggests the importance of innate ability in giftedness. However, researchers have also found that individuals with world-class status in the arts, mathematics, science, and sports all report strong family support and years of training and practice (Bloom, 1985). Deliberate practice is an important characteristic of individuals who become experts in a particular domain.

Developmental Changes and Domain-Specific Giftedness   Can we predict from infancy who will be gifted as children, adolescents, and adults? John Colombo and his colleagues (2004, 2009) have found that measures of infant attention and habituation are not good predictors of high cognitive ability later in development. However, they have discovered a link between assessment with the Home Observation for Measure of the Environment (HOME) at 18 months of age and high cognitive ability in the preschool years. The best predictor at 18 months of high cognitive ability in the preschool years was the provision of materials and a variety of experiences in the home. These findings illustrate the importance of the cognitive environment provided by parents in the development of children's giftedness.

Individuals who are highly gifted are typically not gifted in many domains, and research on giftedness is increasingly focused on domain-specific developmental trajectories (Sternberg & Kaufman, 2018a; Thagard, 2014; Winner, 2009, 2014). During the childhood years, the domain(s) in which individuals are gifted usually emerges. Thus, at some point in the childhood years, the child who is to become a gifted artist or the child who is to become a gifted mathematician begins to show expertise in that domain. Regarding domain-specific giftedness, software genius Bill Gates (1998), the founder of Microsoft and one of the world's richest persons, commented that sometimes you have to be careful when you are good at something and resist the urge to think that you will be good at everything. Gates says that because he has been so successful at software development, people expect him to be brilliant in other domains about which he is far from being a genius.

Identifying an individual's domain-specific talent and providing the person with individually appropriate and optional educational opportunities should

A young Bill Gates, founder of Microsoft and now one of the world's richest persons. Like many highly gifted students, Gates was not especially fond of school. He hacked a computer security system when he was 13, and as a high school student, he was allowed to take some college math classes. He dropped out of Harvard University and began developing a plan for what was to become Microsoft Corporation. *What are some ways that schools can enrich the education of such highly talented students as Gates to make it a more challenging, interesting, and meaningful experience?*
©Doug Wilson/Corbis/Getty Images

be accomplished at the very latest by adolescence (Keating, 2009). During adolescence, individuals who are talented become less reliant on parental support and increasingly pursue their own interests.

Some children who are gifted become gifted adults, but many gifted children do not become gifted and highly creative adults. In Terman's research on children with superior IQs, the children typically became experts in a well-established domain, such as medicine, law, or business. However, they did not become major creators (Winner, 2000). That is, they did not create a new domain or revolutionize an old domain.

One reason that some gifted children do not become gifted adults is that they often have been pushed too hard by overzealous parents and teachers. As a result, they lose their intrinsic (internal) motivation (Winner, 2006). Another reason that gifted children may not become gifted adults is because the criteria for giftedness change—as an adult, an individual has to actually do something special to be labeled gifted.

How Would You...?

If you were an **educator,** how would you structure educational programs for children who are gifted that would challenge and expand their unique cognitive abilities?

Education   An increasing number of experts argue that the education of children who are gifted in the United States requires a significant overhaul (Reis & Renzulli, 2014; Sternberg, 2017c, d; Sternberg & Kaufman, 2018a). Some educators also conclude that the inadequate education of children who are gifted has been compounded by the federal government's No Child Left Behind policy that seeks to raise the achievement level of students who are not doing well academically at the expense of enriching the education of children who are gifted (Clark, 2008; Cloud, 2007).

Ellen Winner (1996, 2006) argues that too often children who are gifted are socially isolated and underchallenged in the classroom. It is not unusual for them to be ostracized and labeled "nerds" or "geeks." A child who is truly gifted often is the only such child in the room and thus lacks the opportunity to learn with students of like ability. Many eminent adults report that school was a negative experience for them, that they were bored and sometimes knew more than their teachers (Bloom, 1985). Winner believes that American education will benefit when standards are raised for all children. When some children are still underchallenged, she recommends that they be allowed to attend advanced classes in their domain of exceptional ability—for example, that some especially precocious middle school students take college classes in their area of expertise. Bill Gates, founder of Microsoft, took college math classes and hacked a computer security system at 13; Yo-Yo Ma, famous cellist, graduated from high school at 15 and attended Juilliard School of Music in New York City.

A final concern is that African American, Latino, and Native American children are underrepresented in gifted programs (Ford, 2012, 2014, 2015a, b; Mills, 2015). Much of the underrepresentation involves the lower test scores for these children compared with non-Latino White and Asian American children, which may be due to factors such as test bias and fewer opportunities to develop language skills such as vocabulary and comprehension (Ford, 2012, 2014, 2015a, b; Mills, 2015).

Review *Connect* Reflect

LG3 Characterize children's intelligence.

Review

- What is intelligence? How can the Binet tests and the Wechsler scales be characterized?
- What are some different views of multiple intelligences? How can the multiple-intelligences approach be evaluated?
- What are some issues in interpreting differences in IQ scores? Explain them.
- What is the nature of children's intellectual disability? How can children's giftedness be described?

Connect

- In this section, you learned how intellectual disability is assessed and classified. What have you learned

about the prevalence of Down syndrome in the population and the factors that might cause a child to be born with Down syndrome?

Reflect *Your Own Personal Journey of Life*

- A computer app called *Children's IQ and Achievement Test* is being sold to parents so they can test their child's IQ. Several parents tell you that they purchased the app and assessed their children's IQ. Why might you be skeptical about giving your children an IQ test and interpreting the results yourself?

4 What Changes in Language Development Occur in Middle and Late Childhood?

LG4 Summarize language development in middle and late childhood.

Knowledge of vocabulary words is a part of virtually all intelligence tests, and this as well as other aspects of language development are important aspects of children's intelligence. As they enter school, children gain new skills that make it possible for them to learn to read and write—these include increasingly using language to talk about things that are not physically present, learning what a word is, and learning how to recognize and talk about sounds (Berko Gleason, 2003). They have to learn the alphabetic principle—that the letters of the alphabet represent sounds of the language. As children develop during middle and late childhood, changes in their vocabulary and grammar also take place (Pace, Hirsh-Pasek, & Golinkoff, 2016).

VOCABULARY, GRAMMAR, AND METALINGUISTIC AWARENESS

During middle and late childhood, changes occur in the way children organize their mental vocabulary. When asked to say the first word that comes to mind when they hear a word, young children typically provide a word that often follows the word in a sentence. For example, when asked to respond to "dog" the young child may say "barks," or to the word "eat" say "lunch." At about 7 years of age, children begin to respond with a word that is the same part of speech as the stimulus word. For example, children may now respond to the word "dog" with "cat" or "horse." To "eat," they now might say "drink." These responses are evidence that children now have begun to categorize their vocabulary by parts of speech (Berko Gleason, 2003).

The process of categorizing becomes easier as children increase their vocabulary (Clark, 2012, 2017). Children's vocabulary grows from an average of about 14,000 words at 6 years of age to an average of about 40,000 words by 11 years of age.

Children make similar advances in grammar (Behrens, 2012). During the elementary school years, children's improvement in logical reasoning and analytical skills helps them understand such constructions as the appropriate use of comparatives (*shorter, deeper*) and subjunctives ("If you were president …"). During the elementary school years, children become increasingly able to understand and use complex grammar, such as the following sentence: *The boy who kissed his mother wore a hat.* They also learn to use language in a more connected way, producing connected discourse. They become able to relate sentences to one another to produce descriptions, definitions, and narratives that make sense. Children must be able to do these things orally before they can be expected to deal with them in written assignments.

These advances in vocabulary and grammar during the elementary school years are accompanied by the development of **metalinguistic awareness,** which is knowledge about language, such as knowing what a preposition is or being able to discuss the sounds of a language (Schiff, Nuri Ben-Shushan, & Ben-Artzi, 2017; Tong, Deacon, & Cain, 2014; Yeon, Bae, & Joshi, 2017). Metalinguistic awareness allows children "to think about their language, understand what words are, and even define them" (Berko Gleason, 2009, p. 4). It improves considerably during the elementary school years (Pan & Uccelli, 2009). Defining words becomes a regular part of classroom discourse, and children increase their knowledge of syntax as they study and talk about the components of sentences, such as subjects and verbs (Crain, 2012). And reading also feeds into metalinguistic awareness as children try to comprehend written text.

Children also make progress in understanding how to use language in culturally appropriate ways—*pragmatics* (Beguin, 2016; Bryant, 2012). By the time they enter adolescence, most children know the rules for the use of language in everyday contexts—that is, what is appropriate to say and what is inappropriate to say.

metalinguistic awareness Knowledge about language, such as knowing what a preposition is or being able to discuss the sounds of a language.

READING AND WRITING

Two key aspects of language development in middle and late childhood are reading and writing.

Reading   Before learning to read, children learn to use language to talk about things that are not present; they learn what a word is; and they learn how to recognize sounds and talk about them. Children who begin elementary school with a robust vocabulary have an advantage in learning to read: vocabulary development plays an important role in reading comprehension.

How should children be taught to read? For many years, the debate focused on the whole-language approach versus the phonics approach (Fisher & Frey, 2016).

The **whole-language approach** stresses that reading instruction should parallel children's natural language learning. In some whole-language classes, beginning readers are taught to recognize whole words or even entire sentences, and to use the context of what they are reading to guess at the meaning of words. Reading materials that support the whole-language approach are whole and meaningful—that is, children are given material in its complete form, such as stories and poems, so that they learn to understand language's communicative function. Reading is connected with listening and writing skills. Although there are variations in whole-language programs, most share the premise that reading should be integrated with other skills and subjects, such as science and social studies, and that it should focus on real-world material. Thus, a class might read newspapers, magazines, or books, and then write about and discuss them.

This teacher is helping a student sound out words. Researchers have found that phonics instruction is a key aspect of teaching students to read, especially beginning readers and students with weak reading skills.
©Gideon Mendel/Corbis/Getty Images

In contrast, the **phonics approach** emphasizes that reading instruction should teach basic rules for translating written symbols into sounds. Early phonics-centered reading instruction should involve simplified materials. Only after children have learned correspondence rules that relate spoken phonemes to the alphabet letters that are used to represent them should they be given complex reading materials, such as books and poems (Cunningham, 2017; Fox & Alexander, 2017; Leu & Kinzer, 2017).

Which approach is better? Research suggests that children can benefit from both approaches, but instruction in phonics needs to be emphasized (Bear & others, 2016; Tompkins, 2017). An increasing number of experts in the field of reading now conclude that direct instruction in phonics is a key aspect of learning to read (Cunningham, 2017; Tompkins, 2017).

Beyond the phonics/whole-language issue in learning to read, becoming a good reader includes learning to read fluently (Allington, 2015; Breen & others, 2016; Fox & Alexander, 2017). Many beginning or poor readers do not recognize words automatically. Their processing capacity is consumed by the demands of word recognition, so they have less capacity to devote to comprehension of groupings of words as phrases or sentences. As their processing of words and passages becomes more automatic, it is said that their reading becomes more *fluent* (Stevens, Walker, & Vaughn, 2017). Metacognitive strategies, such as learning to monitor one's reading progress, getting the gist of what is being read, and summarizing also are important in becoming a good reader (McCormick, Dimmitt, & Sullivan, 2013; Schiff, Nuri Ben-Shushan, & Ben-Artzi, 2017).

whole-language approach An approach to reading instruction based on the idea that instruction should parallel children's natural language learning. Reading materials should be whole and meaningful.

phonics approach The idea that reading instruction should teach basic rules for translating written symbols into sounds.

Writing   Children's writing emerges out of their early scribbles, which appear at around 2 to 3 years of age. In early childhood, children's motor skills usually develop to the point that they can begin printing letters. Most 4-year-olds can print their first names. Five-year-olds can reproduce letters and copy several short words. They gradually learn to distinguish the distinctive characteristics of letters, such as whether the lines are curved or straight, open or closed. Through the early elementary grades, many children continue to reverse letters such as *b* and *d* and *p* and *q* (Temple & others, 2018; Treiman & others, 2014).

At this age, if other aspects of the child's development are normal, letter reversals do not predict literacy problems.

As they begin to write, children often invent spellings. Usually they base these spellings on the sounds of words they hear (Spandel, 2009).

Parents and teachers should encourage children's early writing but not be overly concerned about the formation of letters or spelling. Printing errors are a natural part of the child's growth. Corrections of spelling and printing should be selective and made in positive ways that do not discourage the child's writing and spontaneity.

Like becoming a good reader, becoming a good writer takes many years and lots of practice (Cunningham & Allington, 2016; Graham & Harris, 2016). Children should be given many writing opportunities (Tompkins, 2017). As their language and cognitive skills improve with good instruction, so will their writing skills. For example, developing a more sophisticated understanding of syntax and grammar serves as an underpinning for better writing. So do such cognitive skills as organization and logical reasoning. Through the course of the school years, students develop increasingly sophisticated methods of organizing their ideas. In early elementary school, they narrate and describe or write short poems. In late elementary and middle school, they can combine narration with reflection and analysis in projects such as book reports.

Monitoring one's writing progress is especially important in becoming a good writer (Fidalgo, Harris, & Braaksma, 2016; Graham & Harris, 2017; Harris & Graham, 2017). This includes being receptive to feedback and applying what one learns in writing one paper to making the next paper better. In a recent study, Self-Regulated Strategy Development (SRSD) was implemented with second-grade teachers and their students who were at risk for writing failure (Harris, Graham, & Adkins, 2015). The students were taught a general planning strategy, general writing strategies (a catchy opening, effective vocabulary, clear organization, and an effective ending). The intervention produced positive results for genre elements, story writing quality, motivation, and effort, as well as meaningful generalization to personal writing.

There are increasing concerns about students' writing competence (Graham, 2017; Harris & Graham, 2017; MacArthur, Graham, & Fitzgerald, 2016). One study revealed that 70 to 75 percent of U.S. students in grades 4 through 12 are low-achieving writers (Persky, Dane, & Jin, 2003). Two studies—one of elementary school teachers, the other of high school teachers—raise concerns about the quality of writing instruction in U.S. schools (Gilbert & Graham, 2010; Kiuhara, Graham, & Hawken, 2009). The teachers in both studies reported that their college courses had inadequately prepared them to teach writing. The fourth- through sixth-grade teachers reported that they taught writing only 15 minutes a day. The high school teachers said that their writing assignments infrequently involved analysis and interpretation, and almost 50 percent of them had not assigned any multi-paragraph writing assignments in the span of one month's time.

The metacognitive strategies needed to be a competent writer are linked with those required to be a competent reader because the writing process involves competent reading and rereading during composition and revision (McCormick, Dimmitt, & Sullivan, 2013). Further, researchers have found that strategy instruction involving planning, drafting, revising, and editing improves older elementary school children's metacognitive awareness and writing competence (Harris & others, 2017).

As with reading, teachers play a critical role in students' development of writing skills (Graham & Rijalsardamm, 2016; Troia, Graham, & Harris, 2017). Effective writing instruction provides guidance about planning, drafting, and revising, not only in elementary school but through college (Mayer, 2008). A meta-analysis (use of statistical techniques to combine the results of studies) revealed that the following interventions were the most effective in improving fourth- through twelfth-grade students' writing quality: (1) strategy instruction, (2) summarization, (3) peer assistance, and (4) setting goals (Graham & Perin, 2007).

Beverly Gallagher, a third-grade teacher in Princeton, New Jersey, works with students to stimulate their interest in writing. She created the Imagine the Possibilities program, which brings nationally known poets and authors to her school. She phones each student's parents periodically to describe their child's progress and new interests. She invites students from higher grades to work with small groups in her class so that she can spend more one-on-one time with students. Each student keeps a writer's notebook to record thoughts, inspirations, and special words that intrigue them. Students get special opportunities to sit in an author's chair, where they read their writing to the class.
©Jim Graham Photography

DUAL-LANGUAGE AND SECOND-LANGUAGE LEARNING

Are there sensitive periods in learning a second language? That is, if individuals want to learn a second language, how important is the age at which they begin to learn it? For many years, it was claimed that if individuals did not learn a second language before puberty, they would never reach native-language speakers' proficiency in the second language (Johnson & Newport, 1991). However, recent research indicates a more complex conclusion: Sensitive periods likely vary across different language systems (Thomas & Johnson, 2008). Thus, for late language learners, such as adolescents and adults, new vocabulary is easier to learn than new sounds or new grammar (Neville, 2006; Werker & Tees, 2005). For example, children's ability to pronounce words with a native-like accent in a second language typically decreases with age, with an especially sharp drop occurring after the age of about 10 to 12. Also, adults tend to learn a second language faster than children, but their final level of second-language attainment is not as high as children's.

Some aspects of children's ability to learn a second language are transferred more easily to the second language than others (Bialystok, 2017). Children who are fluent in two languages perform better than their single-language counterparts on tests of control of attention, concept formation, analytical reasoning, cognitive flexibility, and cognitive complexity (Bialystok, 2001, 2007, 2011, 2014, 2015, 2017; Bialystok & Craik, 2010; Genesee & Lindholm-Leary, 2012). Recent research also documented that bilingual children are better at theory of mind tasks (Rubio-Fernandez, 2017). They also are more conscious of the structure of spoken and written language and better at noticing errors of grammar and meaning, skills that benefit their reading ability (Bialystok, 1997; Kuo & Anderson, 2012). A recent study of 6- to 10-year-olds found that early bilingual exposure was a key factor in bilingual children outperforming monolingual children on phonological awareness and word learning (Jasinska & Petitto, 2017).

Students in the United States are far behind their counterparts in many developed countries in learning a second language. For example, in Russia, schools have 10 grades, called *forms,* which roughly correspond to the 12 grades in American schools. Russian children begin school at age 7 and begin learning English in the third form. Because of this emphasis on teaching English, most Russian citizens under the age of 40 today are able to speak at least some English. The United States is the only technologically advanced Western nation that does not have a national foreign language requirement at the high school level, even for students in rigorous academic programs.

American students who do not learn a second language may be missing more than the chance to acquire a skill. *Dual-language learning*—the ability to speak two languages—has a positive effect on children's cognitive development (Gibbons & Ng, 2004).

Thus, overall, bilingualism is linked to more positive outcomes for children's language and cognitive development (Antovich & Graf Estes, 2017; Singh & others, 2017; Wermelinger, Gampe, & Daum, 2017; Yow & others, 2017). An especially important developmental question that many parents of infants and young children have is whether to teach them two languages simultaneously or just teach one language at a time to avoid confusion. The answer is that teaching infants and young children two languages simultaneously (as when a mother's native language is English and her husband's is Spanish) has numerous benefits and few drawbacks (Bialystok, 2014, 2015, 2017).

Most children who learn two languages are not exposed to the same quantity and quality of each language. Nonetheless, bilingual children do not show delays in the rate at which they acquire language overall (Hoff, 2015). In a recent study, by 4 years of age children who continued to learn both Spanish and English languages had a total vocabulary growth that was greater than that of monolingual children (Hoff & others, 2014).

In the United States, many immigrant children go from being monolingual in their home language to being bilingual in that language and in English, only to end up monolingual speakers of English. This *subtractive dual-language learning* can have negative effects on children, who often become ashamed of their home language.

A current controversy related to dual-language learning involves dual-language education. To read about this controversy, see the *Connecting with Diversity* interlude. And to read about an English Language Learning teacher, see *Connecting with Careers.*

What Is the Best Way to Teach English Language Learners?

A current controversy related to dual-language learning involves the millions of U.S. children who come from homes in which English is not the primary language (Echevarria, Vogt, & Short, 2017; Peregoy & Boyle, 2017). What is the best way to teach these English language learners (ELLs), many of whom in the United States are from immigrant families living in poverty (McCabe & others, 2013)?

ELLs have been taught in one of two main ways: (1) instruction in English only, or (2) a *dual-language* (used to be called *bilingual*) approach that involves instruction in their home language and English (Haley & Austin, 2014). In a dual-language approach, instruction is given in both the ELL child's home language and English for varying amounts of time at certain grade levels. One of the arguments for the dual-language approach is the research discussed earlier demonstrating that bilingual children have more advanced information-processing skills than monolingual children do (Genesee & Lindholm-Leary, 2012).

If a dual-language strategy is used, too often it has been thought that immigrant children need only one or two years of this type of instruction. However, in general it takes immigrant children approximately three to five years to develop speaking proficiency and seven years to develop reading proficiency in English (Hakuta, Butler, & Witt, 2001). Also, immigrant children vary in their ability to learn English (Echevarria, Vogt, & Short, 2017). Children who come from lower socioeconomic backgrounds have more difficulty than those from higher socioeconomic backgrounds (Hakuta, 2001; Hoff & Place, 2013). Thus, especially for immigrant children from low socioeconomic backgrounds, more years of dual-language instruction may be needed than they currently are receiving.

What have researchers found regarding outcomes of ELL programs? Drawing conclusions about the effectiveness of ELL programs is difficult because of variations across programs in the number of

A first- and second-grade bilingual English-Cantonese teacher instructing students in Chinese in Oakland, California. *What have researchers found about the effectiveness of bilingual education?*
©Elizabeth Crews

years they are in effect, type of instruction, quality of schooling other than ELL instruction, teachers, children, and other factors. Further, no effective experiments have been conducted that compare bilingual education with English-only education in the United States (Snow & Kang, 2006). Some experts have concluded that the quality of instruction is more important in determining outcomes than the language in which it is delivered (Lesaux & Siegel, 2003).

Nonetheless, other experts, such as Kenji Hakuta (2001, 2005), support the combined home language and English approach because (1) children have difficulty learning a subject when it is taught in a language they do not understand; and (2) when both languages are integrated in the classroom, children learn the second language more readily and participate more actively. In support of Hakuta's view, most large-scale studies have found that the academic achievement of ELLs is higher in dual-language programs than in English-only programs (Genesee & Lindholm-Leary, 2012).

Salvador Tamayo, Teacher of English Language Learners

Salvador Tamayo is an ELL fifth-grade teacher at Turner Elementary School in West Chicago. He recently received a National Educator Award by the Milken Family Foundation for his work in educating ELLs. Tamayo is especially adept at integrating technology into his ELL classes. He and his students have created several award-winning Web sites about the West Chicago City Museum, the local Latino community, and the history of West Chicago. His students also developed an "I Want to Be an American Citizen" Web site to assist family and community members in preparing for the U.S. Citizenship Test. Tamayo also teaches an ELL class at Wheaton College.

Salvador Tamayo works with dual-language education students.
Courtesy of Salvador Tamayo

Review

- What are some changes in vocabulary, grammar, and metalinguistic awareness in the middle and late childhood years?
- What controversy surrounds teaching children to read? What are some positive ways for children to learn how to write competently?
- What characterizes dual-language learning and second-language learning? What issues are involved in dual-language instruction?

Connect

- In an earlier main section in this chapter, you read about

metacognition. Compare that concept with the concept of metalinguistic awareness discussed in this section.

Reflect *Your Own Personal Journey of Life*

- Did you learn a second language as a child? If so, do you think it was beneficial to you? Why or why not? If you did not learn a second language as a child, do you wish you had? Why or why not?

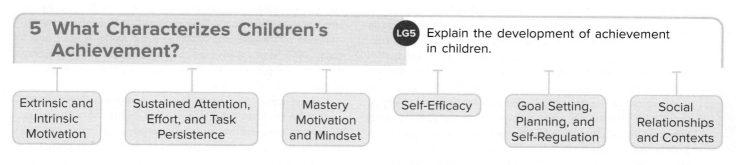

5 What Characterizes Children's Achievement?

LG5 Explain the development of achievement in children.

| Extrinsic and Intrinsic Motivation | Sustained Attention, Effort, and Task Persistence | Mastery Motivation and Mindset | Self-Efficacy | Goal Setting, Planning, and Self-Regulation | Social Relationships and Contexts |

Life is a gift . . . Accept it.

Life is a puzzle . . . Solve it.

Life is an adventure . . . Dare it.

Life is an opportunity . . . Take it.

Life is a mystery . . . Unfold it.

Life is a mission . . . Fulfill it.

Life is a struggle . . . Face it.

Life is a goal . . . Achieve it.

—AUTHOR UNKNOWN

We are a species motivated to do well at what we attempt, to gain mastery over the world in which we live, to explore unknown environments with enthusiasm and curiosity, and to achieve the heights of success. In this section, we explore how children can effectively achieve their potential.

EXTRINSIC AND INTRINSIC MOTIVATION

The behavioral approach emphasizes the importance of **extrinsic motivation,** which involves external incentives such as rewards and punishments (Emmer & Evertson, 2017; Evertson & Emmer, 2017). By contrast, the cognitive approaches stress the importance of intrinsic motivation in achievement (Flannery, 2017; Luyckx & others, 2017; Miele & Scholer, 2016; Ryan & Deci, 2016). **Intrinsic motivation** is based on internal factors such as self-determination, curiosity, challenge, and effort. Some individuals study hard because they want to make good grades or avoid parental disapproval (extrinsic motivation). Others study hard because they are internally motivated to achieve high standards in their work (intrinsic motivation). In a recent study of minority low-SES youth, their intrinsic motivation (but not their extrinsic motivation) predicted their intention to pursue a health-science-related career (Boekeloo & others, 2015).

One view of intrinsic motivation emphasizes self-determination (Ryan & Deci, 2001, 2016; Weinstein, Deci, & Ryan, 2012). In this view, children want to believe that they are doing something because of their own will, not because of external success or rewards (Ryan & Moller, 2017). An overwhelming conclusion of motivation research is that teachers should encourage students to become intrinsically motivated (Harackiewicz & Knogler, 2017). Similarly, teachers should create learning environments that promote students' cognitive engagement, effort, and self-responsibility for learning (Anderman, Gray, & Chang, 2013). Researchers have found that that a number of contextual factors, such as autonomy support, instructor approachability, involvement opportunities, and course material relevance, are

extrinsic motivation Involves external incentives such as rewards and punishments.

intrinsic motivation Involves internal factors such as self-determination, curiosity, challenge, and effort.

linked to situational interest and in turn may support individual interest (Linnenbrink-Garcia & Patall, 2016). That said, the real world includes both intrinsic and extrinsic motivation, and too often intrinsic and extrinsic motivation have been pitted against each other as polar opposites. In many aspects of students' lives, both intrinsic and extrinsic motivation are at work (Anderman, 2012; Cameron & Pierce, 2008). Further, both intrinsic and extrinsic motivation can operate simultaneously. Thus, a student may work hard in a course because she enjoys the content and likes learning about it (intrinsic) and because she wants to earn a good grade (extrinsic) (Schunk, 2016). Keep in mind, though, that many psychologists believe that extrinsic motivation by itself is not a good strategy.

SUSTAINED ATTENTION, EFFORT, AND TASK PERSISTENCE

Of course, it is important not only to perceive that effort is an important aspect of achieving, but it also important to actually engage in sustained attention, effort, and task persistence in school, work, and a career (Wentzel & Miele, 2016). Recall that *sustained attention* is the ability to maintain attention to a selected stimulus for a prolonged period of time. Sustained attention requires effort, and as individuals develop through childhood and adolescence, school tasks, projects, and work become more complex and require longer periods of sustained attention, effort, and task persistence than in childhood.

Might the capacity of children and adolescents to persist at tasks be linked to their career success in adulthood? One study revealed that task persistence at 13 years of age was related to occupational success in middle age (Andersson & Bergman, 2011).

MASTERY MOTIVATION AND MINDSET

Cognitive engagement and efforts toward self-improvement characterize children with a mastery motivation. These children also have a growth mindset—a belief that they can produce positive outcomes if they put forth sufficient effort.

Mastery Motivation Developmental psychologists Valanne Henderson and Carol Dweck (1990) have found that children often show two distinct responses to difficult or challenging circumstances. Individuals who display **mastery motivation** are task-oriented; they concentrate on learning strategies and the process of achievement rather than focusing on their ability or the intended outcome. Those with a **helpless orientation** seem trapped by the experience of difficulty, and they attribute their difficulty to lack of ability. They frequently make comments such as "I'm not very good at this," even though they might earlier have demonstrated their ability through many successes. And, once they view their behavior as failure, they often feel anxious, and their performance worsens even further.

In contrast, mastery-oriented children often instruct themselves to pay attention, to think carefully, and to remember strategies that have worked for them in previous situations. They frequently report feeling challenged and excited by difficult tasks, rather than being threatened by them (Anderman & Mueller, 2010).

Another issue in motivation involves whether to adopt a mastery or a performance orientation. Children with a **performance orientation** are focused on achievement outcomes, believing that winning is what matters most and that happiness results from winning. Does this mean that mastery-oriented individuals do not like to win and that performance-oriented individuals are not motivated to experience the self-efficacy that comes from being able to take credit for one's accomplishments? No. A matter of emphasis or degree is involved, though. For mastery-oriented individuals, winning isn't everything; for performance-oriented individuals, skill development and self-efficacy take a backseat to winning.

A final point needs to be made about mastery and performance goals: They are not always mutually exclusive. Students can be both mastery- and performance-oriented, and researchers have found that mastery goals combined with performance goals often benefit students' success (Anderman & Mueller, 2010).

Mindset Carol Dweck's (2006, 2007, 2012, 2015, 2016) most recent analysis of motivation for achievement stresses the importance of developing a **mindset,** which she defines as

These students were given an opportunity to write and perform their own play. These kinds of self-determining opportunities can enhance students' motivation to achieve.
©Elizabeth Crews/The Image Works

mastery motivation An orientation that focuses on tasks, learning strategies, and the achievement process rather than innate ability.

helpless orientation An orientation in which one seems trapped by the experience of difficulty and attributes one's difficulty to a lack of ability.

performance orientation An orientation in which one focuses on achievement outcomes; winning is what matters most, and happiness is thought to result from winning.

mindset The cognitive view, either fixed or growth, that individuals develop for themselves.

Carol Dweck's Brainology program is designed to cultivate children's growth mindset.

Keep the growth mindset in your thoughts. Then, when you bump up against obstacles, you can turn to it . . . showing you a path into the future.

—CAROL DWECK
Contemporary Psychologist, Stanford University

They can because they think they can.

—VIRGIL
Roman Poet, 1st Century

self-efficacy The belief that one can master a situation and produce favorable outcomes.

the cognitive view individuals develop for themselves. She concludes that individuals have one of two mindsets: (1) a *fixed mindset,* in which they believe that their qualities are carved in stone and cannot change; or (2) a *growth mindset,* in which they believe their qualities can change and improve through their effort. A fixed mindset is similar to a helpless orientation; a growth mindset is much like having a mastery motivation.

In *Mindset,* Dweck (2006) argued that individuals' mindsets influence whether they will be optimistic or pessimistic, shape their goals and how hard they will strive to reach those goals, and affect many aspects of their lives, including achievement and success in school and sports. Dweck says that mindsets begin to be shaped as children and adolescents interact with parents, teachers, and coaches, who themselves have either a fixed mindset or a growth mindset.

In recent research by Dweck and her colleagues, students from lower-income families were less likely to have a growth mindset than their counterparts from wealthier families (Claro, Paunesku, & Dweck, 2016). However, the achievement of students from lower-income families who did have a growth mindset was more likely to be protected from the negative effects of poverty.

Dweck and her colleagues (Blackwell & Dweck, 2008; Blackwell, Trzesniewski, & Dweck, 2007; Dweck, 2012, 2015, 2016) recently incorporated information about the brain's plasticity into their effort to improve students' motivation to achieve and succeed. In one study, they assigned two groups of students to eight sessions of either (1) study skills instruction or (2) study skills instruction plus information about the importance of developing a growth mindset (called *incremental theory* in the research) (Blackwell, Trzesniewski, & Dweck, 2007). One of the exercises in the growth mindset group, titled "You Can Grow Your Brain," emphasized that the brain is like a muscle that can change and grow as it is exercised and develops new connections. Students were informed that the more you challenge your brain to learn, the more your brain cells grow. Both groups had a pattern of declining math scores prior to the intervention. Following the intervention, the group who received only the study skills instruction continued to have declining scores but the group who received a combination of study skills instruction and the growth mindset emphasis on exercising the brain reversed the downward trend and improved their math achievement.

In other work, Dweck has been creating a computer-based workshop, "Brainology," to teach students that their intelligence can change (Blackwell & Dweck, 2008). Students experience six modules about how the brain works and how they can make their brain improve. After the workshop was tested in 20 New York City schools, students strongly endorsed the value of the computer-based brain modules. Said one student, "I will try harder because I know that the more you try the more your brain knows" (Dweck & Master, 2009, p. 137).

Dweck and her colleagues also recently have found that a growth mindset can prevent negative stereotypes from undermining achievement. For example, believing that math ability can be learned counteracted negative gender stereotyping about math (Good, Rattan, & Dweck, 2012). And other research recently indicated that willpower is a virtually unlimited mindset that predicts how long people will work and resist temptations during stressful circumstances (Dweck, 2012, 2015, 2016; Job & others, 2015; Miller & others, 2012).

SELF-EFFICACY

Like having a growth mindset, **self-efficacy**—the belief that one can master a situation and produce favorable outcomes—is an important cognitive view for children to develop. Albert Bandura (2004, 2012, 2015), whose social cognitive theory was discussed earlier, emphasizes that self-efficacy is a critical factor in whether or not students achieve. Self-efficacy has much in common with mastery motivation and intrinsic motivation. Self-efficacy is the belief that

"I can"; helplessness is the belief that "I cannot" (Stipek, 2002). Students with high self-efficacy endorse such statements as "I know that I will be able to learn the material in this class" and "I expect to be able to do well at this activity."

Dale Schunk (2016) has applied the concept of self-efficacy to many aspects of students' achievement. In his view, self-efficacy influences a student's choice of activities. Students with low self-efficacy for learning may avoid many learning tasks, especially those that are challenging. By contrast, their high-self-efficacy counterparts eagerly work at learning tasks (Zimmerman, Schunk, & DiBenedetto, 2017). High-self-efficacy students are more likely to expend effort and persist longer at a learning task than low-self-efficacy students.

Children's achievement is influenced by their parents' self-efficacy. One study revealed a number of positive developmental outcomes, including more daily opportunities for optimal functioning, better peer relations, and fewer problems, for children and adolescents whose parents had high self-efficacy (Steca & others, 2011).

What characterizes students with high self-efficacy?
©Ariel Skelley/Blend Images/Corbis RF

How Would You...?
If you were an **educator,** how would you encourage enhanced self-efficacy in a student who says, "I can't do this work"?

GOAL SETTING, PLANNING, AND SELF-MONITORING/SELF-REGULATION

Goal setting, planning, and self-rmonitoring/self-regulation are important aspects of achievement (Schunk, 2016). Researchers have found that self-efficacy and achievement improve when individuals set goals that are specific, proximal, and challenging (Bandura, 2001). An example of a nonspecific, fuzzy goal is "I want to be successful." A more concrete, specific goal is "I want to do well on my spelling test this week."

Individuals can set both long-term (distal) and short-term (proximal) goals. It is okay for individuals to set some long-term goals, such as "I want to graduate from high school" or "I want to go to college," but they also need to create short-term goals that serve as steps along the way. "Getting an A on the next math test" is an example of a short-term, proximal goal. So is "Doing all of my homework by 4 p.m. Sunday."

Another good strategy is for individuals to set challenging goals (Elliot & Hulleman, 2017; Hofer & Fries, 2016; Senko, 2016). A challenging goal is a commitment to self-improvement. Strong interest and involvement in activities are sparked by challenges. Goals that are easy to reach generate little interest or effort. However, goals should be optimally matched to the individual's skill level. If goals are unrealistically high, the result will be repeated failures that lower the individual's self-efficacy.

It is not enough just to get individuals to set goals. It also is important to encourage them to plan how they will reach their goals. Being a good planner means managing time effectively, setting priorities, and being organized. Younger children will likely need help from parents or teachers to develop goal setting, planning, and organizational skills.

Individuals not only should plan their next week's activities but also should monitor how well they are sticking to their plan (Zimmerman, Schunk, & DiBenedetto, 2017). Once engaged in a task, they need to monitor their progress, judge how well they are doing on the task, and evaluate the outcomes to regulate what they do in the future (Schunk, 2016).

SOCIAL RELATIONSHIPS AND CONTEXTS

Children's relationships with parents, peers, friends, teachers, mentors, and others can profoundly affect their achievement. So can the social contexts of ethnicity and culture.

Parents   Parents' child-rearing practices are linked to children's achievement (Pomerantz, 2017). Here are some positive parenting practices that result in improved motivation and achievement: knowing enough about the child to provide the right amount of challenge and the right amount of support; providing a positive emotional climate that motivates children to internalize their parents' values and goals; and modeling motivated achievement behavior, such as working hard and persisting with effort at challenging tasks.

In addition to general child-rearing practices, parents provide various activities or resources at home that may influence students' interest and motivation to pursue various activities over time (Wigfield & others, 2015). For example, reading to one's preschool children and providing reading materials in the home are positively related to students' later reading achievement and motivation (Wigfield & Asher, 1994).

How Would You...?

If you were an **educator**, how would you describe the importance of teachers in children's achievement?

Teachers Teachers play an important role in students' achievement. When researchers have observed classrooms, they have found that effective, engaging teachers provide support for students to make good progress but also encourage them to become self-regulated achievers (Schunk, 2016). The encouragement takes place in a very positive environment, one in which students are constantly being motivated to try hard and to develop self-efficacy.

Teachers' expectations influence students' motivation and performance (Wigfield, Tonks, & Klauda, 2016). One study revealed that teachers' high expectations can help to buffer the negative effect of parents' low expectations for students' achievement (Wood, Kaplan, & McLoyd, 2007).

Ethnicity The diversity that exists among ethnic minority children is evident in their achievement (Gollnick & Chinn, 2017; Spencer & others, 2017). In addition to recognizing diversity of achievement within every cultural group, it also is important to distinguish between difference and deficiency (Koppelman, 2017). Too often, the achievement levels of ethnic minority students—especially African Americans, Latinos, and Native Americans—have been interpreted as *deficits* by middle-socioeconomic-status White standards, when they simply are *culturally different and distinct* (Jones, 1994). An especially important factor in the lower achievement of students from low-income families is lack of adequate resources, such as unavailability of an up-to-date computer in the home or even any computer at all, to support students' learning (Schunk, 2016).

UCLA educational psychologist Sandra Graham talks with adolescent boys about motivation. She has conducted a number of studies which reveal that middle-socioeconomic-status African American students—like their White counterparts—have high achievement expectations and attribute success to internal factors such as effort rather than external factors such as luck.
Courtesy of Dr. Sandra Graham

Sandra Graham (1986, 1990) has conducted a number of studies that reveal not only the stronger influence of socioeconomic status than ethnic differences in achievement but also the importance of studying ethnic minority student motivation in the context of general motivational theory. Her inquiries fall within the framework of attribution theory and focus on the causes that African American students give for their achievement orientation, such as why they succeed or fail. She is struck by how consistently middle-income African American students do not fit the stereotype of being unmotivated. Like their White middle-income counterparts, they have high achievement expectations and understand that failure is usually due to a lack of effort, rather than bad luck. A longitudinal study revealed that African American children or children from low-income families benefited more than children from higher-income families when they did homework more frequently, had Internet access at home, and had a library card (Xia, 2010). And in a recent research review, it was concluded that increased family income for children in poverty was associated with increased achievement in middle school, as well as greater educational attainment in adolescence and emerging adulthood (Duncan, Magnuson, & Votruba-Drazal, 2017).

Cross-Cultural Comparisons International assessments indicate that the United States has not fared well compared with many other countries in the areas of math and science (DeSilver, 2017). On the Programme for International Student Assessment (PISA) conducted in 2015, 15-year-olds in the United States placed 38th out of 71 countries in math and 24th in science (PISA, 2015). In another recent assessment of fourth- and eighth-grade students on the Trends in International Mathematics and Science Study (TIMMS), U.S. students fared somewhat better, placing 11th out of 48 countries in fourth-grade math and 8th in fourth-grade science (TIMMS, 2015). Also in the TIMMS study, U.S. students placed 8th in math and 8th in science in the 37 countries studied. The top five spots in the international assessments mainly go to East Asian countries, especially Singapore, China, and Japan. The only non-Asian countries to crack the top five in recent years for math and science are Finland and Estonia.

Despite the recent gains by U.S. elementary school students, it is disconcerting that in most comparisons, the rankings for U.S. students in reading, math, and science compared with students in other countries decline as they go from elementary school to high school. Also, U.S. students' achievement scores in math and science are still far below those of students in many East Asian countries.

Asian grade schools intersperse studying with frequent periods of activities. This approach helps children maintain their attention and likely makes learning more enjoyable. Shown here are Japanese fourth-graders making wearable masks. *What are some differences in the way children in many Asian countries are taught compared with children in the United States?*
©Eiji Miyazawa/BlackStar/Stock Photos

Harold Stevenson's (1995, 2000; Stevenson, Hofer, & Randel, 1999; Stevenson & others, 1990) research explores reasons for the poor performance of American students. Stevenson and his colleagues have completed five cross-cultural comparisons of students in the United States, China, Taiwan, and Japan. In these studies, Asian students consistently outperform American students. And, the longer the students are in school, the wider the gap becomes between Asian and American students—the lowest difference is in the first grade, the highest in the eleventh grade (the highest grade studied).

To learn more about the reasons for these large cross-cultural differences, Stevenson and his colleagues spent thousands of hours observing in classrooms as well as interviewing and surveying teachers, students, and parents. They found that the Asian teachers spent more of their time teaching math than did the American teachers. For example, more than one-fourth of total classroom time in the first grade was spent on math instruction in Japan, compared with only one-tenth of the time in the U.S. first-grade classrooms. Also, the Asian students were in school an average of 240 days a year, compared with 178 days in the United States.

In addition to the substantially greater time spent on math instruction in the Asian schools than the American schools, differences were found between the Asian and American parents. The American parents had much lower expectations for their children's education and achievement than did the Asian parents. Also, the American parents were more likely to believe that their children's math achievement was due to innate ability, while the Asian parents were more likely to say that their children's math achievement resulted from effort and training (see Figure 8). The Asian students were more likely to do math homework than were the American students, and the Asian parents were far more likely to help their children with their math homework than were the American parents (Chen & Stevenson, 1989).

A recent study examined factors that might account for the superior academic performance of Asian American children (Hsin & Xie, 2014). In this study, the Asian American advantage was mainly due to children exerting greater academic effort and not to advantages in tested cognitive abilities or sociodemographic factors.

In the *Connecting with Research* interlude, you can read further about efforts to discover why parenting practices are likely to be an important influence on the lower achievement of U.S. children compared with East Asian children and possibly have implications for other aspects of children's development.

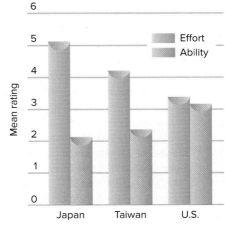

FIGURE **8**

MOTHERS' BELIEFS ABOUT THE FACTORS RESPONSIBLE FOR CHILDREN'S MATH ACHIEVEMENT IN THREE COUNTRIES. In one study, mothers in Japan and Taiwan were more likely to believe that their children's math achievement was due to effort rather than innate ability, whereas U.S. mothers were more likely to believe their children's math achievement was due to innate ability (Stevenson, Lee, & Stigler, 1986). If parents believe that their children's math achievement is due to innate ability and their children are not doing well in math, the implication is that they are less likely to think their children will benefit from putting forth more effort.
Source: Stevenson, Harold W., Shin-ying Lee, James W. Stigler, "Mathematics Achievement of Chinese, Japanese, and American Children" Science, New Series, vol. 231, no. 4739, February 14, 1986, pp. 693–699.

connecting with research

Parenting and Children's Achievement: My Child Is My Report Card, Tiger Moms, and Tiger Babies Strike Back

There is rising concern that U.S. children are not reaching their full potential, which ultimately will reduce the success of the United States in competing with other countries (Pomerantz, 2017; Qu & Pomerantz, 2015; Qu & others, 2016). Eva Pomerantz is interested in identifying how parents can maximize their children's motivation and achievement in school while also maintaining positive emotional adjustment. To this end, Pomerantz and her colleagues are conducting research with children and their parents not only in the United States but also in China, where children often attain higher levels of achievement than their U.S. counterparts (Pomerantz, 2017; Pomerantz, Cheung, & Qin, 2012; Pomerantz & Grolnick, 2017; Pomerantz & Kempner, 2013; Pomerantz, Kim, & Cheung, 2012; Qu & Pomerantz, 2015; Qu & others, 2016).

As indicated earlier regarding Harold Stevenson's research, East Asian parents spend considerably more time helping their children with homework than do U.S. parents (Chen & Stevenson, 1989).

Pomerantz's research indicates that East Asian parental involvement in children's learning is present as early as the preschool years and continues during the elementary school years (Cheung & Pomerantz, 2012; Ng, Pomerantz, & Deng, 2014; Ng, Pomerantz, & Lam, 2013; Siegler & Mu, 2008). In East Asia, children's learning is considered to be a far greater responsibility of parents than in the United States (Ng, Pomerantz, & Lam, 2013; Pomerantz, Kim, & Cheung, 2012). However, researchers have discovered that when U.S. parents are more involved in their children's learning, the children's achievement benefits (Cheung & Pomerantz, 2012). In this study, more than 800 U.S. and Chinese children (average age 12.73 years) reported on their parents' involvement in their learning and their motivation in school every six months from the fall of seventh grade to the end of eighth grade. The researchers also collected data on children's self-regulated learning strategies and grades. Over time, the more

(continued)

(*continued*)

involved parents were in children's learning, the more strongly motivated children were to do well academically for parent-oriented reasons, which improved children's self-regulated learning and grades.

In addition to studying parental involvement in children's learning, Pomerantz and her colleagues also are conducting research on the role of parental control in children's achievement. In a recent study in which the title of the resulting article included the phrase "My Child Is My Report Card," Chinese mothers exerted more control (especially psychological control) over their children than did U.S. mothers (Ng, Pomerantz, & Deng, 2014). Also in this study, Chinese mothers' self-worth was more contingent on their children's achievement than was the case for U.S. mothers.

Pomerantz's research reflects the term "training parents," a variation of authoritarian parenting, in which the parenting strategy of many Asian parents is to train their children to achieve high levels of academic success. In 2011, Amy Chua's book, *Battle Hymn of the Tiger Mom,* sparked considerable interest in the role of parenting in children's achievement. Chua uses the term *Tiger Mom* to mean a mother who engages in strict disciplinary practices. In another recent book, *Tiger Babies Strike Back,* Kim Wong Keltner (2013) argues that the Tiger Mom parenting style can be so demanding and confining that being an Asian American child is like being in an "emotional jail." She says that the Tiger Mom authoritarian style does provide some advantages for children, such as emphasizing the value of going for what you want and not taking no for an answer, but that too often the outcome is not worth the emotional costs that accompany it.

Recent research on Chinese-American immigrant families with first- and second-grade children has found that the children with authoritarian (highly controlling) parents are more aggressive, are more depressed, have a higher anxiety level, and show poorer social skills than children whose parents engaged in non-authoritarian styles

Qing Zhou, who has recently conducted research on authoritarian parenting in immigrant Chinese children, with her children. *What are the results of her research?*
Courtesy of Qing Zhou

(Zhou & others, 2013). Qing Zhou (2013), lead author on the study just described and the director of the University of California's Culture and Family Laboratory, is conducting workshops to teach Chinese mothers positive parenting strategies such as using listening skills, praising their children for good behavior, and spending more time with their children in fun activities. Also, in a recent study in China, young adolescents with authoritative parents showed better adjustment than their counterparts with authoritarian parents (Zhang & others, 2017).

In sum, while an authoritarian, psychologically controlling style of parenting may be associated with higher levels of achievement, especially in Asian children, there are concerns that an authoritarian, highly controlling style also may produce more emotional difficulties in children (Pomerantz & Grolnick, 2017).

Review *Connect* Reflect

LG5 Explain the development of achievement in children.

Review

- How does extrinsic motivation differ from intrinsic motivation?
- What roles do sustained attention, effort, and task persistence play in achievement?
- How does mastery motivation differ from helpless and performance orientations?
- What is mindset, and how does it influence children's achievement?
- What is self-efficacy, and how is it involved in achievement?
- What functions do goal setting, planning, and self-monitoring play in achievement?
- How are social relationships and contexts involved in children's achievement?

Connect

- In this section, you read about extrinsic and intrinsic motivation. Which theory discussed in the "Introduction" chapter places the most emphasis on the importance of extrinsic motivation in children's development?

Reflect *Your Own Personal Journey of Life*

- Think about several of your own past schoolmates who showed low motivation in school. Why do you think they behaved that way? What teaching strategies might have helped them?

reach your **learning goals**

Cognitive Development in Middle and Late Childhood

1 What Is Piaget's Theory of Cognitive Development in Middle and Late Childhood?

LG1 Discuss Piaget's stage of concrete operational thought and apply Piaget's theory to education.

Concrete Operational Thought

Evaluating Piaget's Concrete Operational Stage

Applications to Education

- Concrete operational thought involves operations, conservation, classification, seriation, and transitivity. Thought is not as abstract as it is later in development.

- Critics argue that elements of a stage do not appear at the same time, and that education and culture have more influence on development than Piaget predicted. Neo-Piagetians place more emphasis on how children process information, strategies, speed of information processing, and the division of cognitive problems into more precise steps.

- Application of Piaget's ideas to education especially involves a constructivist approach that focuses on the teacher as a guide rather than a director and turns the classroom into a setting for exploration and discovery.

2 What Is the Nature of Children's Information Processing?

LG2 Describe changes in information processing in middle and late childhood.

Memory

Thinking

- Long-term memory increases in middle and late childhood. Working memory is an important memory process that involves manipulating and assembling information. Knowledge and expertise influence memory. Strategies such as organization, imagery, and elaboration can be used by children to improve their memory. Fuzzy trace theory has been proposed to explain developmental changes in memory.

- Advances in executive function in middle and late childhood include self-control/inhibition, working memory, and cognitive flexibility. Critical thinking involves thinking reflectively and productively, as well as evaluating evidence. Mindfulness is an important aspect of critical thinking. A special concern is the lack of emphasis on critical thinking in many schools.

- Creative thinking is the ability to think in novel and unusual ways and to come up with unique solutions to problems. Guilford distinguished between convergent and divergent thinking. A number of strategies, including brainstorming, can be used to encourage children's creative thinking. Children think like scientists in some ways, but in other ways they don't.

Metacognition

- Metacognition is knowing about knowing, or cognition about cognition. Most metacognitive studies have focused on metamemory. Pressley views the key to education as helping students learn a rich repertoire of strategies.

3 How Can Children's Intelligence Be Described?

LG3 Characterize children's intelligence.

Intelligence and Its Assessment

- Intelligence consists of problem-solving skills and the ability to adapt to and learn from life's everyday experiences. Interest in intelligence often focuses on individual differences and assessment. Widely used intelligence tests today include the Stanford–Binet tests and Wechsler scales. Results on these tests may be reported in terms of an overall IQ or in terms of performance on specific areas of the tests.

Types of Intelligence

- Sternberg proposed that intelligence comes in three main forms: analytical, creative, and practical. Gardner described eight types of intelligence: verbal, math, spatial, bodily-kinesthetic, interpersonal skills, intrapersonal skills, musical skills, and naturalist skills. The multiple-intelligence approaches have expanded our conception of intelligence, but critics argue that the research base for these approaches is not well established.

Interpreting Differences in IQ Scores

- IQ scores are influenced both by genetics and by characteristics of the environment. Parenting, home environments, schools, and intervention programs can influence these scores. Intelligence test scores have risen considerably around the world in recent decades—a phenomenon known as the Flynn effect—and this rise supports the role of environment in intelligence.

- Group differences in IQ scores may reflect many influences, including cultural bias. Tests may be biased against groups that are not familiar with a standard form of English, with the content that is being tested, or with the testing situation.

Extremes of Intelligence

- Intellectual disability involves low IQ and problems in adapting to the demands of everyday life. One classification of intellectual disability distinguishes organic and cultural-familial intellectual disability.

- A child who is gifted has above-average intelligence and/or superior talent for something. Terman contributed to our understanding that gifted children are not more maladjusted than non-gifted children. Three characteristics of gifted children are precocity, individuality, and a passion to master a domain. Critics argue that gifted children have been miseducated.

4 What Changes in Language Development Occur in Middle and Late Childhood?

LG4 Summarize language development in middle and late childhood.

Vocabulary, Grammar, and Metalinguistic Awareness

- In middle and late childhood, children become more analytical and logical in their approach to words and grammar. In terms of grammar, children are better able to understand comparatives and subjunctives. They become increasingly able to use complex grammar and produce narratives that make sense. Improvements in metalinguistic awareness—knowledge about language—are evident during the elementary school years as children increasingly define words, expand their knowledge of syntax, and increase their understanding of how to use language in culturally appropriate ways.

Reading and Writing

- A current debate about reading instruction focuses on the phonics approach versus the whole-language approach. The phonics approach advocates phonetics instruction and simplified reading materials. The whole-language approach stresses that reading instruction should parallel children's natural language learning and recommends giving children whole-language materials, such as books and newspapers. An increasing number of experts now conclude that although both approaches can benefit children, direct instruction in phonics is a key aspect of learning to read.

Dual-Language and Second-Language Learning

- Children's writing emerges out of scribbling. Advances in children's language and cognitive development provide the underpinnings for improved writing.

- Recent research indicates a complex conclusion about whether there are sensitive periods in learning a second language. Children who are fluent in two languages have more advanced information-processing skills than children who use only one language.

- Instruction for English language learners (ELLs) has taken one of two main forms: (1) instruction in English only, or (2) dual-language instruction in the child's home language and English. The majority of large-scale research studies have found a higher level of academic achievement when the dual-language approach is used.

5 What Characterizes Children's Achievement?

LG5 Explain the development of achievement in children.

Extrinsic and Intrinsic Motivation

- Extrinsic motivation involves external incentives such as rewards and punishments. Intrinsic motivation is based on internal factors such as self-determination, curiosity, challenge, and effort. Giving children some choice and providing opportunities for personal responsibility increase intrinsic motivation.

Sustained Attention, Effort, and Task Persistence

- Sustained attention, effort, and task persistence are key aspects of achievement. As children and adolescents develop, school tasks, projects, and work become more complex and require longer periods of sustained attention, effort, and task persistence.

Mastery Motivation and Mindset

- Individuals with a mastery motivation focus on the task rather than their own ability and use solution-oriented strategies. Mastery motivation is preferred over a helpless orientation (in which individuals seem trapped by the experience of difficulty and attribute their difficulty to lack of ability) or a performance orientation (being concerned with achievement outcomes—winning is what matters).

- Mindset is the cognitive view, either fixed or growth, that individuals develop for themselves. Dweck argues that a key aspect of promoting children's development is guiding them in developing a growth mindset.

Self-Efficacy

- Self-efficacy is the belief that one can master a situation and produce positive outcomes. Bandura stresses that self-efficacy is a critical factor in whether children will achieve.

Goal Setting, Planning, and Self-Regulation

- Setting specific, proximal (short-term), and challenging goals benefits children's self-efficacy and achievement. Being a good planner means managing time effectively, setting priorities, and being organized. Self-monitoring is a key aspect of self-regulation that benefits children's learning.

Social Relationships and Contexts

- Among the social relationships and contexts that are linked to children's achievement are those that involve parenting, teachers, ethnicity, and culture. American children are more achievement-oriented than children in many countries but are less achievement-oriented than many children in Asian countries such as China, Taiwan, and Japan.

key terms

brainstorming
convergent thinking
creative thinking
critical thinking
cultural-familial intellectual disability
culture-fair tests
divergent thinking
elaboration
extrinsic motivation

fuzzy trace theory
gifted
helpless orientation
individual differences
intellectual disability
intelligence
intelligence quotient (IQ)
intrinsic motivation
long-term memory
mastery motivation

mental age (MA)
metacognition
metalinguistic awareness
mindfulness
mindset
neo-Piagetians
normal distribution
organic intellectual disability
performance orientation
phonics approach

self-efficacy
seriation
stereotype threat
strategies
transitivity
triarchic theory
   of intelligence
whole-language
   approach
working memory

key **people**

connecting with **improving the lives of children**

STRATEGIES

Supporting Children's Cognitive Development

What are some effective ways to help elementary school children develop their cognitive skills?

- *Facilitate rather than direct children's learning.* Design situations that let children learn by doing and that actively promote their thinking and discovery. Listen, watch, and question children to help them attain a better understanding of concepts.

- *Provide opportunities for children to think critically.* Encourage children to think reflectively, rather than automatically accepting information as correct. Ask children questions about similarities and differences in things. Ask them questions of clarification, such as "What is the main point?" and "Why?" Ask children to justify their opinion. Ask them "what if" questions.

- *Be a good cognitive role model.* Model thinking and self-reflection for the child to see and hear. When children are around people who think critically and reflectively, they incorporate these cognitive styles into their own thinking repertoire.

- *Encourage collaboration with other children.* Children learn not only from adults but from other children as well. Cross-age teaching, in which older children who are competent thinkers interact with younger children, can be especially helpful. Collaborative problem solving teaches children how to work cooperatively with others.

- *Stimulate children's creative thinking.* Encourage children to take risks in their thinking. Don't overcontrol by telling children precisely what to do; let their originality come through. Don't set up grandiose expectations; it can hurt creativity. Encourage the child to think freely and come up with as many different ways of doing something as possible.

RESOURCES

ERIC Database
www.eric.ed.gov

ERIC provides wide-ranging references to many educational topics, including educational practices, parent-school relations, and community programs.

National Association for Gifted Children (NAGC)
www.nagc.org

The NAGC is an association of academics, educators, and librarians. Its goal is to improve the education of gifted children. It publishes periodic reports on the education of gifted children and the journal *Gifted Children Quarterly.*

Mindset (2006)
Carol Dweck
New York: Random House

An outstanding book that emphasizes how important it is for parents, teachers, and other adults to guide children in developing a growth rather than a fixed mindset.

Motivation at School (2016)
Edited by Kathryn Wentzel and David Miele
New York: Routledge

A contemporary look at many aspects of schools that influence students' achievement.

chapter 13

SOCIOEMOTIONAL DEVELOPMENT IN MIDDLE AND LATE CHILDHOOD

chapter outline

① What Is the Nature of Emotional and Personality Development in Middle and Late Childhood?

Learning Goal 1 Discuss emotional and personality development in middle and late childhood.

The Self
Emotional Development
Moral Development
Gender

② What Are Some Changes in Parenting and Families in Middle and Late Childhood?

Learning Goal 2 Describe changes in parenting and families in middle and late childhood.

Developmental Changes in Parent-Child Relationships
Parents as Managers
Stepfamilies

③ What Changes Characterize Peer Relationships in Middle and Late Childhood?

Learning Goal 3 Identify changes in peer relationships in middle and late childhood.

Developmental Changes
Peer Status
Social Cognition
Bullying
Friends

④ What Are Some Important Aspects of Schools?

Learning Goal 4 Characterize contemporary approaches to student learning and sociocultural diversity in schools.

Contemporary Approaches to Student Learning
Socioeconomic Status and Ethnicity

©Will & Deni McIntyre/Corbis/Getty Images

At P.S. 30 in the South Bronx, Mr. Bedrock teaches fifth grade. One student in his class, Serafina, recently lost her mother to AIDS. When author Jonathan Kozol visited the class, he was told that two other children had taken the role of "allies in the child's struggle for emotional survival" (Kozol, 2005, p. 291).

Textbooks are in short supply for the class, and the social studies text is so out of date it claims that Ronald Reagan is the country's president. But Mr. Bedrock told Kozol that it's a "wonderful" class this year. About their teacher, 56-year-old Mr. Bedrock, one student said, "'He's getting old, . . . but we love him anyway'" (p. 292). Kozol found the students orderly, interested, and engaged.

By late childhood, most children, like these students at P.S. 30, have developed friendships, learned to interact with adults other than their parents, and developed ideas about fairness and other moral concepts.

Can children understand such concepts as discrimination, economic inequality, affirmative action, and comparable worth? Probably not, if you use those terms when talking with them. But Phyllis Katz (1987) found that children can understand situations that involve those concepts. Katz (1987) asked elementary-school-age children to pretend that they had taken a long ride on a spaceship to a make-believe planet called Pax. Once there, the children find problematic situations. For example, citizens of Pax who had dotted noses couldn't get jobs. Instead, the jobs went to the people with striped noses. "What would you do in this situation?" Katz asked the children.

She asked them for their opinions about various situations on this faraway planet. For example, what should a teacher do when two students were tied for a prize or when they had been fighting? The elementary school children often came up with interesting solutions to problems. For example, all but two children believed that teachers should earn as much as janitors—the

What are some of the challenges faced by children growing up in the South Bronx?
©Andy Levin/Science Source

--topical **connections**   *looking **back***

In "Socioemotional Development in Early Childhood," you learned that young children are in Erikson's stage of initiative versus guilt, parents continue to play an important role in their development, and a style of authoritative parenting is most likely to have positive outcomes for children. In early childhood, peer relations take on a more significant role as children's social worlds widen. Play has a special place in young children's lives and is an important context for both cognitive and socioemotional development. In the preceding chapter you studied children's cognitive development in middle and late childhood, including Piaget's view of children's thinking, their intelligence, language skills, and achievement. In this chapter, you will explore continuing advances in many aspects of children's socioemotional development.

holdouts said teachers should make less because they stay in one room or because cleaning toilets is more disgusting and therefore deserves higher wages. All but one thought that not giving a job to a qualified applicant who had different physical characteristics (a dotted rather than a striped nose) was unfair. War was mentioned as the biggest problem on Earth, although children were not certain whether it was currently occurring. Overall, the types of rules the children believed a society should abide by were quite sensible—almost all included the need for equitable sharing of resources and work and prohibitions against aggression.

preview

The years of middle and late childhood bring many changes to children's social and emotional lives. The development of their self-concepts, emotions, moral reasoning, and gendered behavior is significant. Transformations in their relationships with parents and peers also occur, and school-ing takes on a more academic flavor.

1 What Is the Nature of Emotional and Personality Development in Middle and Late Childhood?

LG1 Discuss emotional and personality development in middle and late childhood.

The Self   Emotional Development   Moral Development   Gender

In this section, we explore how the self continues to develop during middle and late childhood and the emotional changes that take place during these years. We also discuss children's moral development and many aspects of the role that gender plays in their development in middle and late childhood.

THE SELF

What is the nature of the child's self-understanding, understanding of others, and self-esteem during the elementary school years? What role does self-regulation play in children's achievement?

The Development of Self-Understanding   In middle and late childhood, espe-cially from 8 to 11 years of age, children increasingly describe themselves in terms of psy-chological characteristics and traits, in contrast to the more concrete self-descriptions of younger children. Older children are more likely to describe themselves as "popular, nice, helpful, mean, smart, and dumb" (Harter, 2006, p. 526).

In addition, during the elementary school years, children become more likely to recognize social aspects of the self (Harter, 2006, 2012, 2016). These include references to social groups in their self-descriptions, such as referring to themselves as a Girl Scout, as a Catholic, or as someone who has two close friends (Lively & Bromley, 1973).

Children's self-understanding in the elementary school years also includes increasing refer-ence to social comparison (Harter, 2006, 2012, 2016). At this point in development, children are more likely to distinguish themselves from others in comparative rather than in absolute terms. That is, elementary-school-aged children are no longer as likely to think about what they do or do not do, but are more likely to think about what they can do in comparison with others.

Consider a series of studies in which Diane Ruble (1983) investigated children's use of social comparison in their self-evaluations. Children were given a difficult task and then offered feedback on their performance, as well as information about the performances of other

Children are busy becoming something they have not quite grasped yet, something which keeps changing.

—Alastair Reid
American Poet, 20th Century

How Would You...?
If you were a **psychologist,** how would you explain the role of social comparison in the development of a child's sense of self?

What are some changes in children's understanding of others in middle and late childhood?
©asiseeit/E+/Getty Images RF

children their age. The children were then asked for self-evaluations. Children younger than 7 made virtually no reference to the information about other children's performances. However, many children older than 7 included socially comparative information in their self-descriptions.

In sum, in middle and late childhood, self-description increasingly involves psychological and social characteristics, including social comparison.

Understanding Others Earlier, we described the advances and limitations of young children's understanding of others. In middle and late childhood, children show an increase in *perspective taking,* the ability to take other people's perspectives and understand their thoughts and feelings. In terms of antisocial behavior, recent research indicates that children and adolescents who do not have good perspective-taking skills are more likely to have difficulty in peer relations and engage in more aggressive and oppositional behavior (Morosan & others, 2017; Nilsen & Basco, 2017; O'Kearney & others, 2017).

In Robert Selman's (1980) view, at about 6 to 8 years of age, children begin to understand that others may have a different perspective because some people have more access to information. Then, he says, in the next several years, children become aware that each individual is aware of the other's perspective and that putting oneself in the other's place is a way of judging the other person's intentions, purposes, and actions.

Perspective taking is especially thought to be important in relation to whether children develop prosocial or antisocial attitudes and behavior. In terms of prosocial behavior, taking another's perspective improves children's likelihood of understanding and sympathizing with others who are distressed or in need. A recent study revealed that in children characterized as being emotionally reactive, good perspective-taking skills were linked to being able to regain a neutral emotional state after being emotionally aroused (Bengtsson & Arvidsson, 2011). In this study, children who made gains in perspective-taking skills reduced their emotional reactivity over a two-year period.

In middle and late childhood, children also become more skeptical of others' claims (Heyman, Fu, & Lee, 2013; Mills & Elashi, 2014). Even 4-year-old children show some skepticism of others' claims. In middle and late childhood, children become increasingly skeptical of some sources of information about psychological traits. For example, in one study, 10- to 11-year-olds were more likely to reject other children's self-reports that they were *smart* and *honest* than were 6- to 7-year-olds (Heyman & Legare, 2005). The more psychologically sophisticated 10- to 11-year-olds also showed a better understanding that others' self-reports may involve socially desirable tendencies than did the 6- to 7-year-olds. A recent study of 6- to 9-year-olds revealed that older children were less trusting and more skeptical of others' distorted claims than were younger children (Mills & Elashi, 2014).

How Would You...?
If you were an **educator,** *how would you work with children to help them develop a healthy self-concept concerning their academic ability?*

Self-Esteem and Self-Concept High self-esteem and a positive self-concept are important characteristics of children's well-being (Harter, 2006, 2012, 2016; Kadir & Yeung, 2018). Investigators sometimes use the terms *self-esteem* and *self-concept* interchangeably or do not precisely define them, but there is a meaningful difference between them. **Self-esteem** refers to global evaluations of the self; it is also called self-worth or self-image. For example, a child may perceive that she is not merely a person but a good person. **Self-concept** refers to domain-specific evaluations of the self. Children can make self-evaluations in many domains of their lives—academic, athletic, appearance, and so on. In sum, self-esteem refers to global self-evaluations, self-concept to domain-specific evaluations.

For most children, high self-esteem and a positive self-concept are important aspects of their well-being (Harter, 2012, 2013, 2016). However, for some children, self-esteem reflects perceptions that do not always match reality (Jordan & Zeigler-Hill, 2013). A child's self-esteem might reflect a belief about whether he or she is intelligent and attractive, for example, but that belief is not necessarily accurate. Thus, high self-esteem may refer to accurate, justified perceptions of one's worth as a person and one's successes and accomplishments, but it can also refer to an arrogant, grandiose, unwarranted sense of superiority over others. In the same manner, low self-esteem may reflect either an accurate perception of one's shortcomings or a distorted, even pathological insecurity and inferiority.

What are the consequences of low self-esteem? Low self-esteem has been implicated in overweight and obesity, anxiety, depression, suicide, and delinquency (Hill, 2016; Orth &

self-esteem The global evaluative dimension of the self. Self-esteem is also referred to as self-worth or self-image.

self-concept Domain-specific evaluations of the self.

others, 2016; Paxton & Damiano, 2017; Rieger & others, 2016; Stadelmann & others, 2017). One study revealed that youth with low self-esteem had lower life satisfaction at 30 years of age (Birkeland & others, 2012). Another study found that low and decreasing self-esteem in adolescence were linked to adult depression two decades later (Steiger & others, 2014).

The foundations of self-esteem and self-concept emerge from the quality of parent-child interaction in infancy and childhood. Children with high self-esteem are more likely to be securely attached to their parents and to have parents who engage in sensitive caregiving (Thompson, 2015). And in a longitudinal study, the quality of children's home environment (which involved assessment of parenting quality, cognitive stimulation, and the physical home environment) was linked to their self-esteem in early adulthood (Orth, 2017).

What are some issues involved in understanding children's self-esteem in school?
©Inti St. Clair/Getty Images RF

Although variations in self-esteem have been linked with many aspects of children's development, much of the research is *correlational* rather than *experimental*. Recall that correlation does not equal causation. Thus, if a correlational study finds an association between children's low self-esteem and low academic achievement, low academic achievement could cause the low self-esteem as much as low self-esteem causes low academic achievement. A recent longitudinal study examined whether self-esteem is a cause or consequence of social support in youth (Marshall & others, 2014). In this study, self-esteem predicted subsequent changes in social support but social support did not predict subsequent changes in self-esteem.

In fact, there are only moderate correlations between school performance and self-esteem, and these correlations do not suggest that high self-esteem produces better school performance (Baumeister & others, 2003). Efforts to increase students' self-esteem have not always led to improved school performance (Davies & Brember, 1999).

Children with high self-esteem have greater initiative, but this can produce positive or negative outcomes (Baumeister & others, 2003). High-self-esteem children are prone to both prosocial and antisocial actions. A study revealed that over time aggressive children with high self-esteem increasingly valued the rewards that aggression can bring and belittled their victims (Menon & others, 2007).

In addition, a current concern is that too many of today's children grow up receiving praise for mediocre or even poor performance and as a consequence have inflated self-esteem (Stipek, 2005). They may have difficulty handling competition and criticism. This theme is vividly captured by the title of a book, *Dumbing Down Our Kids: Why American Children Feel Good About Themselves But Can't Read, Write, or Add* (Sykes, 1995). In a series of studies, researchers found that inflated praise, although well intended, may cause children with low self-esteem to avoid important learning experiences such as tackling challenging tasks (Brummelman & others, 2014).

What are some good strategies for effectively increasing children's self-esteem? See the *Caring Connections* interlude for some answers to this question.

Self-Regulation   One of the most important aspects of the self in middle and late childhood is the increased capacity for self-regulation (Blair, 2016; Blair, Raver, & Finegood, 2016; Eisenberg, Smith, & Spinrad, 2016; Schunk & Greene, 2018; Winne, 2018). This increased capacity is characterized by deliberate efforts to manage one's behavior, emotions, and thoughts that lead to increased social competence and achievement (Duncan, McClelland, & Acock, 2017; Eisenberg, Spinrad, & Valiente, 2016; Galinsky & others, 2017; Neuenschwander & Blair, 2017; Usher & Schunk, 2018). For example, one study revealed that children from low-income families who had a higher level of self-regulation earned higher grades in school than their counterparts who had a lower level of self-regulation (Buckner, Mezzacappa, & Beardslee, 2009). Another study found that self-control increased from 4 to 10 years of age and that high self-control was linked to lower levels of deviant behavior (Vazsonyi & Huang, 2010). Also, a recent study of almost 17,000 3- to 7-year-old children revealed that self-regulation was a protective factor for children growing up in low-socioeconomic-status (low-SES) conditions (Flouri, Midouhas, & Joshi, 2014). In this study, 7-year-old children with low self-regulation living in low-SES conditions had more emotional problems than their 3-year-old counterparts.

Increasing Children's Self-Esteem

Four ways children's self-esteem can be improved include identifying the causes of low self-esteem, providing emotional support and social approval, helping children achieve, and helping children cope (Bednar, Wells, & Peterson, 1995; Harter, 2006, 2012, 2016):

- *Identify the causes of low self-esteem.* Intervention should target the causes of low self-esteem. Children have the highest self-esteem when they perform competently in domains that are important to them. Therefore, children should be encouraged to identify and value areas of competence. These areas might include academic skills, athletic skills, physical attractiveness, and social acceptance.
- *Provide emotional support and social approval.* Some children with low self-esteem come from conflicted families or conditions in which they experienced abuse or neglect—situations in which support was not available. In some cases, alternative sources of support can be arranged either informally through the encouragement of a teacher, a coach, or another significant adult, or more formally through programs such as Big Brothers and Big Sisters.
- *Help children achieve.* Achievement also can improve children's self-esteem (Mruk & O'Brien, 2013). For example, the straightforward teaching of real skills to children often results in increased achievement and, thus, in enhanced self-esteem. Children develop higher self-esteem because they know the important tasks that will achieve their goals, and they have performed them or similar behaviors in the past.

How can parents help children develop healthy self-esteem?
©KidStock/Blend Images LLC RF

- *Help children cope.* Self-esteem is often increased when children face a problem and try to cope with it, rather than avoid it. If coping rather than avoidance prevails, children often face problems realistically, honestly, and nondefensively. This produces favorable self-evaluative thoughts, which lead to the self-generated approval that raises self-esteem.

What characterizes Erikson's stage of industry versus inferiority?
©Jim Craigmyle/Corbis/Getty Images

developmental connection

Erikson's Theory

Initiative versus guilt is Erikson's early childhood stage and identity versus identity confusion is his adolescence stage. Connect to "Socioemotional Development in Early Childhood" and "Socioemotional Development in Adolescence."

Thus, low self-regulation was linked to a widening gap in low-SES children's emotional problems over time. And in a recent study, higher levels of self-control assessed at 4 years of age were linked to improvements in the math and reading achievement of early elementary school children living in predominantly rural and low-income contexts (Blair & others, 2015).

The increased capacity for self-regulation is linked to developmental advances in the brain's prefrontal cortex, a topic that was discussed in "Cognitive Development in Middle and Late Childhood" (Bell & others, 2018; Wendelken & others, 2016; Zelazo, 2013). In that discussion, increased focal activation in the prefrontal cortex was linked to improved cognitive control. Such cognitive control includes self-regulation (Schunk & Greene, 2018). An app for iPads has been developed to help children improve their self-regulation (for more information, go to www.selfregulationstation.com/sr-ipad-app/).

Industry Versus Inferiority Earlier, we discussed Erik Erikson's (1968) eight stages of human development. His fourth stage, industry versus inferiority, appears during middle and late childhood. The term *industry* expresses a dominant theme of this period: Children become interested in how things are made and how they work. When children are encouraged in their efforts to make, build, and work—whether they are building a model airplane, constructing a tree house, fixing a bicycle, solving an addition problem, or cooking—their sense of industry increases. However, parents who see their children's efforts at making things as "mischief" or "making a mess" can cause children to develop a sense of inferiority.

Children's social worlds beyond their families also contribute to a sense of industry. School becomes especially important in this regard. Consider children who are slightly below average in intelligence. They are too bright to be in special classes but not bright enough to be in gifted classes. Failing frequently in their academic efforts, they develop a sense of inferiority. By contrast, consider children whose sense of industry is disparaged at home. A series of sensitive and committed teachers may revitalize their sense of industry (Elkind, 1970).

EMOTIONAL DEVELOPMENT

Preschoolers become more adept at talking about their own and others' emotions. They also show a growing awareness of the need to control and manage their emotions to meet social standards. In middle and late childhood, children further develop their understanding and self-regulation of emotion (Calkins & Perry, 2016; Calkins, Perry, & Dollar, 2016; Cole, 2016).

Developmental Changes Developmental changes in emotions during the middle and late childhood years include the following (Denham, Bassett, & Wyatt, 2007, 2015; Denham & others, 2013; Goodvin, Thompson, & Winer, 2015; Kuebli, 1994; Thompson, 2015):

What are some developmental changes in emotion during the middle and late childhood years?
©Kevin Dodge/Corbis

- *Improved emotional understanding.* For example, children in elementary school develop an increased ability to understand such complex emotions as pride and shame. These emotions become less tied to the reactions of other people; they become more self-generated and integrated with a sense of personal responsibility. Also, during middle and late childhood as part of their understanding of emotions, children can engage in "mental time travel," in which they anticipate and recall the cognitive and emotional aspects of events (Kramer & Lagattuta, 2018; Hjortsvang & Lagattuta, 2017; Lagattuta, 2014a, b).

- *Increased understanding that more than one emotion can be experienced in a particular situation.* A third-grader, for example, may realize that achieving something might involve both anxiety and joy.

- *Increased tendency to be aware of the events leading to emotional reactions.* A fourth-grader may become aware that her sadness today is influenced by her friend's moving to another town last week.

- *Ability to suppress or conceal negative emotional reactions.* When one of his classmates irritates him, a fifth-grader has learned to tone down his anger better than he used to.

- *The use of self-initiated strategies for redirecting feelings.* In the elementary school years, children become more reflective about their emotional lives and increasingly use strategies to control their emotions. They become more effective at cognitively managing their emotions, such as soothing themselves after an upset.

- *A capacity for genuine empathy.* For example, a fourth-grader feels sympathy for a distressed person and experiences vicariously the sadness the distressed person is feeling.

Attachment in Middle and Late Childhood You have read about the importance of secure attachment in infancy and the role of sensitive parenting in attachment (Bretherton & Munholland, 2016; Hoffman & others, 2017; Roisman & Cicchetti, 2018; Thompson, 2015, 2016). The attachment process continues to be an important aspect of children's development in the childhood years. In middle and late childhood, attachment becomes more sophisticated and as children's social worlds expand to include peers, teachers, and others, they typically spend less time with parents.

How does attachment change during middle and late childhood?
©Hero Images/Corbis RF

Kathryn Kerns and her colleagues (Movahed Abtahi & Kerns, 2017; Brumariu & Kerns, 2013; Brumariu, Kerns, & Seibert, 2012; Kerns & Brumariu, 2016; Kerns & Seibert, 2012, 2016; Kerns, Siener, & Brumariu, 2011; Siener & Kerns, 2012) have studied links between attachment to parents and various child outcomes in middle and late childhood. They have found that during this period of development, secure attachment is associated with a lower level of internalized symptoms, anxiety, and depression in children (Brumariu & Kerns, 2011, 2013). For example, a recent study revealed that children who were less securely attached to their mothers reported having more anxiety (Brumariu, Kerns, & Seibert, 2012). Also in this study, secure attachment was linked to a higher level of children's emotion regulation and less difficulty in identifying emotions.

Social-Emotional Education Programs An increasing number of social-emotional educational programs have been developed to improve many aspects of children's and adolescents' lives. Two such programs are the Second Step program created by the Committee for Children (2017) and the Collaborative for Academic, Social, and Emotional Learning (CASEL, 2017). Many social-emotional education programs only target young children, but Second Step can be implemented in pre-K through eighth grade and CASEL can used with pre-K through twelfth-grade students.

What characterizes social-emotional programs for children?
©Antonio Perez/MCT/Newscom

- *Second Step* focuses on these aspects of social-emotional learning from pre-K through the eighth grade: (1) pre-K: self-regulation and executive function skills that improve their attention and help them control their behavior; (2) K–grade 5: making friends, self-regulation of emotion, and solving problems; and (3) grades 6–8: communication skills, coping with stress, and decision making to avoid engaging in problem behaviors.
- *CASEL* targets five core social and emotional learning domains: (1) self-awareness (recognizing one's emotions and how they affect behavior, for example); (2) self-management (self-control, coping with stress, and impulse control, for example); (3) social awareness (perspective taking and empathy, for example); (4) relationship skills (developing positive relationships and communicating effectively with individuals from diverse backgrounds, for example); and (5) responsible decision making (engaging in ethical behavior, and understanding the consequences of one's actions, for example).

Coping with Stress   An important aspect of children's lives is learning how to cope with stress (Brenner, 2016; Cicchetti, 2017; Lieberman & Chu, 2016). As children get older, they are able to more accurately appraise a stressful situation and determine how much control they have over it. Older children generate more coping alternatives to stressful conditions and use more cognitive coping strategies (Saarni & others, 2006). For example, older children are better than younger children at intentionally shifting their thoughts to something that is less stressful. Older children are also better at reframing, or changing their perception of a stressful situation. For example, younger children may be very disappointed that their teacher did not say hello to them when they arrived at school. Older children may reframe this type of situation and think, "She may have been busy with other things and just forgot to say hello."

By 10 years of age, most children are able to use cognitive strategies to cope with stress (Saarni & others, 2006). However, in families that have not been supportive and are characterized by turmoil or trauma, children may be so overwhelmed by stress that they do not use such strategies (Thabet & others, 2009).

Disasters can especially harm children's development and produce adjustment problems (Masten, 2017). Among the outcomes for children who experience disasters are acute stress reactions, depression, panic disorder, and post-traumatic stress disorder (Danielson & others, 2017; Lieber, 2017). Proportions of children developing these problems following a disaster depend on factors such as the nature and severity of the disaster, as well as the support available to the children. Also, children who have developed a number of coping techniques have the best chance of adapting and functioning competently in the face of disasters and trauma (Ungar, 2015).

Following are descriptions of recent studies of how various aspects of traumatic events and disasters affect children:

What are some effective strategies to help children cope with traumatic events, such as the terrorist attacks on the United States on 9/11/2001, and the mass shooting at Sandy Hook Elementary School in Connecticut?
©Stephanie Keith/Polaris/Newscom

- In a study of mothers and their children aged 5 years and younger who were directly exposed to the 9/11 attacks in New York City, the mothers who developed post-traumatic stress disorder (PTSD) and depression were less likely to help their children regulate their emotions and behavior than mothers who were only depressed or only had PTSD (Chemtob & others, 2010). This outcome was linked to their children having anxiety, depression, aggression, and sleep problems.
- A study of the effects of the 2004 tsunami in Sri Lanka found that severe exposure to the tsunami combined with more exposure to other adversities, such as an ongoing war and family violence, was linked to poorer adjustment after the tsunami disaster (Catani & others, 2010).
- A research review revealed that children with disabilities are more likely than children without disabilities to live in poverty conditions, which increases their exposure to hazards and disasters (Peek & Stough, 2010). When a disaster occurs, children with disabilities have more difficulty escaping from the disaster.

In research on disasters and trauma, the term *dose-response effects* is often used. A widely supported finding in this research area is that the more severe the disaster or trauma (dose) is, the worse the adaptation and adjustment (response) following the event (Masten, 2017; Masten & others, 2015).

Children who have a number of coping techniques have the best chance of adapting and functioning competently in the face of disasters and traumas. Following are some recommendations for helping children cope with the stress of especially devastating events (Gurwitch & others, 2001, pp. 4–11):

How Would You...?
If you were a **social worker,** how would you counsel a child who had been exposed to a traumatic event?

- *Reassure children of their safety and security.* This step may need to be taken numerous times.
- *Allow children to retell events and be patient in listening to them.*
- *Encourage children to talk about any disturbing or confusing feelings.* Tell them that these are normal feelings after a stressful event.
- *Help children make sense of what happened.* Children may misunderstand what took place. For example, young children "may blame themselves, believe things happened that did not happen, believe that terrorists are in the school, etc. Gently help children develop a realistic understanding of the event" (p. 10).
- *Protect children from reexposure to frightening situations and reminders of the trauma.* This strategy includes limiting conversations about the event in front of the children.

MORAL DEVELOPMENT

Recall our description of Piaget's view of moral development. Piaget proposed that younger children are characterized by *heteronomous morality* but that, by 10 years of age, they have moved into a higher stage called *autonomous morality.* According to Piaget, older children consider the intentions of the individual, believe that rules are subject to change, and are aware that punishment does not always follow wrongdoing. Let's now explore some other views of moral development.

Kohlberg's Theory   A second major perspective on moral development was proposed by Lawrence Kohlberg (1958, 1986). Piaget's cognitive stages of development serve as the underpinnings for Kohlberg's theory, but Kohlberg suggested that there are six stages of moral development. These stages, he argued, are universal. Development from one stage to another, said Kohlberg, is fostered by opportunities to take the perspective of others and to experience conflict between one's current stage of moral thinking and the reasoning of someone at a higher stage.

Kohlberg arrived at his view after 20 years of using a unique interview with children. In the interview, children are presented with a series of stories in which characters face moral dilemmas. The following is the most popular Kohlberg dilemma:

> In Europe a woman was near death from a special kind of cancer. There was one drug that the doctors thought might save her. It was a form of radium that a druggist in the same town had recently discovered. The drug was expensive to make, but the druggist was charging ten times what the drug cost him to make. He paid $200 for the radium and charged $2,000 for a small dose of the drug. The sick woman's husband, Heinz, went to everyone he knew to borrow the money, but he could only get together $1,000, which is half of what it cost. He told the druggist that his wife was dying and asked him to sell it cheaper or let him pay later. But the druggist said, "No, I discovered the drug, and I am going to make money from it." So Heinz got desperate and broke into the man's store to steal the drug for his wife. (Kohlberg, 1969, p. 379)

This story is one of eleven that Kohlberg devised to investigate the nature of moral thought. After reading the story, the interviewee answers a series of questions about the moral dilemma. Should Heinz have stolen the drug? Was stealing it right or wrong? Why? Is it a husband's duty to steal the drug for his wife if he can get it no other way? Would a good husband steal? Did the druggist have the right to charge that much when there was no law setting a limit on the price? Why or why not?

The Kohlberg Stages   Based on the answers interviewees gave for this and other moral dilemmas, Kohlberg described three levels of moral thinking, each of which is characterized by two stages (see Figure 1). A key concept in understanding progression through the levels and stages is that their morality becomes more internal or mature. That is, their reasons for their moral decisions or values begin to go beyond the external or superficial reasons they gave when they were younger. Let's further examine Kohlberg's stages.

Lawrence Kohlberg, the architect of a provocative cognitive developmental theory of moral development. *What is the nature of his theory?*
Harvard University Archives, UAV 605.295.8, Box 7, Kohlberg

LEVEL 1	LEVEL 2	LEVEL 3
Preconventional Level **No Internalization**	**Conventional Level** **Intermediate Internalization**	**Postconventional Level** **Full Internalization**
Stage 1 Heteronomous Morality	**Stage 3** Mutual Interpersonal Expectations, Relationships, and Interpersonal Conformity	**Stage 5** Social Contract or Utility and Individual Rights
Children obey because adults tell them to obey. People base their moral decisions on fear of punishment.	*Individuals value trust, caring, and loyalty to others as a basis for moral judgments.*	*Individuals reason that values, rights, and principles undergird or transcend the law.*
Stage 2 Individualism, Instrumental Purpose, and Exchange	**Stage 4** Social Systems Morality	**Stage 6** Universal Ethical Principles
Individuals pursue their own interests but let others do the same. What is right involves equal exchange.	*Moral judgments are based on understanding and the social order, law, justice, and duty.*	*The person has developed moral judgments that are based on universal human rights. When faced with a dilemma between law and conscience, a personal, individualized conscience is followed.*

FIGURE **1**

KOHLBERG'S THREE LEVELS AND SIX STAGES OF MORAL DEVELOPMENT. Kohlberg argued that people everywhere develop their moral reasoning by passing through these age-based stages. *Where does Kohlberg's theory stand on the nature-nurture and continuity-discontinuity issues?*

preconventional reasoning The lowest level in Kohlberg's theory of moral development. The individual's concept of good and bad is interpreted primarily in terms of external rewards and punishment.

heteronomous morality Kohlberg's first stage in preconventional reasoning in which moral thinking is tied to punishment.

individualism, instrumental purpose, and exchange The second Kohlberg stage in preconventional reasoning. At this stage, individuals pursue their own interests but also let others do the same.

conventional reasoning The second, or intermediate, level in Kohlberg's theory of moral development. At this level, individuals abide by certain standards, but they are standards set by others such as parents or the government.

mutual interpersonal expectations, relationships, and interpersonal conformity Kohlberg's third stage of moral development. At this stage, individuals value trust, caring, and loyalty to others as a basis of moral judgments.

social systems morality The fourth stage in Kohlberg's theory of moral development. Moral judgments are based on understanding the social order, law, justice, and duty.

postconventional reasoning The highest level in Kohlberg's theory of moral development. At this level, the individual recognizes alternative moral courses, explores the options, and then decides on a personal moral code.

Preconventional reasoning is the lowest level of moral reasoning, said Kohlberg. At this level, good and bad are interpreted in terms of external rewards and punishments.

- *Stage 1.* **Heteronomous morality** is the first stage in preconventional reasoning. At this stage, moral thinking is tied to punishment. For example, children think that they must obey because they fear punishment for disobedience.
- *Stage 2.* **Individualism, instrumental purpose, and exchange** is the second stage of preconventional reasoning. At this stage, individuals reason that pursuing their own interests is the right thing to do, but they let others do the same. Thus, they think that what is right involves an equal exchange. They reason that if they are nice to others, others will be nice to them in return.

Conventional reasoning is the second, or intermediate, level in Kohlberg's theory of moral development. At this level, individuals apply certain standards, but they are the standards set by others, such as parents or the government.

- *Stage 3.* **Mutual interpersonal expectations, relationships, and interpersonal conformity** is Kohlberg's third stage of moral development. At this stage, individuals value trust, caring, and loyalty to others as a basis for moral judgments. Children and adolescents often adopt their parents' moral standards at this stage, seeking to be thought of by their parents as a "good girl" or a "good boy."
- *Stage 4.* **Social systems morality** is the fourth stage in Kohlberg's theory of moral development. At this stage, moral judgments are based on understanding the social order, law, justice, and duty. For example, adolescents may reason that in order for a community to work effectively, it needs to be protected by laws that are adhered to by its members.

Postconventional reasoning is the highest level in Kohlberg's theory of moral development. At this level, the individual recognizes alternative moral courses, explores the options, and then decides on a personal moral code.

- *Stage 5.* **Social contract or utility and individual rights** is the fifth Kohlberg stage. At this stage, individuals reason that values, rights, and principles undergird or transcend the law. A person evaluates the validity of actual laws and realizes that social systems can be examined in terms of the degree to which they preserve and protect fundamental human rights and values.
- *Stage 6.* **Universal ethical principles** is the sixth and highest stage in Kohlberg's theory of moral development. At this stage, the person has developed a moral standard

based on universal human rights. When faced with a conflict between law and conscience, the person reasons that conscience should be followed, even though the decision might bring risk.

Kohlberg held that these levels and stages occur in a sequence and are age-related. Before age 9, most children use level 1, preconventional reasoning based on external rewards and punishments, when they consider moral choices. By early adolescence, their moral reasoning is increasingly based on the application of standards set by others. Most adolescents reason at stage 3, with some signs of stages 2 and 4. By early adulthood, a small number of individuals reason in postconventional ways.

What evidence supports this description of development? A 20-year longitudinal investigation found that use of stages 1 and 2 decreased with age (Colby & others, 1983) (see Figure 2). Stage 4, which did not appear at all in the moral reasoning of 10-year-olds, was reflected in the moral thinking of 62 percent of the 36-year-olds. Stage 5 did not appear until age 20 to 22 and never characterized more than 10 percent of the individuals.

Thus, the moral stages appeared somewhat later than Kohlberg initially envisioned, and reasoning at the higher stages, especially stage 6, was rare. Although stage 6 has been removed from the Kohlberg moral judgment scoring manual, it still is considered to be theoretically important in the Kohlberg scheme of moral development.

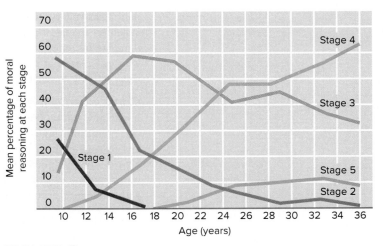

FIGURE 2

AGE AND THE PERCENTAGE OF INDIVIDUALS AT EACH KOHLBERG STAGE. In one longitudinal study of males from 10 to 36 years of age, at age 10 most moral reasoning was at stage 2 (Colby & others, 1983). At 16 to 18 years of age, stage 3 became the most frequent type of moral reasoning, and it was not until the mid-twenties that stage 4 became the most frequent. Stage 5 did not appear until 20 to 22 years of age, and it never characterized more than 10 percent of the individuals. In this study, the moral stages appeared somewhat later than Kohlberg envisioned, and stage 6 was absent. *Do you think it matters that all of the participants in this study were males? Why or why not?*

Influences on the Kohlberg Stages What factors influence movement through Kohlberg's stages? Although moral reasoning at each stage presupposes a certain level of cognitive development, Kohlberg argued that advances in children's cognitive development did not ensure development of moral reasoning. Instead, moral reasoning also reflects children's experiences in dealing with moral questions and moral conflict.

Several investigators have tried to advance individuals' levels of moral development by having a model present arguments that reflect moral thinking one stage above the individuals' established levels. This approach applies the concepts of equilibrium and conflict that Piaget used to explain cognitive development. By presenting arguments slightly beyond the children's level of moral reasoning, the researchers created a disequilibrium that motivated the children to restructure their moral thought. The upshot of studies using this approach is that virtually any plus-stage discussion, for any length of time, seems to promote more advanced moral reasoning (Walker, 1982).

Kohlberg emphasized that peer interaction and perspective taking are critical aspects of the social stimulation that challenges children to change their moral reasoning. Whereas adults characteristically impose rules and regulations on children, the give-and-take among peers gives children an opportunity to take the perspective of another person and to generate rules democratically. Kohlberg stressed that in principle, encounters with any peers can produce perspective-taking opportunities that may advance a child's moral reasoning. A research review of cross-cultural studies involving Kohlberg's theory revealed strong support for a link between perspective-taking skills and more advanced moral judgments (Gibbs & others, 2007).

Kohlberg's Critics Kohlberg's theory has provoked debate, research, and criticism (Graham & others, 2017; Gray & Graham, 2018; Hoover & others, 2018; Killen & Dahl, 2018; Narváez, 2015, 2016, 2017a, b, 2018; Railton, 2017; Turiel & Gingo, 2017). Key criticisms involve the link between moral thought and moral behavior, whether moral reasoning is conscious/deliberative or unconscious/automatic, the role of emotion, the importance of culture and the family in moral development, the significance of concern for others, moral personality, and domain theory.

Moral Thought and Moral Behavior Kohlberg's theory has been criticized for placing too much emphasis on moral thought and not enough emphasis on moral behavior (Walker, 2004). Moral reasons can sometimes be a shelter for immoral behavior. Corrupt CEOs and

How Would You...?
If you were a **human development and family studies professional,** how would you explain the progression of moral reasoning skills that develop during the elementary school years?

developmental **connection**

Peers

Piaget argued that the mutual give-and-take of peer relations is more important than parenting in enhancing children's moral reasoning. Connect to "Socioemotional Development in Early Childhood."

social contract or utility and individual rights The fifth Kohlberg stage. At this stage, individuals reason that values, rights, and principles undergird or transcend the law.

universal ethical principles The sixth and highest stage in Kohlberg's theory of moral development. Individuals develop a moral standard based on universal principles of human rights.

politicians endorse the loftiest of moral virtues in public before their own behavior is exposed. Whatever the latest public scandal, you will probably find that the culprits displayed virtuous thoughts but engaged in immoral behavior. No one wants a nation of cheaters and thieves who can reason at the postconventional level. The cheaters and thieves may know what is right yet still do what is wrong. Heinous actions can be cloaked in a mantle of moral virtue.

Conscious/Deliberative Versus Unconscious/Automatic   Social psychologist Jonathan Haidt (2006, 2013, 2017) argues that a major flaw in Kohlberg's theory is his view that moral thinking is deliberative and that individuals go around all the time contemplating and reasoning about morality. Haidt believes that moral thinking is more often an intuitive gut reaction, with deliberative moral reasoning serving as an after-the-fact justification. Thus, in his view, much of morality begins with rapid evaluative judgments of others rather than with strategic reasoning about moral circumstances (Graham & Valdesolo, 2017).

The Role of Emotion   Kohlberg argued that emotion has negative effects on moral reasoning. However, increasing evidence indicates that emotions play an important role in moral thinking (Gui, Gan, & Liu, 2016; Schalkwijk & others, 2016). Researchers have found that individuals who have damage to a particular region in the brain's prefrontal cortex lose the ability to integrate emotions into their moral judgments (Damasio, 1994). Losing their intuitive feelings about what is right or wrong, they can't adequately decide which actions to take and have trouble making choices involving moral issues.

Research with healthy individuals also has shown that the moral decisions individuals make are linked to the intensity and activation of emotion in the same region of the prefrontal cortex mentioned and in the amygdala (Shenhav & Greene, 2014).

Culture and Moral Reasoning   Kohlberg emphasized that his stages of moral reasoning are universal, but some critics claim his theory is culturally biased (Christen, Narváez, & Gutzwiller, 2017; Graham & Valdesolo, 2017; Gray & Graham, 2018). Both Kohlberg and his critics may be partially correct. One review of 45 studies in 27 cultures around the world, mostly non-European, provided support for the universality of Kohlberg's first four stages (Snarey, 1987). Individuals in diverse cultures developed through these four stages in sequence as Kohlberg predicted. More recent research revealed support for the qualitative shift from stage 2 to stage 3 across cultures (Gibbs & others, 2007). Stages 5 and 6, however, have not been found in all cultures (Gibbs & others, 2007; Snarey, 1987). Furthermore, critics assert that Kohlberg's scoring system does not recognize the higher-level moral reasoning of certain cultures and thus does not acknowledge that moral reasoning is more culture-specific than Kohlberg envisioned (Snarey, 1987).

Darcia Narváez and Tracy Gleason (2013) have described cohort effects regarding moral reasoning. In recent years, postconventional moral reasoning has been declining in college students, not down to the next level (conventional) but to the lowest level (personal interests) (Thoma & Bebeau, 2008). Narváez and Gleason (2013) also argue that declines in prosocial behavior have occurred in recent years and that humans, especially those living in Western cultures, are "on a fast train to demise." They emphasize that the solution to improving people's moral lives lies in better child-rearing strategies and social supports for families and children. In more recent commentary, Narváez and her colleagues (Christen, Narváez, & Gutzwiller, 2017) stress that we need to make better progress in dealing with an increasing array of temptations and possible wrongdoings in a human social world in which complexity is accumulating over time.

In sum, although Kohlberg's approach does capture much of the moral reasoning voiced in various cultures around the world, his approach misses or misconstrues some important moral concepts in particular cultures (Gibbs, 2014; Miller & Bland, 2014).

Families and Moral Development   Kohlberg argued that family processes are essentially unimportant in children's moral development. As noted earlier, he argued that parent-child relationships usually provide children with little opportunity for give-and-take or perspective taking. Rather, Kohlberg said that such opportunities are more likely to be provided by children's peer relations.

Did Kohlberg underestimate the contribution of family relationships to moral development? A number of developmentalists emphasize that *inductive discipline*, which uses reasoning and focuses children's attention on the consequences of their actions for others, positively influences moral development (Grusec & others, 2014). They also stress that parents' moral values influence children's developing moral thoughts (Carlo & others, 2017; Eisenberg, Spinrad, & Knafo-Noam, 2015; Laible & Thompson, 2007). Nonetheless, most developmentalists agree with Kohlberg, and Piaget, that peers play an important role in the development of moral reasoning.

Gender and the Care Perspective   The most publicized criticism of Kohlberg's theory has come from Carol Gilligan (1982, 1992, 1996), who argues that Kohlberg's theory reflects a gender bias. According to Gilligan, Kohlberg's theory is based on a male norm that puts abstract principles above relationships and concern for others and sees the individual as standing alone and independently making moral decisions. It puts justice at the heart of morality. In contrast to Kohlberg's **justice perspective,** which focuses on the rights of the individual, Gilligan argues for a **care perspective,** which is a moral perspective that views people in terms of their connectedness with others and emphasizes interpersonal communication, relationships with others, and concern for others. According to Gilligan, Kohlberg greatly underplayed the care perspective, perhaps because he was a male, because most of his research was with males rather than females, and because he used male responses as a model for his theory.

In extensive interviews with girls from 6 to 18 years of age, Gilligan and her colleagues found that girls consistently interpret moral dilemmas in terms of human relationships and base these interpretations on watching and listening to other people (Gilligan, 1992; Gilligan & others, 2003). However, a meta-analysis (a statistical analysis that combines the results of many different studies) casts doubt on Gilligan's claim of substantial gender differences in moral judgment (Jaffee & Hyde, 2000). A review concluded that girls' moral orientations are "somewhat more likely to focus on care for others than on abstract principles of justice, but they can use both moral orientations when needed (as can boys . . .)" (Blakemore, Berenbaum, & Liben, 2009, p. 132).

Moral Personality   Beyond the development of moral reasoning and specific moral feelings and behaviors, do children also develop a pattern of moral characteristics that is distinctively their own? In other words, do children develop a *moral personality,* and if so, what are its components? Researchers have focused attention on three possible components: (1) moral identity, (2) moral character, and (3) moral exemplars:

- *Moral identity.* Individuals have a moral identity when moral notions and moral commitments are central to their lives (Matsuba, Murazyn, & Hart, 2014; Walker, 2014a, b, 2016). They construct the self with reference to moral categories. Violating their moral commitment would place the integrity of their self at risk (Hardy & others, 2014; Narváez & Lapsley, 2009).

    Daniel Hart and his colleague (Hart, 2005; Hart & Matsuba, 2010; Hart, Matsuba, & Atkins, 2008, 2014; Hart, Richardson, & Wilkenfeld, 2011; Hart & others, 2011; Matsuba, Murazyn, & Hart, 2014) argue that poor urban neighborhoods provide contexts that work against the formation of moral identity and commitment to moral projects. Living in high-poverty contexts often undermines moral attitudes and reduces tolerance for divergent viewpoints. And high-poverty neighborhoods offer fewer opportunities for effective engagement in the community because they lack an extensive network of organizations that support projects connected to moral goals. There are fewer opportunities for volunteering in such contexts. Hart and his colleagues advocate providing more service learning and community opportunities as a way of improving youths' moral attitudes and identity.

- *Moral character.* A person with moral character has the willpower, desires, and integrity to stand up to pressure, overcome distractions and disappointments, and behave morally. A person of good moral character displays moral virtues such as "honesty, truthfulness, and trustworthiness, as well as those of care, compassion, thoughtfulness, and considerateness. Other salient traits revolve around virtues of dependability, loyalty, and conscientiousness" (Walker, 2002, p. 74).

- *Moral exemplars.* Moral exemplars are people who have lived exemplary moral lives (Walker, 2013a, b, 2014a, b, 2016). Their moral personality, identity, character, and set of virtues reflect moral excellence and commitment.

Carol Gilligan. *What is Gilligan's view of moral development?*
Courtesy of Dr. Carol Gilligan

developmental **connection**

Identity
According to James Marcia, what are the four statuses of identity development? Connect to "Socioemotional Development in Adolescence."

justice perspective A moral perspective that focuses on the rights of the individual and in which individuals independently make moral decisions.

care perspective The moral perspective of Carol Gilligan, which views people in terms of their connectedness with others and emphasizes interpersonal communication, relationships with others, and concern for others.

Domain Theory: Moral, Social Conventional, and Personal Reasoning   The **domain theory of moral development** states that there are different domains of social knowledge and reasoning, including moral, social conventional, and personal domains. In domain theory, children's and adolescents' moral, social conventional, and personal knowledge and reasoning emerge from their attempts to understand and deal with different forms of social experience (Jambon & Smetana, 2017; Killen & Dahl, 2017; Mulvey & others, 2016; Nucci, 2014; Smetana, 2011a, b, 2013; Turiel, 2014, 2015; Turiel & Gingo, 2017).

Some theorists and researchers argue that Kohlberg did not adequately distinguish between moral reasoning and social conventional reasoning (Killen & Dahl, 2017; Nucci, 2014; Smetana, 2013; Turiel & Gingo, 2017). **Social conventional reasoning** focuses on conventional rules that have been established by social consensus in order to control behavior and maintain the social system. The rules themselves are arbitrary, such as raising your hand in class before speaking, using one staircase at school to go up, the other to go down, not cutting in front of someone standing in line to buy movie tickets, and stopping at a stop sign when driving. There are sanctions if we violate these conventions, although they can be changed by consensus.

In contrast, moral reasoning focuses on ethical issues and rules of morality. Unlike conventional rules, moral rules are not arbitrary. They are obligatory, widely accepted, and somewhat impersonal (Dahl & Killen, 2017; Mulvey & others, 2016; Turiel, 2015). Rules pertaining to lying, cheating, stealing, and physically harming another person are moral rules because violation of these rules affronts ethical standards that exist apart from social consensus and convention. Moral judgments involve concepts of justice, whereas social conventional judgments are concepts of social organization. Violating moral rules is usually more serious than violating conventional rules.

The social conventional approach is a serious challenge to Kohlberg's approach because Kohlberg argued that social conventions are a stop-over on the road to higher moral sophistication (Jambon & Smetana, 2017; Turiel & Gingo, 2017). For social conventional reasoning advocates, social conventional reasoning is not lower than postconventional reasoning but rather something that needs to be disentangled from the moral thread (Dahl & Killen, 2017; Killen & Dahl, 2017; Killen & Smetana, 2015; Mulvey & others, 2016; Turiel & Gingo, 2017).

Recently, a distinction also has been made between moral and conventional issues, which are viewed as legitimately subject to adult social regulation, and personal issues, which are more likely subject to the child's or adolescent's independent decision making and personal discretion (Killen & Dahl, 2017; Turiel & Gingo, 2017). Personal issues include control over one's body, privacy, and choice of friends and activities. Thus, some actions belong to a *personal* domain, not governed by moral strictures or social norms.

Moral, conventional, and personal domains of reasoning arise in families. Moral issues include actions such as lying to parents about engaging in a deviant behavior or stealing money from a sibling. Conventional issues involve matters such as curfews and who takes out the garbage. Personal issues involve such things as what kinds of music to like, what styles of clothing to wear, what to put on the walls of one's bedroom, and which friends to choose. A recent study of 5- to 9-year-old American and Chinese children found that older children were more likely to say that judgments about personal issues were up to the child to decide (Smetana & others, 2014).

In domain theory, boundaries are developed regarding adult authority, which can produce parent-adolescent conflict. Adolescents have a large personal domain and most parents can live with that; however, parents have a larger moral domain than adolescents think is reasonable (Jambon & Smetana, 2017; Turiel & Gingo, 2017).

Prosocial Behavior
Children engage in both immoral antisocial acts such as lying and cheating and prosocial moral behavior such as showing empathy or acting altruistically (Carlo & others, 2017; Eisenberg & Spinrad, 2016; Laible & others, 2017; Streit & others, 2017). Even during the preschool years children may care for others or comfort others in distress, but prosocial behavior occurs more often in adolescence than in childhood (Eisenberg & Spinrad, 2016).

William Damon (1988) described how sharing develops. During their first years, when children share, it is usually not for reasons of empathy but for the fun of the social play ritual or out of imitation. Then, at about 4 years of age, a combination of empathic awareness and adult encouragement produces a sense of obligation on the part of the child to share with others.

It is one of the beautiful compensations of this life that no one can sincerely try to help another without helping himself.

—**Charles Dudley Warner**
American Essayist, 19th Century

domain theory of moral development Theory that traces social knowledge and reasoning to moral, social conventional, and personal domains. These domains arise from children's and adolescents' attempts to understand and deal with different forms of social experience.

social conventional reasoning Thoughts about social consensus and convention established in order to control behavior and maintain the social system.

Most 4-year-olds are not selfless saints, however. Children believe they have an obligation to share but do not necessarily think they should be as generous to others as they are to themselves.

Children's sharing comes to reflect a more complex sense of what is just and right during middle and late childhood. By the start of the elementary school years, children begin to express objective ideas about fairness (Eisenberg, Fabes, & Spinrad, 2006). It is common to hear 6-year-old children use the word *fair* as synonymous with *equal* or *same*. By the mid to late elementary school years, children understand that equity sometimes means that people with special merit or special needs deserve special treatment.

In sum, moral development is a multifaceted, complex concept. Included in this complexity are thoughts, feelings, behaviors, personality, relationships, domains, and prosocial behavior.

GENDER

Gilligan's claim that Kohlberg's theory of moral development reflects gender bias reminds us of the pervasive influence of gender on development. Long before elementary school, boys and girls show preferences for different toys and activities. Preschool children display a gender identity and gender-typed behavior that reflects biological, cognitive, and social influences. Here we will examine gender stereotypes, gender similarities and differences, and gender-role classification.

How does children's sharing change from the preschool to the elementary school years?
©Norbert Schaefer/Corbis/Getty Images

Gender Stereotypes According to the old ditty, boys are made of "frogs and snails" and girls are made of "sugar and spice and all that's nice." In the past, a well-adjusted boy was supposed to be independent, aggressive, and powerful. A well-adjusted girl was supposed to be dependent, nurturing, and uninterested in power. The masculine characteristics were considered to be healthy and good by society; the feminine characteristics were considered undesirable. These notions reflect **gender stereotypes,** which are broad categories that reflect general impressions and beliefs about females and males.

Gender stereotyping continues to change during middle and late childhood (Brannon, 2017; Halim, 2016; Halim & others, 2016). Research indicates that while gender stereotyping is often a time of gender rigidity, in middle and late childhood boys and girls become more flexible in their gender-typing (Halim, 2016; Halim & others, 2016). In some studies, the increase in gender flexibility characterizes girls more than boys (Halim & others, 2016). For example, a study of 3- to 10-year-old U.S. children revealed that girls and older children used a higher percentage of gender stereotypes (Miller & others, 2009). In this study, appearance stereotypes were more prevalent on the part of girls, whereas activity (sports, for example) and trait (aggressive, for example) stereotyping was more commonly engaged in by boys.

Gender Similarities and Differences What is the reality behind gender stereotypes? Let's examine some of the similarities and differences between the sexes, keeping in mind that (1) the differences are averages—not all females versus all males; (2) even when differences are reported, there is considerable overlap between the sexes; and (3) the differences may be due primarily to biological factors, sociocultural factors, or both. First, we examine physical similarities and differences, and then we will turn to cognitive and socioemotional similarities and differences.

Physical Development Women have about twice the body fat of men, most of it concentrated around breasts and hips. In males, fat is more likely to go to the abdomen. On average, males grow to be 10 percent taller than females. Other physical differences are less obvious. From conception on, females have a longer life expectancy than males, and females are less likely than males to develop physical or mental disorders. The risk of coronary disease is twice as high in males as in females.

Does gender matter when it comes to brain structure and function? Human brains are much alike, whether the brain belongs to a male or a female (Halpern, 2006, 2012; Halpern & others, 2007). However, researchers have found some differences in the brains of males and females (Hofer & others, 2007). Among the differences that have been discovered are the following:

- Female brains are approximately 10 percent smaller than male brains (Giedd, 2012; Giedd & others, 2012). However, female brains have more folds; the larger folds (called convolutions) allow more surface brain tissue within the skulls of females than males (Luders & others, 2004).

gender stereotypes Broad categories that reflect our impressions and beliefs about females and males.

- One part of the hypothalamus responsible for sexual behavior is larger in men than women (Swaab & others, 2001).
- An area of the parietal lobe that functions in visuospatial skills is larger in males than females (Frederikse & others, 2000).
- The areas of the brain involved in emotional expression show more metabolic activity in females than males (Gur & others, 1995).

Although some differences in brain structure and function have been found, either many of these differences are small or research is inconsistent regarding the differences. Also, when sex differences in the brain have been revealed, in many cases they have not been directly linked to psychological differences (Blakemore, Berenbaum, & Liben, 2009). Although research on sex differences in the brain is still in its infancy, it is likely that there are far more similarities than differences in the brains of females and males.

Cognitive Development   No gender differences in general intelligence have been revealed, but gender differences have been found in some cognitive areas (Halpern, 2012). A very large-scale study of more than 7 million U.S. students in grades 2 through 11 revealed no differences in math scores for boys and girls (Hyde & others, 2008). And a recent meta-analysis found no gender differences in math scores for adolescents (Lindberg & others, 2010). A recent research review concluded that girls have more negative math attitudes and that parents' and teachers' expectations for children's math competence are often gender-biased in favor of boys (Gunderson & others, 2012). And in one study, 6- to 12-year-olds reported that math is mainly for boys (Cvencek, Meltzoff, & Greenwald, 2011). The most recent National Assessment of Educational Progress (2016) found that in 2015 girls scored significantly higher than boys in reading, while there were virtually no gender differences in math scores at the fourth-grade level. In 2011, girls had scored significantly higher than boys did in writing (National Assessment of Educational Progress (2012). Also, in a recent international assessment involving 65 countries, in every country girls had higher reading achievement than did boys (Reilly, 2012). Cultural variations occurred in this study, with the gender difference in reading occurring more in countries with less gender equity and lower economic prosperity.

One area of math that has been examined for possible gender differences is visuospatial skills, which include being able to rotate objects mentally and determine what they would look like when rotated. These types of skills are important in courses such as plane and solid geometry and geography. A research review revealed that boys have better visuospatial skills than girls (Halpern & others, 2007). For example, despite equal participation in the National Geography Bee, in most years all 10 finalists were boys (Liben, 1995). A recent research review found that having a stronger masculine gender role was linked to better spatial ability in males and females (Reilly & Neuman, 2013). Some experts argue that the gender difference in visuospatial skills is small (Hyde, 2007a, b, 2014) (see Figure 3).

Socioemotional Development   Five areas of socioemotional development in which gender similarities and differences have been studied extensively are aggression, relationships, emotion, prosocial behavior, and gender in school contexts.

One of the most consistent gender differences is that boys are more physically aggressive than girls are (Hyde, 2014). The difference occurs in all cultures and appears very early in children's development (Dayton & Malone, 2017). The physical aggression difference is especially pronounced when children are provoked. Both biological and environmental factors have been proposed to account for gender differences in aggression. Biological factors include heredity and hormones. Environmental factors include cultural expectations, adult and peer models, and social agents that reward aggression in boys and punish aggression in girls.

Although boys are consistently more physically aggressive than girls, might girls show at least as much verbal aggression, such as yelling, as boys do? When verbal aggression is examined, gender differences often disappear; sometimes, though, verbal aggression is more pronounced in girls (Eagly & Steffen, 1986).

Recently, increased interest has been directed toward *relational aggression,* which involves harming someone by manipulating a relationship (Blakely-McClure & Ostrov, 2016; Casper & Card, 2017; Cooley & Fife, 2016; Orpinas, McNicholas, & Nahapetyan, 2015; Underwood, 2011). Relational aggression includes behaviors such as trying to make others dislike a certain individual by spreading malicious rumors about the person. Mixed findings

What are little boys made of?

Frogs and snails

And puppy dogs' tails.

What are little girls made of?

Sugar and spice

And all that's nice.

—**J. O. Halliwell**

English Author, 19th Century

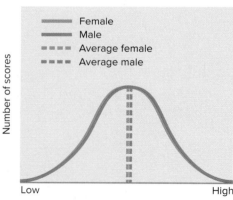

FIGURE **3**

VISUOSPATIAL SKILLS OF MALES AND FEMALES. Notice that, although an average male's visuospatial skills are higher than an average female's, scores for the two sexes almost entirely overlap. Not all males have better visuospatial skills than all females—the overlap indicates that although the average male score is higher, many females outperform most males on such tasks.

have characterized research on whether girls show more relational aggression than boys, but one consistency in findings is that relational aggression comprises a greater percentage of girls' overall aggression than is the case for boys (Putallaz & others, 2007). And a recent research review revealed that girls engage in more relational aggression than boys in adolescence but not in childhood (Smith, Rose, & Schwartz-Mette, 2010).

Gender differences occur in some aspects of emotion (Leaper, 2013). Females express emotion more than do males, are better than males at decoding emotion, smile more, cry more, and are happier (Gross, Frederickson, & Levenson, 1994; LaFrance, Hecht, & Paluck, 2003). Males report experiencing and expressing more anger than do females (Kring, 2000). And a recent meta-analysis found that females are better than males at recognizing nonverbal displays of emotion (Thompson & Voyer, 2014). However, another recent meta-analysis found that overall gender differences in children's emotional expression were small, with girls showing more positive emotions (sympathy, for example) and more internalized emotions (sadness and anxiety, for example) (Chaplin & Aldao, 2013). In this analysis, the gender difference in positive emotions became more pronounced with age as girls more strongly expressed positive emotions than boys in middle and late childhood and in adolescence.

An important skill is to be able to regulate and control one's emotions and behavior (Thompson, Winer, & Goodvin, 2014). Boys usually show less self-regulation than girls do (Eisenberg, Spinrad, & Eggum, 2010). This low self-control can translate into behavior problems.

Researchers have found that girls are more "people oriented" and boys are more "things oriented" (Galambos, Berenbaum, & McHale, 2009; Hyde, 2014). In a recent research review, this conclusion was supported by findings that girls spend more time and energy building relationships, while boys spend more time alone, playing video games, and playing sports; that girls work at part-time jobs that are people-oriented such as waitressing and babysitting, while boys are more likely to take part-time jobs that involve manual labor and using tools; and girls are interested in careers that are more people-oriented, such as teaching and social work, while boys are more likely to be interested in object-oriented careers, such as mechanics and engineering (Perry & Pauletti, 2011).

Are there gender differences in communication in relationships? Sociolinguist Deborah Tannen (1990) distinguishes between rapport talk and report talk:

- **Rapport talk** is the language of conversation and a way of establishing connections and negotiating relationships. Females enjoy rapport talk and conversation that is relationship-oriented more than males do.
- **Report talk** is talk that gives information. Public speaking is an example of report talk. Males hold center stage through report talk with verbal performances such as storytelling, joking, and lecturing with information.

How extensive are the gender differences in communication? Research has yielded somewhat mixed results. Recent studies do reveal some gender differences (Anderson, 2006; Leaper, 2013; Matlin, 2012). Researchers have found that adolescent girls engage in more self-disclosure (communication of intimate details about themselves) in close relationships and are better at actively listening in a conversation than are boys (Leaper, 2015). One study of a sampling of students' e-mails found that people could guess the writer's gender two-thirds of the time (Thompson & Murachver, 2001). Another study revealed that women make 63 percent of phone calls and when talking to another woman stay on the phone longer (7.2 minutes) than men do when talking with other men (4.6 minutes) (Smoreda & Licoppe, 2000). However, meta-analyses suggest that overall gender differences in communication are small in both children and adults (Hyde, 2009; Leaper & Smith, 2004).

What gender differences characterize aggression?
©Corbis RF

How Would You...?
If you were a **psychologist,** how would you discuss gender similarities and differences with a parent or teacher who is concerned about a child's academic progress and social skills?

What are some contexts and activities that indicate girls are more "people oriented" than boys are?
©Rhienna Cutler/Getty Images RF

rapport talk The language of conversation and a way of establishing connections and negotiating relationships; more characteristic of females than of males.

report talk Talk that conveys information; more characteristic of males than females.

Are there gender differences in prosocial behavior? Across childhood and adolescence, females engage in more prosocial behavior (Eisenberg & Spinrad, 2016). The biggest gender difference occurs for kind and considerate behavior, with a smaller difference in sharing.

Are there gender differences in school contexts? With regard to school achievement, girls earn better grades and complete high school at a higher rate than boys (Halpern, 2012). Males are more likely than females to be assigned to special/remedial education classes. Girls are more likely than boys to be engaged with academic material, be attentive in class, put forth more academic effort, and participate more in class (DeZolt & Hull, 2001).

Keep in mind that measures of achievement in school or scores on standardized tests may reflect many factors besides cognitive ability. For example, performance in school may in part reflect attempts to conform to gender roles or differences in motivation, self-regulation, or other socioemotional characteristics (Klug & others, 2016; Wentzel & Miele, 2016; Wigfield & others, 2015).

Some observers have expressed concern that schools and teachers have biases against both boys and girls (Mullola & others, 2012). What evidence exists that the classroom setting is biased against boys? Here are some factors to consider (DeZolt & Hull, 2001):

What are some possible gender biases in the classroom?

©Neustockimages/Getty Images RF

- Compliance, following rules, and being neat and orderly are valued and reinforced in many classrooms. These are behaviors that usually characterize girls more than boys.
- A large majority of teachers are females, especially at the elementary school level. This trend may make it more difficult for boys than for girls to identify with their teachers and model their teachers' behavior. A recent study revealed that male teachers perceived boys more positively and saw them as being more educationally competent than did female teachers (Mullola & others, 2012).
- Boys are more likely than girls to have a learning disability, ADHD, or to drop out of school.
- Boys are more likely than girls to be criticized by their teachers.
- School personnel tend to stereotype boys' behavior as problematic.

What evidence is there that the classroom setting is biased against girls? Consider the views of Myra and David Sadker (2005):

- In a typical classroom, girls are more compliant and boys are more rambunctious. Boys demand more attention, and girls are more likely to quietly wait their turn. Teachers are more likely to scold and reprimand boys, as well as send boys to school authorities for disciplinary action. Educators worry that girls' tendency to be compliant and quiet comes at a cost: diminished assertiveness.
- In many classrooms, teachers spend more time watching and interacting with boys, whereas girls work and play quietly on their own. Most teachers don't intentionally favor boys by spending more time with them, yet somehow the classroom frequently ends up with this type of gendered profile.
- Boys get more instruction than girls and more help when they have trouble with a question. Teachers often give boys more time to answer a question, more hints at the correct answer, and further tries if they give the wrong answer.
- Girls and boys enter first grade with roughly equal levels of self-esteem. Yet by the middle school years, girls' self-esteem is lower than boys'.

What are some recent changes in single-sex education in the United States? What does research say about whether single-sex education is beneficial?

©Rob Crandall/Stock Connection Worldwide/Newscom

Thus, there is evidence of gender bias against both males and females in schools. Many school personnel are not aware of their gender-biased attitudes. These attitudes are deeply entrenched in and supported by the general culture. Increasing awareness of gender bias in schools is clearly an important strategy in reducing such bias.

Might single-sex education be better for children than coeducational schooling? The argument for single-sex education is that it eliminates distraction from the other sex and reduces sexual harassment. Single-sex public education has increased dramatically in recent years. In 2002, only 12 public schools in the U.S. provided single-sex education; in the 2011–2012 school year, 116 public schools were single-sex and an additional 390 provided such experiences (NASSPE, 2012).

The increase in single-sex education has especially been fueled by its inclusion in the No Child Left Behind legislation as a means of improving the educational experiences and academic achievement of low-income students of color. It appears that many of the public schools offering single-sex education have a high percentage of such youth (Klein, 2012). However, two recent research reviews concluded that there have been no documented benefits of single-sex education for low-income students of color (Goodkind, 2013; Halpern & others, 2011). One review, titled "The Pseudoscience of Single-Sex Schooling," by Diane Halpern and her colleagues (2011) concluded that single-sex education is highly misguided, misconstrued, and unsupported by any valid scientific evidence. They emphasize that among the many arguments against single-sex education, the strongest is its reduction in opportunities for boys and girls to work together in a supervised, purposeful environment.

There has been a special call for single-sex public education for one group of adolescents—African American boys—because of their historically poor academic achievement and high dropout rate from school (Mitchell & Stewart, 2013). In 2010, Urban Prep Academy for Young Men became the first all-male, all African American public charter school. One hundred percent of its first graduates enrolled in college, despite the school's location in a section of Chicago where poverty, gangs, and crime predominate. Because so few public schools focus solely on educating African American boys, it is too early to tell whether this type of single-sex education can be effective across a wide range of participants.

Gender in Context   The nature and extent of gender differences may depend on the context (Gershoff, Mistry, & Crosby, 2014; Leaper, 2015; Liben, 2017; Liben, Bigler, & Hilliard, 2014). The importance of considering gender in context is nowhere more apparent than when we examine what is culturally prescribed behavior for females and males in different countries around the world (Chuang & Tamis-Lemonda, 2009). Although there has been greater acceptance of androgyny and similarities in male and female behavior in the United States, in many countries gender roles have remained gender-specific (UNICEF, 2017). For example, in many Middle Eastern countries, the division of labor between males and females is dramatic. Males are socialized and schooled to work in the public sphere, females in the private world of home and child rearing. For example, in many Middle Eastern countries, the dominant view is that the man's duty is to provide for his family and the woman's is to care for her family and household. China and India also have been male-dominant cultures. Although women have made some strides in China and India, especially in urban areas, the male role is still dominant. Most males in China and India do not accept androgynous behavior or gender equity.

In a recent study of eighth-grade students in 36 countries, in every country girls had more egalitarian attitudes about gender roles than boys did (Dotti Sani & Quaranta, 2017). In this study, girls had more egalitarian gender attitudes in countries with higher levels of societal gender equality. In another recent study of 15- to 19-year-olds in the country of Qatar, males had more negative views of gender equality than females did (Al-Ghanim & Badahdah, 2017).

developmental **connection**

Community and Culture

Bronfenbrenner's ecological theory emphasizes the importance of contexts; in his theory, the macrosystem includes cross-cultural comparisons. Connect to "Introduction."

In China, females and males are usually socialized to behave, feel, and think differently. The old patriarchal traditions of male supremacy have not been completely uprooted. Chinese women still make considerably less money than Chinese men do, and, in rural China (such as here in the Lixian Village of Sichuan) male supremacy still governs many women's lives.
©Diego Azubel/EPA/Newscom

Review Connect Reflect

LG1 Discuss emotional and personality development in middle and late childhood.

Review

- What changes take place in the self during the middle and late childhood years?
- How does emotion change during middle and late childhood?
- What is Kohlberg's theory of moral development, and how has it been criticized? How does prosocial behavior develop?

Connect

- What are gender stereotypes, and what are some important gender differences?
- How is the concept of joint attention similar to or different from the concept of perspective taking you learned about in this section?

Reflect *Your Own Personal Journey of Life*

- A young man who had been sentenced to serve 10 years for selling a small amount of marijuana walked away from a prison camp six months after he was sent there. He is now in his fifties and has been a model citizen. Should he be sent back to prison? Why or why not? At which Kohlberg stage should your response be placed? Do you think the stage at which you placed your response accurately captures the level of your moral thinking? Explain.

2 What Are Some Changes in Parenting and Families in Middle and Late Childhood?

 Describe changes in parenting and families in middle and late childhood.

Developmental Changes in Parent-Child Relationships Parents as Managers Stepfamilies

What are some changes in the focus of parent-child relationships in middle and late childhood?

©Radius/Corbis RF

Our discussion of parenting and families in this section focuses on how parent-child interactions typically change in middle and late childhood, the importance of parents being effective managers of children's lives, and how elementary school children are affected by living with stepparents.

DEVELOPMENTAL CHANGES IN PARENT-CHILD RELATIONSHIPS

As children move into the middle and late childhood years, parents spend considerably less time with them (Grusec, 2017; Grusec & others, 2013). In one study, parents spent less than half as much time with their children aged 5 to 12 in caregiving, instruction, reading, talking, and playing as when the children were younger (Hill & Stafford, 1980). Although parents spend less time with their children in middle and late childhood than in early childhood, parents continue to be extremely important in their children's lives. In an analysis of the contributions of parents in middle and late childhood, the following conclusion was reached: "Parents serve as gatekeepers and provide scaffolding as children assume more responsibility for themselves and . . . regulate their own lives" (Huston & Ripke, 2006, p. 422).

Parents especially play an important role in supporting and stimulating children's academic achievement in middle and late childhood (Rowe, Ramani, & Pomerantz, 2016). The value parents place on education can determine whether children do well in school. Parents not only influence children's in-school achievement, but they also make decisions about children's out-of-school activities. Whether children participate in sports, music, and other activities is heavily influenced by the extent to which parents sign up children for such activities or encourage their participation (Simpkins & others, 2006).

Elementary school children tend to receive less physical discipline than they did as preschoolers. Instead of spanking or coercive holding, their parents are more likely to use deprivation of privileges, appeals to the child's self-esteem, comments designed to increase the child's sense of guilt, and statements that the child is responsible for his or her actions.

During middle and late childhood, some control is transferred from parent to child. The process is gradual, and it produces coregulation rather than control by either the child or the parent alone. Parents continue to exercise general supervision and control, while children are allowed to engage in moment-to-moment self-regulation. The major shift to autonomy does not occur until about the age of 12 or later. A key developmental task as children move toward autonomy is learning to relate to adults outside the family on a regular basis—adults such as teachers, who interact with the child much differently from parents.

PARENTS AS MANAGERS

Parents can play important roles as managers of children's opportunities, as monitors of their behavior, and as social initiators and arrangers (Clarke-Stewart & Parke, 2014). Mothers are more likely than fathers to take a managerial role in parenting.

Researchers have found that family management practices are positively related to students' grades and self-responsibility, and negatively to school-related problems (Eccles, 2007; Taylor & Lopez, 2005). Among the most important family management practices in this regard are maintaining a structured and organized family environment, such as establishing routines for homework, chores, meals, bedtime, and so on, and effectively monitoring the child's behavior. A research review of family functioning in African American students' academic achievement found that when African American parents monitored their sons' academic achievement by ensuring that homework was completed, restricted time spent on nonproductive distractions (such as video games and TV), and participated in a consistent, positive dialogue with teachers and school officials, their sons' academic achievement benefited (Mandara, 2006).

STEPFAMILIES

Not only has divorce become commonplace in the United States, so has getting remarried. It takes time for parents to marry, have children, get divorced, and then remarry. Consequently, there are far more elementary and secondary school children than infant or preschool children living in stepfamilies.

How does living in a stepfamily influence a child's development?
©Todd Wright/Blend Images/Getty Images RF

The number of remarriages involving children has grown steadily in recent years. Also, divorces occur at a 10 percent higher rate in remarriages than in first marriages (Cherlin & Furstenberg, 1994). About half of all children whose parents divorce will have a stepparent within four years of the separation.

Remarried parents face some unique tasks (de Jong Gierveld & Merz, 2013; Ganong, Coleman, & Russell, 2015). The couple must define and strengthen their marriage and at the same time renegotiate the biological parent-child relationships and establish stepparent-stepchild and stepsibling relationships (Coleman, Ganong, & Fine, 2004). The complex histories and multiple relationships make adjustment in a stepfamily difficult (Dodson & Davies, 2014; Ganong, Coleman, & Russell, 2015; Hakvoort & others, 2011; Shapiro & Stewart, 2012). Only one-third of stepfamily couples stay remarried.

In some cases, the stepfamily may have been preceded by the death of a spouse. However, by far the largest number of stepfamilies are preceded by divorce rather than death (Pasley & Moorefield, 2004). Three common types of stepfamily structure are (1) stepfather, (2) stepmother, and (3) blended or complex. In stepfather families, the mother typically had custody of the children and remarried, introducing a stepfather into her children's lives. In stepmother families, the father usually had custody and remarried, introducing a stepmother into his children's lives. In a blended or complex stepfamily, both parents bring children from previous marriages to live in the newly formed stepfamily.

In E. Mavis Hetherington's (2006) longitudinal analyses, children and adolescents who had been in a simple stepfamily (stepfather or stepmother) for a number of years were adjusting better than they did in the early years of the remarried family and were functioning well in comparison with children and adolescents in conflicted nondivorced families and children and adolescents in complex (blended) stepfamilies. More than 75 percent of the adolescents in long-established simple stepfamilies described their relationships with their stepparents as "close" or "very close." Hetherington (2006) concluded that in long-established simple stepfamilies adolescents seem to eventually benefit from the presence of a stepparent and the resources provided by the stepparent.

Children often have better relationships with their custodial parents (mothers in stepfather families, fathers in stepmother families) than with simple stepparents (Santrock, Sitterle, & Warshak, 1988). Also, children in simple families (stepmother, stepfather) often show better adjustment than their counterparts in complex (blended) families (Hetherington & Kelly, 2002).

As in divorced families, children in stepfamilies show more adjustment problems than children in nondivorced families (Hetherington & Kelly, 2002). The adjustment problems are similar to those found among children of divorced parents—academic problems and lower self-esteem, for example (Anderson & others, 1999). However, it is important to recognize that a majority of children in stepfamilies do not have problems. In one analysis, 25 percent of children from stepfamilies showed adjustment problems compared with 10 percent in intact, never-divorced families (Hetherington & Kelly, 2002).

Adolescence is an especially difficult time for the formation of a stepfamily (Anderson & others, 1999; Gosselin, 2010). Problems may occur because becoming part of a stepfamily exacerbates normal adolescent concerns about identity, sexuality, and autonomy.

How Would You...?
If you were a **human development and family studies professional,** what advice would you offer to divorced parents about strategies to ease their children's adjustment to remarriage?

3 What Changes Characterize Peer Relationships in Middle and Late Childhood?

 **LG3** Identify changes in peer relationships in middle and late childhood.

| Developmental Changes | Peer Status | Social Cognition | Bullying | Friends |

Having positive relationships with peers is especially important in middle and late childhood (Nesi & others, 2017; Rubin & Barstead, 2018; Rubin & others, 2015; Wentzel & Muenks, 2016; Wentzel & Ramani, 2016). Engaging in positive interactions with peers, resolving conflicts with peers in nonaggressive ways, and having quality friendships in middle and late childhood not only create positive outcomes at this time in children's lives, but also are linked to more positive relationship outcomes in adolescence and adulthood (Huston & Ripke, 2006). For example, in one longitudinal study, being popular with peers and engaging in low levels of aggression at 8 years of age were related to higher levels of occupational status at 48 years of age (Huesmann & others, 2006). Another study found that peer competence (a composite measure that included social contact with peers, popularity with peers, friendship, and social skills) in middle and late childhood was linked to having better relationships with co-workers in early adulthood (Collins & van Dulmen, 2006). And a recent study indicated that low peer status in childhood (low acceptance/likeability) was linked to increased probability of being unemployed and having mental health problems in adulthood (Almquist & Brannstrom, 2014).

DEVELOPMENTAL CHANGES

As children enter the elementary school years, reciprocity becomes especially important in peer interchanges. Researchers estimate that the percentage of time spent in social interaction with peers increases from approximately 10 percent at 2 years of age to more than 30 percent in middle and late childhood (Rubin, Bukowski, & Parker, 2006). In one early study, a typical day in elementary school included approximately 300 episodes with peers (Barker & Wright, 1951). As children move through middle and late childhood, the size of their peer group increases, and peer interaction is less closely supervised by adults (Rubin, Bukowski, & Parker, 2006). Until about 12 years of age, children's preference for same-sex peer groups increases.

PEER STATUS

Which children are likely to be popular with their peers and which ones tend to be disliked? Developmentalists address these and similar questions by examining *sociometric status,* a term that describes the extent to which children are liked or disliked by their peer group (Achterberg & others, 2017; Rubin, Bukowski, & Bowker, 2015). Sociometric status is typically assessed by asking children to rate how much they like or dislike each of their classmates. Or it may be assessed by asking children to nominate the children they like the most and those they like the least.

Developmentalists have distinguished five peer statuses (Wentzel & Asher, 1995):

- **Popular children** are frequently nominated as a best friend and are rarely disliked by their peers.
- **Average children** receive an average number of both positive and negative nominations from their peers.
- **Neglected children** are infrequently nominated as a best friend but are not disliked by their peers.
- **Rejected children** are infrequently nominated as someone's best friend and are actively disliked by their peers.
- **Controversial children** are frequently nominated both as someone's best friend and as being disliked.

What are some statuses that children have with their peers?
©BananaStock RF

Popular children have a number of social skills that contribute to their being well liked. They give out reinforcements, listen carefully, maintain open lines of communication with peers, are happy, control their negative emotions, act like themselves, show enthusiasm and concern for others, and are self-confident without being conceited (Hartup, 1983; Rubin, Bukowski, & Bowker, 2015).

Neglected children engage in low rates of interaction with their peers and are often described as shy by peers. The goal of many training programs for neglected children is to help them attract attention from their peers in positive ways and to hold that attention by asking questions, by listening in a warm and friendly way, and by saying things about themselves that relate to the peers' interests. They also are taught to enter groups more effectively.

Rejected children often have more serious adjustment problems than those who are neglected (Dishion & Piehler, 2009; Prinstein & others, 2009). One study found that in kindergarten, children who were rejected by their peers were less likely to engage in classroom participation, more likely to express a desire to avoid school, and more likely to report being lonely than children who were accepted by their peers (Buhs & Ladd, 2001). The combination of being rejected by peers and being aggressive forecasts problems (Dishion & Piehler, 2009; Rubin, Bukowski, & Bowker, 2015). Peer rejection is consistently linked to the development and maintenance of conduct problems (Chen, Drabick, & Burgers, 2015). A recent study revealed a link between peer rejection and depression in adolescence (Platt, Kadosh, & Lau, 2013). In a recent study of young adolescents, peer rejection predicted increases in aggressive and rule-breaking behavior (Janssens & others, 2017).

John Coie (2004, pp. 252–253) provided three reasons why aggressive peer-rejected boys have problems in social relationships:

How Would You...?

If you were a **social worker**, how would you help a neglected child become more involved in peer activities?

- "First, the rejected, aggressive boys are more impulsive and have problems sustaining attention. As a result, they are more likely to be disruptive of ongoing activities in the classroom and in focused group play.
- Second, rejected, aggressive boys are more emotionally reactive. They are aroused to anger more easily and probably have more difficulty calming down once aroused. Because of this they are more prone to become angry at peers and attack them verbally and physically. . . .
- Third, rejected children have fewer social skills in making friends and maintaining positive relationships with peers."

Not all rejected children are aggressive. Although aggression and its related characteristics of impulsiveness and disruptiveness underlie rejection about half the time, approximately 10 to 20 percent of rejected children are shy.

How can rejected children be trained to interact more effectively with their peers? Rejected children may be taught to more accurately assess whether the intentions of their peers are negative (Fontaine & others, 2010). They may be asked to engage in role playing or to discuss hypothetical situations involving negative encounters with peers, such as when

popular children Children who are frequently nominated as a best friend and are rarely disliked by their peers.

average children Children who receive an average number of both positive and negative nominations from peers.

neglected children Children who are infrequently nominated as a best friend but are not disliked by their peers.

rejected children Children who are infrequently nominated as a best friend and are actively disliked by their peers.

controversial children Children who are frequently nominated both as someone's best friend and as being disliked.

a peer cuts into a line ahead of them. In some programs, children are shown videotapes of appropriate peer interaction and asked to draw lessons from what they have seen (Ladd, Buhs, & Troop, 2004).

SOCIAL COGNITION

A boy accidentally trips and knocks another boy's soft drink out of his hand. The second boy misconstrues the encounter as hostile, and his interpretation leads him to retaliate aggressively against the boy who tripped. Through repeated encounters of this kind, the aggressive boy's classmates come to perceive him as habitually acting in inappropriate ways.

This example demonstrates the importance of *social cognition*—thoughts about social matters, such as the aggressive boy's interpretation of an encounter as hostile and his classmates' perception of his behavior as inappropriate (Carpendale & Lewis, 2015; Vetter & others, 2013). Children's social cognition about their peers becomes increasingly important for understanding peer relationships in middle and late childhood. Of special interest are the ways in which children process information about peer relations and their social knowledge (Dodge 2011a, b; White & Kistner, 2011).

Kenneth Dodge (1983, 2011a, b) argues that children go through five steps in processing information about their social world. They decode social cues, interpret, search for a response, select an optimal response, and enact. Dodge has found that aggressive boys are more likely to perceive another child's actions as hostile when the child's intention is ambiguous. And, when aggressive boys search for cues to determine a peer's intention, they respond more rapidly, less efficiently, and less reflectively than do nonaggressive children. These are among the social cognitive factors believed to be involved in children's conflicts.

Social knowledge also is involved in children's ability to get along with peers (Carpendale & Lewis, 2015). They need to know what goals to pursue in poorly defined or ambiguous situations, how to initiate and maintain a social bond, and what scripts to follow to get other children to be their friends. For example, as part of the script for getting friends, it helps to know that saying nice things, regardless of what the peer does or says, will make the peer like the child more.

BULLYING

Significant numbers of students are victimized by bullies (Campaert, Nocentini, & Menesini, 2017; Connell, Morris, & Piquero, 2016; Hall, 2017; Ladd. Ettekal, & Kochendorfer-Ladd, 2017; Muijs, 2017; Naidoo & others, 2016; Wang & others, 2017; Zarate-Garza & others, 2017). In a national survey of more than 15,000 students in grades 6 through 10, nearly one of every three students said that they had experienced occasional or frequent involvement as a victim or perpetrator in bullying (Nansel & others, 2001). In this study, bullying was defined as verbal or physical behavior intended to disturb someone less powerful (see Figure 4). Boys are more likely to be bullies than girls, but gender differences regarding victims of bullying are less clear (Salmivalli & Peets, 2009).

Who is likely to be bullied? In the study just described, boys and younger middle school students were most likely to be affected (Nansel & others, 2001). Children who said they were bullied reported more loneliness and difficulty in making friends, while those who did the bullying were more likely to have low grades and to smoke and drink alcohol.

Researchers have found that anxious, socially withdrawn, and aggressive children are often the victims of bullying (Hanish & Guerra, 2004; Rubin & Barstead, 2018). Anxious and socially withdrawn children may be victimized because they are nonthreatening and unlikely to retaliate if bullied, whereas aggressive children may be the targets of bullying because their behavior is irritating to bullies (Rubin, Bukowski, & Parker, 2006). Overweight and obese children are often bullied (Puhl & King, 2013). A recent study revealed that having supportive friends was linked to a lower level of bullying and victimization (Kendrick, Jutengren, & Stattin, 2012).

Social contexts such as poverty, family, and peer contexts also influence bullying (Prinstein & Giletta, 2016; Troop-Gordon, 2017). A recent study revealed that ethnic minority children living in poverty who had behavioral problems were more likely to become bullies, as were children whose mothers had suboptimal mental health (Shetgiri & others, 2012).

How Would You...?
If you were a **psychologist,** how would you characterize differences in the social cognition of aggressive children compared with children who behave in less hostile ways?

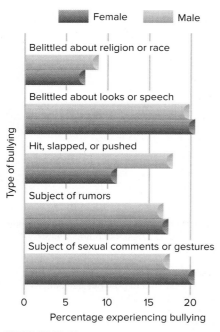

FIGURE 4

BULLYING BEHAVIORS AMONG U.S. YOUTH. This graph shows the types of bullying most often experienced by U.S. youth. The percentages reflect the extent to which bullied students said that they had experienced a particular type of bullying. In terms of gender, note that when they were bullied, boys were more likely to be hit, slapped, or pushed than girls were.

Also in this study, children whose parents talked with them more, had met all or most of their friends, and who always or usually completed their homework were less likely to become bullies. A recent meta-analysis indicated that positive parenting behavior (including having good communication, a warm relationship, being involved, and engaging in supervision of their children) was related to a lesser likelihood that a child would become either a bully/victim or a victim at school (Lereya, Samara, & Wolke, 2013).

The social context of the peer group also plays an important role in bullying (Prinstein & Giletta, 2016; Troop-Gordon, 2017). Recent research indicates that 70 to 80 percent of victims and their bullies are in the same school classroom (Salmivalli & Peets, 2009). Classmates are often aware of bullying incidents and in many cases witness bullying. In many cases, bullies torment victims to gain higher status in the peer group and bullies need others to witness their power displays. Many bullies are not rejected by the peer group. A recent longitudinal study explored the costs and benefits of bullying in the context of the peer group (Reijntjes & others, 2013). In this study children were initially assessed at 10 years of age and then followed into early adolescence. The results indicated that although young bullies may be on a developmental trajectory that over the long run is problematic, in the shorter term personal benefits of bullying often outweigh disadvantages. Frequent bullying was linked to high social status as indexed by perceived popularity in the peer group, and bullies also were characterized by self-perceived personal competence.

Who is likely to be bullied? What are some outcomes of bullying?
©SW Productions/Photodisc/Getty Images RF

What are the outcomes of bullying? Researchers have found that children who are bullied are more likely to experience depression, engage in suicidal ideation, and attempt suicide than their counterparts who have not been the victims of bullying (Arseneault, 2017; Yen & others, 2014; Zarate-Garza & others, 2017). A recent study indicated that peer victimization during the elementary school years was a leading indicator of internalizing problems (depression, for example) in adolescence (Schwartz & others, 2014). Also, a longitudinal study found that children who were bullied at 6 years of age were more likely to have excess weight gain when they were 12 to 13 years of age (Sutin & others, 2016). And three meta-analyses concluded that engaging in bullying during middle school is linked to an increased likelihood of antisocial and criminal behavior later in adolescence and adulthood (Kim & others, 2011; Losel & Bender, 2011; Ttofi & others, 2011). Further, a recent analysis concluded that bullying can have long-term effects, including difficulty in forming lasting relationships and getting along with co-workers (Wolke & Lereya, 2015).

And longitudinal studies have indicated that victims bullied in childhood and adolescence have higher rates of agoropobia (an abnormal fear of being in public, open, and crowded places), depression, anxiety, panic disorder, and suicidality in their early to mid-twenties compared to those who have not been bullied in childhood and adolescence (Arseneault, 2017; Copeland & others, 2013). In addition, another recent study revealed that being a victim of bullying in childhood was linked to increased use of mental health services by the victims five decades later (Evans-Lacko & others, 2017). An increasing concern is peer bullying and harassment on the Internet (called *cyberbullying*) (Vollink, Dehue, & McGuckin, 2016; Wolke, Lee, & Guy, 2017). One study involving third- to sixth-graders revealed that engaging in cyber aggression was related to loneliness, lower self-esteem, fewer mutual friendships, and lower peer popularity (Schoffstall & Cohen, 2011). Another recent study revealed that cyberbullying contributed to depression and suicidal ideation above and beyond the contribution of involvement in traditional types of bullying (physical and verbal bullying in school and in neighborhood contexts, for example) (Bonanno & Hymel, 2013). And a recent meta-analysis concluded that being the victim of cyberbullying was linked to stress and suicidal ideation (Kowalski & others, 2014). Further, a longitudinal study found that adolescents experiencing social and emotional difficulties were more likely to be both cyberbullied and traditionally bullied than traditionally bullied only (Cross, Lester, & Barnes, 2015). In this study, adolescents targeted in both ways stayed away from school more than their counterparts who were traditionally bullied only. And a recent study revealed that adolescents who were bullied both in a direct way and through cyberbullying had more behavioral problems and lower self-esteem than adolescents who were only bullied in one of these two ways (Wolke, Lee, & Guy, 2017). Information about preventing cyberbullying can be found at www.stopcyberbullying.org/.

What leads some children to become bullies and others to fall victim to bullying? To read further about bullying, see the *Connecting with Research* interlude.

How Are Perspective Taking and Moral Motivation Linked to Bullying?

One study explored the roles that perspective taking and moral motivation play in the lives of bullies, bully-victims, victims, and prosocial children (Gasser & Keller, 2009), who are defined as follows:

- *Bullies* are highly aggressive toward other children but are not victims of bullying.
- *Bully-victims* are not only highly aggressive toward other children but also are the recipients of other children's bullying.
- *Victims* are passive, non-aggressive respondents to bullying.
- *Prosocial children* engage in positive behaviors such as sharing, helping, comforting, and empathizing.

Teacher and peer ratings in 34 classrooms were used to classify 212 7- to 8-year-old boys and girls into the aforementioned four categories. On a 5-point scale (from never to several times a week), teachers rated (1) how often the child bullied others and (2) how often the child was bullied. The ratings focused on three types of bullying and being victimized: physical aggression, verbal aggression, and excluding others. On a 4-point scale (from not applicable to very clearly applicable), teachers also rated children's prosocial behavior on three items: "willingly shares with others," "comforts others if necessary," and "empathizes with others." Peer ratings assessed children's nominations of which children in the classroom acted as bullies, were victimized by bullies, and engaged in prosocial behavior. Combining the teacher and peer ratings after eliminating those that did not agree on which children were bullies, victims, or prosocial children, the final sample consisted of 49 bullies, 80 bully-victims, 33 victims, and 50 prosocial children.

Children's perspective-taking skills were assessed using theory of mind tasks, and moral motivation was examined by interviewing children about aspects of right and wrong in stories about children's transgressions. In one theory of mind task, children were tested to see whether they understood that people may have false beliefs about another individual. In another theory of mind task, children were assessed to determine whether they understood that people sometimes hide their emotions by showing an emotion different from what they really feel. A moral interview also was conducted in which children were told four moral transgression stories (with content about being unwilling to share with a classmate, stealing candy from a classmate, hiding a victim's shoes, and verbally bullying a victim) and then asked to judge whether the acts were right or wrong and how the participants in the stories likely felt.

The results of the study indicated that only bully-victims—but not bullies—were deficient in perspective taking. Further analysis revealed that both aggressive groups of children—bullies and bully-victims—had a deficiency in moral motivation. The analyses were consistent with a portrait of bullies as socially competent and knowledgeable in terms of perspective-taking skills and being able to effectively interact with peers. However, bullies use this social knowledge for their own manipulative purposes. The analysis also confirmed the picture of the bully as being morally insensitive. Another recent study also found that bullying was linked to moral disengagement (Obermann, 2011).

What possible solutions to the problem of bullying do these research results suggest? What else would you want to know about the relationship between bullies and their victims before you proposed possible remedies?

Extensive interest is being directed to preventing and treating bullying and victimization (Flannery & others, 2016; Gower, Cousin, & Borowsky, 2017; Hall, 2017; Menesini, Palladino, & Nocentini, 2016; Menesini & Salmivalli, 2017; Muijs, 2017). A research review revealed mixed results for school-based intervention (Vreeman & Carroll, 2007). School-based interventions vary greatly, ranging from involving the whole school in an antibullying campaign to providing individualized social skills training (Strohmeier & Noam, 2012). A recent teacher intervention in elementary and secondary schools to decrease bullying that focused on increasing bullies' empathy and condemning their behavior was effective in increasing the bullies' intent to stop being a bully (Garandeau & others, 2016). In this study, blaming the bully had no effect.

One of the most promising bullying intervention programs has been created by Dan Olweus (2003, 2013). This program focuses on 6- to 15-year-olds, with the goal of decreasing opportunities and rewards for bullying. School staff are instructed in ways to improve peer relations and make schools safer. When properly implemented, the program reduces bullying by 30 to 70 percent (Olweus, 2003). Information on how to implement the program can be obtained from the Center for the Prevention of Violence at the University of Colorado: www.colorado.edu/cspv/blueprints. Also, a recent research review concluded that interventions focused on the whole school, such as Olweus', are more effective than interventions involving classroom curricula or social skills training (Cantone & others, 2015).

How Would You...?

If you were an **educator,** how would you design and implement a bullying-reduction program at your school?

FRIENDS

Like adult friendships, children's friendships are typically characterized by similarity (Rubin & others, 2015). Throughout childhood, friends are more similar than dissimilar in terms of age, sex, race, and many other factors (Prinstein & Giletta, 2016). Friends often have similar attitudes toward school, similar educational aspirations, and closely aligned achievement orientations.

Why are children's friendships important? Willard Hartup (1983, 1996, 2009) has studied peer relations and friendship for more than three decades. He recently concluded that friends can provide cognitive and emotional resources from childhood through old age. Friends can foster self-esteem and a sense of well-being.

More specifically, children's friendships can serve six functions (Gottman & Parker, 1987):

- *Companionship.* Friendship provides children with a familiar partner and playmate, someone who is willing to spend time with them and join in collaborative activities.
- *Stimulation.* Friendship provides children with interesting information, excitement, and amusement.
- *Physical support.* Friendship provides resources and assistance.
- *Ego support.* Friendship provides the expectation of support, encouragement, and feedback, which helps children maintain an impression of themselves as competent, attractive, and worthwhile individuals.
- *Social comparison.* Friendship provides information about where the child stands vis-à-vis others and whether the child is doing okay.
- *Affection and intimacy.* Friendship provides children with a warm, close, trusting relationship with another individual. **Intimacy in friendships** is characterized by self-disclosure and the sharing of private thoughts. Research reveals that intimate friendships may not appear until early adolescence (Berndt & Perry, 1990).

Although having friends can be a developmental advantage, not all friendships are alike (Choukas-Bradley & Prinstein, 2016; Wentzel & Ramani, 2016). People differ in the company they keep—that is, who their friends are. Developmental advantages occur when children have friends who are socially skilled and supportive (Chow, Tan, & Buhrmester, 2015; Kindermann, 2016). However, it is not developmentally advantageous to have coercive and conflict-ridden friendships (Schneider, 2016).

The importance of friendship was underscored in a two-year longitudinal study (Wentzel, Barry, & Caldwell, 2004). Sixth-grade students who did not have a friend engaged in less prosocial behavior (cooperation, sharing, helping others), had lower grades, and were more emotionally distressed (displaying depression, low well-being) than their counterparts who had one or more friends. Two years later, in the eighth grade, the students who did not have a friend in the sixth grade continued to be more emotionally distressed.

What are some characteristics of children's friendships?

©Purestock/Getty Images RF

---

developmental connection

Peers

Beginning in early adolescence, teenagers typically prefer to have a smaller number of friendships that are more intense and intimate. Connect to "Socioemotional Development in Adolescence."

---

intimacy in friendships Self-disclosure and the sharing of private thoughts.

Review Connect Reflect

LG3 Identify changes in peer relationships in middle and late childhood.

Review

- What developmental changes characterize peer relations in middle and late childhood?
- How does children's peer status influence their development?
- How is social cognition involved in children's peer relations?
- What is the nature of bullying?
- What are children's friendships like?

Connect

- Earlier in the chapter you read that most developmentalists agree that peers play an important role in the development of moral reasoning. Of the five peer statuses that you read about in this section, in which group do you think children would have the least opportunity to find answers to their moral reasoning questions, and why would this be the case?

Reflect *Your Own Personal Journey of Life*

- Which of the five peer statuses characterized you as a child? Did your peer status change in adolescence? How do you think your peer status as a child influenced your development?

4 What Are Some Important Aspects of Schools?

LG4 Characterize contemporary approaches to student learning and sociocultural diversity in schools.

Contemporary Approaches to Student Learning

Socioeconomic Status and Ethnicity

The whole art of teaching is the art of awakening the natural curiosity of young minds.

—ANATOLE FRANCE
French Novelist, 20th Century

For most children, entering the first grade signals new obligations. They form new relationships and develop new standards by which to judge themselves. School provides children with a rich source of new ideas to shape their sense of self. They will spend many years in schools as members of small societies in which there are tasks to be accomplished, people to socialize and be socialized by, and rules that define and limit behavior, feelings, and attitudes. By the time students graduate from high school, they will have spent 12,000 hours in the classroom.

CONTEMPORARY APPROACHES TO STUDENT LEARNING

Because there are so many approaches for teaching children, controversy swirls about the best way to teach children (Borich, 2017). There also is considerable interest in finding the best way to hold schools and teachers accountable for whether children are learning (Popham, 2017).

Is this classroom more likely constructivist or direct instruction? Explain.
©Elizabeth Crews

Constructivist and Direct Instruction Approaches

The **constructivist approach** is learner centered and emphasizes the importance of individuals actively constructing their knowledge and understanding with guidance from the teacher. In the constructivist view, teachers should not attempt to simply pour information into children's minds. Rather, children should be encouraged to explore their world, discover knowledge, reflect, and think critically with careful monitoring and meaningful guidance from the teacher (Kauchak & Eggen, 2017). The constructivist belief is that for too long in American education children have been required to sit still, be passive learners, and rotely memorize irrelevant as well as relevant information. Today, constructivism may include an emphasis on collaboration—children working together in their efforts to know and understand (Daniels, 2017; Johnson & others, 2018).

By contrast, the **direct instruction approach** is structured and teacher centered. It is characterized by teacher direction and control, high teacher expectations for students' progress, maximum time spent by students on academic tasks, and efforts by the teacher to keep negative emotional expression to a minimum. An important goal in the direct instruction approach is maximizing student learning time (Parkay, 2016; Webb & Metha, 2017).

Advocates of the constructivist approach argue that the direct instruction approach turns children into passive learners and does not adequately challenge them to think in critical and creative ways (Borich, 2017). The direct instruction enthusiasts say that the constructivist approaches do not give enough attention to the content of a discipline, such as history or science. They also believe that the constructivist approaches are too relativistic and vague.

Some experts in educational psychology believe that many effective teachers use both a constructivist *and* a direct instruction approach rather than relying on either approach exclusively (Johnson & others, 2018; Webb & Metha, 2017). Further, some circumstances may call more for a constructivist approach, others for a direction instruction approach. For example, experts increasingly recommend an explicit, intellectually engaging direct instruction approach when teaching students with a reading or a writing disability (Cunningham, 2017; Temple & others, 2018).

Accountability Since the 1990s, the U.S. public and governments at every level have demanded increased accountability from schools. One result has been the spread of state-mandated tests to measure just what students had or had not learned (Martin, Sargrad, & Batel, 2017;

constructivist approach A learner-centered approach that emphasizes the importance of individuals actively constructing their knowledge and understanding with guidance from the teacher.

direct instruction approach A structured, teacher-centered approach that is characterized by teacher direction and control, mastery of academic skills, high expectations for students' progress, maximum time spent on learning tasks, and efforts to keep negative emotional expression to a minimum.

Popham, 2017). Many states identified objectives for students in their state and created tests to measure whether students were meeting those objectives. This approach became national policy in 2002 when the No Child Left Behind (NCLB) legislation was signed into law.

Advocates argue that statewide standardized testing will have a number of positive effects. These include improved student performance; more time teaching the subjects that are tested; high expectations for all students; identification of poorly performing schools, teachers, and administrators; and improved confidence in schools as test scores rise.

Critics argue that the NCLB legislation is doing more harm than good (Ladd, 2017; Sadker & Zittleman, 2016). One criticism stresses that using a single test as the sole indicator of students' progress and competence presents a very narrow view of students' skills (Lewis, 2007). This criticism is similar to the one leveled at IQ tests, which we described in "Cognitive Development in Middle and Late Childhood." To assess student progress and achievement, many psychologists and educators emphasize that a number of measures should be used, including tests, quizzes, projects, portfolios, classroom observations, and so on. Also, the tests used as part of NCLB don't measure creativity, motivation, persistence, flexible thinking, or social skills (Stiggins, 2008). Critics point out that teachers end up spending far too much class time "teaching to the test" by drilling students and having them memorize isolated facts at the expense of teaching that focuses on thinking skills, which students need for success in life (Ladd, 2017). Also, some individuals are concerned that in the era of No Child Left Behind scant attention is paid to students who are gifted because so much energy is devoted to raising the achievement level of students who are not doing well (Ballou & Springer, 2017).

Consider also the implications of the fact that each state is allowed to have different criteria for what constitutes passing or failing grades on tests designated for NCLB inclusion. An analysis of NCLB data indicated that almost every fourth-grade student in Mississippi knows how to read but only half of Massachusetts' students do (Birman & others, 2007). Clearly, Mississippi's standards for passing the reading test are far below those of Massachusetts. In the recent analysis of state-by-state comparisons, many states have taken the safe route by maintaining low standards for passing tests. Thus, while one of NCLB's goals was to raise standards for achievement in U.S. schools, apparently allowing states to set their own standards has had the opposite effect—reducing achievement standards.

In 2009, the Common Core State Standards Initiative was endorsed by the National Governors Association in an effort to implement more rigorous state guidelines for educating students. The Common Core State Standards specify what students should know and the skills they should develop at each grade level in various content areas (Common Core State Standards Initiative, 2017). A large majority of states have agreed to implement the Standards, but they have generated considerable controversy. Critics argue that they are simply a further effort by the federal government to control education and that they emphasize a "one-size-fits-all" approach that pays little attention to individual variations in students. Supporters say that the Standards provide much-needed detailed guidelines and important milestones for students to achieve.

The most recent initiative in U.S. education is the *Every Student Succeeds Act (ESSA)* that was passed into law in December 2015 and was supposed to be implemented in the 2017-2018 school year (Rothman, 2016). In 2017, the Trump administration still is planning to go forward with ESSA but plans on giving states much more flexibility in implementing the law (Klein, 2017). The law replaced *No Child Left Behind*, in the process modifying but not completely eliminating standardized testing. ESSA retains annual testing for reading and writing success in grades 3 to 8, then once more in high school. The new law also allows states to scale back the role that tests have played in holding schools accountable for student achievement. And schools must use at least one nonacademic factor—such as student engagement—when tracking schools' success.

Other aspects of the new law include still requiring states and districts to improve their lowest-performing schools and to ensure that they improve their work with historically underperforming students, such as English-language learners, ethnic minority students, and students with a disability. Also, states and districts are required to put in place challenging academic standards, although they can opt out of state standards involving *Common Core*. However, with changing political control in the federal government, it remains to be seen if the ESSA educational policy will be enacted.

What are some issues involved in the No Child Left Behind legislation?
©Ocean/Corbis RF

SOCIOECONOMIC STATUS AND ETHNICITY

Children from low-income, ethnic minority backgrounds often have more difficulties in school than do their middle-socioeconomic-status, non-Latino White counterparts. Why? Critics argue that schools have not done a good job of educating low-income, ethnic minority students to overcome the barriers to their achievement (Koppleman, 2017; Troppe & others, 2017). Let's further explore the roles of socioeconomic status and ethnicity in schools.

The Education of Students from Low-Income Backgrounds Many children in poverty face problems that present barriers to their learning (Gardner, Brooks-Gunn, & Chase-Lansdale, 2016; Wadsworth & others, 2016). They might have parents who don't set high educational standards for them, who are incapable of reading to them, or who don't have enough money to pay for educational materials and experiences, such as books and trips to zoos and museums. They might be malnourished or live in areas where crime and violence are a way of life. One study revealed that the longer children experienced poverty, the more detrimental the poverty was to their cognitive development (Najman & others, 2009).

Compared with schools in higher-income areas, schools in low-income areas are more likely to have a high proportion of students with low achievement test scores, low graduation rates, and a smaller proportion of students going to college; they also are more likely to have young teachers with less experience; and they are more likely to encourage rote learning (Curtis & Bandy, 2016; Gollnick & Chinn, 2017). Too few schools in low-income neighborhoods provide students with environments that are conducive to learning (Duncan, Magnuson, & Votruba-Drzal, 2017; Sommer & others, 2016). Many of the schools' buildings and classrooms are old and crumbling. These are the types of undesirable conditions Jonathan Kozol (2005) observed in many inner-city schools, including the South Bronx in New York City, as described at the beginning of the chapter.

Much of the focus on the lives of children living in poverty has emphasized improving their future prospects in educational and economic development. A recent analysis concluded that their social and emotional functioning has often been ignored and should be given more attention (Crosnoe & Leventhal, 2014).

Schools and school programs are the focus of some poverty interventions (Dragoset & others, 2017). In a recent intervention with first-generation immigrant children attending high-poverty schools, the City Connects program was successful in improving children's math and reading achievement at the end of elementary school (Dearing & others, 2016). The program is directed by a full-time school counselor or social worker in each school. Annual reviews of children's needs are conducted during the first several months of the school year. Then site coordinators and teachers collaborate to develop a student support plan that might include an after-school program, tutoring, mentoring, or family counseling. For children identified as having intense needs (about 8 to 10 percent), a wider team of professionals becomes involved, possibly including school psychologists, principals, nurses, and/or community agency staff, to create additional supports.

Further, efforts to intervene in the lives of children living in poverty need to jointly focus on improving schools and neighborhoods (Gershoff & Benner, 2014). To read further about ways to improve the schools and families of children living in poverty, see the *Connecting with Diversity* interlude.

Ethnicity in Schools More than one-third of all African American and almost one-third of all Latino students attend schools in the 47 largest city school districts in the United States, compared with only 5 percent of all non-Latino White and 22 percent of all Asian American students. Many of these inner-city schools are still informally segregated, are grossly underfunded, and do not provide adequate opportunities for children to learn effectively. Thus, the effects of SES and the effects of ethnic minority status are often intertwined (Chaudry & others, 2017; Umana-Taylor & Douglass, 2017).

Even outside inner-city schools, school segregation remains a factor in U.S. education (Gollnick & Chinn, 2017). Almost one-third of all African American and Latino students attend schools in which 90 percent or more of the students are from minority groups (Banks, 2014).

The school experiences of students from different ethnic groups vary considerably (Koppleman, 2017). African American and Latino students are much less likely than non-Latino White or Asian American students to be enrolled in academic, college preparatory programs and are much more likely to be enrolled in remedial and special education programs. Asian American students are far more likely than other ethnic minority groups to take advanced

The New Hope Intervention Program

As we have just discussed, far too many schools in low-income neighborhoods provide students with environments that are not conducive to effective learning (Weisner & Duncan, 2014).

Might intervention with families of children living in poverty improve children's school performance? In an experimental study, Aletha Huston and her colleagues (2006; Gupta, Thornton, & Huston, 2008) evaluated the effects of New Hope—a program designed to increase parental employment and reduce family poverty—on adolescent development. They randomly assigned families with 6- to 10-year-old children living in poverty to the New Hope program or to a control group. New Hope offered adults who were living in poverty and were employed 30 or more hours a week benefits that were designed to increase family income (a wage supplement that ensured that net income increased as parents earned more) and to provide work supports through subsidized child care (for any child under age 13) and health insurance. Management services were provided to New Hope participants to assist them in job searches and other needs. The New Hope program was available to the experimental group families for three years (until the children were 9 to 13 years old).

Five years after the program began and two years after it had ended, the program's effects on the children were examined when they were 11 to 15 years old. Compared with adolescents in the control group, New Hope adolescents were more competent at reading, had better school performance, were less likely to be in special education classes, had more positive social skills, and were more likely to be in formal after-school arrangements. New Hope parents reported better psychological well-being and a greater sense of self-efficacy in managing their adolescents than control group parents did. In further assessment, the influence of the New Hope program on 9- to 19-year-olds after they left the program was evaluated (McLoyd & others, 2011). Positive outcomes especially occurred for African American boys, who became more optimistic about their future employment and career prospects after experiencing the New Hope program.

---

math and science courses in high school. African American students are twice as likely as Latinos, Native Americans, or Whites to be suspended from school.

Following are some effective strategies for improving relationships among ethnically diverse students:

- *Turn the class into a jigsaw classroom.* When Elliot Aronson was a professor at the University of Texas at Austin, the school system contacted him for ideas on how to reduce the increasing racial tension in classrooms. Aronson (1986) developed the concept of a "jigsaw classroom," in which students from different cultural backgrounds are placed in a cooperative group in which they have to construct different parts of a project to reach a common goal. Aronson used the term *jigsaw* because he likened the technique to a group of students cooperating to put different pieces together to complete a jigsaw puzzle. How might this work? Team sports, drama productions, and music performances are examples of contexts in which students participate cooperatively to reach a common goal; however, the jigsaw technique also lends itself to group science projects, history reports, and other learning experiences with a variety of subject matter.

- *Encourage students to have positive personal contact with diverse other students.* Mere contact does not do the job of improving relationships with diverse others. For example, busing ethnic minority students to predominantly non-Latino White schools, or vice versa, has not reduced prejudice or improved interethnic relations. What matters is what happens after children get to school. Especially beneficial in improving interethnic relations is sharing one's worries, successes, failures, coping strategies, interests, and other personal information with people of other ethnicities. When this happens, people tend to look at others as individuals rather than as members of a homogeneous group.

- *Reduce bias.* Teachers can reduce bias by displaying images of children from diverse ethnic and cultural

How Would You...?
If you were an **educator**, how would you attempt to improve the quality of schools with high concentrations of ethnic minority children?

In *The Shame of the Nation,* Jonathan Kozol (2005) criticized the inadequate quality and lack of resources in many U.S. schools, especially those in the poverty areas of inner cities that have high concentrations of ethnic minority children. Kozol praises teachers like Angela Lively (*above*), who keeps a box of shoes in her Indianapolis classroom for students in need.
©Michael Conroy/AP Images

groups, selecting play materials and classroom activities that encourage cultural understanding, helping students resist stereotyping, and working with parents to reduce children's exposure to bias and prejudice at home.

- *View the school and community as a team.* James Comer (1988, 2004, 2006) advocates a
community, team approach as the best way to educate children. Three important aspects
of the Comer Project for Change are (1) a governance and management team that develops a comprehensive school plan, assessment strategy, and staff development plan; (2) a
mental health or school support team; and (3) a parents' program. Comer believes that
the entire school community should have a cooperative rather than an adversarial attitude. The Comer program is currently operating in more than 600 schools in 26 states.
Read further about James Comer's work in the *Connecting with Careers* profile.

- *Be a competent cultural mediator.* Teachers can play a powerful role as cultural mediators
by being sensitive to biased content in materials and classroom interactions, learning more
about different ethnic groups, being sensitive to children's ethnic attitudes, viewing students
of color positively, and thinking of positive ways to get parents of color more involved as
partners with teachers in educating children (Cushner, McClelland, & Safford, 2015).

connecting with careers

James Comer, Child Psychiatrist

James Comer grew up in a low-income neighborhood in East Chicago,
Indiana, and credits his parents with leaving no doubt about the impor-
tance of education. He obtained a BA degree from Indiana University. He
went on to obtain a medical degree from Howard University College of
Medicine, a Master of Public Health degree from the University of Michigan
School of Public Health, and psychiatry training at the Yale University
School of Medicine's Child Study Center. He currently is the Maurice Falk
Professor of Child Psychiatry at the Yale University Child Study Center and
an associate dean at the Yale University Medical School. During his years
at Yale, Comer has concentrated his career on promoting a focus on child
development as a way of improving schools. His efforts in support of
healthy development of young people are known internationally.

Comer is, perhaps, best known for founding the School
Development Program in 1968, which promotes the collaboration of
parents, educators, and community to improve social, emotional, and
academic outcomes for children.

James Comer is shown with some of the inner-city children
who attend a school that became a better learning
environment because of Comer's intervention.
©John Abbott Photography

For more about what child psychiatrists do, see the Careers in Children's Development appendix.

Review *Connect* Reflect

LG4 Characterize contemporary approaches to student learning and sociocultural diversity in schools.

Review

- What are two major contemporary issues in educating children?
- How do socioeconomic status and ethnicity influence schooling?

Connect

- Earlier, you read about Carol Dweck's concept of mindset. How could the concept of mindset be applied to

improving the education of elementary school children?

Reflect *Your Own Personal Journey of Life*

- How would you rate the quality of teachers in your elementary school? Were their expectations for achievement too high or too low? Describe the best elementary school teacher you had and the worst.

topical connections *looking forward*

This chapter concludes the discussion of children's development in middle and late childhood. In "Physical Development in Adolescence" you will read about the dramatic changes of puberty, how the brain changes in adolescence, sexuality, and various aspects of adolescents' health. In "Cognitive Development in Adolescence" you will examine impressive advances in adolescents' thinking and the challenges of educating adolescents effectively. And in "Socioemotional Development in Adolescence" you will learn that adolescents spend far more time thinking about their identity—who they are, what they are all about, and where they are going in life—than they did when they were children. Transformations in relationships with parents and peers also characterize adolescence.

reach your **learning goals**

Socioemotional Development in Middle and Late Childhood

1 What Is the Nature of Emotional and Personality Development in Middle and Late Childhood?	**LG1** Discuss emotional and personality development in middle and late childhood.

The Self

- In middle and late childhood, self-understanding increasingly involves social and psychological characteristics, including social comparison. Children increase their perspective taking in middle and late childhood, and their social understanding shows increasing psychological sophistication as well.

- Self-concept refers to domain-specific evaluations of the self. Self-esteem refers to global evaluations of the self and is also referred to as self-worth or self-image. Self-esteem is only moderately related to school performance but is more strongly linked to initiative. Four ways to increase self-esteem are to (1) identify the causes of low self-esteem, (2) provide emotional support and social approval, (3) help children achieve, and (4) help children cope.

- Erikson's fourth stage of development, industry versus inferiority, characterizes the middle and late childhood years.

Emotional Development

- Developmental changes in emotion include increasing one's understanding of complex emotions such as pride and shame, detecting that more than one emotion can be experienced in a particular situation, taking into account the circumstances that led up to an emotional reaction, improving the ability to suppress or conceal negative emotions, and using self-initiated strategies to redirect feelings.

- In middle and late childhood, attachment becomes more sophisticated as children's social worlds expand. As children get older, they use a greater variety of coping strategies and more cognitive strategies.

Moral Development

- Kohlberg argued that moral development consists of three levels—preconventional, conventional, and postconventional—and six stages (two at each level). Kohlberg maintained that these stages were age-related. Influences on movement through the stages include cognitive development, imitation and cognitive conflict, peer relations, and perspective taking.

- Criticisms of Kohlberg's theory have been made, especially by Gilligan, who advocates a stronger care perspective. Other criticisms focus on the inadequacy of moral reasoning to predict moral behavior, the intuitiveness of moral thought, the role of emotion, and cultural and family influences.

- The moral personality view emphasizes the importance of moral identity, moral character, and moral exemplars. The domain theory of moral development states that there are different domains of social knowledge and reasoning, including moral, social conventional, and personal.

- Prosocial behavior involves positive moral behaviors such as sharing. Most sharing in the first three years is not done for empathy, but at about 4 years of age empathy contributes to sharing. By the start of the elementary school years, children express objective ideas about fairness.

Gender

- Gender stereotypes are broad categories that reflect impressions and beliefs about males and females. A number of physical differences exist between males and females.

- In terms of cognitive skills, girls have better reading and writing skills than do boys. Some experts argue that cognitive differences between males and females have been exaggerated.

- In terms of socioemotional differences, boys are more physically aggressive than girls, while girls are more people oriented and boys are more "things" oriented. Tannen argues that females prefer rapport talk and males prefer report talk, but recent research indicates that gender differences in communication are small. Females regulate their emotions better and engage in more prosocial behavior than males do.

- Gender bias exists in schools, and recent interest has been directed to single-sex schooling. It is important to think about gender in terms of context.

2 What Are Some Changes in Parenting and Families in Middle and Late Childhood?

 LG2 Describe changes in parenting and families in middle and late childhood.

Developmental Changes in Parent-Child Relationships

Parents as Managers

Stepfamilies

- Parents spend less time with children during middle and late childhood than they did in early childhood. Parents especially play an important role in supporting and stimulating children's academic achievement. Discipline changes and control are more coregulatory.

- Parents have important roles as managers of children's opportunities, as monitors of their behavior, and as social initiators and arrangers. Mothers are more likely than fathers to function in these parental management roles.

- As in divorced families, children living in stepparent families have more adjustment problems than their counterparts in nondivorced families. However, a majority of children in stepfamilies do not have adjustment problems. Children in complex (blended) stepfamilies have more problems than children in simple stepfamilies or nondivorced families.

3 What Changes Characterize Peer Relationships in Middle and Late Childhood?

LG3 Identify changes in peer relationships in middle and late childhood.

Developmental Changes

Peer Status

- Among the developmental changes in peer relations in middle and late childhood are increased preference for same-sex groups, increased time spent in peer interaction, expansion in the size of the peer group, and less supervision of the peer group by adults.

- Popular children are frequently nominated as a best friend and are rarely disliked by their peers. Average children receive an average number of both positive and negative nominations from their peers. Neglected children are infrequently nominated as a best friend but are not disliked by their peers. Rejected children are infrequently nominated as a best friend and are actively disliked by their peers. Controversial children are frequently nominated both as a best friend and as being disliked by peers. Rejected children are especially at risk for a number of problems.

- Social information-processing skills and social knowledge are two important dimensions of social cognition in peer relations.

- Significant numbers of children are bullied, and this can result in short-term and long-term negative effects for both the victims and the bullies.

- Like adult friends, children who are friends tend to be similar to each other. Children's friendships serve six functions: companionship, stimulation, physical support, ego support, social comparison, and intimacy/affection.

4 What Are Some Important Aspects of Schools?

LG4 Characterize contemporary approaches to student learning and sociocultural diversity in schools.

- Contemporary approaches to student learning include the constructivist approach (a learner-centered approach) and the direct instruction approach (a teacher-centered approach).

- In the United States, standardized testing of elementary school students was mandated nationally in 2002 by the No Child Left Behind federal legislation. Numerous criticisms of NCLB have been made. Common Core standards have recently been created to improve schools, and the Every Student Succeeds Act has been proposed to replace NCLB in 2017–2018.

- Children in poverty face many barriers to learning at school as well as at home. The effects of SES and ethnicity on schools are intertwined, as many U.S. schools are segregated. Low expectations for ethnic minority children represent one of the barriers to their learning.

key terms

average children
care perspective
constructivist
    approach
controversial children
conventional reasoning
direct instruction approach
domain theory of moral
    development

gender stereotypes
heteronomous morality
individualism, instrumental
    purpose, and exchange
intimacy in friendships
justice perspective
mutual interpersonal
    expectations, relationships,
    and interpersonal conformity

neglected children
popular children
postconventional
    reasoning
preconventional
    reasoning
rapport talk
rejected children
report talk

self-concept
self-esteem
social contract or
    utility and individual rights
social conventional
    reasoning
social systems
    morality
universal ethical principles

key people

Elliot Aronson
John Coie
James Comer
William Damon

Kenneth Dodge
Erik Erikson
Carol Gilligan
Willard Hartup

E. Mavis Hetherington
Aletha Huston
Kathryn Kerns
Lawrence Kohlberg

Jonathan Kozol
Dan Olweus
Diane Ruble
Deborah Tannen

connecting with **improving the lives of children**

STRATEGIES

Guiding Children's Socioemotional Development

What are some good strategies for nourishing children's socioemotional skills?

- *Improve children's self-esteem.* This can be accomplished by identifying the causes of the child's low self-esteem, providing emotional support and social approval, and helping the child achieve.

- *Help children understand their emotions and cope with stress.* When children are experiencing considerable stress, try to remove at least one stressor from their lives. Also help the child learn effective coping strategies.

- *Nurture children's moral development.* Parents can improve their children's morality by being warm and supportive rather than punitive, using reasoning when disciplining, providing opportunities for children to learn about others' perspectives and feelings, involving children in family decision making, and modeling prosocial moral behavior.

- *Adapt to developmental changes in children.* Because parents typically spend less time with children in middle and late childhood, it is important to strengthen children's self-control. As in early childhood, authoritative parenting tends to be more effective than authoritarian, neglectful, or indulgent parenting.

- *Improve children's peer and friendship skills.* Peer and friendship relations become increasingly important to elementary school children. Adults can talk with children about the benefits of being nice, engaging in prosocial behavior, and providing support to peers and friends. Parents also can communicate to children that being aggressive, self-centered, and inconsiderate of others harms peer and friendship relations.

- *Create schools that support children's socioemotional development.* Not only do good teachers know how to challenge and stimulate children's cognitive development, but they also know how to make children feel good about themselves. Too much of elementary school education involves negative feedback. We need more classrooms in which children are excited about learning. This learning should be designed to increase children's self-esteem, not wreck their emotional well-being. Parents need to encourage and support their children's educational accomplishments but not set unrealistic achievement expectations.

RESOURCES

The African American Child (2nd ed.) (2014)
Yvette Harris and James Graham
New York: Springer

An outstanding book by leading experts that provides an in-depth exploration of African American children and their families in many different contexts.

National Stepfamily Resource Center
www.stepfamilies.info

This Web site provides a clearinghouse and support network for stepparents, remarried parents, and their children.

Cyberbullying and the Wild, Wild Web (2016)
J.A. Hitchcock
Lanham, MD: Rowman & Littlefield

An excellent resource for learning more about preventing cyberbullying and what to do if happens.

In no order of things is adolescence the simple time of life.

—Jean Erskine Stewart
American Writer, 20th Century

Adolescence

Adolescents try on one face after another, seeking to find a face of their own. Their generation of young people is the fragile cable by which the best and the worst of their parents' generation is transmitted to the present. In the end, there are only two lasting bequests parents can leave youth— one is roots, the other wings. Section 6 contains three chapters: "Physical Development in Adolescence," "Cognitive Development in Adolescence," and "Socioemotional Development in Adolescence."

chapter 14

PHYSICAL DEVELOPMENT IN ADOLESCENCE

chapter **outline**

① What Is the Nature of Adolescence?

Learning Goal 1 Discuss views and developmental transitions that involve adolescence.

Positive and Negative Views of Adolescence
Developmental Transitions

② What Are the Physical and Psychological Aspects of Puberty?

Learning Goal 2 Describe puberty's characteristics, developmental changes, psychological dimensions, and the development of the brain.

Sexual Maturation, Height, and Weight
Hormonal Changes
Timing and Variations in Puberty
Psychological Dimensions of Puberty
The Brain

③ What Are the Dimensions of Adolescent Sexuality?

Learning Goal 3 Characterize adolescent sexuality.

Developing a Sexual Identity
Timing and Trends in Adolescent Sexual Behavior
Sexual Risk Taking in Adolescence

④ How Can Adolescents' Health and Health-Enhancing Assets Be Characterized?

Learning Goal 4 Summarize adolescents' health and eating disorders.

Adolescent Health
Leading Causes of Death in Adolescence
Substance Use and Abuse
Eating Problems and Disorders

©Kevin Dodge/Corbis/Getty Images

Fifteen-year-old Latisha developed a drinking problem, and recently she was kicked off the cheerleading squad for missing practice too often—but that didn't stop her drinking. She and her friends began skipping school regularly so they could drink.

Fourteen-year-old Arnie is a juvenile delinquent. Last week he stole a TV set, struck his mother and bloodied her face, broke out some streetlights in the neighborhood, and threatened a boy with a wrench and hammer.

Twelve-year-old Katie Bell, more than just about anything else, wanted a playground in her town. She knew that the other kids also wanted one, so she put together a group that generated funding ideas for the playground. They presented their ideas to the town council. Her group got more youth involved, and they raised money by selling candy and sandwiches door-to-door. The playground became a reality—a place where, as Katie says, "People have picnics and make friends." Katie's advice: "You won't get anywhere if you don't try."

Adolescents like Latisha and Arnie are the ones we hear about the most. But there are many adolescents like Katie who contribute in positive ways to their communities and competently make the transition through adolescence. Indeed, for most adolescents, adolescence is not a time of rebellion, crisis, pathology, and deviance. A far more accurate vision of adolescence is that it is a time of evaluation, decision making, commitment, and carving out a place in the world. Most of the problems of today's youth are not with the youth themselves. What adolescents need is access to a range of legitimate opportunities and to long-term support from adults who care deeply about them. In a recent survey, only 20 percent of U.S. 15-year-olds reported that they have had meaningful relationships outside of their family that help them to succeed in life (Search Institute, 2010).

Katie Bell *(front)* and some of her volunteers.
©Ronald Cortes

---

topical **connections** *looking **back***

You have explored the physical, cognitive, and socioemotional development that characterizes children in the elementary school years. In regard to physical development, you learned that growth continues but at a slower pace than in infancy and early childhood. In middle and late childhood, gross motor skills become much smoother and more coordinated, and fine motor skills also improve. Significant advances in the development of the brain's prefrontal cortex also occur in middle and late childhood. In this chapter, you will study how the slower physical growth in middle and late childhood is replaced by the dramatic changes of puberty and continued transformations in the brain.

preview

Adolescence is an important juncture in the lives of many individuals, a time when many health habits—good or bad—are formed and ingrained. In this chapter, we explore what adolescence is, examine its physical and psychological changes, discuss adolescent sexuality, and then describe several adolescent problems and health issues.

1 What Is the Nature of Adolescence?

LG1 Discuss views and developmental transitions that involve adolescence.

> Positive and Negative Views of Adolescence   Developmental Transitions

In youth, we clothe ourselves with rainbows and go brave as the zodiac.

—RALPH WALDO EMERSON
American Poet and Essayist, 19th Century

As in development during childhood, a number of genetic, biological, environmental, and social factors interact in adolescent development. During their first decade of life, adolescents experienced thousands of hours of interactions with parents, peers, and teachers, but now they face dramatic biological changes, new experiences, and new developmental tasks. Relationships with parents take a different form, moments with peers become more intimate, and dating occurs for the first time, as do sexual exploration and possibly intercourse. The adolescent's thoughts are more abstract and idealistic. Biological changes trigger a heightened interest in body image. Adolescence has both continuity and discontinuity with childhood.

POSITIVE AND NEGATIVE VIEWS OF ADOLESCENCE

There is a long history of worrying about how adolescents will turn out. In 1904, G. Stanley Hall proposed the "storm-and-stress" view that adolescence is a turbulent time charged with conflict and mood swings. However, when Daniel Offer and his colleagues (1988) studied the self-images of adolescents in the United States, Australia, Bangladesh, Hungary, Israel, Italy, Japan, Taiwan, Turkey, and West Germany, at least 73 percent of the adolescents displayed a healthy self-image. Although there were differences among them, the adolescents were happy most of the time, they enjoyed life, they perceived themselves as able to exercise self-control, they valued work and school, they expressed confidence about their sexual selves, they expressed positive feelings toward their families, and they felt they had the capability to cope with life's stresses—not exactly a storm-and-stress portrayal of adolescence.

However, in matters of taste and manners, the young people of every generation have seemed radical, unnerving, and different from adults—different in how they look, in how they behave, in the music they enjoy, in their hairstyles, and in the clothing they choose. It would be an enormous error, though, to perceive adolescents' enthusiasm for trying on new identities and enjoying moderate amounts of outrageous behavior as hostility toward parental and societal standards. Acting out and boundary testing are time-honored ways in which adolescents move toward accepting, rather than rejecting, parental values.

Social policy is the course of action designed by the national government to influence the welfare of its citizens. Currently, many researchers in adolescent development are designing studies that ideally will facilitate wise and effective social policy decision making (Duncan, Magnuson, & Votruba-Drzal, 2017; Galinsky & others, 2017; Gonzales & others, 2016; Hall, 2017; Yoshikawa & others, 2016).

Peter Benson and his colleagues (Benson, 2010; Benson & Scales, 2009a, b, 2011; Scales, Benson, & Roehlkepartain, 2011) argue that the United States has a fragmented social

Growing up has never been easy. However, adolescence is not best viewed as a time of rebellion, crisis, pathology, and deviance. A far more accurate vision of adolescence describes it as a time of evaluation, of decision making, of commitment, and of carving out a place in the world. Most of the problems of today's youth are not with the youth themselves. What adolescents need is access to a range of legitimate opportunities and to long-term support from adults who deeply care about them. *What might be some examples of such support and caring?*
©Regine Mahaux/The Image Bank/Getty Images

policy for youth that too often has focused only on the negative developmental deficits of adolescents, especially health-compromising behaviors such as drug use and delinquency, and not enough on positive strength-based approaches. According to Benson and his colleagues (2004), taking a strength-based approach to social policy for youth, also referred to as *positive youth development (PYD)*,

> adopts more of a wellness perspective, places particular emphasis on the existence of healthy conditions, and expands the concept of health to include the skills and competencies needed to succeed in employment, education, and life. It moves beyond the eradication of risk and deliberately argues for the promotion of well-being (Benson & others, 2004, p. 783).

developmental **connection**

Community

Service learning is linked to many positive outcomes for adolescents. Connect to "Cognitive Development in Adolescence."

Research indicates that youth benefit enormously when they have caring adults in their lives in addition to parents or guardians (Lerner & others, 2017). Caring adults—such as coaches, neighbors, teachers, mentors, and after-school leaders—can serve as role models, confidants, advocates, and resources. Relationships with caring adults are powerful when youth know they are respected, that they matter to the adult, and that the adult wants to be a resource in their lives. However, in one survey, only 20 percent of U.S. 15-year-olds reported having meaningful relationships outside of their family that helped them to succeed in life (Search Institute, 2010).

Most adolescents negotiate the lengthy path to adult maturity successfully, but too large a group does not. Ethnic, cultural, gender, socioeconomic, age, and lifestyle factors influence the actual life trajectory of each adolescent (Juster & others, 2016; McQueen, 2017; Ruck, Peterson-Badali, & Freeman, 2017; Spencer & Swanson, 2016). Different portrayals of adolescence emerge, depending on the particular group of adolescents being described. Today's adolescents are exposed to a complex menu of lifestyle options through technology, and many face the temptations of drug use and sexual activity at increasingly young ages. Too many adolescents are not provided with adequate opportunities and support to become competent adults (Andrade & others, 2016; Callina & others, 2017; Lo & others, 2017; Umana-Taylor & Douglass, 2017).

DEVELOPMENTAL TRANSITIONS

Developmental transitions are often important junctures in people's lives. Such transitions include moving from the prenatal period to birth and infancy, from infancy to early childhood, and from early childhood to middle and late childhood. For adolescents, two important transitions are from childhood to adolescence and from adolescence to adulthood. Let's explore these transitions.

Childhood to Adolescence   The transition from childhood to adolescence involves a number of biological, cognitive, and socioemotional changes. Among the biological changes are the growth spurt, hormonal changes, and sexual maturation that come with puberty. In early adolescence, changes take place in the brain that allow for more advanced thinking. Also at this time, adolescents begin to stay up later at night and sleep later in the morning.

Among the cognitive changes that occur during the transition from childhood to adolescence are increases in abstract, idealistic, and logical thinking. As they make this transition, adolescents begin to think in more egocentric ways, often sensing that they are onstage, unique, and invulnerable. In response to these changes, parents place more responsibility for decision making on the young adolescents' shoulders.

Among the socioemotional changes adolescents undergo are a quest for independence, conflict with parents, and a desire to spend more time with peers. Conversations with friends become more intimate and include more self-disclosure. As children enter adolescence, they attend schools that are larger and more impersonal than their neighborhood grade schools. Achievement becomes a more serious business, and academic challenges increase. At this time, increased sexual maturation produces a much greater interest in romantic relationships. Young adolescents also experience greater mood swings than they did when they were children.

In sum, the transition from childhood to adolescence is complex and multidimensional, involving change in many different aspects of an individual's life. Negotiating this transition successfully requires considerable adaptation and thoughtful, sensitive support from caring adults.

Adolescence to Adulthood: Emerging Adulthood   Another important transition occurs from adolescence to adulthood (Arnett. 2015). It has been said that adolescence begins in biology and ends in culture. That is, the transition from childhood to adolescence

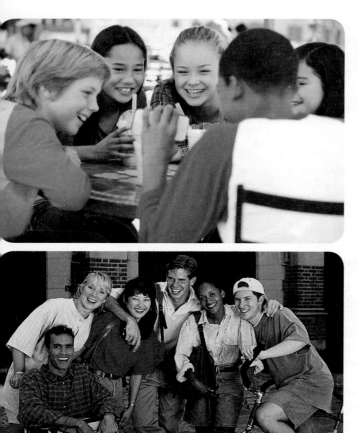

What are some physical, cognitive, and socioemotional changes involved in the transition from childhood to adolescence? What characterizes emerging adulthood?
(*Top*): ©bowdenimages/Getty Images RF; (*bottom*) ©Chuck Savage/Corbis/ Getty Images

begins with the onset of pubertal maturation, whereas the transition from adolescence to adulthood is determined by cultural standards and experiences. Around the world, youth are increasingly expected to delay their entry into adulthood, in large part because the information society in which we now live requires that they obtain more education than their parents' generation received. Thus, the transition between adolescence and adulthood can be a long one as adolescents develop more effective skills to become full members of society.

Recently, the transition from adolescence to adulthood has been referred to as emerging adulthood (Arnett, 2000, 2006, 2007, 2012, 2015). The age range for **emerging adulthood** is approximately 18 to 25 years of age. Experimentation and exploration characterize the emerging adult. At this point in their development, many individuals are still exploring which career path they want to follow, what they want their identity to be, and which lifestyle they want to adopt (for example, single, cohabiting, or married) (Gardner & Chao, 2017; Lapsley & Hardy, 2017; Padilla-Walker & Nelson, 2017).

Jeffrey Arnett (2006) concluded that five key features characterize emerging adulthood:

- *Exploring identity, especially in love and work.* Emerging adulthood is the time during which key changes in identity take place for many individuals.
- *Experiencing instability.* Residential changes peak during early adulthood, a time during which there also is often instability in love, work, and education.
- *Being self-focused.* According to Arnett (2006, p. 10), emerging adults "are self-focused in the sense that they have little in the way of social obligations, little in the way of duties and commitments to others, which leaves them with a great deal of autonomy in running their own lives."
- *Feeling in-between.* Many emerging adults don't consider themselves adolescents or full-fledged adults.
- *Experiencing the age of possibilities, a time when individuals have an opportunity to transform their lives.* Arnett (2006) describes two ways in which emerging adulthood is the age of possibilities. First, many emerging adults are optimistic about their future. Second, for emerging adults who have experienced difficult times while growing up, emerging adulthood presents an opportunity to steer their lives in a more positive direction (Masten, 2011a, b, 2013, 2014, 2015, 2017; Masten & Cicchetti, 2016; Masten & Kalstabakken, 2017).

A recent review and analysis of research on resilience in the transition to adulthood concluded that the increased freedom that is available to emerging adults in Western society places a premium on the capacity to plan ahead, delay gratification, and make positive choices (Burt & Paysnick, 2012). Also emphasized in resilient adaptation during emerging adulthood was the importance of forming positive close relationships—to some degree with parents, but more often with supportive romantic partners, close friends, and mentors.

Joseph and Claudia Allen (2009) wrote a book titled *Escaping the Endless Adolescence: How We Can Help Our Teenagers Grow Up Before They Grow Old*, and opened the book with a chapter titled, "Is Twenty-five the New Fifteen?" They argue that in recent decades adolescents have experienced a world that places more challenges on maturing into a competent adult. In their words (p. 17),

Generations ago, fourteen-year-olds used to drive, seventeen-year-olds led armies, and even average teens contributed labor and income that helped keep their families afloat. While facing other problems, those teens displayed adultlike maturity far more quickly than today's, who are remarkably well kept, but cut off from most of the responsibility, challenge, and growth-producing feedback of the adult world. Parents of twenty-somethings used to lament, "They grow up so fast." But that seems to be replaced with, "Well, . . . Mary's living at home a bit while she sorts things out."

The Allens conclude that what is happening to the current generation of adolescents is that after adolescence, they are experiencing "more adolescence" instead of adequately being launched into the adult years. Even many adolescents who have gotten good grades and then

emerging adulthood Occurring from approximately 18 to 25 years of age, this transitional period between adolescence and adulthood is characterized by experimentation and exploration.

as emerging adults continued to achieve academic success in college later find themselves in their mid-twenties not having a clue about how to find a meaningful job, manage their finances, or live independently.

The Allens offer the following suggestions for helping adolescents become more mature on their way to adulthood:

- *Provide them with opportunities to be contributors.* Help them move away from being consumers by creating more effective work experiences (quality work apprenticeships, for example) or service learning opportunities that allow adolescents to make meaningful contributions.
- *Give candid, quality feedback to adolescents.* Don't just shower praise and material things on them, but let them see how the real world works. Don't protect them from criticism, constructive or negative. Protecting them in this way only leaves them ill-equipped to deal with the ups and downs of the real world of adulthood.
- *Create positive adult connections with adolescents.* Many adolescents deny that they need parental support or attachment to parents, but to help them develop maturity on the way to adulthood, they do. Exploring a wider social world than in childhood, adolescents need to be connected to parents and other adults in positive ways to be able to handle autonomy maturely.
- *Challenge adolescents to become more competent.* Adults need to do fewer things for adolescents that they can accomplish for themselves. Providing adolescents with opportunities to engage in tasks that are just beyond their current level of ability stretches their minds and helps them to make progress along the road to maturity.

developmental connection

Families

Secure attachment to parents increases the likelihood that adolescents will be socially competent. Connect to "Socioemotional Development in Adolescence."

Review Connect Reflect

LG1 Discuss views and developmental transitions that involve adolescence.

Review

- What are some positive and negative views of adolescence?
- What are two key developmental transitions involving adolescence?

Connect

- How could positive youth development (PYD) be incorporated into the nation's social policy?

Reflect *Your Own Personal Journey of Life*

- You likely experienced some instances of stereotyping as an adolescent. What are some examples of circumstances in which you feel that you were stereotyped as an adolescent?

2 What Are the Physical and Psychological Aspects of Puberty?

LG2 Describe puberty's characteristics, developmental changes, psychological dimensions, and the development of the brain.

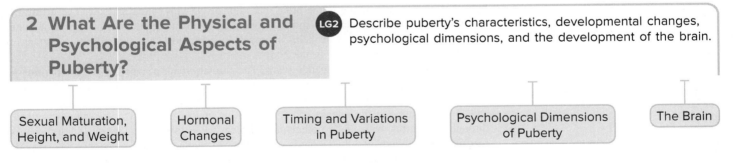

Sexual Maturation, Height, and Weight | Hormonal Changes | Timing and Variations in Puberty | Psychological Dimensions of Puberty | The Brain

One father remarked that the problem with his teenage son was not that he grew, but that he did not know when to stop growing. As we will see, there is considerable variation in the timing of the adolescent growth spurt. In addition to pubertal changes, other physical changes involve sexuality and brain development.

Puberty is not the same as adolescence. For most of us, puberty ends long before adolescence does, although puberty is the most important marker of the beginning of adolescence. **Puberty** is a brain-neuroendocrine process occurring primarily in early adolescence that provides stimulation for the rapid physical changes that take place in this period of development

puberty A brain-neuroendocrine process occurring primarily in early adolescence that provides stimulation for the rapid physical changes that accompany this period of development.

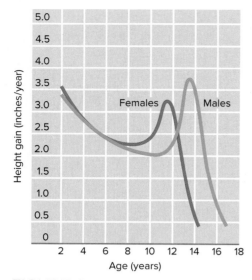

FIGURE 1

PUBERTAL GROWTH SPURT. On average, the peak of the growth spurt during puberty occurs two years earlier for girls (11½) than for boys (13½). *How are hormones related to the growth spurt and to the difference between the average height of adolescent boys and girls?*

menarche A girl's first menstrual period.

hormones Powerful chemical substances secreted by the endocrine glands and carried through the body by the bloodstream.

hypothalamus A structure in the brain that monitors eating and sex.

pituitary gland An important endocrine gland that controls growth and regulates other glands.

gonads The sex glands—the testes in males, the ovaries in females.

gonadotropins Hormones that stimulate the testes or ovaries.

testosterone A hormone associated in boys with the development of the genitals, an increase in height, and a change in voice.

estradiol A hormone associated in girls with breast, uterine, and skeletal development.

(Berenbaum, Beltz, & Corley, 2015; Shalitin & Kiess, 2017; Susman & Dorn, 2013). Rather than a specific event, puberty is a process that unfolds through a series of coordinated neuroendocrine changes. Among the most noticeable changes are signs of sexual maturation and increases in height and weight.

SEXUAL MATURATION, HEIGHT, AND WEIGHT

Male pubertal characteristics typically develop in the following order: increase in penis and testicle size, appearance of straight pubic hair, minor voice change, first ejaculation (which usually occurs through masturbation or a wet dream), appearance of curly pubic hair, onset of maximum growth in height and weight, growth of hair in armpits, more detectable voice changes, and, finally, growth of facial hair.

What is the order of appearance of physical changes in females? First, either the breasts enlarge or pubic hair appears. Later, hair appears in the armpits. As these changes occur, the female grows in height and her hips become wider than her shoulders. **Menarche**—a girl's first menstruation—comes rather late in the pubertal cycle. Initially, her menstrual cycles may be highly irregular. For the first several years, she may not ovulate every menstrual cycle; some girls do not ovulate at all until a year or two after menstruation begins. No voice changes comparable to those in pubertal males occur in pubertal females. By the end of puberty, the female's breasts have become more fully rounded.

Marked weight gains coincide with the onset of puberty. During early adolescence, girls tend to outweigh boys, but by about age 14 boys begin to surpass girls. Similarly, at the beginning of the adolescent period, girls tend to be as tall as or taller than boys of their age, but by the end of the middle school years most boys have caught up or, in many cases, surpassed girls in height.

As indicated in Figure 1, the growth spurt occurs approximately two years earlier for girls than for boys. The mean age at the beginning of the growth spurt in girls is 9; for boys, it is 11. The peak rate of pubertal change occurs at 11½ years for girls and 13½ years for boys. During their growth spurt, girls increase in height about 3½ inches per year, boys about 4 inches. Boys and girls who are shorter or taller than their peers before adolescence are likely to remain so during adolescence; however, as much as 30 percent of an individual's height in late adolescence is unexplained by his or her height in the elementary school years.

HORMONAL CHANGES

Behind the first whisker in boys and the widening of hips in girls is a flood of **hormones,** powerful chemical substances secreted by the endocrine glands and carried through the body by the bloodstream (Herting & Sowell, 2017). The endocrine system's role in puberty involves the interaction of the hypothalamus, the pituitary gland, and the gonads (see Figure 2). The **hypothalamus** is a structure in the brain that is involved with eating and sex. The **pituitary gland** is an important endocrine gland that controls growth and regulates other glands; among these, the **gonads**—the testes in males, the ovaries in females—are particularly important in giving rise to pubertal changes in the body.

How do the gonads, or sex glands, work? The pituitary sends a signal via **gonadotropins**—hormones that stimulate the testes or ovaries—to the appropriate gland to manufacture hormones. These hormones give rise to such changes as the production of sperm in males and menstruation and the release of eggs from the ovaries in females. The pituitary gland, through interaction with the hypothalamus, detects when the optimal level of hormones is reached and responds and maintains it with additional gonadotropin secretion.

Not only does the pituitary gland release gonadotropins that stimulate the testes and ovaries, but through interaction with the hypothalamus the pituitary gland also secretes hormones that either directly lead to growth and skeletal maturation or produce growth effects through interaction with the thyroid gland, located at the base of the throat.

The concentrations of certain hormones increase dramatically during adolescence (Berenbaum, Beltz, & Corley, 2015; Piekarski & others, 2017). **Testosterone** is a hormone associated in boys with genital maturation, an increase in height, and a change in voice. **Estradiol** is a type of estrogen; in girls it is associated with breast, uterine, and skeletal development. In one study, testosterone levels increased eighteenfold in boys but only twofold in girls during

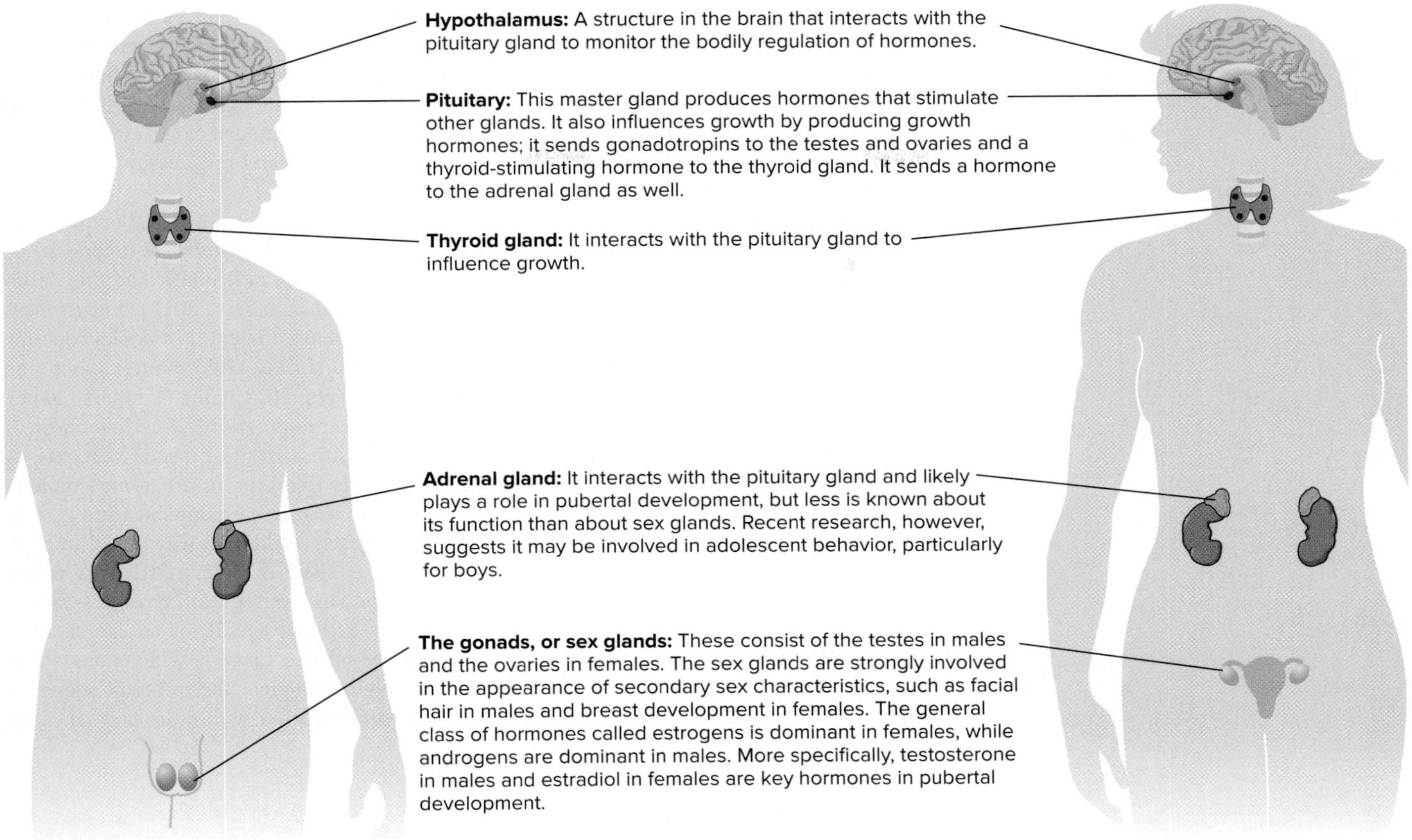

Hypothalamus: A structure in the brain that interacts with the pituitary gland to monitor the bodily regulation of hormones.

Pituitary: This master gland produces hormones that stimulate other glands. It also influences growth by producing growth hormones; it sends gonadotropins to the testes and ovaries and a thyroid-stimulating hormone to the thyroid gland. It sends a hormone to the adrenal gland as well.

Thyroid gland: It interacts with the pituitary gland to influence growth.

Adrenal gland: It interacts with the pituitary gland and likely plays a role in pubertal development, but less is known about its function than about sex glands. Recent research, however, suggests it may be involved in adolescent behavior, particularly for boys.

The gonads, or sex glands: These consist of the testes in males and the ovaries in females. The sex glands are strongly involved in the appearance of secondary sex characteristics, such as facial hair in males and breast development in females. The general class of hormones called estrogens is dominant in females, while androgens are dominant in males. More specifically, testosterone in males and estradiol in females are key hormones in pubertal development.

FIGURE **2**
THE MAJOR ENDOCRINE GLANDS INVOLVED IN PUBERTAL CHANGE

puberty; estradiol increased eightfold in girls but only twofold in boys (Nottelmann & others, 1987). Thus, both testosterone and estradiol are present in the hormonal makeup of both boys and girls, but testosterone dominates in male pubertal development and estradiol in female pubertal development (Benyi & Savendahl, 2017).

The same influx of hormones that grows hair on a male's chest and increases the fatty tissue in a female's breasts may also contribute to psychological development in adolescence (Wang & others, 2017). In one study of boys and girls ranging in age from 9 to 14, a higher concentration of testosterone was present in boys who rated themselves as more socially competent (Nottelmann & others, 1987). However, a recent research review concluded that there is insufficient quality research to confirm that changing testosterone levels during puberty are linked to mood and behavior in adolescent males (Duke, Balzer, & Steinbeck, 2014); hormonal effects by themselves do not account for adolescent development (Graber, 2013). For example, in one study, social factors were much better predictors of young adolescent girls' depression and anger than hormonal factors (Brooks-Gunn & Warren, 1989). Behavior and moods also can affect hormones. Stress, eating patterns, exercise, sexual activity, tension, and depression can activate or suppress various aspects of the hormonal system (Sontag & others, 2008). In sum, the hormone-behavior link is complex (Berenbaum, Beltz, & Corley, 2015; Susman & Dorn, 2013).

TIMING AND VARIATIONS IN PUBERTY

In the United States—where children mature up to a year earlier than children in European countries—the average age of menarche has declined significantly since the mid-nineteenth century. Fortunately, however, we are unlikely to see pubescent toddlers, since what has happened in the past century is likely the result of improved nutrition and health.

Why do the changes of puberty occur when they do, and how can variations in their timing be explained? Puberty is not an environmental accident. Programmed into the genes of every human being is the timing for the emergence of puberty (Day & others, 2017; Kiess & others, 2016). Puberty does not take place at 2 or 3 years of age and it does not occur in the twenties. Recently, scientists have begun to conduct molecular genetic studies in an attempt to identify specific genes that are linked to the onset and progression of puberty (Macedo & others, 2016).

However, puberty is not determined by genes alone. Nutrition, health, family stress, and other environmental factors also affect puberty's timing and makeup (Bratke & others, 2017; Villamor & Jansen, 2016). For example, a recent study of Chinese girls confirmed that childhood obesity contributed to an earlier onset of puberty (Zhai & others, 2015). Experiences that are linked to earlier pubertal onset also include an urban environment, low socioeconomic status, adoption, father absence, family conflict, maternal harshness, child maltreatment, and early substance use (Arim & others, 2011; Deardorff & others, 2011; Ellis & others, 2011). In many cases, puberty comes months earlier in these situations, and this earlier onset of puberty is likely explained by high rates of conflict and stress in these social contexts. A study of more than 15,000 girls in China revealed that girls living in an urban environment started puberty earlier than their counterparts who lived in a rural environment (Sun & others, 2012). One study revealed that maternal harshness in early childhood was linked to early maturation as well as sexual risk taking in adolescence (Belsky & others, 2010). A recent study found that child sexual abuse was linked to earlier pubertal onset (Noll & others, 2017).

For most boys, the pubertal sequence may begin as early as age 10 or as late as 13½, and may end as early as age 13 or as late as 17. Thus, the normal range is wide enough that, given two boys of the same chronological age, one might complete the pubertal sequence before the other one has begun it. For girls, menarche is considered within the normal range if it appears between the ages of 9 and 15.

PSYCHOLOGICAL DIMENSIONS OF PUBERTY

A host of psychological changes accompanies pubertal development. These changes involve body image and early and late maturation (Senin-Calderon & others, 2017; Solomon-Krakus & others, 2017).

Body Image Preoccupation with body image is strong throughout adolescence, but it is especially acute during early adolescence, a time when adolescents are more dissatisfied with their bodies than in late adolescence (Leone & others, 2014; Voelker, Reel, & Greenleaf, 2015).

Gender differences characterize adolescents' perceptions of their bodies (de Guzman & Nishina, 2014; Hoffman & Warschburger, 2017). In general, throughout puberty girls are less happy with their bodies and have more negative body images than boys do (Benowitz-Fredericks & others, 2012; Griffiths & others, 2017). As pubertal change proceeds, girls often become more dissatisfied with their bodies, probably because their body fat increases (Yuan, 2010). In contrast, boys become more satisfied as they move through puberty, probably because their muscle mass increases. However, when the entirety of adolescence is considered, rather than just puberty, researchers found that both boys' and girls' body images became more positive as they moved from the beginning to the end of adolescence (Holsen, Carlson Jones, & Skogbrott Birkeland, 2012).

Early and Late Maturation Some people enter puberty early, others late, and still others on time. Adolescents who mature earlier or later than their peers perceive themselves differently (Bralic & others, 2012; de Rose & others, 2011; Lee & others, 2017; Negriff, Susman, & Trickett, 2011; Wang & others, 2017). In the Berkeley Longitudinal Study conducted some years ago, early-maturing boys perceived themselves more positively and had more successful peer relations than did their late-maturing counterparts (Jones, 1965). When the late-maturing boys were in their thirties, however, they had developed a stronger sense of identity than the early-maturing boys had (Peskin, 1967). This may have occurred because the late-maturing boys had more time to explore life's options, or because the

How does early and late maturation influence adolescent development?
©Fuse/Getty Images RF

early-maturing boys continued to focus on their advantageous physical status instead of on career development and achievement. More recent research confirms, though, that at least during adolescence it is advantageous to be an early-maturing rather than a late-maturing boy (Graber, Brooks-Gunn, & Warren, 2006).

For girls, early and late maturation have been linked with body image. In the sixth grade, early-maturing girls show greater satisfaction with their figures than do late-maturing girls, but by the tenth grade late-maturing girls are more satisfied (Simmons & Blyth, 1987) (see Figure 3). One possible reason for this developmental change is that in late adolescence early-maturing girls are shorter and stockier, whereas late-maturing girls are taller and thinner. Thus, late-maturing girls in late adolescence have bodies that more closely approximate the current American ideal of feminine beauty—tall and thin. Also, a recent study found that in the early high school years, late-maturing boys had a more negative body image than early-maturing boys (de Guzman & Nishina, 2014).

An increasing number of researchers have found that early maturation increases girls' vulnerability to a number of problems (Cheong & others, 2015; Graber, 2013; Hamilton & others, 2014). Early-maturing girls are more likely to smoke, drink, be depressed, have an eating disorder, engage in delinquency, struggle for earlier independence from their parents, and have older friends; and their bodies are likely to elicit responses from males that lead to earlier dating and earlier sexual experiences (Copeland & others, 2010; Ibitoye & others, 2017; Negriff, Susman, & Trickett, 2011; Pomerantz & others, 2017; Verhoef & others, 2014; Wang & others, 2017). For example, in a recent Korean study, early menarche was associated with risky sexual behavior in females (Cheong & others, 2015). Researchers also have found that early-maturing girls tend to engage in sexual intercourse earlier, have more unstable sexual relationships, and are more at risk for physical and verbal abuse in dating (Chen, Rothman, & Jaffee, 2017; Moore, Harden, & Mendle, 2014). Further, a recent study revealed that early-maturing Chinese girls and boys engaged in delinquency more than their on-time or late-maturing counterparts (Chen & others, 2015). A recent study found that early maturation predicted a stable higher level of depression for adolescent girls (Rudolph & others, 2014). And early-maturing girls are less likely to graduate from high school, and they tend to cohabit and marry earlier (Cavanagh, 2009). Apparently as a result of their social and cognitive immaturity, combined with early physical development, early-maturing girls are easily lured into problem behaviors, not recognizing the possible long-term effects on their development.

In the short term, early maturation often has more favorable outcomes for boys, especially in early adolescence. However, late-maturing boys may do better in the long term, especially in terms of identity and career development. Research increasingly has found that early-maturing girls are more vulnerable to a number of problems.

THE BRAIN

Along with the rest of the body, the brain is changing during adolescence, but the study of adolescent brain development is in its infancy. As advances in technology take place, significant strides will also likely be made in charting developmental changes in the adolescent brain (Cohen & Casey, 2017; Crone, 2017; Galvan & Tottenham, 2016; Monahan & others, 2016). What do we know now?

The dogma of the unchanging brain has been discarded and researchers are mainly focused on context-induced plasticity of the brain over time (Aoki, Romeo, & Smith, 2017; Zelazo, 2013). The development of the brain mainly changes in a bottom-up, top-down sequence with sensory, appetitive (eating, drinking), sexual, sensation-seeking, and risk-taking brain linkages maturing first and higher-level brain linkages such as self-control, planning, and reasoning maturing later (Zelazo, 2013).

Using fMRI brain scans, scientists have recently discovered that adolescents' brains undergo significant structural changes (Casey, Galvan, & Somerville, 2016; Cohen & others, 2016; Goddings & Mills, 2017; Steinberg & others, 2017). The **corpus callosum**, where fibers connect the brain's left and right hemispheres, thickens in adolescence, and this change improves adolescents' ability to process information (Chavarria & others, 2014). We have discussed advances in the development of the *prefrontal cortex*—the highest level of the frontal lobes involved in reasoning, decision making, and self-control. However, the prefrontal cortex does not finish maturing until the emerging adult years, approximately 18 to 25 years of age, or later (Casey, Galvan, & Somerville, 2016; Juraska & Willing, 2017).

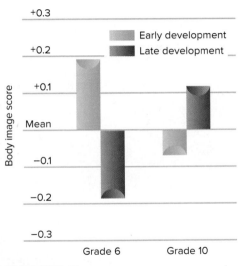

FIGURE 3

EARLY- AND LATE-MATURING ADOLESCENT GIRLS' PERCEPTIONS OF BODY IMAGE IN EARLY AND LATE ADOLESCENCE. The sixth-grade girls in this study had positive body image scores if they were early maturers but negative body image scores if they were late maturers (Simmons & Blyth, 1987). Positive body image scores indicated satisfaction with their figures. By the tenth grade, however, it was the late maturers who had positive body image scores.

corpus callosum The location where fibers connect the brain's left and right hemispheres.

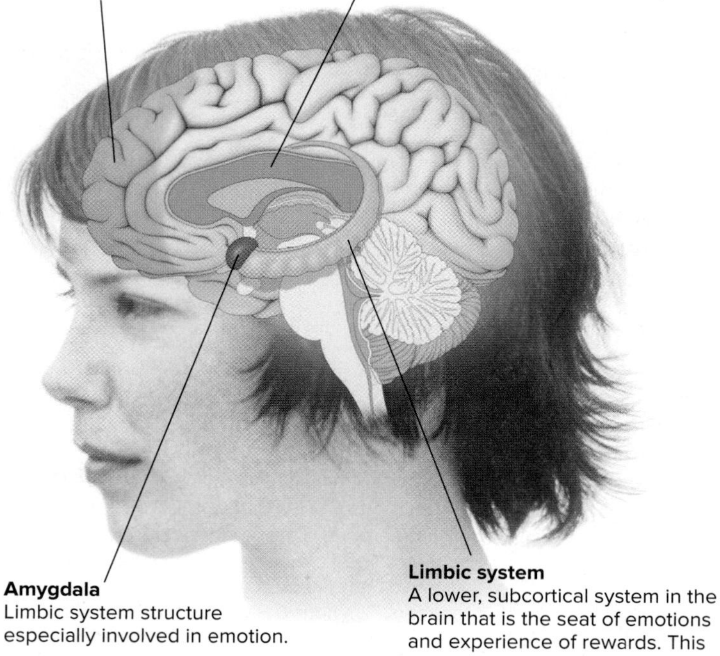

Prefrontal cortex
This "judgment" region reins in intense emotions but doesn't finish developing until at least emerging adulthood.

Corpus callosum
These nerve fibers connect the brain's two hemispheres; they thicken in adolescence to process information more effectively.

Amygdala
Limbic system structure especially involved in emotion.

Limbic system
A lower, subcortical system in the brain that is the seat of emotions and experience of rewards. This system is almost completely developed by early adolescence.

FIGURE 4

THE PREFRONTAL CORTEX, LIMBIC SYSTEM, AMYGDALA, AND CORPUS CALLOSUM

limbic system A lower, subcortical system in the brain that is the seat of emotions and experience of rewards.

amygdala A part of the brain that is the seat of emotions.

At a lower, subcortical level, the **limbic system**, which is the seat of emotions and where rewards are experienced, matures much earlier than the prefrontal cortex and is almost completely developed by early adolescence (Shulman & others, 2016a). The limbic system structure that is especially involved in emotion is the **amygdala.** Figure 4 shows the locations of the prefrontal cortex, limbic system, amygdala, and corpus callosum.

With the onset of puberty, the levels of neurotransmitters change (Cohen & Casey, 2017; Monahan & others, 2016). For example, an increase in the neurotransmitter dopamine occurs in both the prefrontal cortex and the limbic system during adolescence (Casey, 2015; Cohen & Casey, 2017). Increases in dopamine have been linked to increased risk taking and the use of addictive drugs (Steinberg, 2016; Steinberg & others, 2017; Webber & others, 2017). Researchers have found that dopamine plays an important role in reward seeking during adolescence (Leyton & Vezina, 2014).

Earlier, we described the increased focal activation that is linked to synaptic pruning in a specific region, such as the prefrontal cortex. In middle and late childhood, while there is increased focal activation within a specific brain region such as the prefrontal cortex, there also are only limited connections across distant brain regions. By the time individuals reach emerging adulthood, there are increased connections across brain areas (Markant & Thomas, 2013). The increased connections (referred to as brain networks) are especially prevalent across more distant brain regions (Markant & Thomas, 2013). Thus, as children develop, greater efficiency and focal activation occurs in local areas of the brain, and simultaneously there is an increase in brain networks across different brain regions (Markant & Thomas, 2013).

Many of the changes in the adolescent brain that we have described involve the rapidly emerging fields of *cognitive developmental neuroscience* and *social developmental neuroscience,* which involve connections between development, the brain, and cognitive or socioemotional processes (Shulman & others, 2016b; Steinberg & others, 2017). For example, consider leading researcher Charles Nelson's (2003) view that although adolescents are capable of very strong emotions their prefrontal cortex has not adequately developed to the point at which they can control these passions. It is as if their brain does not have the brakes to slow down their emotions. Or consider this interpretation of the development of emotion and cognition in adolescents: "early activation of strong 'turbo-charged' feelings with a relatively un-skilled set of 'driving skills' or cognitive abilities to modulate strong emotions and motivations" (Dahl, 2004, p. 18).

Of course, a major issue is which comes first, biological changes in the brain or experiences that stimulate these changes (Lerner, Boyd, & Du, 2008). In a longitudinal study, 11- to 18-year-olds who lived in poverty conditions had diminished brain functioning at 25 years of age (Brody & others, 2017). However, the adolescents from poverty backgrounds whose families participated in a supportive parenting intervention did not show this diminished brain functioning in adulthood. Another study found that the prefrontal cortex thickened and more brain connections formed when adolescents resisted peer pressure (Paus & others, 2008). Scientists have yet to determine whether the brain changes come first or whether the brain changes are the result of experiences with peers, parents, and others (Webber & others, 2017). Once again, we encounter the nature-nurture issue that is so prominent in examining development through the life span. Nonetheless, there is adequate evidence that environmental experiences make important contributions to the brain's development (Monahan & others, 2016; Steinberg & others, 2017).

In closing this section on the development of the brain in adolescence a further caution is in order. Much of the research on neuroscience and the development of the brain in adolescence is correlational in nature, and thus causal statements need to be scrutinized.

Review Connect Reflect

LG2 Describe puberty's characteristics, developmental changes, psychological dimensions, and the development of the brain.

Review

- What is puberty? What characterizes sexual maturation and the pubertal growth spurt?
- What are some hormonal changes in puberty?
- How has the timing of puberty changed, and what are some variations in puberty?
- What are some psychological dimensions of pubertal change?
- What developmental changes occur in the brain during adolescence?

Connect

- What developmental changes in the brain occur in middle and late childhood?

Reflect *Your Own Personal Journey of Life*

- Did you experience puberty early, late, or on time? How do you think the timing of your puberty influenced your development?

3 What Are the Dimensions of Adolescent Sexuality?

LG3 Characterize adolescent sexuality.

Developing a Sexual Identity

Timing and Trends in Adolescent Sexual Behavior

Sexual Risk Taking in Adolescence

Not only are adolescents characterized by substantial changes in physical growth and the development of the brain, but adolescence also is a bridge between the asexual child and the sexual adult (Diamond & Alley, 2018; Diamond & Savin-Williams, 2015; Savin-Williams, 2016, 2017, 2018). Adolescence is a time of sexual exploration and experimentation, of sexual fantasies and realities, of incorporating sexuality into one's identity. Adolescents have an almost insatiable curiosity about sexuality. They are concerned about whether they are sexually attractive, how to do sex, and what the future holds for their sexual lives. Although most adolescents experience times of vulnerability and confusion, the majority will eventually develop a mature sexual identity.

Every society gives some attention to adolescent sexuality. In some societies, adults resolutely protect adolescent females from males by chaperoning them, while other societies promote very early marriage. Then there are societies that allow some sexual experimentation.

In the United States, the sexual culture is widely available to adolescents. In addition to any advice adolescents get from parents, they learn a great deal about sex from television, videos, magazines, the lyrics of popular music, and the Internet (Bleakley & others, 2017; van Oosten & Vandenbosch, 2017). In some schools, sexting occurs more frequently, as indicated in a recent study of 656 high school students at one school in which 15.8 percent of males and 13.6 percent of females reported sending and 40.5 percent of males and 30.6 percent of females reported receiving explicit sexual pictures on cell phones (Strassberg, Cann, & Velarde, 2017). And in another recent study of 13- to 21-year-old Latinos, engaging in sexting was linked to engaging in penetrative sex (oral, vaginal, and anal sex) (Romo & others, 2017).

> Sexual arousal emerges as a new phenomenon in adolescence and it is important to view sexuality as a normal aspect of adolescent development.
>
> —**SHIRLEY FELDMAN**
> *Contemporary Psychologist, Stanford University*

DEVELOPING A SEXUAL IDENTITY

Mastering emerging sexual feelings and forming a sense of sexual identity are multifaceted and lengthy processes (Diamond & Alley, 2018; Merrill, Stief, & Savin-Williams, 2016; Savin-Williams, 2016, 2017, 2018). They involve learning to manage sexual feelings (such as sexual arousal and attraction), developing new forms of intimacy, and learning the skills to regulate sexual behavior to avoid undesirable consequences. Developing a sexual identity also involves more than just sexual behavior. Sexual identities emerge in the context of physical factors, social factors, and cultural factors, with most societies placing constraints on the sexual behavior of adolescents.

An adolescent's sexual identity involves activities, interests, styles of behavior, and an indication of sexual orientation (whether an individual has same-sex or other-sex attractions) (Goldberg & Halpern, 2017). For example, some adolescents have a high anxiety level about sex, others a low level. Some adolescents are strongly aroused sexually, others less so. Some adolescents are very active sexually, others not at all. Some adolescents are sexually inactive in response to their strong religious upbringing; others go to church regularly, yet their religious training does not inhibit their sexual activity.

It is commonly believed that most gays and lesbians quietly struggle with same-sex attractions in childhood, do not engage in heterosexual dating, and gradually recognize that they are gay or lesbian in mid to late adolescence. Many youth do follow this developmental pathway, but others do not (Diamond & Alley, 2018; Diamond & Savin-Williams, 2015; Savin-Williams, 2016, 2017, 2018). Gay and lesbian youth have diverse patterns of initial attraction, often have bisexual attractions, and may have physical or emotional attraction to same-sex individuals but do not always fall in love with them.

Further, the majority of sexual minority (gay, lesbian, and bisexual) adolescents have competent and successful paths of development through adolescence and become healthy and productive adults. However, in a recent large-scale study, sexual minority adolescents did engage in a higher prevalence of health-risk behaviors (greater drug use and sexual risk taking, for example) compared with heterosexual adolescents (Kann & others, 2016b).

TIMING AND TRENDS IN ADOLESCENT SEXUAL BEHAVIOR

The timing of sexual initiation varies by country as well as by gender and other socioeconomic characteristics. In one cross-cultural study, the proportion of females having first intercourse by age 17 ranged from 72 percent in Mali to 47 percent in the United States and 45 percent in Tanzania (Singh & others, 2000). The percentage of males who had their first intercourse by age 17 ranged from 76 percent in Jamaica to 64 percent in the United States and 63 percent in Brazil.

What is the current profile of sexual activity of adolescents? In a U.S. national survey conducted in 2015, 58 percent of twelfth-graders reported having experienced sexual intercourse, compared with 24 percent of ninth-graders (Kann & others, 2016a). By age 20, 77 percent of U.S. youth report having engaged in sexual intercourse (Dworkin & Santelli, 2007). Nationally, 46 percent of twelfth-graders, 33.5 percent of eleventh-graders, 25.5 percent of tenth-graders, and 16 percent of ninth-graders recently reported that they were currently sexually active (Kann & others, 2016a). An analysis of more than 12,000 adolescents in the Longitudinal Study of Adolescent Health found a predominant overall pattern of vaginal sex first, average age of sexual initiation of 16 years, and spacing of more than one year between initiation of first and second sexual behaviors (Haydon & others, 2012). In this study, about a third of the adolescents initiated sex slightly later but initiated oral-genital and vaginal sex within the same year. Further, compared with non-Latino white adolescents, African American adolescents were more likely to engage in vaginal sex first. Also, adolescents from low-SES backgrounds were characterized by earlier sexual initiation.

What trends in adolescent sexual activity have occurred in the last two decades? From 1991 to 2015, fewer adolescents reported any of the following: ever having had sexual intercourse, currently being sexually active, having had sexual intercourse before the age of 13, and having had sexual intercourse with four or more persons during their lifetime (Kann & others, 2016a) (see Figure 5).

Until very recently, at all grade levels adolescent males have been more likely than adolescent females to report having had sexual intercourse and being sexually active. However, the 2009 national survey was the first time that a higher percentage of twelfth-grade females than twelfth-grade males reported having experienced sexual intercourse (Eaton & others, 2010). This reversal continued through 2015 (Kann & others, 2016a). Also in 2015, the reversal also occurred at the eleventh grade with more eleventh-grade females

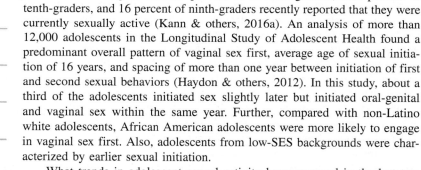

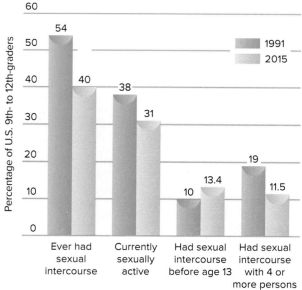

FIGURE 5

SEXUAL ACTIVITY OF U.S. ADOLESCENTS FROM 1991 TO 2015 (KANN & OTHERS, 2016a).

reporting they had experienced sexual intercourse than eleventh-grade males (Kann & others, 2016a) (see Figure 6). However, a higher percentage of ninth- and tenth-grade males reported they had experienced sexual intercourse than their female counterparts (Kann & others, 2016a). Adolescent males also are more likely than their female counterparts to describe sexual intercourse as an enjoyable experience.

Sexual initiation varies by ethnic group in the United States (Kann & others, 2016a). African Americans are likely to engage in sexual behavior earlier than other ethnic groups, whereas Asian Americans are likely to engage in it later (Feldman, Turner, & Araujo, 1999). In a recent national U.S. survey (2015) of ninth- to twelfth-graders, 49 percent of African Americans, 43 percent of Latinos, and 40 percent of non-Latino Whites said they had experienced sexual intercourse (Kann & others, 2016a). In this study, 8 percent of African Americans (compared with 5 percent of Latinos and 3 percent of non-Latino Whites) said they had their first sexual experience before 13 years of age. All of these figures represent a significant decrease in sexual intercourse since 2011 for African American and Latino adolescents (Eaton & others, 2012; Kann & others, 2016a).

Recent research indicates that oral sex is now a common occurrence for U.S. adolescents (Halpern & Haydon, 2012). In a national survey, 51 percent of U.S. 15- to 19-year-old boys and 47 percent of girls in the same age range said they had engaged in oral sex (Child Trends, 2015). Thus, more U.S. youth engage in oral sex than vaginal sex, likely because they perceive oral sex to be more acceptable and produce fewer health risks. Researchers have found that among female adolescents who reported having vaginal sex first, 31 percent reported having a teen pregnancy, whereas among those who initiated oral-genital sex first, only 8 percent reported having a teen pregnancy (Reese & others, 2013). Thus, how adolescents initiate their sex lives may have positive or negative consequences for their sexual health.

SEXUAL RISK TAKING IN ADOLESCENCE

Many adolescents are not emotionally prepared to handle sexual experiences, especially in early adolescence. Early sexual activity is linked with risky behaviors such as drug use, delinquency, and school-related problems (Chan & others, 2015; Letourneau & others, 2017). A recent study of more than 3,000 Swedish adolescents revealed that sexual intercourse before age 14 was linked to risky behaviors such as an increased number of sexual partners, experience of oral and anal sex, negative health behaviors (smoking, drug and alcohol use), and antisocial behavior (being violent, stealing, running away from home) at 18 years of age (Kastbom & others, 2015). Further, a recent study found that early sexual debut (first sexual intercourse before age 13) was associated with sexual risk taking, substance use, violent victimization, and suicidal thoughts/attempts in both sexual minority (in this study, gay, lesbian, and bisexual) adolescents and heterosexual youth (Lowry & others, 2017). And in a recent study of Korean adolescent girls, early menarche was linked to earlier initiation of sexual intercourse (Kim & others, 2017).

A number of family factors are associated with sexual risk taking (Ashcraft & Murray, 2017; de Looze & others, 2015; Johnson-Motoyama & others, 2016; Simons & others, 2016). For example, a recent study revealed that adolescents who in the eighth grade reported greater parental knowledge and more family rules about dating were less likely to initiate sex from the eighth to tenth grade (Ethier & others, 2016). In another recent study, difficulties and disagreements between Latino adolescents and their parents were linked to the adolescents' early sexual initiation (Cordova & others, 2014). And a recent study revealed that the parenting practice associated most closely with a lower level of risky sexual behavior by adolescents was supportive parenting (Simons & others, 2016). Also, having older sexually active siblings or pregnant/parenting teenage sisters placed adolescent girls at increased risk for pregnancy (Miller, Benson, & Galbraith, 2001).

Socioeconomic status/poverty, peer, school, and sport contexts provide further information about sexual risk taking in adolescents (Choukas-Bradley & Prinstein, 2016;

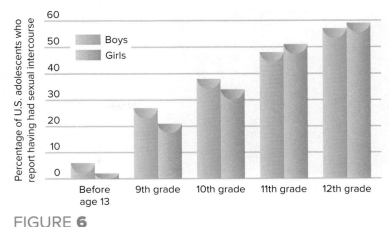

FIGURE **6**

TIMING OF SEXUAL INTERCOURSE AMONG U.S. ADOLESCENTS (KANN & OTHERS, 2016a).

How Would You...?

If you were a **psychologist,** how would you describe the ethnic differences in the timing of an adolescent's first sexual experience?

developmental **connection**

Self and Identity

One of the most important aspects of the self in middle and late childhood is the increased capacity for self-regulation. Connect to "Socioemotional Development in Middle and Late Childhood."

What are some risks for early initiation of sexual intercourse?
©Stockbyte/Punchstock RF

Psychologists are exploring ways to encourage adolescents to make less risky sexual decisions. Here an adolescent participates in an interactive video session developed by Julie Downs and her colleagues at the Department of Social and Decision Making Sciences at Carnegie Mellon University. The videos help adolescents evaluate their responses and decisions in high-risk sexual contexts.
©Michael Ray

How Would You...?

If you were a **social worker**, how would you design an educational campaign to increase adolescents' effective use of contraception?

sexually transmitted infections (STIs) Diseases that are contracted primarily through sexual contact. This contact is not limited to vaginal intercourse but includes oral-genital contact and anal-genital contact as well.

A 13-year-old boy pushes his friends around in his barrow during a break from his work as a barrow boy in a community in sub-Saharan Africa. He became the breadwinner in the family after both of his parents died of AIDS.
©Louise Gubb/Corbis/Getty Images

Widman & others, 2016). The percentage of sexually active young adolescents is higher in low-income areas of inner cities (Morrison-Beedy & others, 2013). One study found that adolescents who associated with more deviant peers in early adolescence were likely to have more sexual partners at age 16 (Lansford & others, 2010). Further, a research review found that school connectedness was linked to positive sexuality outcomes (Markham & others, 2010). Also, a study of middle school students revealed that better academic achievement was a protective factor in keeping boys and girls from engaging in early initiation of sexual intercourse (Laflin, Wang, & Barry, 2008). And a recent study found that adolescent males who play sports engage in a higher level of sexual risk taking, while adolescent females who play sports engage in a lower level of sexual risk taking (Lipowski & others, 2016).

Weak self-regulation (difficulty controlling one's emotions and behavior) is increasingly being implicated in sexual risk taking. For example, a longitudinal study found that weak self-regulation at 8 to 9 years of age and risk proneness (tendency to seek sensation and make poor decisions) at 12 to 13 years of age set the stage for sexual risk taking at 16 to 17 years of age (Crockett, Raffaelli, & Shen, 2006). Also, another study revealed that a high level of impulsiveness was linked to early adolescent sexual risk taking (Khurana & others, 2012).

Contraceptive Use Are adolescents increasingly using condoms? A recent national study revealed a substantial increase in the use of a contraceptive (57 percent in 2015 compared with 46 percent in 1991 but down from 60 percent in 2011) by U.S. high school students the last time they had sexual intercourse (Eaton & others, 2012; Kann & others, 2016a).

Too many sexually active adolescents still do not use contraceptives, use them inconsistently, or use contraceptive methods that are not highly effective (Diedrich, Klein, & Peipert, 2017; Francis & Gold, 2017; Jaramillo & others, 2017; Salam & others, 2016). In 2015, 14 percent of sexually active adolescents did not use any contraceptive method the last time they had sexual intercourse (Kann & others, 2016a). Younger adolescents are less likely than older adolescents to take contraceptive precautions. Also, researchers found that a greater age difference between sexual partners in adolescence is associated with less consistent condom use (Volpe & others, 2013).

Recently, a number of leading medical organizations and experts have recommended that adolescents use long-acting reversible contraception (LARC). These include the Society for Adolescent Health and Medicine (2017), the American Academy of Pediatrics and American College of Obstetrics and Gynecology (Allen & Barlow, 2017), and the World Health Organization (2017). LARC includes intrauterine devices (IUDs) and contraceptive implants, which are much more effective than birth control pills and condoms in preventing unwanted pregnancies (Diedrich, Klein, & Peipert, 2017; Francis & Gold, 2017; Society for Adolescent Health and Medicine, 2017).

Sexually Transmitted Infections Some forms of contraception, such as birth control pills or implants, do not protect against sexually transmitted infections, or STIs. **Sexually transmitted infections (STIs)** are diseases that are contracted primarily through sexual contact. This contact is not limited to vaginal intercourse but includes oral-genital and anal-genital contact as well. STIs are an increasing health problem. Approximately 25 percent of sexually active adolescents are estimated to become infected with an STI each year. Among the main STIs adolescents can get are bacterial infections (such as gonorrhea, syphilis, and chlamydia), and STIs caused by viruses—genital herpes, genital warts, and **AIDS** (acquired immune deficiency syndrome). Figure 7 describes these sexually transmitted infections.

No single STI has had a greater impact on sexual behavior, or created more fear, in the last two decades than AIDS. AIDS is caused by the human immunodeficiency virus (HIV), which destroys the body's immune system. Following exposure to HIV, an individual is vulnerable to germs that a normal immune system could destroy.

In 2014, 22 percent of all new HIV infections in the United States occurred among individuals 13 to 24 years of age (Centers for Disease Control and Prevention, 2016). Worldwide, the greatest concern about AIDS is in sub-Saharan Africa, where it has reached epidemic proportions (UNICEF, 2017). Adolescent girls in many African countries are especially vulnerable to infection with the HIV virus by adult men. Approximately six times as many adolescent girls as boys have AIDS in these countries. In Kenya, 25 percent of the 15- to 19-year-old girls are HIV-positive, compared with only 4 percent of boys in this

STI	Description/cause	Incidence	Treatment
Gonorrhea	Commonly called the "drip" or "clap." Caused by the bacterium *Neisseria gonorrhoeae*. Spread by contact between infected moist membranes (genital, oral-genital, or anal-genital) of two individuals. Characterized by discharge from penis or vagina and painful urination. Can lead to infertility.	500,000 cases annually in U.S.	Penicillin, other antibiotics
Syphilis	Caused by the bacterium *Treponema pallidum*. Characterized by the appearance of a sore where syphilis entered the body. The sore can be on the external genitals, vagina, or anus. Later, a skin rash breaks out on palms of hands and bottom of feet. If not treated, can eventually lead to paralysis or even death.	100,000 cases annually in U.S.	Penicillin
Chlamydia	A common STI named for the bacterium *Chlamydia trachomatis*, an organism that spreads by sexual contact and infects the genital organs of both sexes. A special concern is that females with chlamydia may become infertile. It is recommended that adolescent and young adult females have an annual screening for this STI.	About 3 million people in U.S. annually	Antibiotics
Genital herpes	Caused by a family of viruses with different strains. Involves an eruption of sores and blisters. Spread by sexual contact.	One of five U.S. adults	No known cure but antiviral medications can shorten outbreaks
AIDS	Caused by the human immunodeficiency virus (HIV), which destroys the body's immune system. Semen and blood are the main vehicles of transmission. Common symptoms include fevers, night sweats, weight loss, chronic fatigue, and swollen lymph nodes.	More than 300,000 cumulative cases of HIV virus in U.S. 25–34-year-olds; epidemic incidence in sub-Saharan countries	New treatments have slowed the progression from HIV to AIDS; no cure
Genital warts	Caused by the human papillomavirus, which does not always produce symptoms. Usually appear as small, hard painless bumps in the vaginal area, or around the anus. Very contagious. Certain high-risk types of this virus cause cervical cancer and other genital cancers. May recur despite treatment. A new HPV preventive vaccine, Gardasil, has been approved for girls and women 9–26 years of age.	About 5.5 million new cases annually; considered the most common STI in the U.S.	A topical drug, freezing, or surgery

FIGURE 7

SEXUALLY TRANSMITTED INFECTIONS

age group. In Botswana, more than 30 percent of the adolescent girls who are pregnant are infected with the HIV virus. In some sub-Saharan countries, less than 20 percent of women and 40 percent of 15- to 19-year-olds reported having used a condom the last time they had sexual intercourse (Singh & others, 2004).

There continues to be great concern about AIDS in many parts of the world, not just sub-Saharan Africa. In the United States, prevention is especially targeted at groups that show the highest incidence of AIDS. These include drug users, individuals with other STIs, young gay males, individuals living in low-income circumstances, Latinos, and African Americans (Centers for Disease Control and Prevention, 2017).

Adolescent Pregnancy   Adolescent pregnancy is another problematic outcome of sexuality in adolescence and requires major efforts to reduce its occurrence (Brindis, 2017; Romero & others, 2017; Tevendale & others, 2017). In cross-cultural comparisons, the United States continues to have one of the highest adolescent pregnancy and childbearing rates in the industrialized world, despite a considerable decline during the 1990s. The U.S. adolescent pregnancy rate is four times as high as that in the Netherlands (Sedgh & others, 2015). Although U.S. adolescents are no more sexually active than their counterparts in the Netherlands, their adolescent pregnancy rate is dramatically higher. In the United States, 82 percent of pregnancies to mothers 15 to 19 years of age are unintended (Koh, 2014). A cross-cultural comparison conducted in 2011 found that among 21 countries, the United States had the highest adolescent pregnancy rate among 15- to 19-year-olds and Switzerland the lowest (Sedgh & others, 2015). However, as you will see shortly, the adolescent pregnancy rate in the United States has dropped considerably in the last few years.

Despite the negative comparisons of the United States with many other developed countries, there have been some encouraging trends in U.S. adolescent pregnancy rates. In 2014,

AIDS AIDS, or acquired immune deficiency syndrome, is caused by the human immunodeficiency virus (HIV), which destroys the body's immune system.

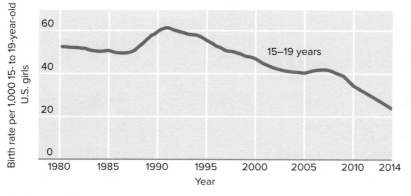

FIGURE **8**

BIRTH RATES FOR U.S. 15- TO 19-YEAR-OLD GIRLS FROM 1980 TO 2014 (MARTIN, HAMILTON, & OSTERMAN, 2015).

the U.S. birth rate for 15- to 19-year-olds was 24 births per 1,000 females, the lowest rate ever recorded, which represents a substantial decrease from 62 births per 1,000 females for the same age range in 1991 (Martin, Hamilton, & Osterman, 2015) (see Figure 8). Reasons for the decline include school/community health classes, increased contraceptive use, and fear of sexually transmitted infections such as AIDS.

Ethnic variations characterize adolescent pregnancy (Bartlett & others, 2014). Latina adolescents are more likely than African American and non-Latina White adolescents to become pregnant (Martin, Hamilton, & Osterman, 2015). For 15- to 19-year-old U.S. females in 2014, per 1,000 females the birth rate for Latinas was 38, for African Americans 35, for non-Latina Whites 17, and for Asian Americans 8 (Martin, Hamilton, & Osterman, 2015). These figures represent substantial decreases (approximately a 70 percent decrease just since 2011) in adolescent pregnancy rates for Latina and African American teens. However, Latina and African American adolescent girls who have a child are more likely to have a second child than are non-Latina White adolescent girls (Rosengard, 2009). And daughters of teenage mothers are at risk for teenage childbearing, thus perpetuating an intergenerational cycle. A study using data from the National Longitudinal Survey of Youth revealed that daughters of teenage mothers were 66 percent more likely to become teenage mothers themselves (Meade, Kershaw, & Ickovics, 2008). In this study, conditions that increased the likelihood that daughters of the teenage mothers would become pregnant included low parental monitoring and poverty.

Why are U.S. adolescent pregnancy rates so high? We discuss possible answers to this question in the following *Connecting with Diversity* interlude.

The consequences of America's high adolescent pregnancy rate are cause for great concern (Barbee & others, 2016; Brindis, 2017; Gelfand & others, 2016; Romero & others, 2017; Tevendale & others, 2017). Adolescent pregnancy creates health risks for both the baby and the mother (Leftwich & Alves, 2017). Adolescent mothers are more likely to be depressed and drop out of school than their peers (Siegel & Brandon, 2014). Infants born to adolescent mothers are more likely to have low birth weights—a prominent factor in infant mortality—as well as neurological problems and childhood illness (Leftwich & Alves, 2017). Although many adolescent mothers resume their education later in life, they generally never catch up economically with women who postpone childbearing until their twenties. One longitudinal study found that the children of women who had their first birth during their teens had lower achievement test scores and more behavioral problems than did children whose mothers had their first birth as adults (Hofferth & Reid, 2002). Also, a recent study of African American urban youth found that at 32 years of age, women who had been teenage mothers were more likely to be unemployed, live in poverty, depend on welfare, and not have completed college than were women who had not been teenage mothers (Assini-Meytin & Green, 2015). In this study, at 32 years of age, men who had been teenage fathers were more likely to not have a job than were men who had not been teenage fathers.

A special concern is repeated adolescent pregnancy. In a recent national study, the percentage of teen births that were repeat births decreased from 21 percent in 2004 to 17 percent in 2015 (Dee & others, 2017). In a recent meta-analysis, use of effective contraception, especially LARC, and education-related factors (higher level of education and school continuation) resulted in a lower incidence of repeated teen pregnancy, while depression and a history of abortion were linked to a higher percentage of repeated teen pregnancy (Maravilla & others, 2017).

Researchers have found that adolescent mothers interact less effectively with their infants than do adult mothers (Leftwich & Alves, 2017). A study revealed that adolescent mothers spent more time negatively interacting and less time in play and positively interacting with their infants than did adult mothers (Riva Crugnola & others, 2014). A recent intervention, "My Baby and Me," that involved frequent, intensive home visitation coaching sessions with

How Would You...?
If you were an **educator**, how would you incorporate sex education throughout the curriculum to encourage adolescents' healthy, responsible sexual development?

Cross-Cultural Comparisons of Adolescent Pregnancy

Three reasons U.S. adolescent pregnancy rates are so high can be found in cross-cultural studies (Boonstra, 2002, pp. 9–10):

- *"Childbearing regarded as adult activity."* European countries, as well as Canada, give a strong consensus that childbearing belongs in adulthood "when young people have completed their education, have become employed and independent from their parents and are living in stable relationships. . . . In the United States, this attitude is much less strong and much more variable across groups and areas of the country."

- *"Clear messages about sexual behavior.* While adults in other countries strongly encourage teens to wait until they have established themselves before having children, they are generally more accepting than American adults of teens having sex. In France and Sweden, in particular, teen sexual expression is seen as normal and positive, but there is also widespread expectation that sexual intercourse will take place within committed relationships. In fact, relationships among U.S. teens tend to be more sporadic and of shorter duration. Equally strong is the expectation that young people who are having sex will take actions to protect themselves and their partners from pregnancy

and sexually transmitted infections," an expectation that is much stronger in Europe than in the United States. "In keeping with this view, . . . schools in Great Britain, France, Sweden, and most of Canada" have sex education programs that provide more comprehensive information about prevention than U.S. schools do. In addition, these countries use the media more often in "government-sponsored campaigns for promoting responsible sexual behavior."

- *"Access to family-planning services.* In countries that are more accepting of teenage sexual relationships, teenagers also have easier access to reproductive health services. In Canada, France, Great Britain, and Sweden, contraceptive services are integrated into other types of primary health care and are available free or at low cost for all teenagers. Generally, teens [in these countries] know where to obtain information and services and receive confidential and nonjudgmental care. . . . In the United States, where attitudes about teenage sexual relationships are more conflicted, teens have a harder time obtaining contraceptive services. Many do not have health insurance or cannot get birth control as part of their basic health care."

---

adolescent mothers across three years resulted in improved maternal behavior and child outcomes (Guttentag & others, 2014). And a recent study assessed the reading and math achievement trajectories of children born to adolescent and non-adolescent mothers with different levels of education (Tang & others, 2016). In this study, higher levels of maternal education were linked to growth in their children's achievement through the eighth grade. Nonetheless, the achievement of children born to the adolescent mothers never reached the levels of children born to adult mothers.

Though the consequences of America's high adolescent pregnancy rate are cause for great concern, it often is not pregnancy alone that leads to negative consequences for an adolescent mother and her offspring. Adolescent mothers are more likely to come from low-SES backgrounds (Molina & others, 2010; Mollborn, 2017). Many adolescent mothers also were not good students before they became pregnant. However, not every adolescent female who bears a child lives a life of poverty and low achievement. Thus, although adolescent pregnancy is a high-risk circumstance, and adolescents who do not become pregnant generally fare better than those who do, some adolescent mothers do well in school and have positive outcomes (Leadbeater & Way, 2001).

Serious, extensive efforts are needed to help pregnant adolescents and young mothers enhance their educational and occupational opportunities (Asheer & others, 2014; Tang & others, 2017). Adolescent mothers also need help in obtaining competent child care and in planning for the future.

What are some consequences of adolescent pregnancy?
©Geoff Manasse/Getty Images RF

All adolescents can benefit from age-appropriate family-life education (Barfield, Warner, & Kappeler, 2017; Mueller & others, 2017; Tang & others, 2016). Family and consumer science educators teach life skills, such as effective decision making, to adolescents. To read about the work of one family and consumer science educator, see the *Connecting with Careers* profile. And to learn more about ways to reduce adolescent pregnancy, see the *Caring Connections* interlude.

Lynn Blankinship, Family and Consumer Science Educator

Lynn Blankinship is a family and consumer science educator. She has an undergraduate degree in this field from the University of Arizona. She has taught for more than 20 years, the last 14 at Tucson High Magnet School.

Blankinship was honored by the Tucson Federation of Teachers as Educator of the Year in 1999–2000 and was named Arizona Teacher of the Year in 1999.

Blankinship especially enjoys teaching life skills to adolescents. One of her favorite activities is having students care for an automated baby that imitates the needs of real babies. She says that this program has a profound impact on students because the baby must be cared for around the clock for the duration of the assignment. Blankinship also coordinates real-world work experiences and training for students in several child-care facilities in the Tucson area.

Lynn Blankinship (*center*) teaching life skills to students.
Courtesy of Lynn Blankinship

For more about what family and consumer science educators do, see the Careers in Children's Development appendix.

Reducing Adolescent Pregnancy

One strategy for reducing adolescent pregnancy, called the Teen Outreach Program (TOP), focuses on engaging adolescents in volunteer community service and initiating discussions that help adolescents appreciate the lessons they learn through volunteerism. In one study, 695 adolescents in grades 9 to 12 were randomly assigned to either a Teen Outreach group or a control group (Allen & others, 1997). They were assessed both at program entry and at program exit nine months later. The rate of pregnancy was substantially lower for the Teen Outreach adolescents. These adolescents also had lower rates of school failure and academic suspension.

Another organization, Girls Inc., offers four programs that are intended to increase adolescent girls' motivation to avoid pregnancy until they are mature enough to make responsible decisions about motherhood (Roth & others, 1998). "Growing Together," a series of five two-hour workshops for mothers and adolescents, and "Will Power/Won't Power," a series of six two-hour sessions that focus on assertiveness training, are geared toward 12- to 14-year-old girls. For older adolescent girls, "Taking Care of Business" provides nine sessions that emphasize career planning as well as information about sexuality, reproduction, and contraception. "Health Bridge" coordinates health and education services—girls can participate in this program as one of their club activities. Girls who participated in these programs were less likely to get pregnant than girls who did not participate (Girls Inc., 1991).

In 2010, the U.S. government launched the Teen Pregnancy Prevention (TPP) program under the direction of the newly created Office of Adolescent Health (Koh, 2014). Currently, a number of studies are being funded by the program in an effort to find ways to reduce the rate of adolescent pregnancy.

Currently, a major controversy in sex education is whether schools should have an abstinence-only program or a program that emphasizes contraceptive knowledge (Erkut & others, 2013; MacKenzie, Hedge, & Enslin, 2017). A number of leading experts on adolescent sexuality now conclude that sex education programs that emphasize contraceptive knowledge do not increase the incidence of sexual intercourse and are more likely to reduce the risk of adolescent pregnancy and sexually transmitted infections than abstinence-only programs (Donovan, 2017; Eisenberg & others, 2008, 2013; Jaramillo & others, 2017). Despite the evidence that favors comprehensive sex education, there recently has been an increase in government funding for abstinence-only programs (Donovan, 2017). Also, in some states (Texas and Mississippi, for example), many students still get abstinence-only instruction or no sex education at all (Campbell, 2016; Pollock, 2017).

Some sex education programs are starting to adopt an abstinence-plus sexuality approach that promotes abstinence while providing information on contraceptive use (Realini & others, 2010). One study found that sex education about abstinence and birth control was associated with healthier sexual behaviors, such as using some form of contraception at first sex, than no instruction at all (Lindberg & Maddow-Zimet, 2012). For girls whose behavior was tracked in this study, condom use at first sex was more likely among those who received instruction about both abstinence and birth control.

4 How Can Adolescents' Health and Health-Enhancing Assets Be Characterized?

LG4 Summarize adolescents' health and eating disorders.

| Adolescent Health | Leading Causes of Death in Adolescence | Substance Use and Abuse | Eating Problems and Disorders |

To improve adolescent health, adults should aim (1) to increase adolescents' *health-enhancing behaviors*, such as eating nutritious foods, exercising, wearing seat belts, and getting adequate sleep; and (2) to reduce adolescents' *health-compromising behaviors*, such as drug abuse, violence, unprotected sexual intercourse, and dangerous driving.

How Would You...?
If you were a **health-care professional,** how would you explain the benefits of physical fitness in adolescence to adolescents, parents, and teachers?

ADOLESCENT HEALTH

Adolescence is a critical juncture in the adoption of behaviors that are relevant to health (Coore Desai, Reece, & Shakespeare-Pellington, 2017; Devenish, Hooley, & Mellor, 2017; Griesler, Hu, & Kandel, 2016; Yap & others, 2017). Many of the behaviors that are linked to poor health habits and early death in adults begin during adolescence (Blackstone & Hermann, 2016; Blake, 2017; Donatelle, 2017). Conversely, the early formation of healthy behavior patterns, such as regular exercise and a preference for foods low in fat and cholesterol, not only has immediate health benefits but also helps in adulthood to delay or prevent disability and mortality from heart disease, stroke, diabetes, and cancer (Blake, Munoz, & Volpe, 2016; Hales, 2018).

Nutrition and Weight Concerns are growing about adolescents' nutrition and exercise habits (Powers & Dodd, 2017; Schiff, 2017). National data indicated that the percentage of obese U.S. 12- to 19-year-olds increased from 11 percent in the early 1990s to nearly 21 percent in 2013–2014 (Centers for Disease Control and Prevention, 2015).

Being obese in adolescence predicts obesity in emerging adulthood. For example, a study of more than 8,000 12- to 21-year-olds found that obese adolescents were more likely to develop severe obesity in emerging adulthood than were overweight or normal-weight adolescents (The & others, 2010).

And more emerging adults are overweight or obese than are adolescents. A recent longitudinal study tracked more than 1,500 adolescents who were classified as not overweight, overweight,

These adolescent girls are attending a weight-management camp. *What types of interventions have been most successful in helping overweight adolescents lose weight?*
©Richard Walker/Alamy

What are some characteristics of adolescents' exercise patterns?
©Tom Stewart/Corbis/Getty Images

- - - - - - - ➤

developmental connection

Nutrition and Weight

Being overweight at age 3 is a risk factor for subsequently being overweight at age 12. Connect to "Physical Development in Early Childhood."

◄ - - - - - - - -

or obese when they were 14 years of age (Patton & others, 2011). Across the 10-year period of the study, the percentage of overweight individuals increased from 20 percent at 14 years of age to 33 percent at 24 years of age. Obesity increased from 4 percent to 7 percent across the 10 years. A recent national survey found that for 18- to 23-year-olds, the percent of individuals who were obese increased from 13.9 percent to 14.4 percent (Gallup Poll, 2012).

What types of interventions and activities have been successful in reducing overweight in adolescents and emerging adults? Research indicates that dietary changes and regular exercise are key components of weight reduction in adolescence and emerging adulthood (Fulkerson & others, 2017; Goldfield & others, 2017; Kumar & Kelly, 2017; Lipsky & others, 2017). For example, a recent study found that a combination of regular exercise and a diet plan promoted weight loss and enhanced executive function in adolescents (Xie & others, 2017). Also, a recent meta-analysis concluded that supervised exercise, especially aerobic exercise, was linked to a reduction of abdominal fat in adolescents (Gonzalez-Ruiz & others, 2017). Further, a three-month experimental study found that both aerobic exercise and resistance exercise without caloric restriction were effective in reducing abdominal fat and insulin sensitivity in obese adolescent boys compared with a no-exercise control group (Lee & others, 2012). Another study revealed that playing on a sports team was an important factor in adolescents' weight. In this study, among a wide range of activities (other physical activity, physical education, screen time, and diet quality, for example), team sports participation was the strongest predictor of lower risk for being overweight or obese (Drake & others, 2012). And a recent study found that family meals during adolescence protected against the development of being overweight or obese in adulthood (Berge & others, 2015).

Exercise   There also is major concern about the low level of exercise by U.S. adolescents. In a cross-cultural study, just two-thirds of U.S. adolescents exercised at least twice a week, compared with 80 percent or more of adolescents in Ireland, Austria, Germany, and the Slovak Republic (World Health Organization, 2000).

Individuals tend to become less active as they reach and progress through adolescence (Pate & others, 2009). A national study of U.S. 9- to 15-year-olds revealed that almost all 9- and 11-year-olds met the federal government's moderate to vigorous exercise recommendations per day (a minimum of 60 minutes a day), but only 31 percent of 15-year-olds met the recommendations on weekdays, and on weekends only 17 percent met the recommendations (Nader & others, 2008). The same study also found that adolescent boys were more likely to engage in moderate to vigorous exercise than girls. Figure 9 shows the average amount of exercise among U.S. boys and girls from 9 to 15 years of age on weekdays and weekends. A recent national study also found that adolescent girls were much less likely to engage in 60 minutes or more of vigorous exercise per day in 5 of the last 7 days (61 percent) than were boys (42 percent) (YRBSS, 2016). Yet another national study of U.S. adolescents revealed that physical activity increased until 13 years of age in boys and girls but then declined through 18 years of age (Kahn & others, 2008). In this study, adolescents were more likely to engage in regular exercise when they wanted to present a positive body image to their friends and when exercise was important to their parents.

Ethnic differences in exercise participation rates of U.S. adolescents also occur and these rates vary by gender. As indicated in Figure 10, in the National Youth Risk Survey, non-Latino White boys exercised the most, African American and Latina girls the least (Kann & others, 2016a). Do U.S. adolescents exercise less than their counterparts in other countries? A comparison of adolescents in 28 countries found that U.S.

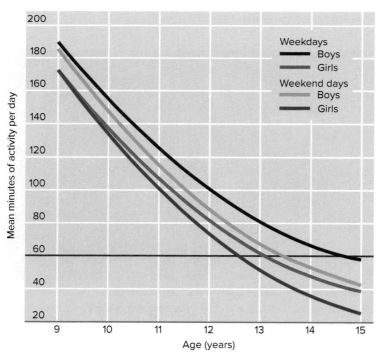

FIGURE 9

AVERAGE AMOUNT OF MODERATE TO VIGOROUS EXERCISE ENGAGED IN BY U.S. 9- TO 15-YEAR-OLDS ON WEEKDAYS AND WEEKENDS.

Note: The federal government recommends 60 minutes of moderate to vigorous physical activity per day.

adolescents exercised less and ate more junk food than did adolescents in most of the other countries (World Health Organization, 2000). Just two-thirds of U.S. adolescents exercised at least twice a week compared with 80 percent or more of adolescents in Ireland, Austria, Germany, and the Slovak Republic. U.S. adolescents were more likely to eat fried food and less likely to eat fruits and vegetables than were adolescents in most other countries studied. U.S. adolescents' eating choices were similar to those of adolescents in England.

Exercise is linked with a number of positive outcomes in adolescence (Barton & others, 2017; Ten Hoor & others, 2016). Regular exercise has a positive effect on adolescents' weight status (Xie & others, 2017). One study revealed that regular exercise from 9 to 16 years of age especially was associated with normal weight in girls (McMurray & others, 2008). Another study found that adolescents high in physical fitness had better connectivity between brain regions than adolescents low in physical fitness (Herting & others, 2014). Additional positive outcomes of exercise in adolescence are reduced triglyceride levels, lower blood pressure, and a lower incidence of type 2 diabetes (Anyaegbu & Dharnidharka, 2014; Son & others, 2017). Other research indicated that eighth-, tenth-, and twelfth-grade students who engaged in higher levels of exercise had lower levels of alcohol, cigarette, and marijuana use (Terry-McElrath, O'Malley, & Johnston, 2011). Also in a recent study, an exercise program of 180 minutes per week improved the sleep patterns of obese adolescents (Mendelson & others, 2016). In further research, a high-intensity exercise program reduced depressive symptoms and improved the moods of depressed adolescents (Carter & others, 2016). And in a recent research review, among a number of cognitive factors, memory was the factor most often improved by exercise in adolescence (Li & others, 2017).

Adolescents' exercise is increasingly being found to be associated with parenting and peer relationships (Mason & others, 2017; Michaud & others, 2017). For example, one study revealed that female adolescents' physical activity was linked to their male and female friends' physical activity while male adolescents' physical activity was associated with their female friends' physical activity (Sirard & others, 2013). In a recent research review, peer/friend support of exercise, presence of peers and friends, peer norms, friendship quality and acceptance, peer crowds, and peer victimization were linked to adolescents' physical activity (Fitzgerald, Fitzgerald, & Aherne, 2012).

Researchers have found that screen time is associated with a number of adolescent health problems, including a lower rate of exercise and a higher rate of sedentary behavior (Pearson & others, 2017). In one research review, a higher level of screen-based sedentary behavior was associated with being overweight, having sleep problems, being depressed, and having lower levels of physical activity/fitness and psychological well-being (higher stress levels, for example) (Costigan & others, 2013).

Sleep Might changing sleep patterns in adolescence contribute to adolescents' health-compromising behaviors? Recently there has been a surge of interest in adolescent sleep patterns (Agostini & others, 2017; Gariepy & others, 2017; Hysing & others, 2015; Meltzer, 2017; Reddy & others, 2017; Seo & others, 2017). A longitudinal study in which adolescents completed daily diaries every 14 days in ninth, tenth, and twelfth grades found that regardless of how much students studied each day, when the students sacrificed sleep time to study more than usual, they had difficulty understanding what was taught in class and were more likely to struggle with class assignments the next day (Gillen-O'Neel, Huynh, & Fuligni, 2013). Also, a recent experimental study indicated that when adolescents' sleep was restricted to five hours for five nights, then returned to ten hours for two nights, their sustained attention was negatively affected (especially in the early morning) and did not return to baseline levels during recovery (Agostini & others, 2017). Further, researchers have found that adolescents who get less than 7.7 hours of sleep per night on average have more emotional and peer-related problems, higher anxiety, and a higher level of suicidal ideation (Sarchiapone & others, 2014). And a recent national study of more than 10,000 13- to 18-year-olds revealed that later

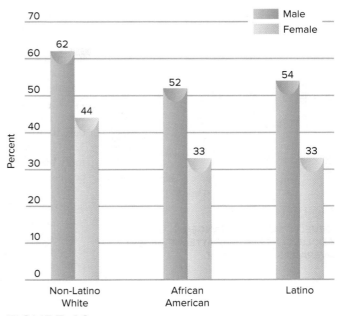

FIGURE **10**

EXERCISE RATES OF U.S. HIGH SCHOOL STUDENTS IN 2015: GENDER AND ETHNICITY (KANN & OTHERS, 2016a).
Note: Data are for high school students who were physically active doing any kind of physical activity that increased their heart rate and made them breathe hard some of the time for a total of at least 60 minutes per day on five or more of the seven days preceding the survey.

developmental **connection**

Exercise

Researchers have found that children who participate in sports are less likely to be overweight or obese than those who don't. Connect to "Physical Development in Middle and Late Childhood."

In 2007, Texas became the first state to test students' physical fitness. This student is performing the trunk lift. Other assessments include aerobic exercise, muscle strength, and body fat. Assessments are done annually.
©Vernon Bryant/Dallas Morning News

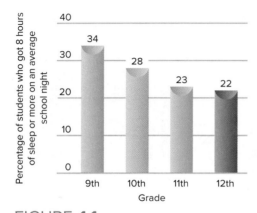

FIGURE 11

DEVELOPMENTAL CHANGES IN U.S. ADOLESCENTS' SLEEP PATTERNS ON AN AVERAGE SCHOOL NIGHT

developmental **connection**

Sleep

Experts recommend that young children get 11 to 13 hours of sleep each night. Connect to "Physical Development in Early Childhood."

In Mary Carskadon's sleep laboratory at Brown University, an adolescent girl's brain activity is being monitored. Carskadon (2005) says that in the morning, sleep-deprived adolescents' "brains are telling them it's night time . . . and the rest of the world is saying it's time to go to school" (p. 19).
©Jim LoScalzo

How Would You...?
If you were an **educator,** how would you use developmental research to convince your school board to change the starting time of high school?

melatonin A sleep-inducing hormone that is produced in the brain's pineal gland.

weeknight bedtime, shorter weekend bedtime delay, and both short and long periods of weekend oversleep were linked to increased rates of anxiety, mood, substance abuse, and behavioral disorders (Zhang & others, 2017). Further, in a four-year longitudinal study beginning at 12 years of age, poor sleep patterns (for example, shorter sleep duration and greater daytime sleepiness) at age 12 were associated with an increased likelihood of drinking alcohol and using marijuana at 16 years of age (Miller, Janssen, & Jackson, 2017). Also, recent Swedish studies revealed that adolescents with a shorter sleep duration were likely to have more school absences, while shorter sleep duration and greater sleep deficits were linked to lower grade point averages (Hysing & others, 2015, 2016).

In a recent national survey of youth, only 27 percent of U.S. adolescents got eight or more hours of sleep on an average school night (Kann & others, 2016a). In this study, the percentage of adolescents getting this much sleep on an average school night decreased as they got older (see Figure 11). Also, in other research with more than 270,000 U.S. adolescents from 1991–2012, the amount of sleep they get has been decreasing in recent years (Keyes & others, 2015).

Mary Carskadon and her colleagues (2002, 2004, 2006, 2011a, b; Crowley & Carskadon, 2010; Kurth & others, 2010; Tarokh, Carskadon, & Achermann, 2010) have conducted a number of research studies on adolescent sleep patterns. They found that when given the opportunity, adolescents will sleep an average of nine hours and 25 minutes a night. Most get considerably less than nine hours of sleep, especially during the week. This shortfall creates a sleep deficit, which adolescents often attempt to make up on the weekend. The researchers also found that older adolescents tend to be more sleepy during the day than younger adolescents. They theorized that this sleepiness was not due to academic work or social pressures. Rather, their research suggests that adolescents' biological clocks undergo a shift as they get older, delaying their period of wakefulness by about one hour. A delay in the nightly release of the sleep-inducing hormone **melatonin,** which is produced in the brain's pineal gland, seems to underlie this shift. Melatonin is secreted at about 9:30 p.m. in younger adolescents and approximately an hour later in older adolescents.

Carskadon has suggested that early school starting times may cause grogginess, inattention in class, and poor performance on tests. Based on her research, school officials in Edina, Minnesota, decided to start classes at 8:30 a.m. rather than the usual 7:25 a.m. Since then there have been fewer referrals for discipline problems, and the number of students who report being ill or depressed has decreased. The school system reports that test scores have improved for high school students, but not for middle school students. This finding supports Carskadon's suspicion that early start times are likely to be more stressful for older than for younger adolescents. Also, researchers found that just a 30-minute delay in school start time was linked to improvements in adolescents' sleep, alertness, mood, and health (Owens, Belon, & Moss, 2010). In another study, early school start times were linked to a higher vehicle crash rate in adolescent drivers (Vorona & others, 2014). Recently, the American Academy of Pediatrics recommended that schools institute start times from 8:30 to 9:30 a.m. to improve adolescents' academic performance and quality of life (Adolescent Sleep Working Group, AAP, 2014).

Do sleep patterns change in emerging adulthood? Research indicates that they do (Galambos, Howard, & Maggs, 2011). One study categorized more than 60 percent of college students as poor-quality sleepers (Lund & others, 2010). In this study, the weekday bedtimes and rise times of first-year college students were approximately 1 hour and 15 minutes later than those of seniors in high school (Lund & others, 2010). However, the first-year college students had later bedtimes and rise times than third- and fourth-year college students, indicating that at about 20 to 22 years of age, a reverse in the timing of bedtimes and rise times occurs.

LEADING CAUSES OF DEATH IN ADOLESCENCE

The three leading causes of death in adolescence and emerging adulthood are accidents, homicide, and suicide (National Center for Health Statistics, 2017). Almost half of all deaths at 15 to 24 years of age are due to unintentional injuries, approximately three-fourths of them involving motor vehicle accidents. Risky driving habits, such as speeding, tailgating, and driving under the influence of alcohol or other drugs, may be more important contributors to these accidents than lack of driving experience. In about 50 percent of motor vehicle fatalities involving adolescents, the driver has a blood alcohol level of 0.10 percent—twice the level needed to be designated as "under the influence" in some states. A high rate of intoxication is also found in adolescents who die as pedestrians or while using recreational vehicles.

Homicide is another leading cause of death in adolescence and emerging adulthood, especially among African American males, who are three times more likely to be killed by guns than by natural causes.

Suicide is the third leading cause of death in adolescence and emerging adulthood. The suicide rate among U.S. adolescents and emerging adults tripled during the second half of the twentieth century, but it has declined in recent years (Ash, 2008).

- - - - - - - - →

developmental connection

Problems, Diseases, and Disorders
Both earlier and later experiences may be involved in adolescent suicide attempts. Connect to "Socioemotional Development in Adolescence."

← - - - - - - - - - - -

SUBSTANCE USE AND ABUSE

Among the significant problems that can develop in adolescence are substance use and abuse, which we will discuss here. In the chapter on "Socioemotional Development in Adolescence" we will explore the adolescent problems of juvenile delinquency, depression, and suicide.

Trends in Substance Use and Abuse   Each year since 1975, Lloyd Johnston and his colleagues at the Institute for Social Research at the University of Michigan have monitored the drug use of America's high school seniors in a wide range of public and private high schools. Since 1991, they also have surveyed drug use by eighth- and tenth-graders. In 2016, the study surveyed 45,000 secondary school students in 380 public and private schools (Johnston & others, 2017).

According to this study, the proportions of eighth-, tenth-, and twelfth-grade U.S. students who used any illicit drug declined during the late 1990s and the first two decades of the twenty-first century (Johnston & others, 2017) (see Figure 12). The use of drugs among U.S. secondary school students had declined in the 1980s but had begun to increase in the early 1990s (Johnston & others, 2017). The overall decline in the use of illicit drugs since the late 1990s is approximately one-third for eighth-graders, one-fourth for tenth-graders, and one-eighth for twelfth-graders. The most notable declines in drug use by U.S. adolescents in the twenty-first century have occurred for LSD, cocaine, cigarettes, sedatives, tranquilizers, and Ecstasy.

As shown in Figure 12, in which marijuana use is included, an increase in illicit drug use by U.S. adolescents occurred from 2008 to 2013. However, when marijuana use is subtracted from the illicit drug index, no increase in U.S. adolescent drug use occurred in this time frame (Johnston & others, 2017). Illicit drug use by adolescents began decreasing again in 2014 and 2015, and then an even greater decrease in U.S. adolescents' use of illicit drugs

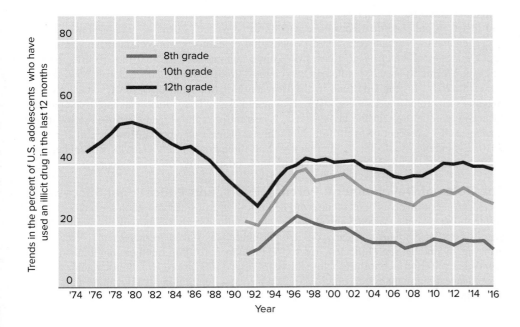

FIGURE **12**

TRENDS IN DRUG USE BY U.S. EIGHTH-, TENTH-, AND TWELFTH-GRADE STUDENTS. This graph shows the percentage of U.S. eighth-, tenth-, and twelfth-grade students who reported having taken an illicit drug in the last 12 months from 1991 to 2016 (for eighth- and tenth-graders) and from 1975 to 2016 (for twelfth-graders) (Johnston & others, 2017).

What are some trends in alcohol use by U.S. adolescents?
©Bill Aron/PhotoEdit

occurred in 2016, with the greatest declines occurring for eighth- and tenth-grade students (Johnston & others, 2017). The United States still has one of the highest rates of adolescent drug use among industrialized nations.

How extensive is alcohol use by U.S. adolescents? Sizable declines in adolescent alcohol use have occurred in recent years (Johnston & others, 2017). The percentage of U.S. eighth-graders who reported having had any alcohol to drink in the past 30 days fell from a 1996 high of 26 percent to 7.3 percent in 2016 (down from 10 percent in 2013). The 30-day prevalence fell among tenth-graders from 39 percent in 2001 to 20 percent in 2016 (down from 20 percent in 2013) and among high school seniors from 72 percent in 1980 to 33 percent in 2016 (down from 39 percent in 2013). Binge drinking (defined in the University of Michigan surveys as having five or more drinks in a row in the last two weeks) in a 30-day period by high school seniors declined from 41 percent in 1980 to 20.4 percent in 2016 (down from 26 percent in 2013). Binge drinking by eighth- and tenth-graders also has dropped in recent years. A consistent gender difference occurs in binge drinking, with males engaging in this behavior more than females do (Johnston & others, 2017).

A special concern is adolescents who drive while they are under the influence of alcohol or other substances (Sanem & others, 2015). In a recent national study, one in four twelfth-graders reported that they had consumed alcohol mixed with energy drinks in the last 12 months, and this combination was linked to their unsafe driving (Martz, Patrick, & Schulenberg, 2015).

Cigarette smoking (in which the active drug is nicotine) is one of the most serious yet preventable health problems among adolescents and emerging adults (McKelvey & Halpern-Felsher, 2017). Smoking is likely to begin in grades 7 through 9, although sizable proportions of youth are still establishing regular smoking habits during high school and college. Risk factors for becoming a regular smoker in adolescence include having a friend who smokes, a weak academic orientation, and low parental support (Tucker, Ellickson, & Klein, 2003).

The peer group plays an especially influential role in smoking (Strong & others, 2017; Valente & others, 2013). In one study, the risk of current smoking was linked with peer networks in which at least half of the members smoked, one or two best friends smoked, and smoking was common in the school (Alexander & others, 2001). And in another study, early smoking was predicted better by sibling and peer smoking than by parental smoking (Kelly & others, 2011).

Cigarette smoking among U.S. adolescents peaked in 1996 and 1997 and has declined since then (Johnston & others, 2017). Following peak use in 1996, smoking rates for U.S. eighth-graders have fallen by 50 percent. In 2016, the percentages of adolescents who said they had smoked cigarettes in the last 30 days were 10.5 percent among twelfth-graders (down from 16 percent in 2013), 4.9 percent among tenth-graders (down from 9 percent in 2013), and 2.6 percent among eighth-graders (down from 4.5 percent in 2013). Since the mid-1990s a growing percentage of adolescents have reported that they perceive cigarette smoking as dangerous, that they disapprove of it, that they are less accepting of being around smokers, and that they prefer to date nonsmokers (Johnston & others, 2017).

E-cigarettes are battery-powered devices that contain a heating element and produce a vapor that users inhale. In most cases the vapor contains nicotine, but the specific contents of "vape" formulas are not regulated (Barrington-Trimis & others, 2017; Gorukanti & others, 2017). In 2014, for the first time in the University of Michigan drug study, E-cigarette use was assessed (Johnston & others, 2015). E-cigarette use by U.S. adolescents in 2014 surpassed tobacco cigarette use—in the last 30 days, 9 percent of eighth-graders, 16 percent of tenth-graders, and 17 percent of twelfth-graders reported using E-cigarettes. However, in 2015 and 2016, E-cigarette use declined significantly at all three grade levels, but was still higher than cigarette use at all three grade levels (Johnston & others, 2017).

The Roles of Development, Parents, Peers, and Educational Success

A special concern involves adolescents who begin to use drugs early in adolescence or even in childhood (Donatelle & Ketcham, 2018). A longitudinal study of individuals from 8 to 42 years of age also found that early onset of drinking was linked to increased risk of heavy drinking in middle age (Pitkanen, Lyyra, & Pulkkinen, 2005). Another longitudinal study found that onset of alcohol use before 11 years of age was linked to increased adult alcohol dependence (Guttmannova & others, 2012). Further, a longitudinal study found that earlier age at first use of alcohol was linked to risk of heavy alcohol use in early adulthood (Liang & Chikritzhs, 2015). And another recent study indicated that early- and rapid-onset trajectories

How Would You...?
If you were a **human development and family studies professional,** how would you explain to parents the importance of parental monitoring in preventing adolescent substance abuse?

of alcohol, marijuana, and substance use were associated with substance abuse in early adulthood (Nelson, Van Ryzin, & Dishion, 2015).

Parents play an important role in preventing adolescent drug abuse (Pena & others, 2017). Positive relationships with parents and others can reduce adolescents' drug use (Chassin & others, 2016; Zucker, Hicks, & Heitzeg, 2016). Researchers have found that parental monitoring is linked with a lower incidence of drug use (Wang & others, 2014). A research review concluded that the more frequently adolescents ate dinner with their family, the less likely they were to have substance abuse problems (Sen, 2010). Negative interactions with parents are linked to increased adolescent drinking and smoking, while positive interactions with parents are related to declines in use of these substances (Gutman & others, 2011). Further, in one study, a higher level of parental monitoring during the last year of high school was linked to a lower risk of dependence on alcohol, but not marijuana, in the first year of college (Kaynak & others, 2013). Another study revealed that having friends in their school's social network and having fewer friends who use substances were related to a lower level of substance use by middle school students (Ennett & others, 2006).

Peer relations influence whether adolescents engage in substance use (Choukas-Bradley & Prinstein, 2016; Prinstein & Giletta, 2016; Strong & others, 2017). One study indicated that among numerous risk factors the strongest predictors of adolescent substance use involved peers (Patrick & Schulenberg, 2010).

Educational success is also a strong buffer for the emergence of drug problems in adolescence. An analysis by Jerald Bachman and his colleagues (2008) revealed that early educational achievement considerably reduced the likelihood that adolescents would develop drug problems, including those involving alcohol abuse, smoking, and abuse of various illicit drugs.

Can special programs effectively reduce adolescent drinking and smoking? See the *Connecting with Research* interlude for a description of one study that addressed this question.

What are ways that parents have been found to influence whether their adolescents take drugs?
©Charles Gullung/Corbis/Getty Images

EATING PROBLEMS AND DISORDERS

Eating disorders have become increasingly common among adolescents (Schiff, 2017). Here are some research findings involving adolescent eating disorders:

- *Body image.* Body dissatisfaction and distorted body image play important roles in adolescent eating disorders (Gadsby, 2017; Senin-Calderon & others, 2017). One study revealed that in general, adolescents were dissatisfied with their bodies, with males desiring to increase their upper body and females wanting to decrease the overall size of their body (Ata, Ludden, & Lally, 2007). In this study, low self-esteem and social support, weight-related teasing, and pressure to lose weight were linked to adolescents' negative body images. In another study, girls who felt negatively about their bodies in early adolescence were more likely to develop eating disorders two years later than their counterparts who did not feel negatively about their bodies (Attie & Brooks-Gunn, 1989). And in yet another study, the key link for explaining depression in overweight adolescents involved body dissatisfaction (Mond & others, 2011).

- *Parenting.* Adolescents who reported observing more healthy eating patterns and exercise by their parents had more healthy eating patterns and exercised more themselves (Pakpreo & others, 2005). Negative parent-adolescent relationships were linked with increased dieting by girls over a one-year period (Archibald, Graber, & Brooks-Gunn, 1999).

- *Sexual activity.* Girls who were both sexually active with their boyfriends and in pubertal transition were the most likely to be dieting or engaging in disordered eating patterns (Cauffman, 1994).

- *Role models and the media.* Girls who were highly motivated to look like female celebrities were more likely than their peers to become very concerned about their weight (Field & others, 2001). Watching commercials with idealized thin female images increased adolescent girls' dissatisfaction with their bodies (Hargreaves & Tiggemann, 2004).

Earlier in the chapter we examined the health risks and emotional consequences of being overweight or obese in adolescence. Let's now examine two other eating problems—anorexia nervosa and bulimia nervosa. Researchers consistently have discovered that the onset of anorexia nervosa and bulimia nervosa occurs in adolescence and that adult onset of these conditions is

Evaluation of a Family Program Designed to Reduce Drinking and Smoking in Young Adolescents

Few experimental studies have been conducted to determine whether family programs can reduce drinking and smoking in young adolescents. In one experimental study, 1,326 families throughout the United States with 12- to 14-year-old adolescents were interviewed (Bauman & others, 2002). After the baseline interviews, participants were randomly assigned either to go through the Family Matters program (experimental group) or not to experience the program (control group) (Bauman & others, 2002).

The families assigned to the Family Matters program received four mailings of booklets. Each mailing was followed by a telephone call from a health educator to "encourage participation by all family members, answer any questions, and record information" (Bauman & others, 2002, pp. 36–37). The first booklet focused on the negative consequences of adolescent substance abuse to the family. The second booklet emphasized "supervision, support, communication skills, attachment, time spent together, educational achievement, conflict reduction, and how well adolescence is understood." The third booklet asked parents to "list things that they do that might inadvertently encourage their child's use of tobacco or alcohol, identify rules that might influence the child's use, and consider ways to monitor use. Then adult family members and the child meet to agree upon rules and sanctions related to adolescent use." Booklet four deals with what "the child can do to resist peer and media pressures for use."

Two follow-up interviews with the parents and adolescents were conducted three months and one year after the experimental group completed the program. Adolescents in the Family Matters program

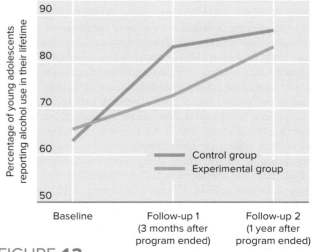

FIGURE 13

YOUNG ADOLESCENTS' REPORTS OF ALCOHOL USE IN THE FAMILY MATTERS PROGRAM.
Note that at baseline (before the program started) the young adolescents in the Family Matters program (experimental group) and their counterparts who did not go through the program (control group) reported approximately the same lifetime use of alcohol (slightly higher use by the experimental group). However, three months after the program ended, the experimental group reported lower alcohol use, and this reduction was still present one year after the program ended, although at a reduced level.

reported lower rates of alcohol and cigarette use both at three months and again one year after the program had been completed. Figure 13 shows the results for alcohol.

What other types of research efforts might help identify or design programs that are effective in reducing adolescent drinking and smoking?

---

rare (Hebebrand & Bulik, 2011). They also have found that eating disorders, including anorexia nervosa and bulimia nervosa, are far more likely to characterize females than males.

Anorexia Nervosa   **Anorexia nervosa** is an eating disorder that involves the relentless pursuit of thinness through starvation. It is a serious disorder that can lead to death (Westmoreland, Krantz, & Mehler, 2016). Anorexia nervosa is about 10 times more likely to occur in females than males. Although most U.S. girls have been on a diet at some point, slightly less than 1 percent ever develop anorexia nervosa.

Three main characteristics of anorexia nervosa are (1) weighing less than 85 percent of what is considered normal for a person's age and height, (2) having an intense fear of gaining weight—a fear that does not decrease with weight loss, and (3) having a distorted image of body shape (Pinhas & others, 2017; Reville, O'Connor, & Frampton, 2016). Obsessive thinking about weight and compulsive exercise also are linked to anorexia nervosa (Simpson & others, 2013). Even when they are extremely thin, anorexics see themselves as too fat. They never think they are thin enough, especially in the abdomen, buttocks, and thighs. They usually weigh themselves frequently, often take their body measurements, and gaze critically at themselves in mirrors.

Anorexia nervosa typically begins in the early to middle teenage years, often following an episode of dieting and some type of life stress. When anorexia nervosa does occur in males, the symptoms and other characteristics (such as a distorted body image and family conflict) are usually similar to those reported by females who have the disorder (Ariceli & others, 2005).

anorexia nervosa An eating disorder that involves the relentless pursuit of thinness through starvation.

Most anorexics are non-Latino White adolescent or emerging adult females from well-educated, middle- and upper-income families, and they are competitive and high-achieving (Schmidt, 2003). They become stressed about not being able to reach their high expectations and shift their focus to something they can control: their weight (Murray & others, 2017; Stice & others, 2017). Offspring of mothers with anorexia nervosa are at risk for becoming anorexic themselves (Striegel-Moore & Bulik, 2007). Problems in family functioning are increasingly being found to be linked to the appearance of anorexia nervosa in adolescent girls (Machado & others, 2014), and family therapy is often the most effective treatment (Espie & Eisler, 2015; Hughes & others, 2017).

Biology and culture are involved in anorexia nervosa. Genes play an important role in anorexia nervosa (Boraska & others, 2014). Also, the physical effects of dieting may change neural networks and thus sustain the disordered pattern (Kaye & others, 2013; Scaife & others, 2017). The fashion image in U.S. culture likely contributes to the incidence of anorexia nervosa (Cazzato & others, 2016). The media portray thin as beautiful in their choice of fashion models, whom many adolescent girls strive to emulate (Carr & Peebles, 2012). A recent study found that having an increased number of Facebook friends across two years was linked to enhanced motivation to be thin (Tiggemann & Slater, 2017). And many adolescent girls who strive to be thin hang out together in person and online.

Bulimia Nervosa Whereas anorexics control their eating by restricting it, most bulimics do not (Castillo & Weiselberg, 2017). **Bulimia nervosa** is an eating disorder in which the individual consistently follows a binge-and-purge pattern. The bulimic goes on an eating binge and then purges by self-induced vomiting or use of a laxative. Many people binge and purge occasionally and some experiment with it, but a person is considered to have a serious bulimic disorder if the episodes occur at least twice a week for three months (Cuzzolaro, 2014).

About 90 percent of bulimics are females, and approximately 1 to 2 percent of U.S. females are estimated to develop bulimia nervosa. Bulimia nervosa typically begins in late adolescence or early adulthood. Many women who develop bulimia nervosa were somewhat overweight before the onset of the disorder, and the binge eating often began during an episode of dieting. Unlike anorexics, people who binge-and-purge typically fall within a normal weight range, which makes bulimia more difficult to detect.

As with anorexics, most bulimics are preoccupied with food, have a strong fear of becoming overweight, and are depressed or anxious (Murray & others, 2017; Stice & others, 2017). One study found that bulimics have difficulty controlling their emotions (Lavender & others, 2014). Like anorexics, bulimics are highly perfectionistic (Lampard & others, 2012). Unlike anorexics, people who binge and purge typically fall within a normal weight range, a characteristic that makes bulimia more difficult to detect.

As with anorexia nervosa, about 70 percent of individuals who develop bulimia nervosa eventually recover from the disorder (Agras & others, 2004). Drug therapy and psychotherapy have been effective in treating anorexia nervosa and bulimia nervosa (Harrington & others, 2015). Cognitive behavior therapy has especially been helpful in treating bulimia nervosa (Abreu & Filho, 2017; Agras & others, 2017; Dalle Grave & others, 2016; Peterson & others, 2017).

Anorexia nervosa has become an increasing problem for adolescent girls and young adult women. *What are some possible causes of anorexia nervosa?*
©Ian Thraves/Alamy

How Would You...?
If you were a **health-care professional,** how would you educate parents to identify the signs and symptoms that may signal an eating disorder?

bulimia nervosa An eating disorder in which the individual consistently follows a binge-and-purge eating pattern.

Review Connect Reflect

LG4 Summarize adolescents' health and eating disorders.

Review
- What are key concerns about the health of adolescents?
- What are the leading causes of death in adolescence and emerging adulthood?
- What are some characteristics of adolescents' substance use and abuse?
- What are the characteristics of the major eating disorders?

Connect
- How might eating patterns in childhood possibly contribute to eating problems in adolescence?

Reflect *Your Own Personal Journey of Life*
- What were your health habits like from the time you entered puberty to the time you completed high school? Describe your health-compromising and health-enhancing behaviors during this time. Since high school, have you reduced your health-compromising behaviors? Explain.

In this chapter, you examined some significant changes that occur in the adolescent's brain—the early development of the amygdala and the delayed development of the prefrontal cortex—that may contribute to risk taking and sensation seeking. Next, you will read about how adolescent thinking becomes more abstract, idealistic, and logical—which Piaget described as the key aspects of formal operational thought. Other topics you will explore in the next chapter include adolescents' decision making and the influence of schools in their lives.

reach your **learning goals**

Physical Development in Adolescence

1 What Is the Nature of Adolescence? **LG1** Discuss views and developmental transitions that involve adolescence.

Positive and Negative Views of Adolescence

- Many stereotypes about adolescents are negative. Today, however, the majority of adolescents successfully negotiate the path from childhood to adulthood, although too many are not provided with adequate support and opportunities.

- It is important to view adolescents as a heterogeneous group. Acting out and boundary testing by adolescents move them toward accepting, rather than rejecting, parental values. Recent interest has focused on a strength-based approach that emphasizes positive youth development.

Developmental Transitions

- Two important transitions in development are those from childhood to adolescence and from adolescence to adulthood. In the transition from childhood to adolescence, pubertal change is prominent, although cognitive and socioemotional changes occur as well.

- The concept of emerging adulthood recently has been proposed to describe the transition from adolescence to adulthood. Five key characteristics of emerging adulthood are identity exploration (especially in love and work), instability, being self-focused, feeling in-between, and experiencing opportunities to transform one's life.

2 What Are the Physical and Psychological Aspects of Puberty? **LG2** Describe puberty's characteristics, developmental changes, psychological dimensions, and the development of the brain.

Sexual Maturation, Height, and Weight

- Puberty is a brain-neuroendocrine process occurring primarily in early adolescence that provides stimulation for the rapid physical change involved in this period of development. A number of changes occur in sexual maturation, including increased size of the penis and testicles in boys and breast growth and menarche in girls. The growth spurt involves height and weight and occurs about two years earlier for girls than for boys.

Hormonal Changes

- Extensive hormonal changes characterize puberty. The pituitary gland plays an important role in these hormonal changes. During puberty, testosterone concentrations increase considerably in boys, and estradiol increases considerably in girls.

Timing and Variations in Puberty

- In the United States, the age of menarche (a girl's first menstrual period) has declined since the mid-1800s. The basic genetic program for puberty is wired into the species, but nutrition, health, and other environmental factors affect puberty's timing and makeup. Menarche typically appears between 9 and 15 years of age. Boys can start the pubertal sequence as early as 10 years of age or as late as 17.

Psychological Dimensions of Puberty

- Adolescents show heightened interest in their bodies and body images. Younger adolescents are more preoccupied with these images than are older adolescents. Adolescent girls often have a more negative body image than do adolescent boys.

- The Brain

- Early maturation often favors boys, at least during early adolescence, but as adults, late-maturing boys have a more positive identity than early-maturing boys. Early-maturing girls are at risk for a number of developmental problems. They are more likely to smoke and drink and have an eating disorder and are likely to have earlier sexual experiences than later-maturing girls.
- The thickening of the corpus callosum in adolescence is linked to improved processing of information. The limbic system and the amygdala, which are involved in emotions such as anger, mature earlier than the prefrontal cortex, which functions in reasoning and self-regulation. This gap in development may help to explain the increase in risk-taking behavior that often characterizes adolescence.

3 What Are the Dimensions of Adolescent Sexuality?

LG3 Characterize adolescent sexuality.

Developing a Sexual Identity

Timing and Trends in Adolescent Sexual Behavior

Sexual Risk Taking in Adolescence

- Adolescence is a time of sexual exploration and sexual experimentation. Mastering emerging sexual feelings and forming a sense of sexual identity are multifaceted. An adolescent's sexual identity includes sexual orientation, activities, interests, and styles of behavior.
- The timing of sexual initiation in adolescence varies by country, gender, and socioeconomic characteristics. In a 2009 study, 62 percent of twelfth-graders reported that they had experienced sexual intercourse. Also, recently there has been a decline in the number of adolescents who say they have experienced various aspects of sexuality. However, a dramatic increase in oral sex has occurred recently among adolescents.
- Having sexual intercourse in early adolescence, as well as various contextual and family factors, is associated with sexual problems and negative developmental outcomes. Adolescents are increasing their use of contraceptives, but large numbers still do not use them. Recently, there has been increased emphasis on having adolescents use long-acting reversible contraception.
- Sexually transmitted infections (STIs) are contracted primarily through sexual contact. Approximately one in four sexually active adolescents have an STI. Among the STIs are bacterial infections such as gonorrhea, syphilis, and chlamydia, and viral infections such as genital herpes, genital warts, and AIDS.
- Although the U.S. adolescent pregnancy rate is still among the highest in the developed world, the rate declined considerably in the last two decades. Adolescent pregnancy often increases health risks for the mother and the offspring, although it often is not pregnancy alone that places adolescents at risk. Easy access to family-planning services and sex education programs in schools can help reduce the U.S. adolescent pregnancy rate.

4 How Can Adolescents' Health and Health-Enhancing Assets Be Characterized?

LG4 Summarize adolescents' health and eating disorders.

Adolescent Health

Leading Causes of Death in Adolescence

Substance Use and Abuse

Eating Problems and Disorders

- Adolescence is a critical juncture in health because many of the factors related to poor health habits and early death in the adult years begin during adolescence. Poor nutrition, lack of exercise, and inadequate sleep are concerns.
- The three leading causes of death in adolescence and emerging adulthood are accidents, homicide, and suicide.
- Despite recent declines in use, the United States has one of the highest rates of adolescent drug use of any industrialized nation. Alcohol abuse is a major adolescent problem, although its rate has been dropping in recent years, as has the rate of cigarette smoking. Drug use in childhood or early adolescence has more negative outcomes than drug use that begins in late adolescence. Parents and peers play important roles in whether adolescents take drugs.
- Eating disorders have increased in adolescence, with a substantial increase in the percentage of adolescents who are overweight. Three eating disorders that may occur in adolescence are obesity, anorexia nervosa, and bulimia nervosa.
- A combination of behavioral therapy, calorie restriction, exercise, and reduction of sedentary activities such as TV watching has been more effective for overweight adolescents than school-based approaches.

- Anorexia nervosa is an eating disorder that involves the relentless pursuit of thinness through starvation. Anorexics are intensely afraid of weight gain, have a distorted body image, and weigh less than 85 percent of what would be considered normal for their height.
- Bulimia nervosa is an eating disorder in which a binge-and-purge pattern is consistently followed. Most bulimics are depressed or anxious and fearful of becoming overweight, and their weight typically falls within a normal range. About 70 percent of bulimics and anorexics eventually recover.

key terms

AIDS	emerging adulthood	hypothalamus	puberty
amygdala	estradiol	limbic system	sexually transmitted infections
anorexia nervosa	gonadotropins	melatonin	(STIs)
bulimia nervosa	gonads	menarche	testosterone
corpus callosum	hormones	pituitary gland	

key people

Claudia Allen	Peter Benson	G. Stanley Hall	Charles Nelson
Joseph Allen	Mary Carskadon	Lloyd Johnston	Daniel Offer
Jeffrey Arnett			

connecting with improving the lives of children

STRATEGIES

Supporting Adolescent Physical Development and Health

What are some strategies for supporting and guiding adolescent physical development and health?

- Develop positive expectations for adolescents. Adolescents often are negatively stereotyped. These negative expectations have a way of becoming self-fulfilling prophecies and harming adult-adolescent communication. Don't view adolescence as a time of crisis and rebellion. View it instead as a time of evaluation, decision making, commitment, and the carving out of a place in the world.

- Understand the many physical changes adolescents are going through. The physical changes adolescents go through can be very perplexing to them. They are not quite sure what they are going to change into, and this can create considerable uncertainty for them.

- Be a good health role model for adolescents. Adolescents benefit from being around adults who are good health role models: individuals who exercise regularly, eat healthily, and don't take drugs or smoke.

- Communicate effectively with adolescents about sexuality. Emphasize that young adolescents should abstain from sex. If adolescents are going to be sexually active, they need to take contraceptive precautions. Adolescents also need to learn about sexuality and human reproduction before they become sexually active.

RESOURCES

Search Institute

www.search-institute.org

The Search Institute has available a large number of resources for improving the lives of adolescents. Brochures and books include resource lists and address topics such as school improvement, adolescent literacy, parent education, program planning, and adolescent health. A free quarterly newsletter is also available.

The Society for Adolescent Medicine (SAM)

www.adolescenthealth.org

SAM is a valuable source of information about competent physicians who specialize in treating adolescents. It maintains a list of recommended adolescence specialists across the United States. SAM publishes an excellent research journal, *Journal of Adolescent Health,* that provides up-to-date coverage of many problems adolescents can develop.

KidsHealth

kidshealth.org/en/parents/adolescence.html#

This website provides excellent advice to help parents understand, guide, and converse with their teens about many topics, including puberty, sleep problems, body image, and drugs.

Escaping the Endless Adolescence (2009)

Joe Allen and Claudia Allen
New York: Ballantine

A superb, well-written book on the lives of emerging adults, including extensive recommendations for parents on how to effectively guide their children through the transition from adolescence to adulthood.

The Path to Purpose (2008)

William Damon
New York: Free Press

A provocative book by leading expert William Damon on helping adolescents find their calling in life.

chapter 15

COGNITIVE DEVELOPMENT IN ADOLESCENCE

chapter outline

Kim-Chi Trinh was only 9 years old in Vietnam when her father used his savings to buy passage for her on a fishing boat. It was a costly and risky sacrifice for the family, who placed Kim-Chi on the small boat, among strangers, in the hope that she eventually would reach the United States, where she would get a good education and enjoy a better life.

Kim-Chi made it to the United States and coped with a succession of three foster families. When she graduated from high school in San Diego, she had a straight-A average and a number of college scholarship offers. When asked why she excelled in school, Kim-Chi says that she had to do well because she owed it to her parents, who were still in Vietnam.

Kim-Chi is one of a wave of bright, highly motivated Asians who are immigrating to America. Percentage-wise, Asian Americans are the fastest-growing ethnic minority group in the United States—from 2010 to 2015, the Asian American immigrant population grew 17 percent (compared with 11 percent for the Latino population) (U.S. Census Bureau, 2016).

Not all Asian American youth do this well, however. Poorly educated Vietnamese, Cambodian, and Hmong refugee youth especially have been at risk for school-related problems. Many refugee children's histories are replete with losses and trauma.

topical connections   *looking **back***

You have explored how early adolescence is a time of dramatic physical change as puberty unfolds. Pubertal change also brings considerable interest in one's body image. And pubertal change ushers in an intense interest in sexuality. Adolescence also is a critical time in the development of behaviors related to health, such as good nutrition and regular exercise, which are health enhancing, and drug abuse, which is health compromising. Significant changes occur in the adolescent's brain—the early development of the limbic system/amygdala and the delayed development of the prefrontal cortex—that may contribute to risk taking and decision making. You have read about cognitive advances in middle childhood, including improved thinking strategies and reading skills. This chapter examines continued advances in thinking skills, moral development and values, and schools.

preview

When people think of the changes that characterize adolescents, they often focus on puberty and adolescent problems. However, some impressive cognitive changes occur during adolescence. We begin this chapter by focusing on these cognitive changes and then turn our attention to adolescents' values, moral education, and religion. In the last section of the chapter, we study the characteristics of schools for adolescents.

1 How Do Adolescents Think and Process Information?

LG1 Discuss different approaches to adolescent cognition.

Piaget's Theory   Adolescent Egocentrism   Information Processing

Adolescents' developing power of thought opens up new cognitive and social horizons. Let's examine the characteristics of this developing power of thought, beginning with Piaget's theory (1952).

PIAGET'S THEORY

Jean Piaget proposed that at about 7 years of age children enter the *concrete operational stage* of cognitive development. They can reason logically about concrete events and objects, and they make gains in their ability to classify objects and to reason about the relationships between classes of objects. According to Piaget, the concrete operational stage lasts until the child is about 11 years old, when the fourth and final stage of cognitive development begins—the formal operational stage.

The Formal Operational Stage   What are the characteristics of the formal operational stage? Formal operational thought is more abstract than concrete operational thought. Adolescents are no longer limited to actual experiences as anchors for thought. They can conjure up make-believe situations—events that are purely hypothetical possibilities or abstract propositions—and can try to reason logically about them.

The abstract quality of thinking during the formal operational stage is evident in the adolescent's verbal problem-solving ability. Whereas the concrete operational thinker needs to see the concrete elements A, B, and C to be able to make the logical inference that if A = B and B = C, then A = C, the formal operational thinker can solve this problem merely through verbal presentation.

Another indication of the abstract quality of adolescents' thought is their increased tendency to think about thought itself. One adolescent commented, "I began thinking about why I was thinking what I was. Then I began thinking about why I was thinking about what I was thinking about what I was." If this sounds abstract, it is, and it characterizes the adolescent's enhanced focus on thought and its abstract qualities.

Accompanying the abstract nature of formal operational thought is thought full of idealism and possibilities, especially during the beginning of the formal operational stage, when assimilation dominates. Adolescents engage in extended speculation about ideal characteristics—qualities they desire in themselves and in others. Such thoughts often lead adolescents to compare themselves with others in regard to such ideal standards.

→ developmental **connection**

Cognitive Development

Piaget's first three stages are sensorimotor, preoperational, and concrete operational. Connect to "Cognitive Development in Infancy," "Cognitive Development in Early Childhood," and "Cognitive Development in Middle and Late Childhood."

Might adolescents' ability to reason hypothetically and to evaluate what is ideal versus what is real lead them to engage in demonstrations, such as this protest related to improving education? What other causes might be attractive to adolescents' newfound cognitive abilities of hypothetical-deductive reasoning and idealistic thinking?
©Jim West/Alamy

developmental **connection**

Cognitive Development

Neo-Piagetians are developmentalists who have elaborated on Piaget's theory, arguing that cognitive development is more specific than Piaget envisioned and that it gives more emphasis to information processing. Connect to "Cognitive Development in Middle and Late Childhood."

And their thoughts are often fantasy flights into future possibilities. It is not unusual for the adolescent to become impatient with these newfound ideal standards and to become perplexed over which of many ideal standards to adopt.

At the same time that adolescents think more abstractly and idealistically, they also think more logically about abstract concepts. Children are likely to solve problems through trial-and-error; adolescents begin to think more as a scientist thinks, devising plans to solve problems and systematically testing solutions. This type of problem solving requires **hypothetical-deductive reasoning.** Such reasoning involves creating a hypothesis and deducing its implications, which provide ways to test the hypothesis. Thus, formal operational thinkers develop hypotheses about ways to solve problems and then systematically deduce the best path to follow to solve the problem.

Evaluating Piaget's Theory   Some of Piaget's ideas on the formal operational stage have been challenged. The stage includes much more individual variation than Piaget envisioned. Only about one in three young adolescents is a formal operational thinker. Many American adults never become formal operational thinkers, and neither do many adults in other cultures.

Furthermore, education in the logic of science and mathematics promotes the development of formal operational thinking. This point recalls a criticism of Piaget's theory: Culture and education exert stronger influences on cognitive development than Piaget maintained (Gauvain & Perez, 2015; Petersen & others, 2017; Wagner, 2018).

Piaget's theory of cognitive development has been challenged on other points as well. Piaget conceived of stages as unitary structures of thought, with various aspects of a stage emerging at the same time. However, most contemporary developmentalists agree that cognitive development is not as stage-like as Piaget envisioned. Furthermore, children can be trained to reason at a higher cognitive stage, and some cognitive abilities emerge earlier than Piaget predicted (Baillargeon, 2014; Spelke, Bernier, & Snedeker, 2013). For example, even 2-year-olds are nonegocentric in some contexts. When they realize that another person will not see an object, they investigate whether the person is blindfolded or looking in a different direction. Some understanding of the conservation of number has been demonstrated as early as age 3, although Piaget did not think it emerged until 7. Other cognitive abilities can emerge later than Piaget expected (Kuhn, 2011). As we have discussed, many adolescents still think in concrete operational ways or are just beginning to master formal operations. Even many adults are not formal operational thinkers.

Despite these challenges to Piaget's ideas, we owe him a tremendous debt. Piaget was the founder of the present field of cognitive development, and he established a long list of masterful concepts of enduring power and fascination: assimilation, accommodation, object permanence, egocentrism, conservation, and others. Psychologists also owe him the current vision of children as active, constructive thinkers. And they are indebted to him for creating a theory that generated a huge volume of research on children's cognitive development (Miller, 2016).

Piaget was a genius when it came to observing children. His careful observations demonstrated inventive ways to discover how children act on and adapt to their world. He also showed us how children need to make their experiences fit their schemes yet simultaneously adapt their schemes to reflect their experiences. Piaget revealed how cognitive change is likely to occur if the context is structured to allow gradual movement to the next higher level. Concepts do not emerge suddenly, full-blown, but instead develop through a series of partial accomplishments that lead to increasingly comprehensive understanding (Birch & others, 2017; Blair, 2017; Fourneret & des Portes, 2017; Gelman, 2013).

ADOLESCENT EGOCENTRISM

In addition to thinking more logically, abstractly, and idealistically—characteristics of Piaget's formal operational thought stage—in what other ways do adolescents change cognitively? David Elkind (1978) described how adolescent egocentrism governs the way that adolescents think about social matters. **Adolescent egocentrism** is the heightened self-consciousness of adolescents, which is reflected in their belief that others are as interested in them as they are themselves, as well as in their sense of personal uniqueness and invincibility. Elkind argued that adolescent egocentrism can be dissected into two types of social thinking—imaginary audience and personal fable.

hypothetical-deductive reasoning Piaget's formal operational concept that adolescents have the cognitive ability to develop hypotheses, or best guesses, about ways to solve problems.

adolescent egocentrism The heightened self-consciousness of adolescents that is reflected in their belief that others are as interested in them as they are in themselves, and in their sense of personal uniqueness and invincibility.

The **imaginary audience** refers to the aspect of adolescent egocentrism that involves feeling one is the center of everyone's attention and sensing that one is on stage. An adolescent boy might think that others are as aware of a few hairs that are out of place as he is. An adolescent girl walks into her classroom and thinks that all eyes are riveted on her complexion. Adolescents especially sense that they are "on stage" in early adolescence, believing they are the main actors and all others are the audience.

Might today's teens be drawn to social media to express their imaginary audience and sense of uniqueness? A recent analysis concluded that amassing a large number of friends (audience) may help to validate adolescents' perception that everyone is watching them (Psychster Inc., 2010). A look at a teen's home Twitter comments may suggest to many adults that what teens are reporting is often rather mundane and uninteresting as they update to the world at large what they are doing and having, such as: "Studying heavy. Not happy tonight." or "At Starbucks with Jesse. Lattes are great." Possibly for adolescents, though, such tweets are not trivial but rather an expression of each teen's sense of uniqueness. A recent study found that Facebook use does indeed increase self-interest (Chiou, Chen, & Liao, 2014). And a recent meta-analysis concluded that greater use of social networking sites was linked to higher levels of narcissism (Gnambs & Appel, 2017).

According to Elkind, the **personal fable** is the part of adolescent egocentrism that involves an adolescent's sense of personal uniqueness and invincibility. Adolescents' sense of personal uniqueness makes them believe that no one can understand how they really feel. For example, an adolescent girl thinks that her mother cannot possibly sense the hurt she feels because her boyfriend has broken up with her. As part of their effort to retain a sense of personal uniqueness, adolescents might craft stories about themselves that are filled with fantasy, immersing themselves in a world that is far removed from reality. Personal fables frequently show up in adolescent diaries.

Many adolescent girls spend long hours in front of the mirror, depleting cans of hairspray, tubes of lipstick, and jars of cosmetics. *How might this behavior be related to changes in adolescent cognitive and physical development?*
©Image Source/JupiterImages RF

Research studies, however, suggest that rather than perceiving themselves to be invulnerable, many adolescents portray themselves as vulnerable (Reyna & Rivers, 2008). For example, in a recent study, 12- to 18-year olds were asked about their chances of dying in the next year and prior to age 20 (Fischhoff & others, 2010). The adolescents greatly overestimated their chances of dying.

Some researchers have questioned the view that invulnerability is a unitary concept and argued rather that it consists of two dimensions (Duggan, Lapsley, & Norman, 2000; Lapsley & Hill, 2010):

Are social media, such as Facebook and Twitter, amplifying the expression of adolescents' imaginary audience and personal fable sense of uniqueness?
©Garo/Phanie/age fotostock

- *Danger invulnerability,* which involves adolescents' sense of indestructibility and tendency to take on physical risks (driving recklessly at high speeds, for example)
- *Psychological invulnerability*, which captures an adolescent's felt invulnerability related to personal or psychological distress (getting one's feelings hurt, for example)

One study revealed that adolescents who scored high on a danger invulnerability scale were more likely to engage in juvenile delinquency or substance abuse, or to be depressed (Lapsley & Hill, 2010). In this study, adolescents who scored high on psychological invulnerability were less likely to be depressed, had higher self-esteem, and engaged in better interpersonal relationships. In terms of psychological invulnerability, adolescents often benefit from the normal developmental challenges of exploring identity options, making new friends, asking someone to go out on a date, and learning a new skill. All of these important adolescent tasks involve a risk of failure as well as a potential for enhanced self-image following a successful outcome.

INFORMATION PROCESSING

In Deanna Kuhn's (2009) view, in the later years of childhood and continuing in adolescence, individuals approach cognitive levels that may or may not be achieved, in contrast with the

imaginary audience Refers to adolescents' belief that others are as interested in them as they themselves are, as well as their attention-getting behavior motivated by a desire to be noticed, visible, and "on stage."

personal fable The part of adolescent egocentrism that involves an adolescent's sense of uniqueness and invincibility.

largely universal cognitive levels that young children attain. By adolescence, considerable variation in cognitive functioning is present across individuals. This variability supports the argument that adolescents are producers of their own development to a greater extent than are children.

developmental **connection**

The Brain

The prefrontal cortex is the location in the brain where much of executive function occurs. Connect to "Physical Development in Early Childhood," "Physical Development in Middle and Late Childhood," and "Physical Development in Adolescence."

Executive Function   Kuhn (2009) further argues that the most important cognitive change in adolescence is improvement in *executive function.* Recall our description of *executive function* as an umbrella-like concept that consists of a number of higher-level cognitive processes linked to the development of the prefrontal cortex. Executive function involves managing one's thoughts to engage in goal-directed behavior and to exercise self-control. Executive function in early childhood especially involves developmental advances in cognitive inhibition, cognitive flexibility, and goal setting (Bardikoff & Sabbagh, 2017; Knapp & Morton, 2017). We have described executive function advances in cognitive inhibition, as well as progress in working memory (Gerst & others, 2017).

It is increasingly thought that executive function strengthens during adolescence (Kuhn, 2009). This executive function "assumes a role of monitoring and managing the deployment of cognitive resources as a function of task demands. As a result, cognitive development and learning itself become more effective. . . . Emergence and strengthening of this executive (function) is arguably the single most important and consequential intellectual development to occur in the second decade of life" (Kuhn & Franklin, 2006, p. 987). Our further coverage of executive function in adolescence focuses on working memory, cognitive control, decision making, critical thinking, and metacognition.

Cognitive Control   Cognitive control involves exercising effective control in a number of areas, including focusing attention, reducing interfering thoughts, and being cognitively flexible (Diamond, 2013; Stewart & others, 2017). Cognitive control increases in adolescence and emerging adulthood (Chevalier, Dauvier, & Blaye, 2017; Somerville, 2016).

Think about all the times adolescents need to engage in cognitive control, such as the following situations (Galinsky, 2010):

- Making a real effort to stick with a task, avoiding interfering thoughts or environmental events, and instead doing what is most effective.
- Stopping and thinking before acting to avoid blurting out something that a minute or two later they wished they hadn't said.
- Continuing to work on something that is important but boring when there is something a lot more fun to do, inhibiting their behavior and doing the boring but important task, saying to themselves, "I have to show the self-discipline to finish this."

Working Memory   Recall that *working memory* is a kind of "mental workbench" where people manipulate and assemble information to help them make decisions, solve problems, and comprehend written and spoken language (Baddeley, 2013, 2015). Working memory is an important aspect of executive function and is linked to many aspects of children's and adolescents' development (Cassidy, 2016; Moriguchi, Chevalier, & Zelazo, 2016; Ogino & others, 2017; Tsubomi & Watanabe, 2017). For example, a recent study found that adolescent binge drinkers had working memory deficits (Carbia & others, 2017).

In one study, the performances of individuals from 6 to 57 years of age were examined on both verbal and visuospatial working memory tasks (Swanson, 1999). The two verbal tasks were auditory digit sequence (the ability to remember numerical information embedded in a short sentence, such as "Now suppose somebody wanted to go to the supermarket at 8651 Elm Street") and semantic association (the ability to organize words into abstract categories) (Swanson, 1999, p. 988).

In the semantic association task, the participant was presented with a series of words (such as *shirt, saw, pants, hammer, shoes,* and *nails*) and then asked to remember how they go together. The two visuospatial tasks involved mapping/directions and a visual matrix. In the mapping/directions task, the participant was shown a street map indicating the route a bicycle (child/young adolescent) or car (adult) would take through a city. After briefly looking at the map, participants were asked to redraw the route on a blank map. In the visual matrix task, participants were asked to study a matrix showing a series of dots. After looking at the matrix for five seconds, they were asked to answer questions about the location of the dots. As shown in Figure 1, working memory increased substantially from 8 through 24 years of age—that is, through the transition to adulthood and beyond—no matter what the task. Thus, the adolescent years are likely to be an important developmental period for improvement in working memory (Swanson, 1999).

Cognitive Control   **Cognitive control** involves effective control and flexible thinking in a number of areas, including controlling attention, reducing interfering thoughts, and being cognitively flexible (Stewart & others, 2017). Cognitive control also has been referred to as *inhibitory control* or *effortful control* to emphasize the ability to resist a strong inclination to do one thing but instead to do what is most effective.

Across childhood and adolescence, cognitive control increases with age (Chevalier, Dauvier, & Blaye, 2017; Steinberg, 2016). The increase in cognitive control is thought to be due to the maturation of brain pathways and circuitry, especially those involving the prefrontal cortex (Monahan & others, 2016). For example, one study found less diffusion and more focal activation in the prefrontal cortex from 7 to 30 years of age (Durston & others, 2006). The activation change was accompanied by increased efficiency in cognitive performance, especially in *cognitive control*.

Think about all the times adolescents and emerging adults need to engage in cognitive control, such as the following situations (Galinsky, 2010):

- making a real effort to stick with a task, avoiding interfering thoughts or environmental events, and instead doing what is most effective;
- stopping and thinking before acting to avoid blurting out something they might wish they hadn't said; and
- continuing to work on something that is important but boring when there is something a lot more fun to do.

A longitudinal study of an important dimension of executive function—inhibitory control—found that 3- to 11-year-old children who early in development had better inhibitory control (waiting their turn, not getting easily distracted, showing more persistence, and being less impulsive) were more likely to still be in school, less likely to engage in risk-taking behavior, and less likely to be taking drugs in adolescence (Moffitt & others, 2011). Thirty years after they were initially assessed, the children with better inhibitory control had better physical and mental health (they were less likely to be overweight, for example), had better earnings in their career, were more law-abiding, and were happier (Moffitt, 2012; Moffitt & others, 2011).

Controlling Attention and Reducing Interfering Thoughts   Controlling attention is a key aspect of learning and thinking in adolescence and emerging adulthood (Lau & Waters, 2017). Distractions that can interfere with attention in adolescence and emerging adulthood come from the external environment (other students talking while the student is trying to listen to a lecture, or the student switching on a laptop during a lecture and looking at a new friend request on Facebook, for example) or intrusive distractions from competing thoughts in the individual's mind. Self-oriented thoughts, such as worrying, self-doubt, and intense emotionally laden thoughts may especially interfere with focusing attention on thinking tasks.

Being Cognitively Flexible   *Cognitive flexibility* involves being aware that options and alternatives are available and adapting to the situation (Wang, Ye, & Degol, 2017). Before adolescents and emerging adults adapt their behavior in a situation, they must become aware

	TASK			
	VERBAL		**VISUOSPATIAL**	
Age	**Semantic Association**	**Digit/ Sentence**	**Mapping/ Directions**	**Visual Matrix**
8	1.33	1.75	3.13	1.67
10	1.70	2.34	3.60	2.06
13	1.86	2.94	4.09	2.51
16	2.24	2.98	3.92	2.68
24	2.60	3.71	4.64	3.47

Highest Working Memory Performance

3.02 (age 45)	3.97 (age 35)	4.90 (age 35)	3.47 (age 24)

FIGURE 1

DEVELOPMENTAL CHANGES IN WORKING MEMORY.

Note: The scores shown here are the means for each age group, and the age also represents a mean age. Higher scores reflect superior working memory performance.

The error of youth is to believe that intelligence is a substitute for experience, while the error of age is to believe that experience is a substitute for intelligence.

—LYMAN BRYSON
American Author, 20th Century

cognitive control Involves effective control and flexible thinking in a number of areas, including controlling attention, reducing interfering thoughts, and being cognitively flexible.

CIRCLE THE NUMBER THAT BEST REFLECTS HOW YOU THINK FOR EACH OF
THE FOUR ITEMS:

	Exactly Like You	Very Much Like You	Somewhat Like You	Not Too Much Like You	Not At All Like You
1. When I try something that doesn't work, it's hard for me to give it up and try another solution.	1	2	3	4	5
2. I adapt to change pretty easily.	5	4	3	2	1
3. When I can't convince someone of my point of view, I can usually understand why not.	5	4	3	2	1
4. I am not very quick to take on new ideas.	1	2	3	4	5

Add your numbers for each of the four items: Total Score: _____
If your overall score is between 20 and 15, then you rate high on cognitive flexibility. If you scored between 9 and 14, you are in the middle category, and if you scored 8 or below, you likely could improve.

FIGURE 2

HOW COGNITIVELY FLEXIBLE ARE YOU?

that they need to change their way of thinking and be motivated to do so. Having confidence in their ability to adapt their thinking to a particular situation, an aspect of *self-efficacy,* also is important in being cognitively flexible (Bandura, 2012). To evaluate how cognitively flexible you are, take the quiz in Figure 2 (Galinsky, 2010).

How Would You...?

If you were an **educator,** how would you incorporate decision-making exercises into the school curriculum for adolescents?

Decision Making   Adolescence is a time of increased decision making—which friends to choose, which person to date, whether to have sex, buy a car, go to college, and so on (Steinberg & others, 2017; van den Bos & Hertwig, 2017). How competent are adolescents at making decisions? In some reviews, older adolescents are described as more competent than younger adolescents, who in turn are more competent than children (Keating, 2004). Compared with children, young adolescents are more likely to generate different options, examine a situation from a variety of perspectives, anticipate the consequences of decisions, and consider the credibility of sources.

However, older adolescents' (as well as adults') decision-making skills are far from perfect, and having the capacity to make competent decisions does not guarantee they will be made in everyday life, where breadth of experience often comes into play (Kuhn, 2009). As an example, driver-training courses improve adolescents' cognitive and motor skills to levels equal to, or sometimes superior to, those of adults. However, driver training has not been effective in reducing adolescents' high rate of traffic accidents, although recently researchers have found that implementing a graduated driver licensing (GDR) program can reduce crash and fatality rates for adolescent drivers (Keating, 2007). GDR components include a learner's holding period, practice-driving certification, night-driving restriction, and passenger restriction.

Most people make better decisions when they are calm than when they are emotionally aroused, which often is the case for adolescents (Duell & others, 2016; Steinberg & others, 2017). Recall from our discussion of brain development in "Physical Development in Adolescence" that adolescents have a tendency to be emotionally intense (Cohen & Casey, 2017; Galvan & Tottenham, 2016). Thus, the same adolescent who makes a wise decision when calm may make an unwise decision when emotionally aroused. In the heat of the moment, then, adolescents' emotions may especially overwhelm their decision-making ability (Goddings & Mills, 2017).

The social context plays a key role in adolescent decision making (Steinberg & others, 2017). For example, adolescents' willingness to make risky decisions is more likely

What are some of the decisions adolescents have to make? What characterizes their decision making?
©Big Cheese Photo/SuperStock RF

to occur in contexts where alcohol, drugs, and other temptations are readily available (Reyna & Rivers, 2008). Recent research reveals that the presence of peers in risk-taking situations increases the likelihood that adolescents will make risky decisions (Shulman, 2016a, b). In one study of risk taking involving a simulated driving task, the presence of peers increased an adolescent's decision to engage in risky driving by 50 percent but had no effect on adults (Gardner & Steinberg, 2005). In a recent study, adolescents took greater risks and showed stronger preference for immediate rewards when they were with three same-aged peers than when they were alone (Silva, Chein, & Steinberg, 2016). One view is that the presence of peers activates the brain's reward system, especially its dopamine pathways (Steinberg & others, 2017).

How do emotions and social contexts influence adolescents' decision making?
©JodiJacobson/E+/Getty Images RF

Adolescents need more opportunities to practice and discuss realistic decision making. Many real-world decisions on matters such as sex, drugs, and daredevil driving occur in an atmosphere of stress that includes time constraints and emotional involvement. One strategy for improving adolescent decision making in such circumstances is to provide more opportunities for them to engage in role playing and group problem solving. Another strategy is for parents to involve adolescents in appropriate decision-making activities.

To better understand adolescent decision making, Valerie Reyna and her colleagues (Reyna & others, 2011, 2015) have proposed the **fuzzy-trace theory dual-process model,** which states that decision making is influenced by two cognitive systems—"verbatim" analytical (literal and precise) and gist-based intuitional (simple bottom-line meaning)—which operate in parallel. Basing judgments and decisions on simple gist is viewed as more beneficial than analytical thinking to adolescents' decision making. In this view, adolescents don't benefit from engaging in reflective, detailed, higher-level cognitive analysis about a decision, especially in high-risk, real-world contexts where they would get bogged down in trivial detail. In such contexts, adolescents need to rely on their awareness that some circumstances are simply so dangerous that they must be avoided at all costs.

In the experiential system, in risky situations it is important for an adolescent to quickly get the *gist,* or meaning, of what is happening and glean that the situation is a dangerous context, which can cue personal values that will protect the adolescent from making a risky decision (Brust-Renck & others, 2017; Reyna & others, 2015; Rahimi-Golkhandan & others, 2017). A recent experiment showed that encouraging gist-based thinking about risks (along with factual information) reduced self-reported risk taking up to one year after exposure to the curriculum (Reyna & Mills, 2014). However, some experts on adolescent cognition argue that in many cases adolescents benefit from both analytical and experiential systems (Kuhn, 2009).

Critical Thinking   In "Cognitive Development in Middle and Late Childhood" we defined *critical thinking* as thinking reflectively and productively and evaluating evidence. Here we discuss how critical thinking changes in adolescence. In one study of fifth-, eighth-, and eleventh-graders, critical thinking increased with age but still occurred only in 43 percent of eleventh-graders (Klaczynski & Narasimham, 1998). Among the factors that provide a basis for improvement in critical thinking during adolescence are (Keating, 1990):

- Increased speed, automaticity, and capacity of information processing, which free cognitive resources for other purposes
- Greater breadth of content knowledge in a variety of domains
- Increased ability to construct new combinations of knowledge
- A greater range and more spontaneous use of strategies and procedures for obtaining and applying knowledge, such as planning, considering the alternatives, and cognitive monitoring

Although adolescence is an important period in the development of critical-thinking skills, if an individual has not developed a solid basis of fundamental skills (such as literacy and math skills) during childhood, critical-thinking skills are unlikely to mature in adolescence. For the subset of adolescents who lack such fundamental skills, potential gains

developmental **connection**

Cognitive Processes

Mindfulness is an important aspect of critical thinking. Connect to "Cognitive Development in Middle and Late Childhood."

fuzzy-trace theory dual-process model States that decision making is influenced by two systems—"verbatim" analytical (literal and precise) and gist-based intuition (simple bottom-line meaning)—which operate in parallel; in this model, gist-based intuition benefits adolescent decision making more than analytical thinking does.

Laura Bickford, Secondary School Teacher

Laura Bickford teaches English and journalism in grades 9 to 12, and she is chair of the English Department at Nordhoff High School in Ojai, California.

Bickford especially believes it is important to encourage students to think. Indeed, she says that "the call to teach is the call to teach students how to think." She believes teachers need to show students the value of asking their own questions, having discussions, and engaging in stimulating intellectual conversations. Bickford says that she also encourages students to engage in metacognitive strategies (knowing about knowing). For example, she asks students to comment on their learning after particular pieces of projects have been completed. She requires students to keep logs so they can observe their own thinking as it happens.

Laura Bickford working with students writing papers.
Courtesy of Laura Bickford

---

developmental connection

Cognitive Processes

Developing effective strategies is a key aspect of metacognition. Connect to "Cognitive Development in Middle and Late Childhood."

in adolescent thinking are not likely. Laura Bickford is a secondary school teacher who encourages her students to think critically. To read about her work, see the *Connecting with Careers* profile.

Metacognition   Recall from the chapter on "Cognitive Development in Middle and Late Childhood" that *metacognition* involves cognition about cognition, or "knowing about knowing" (Allen & others, 2017; Fergus & Bardeen, 2017). Metacognition helps people to perform many cognitive tasks more effectively (Fitzgerald, Arvaneh, & Dockree, 2017; Norman, 2017). Metacognition is increasingly recognized as a very important cognitive skill not only in adolescence but also in emerging adulthood (Jaleel & Premachandran, 2016). In comparison with children, adolescents have a greater capacity to monitor and manage cognitive resources to effectively meet the demands of a learning task (Kuhn, 2009). This increased metacognitive ability results in improved cognitive functioning and learning. A longitudinal study revealed that from 12 to 14 years of age, young adolescents increasingly used metacognitive skills and used them more effectively in math and history classes (van der Stel & Veenman, 2010). For example, 14-year-olds monitored their own text comprehension more frequently and more effectively than their younger counterparts did. Another study documented the importance of metacognitive skills, such as planning, strategizing, and monitoring, in college students' ability to think critically (Magno, 2010).

Review *Connect* Reflect

LG1 Discuss different approaches to adolescent cognition.

Review

- What is Piaget's view of adolescent cognitive development?
- What is adolescent egocentrism?
- How does information processing change during adolescence?

Connect

- Egocentrism has been mentioned in the context of early childhood cognitive development. How is egocentrism in adolescence similar to or different from egocentrism in early childhood?

Reflect *Your Own Personal Journey of Life*

- Think back to your early adolescent years. How would you describe the level of your thinking at that point in your development? Has your cognitive development changed since you were a young adolescent? Explain.

2 What Characterizes Adolescents' Values, Moral Development and Education, and Religion?

LG2 Describe adolescents' values, moral development and education, and religion.

Values | Moral Development and Education | Religion

What are the values of adolescents today? How can moral education be characterized? How powerful is the influence of religion in adolescents' lives?

VALUES

Values are beliefs and attitudes about the way things should be. They involve what is important to us. We attach values to all sorts of things: politics, religion, money, sex, education, helping others, family, friends, career, cheating, self-respect, and so on.

Changing Values One way of measuring what people value is to ask them what their goals are. Over the past four decades, traditional-aged college students have shown an increased concern for personal well-being and a decreased concern for the well-being of others, especially for the disadvantaged (Eagan & others, 2016). As shown in Figure 3, today's college freshmen are more strongly motivated to be well-off financially and less motivated to develop a meaningful philosophy of life than were their counterparts of 20 or even 10 years ago. In 2015, 82 percent of students (the highest percent ever in this survey) viewed becoming well-off financially as an "essential" or a "very important" objective compared with only 42 percent in 1971.

There are, however, some signs that U.S. college students are shifting toward a stronger interest in the welfare of society. In the survey just described, interest in developing a meaningful philosophy of life increased from 39 percent to 46.5 percent of U.S. college freshmen from 2003 through 2015 (Eagan & others, 2016) (see Figure 3).

How Would You...?

If you were an **educator,** how would you devise a program to increase adolescents' motivation to participate in service learning?

values Beliefs and attitudes about the way things should be.

service learning A form of education that promotes social responsibility and service to the community.

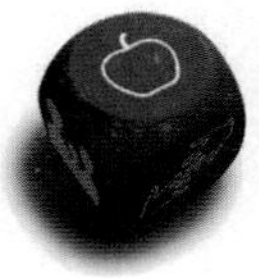

Service Learning **Service learning** is a form of education that promotes social responsibility and service to the community. In service learning, adolescents engage in activities such as tutoring, helping older adults, working in a hospital, assisting at a child-care center, or cleaning up a vacant lot to make a play area. An important goal of service learning is for adolescents to become less self-centered and more strongly motivated to help others (Hart, Matsuba, & Atkins, 2014; Hart & others, 2017). Service learning is often more effective when two conditions are met (Nucci, 2006): (1) students have some degree of choice in the service activities in which they participate, and (2) students have opportunities to reflect about their participation.

Service learning takes education out into the community (Gaylord, Chyka, & Lawley, 2012; Hart & others, 2017). Adolescent volunteers tend to be extraverted and committed to others, and to have a high level of self-understanding (Eisenberg & others, 2009). Also, one study revealed that adolescent girls participated in service learning more than adolescent boys did (Webster & Worrell, 2008).

Researchers have found that service learning benefits adolescents in a number of ways (Hart, Goel, & Atkins, 2017; Hart & others, 2017; Miller,

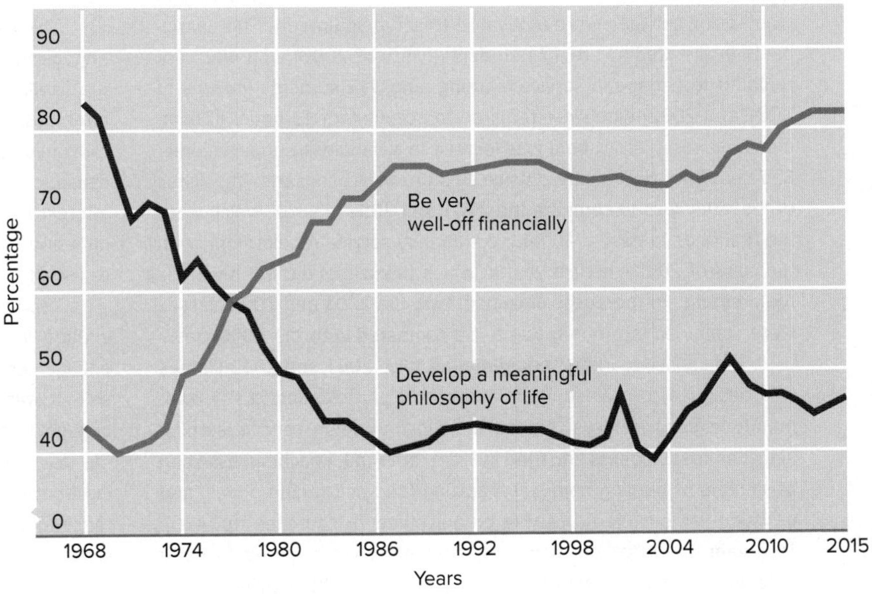

FIGURE 3

CHANGING FRESHMAN LIFE GOALS, 1968 TO 2015. In the last four decades, a significant change has occurred in freshman students' life goals. A far greater percentage of today's college freshmen state that an "essential" or "very important" life goal is to be well-off financially, and far fewer state that developing a meaningful philosophy of life is an "essential" or "very important" life goal.

What are some of the positive effects of service learning?

©Hero Images/Getty Images RF

2013; Waldner, McGorry, & Widener, 2012). These improvements in adolescent development include higher grades in school, increased goal setting, higher self-esteem, a greater sense of being able to make a difference for others, and an increased likelihood that they will serve as volunteers in the future. A recent study of more than 4,000 high school students revealed that those who worked directly with individuals in need were better adjusted academically, whereas those who worked for organizations had better civic outcomes (Schmidt, Shumow, & Kackar, 2007).

Recently, researchers have explored the role that civic engagement might play in adolescents' identity and moral development (Hart & van Goethem, 2017). A recent study found that compared with adolescents who had a diffused identity status, those who were identity achieved were more involved in volunteering in their community (Crocetti, Jahromi, & Meeus, 2012). (Identity statuses of adolescents are further discussed in the chapter on "Socioemotional Development in Adolescence.") In this study, adolescents' volunteer activity also was linked to their values, such as social responsibility, and the view that they, along with others, could make an impact on their community. Another recent study revealed that adolescents' volunteer activities provided opportunities to explore and reason about moral issues (van Goethem & others, 2012).

One analysis revealed that 26 percent of U.S. public high schools require students to participate in service learning (Metz & Youniss, 2005). The benefits of service learning, for both the volunteer and the recipient, suggest that more adolescents should be required to participate in such programs (Enfield & Collins, 2008). What are some of these positive outcomes? See the *Connecting with Research* interlude for the results of one study that asked this question.

connecting with research

Evaluating a Service-Learning Program Designed to Increase Civic Engagement

In one study, the possible benefits of a service-learning requirement for high school students were explored (Metz & Youniss, 2005). One group of students had a service-learning requirement, while the other group did not. Each group of students was also divided according to whether or not they were motivated to serve voluntarily. The participants in the study were 174 students (class of 2000) who were not required to engage in service learning, and 312 students (classes of 2001 and 2002) who were required to accumulate 40 hours of community service. The school was located in a middle- to upper-middle-SES suburban community outside Boston, Massachusetts. The focus of the study was to compare the 2001 and 2002 classes, which were the first ones to have a 40-hour community service requirement, with the class of 2000, the last year in which the school did not have this requirement. For purposes of comparison, the 2001 and 2002 classes were combined into one group to be compared with the 2000 class.

The service-learning requirement for the 2001 and 2002 classes was designed to give students a sense of participating in the community in positive ways. Among the most common service-learning activities that students engaged in were "tutoring, coaching, assisting at shelters or nursing homes, organizing food or clothing drives, and assisting value-centered service organizations or churches" (p. 420). To obtain credit for the activities, students were required to write reflectively about the activities and describe how the activities benefited both the recipients and themselves. Students also had to obtain an adult's or supervisor's signature to document their participation.

Detailed self-reported records of students' service in grades 10 through 12 were obtained. In addition to describing the number of

service hours they accumulated toward their requirement, they also were asked to indicate any voluntary services they provided in addition to the required 40 hours. Since students in the 2000 class had no required service participation, all of their service was voluntary.

The students rated themselves on four 5-point scales of civic engagement: (1) their likelihood of voting when reaching 18; (2) the likelihood they would "volunteer" or "join a civic organization" after graduating from high school; (3) their future unconventional civic involvement (such as boycotting a product, demonstrating for a cause, or participating in a political campaign); and (4) their political interest and understanding (how much they discuss politics with parents and friends, read about politics in magazines and newspapers, or watch the news on TV).

The results indicated that students who were already inclined to engage in service learning scored high on the four scales of civic engagement throughout high school and showed no increase in service after it was required. However, students who were less motivated to engage in service learning increased their civic engagement on three of the four scales (future voting, joining a civic organization after graduating from high school, and interest and understanding) after they were required to participate. In sum, this research documented that a required service-learning program can especially benefit the civic engagement of students who are inclined not to engage in service learning.

How might you design a study to identify positive outcomes of service learning that did not rely on self-reports?

MORAL DEVELOPMENT AND EDUCATION

What are some changes that occur in moral development during adolescence? What characterizes moral education?

Moral Stages   Recall that Lawrence Kohlberg argues that adolescents' moral reasoning is more likely to be at the conventional level of moral development and that some adolescents, emerging adults, and adults reach the highest level of moral development—post-conventional reasoning. Also recall that Kohlberg's theory has been criticized for a number of reasons, including its cultural and gender bias, inadequate attention to parenting influences, and other shortcomings (Lapsley & Yeager, 2013; Narváez, 2014; Walker, 2014a, b). Darcia Narváez and Tracy Gleason (2013) recently described cohort effects regarding moral reasoning. In recent years, post-conventional moral reasoning has been declining in college students, not down to the next level (conventional), but to the lowest level (personal interests) (Thoma & Bebeau, 2008). Narváez and Gleason (2013) also argue that declines in prosocial behavior have occurred in recent years and that humans, especially those living in Western cultures, are "on a fast train to demise." They believe the solution to improving people's moral lives lies in better childrearing strategies and social supports for families and children. And they emphasize the importance of expanding and improving moral education.

Prosocial Behavior   Prosocial behavior increases in adolescence. Why might this happen? Cognitive changes involving advances in abstract, idealistic, and logical reasoning as well as increased empathy and emotional understanding likely are involved. With such newfound cognitive abilities, young adolescents increasingly sympathize with members of abstract groups with whom they have little experience, such as people living in poverty in other countries (Eisenberg, Spinrad, & Morris, 2013). The increase in volunteer opportunities in adolescence also contributes to more frequent prosocial behavior.

Two aspects of prosocial behavior that have increasingly been studied in adolescence are forgiveness and gratitude. **Forgiveness** is an aspect of prosocial behavior that occurs when the injured person releases the injurer from possible behavioral retaliation (Flanagan & others, 2012; Klatt & Enright, 2009). In one investigation, individuals from the fourth grade through college and adulthood were asked questions about forgiveness (Enright, Santos, & Al-Mabuk, 1989). The adolescents were especially swayed by peer pressure in their willingness to forgive others. Also, a recent study revealed that when adolescents encountered hurtful experiences in school settings, if they disliked the transgressor they had more hostile thoughts, feelings of anger, and avoidance/revenge tendencies than they did when they liked the transgressing peer (Peets, Hodges, & Salmivalli, 2013).

Gratitude is a feeling of thankfulness and appreciation, especially in response to someone doing something kind or helpful (Grant & Gino, 2010). Interest in studying adolescents' gratitude or lack thereof is increasing. Consider the following recent studies:

- Coverage of a recent study of young adolescent Chinese students that revealed when they engaged in more gratitude their well-being at school was better (Ekema-Agba, McCutchen, & Geller, 2016).
- Gratitude was linked to a number of positive aspects of development in young adolescents, including satisfaction with one's family, optimism, and prosocial behavior (Froh, Yurkewicz, & Kashdan, 2009).
- Adolescents' expression of gratitude was linked to having fewer depressive symptoms (Lambert, Fincham, & Stillman, 2012).
- Chinese adolescents who had a higher level of gratitude were less likely to engage in suicidal ideation and attempts (Li & others, 2012).
- A longitudinal study assessed the gratitude of adolescents at 10 to 14 years of age (Bono, 2012). Four years later, the most grateful adolescents (top 20 percent) had a stronger sense of the meaning of life, were more satisfied with their life, were happier and more hopeful, and had a lower level of negative emotions and were less depressed than the least grateful students (bottom 20 percent).

forgiveness An aspect of prosocial behavior that occurs when an injured person releases the injurer from possible behavioral retaliation.

gratitude A feeling of thankfulness and appreciation, especially in response to someone doing something kind or helpful.

What are characteristics of gratitude in adolescence?
©Pamela Moore/Getty Images RF

Compared with antisocial behavior such as juvenile delinquency, less attention has been given to prosocial behavior in adolescence. We still do not have adequate research information about such topics as how youth perceive prosocial norms and how school policies and peers influence prosocial behavior (Siu, Shek, & Law, 2012).

Moral Education   Two views on moral education involve (1) the hidden curriculum and (2) character education.

The Hidden Curriculum   More than 70 years ago, educator John Dewey (1933) recognized that, even when schools do not offer specific programs in moral education, they provide moral education through a "hidden curriculum." The **hidden curriculum** is conveyed by the moral atmosphere that is a part of every school. The moral atmosphere is created by school and classroom rules, the moral orientation of teachers and school administrators, and text materials. Teachers serve as models of ethical or unethical behavior. Classroom rules and peer relations at school transmit attitudes about cheating, lying, stealing, and consideration for others. And, by creating and enforcing rules and regulations, the school administration infuses the school with a value system.

Recently, increasing interest has been directed toward the role of classroom and school climates as part of the hidden curriculum. Darcia Narváez (2010a) argues that attention should be given to the concept of "sustaining climates." In her view, a sustaining classroom climate is more than a positive learning environment and more than a caring context. Sustaining climates involve focusing on students' sense of purpose, social engagement, community connections, and ethics. In sustaining classroom and school climates, students learn skills for flourishing and reaching their potential and help others to do so as well.

Character Education   Currently 40 of 50 states have mandates regarding **character education,** a direct education approach that involves teaching students a basic moral literacy to prevent them from engaging in immoral behavior and doing harm to themselves or others (Nucci & Narváez, 2008). The argument is that behaviors such as lying, stealing, and cheating are wrong, and students should be taught this throughout their education (Berkowitz, Battistich, & Bier, 2008).

In the character education approach, every school is expected to have an explicit moral code that is clearly communicated to students. According to traditional views of character education, any violations of the code should be met with sanctions, although more recent approaches advocate a more democratic solution. Instruction in specified moral concepts, such as cheating, can take the form of example and definition, class discussions and role playing, or rewarding students for proper behavior. More recently, an emphasis on the importance of encouraging students to develop a care perspective has been accepted as a relevant aspect of character education (Noddings, 2008). Rather than just instructing adolescents to refrain from engaging in morally deviant behavior, a care perspective emphasizes educating students about the importance of engaging in prosocial behaviors such as considering others' feelings, being sensitive to others, and helping others (Carlo & others, 2011).

Cheating   A concern involving moral education is whether students cheat and how to handle cheating if it is discovered (Cheung, Wu, & Huang, 2016; Miller, 2017; Popoola & others, 2017). Academic cheating can take many forms, including plagiarism, using "cheat sheets" during an exam, copying from a neighbor during a test, purchasing papers, and falsifying lab results. A 2006 survey revealed that 60 percent of secondary school students said they had cheated on a test in school during the past year, and one-third of the students reported that they had plagiarized information from the Internet in the past year (Josephson Institute of Ethics, 2006).

Why do students cheat? Among the reasons students give for cheating are pressure to get high grades, time constraints, poor teaching, and lack of interest (Stephens, 2008). In terms of

How Would You...?
If you were an **educator,** how would you try to reduce the incidence of cheating in your school?

hidden curriculum Dewey's concept that every school has a pervasive moral atmosphere, even if it doesn't have an official program of moral education.

character education A direct education approach that involves teaching students a basic moral literacy to prevent them from engaging in immoral behavior and doing harm to themselves and others.

Why do students cheat? What are some strategies teachers can adopt to prevent cheating?
©Eric Audras/PhotoAlto/Getty Images RF

poor teaching, "students are more likely to cheat when they perceive their teacher to be incompetent, unfair, and uncaring" (Stephens, 2008, p. 140).

A long history of research also implicates the power of the situation in determining whether students will cheat (Hartshorne & May, 1928–1930; Cheung, Wu, & Huang, 2016; Murdock, Miller, & Kohlhardt, 2004; Vandehey, Diekhoff, & LaBeff, 2007). For example, students are more likely to cheat when they are not being closely monitored during a test, when they know their peers are cheating, when they know whether another student has been caught cheating, and when student scores are made public (Anderman & Murdock, 2007; Carrell, Malmstrom, & West, 2008; Harmon, Lambrinos, & Kennedy, 2008).

Certain personality traits also are linked to cheating. For example, a recent study revealed that college students who engaged in academic cheating were characterized by the personality traits of low conscientiousness and low agreeableness (Williams, Nathanson, & Paulhus, 2010).

Among the strategies for decreasing academic cheating are preventive measures such as making sure students are aware of what constitutes cheating and what the consequences will be if they cheat, closely monitoring students' behavior while they are taking tests, and emphasizing the importance of being a moral, responsible individual who practices academic integrity. In promoting academic integrity, many colleges have instituted an honor code policy that emphasizes self-responsibility, fairness, trust, and scholarship (Popoola & others, 2017). However, few secondary schools have developed honor code policies. The Center for Academic Integrity (www.academicintegrity.org) offers an extensive selection of materials to help schools develop academic integrity policies.

An Integrative Approach   Darcia Narváez (2006, 2008, 2010a, b; Narváez, 2016, 2017, 2018) emphasizes an *integrative approach* to moral education that encompasses the reflective moral thinking and commitment to justice advocated in Kohlberg's approach along with an emphasis on developing a particular moral character as advocated in the character education approach. She highlights the Child Development Project as an excellent example of an integrative moral education approach. In the Child Development Project, students are given multiple opportunities to discuss other students' experiences, which encourages empathy and perspective taking, and they participate in exercises that encourage them to reflect on their own behaviors in terms of values such as fairness and social responsibility (Battistich, 2008). Adults coach students in ethical decision making and guide them in becoming more caring individuals. Students experience a caring community, not only in the classroom, but also in after-school activities and through parental involvement in the program. Research evaluations of the Child Development Project indicate that it is related to an improved sense of community, an increase in prosocial behavior, better interpersonal understanding, and an increase in social problem solving (Battistich, 2008; Solomon & others, 1990).

RELIGION

Can religion, religiousness, and spirituality be distinguished from each other? A recent analysis by Pamela King and her colleagues (2011) makes the following distinctions:

- **Religion** is an organized set of beliefs, practices, rituals, and symbols that increases an individual's connection to a sacred or transcendent other (God, higher power, or ultimate truth).
- **Religiousness** refers to the degree of affiliation with an organized religion, participation in its prescribed rituals and practices, connection with its beliefs, and involvement in a community of believers.
- **Spirituality** involves experiencing something beyond oneself in a transcendent manner and living in a way that benefits others and society.

Religious issues are important to adolescents (King & Boyatzis, 2015). In one survey, 95 percent of 13- to 18-year-olds said that they believe in God or a universal spirit (Gallup & Bezilla, 1992). Almost three-fourths of adolescents said that they pray, and about one-half indicated that they had attended religious services within the past week. Almost half of the youth said that it is very important for a young person to learn religious faith.

One developmental study revealed that religiousness declined in U.S. adolescents between age 14 and age 20 (Koenig, McGue, & Iacono, 2008) (see Figure 4). In this

religion An organized set of beliefs, practices, rituals, and symbols that increases an individual's connection to a sacred or transcendent other (God, higher power, or higher truth).

religiousness Degree of affiliation with an organized religion, participation in prescribed rituals and practices, connection with its beliefs, and involvement in a community of believers.

spirituality Experiencing something beyond oneself in a transcendent manner and living in a way that benefits others and society.

Religion enlightens, terrifies, subdues; it gives faith, inflicts remorse, inspires resolutions, and inflames devotion.

—HENRY NEWMAN
English churchman and writer, 19th century

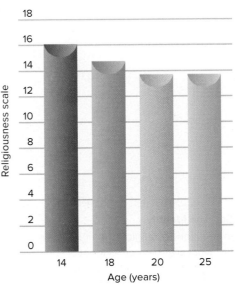

FIGURE 4

DEVELOPMENTAL CHANGES IN RELIGIOUSNESS FROM 14 TO 25 YEARS OF AGE.
Note: The religiousness scale ranged from 0 to 32, with higher scores indicating stronger religiousness (Koenig, McGue, & Iacono, 2008).

study, religiousness was assessed on the basis of criteria such as frequency of prayer, frequency of discussing religious teachings, frequency of deciding moral actions for religious reasons, and the overall importance of religion in everyday life. As indicated in Figure 4, more change in religiousness occurred from 14 to 18 years of age than from 20 to 25 years of age. Also, the researchers found that frequency of attending religious services was highest at 14 years of age, declined from 14 to 18 years of age, and increased at 20 years of age.

The Positive Role of Religion in Adolescents' Lives
Researchers have found that various aspects of religion are linked with positive outcomes for adolescents (King & Boyatzis, 2015; Longo, Bray, & Kim-Spoon, 2017; Talib & Abdollahi, 2017). A recent study revealed that a higher level of church engagement (based on years of attendance, choice in attending, and participation in activities) was related to higher grades for male adolescents (Kang & Romo, 2011). Churchgoing may benefit students because religious communities encourage socially acceptable behavior, which includes doing well in school. Churchgoing also may benefit students because churches often offer positive role models for students.

What are some positive influences of religion on adolescents' development?
©Christopher Futcher/Getty Images RF

Religion also plays a role in adolescents' health and whether they engage in problem behaviors (Holmes & Kim-Spoon, 2016a, b). A meta-analysis found that spirituality/religiosity was positively related to well-being, self-esteem, and three of the Big Five factors of personality (conscientiousness, agreeableness, openness) (Yonker, Schnabelrauch, & DeHaan, 2012). In this meta-analysis, spirituality/religion was negatively associated with risk behavior and depression. Also, in a recent study, adolescents who had a lower level of spirituality were more likely to have a higher level of substance use (Debnam & others, 2016). Many religious adolescents also internalize their religion's message about caring and concern for people (Lerner & others, 2013; Saroglou, 2013). For example, in one survey, religious youth were almost three times as likely to engage in community service as nonreligious youth (Youniss, McLellan, & Yates, 1999).

Developmental Changes
Adolescence can be an important juncture in religious development (Scarlett & Warren, 2010). Even if children have been indoctrinated into a religion by their parents, because of advances in their cognitive development they may begin to question what their own religious beliefs truly are.

Cognitive Changes
Many of the cognitive changes thought to influence religious development involve Piaget's cognitive developmental theory, which we discussed earlier in this chapter. In comparison with children, adolescents think more abstractly, idealistically, and logically. The increase in abstract thinking lets adolescents consider various ideas about religious and spiritual concepts. For example, an adolescent might ask how a loving God can possibly exist given the extensive suffering of many people in the world (Good & Willoughby, 2008). Adolescents' increased idealistic thinking provides a foundation for thinking about whether religion provides the best route to a better, more ideal world in the future. And adolescents' increased logical reasoning gives them the ability to develop hypotheses and systematically sort through different answers to spiritual questions (Good & Willoughby, 2008).

Erikson's Theory and Identity
During adolescence, especially in late adolescence and the college years, identity development becomes a central focus. In Erik Erikson's (1968) theory, adolescents seek answers to questions like "Who am I?" "What am I all about as a person?" and "What kind of life do I want to lead?" As part of their search for identity, adolescents begin to grapple in more sophisticated, logical ways with such questions as "Why am I on this planet?" "Is there really a God or higher spiritual being, or have I just been believing what my parents and the church imprinted in my mind?" "What really are my religious views?" An analysis of the link between identity and spirituality concluded that adolescence and emerging adulthood can serve as gateways to a spiritual identity that "transcends, but not necessarily excludes, the assigned religious identity in childhood" (Templeton & Eccles, 2005, p. 261).

A recent study of Latino, African American, Asian, and non-Latino White adolescents revealed that their religious identity remained stable across high school grades but that religious participation declined (Lopez, Huynh, & Fuligni, 2011). In this study, Latino and Asian

- - - - - - - - →
developmental **connection**

Self and Identity

In addition to religious/spiritual identity, what are some other identity components? Connect to "Socioemotional Development in Adolescence."

← - - - - - - - -

adolescents had the highest levels of religious identity, while Latino adolescents had the highest level of religious participation.

Religious Beliefs and Parenting Religious institutions created by adults are designed to introduce certain beliefs to children and thereby ensure that they will carry on a religious tradition. Various societies utilize Sunday schools, parochial education, tribal transmission of religious traditions, and parental teaching of children at home to further this aim.

Does this socialization work? In many cases it does (Paloutzian, 2000). In general, adults tend to adopt the religious teachings of their upbringing. A recent study revealed that parents' religiousness assessed during youths' adolescence was positively related to youths' own religiousness during adolescence, which in turn was linked to their religiousness following the transition to adulthood (Spilman & others, 2013).

However, when examining religious beliefs and adolescence, it is important to consider the quality of the parent-adolescent relationship (Brelsford & Mahoney, 2008). Adolescents who have a positive relationship with their parents or are securely attached to them are likely to adopt their parents' religious affiliation. But when conflict or insecure attachment characterizes parent-adolescent relationships, adolescents may seek a religious affiliation that is different from that of their parents (Streib, 1999).

Peers also play a role in adolescents' religious interest. A recent study of Indonesian adolescents found that adolescents were similar to their friends in religiosity, and the religiosity of friends and others in the peer network increased adolescents' self-religiosity in predicting whether they engaged in antisocial behavior (French, Purwono, & Rodkin, 2012).

Religiousness and Sexuality in Adolescence and Emerging Adulthood One area of religion's influence on adolescent and emerging adult development involves sexual activity. Although variability and change in church teachings make it difficult to generalize about religious doctrines, most churches discourage premarital sex. Thus, the degree of adolescent and emerging adult participation in religious organizations may be more important than affiliation with a specific religion as a determinant of premarital sexual attitudes and behavior. Adolescents and emerging adults who frequently attend religious services are likely to hear messages about abstaining from sex. Involvement of adolescents and emerging adults in religious organizations also enhances the probability that they will become friends with adolescents who have restrictive attitudes toward premarital sex. A recent study revealed that adolescents with high religiosity were less likely to have had sexual intercourse (Gold & others, 2010).

One study found that parents' religiosity was linked to a lower level of risky sexual behavior among adolescents, in part because of friendships with less sexually permissive peers (Landor & others, 2011). Also, a recent research review concluded that *spirituality* (being spiritual, religious, or believing in a higher power, for example) was linked to the following positive adolescent outcomes: reduced likelihood of intending to have sex, refraining from early sex, having sex less frequently, and not becoming pregnant (House & others, 2010). And in a recent study of African American adolescent girls, those who reported that religion was of low or moderate importance to them had a younger sexual debut than their counterparts who indicated that religion was extremely important to them (George Dalmida & others, 2017).

Review Connect Reflect

LG2 Describe adolescents' values, moral development and education, and religion.

Review
- What characterizes adolescents' values? What is service learning?
- What are some variations in moral education?
- What are adolescents' religious views and experiences?

Connect
- Earlier, we described five characteristics of emerging adults. Might some of those characteristics

be linked to an individual's religiousness and spirituality? Explain.

Reflect *Your Own Personal Journey of Life*
- What were your values, religious beliefs, and spiritual interests in middle school and high school? Have they changed since then? If so, how?

The American Middle School | The American High School | High School Dropouts

The impressive changes in adolescents' cognition lead us to examine the nature of schools for adolescents. Earlier, we discussed various ideas about the effects of schools on children's development. Here, we focus more exclusively on the nature of secondary schools.

THE AMERICAN MIDDLE SCHOOL

One worry expressed by educators and psychologists is that middle schools (most often consisting of grades 6 through 8) tend to be watered-down versions of high schools, mimicking their curricular and extracurricular schedules. The critics argue that unique curricular and extracurricular activities reflecting a wide range of individual differences in biological and psychological development in early adolescence should be incorporated into junior high and middle schools. The critics also stress that many high schools foster passivity rather than autonomy, and they urge schools to create a variety of pathways on which students can achieve an identity.

The Transition to Middle or Junior High School   The transition to middle school from elementary school interests developmentalists because, even though it is a normative experience for virtually all children, the transition can be stressful (Wigfield & others, 2015; Wigfield, Tonks, & Klauda, 2016). Why? The transition takes place at a time when many changes—in the individual, in the family, and in school—are occurring simultaneously. These changes include puberty and related concerns about body image; the emergence of at least some aspects of formal operational thought, including accompanying changes in social cognition; increased responsibility and independence in association with decreased dependence on parents; moving from a small, contained classroom structure to a larger, more impersonal school structure; switching from one teacher to many teachers and from a small, homogeneous set of peers to a larger, more heterogeneous set of peers; and adjusting to an increased focus on achievement and performance.

This list includes a number of negative, stressful features, but there can be positive aspects to the transition from elementary school to middle school or junior high. Students are more likely to feel grown up, to have more subjects from which to select, to have more opportunities to spend time with peers and to locate compatible friends, and to enjoy increased independence from direct parental monitoring—and they may be more challenged intellectually by academic work.

When students make the transition from elementary school to middle or junior high school, they experience the **top-dog phenomenon,** the circumstance of moving from the top position (in elementary school, being the oldest, biggest, and most powerful students in the school) to the lowest position (in middle or junior high school, being the youngest, smallest, and least powerful students in the school). Researchers who have charted the transition from elementary to middle school find that the first year of middle school can be difficult for many students (Hawkins & Berndt, 1985). A recent study in North Carolina schools revealed that sixth-grade students attending middle schools were far more likely to be cited for discipline problems than their counterparts who were attending elementary schools (Cook & others, 2008).

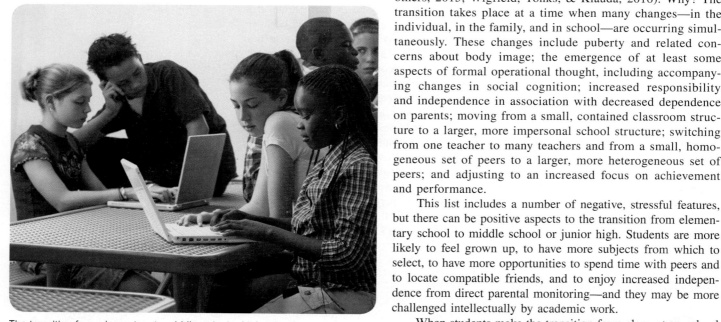

The transition from elementary to middle or junior high school occurs at the same time as a number of other developmental changes. *What are some of these other developmental changes?*
©Creatas/PunchStock RF

top-dog phenomenon The circumstance of moving from the top position (in elementary school, being the oldest, biggest, and most powerful students) to the lowest position (in middle or junior high school, being the youngest, smallest, and least powerful students).

Effective Middle Schools How effective are the middle schools U.S. students attend? The Carnegie Council on Adolescent Development (1989) issued an extremely negative evaluation of U.S. middle schools. In the report—*Turning Points: Preparing American Youth for the Twenty-First Century*—the conclusion was reached that most young adolescents attend massive, impersonal schools; learn from seemingly irrelevant curricula; trust few adults in school; and lack access to health care and counseling. The Carnegie report recommended the following changes:

- Developing smaller "communities" or "houses" to lessen the impersonal nature of large middle schools
- Lowering student-to-counselor ratios from several-hundred-to-1 to 10-to-1
- Involving parents and community leaders in schools
- Developing curricula that produce students who are literate, understand the sciences, and have a sense of health, ethics, and citizenship
- Having teachers team-teach in more flexibly designed curriculum blocks that integrate several disciplines, instead of presenting students with disconnected, rigidly separated 50-minute segments
- Boosting students' health and fitness with more in-school programs and helping students who need public health care to get it

Turning Points 2000 (Jackson & Davis, 2000) continued to endorse the recommendations set forth in *Turning Points 1989*. One new recommendation in the 2000 report stated that it is important to teach a curriculum grounded in rigorous academic standards for what students should know and should be able to learn. A second new recommendation was to engage in instruction that encourages students to achieve higher standards and become lifelong learners. These new recommendations reflect the increasing emphasis on challenging students to meet higher standards (Manzo, 2008).

To read about one individual whose main career focus is improving middle school students' learning and education, see *Connecting with Careers*.

How Would You...?
If you were an **educator,** how would you improve middle schools?

Extracurricular Activities Adolescents in U.S. schools usually have a wide array of extracurricular activities they can participate in beyond their academic courses. These activities include such diverse programs as sports, academic clubs, band, drama, and math clubs. Researchers have found that participation in extracurricular activities is linked to higher grades, increased school engagement, a reduced likelihood of dropping out of school, improved probability of going to college, higher self-esteem, and lower rates of depression, delinquency, and substance abuse (Barber, Stone, & Eccles, 2010; Fischer & Theis, 2014; Guevremont, Findlay, & Kohen, 2014; Mahoney, Parente, & Zigler, 2010). Further, one study revealed that intensive participation in after-school programs or extracurricular activities was linked to fewer internalized problems

connecting with careers

Katherine McMillan Culp, Research Scientist at an Educational Center

Katherine McMillan Culp wanted mainly to live in New York City when she graduated from college and became a receptionist at a center that focused on children and technology. More than 20 years later she is leading research projects at the center (Center for Children and Technology). Not long after leaving her receptionist job, she combined work at the center with graduate school at Columbia University. Culp became especially interested in how content and instruction can best be created to link with the developmental level of children and adolescents.

Today she holds the position of principal research scientist at Education Development Center, directing a number of projects. One of her main current interests is middle-school students' science learning. In this area, she consults with game designers, teachers, and policy makers to improve their understanding of how adolescents think and learn.

Her advice to anyone wanting to do this type of work outside of academia is to get the best education and training possible, then get connected with schools, work with teachers, and get experience related to practical problems involved with schools and learning.

Source: Culp, K.M (2012).

©Comstock Images/SuperStock RF

(depression, for example) in adolescents living in homes characterized by domestic violence (Gardner, Browning, & Brooks-Gunn, 2012). Another study also revealed that the more adolescents participated in organized out-of-school activities, the more likely they were to experience positive outcomes—educational attainment, civic engagement, and psychological flourishing—in emerging adulthood (Mahoney & Vest, 2012). A recent study revealed that immigrant adolescents who participated in extracurricular activities improved their academic achievement and increased their school engagement (Camacho & Fuligni, 2015). Also, an Australian study found that extracurricular participation in the eighth grade was linked to a lower likelihood of binge drinking through the eleventh grade (Modecki, Barber, & Eccles, 2014). Adolescents benefit from a breadth of extracurricular activities more than focusing on a single extracurricular activity.

THE AMERICAN HIGH SCHOOL

Many high school graduates not only are poorly prepared for college but also are poorly prepared to meet the demands of the modern, high-performance workplace (Lauff, Ingels, & Christopher, 2014). In a review of hiring practices at major companies, it was concluded that many companies now want their employees to possess certain basic skills. These include the ability to read at relatively high levels, do at least elementary algebra, use personal computers for straightforward tasks such as word processing, solve semistructured problems in which hypotheses must be formulated and tested, communicate effectively (orally and in writing), and work effectively in groups with persons of various backgrounds (Murnane & Levy, 1996).

The transition to high school can be problematic for adolescents, just as the transition to middle school can. These problems may include the following (Eccles & Roeser, 2015): high schools are often even larger, more bureaucratic, and more impersonal than middle schools are; there isn't much opportunity for students and teachers to get to know each other, which can lead to distrust; and teachers too infrequently choose content that is relevant to students' interests. Such experiences likely undermine the motivation of students.

Robert Crosnoe's (2011) book, *Fitting In, Standing Out,* highlighted another major problem with U.S. high schools: how the negative social aspects of adolescents' lives undermine their academic achievement. In his view, adolescents become immersed in complex peer group cultures that demand conformity. High school is supposed to be about getting an education, but for many youth it involves navigating the social worlds of peer relations that may or may not value education and academic achievement. Adolescents who fail to fit in, especially those who are obese or gay, become stigmatized.

The National Research Council (2004) made a number of recommendations for improving U.S. high schools. They especially emphasized the importance of finding ways to get students more engaged in learning. The council concluded that the best way to do this is to address the psychological factors involved in motivation. To increase students' engagement in learning, schools should promote a sense of belonging "by personalizing instruction, showing an interest in students' lives, and creating a supportive, caring social environment" (National Research Council, 2004, p. 3). The council said that this description of engaging students applies to very few urban high schools, which often are characterized by low expectations, alienation, and low achievement. A recent study examined school transitions of multiethnic urban adolescents from the seventh through the tenth grade (Benner & Graham, 2009). The transition to high school was especially challenging for African American and Latino youth when the number of students in their own ethnic groups declined from middle to high school.

A special concern regarding secondary schools—middle and high schools—involves adolescents who are growing up in economically disadvantaged contexts (McLoyd & others, 2011). Although relevant studies are few, those that have been conducted indicate that living in economically disadvantaged families during adolescence may have more negative achievement outcomes than corresponding circumstances in childhood (McLoyd & others, 2009). The possible timing difference in poverty effects might be due to adolescents' awareness of barriers to their success and the difficulties they will encounter in becoming successful.

What are some concerns about the American high school?
©Spencer Grant/PhotoEdit

Some innovative programs indicate that improving certain characteristics of schools raises achievement levels for adolescents from economically disadvantaged backgrounds (McLoyd & others, 2009). For example, a study of pilot schools in Boston revealed that the following changes were linked with higher levels of achievement in high school: having smaller class sizes and longer class periods, creating more advisory sessions, and allotting more time for teachers to explore teaching methods (Tung & Ouimette, 2007).

Are American secondary schools different from those in other countries? To explore this question, see the *Connecting with Diversity* interlude.

developmental **connection**

Schools

The New Hope intervention program is designed to enhance the development of children and adolescents growing up in poverty. Connect to "Socioemotional Development in Middle and Late Childhood."

connecting with diversity

Cross-Cultural Comparisons of Secondary Schools

Many countries recognize that quality, universal education of children and youth is critical for the success of any country. However, countries vary considerably in their ability to fulfill this mission. More than 100 million adolescents, mostly in sub-Saharan Africa, India, and southern Asia, don't even attend secondary schools (Paris & others, 2012). In developing countries, adolescent girls are less likely to be enrolled in school than are boys.

Secondary schools in different countries share a number of features but differ in many ways. Let's explore the similarities and differences in secondary schools in seven countries: Australia, Brazil, Germany, Japan, China, Russia, and the United States.

Most countries mandate that children begin school at 6 to 7 years of age and stay in school until they are 14 to 17 years of age. Brazil requires students to go to school only until they are 14 years old, whereas Russia mandates that students stay in school until they are 17. Germany, Japan, Australia, and the United States require school attendance until at least 15 to 16 years of age, with some states, such as California, recently raising the mandatory age to 18.

Most secondary schools around the world are divided into two or more levels, such as middle school (or junior high school) and high school. However, Germany's schools are divided according to three educational ability tracks: (1) the main school provides a basic level of education, (2) the middle school gives students a more advanced education, and (3) the academic school prepares students for entrance to a university. German schools, like most European schools, offer a classical education, which includes courses in Latin and Greek. Japanese secondary schools have an entrance exam, but secondary schools in the other five countries do not. Only Australia and Germany have comprehensive exit exams.

The United States and Australia are among the few countries in the world in which sports are an integral part of the public school system. Only a few private schools in other countries have their own sports teams, sports facilities, and highly organized sports events.

In Brazil, students are required to take Portuguese (the native language) and four foreign languages (Latin, French, English, and Spanish). Brazil requires these languages because of the country's international character and emphasis on trade and commerce. Seventh-grade students in Australia take courses in sheep husbandry and weaving, two areas of economic and cultural interest in the country. In Japan, students take a number of Western courses in addition to their basic Japanese courses; these courses include Western literature and languages (in addition to Japanese literature and language), Western physical education (in addition to Japanese martial arts classes), and

The juku, or "cramming school," is available to Japanese children and adolescents in the summer and after school. It provides coaching to help them improve their grades and entrance exam scores for high schools and universities. The Japanese practice of requiring an entrance exam for high school is a rarity among the nations of the world.
©Fujifotos/The Image Works

Western sculpture and handicrafts (in addition to Japanese calligraphy). The Japanese school year is also much longer than that of other countries (225 days versus 180 days in the United States, for example).

I recently visited China and interviewed parents about their adolescents' education. Several aspects of education in China are noteworthy, especially in comparison with the United States. Parents' comments reflected motivation to provide adolescents with the best possible education and to ensure that they work extremely hard in school and on homework. Also, when I asked parents if there are disciplinary problems in Chinese schools, they responded that if an adolescent acts up in school, the school immediately sends the adolescent home. In China, it is considered the parents' responsibility to orient their adolescents to behave in school and focus on schoolwork. When Chinese adolescents are sent home because of discipline problems, they are not allowed to return until parents work with the adolescent to ensure that the discipline problems will not recur. In China, classroom sizes are often large, sometimes having as many as 50 to 70 students, yet observers describe such classes as orderly and disciplined (Cavanagh, 2007).

HIGH SCHOOL DROPOUTS

Dropping out of high school has been viewed as a serious educational and societal problem for many decades. When adolescents leave high school before graduating, they approach adult life with educational deficiencies that severely curtail their economic and social well-being (Vaughn & others, 2010). In this section, we study the scope of the problem, the causes of dropping out, and ways to reduce dropout rates.

Dropout Rates   In the last half of the twentieth century and the first decade of the twenty-first century, U.S. high school dropout rates declined (National Center for Education Statistics, 2016). In the 1940s, more than half of U.S. 16- to 24-year-olds had dropped out of school; by 1990, this rate had dropped to 12 percent. In 2014, this figure had decreased further to 6.5 percent. The dropout rate of Latino adolescents remains high, although it has been decreasing considerably in the twenty-first century (from 28 percent in 2000 to 15 percent in 2010 to 12 percent in 2014). The lowest dropout rate in 2014 occurred for Asian American adolescents (1 percent), followed by non-Latino White adolescents (5 percent), African American adolescents (7 percent), and Latino adolescents (11 percent) (National Center for Education Statistics, 2016). Gender differences characterize U.S. dropout rates, with males more likely to drop out than females (7.1 versus 5.9 percent) (National Center for Education Statistics, 2016).

National data on Native American adolescents have been collected inadequately—sporadically and/or based on small samples. However, there are some indications that Native American adolescents likely have the highest school dropout rate. Also, the average U.S. high school dropout rates just described mask some very high dropout rates in low-income areas of inner cities. For example, in cities such as Detroit, Cleveland, and Chicago, dropout rates are higher than 50 percent. Also, the percentages cited here are for 16- to 24-year-olds. When dropout rates are calculated in terms of students who do not graduate from high school in four years, the percentage of students is also much higher. Thus, in considering high school dropout rates, it is important to examine age, the number of years it takes to complete high school, and various contexts including ethnicity, gender, and school location.

How Would You...?

If you were an **educator,** how would you reduce the school dropout rate of high-risk adolescents?

Causes of Dropping Out of School   Students drop out of school for school-related, economic, family-related, peer-related, and personal reasons. School-related problems are consistently associated with dropping out of school (Dupere & others, 2015). In one investigation, almost 50 percent of the dropouts cited school-related reasons for leaving school, such as not liking school, being suspended, or being expelled (Rumberger, 1995). Twenty percent of the dropouts (but 40 percent of the Latino students) cited economic reasons for dropping out. Many of these students quit school and go to work to help support their families. A recent study revealed that when children's parents were involved in their school in middle and late childhood, and when parents and adolescents had good relationships in early adolescence, a positive trajectory toward academic success was the likely outcome (Englund, Egeland, & Collins, 2008). By contrast, those who had poor relationships with their parents were more likely to drop out of high school despite doing well academically and behaviorally. Many school dropouts have friends who also are school dropouts. Approximately one-third of the girls who drop out of school do so for personal reasons, such as pregnancy or marriage.

An important educational goal is to increase the high school graduation rate of Native youth. An excellent strategy to accomplish this goal is high quality early childhood educational programs such as this one at St. Bonaventure Indian School on the Navajo Nation in Thoreau, New Mexico.
©Jim West/Alamy

Reducing the Dropout Rate   A review of school-based dropout prevention programs found that the most effective programs provided early reading support, tutoring, counseling, and mentoring (Lehr & others, 2003). They also emphasized the importance of creating caring environments and relationships and offered community-service opportunities.

Clearly, then, early detection of children's school-related difficulties, and getting children engaged with school in positive ways, are important strategies for reducing the dropout rate (Jimerson, 2009). Also, the Bill and Melinda Gates Foundation (2008) has provided funding for efforts to reduce the dropout rate in schools where dropout rates are high. One strategy that is being emphasized in the Gates' funding is keeping students who are at risk for dropping out of school with the same teachers through their high

caring connections

The "I Have a Dream" Program

"I Have a Dream" (IHAD) is an innovative, comprehensive, long-term dropout prevention program administered by the National "I Have a Dream" Foundation in New York. Since the National IHAD Foundation was created in 1986, it has grown to encompass more than 180 projects in 64 cities and 28 states plus Washington, DC, and New Zealand, serving more than 16,000 children ("I Have a Dream" Foundation, 2017). Local IHAD projects around the country "adopt" entire grades (usually the third or fourth) from public elementary schools, or corresponding age cohorts from public housing developments. These children—"Dreamers"—are then provided with a program of academic, social, cultural, and recreational activities throughout their elementary, middle school, and high school years. An important part of this program is that it is personal rather than institutional: IHAD sponsors and staff develop close, long-term relationships with the children. When participants complete high school, IHAD provides the tuition assistance necessary for them to attend a state or local college or vocational school.

The IHAD program was created in 1981 when philanthropist Eugene Lang made an impromptu offer of college tuition to a class of graduating sixth-graders at P.S. 121 in East Harlem. Statistically, 75 percent of the students should have dropped out of school; instead, 90 percent graduated and 60 percent went on to college. Other evaluations of IHAD programs have found dramatic improvements in grades, test scores, and school attendance, as well as a reduction in behavioral problems of Dreamers. For example, in Portland, Oregon, twice as many Dreamers as control-group students had reached a

These adolescents are participating in the "I Have a Dream" (IHAD) Program, a comprehensive, long-term dropout prevention program that has been very successful. *What are some other strategies for reducing high school dropout rates?*
Courtesy of "I Have a Dream" Foundation of Boulder County (www.ihadboulder.org)

math standard, and the Dreamers were less likely to be referred to the juvenile justice system (Davis, Hyatt, & Arrasmith, 1998). And in an analysis of the "I Have a Dream" program in Houston, 91 percent of the participants received passing grades in reading/English, 83 percent said they liked school, 98 percent said getting good grades is important to them, 100 percent said they plan to graduate from high school, and 94 percent reported they plan to go to college ("I Have a Dream" Foundation, 2017).

school years. The hope is that the teachers will get to know these students much better, their relationship with the students will improve, and they will be able to monitor and guide the students toward graduating from high school. Recent initiatives by the Bill and Melinda Gates Foundation (2011, 2016) involve creating a new generation of courseware that adapts to students' learning needs and blending face-to-face instruction with digital tools that help students to learn independently.

One program that has been very effective in reducing school dropout rates is described in the *Caring Connections* interlude above.

Review *Connect* Reflect

LG3 Characterize schools for adolescents.

Review

- What is the transition from elementary to middle school like? What are some criticisms of, and recommendations for improving, U.S. middle schools?
- How can the American high school be improved so that students are better prepared for the demands of the modern workplace?
- What are some of the reasons why adolescents drop out of school?

Connect

- What impact might the concept of parents as "managers" have on reducing the high school dropout rate?

Reflect *Your Own Personal Journey of Life*

- What was your own middle or junior high school like? How did it measure up to the recommendations made by the Carnegie Foundation?

The next chapter concludes our exploration of the journey through childhood and adolescence. You will read about how adolescents spend more time thinking about their identity—who they are, what they are all about, and where they are going in life—than they did when they were children. Time spent with peers increases in adolescence, and friendships become more intense and intimate. Dating and romantic relationships also become more central to the lives of most adolescents. Parents continue to have an important influence on adolescent development. Having good relationships with parents provides support for adolescents as they seek greater autonomy and explore a widening social world. Problems that adolescents can develop include juvenile delinquency, depression, and suicide.

reach your **learning goals**

Cognitive Development in Adolescence

1 How Do Adolescents Think and Process Information?

LG1 Discuss different approaches to adolescent cognition.

Piaget's Theory

- During the formal operational stage, Piaget's fourth stage of cognitive development, thinking is more abstract, idealistic, and logical than during the concrete operational stage. Adolescents become capable of hypothetical-deductive reasoning. However, many adolescents are not formal operational thinkers but are consolidating their concrete operational thought. Piaget made a number of important contributions to understanding children's development, but his theory has undergone considerable criticism.

Adolescent Egocentrism

- Elkind proposed that adolescents, especially young adolescents, develop an egocentrism that includes both an imaginary audience (the belief that others are as interested in the adolescent as the adolescent is) and a personal fable (a sense of uniqueness and invincibility).

Information Processing

- Key changes in information processing especially involve executive function. These changes focus on working memory, cognitive control, decision making, critical thinking, and metacognition. It is increasingly thought that executive function strengthens during adolescence.

- Adolescence is a time of increased decision making. Older adolescents make better decisions than younger adolescents, who in turn are better at this skill than children are. Being able to make competent decisions, however, does not mean adolescents actually will make such decisions in everyday life, where breadth of experience comes into play. One proposal to explain effective adolescent decision making is the dual-process model.

- Adolescence is an important transitional period in critical thinking because of cognitive changes such as increased speed, automaticity, and capacity of information processing; greater breadth of content knowledge; increased ability to construct new combinations of knowledge; and increased use of spontaneous strategies.

2 What Characterizes Adolescents' Values, Moral Development and Education, and Religion?

LG2 Describe adolescents' values, moral development and education, and religion.

Values

- Values are beliefs and attitudes about the way things should be. Over the past four decades, traditional-aged college students have shown an increased concern for personal well-being and a decreased interest in the welfare of others. Recently, U.S. college freshmen have shown an increased interest in developing a meaningful philosophy of life.

- Service learning is a form of education that promotes social responsibility and service to the community. Service learning is increasingly required by schools and has positive effects on adolescent development.

Moral Development and Education

- Recent research indicates that cohort effects characterize adolescents' moral reasoning with more adolescents today reasoning at a lower moral level than in the past. Adolescents engage in more prosocial behavior than do children.

- Two important aspects of adolescents' prosocial behavior that are increasingly being studied are forgiveness and gratitude. Aspects of moral education include Dewey's hidden curriculum and character education.

- Cheating is a moral education concern and can take many forms. Various aspects of the situation influence whether students will cheat or not. Recently, an integrative moral education approach has been advocated for preventing academic cheating in schools.

Religion

- Distinctions have been made between the concepts of religion, religiousness, and spirituality. Religious issues are important to adolescents. Adolescence may be a special juncture in religious development for many individuals.

- Various aspects of religion are linked with positive outcomes in adolescent development. Religious affiliation is linked to lower drug use and delinquency rates, less school truancy, and lower rates of depression.

- Erikson's ideas on identity can be applied to understanding the increased interest in religion during adolescence. Piaget's theory provides a theoretical foundation for understanding developmental changes in religion. When adolescents have a positive relationship with their parents, and/or are securely attached to them, they often adopt their parents' religious beliefs. Links have been found between adolescents' sexual behavior and their religiousness.

3 What Is the Nature of Schools for Adolescents?

LG3 Characterize schools for adolescents.

The American Middle School

- The transition to middle or junior high school coincides with many physical, cognitive, and socioemotional changes. The transition involves moving from the top-dog position to the lowest position, and this transition is difficult for many children.

- U.S. middle schools have been criticized as too massive and impersonal, with curricula that are often irrelevant. Recommendations for improving U.S. middle schools include developing small communities of students within the schools, maintaining lower student-to-counselor ratios, and raising academic standards.

- Participation in extracurricular activities is associated with positive academic and psychological outcomes.

The American High School

- The American high school needs to prepare students for today's workplace by providing them with an education that gives them skills in computer use, effective written and oral communication, high-level reading comprehension, and working in groups with diverse others.

High School Dropouts

- Many school dropouts have educational deficiencies that limit their economic and social well-being for much of their adult lives. Progress has been made in lowering the dropout rate for African American youth, but the dropout rates for Native American and Latino youth remain very high. Native American youth have the highest dropout rate. Males are more likely to drop out of high school than females. Dropping out of school is associated with demographic, family-related, peer-related, school-related, economic, and personal factors.

key **terms**

adolescent egocentrism
character education
cognitive control
forgiveness
fuzzy-trace theory dual-process
  model

gratitude
hidden curriculum
hypothetical-deductive
  reasoning

imaginary audience
personal fable
religion
religiousness

service learning
spirituality
top-dog phenomenon
values

key **people**

Robert Crosnoe
John Dewey
David Elkind

Erik Erikson
Pamela King

Lawrence Kohlberg
Deanna Kuhn

Darcia Narváez
Jean Piaget

connecting with **improving the lives of children**

STRATEGIES

Supporting Adolescents' Cognitive Development

What are some good strategies for nourishing adolescents' cognitive development?

· *Provide support for adolescents' information processing.* Provide opportunities and guide adolescents to develop their executive function skills such as cognitive control; to gain practice in making good decisions, especially in real-world settings; to think critically; and to engage in self-regulatory learning.

· *Give adolescents opportunities to discuss moral dilemmas.* Provide adolescents with group opportunities to discuss the importance of cooperation, trust, and caring.

· *Create better schools for adolescents.* Schools for adolescents need to emphasize socioemotional development as well as cognitive development.

· *Take individual variation in adolescents seriously.*

· *Develop curricula that involve high expectations for success and the support to attain that success.*

· *Develop smaller communities within each school.*

· *Involve parents and community leaders more.*

· *Break down the barriers between school and work to reduce the high school dropout rate.*

· *Provide adolescents with information about careers.* Adolescents do not get adequate information about careers. Career decision making needs to be given a higher priority in schools.

RESOURCES

Adolescent Thinking (2009)
Deanna Kuhn
In R. M. Lerner & L. Steinberg (Eds.), *Handbook of Adolescent Psychology* (3rd ed.).
New York: Wiley

An in-depth examination of the important changes in executive function and other aspects of cognitive development in adolescence.

Schools as Developmental Contexts During Adolescence (2013)
Jacquelynne Eccles and Robert Roeser
In I.B. Weiner & others (Eds.), *Handbook of Psychology* (2nd ed., Vol. 6).
New York: Wiley

Leading experts provide up-to-date discussions of a wide range of topics, including academic expectations, teacher–student relationships, peer influences, and extracurricular activities.

APA Educational Psychology Handbook (Volumes 1–3) (2012)
Edited by Karen Harris and others
Washington, DC: American Psychological Association

Leading experts in educational psychology provide an up-to-date account of a wide-ranging set of topics related to improving the education of children and adolescents.

National Dropout Prevention Center
www.dropoutprevention.org

Acts as a clearinghouse for information about dropout prevention and at-risk youth and publishes the *National Dropout Prevention Newsletter*.

Turning Points 2000 (2000)
Gayle Davis and Anthony Jackson
New York: Teachers College Press

This follow-up to earlier Turning Points recommendations includes a number of strategies for meeting the educational needs of adolescents, especially young adolescents.

©John Giustina/The Image Bank/Getty Images

The mayor of the city said that she was "everywhere." She persuaded the city's school committee to consider ending the practice of locking tardy students out of their classrooms. She also swayed a neighborhood group to support her proposal for a winter jobs program. According to one city councilman, "People are just impressed with the power of her arguments and the sophistication of the argument" (Silva, 2005, pp. B1, B4). She is Jewel E. Cash, and she did all these things while she was a teenager attending the prestigious Boston Latin Academy.

Jewel Cash and her mother participate in a crime watch meeting at a community center.
©Matthew J. Lee/The Boston Globe/Getty Images

Jewel was raised in one of Boston's housing projects by her mother, a single parent. During high school she was a member of the Boston Student Advisory Council, mentored children, volunteered at a women's shelter, managed and danced in two troupes, and participated in a neighborhood watch group—among other activities. Jewel's high school experiences are far from typical, but her activities illustrate that cognitive and socioemotional development allows adolescents—including adolescents from disadvantaged backgrounds—to be capable, effective individuals. As an emerging adult, Jewel now works with a public consulting group and has continued helping others as a mentor and community organizer.

-topical **connections**   *looking **back***

In other chapters, you explored changes in the physical and cognitive development of adolescents. You read about socioemotional development in middle and late childhood, including how self-understanding and understanding others becomes more sophisticated, emotional understanding improves, and moral reasoning advances. In Erikson's view, in middle and late childhood, children are in the industry versus inferiority stage. Children at this developmental stage spend more time with peers, but parents continue to play important roles in their development, especially in guiding their academic achievement and managing their opportunities. Peer status and friendship become more important in children's peer relations, and school takes on a stronger academic focus. In this chapter, we will examine a key feature of adolescent development—exploring an identity. We will also look at changing relationships with parents and peers, then consider some problems that can develop during adolescence, such as delinquency.

preview

Significant changes characterize socioemotional development in adolescence. These changes include increased efforts to understand oneself, a search for identity, and emotional fluctuations. Changes also occur in the social contexts of adolescents' lives, with transformations occurring in relationships with families and peers. Adolescents are also at risk for developing socioemotional problems such as delinquency and depression.

---

1 What Characterizes Identity, Emotional Development, and Gender Classification in Adolescence?

LG1 Discuss identity, emotional development, and gender classification during adolescence.

> Identity — Emotional Development — Gender Classification

Jewel Cash told an interviewer from the *Boston Globe,* "I see a problem and I say, 'How can I make a difference?' . . . I can't take on the world, even though I can try. . . . I'm moving forward but I want to make sure I'm bringing people with me" (Silva, 2005, pp. B1, B4). Jewel's confidence, positive identity, and emotional maturity sound at least as impressive as her activities. In this section, we examine how adolescents develop characteristics like these.

IDENTITY

"Who am I? What am I all about? What am I going to do with my life? What is different about me? How can I make it on my own?" These questions reflect the search for an identity. By far the most comprehensive and provocative theory of identity development is Erik Erikson's. In this section, we examine his views on identity. We also discuss contemporary research on how identity develops and how social contexts influence that development.

What Is Identity?   Identity is a self-portrait composed of many pieces, including these:

- The career and work path the person wants to follow (vocational/career identity)
- Whether the person is conservative, liberal, or middle-of-the-road (political identity)
- The person's spiritual beliefs (religious identity)
- Whether the person is single, married, divorced, and so on (relationship identity)
- The extent to which the person is motivated to achieve and is intellectual (achievement, intellectual identity)
- Whether the person is heterosexual, homosexual, bisexual, or transgendered (sexual identity)
- Which part of the world or country a person is from and how intensely the person identifies with his or her cultural heritage (cultural/ethnic identity)
- The kinds of things a person likes to do, which can include sports, music, hobbies, and so on (interests)
- The individual's personality characteristics (such as being introverted or extraverted, anxious or calm, friendly or hostile, and so on) (personality)
- The individual's body image (physical identity)

Synthesizing the identity components can be a lengthy process, with many negations and affirmations of various roles and facets (Maher, Winston, & Ur, 2017; Meeus, 2017; Reece & others, 2017). Decisions are not made once and for all, but have to be made again and again. Identity development does not happen neatly, and it does not happen cataclysmically (Adler & others, 2017; Beyers & Luyckx, 2016; Galliher, McLean, & Syed, 2017).

Who are you?" said the Caterpillar. Alice replied, rather shyly, "I—I hardly know, Sir, just at present—at least I know who I was when I got up this morning, but I must have changed several times since then."

—LEWIS CARROLL
English Writer, 19th Century

What are some important dimensions of identity?
©Art Grafts/The Image Bank/Getty Images

Erik Erikson
©Bettmann/Getty Images

Erikson's View   Questions about identity surface as common, virtually universal, concerns during adolescence. Some decisions made during adolescence might seem trivial: whether to study or play, whether to take a part-time job after school, whom to date, whether to break up with someone or stay in the relationship, whether or not to be politically active, and so on. Over the years of adolescence, however, such decisions begin to form the core of what the individual is all about as a human being—what is called his or her identity.

It was Erik Erikson (1950, 1968) who first understood the importance of questions about identity in understanding adolescent development. The fact that identity is now believed to be a key aspect of adolescent development is a result of Erikson's masterful thinking and analysis.

We discussed Erikson's theory in the "Introduction" chapter. Recall that his fifth developmental stage, which individuals experience during adolescence, is **identity versus identity confusion.** During this time, said Erikson, adolescents are faced with deciding who they are, what they are all about, and where they are going in life.

The search for an identity during adolescence is aided by a **psychosocial moratorium,** which is Erikson's term for the gap between childhood security and adult autonomy. During this period, society leaves adolescents relatively free of responsibilities and able to try out different identities. Adolescents in effect search their culture's identity files, experimenting with different roles and personalities. They may want to pursue one career one month (lawyer, for example) and another career the next month (doctor, actor, teacher, social worker, or astronaut, for example). They may dress neatly one day, sloppily the next. This experimentation is a deliberate effort on the part of adolescents to find out where they fit into the world. Most adolescents eventually discard undesirable roles.

Youth who successfully cope with conflicting identities emerge with a new sense of self that is both refreshing and acceptable. Adolescents who do not successfully resolve this identity crisis suffer what Erikson calls *identity confusion.* The confusion takes one of two courses: Individuals withdraw, isolating themselves from peers and family, or they immerse themselves in the world of peers and lose their identity in the crowd.

Some critics argue that the identity status approach does not produce enough depth in understanding identity development (Klimstra & others, 2017). One way that researchers are now examining identity changes in depth is to use a *narrative approach.* This involves asking individuals to tell their life stories and evaluate the extent to which their stories are meaningful and integrated (Adler & others, 2017; Maher, Winston, & Ur, 2017). The term *narrative identity* "refers to the stories people construct and tell about themselves to define who they are for themselves and others. Beginning in adolescence and young adulthood, our narrative identities are the stories we live by" (McAdams, Josselson, & Lieblich, 2006, p. 4).

A recent study used both identity status and narrative approaches to examine college students' identity domains. In both approaches, the interpersonal domain was most frequently described (McLean & others, 2016). In the interpersonal domain, dating and friendships were frequently mentioned, although there was no mention of gender roles. In the narrative domain, family stories were common.

Developmental Changes   Although questions about identity may be especially important during adolescence, identity formation neither begins nor ends during these years. It begins with the appearance of attachment, the development of the sense of self, and the emergence of independence in infancy; the process reaches its final phase with a life review and integration in old age. What is important about identity development in adolescence, especially late adolescence, is that for the first time, physical development, cognitive development, and socioemotional development advance to the point at which the individual can sort through and synthesize childhood identities and identifications to construct a viable path toward adult maturity.

How do individual adolescents go about the process of forming an identity? Eriksonian researcher James Marcia (1980, 1994) argues that Erikson's theory of identity development contains four identity statuses, or ways of resolving the identity crisis: identity diffusion, identity foreclosure, identity moratorium, and identity achievement. What determines an individual's identity status? Marcia classifies individuals based on the existence or extent of their crisis or commitment (see Figure 1). **Crisis** is defined as a period of identity development during which the individual is exploring alternatives.

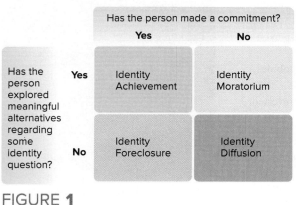

		Has the person made a commitment?	
		Yes	**No**
Has the person explored meaningful alternatives regarding some identity question?	**Yes**	Identity Achievement	Identity Moratorium
	No	Identity Foreclosure	Identity Diffusion

FIGURE 1

MARCIA'S FOUR STATUSES OF IDENTITY

Most researchers use the term *exploration* rather than *crisis*. **Commitment** is a personal investment in identity. The four statuses of identity are as follows:

- **Identity diffusion,** the status of individuals who have not yet experienced a crisis or made any commitments. Not only are they undecided about occupational and ideological choices, but they are also likely to show little interest in such matters.

- **Identity foreclosure** is the status of individuals who have made a commitment but have not experienced a crisis. This occurs most often when parents hand down commitments to their adolescents, usually in an authoritarian way, before adolescents have had a chance to explore different approaches, ideologies, and vocations on their own.

- **Identity moratorium** is the status of individuals who are in the midst of a crisis but whose commitments are either absent or only vaguely defined.

- **Identity achievement** is the status of individuals who have undergone a crisis and have made a commitment.

How Would You...?

If you were a **psychologist,** how would you apply Marcia's theory of identity formation to describe your current identity status or the identity status of adolescents you know?

Emerging Adulthood and Beyond One study found that as individuals aged from early adolescence to emerging adulthood, they increasingly explored their identity in depth (Klimstra & others, 2010). And a recent meta-analysis of 124 studies by Jane Kroger and her colleagues (2010) revealed that during adolescence and emerging adulthood, identity moratorium status rose steadily to age 19 and then declined; identity achievement rose across late adolescence and emerging adulthood; and foreclosure and diffusion statuses declined across the high school years but fluctuated during the late teens and emerging adulthood.

How does identity change in emerging adulthood?
©Tom Grill/Corbis RF

The studies also found that a large proportion of individuals were not identity achieved by the time they reached their twenties.

Indeed, developmental experts are moving toward a consensus that the key changes in identity are more likely to take place in emerging adulthood (18 to 25 years of age) or later than in adolescence (Kroger, 2015; Schwartz & others, 2015). For example, Alan Waterman (1985, 1999) has found that from the years preceding high school through the last few years of college, the number of individuals who are identity achieved increases, while the number who are identity diffused decreases. College upperclassmen are more likely to be identity achieved than college freshmen or high school students. Many young adolescents, on the other hand, are identity diffused. These developmental changes are especially true for vocational choice. In terms of religious beliefs and political ideology, fewer college students reach the identity-achieved status; a substantial number are characterized by foreclosure and diffusion. Thus, the timing of identity development may depend on the specific dimension examined.

Why might college produce some key changes in identity? Increased complexity in the reasoning skills of college students combined with a wide range of new experiences that highlight contrasts between home and college and between themselves and others stimulates them to reach a higher level of integrating various dimensions of their identity (Phinney, 2008). College serves as a virtual "laboratory" for identity development through such experiences as diverse coursework and exposure to peers from diverse backgrounds. Also, one of emerging adulthood's themes is not having many social commitments, which gives individuals considerable independence in developing a life path (Arnett, 2015).

Resolution of the identity issue during adolescence and emerging adulthood does not mean that a person's identity will be stable through the remainder of life (McAdams & Zapata-Gietl, 2015). Many individuals who develop positive identities follow what are called "MAMA" cycles—that is, their identity status changes from *m*oratorium to *a*chievement to *m*oratorium to *a*chievement (Marcia, 1994). These cycles may be repeated throughout life (Francis, Fraser, & Marcia, 1989). Marcia (2002) argues that the first identity is just that—it should not be viewed as the final product.

identity versus identity confusion Erikson's fifth developmental stage, which occurs at about the time of adolescence. At this time, adolescents are faced with deciding who they are, what they are all about, and where they are going in life.

psychosocial moratorium Erikson's term for the gap between childhood security and adult autonomy.

crisis Marcia's term for a period of identity development during which the individual is exploring alternatives.

commitment Marcia's term for the part of identity development in which individuals show a personal investment in identity.

identity diffusion Marcia's term for the status of individuals who have not yet experienced a crisis (explored alternatives) or made any commitments.

identity foreclosure Marcia's term for the status of individuals who have made a commitment but have not experienced a crisis.

identity moratorium Marcia's term for the status of individuals who are in the midst of a crisis, but their commitments are either absent or vaguely defined.

identity achievement Marcia's term for the status of individuals who have undergone a crisis and have made a commitment.

In short, questions about identity come up throughout life. An individual who develops a healthy identity is flexible and adaptive, open to changes in society, in relationships, and in careers. This openness ensures numerous reorganizations of identity throughout the individual's life.

Family Influences   Parents are important figures in the adolescent's development of identity (Crocetti & others, 2017; Smokowski & others, 2017; Tang, McLoyd, & Hallman, 2016). Researchers have found that a family atmosphere that promotes both individuality and connectedness is important to the adolescent's identity development (Cooper & Grotevant, 1989):

- **Individuality** consists of two dimensions: self-assertion (the ability to have and communicate a point of view) and separateness (the use of communication patterns to express how one is different from others).
- **Connectedness** also consists of two dimensions: mutuality, which involves sensitivity to and respect for others' views, and permeability, which involves openness to others' views.

In general, then, research indicates that identity formation is enhanced by family relationships that sustain both individuation, which encourages adolescents to develop their own point of view, and connectedness, which provides a secure base from which adolescents can explore their widening social worlds (Cooper, 2011; Cooper, Gonzales, & Wilson, 2015). When connectedness is strong and individuation weak, adolescents often have an identity foreclosure status. When connectedness is weak, adolescents often experience identity confusion.

Peer/Romantic Relationships   Researchers have recently found that the capacity to explore one's identity during adolescence and emerging adulthood is linked to the quality of friendships and romantic relationships (Douglass, Mirpuri, & Yip, 2017; Kornienko & others, 2016; Rivas-Drake & others, 2017). In a recent research review, it was concluded that good peer relationships were an important factor in achieving a positive identity (Rageliené, 2016). One study found that an open, active exploration of identity with the support of close friends contributes to the positive quality of the friendship (Doumen & others, 2012). In another study, friends were often a safe context for exploring identity-related experiences, serving as a testing ground for how self-disclosing comments are viewed by others (McLean & Jennings, 2012).

In terms of links between identity and romantic relationships in adolescence and emerging adulthood, two individuals in a romantic relationship are both in the process of constructing their own identities and each person provides the other with a context for identity exploration (Pittman & others, 2012). The extent of their secure attachment with each other can influence how each partner constructs his or her own identity.

Cultural and Ethnic Identity   Identity developments is influenced by culture and ethnicity (Yoon & others, 2017). Most research on identity development has historically been based on data obtained from adolescents and emerging adults in the United States and Canada, especially those who are non-Latino Whites (Schwartz & others, 2015). Many of these individuals have grown up in cultural contexts that value individual autonomy. However, in many countries around the world, adolescents and emerging adults have grown up influenced by a collectivist emphasis on fitting in with the group and connecting with others. The collectivist emphasis is especially prevalent in East Asian countries such as China. Researchers have found that self-oriented identity exploration may not be the main process through which identity achievement is attained in East Asian countries (Schwartz & others, 2012). Rather, East Asian adolescents and emerging adults may develop their identity through identification with and imitation of others in the cultural group (Bosma & Kunnen, 2001). This emphasis on interdependence in East Asian cultures includes an emphasis on adolescents and emerging adults accepting and embracing social and family roles (Berman & others, 2011). Thus, some patterns of identity development, such as the foreclosed status, may be more adaptive in East Asian countries than in North American countries (Chen & Berman, 2012).

individuality Characteristic consisting of two dimensions: self-assertion (the ability to have and communicate a point of view) and separateness (the use of communication patterns to express how one is different from others).

connectedness Characteristic consisting of two dimensions: mutuality (sensitivity to and respect for others' views) and permeability (openness to others' views).

One adolescent girl, 16-year-old Michelle Chin, made these comments about ethnic identity development: "My parents do not understand that teenagers need to find out who they are, which means a lot of experimenting, a lot of mood swings, a lot of emotions and awkwardness. Like any teenager, I am facing an identity crisis. I am still trying to figure out whether I am a Chinese American or an American with Asian eyes."
©Red Chopsticks/Getty Images RF

Identity development may take longer in some countries than in others (Schwartz & others, 2015). For example, research indicates that Italian youth may postpone significant identity exploration beyond adolescence and emerging adulthood, not settling on an identity until their mid- to late-twenties (Crocetti, Rabaglietti, & Sica, 2012). This delayed identity development is strongly influenced by many Italian youth living at home with their parents until 30 years of age and older.

Seth Schwartz and his colleagues (2012) recently pointed out that while everyone identifies with a particular "culture," many individuals in cultural majority groups take their cultural identity for granted. Thus, many adolescents and emerging adults in the cultural majority of non-Latino Whites in the United States likely don't spend much time thinking of themselves as "White American." However, for many adolescents and emerging adults who have grown up as a member of an ethnic minority group in the United States or emigrated from another country, cultural dimensions likely are an important aspect of their identity. Researchers have found that at both the high school and college level, Latino students are more likely than non-Latino White students to indicate that their cultural identity is an important dimension of their overall self-concept (Urdan, 2012).

Throughout the world, ethnic minority groups have struggled to maintain their ethnic identities while blending in with the dominant culture (Erikson, 1968). **Ethnic identity** is an enduring aspect of the self that includes a sense of membership in an ethnic group as well as alignment with the attitudes and feelings related to that membership (Douglass & Umana-Taylor, 2017; Meeus, 2017; Tang, McLoyd, & Hallman, 2016; Umana-Taylor & Douglass, 2017; White & others, 2017; Yoon & others, 2017). Thus, for adolescents from ethnic minority groups, the process of identity formation has an added dimension: the choice between two or more sources of identification—their own ethnic group and the mainstream, or dominant, culture (Gonzales & others, 2017; Tang, McLoyd, & Hallman, 2016). Many adolescents resolve this choice by developing a **bicultural identity.** That is, they identify in some ways with their ethnic group and in other ways with the majority culture (Cooper, Gonzales, & Wilson, 2015; Fleischmann & Verkuylen, 2016).

Recent research indicates that pride in one's ethnic identity group has positive outcomes (Ikram & others, 2016). For example, in a recent study, having pride in one's ethnic group and a strong ethnic identity were linked to lower rates of substance use in adolescents (Grindal & Nieri, 2016). And in another recent study, strong ethnic group affiliation and connection served a protective function in reducing risk for psychiatric problems (Anglin & others, 2016). Recent longitudinal studies document that the ethnic identity of adolescents is influenced by positive and diverse friendships (Rivas-Drake & others, 2017; Santos & others, 2017).

For ethnic minority individuals, adolescence and emerging adulthood are often special junctures in their development (Douglass & Umana-Taylor, 2017; Espinosa & others, 2017; Meeus, 2017). Although children are aware of some ethnic and cultural differences, individuals consciously confront their ethnicity for the first time in adolescence or emerging adulthood. Unlike children, adolescents and emerging adults are able to interpret ethnic and cultural information, to reflect on the past, and to speculate about the future.

The indicators of changing identity often differ for each succeeding generation (Phinney & Vedder, 2013). First-generation immigrants are likely to be secure in their identities and unlikely to change much; they may or may not develop a new identity. The degree to which they begin to feel "American" appears to be related to whether or not they learn English, develop social networks beyond their ethnic group, and become culturally competent in their new country. Second-generation immigrants are more likely to think of themselves as "American," possibly because citizenship is granted at birth. Their ethnic identity is likely to be linked to retention of their ethnic language and social networks. In the third and later generations, the issues become more complex. Historical, contextual, and political factors that are unrelated to acculturation may affect the extent to which members of this generation retain their ethnic identities.

EMOTIONAL DEVELOPMENT

Adolescence has long been described as a time of emotional turmoil (Hall, 1904). In its extreme form, this view is inaccurate because adolescents are not constantly in a state of "storm and stress." Nonetheless, early adolescence is a time when emotional highs and lows increase (Rosenblum & Lewis, 2003). Young adolescents can be on top of the world one moment and down in the dumps the next. In many instances, the intensity of their emotions

How Would You...?
If you were a **human development and family studies professional,** how would you design a community program that assists ethnic minority adolescents to develop a healthy bicultural identity?

ethnic identity An enduring, basic aspect of the self that includes a sense of membership in an ethnic group and the attitudes and feelings related to that membership.

bicultural identity Identity formation that occurs when adolescents identify in some ways with their ethnic group and in other ways with the majority culture.

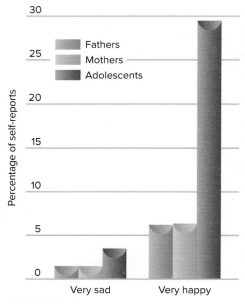

FIGURE 2

SELF-REPORTED EXTREMES OF EMOTION BY ADOLESCENTS, MOTHERS, AND FATHERS USING THE EXPERIENCE SAMPLING METHOD. In the study by Reed Larson and Maryse Richards (1994), adolescents and their mothers and fathers were beeped at random times by researchers using the experience sampling method. The researchers found that adolescents were more likely to report emotional extremes than their parents were.

seems out of proportion to the events that elicit them (Guyer, Silk, & Nelson, 2016). Young adolescents might sulk a lot, not knowing how to adequately express their feelings. With little or no provocation, they might blow up at their parents or siblings or use defense mechanisms to displace their feelings onto another person.

Reed Larson and Maryse Richards (1994) found that adolescents reported more extreme emotions and more fleeting emotions than their parents did. For example, adolescents were five times more likely to report being "very happy" and three times more likely to report being "very sad" than their parents were (see Figure 2). These findings lend support to the perception of adolescents as moody and changeable (Rosenblum & Lewis, 2003).

Researchers have also found that from the fifth through the ninth grades, both boys and girls experience a 50 percent decrease in being "very happy" (Larson & Lampman-Petraitis, 1989). In this same study, adolescents were more likely than preadolescents to report mildly negative mood states.

It is important for adults to recognize that moodiness is a *normal* aspect of early adolescence and that most adolescents make it through these moody times to become competent adults. Nonetheless, for some adolescents, such emotions can reflect serious problems.

The ability to effectively manage and control one's emotions is a key dimension of positive outcomes in adolescent development, just as it is in children's development. Emotion regulation consists of effectively managing arousal to adapt to changing conditions and reach a goal (Calkins & Brown, 2016). Arousal involves a state of alertness or activation, which can reach levels that are too high for effective functioning in adolescence. Anger, for example, often requires regulation.

With increasing age, adolescents are more likely to improve their use of cognitive strategies for regulating emotion, to modulate their emotional arousal, to become more adept at managing situations to minimize negative emotion, and to choose effective ways to cope with stress. Of course, there are wide variations in individuals' ability to modulate their emotions (Denham, Bassett, & Wyatt, 2015; Thompson, 2015). Indeed, a prominent feature of adolescents with problems is that they often have difficulty managing their emotions.

One study found that young adolescents in Taiwan who used a cognitive reappraisal strategy rather than a suppression strategy were more likely to have a positive self-concept, which in turn was associated with having fewer internalizing problems such as depression (Hsieh & Stright, 2012). Cognitive reappraisal is a coping strategy that actively involves changing how one thinks about a situation to regulate the emotional impact.

GENDER CLASSIFICATION

Not long ago, it was accepted that boys should grow up to be masculine (powerful, assertive, for example) and girls to be feminine (sensitive to others, caring, for example). In the 1970s, however, as both females and males became dissatisfied with the burdens imposed by their stereotypic roles, alternatives to femininity and masculinity were proposed. Instead of describing masculinity and femininity as a continuum in which more of one means less of the other, it was proposed that individuals could have both masculine and feminine traits.

This thinking led to the development of the concept of **androgyny,** the presence of positive masculine and feminine characteristics in the same person (Bem, 1977; Spence & Helmreich, 1978). The androgynous boy might be assertive (masculine) and nurturing (feminine). The androgynous girl might be powerful (masculine) and sensitive to others' feelings (feminine). Measures have been developed to assess androgyny, such as the Bem Sex Role Inventory (Bem, 1997).

Gender experts such as Sandra Bem (1977) argue that androgynous individuals are more flexible, competent, and mentally healthy than their masculine or feminine counterparts. To some degree, though, which gender-role classification is best depends on the context involved. For example, in close relationships, feminine and androgynous orientations might be more desirable. One study found that girls and individuals high in femininity showed a stronger interest in caring than did boys and individuals high in masculinity (Karniol, Grosz, & Schorr, 2003). However, masculine and androgynous orientations might be more desirable in traditional academic and work settings because of the achievement demands in these contexts.

Despite talk about the "sensitive male," William Pollack (1999) argues that little has been done to change traditional ways of raising boys. He says that the "boy code" tells boys that they should show little if any emotion and should act tough. Boys learn the boy code in many contexts—sandboxes, playgrounds, schoolrooms, camps, hangouts. The result, according to Pollack, is a

androgyny The presence of positive masculine and feminine characteristics in the same individual.

"national crisis of boyhood." Pollack and others suggest that boys would benefit from being socialized to express their anxieties and concerns and to better regulate their aggression.

Recently, considerable interest has been generated about a new category of gender classification, **transgender,** a broad term that refers to individuals who adopt a gender identity that differs from the one assigned to them at birth (Budge & Orovecz, 2017; Budge & others, 2017; Moradi & others, 2016; Sangganjanavanich, 2016). For example, an individual may have a female body but identify more strongly with being masculine than being feminine, or have a male body but identify more strongly with being feminine than masculine. A transgender identity of being born male but identifying with being a female is much more common than the reverse (Zucker, Lawrence, & Kreukels, 2016). Transgender persons also may not want to be labeled "he" or "she" but prefer a more neutral label such as "they" or "ze" (Scelfo, 2015).

Because of the nuances and complexities involved in such gender categorizations, some experts have recently argued that a better overarching umbrella term might be *trans* to identify a variety of gender identities and expressions different from the gender identity they were assigned at birth (Moradi & others, 2016). The variety of gender identities might include transgender, gender queer (also referred to as gender expansive, this broad gender identity category encompasses individuals who are not exclusively masculine or exclusively feminine), and gender nonconforming (individuals whose behavior/appearance does not conform to social expectations for what is appropriate for their gender). Another recently generated term, *cisgender,* can be used to describe individuals whose gender identity and expression corresponds with the gender identity assigned at birth (Moradi & others, 2016).

Transgender individuals can be straight, gay, lesbian, or bisexual. A recent research review concluded that transgender youth have higher rates of depression, suicide attempts, and eating disorders than their non-transgender peers (Connolly & others, 2016). Among the explanations for this higher rate of disorders are the distress of living in the wrong body and the discrimination and misunderstanding they experience as a gender minority individual (Budge, Chin, & Minero, 2017; Zucker, Lawrence, & Kreukels, 2016).

Among youth who identify themselves as transgender persons, the majority eventually adopt a gender identity in line with the body into which they were born (Byne & others, 2012; King, 2017). Some transgender individuals seek transsexual surgery to go from a male body to a female body or vice versa, but most do not. Some choose just to have hormonal treatments, such as biological females who use testosterone to enhance their masculine characteristics, or biological males who use estrogen to increase their feminine characteristics. Yet other transgender individuals opt for another, broader strategy that involves choosing a lifestyle that challenges the traditional view by having a gender identity that does not fit within one of two opposing categories (King, 2017).

transgender A broad term that refers to individuals who adopt a gender identity that differs from the one assigned to them at birth.

Mack Beggs, a 17-year-old high school student who is transitioning from female to male, won the Texas state wrestling championship for girls in the 110-pound weight class in 2017. The transgender wrestler is taking testosterone treatments as part of the gender transition to enhance male characteristics. Some of the wrestler's opponents have said that Mack has an unfair advantage among girls because of the testosterone treatments. Mack never lost a wrestling match during the 2016–2017 school year, going 52-0 in matches, all in the female division. *What do you think? Should Mack have been allowed to wrestle in the girls' division?*
©Leslie Plaza Johnson/Icon Sportswire/Getty Images

Review *Connect* Reflect

LG1 Discuss identity, emotional development, and gender classification during adolescence.

Review
- How does identity develop in adolescence?
- What factors affect emotional development in adolescence?
- What are different ways that gender classification occurs?

Connect
- What characterizes emotional development in middle and late childhood? How do those changes compare with what you have just read about emotional development in adolescence?

Reflect *Your Own Personal Journey of Life*
- Where are you in your identity development? Get out a sheet of paper and list each of the pieces of identity (vocational, political, religious, relationship, achievement/intellectual, sexual, cultural/ethnic, interests, personality, and physical) in a column on the left side of the paper. Then write the four identity statuses (diffused, foreclosed, moratorium, and achieved) across the top of the page. For each dimension of identity, place a check mark in the column that reflects your identity status. If you checked "diffused" or "foreclosed" for any of the dimensions, think about what you need to do to move to a moratorium status in those areas.

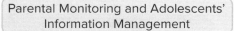

2 What Is the Nature of Parent-Adolescent Relationships?

LG2 Describe changes that take place in adolescents' relationships with their parents.

Parental Monitoring and Adolescents' Information Management

Autonomy and Attachment

Parent-Adolescent Conflict

In case you're worried about what's going to become of the younger generation, it's going to grow up and start worrying about the younger generation.

—ROGER ALLEN
Contemporary American Writer

As you read about parent-adolescent relationships in this section, keep in mind that a positive family climate for adolescents involves not only effective parenting but also a positive relationship between adolescents' parents, whether they are married or divorced. For example, a longitudinal study found that a positive family climate (based on positive interaction between spouses and between parents and their seventh-grader) was linked to the degree of positive engagement the adolescents showed toward their own spouses almost 20 years later during early adulthood (Ackerman & others, 2013).

Adolescence typically alters the relationship between parents and their children. Among the most important aspects of family relationships that change during adolescence are those that involve parental monitoring, autonomy, attachment, and parent-adolescent conflict.

PARENTAL MONITORING AND ADOLESCENTS' INFORMATION MANAGEMENT

We have discussed the important role that parents play as managers of their children's development. A key aspect of the managerial role of parenting is effective monitoring, which is especially important as children move into the adolescent years (Cope & others, 2017; Donaldson, Handren, & Crano, 2016; Kuntsche & Kuntsche, 2016; Low & Shortt, 2017; Top, Liew, & Luo, 2017). A current interest also focuses on adolescents' management of their parents' access to information, especially the extent to which adolescents disclose or conceal information about their activities (Smetana, Robinson, & Rote, 2015).

A key aspect of the managerial role of parenting is parental monitoring, which is especially important as children move into the adolescent years (Clark & others, 2015). Parental monitoring includes supervising adolescents' choice of social settings, activities, and friends, as well as their academic efforts (Low & Shortt, 2017; Sajber & others, 2016). In a recent study of fifth- to eighth-graders, a higher level of parental monitoring was associated with students' having higher grades (Top, Liew, & Luo, 2017). In another recent study, low parental monitoring was a key factor in predicting a developmental trajectory of delinquency and substance use in adolescence (Wang & others, 2014). Further, in another recent study, higher parental monitoring reduced negative peer influence on adolescent risk-taking (Wang & others, 2016a). And in a recent meta-analysis, a higher level of parental monitoring and rule enforcement were linked to later initiation of sexual intercourse and a greater use of condoms by adolescents (Dittus & others, 2015).

A current interest involving parental monitoring focuses on adolescents' management of their parents' access to information, especially strategies for disclosing or concealing information about their activities (Donaldson, Handren, & Crano, 2016; Hawk, 2017; Rote & Smetana, 2016; Smetana, Robinson, & Rote, 2015). When parents engage in positive parenting practices, adolescents are more likely to disclose information. For example, disclosure increases when parents ask adolescents questions and when adolescents' relationship with parents is characterized by a high level of trust, acceptance, and quality (McElvaney, Greene, & Hogan, 2014). Researchers have found that adolescents' disclosure to parents about their whereabouts, activities, and friends is linked to positive adolescent adjustment. A recent study of 10- to 18-year-olds found that lower adolescent disclosure to parents was linked to antisocial behavior (Criss & others, 2015).

Three ways that parents can engage in parental monitoring are solicitation (asking questions), control (disclosure rules), and when youth don't

What roles do parental monitoring and adolescents' information management play in adolescent development?
©Wavebreakmedia/Getty Images RF

comply, snooping. In a recent study, snooping was perceived by both adolescents and parents as the most likely of these three strategies to violate youths' privacy rights (Hawk, Becht, & Branje, 2016). Also, in this study, snooping was a relatively infrequent parental monitoring tactic but was a better indicator of problems in adolescent and family functioning than were solicitation and control.

AUTONOMY AND ATTACHMENT

With most adolescents, parents are likely to find themselves engaged in a delicate balancing act, weighing competing needs for autonomy and control, for independence and connection.

The Push for Autonomy   The typical adolescent's push for autonomy and responsibility puzzles and angers many parents. As parents see their teenager slipping from their grasp, they may have an urge to take stronger control. Heated emotional exchanges may ensue, with either side calling names, making threats, and doing whatever seems necessary to gain control. Parents may seem frustrated because they *expect* their teenager to heed their advice, to want to spend time with the family, and to grow up to do what is right. Most parents anticipate that their teenager will have some difficulty adjusting to the changes that adolescence brings, but few parents imagine and predict just how strong an adolescent's desires will be to spend time with peers or how intensely adolescents will want to show that it is they—not their parents—who are responsible for their successes and failures.

Adolescents' ability to attain autonomy and gain control over their behavior is acquired through appropriate adult reactions to their desire for control (Steinberg & Collins, 2011). At the onset of adolescence, the average individual does not have the knowledge to make appropriate or mature decisions in all areas of life. As the adolescent pushes for autonomy, the wise adult relinquishes control in those areas where the adolescent can make reasonable decisions, but continues to guide the adolescent to make reasonable decisions in areas in which the adolescent's knowledge is more limited. Gradually, adolescents acquire the ability to make mature decisions on their own. A recent study also found that from 16 to 20 years of age, adolescents perceived that they had increasing independence and improved relationships with their parents (Hadiwijaya & others, 2017).

Gender differences characterize autonomy-granting in adolescence. Boys are given more independence than girls. In one study, this tendency was especially true in U.S. families with a traditional gender-role orientation (Bumpus, Crouter, & McHale, 2001).

In contexts where adolescents experience a high level of risk, such as high-crime communities, and in cultural groups that place a high value on family solidarity and deference to parents, parental control either has not been linked to problem behaviors or has been shown to benefit adolescent outcomes (McElhaney & Allen, 2012). And expectations about the appropriate timing of adolescent autonomy often vary across cultures, parents, and adolescents (McElhaney & Allen, 2012). For example, expectations for early autonomy on the part of adolescents are more prevalent in non-Latino Whites, single parents, and adolescents themselves than they are in Asian Americans or Latinos, married parents, and parents themselves (Feldman & Rosenthal, 1999; Romo, Mireles-Rios, & Lopez-Tello, 2014). Nonetheless, although Latino cultures may place a stronger emphasis on parental authority and restrict adolescent autonomy, a recent study revealed that regardless of where they were born, Mexican-origin adolescent girls living in the United States expected autonomy at an earlier age than their mothers preferred (Bamaca-Colbert & others, 2012). Another recent study of Mexican immigrant mothers and their U.S.-raised 13- to 14-year-old daughters explored future autonomy expectations when the daughters reach 15 years of age (Romo, Mireles-Rios, & Lopez-Tello, 2014). In this study, the daughters hoped for less strict rules regarding social activities while mothers reported that they still expected to exert control, although they were willing to allow more autonomy in personal matters such as physical appearance and to allow the daughter to group date.

The Role of Attachment   Recall that one of the most widely discussed aspects of socioemotional development in infancy is secure attachment to caregivers (Jones & others, 2017; Meins, Bureau, & Fernyhough, 2017; Pasco-Fearon & others, 2016; Thompson, 2015, 2016). In the past decade, researchers have explored whether secure attachment also might be an important concept in adolescents' relationships with their parents (Kobak & Kerig,

When I was a boy of 14, my father was so ignorant I could hardly stand to have the man around. But when I got to be 21, I was astonished at how much he had learnt in 7 years.

—MARK TWAIN
American Writer and Humorist, 20th Century

Stacey Christensen, age 16: "I am lucky enough to have open communication with my parents. Whenever I am in need or just need to talk, my parents are there for me. My advice to parents is to let your teens grow at their own pace, be open with them so that you can be there for them. We need guidance; our parents need to help but not be too overwhelming."
©Stockbyte/Getty Images RF

developmental connection

Attachment

In secure attachment, babies use the caregiver as a secure base from which to explore the environment. Connect to "Socioemotional Development in Infancy."

It is not enough for parents to understand children. They must accord children the privilege of understanding them.

—MILTON SAPIRSTEIN
American Psychiatrist, 20th Century

Conflict with parents increases in early adolescence. *What is the nature of this conflict in a majority of American families?*
©Wavebreakmedia/age fotostock RF

2015; Lockhart & others, 2017). For example, Joseph Allen and his colleagues (Allen, 2007, 2008; Allen & Tan, 2017; Allen & others, 2007, 2009) found that securely attached adolescents were less likely than those who were insecurely attached to engage in problem behaviors such as juvenile delinquency and drug abuse. In a recent longitudinal study, Allen and colleagues (2009) found that secure attachment at 14 years of age was linked to a number of positive outcomes at 21 years of age, including relationship competence, financial/career competence, and fewer problematic behaviors. A recent study involving adolescents and emerging adults from 15 to 20 years of age found that insecure attachment to mothers was linked to becoming depressed and remaining depressed (Agerup & others, 2015). Also, a recent study found that adolescents who had attempted suicide were less securely attached to their mothers and fathers (Sheftall & others, 2013). Further, in a recent study of Latino families, a higher level of secure attachment with mothers was associated with less heavy drug use by adolescents (Gattamorta & others, 2017). And in a recent research review, it was concluded that the most consistent outcomes of secure attachment in adolescence involve positive peer relations and development of the adolescent's emotion regulation capacities (Allen & Miga, 2010).

Might secure attachment be linked to parenting styles in adolescence? A recent study of Chinese adolescents revealed that authoritative parenting positively predicted parent-adolescent attachment, which in turn was associated with a higher level of adolescent self-esteem and positive attachment to peers (Cai & others, 2013). And a longitudinal study revealed that secure attachment in adolescence and emerging adulthood was predicted by observations of maternal sensitivity across childhood and adolescence (Waters, Ruiz, & Roisman, 2017).

PARENT-ADOLESCENT CONFLICT

Although parent-adolescent conflict increases in early adolescence, it does not reach the tumultuous proportions G. Stanley Hall envisioned at the beginning of the twentieth century (Juang & Umana-Taylor, 2012). Rather, much of the conflict involves the everyday expectations of family life, such as keeping a bedroom clean, dressing neatly, getting home by a certain time, and not talking for hours on the phone. The conflicts rarely involve major dilemmas such as drugs or delinquency.

Conflict with parents often escalates during early adolescence, remains somewhat stable during the high school years, and then lessens in emerging adulthood. Parent-adolescent relationships become more positive if adolescents go away to college than if they attend college while living at home (Sullivan & Sullivan, 1980).

The everyday conflicts that characterize parent-adolescent relationships may actually serve a positive developmental function. These minor disputes and negotiations facilitate the adolescent's transition from being dependent on parents to becoming an autonomous individual.

The old model of parent-adolescent relationships suggested that as adolescents mature they detach themselves from parents and move into a world of autonomy apart from parents. The old model also suggested that parent-adolescent conflict is intense and stressful throughout adolescence. The new model emphasizes that parents serve as important attachment figures and support systems while adolescents explore a wider, more complex social world. The new model also emphasizes that, in most families, parent-adolescent conflict is moderate rather than severe and that the everyday negotiations and minor disputes not only are normal but also can serve the positive developmental function of helping the adolescent make the transition from childhood dependency to adult independence (see Figure 3).

Still, a high degree of conflict characterizes some parent-adolescent relationships (Moed & others, 2015; Skinner & McHale, 2016). One estimate of the proportion of parents and adolescents who engage in prolonged, intense, repeated, unhealthy conflict is about one in five families (Montemayor, 1982). This prolonged, intense conflict is associated with various adolescent problems: moving out of the home, juvenile delinquency, school dropout, pregnancy and early marriage, membership in religious cults, and drug abuse. For example, a recent study found that a higher level of parent-adolescent conflict was associated with higher levels of adolescent anxiety, depression, and aggression, and lower levels of self-esteem (Smokowski & others, 2015). Also, a recent study found that higher levels of parent-adolescent

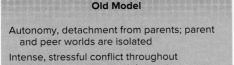

Old Model

Autonomy, detachment from parents; parent and peer worlds are isolated

Intense, stressful conflict throughout adolescence; parent-adolescent relationships are filled with storm and stress on virtually a daily basis

New Model

Attachment and autonomy; parents are important support systems and attachment figures; adolescent-parent and adolescent-peer worlds have some important connections

Moderate parent-adolescent conflict is common and can serve a positive developmental function; conflict greater in early adolescence

FIGURE 3

OLD AND NEW MODELS OF PARENT-ADOLESCENT RELATIONSHIPS

©Martin Barraud/Caia Image/Glow Images RF

conflict were associated with lower levels of empathy in adolescents from 13 to 18 years of age (Van Lissa & others, 2015).

Cross-cultural studies reveal that parent-adolescent conflict is lower in some countries than in the United States. Two countries where parent-adolescent conflict is lower than in the United States are Japan and India (Larson & Verma, 1999; Rothbaum & others, 2000).

When families emigrate to another country, adolescents typically acculturate more quickly to the norms and values of their new country than do their parents (Fuligni, 2012). This likely occurs because of immigrant adolescents' exposure in school to the language and culture of the host country. The norms and values immigrant adolescents experience are especially likely to diverge from those of their parents in areas such as autonomy and romantic relationships. Such divergences are likely to increase parent-adolescent conflict in immigrant families. Andrew Fuligni (2012) argues that these conflicts aren't always expressed openly but are often present in underlying, internal feelings. For example, immigrant adolescents may feel that their parents want them to give up their personal interests for the sake of the family, but the adolescents don't think this is fair. Such acculturation-based conflict focuses on issues related to core cultural values and is likely to occur in immigrant families, such as Latino and Asian American families, who come to the United States to live (Juang & Umana-Taylor, 2012). In a recent study of Chinese American families, parent-adolescent conflict was linked to a sense of alienation between parents and adolescents, which in turn was related to more depressive symptoms, delinquent behavior, and lower academic achievement (Hou, Kim, & Wang, 2016).

To read about some effective strategies for parenting adolescents, see the *Caring Connections* interlude.

How Would You...?

If you were a **social worker**, how would you counsel parents who are experiencing stress about anticipated family conflicts as their child enters adolescence?

caring connections

Strategies for Parenting Adolescents

Competent adolescent development is most likely when adolescents have parents who:

- *Show them warmth and respect, and avoid the tendency to be too controlling or too permissive.*
- *Serve as positive role models for adolescents.*
- *Demonstrate sustained interest in their lives.* Parents need to spend time with their adolescents and monitor their lives.
- *Understand and adapt to the adolescents' cognitive and socioemotional development.*

- *Communicate expectations for high standards of conduct and achievement.*
- *Display constructive ways of dealing with problems and conflict.* Moderate conflict is a normal expression of the adolescent's desire for independence and search for an identity.
- *Understand that adolescents don't become adults overnight.* Adolescence is a long journey.

3 What Aspects of Peer Relationships Are Important in Adolescence?

LG3 Characterize the changes that occur in peer relations during adolescence.

Friendship   Peer Groups   Dating and Romantic Relationships

Peers play powerful roles in the lives of adolescents (Nesi & others, 2017; Rubin & Barstead, 2018; Wentzel & Munecks, 2016; Wentzel & Ramani, 2016). Peer relations undergo important changes in adolescence, including changes in friendships and in peer groups and the beginning of romantic relationships. In middle and late childhood, the focus of peer relations is on being liked by classmates and on being included in games or lunchroom conversations. Being overlooked or, worse yet, being rejected can have damaging effects on children's development that sometimes are carried forward to adolescence.

FRIENDSHIP

What changes take place in friendship during the adolescent years?
©SW Productions/Getty Images RF

For most children, being popular with their peers is a strong motivator. In early adolescence, being popular with peers continues to be important but teenagers also typically begin to prefer to have a smaller number of friendships that are more intense and intimate than those of young children.

Harry Stack Sullivan (1953) was the most influential theorist to discuss the importance of adolescent friendships. In contrast with other psychoanalytic theorists who focused almost exclusively on parent-child relationships, Sullivan argued that friends are also important in shaping the development of children and adolescents. Everyone, said Sullivan, has basic social needs, such as the need for tenderness (secure attachment), playful companionship, social acceptance, intimacy, and sexual relations. Whether or not these needs are fulfilled largely determines our emotional well-being. For example, if the need for playful companionship goes unmet, then we become bored and depressed; if the need for social acceptance is not met, we suffer a diminished sense of self-worth.

During adolescence, said Sullivan, friends become increasingly important in meeting social needs. In particular, Sullivan argued, the need for intimacy intensifies during early adolescence and motivates teenagers to seek out close friends. If adolescents fail to forge such close friendships, they experience loneliness and a reduced sense of self-worth.

Many of Sullivan's ideas have withstood the test of time (Buhrmester & Chong, 2009). For example, adolescents report disclosing intimate and personal information to their friends more often than do younger children (Buhrmester, 1998) (see Figure 4). Adolescents also say they depend more on friends than on parents to satisfy their needs for companionship, reassurance of worth, and intimacy. The ups and downs of experiences with friends shape adolescents' well-being (Nesi & others, 2017; Prinstein & Giletta, 2016).

People differ in the company they keep—that is, who their friends are. Although having friends can be a developmental advantage, not all friendships are alike and the quality of friendship is also important to consider (Choukas-Bradley & Prinstein, 2016; Nesi & others, 2017; Rubin & others, 2016). Developmental advantages occur when adolescents have friends who are socially skilled, supportive, and oriented toward academic achievement (Graber, Turner, & Madill, 2016; Jones & Magee, 2014; Witkow, Rickert, & Cullen, 2017). It is a developmental disadvantage to have coercive, conflict-ridden, and poor-quality friendships. A recent study revealed that having friends who engage in delinquent behavior is associated with early onset and more persistent delinquency (Evans, Simons, & Simons, 2016). Another recent study found that adolescents adapted their smoking and drinking behavior to that of their best friends (Wang & others, 2016b). Further, a recent study of adolescent girls revealed that friends' dieting predicted whether adolescent girls would engage in dieting or extreme dieting (Balantekin, Birch, & Savage, 2017).

Although most adolescents develop friendships with individuals who are close to their own age, some adolescents become best friends with younger or older individuals. Do older friends encourage adolescents to engage in delinquent behavior or early sexual behavior? Adolescents who interact with older youth engage in these behaviors more frequently (Billy, Rodgers, & Udry, 1984).

PEER GROUPS

How extensive is peer pressure in adolescence? What roles do cliques and crowds play in adolescents' lives? As we see next, researchers have found that the standards of peer groups and the influence of crowds and cliques become increasingly important during adolescence.

Peer Pressure Young adolescents conform more to peer standards than children do (Choukas-Bradley & Prinstein, 2016; Nesi & others, 2017). Around the eighth and ninth grades, conformity to peers—especially to their antisocial standards—peaks (Brown & Larson, 2009). At this point, adolescents are most likely to go along with a peer to steal hubcaps off a car, draw graffiti on a wall, or steal cosmetics from a store counter.

Which adolescents are most likely to conform to peers? Mitchell Prinstein and his colleagues (Cohen & Prinstein, 2006; Prinstein, 2007; Prinstein & Giletta, 2016; Prinstein & others, 2009) have conducted research and analysis addressing this question. They conclude that adolescents who are uncertain about their social identity, which can appear in the form of low self-esteem and high social anxiety, are most likely to conform to peers. This uncertainty often increases during times of change, such as school and family transitions. Also, adolescents are more likely to conform when they are in the presence of someone they perceive to have higher status than themselves. And a recent study found that boys were more likely to be influenced by peer pressure involving sexual behavior than were girls (Widman & others, 2016).

Cliques and Crowds Cliques and crowds assume more important roles in the lives of adolescents than in the lives of children (Brown, 2011). **Cliques** are small groups that range from 2 to about 12 individuals and average about 5 or 6 individuals. The clique members are usually of the same sex and about the same age.

Cliques can form because adolescents engage in similar activities, such as being in a club or on a sports team (Brown, 2011; Brown & Dietz, 2009). Several adolescents may form a clique because they have spent time with each other, share mutual interests, and enjoy each other's company. Not necessarily friends, they often develop a friendship if they stay in the clique. What do adolescents do in cliques? They share ideas and hang out together. Often they develop an in-group identity in which they believe that their clique is better than other cliques.

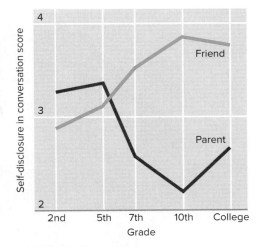

FIGURE 4

DEVELOPMENTAL CHANGES IN SELF-DISCLOSING CONVERSATIONS. Self-disclosing conversations with friends increased dramatically in adolescence while declining in an equally dramatic fashion with parents. However, self-disclosing conversations with parents began to pick up somewhat during the college years. The measure of self-disclosure involved a 5-point rating scale completed by the children and youth, with a higher score representing greater self-disclosure. The data shown represent the means for each age group.

clique A small group that ranges from 2 to about 12 individuals, averaging about 5 or 6 individuals, and may form because adolescents engage in similar activities.

What characterizes peer pressure in adolescence?
©Christin Rose/Getty Images RF

Crowds are larger than cliques and less personal. Adolescents are usually members of a crowd based on reputation, and they may or may not spend much time together. Many crowds are defined by the activities adolescents engage in (such as "jocks" who are good at sports or "druggies" who take drugs) (Brown, 2011). Reputation-based crowds often appear for the first time in early adolescence and usually become less prominent in late adolescence (Collins & Steinberg, 2006).

In one study, crowd membership was associated with adolescent self-esteem (Brown & Lohr, 1987). The crowds included jocks (athletically oriented students), populars (well-known students who led social activities), normals (middle-of-the-road students who made up the masses), druggies or toughs (students who are known for illicit drug use or other delinquent activities), and nobodies (students who are low in social skills or intellectual abilities). The self-esteem of the jocks and the populars was highest, whereas that of the nobodies was lowest. One group of adolescents not in a crowd had self-esteem equivalent to that of the jocks and the populars; this group was the independents, who indicated that crowd membership was not important to them. Keep in mind that these data are correlational; self-esteem could increase an adolescent's probability of becoming a crowd member, just as crowd membership could increase the adolescent's self-esteem.

What characterizes adolescents' cliques and crowds?

©Rolf Bruderer/Corbis/Getty Images

crowd A larger group than a clique, one that is usually formed based on reputation; members may or may not spend much time together.

DATING AND ROMANTIC RELATIONSHIPS

Adolescents spend considerable time either dating or thinking about dating (Davila, Capaldi, & La Greca, 2016; Furman & Rose, 2015; Lantagne & Furman, 2017). Dating can be a form of recreation, a source of status, and a setting for learning about close relationships, as well as a way of finding a mate.

Types of Dating and Developmental Changes   A number of dating variations and developmental changes characterize dating and romantic relationships. First, we examine heterosexual romantic relationships, and then we turn to romantic relationships among sexual minority youth (gay and lesbian adolescents).

Heterosexual Romantic Relationships   Three stages characterize the development of romantic relationships in adolescence (Connolly & McIsaac, 2009):

- *Entering into romantic attractions and affiliations at about 11 to 13 years of age.* This initial stage is triggered by puberty. From 11 to 13, adolescents become intensely interested in romance, and it dominates many conversations with same-sex friends. Developing a crush on someone is common, and the crush often is shared with a same-sex friend. Young adolescents may or may not interact with the individual who is the object of their infatuation. When dating occurs, it usually occurs in a group setting.

- *Exploring romantic relationships at approximately 14 to 16 years of age.* At this point in adolescence, two types of romantic involvement occur: casual dating and group dating. *Casual dating* emerges between individuals who are mutually attracted. These dating experiences are often short-lived, last a few months at best, and usually endure for only a few weeks. Dating in groups is common and reflects embeddedness in the peer context. Friends often act as a third-party facilitator of a potential dating relationship by communicating their friend's romantic interest and determining whether this attraction is reciprocated.

- *Consolidating dyadic romantic bonds at about 17 to 19 years of age.* At the end of the high school years, more serious romantic relationships develop. This is characterized by strong emotional bonds more

What are some developmental changes in romantic relationships in adolescence?

©Digital Vision/Getty Images RF

closely resembling those in adult romantic relationships. These bonds often are more stable and enduring than earlier bonds, typically lasting one year or more.

Two variations on these stages in the development of romantic relationships in adolescence involve early and late bloomers (Connolly & McIsaac, 2009). *Early bloomers* include 15 to 20 percent of 11- to 13-year-olds who say that they currently are in a romantic relationship and 35 percent who indicate that they have had some prior experience in romantic relationships. A recent study found that early bloomers externalized problem behaviors through adolescence to a greater extent than their on-time and late-bloomer counterparts (Connolly & others, 2013). *Late bloomers* comprise approximately 10 percent of 17- to 19-year-olds who say that they have had no experience with romantic relationships and another 15 percent who report that they have not engaged in any romantic relationships that lasted more than four months.

Romantic Relationships in Sexual Minority Youth Recently, researchers have begun to study romantic relationships in gay and lesbian youth (Savin-Williams, 2016, 2017). Many sexual minority youth date other-sex peers, a practice that can help them to clarify their sexual orientation or disguise it from others. Most gay and lesbian youth have had some same-sex sexual experience, often with peers who are "experimenting," and then go on to a primarily heterosexual orientation (Savin-Williams, 2016); however, relatively few gay and lesbian youth have had same-sex romantic relationships.

What characterizes romantic relationships in sexual minority youth?
©Pinto/Corbis/Getty Images

Sociocultural Contexts and Dating The sociocultural context exerts a powerful influence on adolescents' dating patterns (Yoon & others, 2017). This influence may be seen in differences in dating patterns among ethnic groups within the United States.

Values, religious beliefs, and traditions often dictate at what age dating begins, how much freedom in dating is allowed, whether dates must be chaperoned by adults or parents, and the roles of males and females in dating. For example, Latino and Asian American cultures have more conservative standards regarding adolescent dating than does the Anglo-American culture. Dating may become a source of conflict within a family if the parents have immigrated from cultures in which dating begins at a late age, little freedom in dating is allowed, dates are chaperoned, and dating by adolescent girls is especially restricted. When immigrant adolescents choose to adopt the ways of the dominant U.S. culture (such as unchaperoned dating), they often clash with parents and extended-family members who have more traditional values.

In one study, Latina young adults in the midwestern United States reflected on their experiences in dating during adolescence (Raffaelli & Ontai, 2004). They said that their parents placed strict boundaries on their romantic involvement. As a result, the young women said that their adolescent dating experiences were filled with tension and conflict. Over half of the Latinas engaged in "sneak dating" without their parents' knowledge. Also, a recent study found that mother-daughter conflict in Mexican American families was linked to an increase in daughters' romantic involvement (Tyrell & others, 2016).

Dating and Adjustment Researchers have linked dating and romantic relationships with how well adjusted adolescents are (Davila, Capaldi, & La Greca, 2016; Moosmann & Roosa, 2015; Soller, 2014). For example, a study of 200 tenth-graders revealed that the greater the number of romantic experiences they had, the higher were their reported levels of social acceptance, friendship competence, and romantic competence—however, having more romantic experience also was linked to a higher level of substance use, delinquency, and sexual behavior (Furman, Low, & Ho, 2009). In another study, for adolescent girls but not adolescent boys, having an older romantic partner was linked to an increase in depressive symptoms, largely influenced by an increase in substance use (Haydon & Halpern, 2010). However, in some cases, romantic relationships in adolescence are linked with positive developmental changes. For example, in a recent study, having a supportive romantic relationship in adolescence was linked to positive outcomes for adolescents who had a negative relationship with their mother (Szwedo, Hessel, & Allen, 2017). In another study, adolescents who engaged in a higher level of intimate disclosure at age 10 reported a higher level of companionship in

How Would You...?
If you were a **human development and family studies professional,** how would you explain to parents the developmental challenges faced by a gay or lesbian adolescent?

romantic relationships at 12 and 15 years of age (Kochendorfer & Kerns, 2017). In this study, those who reported more conflict in friendships had a lower level of companionship in romantic relationships at 15 years of age.

Dating and romantic relationships at an unusually early age also have been linked with several problems (Furman & Rose, 2015). For example, early dating and "going with" someone are associated with adolescent pregnancy and problems at home and school (Furman & Collins, 2009). In one study, girls' early romantic involvement was linked with lower grades, less active participation in class discussions, and other school-related problems (Buhrmester, 2001).

Recently, romantic attraction has not only taken place in person but also over the Internet. Some critics argue that online romantic relationships lose the interpersonal connection, whereas others emphasize that the Internet may benefit shy or anxious individuals who find it difficult to meet potential partners in person (Holmes, Little, & Welsh, 2009). One problem with online matchmaking is that many individuals misrepresent their characteristics, such as how old they are, how attractive they are, and their occupation. Despite such dishonesty, researchers have found that romantic relationships initiated on the Internet are more likely than relationships established in person to last for more than two years (Bargh & McKenna, 2004).

Connecting Online   Is looking for love online likely to work out? It didn't work out well in 2012 for Notre Dame linebacker Manti Te'o, whose online girlfriend turned out to be a "catfish," someone who fakes an identity online. However, a national study of more than 19,000 individuals found that more than one-third of marriages now begin online (Cacioppo & others, 2013). Also in this study, marriages that began online were slightly less likely to break up and were characterized by slightly higher marital satisfaction than those that started in traditional offline contexts.

Connecting online for love turned out positively for two Columbia University graduate students, Michelle Przybyksi and Andy Lalinde (Steinberg, 2011). They lived several blocks away from each other, so soon after they communicated online through Datemyschool.com, an online dating site exclusively for college students, they met in person, really hit it off, applied for a marriage license 10 days later, and eventually got married.

However, a recent editorial by Samantha Nickalls (2012) in *The Tower,* the student newspaper at Arcadia University in Philadelphia, argued that online dating sites might be okay for people in their thirties and older but not for college students. She commented:

> The dating pool of our age is huge. Huge. After all, marriage is not on most people's minds when they're in college, but dating (or perhaps just hooking up) most certainly is. A college campus, in fact, is like living a dating service because the majority of people are looking for the same thing you are. As long as you put yourself out there, flirt a bit, and be friendly, chances are that people will notice.

(*Left*) Manti Te'o; (*right*) Michelle Przybyksi and Andy Lalinde.

(*Left*): ©John Biever/Sports Illustrated/Getty Images; (*right*): Courtesy of Michelle and Andres Lalinde.

If this doesn't work for you right away, why should it really matter? As a college student, you have so many other huge things going on in your life—your career choice, your transition from kid to adult, your crazy social life. Unless you are looking to get married at age 20 (which is a whole other issue that I could debate for hours), dating shouldn't be the primary thing on your mind anyway. Besides, as the old saying goes, the best things come when you least expect them.

Oftentimes, you find the best dates by accident—not by hunting them down.

What do you think? Is it a good idea to search online for romantic relationships? What are some cautions that need to be taken if you pursue an online romantic relationship?

Review Connect Reflect

LG3 Characterize the changes that occur in peer relations during adolescence.

Review
- What changes take place in friendship during adolescence?
- What are adolescents' peer groups like?
- What is the nature of adolescent dating and romantic relationships?

Connect
- Piece together the information discussed earlier about sexual development in adolescence with the coverage of dating and romantic relationships in this chapter to construct a profile of positive adolescent development.

Reflect *Your Own Personal Journey of Life*
- What were your peer relationships like during adolescence? What peer groups were you involved in? How did they influence your development? What were your dating and romantic relationships like in adolescence? If you could change anything about the way you experienced peer relations in adolescence, what would it be?

4 Why Is Culture an Important Context for Adolescent Development?

LG4 Explain how culture influences adolescent development.

Cross-Cultural Comparisons   Ethnicity   Media and Technology

We live in an increasingly diverse world, one in which there is increasing contact between adolescents from different cultures and ethnic groups. In this section, we explore these differences as they relate to adolescents, and then examine media influences on adolescents.

CROSS-CULTURAL COMPARISONS

What traditions remain for adolescents around the globe? What circumstances are changing adolescents' lives?

Traditions and Changes in Adolescence Around the Globe   Consider some of the variations of adolescence around the world (Brown & Larson, 2002):

- Two-thirds of Asian Indian adolescents accept their parents' choice of a marital partner for them.
- In the Philippines, many female adolescents sacrifice their own futures by migrating to the city to earn money that they send home to their families.
- In the Middle East, many adolescents are not allowed to interact with the other sex, even in school.
- Street youth in Kenya and other parts of the world learn to survive under highly stressful circumstances. In some cases abandoned by their parents, they may engage in delinquency or prostitution to provide for their economic needs.

(a)

(b)

(c)

(*a*) Asian Indian adolescents in a marriage ceremony. (*b*) Muslim school in Middle East with boys only. (*c*) Street youth in Rio de Janeiro.

(a): ©PhotosIndia/age fotostock; (b): ©Yvan Cohen/LightRocket/Getty Images; (c): ©Tom Stoddart/Getty Images.

- Whereas individuals in the United States are marrying later than in past generations, youth in Russia are marrying earlier to legitimize sexual activity.

Thus, depending on the culture being observed, adolescence may involve many different experiences (Jackson, Jiang, & Chen, 2016; Larson, Shernoff, & Bempechat, 2014; Mackinnon & others, 2017; UNICEF, 2017; Verloigne & others, 2016; Vignoles & others, 2016). Some cultures have retained their traditions regarding adolescence, but rapid global change is altering the experience of adolescence in many places, presenting new opportunities and challenges to young people's health and well-being. Around the world, adolescents' experiences may differ significantly.

Gender   The experiences of male and female adolescents in many cultures continue to be quite different (Brown & Larson, 2002; Peitzmeier & others, 2016). Except in a few regions, such as Japan, the Philippines, and Western countries, males have far greater access to educational opportunities than females do (UNICEF, 2017). In many countries, adolescent females have less freedom than males to pursue a variety of careers and engage in various leisure activities. Gender differences in sexual expression are widespread, especially in India, Southeast Asia, Latin America, and Arab countries, where there are far more restrictions on the sexual activity of adolescent females than on that of males. These gender differences do appear to be narrowing over time, however. In some countries, educational and career opportunities for women are expanding, and control over adolescent girls' romantic and sexual relationships is weakening.

Family   In some countries, adolescents grow up in closely knit families with extensive extended-kin networks that retain a traditional way of life. For example, in Arab countries, adolescents are taught strict codes of conduct and loyalty (Brown & Larson, 2002). However, in Western countries such as the United States, parenting is less authoritarian than in the past, and much larger numbers of adolescents are growing up in divorced families and stepfamilies.

In many countries around the world, current trends "include greater family mobility, migration to urban areas, family members working in distant cities or countries, smaller families, fewer extended-family households, and increases in mothers' employment" (Brown & Larson, 2002, p. 7). Unfortunately, many of these changes may reduce the ability of families to spend time with their adolescents.

Peers   Some cultures give peers a stronger role in adolescence than others do (Brown & Larson, 2002). In most Western nations, peers figure prominently in adolescents' lives, in some cases taking on roles that would otherwise be assumed by parents. Among street youth in South America, the peer network serves as a surrogate family that supports survival in dangerous and stressful settings. In other regions of the world, such as in Arab countries, peer relations are restricted, especially for girls (Booth, 2002).

To read about how adolescents around the world spend their time, see the *Connecting with Diversity* interlude.

Rites of Passage   Another variation in the experiences of adolescents in different cultures is whether the adolescents go through a rite of passage. Some societies have elaborate ceremonies that signal the adolescent's move to maturity and achievement of adult status (Miller, 2017). A **rite of passage** is a ceremony or ritual that marks an individual's transition from one status to another. Most rites of passage focus on the transition to adult status. In some traditional cultures, rites of passage are the avenue through which adolescents gain access to sacred adult practices, to knowledge, and to sexuality. These rites often involve dramatic practices intended to facilitate the adolescent's separation from the immediate family, especially the mother. The transformation is usually characterized by some form of ritual death and rebirth, or by contact with the spiritual world. Bonds are forged between the adolescent and the adult instructors through shared rituals, hazards, and secrets to allow the adolescent to enter the adult world. This kind of ritual provides a forceful and discontinuous entry into the adult world at a time when the adolescent is perceived to be ready for the change.

An especially rich tradition of rites of passage for adolescents has prevailed in African cultures, especially sub-Saharan Africa (Scupin & DeCorse, 2017). Under the influence of Western industrialized culture, many of these rites are disappearing today, although they are still prevalent in locations where formal education is not readily available.

How Adolescents Around the World Spend Their Time

Reed Larson and Suman Verma (Larson, 2001; Larson & Verma, 1999) have examined how adolescents spend their time in work, play, and developmental activities such as school. U.S. adolescents spend about 60 percent as much time on schoolwork as East Asian adolescents do, mainly because U.S. adolescents do less homework than East Asians do (Larson & Verma, 1999).

What U.S. adolescents have in greater quantities than do adolescents in other industrialized countries is discretionary time (Larson, McGovern, & Orson, 2018; Larson, Walker, & McGovern, 2018; Larson & Wilson, 2004). About 40 to 50 percent of U.S. adolescents' waking hours (not counting summer vacations) is spent in discretionary activities, compared with 25 to 35 percent in East Asia and 35 to 45 percent in Europe. Whether this additional discretionary time is a liability or an asset for U.S. adolescents, of course, depends on how they use it.

According to Larson (2001), U.S. adolescents may have more unstructured time than is beneficial for their development. Indeed, when adolescents are allowed to choose what to do with their time, they typically engage in unchallenging activities such as hanging out and watching TV. Although relaxation and social interaction are important aspects of adolescence, it seems unlikely that spending large numbers

How do East Asian and U.S. adolescents spend their time differently?
©DragonImages/Getty Images RF

of hours per week in unchallenging activities fosters development. Structured voluntary activities may provide more promise for adolescent development than unstructured time, especially if adults give responsibility to adolescents, challenge them, and provide competent guidance in these activities (Larson & Dawes, 2015; Larson, McGovern, & Orson, 2018; Larson, Orson, & Bowers, 2017; Larson & Walker, 2010; Larson & others, 2009; Larson, Walker, & McGovern, 2018).

Do we have such rites of passage for American adolescents? We certainly do not have universal formal ceremonies that mark the passage from adolescence to adulthood. Certain religious and social groups do, however, have initiation ceremonies that indicate that an advance in maturity has been reached: the Jewish bar and bat mitzvah, the Catholic confirmation, and social debuts, for example. School graduation ceremonies come the closest to being culture-wide rites of passage in the United States. The high school graduation ceremony has become nearly universal for middle-class adolescents and increasing numbers of adolescents from low-income backgrounds.

ETHNICITY

Earlier in this chapter, we explored the identity development of ethnic minority adolescents. Here we further examine immigration and the relationship between ethnicity and socioeconomic status.

Immigration Relatively high rates of immigration are contributing to the growing proportion of ethnic minority adolescents and emerging adults in the United States (Kane & others, 2016; Yoon & others, 2017). Immigrant families are those in which at least one of the parents is born outside of the country of residence. Variations in immigrant families involve whether one or both parents are foreign born, whether the child was born in the host country, and the ages at which immigration took place for both the parents and the children (Kim & others, 2015).

Different models have been proposed as to whether children and adolescents in immigrant families are more vulnerable or more successful in relation to the general population of children and adolescents (Crosnoe & Fuligni, 2012). Historically, an *immigrant risk model* was emphasized, concluding that youth of immigrants had a lower level of well-being and were

These Congolese Kota boys painted their faces as part of the rite of passage to adulthood. *What rites of passage do American adolescents have?*
©Daniel Laine/Gamma Rapho

rite of passage A ceremony or ritual that marks an individual's transition from one status to another. Most rites of passage focus on the transition to adult status.

What are some cultural adaptations that many immigrant adolescents who come to the United States likely need to make?
©Caroline Woodham/Getty Images RF

How Would You...?

If you were an **educator**, how would you modify high school graduation to be a more meaningful rite of passage for adolescents in the United States?

Consider the flowers of a garden: Though differing in kind, color, form, and shape, yet, inasmuch as they are refreshed by the waters of one spring, revived by the breath of one wind, invigorated by the rays of one sun, this diversity increases their charm and adds to their beauty. . . . How unpleasing to the eye if all the flowers and plants, the leaves and blossoms, the fruits, the branches, and the trees of that garden were all of the same shape and color! Diversity of hues, form, and shape enriches and adorns the garden and heightens its effect.

—ABDU'L BAHA
Persian Baha'i Religious Leader, 19th/20th Century

at risk for more problems. For example, one study found that the longer immigrant youth from the Dominican Republic lived in the United States the higher their risk for suicide or suicide attempts (Pena & others, 2012).

More recently, an *immigrant paradox model* has been proposed, emphasizing that despite the many cultural, socioeconomic, language, and other obstacles that immigrant families face, their youth show a higher level of well-being and fewer problems than native-born youth (Garcia Coll & others, 2012). Based on current research, some support exists for each model. As concluded by Robert Crosnoe and Andrew Fuligni (2012, p. 1473):

> Some children from immigrant families are doing quite well, some less so, depending on the characteristics of migration itself (including the nation of origin) and their families' circumstances in their new country (including their position in socioeconomic and race-ethnic stratification systems).

What are some of the circumstances immigrants face that challenge their adjustment? Immigrants often experience stressors uncommon to or less prominent among longtime residents, such as language barriers, dislocations and separations from support networks, the dual struggle to preserve identity and to acculturate, and changes in SES status (Chaudry & others, 2017; Kao & Huang, 2015). In a recent study comparing Asian, Latino, and non-Latino White immigrant adolescents, immigrant Asian adolescents had the highest level of depression, the lowest self-esteem, and were the most likely to report experiencing discrimination (Lo & others, 2017).

Many individuals in immigrant families are dealing with the problem of being undocumented. Living in an undocumented family can affect children's and adolescents' developmental outcomes through parents being unwilling to sign up for services for which they may be eligible, through conditions linked to low-wage work and lack of benefits, through stress, and through a lack of cognitive stimulation in the home (Yoshikawa & others, 2016, 2017). Consequently, when working with adolescents and their immigrant families, counselors need to adapt intervention programs to optimize cultural sensitivity (Gonzales & others, 2016; Sue, Sue, & Sue, 2017).

The ways in which ethnic minority families deal with stress depend on many factors (Spencer & Swanson, 2016). Whether the parents are native-born or immigrants, how long the family has been in the United States, its socioeconomic status, and its national origin all make a difference. One study revealed that parents' education before migrating was strongly linked to their children's academic achievement (Pong & Landale, 2012). Another study found that first-generation immigrant adolescents had more internalizing problems (anxiety and depression, for example) than second-generation immigrants did (Katsiaficas & others, 2013).

Ethnicity and Socioeconomic Status   Too often the research on ethnic minority adolescents has failed to tease apart the influences of ethnicity and socioeconomic status. These two factors can interact in ways that exaggerate the influence of ethnicity because ethnic minority individuals are overrepresented in the lower socioeconomic levels of American society (Golnick & Chinn, 2017). Consequently, researchers too often have given ethnic explanations for aspects of adolescent development that were largely due instead to socioeconomic status.

Not all ethnic minority families are poor. However, poverty contributes to the stressful life experiences of many ethnic minority adolescents (Gonzales & others, 2016). Thus, many ethnic minority adolescents experience a double disadvantage: (1) prejudice, discrimination, and bias because of their ethnic minority status; and (2) the stressful effects of poverty (Golnick & Chinn, 2017; Koppelman, 2017).

Jason Leonard, age 15: "I want America to know that most of us black teens are not troubled people from broken homes and headed to jail. . . . In my relationships with my parents, we show respect for each other and we have values in our house. We have traditions we celebrate together, including Christmas and Kwanzaa."
©Comstock/Getty Images RF

MEDIA AND TECHNOLOGY

Earlier, we discussed the role of television in children's development. Here we examine changes in TV watching from childhood to adolescence and the dramatically increasing influence of a number of other media in adolescence.

Media Use   If the amount of time spent in an activity is any indication of its importance, there is no doubt that media play important roles in adolescents' lives (Calvert, 2015; Lever-Duffy & McDonald, 2018; Maloy & others, 2017). To better understand various aspects of U.S. adolescents' media use, the Kaiser Family Foundation funded national surveys in 1999, 2004, and 2009. The 2009 survey included more than 2,000 young people 8 to 18 years old and documented that adolescent media use has increased dramatically in the last decade (Rideout, Foehr, & Roberts, 2010). Today's youth live in a world in which they are encapsulated by media. In this survey, in 2009, 8- to 10-year-olds used media 5 hours and 29 minutes a day, but 11- to 14-year-olds used media an average of 8 hours and 40 minutes a day, and 15- to 18-year-olds an average of 7 hours and 58 minutes a day (see Figure 5). Thus, media use jumps more than 3 hours per day in early adolescence! The largest increase in media use in early adolescence comprises TV viewing and video game playing. TV use by youth increasingly has involved watching TV on the Internet, on an iPod/MP3 player, or on a cell phone. As indicated in Figure 5, listening to music and using computers also increase considerably in 11- to 14-year-old adolescents. And in the 2009 survey, adding up the daily media use figures to obtain weekly media use leads to the staggering levels of more than 60 hours a week of media use by 11- to 14-year-olds and almost 56 hours a week by 15- to 18-year-olds!

A major trend in the use of technology is the dramatic increase in media multitasking (Calvert, 2015; Lever-Duffy & McDonald, 2018; Maloy & others, 2017). In the 2009 survey, when the amount of time spent multitasking was included in computing total media use, 11- to 14-year-olds spent nearly 12 hours a day (compared with almost 9 hours a day when multitasking was not included) exposed to media (Rideout, Foehr, & Roberts, 2010)! In this survey, 39 percent of seventh- to twelfth-graders said "most of the time" they use two or more media concurrently, such as surfing the Web while listening to music. In some cases, media multitasking—such as text messaging, listening to an iPod, and updating a YouTube site—is engaged in at the same time as doing homework. It is hard to imagine that this allows a student to do homework efficiently.

Consider the following recent studies that involve media multitasking:

- Heavy multimedia multitaskers were less likely than light media multitaskers to delay gratification and more likely to endorse intuitive, but wrong, answers on a cognitive reflection task (Schutten, Stokes, & Arnell, 2017).

- In a recent research review, a higher level of media multitasking was linked to lower levels of school achievement, executive function, and growth mindset in adolescents (Cain & others, 2016).

- For 8- to 12-year-old girls, a higher level of media multitasking was linked to negative social well-being, while a higher level of face-to-face communication was associated with positive social-well-being indicators, such as greater social success, feeling more normal, and having fewer friends whom parents thought were a bad influence (Pea & others, 2012).

- Heavy media multitaskers were more likely to be depressed and have social anxiety than their counterparts who engaged in a lower incidence of media multitasking (Becker, Alzahabi, & Hopwood, 2013).

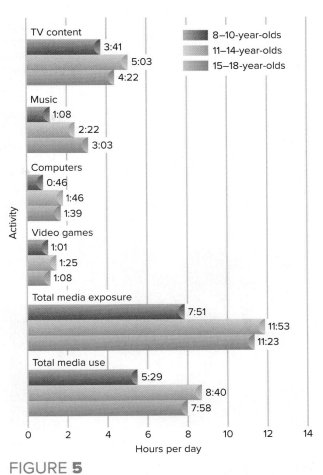

FIGURE 5

DEVELOPMENTAL CHANGES IN THE AMOUNT OF TIME U.S. 8- TO 18-YEAR-OLDS SPEND WITH DIFFERENT TYPES OF MEDIA

How much time do adolescents spend using different types of media?
© Antonio Guillem/Shutterstock RF

Technology and Digitally Mediated Communication   Culture involves change, and nowhere is that change more apparent than in the technological revolution individuals are experiencing with increased use of computers and the Internet (Lever-Duffy & McDonald, 2018; Maloy & others, 2017; Smaldino & others, 2015). Society still relies on some basic nontechnological competencies—for example, good communication skills, positive attitudes, and the ability to solve problems and to think deeply and creatively. But how people pursue these competencies is changing in ways and at a speed that few people had to cope with in previous eras. For youth to be adequately prepared for tomorrow's jobs, technology needs to become an integral part of their lives.

Mobile media, such as cell phones and iPads, are mainly driving the increased media use by adolescents. For example, in 2004, 39 percent of U.S. adolescents owned a cell phone, a figure that had jumped to 66 percent in 2009 and then to 87 percent in 2016, with a prediction of 92 percent by 2019 (eMarketeer.com, 2016; Rideout, Foehr, & Roberts, 2010).

A recent national survey revealed dramatic increases in adolescents' use of social media and text messaging (Lenhart, 2015a). In 2015, 92 percent of U.S. 13- to 17-year-olds reported using social networking sites daily. Twenty-four percent of the adolescents said they go online almost constantly. Much of this increase in going online has been fueled by smartphones and mobile devices. Facebook is the most popular and frequently used social networking site—71 percent reported using Facebook and half said they use Instagram. A recent study found that less screen time was linked to adolescents' better health-related quality of life (Wong & others, 2017). Another recent study indicated that a higher level of social media use was associated with a higher level of heavy drinking by adolescents (Brunborg, Andreas, & Kvaavik, 2017).

Text messaging has become the main way that adolescents connect with their friends, surpassing face-to-face contact, e-mail, instant messaging, and voice calling (Lenhart, 2015; Lenhart & others, 2015). In the national survey and a further update (Lenhart & others, 2015), daily text

What characterizes the online social environment of adolescents and emerging adults?
©Digital Vision/Alamy RF

messaging increased from 38 percent who texted friends daily in 2008 to 55 percent in 2015. However, voice mail was the primary way that most adolescents preferred to connect with parents.

Clearly, parents need to monitor and regulate adolescents' use of the Internet (Padilla-Walker, Coyne, & Collier, 2016). Consider Bonita Williams, who began to worry about how obsessed her 15-year-old daughter, Jade, had become with MySpace (Kornblum, 2006). She became even more concerned when she discovered that Jade was posting suggestive photos of herself and had given her cell phone number to people in different parts of the United States. Bonita grounded her daughter, blocked MySpace at home, and moved Jade's computer from her bedroom to the family room.

Review Connect Reflect

LG4 Explain how culture influences adolescent development.

Review

- What are some differences in the lives of adolescents in various cultures? How do adolescents around the world spend their time? What are some examples of rites of passage?
- How does ethnicity influence adolescent development?
- What characterizes adolescents' use of media and technology?

Connect

- How do ethnicity and poverty influence children's development?

Reflect *Your Own Personal Journey of Life*

- What is your ethnicity? Have you ever been stereotyped because of your ethnicity? In what ways is your ethnic identity similar to or different from the mainstream culture?

5 What Are Some Socioemotional Problems in Adolescence?

LG5 Identify adolescent problems in socioemotional development and strategies for helping adolescents with problems.

| Juvenile Delinquency | Depression and Suicide | The Interrelation of Problems and Successful Prevention/Intervention Programs |

Earlier, we described several adolescent problems: substance abuse, sexually transmitted infections, and eating disorders. In this chapter, we examine the problems of juvenile delinquency, depression, and suicide. We also explore interrelationships among adolescent problems and describe how such problems can be prevented or remedied.

JUVENILE DELINQUENCY

The label **juvenile delinquent** is applied to an adolescent who breaks the law or engages in behavior that is considered illegal. Like other categories of disorders, juvenile delinquency is a broad concept, encompassing legal infractions that range from littering to murder. For both male and female delinquents, rates for property offenses are higher than rates for other offenses (such as offenses against persons, drug offenses, and public order offenses). Arrest rates of adolescent males for delinquency continue to be much higher than arrest rates among adolescent females (Puzzanchera & Robson, 2014).

One issue in juvenile justice is whether an adolescent who commits a crime should be tried as an adult (Cauffman & others, 2015; Fine & others, 2017a, b, c). Some psychologists have proposed that individuals 12 and under should not be evaluated under adult criminal laws and that those 17 and older should be (Cauffman & others, 2015; Fine & others, 2017a, b, c; Shulman & Steinberg, 2015). They also recommend that individuals 13 to 16 years of age be given some type of individualized assessment to determine whether they will be tried in a juvenile court or an adult criminal court. This framework argues strongly against court placement based solely on the nature of an offense and takes into account the offender's developmental maturity. The Society for Adolescent Medicine has argued that the death penalty should not be used with adolescents.

A distinction is made between early-onset—before age 11—and late-onset—after 11—antisocial behavior of minors. Early-onset antisocial behavior is associated with more negative developmental outcomes than late-onset antisocial behavior (Schulenberg & Zarrett, 2006). Early-onset antisocial behavior is more likely to persist into emerging adulthood and is more frequently associated with mental health and relationship problems than is late-onset antisocial behavior (Burke, 2011; Burke & Loeber, 2015; Loeber & Burke, 2011; Pechorro & others, 2014).

Causes of Delinquency What causes delinquency? Although delinquency is less exclusively a phenomenon of lower socioeconomic status (SES) than it was in the past, some characteristics of lower-SES culture might promote delinquency (Dawson-McClure & others, 2015; Macionis, 2017). A recent study of more than 10,000 children and adolescents found that having a family environment characterized by poverty and child maltreatment was linked to entering the juvenile justice system in adolescence (Vidal & others, 2017). The norms of many lower-SES peer groups and gangs are antisocial, or counterproductive, to the goals and norms of society at large. Getting into and staying out of trouble are prominent features of life for some adolescents in low-income neighborhoods. Also, adolescents in communities with high crime rates observe many models who engage in criminal activities (Loeber & Burke, 2011). These communities may be characterized by poverty, unemployment, and feelings of alienation toward the middle class (Henslin, 2017). Quality schooling, educational funding, and organized neighborhood activities may be lacking in these communities (Crosnoe & Leventhal, 2014). One study revealed that engaged parenting and mothers' social network support were linked to a lower level of delinquency in low-income families (Ghazarian & Roche, 2010). And

juvenile delinquent An adolescent who breaks the law or engages in behavior that is considered illegal.

What are some factors that are linked to whether adolescents engage in delinquent acts?
©Bill Aron/PhotoEdit

another study found that youth whose families had experienced repeated poverty were more than twice as likely to be delinquent at 14 and 21 years of age (Najman & others, 2010).

Certain characteristics of family support systems are also associated with delinquency (Dishion & Patterson, 2016; Evans, Simon, & Simon, 2016; Ray & others, 2017). Parental monitoring of adolescents is especially important in determining whether an adolescent becomes a delinquent (Bendezu & others, 2017). Also, a recent study found that for both African American and non-Latino White youth, low parental control predicted delinquency, indirectly through its link to deviant peer affiliation (Deutsch & others, 2012). Further, in one study, authoritative parenting increased adolescents' perception of the legitimacy of parents' authority, while authoritarian parenting reduced the perception of legitimacy of parental authority (Trinkner & others, 2012). In this study, youths' perception of the legitimacy of parental authority was linked to a lower level of future delinquency. And another study found that low rates of delinquency from 14 to 23 years of age were associated with an authoritative parenting style (Murphy & others, 2012).

Family discord and inconsistent and inappropriate discipline are also associated with delinquency (Dishion & Patterson, 2016). Further, recent research indicates that family therapy is often effective in reducing delinquency (Baldwin & others, 2012; Darnell & Schuler, 2015). A meta-analysis found that of five program types (case management, individual treatment, youth court, restorative justice, and family treatment), family treatment was the only one that was linked to reduced recidivism among juvenile offenders (Schwalbe & others, 2012). Also, in a recent study, family therapy improved juvenile court outcomes beyond what was achieved in non-family-based treatment, especially in reducing criminal behavior and rearrests (Dakof & others, 2015).

Siblings also can influence delinquency (Tucker & others, 2015). In one study, high levels of hostile sibling relationships and older sibling delinquency were linked with younger sibling delinquency in both brother and sister pairs (Slomkowski & others, 2001). Peer relations also can influence delinquency (Dong & Krohn, 2016; Ray & others, 2017). Adolescents who begin to hang out with delinquent peers are more likely to become delinquent themselves (Yu & others, 2013).

Lack of academic success is associated with delinquency (Mercer & others, 2016). And a number of cognitive factors such as low self-control, low intelligence, and lack of sustained attention are linked to delinquency (Fine & others, 2017c). Further, recent research indicates that having callous-unemotional personality traits predicts an increased risk of engaging in delinquency for adolescent males (Ray & others, 2017).

One individual whose goal is to help at-risk adolescents, such as juvenile delinquents, cope more effectively with their lives is Rodney Hammond. Read about his work in the *Connecting with Careers* profile.

DEPRESSION AND SUICIDE

What is the nature of depression in adolescence? What causes an adolescent to commit suicide?

Depression   Depression is more likely to occur in adolescence than in childhood and more likely to occur in adulthood than adolescence. Researchers have found a linear increase in major depressive disorder from 15 to 22 years of age (Kessler & Waters, 1988). However, an early onset of a mood disorder, such as major depressive disorder in adolescence, is linked with more negative outcomes than late onset of a mood disorder (Schulenberg & Zarrett, 2006). For example, the early onset is associated with further recurrences of depression and with an increased risk of being diagnosed with an anxiety disorder, substance abuse, eating disorder, suicide attempt, and unemployment at a future point in development (Graber, 2004).

How serious a problem is depression in adolescence? Rates of ever experiencing a major depressive disorder range from 1.5 to 2.5 percent in school-age children and 15 to 20 percent for adolescents (Graber & Sontag, 2009). Adolescents who are experiencing a high level of stress and/or a loss of some type are at increased risk for developing depression (Rice & others, 2017). Also, a recent study found that adolescents who became depressed were characterized by a sense of hopelessness (Weersing & others, 2016).

Adolescent females are far more likely to develop depression than are their male counterparts. In a recent study, at 12 years of age, 5.2 percent of females and 2 percent of males had experienced first-onset depression (Breslau & others, 2017). In this study, the cumulative incidence of depression from 12 to 17 years of age was 36 percent for females and 14 percent

How Would You...?
If you were a **psychologist**, how would you seek to lower the risk of juvenile delinquency?

What are some characteristics of adolescents who become depressed? What are some factors that are linked with suicide attempts by adolescents?
©Science Photo Library/age fotostock RF

Rodney Hammond, Health Psychologist

In describing his college experiences, Rodney Hammond said, "When I started as an undergraduate at the University of Illinois, Champaign-Urbana, I hadn't decided on my major. But to help finance my education, I took a part-time job in a child development research program sponsored by the psychology department. There, I observed inner-city children in settings designed to enhance their learning. I saw firsthand the contribution psychology can make, and I knew I wanted to be a psychologist" (American Psychological Association, 2003, p. 26).

Rodney Hammond went on to obtain a doctorate in school and community psychology with a focus on children's development. For a number of years, he trained clinical psychologists at Wright State University in Ohio and directed a program to reduce violence in ethnic minority youth. Hammond and his associates taught at-risk youth how to use social skills to effectively manage conflict and how to recognize situations that could lead to violence. Hammond became the first Director of the Division of Violence Prevention at the Centers for Disease Control and Prevention in Atlanta. He is currently Adjunct Professor of Human Development and Counseling at the University of Georgia, following his retirement from CDC.

Rodney Hammond counsels an adolescent girl about the risks of adolescence and how to effectively cope with them.

Courtesy of Dr. Rodney Hammond

for males. Among the reasons for this gender difference are that females tend to ruminate in their depressed mood and amplify it; females' self-images, especially their body images, are more negative than males'; females face more discrimination than males do; and puberty occurs earlier for girls than for boys (Kouros, Morris, & Garber, 2016). As a result, girls experience a confluence of changes and life experiences in the middle school years that can increase depression (Chen & others, 2015).

Do gender differences in adolescent depression hold for other cultures? In many cultures the gender difference of females experiencing more depression does hold, but a study of more than 17,000 Chinese 11- to 22-year-olds revealed that the male adolescents and emerging adults experienced more depression than their female counterparts did (Sun & others, 2010). Explanations of the higher rates of depression among males in China focused on stressful life events and a less positive coping style.

Is adolescent depression linked to problems in emerging and early adulthood? A recent study initially assessed U.S. adolescents when they were 16 to 17 years of age and then again every two years until they were 26 to 27 years of age (Naicker & others, 2013). In this study, significant effects that persisted after 10 years were depression recurrence, stronger depressive symptoms, migraine headaches, poor self-rated health, and low levels of social support. Adolescent depression was not associated with employment status, personal income, marital status, and educational attainment a decade later. In another longitudinal study involving individuals from 14 to 24 years of age, mild to moderate levels of early adolescent depressive behaviors were linked to lower maternal relationship quality, less positive romantic relationships, and greater loneliness in emerging adulthood (Allen & others, 2014).

Certain family factors place adolescents at increased risk for depression (Kelly & others, 2016; Olino & others, 2016). These include having a depressed parent, emotionally unavailable parents, parents with high marital conflict, and parents with financial problems. A recent study revealed that mother-daughter co-rumination (extensively discussing, rehashing, and speculating about problems) was linked to increased anxiety and depression in adolescent daughters (Waller & Rose, 2010). Another study found that exposure to maternal depression by age 12 predicted risk processes during development (higher stress and difficulties in family relationships), which set the course for the development of the adolescent's depression

(Garber & Cole, 2010). Also, a recent study found that positive parenting characteristics such as emotional and educational support were associated with less depression in adolescents (Smokowski & others, 2015).

Poor peer relationships also are associated with adolescent depression (Stewart & others, 2017). A recent study found that adolescents who were isolated from their peers and whose caregivers emotionally neglected them were at significant risk for developing depression (Christ, Kwak, & Lu, 2017). Not having a close relationship with a best friend, having less contact with friends, and being rejected by peers increase depressive tendencies in adolescents (Platt & others, 2013; Vernberg, 1990). A recent study revealed that adolescent bullies, victims, and bully-victims, as well as victims of cyberbullying, had higher rates of depression than adolescents not involved in bullying (Wang, Nansel, & Iannotti, 2011). Problems in adolescent romantic relationships also can trigger depression (Steinberg & Davila, 2008).

Friendship often provides social support. One study found that friendship prevented an increase in depressive symptoms in adolescents who had avoided peer relations or been excluded from them as children (Bukowski, Laursen, & Hoza, 2010). However, a study of third- through ninth-graders revealed that one aspect of social support in friendship may have costs as well as benefits (Rose, Carlson, & Waller, 2007). In the study, girls' co-rumination predicted not only an increase in positive friendship quality but also an increase in further co-rumination as well as an increase in depressive and anxiety symptoms. However, for boys, co-rumination predicted only an increase in positive friendship quality and no increase in depressive and anxiety symptoms. One implication of the research is that some girls who are vulnerable to developing internalized problems may go undetected because they have supportive friendships.

A recent meta-analysis found that adolescent females who are obese were more likely to have depression (Quek & others, 2017). Stress involving weight-related concerns is increasingly thought to contribute to the greater incidence of depression in adolescent girls than in adolescent boys (Rankin & others, 2016). One study revealed that one explanation for adolescent girls' higher level of depressive symptoms is a heightened tendency to perceive oneself as overweight and to diet (Vaughan & Halpern, 2010).

What type of treatment is most effective in reducing depression in adolescence? A research review concluded that treatment of adolescent depression needs to take into account the severity of the depression, suicidal tendencies, and social factors (Clark, Jansen, & Cloy, 2012). In this review, cognitive behavioral therapy and interpersonal therapy were recommended for adolescents with mild depression and in combination with drug therapy for adolescents experiencing moderate or severe depression. However, caution needs to be exercised when prescribing antidepressants, such as Prozac (fluoxetine) for adolescents, and in 2004 the U.S. Food and Drug Administration assigned warnings to such drugs stating that they slightly increase the risk of suicidal behavior in adolescents. However, a recent research review concluded that Prozac and other SSRIs (selective serotonin reuptake inhibitors) show clinical benefits for adolescents at risk for moderate and severe depression (Cousins & Goodyer, 2015).

Suicide Suicidal behavior is rare in childhood but escalates in adolescence and then increases further in emerging adulthood (Park & others, 2006). Suicide is the third leading cause of death in 10- to 19-year-olds today in the United States (National Center for Health Statistics, 2017). Emerging adults have triple the rate of suicide of adolescents (Park & others, 2006).

Although a suicide threat should always be taken seriously, far more adolescents contemplate or attempt it unsuccessfully than actually commit it (Castellvi & others, 2017). A recent national study found that in the last two decades there has been a considerable decline in the percentage of adolescents who think seriously about committing suicide, although from 2009 to 2015 this percentage increased from 14 to 18 percent (Kann & others, 2016a). In this study, in 2015, 8.6 percent attempted suicide and 2.8 percent engaged in suicide attempts that required medical attention.

Females are more likely to attempt suicide than males, but males are more likely to succeed in committing suicide (Hamilton & Klimes-Dougan, 2015). Males use more lethal means, such as guns, in their suicide attempts, whereas adolescent females are more likely to cut their wrists or take an overdose of sleeping pills—methods less likely to result in death.

Both early and later experiences may be involved in suicide attempts (Bjorkenstam, Kosidou, & Bjorkenstam, 2017). The adolescent might have a long-standing history of family instability and unhappiness. Lack of affection and emotional support, high control, and pressure for achievement by parents during childhood are likely to show up as factors in suicide attempts.

Adolescents who have experienced abuse also are at risk for suicidal ideation and attempts. For example, in a recent study, child maltreatment was linked to adolescent suicide attempts (Hadland & others, 2015). Further, in two recent studies, maltreatment during the childhood years was linked with suicide attempts in adulthood (Park, 2017; Turner & others, 2017). Family relationships can be involved in adolescent suicide (J. D. King & others, 2017). For example, a recent study revealed that adolescents who engaged in suicidal ideation perceived their family functioning to be significantly worse than did their caregivers (Lipschitz & others, 2012). Another recent study found that family discord and negative relationships with parents were associated with increased suicide attempts by depressed adolescents (Consoli & others, 2013). Further, a recent study indicated that adolescents who were being treated in a suicide clinic experienced lower family cohesion than nonclinical adolescents and adolescents being treated at a general psychiatric clinic (Jakobsen, Larsen, & Horwood, 2017).

Recent and current stressful circumstances, such as getting poor grades in school or experiencing the breakup of a romantic relationship, may trigger suicide attempts (Antai-Otong, 2003; Im, Oh, & Suk, 2017; Thompson & others, 2012). Peer victimization is linked to adolescent suicide (Barzilay & others, 2017; Stewart & others, 2017). For example, a recent study found that peer victimization was linked to suicidal ideation and suicide attempts, with cyberbullying more strongly associated with suicidal ideation than traditional bullying (van Geel, Vedder, & Tanilon, 2014). By contrast, higher levels of school connectedness were associated with decreased suicidal ideation in female and male adolescents and with lower rates of suicide attempts in female adolescents (Langille & others, 2015). Another study revealed that playing sports predicted lower suicidal ideation in boys and venting by talking to others was associated with lower suicidal ideation in girls (Kim & others, 2014).

Cultural contexts also are linked to suicide attempts, and adolescent suicide attempts vary across ethnic groups in the United States. As indicated in Figure 6, more than 20 percent of Native American/Alaska Native (NA/AN) female adolescents reported that they had attempted suicide in the previous year, and suicide accounts for almost 20 percent of NA/AN deaths in 15- to 19-year-olds (Goldston & others, 2008). African American and non-Latino White males reported the lowest incidence of suicide attempts. A major risk factor in the high rate of suicide attempts by NA/AN adolescents is their elevated rate of alcohol abuse.

Just as genetic factors are associated with depression, they also are associated with suicide (De la Cruz-Cano, 2017; Rao & others, 2017). The closer a person's genetic relationship is to someone who has committed suicide, the more likely that person is to commit suicide.

What is the psychological profile of the suicidal adolescent? Suicidal adolescents often have depressive symptoms (Thompson & Swartout, 2017). Although not all depressed adolescents are suicidal, depression is the most frequently cited factor associated with adolescent suicide (du Roscoat & others, 2016). A recent study also found that both depression and hopelessness were predictors of whether adolescents repeated a suicide attempt over a six-month period (Consoli & others, 2015). In another recent study, the most significant factor in a first suicide attempt during adolescence was a major depressive episode, while for children it was child maltreatment (Peyre & others, 2017). A sense of hopelessness, low self-esteem, and high self-blame also are associated with adolescent suicide (Chang, 2017; O'Donnell & others, 2004).

How Would You...?
If you were a **psychologist**, how would you talk with someone who has just threatened suicide?

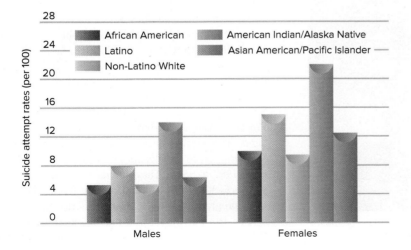

FIGURE 6

SUICIDE ATTEMPTS BY U.S. ADOLESCENTS FROM DIFFERENT ETHNIC GROUPS.
Note: Data shown are for one-year rates of self-reported suicide attempts (Goldston & others, 2008).

THE INTERRELATION OF PROBLEMS AND SUCCESSFUL PREVENTION/INTERVENTION PROGRAMS

Earlier, we discussed many adolescent problems: substance abuse; juvenile delinquency; school-related problems, such as dropping out of high school; adolescent pregnancy and sexually transmitted infections; eating disorders; depression; and suicide. The four problems that affect the most adolescents are (1) drug abuse, (2) juvenile delinquency, (3) sexual problems, and (4) school-related problems (Dryfoos, 1990; Dryfoos & Barkin, 2006). The adolescents most at risk have more than one of these problems. Researchers are increasingly finding that problem behaviors in adolescence are interrelated (Feldstein Ewing & others, 2016). For example, heavy substance abuse is related to early sexual activity, lower grades, dropping out of school, and delinquency (Swartzendruber & others, 2016). Early initiation of sexual activity is associated with the use of cigarettes and alcohol, use of marijuana and other illicit drugs, lower grades, dropping out of school, and delinquency (Chan & others, 2015). Delinquency is related to early sexual activity, early pregnancy, substance abuse, and dropping out of school (Liddon & others, 2016). As much as 10 percent of the adolescent population in the United States have serious multiple-problem behaviors (adolescents who have dropped out of school, or are behind in their grade level, are users of heavy drugs, regularly use cigarettes and marijuana, and are sexually active but do not use contraception). Many, but not all, of these very high-risk youth "do it all." In 1990, it was estimated that another 15 percent of adolescents participate in many of these same behaviors but with slightly lower frequency and less deleterious consequences (Dryfoos, 1990). These high-risk youth often engage in two or three problem behaviors (Dryfoos, 1990). In 2005 it was estimated that the proportion of high-risk youth had increased to 20 percent of all U.S. adolescents (Dryfoos & Barkin, 2006).

A review of the programs that have been successful in preventing or reducing adolescent problems found the following common components (Dryfoos, 1990; Dryfoos & Barkin, 2006):

1. *Intensive individualized attention.* In successful programs, high-risk adolescents are attached to a responsible adult who gives the adolescent attention and deals with the adolescent's specific needs. This theme occurs in a number of programs. In a successful substance-abuse program, a student assistance counselor is available full-time for individual counseling and referral for treatment.

2. *Community-wide multiagency collaborative approaches.* The basic philosophy of community-wide programs is that a number of different programs and services have to be in place. In one successful substance-abuse program, a community-wide health promotion campaign has been implemented that uses local media and community education, in concert with a substance-abuse curriculum in the schools.

3. *Early identification and intervention.* Reaching younger children and their families before children develop problems, or at the beginning of their problems, is a successful strategy (Almy & Cicchetti, 2018; Cicchetti, 2017). One preschool program served as an excellent model for the prevention of delinquency, pregnancy, substance abuse, and dropping out of school. Operated by the High/Scope Foundation in Ypsilanti, Michigan, the Perry Preschool had a long-term positive impact on its students. This enrichment program, directed by David Weikart, served disadvantaged African American children from 1962 to 1967. They attended a high-quality two-year preschool program and receive weekly home visits from program personnel. Based on official police records, by age 19, individuals who had attended the Perry Preschool program were less likely to have been arrested

What are some strategies for preventing and intervening in adolescent problems?
©Image Source/Alamy RF

Fast Track

A program that attempts to lower the risk of juvenile delinquency and other problems is Fast Track (Conduct Problems Prevention Research Group, 2007, 2010, 2011, 2013, 2016; Dodge, Godwin, & Conduct Problems Prevention Research Group, 2013; Dodge & McCourt, 2010; Jones & others, 2010; K. M. King & others, 2017; Miller & others, 2010; Sorensen, Dodge, & Conduct Problems Prevention Research Group, 2016; Zheng & others, 2017). Schools in four areas (Durham, North Carolina; Nashville, Tennessee; Seattle, Washington; and rural central Pennsylvania) were identified as high-risk based on neighborhood crime and poverty data. Researchers screened more than 9,000 kindergarten children in the four schools and randomly assigned 891 of the highest-risk and moderate-risk children to intervention or control conditions. The average age of the children when the intervention began was 6.5 years of age. The 10-year intervention consisted of behavior management training of parents, social cognitive skills training of children, reading tutoring, home visitations, mentoring, and a revised classroom curriculum that was designed to increase socioemotional competence and decrease aggression.

The extensive intervention was most successful for children and adolescents who were identified as the highest risk in kindergarten, lowering their incidence of conduct disorder, attention deficit hyperactivity disorder, any externalized disorder, and antisocial behavior.

Positive outcomes for the intervention occurred as early as the third grade and continued through the ninth grade. For example, in the ninth grade the intervention reduced the likelihood that the highest-risk kindergarten children would develop conduct disorder by 75 percent, attention deficit hyperactivity disorder by 53 percent, and any externalized disorder by 43 percent. Data have been reported through age 19 (Miller & others, 2010). Findings indicate that the comprehensive Fast Track intervention was successful in reducing youth arrest rates (Conduct Problems Prevention Research Group, 2010). Also, one study found that the intervention's impact on adolescents' antisocial behavior was linked to three social cognitive processes: reducing hostile-attribution biases, improving responses to social problems, and devaluing aggression (Dodge, Godwin, & Conduct Problems Prevention Research Group, 2013). And in the most recent research analysis involving this project, approximately one-third of Fast Track's reduction in later crime outcomes in emerging adulthood was attributed to improvements in social and self-regulation skills, such as prosocial behavior, emotion regulation, and problem solving, at 6 to 11 years of age (Sorensen, Dodge, & Conduct Problems Prevention Research Group, 2016).

How might educators apply the results of this research to their daily work with adolescents in school settings?

and reported fewer adult offenses than a control group did. The Perry Preschool students also were less likely to drop out of school, and teachers rated their social behavior as more competent than that of a control group who had not received the enriched preschool experience (Schweinhart & others, 2005).

What other effects can intervention programs achieve? For a description of one successful program, see the *Connecting with Research* interlude.

Review *Connect* Reflect

LG5 Identify adolescent problems in socioemotional development and strategies for helping adolescents with problems.

Review
- What is juvenile delinquency? What causes it?
- What is the nature of depression and suicide in adolescence?
- How are adolescent problems interrelated? What are some components of successful prevention/intervention programs for adolescents?

Connect
- What have you learned about the connection between bullying and the development of problems in bullies and victims?

Reflect *Your Own Personal Journey of Life*
- As an adolescent, did you have any of the problems discussed in this chapter? If you had one or more of the problems, why do you think you developed the problem(s)? If you did not have any of the problems, what prevented you from developing them?

Socioemotional Development in Adolescence

1 What Characterizes Identity, Emotional Development, and Gender Classification in Adolescence?

LG1 Discuss identity, emotional development, and gender classification during adolescence.

Identity

- Identity development is a complex process that happens in bits and pieces. Erikson argues that identity versus identity confusion is the fifth stage of the human life span, which individuals experience during adolescence. A psychosocial moratorium during adolescence allows the personality and role experimentation that are important aspects of identity development.

- James Marcia proposed four identity statuses—identity diffusion, foreclosure, moratorium, and achievement—that are based on crisis (exploration) and commitment. Increasingly, experts argue that major changes in identity occur in emerging adulthood rather than adolescence. Individuals often follow moratorium-achievement-moratorium-achievement ("MAMA") cycles in their lives.

- Parents are important figures in adolescents' identity development. Identity development is facilitated by family relations that promote both individuality and connectedness. Adolescents who belong to ethnic minority groups struggle to maintain their identities while blending into the majority culture.

Emotional Development

- Adolescents report more extreme and fleeting emotions than their parents, and as individuals go through early adolescence they are less likely to report being very happy. However, it is important to view moodiness as a normal aspect of early adolescence.

- Although pubertal change is associated with an increase in negative emotions, hormonal influences are often small, and environmental experiences may contribute more to the emotions of adolescence than hormonal changes do. Emotion regulation helps to prevent the development of problems in adolescence.

Gender Classification

- Gender-role classification focuses on the degree to which individuals are masculine, feminine, or androgynous. Androgyny means having positive feminine and masculine characteristics.

- Recently, considerable research interest has been directed to the gender category of transgender, which refers to individuals who adopt a gender identity that differs from the one assigned to them at birth.

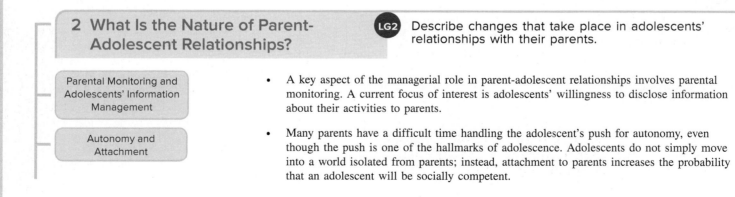

2 What Is the Nature of Parent-Adolescent Relationships?

LG2 Describe changes that take place in adolescents' relationships with their parents.

Parental Monitoring and Adolescents' Information Management

- A key aspect of the managerial role in parent-adolescent relationships involves parental monitoring. A current focus of interest is adolescents' willingness to disclose information about their activities to parents.

Autonomy and Attachment

- Many parents have a difficult time handling the adolescent's push for autonomy, even though the push is one of the hallmarks of adolescence. Adolescents do not simply move into a world isolated from parents; instead, attachment to parents increases the probability that an adolescent will be socially competent.

| Parent-Adolescent Conflict | • Parent-adolescent conflict increases in early adolescence. The conflict is usually moderate rather than severe, and the increased conflict may serve the positive developmental function of promoting autonomy and identity. A subset of adolescents experience high parent-adolescent conflict, which is linked with negative outcomes. |

3 What Aspects of Peer Relationships Are Important in Adolescence? LG3 Characterize the changes that occur in peer relations during adolescence.

| Friendship | • Harry Stack Sullivan was the most influential theorist to discuss the importance of adolescent friendships. He argued that there is a dramatic increase in the psychological importance and intimacy of close friendships in early adolescence. |

| Peer Groups | • Groups of children are less formal and less heterogeneous than groups of adolescents. The pressure to conform to peers is strong during adolescence, especially during the eighth and ninth grades. Cliques and crowds assume more importance in the lives of adolescents than in the lives of children. Membership in certain crowds—especially jocks and populars—is associated with increased self-esteem. Independents also show high self-esteem. |

| Dating and Romantic Relationships | • Three stages characterize the development of romantic relationships in adolescence: (1) entry into romantic attractions and affiliations at about 11 to 13 years of age, (2) exploring romantic relationships at approximately 14 to 16 years of age, and (3) consolidating dyadic romantic bonds at about 17 to 19 years of age. A special concern is early dating, which is associated with a number of problems. |

• Most sexual minority youth (gays and lesbians) have had some same-sex sexual experience, but relatively few have had same-sex romantic relationships. Many sexual minority youth date other-sex peers, which can help them to clarify their sexual orientation or disguise it from others.

• Adolescents who date have more problems, such as substance abuse, than those who do not date, but they also have greater acceptance from peers. Culture can exert a powerful influence on dating. Many adolescents from immigrant families face conflicts with their parents about dating.

4 Why Is Culture an Important Context for Adolescent Development? LG4 Explain how culture influences adolescent development.

| Cross-Cultural Comparisons | • There are similarities and differences in adolescents across different countries. In some countries, traditions are being continued in the socialization of adolescents, whereas in others, the experiences of adolescents are changing substantially. The ways in which adolescents fill their time vary, depending on the culture in which they live. |

• Rites of passage are ceremonies that mark an individual's transition from one status to another, especially into adulthood. In primitive cultures, rites of passage are often well defined. In contemporary America, universal, formal rites of passage to adulthood are ill-defined, but certain religious groups have initiation ceremonies, such as the Jewish bat and bar mitzvah and the Catholic confirmation. The high school graduation ceremony has become a nearly universal rite of passage for U.S. adolescents.

| Ethnicity | • Many of the families that have immigrated to the United States in recent decades come from collectivist cultures in which there is a strong sense of family obligation. Much of the research on ethnic minority adolescents has not teased apart the influences of ethnicity and socioeconomic status. Because of this failure, too often researchers have given ethnic explanations for characteristics that were largely due to socioeconomic factors. Although not all ethnic minority families are poor, poverty contributes to the stress of many ethnic minority adolescents. |

Media and Technology

- In terms of exposure, a significant increase in media use occurs in 11- to 14-year-olds. Adolescents are spending more time in media multitasking. The social environment of adolescents has increasingly become digitally mediated. The Internet continues to serve as the main focus of digitally mediated social interaction for adolescents but now encompasses a variety of digital devices, including cell phones (especially smartphones).

- Adolescents' online time can have positive or negative outcomes. Large numbers of adolescents and college students engage in social networking on sites such as Facebook. A special concern is the difficulty parents face in monitoring the information their children are accessing.

5 What Are Some Socioemotional Problems in Adolescence?

LG5 Identify adolescent problems in socioemotional development and strategies for helping adolescents with problems.

Juvenile Delinquency

- A juvenile delinquent is an adolescent who breaks the law or engages in conduct that is considered illegal. Heredity, identity problems, community influences, and family experiences have been proposed as causes of juvenile delinquency.

Depression and Suicide

- Adolescents and emerging adults have higher rates of depression than children do. Female adolescents and emerging adult women are more likely to have mood and depressive disorders than their male counterparts. Adolescent suicide is the third leading cause of death in U.S. 10- to 19-year-olds. Both early and later factors are likely involved in suicide's causes.

The Interrelation of Problems and Successful Prevention/Intervention Programs

- Researchers are increasingly finding that problem behaviors in adolescence are interrelated. A number of common components are found in programs that successfully prevent or reduce adolescent problems: providing individual attention to high-risk adolescents, developing community-wide intervention, and providing early identification and intervention.

key terms

androgyny	crisis	identity foreclosure	juvenile delinquent
bicultural identity	crowd	identity moratorium	psychosocial
clique	ethnic identity	identity versus	moratorium
commitment	identity achievement	identity confusion	rite of passage
connectedness	identity diffusion	individuality	transgender

key people

Erik Erikson	Reed Larson	Maryse Richards	Harry Stack Sullivan
Andrew Fuligni	James Marcia	Seth Schwartz	Alan Waterman

connecting with **improving the lives of children**

STRATEGIES

Supporting Adolescents' Socioemotional Development

What are some good strategies for helping adolescents improve their socioemotional competencies?

- *Let adolescents explore their identity.* Adolescence is a time of identity exploration. Adults should encourage adolescents to try out different options as they seek to identify what type of life they want to pursue.

- *Engage in effective monitoring of adolescents' activities.* Especially important is using strategies for getting adolescents to disclose information about their activities.

- *Understand the importance of autonomy and attachment.* A common stereotype is that parents are less important in adolescent development than in child development. However, parents continue to play a crucial role in adolescents' development by serving as a resource and support system, especially in stressful times. Value the adolescent's motivation for independence. However, continue to monitor the adolescent's whereabouts, although less intrusively and directly than in childhood.

- *Keep parent-adolescent conflict from being turbulent, and use good communication skills with the adolescent.* Adolescents' socioemotional development benefits when conflict with parents is either low or moderate. Keep communication channels open with the adolescent. Be an active listener and show respect for the adolescent's advancing developmental status. As it was during childhood, authoritative parenting is the best choice in most situations. Communicate expectations for high standards of achievement and conduct.

- *Recognize the importance of peers, youth organizations, and mentors.* Respected peers need to be used more frequently in programs that promote health and education. Adolescents need greater access to youth organizations staffed by caring peers and adults. Mentors can play a strong role in supporting adolescents' socioemotional development.

- *Help adolescents better understand the nature of differences, diversity, and value conflicts.* Adolescents need to be encouraged to take the perspective of adolescents from diverse ethnic backgrounds.

- *Give adolescents individualized attention.* One of the reasons adolescents develop problems is that they have not received adequate attention.

- *Provide better community-wide collaboration for helping youth.* In successful programs, a number of different services and programs cooperate to help adolescents.

- *Prevent adolescent problems through early identification and intervention.* The seeds of many adolescent problems are already in place in childhood.

RESOURCES

Adolescence: Growing Up in America Today **(2006)**
Joy Dryfoos and Carol Barkin
New York: Oxford University Press

Dryfoos' update of her 1990 book on at-risk adolescents contains extensive information about programs and strategies for improving adolescents' lives.

101 Insights and Strategies for Parenting Teenagers **(2010)**
Sheryl Feinstein
Monterey, CA: Healthy Learning

An excellent, easy-to-read book for parents that provides valuable strategies for guiding adolescents through the transition from childhood to emerging adulthood.

Age of Opportunity **(2014)**
Laurence Steinberg
Boston: Houghton Mifflin Harcourt

An outstanding book by a leading expert on adolescent development with valuable information for adults who parent, teach, or counsel adolescents.

Realizing the Potential of Immigrant Youth **(2012)**
Edited by Ann Masten and others
New York: Cambridge University Press

Leading international researchers describe contemporary research on immigrant youth and the most promising strategies for supporting their development.

National Adolescent Suicide Hotline
800-621-4000

This hotline can be used 24 hours a day by teenagers contemplating suicide, as well as by their parents.

National Clearinghouse for Alcohol Information
www.health.org

This clearinghouse provides information about a wide variety of issues related to drinking problems, including adolescent drinking.

glossary

A

A-not-B error This occurs when infants make the mistake of selecting the familiar hiding place (A) rather than the new hiding place (B) of an object as they progress into substage 4 in Piaget's sensorimotor stage.

accommodation Piagetian concept of adjusting schemes to fit new information and experiences.

active (niche-picking) genotype-environment correlations Correlations that exist when children seek out environments they find compatible and stimulating. *Niche-picking* refers to finding a setting that is suited to one's genetically influenced abilities.

adolescence The developmental period of transition from childhood to early adulthood, entered at approximately 10 to 12 years of age and ending at 18 to 22 years of age.

adolescent egocentrism The heightened self-consciousness of adolescents that is reflected in their belief that others are as interested in them as they are in themselves, and in their sense of personal uniqueness and invincibility.

adoption study A study in which investigators seek to discover whether, in behavior and psychological characteristics, adopted children are more like their adoptive parents, who provided a home environment, or more like their biological parents, who contributed their heredity. Another form of the adoption study compares adopted and biological siblings.

affordances Opportunities for interaction offered by objects that fit within our capabilities to perform functional activities.

afterbirth The third stage of birth, when the placenta, umbilical cord, and other membranes are detached and expelled from the uterus.

AIDS AIDS, or acquired immune deficiency syndrome, is caused by the human immunode-ficiency virus (HIV), which destroys the body's immune system.

amnion The fetal life-support system, which consists of a thin bag or envelope that contains a clear fluid in which the developing embryo floats.

amygdala A part of the brain that is the seat of emotions.

analgesics Drugs used to alleviate pain, such as tranquilizers, barbiturates, and narcotics.

androgyny The presence of positive masculine and feminine characteristics in the same individual.

anesthesia Drugs used in late first-stage labor and during expulsion of the baby to block sensation in an area of the body or to block consciousness.

anger cry A cry similar to the basic cry, with more excess air forced through the vocal cords.

animism The belief that inanimate objects have lifelike qualities and are capable of action.

anorexia nervosa An eating disorder that involves the relentless pursuit of thinness through starvation.

Apgar Scale A widely used method to assess newborn's chances of survival and determine whether medical attention is needed.

aphasia A loss or impairment of language processing caused by brain damage in Broca's area or Wernicke's area.

articulation disorders Problems in pronouncing sounds correctly.

Asperger syndrome A relatively mild autism spectrum disorder in which the child has relatively good verbal language skills, milder nonverbal language problems, and a restricted range of interests and relationships.

assimilation Piagetian concept involving incorporation of new information into existing schemes.

asthma A chronic lung disease that involves episodes of airflow obstruction.

attachment A close emotional bond between two people.

attention The focusing of mental resources on select information.

attention deficit hyperactivity disorder (ADHD) A disability in which children consistently show one or more of the following characteristics: (1) inattention, (2) hyperactivity, and (3) impulsivity.

authoritarian parenting A restrictive, punitive parenting style in which parents exhort the child to follow their directions and to respect their work and effort. The authoritarian parent places firm limits and controls on the child and allows little verbal exchange. Authoritarian parenting is associated with children's social incompetence.

authoritative parenting A parenting style in which parents encourage their children to be independent but still place limits and controls on their actions. Extensive verbal give-and-take is allowed, and parents are warm and nurturant toward the child. Authoritative parenting is associated with children's social competence.

autism spectrum disorders (ASDs) Also called pervasive developmental disorders, this category ranges from the severe disorder labeled autistic disorder to the milder disorder called Asperger syndrome. Children with these disorders are characterized by problems with social interaction, verbal and nonverbal communication, and repetitive behaviors.

autistic disorder A severe autism spectrum disorder that has its onset in the first three years of life and includes deficiencies in social relationships, abnormalities in communication, and restricted, repetitive, and stereotyped patterns of behavior.

autonomous morality The second stage of moral development in Piaget's theory, displayed by older children (about 10 years of age and older). The child becomes aware that rules and laws are created by people and that, in judging an action, one should consider the actor's intentions as well as the consequences.

average children Children who receive an average number of both positive and negative nominations from peers.

basic cry A rhythmic pattern usually consisting of a cry, a briefer silence, a shorter inspiratory whistle that is higher pitched than the main cry, and then a brief rest before the next cry.

B

Bayley Scales of Infant Development Scales developed by Nancy Bayley that are widely used in assessing infant development. The current version, the Bayley Scales of Infant and Toddler Development—Third Edition (Bayley-III), has five components: a cognitive scale, a language scale, a motor scale, a socio-emotional scale, and an adaptive scale.

behavior genetics The field that seeks to discover the influence of heredity and environment on individual differences in human traits and development.

bicultural identity Identity formation that occurs when adolescents identify in some ways with their ethnic group and in other ways with the majority culture.

biological processes Changes in an individual's body.

blastocyst The inner mass of cells that develops during the germinal period. These cells later develop into the embryo.

bonding A close connection, especially a physical bond, between parents and their newborn in the period shortly after birth.

brainstorming A technique in which individuals are encouraged to come up with creative ideas in a group, play off each other's ideas, and say practically whatever comes to mind.

Brazelton Neonatal Behavioral Assessment Scale (NBAS) A test performed within 24 to 36 hours after birth to assess newborns' neurological development, reflexes, and reactions to people.

breech position Position of the baby within the uterus that causes the buttocks to be the first part to emerge from the vagina.

Broca's area An area in the brain's left frontal lobe that is involved in speech production.

Bronfenbrenner's ecological theory An environmental systems theory that focuses on five environmental systems: microsystem, mesosystem, exosystem, macrosystem, and chronosystem.

bulimia nervosa An eating disorder in which the individual consistently follows a binge-and-purge eating pattern.

C

care perspective The moral perspective of Carol Gilligan, which views people in terms of their connectedness with others and emphasizes interpersonal communication, relationships with others, and concern for others.

case study An in-depth look at a single individual.

centration The focusing of attention on one characteristic to the exclusion of all others.

cephalocaudal pattern The sequence in which the earliest growth always occurs at the top—the head—with physical growth and feature differentiation gradually working from top to bottom.

cerebral cortex Tissue that covers the forebrain like a wrinkled cap and includes two halves, or hemispheres.

cerebral palsy A disorder that involves a lack of muscular coordination, shaking, and unclear speech.

cesarean delivery Delivery in which the baby is removed from the mother's uterus through an incision made in her abdomen. This also is sometimes referred to as a cesarean section.

character education A direct education approach that involves teaching students a basic moral literacy to prevent them from engaging in immoral behavior and doing harm to themselves and others.

child-centered kindergarten Education that involves the whole child by considering the child's physical, cognitive, and socioemotional development and addressing the child's needs, interests, and learning styles.

child-directed speech Language spoken in a higher pitch than normal, with simple words and sentences.

chromosomes Threadlike structures made up of deoxyribonucleic acid, or DNA.

clique A small group that ranges from 2 to about 12 individuals, averaging about 5 or 6 individuals, and may form because adolescents engage in similar activities.

cognitive control Involves effective control and flexible thinking in a number of areas, including controlling attention, reducing interfering thoughts, and being cognitively flexible.

cognitive processes Changes in an individual's thought, intelligence, and language.

cohort effects Effects due to a person's time of birth, era, or generation but not to actual age.

commitment Marcia's term for the part of identity development in which individuals show a personal investment in identity.

concepts Cognitive groupings of similar objects, events, people, or ideas.

connectedness Characteristic consisting of two dimensions: mutuality (sensitivity to and respect for others' views) and permeability (openness to others' views).

conscience An internal regulator of standards of right and wrong that involves an integration of moral thought, feeling, and behavior.

conservation The concept that an object's or substance's basic properties stay the same even if its appearance has been altered.

constructive play Play that combines sensorimotor/practice play with symbolic representation. Constructive play occurs when children engage in self-regulated creation or construction of a product or a solution.

constructivist approach A learner-centered approach that emphasizes the importance of individuals actively constructing their knowledge and understanding with guidance from the teacher.

context The settings, influenced by historical, economic, social, and cultural factors, in which development occurs.

continuity-discontinuity issue The issue regarding whether development involves gradual, cumulative change (continuity) or distinct stages (discontinuity).

controversial children Children who are frequently nominated both as someone's best friend and as being disliked.

conventional reasoning The second, or intermediate, level in Kohlberg's theory of moral development. At this level, individuals abide by certain standards, but they are standards set by others such as parents or the government.

convergent thinking Thinking that produces one correct answer and is characteristic of the kind of thinking tested by standardized intelligence tests.

coordination of secondary circular reactions Piaget's fourth sensorimotor substage, which develops between 8 and 12 months of age. Actions become more outwardly directed, and infants coordinate schemes and act with intentionality.

core knowledge approach View that infants are born with domain-specific innate knowledge systems.

corpus callosum The location where fibers connect the brain's left and right hemispheres.

correlation coefficient A number based on statistical analysis that is used to describe the degree of association between two variables.

correlational research A research design whose goal is to describe the strength of the relationship between two or more events or characteristics.

creative thinking The ability to think in novel and unusual ways and to come up with unique solutions to problems.

crisis Marcia's term for a period of identity development during which the individual is exploring alternatives.

critical thinking The ability to think reflectively and productively, as well as to evaluate the evidence.

cross-cultural studies Comparisons of one culture with one or more other cultures. These comparisons provide information about the degree to which children's development is similar, or universal, across cultures, and the degree to which it is culture-specific.

cross-sectional approach A research strategy in which individuals of different ages are compared at one time.

crowd A larger group than a clique, one that is usually formed based on reputation; members may or may not spend much time together.

cultural-familial intellectual disability Condition in which there is no evidence of organic brain damage but the individual's IQ generally is between 50 and 70.

culture The behavior patterns, beliefs, and all other products of a group that are passed on from generation to generation.

culture-fair tests Tests of intelligence that are designed to be free of cultural bias.

D

deferred imitation Imitation that occurs after a delay of hours or days.

Denver Developmental Screening Test II A test used to diagnose developmental delay in children from birth to 6 years of age; includes separate assessments of gross and fine motor skills, language, and personal-social ability.

descriptive research A research design that has the purpose of observing and recording behavior.

design stage Kellogg's term for 3- to 4-year-olds' drawings that mix two basic shapes into more complex designs.

development The pattern of movement or change that begins at conception and continues through the human life span.

developmental cascade model Involves connections across domains over time that influence developmental pathways and outcomes.

developmental quotient (DQ) An overall score that combines subscores in motor, language, adaptive, and personal-social domains in the Gesell assessment of infants.

developmentally appropriate practice (DAP) Education that focuses on the typical developmental patterns of children (age appropriateness) as well as the uniqueness of each child (individual appropriateness). Such practice contrasts with *developmentally inappropriate practice,* which ignores the concrete, hands-on approach to learning. For example, direct teaching largely through abstract paper-and-pencil activities presented to large groups of young children is believed to be developmentally inappropriate.

difficult child A child who tends to react negatively and cry frequently, who engages in irregular daily routines, and who is slow to accept new experiences.

direct instruction approach A structured, teacher-centered approach that is characterized by teacher direction and control, mastery of academic skills, high expectations for students' progress, maximum time spent on learning tasks, and efforts to keep negative emotional expression to a minimum.

dishabituation Recovery of a habituated response after a change in stimulation.

divergent thinking　Thinking that produces many different answers to the same question and is characteristic of creativity.

DNA　A complex molecule with a double helix shape; contains genetic information.

domain theory of moral development　Theory that traces social knowledge and reasoning to moral, social conventional, and personal domains. These domains arise from children's and adolescents' attempts to understand and deal with different forms of social experience.

doula　A caregiver who provides continuous physical, emotional, and educational support to the mother before, during, and after childbirth.

Down syndrome　A form of intellectual disability that is caused by the presence of an extra copy of chromosome 21.

dynamic systems theory　The perspective on motor development that seeks to explain how motor skills are assembled for perceiving and acting.

dyscalculia　Also known as developmental arithmetic disorder; a learning disability that involves difficulty in math computation.

dysgraphia　A learning disability that involves difficulty in handwriting.

dyslexia　A category of learning disabilities involving a severe impairment in the ability to read and spell.

E

early childhood　The developmental period that extends from the end of infancy to about 5 to 6 years of age; sometimes called the preschool years.

early-later experience issue　The issue of the degree to which early experiences (especially infancy) or later experiences are the key determinants of the child's development.

easy child　A child who is generally in a positive mood, who quickly establishes regular routines in infancy, and who adapts easily to new experiences.

eclectic theoretical orientation　An orientation that does not follow any one theoretical approach but rather selects from each theory whatever is considered the best in it.

ecological view　The view that perception functions to bring organisms in contact with the environment and to increase adaptation.

ectoderm　The outermost layer of cells, which becomes the nervous system and brain, sensory receptors (ears, nose, and eyes, for example), and skin parts (hair and nails, for example).

educationally blind　Unable to use one's vision in learning and needing to use hearing and touch to learn.

egocentrism　Piaget's concept that describes the inability to distinguish between one's own perspective and someone else's perspective.

elaboration　An important strategy that involves engaging in more extensive processing of information.

embryonic period　The period of prenatal development that occurs two to eight weeks after conception. During the embryonic period, the rate of cell differentiation intensifies, support systems for the cells form, and organs appear.

emerging adulthood　Occurring from approximately 18 to 25 years of age, this transitional period between adolescence and adulthood is characterized by experimentation and exploration.

emotion　Feeling, or affect, that occurs when a person is in a state or interaction that is important to him or her. Emotion can be characterized as positive (enthusiasm, joy, love, for example) or negative (anxiety, guilt, or sadness, for example).

emotional and behavioral disorders　Serious, persistent problems that involve relationships, aggression, depression, fears associated with personal or school matters, as well as other inappropriate socioemotional characteristics.

empathy　An affective response to another's feelings with an emotional response that is similar to the other's feelings.

endoderm　The inner layer of cells, which develops into digestive and respiratory systems.

epigenetic view　Emphasizes that development reflects an ongoing, bidirectional interchange between heredity and environment.

equilibration　A mechanism that Piaget proposed to explain how children shift from one stage of thought to the next.

Erikson's theory　Includes eight stages of human development. Each stage consists of a unique developmental task that confronts individuals with a crisis that must be resolved.

estradiol　A hormone associated in girls with breast, uterine, and skeletal development.

ethnic gloss　The use of an ethnic label such as African American or Latino in a superficial way that portrays an ethnic group as being more homogeneous than it really is.

ethnic identity　An enduring, basic aspect of the self that includes a sense of membership in an ethnic group and the attitudes and feelings related to that membership.

ethnicity　A characteristic based on cultural heritage, nationality, race, religion, and language.

ethology　Stresses that behavior is strongly influenced by biology, is tied to evolution, and is characterized by critical or sensitive periods.

evocative genotype-environment correlations　Correlations that exist when the child's genetically influenced characteristics elicit certain types of physical and social environments.

evolutionary psychology　Branch of psychology that emphasizes the importance of adaptation, reproduction, and "survival of the fittest" in shaping behavior.

executive attention　Involves planning actions, allocating attention to goals, detecting and compensating for errors, monitoring progress on tasks, and dealing with novel or difficult circumstances.

executive function　An umbrella-like concept that consists of a number of higher-level cognitive processes linked to the development of the brain's prefrontal cortex. Executive function involves managing one's thoughts to engage in goal-directed behavior and exercise self-control.

experiment　A carefully regulated procedure in which one or more of the factors believed to influence the behavior being studied are manipulated, while all other factors are held constant.

explicit memory　Conscious memory of facts and experiences.

extrinsic motivation　Involves external incentives such as rewards and punishments.

F

fast mapping　A process that helps to explain how young children learn the connection between a word and its referent so quickly.

fertilization　A stage in reproduction when an egg and a sperm fuse to create a single cell, called a zygote.

fetal alcohol spectrum disorders (FASD)　A cluster of abnormalities and problems that appears in the offspring of mothers who drink alcohol heavily during pregnancy.

fetal period　The prenatal period of development that begins two months after conception and lasts for seven months on average.

fine motor skills　Motor skills that involve finely tuned movements, such as finger dexterity.

first habits and primary circular reactions　Piaget's second sensorimotor substage, which develops between 1 and 4 months of age. In this substage, the infant coordinates sensation and two types of schemes: habits and primary circular reactions.

fluency disorders　Various disorders that involve what is commonly called "stuttering."

forebrain　The region of the brain that is farthest from the spinal cord and includes the cerebral cortex and several structures beneath it.

forgiveness　An aspect of prosocial behavior that occurs when an injured person releases the injurer from possible behavioral retaliation.

fragile X syndrome　A genetic disorder involving an abnormality in the X chromosome, which becomes constricted and often breaks.

fuzzy trace theory　A theory stating that memory is best understood by considering two types of memory representations: (1) verbatim memory trace and (2) gist. In this theory, older children's better memory is attributed to the fuzzy traces created by extracting the gist of information.

fuzzy-trace theory dual-process model　States that decision making is influenced by two systems—"verbatim" analytical (literal and precise) and gist-based intuition (simple bottom-line meaning)—which operate in parallel; in this model, gist-based intuition benefits adolescent decision making more than analytical thinking does.

G

games　Activities engaged in for pleasure that include rules and often competition with one or more individuals.

gender　The characteristics of people as females or males.

gender identity   The sense of one's own gender, including knowledge, understanding, and acceptance of being male or female.

gender role   A set of expectations that prescribes how females or males should think, act, and feel.

gender schema theory   The theory that gender typing emerges as children gradually develop gender schemas of what is considered gender-appropriate and gender-inappropriate in their culture.

gender stereotypes   Broad categories that reflect our impressions and beliefs about females and males.

gender typing   Acquisition of a traditional masculine or feminine role.

genes   Units of hereditary information composed of DNA. Genes help cells to reproduce themselves and help manufacture the proteins that maintain life.

gene × environment (G × E) interaction   The interaction of a specific measured variation in the DNA and a specific measured aspect of the environment.

genotype   A person's genetic heritage; the actual genetic material.

germinal period   The period of prenatal development that takes place in the first two weeks after conception. It includes the creation of the zygote, continued cell division, and the attachment of the zygote to the uterine wall.

gifted   Having above-average intelligence (an IQ of 130 or higher) and/or superior talent for something.

gonadotropins   Hormones that stimulate the testes or ovaries.

gonads   The sex glands—the testes in males, the ovaries in females.

goodness of fit   Refers to the match between a child's temperament and the environmental demands with which the child must cope.

grasping reflex   A neonatal reflex that occurs when something touches the infant's palms. The infant responds by grasping tightly.

gratitude   A feeling of thankfulness and appreciation, especially in response to someone doing something kind or helpful.

gross motor skills   Motor skills that involve large-muscle activities, such as walking.

growth hormone deficiency   The absence or deficiency of growth hormone produced by the pituitary gland to stimulate the body to grow.

H

habituation   Decreased responsiveness to a stimulus after repeated presentations of the stimulus.

helpless orientation   An orientation in which one seems trapped by the experience of difficulty and attributes one's difficulty to a lack of ability.

heteronomous morality   Kohlberg's first stage in preconventional reasoning in which moral thinking is tied to punishment.

heteronomous morality   The first stage of moral development in Piaget's theory, occurring from approximately 4 to 7 years of age. Justice and rules are conceived of as unchangeable properties of the world, removed from the control of people.

hidden curriculum   Dewey's concept that every school has a pervasive moral atmosphere, even if it doesn't have an official program of moral education.

hormones   Powerful chemical substances secreted by the endocrine glands and carried through the body by the bloodstream.

hypothalamus   A structure in the brain that monitors eating and sex.

hypothesis   A specific assumption or prediction that can be tested to determine its accuracy.

hypothetical-deductive reasoning   Piaget's formal operational concept that adolescents have the cognitive ability to develop hypotheses, or best guesses, about ways to solve problems.

I

identity achievement   Marcia's term for the status of individuals who have undergone a crisis and have made a commitment.

identity diffusion   Marcia's term for the status of individuals who have not yet experienced a crisis (explored alternatives) or made any commitments.

identity foreclosure   Marcia's term for the status of individuals who have made a commitment but have not experienced a crisis.

identity moratorium   Marcia's term for the status of individuals who are in the midst of a crisis, but their commitments are either absent or vaguely defined.

identity versus identity confusion   Erikson's fifth developmental stage, which occurs at about the time of adolescence. At this time, adolescents are faced with deciding who they are, what they are all about, and where they are going in life.

imaginary audience   Refers to adolescents' belief that others are as interested in them as they themselves are, as well as their attention-getting behavior motivated by a desire to be noticed, visible, and "on stage."

immanent justice   The expectation that, if a rule is broken, punishment will be meted out immediately.

implicit memory   Memory without conscious recollection; involves skills and routine procedures that are automatically performed.

inclusion   Educating a child with special educational needs full-time in the regular classroom.

individual differences   The stable, consistent ways in which people differ from each other.

individualism, instrumental purpose, and exchange   The second Kohlberg stage in preconventional reasoning. At this stage, individuals pursue their own interests but also let others do the same.

individuality   Characteristic consisting of two dimensions: self-assertion (the ability to have and communicate a point of view) and separateness (the use of communication patterns to express how one is different from others).

individualized education plan (IEP)   A written statement that spells out a program tailored to a child with a disability. The plan should be (1) related to the child's learning capacity, (2) specially constructed to meet the child's individual needs and not merely a copy of what is offered to other children, and (3) designed to provide educational benefits.

Individuals with Disabilities Education Act (IDEA)   The IDEA spells out broad mandates for providing services to all children with disabilities (IDEA is a renaming of Public Law 94-142); these include evaluation and eligibility determination, appropriate education and an individualized education plan (IEP), and education in the least restrictive environment (LRE).

indulgent parenting   A style of parenting in which parents are highly involved with their children but place few demands or controls on them. Indulgent parenting is associated with children's social incompetence, especially a lack of self-control.

infancy   The developmental period that extends from birth to 18 to 24 months of age.

infinite generativity   The ability to produce an endless number of meaningful sentences using a finite set of words and rules.

information-processing theory   Emphasizes that individuals manipulate information, monitor it, and strategize about it. Central to this theory are the processes of memory and thinking.

insecure avoidant babies   Babies that show insecurity by avoiding the caregiver.

insecure disorganized babies   Babies that show insecurity by being disorganized and disoriented.

insecure resistant babies   Babies that often cling to the caregiver, then resist her by fighting against the closeness, perhaps by kicking or pushing away.

intellectual disability   A condition of limited mental ability in which an individual has a low IQ, usually below 70 on a traditional test of intelligence, and has difficulty adapting to the demands of everyday life.

intelligence   Problem-solving skills and the ability to learn from and adapt to the experiences of everyday life.

intelligence quotient (IQ)   A person's mental age divided by chronological age, multiplied by 100.

intermodal perception   The ability to relate and integrate information from two or more sensory modalities, such as vision and hearing.

internalization of schemes   Piaget's sixth and final sensorimotor substage, which develops between 18 and 24 months of age. In this substage, the infant develops the ability to use primitive symbols.

intimacy in friendships   Self-disclosure and the sharing of private thoughts.

intrinsic motivation   Involves internal factors such as self-determination, curiosity, challenge, and effort.

intuitive thought substage   Piaget's second substage of preoperational thought, in which children begin to use primitive reasoning and want to know the answers to all sorts of questions (occurs between about 4 and 7 years of age).

involution The process by which the uterus returns to its prepregnant size.

J

joint attention Occurs when individuals focus on the same object or event and are able to track each other's behavior; one individual directs another's attention, and reciprocal interaction is present.

justice perspective A moral perspective that focuses on the rights of the individual and in which individuals independently make moral decisions.

juvenile delinquent An adolescent who breaks the law or engages in behavior that is considered illegal.

K

kangaroo care A way of holding a preterm infant so that there is skin-to-skin contact.

Klinefelter syndrome A chromosomal disorder in which males have an extra X chromosome, making them XXY instead of XY.

kwashiorkor A condition caused by a severe deficiency in protein in which the child's abdomen and feet become swollen with water; usually appears between 1 and 3 years of age.

L

laboratory A controlled setting in which many of the complex factors of the "real world" are absent.

language A form of communication, whether spoken, written, or signed, that is based on a system of symbols.

language acquisition device (LAD) Chomsky's term describing a biological endowment that enables the child to detect the features and rules of language, including phonology, syntax, and semantics.

lateralization Specialization of function in one hemisphere of the cerebral cortex or the other.

learning disability Disability in which a child has difficulty in learning that involves understanding or using spoken or written language, and the difficulty can appear in listening, thinking, reading, writing, or spelling. A learning disability also may involve difficulty in doing mathematics. To be classified as a learning disability, the learning problem is not primarily the result of visual, hearing, or motor disabilities; intellectual disabilities; emotional disorders; or environmental, cultural, or economic disadvantage.

least restrictive environment (LRE) The concept that a child with a disability must be educated in a setting that is as similar as possible to the one in which children who do not have a disability are educated.

limbic system A lower, subcortical system in the brain that is the seat of emotions and experience of rewards.

long-term memory A relatively permanent type of memory that holds huge amounts of information for a long period of time.

longitudinal approach A research strategy in which the same individuals are studied over a period of time, usually several years or more.

low birth weight infants Babies that weigh less than 5½ pounds at birth.

low vision Visual acuity between 20/70 and 20/2000.

M

manual approaches Educational approaches to help hearing-impaired children, including sign language and finger spelling.

marasmus A wasting away of body tissues in the infant's first year, caused by severe protein-calorie deficiency.

mastery motivation An orientation that focuses on tasks, learning strategies, and the achievement process rather than innate ability.

meiosis A specialized form of cell division that occurs to form eggs and sperm (also known as *gametes*).

melatonin A sleep-inducing hormone that is produced in the brain's pineal gland.

memory A central feature of cognitive development, involving the retention of information over time.

menarche A girl's first menstrual period.

mental age (MA) Binet's measure of an individual's level of mental development, compared with that of others.

mesoderm The middle layer of cells, which becomes the circulatory system, bones, muscles, excretory system, and reproductive system.

metacognition Cognition about cognition, or knowing about knowing.

metalinguistic awareness Knowledge about language, such as knowing what a preposition is or being able to discuss the sounds of a language.

middle and late childhood The developmental period that extends from about 6 to 11 years of age; sometimes called the elementary school years.

Millennials The generation born after 1980, which is the first generation to come of age and enter emerging adulthood in the new millennium; members of this generation are characterized by their ethnic diversity and their connection to technology.

mindfulness Being alert, mentally present, and cognitively flexible while going through life's everyday activities and tasks.

mindset The cognitive view, either fixed or growth, that individuals develop for themselves.

mitosis Cellular reproduction in which the cell's nucleus duplicates itself with two new cells being formed, each containing the same DNA as the parent cell, arranged in the same 23 pairs of chromosomes.

Montessori approach An educational philosophy in which children are given considerable freedom and spontaneity in choosing activities and specially designed curriculum materials.

moral development Development that involves thoughts, feelings, and behaviors regarding rules and conventions about what people should do in their interactions with other people.

Moro reflex A neonatal startle response that occurs in reaction to a sudden, intense noise or movement. When startled, newborns arch their back, throw their head back, and fling out their arms and legs. Then they rapidly close their arms and legs, bringing them close to the center of the body.

morphology Units of meaning involved in word formation.

mutual interpersonal expectations, relationships, and interpersonal conformity Kohlberg's third stage of moral development. At this stage, individuals value trust, caring, and loyalty to others as a basis of moral judgments.

myelination The process in which the nerve cells are covered and insulated with a layer of fat cells, which increases the speed at which information travels through the nervous system.

N

natural childbirth Method developed in 1914 by English obstetrician Grantly Dick-Read that attempts to reduce the mother's pain by decreasing her fear through education about childbirth and breathing methods and relaxation techniques during delivery.

naturalistic observation Observing behavior in real-world settings.

nature-nurture issue The issue regarding whether development is primarily influenced by nature or nurture. The "nature" proponents claim that biological inheritance is the more important influence on development; the "nurture" proponents assert that environmental experiences are more important.

neglected children Children who are infrequently nominated as a best friend but are not disliked by their peers.

neglectful parenting A style of parenting in which the parent is very uninvolved in the child's life; it is associated with children's social incompetence, especially a lack of self-control.

neo-Piagetians Developmentalists who have elaborated on Piaget's theory, giving more emphasis to information processing, strategies, and precise cognitive steps.

Neonatal Intensive Care Unit Network Neurobehavioral Scale (NNNS) An "offspring" of the NBAS, the NNNS provides a more comprehensive analysis of the newborn's behavior, neurological and stress responses, and regulatory capacities.

neuroconstructivist view In this view, biological processes and environmental conditions influence the brain's development; the brain has plasticity and is context dependent; and brain development is closely linked with cognitive development.

neurogenesis The formation of new neurons.

neurons The term for nerve cells, which handle information processing at the cellular level.

night terrors Incidents characterized by sudden arousal from sleep, intense fear, and usually physiological reactions such as rapid heart rate and breathing, loud screams, heavy perspiration, and physical movement.

nightmares   Frightening dreams that awaken the sleeper.

normal distribution   A symmetrical distribution with most scores falling in the middle of the possible range of scores and few scores appearing toward the extremes of the range.

O

object permanence   Piagetian term for understanding that objects continue to exist, even when they cannot directly be seen, heard, or touched.

operations   In Piaget's theory, reversible mental actions that allow children to do mentally what they formerly did physically.

oral approaches   Educational approaches to help hearing-impaired children, including lip reading, speech reading, and use of whatever hearing the child has.

organic intellectual disability   Involves physical causes such as a genetic disorder or brain damage.

organization   Piaget's concept of grouping isolated behaviors and thoughts into a higher-order system, a more smoothly functioning cognitive system.

organogenesis   Process of organ formation that takes place during the first two months of prenatal development.

orthopedic impairments   Restrictions in movement abilities due to muscle, bone, or joint problems.

oxytocin   A hormone that is sometimes administered during labor to stimulate contractions.

P

pain cry   A sudden appearance of a long, initial loud cry without preliminary moaning, followed by breath holding.

passive genotype-environment correlations Correlations that exist when the biological parents, who are genetically related to the child, provide a rearing environment for the child.

perception   The interpretation of what is sensed.

performance orientation   An orientation in which one focuses on achievement outcomes; winning is what matters most, and happiness is thought to result from winning.

personal fable   The part of adolescent egocentrism that involves an adolescent's sense of uniqueness and invincibility.

perspective taking   The social cognitive process involved in assuming the perspective of others and understanding their thoughts and feelings.

phenotype   The way an individual's genotype is expressed in observed and measurable characteristics.

phenylketonuria (PKU)   A genetic disorder in which the individual cannot properly metabolize phenylalanine, an amino acid. PKU is now easily detected—but if left untreated, results in intellectual disability and hyperactivity.

phonics approach   The idea that reading instruction should teach basic rules for translating written symbols into sounds.

phonology   The sound system of the language, including the sounds that are used and how they may be combined.

Piaget's theory   States that children actively construct their understanding of the world and go through four stages of cognitive development.

pictorial stage   Kellogg's term for 4- to 5-year-olds' drawings depicting objects that adults can recognize.

pituitary gland   An important endocrine gland that controls growth and regulates other glands.

placement stage   Kellogg's term for 2- to 3-year-olds' drawings that are drawn on a page in placement patterns.

placenta   A disk-shaped group of tissues in which small blood vessels from the mother and the offspring intertwine but don't join.

popular children   Children who are frequently nominated as a best friend and are rarely disliked by their peers.

postconventional reasoning   The highest level in Kohlberg's theory of moral development. At this level, the individual recognizes alternative moral courses, explores the options, and then decides on a personal moral code.

postpartum depression   Involves a major depressive episode characterized by strong feelings of sadness, anxiety, or despair in new mothers, making it difficult for them to carry out daily tasks.

postpartum period   The period after childbirth when the mother adjusts, both physically and psychologically, to the process of childbearing. This period lasts for about six weeks, or until her body has completed its adjustment and has returned to a near-prepregnant state.

practice play   Play that involves repetition of behavior when new skills are being learned or when physical or mental mastery and coordination of skills are required for games or sports.

pragmatics   The appropriate use of language in different contexts.

preconventional reasoning   The lowest level in Kohlberg's theory of moral development. The individual's concept of good and bad is interpreted primarily in terms of external rewards and punishment.

prenatal period   The time from conception to birth.

preoperational stage   Piaget's second stage, lasting from 2 to 7 years of age, when children begin to represent the world with words, images, and drawings. In this stage, they also form stable concepts and begin to reason. At the same time, their cognitive world is dominated by egocentrism and magical beliefs.

prepared childbirth   Developed by French obstetrician Ferdinand Lamaze, this childbirth method is similar to natural childbirth but teaches a special breathing technique to control pushing in the final stages of labor and also provides a more detailed anatomy and physiology course.

pretense/symbolic play   Play in which the child transforms aspects of the physical environment into symbols.

preterm infants   Babies born three weeks or more before the pregnancy has reached its full term.

primary circular reaction   A scheme based on the attempt to reproduce an event that initially occurred by chance.

primary emotions   Emotions that are present in humans and other animals, and emerge early in life; examples are joy, anger, sadness, fear, and disgust.

Project Head Start   Compensatory education designed to provide children from low-income families the opportunity to acquire skills and experiences that are important for school success.

proximodistal pattern   The sequence in which growth starts at the center of the body and moves toward the extremities.

psychoanalytic theories   Describe development as primarily unconscious and heavily colored by emotion. Behavior is merely a surface characteristic, and the symbolic workings of the mind have to be analyzed to understand behavior. Early experiences with parents are emphasized.

psychoanalytic theory of gender   A theory deriving from Freud's view that the preschool child develops a sexual attraction to the opposite-sex parent, by approximately 5 or 6 years of age renounces this attraction because of anxious feelings, and subsequently identifies with the same-sex parent, unconsciously adopting the same-sex parent's characteristics.

psychosocial moratorium   Erikson's term for the gap between childhood security and adult autonomy.

puberty   A brain-neuroendocrine process occurring primarily in early adolescence that provides stimulation for the rapid physical changes that accompany this period of development.

Public Law 94-142   The Education for All Handicapped Children Act, created in 1975, which requires that all children with disabilities be given a free, appropriate public education and which provides the funding to help with the costs of implementing this education.

R

rapport talk   The language of conversation and a way of establishing connections and negotiating relationships; more characteristic of females than of males.

reciprocal socialization   Socialization that is bidirectional; children socialize parents, just as parents socialize children.

reflexes   Built-in reactions to stimuli that govern the newborn's movements, which are automatic and beyond the newborn's control.

reflexive smile   A smile that does not occur in response to external stimuli. It happens during the month after birth, usually during sleep.

rejected children   Children who are infrequently nominated as a best friend and are actively disliked by their peers.

religion An organized set of beliefs, practices, rituals, and symbols that increases an individual's connection to a sacred or transcendent other (God, higher power, or higher truth).

religiousness Degree of affiliation with an organized religion, participation in prescribed rituals and practices, connection with its beliefs, and involvement in a community of believers.

report talk Talk that conveys information; more characteristic of males than females.

rite of passage A ceremony or ritual that marks an individual's transition from one status to another. Most rites of passage focus on the transition to adult status.

rooting reflex A newborn's built-in reaction that occurs when the infant's cheek is stroked or the side of the mouth is touched. In response, the infant turns its head toward the side that was touched in an apparent effort to find something to suck.

S

scaffolding In regard to cognitive development, Vygotsky used this term to describe the changing level of support provided over the course of a teaching session, with the more-skilled person adjusting guidance to fit the child's current performance level.

schemes In Piaget's theory, actions or mental representations that organize knowledge.

scientific method An approach that can be used to obtain accurate information. It includes these steps: (1) conceptualize the problem, (2) collect data, (3) draw conclusions, and (4) revise research conclusions and theory.

secondary circular reactions Piaget's third sensorimotor substage, which develops between 4 and 8 months of age. In this substage, the infant becomes more object-oriented, moving beyond preoccupation with the self.

securely attached babies Babies that use the caregiver as a secure base from which to explore their environment.

self-concept Domain-specific evaluations of the self.

self-conscious emotions Emotions that require self-awareness, especially consciousness and a sense of "me"; examples include jealousy, empathy, and embarrassment.

self-efficacy The belief that one can master a situation and produce favorable outcomes.

self-esteem The global evaluative dimension of the self. Self-esteem is also referred to as self-worth or self-image.

self-understanding The child's cognitive representation of self; the substance and content of the child's self-conceptions.

semantics The meaning of words and sentences.

sensation The product of the interaction between information and the sensory receptors—the eyes, ears, tongue, nostrils, and skin.

sensorimotor play Behavior engaged in by infants to derive pleasure from exercising their existing sensorimotor schemas.

sensorimotor stage The first of Piaget's stages, which lasts from birth to about 2 years of age, in which infants construct an understanding of the world by coordinating sensory experiences with motoric actions.

separation protest An infant's distressed reaction when the caregiver leaves.

seriation The concrete operation that involves ordering stimuli along a quantitative dimension (such as length).

service learning A form of education that promotes social responsibility and service to the community.

sexually transmitted infections (STIs) Diseases that are contracted primarily through sexual contact. This contact is not limited to vaginal intercourse but includes oral-genital contact and anal-genital contact as well.

shape constancy The recognition that an object's shape remains the same even though its orientation to us changes.

shape stage Kellogg's term for 3-year-olds' drawings consisting of diagrams in different shapes.

short-term memory The memory component in which individuals retain information for up to 30 seconds, assuming there is no rehearsal.

sickle-cell anemia A genetic disorder that affects the red blood cells and occurs most often in people of African descent.

simple reflexes Piaget's first sensorimotor substage, which corresponds to the first month after birth. In this substage, sensation and action are coordinated primarily through reflexive behaviors.

size constancy The recognition that an object remains the same even though the retinal image of the object changes as you move toward or away from the object.

slow-to-warm-up child A child who has a low activity level, is somewhat negative, and displays a low intensity of mood.

small for date (small for gestational age) infants Babies whose birth weight is below normal when the length of pregnancy is considered.

social cognitive theory of gender A theory that emphasizes that children's gender development occurs through the observation and imitation of gender behavior and through the rewards and punishments children experience for gender-appropriate and gender-inappropriate behavior.

social cognitive theory The view of psychologists who emphasize behavior, environment, and cognition as the key factors in development.

social constructivist approach An approach that emphasizes the social contexts of learning and the fact that knowledge is mutually built and constructed; Vygotsky's theory is a social constructivist approach.

social contract or utility and individual rights The fifth Kohlberg stage. At this stage, individuals reason that values, rights, and principles undergird or transcend the law.

social conventional reasoning Thoughts about social consensus and convention established in order to control behavior and maintain the social system.

social play Play that involves social interactions with peers.

social policy A government's course of action designed to promote the welfare of its citizens.

social referencing "Reading" emotional cues in others to help determine how to act in a particular situation.

social role theory A theory that gender differences arise from the contrasting roles of men and women.

social smile A smile in response to an external stimulus, which, early in development, typically is a face.

social systems morality The fourth stage in Kohlberg's theory of moral development. Moral judgments are based on understanding the social order, law, justice, and duty.

socioeconomic status (SES) An individual's position within society based on occupational, educational, and economic characteristics.

socioemotional processes Changes in an individual's relationships with other people, changes in emotions, and changes in personality.

somnambulism Sleepwalking; occurs in the deepest stage of sleep.

spirituality Experiencing something beyond oneself in a transcendent manner and living in a way that benefits others and society.

standardized test A test with uniform procedures for administration and scoring. Many standardized tests allow a person's performance to be compared with the performance of other individuals.

stereotype threat Anxiety that one's behavior might confirm a negative stereotype about one's group.

Strange Situation An observational measure of infant attachment that requires the infant to move through a series of introductions, separations, and reunions with the caregiver and an adult stranger in a prescribed order.

stranger anxiety An infant's fear and wariness of strangers; it tends to appear in the second half of the first year of life.

strategies Deliberate mental activities designed to improve the processing of information.

sucking reflex A newborn's built-in reaction to automatically suck an object placed in the mouth. The sucking reflex enables the infant to get nourishment before he or she has associated a nipple with food and also serves as a self-soothing or self-regulating mechanism.

sudden infant death syndrome (SIDS) A condition that occurs when an infant stops breathing, usually during the night, and suddenly dies without an apparent cause.

sustained attention Focused and extended engagement with an object, task, event, or other aspect of the environment.

symbolic function substage Piaget's first substage of preoperational thought, in which the child gains the ability to mentally represent an object that is not present (occurs roughly between 2 and 4 years of age).

sympathy An emotional response to another person in which the observer feels sad or concerned about the individual's well-being.

syntax The ways words are combined to form acceptable phrases and sentences.

T

telegraphic speech The use of content words without grammatical markers such as articles, auxiliary verbs, and other connectives.

temperament An individual's behavioral style and characteristic way of emotionally responding.

teratogen Any agent that can potentially cause a physical birth defect. The field of study that investigates the causes of birth defects is called *teratology*.

tertiary circular reactions, novelty, and curiosity Piaget's fifth sensorimotor substage, which develops between 12 and 18 months of age. In this substage, infants become intrigued by the many properties of objects and by the many things that they can make happen to objects.

testosterone A hormone associated in boys with the development of the genitals, an increase in height, and a change in voice.

theory An interrelated, coherent set of ideas that helps to explain and make predictions.

theory of mind A concept that refers to awareness of one's own mental processes and the mental processes of others.

top-dog phenomenon The circumstance of moving from the top position (in elementary school, being the oldest, biggest, and most powerful students) to the lowest position (in middle or junior high school, being the youngest, smallest, and least powerful students).

transgender A broad term that refers to individuals who adopt a gender identity that differs from the one assigned to them at birth.

transitivity The ability to logically combine relations to understand certain conclusions.

triarchic theory of intelligence Sternberg's theory that intelligence consists of analytical intelligence, creative intelligence, and practical intelligence.

trophoblast The outer layer of cells that develops in the germinal period. These cells later provide nutrition and support for the embryo.

Turner syndrome A chromosomal disorder in females in which either an X chromosome is missing, making the person XO instead of XX, or the second X chromosome is partially deleted.

twin study A study in which the behavioral similarity of identical twins is compared with the behavioral similarity of fraternal twins.

type 1 diabetes An autoimmune disease in which the body's immune system destroys insulin-producing cells.

type 2 diabetes The most common type of diabetes, in which the body is able to produce insulin, but the amount may be insufficient or the body's cells may be unable to use it.

U

umbilical cord Contains two arteries and one vein, and connects the baby to the placenta.

universal ethical principles The sixth and highest stage in Kohlberg's theory of moral development. Individuals develop a moral standard based on universal principles of human rights.

V

values Beliefs and attitudes about the way things should be.

visual preference method A method used to determine whether infants can distinguish one stimulus from another by measuring the length of time they attend to different stimuli.

voice disorders Disorders reflected in speech that is hoarse, harsh, too loud, too high-pitched, or too low-pitched.

Vygotsky's theory A sociocultural cognitive theory that emphasizes how culture and social interaction guide cognitive development.

W

Wernicke's area An area of the brain's left hemisphere that is involved in language comprehension.

whole-language approach An approach to reading instruction based on the idea that instruction should parallel children's natural language learning. Reading materials should be whole and meaningful.

working memory A mental "workbench" where individuals manipulate and assemble information when making decisions, solving problems, and comprehending written and spoken language.

X

XYY syndrome A chromosomal disorder in which males have an extra Y chromosome.

Z

zone of proximal development (ZPD) Vygotsky's term for the range of tasks that are too difficult for children to achieve alone but can be achieved with the guidance and assistance of adults or more-skilled children.

zygote A single cell formed through fertilization.

references

A

Abbasi, M., & others (2010). The effect of hypnosis on pain relief during labor and childbirth in Iranian pregnant women. *International Journal of Clinical and Experimental Hypnosis, 57,* 174–183.

ABC News (2005, December 12). Larry Page and Sergey Brin. Retrieved June 24, 2006, from www. Montessori.org/enews/barbara_Walters.html

Abelsohn, A.R., & Sanborn, M. (2010). Lead and children: Clinical management for family physicians. *Canadian Family Physician, 56,* 531–535.

Abreu, C.N., & Filho, R.C. (2017). Anorexia nervosa and bulimia nervosa—a psychotherapeutic cognitive-constructivist approach. *International Review of Psychiatry, 29,* 248–253.

Abulizi, X., & others (2017). Temperament in infancy and behavioral and emotional problems at age 5.5: The EDEN mother-child cohort. *PLoS One, 12*(2), 0171971.

Achterberg, M., & others (2017). The neural and behavioral correlates of social evaluation in childhood. *Developmental Cognitive Neuroscience, 24,* 107–117.

Ackerman, J.P., Riggins, T., & Black, M.M. (2010). A review of the effects of prenatal cocaine exposure among school-aged children. *Pediatrics, 125,* 554–565.

Ackerman, R.A., & others (2013). The interpersonal legacy of a positive family climate in adolescence. *Psychological Science, 24,* 243–250.

Adams, A. (2015). A cultural historical theoretical perspective of discourse and design in the science classroom. *Cultural Studies of Science Education, 10,* 329–338.

Adams, K.A., & others (2017, in press). Caregiver talk and medical risk as predictors of language outcomes in full term and preterm toddlers. *Child Development.*

Adams, T., Keisberg, G., & Safranek, S. (2016). Clinical inquiry: Does caffeine intake during pregnancy affect birth weight? *Journal of Family Practice, 65,* 205–213.

Adamson, L., & Frick, J. (2003). The still face: A history of a shared experimental paradigm. *Infancy, 4,* 451–473.

Adler, J.M., & others (2017, in press). Research methods in studying narrative identity: A primer. *Social Psychology and Personality Science.*

Administration for Children & Families (2008). Statistical fact sheet fiscal year 2008. Washington, DC: Author.

Adolescent Sleep Working Group, AAP (2014). School start times for adolescents. *Pediatrics, 134,* 642–649.

Adolph, K.E. (1997). Learning in the development of infant locomotion. *Monographs of the Society for Research in Child Development, 62*(3, Serial No. 251).

Adolph, K.E. (2018, in press). Motor development. In M.H. Bornstein & others (Eds.), *SAGE encyclopedia of lifespan development.* Thousand Oaks, CA: Sage.

Adolph, K.E., & Berger, S.E. (2005). Physical and motor development. In M.H. Bornstein & M.E. Lamb (Eds.), *Developmental psychology* (5th ed.). Mahwah, NJ: Erlbaum.

Adolph, K.E., & Berger, S.E. (2015). Physical and motor development. In M.H. Bornstein & M.E. Lamb (Eds.), *Developmental science* (7th ed.). New York: Psychology Press.

Adolph, K.E., Karasik, L.B., & Tamis-LeMonda, C.S. (2010). Motor skills. In M. Bornstein (Ed.), *Handbook of cultural developmental science.* New York: Psychology Press.

Adolph, K.E., Kretch, K.S., & LoBue, V. (2014). Fear of height in infants? *Current Directions in Psychological Science, 23,* 60–66.

Adolph, K.E., & Robinson, S.R. (2013). The road to walking: What learning to walk tells us about development. In P. Zelazo (Ed.), *Oxford handbook of developmental psychology.* New York: Oxford University Press.

Adolph, K.E., & Robinson, S.R. (2015). Motor development. In R.M. Lerner (Eds.), *Handbook of child psychology and developmental science* (7th ed.). New York: Wiley.

Adolph, K.E., & others (2012). How do you learn to walk? Thousands of steps and dozens of falls per day. *Psychological Science, 23,* 1387–1394.

Afifi, T.O., & others (2017a, in press). Spanking and adult mental health impairment: The case for the designation of spanking as an adverse childhood experience. *Child Abuse and Neglect.*

Afifi, T.O., & others (2017b). The relationships between harsh physical punishment and child maltreatment in childhood and intimate partner violence in adulthood. *BMC Public Health, 17*(1), 493.

Agency for Healthcare Research and Quality (2007). Breastfeeding and maternal and infant health outcomes in developed countries. *Evidence Report/Technology Assessment, 153,* 1–186. Rockville, MD: U.S. Department of Health and Human Services.

Agerup, T., Lydersen, S., Wallander, J., & Sund, A.M. (2015). Associations between parental attachment and course of depression between adolescence and young adulthood. *Child Psychiatry and Human Development, 46,* 632–642.

Agostini, A., & others (2017, in press). An experimental study of adolescent sleep restriction during a simulated school week: Changes in phase, sleep staging, performance, and sleepiness. *Journal of Sleep Research.*

Agras, W.S., Fitzsimmons-Craft, E.E., & Wilfley, D.E. (2017). Evolution of cognitive-behavior therapy for eating disorders. *Behavior Research and Therapy, 88,* 26–36.

Agras, W.S., Hammer, L.D., McNicholas, F., & Kraemer, H.C. (2004). Risk factors for childhood overweight: A prospective study from birth to 9.5 years. *Journal of Pediatrics, 145,* 20–25.

Agras, W.S., & others (2004). Report of the National Institutes of Health workshop on overcoming barriers to treatment research in anorexia nervosa. *International Journal of Eating Disorders, 35,* 509–521.

Agricola, E., & others (2016). Investigating paternal preconception risk factors for adverse pregnancy outcomes in a population of Internet users. *Reproductive Health, 13,* 37.

Ahamed, M., Verma, S., Kumar, A., & Siddiqui, M.K. (2005). Environmental exposure to lead and its correlation with biochemical indices in children. *Science of the Total Environment, 346,* 48–55.

Ahluwalia, I.B., Tessaro, I., Grumer-Strawn, L.M., MacGowan, C., & Benton-Davis, S. (2000). Georgia's breastfeeding promotion program for low-income women. *Pediatrics, 105,* E85–E87.

Ahrens, B., Beyer, K., Wahn, U., & Niggemann, B. (2008). Differential diagnosis of food-induced symptoms. *Pediatric Allergy & Immunology, 19,* 92–96.

Ahrons, C. (2004). *We're still family.* New York: Harpercollins.

Ainsworth, M.D.S. (1979). Infant-mother attachment. *American Psychologist, 34,* 932–937.

Aires, L., & others (2016). Exercise intervention and cardiovascular risk factors in obese children. Comparison between obese youngsters taking part in a physical activity school-based program with and without individualized diet counseling: The ACORDA project. *Annals of Human Biology, 43,* 183–190.

Ajetunmobi, O.M., & others (2015). Breastfeeding is associated with reduced childhood hospitalization: Evidence from a Scottish birth cohort (1997–2009). *Journal of Pediatrics, 166,* 620–625.

Akbari, A., & others (2011). Parity and breastfeeding are preventive measures against breast cancer in Iranian women. *Breast Cancer, 18,* 51–55.

Akhutina, T., & Romanova, A. (2017). Games as a tool for facilitating cognitive development. In T. Bruce & others (Eds.), *Routledge international handbook of early childhood play.* New York: Routledge.

Akinsanya, A., Marwaha, R., & Tampi, R.R. (2017). Prazosin in children and adolescents with posttraumatic stress disorder who have nightmares: A systematic review. *Journal of Clinical Psychopharmacology, 37,* 84–88.

Aksglaede, L., & others (2013). 47, XXY Klinefelter syndrome: Clinical characteristics and age-specific recommendations for medical management. *American Journal of Medical Genetics C: Seminars in Medical Genetics, 163,* 55–63.

Alberico, S., & others (2014). The role of gestational diabetes, pre-pregnancy body mass index, and gestational weight gain on the risk of newborn macrosoma: Results from a prospective multicenter study. *BMC Pregnancy and Childbirth, 14*(1), 23.

Alberto, P.A., & Troutman, A.C. (2017). *Applied behavior analysis for teachers* (9th ed.). Upper Saddle River, NJ: Pearson.

Alby, C., & others (2016). Clinical, medical, and neuropathological findings in a series of 138 fetuses with a corpus callosum malformation. *Birth Defects Research A: Clinical and Molecular Teratology, 106,* 36–46.

Aldercotte, A., White, N., & Hughes, C. (2016). Sibling and peer relationships in early childhood. In L. Balter & C.S. Tamis-LeMonda (Eds.), *Child psychology* (3rd ed.). New York: Routledge.

Alderson-Day, B., & Fernyhough, C. (2014). More than one voice: Investigating the phenomenological properties of inner speech requires a variety of methods. *Consciousness and Cognition, 24,* 113–114.

Alegria, A.A., & others (2017, in press). Real-time fMRI neurofeedback in adolescents with attention deficit hyperactivity disorder. *Human Brain Mapping.*

Alexander, C., Piazza, M., Mekos, D., & Valente, T. (2001). Peers, schools, and cigarette smoking. *Journal of Adolescent Health, 29,* 22–30.

Alexander, C.P., & others (2017, in press). Fathers make a difference: Positive relationships with mother and baby in relation to infant colic. *Child Care, Health, and Development.*

Al-Ghanim, & Badahdah, A.M. (2017, in press). Gender roles in the Arab world: Development and psychometric properties of the Arab Adolescents Gender Roles Attitude Scale. *Sex Roles.*

Allameh, Z., Tehrani, H.G., & Ghasemi, M. (2015). Comparing the impact of acupuncture and pethidine on reducing labor pain. *Advanced Biomedical Research, 4,* 46.

Allen, J., & Allen, C. (2009). *Escaping the endless adolescence.* New York: Ballantine.

Allen, J.P. (2007, March). *A transformational perspective on the attachment system in adolescence.* Paper presented at the meeting of the Society for Research in Child Development, Boston.

Allen, J.P. (2008). The attachment system in adolescence. In J. Cassidy & P.R. Shaver (Eds.), *Handbook of attachment* (2nd ed.). New York: Guilford.

Allen, J.P., Chango, J., Szwedo, D., & Schad, M. (2014). Long-term sequelae of subclinical depressive symptoms in early adolescence. *Development and Psychopathology, 26,* 171–180.

Allen, J.P., & Miga, E.M. (2010). Attachment in adolescence: A move to the level of emotion regulation. *Journal of Social and Personal Relationships, 27,* 181–190.

Allen, J.P., Philliber, S., Herring, S., & Kuperminc, G.P. (1997). Preventing teen pregnancy and academic failure: Experimental evaluation of a developmentally based approach. *Child Development, 68,* 729–742.

Allen, J.P., Porter, M., McFarland, C., Boykin McElhaney, K., & Marsh, P. (2007). The relation of attachment security to adolescents' paternal and peer relationships, depression, and externalizing behavior. *Child Development, 78,* 1222–1239.

Allen, J.P., & Tan, J. (2016). The multiple facts of attachment in adolescence. In J. Cassidy & P.R. Shaver (Eds.), *Handbook of attachment* (3rd ed.). New York: Guilford.

Allen, J.P., & others (2009, April). *Portrait of the secure teen as an adult.* Paper presented at the meeting of the Society for Research in Child Development, Denver.

Allen, M., & others (2017). Metacognitive ability correlates with hippocampal and prefrontal microstructure. *NeuroImage, 149,* 415–423.

Allen, S., & Barlow, E. (2017). Long-acting reversible contraception: An essential guide for pediatric primary care. *Pediatric Clinics of North America, 64,* 359–369.

Allington, R.L. (2015). *What really matters for middle school readers.* Upper Saddle River, NJ: Pearson.

Alm, B., Wennergren, G., Mollborg, P., & Lagercrantz, H. (2016). Breastfeeding and dummy use have a protective effect on sudden infant death syndrome. *Acta Pediatrica, 105,* 31–38.

Almeida, N.D., & others (2016). Risk of miscarriage in women receiving antidepressants in early pregnancy, correcting for induced abortions. *Epidemiology, 27,* 538–546.

Almquist, Y.B., & Brannstrom, L. (2014). Childhood peer status and the clustering of social, economic, and health-related circumstances in adulthood. *Social Science & Medicine, 105,* 67–75.

Almy, B., & Cicchetti, D. (2018, in press). Developmental cascades. In M.H. Bornstein & others (Eds.), *SAGE encyclopedia of lifespan development.* Thousand Oaks, CA: Sage.

Alnababtah, K., Khan, S., & Ashford, R. (2016). Socio-demographic factors and the prevalence of burns in children: An overview of the literature. *Pediatric and International Child Health, 36,* 45–51.

Alonzo, D., Thompson, R.G., Stohl, M., & Hasin, D. (2014). The influence of parental divorce and alcohol abuse on adult offspring risk of lifetime suicide attempt in the United States. *American Journal of Orthopsychiatry, 84,* 316–320.

Altug, H., & others (2013). Effects of air pollution on lung function and symptoms of asthma, rhinitis, and eczema in primary school children. *Environmental Science and Pollution Research International, 20*(9), 6455.

Amabile, T. (1993). Commentary. In D. Goleman, P. Kaufman, & M. Ray (Eds.), *The creative spirit.* New York: Plume.

Amare, A.T., & others (2017). The genetic overlap between mood disorders and cardiometabolic disease: A systematic review of genome wide and candidate gene studies. *Translational Psychiatry, 7,* e1007.

Amato, P.R. (2006). Marital discord, divorce, and children's well-being: Results from a 20-year longitudinal study of two generations. In A. Clarke-Stewart & J. Dunn (Eds.), *Families count.* New York: Cambridge University Press.

Amato, P.R., & Anthony, C.J. (2014). Estimating the effects of parental divorce and death with fixed effects. *Journal of Marriage and the Family, 76,* 370–386.

Amato, P.R., & Booth, A. (1996). A prospective study of divorce and parent-child relationships. *Journal of Marriage and the Family, 58,* 356–365.

Ambrose, D., & Sternberg, R.J. (2016a). *Giftedness and talent in the 21st century.* Rotterdam, The Netherlands: Sense Publishers.

Ambrose, D., & Sternberg, R.J. (2016b). Previewing a collaborative exploration of giftedness and talent in the 21st century. In D. Ambrose & R.J. Sternberg (Eds.), *Giftedness and talent in the 21st century.* Rotterdam, The Netherlands.

American Academy of Pediatrics (2001). Committee on Public Education: Children, adolescents, and television. *Pediatrics, 107,* 423–426.

American Academy of Pediatrics (2016). *American Academy of Pediatrics announces new recommendations for children's media use.* Elk Grove Village, IL: AAP.

American Academy of Pediatrics Task Force on Infant Positioning and SIDS (AAPTFIPS) (2000). Changing concepts of sudden infant death syndrome. *Pediatrics, 105,* 650–656.

American Academy of Pediatrics: Section on Breastfeeding (2012). Breastfeeding and the use of human milk. *Pediatrics, 129,* e827–e841.

American College of Obstetricians and Gynecologists (2008). *Exercise during pregnancy.* Retrieved October 13, 2008, from http://www.acog.org/publications/patient_education/bp119.cfm

American Pregnancy Association (2017). *Mercury levels in fish.* Retrieved January 10, 2017, from http://www.americanpregnancy.org/pregnancyhealth/fishmercury.htm

American Psychological Association (2003). *Psychology: Scientific problem solvers.* Washington, DC: Author.

American Public Health Association (2006). *Understanding the health culture of recent immigrants to the United States.* Retrieved July 28, 2006, from http://www.apha.org/ppp/red/Intro.htm

Amole, M.C., Cyranowski, J.M., Wright, A.G.C., & Swartz, H.A. (2017). Depression impacts the physiological responsiveness of mother-daughter dyads during social interaction. *Depression Anxiety, 34,* 118–126.

Amrithraj, A.I., & others (2017, in press). Gestational diabetes alters functions in offspring's umbilical cord cells with implications for cardiovascular health.

Amsterdam, R.K. (1968). *Mirror behavior in children under two years of age.* Unpublished doctoral dissertation. University of North Carolina, Chapel Hill.

Amuna, P., & Zotor, F.B. (2008). Epidemiological and nutrition transition in developing countries: Impact on human health and development. *Proceedings of the Nutrition Society, 67,* 82–90.

Anastasi, A., & Urbina, S. (1997). *Psychological testing* (11th ed.). Upper Saddle River, NJ: Prentice Hall.

Anderman, E.M. (2012). Adolescence. In K. Harris, S. Graham, & T. Urdan (Eds.), *APA handbook of educational psychology.* Washington, DC: American Psychological Association.

Anderman, E.M., Gray, D.L., & Chang, Y. (2013). Motivation and classroom learning. In I.B. Weiner & others (Eds.), *Handbook of psychology* (2nd ed.) (Vol. 7). New York: Wiley.

Anderman, E.M., & Mueller, C.E. (2010). Middle school transitions and adolescent development: Disentangling psychological, social, and biological effects. In J. Meece & J. Eccles (Eds.). *Handbook of research on schools, schooling, and human development.* Clifton, NJ: Psychology Press.

Anderman, E.M., & Murdock, T.B. (Eds.). (2007). *Psychology of academic cheating.* San Diego: Academic Press.

Anderson, B.L., & Cu-Uvin, S. (2009). Pregnancy and optimal care of HIV-infected patients. *Clinical Infectious Diseases, 48,* 449–435.

Anderson, D.R., Huston, A.C., Schmitt, K., Linebarger, D.L., & Wright, J.C. (2001). Early childhood viewing and adolescent behavior: The recontact study. *Monographs of the Society for Research in Child Development, 66*(1), Serial No. 264.

Anderson, D.R., Torch, E.P., Held, D.E., Collins, P.A., & Nathan, J.G. (1985, April). *Television viewing at home: Age trends in visual attention and time with TV.* Paper presented at the biennial meeting of the Society for Research in Child Development, Toronto.

Anderson, E., Greene, S.M., Hetherington, E.M., & Clingempeel, W.G. (1999). The dynamics of parental remarriage. In E.M. Hetherington (Ed.), *Coping with divorce, single parenting, and remarriage.* Mahwah, NJ: Erlbaum.

Anderson, P.A. (2006). The evolution of biological sex differences in communication. In K. Dindia & D. J. Canary (Eds.), *Sex differences and similarities in communication.* Mahwah, NJ: Erlbaum.

Anderson, S.E., Gooze, R.A., Lemeshow, S., & Whitaker, R.C. (2012). Quality of early maternal-child relationship and risk of adolescent obesity. *Pediatrics, 129,* 132–140.

Andersson, H., & Bergman, L.R. (2011). The role of task persistence in young adolescence for successful educational and occupational attainment in middle adulthood. *Developmental Psychology, 47,* 950–960.

Andescavage, N.N., & others (2017, in press). Complex trajectories of brain development in the healthy human fetus. *Cerebral Cortex.*

Anding, J.E., & others (2016). Couple comorbidity and correlates of postnatal depressive symptoms in mothers and fathers in the first two weeks following delivery. *Journal of Affective Disorders, 190,* 300–309.

Andrade, E., & others (2016, Fall). Where PYD meets CBPR: A photovoice program for Latino immigrant youth. *Journal of Youth Development, 11*(2).

Andrews, N.C.Z., & others (2016). Development of expectancies for own- and other-gender group interactions and their school-related consequences. *Child Development, 87,* 1423–1435.

Andrews, S.J., & Lamb, M.E. (2017). The structural linguistic complexity of lawyers' questions and children's responses in Scottish criminal courts. *Child Abuse and Neglect, 65,* 182–193.

Andriani, H., Liao, C.Y., & Kuo, H.W. (2015). Parental weight changes as key predictors of child weight changes. *BMC Public Health, 15,* 645.

Ang, S., Rodgers, J.L., & Wanstrom, L. (2010). The Flynn effect within subgroups in the U.S.: Gender, race, income, education, and urbanization differences in the NYLS-children data. *Intelligence, 38,* 367–384.

Anglin, D.M., & others (2017, in press). Ethnic identity, racial discrimination, and attenuated psychotic symptoms in an urban population of emerging adults. *Early Intervention in Psychiatry.*

Annas, J., Narváez, D., & Snow, N. (Eds.) (2016). *Developing the virtues: Integrating perspectives.* New York: Oxford University Press.

Ansari, A., & Gershoff, E. (2016). Parent involvement in Head Start and children's development: Indirect effects through parenting. *Journal of Marriage and the Family, 78,* 562–579.

Ansari, A., & Winsler, A. (2014). Montessori public school pre-K programs and the school readiness of low-income Black and Latino children. *Journal of Educational Psychology, 106,* 1066–1079.

Ansari, J., Carvalho, B., Shafer, S.L., & Flood, P. (2016). Pharmacokinetics and pharmacodynamics of drugs commonly used in pregnancy and parturition. *Anesthesia and Analgesia, 122,* 786–804.

Antai-Otong, D. (2003). Suicide: Life span considerations. *Nursing Clinics of North America, 38,* 137–150.

Antfolk, J. (2017, in press). Age limits. *Evolutionary Psychology.*

Antonogeorgos, G., & others (2011). Association of extracurricular sports participation with obesity in Greek children. *Journal of Sports Medicine and Physical Fitness, 51,* 121–127.

Antonopoulos, C., & others (2011). Maternal smoking during pregnancy and childhood lymphoma: A meta-analysis. *International Journal of Cancer, 129,* 2694–2703.

Antonucci, T.C, & others (2016). Society and the individual at the dawn of the twenty-first century. In K.W. Schaie & S.L. Willis (Eds.), *Handbook of the psychology of aging* (8th ed.). New York: Elsevier.

Antovich, D.M., & Graf Estes, K. (2017, in press). Learning across languages: Bilingual experience supports dual language statistical word segmentation. *Developmental Science.*

Anyaegbu, E., & Dharnidharka, V.R. (2014). Hypertension in the teenager. *Pediatric Clinics of North America, 61,* 131–151.

Anzures, G., Goyet, L., Ganea, N., & Johnson, M.H. (2016). Enhanced ERPs to visual stimuli in unaffected male siblings of ASD children. *Child Neuropsychology, 22,* 220–227.

Aoki, C., Romeo, R.D., & Smith, S.S. (2017). Adolescence as a critical period for developmental plasticity. *Brain Research, 1654 (Pt. B),* 85–86.

Archibald, A.B., Graber, J.A., & Brooks-Gunn, J. (1999). Associations among parent-adolescent relationships, pubertal growth, dieting, and body image in young adolescent girls: A short-term longitudinal study. *Journal of Research on Adolescence, 9,* 395–415.

Ariceli, G., Castro, J., Cesena, J., & Toro, J. (2005). Anorexia nervosa in male adolescents: Body image, eating attitudes, and psychological traits. *Journal of Adolescent Health, 36,* 221–226.

Arim, R.G., & others (2011). The family antecedents and the subsequent outcomes of early puberty. *Journal of Youth and Adolescence, 40,* 1423–1435.

Arkes, J. (2015). The temporal effects of divorces and separations on children's academic achievement and problem behavior. *Journal of Divorce and Remarriage, 56,* 25–42.

Arnett, J.J. (2000). Emerging adulthood. *American Psychologist, 55,* 469–480.

Arnett, J.J. (2006). Emerging adulthood: Understanding the new way of coming of age. In J.J. Arnett & J.L. Tanner (Eds.), *Emerging adults in America.* Washington, DC: American Psychological Association.

Arnett, J.J. (2007). Socialization in emerging adulthood. In J.E. Grusec & P.D. Hastings (Eds.), *Handbook of socialization.* New York: Guilford.

Arnett, J.J. (Ed.) (2012). *Adolescent psychology around the world.* New York: Psychology Press.

Arnett, J.J. (2015). *Emerging adulthood* (2nd ed.). New York: Oxford University Press.

Aron, A., Aron, E., & Coups, E. (2017). *REVEL for statistics for psychology* (6th ed.). Upper Saddle River, NJ: Pearson.

Aronson, E. (1986, August). *Teaching students things they think they already know about: The case of prejudice and desegregation.* Paper presented at the meeting of the American Psychological Association, Washington, DC.

Aronson, J. (2002). Stereotype threat: Contending and coping with unnerving expectations. *Improving academic achievement.* San Diego: Academic Press.

Arseneault, L. (2017). The long-term impact of bullying victimization on mental health. *World Psychiatry, 16,* 27–28.

Asendorph, J.B. (2008). Shyness. In M.M. Haith & J.B. Benson (Eds.), *Encyclopedia of infant and early childhood development.* Oxford, UK: Elsevier.

Ash, P. (2008). Suicidal behavior in children and adolescents. *Journal of Psychosocial Nursing and Mental Health Services, 46,* 26–30.

Ashcraft, A.M., & Murray, P.J. (2017). Talking to parents about adolescent sexuality. *Pediatric Clinics of North America, 64,* 305–320.

Asheer, S., & others (2014). Engaging pregnant and parenting teens: Early challenges and lessons learned from the evaluation of adolescent pregnancy prevention approaches. *Journal of Adolescent Health, 54*(3, Suppl.), S84–S91.

Askeland, K.G., & others (2017). Mental health in internationally adopted adolescents: A meta-analysis. *Journal of the American Academy of Child and Adolescent Psychiatry, 56,* 202–213.

Aslin, R.N. (2009). The role of learning in cognitive development. In A. Woodward & A. Needham (Eds.), *Learning and the infant mind.* New York: Oxford University Press.

Aslin, R.N. (2012). Infant eyes: A window on cognitive development. *Infancy, 17,* 126–140.

Aslin, R.N., Jusczyk, P.W., & Pisoni, D.B. (1998). Speech and auditory processing during infancy: Constraints on and precursors to language. In W. Damon (Ed.), *Handbook of child psychology* (5th ed., Vol. 2). New York: Wiley.

Aslin, R.N., & Lathrop, A.L. (2008). Visual perception. In M.M. Haith & J.B. Benson (Eds.), *Encyclopedia of infant and early childhood development.* Oxford, UK: Elsevier.

Aspen Institute (2013). *Two generations, one future.* Washington, DC: Aspen Institute.

Aspen Institute (2017). *Making tomorrow better together.* Washington, DC: Aspen Institute.

Assanand, S., Dias, M., Richardson, E., & Waxler-Morrison, N. (1990). The South Asians. In N. Waxler-Morrison, J.M. Anderson, & E. Richardson (Eds.), *Cross-cultural caring.* Vancouver, BC: UBC Press.

Assini-Meytin, L.C., & Green, K.M. (2015). Long-term consequences of adolescent parenthood among African-American youth: A propensity score matching approach. *Journal of Adolescent Health, 56,* 529–535.

Astington, J.W., & Hughes, C. (2013). Theory of mind: Self-reflection and social understanding. In P.D. Zelazo (Ed.), *Oxford handbook of developmental psychology.* New York: Oxford University Press.

Ata, R.N., Ludden, A.B., & Lally, M.M. (2007). The effect of gender and family, friend, and media influences on eating behaviors and body image during adolescence. *Journal of Youth and Adolescence, 36,* 1024–1037.

Atkinson, J., & Braddick, O. (2013). Visual development. In P.D. Zelazo (Ed.), *Handbook of developmental psychology.* New York: Oxford University Press.

Atta, C.A., & others (2016). Global birth prevalence of spina bifida by folic acid fortification status: A systematic review and meta-analysis. *American Journal of Public Health, 106,* e24–e34.

Attie, I., & Brooks-Gunn, J. (1989). Development of eating problems in adolescent girls: A longitudinal study. *Developmental Psychology, 25,* 70–79.

Au, C.H., & others (2016). Clinical evaluation of panel testing by next-generation sequencing (NGS) for gene mutations in myeloid neoplasms. *Diagnostic Pathology, 22,* 11.

Aubuchon-Endsley, N., & others (2017, in press). Maternal pre-pregnancy obesity and gestational weight gain influence neonatal neurobehavior. *Maternal and Child Nutrition.*

Audesirk, G., Audesirk, T., & Byers, B.E. (2017). *Biology* (11th ed.). Upper Saddle River, NJ: Pearson.

Auerbach, J.G., Zilberman-Hayun, U., Atzaba-Poria, N., & Berger, A. (2017). The contribution of maternal ADHD symptomatology, maternal DAT1, and home atmosphere to child ADHD symptomatology at 7 years of age. *Journal of Abnormal Child Psychology, 45,* 415–427.

Autism Research Institute (2013). *DSM-V: What changes may mean.* Retrieved May 7, 2013, from www.autism.com/index.php/news_dsmV

Auyeung, B., & others (2009). Fetal testosterone predicts sexually differentiated childhood behavior in girls and in boys. *Psychological Science, 20,* 144–148.

Awwad, J., & others (2015). A randomized controlled double-blind clinical trial of 17-hydroxyprogesterone caproate for the prevention of preterm birth in twin gestation (PROGESTWIN): Evidence for reduced neonatal morbidity. *BJOG, 122*(1), 71–79.

Ayoub, C., Vallotton, C.D., & Mastergeorge, A.M. (2011). Developmental pathways to integrated social skills: The role of parenting and early intervention. *Child Development, 82,* 583–600.

Azar, S., & Wong, T.E. (2017). Sickle cell disease: A brief update. *Medical Clinics of North America, 101,* 375–393.

B

Babbie, E.R. (2017). *The basics of social research* (7th ed.). Boston: Cengage.

Bacchi, M., & others (2017, in press). Aquatic activities during pregnancy prevent excessive maternal weight gain and preserve birthweight. *American Journal of Health Promotion.*

Bachman, J.G., & others (2008). *The education–drug use connection.* Clifton, NJ: Psychology Press.

Bachmann, N., & others (2017, in press). Novel deletion of 11p15.5 imprinting center region 1 in a patient with Beckwith-Wiedemann syndrome provides insight into distal enhancer regulation and tumorigenesis. *Pediatric and Blood Cancer.*

Bacikova-Sleskova, M., Benka, J., & Orosova, O. (2015). Parental employment status and adolescents' health: The role of financial situation, parent-adolescent relationship, and adolescents' resilience. *Psychology and Health, 30,* 400–422.

Bacon, J.L., & Temich, P. (2017). *Obstetrics and gynecology.* New York: Elsevier.

Baddeley, A.D. (2007). *Working memory, thought, and action.* New York: Oxford University Press.

Baddeley, A.D. (2010a). Working memory. *Current Biology, 20,* 136–140.

Baddeley, A.D. (2010b). Long-term and working memory: How do they interact? In L. Backman & L. Nyberg (Eds.), *Memory, aging, and the brain.* New York: Psychology Press.

Baddeley, A.D. (2012). Prefatory. *Annual Review of Psychology* (Vol. 63). Palo Alto, CA: Annual Reviews.

Baddeley, A.D. (2013). On applying cognitive psychology. *British Journal of Psychology, 104,* 443–456.

Baddeley, A.D. (2015). Origins of multicomponent working memory model. In M. Eysenck & D. Groome (Eds.), *Cognitive psychology.* London: Sage.

Badeli, H., & others (2016). Prevalence of hypertension and obesity-related hypertension in urban school-aged children in Rasht. *Iranian Journal of Kidney Diseases, 10,* 364–368.

Baer, J. (2016). Creativity doesn't develop in a vacuum. *New Directions in Child and Adolescent Development, 151,* 9–20.

Bahrick, L.E. (2010). Intermodal perception and selective attention to intersensory redundancy: Implications for social development and autism. In J.G. Bremner & T.D. Wachs (Eds.), *Wiley-Blackwell handbook of infant development* (2nd ed.). New York: Wiley.

Bahrick, L.E., & Hollich, G. (2008). Intermodal perception. In M.M. Haith & J.B. Benson (Eds.), *Encyclopedia of infant and early childhood development.* Oxford, UK: Elsevier.

Bailey, A.L., Osipova, A., & Kelly, K.R. (2016). Language development. In L. Corno & E.M. Anderman (Eds.), *Handbook of educational psychology* (3rd ed.). New York: Routledge.

Baillargeon, R. (1995). The object concept revisited: New directions in the investigation of infants' physical knowledge. In C.E. Granrud (Ed.), *Visual perception and cognition in infancy.* Hillsdale, NJ: Erlbaum.

Baillargeon, R. (2004). The acquisition of physical knowledge in infancy: A summary in eight lessons. In U. Goswami (Ed.), *Blackwell handbook of childhood cognitive development.* Malden, MA: Blackwell.

Baillargeon, R. (2008). Innate ideas revisited: For a principle of persistence in infants' physical reasoning. *Perspectives on Psychological Science, 3,* 2–13.

Baillargeon, R. (2014). Cognitive development in infancy. *Annual Review of Psychology* (Vol. 65). Palo Alto, CA: Annual Reviews.

Baillargeon, R. (2016). Cognitive development in infancy. *Annual Review of Psychology* (Vol. 67). Palo Alto, CA: Annual Reviews.

Baillargeon, R., & DeVos, J. (1991). Object permanence in young children: Further evidence. *Child Development, 62,* 1227–1246.

Baillargeon, R., Li, J., Gertner, Y., & Wu, D. (2011). How do infants reason about physical events? In U. Goswami (Ed.), *Wiley-Blackwell handbook of childhood cognitive development* (2nd ed.). New York: Wiley.

Baillargeon, R., & others (2012). Object individuation and physical reasoning in infancy: An integrative account. *Language, Learning, and Development, 8*(1), 4–46.

Bakeman, R., & Brown, J.V. (1980). Early interaction: Consequences for social and mental development at three years. *Child Development, 51,* 437–447.

Baker, J., & others (Eds.) (2017). *Routledge handbook of talent identification and development in sport.* New York: Routledge.

Baker, J.H., Rothenberger, S.D., Kline, C.E., & Okun, M.L. (2017, in press). Exercise during pregnancy is associated with greater sleep continuity. *Behavioral Sleep Medicine.*

Baker, J.K., Fenning, R.M., & Crnic, K.A. (2011). Emotion socialization by mothers and fathers: Coherence among behaviors and associations with parent attitudes and children's competence. *Social Development, 20,* 412–430.

Baker, R.K., Pettigrew, T.L., & Poulin-Dubois, D. (2014). Infants' ability to associate motion paths with object kinds. *Infant Behavior and Development, 37,* 119–129.

Bakermans-Kranenburg, M.J., & van IJzendoorn, M.H. (2011). Differential susceptibility to rearing environment depending on dopamine-related genes: New evidence and a meta-analysis. *Development and Psychopathology, 23,* 39–52.

Bakermans-Kranenburg, M.J., & van IJzendoorn, M.H. (2016). Attachment, parenting, and genetics. In J. Cassidy & P.R.Shaver (Eds.), *Handbook of parenting* (3rd ed.). New York: Guilford.

Bakusic, J., & others (2017). Stress, burnout, and depression: A systematic review on DNA methylation mechanisms. *Journal of Psychosomatic Research, 92,* 34–44.

Balantekin, K.N., Birch, L.L., & Savage, J.S. (2017, in press). Family, friend, and media factors are associated with patterns of weight-control behavior among adolescent girls. *Eating and Weight Disorders.*

Baldwin, S.A., Christian, S., Berkeljon, A., & Shadish, W.R. (2012). The effects of family therapies for adolescent delinquency and substance abuse: A meta-analysis. *Journal of Marital and Family Therapy, 38,* 281–304.

Ball, J.W., Bindler, R.C., & Cowen, K.J. (2014). *Child health nursing* (3rd ed.). Upper Saddle River, NJ: Pearson.

Ballou, D., & Springer, M.G. (2017). Has NCLB encouraged educational triage? Accountability and the distribution of achievement gains. *Education Finance and Policy, 12,* 77–106.

Bamaca-Colbert, M., Umana-Taylor, A.J., Espinosa-Hernandez, G., & Brown, A.M. (2012). Behavioral autonomy expectations among Mexican-origin mother-daughter dyads: An examination of within-group variability. *Journal of Adolescence, 35,* 691–700.

Ban, L., Gibson, J.E., West, J., & Tata, L.J. (2010). Association between perinatal depression in mothers and the risk of infections in offspring: A population-based cohort study. *BMC Public Health, 10,* 799–806.

Bandura, A. (1998, August). *Swimming against the mainstream: Accentuating the positive aspects of humanity.* Paper presented at the meeting of the American Psychological Association, San Francisco.

Bandura, A. (2001). Social cognitive theory. *Annual Review of Psychology* (Vol. 52). Palo Alto, CA: Annual Reviews.

Bandura, A. (2004, May). *Toward a psychology of human agency.* Paper presented at the meeting of the American Psychological Society, Chicago.

Bandura, A. (2007). Self-efficacy in health functioning. In S. Ayers & others (Eds.), *Cambridge handbook of psychology, health and medicine* (2nd ed.). New York: Cambridge University Press.

Bandura, A. (2010a). Self-efficacy. In D. Matsumoto (Ed.), *Cambridge dictionary of psychology.* New York: Cambridge University Press.

Bandura, A. (2010b). Self-reinforcement. In D. Matsumoto (Ed.), *Cambridge dictionary of psychology.* New York: Cambridge University Press.

Bandura, A. (2012). Social cognitive theory. *Annual Review of Clinical Psychology* (Vol. 8). Palo Alto, CA: Annual Reviews.

Bandura, A. (2015). *Moral disengagement.* New York: Worth.

Banks, J.A. (2014). *Introduction to multicultural education* (5th ed.). Upper Saddle River, NJ: Pearson.

Baptista, J., Belsky, J., Mesquita, A., & Soares, I. (2017). Serotonin transporter polymorphism moderates the effects of caregiver intrusiveness on ADHD symptoms among institutionalized preschoolers. *European Child and Adolescent Psychiatry, 26,* 303–313.

Barakat, R., & others (2016). Exercise during pregnancy protects against hypertension and macrosomia: Randomized clinical trial. *American Journal of Obstetrics and Gynecology, 214* (5), 649e1–18.

Barakat, R., & others (2017, in press). Influence of land and water exercise in pregnancy on outcomes: A cross-sectional study. *Medicine and Science in Sports and Exercise.*

Barbaro, N., Boutwell, B.B., Barnes, J.C., & Shackelford, T.K. (2017). Rethinking the transmission gap: What behavioral genetics and evolutionary psychology mean for attachment theory: A comment on Verhage et al. (2016). *Psychological Bulletin, 143,* 107–113.

Barbee, A.P., & others (2016). Impact of two adolescent pregnancy prevention interventions on risky sexual behavior: A three-arm cluster randomized control trial. *American Journal of Public Health, 106,* S85–S90.

Barber, B., Stone, M., & Eccles, J. (2010). Protect, prepare, support, and engage: The roles of school-based extracurricular activities in students' development. In J. Meece & J. Eccles (Eds.), *Handbook of research on schools, schooling, and human development.* New York: Routledge.

Barbot, B., & Tinio, P.P. (2015). Where is the "g" in creativity? A specialization-differentiation hypothesis. *Frontiers in Human Neuroscience, 8,* 1041.

Bardak, H., & others (2017, in press). Next-generation sequencing analysis of the ARMS2 gene in Turkish exudative age-related macular degeneration patients. *Genetics and Molecular Research.*

Bardid, F., & others (2017a). The effectiveness of a community-based fundamental motor skill intervention in children aged 3–8 years: Results of the "Multimove for Kids" project. *Journal of Science and Medicine in Sport, 20,* 184–189.

Bardid, F., & others (2017b, in press). Configurations of actual and perceived motor competence among children: Associations with motivation for sports and global self-worth. *Human Movement Science.*

Bardikoff, N., & Sabbagh, M. (2017). The differentiation of executive function over development: Insights from developmental cognitive neuroscience. In N. Buwig & others (Eds.), *New perspectives on human development.* New York: Cambridge University Press.

Barfield, W.D., Warner, L., & Kappeler, E. (2017). Why we need evidence-based, community-wide prevention of teen pregnancy. *Journal of Adolescent Health, 60* (Suppl. 3), S3–S6.

Bargh, J.A., & McKenna, K.Y.A. (2004). The Internet and social life. *Annual Review of Psychology* (Vol. 55). Palo Alto, CA: Annual Reviews.

Barker, R., & Wright, H.F. (1951). *One boy's day.* New York: Harper & Row.

Barnett, L.M., Salmon, J., & Hesketh, K.D. (2016). More active pre-school children have better motor coordination at school starting age: An observational cohort study. *BMC Public Health, 16,* 1068.

Baron, N.S. (1992). *Growing up with language.* Reading, MA: Addison-Wesley.

Baron-Cohen, S. (2008). Autism, hypersystemizing, and truth. *Quarterly Journal of Experimental Psychology, 61,* 64–75.

Baron-Cohen, S. (2011). The empathizing-systemizing (E-S) theory of autism: A cognitive developmental account. In U. Goswami (Ed.), *Wiley-Blackwell handbook of childhood cognitive development* (2nd ed.). New York: Wiley-Blackwell.

Baron-Cohen, S., Golan, O., Chapman, E., & Granader, Y. (2007). Transported to a world of emotion. *The Psychologist, 20,* 76–77.

Barone, L., Lionetti, F., & Green, J. (2017, in press). A matter of attachment? How adoptive parents foster post-institutionalized children's social and emotional adjustment. *Attachment and Human Development.*

Barrington-Trimis, J.L., & others (2017, in press). Type of e-cigarette device used by adolescents and young adults: Findings from a pooled analysis of 8 studies of 2,166 vapers. *Nicotine and Tobacco Research.*

Bartlett, J.D., & others (2014). An ecological analysis of infant neglect by adolescent mothers. *Child Abuse and Neglect, 38,* 723–734.

Barton, M., & others (2017). Better health-related fitness in youth: Implications for public health guidelines. *International Journal of Exercise Science, 10,* 379–389.

Bartsch, K., & Wellman, H.M. (1995). *Children talk about the mind.* New York: Oxford University Press.

Bartschat, S., Richter, C., Stiller, D., & Banshak, S. (2016). Long-term outcome in a case of shaken baby syndrome. *Medicine, Science, and the Law, 56,* 147–149.

Barzilay, S., & others (2017, in press). Bullying victimization and suicide ideation and behavior among adolescents in Europe: A 10-country study. *Journal of Adolescent Health.*

Bascandziev, I., & Harris, P.L. (2011). The role of testimony in young children's solution of a gravity-driven invisible displacement task. *Cognitive Development, 25,* 233–246.

Bas-Sarmiento, P., & others (2017). Mental health in immigrants versus native population: A systematic review of the literature. *Archives of Psychiatric Nursing, 31,* 111–121.

Basterfield, L., & others (2015). Longitudinal associations between sports participation, body composition, and physical activity from childhood to adolescence. *Journal of Science and Medicine in Sport, 18,* 178–182.

Bateman, B.T., & Simpson, L.L. (2006). Higher rate of stillbirth at the extremes of reproductive age: A large nationwide sample of deliveries in the United States. *American Journal of Obstetrics and Gynecology, 194,* 840–845.

Bates, J.E. (2008). Unpublished review of J.W. Santrock's *Children,* 11th ed. New York: McGraw-Hill.

Bates, J.E. (2012a). Behavioral regulation as a product of temperament and environment. In S.L. Olson & A.J. Sameroff (Eds.), *Biopsychosocial regulatory processes in the development of childhood behavioral problems.* New York: Cambridge University Press.

Bates, J.E. (2012b). Temperament as a tool in promoting early childhood development. In S.L. Odom, E.P. Pungello, & N. Gardner-Neblett (Eds.), *Infants, toddlers, and families in poverty.* New York: Guilford University Press.

Bates, J.E., & Pettit, G.S. (2015). Temperament, parenting, and social development. In J.E. Grusec & P.D. Hastings (Eds.), *Handbook of socialization* (2nd ed.). New York: Guilford.

Battistich, V.A. (2008). The Child Development Project: Creating caring school communities. In L. Nucci & D. Narváez (Eds.), *Handbook of moral and character education.* Clifton, NJ: Psychology Press.

Bauer, A., Knapp, M., & Parsonage, M. (2016). Lifetime costs of perinatal anxiety and depression. *Journal of Affective Disorders, 192,* 83–90.

Bauer, P.J. (2009a). Learning and memory: Like a horse and carriage. In A. Needham & A. Woodward (Eds.), *Learning and the infant mind.* New York: Oxford University Press.

Bauer, P.J. (2009b). Neurodevelopmental changes in infancy and beyond: Implications for learning and memory. In O.A. Barbarin & B.H. Wasik (Eds.), *Handbook of child development and early education.* New York: Oxford University Press.

Bauer, P.J. (2013). Memory. In P.D. Zelazo (Ed.), *Oxford handbook of developmental psychology.* New York: Oxford University Press.

Bauer, P.J. (2015). A complementary processes account of the development of childhood amnesia and a personal past. *Psychological Review, 122,* 204–231.

Bauer, P.J., & Fivush, R. (Eds.) (2014). *Wiley-Blackwell handbook of children's memory.* New York: Wiley.

Bauer, P.J., Hattenschwiler, N., & Larkina, M. (2016). "Owning" the personal past: Adolescents' and adults' autobiographical narratives and ratings of memory of recent and distant events. *Memory, 24,* 165–183.

Bauer, P.J., & Larkina, M. (2014). The onset of childhood amnesia in childhood: A prospective investigation of the course and determinants of forgetting of early-life events. *Memory, 22,* 907–924.

Bauer, P.J., & Larkina, M. (2016). Predicting and remembering and forgetting of autobiographical memories in children and adults: A 4-year prospective study. *Memory, 24,* 1345–1368.

Bauer, P.J., Larkina, M., & Deocampo, J. (2011). Early memory development. In U. Goswami (Ed.), *Wiley-Blackwell handbook of childhood cognitive development* (2nd ed.). New York: Wiley-Blackwell.

Bauer, P.J., & Leventon, S.J. (2015). The development of declarative memory in infancy and implications for social learning. In S.D. Calkins (Ed.), *Handbook of biopsychosocial development.* New York: Guilford.

Bauer, P.J., Wenner, J.A., Dropik, P.I., & Wewerka, S.S. (2000). Parameters of remembering and forgetting in the transition from infancy to early childhood. *Monographs of the Society for Research in Child Development, 65*(4, Serial No. 263).

Bauer, P.J., & others (2003). Developments in long-term explicit memory late in the first year of life: Behavioral and electrophysiological indices. *Psychological Science, 14,* 629–635.

Baugh, N., & others (2017, in press). The impact of maternal obesity and excessive gestational weight gain on maternal and infant outcomes in Maine: Analysis of pregnancy risk assessment monitoring results from 2000 to 2010. *Journal of Pregnancy.*

Bauman, K.E., & others (2002). Influence of a family program on adolescent smoking and drinking prevalence. *Prevention Science, 3,* 35–42.

Baumeister, R.F., Campbell, J.D., Krueger, J.I., & Vohs, K.D. (2003). Does high self-esteem cause better performance, interpersonal success, happiness, or healthier lifestyles? *Psychological Science in the Public Interest, 4*(1), 1–44.

Baumrind, D. (1971). Current patterns of parental authority. *Developmental Psychology Monographs, 4*(1, Pt. 2).

Baumrind, D. (2012). Authoritative parenting revisited: History and current status. In R. Larzelere, A.S. Morris, & A.W. Harist (Eds.), *Authoritative parenting.* Washington, DC: American Psychological Association.

Baxley, F., & Miller, M. (2006). Parental misperceptions about children and firearms. *Archives of Pediatric and Adolescent Medicine, 160,* 542–547.

Bayley, N. (1969). *Manual for the Bayley Scales of Infant Development.* New York: Psychological Corporation.

Bayley, N. (2005). *Bayley Scales of Infant and Toddler Development* (3rd ed.). San Antonio: Harcourt Assessment.

Bear, D.R., & others (2016). *Words their way* (6th ed.). Upper Saddle River, NJ: Pearson.

Beart, P.M. (2016). Synaptic signaling and its interface with neuropathologies: Snapshots from the past, present, and future. *Journal of Neurochemistry, 139*(Suppl. 2), 76–90.

Beauchamp, G., & Mennella, J.A. (2009). Early flavor learning and its impact on later feeding behavior. *Journal of Pediatric Gastroenterology and Nutrition, 48*(Suppl. 1), S25–S30.

Beaver, N., Wyatt, S., & Jackman, H. (2018). *Early education curriculum* (7th ed.). Boston: Cengage.

Bechtold, A.G., Bushnell, E.W., & Salapatek, P. (1979, April). *Infants' visual localization of visual and auditory targets.* Paper presented at the meeting of the Society for Research in Child Development, San Francisco.

Beck, D. (2017) A typology of morphological processes: Form and function. In A.Y. Aikhenvald & R.M.W. Dixon (Eds.), *Cambridge handbook of linguistic typology.* New York: Cambridge University Press.

Becker, D.R., Miao, A., Duncan, R., & McClelland, M.M. (2014). Behavioral self-regulation and executive function both predict visuomotor skills and early academic achievement. *Early Childhood Research Quarterly, 29,* 411–424.

Becker, M.W., Alzahabi, R., & Hopwood, C.J. (2013). Media multitasking is associated with symptoms of depression and social anxiety. *Cyberpsychology, Behavior, and Social Networking, 16,* 132–136.

Bedford, R., & others (2017, in press). The role of infants' mother-directed gaze, maternal sensitivity, and emotion regulation in childhood. *European Child and Adolescent Psychiatry.*

Bednar, R.L., Wells, M.G., & Peterson, S. (1995). *Self-esteem* (2nd ed.). Washington, DC: American Psychological Association.

Beebe, B., & others (2016). A systematic view of mother-infant face-to-face communication. *Developmental Psychology, 52,* 556–571.

Beeghly, M., & others (2006). Prenatal cocaine exposure and children's language functioning at 6 and 9.5 years: Moderating effects of child age, birthweight, and gender. *Journal of Pediatric Psychology, 31,* 98–115.

Beets, M.W., & Foley, J.T. (2008). Association of father involvement and neighborhood quality with kindergarteners' physical activity: A multilevel structural equation model. *American Journal of Health Promotion, 22,* 195–203.

Beghetto, R.A., & Kaufman, J.C. (Eds.) (2017). *Nurturing creativity in the classroom* (2nd ed.). New York: Cambridge University Press.

Beguin, M. (2016). Object pragmatics and language development. *Integrative Psychological and Behavioral Science, 50,* 603–620.

Behrens, H. (2012). Grammatical categories. In E.L. Bavin (Ed.), *Cambridge handbook of child language.* New York: Cambridge University Press.

Bell, M.A. (2015). Bringing the field of infant cognition and perception toward a biopsychosocial perspective. In S.D. Calkins (Ed.), *Handbook of infant biopsychosocial development.* New York: Guilford.

Bell, M.A., & Cuevas, K. (2012). Using EEG to study cognitive development: Issues and practices. *Journal of Cognition and Development, 13,* 281–294.

Bell, M.A., & Cuevas, K. (2015). Psychobiology of executive function in early development. In J.A. Griffin, L.S. Freund, & P. McCardle (Eds.), *Executive function in preschool children.* Washington, DC: American Psychological Association.

Bell, M.A., Ross, A.P., & Patton, L.K. (2017, in press). Emotion regulation. In M.H. Bornstein & others (Eds.), *SAGE encyclopedia of lifespan development.* Thousand Oaks, CA: Sage.

Bell, M.A., Wolfe, C.D., & Adkins, D.R. (2007). Frontal lobe development during infancy and childhood.

In D.J. Coch, G. Dawson, & K.W. Fischer (Eds.), *Human behavior, learning, and the developing brain.* New York: Guilford.

Bell, M.A., & others (2018, in press). Brain development. In M.H. Bornstein & others (Eds.), *SAGE encyclopedia of lifespan development.* Thousand Oaks, CA: Sage.

Bell, S.M., & Ainsworth, M.D.S. (1972). Infant crying and maternal responsiveness. *Child Development, 43,* 1171–1190.

Bellieni, C.V., & others (2016). How painful is a heelprick or a venipuncture in a newborn? *Journal of Maternal-Fetal and Neonatal Medicine, 29,* 202–206.

Bellinger, D.C. (2008). Very low lead exposures and children's neurodevelopment. *Current Opinion in Pediatrics, 20,* 172–177.

Belsky, J. (1981). Early human experience: A family perspective. *Developmental Psychology, 17,* 3–23.

Belsky, J. (2009). Classroom composition, childcare history, and social development: Are childcare effects disappearing or spreading? *Social Development, 18,* 230–238.

Belsky, J., & Pluess, M. (2016). Differential susceptibility to environmental influences. In D. Cicchetti (Ed.), *Developmental psychopathology* (3rd ed.). New York: Wiley.

Belsky, J., & van IJzendoorn, M.H. (2017, in press). What works for whom? Genetic moderation of intervention efficacy. *Development and Psychopathology.*

Belsky, J., & others (2010). The development of reproductive strategy in females: Early maternal harshness, earlier menarche, increased sexual risk. *Developmental Psychology, 46,* 120–128.

Belsky, J., & others (2015). Differential susceptibility to effects of maternal sensitivity? A study of candidate plasticity genes. *Development and Psychopathology, 27,* 725–746.

Bem, S.I. (1977). On the utility of alternative procedures for assessing psychological androgyny. *Journal of Consulting and Clinical Psychology, 45,* 196–205.

Bendersky, M., & Sullivan, M.W. (2007). Basic methods in infant research. In A. Slater & M. Lewis (Eds.), *Introduction to infant development* (2nd ed.). New York: Oxford University Press.

Bendezu, J.J., & others (2017, in press). Longitudinal relations among parental monitoring strategies, knowledge, and adolescent delinquency in a racially diverse at-risk sample. *Journal of Clinical Child and Adolescent Psychology.*

Benediktsson, I., & others (2013). Comparing CenteringPregnancy to standard prenatal care plus prenatal education. *BMC Pregnancy and Childbirth,* Suppl. 1, S5.

Bengtsson, H., & Arvidsson, A. (2011). The impact of developing social perspective-taking skills on emotionality in middle and late childhood. *Social Development, 20,* 353–375.

Benitez, V.L., & others (2017). Sustained selective attention predicts flexible switching in preschoolers. *Journal of Experimental Child Psychology, 156,* 29–42.

Benner, A.D., & Graham, S. (2009). The transition to high school as a developmental process among multiethnic urban youth. *Child Development, 80,* 356–376.

Benowitz-Fredericks, C.A., Garcia, K., Massey, M., Vassagar, B., & Borzekowski, D.L. (2012). Body image, eating disorders, and the relationship to adolescent media use. *Pediatric Clinics of North America, 59,* 693–704.

Benson, J.E., & Sabbagh, M.A. (2017). Executive function helps children think about and learn about others' mental states. In M.J. Hoskyns & others (Eds.), *Executive functions in children's everyday lives.* New York: Oxford University Press.

Benson, L., Baer, H.J., & Kaelber, D.C. (2009). Trends in the diagnosis of overweight and obesity in children and adolescents: 1999–2007. *Pediatrics, 123,* e153–e158.

Benson, P.L. (2010). *Parent, teacher, mentor, friend: How every adult can change kids' lives.* Minneapolis: Search Institute Press.

Benson, P.L., Mannes, M., Pittman, K., & Ferber, T. (2004). Youth development, developmental assets, and public policy. In R. Lerner & L. Steinberg (Eds.), *Handbook of adolescent psychology* (2nd ed.). New York: Wiley.

Benson, P.L., & Scales, P.C. (2009a). The definition and preliminary measurement of thriving in adolescence. *Journal of Positive Psychology, 4,* 85–104.

Benson, P.L., & Scales, P.C. (2009b). Positive youth development and the prevention of youth aggression and violence. *European Journal of Developmental Science, 3*(3), 218–234.

Benson, P.L., & Scales, P.C. (2011). Thriving and sparks: Development and emergence of new core concepts in positive youth development. In R.J.R. Levesque (Ed.), *Encyclopedia of adolescence.* Berlin: Springer.

Benyi, E., & Savendahl, L. (2017, in press). The physiology of child growth: Hormonal regulation. *Hormone Research in Pediatrics.*

Bera, A., & others (2014). Effects of kangaroo care on growth and development of low birthweight babies up to 12 months of age: A controlled clinical trial. *Acta Pediatrica, 103,* 643–650.

Berenbaum, S.A., Beltz, A.M., & Corley, R. (2015). The importance of puberty for adolescent development: Conceptualization and measurement. *Advances in Child Development and Behavior, 48,* 53–92.

Berenson, G.S. (2005). Obesity—A critical issue in preventive cardiology: The Bogalusa Heart Study. *Preventive Cardiology, 8,* 234–241.

Berenson, G.S., & Bogalusa Heart Study Group (2012). Health consequences of obesity. *Pediatric Blood and Cancer, 58,* 117–121.

Berenson, G.S., Srinivasan, S.R., Xu, J.H., & Chen, W. (2016). Adiposity and cardiovascular risk factor variables in childhood are associated with premature death from coronary heart disease in adults: The Bogalusa Heart Study. *American Journal of Medical Science, 352,* 448–454.

Berge, J.M., & others (2015). The protective role of family dinners for youth obesity: 10-year longitudinal associations. *Journal of Pediatrics, 166,* 296–301.

Bergen, D. (1988). Stages of play development. In D. Bergen (Ed.), *Play as medium for learning and development.* Portsmouth, NH: Heinemann.

Bergen, D. (2015). Psychological approaches to the study of play. In J.E. Johnson & others (Eds.), *Handbook of the study of play.* Blue Ridge Summit, PA: Rowman & Littlefield.

Bergman, J.E., Otten, E., Verheij, J.B., & de Walls, H.E. (2016). Folic acid supplementation influences the distribution of neural tube defect subtypes: A registry-based study. *Reproductive Toxicology, 59,* 96–100.

Berk, L.E. (1994). Why children talk to themselves. *Scientific American, 271*(5), 78–83.

Berk, L.E., & Spuhl, S.T. (1995). Maternal interaction, private speech, and task performance in preschool children. *Early Childhood Research Quarterly, 10,* 145–169.

Berko, J. (1958). The child's learning of English morphology. *Word, 14,* 150–177.

Berko Gleason, J. (2003). Unpublished review of J.W. Santrock's *Life-span development,* 9th ed. (New York: McGraw-Hill).

Berko Gleason, J. (2009). The development of language: An overview. In J. Berko Gleason & N.B. Ratner (Eds.), *The development of language* (7th ed.). Boston: Allyn & Bacon.

Berkowitz, M.W., Battistich, V.A., & Bier, M. (2008). What works in character education: What is known and what needs to be known. In L. Nucci & D. Narváez (Eds.), *Handbook of moral and character education.* Clifton, NJ: Psychology Press.

Berlin, L.J., & others (2009). Correlates and consequences of spanking and verbal punishment for low-income White, African-American, and Mexican American toddlers. *Child Development, 80,* 1403–1420.

Berlyne, D.E. (1960). *Conflict, arousal, and curiosity.* New York: McGraw-Hill.

Berman, M.G., & others (2013). Dimensionality of brain networks linked to life-long individual differences in self-control. *Nature Communications, 4,* 1373.

Berman, S.L., You, Y., Schwartz, S., Teo, G., & Mochizuki, K. (2011). Identity exploration, commitment, and distress: A cross national investigation in China, Taiwan, Japan, and the United States. *Child Youth Care Forum, 40,* 65–75.

Bernard, K., & Dozier, M. (2008). Adoption and foster placement. In M.M. Haith & J.B. Benson (Eds.), *Encyclopedia of infant and early childhood development.* Oxford, UK: Elsevier.

Berndt, T.J., & Perry, T.B. (1990). Distinctive features and effects of early adolescent friendships. In R. Montemayor (Ed.), *Advances in adolescent research.* Greenwich, CT: JAI Press.

Bernier, A., & others (2013). Sleep and cognition in preschool years: Specific links to executive functioning. *Child Development, 84*(5), 1542–1553.

Bernier, A., & others (2017). Parenting and young children's executive function development. In M.J. Hoskyn & others (Eds.), *Executive functions in* children's everyday lives. New York: Oxford University Press.

Bernier, A., Beauchamp, M.H., Carlson, S.M., & Lalonde, G. (2015). A secure base from which to regulate: Attachment security in toddlerhood is a predictor of executive functioning at school entry. *Developmental Psychology, 51,* 1177–1189.

Bernier, A., Calkins, S.D., & Bell, M.A. (2016). Longitudinal associations between the quality of mother-infant interactions and brain development across infancy. *Child Development, 87,* 1159–1174.

Bernier, A., Carlson, S.M., & Whipple, N. (2010). From external regulation to self-regulation: Early parenting precursors of young children's executive functioning. *Child Development, 81,* 326–339.

Bernier, R., & Dawson, G. (2016). Autism spectrum disorders. In D. Cicchetti (Ed.), *Developmental psychopathology* (3rd ed.). New York: Wiley.

Berninger, V.W., & O'Malley, M.M. (2011). Evidence-based diagnosis and treatment for specific learning disabilities involving impairments in written and/or oral language. *Journal of Learning Disabilities, 44,* 167–183.

Bernthal, J.E., Bankson, N.W., & Flipsen, P. (2017). *Articulation and phonological disorders* (8th ed.). Upper Saddle River, NJ: Pearson.

Berry, J.W. (2015). Acculturation. In J.E. Grusec & P.D. Hastings (Eds.), *Handbook of socialization* (2nd ed.). New York: Guilford.

Bertenthal, B.I. (2008). Perception and action. In M.M. Haith & J.B. Benson (Eds.), *Encyclopedia of infant and early childhood development.* Oxford, UK: Elsevier.

Bertenthal, B.I., Longo, M.R., & Kenny, S. (2007). Phenomenal permanence and the development of predictive tracking in infancy. *Child Development, 78,* 350–363.

Besser, A.G., & Mounts, E.L. (2017, in press). Counseling considerations for chromosomal mosaicism detected by preimplantation genetic screening. *Reproductive Biomedicine Online.*

Best, J.R. (2010). Effects of physical activity on children's executive function: Contributions of experimental research on aerobic exercise. *Developmental Review, 30,* 331–351.

Betts, K.S., Williams, G.M., Najman, J.M., & Alati, R. (2014). Maternal depressive, anxious, and stress symptoms during pregnancy predict internalizing problems in adolescence. *Depression and Anxiety, 31,* 9–18.

Beuker, K.T., Rommelse, N.N., Donders, R., & Buitelaar, J.K. (2013). Development of early communication skills in the first two years of life. *Infant Behavior and Development, 36,* 71–83.

Bevan, D., Wittkowski, A., & Wells, A. (2013). A multiple-baseline study of the effects associated with metacognitive therapy in postpartum depression. *Journal of Midwifery and Women's Health, 58,* 69–75.

Beyers, W., & Luyckx, K. (2016). Ruminative exploration and reconsideration of commitment as risk factors for suboptimal identity development in adolescence and emerging adulthood. *Journal of Adolescence, 47,* 169–178.

Bialystok, E. (1997). Effects of bilingualism and biliteracy on children's emerging concepts of print. *Developmental Psychology, 33,* 429–440.

Bialystok, E. (2001). *Bilingualism in development: Language, literacy, and cognition.* New York: Cambridge University Press.

Bialystok, E. (2007). Acquisition of literacy in preschool children: A framework for research. *Language Learning, 57,* 45–77.

Bialystok, E. (2010). Global-local and trail-making tasks by monolingual and bilingual children: Beyond inhibition. *Developmental Psychology, 46,* 93–105.

Bialystok, E. (2011, April). *Becoming bilingual: Emergence of cognitive outcomes of bilingualism in immersion education.* Paper presented at the meeting of the Society for Research in Child Development, Montreal.

Bialystok, E. (2014). Language experience changes language and cognitive ability: Implications for social policy. In B. Spolsky, O. Inbar-Lourie, & M. Tannenbaum (Eds.), *Challenges for language education and policy.* New York: Routledge.

Bialystok, E. (2015). The impact of bilingualism on cognition. In R. Scott & S. Kosslyn (Eds.), *Emerging trends in the social and behavioral sciences.* New York: Wiley.

Bialystok, E. (2017). The bilingual adaptation: How minds accommodate experience. *Psychological Bulletin, 143,* 233–262.

Bialystok, E., & Craik, F.I.M. (2010). Cognitive and linguistic processing in the bilingual mind. *Current Directions in Psychological Science, 19,* 19–23.

Bick, J., & Nelson, C.A. (2017, in press). Early experience and brain development. *Wiley Interdisciplinary Review of Cognitive Science.*

Bick, J., & others (2017). Early deprivation, atypical brain development, and internalizing symptoms in late childhood. *Neuroscience, 342,* 140–153.

Biddle, S.J., Garcia Bengoechea, E., & Wiesner, G. (2017). Sedentary behavior and adiposity in youth: A systematic review of reviews and analysis of causality. *Journal of Behavioral Nutrition and Physical Activity, 14*(1), 43.

Biehle, S.N., & Mickelson, K.D. (2012). First-time parents' expectations about the division of childcare and play. *Journal of Family Psychology, 26,* 36–45.

Bierman, K.L., & others (2014). Effects of Head Start REDI on children's outcomes 1 year later in different kindergarten contexts. *Child Development, 85*(1), 140–159.

Bill and Melinda Gates Foundation (2008). America's newest high school graduates earn diplomas, celebrate individual achievements. Retrieved June 28, 2017, from http://www.gatesfoundation.org/Media-Center/Press-Releases/2008/06/ . . .

Bill and Melinda Gates Foundation (2011). *College-ready education.* Retrieved August 21, 2011, from www.gatesfoundation.org/college-ready-education/Pages/default.aspx

Bill and Melinda Gates Foundation (2016). *K-12 education.* Retrieved December 20, 2016, from www.gatesfoundation.org/What-We-Do/US-Programs/K-12-Edu . . .

Billy, J.O.G., Rodgers, J.L., & Udry, J.R. (1984). Adolescent sexual behavior and friendship choice. *Social Forces, 62,* 653–678.

Bindler, R.C., & others (2017). *Clinical manual for maternity and pediatric nursing* (5th ed.). Upper Saddle River, NJ: Pearson.

Birch, S., & Bloom, P. (2003). Children are cursed: An asymmetric bias in mental state attribution. *Psychological Science, 14,* 283–286.

Birch, S.A., & others (2017). Perspectives on perspective taking: How children think about the minds of others. *Advances in Child Development and Behavior, 52,* 185–226.

Bird, A.L., & others (2017). Maternal health in pregnancy and associations with adverse birth outcomes: Evidence from Growing Up in New Zealand. *Australia and New Zealand Obstetrics and Gynecology, 57,* 16–24.

Birkeland, M.S., Melkevick, O., Holsen, I., & Wold, B. (2012). Trajectories of global self-esteem development during adolescence. *Journal of Adolescence, 35,* 43–54.

Birman, B.F., & others (2007). *State and local implementation of the "No Child Left Behind Act." Volume II—Teacher quality under "NCLB": Interim report.* Jessup, MD: U.S. Department of Education.

Birnbach, D.J., & Ranasinghe, J.S. (2008). Anesthesia complications in the birthplace: Is the neuraxial block always to blame? *Clinical Perinatology, 35,* 35–52.

Bjorkenstam, C., Kosidou, K., & Bjorkenstam, E. (2017). Childhood adversity and risk of suicide: Cohort study of 548,721 adolescents and young adults in Sweden. *BMJ, 357,* 1334.

Bjorklund, D.F. (2012). *Children's thinking* (5th ed.). Boston: Cengage.

Bjorklund, D.F., & Pellegrini, A.D. (2011). Evolutionary perspectives on social development. In P.K. Smith & C.H. Hart (Eds.), *Wiley-Blackwell handbook of childhood social development* (2nd ed.). New York: Wiley.

Black, M.M., & Hurley, K.M. (2007). Helping children develop healthy eating habits. In R.E. Tremblay, R.G. Barr, R. Peters, & M. Boivin (Eds.), *Encyclopedia of early childhood development* (Rev. Ed.). Retrieved March 11, 2008, from http://www.child-encyclopedia.com/documents/Black-Hurley ANGxp_rev-Eating.pdf

Black, M.M., & Hurley, K.M. (2017). Responsive feeding: Strategies to promote healthy mealtime interactions. *Nestle Nutrition Institute Workshop Series, 87,* 153–165.

Black, M.M., & others (2017). Early childhood development coming of age: Science through the life course. *Lancet, 389,* 77–90.

Black, R.E., & others (2013). Maternal and child undernutrition in low-income and middle-income countries. *Lancet, 382,* 427–451.

Blackowicz, M.J., & others (2017, in press). The impact of low-level lead toxicity on school performance among Hispanic subgroups in the Chicago public schools. *International Journal of Environmental Research and Public Health.*

Blackstone, S.R., & Herrmann, L.K. (2016). Relationships between illicit drug use and body mass index among adolescents. *Health Education and Behavior, 43,* 21–24.

Blackwell, L.S., & Dweck, C.S. (2008). *The motivational impact of a computer-based program that teaches how the brain changes with learning.* Unpublished manuscript, Department of Psychology, Stanford University, Palo Alto, CA.

Blackwell, L.S., Trzesniewski, K.H., & Dweck, C.S. (2007). Implicit theories of intelligence predict achievement across an adolescent transition: A longitudinal study and an intervention. *Child Development, 78,* 246–263.

Blaga, O.M., & others (2009). Structure and continuity of intellectual development in early childhood. *Intelligence, 37,* 106–113.

Blair, C. (2016). The development of executive functions and self-regulation: A bidirectional psychobiological model. In K.D. Vohs & R. Baumeister (Eds.), *Handbook of self-regulation* (3rd ed.). New York: Guilford.

Blair, C. (2017, in press). Educating executive function. *Wiley Interdisciplinary Reviews. Cognitive Science.*

Blair, C., & Raver, C.C. (2012). Child development in the context of poverty: Experiential canalization of brain and behavior. *American Psychologist, 67,* 309–318.

Blair, C., & Raver, C.C. (2014). Closing the achievement gap through modification and neuroendocrine function: Results from a cluster randomized controlled trial of an innovative approach for the education of children in kindergarten. *PLoS One, 9*(11), e112393.

Blair, C., & Raver, C.C. (2015). School readiness and self-regulation: A developmental psychobiological approach. *Annual Review of Psychology* (Vol. 66). Palo Alto, CA: Annual Reviews.

Blair, C., Raver, C.C., & Berry, D.J. (2014). Two approaches estimating the effect of parenting on the development of executive function in early childhood. *Developmental Psychology, 50,* 554–565.

Blair, C., Raver, C.C., & Finegood, E.D. (2016). Self-regulation and developmental psychopathology: Experiential canalization of brain and behavior. In D. Cicchetti (Ed.), *Developmental psychopathology* (3rd ed.). New York: Wiley.

Blair, C., & others (2015). Multiple aspects of self-regulation uniquely predict mathematics but not letter-word knowledge in the early elementary grades. *Developmental Psychology, 5,* 459–472.

Blake, J.S. (2017). *Nutrition and you* (4th ed.). Upper Saddle River, NJ: Pearson.

Blake, J.S., Munoz, K.D., & Volpe, S. (2016). *Nutrition: From science to you plus mastering nutrition with MyDietAnalysis with etext* (3rd ed.). Upper Saddle River, NJ: Pearson.

Blakely-McClure, S.J., & Ostrov, J.M. (2016). Relational aggression, victimization, and self-concept: Testing pathways from middle childhood to adolescence. *Journal of Youth and Adolescence, 45,* 376–390.

Blakemore, J.E.O., Berenbaum, S.A., & Liben, L.S. (2009). *Gender development.* New York: Psychology Press.

Blakey, J. (2011). Normal births or spontaneous vertex delivery? *Practicing Midwife, 14,* 12–13.

Blandthorn, J., Forster, D.A., & Love, V. (2011). Neonatal and maternal outcomes following maternal use of buprenorphine or methadone during pregnancy: Findings of a retrospective audit. *Women and Birth, 24,* 32–39.

Blankenship, S.L., Redcay, E., Dougherty, L.R., & Riggins, T. (2017). Development of hippocampal functional connectivity during childhood. *Human Brain Mapping, 38,* 182–201.

Blankenship, T.L., O'Neill, M., Deater-Deckard, K., Diana, R.A., & Bell, M.A. (2016). Frontotemporal functional connectivity and executive functions contribute to episodic memory performance. *International Journal of Psychophysiology, 107,* 72–82.

Blass, E. (2008). Suckling. In M.M. Haith & J.B. Benson (Eds.), *Encyclopedia of infant and early childhood development.* Oxford, UK: Elsevier.

Blatny, M., Millova, K., Jelinek, M., & Osecka, T. (2015). Personality predictors of successful development: Toddler temperament and adolescent personality traits predict well-being and career stability in middle adulthood. *PLoS One, 10*(4), e0126032.

Bleakley, A., & others (2017, in press). Alcohol, sex, and screens: Modeling media influence on adolescent alcohol and sex co-occurrence. *Journal of Sex Research.*

Blood, J.D., & others (2015). The variable heart: High frequency and very low frequency correlates of depressive symptoms in children and adolescents. *Journal of Affective Disorders, 186,* 119–126.

Bloom, B. (1985). *Developing talent in young people.* New York: Ballantine.

Bloom, L., Lifter, K., & Broughton, J. (1985). The convergence of early cognition and language in the second year of life: Problems in conceptualization and measurement. In M. Barrett (Ed.), *Single word speech.* London: Wiley.

Bloom, P., & German, T.P. (2000). Two reasons to abandon the false belief task as a test of theory of mind. *Cognition, 77,* B25–B31.

Blum, J.W., Beaudoin, C.M., & Caton-Lemos, L. (2005). Physical activity patterns and maternal well-being in postpartum women. *Maternal and Child Health Journal, 8,* 163–169.

Boardman, J.P., & Fletcher-Watson, S. (2017, in press). What can eye-tracking tell us? *Archives of Disease in Childhood.*

Bodrova, E., & Leong, D.J. (2007). *Tools of the mind (2nd ed.).* Geneva, Switzerland: International Bureau of Education, UNESCO.

Bodrova, E., & Leong, D.J. (2015). Vygotskian and post-Vygotskian views of children's play. *American Journal of Play, 7,* 371–388.

Boekeloo, B.O., & others (2015). The role of intrinsic motivation in the pursuit of health science-related careers among youth from underrepresented low socioeconomic populations. *Journal of Urban Health, 92,* 980–994.

Bohlin, G., & Hagekull, B. (2009). Socio-emotional development: From infancy to young adulthood. *Scandinavian Journal of Psychology, 50,* 592–601.

Bonanno, R.A., & Hymel, S. (2013). Cyber bullying and internalizing difficulties: Above and beyond the impact of traditional forms of bullying. *Journal of Youth and Adolescence, 42,* 685–697.

Bond, V.L. (2015). Sounds to share: The state of music education in three Reggio-Emilia inspired North American preschools. *Journal of Research in Music Education, 62,* 462–484.

Bonney, C.R., & Sternberg, R.J. (2017). Learning to think critically. In R.E. Mayer & P.A. Alexander (Eds.), *Handbook of learning and instruction (2nd ed.).* New York: Routledge.

Bono, G. (2012, August 5). *Searching for the developmental role of gratitude: A 4-year longitudinal analysis.* Paper presented at the American Psychological Association, Orlando.

Boonstra, H. (2002, February). Teen pregnancy: Trends and lessons learned. *The Guttmacher Report on Public Policy,* pp. 7–10.

Booth, M. (2002). Arab adolescents facing the future: Enduring ideals and pressures to change. In B.B. Brown, R.W. Larson, & T.S. Saraswathi (Eds.), *The world's youth.* New York: Cambridge University Press.

Boraska, V., & others (2014). A genome-wide study of anorexia nervosa. *Molecular Psychiatry, 19,* 1085–1094.

Bordoni, L., & others (2017). Obesity-related genetic polymorphisms and adiposity indices in a young Italian population. *IUBMB Life, 69,* 98–105.

Borich, G.D. (2017). *Effective teaching methods* (9th ed.). Upper Saddle River, NJ: Pearson.

Bornstein, M.H. (1975). Qualities of color vision in infancy. *Journal of Experimental Child Psychology, 19,* 401–409.

Bornstein, M.H. (2016). Determinants of parenting. In D. Cicchetti (Ed.), *Developmental psychopathology* (3rd ed.). New York: Wiley.

Bornstein, M.H., Arterberry, M., & Mash, C. (2015). Perceptual development. In M.H. Bornstein & M.E. Lamb (Eds.), *Developmental science* (7th ed.). New York: Psychology Press.

Bornstein, M.H., & Zlotnik, D. (2008). Parenting styles and their effects. In M.M. Haith & J.B. Benson (Eds.), *Encyclopedia of infant and early childhood development.* Oxford, UK: Elsevier.

Bornstein, M.H., & others (Eds.) (2018, in press). *SAGE encyclopedia of lifespan development.* Thousand Oaks, CA: Sage.

Bos, D.J., & others (2017, in press). Structural and functional connectivity in children and adolescents with and without attention deficit/hyperactivity disorder. *Journal of Child Psychology and Psychiatry.*

Bosma, H.A., & Kunnen, E.S. (2001). Determinants and mechanisms in ego identity development: A review and synthesis. *Developmental Review, 21,* 39–66.

Botkin, J.R. (2016). Ethical issues in pediatric genetic testing and screening. *Current Opinion in Pediatrics, 28,* 700–704.

Bouchard, T.J. (1995, August). *Heritability of intelligence.* Paper presented at the meeting of the American Psychological Association, New York.

Bouchard, T.J. (2008). Genes and human psychological traits. In P. Carruthers, S. Laurence, & S. Stich (Eds.), *The innate mind: Foundations for the future* (Vol. 3). Oxford: Oxford University Press.

Boukhris, T., Sheehy, O., Mottron, L., & Berard, A. (2016). Antidepressant use during pregnancy and the risk of autism spectrum disorder in children. *JAMA Pediatrics, 170,* 117–124.

Boundy, E.O., & others (2017, in press). Kangaroo care and neonatal outcomes: A meta-analysis. *Pediatrics.*

Boutot, E.A. (2017). *Autism spectrum disorders* (2nd ed.). Upper Saddle River, NJ: Pearson.

Bovbjerg, M.L., Cheyney, M., & Everson, C. (2016). Maternal and newborn outcomes following waterbirth: The Midwives Alliance of North America Statistics Project, 2004 to 2009 cohort. *Journal of Midwifery and Women's Health, 61,* 11–20.

Bower, T.G.R. (1966). Slant perception and shape constancy in infants. *Science, 151,* 832–834.

Bowlby, J. (1969). *Attachment and loss* (Vol. 1). London: Hogarth Press.

Bowlby, J. (1989). *Secure and insecure attachment.* New York: Basic Books.

Boyer, K., & Diamond, A. (1992). Development of memory for temporal order in infants and young children. In A. Diamond (Ed.), *Development and neural bases of higher cognitive function.* New York: Academy of Sciences.

Boyle, J., & Cropley, M. (2004). Children's sleep: Problems and solutions. *Journal of Family Health Care, 14,* 61–63.

Braccio, S., Sharland, M., & Ladhani, S.N. (2016). Prevention and treatment of mother-to-child syphilis. *Current Opinion on Infectious Diseases, 29,* 268–274.

Bracken, M.B., & others (1990). Association of cocaine use with sperm concentration, motility, and morphology. *Fertility and Sterility, 53,* 315–322.

Brady, K.W., & Goodman, J.C. (2014). The type, but not the amount, of information available influences toddlers' fast mapping and retention of new words. *American Journal of Speech and Language Pathology, 23,* 120–123.

Brainerd, C.J., & Reyna, V.E. (1993). Domains of fuzzy-trace theory. In M.L. Howe & R. Pasnak (Eds.), *Emerging themes in cognitive development.* New York: Springer.

Brainerd, C.J., & Reyna, V.E. (2014). Dual processes in memory development: Fuzzy-trace theory. In P. Bauer & R. Fivush (Eds.), *Wiley-Blackwell handbook of children's memory.* New York: Wiley.

Braithwaite, E.C., & others (2017). Maternal prenatal cortisol predicts infant negative emotionality in a sex-dependent manner. *Physiology and Behavior, 175,* 31–36.

Bralic, I., & others (2012). Association of early menarche age and overweight/obesity. *Journal of Pediatric Endocrinology and Metabolism, 25,* 57–62.

Brams, H., Mao, A.R., & Doyle, R.L. (2009). Onset of efficacy of long-lasting psychostimulants in pediatric attention-deficit/hyperactivity disorder. *Postgraduate Medicine, 120,* 69–88.

Brand, S.R., & Brennan, P.A. (2009). Impact of antenatal and postpartum maternal mental illness: How are the children? *Clinical Obstetrics and Gynecology, 52,* 441–455.

Brannon, L. (2017). *Gender.* New York: Routledge.

Bratke, H., & others (2017). Timing of menarche in Norwegian girls: Associations with body mass, waist circumference, and skinfold thickness. *BMC Pediatrics, 17,* 138.

Braun, S.S., & Davidson, A.J. (2017, in press). Gender (non)conformity in middle childhood: A mixed methods approach to understanding gender-typed behavior, friendship, and peer preference. *Sex Roles.*

Braver, S.L., & Lamb, M.E. (2013). Marital dissolution. In G.W. Peterson & K.R. Bush (Eds.), *Handbook of marriage and the family* (3rd ed.). New York: Springer.

Bredekamp, S. (2017). *Effective practices in early childhood education* (3rd ed.). Upper Saddle River, NJ: Pearson.

Breen, M., & others (2016). Imitated prosodic fluency predicts reading comprehension ability in good and poor high school readers. *Frontiers in Psychology, 7,* 1026.

Brelsford, G.M., & Mahoney, A. (2008). Spiritual disclosure between older adolescents and their mothers. *Journal of Family Psychology, 22,* 62–70.

Bremner, A.J., & Spence, C. (2017). The development of tactile stimulation. *Advances in Child Development and Behavior, 52,* 227–268.

Bremner, J.G., Slater, A.M., Johnson, S.P., Mason, U.C., & Spring, J. (2012). The effects of auditory information on 4-month-old infants' perception of trajectory continuity. *Child Development, 83*(3), 954–964.

Bremner, J.G., & others (2017). Limits of object persistence: Young infants perceive continuity of vertical and horizontal trajectories but not 45-degree oblique trajectories. *Infancy, 22,* 303–322.

Brenner, J.D. (2016). Traumatic stress from a multi-level developmental psychopathology perspective. In D. Cicchetti (Ed.), *Developmental psychopathology* (3rd ed.). New York: Wiley.

Brent, R.L. (2009). Saving lives and changing family histories: Appropriate counseling of pregnant women and men and women of reproductive age concerning the risk of diagnostic radiation exposure during and before pregnancy. *American Journal of Obstetrics and Gynecology, 200,* 4–24.

Brent, R.L. (2011). The pulmonologist's role in caring for pregnant women with regard to the reproductive risks of diagnostic radiological studies or radiation therapy. *Clinics in Chest Medicine, 32*(1), 33–42.

Brentari, D., & Goldin-Meadow, S. (2017, in press). Language emergence. *Annual Review of Linguistics.*

Breslau, J., & others (2017). Sex differences in recent first-onset depression in an epidemiological sample of adolescents. *Translational Psychiatry, 7*(5), e1139.

Bretherton, I., & Munholland, K.A. (2016). The internal working model construct in light of contemporary neuroimaging research. In J. Cassidy & P.R. Shaver (Eds.), *Handbook of attachment* (3rd ed.). New York: Guilford.

Breveglieri, G., & others (2016). Y-chromosome identification in circulating cell-free DNA using surface plasmon resonance. *Prenatal Diagnosis, 36,* 353–361.

Bridgett, D.J., Laake, L.M., Gartstein, M.A., & Dorn, D. (2013). Development of infant positive emotionality: The contribution of maternal characteristics and effects on subsequent parenting. *Infant and Child Development, 22*(4), 362–382.

Brindis, C.D. (2017). Advancing the field of teenage pregnancy prevention through community-wide pregnancy prevention initiatives. *Journal of Adolescent Health, 60*(Suppl. 3), S1–S2.

Brinksma, D.M., & others (2017). Age-dependent role of pre- and perinatal factors in interaction with genes on ADHD symptoms across adolescence. *Journal of Psychiatric Research, 90,* 110–117.

Brion, M., & others (2012). Sarcomeric gene mutations in sudden infant death syndrome (SIDS). *Forensic Science International, 219*(1), 278–281.

Brock, R.L., & Kochanska, G. (2016). Interparental conflict, children's security with parents, and long-term risk of internalizing problems: A longitudinal study from ages 2 to 10. *Development and Psychopathology, 28,* 45–54.

Brodsky, J.L., Viner-Brown, S., & Handler, A.S. (2009). Changes in maternal cigarette smoking among pregnant WIC participants in Rhode Island. *Maternal and Child Health Journal, 13,* 822–831.

Brody, G.H., & others (2017). Protective prevention effects on the association of poverty with brain development. *JAMA Pediatrics, 17,* 46–52.

Brody, N. (2000). Intelligence. In A. Kazdin (Ed.), *Encyclopedia of psychology.* New York: Oxford University Press.

Brody, N. (2007). Does education influence intelligence? In P.C. Kyllonen, R.D. Roberts, & L. Stankov (Eds.), *Extending intelligence.* Mahwah, NJ: Erlbaum.

Brodzinsky, D.M., & Pinderhughes, E. (2002). Parenting and child development in adoptive families. In M.H. Bornstein (Ed.), *Handbook of parenting* (Vol. I). Mahwah, NJ: Erlbaum.

Broekhof, E., & others (2015). The understanding of intentions, desires, and beliefs in young children with autism spectrum disorder. *Journal of Autism and Developmental Disorders, 45,* 2035–2045.

Broesch, T., & Bryant, G.A. (2017, in press). Fathers' infant-directed speech in a small-scale society. *Child Development.*

Bronfenbrenner, U. (1986). Ecology of the family as a context for human development: Research perspectives. *Developmental Psychology, 22,* 723–742.

Bronfenbrenner, U. (2000). Ecological theory. In A. Kazdin (Ed.), *Encyclopedia of psychology.* New York: Oxford University Press.

Bronfenbrenner, U., & Morris, P.A. (2006). The ecology of developmental processes. In W. Damon & R. Lerner (Eds.), *Handbook of child psychology* (6th ed.). New York: Wiley.

Bronstein, P. (2006). The family environment: Where gender role socialization begins.

In J. Worell & C.D. Goodheart (Eds.), *Handbook of girls' and women's psychological health*. New York: Oxford University Press.

Brook, J.S., Balka, E.B., Zhang, C., & Brook, D.W. (2014). ADHD, conduct disorder, substance use disorder, and non-prescription stimulant use. *Journal of Attention Disorders, 21,* 776–782.

Brooks, J.G., & Brooks, M.G. (2001). *The case for constructivist classrooms* (2nd ed.). Upper Saddle River, NJ: Erlbaum.

Brooks, R., & Meltzoff, A.N. (2005). The development of gaze in relation to language. *Developmental Science, 8,* 535–543.

Brooks, R., & Meltzoff, A.N. (2008). Infant gaze following and pointing predict accelerated vocabulary growth through two years of age: A longitudinal, growth curve modeling study. *Journal of Child Language, 35,* 207–220.

Brooks, R., & Meltzoff, A.N. (2014). Gaze following: A mechanism for building social connections between infants and adults. In M. Mikulincer & P.R. Shaver (Eds.), *Mechanisms of social connection*. Washington, DC: American Psychological Association.

Brooks-Gunn, J., Han, W-J., & Waldfogel, J. (2010). First-year maternal employment and child development in the first seven years. *Monographs of the Society for Research in Child Development (SRCD), 75*(2), 1–147.

Brooks-Gunn, J., & Warren, M.P. (1989). The psychological significance of secondary sexual characteristics in 9- to 11-year-old girls. *Child Development, 59,* 161–169.

Brown, B.B. (2011). Popularity in peer group perspective: The role of status in adolescent peer systems. In A.H.N. Cillessen, D. Schwartz, & L. Mayeux (Eds.), *Popularity in the peer system*. New York: Guilford.

Brown, B.B., & Bakken, J.P. (2011). Parenting and peer relationships: Reinvigorating research on family-peer linkages in adolescence. *Journal of Research on Adolescence, 21,* 153–165.

Brown, B.B., & Dietz, E.L. (2009). Informal peer groups in middle childhood and adolescence. In K.H. Rubin, W.M. Bukowski, & B. Laursen (Eds.), *Handbook of peer interaction, relationships, and groups*. New York: Guilford.

Brown, B.B., & Larson, J. (2009). Peer relationships in adolescence. In R.M. Lerner & L. Steinberg (Eds.), *Handbook of adolescent development* (3rd ed.). New York: Wiley.

Brown, B.B., & Larson, R.W. (2002). The kaleidoscope of adolescence: Experiences of the world's youth at the beginning of the 21st century. In B.B. Brown, R.W. Larson, & T.S. Saraswathi (Eds.), *The world's youth*. New York: Cambridge University Press.

Brown, B.B., & Lohr, M.J. (1987). Peer-group affiliation and adolescent self-esteem: An integration of ego-identity and symbolic-interaction theories. *Journal of Personality and Social Psychology, 52,* 47–55.

Brown, D.A., & Lamb, M.E. (2015). Can children be useful witnesses? It depends how they are questioned. *Child Development Perspectives, 9,* 250–255.

Brown, E.C., & others (2016). A systematized review of primary school whole class child obesity interventions: Effectiveness, characteristics, and strategies. *BioMed Research International. 2016,* 4902714.

Brown, H.L., & Graves, C.R. (2013). Smoking and marijuana in pregnancy. *Clinical Obstetrics and Gynecology, 56,* 107–113.

Brown, J.E. (2017). *Nutrition through the life cycle* (6th ed.). Boston: Cengage.

Brown, Q.L., & others (2016). Trends in marijuana use among pregnant and non-pregnant reproductive-aged women 2002–2014. *JAMA, 317,* 207–209.

Brown, R. (1958). *Words and things*. Glencoe, IL: Free Press.

Brown, R. (1973). *A first language: The early stages*. Cambridge, MA: Harvard University Press.

Brown, S.M., & others (2017, in press). Systematic medications used in treatment of common dermatological conditions: Safety profile with respect to pregnancy, breast feeding, and content in seminal fluid. *Journal of Dermatological Treatment*.

Brown, W.H., & others (2009). Social and environmental factors associated with preschoolers' nonsedentary physical activity. *Child Development, 80,* 45–58.

Browne, T.K. (2017). Why parents should not be told the sex of their fetus. *Journal of Medical Ethics, 43,* 5–10.

Brownell, C. (2011). Early Social Development Lab. Retrieved March 24, 2011, from http://www.pitt.edu/~toddlers/ESDL/brownell.html

Brownell, C., Nichols, S., Svetlova, M., Zerwas, S., & Ramani, G. (2009). The head bone's connected to the neck bone: When do toddlers represent their own body topography? *Child Development, 81*(3), 797–810.

Brownell, C.A., Lemerise, E.A., Pelphrey, K.A., & Roisman, G.I. (2015). Measuring socioemotional behavior and development. In R.M. Lerner (Ed.), *Handbook of child psychology and developmental science* (7th ed.). New York: Wiley.

Brownell, C.A., Ramani, G.B., & Zerwas, S. (2006). Becoming a social partner with peers: Cooperation and social understanding in one- and two-year-olds. *Child Development, 77,* 803–821.

Brownell, C.A., Svetlova, M., Anderson, R., Nichols, S.R., & Drummond, J. (2013). Socialization of early prosocial behavior: Parents' talk about emotions is associated with sharing and helping in toddlers. *Infancy, 18*(1), 91–119.

Bruchmiller, K., Margraf, J., & Schneider, S. (2012). Is ADHD diagnosed in accord with diagnostic criteria? Overdiagnosis and influence of client gender on diagnosis. *Journal of Consulting and Clinical Psychology, 80,* 128–138.

Bruck, M., & Ceci, S.J. (1999). The suggestibility of children's memory. *Annual Review of Psychology, 50,* 419–439.

Bruck, M., & Ceci, S.J. (2012). Forensic developmental psychology in the courtroom. In D. Faust & M. Ziskin (Eds.), *Coping with psychiatric and psychological testimony*. New York: Cambridge University Press.

Bruck, M., & Melnyk, L. (2004). Individual differences in children's suggestibility: A review and a synthesis. *Applied Cognitive Psychology, 18,* 947–996.

Bruckner, S., & Kammer, T. (2017). Both anodal and cathodal transcranial direct current stimulation improves semantic processing. *Neuroscience, 343,* 269–275.

Brumariu, L.E., & Kerns, K.A. (2011). Parent-child attachment in early and middle childhood. In P.K. Smith & C.H. Hart (Eds.), *Wiley-Blackwell handbook of social development* (2nd ed.). New York: Wiley.

Brumariu, L.E., & Kerns, K.A. (2013). Pathways to anxiety: Contributions to attachment history, temperament, peer competence, and ability to manage intense emotions. *Child Psychiatry and Human Development, 44,* 504–515.

Brumariu, L.E., Kerns, K.A., & Seibert, A.C. (2012). Mother-child attachment, emotion regulation, and anxiety symptoms in middle childhood. *Personal Relationships, 19*(3), 569–585.

Brummelman, J.E., Thomaes, S., Orbobio de Castro, B., Overbeek, G., & Bushman, B.J. (2014). "That's not just beautiful—that's incredibly beautiful!": The adverse impact of inflated praise on children with low self-esteem. *Psychological Science, 25,* 728–735.

Brummelte, S., & Galea, L.A. (2016). Postpartum depression: Etiology, treatment, and consequences for maternal care. *Hormones and Behavior, 77,* 153–166.

Brunborg, G.S., Andreas, J.B., & Kvaavik, E. (2017). Social media use and episodic heavy drinking among adolescents. *Psychological Reports, 120,* 475–490.

Brust-Renck, P.G., Reyna, V.F., Wilhelms, E.A., & Lazar, A.N. (2017). A fuzzy-trace theory of judgment and decision-making in healthcare: Explanations, predictions, and applications. In M.A., Diefenbach & others (Eds.), *Handbook of health and decision science*. New York: Springer.

Bryant, J.B. (2012). Pragmatic development. In E.L. Bavin (Ed.), *Cambridge handbook of child language*. New York: Cambridge University Press.

Buckingham-Howes, S., Berger, S.S., Scaletti, L.A., & Black, M.M. (2013). Systematic review of prenatal cocaine exposure and adolescent development. *Pediatrics, 131,* e1917–e1936.

Buckner, J.C., Mezzacappa, E., & Beardslee, W.R. (2009). Self-regulation and its relations to adaptive functioning in low-income youths. *American Journal of Orthopsychiatry, 79,* 19–30.

Budge, S.L., Chin, M.Y., & Minero, L.P. (2017, in press). Trans individuals' facilitative coping: An analysis of internal and external processes. *Journal of Counseling Psychology*.

Budge, S.L., & Orovecz, J.J. (2018, in press). Gender fluidity. In K. Nadal (Ed.), *SAGE encyclopedia of psychology and gender*. Thousand Oaks, CA: Sage.

Budge, S.L., Orovecz, J.J., Owen, J.J., & Sherry, A.R. (2017, in press). The relationship between conformity to gender norms, sexual orientation, and gender identity for sexual minorities. *Counseling Psychology Quarterly*.

Buhrmester, D. (1998). Need fulfillment, interpersonal competence, and the developmental contexts of early adolescent friendship. In W.M. Bukowski & A.F. Newcomb (Eds.), *The company they keep: Friendship in childhood and adolescence*. New York: Cambridge University Press.

Buhrmester, D. (2001, April). *Does age at which romantic involvement starts matter?* Paper presented at the meeting of the Society for Research in Child Development, Minneapolis.

Buhrmester, D., & Chong, C.M. (2009). Friendship in adolescence. In H. Reis & S. Sprecher (Eds.), *Encyclopedia of human relationships*. Thousand Oaks, CA: Sage.

Buhs, E.S., & Ladd, G.W. (2001). Peer rejection as an antecedent of young children's school adjustment: An examination of mediating processes. *Developmental Psychology, 37,* 550–560.

Buitelaar, J., Karr, C., & Asherton, P. (2010). *ADHD in adulthood*. New York: Cambridge University Press.

Bukowski, R., & others (2008, January). *Folic acid and preterm birth*. Paper presented at the meeting of the Society for Maternal-Fetal Medicine, Dallas.

Bukowski, W.M., Laursen, B., & Hoza, B. (2010). The snowball effect: Friendship moderates escalations in depressed affect among avoidant and excluded children. *Development and Psychopathology, 22,* 749–757.

Bukowski, W.M., Laursen, B., & Rubin, K.H. (Eds.) (2018). *Handbook of peer interaction, relationships, and groups* (2nd ed.). New York: Guilford.

Bullard, J. (2014). *Creating environments for learning* (2nd ed.). Upper Saddle River, NJ: Pearson.

Bullock, M., & Lutkenhaus, P. (1990). Who am I? Self-understanding in toddlers. *Merrill-Palmer Quarterly, 36,* 217–238.

Bumpus, M.F., Crouter, A.C., & McHale, M. (2001). Parental autonomy granting during adolescence: Exploring gender differences in context. *Developmental Psychology, 37,* 163–173.

Buratti, S., Allwood, C.M., & Johansson, M. (2014). Stability in the metamemory realism of eyewitness confidence judgments. *Cognitive Processing, 15,* 39–53.

Burchinal, M., Magnuson, K., Powell, D., & Hong, S.S. (2015). Early child care and education. In R.M. Lerner (Ed.), *Handbook of child psychology and developmental science* (7th ed.). New York: Wiley.

Burger, S. (2010). A cost consequence analysis of outreach strategies for high-risk pregnant women. *Journal of Community Health Nursing, 27,* 137–145.

Burgette, J.M., & others (2017). Impact of Early Head Start in North Carolina on dental care use among children younger than 3 years. *American Journal of Public Health, 107,* 614–620.

Buriel, R. (2011). Historical origins of the immigrant paradox in the Mexican-origin population. In C. Garcia Coll & A.K. Marks (Eds.), *The immigrant paradox in children and adolescents: Is becoming an American a risk?* Washington, DC: American Psychological Association.

Burke, J.D. (2011). The relationship between conduct disorder and oppositional defiant disorder and their continuity with antisocial behaviors.

In D. Shaffer, E. Leibenluft, & L.A. Rohde (Eds.), *Externalizing disorders of childhood: Refining the research agenda for DSM-V*. Arlington, VA: American Psychiatric Association.

Burke, J.D., & Loeber, R. (2015). The effectiveness of the Stop Now And Plan (SNAP) program for boys at risk for violence and delinquency. *Prevention Science, 16,* 242–253.

Burkhart, J.M., Schubiger, M.N., & van Schaik, C.P. (2017, in press). The evolution of general intelligence. *Behavioral and Brain Sciences.*

Burnette, J. (1998). Reducing the disproportionate representation of minority students in special education. *ERIC/OSEP Digest,* No. E566.

Burnham, D., & Mattock, K. (2010). Auditory development. In J.G. Bremner & T.D. Wachs (Eds.), *Wiley-Blackwell handbook of infant development* (2nd ed.). New York: Wiley.

Burnham, M.M. (2014). Co-sleeping and self-soothing during infancy. In A.R. Wolfson & H.E. Montgomery-Downs (Eds.), *Oxford handbook of infant, child, and adolescent sleep and behavior*. New York: Oxford University Press.

Burns, L., Mattick, R.P., Lim, K., & Wallace, C. (2007). Methadone in pregnancy: Treatment retention and neonatal outcomes. *Addiction, 102,* 264–270.

Burt, K.B., & Paysnick, A.A. (2012). Resilience in the transition to adulthood. *Development and Psychopathology, 24,* 493–505.

Bush, K.R., & Peterson, G.W. (2013). Parent-child relationships in diverse contexts. In G.W. Peterson & K.R. Bush (Eds.), *Handbook of marriage and the family* (3rd ed.). New York: Springer.

Bushnell, I.W.R. (2003). Newborn face recognition. In O. Pascalis & A. Slater (Eds.), *The development of face processing in infancy and early childhood*. New York: NOVA Science.

Buss, D.M. (1995). Psychological sex differences: Origins through sexual selection. *American Psychologist, 50,* 164–168.

Buss, D.M. (2008). *Evolutionary psychology* (3rd ed.). Boston: Allyn & Bacon.

Buss, D.M. (2012). *Evolutionary psychology* (4th ed.). Boston: Allyn & Bacon.

Buss, D.M. (2015). *Evolutionary psychology* (5th ed.). Upper Saddle River, NJ: Pearson.

Buss, K.A., & Goldsmith, H.H. (2007). Biobehavioral approaches to early socioemotional development. In C.A. Brownell & C.B. Kopp (Eds.), *Socioemotional development in the toddler years*. New York: Guilford.

Bussey, K., & Bandura, A. (1999). Social cognitive theory of gender development and differentiation. *Psychological Review, 106,* 676–713.

Bustos, N., & others (2016). Impact of a school-based intervention on nutritional education and physical activity in primary public schools in Chile (KIND) program study protocol: Cluster randomized controlled trial. *BMC Public Health, 16*(1), 1217.

Busuito, A., & Moore, G.A. (2017). Dyadic flexibility mediates the relation between parent conflict and infants' vagal reactivity during the

Face-to-Face Still-Face. *Development and Psychopathology.*

Butte, N.F. (2006). Energy requirements of infants and children. *Nestle Nutrition Workshop Series: Pediatric Program, 58,* 19–32.

Butts, B., & others (2017, in press). ASC methylation and interleukin-1*B* are associated with aerobic capacity in heart failure. *Medicine and Science in Sports and Exercise.*

Byard, R.W. (2012a). Should infants and adults sleep in the same bed together? *Medical Journal of Australia, 196,* 10–11.

Byard, R.W. (2012b). The triple risk model for shared sleeping. *Journal of Pediatric Child Health, 48,* 947–948.

Byard, R.W. (2013). Breastfeeding and sudden infant death syndrome. *Journal of Pediatrics and Child Health, 49,* E353.

Byne, W., & others (2012). Report of the American Psychiatric Association Task Force on the treatment of gender identity disorder. *Archives of Sexual Behavior, 41,* 759–796.

Byrd-Bredbenner, C., Moe, G., Beshgetoor, D., Berning, J., & Kelley, D. (2014). *Wardlaw's perspectives in nutrition*. New York: McGraw-Hill.

Byrne, J.L., & others (2017, in press). A brief eHealth tool delivered in primary care to help parents prevent childhood obesity: A randomized controlled trial. *Pediatric Obesity.*

Byrnes, J.P. (2008). Piaget's cognitive developmental theory. In M.M. Haith & J.B. Benson (Eds.), *Encyclopedia of infant and early childhood development*. Oxford, UK: Elsevier.

C

Cabeza, R., Nyberg, L., & Park, D.C. (Eds.) (2017). *Cognitive neuroscience of aging* (2nd ed.). New York: Oxford University Press.

Cabrera, N.J., Hofferth, S.L., & Chae, S. (2011). Patterns and predictors of father-infant engagement across race/ethnic groups. *Early Childhood Research Quarterly, 26,* 365–375.

Cacioppo, J.T., Cacioppo, S., Gonzaga, G.C., Ogburn, E.L., & VanderWheele, T.J. (2013). Marital satisfaction and break-ups differ across on-line and off-line meeting venues. *Proceedings of the National Academy of Sciences, 110*(25), 10135–10140.

Cai, M., & others (2013). Adolescent-parent attachment as a mediator of relationships between parenting and adolescent social behavior and wellbeing in China. *International Journal of Psychology, 48,* 1185–1190.

Cain, M.A., Bornick, P., & Whiteman, V. (2013). The maternal, fetal, and neonatal effects of cocaine exposure in pregnancy. *Clinical Obstetrics and Gynecology, 56,* 124–132.

Cain, M.S., Leonard, J.A., Gabrieli, J.D., & Finn, A.S. (2016). Media multitasking in adolescence. *Psychonomic Bulletin and Review, 23,* 1932–1941.

Caino, S., & others (2010). Short-term growth in head circumference and its relationship with supine length in healthy infants. *Annals of Human Biology, 37,* 108–116.

Cairncross, M., & Miller, C.J. (2017, in press). The effectiveness of mindfulness-based therapies for ADHD: A meta-analytic review. *Journal of Attention Disorders.*

Caldwell, B.A., & Redeker, N.S. (2015). Maternal stress and psychological status and sleep in minority preschool children. *Public Health Nursing, 32,* 101–111.

Calkins, S.D. (2015). Introduction to the volume: Seeing infant development through a biopsychosocial lens. In S.D. Calkins (Ed.), *Handbook of infant biopsychosocial development.* New York: Guilford.

Calkins, S.D., & Brown, N. (2016). The development of emotion regulation: Implications for child adjustment. In D. Cicchetti (Ed.), *Handbook of developmental psychopathology.* New York: Wiley.

Calkins, S.D., & Perry, N.B. (2016). The development of emotion regulation. In D. Cicchetti (Ed.), *Developmental psychopathology* (3rd ed.). New York: Wiley.

Calkins, S.D., Perry, N.B., & Dollar, J. (2016). A biopsychological model of self-regulation in infancy. In L. Balter & C.S. Tamis-LeMonda (Eds.), *Child psychology* (3rd ed.). New York: Psychology Press.

Callaghan, T. (2013). Symbols and symbolic thought. In P.D. Zelazo (Ed.), *Oxford handbook of developmental psychology.* New York: Oxford University Press.

Callaway, L.K., Lust, K., & McIntyre, H.D. (2005). Pregnancy outcomes in women of very advanced maternal age. *Obstetrics and Gynecology Survey, 60,* 562–563.

Callina, K., & others (2017). The positive youth development perspective: Theoretical and empirical bases of a strengths-based approach to adolescent development. In S.J. Lopez & others (Eds.), *Oxford handbook of positive psychology* (3rd ed.). New York: Oxford University Press.

Calvert, S.L. (2015). Children and digital media. In R.M. Lerner (Ed.), *Handbook of child psychology and developmental science* (7th ed.). New York: Wiley.

Calvo-Garcia, M.A. (2016). Guidelines for scanning twins and triplets with US and MRI. *Pediatric Radiology, 46,* 156–166.

Camacho, D.E., & Fuligni, A.J. (2015). Extracurricular participation among adolescents from immigrant families. *Journal of Youth and Adolescence, 44,* 1251–1262.

Cameron, C.M., & others (2017, in press). Recurrent episodes of injury in children: An Australian cohort study. *Australian Health Review.*

Cameron, J., & Pierce, D. (2008). Intrinsic versus extrinsic motivation. In N.J. Salkind (Ed.), *Encyclopedia of educational psychology.* Thousand Oaks, CA: Sage.

Campaert, K., Nocentini, A., & Menesini, E. (2017). The efficacy of teachers' responses to incidents of bullying and victimization: The mediational role of moral disengagement for bullying. *Aggressive Behavior.*

Campbell, F.A. (2007). The malleability of the cognitive development of children of low-income African-American families: Intellectual test performance over twenty-one years. In P.C. Kyllonen, R.D. Roberts, & L. Stankov (Eds.), *Extending intelligence.* Mahwah, NJ: Erlbaum.

Campbell, F.A., Pungello, E.P., Miller-Johnson, S., Burchinal, M., & Ramey, C.T. (2001). The development of cognitive and academic abilities: Growth curves from an early childhood educational experiment. *Developmental Psychology, 37,* 231–243.

Campbell, F.A., & others (2012). Adult outcomes as a function of an early childhood educational program: An Abecedarian Project follow-up. *Developmental Psychology, 48,* 1033–1043.

Campbell, L. (2016, March 29). Mississippi extends abstinence-based sex-ed. *Mississippi Today.* Retrieved June 25, 2017, from https://mississippitoday.org/2016/03/29.

Campbell, L., Campbell, B., & Dickinson, D. (2004). *Teaching and learning through multiple intelligence* (3rd ed.). Boston: Allyn & Bacon.

Campione-Barr, N., Greer, K.B., & Kruse, A. (2013). Differential associations between domains of sibling conflict and adolescent emotional adjustment. *Child Development, 84*(3), 938–954.

Campos, J.J. (2005). Unpublished review of J.W. Santrock's *Life-span development* (10th ed.). New York: McGraw-Hill.

Campos, J.J. (2009). Unpublished review of J.W. Santrock's *Life-span development* (13th ed.). New York: McGraw-Hill.

Canfield, R.L., & Jusko, T.A. (2008). Lead poisoning. In M.M. Haith & J.B. Benson (Eds.), *Encyclopedia of infancy and early childhood.* Oxford, UK: Elsevier.

Canfield, R.L., Gendle, M.H., & Cory-Slechta, D.A. (2004). Impaired neuropsychological functioning in lead-exposed children. *Developmental Neuropsychology, 26,* 513–540.

Canivez, G.L., Watkins, M.W., & Dombrowski, S.C. (2017, in press). Structural validity of the Wechsler Intelligence Scale for Children—Fifth Edition: Confirmatory factor analysis with the 16 primary and secondary subtests. *Psychological Assessment.*

Cano, M.A., & others (2017). Immigration stress and alcohol use severity among recently immigrated Hispanic adults: Examining moderating effects of gender, immigration status, and social support. *Journal of Clinical Psychology, 73,* 294–307.

Canterino, J.C., Ananth, C.V., Smulian, J., Harrigan, J.T., & Vintzileos, A.M. (2004). Maternal age and risk of fetal death in singleton gestation, United States, 1995–2000. *Obstetrics and Gynecology Survey, 59,* 649–650.

Cantone, E., & others (2015). Interventions on bullying and cyberbullying in schools: A systematic review. *Clinical Practice and Epidemiology in Mental Health, 11*(Suppl. 1), S58–S76.

Carbajal-Valenzuela, C.C., & others (2017). Development of emotional face processing in premature and full-term infants. *Clinical EEG and Neuroscience, 48,* 88–95.

Carbia, C., & others (2017, in press). Working memory over a six-year period in young binge drinkers. *Alcohol, 61,* 17–23.

Carlin, R.E., & Moon, R.Y. (2017). Risk factors, protective factors, and current recommendations to reduce sudden infant death syndrome: A review. *JAMA Pediatrics, 17,* 175–180.

Carling, S.J., Demment, M.M., Kjolhede, C.L., & Olson, C.M. (2015). Breastfeeding duration and weight gain in infancy. *Pediatrics, 135,* 111–119.

Carlo, G., Mestre, M.V., Samper, P., Tur, A., & McGinley, M. (2011, March). *Emotional instability and empathy as mediators of the links between coping and prosocial and aggressive behaviors.* Paper presented at the meeting of the Society for Research in Child Development, Montreal, Canada.

Carlo, G., & others (2017, in press). Longitudinal relations among parenting styles, prosocial behaviors, and academic outcomes in U.S. Mexican adolescents. *Child Development.*

Carlson, N.S., Corwin, E.J., & Lowe, N.K. (2017, in press). Oxytocin augmentation in spontaneously laboring, nulliparous women. *Biological Research in Nursing.*

Carlson, S.M. (2010). Development of conscious control and imagination. In R.F. Baumeister, A.R. Mele, & K.D. Vohs (Eds.), *Free will and consciousness: How might they work?* New York: Oxford University Press.

Carlson, S.M. (2011). Introduction to the special issue: Executive function. *Journal of Experimental Child Psychology, 108,* 411–413.

Carlson, S.M., Claxton, L.J., & Moses, L.J. (2015). The relation between executive function and theory of mind is more than skin deep. *Journal of Cognition and Development, 16,* 186–197.

Carlson, S.M., Davis, A.C., & Leach, J.G. (2005). Executive function and symbolic representation in preschool children. *Psychological Science, 16,* 609–616.

Carlson, S.M., & White, R. (2011). Unpublished research. Minneapolis: Institute of Child Development, University of Minnesota.

Carlson, S.M., & White, R. (2013). Executive function and imagination. In M. Taylor (Ed.), *Handbook of imagination.* New York: Oxford University Press.

Carlson, S.M., White, R., & Davis-Unger, A.C. (2014). Evidence for a relation between executive function and pretense representation in preschool children. *Cognitive Development, 29,* 1–16.

Carlson, S.M., Zelazo, P.D., & Faja, S. (2013). Executive function. In P.D. Zelazo (Ed.), *Oxford handbook of developmental psychology.* New York: Oxford University Press.

Carnegie Council on Adolescent Development (1989). *Turning points: Preparing American youth for the twenty-first century.* New York: Carnegie Foundation.

Carpendale, J.I., & Chandler, M.J. (1996). On the distinction between false belief understanding and subscribing to an interpretive theory of mind. *Child Development, 67,* 1686–1706.

Carpendale, J.I., & Hammond, S.I. (2016). The development of moral sense and moral thinking. *Current Opinion in Pediatrics, 28,* 743–747.

Carpendale, J.I.M., & Lewis, C. (2015). The development of social understanding. In R.M. Lerner (Ed.), *Handbook of child psychology and developmental science* (7th ed.). New York: Wiley.

Carpenter, M. (2011). Social cognition and social motivations in infancy. In U. Goswami (Ed.), *Wiley-Blackwell handbook of childhood cognitive development* (2nd ed.). New York: Wiley.

Carr, R., & Peebles, R. (2012). Developmental considerations of media exposure risk for eating disorders. In J. Lock (Ed.), *Oxford handbook of child and adolescent eating disorders: Developmental perspectives.* New York: Oxford University Press.

Carrell, S.E., Malmstrom, F.V., & West, J.E. (2008). Peer effects in academic cheating. *Journal of Human Resources, 43,* 173–207.

Carskadon, M.A. (2004). Sleep difficulties in young people. *Archives of Pediatric and Adolescent Health, 158,* 597–598.

Carskadon, M.A. (2005). Sleep and circadian rhythms in children and adolescents: Relevance for athletic performance of young people, *Clinical Sports Medicine, 24,* 319–328.

Carskadon, M.A. (2006, April). *Adolescent sleep: The perfect storm.* Paper presented at the meeting of the Society for Research on Adolescence, San Francisco.

Carskadon, M.A. (2011a). Sleep in adolescents: The perfect storm. *Pediatric Clinics of North America, 58,* 637–647.

Carskadon, M.A. (2011b). Sleep's effects on cognition and learning in adolescence. *Progress in Brain Research, 190,* 137–143.

Carskadon, M.A. (Ed.). (2002). *Adolescent sleep patterns.* New York: Cambridge University Press.

Carson, V., & others (2015). Systematic review of sedentary behavior and cognitive development in early childhood. *Preventive Medicine, 78,* 15–22.

Carter, T., Morres, I., Repper, J., & Callaghan, P. (2016). Exercise for adolescents with depression: Valued aspects and perceived change. *Journal of Psychiatric and Mental Health Nursing, 23,* 37–44.

Cartwright, R., Agargun, M.Y., Kirkby, J., & Friedman, J.K. (2006). Relation of dreams to waking concerns. *Psychiatry Research, 141,* 261–270.

Caruthers, A.S., Van Ryzin, M.J., & Dishion, T.J. (2014). Preventing high-risk sexual behavior in early adulthood with family interventions in adolescence: Outcomes and developmental processes. *Prevention Science, 15*(Suppl. 1), S59–S69.

Carvalho Bos, S., & others (2009). Sleep and behavioral/emotional problems in children: A population-based study. *Sleep Medicine, 10,* 66–74.

Carver, L.J., & Bauer, P.J. (2001). The dawning of the past: The emergence of long-term explicit memory in infancy. *Journal of Experimental Psychology: General, 130,* 726–745.

Case, R., & Mueller, M.P. (2001). Differentiation, integration, and covariance mapping as fundamental processes in cognitive and neurological growth. In J.L. McClelland & R.S. Siegler (Eds.), *Mechanisms of cognitive development.* Mahwah, NJ: Erlbaum.

CASEL (2017). *Collaborative for Academic, Social, and Emotional Learning.* Retrieved June 3, 2017, from www.casel.org

Casey, B.J. (2015). The adolescent brain and self-control. *Annual Review of Psychology* (Vol. 66). Palo Alto, CA: Annual Reviews.

Casey, B.J., Galvan, A., & Somerville, L.H. (2016). Beyond simple models of adolescence to an integrated circuit-based account: A commentary. *Developmental Cognitive Neuroscience, 17,* 128–130.

Casey, E.C., & others (2016). Promoting resilience through executive function training for homeless and highly mobile preschoolers. In S. Prince-Embury & D. Saklofske (Eds.). *Resilience intervention for diverse populations.* New York: Springer.

Casper, D.M., & Card, N.A. (2017). Overt and relational victimization: A meta-analytic review of their overlap and associations with social-psychological adjustment. *Child Development, 88,* 466–483.

Caspers, K.M., & others (2009). Association between the serotonin transporter polymorphism (5-HTTLPR) and adult unresolved attachment. *Developmental Psychology, 45,* 64–76.

Caspi, A., & others (2003). Influence of life stress on depression: Moderation by a polymorphism in the 5-HTT gene. *Science, 301,* 386–389.

Cassidy, A.R. (2016). Executive function and psychosocial adjustment in healthy children and adolescents: A latent variable modeling investigation. *Child Neuropsychology, 22,* 292–317.

Cassidy, J. (2016). The nature of the child's ties. In J. Cassidy & P.R. Shaver (Eds.), *Handbook of attachment* (3rd ed.). New York: Guilford.

Cassina, M., & others (2017). Human teratogens and genetic phenocopies. Understanding pathogenesis through human genes mutation. *European Journal of Medical Genetics, 60,* 22–31.

Castellvi, P., & others (2017). Longitudinal association between self-injurious thoughts and behaviors and suicidal behavior in adolescents and young adults: A systematic review and meta-analysis. *Journal of Affective Disorders, 215,* 37–48.

Castillo, M., & Weiselberg, E. (2017). Bulimia nervosa/purging disorder. *Current Problems in Pediatric and Adolescent Health Care, 47,* 85–94.

Castle, J., & others (2010). Parents' evaluation of adoption success: A follow-up study of intercountry and domestic adoptions. *American Journal of Orthopsychiatry, 79,* 522–531.

Catani, C., & others (2010). Tsunami, war, and cumulative risk in the lives of Sri Lankan school children. *Child Development, 81,* 1176–1191.

Cauffman, B.E. (1994, February). *The effects of puberty, dating, and sexual involvement on dieting and disordered eating in young adolescent girls.* Paper presented at the meeting of the Society for Research on Adolescence, San Diego.

Cauffman, E., Shulman, E., Bechtold, J., & Steinberg, L. (2015). Children and the law. In R.M. Lerner (Ed.), *Handbook of child psychology* (7th ed.). New York: Wiley.

Causadias, J.M., Telzer, E.H., & Lee, R.M. (2017, in press). Culture and biology interplay: An introduction. *Cultural Diversity and Ethnic Minority Psychology.*

Cavanagh, S. (2007, October 3). U.S.-Chinese exchanges nurture ties between principals. *Education Week.* Retrieved July 15, 2008, from http://www.edweek.org

Cavanagh, S.E. (2009). Puberty. In D. Carr (Ed.), *Encyclopedia of the life course and human development.* Boston: Gale Cengage.

Cazzato, V., & others (2016). The effects of body exposure on self-body image and esthetic appreciation in anorexia nervosa. *Experimental Brain Research, 234,* 695–709.

Ceci, S.J., & Gilstrap, L.L. (2000). Determinants of intelligence: Schooling and intelligence. In A. Kazdin (Ed.), *Encyclopedia of psychology.* New York: Oxford University Press.

Ceci, S.J., Hritz, A., & Royer, C.E. (2016). Understanding suggestibility. In W. O'Donohue & M. Fanetti (Eds.), *A guide to evidence-based practice.* New York: Springer.

Ceci, S.J., Papierno, P.B., & Kulkofsky, S. (2007). Representational constraints on children's suggestibility. *Psychological Science, 18,* 503–509.

Cecil, C.A., Walton, E., & Barker, E.D. (2016). Prenatal diet and childhood ADHD: Exploring the role of IGF2 methylation. *Epigenomics, 8,* 1573–1576.

Center for Science in the Public Interest (2008). Obesity on the kids' menu at top chains. Retrieved October 24, 2008, from http://www.cspinet.org/new/200808041.html

Centers for Disease Control and Prevention (2000). *CDC growth charts: United States.* Atlanta: Author.

Centers for Disease Control and Prevention (2012). CDC estimates 1 in 88 children in the United States has been identified as having an autism spectrum disorder. *CDC Division of News & Electronic Media.* Retrieved June 24, 2017, from https://www.cdc.gov/media/releases/2014/p0327-autism-spectrum-disorder.html

Centers for Disease Control and Prevention (2015). *Health, United States, 2015.* Atlanta: Author.

Centers for Disease Control and Prevention (2016). *ADHD.* Retrieved January 12, 2016, from www.cdc.gov/ncbddd/adhd/data.html

Centers for Disease Control and Prevention (2016). *Breastfeeding rates continue to rise in the U.S.* Atlanta: Author.

Centers for Disease Control and Prevention (2016). *HIV among youth/age/HIV by group.* Atlanta: Author.

Centers for Disease Control and Prevention (2017). *Body mass index for children and teens.* Atlanta: Author.

Centers for Disease Control and Prevention (2017). *Sexually transmitted disease surveillance.* Atlanta, GA: U.S. Department of Health and Human Services.

Cercignani, M., & others (2017). Characterizing axonal myelination within the healthy population: A tract-by-tract mapping of effects of age and gender on the fiber-g ratio. *Neurobiology of Aging, 49,* 109–118.

Cerrillo-Urbina, A.J., & others (2015). The effects of physical exercise in children with attention deficit hyperactivity disorder: A systematic review and meta-analysis of randomized controlled trials. *Child Care, Health, and Development, 41,* 779–788.

Chaco, A., & others (2017, in press). Engaging fathers in effective parenting for preschool children using shared book reading: A randomized controlled trial. *Journal of Clinical Child and Adolescent Psychology.*

Chae, S.Y., & others (2017). Promoting improved social support and quality of life with the Centering Pregnancy group model of prenatal care. *Archives of Women's Mental Health, 20,* 209–220.

Challacombe, F.L., & others (2017, in press). A pilot randomized controlled trial of time-intensive cognitive-behavior therapy for postpartum obsessive-compulsive disorder: Effects on maternal symptoms, mother-infant interactions, and attachment. *Psychological Medicine.*

Chan, C.H., & others (2015). Sexual initiation and emotional/behavior problems in Taiwanese adolescents: A multivariate response profile analysis. *Archives of Sexual Behavior, 44,* 717–727.

Chandra-Mouli, V., Camacho, A.V., & Michaud, P.A. (2013). WHO guidelines on preventing early pregnancy and poor reproductive outcomes among adolescents in developing countries. *Journal of Adolescent Research, 52,* 517–522.

Chang, E.C. (2017, in press). Hope and hopelessness as predictors of suicide ideation in Hungarian college students. *Death Studies.*

Chang, H.Y., & others (2014). Prenatal maternal depression is associated with low birth weight through shorter gestational age in term infants in Korea. *Early Human Development, 90,* 15–20.

Chang, M.W., Brown, R., & Nitzke, S. (2017). Results and lessons learned from a prevention of weight gain program for low-income overweight and obese young mothers: Mothers in motion. *BMC Public Health, 17,* 182.

Chang, M.Y., Chen, C.H., & Huang, K.F. (2006). A comparison of massage effects on labor pain using the McGill Pain Questionnaire. *Journal of Nursing Research, 14,* 190–197.

Chang, Y.K., Liu, S., Yu, H.H., & Lee, Y.H. (2012). Effect of acute exercise on executive function in children with attention deficit hyperactivity disorder. *Archives of Clinical Neuropsychology, 27,* 225–237.

Chao, R.K. (2005, April). *The importance of Guan in describing control of immigrant Chinese.* Paper presented at the meeting of the Society for Research in Child Development, Atlanta.

Chao, R.K. (2007, March). *Research with Asian Americans. Looking back and moving forward.* Paper presented at the meeting of the Society for Research in Child Development, Boston.

Chaplin, J.E., & others (2011). Improvements in behavior and self-esteem following growth hormone treatment in short prepubertal children. *Hormone Research in Pediatrics, 75*(4), 291–303.

Chaplin, T.M., & Aldao, A. (2013). Gender differences in emotion in children: A meta-analytic review. *Psychological Bulletin, 139*(4), 735–765.

Charlet, J., Schnekenburger, M., Brown, K.W., & Diederich, M. (2012). DNA demethylation increases sensitivity of neuroblastoma cells to chemotherapeutic drugs. *Biochemical Pharmacology, 83,* 858–865.

Charpak, N., & others (2017, in press). Twenty-year follow-up of kangaroo mother care versus traditional care. *Pediatrics.*

Chasnoff, I.J. (2017). Medical marijuana laws and pregnancy: Implications for public health policy. *American Journal of Obstetrics and Gynecology, 216,* 27–30.

Chassin, L., Colder, C.R., Hussong, A., & Sher, K.J. (2016). Substance use and substance use disorders. In D. Cicchetti (Ed.), *Developmental psychopathology (3rd ed.).* New York: Wiley.

Chatterton, Z., & others (2017, in press). In utero exposure to maternal smoking is associated with DNA methylations and reduced neuronal content in the developing fetal brain. *Epigenetics and Chromatin.*

Chattin-McNichols, J. (1992). *The Montessori controversy.* Albany, NY: Delmar.

Chaturvedi, S., & others (2014). Pharmacological interventions for hypertension in children. *Cochrane Database of Systematic Reviews, 2,* CD008117.

Chaudry, A., & others (2017). *Cradle to kindergarten: A new plan to combat inequality.* New York: Russell Sage Foundation.

Chavarria, M.C., & others (2014). Puberty in the corpus callosum. *Neuroscience, 265,* 1–8.

Chemtob, C.M., & others (2010). Impact of maternal posttraumatic stress disorder and depression following exposure to the September 11 attacks on preschool children's behavior. *Child Development, 81,* 1129–1141.

Chen, C., & Stevenson, H.W. (1989). Homework: A cross-cultural examination. *Child Development, 60,* 551–561.

Chen, D., Drabick, D.A., & Burgers, D.E. (2015). A developmental perspective on peer rejection, deviant peer affiliation, and conduct problems among youth. *Child Psychiatry and Human Development, 46,* 823–838.

Chen, F.R., Rothman, E.F., & Jaffee, S.R. (2017, in press). Early puberty, friendship, group characteristics, and dating abuse in U.S. girls. *Pediatrics.*

Chen, J., Yu, J., Wu, Y., & Zhang, J. (2015). The influence of pubertal timing and stressful life events on depression and delinquency among Chinese adolescents. *Psychology Journal, 4,* 88–97.

Chen, L.W., & others (2016). Maternal caffeine intake during pregnancy and risk of pregnancy loss: A categorical and dose-response meta-analysis of prospective studies. *Public Health Nutrition 19,* 1233–1244.

Chen, M., & Berman, S.L. (2012). Globalization and identity development: A Chinese perspective. *New Directions in Child and Adolescent Development, 138,* 103–121.

Chen, P.J., & others (2017). Effects of prenatal yoga on women's stress and immune function across pregnancy: A randomized controlled trial. *Complementary Therapies in Medicine, 31,* 109–117.

Chen, R., Hughes, A.C., & Austin, J.P. (2017, in press). The use of theory in family therapy research: Content analysis. *Journal of Marital and Family Therapy.*

Chen, T.Y., & others (2015). Effects of a selective educational system on fatigue, sleep problems, daytime sleepiness, and depression among senior high school adolescents in Taiwan. *Neuropsychiatric Disease and Treatment, 11,* 741–750.

Chen, W., & others (2015). Secondhand smoke exposure is associated with increased carotid intima-media thickness: The Bogalusa Heart Study, *240,* 374–379.

Chen, X., Fu, R., & Zhao, S. (2015). Culture and socialization. In J.E. Grusec & P.D. Hastings (Eds.), *Handbook of socialization* (2nd ed.). New York: Guilford.

Chen, X., & Liu, C. (2016). Culture, peer relationships, and developmental psychopathology. In D. Cicchetti (Ed.), *Developmental psychopathology* (3rd ed.). New York: Wiley.

Chen, X., & Schmidt, L.A. (2015). Temperament and personality. In R.M. Lerner (Ed.), *Handbook of child psychology and developmental science* (7th ed.). New York: Wiley.

Chen, X., & others (1998). Childrearing attitudes and behavioral inhibition in Chinese and Canadian toddlers: A cross-cultural study. *Developmental Psychology, 34,* 677–686.

Chen, X.K., Wen, S.W., Yang, Q., & Walker, M.C. (2007). Adequacy of prenatal care and neonatal mortality in infants born to mothers with and without antenatal high-risk conditions. *Australian and New Zealand Journal of Obstetrics and Gynecology, 47,* 122–127.

Cheng, C.A., & others (2017, in press). Pregnancy increases stroke risk up to 1 year postpartum and reduces long-term risk. *Quarterly Journal of Medicine.*

Cheng, S., & others (2010). Early television exposure and children's behavioral and social outcomes at age 30 months. *Journal of Epidemiology, 20*(Suppl. 2), S482–S489.

Cheong, J.I., & others (2015). The effect of early menarche on the sexual behaviors of Korean female adolescents. *Annals of Pediatric Endocrinology and Metabolism, 20,* 130–135.

Cherlin, A.J., & Furstenberg, F.F. (1994). Stepfamilies in the United States: A reconsideration. In J. Blake & J. Hagen (Eds.), *Annual review of sociology.* Palo Alto, CA: Annual Reviews.

Cheron, C., Le Scanff, C., & Leboeuf-Yde, C. (2016). Association between sports type and overuse injuries of extremities in children and adolescents: Systematic review. *Chiropractic and Manual Therapies, 24,* 41.

Chess, S., & Thomas, A. (1977). Temperamental individuality from childhood to adolescence. *Journal of Child Psychiatry, 16,* 218–226.

Cheung, C.S., & Pomerantz, E.M. (2012). Why does parental involvement in children's learning enhance children's achievement? The role of parent-oriented motivation. *Journal of Educational Psychology, 104,* 820–832.

Cheung, H.Y, Wu, J., & Huang, Y. (2016). Why do Chinese students cheat? Initial findings based on the self-reports of high school students in China. *Australian Educational Researcher, 43,* 245–271.

Chevalier, N., Dauvier, B., & Blaye, A. (2017, in press). From prioritizing objects to prioritizing cues: A developmental shift for cognitive control. *Developmental Science.*

Chevalier, N., & others (2015). Myelination is associated with processing speed in early childhood: Preliminary insights. *PLoS One, 10,* e0139897.

Chi, M.T. (1978). Knowledge structures and memory development. In R.S. Siegler (Ed.), *Children's thinking: What develops?* Hillsdale, NJ: Erlbaum.

Child Trends (2015, November). *Oral sex behaviors among teens.* Washington, DC: Child Trends.

Childers, J.B., & Tomasello, M. (2002). Two-year-olds learn novel nouns, verbs, and conventional actions from massed or distributed exposures. *Developmental Psychology, 38,* 967–978.

Chiocca, E.M. (2017). American parents' attitudes and beliefs about corporal punishment: An integrative literature review. *Journal of Pediatric Health Care, 31,* 372–383.

Chiou, W.B., Chen, S.W., & Liao, D.C. (2014). Does Facebook promote self-interest? Enactment of indiscriminate one-to-many communication on online social networking sites decreases prosocial behavior. *Cyberpsychology, Behavior, and Social Networking, 17,* 68–73.

Cho, E.S., & others (2016). The effects of kangaroo care for the neonatal intensive care unit on the physiological functions of preterm infants, maternal-infant attachment, and maternal stress. *Journal of Pediatric Nursing, 31,* 430–438.

Cho, M., & Suh, Y. (2016). Genetics of aging. In M. Kaeberlein & G.A. Martin (Eds.), *Handbook of the biology of aging* (8th ed.). New York: Elsevier.

Choi, Y.J., & Luo, Y. (2015). 13-month-olds' understanding of social interaction. *Psychological Science, 26,* 274–283.

Chomsky, N. (1957). *Syntactic structures.* The Hague: Mouton.

Chou, C.C., & Huang, C.J. (2017). Effects of an 8-week yoga program on sustained attention and discrimination function in children with attention deficit hyperactivity disorder. *PeerJ, 5,* e2883.

Choudhary, M., & others (2016). To study the effect of kangaroo mother care on pain response in preterm neonates and to determine the behavioral and physiological responses to painful stimuli in preterm neonates: A study from western Rajasthan. *Journal of Maternal-Fetal and Neonatal Medicine, 29,* 826–831.

Choukas-Bradley, S., & Prinstein, M.J. (2016). Peer relationships and the development of psychopathology. In M. Lewis & D. Rudolph (Eds.), *Handbook of developmental psychopathology* (3rd ed.). New York: Springer.

Chow, C.M., Tan, C.C., & Buhrmester, D. (2015). Interdependence of depressive symptoms, school involvement, and academic performance between adolescent friends: A dyadic analysis. *British Journal of Educational Psychology, 85,* 316–331.

Christ, S.L., Kwak, Y.Y., & Lu, T. (2017). The joint impact of parental psychological neglect and peer isolation on adolescents' depression. *Child Abuse and Neglect, 69,* 151–162.

Christakis, D.A., Zimmerman, F.J., DiGiuseppe, D.L., & McCarty, C.A. (2004). Early television exposure and subsequent attentional problems in children. *Pediatrics, 113,* 708–713.

Christakis, D.A., & others (2009). Audible television and decreased adult words, infant vocalizations, and conversational turns. *Archives of Pediatric & Adolescent Medicine, 163,* 554–558.

Christen, M., Narváez, D., & Gutzwiller, E. (2017, in press). Comparing and integrating biological and cultural moral progress. *Ethical Theory and Moral Practice.*

Christensen, D.L., & others (2016). *Prevalence and characteristics of autism spectrum disorder among children aged 8 years—Autism and Developmental Disabilities Monitoring Network, 11 sites, United States 2012.* Atlanta: Centers for Disease Control and Prevention.

Christensen, L.F., & Overgaard, C. (2017, in press). Are freestanding midwifery units a safe alternative to obstetric units for low-risk, primiparous childbirth? An analysis of effect differences by parity in a matched cohort study. *BMC Pregnancy and Childbirth.*

Chua, A. (2011). *Battle hymn of the tiger mom.* New York: Penguin.

Chuang, S.S., & Tamis-Lemonda, C. (2009). Gender roles in immigrant families: Parenting views, practices, and child development. *Sex Roles, 60,* 451–455.

Cicchetti, D. (2017, in press). A multilevel developmental approach to the prevention of psychopathology in children and adolescents. In J.N. Butcher & others (Eds.), *APA handbook of psychopathology.* Washington, DC: APA Books.

Cicchetti, D., & Toth, S.L. (2016). Child maltreatment and developmental psychopathology: A multi-level perspective. In D. Cicchetti (Ed.), *Developmental psychopathology* (3rd ed.). New York: Wiley.

Cicchetti, D., & Toth, S.L. (2017, in press). Using the science of developmental psychopathology to inform child and adolescent psychotherapy. In A.E. Kazdin & I.R. Weisz (Eds.), *Evidence-based psychotherapies for children and adolescents.* Thousand Oaks, CA: Sage.

Cicchetti, D., Toth, S.L., & Rogosch, F.A. (2005). *A prevention program for child maltreatment.* Unpublished manuscript. Rochester, NY: University of Rochester.

Cillessen, A.H.N., & Bellmore, A.D. (2011). Social skills and social competence in interactions with peers. In P.K. Smith & C.H. Hart (Eds.), *Wiley-Blackwell handbook of childhood social development* (2nd ed.). New York: Wiley.

Cisneros-Cohernour, E.J., Moreno, R.P., & Cisneros, A.A. (2000). Curriculum reform in Mexico: Kindergarten teachers' challenges and dilemmas. Proceedings of the Lilian Katz Symposium. In D. Rothenberg (Ed.), *Issues in early childhood education: Curriculum reform, teacher education, and dissemination of information.* Urbana-Champaign, IL: University of Illinois.

Clara, M. (2017). How instruction influences conceptual development: Vygotsky's theory revisited. *Educational Psychologist, 52,* 50–62.

Clark, B. (2008). *Growing up gifted* (7th ed.). Upper Saddle River, NJ: Prentice Hall.

Clark, C.D. (2015). Play interventions and therapy. In J.E. Johnson & others (Eds.), *Handbook of the study of play.* Blue Ridge Summit, PA: Rowman & Littlefield.

Clark, C.D. (2016). *Play and well-being.* New York: Routledge.

Clark, D.A., Donnellan, M.B., Robins, R.W., & Conger, R.D. (2015). Early adolescent temperament, parental monitoring, and substance use in Mexican-origin adolescents. *Journal of Adolescence, 41,* 121–130.

Clark, E.V. (1993). *The lexicon in acquisition.* New York: Cambridge University Press.

Clark, E.V. (2012). Lexical meaning. In E.L. Bavin (Ed.), *Cambridge handbook of child language.* New York: Cambridge University Press.

Clark, E.V. (2014). Pragmatics in acquisition. *Journal of Child Language, 41*(Suppl. 1), S105–S116.

Clark, E.V. (2017). *Language in children.* New York: Psychology Press.

Clark, M.S., Jansen, K.L., & Cloy, J.A. (2012). Treatment of childhood and adolescent depression. *American Family Physician, 86,* 442–446.

Clarke-Stewart, A.K., & Miner, J.L. (2008). Effects of child and day care. In M.M. Haith & J.B. Benson (Eds.), *Encyclopedia of infant and early childhood development.* Oxford, UK: Elsevier.

Clarke-Stewart, A.K., & Parke, R.D. (2014). *Social development* (2nd ed.). New York: Wiley.

Claro, S., Paunesku, D., & Dweck, C.S. (2016). Growth mindset tempers the effect of poverty on academic achievement. *Proceedings of the National Academy of Sciences USA, 113,* 8664–8868.

Clauss, J.A., Avery, S.N., & Blackford, J.U. (2015). The nature of individual differences in inhibited temperament and risk for psychiatric disease: A review and meta-analysis. *Progress in Neurobiology, 127–128,* 23–45.

Clay, R. (2001, February). Fulfilling an unmet need. Copy edition. *Monitor on Psychology,* No. 2 (no page number available).

Clearfield, M.W., Diedrich, F.J., Smith, L.B., & Thelen, E. (2006). Young infants reach correctly in A-not-B tasks: On the development of stability and perseveration. *Infant Behavior and Development, 29,* 435–444.

Clifton, R.K., Morrongiello, B.A., Kulig, J.W., & Dowd, J.M. (1981). Developmental changes in auditory localization in infancy. In R.N. Aslin, J.R. Alberts, & M. Petersen (Eds.), *Development of perception* (Vol. 1). Orlando, FL: Academic Press.

Clifton, R.K., Muir, D.W., Ashmead, D.H., & Clarkson, M.G. (1993). Is visually guided reaching in early infancy a myth? *Child Development, 64,* 1099–1110.

Cloud, J. (2007, August 27). Failing our geniuses. *Time,* 40–47.

Cnattingius, S., & others (2013). Maternal obesity and risk of preterm delivery. *Journal of the American Medical Association, 309,* 2362–2370.

Coan, J.A. (2016). Toward a neuroscience of attachment. In J. Cassidy & P.R. Shaver (Eds.), *Handbook of attachment* (3rd ed.). New York: Guilford.

Coard, S. (2017). *Black adolescent development.* New York: Psychology Press.

Cochet, H., & Byrne, R.W. (2016). Communication in the second and third year of life: Relationships between nonverbal social skills and language. *Infant Behavior and Development, 44,* 189–198.

CogMed (2013). *CogMed: Working memory is the engine of learning.* Upper Saddle River, NJ: Pearson.

Cohen, A.O., & Casey, B.J. (2017). The neurobiology of adolescent self-control. In T. Egner (Ed.), *Wiley handbook of cognitive control.* New York: Wiley.

Cohen, A.O., & others (2016). When is an adolescent an adult? Assessing cognitive control in emotional and nonemotional contexts. *Psychological Science, 27,* 549–562.

Cohen, G.L., & Prinstein, M.J. (2006). Peer contagion of aggression and health-risk behavior among adolescent males: An experimental investigation of effects of public conduct and private attitudes. *Child Development, 77,* 967–983.

Cohen, J., Golub, G., Kruk, M.E., & McCornnell, M. (2016). Do active patients seek higher-quality prenatal care? A panel data analysis from Nairobi, Kenya. *Preventive Medicine, 92,* 74–81.

Coie, J. (2004). The impact of negative social experiences on the development of antisocial behavior. In J.B. Kupersmidt & K.A. Dodge (Eds.), *Children's peer relations: From development to intervention.* Washington, DC: American Psychological Association.

Coker, T.R., & others (2015). Media violence exposure and physical aggression in fifth-grade children. *Academic Pediatrics, 15,* 82–88.

Colby, A., Kohlberg, L., Gibbs, J., & Lieberman, M. (1983). A longitudinal study of moral judgment. *Monographs of the Society for Research in Child Development* (Serial No. 201).

Colby, S.L., & Ortman, J.M. (2015, March). Projections of the size and composition of the U.S. population: 2014 to 2060. *Current Population Reports.* Washington, DC: United States Census Bureau.

Cole, P.M (2016). Emotion and the development of psychopathology. In D. Cicchetti (Ed.), *Developmental psychopathology* (3rd ed.). New York: Wiley.

Cole, P.M., Dennis, T.A., Smith-Simon, K.E., & Cohen, L.H. (2009). Preschoolers' emotion regulation strategy understanding: Relations with emotion socialization and child self-regulation. *Social Development, 18*(2), 324–352.

Cole, P.M., & Tan, P.Z. (2007). Emotion socialization from a cultural perspective. In J.E. Grusec & P.D. Hastings (Eds.), *Handbook of socialization.* New York: Guilford.

Cole, W.G., Robinson, S.R., & Adolph, K.E. (2016). Bouts of steps: The organization of infant exploration. *Developmental Psychobiology, 58,* 341–354.

Coleman, M., Ganong, L., & Fine, M. (2004). Communication in stepfamilies. In A.L. Vangelisti (Ed.), *Handbook of family communication.* Mahwah, NJ: Erlbaum.

Coleman-Phox, K., Odouli, R., & Li, D-K. (2008). Use of a fan during sleep and the risk of sudden infant death syndrome. *Archives of Pediatric and Adolescent Medicine, 162,* 963–968.

Colemenares, F., & Hernandez-Lloreda, M.V. (2017). Cognition and culture in evolutionary context. *Spanish Journal of Psychology, 19,* E101.

Colen, C.G., & Ramey, D.M. (2014). Is breast truly best? Estimating the effects of breastfeeding on long-term health and well-being in the United States using sibling comparisons. *Social Science and Medicine, 109C,* 55–65.

Coles, C.D., & others (2016). A comparison of 5 methods for the clinical diagnosis of fetal alcohol spectrum disorders. *Alcoholism: Clinical and Experimental Research, 40,* 1000–1009.

Coley, R.L., & others (2017, in press). Locating economic risks for adolescent mental and behavioral health: Poverty and affluence in families, neighborhoods, and schools. *Child Development.*

Collins, C.E., & others (2011). Parent diet modification, child activity, or both in obese children: An RCT. *Pediatrics, 127,* 619–627.

Collins, W.A., & Steinberg, L. (2006). Adolescent development in interpersonal context. In W. Damon & R. Lerner (Eds.), *Handbook of child psychology* (6th ed.). New York: Wiley.

Collins, W.A., & van Dulmen, M. (2006). The significance of middle childhood peer competence for work and relationships in early childhood. In A.C. Huston & M.N. Ripke (Eds.), *Developmental contexts in middle childhood.* New York: Cambridge University Press.

Colombo, J., & Mitchell, D.W. (2009). Infant visual habituation. *Neurobiology of Learning and Memory, 92,* 225–234.

Colombo, J., & Salley, B. (2015). Biopsychosocial perspectives on attention in infancy. In S.D. Calkins (Ed.), *Handbook of infant biopsychosocial development.* New York: Guilford.

Colombo, J., Shaddy, D.J., Blaga, O.M., Anderson, C.J., & Kannass, K.N. (2009). High cognitive ability in infancy and early childhood. In F.D. Horowitz, R.F. Subotnik, & D.J. Matthews (Eds.), *The development of giftedness and talent across the life span.* Washington, DC: American Psychological Association.

Colombo, J., Shaddy, D.J., Richman, W.A., Maikranz, J.M., & Blaga, O.M. (2004). The developmental course of attention in infancy and preschool cognitive outcome. *Infancy, 4,* 1–38.

Colonnesi, C., Stams, G.J., Koster, I., & Noom, M.J. (2011). The relation between pointing and language development: A meta-analysis. *Developmental Review, 30,* 352–366.

Colunga, E., & Sims, C.E. (2017). Not only size matters: Early-talker and later-talker vocabularies support different word-learning biases in babies and networks. *Cognitive Science, 41*(Suppl. 1), 73–95.

Comalli, D.M., Persand, D., & Adolph, K.E. (2017, in press). Motor decisions are not black and white: Selecting actions in the "gray zone." *Experimental Brain Research.*

Comer, J. (2004). Leave no child behind. New Haven, CT: Yale University Press.

Comer, J. (2006). Child development: The underweighted aspect of intelligence. In P.C. Kyllonen, R.D. Roberts, & L. Stankov (Eds.), *Extending intelligence.* Mahwah, NJ: Erlbaum.

Comer, J.P. (1988). Educating poor minority children. *Scientific American, 259,* 42–48.

Committee for Children (2017). *Second Step.* Retrieved June 3, 2017, from www.cfchildren.org/second-step

Committee on the Rights of the Child (2014). *The Convention on the Rights of the Child and Its Treaty Body—the Committee on the Rights of the Child.* Retrieved April 14, 2015, from http://endcorporalpunishment.org/pages/hrlaw/crc_session.html

Common Core State Standards Initiative (2017). *Common Core.* Retrieved January 7, 2017, from www.core standards.org/

Common Sense Media (2011). *Zero to eight: Children's media use in America.* Retrieved June 21, 2012, from www.commonsensemedia.org/research

Common Sense Media (2013). *Zero to eight: Children's media use in America 2013.* San Francisco: Common Sense Media.

Commoner, B. (2002). Unraveling the DNA myth: The spurious foundation of genetic engineering. *Harper's Magazine, 304,* 39–47.

Compton, R.J. (2016). *Adoption beyond borders.* New York: Oxford University Press.

Comstock, G., & Scharrer, E. (2006). Media and popular culture. In W. Damon & R. Lerner (Eds.), *Handbook of child psychology* (6th ed.). New York: Wiley.

Comuk-Balci, N., & others (2016). Screening preschool children for fine motor skills: Environmental influence. *Journal of Physical Therapy Science, 28,* 1026–1031.

Conant-Norville, D.O. (2016). Child and adolescent sports psychiatry in the U.S. *International Review of Psychiatry, 28,* 556–563.

Conboy, B.T., Brooks, R., Meltzoff, A.N., & Kuhl, P.K. (2015). Social interaction in infants' learning of second-language phonetics: An exploration of brain-behavior relations. *Developmental Neuropsychology, 40,* 216–229.

Condition of Education (2015). *Participation in education.* Washington, DC: U.S. Office of Education.

Condition of Education (2016). *Participation in education.* Washington, DC: U.S. Office of Education.

Conduct Problems Prevention Research Group (2007). The Fast Track randomized controlled trial to prevent externalizing psychiatric disorders: Findings from grades 3 to 9. *Journal of the American Academy of Child and Adolescent Psychiatry, 46,* 1250–1262.

Conduct Problems Prevention Research Group (2010). The difficulty of maintaining positive intervention effects: A look at disruptive behavior, deviant peer relations, and social skills during the middle school years. *Journal of Early Adolescence, 30*(4), 593–624.

Conduct Problems Prevention Research Group (2011). The effects of Fast Track preventive intervention on the development of conduct disorder across childhood. *Child Development, 82,* 331–345.

Conduct Problems Prevention Research Group (2013). Assessing findings from the Fast Track Study. *Journal of Experimental Criminology, 9,* 119–126.

Conduct Problems Prevention Research Group (2016). The Fast Track Project effects on violence/aggression and selected outcomes. In P. Sturmey (Ed.), *Wiley handbook of violence and aggression.* New York: Wiley.

Connell, N.M., Morris, R.G., & Piquero, A.R. (2016). Predicting bullying: Exploring the contribution of negative life experiences in predicting adolescent bullying behavior. *International Journal of Offender Therapy and Comparative Criminology, 60,* 1082–1096.

Connolly, J.A., & McIsaac, C. (2009). Romantic relationships in adolescence. In R.M. Lerner & L. Steinberg (Eds.), *Handbook of adolescent psychology* (3rd ed.). New York: Wiley.

Connolly, J.A., Nguyen, H.N., Pepler, D., Craig, W., & Jiang, D. (2013). Developmental trajectories of romantic stages and associations with problem behaviors during adolescence. *Journal of Adolescence, 36,* 1013–1024.

Connolly, M.D., & others (2016). The mental health of transgender youth: Advances in understanding. *Journal of Adolescent Health, 59,* 489–495.

Connolly, S., Anney, R., Gallagher, L., & Heron, E.A. (2017). A genome-wide investigation into parent-of-origin effects in autism spectrum disorder identifies previously associated genes including SHANK3. *European Journal of Human Genetics, 25,* 234–239.

Conry-Murray, C., Kim, J.M., & Turiel, E. (2012, April). *U.S. and Korean children's judgments of gender norm violations.* Paper presented at the Gender Development Research conference, San Francisco.

Consoli, A., & others (2013). Suicidal behaviors in depressed adolescents: Role of perceived relationships in the family. *Child and Adolescent Psychiatry and Mental Health, 7*(1), 8.

Consoli, A., & others (2015). Risk and protective factors for suicidality at 6-month follow-up in adolescent inpatients who attempted suicide: An exploratory model. *Canadian Journal of Psychiatry, 60*(2, Suppl 1), S27–S36.

Contant, T.L., & others (2018). *Teaching science through inquiry-based instruction* (13th ed.). Upper Saddle River, NJ: Pearson.

Conway, A., Modrek, A., & Gorroochum, P. (2017, in press). Maternal sensitivity predicts fewer sleep problems at early adolescence for toddlers with negative emotionality: A case of differential susceptibility. *Child Psychiatry and Human Development.*

Cook, J.L., & others (2016). Fetal alcohol spectrum disorder: A guideline for diagnosis across the lifespan. *CMAJ, 168,* 191–197.

Cook, M., & Birch, R. (1984). Infant perception of the shapes of tilted plane forms. *Infant Behavior and Development, 7,* 389–402.

Cook, P.J., MacCoun, R., Muschkin, C., & Vigdoi, J. (2008). The negative impacts of starting middle school in the sixth grade. *Journal of Policy Analysis and Management, 27,* 104–121.

Cook, R.E., & Richardson-Gibbs, A M. (Eds.) (2018). *Strategies for including children with special needs in early childhood settings* (2nd ed.). Boston: Cengage.

Cooley, J.L., & Fife, P.J. (2016). Peer victimization and forms of aggression during middle childhood: The role of emotion regulation. *Journal of Abnormal Child Psychology, 44,* 535–547.

Cooper, C.R. (2011). *Bridging multiple worlds: Cultures, identities, and pathways to college.* New York: Oxford University Press.

Cooper, C.R., Gonzales, E., & Wilson, A.R. (2015). Identities, cultures, and schooling: How students navigate racial-ethnic, indigenous, immigrant, social class, and gender identities on their pathways through school. In K.C. McLean & M. Syed (Eds.), *Oxford handbook of identity development.* New York: Oxford University Press.

Cooper, C.R., & Grotevant, H.D. (1989, April). *Individuality and connectedness in the family and adolescents' self and relational competence.* Paper presented at the meeting of the Society for Research in Child Development, Kansas City.

Cooperrider, K., & Goldin-Meadow, S. (2017, in press). Gesture, language, and cognition. In B. Dancygier (Ed.), *Cambridge handbook of cognitive linguistics.* New York: Cambridge University Press.

Coore Desai, C., Reece, J.A., & Shakespeare-Pellington, S. (2017, in press). The prevention of violence in childhood through parenting programs: A global review. *Psychology, Health, and Medicine.*

Coovadia, H., & Moodley, D. (2016). Improving HIV pre-exposure prophylaxis for infants. *Lancet, 387,* 513–514.

Cope, L.M., & others (2017). Effects of serotonin transporter gene, sensitivity of response to alcohol, and parental monitoring on risk for problem alcohol use. *Alcohol, 59,* 7–16.

Copeland, W., & others (2010). Outcomes of early pubertal timing in young women: A prospective. *American Journal of Psychiatry, 167,* 1218–1225.

Copeland, W.E., & others (2013). Adult psychiatric outcomes of bullying and being bullied by peers in childhood and adolescence. *JAMA Psychiatry, 70,* 419–426.

Corbetta, D. (2009). Brain, body, and mind: Lessons from infant development. In J.P. Spencer, M. Thomas, & J. McClelland (Eds.), *Connectionism and dynamic systems theory reconsidered.* New York: Oxford University Press.

Cordier, S. (2008). Evidence for a role of paternal exposure in developmental toxicity. *Basic and Clinical Pharmacology and Toxicology, 102,* 176–181.

Cordova, D., Huang, S., Lally, M., Estrada, Y., & Prado, G. (2014). Do parent-adolescent discrepancies in family functioning increase the risk of Hispanic adolescent HIV risk behaviors? *Family Process, 53,* 348–363.

Costigan, S.A., Barnett, L., Plotnikoff, R.C., & Lubans, D.R. (2013). The health indicators associated with screen-based sedentary behavior among adolescent girls: A systematic review. *Journal of Adolescent Health, 52*(4), 382–392.

Coubart, A., & others (2014). Dissociation between small and larger numerosities in newborn infants. *Developmental Science, 17,* 11–22.

Coulson, S. (2017). Language and the brain. In B. Dancygier (Ed.), *Cambridge handbook of cognitive linguistics.* New York: Cambridge University Press.

Courage, M.L., & Richards, J.E. (2008). Attention. In M.M. Haith & J.B. Benson (Eds.), *Encyclopedia of infant and early childhood development.* Oxford, UK: Elsevier.

Cousins, L., & Goodyer, I.M. (2015). Antidepressants and the adolescent brain. *Journal of Psychopharmacology, 29,* 545–555.

Cowan, C.P., & Cowan, P.A. (2000). *When partners become parents.* Mahwah, NJ: Erlbaum.

Cowan, M.K., & Bunn, J. (2016). *Microbiology fundamentals* (2nd ed.). New York: McGraw-Hill.

Cowan, P., Cowan, C., Ablow, J., Johnson, V.K., & Measelle, J. (2005) *The family context of parenting in children's adaptation to elementary school.* Mahwah, NJ: Erlbaum.

Craciunoiu, O., & Holsti, L. (2017). A systematic review of the predictive validity of neurobehavioral assessments during the preterm period. *Physical and Occupational Therapy in Pediatrics, 37,* 292–307.

Craig, F., & others (2016). A review of executive function deficits in autism spectrum disorder and attention-deficit/hyperactivity disorder. *Neuropsychiatric Disease and Treatment, 12,* 1191–1202.

Craik, F.I.M. (2006). Brain-behavior relations across the lifespan: A commentary. *Neuroscience and Biobehavioral Reviews, 30,* 885–892.

Crain, S. (2012). Sentence scope. In E.L. Bavin (Ed.), *Cambridge handbook of child language.* New York: Cambridge University Press.

Crain, T.L., Schonert-Reichl, K.A., & Roeser, R.W. (2017, in press). Cultivating teacher mindfulness: Effects of a randomized controlled trial on work, home, and sleep outcomes. *Journal of Occupational Health Psychology.*

Craswell, A., Kearney, L., & Reed, R. (2016). 'Expecting and connecting' group pregnancy care: Evaluation of a collaborative clinic. *Women and Birth, 29,* 416–422.

Criss, M.M., & others (2015). Link between monitoring behavior and adolescent adjustment: An analysis of direct and indirect effects. *Journal of Child and Family Studies.*

Crocetti, E., Jahromi, P., & Meeus, W. (2012). Identity and civic engagement in adolescence. *Journal of Adolescence, 35,* 521–532.

Crocetti, E., Rabaglietta, E., & Sica, L.S. (2012). Personal identity in Italy. *New Directions in Child and Adolescent Development, 138,* 87–102.

Crocetti, E., & others (2017). Identity processes and parent-child and sibling relationships in adolescence: A five-wave multi-informant longitudinal study. *Child Development, 88,* 210–228.

Crockenberg, S.B., & Leerkes, E.M. (2006). Infant and maternal behaviors moderate reactivity to novelty to predict anxious behavior at 2.5 years. *Development and Psychopathology, 18,* 17–24.

Crockett, A., & others (2017). Investing in CenteringPregnancy group prenatal care reduces newborn hospitalization costs. *Women's Health Issues, 27,* 60–66.

Crockett, L.J., Raffaeli, M., & Shen, Y-L. (2006). Linking self-regulation and risk proneness to risky sexual behavior: Pathways through peer pressure and early substance use. *Journal of Research on Adolescence, 16,* 503–525.

Crone, E. (2017). *The adolescent brain.* New York: Routledge.

Crosnoe, R. (2011). *Fitting in, standing out.* New York: Cambridge University Press.

Crosnoe, R., & Fuligni, A.J. (2012). Children from immigrant families: Introduction to the special section. *Child Development, 83,* 1471–1476.

Crosnoe, R., & Leventhal, T. (2014). School- and neighborhood-based interventions to improve the lives of disadvantaged children. In E.T. Gershoff, R.S. Mistry, & D.A. Crosby (Eds.), *The societal context of child development.* New York: Oxford University Press.

Cross, D., Lester, L., & Barnes, A. (2015). A longitudinal study of the social and emotional predictors and consequences of cyber and traditional bullying victimization. *International Journal of Public Health, 60,* 207–217.

Croteau-Chonka, E.C., & others (2016). Examining the relationships between cortical maturation and white matter myelination throughout early childhood. *Neuroimage, 125,* 413–421.

Crouter, A.C. (2006). Mothers and fathers at work. In A. Clarke-Stewart & J. Dunn (Eds.), *Families count.* New York: Cambridge University Press.

Crowley, K., Callahan, M.A., Tenenbaum, H.R., & Allen, E. (2001). Parents explain more to boys than to girls during shared scientific thinking. *Psychological Science, 12,* 258–261.

Crowley, S.J., & Carskadon, M.A. (2010). Modifications to weekend recovery sleep delay circadian phase in older adolescents. *Chronobiology International, 27,* 1469–1492.

Cucina, J.M., Peyton, S.T., Su, C., & Byle, K.A. (2016). Role of mental abilities and mental tests in explaining school grades. *Intelligence, 54,* 90–104.

Cuevas, K., & Bell, K.A. (2014). Infant attention and early childhood executive function. *Child Development, 85*(2), 397–404.

Cuevas, K., & others (2014). What's mom got to do with it? Contributions of maternal executive function and caregiving to the development of executive function across early childhood. *Developmental Science, 17,* 224–238.

Cuffe, J.S., & others (2017, in press). Review: Placental derived biomarkers of pregnancy disorders. *Placenta.*

Culen, C., & others (2017, in press). Care of girls and women with Turner syndrome: Beyond growth and hormones. *Endocrine Connections.*

Culp, K.M. (2012). *An interesting career in psychological science: Research scientist at an education research organization.* Retrieved July 30, 2013, from www.apa.org/science/about/psa/2012/10/education-research.aspx

Cummings, E.M., Bergman, K.N., & Kuznicki, K.A. (2014). Emerging methods for studying family systems. In S. McHale, P. Amato, & A. Booth (Eds.), *Emerging methods for family research.* New York: Springer.

Cummings, E.M., & Davies, P.T. (2010). *Marital conflict and children: An emotional security perspective.* New York: Guilford.

Cummings, E.M., El-Sheikh, M., & Kouros, C.D. (2009). Children and violence: The role of children's regulation in the marital aggression–child adjustment link. *Clinical Child and Family Psychology Review, 12*(1), 3–15.

Cummings, E.M., George, M.R.W., McCoy, K.P., & Davies, P.T. (2012). Interparental conflict in kindergarten and adolescent adjustment: Prospective investigation of emotional security as an explanatory mechanism. *Child Development, 83,* 1703–1715.

Cummings, E.M., Koss, K.J., & Cheung, R.Y.M. (2015). Interparental conflict and children's mental health: Emerging directions in emotional security theory. In C.R. Agnew & S.C. South (Eds.), *Interpersonal relationships and health.* New York: Oxford University Press.

Cummings, E.M., & Merrilees, C.E. (2009). Identifying the dynamic processes underlying links between marital conflict and child adjustment. In M.S. Schulz, P.K. Kerig, M.K. Pruett, & R.D. Parke (Eds.), *Feathering the nest.* Washington, DC: American Psychological Association.

Cummings, E.M., & Miller, L.M. (2015). Emotional security theory: An emerging theoretical model for youths' psychological and physiological responses across multiple developmental contexts. *Current Directions in Psychological Science, 24,* 208–213.

Cummings, E.M., & Valentino, K.V. (2015). Developmental psychopathology. In R.M. Lerner (Ed.), *Handbook of child psychology and developmental science* (7th ed.). New York: Wiley.

Cummings, E.M., & others (2017, in press). Emotional insecurity about the community: A dynamic, within-person mediator of child adjustment in contexts of political violence. *Development and Psychopathology.*

Cunha, A.B., & others (2016). Effect of short-term training on reaching behavior in infants: A randomized controlled trial. *Journal of Motor Behavior, 48,* 132–142.

Cunningham, P.M. (2017). *Phonics they use* (7th ed.). Upper Saddle River, NJ: Pearson.

Cunningham, P.M., & Allington, R.L. (2016). *Classrooms that work* (6th ed.). Upper Saddle River, NJ: Pearson.

Cunningham, S.A., Kramer, M.R., & Narayan, K.M. (2014). Incidence of childhood obesity in the United States. *New England Journal of Medicine, 370,* 403–411.

Curran, K., DuCette, J., Eisenstein, J., & Hyman, I.A. (2001, August). *Statistical analysis of the cross-cultural data: The third year.* Paper presented at the meeting of the American Psychological Association, San Francisco.

Curtis, L.A., & Bandy, T. (2016). *The Quantum Opportunities Program: A randomized controlled evaluation.* Washington, DC: Milton S. Eisenhower Foundation.

Cushner, K.H., McClelland, A., & Safford, P. (2015). *Human diversity in education* (8th ed.). New York: McGraw-Hill.

Cuzzolaro, M. (2014). Eating and weight disorders: Studies on anorexia, bulimia, and obesity turn 19. *Eating and Weight Disorders, 19,* 1–2.

Cvencek, D., Meltzoff, A.N., & Greenwald, A.G. (2011). Math-gender stereotypes in elementary school children. *Child Development, 82,* 766–779.

D

Dahl, A., & Killen, M. (2017). The development of moral reasoning from infancy to adulthood. In J. Wixted (Ed.), *Stevens' handbook of experimental psychology and cognitive neuroscience.* New York: Wiley.

Dahl, A., & others (2017). Explicit scaffolding increases simple helping in younger infants. *Developmental Psychology, 53,* 407–416.

Dahl, R.E. (2004). Adolescent brain development: A period of vulnerabilities and opportunities. *Annals of the New York Academy of Sciences, 1021,* 1–22.

Daigneault, I., & others (2017, in press). Physical and mental health of children with substantiated sexual abuse: Gender comparisons from a matched-control cohort study. *Child Abuse and Neglect.*

Dakof, G.A., & others (2015). A randomized clinical trial of family therapy in juvenile drug court. *Journal of Family Psychology, 29,* 232–241.

Dale, B., & others (2014). Utility of the Stanford-Binet Intelligence Scales, Fifth Edition, with ethnically diverse preschoolers. *Psychology in the Schools, 51,* 581–590.

Daley, A.J., Macarthur, C., & Winter, H. (2007). The role of exercise in treating postpartum depression: A review of the literature. *Journal of Midwifery and Women's Health, 52,* 56–62.

Dalke, K.B., Wenzel, A., & Kim, D.R. (2016). Depression and anxiety during pregnancy: Evaluating the literature in support of clinical risk-benefit decision-making. *Current Psychiatry Reports, 18,* 59.

Dalle Grave, R., El Ghoch, M., Sartriana, M., & Calugi, S. (2016). Cognitive behavioral therapy for anorexia nervosa: An update. *Current Psychiatry Reports, 18*(1), 2.

Damasio, A.R. (1994). Descartes' error and the future of human life. *Scientific American, 271,* 144.

Damon, W. (1988). *The moral child.* New York: Free Press.

Daniels, H. (2017). *Introduction to Vygotsky* (3rd ed.). New York: Routledge.

Danielson, C.K., & others (2017). Clinical decision-making following disasters: Efficient identification of PTSD risk in adolescents. *Journal of Abnormal Child Psychology, 48,* 117–128.

Danis, A., & others (2008). A continuous performance task in preschool children: Relations between attention and performance. *European Journal of Developmental Psychology, 43,* 576–589.

Dariotis, J.K., & others (2016). A qualitative evaluation of student learning and skills use in a school-based mindfulness and yoga program. *Mindfulness, 7,* 76–89.

Darnell, A.J., & Schuler, M.S. (2015). Quasi-experimental study of functional family therapy effectiveness for juvenile justice aftercare in a racially and ethnically diverse community sample. *Children and Youth Services Review, 50,* 75–82.

Darwin, C. (1859). *On the origin of species.* London: John Murray.

Darwom, Z., & others (2017). Fathers' views and experiences of their own mental health during pregnancy and the first postnatal year: A qualitative interview study of men participating in the UK Born and Bred in Yorkshire (BaBY) cohort. *BMC Pregnancy and Childbirth, 17*(1), 45.

Das, S., & Red-Horse, K. (2017, in press). Cellular plasticity in cardiovascular development and disease. *Developmental Dynamics.*

Dasen, P.R. (1977). Are cognitive processes universal? A contribution to cross-cultural Piagetian psychology. In N. Warren (Ed.), *Studies in cross-cultural psychology* (Vol.1). London: Academic Press.

Datar, A., & Nicosia, N. (2017). The effect of state competitive food and beverage regulations on childhood overweight and obesity. *Journal of Adolescent Health, 60,* 520–527.

Dau, A.L., & others (2017). Postpartum depressive symptoms and maternal sensitivity: An exploration of possible social media-based measures. *Archives of Women's Mental Health, 20,* 221–224.

Davids, I., & Mayo, A.M. (2017). Windows of optimal development. In J. Baker & others (Eds.), *Routledge handbook of talent identification in sport.* New York: Routledge.

Davidson, J. (2000). Giftedness. In A. Kazdin (Ed.), *Encyclopedia of psychology.* Washington, DC, & New York: American Psychological Association and Oxford University Press.

Davies, G., & others (2011). Genome-wide association studies establish that human intelligence is highly heritable and polygenic. *Molecular Psychiatry, 16,* 996–1005.

Davies, G., & others (2016). Genome-wide association study of cognitive functions and educational attainment in UK Biobank. *Molecular Psychiatry, 21,* 758–767.

Davies, J., & Brember, I. (1999). Reading and mathematics attainments and self-esteem in years 2 and 6—an eight-year cross-sectional study. *Educational Studies, 25,* 145–157.

Davies, P.T., Martin, M.J., Coe, J.L., & Cummings, E.M. (2016a). Transactional cascades of destructive interparental conflict, children's emotional insecurity, and psychological problems across childhood and adolescence. *Development and Psychopathology, 27,* 653–671.

Davies, P.T., Martin, M.J., & Sturge-Apple, M.L. (2016). Emotional security theory and developmental psychopathology. In D. Cicchetti (Ed.), *Developmental psychopathology* (3rd ed.). New York: Wiley.

Davies, P.T., & others (2016b). The multiple faces of interparental conflict: Implications for cascades of children's insecurity and externalizing problems. *Journal of Abnormal Psychology, 125,* 664–676.

Davies, R., Davis, D., Pearce, M., & Wong, N. (2015). The effect of waterbirth on neonatal mortality and morbidity: A systematic review and meta-analysis. *JBI Database of Systematic Reviews and Implementation Reports, 13,* 180–231.

Davila, J., Capaldi, D.M., & La Greca, A.M. (2016). Adolescent/young adult romantic relationships and psychopathology. In D. Cicchetti (Ed.), *Developmental psychopathology* (3rd ed.). New York: Wiley.

Davis, A.E., Hyatt, G., & Arrasmith, D. (1998, February). *"I Have a Dream" program. Class One Evaluation Report.* Portland, OR: Northwest Regional Education Laboratory.

Davis, B.E., Moon, R.Y., Sachs, M.C., & Ottolini, M.C. (1998). Effects of sleep position on infant motor development. *Pediatrics, 102,* 1135–1140.

Davis, C.L., & Cooper, S. (2011). Fitness, fatness, cognition, behavior, and academic achievement among overweight children: Do cross-sectional associations correspond to exercise trial outcomes? *Preventive Medicine, 52*(Suppl. 1), S65–S69.

Davis, C.L., & others (2007). Effects of aerobic exercise on overweight children's cognitive functioning: A randomized controlled trial. *Research Quarterly for Exercise and Sport, 78,* 510–519.

Davis, C.L., & others (2011). Exercise improves executive function and achievement and alters neural activation in overweight children. *Health Psychology, 30*(1), 91–98.

Davis, D.K. (2005). Leading the midwifery renaissance. *RCM Midwives, 8,* 264–268.

Davis, R.E., & others (2016). Eat, play, view, sleep: Exploring Mexican American mothers' perceptions of decision making for four behaviors associated with childhood obesity risk. *Appetite, 101,* 104–113.

Davison, K.K., & Birth, L.L. (2001). Weight status, parent reaction, and self-concept in five-year-old girls. *Pediatrics, 107,* 46–53.

Davison, S.M., & others (2013). CHILE: An evidence-based preschool intervention for obesity prevention in Head Start. *Journal of School Health, 83,* 223–229.

Dawson-McClure, S., & others (2015). A population-level approach to promoting healthy child development and school success in low-income, urban neighborhoods: Impact on parenting and child conduct problems. *Prevention Science, 16,* 279–290.

Day, F.R., & others (2017). Genomic analyses identify hundreds of variants associated with age at menarche and support a role for puberty timing on cancer risk. *Nature Genetics, 49,* 834–841.

Day, N.L., Goldschmidt, L., & Thomas, C.A. (2006). Prenatal marijuana exposure contributes to the prediction of marijuana use at age 14. *Addiction, 101,* 1313–1322.

Day, R.H., & McKenzie, B.E. (1973). Perceptual shape constancy in early infancy. *Perception, 2,* 315–320.

Dayton, C.J., & Malone, J.C. (2017). Development and socialization of physical aggression in very young boys. *Infant Mental Health, 38,* 150–165.

Dayton, C.J., Walsh, T.B., Oh, W., & Volling, B. (2015). Hush now baby: Mothers' and fathers' strategies for soothing their infants and associated parenting outcomes. *Journal of Pediatric Health Care, 29,* 145–155.

De Bruyne, L.K., & Pinna, K. (2017). *Nutrition for health and healthcare* (6th ed.). Boston: Cengage.

De Genna, N.M., Goldschmidt, L., Day N.L., & Cornelius, M.D. (2016). Prenatal and postnatal maternal trajectories of cigarette use predict adolescent cigarette use. *Nicotine and Tobacco Research, 18,* 988–992.

De Giovanni, N., & Marchetti, D. (2012). Cocaine and its metabolites in the placenta: A systematic review of the literature. *Reproductive Toxicology, 33*(1), 1–14.

de Guzman, N.S., & Nishina, A. (2014). A longitudinal study of body dissatisfaction and pubertal timing in an ethnically diverse adolescent sample. *Body Image, 11,* 68–71.

de Haan, M. (2015). Neuroscientific methods with children. In R.M. Lerner (Ed.), *Handbook of child psychology and developmental science* (7th ed.). New York: Wiley.

de Haan, M., & Gunnar, M.R. (Eds.). (2009). *Handbook of developmental social neuroscience.* New York: Guilford.

de Haan, M., & Johnson, M.H. (2016). Typical and atypical human functional brain development. In D. Cicchetti (Ed.), *Developmental psychopathology* (3rd ed.). New York: Wiley.

de Heer, H.D., & others (2017). Let's move together. *Health Education and Behavior, 44,* 141–152.

de Jong Gierveld, J., & Merz, E-M. (2013). Parents' partnership decision making after divorce or widowhood: The role of (step) children. *Journal of Marriage and Family, 75,* 1098–1113.

de Koning, L., Denhoff, E., Kellogg, M.D., & de Ferranti, S.D. (2015). Associations of total and abdominal adiposity with risk marker patterns in children at high risk for cardiovascular disease. *BMC Obesity, 2,* 15.

De la Cruz-Cano, E. (2017). Association between FKBP5 and CRHR1 genes with suicidal behavior: A systematic review. *Behavioral Brain Research, 317,* 446–461.

de la Rocheborchard, E., & Thonneau, F. (2002). Paternal age and maternal age are risk factors for miscarriage: Results of a multicentre European study. *Human Reproduction, 17,* 1649–1656.

de Looze, M., & others (2015). Parent-adolescent sexual communication and its association with adolescent sexual behaviors: A nationally representative analysis in the Netherlands. *Journal of Sex Research, 52,* 257–268.

de Medeiros, T.S., & others (2017, in press). Caffeine intake during pregnancy in different intrauterine environments and its association with infant anthropometric measurements at 3 and 6 months of age. *Maternal and Child Health Journal.*

de Rose, L.M., Shiyko, M.P., Foster, H., & Brooks-Gunn, J. (2011). Associations between menarcheal timing and behavioral developmental trajectories for girls from age 6 to age 15. *Journal of Youth and Adolescence, 40(10),* 1329–1342.

de Villiers, J., & de Villiers, P. (2013). Syntax acquisition. In P.D. Zelazo (Ed.), *Oxford handbook of developmental psychology*. New York: Oxford University Press.

De, R., & others (2017). Identifying gene-gene interactions that are highly associated with four quantitative lipid traits across multiple cohorts. *Human Genetics, 136,* 165–178.

Deardorff, J., & others (2011). Father absence, body mass index, and pubertal timing in girls: Differential effects by family income and ethnicity. *Journal of Adolescent Health, 48,* 441–447.

Dearing, E., & others (2016). Can community and school-based supports improve the achievement of first-generation immigrant children attending high-poverty schools? *Child Development, 87,* 883–897.

Deater-Deckard, K. (2013). The social environment and the development of psychopathology. In P.D. Zelazo (Ed.), Handbook of developmental psychology. New York: Oxford University Press.

Deater-Deckard, K. (2016). Is self-regulation "all in the family"? Testing environmental effects using within-family quasi-experiments. *International Journal of Behavioral Development, 40,* 224–233.

Debnam, K., Milam, A.J., Furr-Holden, C.D., & Bradshaw, C. (2016). The role of stress and spirituality in adolescent substance use. *Substance Use and Misuse, 51,* 733–741.

DeCasper, A.J., & Spence, M.J. (1986). Prenatal maternal speech influences newborns' perception of speech sounds. *Infant Behavior and Development, 9,* 133–150.

Decety, J., & Cowell, J. (2016). Developmental social neuroscience. In D. Cicchetti (Ed.), *Developmental psychopathology* (3rd ed.). New York: Wiley.

Decety, J., Meidenbauer, K.L., & Cowell, J.M. (2017, in press). The development of cognitive empathy and concern in preschool children: A behavioral neuroscience investigation. *Developmental Science.*

Dee, D.L., & others (2017). Trends in repeat births and use of postpartum contraception among teens—United States 2004–2015. *MMWR Monthly Mortality Weekly Reports, 66,* 422–426.

Deevy, P., Leonard, L.B., & Marchman, V.A. (2017, in press). Sensitivity to morphosyntactic information in 3-year-old children with typical language development: A feasibility study. *Journal of Speech, Language, and Hearing Research.*

Dehcheshmeh, F.S., & Rafiei, H. (2015). Complementary and alternative therapies to relieve labor pain: A comparative study between music therapy and Hoku point ice massage. *Complementary Therapies in Clinical Practice, 21,* 229–232.

Del Campo, M., & Jones, K.L. (2017). A review of the physical features of the fetal alcohol syndrome disorders. *European Journal of Medical Genetics, 60,* 55–64.

Del Giudice, M., & Ellis, B.J. (2016). Evolutionary foundations of developmental psychopathology. In D. Cicchetti (Ed.), *Developmental psychopathology* (3rd ed.). New York: Wiley.

DeLisi, R. (2015). Piaget's sympathetic but unromantic account of children's play. In J.E. Johnson & others (Eds.), *Handbook of the study of play*. Blue Ridge Summit, PA: Rowman & Littlefield.

DeLoache, J.S. (2011). Early development of the understanding and use of symbolic artifacts. In U. Goswami (Ed.), *Wiley-Blackwell handbook of childhood cognitive development* (2nd ed.). New York: Wiley.

DeLoache, J.S., Simcock, G., & Macari, S. (2007). Planes, trains, automobiles and tea-sets: Extremely intense interests in very young children. *Developmental Psychology, 43,* 1579–1586.

Demanchick, S.P. (2015). The interpretation of play: Psychoanalysis and beyond. In J.E. Johnson & others (Eds.), *Handbook of the study of play*. Blue Ridge Summit, PA: Rowman & Littlefield.

DeMarie, D., & Lopez, L. (2014). Memory in school. In R. Fivush & P. Bauer (Eds.), *Wiley-Blackwell handbook of the development of children's memory*. New York: Wiley.

Demby, S.L. (2016). Parenting coordination: Applying clinical thinking to the management of post-divorce conflict. *Journal of Clinical Psychology, 72,* 458–468.

Dempster, F.N. (1981). Memory span: Sources of individual and developmental differences. *Psychological Bulletin, 80,* 63–100.

Den Heijer, A.E., & others (2017). Sweat it out? The effects of physical exercise on cognition and behavior in children and adults with ADHD: A systematic literature review. *Journal of Neural Transmission, 124* (Suppl. 1), S3–S26.

Denault, A.S., & Guay, F. (2017). Motivation toward extracurricular activities and motivation at school: A test of the generalization effect hypothesis. *Journal of Adolescence, 54,* 94–103.

DeNavas-Walt, C., & Proctor, B.D. (2015). Income and poverty in the United States: 2014. Washington, DC: U.S. Census Bureau.

Denes, G. (2016). *Neural plasticity across the lifespan*. New York: Psychology Press.

Denham, S.A., Bassett, H.H., & Wyatt, T. (2007). The socialization of emotional competence. In J.E. Grusec & P.D. Hastings (Eds.), *Handbook of socialization*. New York: Guilford.

Denham, S.A., Bassett, H.H., & Wyatt, T. (2015). The socialization of emotional competence. In J.E. Grusec & P.D. Hastings (Eds.), *Handbook of socialization* (2nd ed.). New York: Guilford.

Denham, S.A., & others (2013). Social and emotional information processing in preschoolers: Indicators of early social success? *Early Child Development and Care, 183,* 667–688.

Denmark, F.L., Russo, N.F., Frieze, I.H., & Eschuzur, J. (1988). Guidelines for avoiding sexism in psychological research: A report of the ad hoc committee on nonsexist research. *American Psychologist, 43,* 582–585.

Dennis, C.L. (2017). Psychological treatment is one of the several important components to the effective management of postpartum depression. *Evidence Based Nursing, 20*(1), 9.

Deoni, S.C., & others (2016). White matter maturation profiles through early childhood predict general cognitive ability. *Brain Structure and Function, 22,* 1189–1203.

DeRosa, D.A., & Abruscato, J. (2015). *Teaching children science* (8th ed.). Upper Saddle River, NJ: Pearson.

DeSantis, L. (1998). Building healthy communities with immigrants and refugees. *Journal of Transcultural Nursing, 9,* 20–31.

DeSilver, D. (2017). *U.S. students' academic achievement still lags that of their peers in many other countries*. Washington, DC: Pew Research Center.

Dette-Hagenmeyer, D.E., Erzinger, A.G., & Reichle, B. (Eds.) (2016). *Fathers in families*. New York: Psychology Press.

Deutsch, A.R., Crockett, L.J., Wolff, J.M., & Russell, S.T. (2012). Parent and peer pathways to adolescent delinquency: Variations by ethnicity and neighborhood context. *Journal of Youth and Adolescence, 41,* 1078–1094.

Deutsch, R., & Pruett, M.K. (2009). Child adjustment and high-conflict divorce. In R.M. Galatzer-Levy & L. Kraus (Eds.), *The scientific basis of custody decisions* (2nd ed.). New York: Wiley.

Devaney, S.A., Palomaki, G.E., Scott, J.A., & Bianchi, D.W. (2011). Noninvasive fetal sex determination using cell-free fetal DNA: A systematic review and meta-analysis. *Journal of the American Medical Association, 306,* 627–636.

Devine, R.T., & Hughes, C. (2017, in press). Family correlates of false belief understanding in early childhood: A meta-analysis. *Child Development.*

Devine, R.T., White, N., Ersor, R., & Hughes, C. (2016). Theory of mind in middle childhood: Longitudinal associations with executive function. *Developmental Psychology, 52,* 758–771.

Devinish, B., Hooley, M., & Mellor, D. (2017, in press). The pathways between socioeconomic status and adolescent outcomes: A systematic review. *American Journal of Community Psychology.*

Dewey, J. (1933). *How we think*. Lexington, MA: D.C. Heath.

DeZolt, D.M., & Hull, S.H. (2001). Classroom and school climate. In J. Worell (Ed.), *Encyclopedia of women and gender*. San Diego: Academic Press.

Di Florio, A., & others (2014). Mood disorders and parity—a clue to the etiology of the postpartum trigger. *Journal of Affective Disorders, 152,* 334–349.

Di Mascio, D., & others (2016). Exercise during pregnancy in normal-weight women and risk of preterm birth: A systematic review and meta-analysis of randomized controlled trials. *American Journal of Obstetrics and Gynecology, 215,* 561–571.

Diamond, A. (2001). A model system for studying the role of dopamine in the prefrontal cortex during early development in humans: Early and continuously treated phenylketonuria. In C. Nelson & M. Luciana (Eds.), *Handbook of developmental cognitive neuroscience*. Cambridge, MA: MIT Press.

Diamond, A. (2013). Executive functions. *Annual Review of Psychology* (Vol. 64). Palo Alto, CA: Annual Reviews.

Diamond, A., & Lee, K. (2011). Interventions shown to aid executive function development in children 4 to 12 years old. *Science, 333,* 959–964.

Diamond, A.D. (1985). Development of the ability to use recall to guide action, as indicated by infants' performance on AB. *Child Development, 56,* 868–883.

Diamond, L.M., & Alley, J. (2018, in press). The dynamic expression of same-sex sexuality from childhood to young adulthood. In S. Lamb & D. Gilbert (Eds.), *Cambridge handbook of sexuality: Childhood and adolescence.* New York: Cambridge University Press.

Diamond, L.M., & Savin-Williams, R.C. (2015). Same-sex activity in adolescence: Multiple meanings and implications. In R.F. Fassinger & S.L. Morrow (Eds.), *Sex in the margins.* Washington, DC: American Psychological Association.

Diaz, G., & McClelland, M.M. (2017, in press). The influence of parenting on Mexican American children's executive function. *PsyCh Journal.*

Diedrich, J.T., Klein, D.A., & Peipert, J.F. (2017). Long-acting reversible contraception in adolescents: A systematic review and meta-analysis. *American Journal of Obstetrics and Gynecology, 364,* e1–e12.

Diego, M.A., Field, T., & Hernandez-Reif, M. (2008). Temperature increases in preterm infants during massage therapy. *Infant Behavior and Development, 31,* 149–152.

Diego, M.A., Field, T., & Hernandez-Reif, M. (2014). Preterm infant weight gain is increased by massage therapy and exercise via different underlying mechanisms. *Early Human Development, 90,* 137–140.

Dillon, M.R., Pires, A.C., Hyde, D.C., & Spelke, E.S. (2015). Children's expectations about training the approximate number system. *British Journal of Developmental Psychology, 33,* 411–418.

DiLonardo, M.J. (2013). *Talking about weight with your child.* Retrieved February 21, 2013, from www.webmd.com/parenting/raising-fit-kids/weight/talk-child-obesity

Ding, L., Zhu, D., Peng, D., & Zhao, Y. (2017). Air pollution and asthma attacks in children: A case-crossover analysis in the city of Chongqing. *Environmental Pollution, 22* (Pt. A), 348–353.

Dinger, J., & others (2017, in press). Methamphetamine consumption during pregnancy—effects on child health. *Pharmacopsychiatry.*

DiPietro, J. (2008). Unpublished review of J.W. Santrock's *Children,* 11th ed. (New York: McGraw-Hill).

Dishion, T.J., & Patterson, G.R. (2016). The development and ecology of antisocial behavior. In D. Cicchetti (Ed.), *Developmental psychopathology* (3rd ed.). New York: Wiley.

Dishion, T.J., & Piehler, T.F. (2009). Deviant by design: Peer contagion in development, interventions, and schools. In K.H. Rubin, W.M. Bukowski, & B. Laursen (Eds.), *Handbook of peer interactions, relationships, and groups.* New York: Guilford.

Dittus, P.J., & others (2015). Parental monitoring and its associations with adolescent sexual risk behavior: A meta-analysis. *Pediatrics, 136,* e1587–e1599.

Diwadkar, V.A., & others (2013). Differences in cortico-striatal-cerebellar activation during working memory in syndromal and nonsyndromal children with prenatal exposure to alcohol. *Human Brain Mapping, 34,* 1931–1945.

Dixon, S.V., Graber, J.A., & Brooks-Gunn, J. (2008). The roles of respect for parental authority and parenting practices in parent-child conflict among African American, Latino, and European American families. *Journal of Family Psychology, 22,* 1–10.

Dodge, K.A. (1983). Behavioral antecedents of peer social status. *Child Development, 54,* 1386–1399.

Dodge, K.A. (2011a). Context matters in child and family policy. *Child Development, 82,* 433–442.

Dodge, K.A. (2011b). Social information processing models of aggressive behavior. In M. Mikulincer & P. R. Shaver (Eds.), *Understanding and reducing aggression, violence, and their consequences.* Washington, DC: American Psychological Association.

Dodge, K.A., Godwin, J., & Conduct Problems Prevention Research Group (2013). Social-information-processing patterns mediate the impact of preventive intervention on adolescent antisocial behavior. *Psychological Science, 24,* 456–465.

Dodge, K.A., & McCourt, S.N. (2010). Translating models of antisocial behavioral development into efficacious intervention policy to prevent adolescence violence. *Developmental Psychobiology, 52,* 277–285.

Dodington, J., Violano, P., Baum, C.R., & Bechtel, K. (2017). Drugs, guns, and cars: How far we have come to improve safety in the United States, yet we still have far to go. *Pediatric Research, 81,* 227–232.

Dodson, L.J., & Davies, A.P.C. (2014). Different challenges, different well-being: A comparison of psychological well-being across stepmothers and biological mothers and across four categories of stepmothers. *Journal of Divorce & Remarriage, 55,* 49–63.

Doering, J.J., Sims, D.A., & Miller, D.D. (2017, in press). How postpartum women with depressive symptoms manage sleep disruption and fatigue. *Research in Nursing & Health.*

Dohla, D., & Heim, S. (2016). Developmental dyslexia and dysgraphia: What can we learn from one about the other? *Frontiers in Psychology, 6,* 2045.

Domsch, H., Lohaus, A., & Thomas, H. (2009). Influences of information processing and disengagement on infants' looking behavior. *Infant and Child Development, 19,* 161–174.

Donaldson, C.D., Handren, L.M., & Crano, W.D. (2016). The enduring impact of parents' monitoring, warmth, expectancies, and alcohol use on their children's future binge drinking and arrests: A longitudinal analysis. *Prevention Science, 17,* 606–614.

Donatelle, R.J. (2017). *Health* (12th ed.). Upper Saddle River, NJ: Pearson.

Donatelle, R.J., & Ketcham, P. (2018). *Access to health* (15th ed.). Upper Saddle River, NJ: Pearson.

Dondi, M., Simion, F., & Caltran, G. (1999). Can newborns discriminate between their own cry and the cry of another newborn infant? *Developmental Psychology, 35*(2), 418–426.

Done, A.J., & Traustadottir, T. (2016). Nrf2 mediates redox adaptations to exercise. *Redox Biology, 10,* 191–199.

Dong, B., & Krohn, M.D. (2016). Dual trajectories of gang affiliation and delinquent peer association during adolescence: An examination of long-term offending outcomes. *Journal of Youth and Adolescence, 45,* 746–762.

Dong, B., Ma., J., Wang, H.J., & Wang, Z.Q. (2013). The association of overweight and obesity with blood pressure among Chinese children and adolescents. *Biomedical and Environmental Sciences, 26,* 437–444.

Dong, B., Wang, Z., Wang, H.J., & Ma, J. (2015). Population attributable risk of overweight and obesity for high blood pressure in Chinese children. *Blood Pressure, 24,* 230–236.

Donnegan, S., & others (2010). Two food-assisted maternal and child health nutrition programs helped mitigate the impact of economic hardship on child stunting in Haiti. *Journal of Nutrition, 140,* 1139–1145.

Donovan, M.K. (2017). The looming threat to sex education: A resurgence of federal funding for abstinence-only programs? *Guttmacher Policy Review, 20,* 44–47.

Doob, C.B. (2013). *Social inequality and social stratification in U.S. society.* Upper Saddle River, NJ: Pearson.

Dosso, J.A., Herrera, S.V., & Boudreau, J.P. (2017). A study of reaching actions in walking infants. *Infant Behavior and Development, 47,* 112–120.

Dotti Sani, G.M., & Quaranta, M. (2017, in press). The best is yet to come? Attitudes toward gender roles among adolescents in 36 countries. *Sex Roles.*

Doty, R.L., & Shah, M. (2008). Taste and smell. In M.M. Haith & J.B. Benson (Eds.), *Encyclopedia of infant and early childhood development.* Oxford, UK: Elsevier.

Douglass, S., Mirpuri, S., & Yip, T. (2017). Considering friends within the context of peers in school for the development of ethnic/racial identity. *Journal of Youth and Adolescence, 46,* 300–316.

Douglass, S., & Umana-Taylor, A.J. (2017). Examining discrimination, ethnic-racial identity status, and youth public regard among Black, Latino, and White adolescents. *Journal of Research on Adolescence, 27,* 155–172.

Doumen, S., & others (2012). Identity and perceived peer relationship quality in emerging adulthood: The mediating role of attachment-related emotions. *Journal of Adolescence, 35,* 1417–1425.

Dovey, T.M., Staples, P.A., Gibson, E.L., & Halford, J.C. (2008). Food neophobia and "picky/fussy" eating in children: A review. *Appetite, 50,* 181–193.

Dowda, M., & others (2017). Physical activity and changes in adiposity in the transition from elementary to middle school. *Child Obesity, 13,* 53–62.

Doyle, C., & Cicchetti, D. (2018, in press). Child maltreatment. In M.H. Bornstein & others (Eds.), *SAGE encyclopedia of lifespan development.* Thousand Oaks, CA: Sage.

Dozier, M., Stovall-McClough, K.C., & Albus, K.E. (2009). Attachment and psychopathology in adulthood. In J. Cassidy & P.R. Shaver (Eds.), *Handbook of attachment* (2nd ed.). New York: Guilford.

Dragoset, L., & others (2017). School improvement grants: Implementation and effectiveness. NCEE 2017-4013. *ERIC*, ED572215.

Drake, K.M., & others (2012). Influence of sports, physical education, and active commuting to school on adolescent weight status. *Pediatrics, 130,* e296–e304.

Dreby, J. (2010). *Divided by borders.* Berkeley: University of California Press.

Dryfoos, J.G. (1990). *Adolescents at risk: Prevalence and prevention.* New York: Oxford University Press.

Dryfoos, J.G., & Barkin, C. (2006). *Adolescence.* New York: Oxford University Press.

D'Souza, H., & Karmiloff-Smith, A. (2017, in press). Neurodevelopmental disorders. *Wiley Interdisciplinary Reviews. Cognitive Science.*

D'Souza, H., & others (2017, in press). Specialization of the motor system in infancy: From broad tuning to selectively specialized purposeful actions. *Developmental Science.*

du Roscoat, E., & others (2016). Risk factors for suicide attempts and hospitalizations in a sample of 39,542 French adolescents. *Journal of Affective Disorders, 190,* 517–521.

Duell, N., & others (2016). Interaction of reward seeking and self-regulation in the prediction of risk taking: A cross-national test of the dual systems model. *Developmental Psychology, 52,* 1593–1605.

Duff, D., Tomblin, J.B., & Catts, H. (2015). The influence of reading on vocabulary growth: A case for a Matthew effect. *Journal of Speech, Language, and Hearing Research, 58,* 853–864.

Duggan, K.A., & Friedman, H.S. (2014). Lifetime biopsychosocial trajectories of the Terman gifted children: Health, well-being, and longevity. In D.K. Simonton (Ed.), *Wiley-Blackwell handbook of genius.* New York: Oxford University Press.

Duggan, P.M., Lapsley, D.K., & Norman, K. (2000, April). *Adolescent invulnerability and personal uniqueness: Scale development and initial contact validation.* Paper presented at the biennial meeting of the Society for Research in Child Development, Chicago.

Duke, S.A., Balzer, B.W., & Steinbeck, K.S. (2014). Testosterone and its effects on human male adolescent mood and behavior: A systematic review. *Journal of Adolescent Health, 55,* 315–322.

Dumuid, D., & others (2017, in press). Health-related quality of life and lifestyle behavior clusters in school-aged children from 12 countries. *Journal of Pediatrics.*

Duncan, G.J., Magnuson, K., & Votruba-Drzal, E. (2017). Moving beyond correlations in assessing the consequences of poverty. *Annual Review of Psychology* (Vol. 68). Palo Alto, CA: Annual Reviews.

Duncan, G.J., & others (2007). School readiness and later achievement. *Developmental Psychology, 43,* 1428–1446.

Duncan, R., McClelland, M.M., & Acock, A.C. (2017, in press). Relations between executive function, behavioral regulation, and achievement: Moderation by family income. *Journal of Applied Developmental Psychology.*

Dundek, L.H. (2006). Establishment of a Somali doula program at a large metropolitan hospital. *Journal of Perinatal and Neonatal Nursing, 20,* 128–137.

Dunkel Schetter, C. (2011). Psychological science in the study of pregnancy and birth. *Annual Review of Psychology* (Vol. 62). Palo Alto, CA: Annual Reviews.

Dunn, E.C., McLaughlin, K.A., Slopen, N., Rosand, J., & Smoller, J.W. (2013). Developmental timing of child maltreatment and symptoms of depression and suicidal ideation in young adulthood: Results from the National Longitudinal Study of Adolescent Health. *Depression and Anxiety, 30,* 955–964.

Dunn, J. (2007). Siblings and socialization. In J.E. Grusec & P.D. Hastings (Eds.), *Handbook of socialization.* New York: Guilford.

Dunn, J. (2015). Siblings. In J.E. Grusec & P.D. Hastings (Eds.), *Handbook of socialization* (2nd ed.). New York: Guilford.

Dunn, J., & Kendrick, C. (1982). *Siblings.* Cambridge, MA: Harvard University Press.

Dunsmore, J.C., Booker, J.A., & Ollendick, T.H. (2013). Parental emotion coaching and child emotion regulation as protective factors for children with oppositional defiant disorder. *Social Development, 22,* 444–466.

Dunson, D.B., Baird, D.D., & Colombo, B. (2004). Increased fertility with age in men and women. *Obstetrics and Gynecology, 103,* 51–56.

Dupere, V., & others (2015). Stressors and turning points in high school and dropout: A stress process, life course framework. *Review of Educational Research, 85,* 591–629.

Durham, R., & Chapman, L. (2014). *Maternal-newborn nursing* (2nd ed.). Philadelphia: F.A. Davis.

Durrant, J.E. (2008). Physical punishment, culture, and rights: Current issues for professionals. *Journal of Developmental and Behavioral Pediatrics, 29,* 55–66.

Durston, S., & others (2006). A shift from diffuse to focal cortical activity with development. *Developmental Science, 9,* 1–8.

Dursun, A., & others (2016). Maternal risk factors associated with lead, mercury, and cadmium levels in umbilical cord blood, breast milk, and newborn hair. *Journal of Maternal-Fetal and Neonatal Medicine, 29,* 954–961.

Dweck, C. (2006). *Mindset.* New York: Random House.

Dweck, C.S. (2007). Boosting achievement with messages that motivate. *Education Canada, 47,* 6–10.

Dweck, C.S. (2012). Mindsets and human nature: Promoting change in the Middle East, the school yard, the racial divide, and willpower. *American Psychologist, 67,* 614–622.

Dweck, C.S. (2015, September 23). Carol Dweck revisits the 'growth mindset'. *Education Week, 35*(5), 24–26.

Dweck, C.S. (2016, March 11). *Growth mindset revisited.* Invited presentation at Leaders to Learn From Washington, DC: Education Week.

Dweck, C.S., & Master, A. (2009). Self-theories and motivation: Students' beliefs about intelligence. In K.R. Wentzel & A. Wigfield (Eds.), *Handbook of motivation at school.* New York: Routledge.

Dworkin, S.L., & Santelli, J. (2007). Do abstinence-plus interventions reduce sexual risk behavior among youth? *PLoS Medicine, 4,* 1437–1439.

E

Eagan, K., & others (2016). *The American freshman: National norms fall 2015.* Los Angeles: Higher Education Research Institute, UCLA.

Eagly, A.H. (2001). Social role theory of sex differences and similarities. In J. Worrell (Ed.), *Encyclopedia of women and gender.* San Diego: Academic Press.

Eagly, A.H. (2010). Gender roles. In J. Levine & M. Hogg (Eds.), *Encyclopedia of group process and intergroup relations.* Thousand Oaks, CA: Sage.

Eagly, A.H. (2012). Women as leaders: Paths through the labyrinth. In M.C. Bligh & R. Riggio (Eds.), *When near is far and far is near: Exploring distance in leader-follower relationships.* New York: Wiley-Blackwell.

Eagly, A.H., & Steffen, V.J. (1986). Gender and aggressive behavior: A meta-analytic review of the social psychological literature. *Psychological Bulletin, 100,* 309–330.

Eagly, A.H., & Wood, W. (2016). Social role theory of sex differences and similarities. In N. Naples & others (Eds.), *Wiley-Blackwell encyclopedia of gender and sexuality studies.* New York: Wiley-Blackwell.

Eaton, D.K., & others (2010). Youth risk behavior surveillance—United States, 2009. *MMWR Surveillance Summary, 59,* 1–142.

Eaton, D.K., & others (2012). Youth risk behavior surveillance—United States, 2011. *MMWR Surveillance Summary, 61,* 1–162.

Eaton, W.O. (2008). Milestones: Physical. In M.M. Haith & J.B. Benson (Eds.), *Encyclopedia of infant and early childhood development.* Oxford, UK: Elsevier.

Eccles, J.S. (2007). Families, schools, and developing achievement-related motivations and engagement. In J.E. Grusec & P.D. Hastings (Eds.), *Handbook of socialization.* New York: Guilford.

Eccles, J.S., & Roeser, R.W. (2015). School and community influences on human development. In M.H. Bornstein & M.E. Lamb (Eds.), *Developmental science* (7th ed.). New York: Psychology Press.

Echevarria, J.J., Vogt, M.J., & Short, D.J. (2017). *Making content comprehensible for English learners: The SIOP model* (5th ed.). Upper Saddle River, NJ: Pearson.

Ecker, C. (2017). The neuroanatomy of autism spectrum disorder: An overview of structural neuroimaging findings and their translatability to the clinical setting. *Autism, 21,* 18–28.

Eckstein, K.C., & others (2006). Parents' perceptions of their child's weight and health. *Pediatrics, 117,* 681–690.

Edel, M.A., & others (2017). A comparison of mindfulness-based group training and skills group training in adults with ADHD. *Journal of Attention Disorders, 21,* 533–539.

Edmiston, B. (2017). Across the universe: Dialogic dramatic play with young children. In T. Bruce (Ed.), *Routledge international handbook of early childhood play.* New York: Routledge.

Ednick, M., & others (2010). Sleep-related respiratory abnormalities and arousal pattern in achondroplasia during early infancy. *Journal of Pediatrics, 155,* 510–515.

Edwards, M.L., & Jackson, A.D. (2017). The historical development of obstetric anesthesia and its contributions to perinatology. *American Journal of Perinatology, 34,* 211–216.

Edwardson, C.L., & Gorely, T. (2010). Activity-related parenting practices and children's objectively measured physical activity. *Pediatric Exercise Science, 22,* 105–113.

Egeland, B., Jacobvitz, D., & Sroufe, L.A. (1988). Breaking the cycle of abuse. *New Directions for Child Development, 11,* 77–92.

Ehehalt, S., & others (2017). Diabetes screening in overweight and obese children and adolescents: Choosing the right test. *European Journal of Pediatrics, 176,* 89–97.

Eijkemans, M., Mommers, M., Draaisma, J.M., Thijs, C., & Prins, M.H. (2012). Physical activity and asthma: A systematic review and meta-analysis. *PLoS One, 7*(12), e50775.

Eilertsen, T., & others (2016). Parental socioeconomic status and child intellectual functioning in a Norwegian sample. *Scandinavian Journal of Psychology, 57,* 399–405.

Einziger, T., & others (2017, in press). Predicting ADHD symptoms in adolescence from early childhood temperament traits. *Journal of Abnormal Child Psychology.*

Eisenberg, M.E., Bernat, D.H., Bearinger, L.H., & Resnick, M.D. (2008). Support for comprehensive sexuality education: Perspectives from parents of school-aged youth. *Journal of Adolescent Research, 42,* 352–359.

Eisenberg, N., Fabes, R.A., & Spinrad, T L. (2006). Prosocial development. In W. Damon & R. Lerner (Eds.), *Handbook of child psychology* (6th ed.). New York: Wiley.

Eisenberg, M.E., Madsen, N., Oliphant, J.A., & Sieving, R.E. (2013). Barriers to providing sexuality education that teachers believe students need. *Journal of School Health, 83,* 335–342.

Eisenberg, N., Morris, A.S., McDaniel, B., & Spinrad, T.L. (2009). Moral cognitions and prosocial responding in adolescence. In R.M. Lerner & L. Steinberg (Eds.), *Handbook of adolescent psychology* (3rd ed.). New York: Wiley.

Eisenberg, N., Smith, C.L., & Spinrad, T.L. (2016). Effortful control: Relations with emotion regulation, adjustment, and socialization in childhood. In K.D. Vohs & R.F. Baumeister (Eds.), *Handbook of self-regulation* (3rd ed.). New York: Guilford.

Eisenberg, N., & Spinrad, T.L. (2014). Multidimensionality of prosocial behavior: Rethinking the conceptualization and development of prosocial behavior. In L. Padilla-Walker & G. Carlo (Eds.), *Prosocial development: A multidimensional approach.* New York: Oxford University Press.

Eisenberg, N., & Spinrad, T.L. (2016). Multidimensionality of prosocial behavior: Rethinking the conceptualization and development of prosocial behavior. In L. Padilla-Walker & G. Carlo (Eds.), *Prosocial development: A multidimensional approach* (2nd ed.). New York: Oxford University Press.

Eisenberg, N., Spinrad, T. R., & Eggum, N. D. (2010). Emotion-focused self-regulation and its relation to children's maladjustment. *Annual Review of Clinical Psychology* (Vol. 6). Palo Alto, CA: Annual Reviews.

Eisenberg, N., Spinrad, T.L., & Knafo-Noam, A. (2015). Prosocial development. In R.M. Lerner (Ed.), *Handbook of child psychology and developmental science* (7th ed.). New York: Wiley.

Eisenberg, N., Spinrad, T.L., & Morris, A.S. (2013). Prosocial development. In P.D. Zelazo (Ed.), *Oxford handbook of developmental psychology.* New York: Oxford University Press.

Eisenberg, N., Spinrad, T.L., & Valiente, C. (2016). Emotion-related self-regulation and children's social, psychological, and academic functioning. In L. Balter & C.S. Tamis-LeMonda (Eds.), *Child psychology* (3rd ed.). New York: Routledge.

Eisharkawy, H., Sonny, A., & Chin, K.J. (2017). Localization of epidural space: A review of available technologies. *Journal of Anesthesiology, Clinical Pharmacology, 33,* 16–37.

Ekema-Agbaw, M.L., McCutchen, J.A., & Geller, E.S. (2016). Intervening to promote statements of gratitude: Informative incongruity between intention and behavior. *Journal of Prevention and Intervention in the Community, 44,* 144–154.

Eklund, K., Tanner, N., Stoll, K., & Anway, L. (2015). Identifying emotional and behavioral risk among gifted and nongifted children: A multi-gate, multi-informant approach. *School Psychology Quarterly, 30,* 197–211.

Elkind, D. (1970, April 5). Erik Erikson's eight ages of man. *New York Times Magazine.*

Elkind, D. (1976). *Child development and education: A Piagetian perspective.* New York: Oxford University Press.

Elkind, D. (1978). Understanding the young adolescent. *Adolescence, 13,* 127–134.

Elliot, A.J., & Hulleman, C.S. (2017). Achievement goals. In A.J. Elliot, C.S. Dweck, and D.S. Yeager (Eds.), *Handbook of competence and motivation* (2nd ed.). New York: Guilford.

Ellis, B.J., Shirtcliff, E.A., Boyce, W.T., Deardorff, J., & Essex, M.J. (2011). Quality of early family relationships and the timing and tempo of puberty: Effects depend on biological sensitivity to context. *Development and Psychopathology, 23,* 85–99.

Ellison, A., & others (2014). Functional interaction between right parietal and bilateral frontal cortices during visual search tasks revealed using functional magnetic imaging and transcranial direct current stimulation. *PLoS One, 9*(4), e93767.

El-Sheikh, M. (2013). *Auburn University Child Sleep, Health, and Development Center.* Auburn, AL: Auburn University.

El-Sheikh, M., & Buckhalt, J.A. (2015). Moving sleep and child development research forward: Priorities and recommendations from the SRCD-sponsored forum on sleep and child development. In M. El-Sheikh & A. Sadeh (Eds.), Sleep and development: Advancing theory and research. *Monographs of the Society for Research in Child Development, 80,* 15–32.

El-Sheikh, M., Hinnant, J.B., & Philbrook. L.E. (2017, in press). Trajectories of sleep and cardiac sympathetic activity indexed by pre-ejection period in childhood. *Journal of Sleep Research.*

El-Sheikh, M., & Sadeh (Eds.) (2015). Sleep and development: Advancing theory and research. *Monographs of the Society for Research in Child Development, 80,* 1–215.

El-Sheikh, M., & others (2013). Economic adversity and children's sleep problems: Multiple indicators and moderation of health. *Health Psychology, 32,* 849–859.

Eltonsy, S., Martin, B., Ferreira, E., & Blais, L. (2016). Systematic procedure for the classification of proven and potential teratogens for use in research. *Birth Defects Research A: Clinical and Molecular Teratology, 106,* 285–297.

eMarketeer.com (2016). *Mobile phone, smartphone usage.* New York: Author.

Emberson, L.L. (2017). How does experience shape early development? Considering the role of top-down mechanisms. *Advances in Child Development and Behavior, 52,* 1–41.

Emberson, L.L., & others (2017a). Using fNIRS to examine occipital and temporal responses to stimulus repetition in young infants: Evidence of selective frontal cortex involvement. *Developmental Cognitive Neuroscience, 23,* 26–38.

Emberson, L.L., & others (2017b). Deficits in top-down sensory prediction in infants at risk due to premature birth. *Current Biology, 27,* 431–436.

Emery, R.E. (1994). *Renegotiating family relationships.* New York: Guilford.

Emery, R.E. (2014). Families as systems: Some thoughts on methods and theory. In S. McHale, P. Amato, & A. Booth (Eds.), *Emerging methods in family research.* New York: Springer.

Emmer, E.T., & Evertson, C.M. (2017). *Classroom management for middle and high school teachers* (7th ed.). Upper Saddle River, NJ: Pearson.

Emond, A., & others (2017). Developmental and behavioral associations of burns and scalds in children: A prospective population-based study. *Archives of Disease in Childhood, 102,* 428–483.

Endendijk, J.J., & others (2017). Gender differences in child aggression: Relations with gender-differentiated parenting and parents' gender-role stereotypes. *Child Development, 88,* 299–316.

Enfield, A., & Collins, D. (2008). The relationship of service-learning, social justice, multicultural competence, and civic engagement. *Journal of College Student Development, 49,* 95–109.

Engels, A.C., & others (2016). Sonographic detection of central nervous system in the first trimester of pregnancy. *Prenatal Diagnosis, 36,* 266–273.

Englund, M.M., Egeland, B., & Collins, W.A. (2008). Exceptions to high school dropout predictions in a low-income sample: Do adults make a difference? *Journal of Social Issues, 64,* 1, 77–93.

Ennett, S.T., & others (2006). The peer context of adolescent substance use: Findings from social network analysis. *Journal of Research on Adolescence, 16,* 159–186.

Enright, R.D., Santos, M.J.D., & Al-Mabuk, R. (1989). The adolescent as forgiver. *Journal of Adolescence, 12,* 95–110.

Ensembl Human (2008). *Explore the Homo sapiens genome.* Retrieved October 10, 2008, from http://www.ensembl.org/Homo_sapiens/index.html

Ensor, R., Spencer, D., & Hughes, C. (2010). "You feel sad?" Emotional understanding mediates effects of verbal ability and mother-child mutuality on prosocial behaviors: Findings from 2 to 4 years. *Social Development, 20,* 93–110.

Erickson, S.J., & others (2013). Differential associations between maternal scaffolding and toddler emotion regulation in toddlers born preterm and full term. *Early Human Development, 89,* 699–704.

Ericsson, K.A. (2017, in press). Expertise and individual differences: The search for the structure and acquisition of experts' superior performance. *Wiley Interdisciplinary Reviews: Cognitive Science.*

Ericsson, K.A., Charness, N., Feltovich, P.J., & Hoffman, R.R. (Eds.). (2006). *The Cambridge handbook of expertise and expert performance.* New York: Cambridge University Press.

Ericsson, K.A., & others (Eds.) (2016). *Cambridge handbook of expertise and expert performance* (3rd ed.). New York: Cambridge University Press.

Erikson, E.H. (1950). *Childhood and society.* New York: W.W. Norton.

Erikson, E.H. (1968). *Identity: Youth and crisis.* New York: W.W. Norton.

Eriksson, U.J. (2009). Congenital malformations in diabetic pregnancy. *Seminar in Fetal and Neonatal Medicine, 14,* 85–93.

Erkut, S., & others (2013). Can sex education delay early sexual debut? *Journal of Early Adolescence, 33*(4), 482–497.

Erlich, K.B., Miller, G.E., Jones, J.D., & Cassidy, J. (2016). Attachment and psychoneuroimmunology. In J. Cassidy & P.R. Shaver (Eds.), *Handbook of attachment* (3rd ed.). New York: Guilford.

Erskine, H.E., & others (2016). Long-term outcomes of attention-deficit/hyperactivity disorder and conduct disorder: A systematic review and meta-analysis. *Journal of the American Academy of Child and Adolescent Psychiatry, 55,* 841–850.

Espie, J., & Eisler, I. (2015). Focus on anorexia nervosa: Modern psychological treatment and guidelines for the adolescent patient. *Adolescent Health, Medicine, and Therapeutics, 29,* 9–16.

Espinosa, A., & others (2017, in press). Ethnic identity and perceived stress among ethnically diverse immigrants. *Journal of Immigrant and Minority Health.*

Esposito, G., & others (2017a). Response to infant cry in clinically depressed and non-depressed mothers. *PLoS One, 12*(1), e0169066.

Esposito, G., & others (2017b). The development of attachment: Integrating genes, brain, behavior, and environment. *Behavioral Brain Research, 325*(Pt. B), 87–89.

Estes, K.G., & Lew-Williams, C. (2015). Listening through voices: Infant statistical word segmentation across multiple speakers. *Developmental Psychology, 51,* 1517–1528.

Estrada, E., & others (2017, in press). Separating power and speed components of standardized intelligence measures. *Intelligence.*

Ethier, K.A., Harper, C.R., Hoo, E., & Ditts, P.J. (2016). The longitudinal impact of perceptions of parental monitoring on adolescent initiation of sexual activity. *Journal of Adolescent Health, 59,* 570–576.

Etzel, R. (1988, October). *Children of smokers.* Paper presented at the American Academy of Pediatrics meeting, New Orleans.

Evans, C.E. (2017). Sugars and health: A review of current evidence and future policy. *Proceedings of the Nutrition Society.*

Evans, G.W., & English, G.W. (2002). The environment of poverty. *Child Development, 73,* 1238–1248.

Evans, G.W., & Kim, P. (2007). Childhood poverty and health: Cumulative risk exposure and stress dysregulation. *Psychological Science, 18,* 953–957.

Evans, G.W., Li, D., & Sepanski Whipple, S. (2013). Cumulative risk and child development. *Psychological Bulletin, 139*(6), 1342–1396.

Evans, S.Z., Simons, L.G., & Simons, R.L. (2016). Factors that influence trajectories of delinquency throughout adolescence. *Journal of Youth and Adolescence, 45,* 156–171.

Evans-Lacko, S., & others (2017). Childhood bullying victimization is associated with the use of mental health services over five decades: A longitudinal nationally representative study. *Psychological Medicine, 47,* 127–135.

Evereklian, M., & Posmontier, B. (2017, in press). The impact of kangaroo care on premature infant weight gain. *Journal of Pediatric Nursing.*

Evertson, C.M., & Emmer, E.T. (2017). *Classroom management for elementary teachers* (10th ed.). Upper Saddle River, NJ: Pearson.

Ezkurdia, L., & others (2014). The shrinking human protein coding complement: Are there fewer than 20,000 genes? *bioRxiv,* doi:10.1101/001909

F

Fabiano, G.A., & others (2009). A meta-analysis of behavioral treatments for attention deficit/ hyperactivity disorder. *Clinical Psychology Review, 29*(2), 129–140.

Fabricius, W.V., Braver, S.L., Diaz, P., & Schenck, C. (2010). Custody and parenting time: Links to family relationships and well-being after divorce. In M.E. Lamb (Ed.), *The role of the father in child development* (5th ed.). New York: Wiley.

Fagan, J.F. (1992). Intelligence: A theoretical viewpoint. *Current Directions in Psychological Science, 1,* 82–86.

Fagan, J.F., Holland, C.R., & Wheeler, K. (2007). The prediction, from infancy, of adult IQ and achievement. *Intelligence, 35,* 225–231.

Fagot, B.I., Rodgers, C.S., & Leinbach, M.D. (2000). Theories of gender socialization. In T. Eckes & H.M. Trautner (Eds.), *The developmental social psychology of gender.* Mahwah, NJ: Erlbaum.

Fairclough, S.J., & others (2017). Fitness, fatness, and the reallocation of time between children's daily movement behaviors: An analysis of compositional data. *International Journal of Behavioral Nutrition and Physical Activity, 14*(1), 64.

Falbo, T., & Poston, D.L. (1993). The academic, personality, and physical outcomes of only children in China. *Child Development, 64,* 18–35.

Fantz, R.L. (1963). Pattern vision in newborn infants. *Science, 140,* 286–297.

Farr, R.H. (2017). Does parental sexual orientation matter? A longitudinal follow-up of adoptive families with a school-age child. *Developmental Psychology, 53,* 252–264.

Farr, R.H., Crain, E.E., Oakley, M.K., Cashen, K.K., & Garber, K.J. (2016). Microaggression, feelings of difference, and resilience among adoptive children with sexual minority parents. *Journal of Youth and Adolescence, 45,* 85–104.

Farr, R.H., Grant-Marsney, H.A., & Grotevant, H.D. (2014). Adoptees' contact with birth parents in emerging adulthood: The role of adoption communication and attachment to adoptive parents. *Family Process, 53,* 656–671.

Farr, R.H., Oakley, M.K., & Ollen, E.W. (2017, in press). School experiences of young children and their lesbian and gay adoptive parents. *Psychology of Sexual Orientation and Gender Diversity.*

Farr, R.H., & Patterson, C.J. (2013). Coparenting among lesbian, gay, and heterosexual couples: Associations with adopted children's outcomes. *Child Development, 84,* 1226–1240.

Fasano, R.M. (2017). Hemolytic disease of the fetus and newborn in the molecular era. *Seminars in Fetal and Neonatal Medicine, 21,* 28–34.

Fasig, L. (2000). Toddlers' understanding of ownership: Implications for self-concept development. *Social Development, 9,* 370–382.

Fatima, M., Srivastav, S., & Mondal, A.C. (2017, in press). Prenatal stress and depression associated neuronal development in neonates. *International Journal of Developmental Neuroscience.*

Faucher, M.A. (2017, in press). Updates from the literature, September/October 2016. *Journal of Midwifery and Women's Health.*

Faye, P.M., & others (2016). Kangaroo care for low birth weight infants at Albert-Royer National Children Hospital Center of Dakar. *Archives of Pediatrics, 23,* 268–274.

Fazio, L.K., DeWolf, M., & Siegler, R.S. (2016). Strategy use and strategy choice in fraction magnitude comparison. *Journal of Experimental Psychology: Learning, Memory, and Cognition, 42,* 1–16.

Fear, N.T., Hey, K., Vincent, T., & Murphy, M. (2007). Paternal occupation and neural tube defects: A case-control study based on the Oxford Record Linkage Study register. *Pediatric and Perinatal Epidemiology, 21,* 163–168.

Fearon, R.P., & others (2010). The significance of insecure attachment and disorganization in the development of children's externalizing behavior: A meta-analytic study. *Child Development, 81,* 435–456.

Feeney, S., Moravcik, E., & Nolte, S. (2016). *Who am I in the lives of children?* (10th ed.). Upper Saddle River, NJ: Pearson.

Fein, G.G. (1986). Pretend play. In D. Görlitz & J.E. Wohlwill (Eds.), *Curiosity, imagination, and play.* Hillsdale, NJ: Erlbaum.

Feldman, R. (2017). The neurobiology of human attachments. *Trends in Cognitive Science, 21,* 80–89.

Feldman, S.S., & Rosenthal, D.A. (1999). *Factors influencing parents' and adolescents' evaluations of parents as sex communicators.* Unpublished manuscript, Stanford Center on Adolescence, Stanford University.

Feldman, S.S., Turner, R., & Araujo, K. (1999). Interpersonal context as an influence on sexual timetables of youths: Gender and ethnic effects. *Journal of Research on Adolescence, 9,* 25–52.

Feldstein Ewing, S.W., & others (2016). Developmental cognitive neuroscience of adolescent sexual risk and alcohol use. *AIDS Behavior, 20*(Suppl. 1), S97–S108.

Feleszko, W., & others (2006). Parental tobacco smoking is associated with IL-13 secretion in children with allergic asthma. *Journal of Allergy and Clinical Immunology, 117,* 97–102.

Fenson, L., & others (2007). *The MacArthur-Bates communicative development inventories user's guide and technical manual* (2nd ed.). Baltimore: Paul H. Brookes.

Fergus, T.A., & Bardeen, J.R. (2017, in press). The metacognitions questionnaire—30. *Assessment.*

Ferguson, C.J. (2013). Spanking, corporal punishment, and negative long-term outcomes: A meta-analytic review of longitudinal studies. *Clinical Psychology Review, 33,* 196–208.

Fergusson, D.M., Harwood, L.J., & Shannon, F.T. (1987). Breastfeeding and subsequent social adjustment in 6- to 8-year-old children. *Journal of Child Psychology and Psychiatry, 28,* 378–386.

Fergusson, D.M., McLeod, G.F., & Horwood, L.J. (2014). Parental separation/divorce in childhood and partnership outcomes at age 30. *Journal of Child Psychology and Psychiatry, 55,* 352–360.

Fernald, A., Marchman, V.A., & Weisleder, A. (2013). SES differences in language processing skill and vocabulary are evident at 18 months. *Developmental Science, 16,* 234–248.

Fernandez-Jaen, A., & others (2015). Cortical thickness differences in the prefrontal cortex in children and adolescents with ADHD in relation to dopamine transporter (DAT1) genotype. *Psychiatry Research, 233,* 409–117.

Ferriby, M., Kotila, L., Kamp Dush, G.K., & Schoppe-Sullivan, S. (2015). Dimensions of attachment and commitment across the transition to parenthood. *Journal of Family Psychology, 29,* 938–944.

Fertig, A.R. (2010). Selection and the effect of prenatal smoking. *Health Economics, 19,* 209–226.

Fidalgo, R., Harris, K.R., & Braaksma, M. (2016). *Design principles for teaching effective writing.* Leiden, The Netherlands: Brill.

Field, A.E., & others (2001). Peer, parent, and media influences on the development of weight concerns and frequent dieting among preadolescent and adolescent girls and boys. *Pediatrics, 107,* 54–60.

Field, T.M. (2001). Massage therapy facilitates weight gain in preterm infants. *Current Directions in Psychological Science, 10,* 51–55.

Field, T.M. (2007). *The amazing infant.* Malden, MA: Blackwell.

Field, T.M. (2010). Postpartum depression effects on early interactions, parenting, and safety practices: A review. *Infant Behavior and Development, 33,* 1–6.

Field, T.M. (2012). Prenatal exercise research. *Infant Behavior and Development, 35,* 397–407.

Field, T.M. (2016). Massage therapy research review. *Complementary Therapies in Clinical Practice, 24,* 19–31.

Field, T.M., Delgado, J., Diego, M., & Medina, L. (2013). Tai chi/yoga reduces prenatal depression, anxiety, and sleep disturbances. *Complementary Therapies in Clinical Practice, 19,* 6–10.

Field, T.M., Diego, M., & Hernandez-Reif, M. (2008). Prematurity and potential predictors. *International Journal of Neuroscience, 118,* 277–289.

Field, T.M., Diego, M., & Hernandez-Reif, M. (2010). Preterm infant massage therapy research: A review. *Infant Behavior and Development, 33,* 115–124.

Field, T.M., Grizzle, N., Scafidi, F., & Schanberg, S. (1996). Massage and relaxation therapies' effects on depressed adolescent mothers. *Adolescence, 31,* 903–911.

Field, T.M., Hernandez-Reif, M., & Freedman, J. (2004, Fall). Stimulation programs for preterm infants. *SRCD Social Policy Reports, XVIII* (No. 1), 1–20.

Fillo, J., Simpson, J.A., Rholes, W.S., & Kohn, J.L. (2015). Dads doing diapers: Individual and relational systems associated with the division of childcare across the transition to parenthood. *Journal of Personality and Social Psychology, 108,* 298–316.

Finch, K.H., & others (2017). Lateralization of ERPs to speech and handedness in the early development of autism spectrum disorder. *Journal of Neurodevelopmental Disorders.*

Fine, A., Steinberg, L., Frick, P.J., & Cauffman, E. (2017c, in press). Self-control assessments and implications for predicting adolescent offending. *Journal of Youth and Adolescence.*

Fine, A., & others (2017a). And justice for all: Determinants and effects of probation among first-time offenders. *Law and Human Behavior.*

Fine, A., & others (2017b, in press). Is the effect of justice system attitudes on recidivism stable after youths' first arrests? *Race and Legal Socialization.*

Finger, B., Hans, S.L., Bernstein, V.J., & Cox, S.M. (2009). Parent relationship quality and infant-mother attachment. *Attachment and Human Development, 11,* 285–306.

Fingerman, K.L., & others (2017, in press). Coresident and noncoresident emerging adults' daily experiences with parents. *Emerging Adulthood.*

Finke, E.H., Wilkinson, K.M., & Hickerson, B.D. (2017). Social referencing gaze behavior during a videogame task: Eye tracking evidence from children with and without ASD. *Journal of Autism Spectrum Disorders, 47,* 415–423.

Finnane, J.M., Jansen, E., Mallan, K.M., & Daniels, L.A. (2017). Mealtime structure and responsive feeding practices are associated with less food fussiness and more food enjoyment in children. *Journal of Nutrition Education and Behavior, 49,* 11–18.

Fischer, N., & Theis, D. (2014). Extracurricular participation and the development of school attachment and learning goal orientation: The impact of school quality. *Developmental Psychology, 50,* 1788–1793.

Fischhoff, B., Bruine de Bruin, W., Parker, A.M., Millstein, S.G., & Halpern-Felsher, B.L. (2010). Adolescents' perceived risk of dying. *Journal of Adolescent Health, 46,* 265–269.

Fisher, D., & Frey, N. (2016). *Improving adolescent literacy* (4th ed.). Upper Saddle River, NJ: Pearson.

Fisher, K.R., Hirsh-Pasek, K., Newcombe, N., & Golinkoff, R.M. (2013). Taking shape: Supporting preschoolers' acquisition of geometric knowledge through guided play. *Child Development, 84*(6), 1872–1878.

Fisher, P.A. (2005, April). *Translational research on underlying mechanisms of risk among foster children: Implications for prevention science.* Paper presented at the meeting of the Society for Research in Child Development, Washington, DC.

Fitzgerald, A., Fitzgerald, N., & Aherne, C. (2012). Do peers matter? A review of peer and/or friends' influence on physical activity among American adolescents. *Journal of Adolescence, 35,* 941–958.

Fitzgerald, L.M., Arvaneh, M., & Dockree, P.M. (2017). Domain-specific and domain-general processes underlying metacognitive judgments. *Consciousness and Cognition, 49,* 264–277.

Fivush, R. (2010). The development of autobiographical memory. *Annual Review of Psychology* (Vol. 62). Palo Alto, CA: Annual Reviews.

Fivush, R., & Haden, C.A. (1997). Narrating and representing experience: Preschoolers' developing autobiographical accounts. In P. van den Broek, P.J. Bauer, & T. Bourg (Eds.), *Developmental spans in event representations and comprehension: Bridging fictional and actual events.* Mahwah, NJ: Erlbaum.

Flam, K.K., Sandler, I., Wolchik, S., & Tein, J.Y. (2016). Non-residential father-child involvement, interparental conflict, and mental health of children following divorce: A person-focused approach. *Journal of Youth and Adolescence, 45,* 581–593.

Flanagan, J.C., Gordon, K.C., Moore, T.M., & Stuart, G.L. (2015). Women's stress, depression, and relationship adjustment profiles as they relate to intimate partner violence and mental health during pregnancy and postpartum. *Psychology of Violence, 5*, 66–71.

Flanagan, K.S., Vanden Hoek, K.K., Ranter, J.M., & Reich, H.A. (2012). The potential of forgiveness as a response for coping with negative peer experiences. *Journal of Adolescence, 35*, 1215–1223.

Flannery, D.J., & others (2016). Bullying prevention: A summary of the report of the National Academies of Sciences, Engineering, and Medicine: Committee on the Biological and Psychological Effects of Peer Victimization: Lessons for bullying prevention. *Prevention Science, 17*, 1044–1053.

Flannery, M. (2017). Self-determination theory: Intrinsic motivation and behavior change. *Oncology Nursing Forum, 44*, 155–156.

Flavell, J.H. (2004). Theory-of-mind development: Retrospect and prospect. *Merrill-Palmer Quarterly, 50*, 274–290.

Flavell, J.H., Friedrichs, A., & Hoyt, J. (1970). Developmental changes in memorization processes. *Cognitive Psychology, 1*, 324–340.

Flavell, J.H., Green, F.L., & Flavell, E.R. (1993). Children's understanding of the stream of consciousness. *Child Development, 64*, 95–120.

Flavell, J.H., Green, F.L., & Flavell, E.R. (1995). The development of children's knowledge about attentional focus. *Developmental Psychology, 31*, 706–712.

Flavell, J.H., Green, F.L., & Flavell, E.R. (1998). The mind has a mind of its own: Developing knowledge about mental uncontrollability. *Cognitive Development, 13*, 127–138.

Flavell, J.H., Green, F.L., & Flavell, E.R. (2000). Development of children's awareness of their own thoughts. *Journal of Cognition and Development, 1*, 97–112.

Flavell, J.H., Mumme, D., Green, F., & Flavell E. (1992). Young children's understanding of different types of beliefs. *Child Development, 63*, 960–977.

Flensborg-Madsen, T., & Mortensen, E.L. (2017). Predictors of motor developmental milestones during the first year of life. *European Journal of Pediatrics, 176*, 109–119.

Fletcher, P., & Frizelle, P. (2017). Syntax in child language disorders. In R. Schwarz (Ed.), *Handbook of child language disorders* (2nd ed.). New York: Routledge.

Fletcher, S., & others (2017, in press). Tracking of toddler fruit and vegetable preferences to intake and adiposity later in childhood. *Maternal and Child Health.*

Fletcher-Watson, S., McConnell, F., Manola, E., & McConachie, H. (2014). Interventions based on the theory of mind cognitive model for autism spectrum disorder. *Cochrane Database of Systematic Reviews, 3*, CD008785.

Flicek, P., & others (2013). Ensembl 2013. *Nucleic Acids Research 41*, D48–D55.

Flint, M.S., Baum, A., Chambers, W.H., & Jenkins, F.J. (2007). Induction of DNA damage, alteration of DNA repair, and transcriptional activation by stress hormones. *Psychoneuroendocrinology, 32*, 470–479.

Flores, G., Abreu, M., & Tomany-Korman, S.C. (2005). Limited English proficiency, primary language at home, and disparities in children's health care: How language barriers are measured matters. *Public Health Reports, 120*, 418–420.

Flouri, E., Midouhas, E., & Joshi, H. (2014). Family poverty and trajectories of children's emotional and behavioral problems: The moderating role of self-regulation and verbal cognitive ability. *Journal of Abnormal Child Psychology, 42*, 1043–1056.

Flynn, J.R. (1999). Searching for justice: The discovery of IQ gains over time. *American Psychologist, 54*, 5–20.

Flynn, J.R. (2007). The history of the American mind in the 20th century: A scenario to explain IQ gains over time and a case for the relevance of g. In P.C. Kyllonen, R.D. Roberts, & L. Stankov (Eds.), *Extending intelligence.* Mahwah, NJ: Erlbaum.

Flynn, J.R. (2011). Secular changes in intelligence. In R.J. Sternberg & S.B. Kaufman (Eds.), *Cambridge handbook of intelligence.* New York: Cambridge University Press.

Flynn, J.R. (2013). *Are we getting smarter?* New York: Cambridge University Press.

Follari, L. (2015). *Foundations and best practices in early childhood education* (3rd ed.). Upper Saddle River, NJ: Pearson.

Fonseca-Machado Mde, O., & others (2015). Depressive disorder in Latin women: Does intimate partner violence matter? *Journal of Clinical Nursing, 24*, 1289–1299.

Fontaine, R.G., & others (2010). Does response evaluation and decision (RED) mediate the relation between hostile attributional style and antisocial behavior in adolescence? *Journal of Abnormal Child Psychology, 38*, 615–626.

Ford, D.Y. (2012). Gifted and talented education: History, issues, and recommendations. In K.R. Harris, S. Graham, & T. Urdan (Eds.), *APA handbook of educational psychology.* Washington, DC: American Psychological Association.

Ford, D.Y. (2014). Why education must be multicultural: Addressing a few misperceptions with counterarguments. *Gifted Child Today, 37*, 59–62.

Ford, D.Y. (2015a). Multicultural issues: Recruiting and retaining Black and Hispanic students in gifted education: Equality versus equity in schools. *Gifted Child Today, 38*, 187–191.

Ford, D.Y. (2015b). Culturally responsive gifted classrooms for culturally different students: A focus on invitational learning. *Gifted Child Today, 38*, 67–69.

Foster, B.A., & others (2016). A pilot study of parent mentors for early childhood obesity. *Obesity, 2016*, 2609504.

Fourneret, P., & des Portes, V. (2017). Developmental approach of executive functions: From infancy to adolescence. *Archives of Pediatrics, 24*, 66–72.

Fouts, H.N., & Bader, L.R. (2017). Transitions in siblinghood: Integrating developments, cultural, and evolutionary perspectives. In D. Narváez & others (Eds.), *Contexts for young child flourishing.* New York: Oxford University Press.

Fox, E., & Alexander, R.A. (2017). Learning to read. In R.E. Mayer & P.A. Alexander (Eds.), *Handbook of research on learning and instruction* (2nd ed.). New York: Routledge.

Fox, M.K., Condon, E., Briefel, R.R., Reidy, K.C., & Deming, D.M. (2010). Food consumption patterns of young preschoolers: Are they starting off on the right path? *Journal of the American Dietetic Association, 110*(Suppl. 12), S52–S59.

Fox, M.K., Pac, S., Devaney, B., & Jankowski, L. (2004). Feeding infants and toddlers study: What foods are infants and toddlers eating? *American Dietetic Association Journal, 104*(Suppl.), S22–S30.

Fraley, R.C., Roisman, G.I., Booth-LaForce, C., Owen, M.T., & Holland, A.S. (2013). Intrapersonal and genetic origins of adult attachment styles: A longitudinal study from infancy to early adulthood. *Journal of Personality and Social Psychology, 104*, 817–838.

Franchak, J.M., & Adolph, K.E. (2014). Affordances as probabilistic functions: Implications for development, perception, and decisions for action. *Ecological Psychology, 26*, 109–124.

Franchak, J.M., Heeger, D.J., Hasson, U., & Adolph, K.E. (2016). Free viewing gaze behavior in infants and adults. *Infancy 21*, 262–287.

Francis, J., Fraser, G., & Marcia, J.E. (1989). *Cognitive and experimental factors in moratorium-achievement (MAMA) cycles.* Unpublished manuscript. Department of Psychology, Simon Fraser University, Burnaby, British Columbia.

Francis, J.K.R., & Gold, M.A. (2017, in press). Long-acting reversible contraception for adolescents: A review. *JAMA Pediatrics.*

Franco, P., & others (2010). Arousal from sleep mechanisms in infants. *Sleep Medicine, 11*, 603–614.

Franklin, A., Vevis, L., Ling, Y., & Hurlbert, A. (2010). Biological components of color preference in infancy. *Developmental Science, 13*, 346–354.

Frawley, J., & others (2016). Complementary and alternative medicine practitioner use prior to pregnancy predicts use during pregnancy. *Women's Health, 56*, 926–939.

Frederikse, M., & others (2000). Sex differences in inferior lobule volume in schizophrenia. *American Journal of Psychiatry, 157*, 422–427.

Freedman, D.G. (2017). *Human infancy: An evolutionary approach.* New York: Routledge.

Freedman, D.S., & others (2005). The relation of childhood BMI to adult adiposity: The Bogalusa Heart Study. *Pediatrics, 115*, 22–27.

Freeman, S., & others (2017). *Biological science* (6th ed.). Upper Saddle River, NJ: Pearson.

French, D.C., Purwono, U., & Rodkin, P.C. (2012). Religiosity of adolescents and their friends and network associates: Homophily and associations with antisocial behavior. *Journal of Research on Adolescence, 22*, 326–332.

Frenkel, T.I., & Fox, N.A. (2015). Caregiver socialization factors influencing socioemotional development in infancy and childhood: A neuroscience perspective. In J.E. Grusec & P.D. Hastings (Eds.), *Handbook of socialization* (2nd ed.). New York: Guilford.

Freud, S. (1917). *A general introduction to psychoanalysis.* New York: Washington Square Press.

Friedman, J. (2013). Twin separation. Retrieved February 14, 2013, from http://christinabaglivitinglof.com/twin-pregnancy/six-twin-experts-tell-all/

Friedman, N.P., & others (2009). Individual differences in childhood sleep problems predict later cognitive control. *Sleep, 32,* 323–333.

Friedman, S.L., Melhuish, E., & Hill, C. (2010). Childcare research at the dawn of a new millennium: An update. In G. Bremner & T. Wachs (Eds.), *Wiley-Blackwell handbook of infant development* (2nd ed.). Oxford, UK: Wiley-Blackwell.

Friend, M. (2018). *Special education* (5th ed.). Upper Saddle River, NJ: Pearson.

Froh, J.J., Yurkewicz, C., & Kashdan, T.B. (2009). Gratitude and subjective well-being in early adolescence: Examining gender differences. *Journal of Adolescence, 32,* 633–650.

Fuchs, L.S., & others (2016). Supported self-explaining during fraction intervention. *Journal of Educational Psychology, 108,* 493–508.

Fuhs, M.W., Nesbitt, K.T., Farran, D.C., & Dong, N. (2014). Longitudinal associations between executive functioning and academic skills across content areas. *Developmental Psychology, 50,* 1698–1709.

Fujiki, M., & Brinton, B. (2017). Pragmatics and social communication in child language disorders. In R. Schwartz (Ed.), *Handbook of child language disorders* (2nd ed.). New York: Routledge.

Fukushima, A., & others (2015). A proposal for improvement of genotyping performance for ethnically homogeneous population using DNA microarray. *Conference Proceedings of the Annual International Conference of the IEEE Engineering in Medicine and Biology Society, 2015,* 6816–6818.

Fuligni, A.J. (2012). Gaps, conflicts, and arguments between adolescents and their parents. *New Directions for Child and Adolescent Development, 135,* 105–110.

Fulkerson, J.A., & others (2017, in press). Family home food environment and nutrition-related parent and child personal and behavioral outcomes of the Healthy Home Offerings via the Mealtime Environment (HOME) Plus Program: A randomized controlled trial. *Journal of the Academy of Nutrition and Dietetics.*

Fung, H. (2011). Cultural psychological perspectives on social development. In P.K. Smith & C.H. Hart (Eds.), *Wiley-Blackwell handbook of childhood social development* (2nd ed.). New York: Wiley.

Funk, C.M., & others (2016). Local slow waves in superficial layers of primary cortical areas during REM sleep. *Current Biology, 26,* 396–403.

Furman, L. (2017, in press). Kangaroo care 20 years late: Connecting infants and families. *Pediatrics.*

Furman, W., & Collins, W.A. (2009). Adolescent romantic relationships and experiences. In K.H. Rubin, W.M. Bukowksi, & B. Laursen (Eds.), *Handbook of peer interactions, relationships, and groups.* New York: Wiley.

Furman, W., Low, S., & Ho, M.J. (2009). Romantic experience and psychosocial adjustment in middle adolescence. *Journal of Clinical Child and Adolescent Psychology, 38,* 75–90.

Furman, W., & Rose, A.J. (2015). Friendships, romantic relationships, and other dyadic peer relationships in childhood and adolescence: A united relational perspective. In R.M. Lerner (Ed.), *Handbook of child psychology and developmental science* (7th ed.). New York: Wiley.

Furth, H.G., & Wachs, H. (1975). *Thinking goes to school.* New York: Oxford University Press.

G

Gadsby, S. (2017). Distorted body representations in anorexia nervosa. *Consciousness and Cognition, 51,* 17–33.

Gaias, L.M., & others (2012). Cross-cultural temperamental differences in infants, children, and adults in the United States of America and Finland, 53, 119–128.

Gaillard, A., & others (2014). Predictors of postpartum depression: Prospective study of 264 women followed during pregnancy and postpartum. *Psychiatry Research, 215,* 341–346.

Gaither, S.E., Pauker, K., & Johnson, S.P. (2012). Biracial and monoracial infant own-race face perception: An eye tracking study. *Developmental Science, 15*(6), 775–782.

Galambos, N.L., Berenbaum, S.A., & McHale, S.M. (2009). Gender development in adolescence. In R.M. Lerner & L. Steinberg (Eds.), *Handbook of adolescent psychology.* New York: Wiley.

Galambos, N.L., Howard, A.L., & Maggs, J.L. (2011). Rise and fall of sleep quality with student experiences across the first year of the university. *Journal of Research on Adolescence, 21,* 342–349.

Galbally, M., Lewis, A.J., IJzendoorn, M., & Permezel, M. (2011). The role of oxytocin in mother-infant relations: A systematic review of human studies. *Harvard Review of Psychiatry, 19,* 1–14.

Galdiolo, S., & Roskam, I. (2016). From me to us: The construction of family alliance. *Infant Mental Health, 37,* 29–44.

Galinksy, E. (2010). *Mind in the making.* New York: Harpercollins.

Galinsky, E., & David, J. (1988). *The preschool years: Family strategies that work—from experts and parents.* New York: Times Books.

Galinsky, E., & others (2017, in press). Civic science for public use: Mind in the Making and Vroom. *Child Development.*

Galland, B.C., Taylor, B.J., Edler, D.E., & Herbison, P. (2012). Normal sleep patterns in infants and children: A systematic review of observational studies. *Sleep Medicine Review, 16,* 213–222.

Gallant, S.N. (2016). Mindfulness meditation practice and executive functioning: Breaking down the benefit. *Consciousness and Cognition, 40,* 116–130.

Galler, J.R., & others (2012). Infant malnutrition is associated with persisting attention deficits in middle childhood. *Journal of Nutrition, 142,* 788–794.

Galliano, D., & Bellver, J. (2013). Female obesity: Short- and long-term consequences on the offspring. *Gynecological Endocrinology, 29,* 626–631.

Galliher, R.V., McLean, K.C., & Syed, M. (2017, in press). An integrated model for studying identity content in context. *Developmental Psychology.*

Gallo, E.F., & Posner, J. (2016). Moving towards causality in attention-deficit hyperactivity disorder: Overview of neural and genetic mechanisms. *Lancet Psychiatry, 3,* 555–567.

Galloway, J.C., & Thelen, E. (2004). Feet first: Object exploration in young infants. *Infant Behavior & Development, 27,* 107–112.

Gallup Poll (2012, October 24). *In U.S., obesity up in nearly all age groups since 2008.* Retrieved June 25, 2017, from www.gallup.com/poll/158351/obesity-nearly-age-groups-2008.aspx

Gallup, G.W., & Bezilla, R. (1992). *The religious life of young Americans.* Princeton, NJ: Gallup Institute.

Galvan, A., & Tottenham, N. (2016). Adolescent brain development. In D. Cicchetti (Ed.), *Developmental psychopathology* (3rd ed.). New York: Wiley.

Ganguli, M. (2017, in press). The times they are a-changin': Cohort effects in aging, cognition, and dementia. *International Psychogeriatrics.*

Ganong, L., Coleman, M., & Russell, L. (2015). Children in diverse families. In R.M. Lerner (Ed.), *Handbook of child psychology and developmental science* (7th ed.). New York: Wiley.

Gao, W., Lin, W., Grewen, K., & Gilmore, J.H. (2016). Functional connectivity of the infant human brain: Plastic and modifiable. *Neuroscientist.* doi:10.1177/1073858416635986

Garandeau, C.F., Vartio, A., Poskiparta, E., & Salmivalli, C. (2016). School bullies' intention to change behavior following teacher interventions: Effects of empathy arousal, condemning of bullying, and blaming the perpetrator. *Prevention Science, 17,* 1034–1043.

Garber, J., & Cole, D.A. (2010). Intergenerational transmission of depression: A launch and grow model of change across adolescence. *Development and Psychopathology, 22*(4), 819–830.

Garcia Coll, C., & others (2012). Understanding the immigrant paradox in youth: Developmental and contextual considerations. In A.S. Masten (Ed.), *Realizing the potential of immigrant youth.* New York: Cambridge University Press.

Garcia-Hermoso, A., Saavedra, J.M., & Escalante, Y. (2013). Effects of exercise on resting blood pressure in obese children: A meta-analysis of randomized controlled trials. *Obesity Reviews, 14*(11), 919–928.

Gardner, H. (1983). *Frames of mind.* New York: Basic Books.

Gardner, H. (1993). *Multiple intelligences.* New York: Basic Books.

Gardner, H. (2002). The pursuit of excellence through education. In M. Ferrari (Ed.), *Learning from extraordinary minds.* Mahwah, NJ: Erlbaum.

Gardner, H. (2016). *Multiple intelligences: Prelude, theory, and aftermath.* In R.J. Sternberg,

S.T. Fiske, & J. Foss (Eds.), *Scientists making a difference*. New York: Cambridge University Press.

Gardner, M., Brooks-Gunn, J., & Chase-Lansdale, P.L. (2016). The two-generation approach to building human capital: Past, present, and future. In E. Votruba-Drzal & E. Dearing (Eds.), *Handbook of early childhood development programs, practices, and policies*. New York: Wiley.

Gardner, M., Browning, C., & Brooks-Gunn, J. (2012). Can organized youth activities protect against internalizing problems among adolescents living in violent homes? *Journal of Research in Adolescence, 22,* 662–677.

Gardner, M., & Steinberg, L. (2005). Peer influence on risk taking, risk preference, and risky decision making in adolescence and adulthood: An experimental study. *Developmental Psychology, 41,* 625–635.

Gardner, P., & Chao, G. (2017). Healthy transitions to work. In L.M. Padilla & L. Walker (Eds.), *Flourishing in emerging adulthood*. New York: Oxford University Press.

Gardosi, J., & others (2013). Maternal and fetal risk factors for stillbirth: Population-based study. *British Medical Journal, 346,* f108.

Gareau, S., & others (2016). Group prenatal care results in Medicaid savings with better outcomes: A propensity score analysis of Centering Pregnancy participation in South Carolina. *Maternal and Child Health Journal, 20,* 1384–1393.

Garfield, C.F., & others (2012). Trends in attention deficit hyperactivity disorder ambulatory diagnosis and medical treatment in the United States 2000–2010. *Academic Pediatrics, 12,* 110–116.

Gariepy, G., Janssen, I., Sentenac, M., & Elgar, F.J. (2017). School start time and sleep in Canadian adolescents. *Journal of Sleep Research, 26,* 195–201.

Garrison, M.M., Liekweg, K., & Christakis, D.A. (2011). Media use and child sleep: The impact of content, timing, and environment. *Pediatrics, 128,* 29–35.

Gartstein, M.A., Putnam, S., & Kliewer, R. (2016). Do infant temperament characteristics predict core academic abilities in preschool-aged children? *Learning and Individual Differences, 45,* 299–306.

Garvey, C. (2000). *Play* (Enlarged Ed.). Cambridge, MA: Harvard University Press.

Gaskins, S. (2016). Childhood practices across cultures: Play and household work. In L.J. Arnett (Ed.), *Oxford handbook of human development and culture*. New York: Oxford University Press.

Gasser, L., & Keller, M. (2009). Are the competent morally good? Perspective taking and moral motivation of children involved in bullying. *Social Development, 18*(4), 798–816.

Gates, G.J. (2013, February). *LGBT parenting in the United States*. Los Angles: The Williams Institute, UCLA.

Gates, W. (1998, July 20). Charity begins when I'm ready (interview). *Fortune Magazine*.

Gattamorta, K.A., & others (2017). Psychiatric symptoms, parental attachment, and reasons for use as correlates of heavy substance use among treatment-seeking Hispanic adolescents. *Substance Use and Misuse, 52,* 392–400.

Gauvain, M. (2013). Sociocultural contexts of development. In P.D. Zelazo (Ed.), *Oxford handbook of developmental psychology*. New York: Oxford University Press.

Gauvain, M. (2016). Peer contributions to cognitive development. In K. Wentzel & G.B. Ramani (Eds.), *Handbook of social influences in school contexts*. New York: Routledge.

Gauvain, M., & Perez, S. (2015). Cognitive development in the context of culture. In R.M. Lerner (Ed.), *Handbook of child psychology and developmental science* (7th ed.). New York: Wiley.

Gawlik, S., & others (2014). Prevalence of paternal perinatal depressiveness and its link to partnership satisfaction and birth concerns. *Archives of Women's Mental Health, 17,* 49–56.

Gaylord, N., Chyka, D.L., & Lawley, G. (2012). Developmental evaluation of preschool children: A service-learning experience for nursing students. *Journal of Nursing Education, 51,* 710–713.

Gebremariam, M.K., & others (2017). Screen-based sedentary time: Association with soft drink consumption and the moderating effect of parental education in European children: The ENERGY study. *PLoS One, 12*(2), e017157.

Gee, C.L., & Heyman, G.D. (2007). Children's evaluations of other people's self-descriptions. *Social Development, 16,* 800–818.

Gelfand, J., Dierschke, N., Lowe, D., & Plastino, K. (2016). Preventing pregnancy in high school students: Observations from a 3-year longitudinal quasi-experimental study. *American Journal of Public Health, 106,* S97–S102.

Gelman, R. (1969). Conservation acquisition: A problem of learning to attend to relevant attributes. *Journal of Experimental Child Psychology, 7,* 67–87.

Gelman, S.A. (2013). Concepts in development. In P. Zelazo (Ed.), *Oxford handbook of developmental psychology*. New York: Oxford University Press.

Gelman, S.A., & Kalish, C.W. (2006). Conceptual development. In W. Damon & R. Lerner (Eds.), *Handbook of child psychology* (6th ed.). New York: Wiley.

Genesee, F., & Lindholm-Leary, K. (2012). The education of English language learners. In K. Harris, S. Graham, & T. Urdan (Eds.), *APA educational psychology handbook*. Washington, DC: American Psychological Association.

Gennetian, L.A., & Miller, C. (2002). Children and welfare reform: A view from an experimental welfare reform program in Minnesota. *Child Development, 73,* 601–620.

Gentile, D.A. (2011). The multiple dimensions of video game effects. *Child Development Perspectives, 5,* 75–81.

George Dalmida, S., & others (2017, in press). Sexual risk behaviors of African American adolescent females: The role of cognitive and risk factors. *Journal of Transcultural Nursing*.

Gerenser, J., & Lopez, K. (2017). Autism spectrum disorder. In R. Schwartz (Ed.), *Handbook of child language disorders* (2nd ed.). New York: Routledge.

Gernhardt, A., Keller, H., & Rubeling, H. (2016). Children's family drawings as expressions of attachment representations across cultures: Possibilities and limitations. *Child Development, 87,* 1069–1078.

Gershoff, E.T. (2013). Spanking and development: We know enough now to stop hitting our children. *Child Development Perspectives, 7,* 133–137.

Gershoff, E.T., & Benner, A.D. (2014). Neighborhood and school contexts in the lives of children. In E.T. Gershoff, R.S. Mistry, & D.A. Crosby (Eds.), *The societal contexts of child development*. New York: Oxford University Press.

Gershoff, E.T., & Grogan-Kaylor, A. (2016). Spanking and child outcomes: Old controversies and new meta-analyses. *Journal of Family Psychology, 30,* 453–469.

Gershoff, E.T., Lansford, J.E., Sexton, H.R., Davis-Kean, P., & Sameroff, A. (2012). Longitudinal links between spanking and children's externalizing behaviors in a national sample of White, Black, Hispanic, and Asian American families. *Child Development, 83,* 838–843.

Gershoff, E.T., Lee, S.J., & Durrant, J.E. (2017, in press). Promising intervention strategies for reducing parents' use of physical punishment. *Child Abuse and Neglect*.

Gershoff, E.T., Mistry, R.S., & Crosby, D.A. (Eds.) (2014). *The societal contexts of child development*. New York: Oxford University Press.

Gerson, S.A., & Woodward, A.L. (2014). The joint role of trained, untrained, and observed actions at the origins of goal recognition. *Infant Behavior and Development, 37,* 94–104.

Gerst, E.H., Dirino, P.T., Fletcher, J.M., & Yoshida, H. (2017). Cognitive and behavioral rating measures of executive function predictors of academic outcomes in children. *Child Neuropsychology, 23*(4), 381–407.

Gesell, A.L. (1934a). *An atlas of infant behavior*. New Haven, CT: Yale University Press.

Gesell, A.L. (1934b). *Infancy and human growth*. New York: Macmillan.

Gestwicki, C. (2017). *Developmentally appropriate practice* (6th ed.). Boston: Cengage.

Geva, R., Yaron, H., & Kuint, J. (2016). Neonatal sleep predicts attention orienting and distractibility. *Journal of Attention Disorders, 20,* 138–150.

Gewirtz, J. (1977). Maternal responding and the conditioning of infant crying: Directions of influence within the attachment-acquisition process. In B.C. Etzel, J.M. LeBlanc, & D.M. Baer (Eds.), *New developments in behavioral research*. Hillsdale, NJ: Erlbaum.

Ghazarian, S.R., & Roche, K.M. (2010). Social support and low-income, urban mothers: Longitudinal associations with delinquency. *Journal of Youth and Adolescence, 39,* 1097–1108.

Ghetti, S., & Alexander, K.W. (2004). "If it happened, I would remember it": Strategic use of event memorability in the rejection of false autobiographical events. *Child Development, 75,* 542–561.

Ghosh, S., Feingold, E., Chakraborty, S., & Dey, S.K. (2010). Telomere length is associated with types of chromosome 21 nondisjunction: A new insight into the maternal age effect on Down syndrome birth. *Human Genetics, 127,* 403.

Gialamas, A., & others (2014). Quality of childcare influences children's attentiveness and emotional regulation at school entry. *Journal of Pediatrics, 165,* 813–819.

Gibbons, J., & Ng, S.H. (2004). Acting bilingual and thinking bilingual. *Journal of Language & Social Psychology, 23,* 4–6.

Gibbs, J.C. (2014). *Moral development and reality: Beyond the theories of Kohlberg and Hoffman* (3rd ed.). Upper Saddle River, NJ: Pearson.

Gibbs, J.C., Basinger, K.S., Grime, R.L., & Snarey, J.R. (2007). Moral judgment development across cultures: Revisiting Kohlberg's universality claims. *Developmental Review, 27,* 443–500.

Gibson, E.J. (1969). *Principles of perceptual learning and development.* New York: Appleton-Century-Crofts.

Gibson, E.J. (1989). Exploratory behavior in the development of perceiving, acting, and the acquiring of knowledge. *Annual Review of Psychology* (Vol. 39). Palo Alto, CA: Annual Reviews.

Gibson, E.J. (2001). *Perceiving the affordances.* Mahwah, NJ: Erlbaum.

Gibson, E.J., & others (1987). Detection of the traversability of surfaces by crawling and walking infants. *Journal of Experimental Psychology: Human Perception and Performance, 13,* 533–544.

Gibson, E.J., & Walk, R.D. (1960). The "visual cliff." *Scientific American, 202,* 64–71.

Gibson, J.J. (1966). *The senses considered as perceptual systems.* Boston: Houghton Mifflin.

Gibson, J.J. (1979). *The ecological approach to visual perception.* Boston: Houghton Mifflin.

Giedd, J.N. (2012). The digital revolution and the adolescent brain. *Journal of Adolescent Health, 51,* 101–105.

Giedd, J.N., & others (2012). Automatic magnetic resonance imaging of the developing child and adolescent brain. In V.F. Reyna & others (Eds.), *The adolescent brain.* Washington, DC: American Psychological Association.

Gilbert, G., & Graham, S. (2010). Teaching writing to students in grades 4–6: A national survey. *Elementary School Journal, 110,* 494–518.

Giles, E.D., & others (2016). Exercise decreases lipogenic gene expression in adipose tissue and alters adipocyte cellularity during weight regain after weight loss. *Frontiers in Physiology, 7,* 32.

Gillen-O'Neel, C., Huynh, V.W., & Fuligni, A.J. (2013). To study or to sleep? The academic costs of extra studying at the expense of sleep. *Child Development, 84*(1), 133–142.

Gilligan, C. (1982). *In a different voice.* Cambridge, MA: Harvard University Press.

Gilligan, C. (1992, May). *Joining the resistance: Girls' development in adolescence.* Paper presented at the symposium on development and vulnerability in close relationships, Montreal, Quebec.

Gilligan, C. (1996). The centrality of relationships in psychological development: A puzzle, some

evidence, and a theory. In G.G. Noam & K.W. Fischer (Eds.), *Development and vulnerability in close relationships.* Hillsdale, NJ: Erlbaum.

Gilligan, C., Spencer, R., Weinberg, M.K., & Bertsch, T. (2003). On the listening guide: A voice-centered relational model. In P.M. Carnic & J.E. Rhodes (Eds.), *Qualitative research in psychology.* Washington, DC: American Psychological Association.

Giofre, D., & others (2017, in press). Intelligence measures as diagnostic tools for children with specific learning disabilities. *Intelligence.*

Girling, A. (2006). The benefits of using the Neonatal Behavioral Assessment Scale in health visiting practice. *Community Practice, 79,* 118–120.

Girls Inc. (1991). *Truth, trusting and technology: New research on preventing adolescent pregnancy.* Indianapolis: Author.

Giuntella, O. (2017, in press). Why does the health of Mexican Americans deteriorate? New evidence from linked birth records. *Journal of Health Economics.*

Gleason, T., & others (2017). Well-being and sociomoral development in preschoolers: The relation of maternal parenting attitudes consistent with the evolved developmental niche. In D. Narváez & others (Eds.), *Contexts for young child flourishing.* New York: Oxford University Press.

Gliga, T., & others (2017, in press). Early visual foraging in relationship to familial risk for autism and hyperactivity/inattention. *Journal of Attention Disorders.*

Gnambs, T., & Appel, M. (2017, in press). Narcissism and social networking behavior: A meta-analysis. *Journal of Personality.*

Goad, H. (2017). Phonological processes in children's production: Convergence and divergence from adult grammars. In J. Lidz, W. Snyder, & J. Pater (Eds.), *Oxford handbook of developmental linguistics.* New York: Oxford University Press.

Gockley, A.A., & others (2016). The effect of adolescence and advanced maternal age on the incidence of partial molar pregnancy. *Gynecology and Oncology, 140,* 470–473.

Godding, V., & others. (2004). Does in utero exposure to heavy maternal smoking induce nicotine withdrawal symptoms in neonates? *Pediatric Research, S5,* 645–651.

Goddings, A-L., & Mills, K. (2017). *Adolescence and the brain.* New York: Psychology Press.

Godfrey, K.M., & others (2017). Influence of maternal obesity on the long-term health of offspring. *Lancet. Diabetes and Endocrinology, 5,* 53–64.

Goffin, S.G., & Wilson, C.S. (2001). *Curriculum models and early childhood education: Appraising the relationship* (2nd ed.). Upper Saddle River, NJ: Prentice Hall.

Gogtay, N., & Thompson, P.M. (2010). Mapping gray matter development: Implications for typical development and vulnerability to psychopathology. *Brain and Cognition, 72,* 6–15.

Goh, S.N., & others (2016). Sociodemographic, home environment, and parental influences on total

and device-specific screen viewing in children aged 2 years and below: An observational study. *BMJ Open, 6*(1), e009113.

Goksan, S., & others (2015). fMRI reveals neural activity overlap between adult and infant pain. *eLife, 4,* e06356.

Gold, A.L., & others (2016). Comparing brain morphometry across multiple childhood psychiatric disorders. *Journal of the American Academy of Child and Adolescent Psychiatry, 55,* 1027–1037.

Gold, M.A., & others. (2010). Associations between religiosity and sexual and contraceptive behaviors. *Journal of Pediatric and Adolescent Gynecology, 23,* 290–297.

Goldberg, E. (2017). *Creativity.* New York: Oxford University Press.

Goldberg, S.K., & Halpern, C.T. (2017). Sexual initiation patterns of U.S. sexual minority youth: A latent class analysis. *Perspectives on Sex and Reproductive Health, 49,* 55–67.

Goldberg, W.A., & Lucas-Thompson, R. (2008). Maternal and paternal employment, effects of. In M.M. Haith & J.B. Benson (Eds.), *Encyclopedia of infant and early childhood development.* Oxford, UK: Elsevier.

Goldenberg, R.L., & Culhane, J.F. (2007). Low birth weight in the United States. *American Journal of Clinical Nutrition, 85*(Suppl.), S584–S590.

Goldfield, G.S. (2012). Making access to TV contingent on physical activity: Effects on liking and relative reinforcing value of TV and physical activity in overweight and obese children. *Journal of Behavioral Medicine, 35*(1), 1–7.

Goldfield, G.S., & others (2017). Effects of aerobic or resistance training or both on health-related quality of life in youth with obesity: The HEARTY Trial. *Applied Physiology, Nutrition, and Metabolism, 42,* 361–370.

Goldin-Meadow, S. (2014a). Widening the lens: What the manual modality reveals about language, learning, and cognition. *Philosophical Transactions of the Royal Society, Series B, 369,* 20130295.

Goldin-Meadow, S. (2014b). Language and the manual modality: How our hands help us talk and think. In N.J. Enfield & others (Eds.), *Cambridge handbook of linguistic anthropology.* New York: Cambridge University Press.

Goldin-Meadow, S. (2015). Nonverbal communication: The hand's role in talking and thinking. In R.M. Lerner (Ed.), *Handbook of child psychology and developmental science* (7th ed.). New York: Wiley.

Goldin-Meadow, S. (2017a, in press). Using our hands to change our minds. *Wiley Interdisciplinary Reviews. Cognitive Science.*

Goldin-Meadow, S. (2017b). What the hands can tell us about language emergence. *Psychonomic Bulletin & Review, 24,* 213–218.

Golding, J., & others (2016). Associations between prenatal mercury exposure and early child development in the ALSPAC study. *Neurotoxicology, 53,* 215–222.

Goldschmidt, L., Richardson, G.A., Willford, J., & Day, N.N. (2008). Prenatal marijuana exposure and intelligence test performance at age 6. *Journal of the American Academy of Child and Adolescent Psychiatry, 47,* 254–263.

Goldstein, M.H., King, A.P., & West, M.J. (2003). Social interaction shapes babbling: Testing parallels between birdsong and speech. *Proceedings of the National Academy of Sciences, 100*(13), 8030–8035.

Goldston, D.B., & others (2008). Cultural considerations in adolescent suicide prevention and psychosocial treatment. *American Psychologist, 63,* 14–31.

Goleman, D., Kaufman, P., & Ray, M. (1993). *The creative spirit.* New York: Plume.

Golinkoff, R.M., Can, D.D., Soderstrom, M., & Hirsh-Pasek, K. (2015). (Baby) talk to me: The social context of infant-directed speech and its effect on early language acquisition. *Current Directions in Psychological Science, 24,* 339–344.

Golinkoff, R.M., & Hirsh-Pasek, K. (2000). *How babies talk: The magic and mystery of language in the first three years of life.* New York: Penguin.

Gollnick, D.M., & Chinn, P.C. (2017). *Multicultural education in a pluralistic society* (10th ed.). Upper Saddle River, NJ: Pearson.

Golomb, C. (2002). *Child art in context.* Washington, DC: American Psychological Association.

Golomb, C. (2008). Artistic development. In M.M. Haith & J.B. Benson (Eds.), *Encyclopedia of infant and early childhood development.* Oxford, UK: Elsevier.

Golomb, C. (2011). *The creation of imaginary worlds.* London: Jessica Kingsley.

Golomb, C. (2016). *The development of artistically gifted children.* New York: Psychology Press.

Golombok, S. (2011a). Children in new family formations. In R. Gross (Ed.), *Psychology* (6th ed.). London: Holder Education.

Golombok, S. (2011b). Why I study lesbian families. In S. Ellis, V. Clarke, E. Peel, & D. Riggs (Eds.), *LGBTQ Psychologies.* New York: Cambridge University Press.

Golombok, S., MacCallum, F., & Goodman, E. (2001). The "test-tube" generation: Parent-child relationships and the psychological well-being of in vitro fertilization children at adolescence. *Child Development, 72,* 599–608.

Golombok, S., & Tasker, F. (2010). Gay fathers. In M.E. Lamb (Ed.), *The role of the father in child development* (5th ed.). New York: Wiley.

Golombok, S., & others (2008). Developmental trajectories of sex-typed behavior in boys and girls: A longitudinal general population study of children aged 2.5–8 years. *Child Development, 79,* 1583–1593.

Golombok, S., & others (2014). Adoptive gay father families: Parent-child relationships and children's psychological adjustment. *Child Development, 85,* 456–468.

Gomez, R.L. (2017). Do infants retain the statistics of statistical learning experience? Insights from a developmental cognitive neuroscience perspective. *Philosophical Transactions of the Royal Society of London, 372,* 1711.

Gomez, S.H., & others (2017, in press). Are there sensitive periods when child maltreatment substantially elevates suicide risk? Results from a nationally representative sample of adolescents. *Depression and Anxiety.*

Gomez-Bruton, A., & others (2017, in press). Plyometric exercise and bone health in children and adolescents: A systematic review. *World Journal of Pediatrics.*

Gomez-Moya, R., Diaz, R., & Fernandez-Ruiz, J. (2016). Different visuomotor processes maturation rates in children support dual visuomotor learning systems. *Human Motivation Science, 46,* 221–228.

Gonçalves, L.F. (2016). Three-dimensional ultrasound of the fetus: How does it help? *Pediatric Radiology, 46,* 177–189.

Goncu, A., & Gauvain, M. (2011). Sociocultural approaches to educational psychology: Theory, research, and application. In K.R. Harris, S. Graham, & T. Urdan (Eds.), *APA educational psychology handbook.* Washington, DC: American Psychological Association.

Gonzales, N.A., & others (2016). Culturally adaptive preventive interventions for children and adolescents. In D. Cicchetti (Ed.), *Developmental psychopathology* (3rd ed.). New York: Wiley.

Gonzales, R., & others (2017). Ethnic identity development and acculturation preferences among minority and majority youth: Group norms and contact. *Child Development, 88,* 743–760.

Gonzalez, A., Atkinson, L., & Fleming, A.S. (2009). Attachment and the comparative psychobiology of mothering. In M. De Haan & M.R. Gunnar (Eds.), *Handbook of developmental social neuroscience.* New York: Guilford.

Gonzalez-Echavarri, C., & others (2015). Prevalence and significance of persistently positive antiphospholipid antibodies in women with preeclampsia. *Journal of Rheumatology, 42,* 210–213.

González-Ruiz, K., & others (2017, in press). The effects of exercise on abdominal fat and liver enzymes in pediatric obesity: A systematic review and meta-analysis. *Child Obesity.*

Good, C., Rattan, A., & Dweck, C.S. (2012). Why do women opt out? Sense of belonging and women's representation in mathematics. *Journal of Personality and Social Psychology, 102,* 700–717.

Good, M., & Willoughby, T. (2008). Adolescence as a sensitive period for spiritual development. *Child Development Perspectives, 2,* 32–37.

Goodenough, J., & McGuire, B.A. (2017). *Biology of humans* (6th ed.). Upper Saddle River, NJ: Pearson.

Goodkind, S. (2013). Single-sex public education for low-income youth of color: A critical theoretical review. *Sex Roles, 69,* 393–402.

Goodnough, L.T., & others (2011). How we treat: Transfusion medicine support of obstetric services. *Transfusion, 51*(12), 2540–2548.

Goodvin, R., Meyer, S., Thompson, R.A., & Hayes, R. (2008). Self-understanding in early childhood: Associations with child attachment security and maternal negative affect. *Attachment and Human Development, 10,* 433–450.

Goodvin, R., Winer, A.C., & Thompson, R.A. (2015). The individual child: Temperament, emotion, self, and personality. In M. Bornstein & M.E. Lamb (Eds.), *Developmental science* (7th ed.). New York: Psychology Press.

Gopnik, A. (2010). Commentary. In R.E. Gitlivsky, *Mind in the making.* New York: HarperCollins.

Gordon, A.M., & Browne, K.W. (2017). *Beginnings and beyond* (10th ed.). Boston: Cengage.

Gordon, I., Zagoory-Sharon, O., Leckman, J.F., & Feldman, R. (2010). Oxytocin and the development of parenting in humans. *Biological Psychiatry, 68,* 377–382.

Gorukanti, A., & others (2017). Adolescents' attitudes towards e-cigarette ingredients, safety, addictive properties, social norms, and regulation. *Preventive Medicine.*

Gosselin, J. (2010). Individual and family factors related to psychosocial adjustment in stepmother families with adolescents. *Journal of Divorce and Remarriage, 51,* 108–123.

Goswami, U.C., & Bryant, P. (2016). *Phonological skills and learning to read.* New York: Psychology Press.

Gotlieb, R., Jahner, E., Immordino-Yang, M.H., & Kaufman, S.B. (2017). How social-emotional imagination facilitates deep learning and creativity in the classroom. In R.A. Beghetto & J.C. Kaufman (Eds.), *Nurturing creativity in the classroom.* New York: Cambridge University Press.

Gottlieb, A., & DeLoache, J. (2017). *A world of babies* (2nd ed.). New York: Cambridge University Press.

Gottlieb, G. (2007). Probabilistic epigenesis. *Developmental Science, 10,* 1–11.

Gottlieb, G., Wahlsten, D., & Lickliter, R. (2006). The significance of biology for human development: A developmental psychobiological systems view. In W. Damon & R. Lerner (Eds.), *Handbook of child psychology* (6th ed.). New York: Wiley.

Gottman, J.M. (2014). *Research on parenting.* Retrieved February 25, 2014, from www.gottman.com/parenting/research

Gottman, J.M. (2017). *Research on parenting.* Retrieved January 5, 2017, from www.gottman.com/parenting/research

Gottman, J.M., & DeClaire, J. (1997). *The heart of parenting: Raising an emotionally intelligent child.* New York: Simon & Schuster.

Gottman, J.M., & Parker, J.G. (Eds.). (1987). *Conversations of friends.* New York: Cambridge University Press.

Gottman, J.M., Shapiro, A.F., & Parthemer, J. (2004). Bringing baby home: A preventative intervention program for expectant couples. *International Journal of Childbirth Education, 19,* 28–30.

Gouin, K., & others (2011). Effects of cocaine use during pregnancy on low birthweight and preterm birth: Systematic review and meta analyses. *American Journal of Obstetrics and Gynecology, 204*(4), 340.e1–e12.

Gould, J.F. (2017). Complementary feeding, micronutrients, and developmental outcomes in children. *Nestle Nutrition Institute Workshop Series, 87,*13–28.

Gould, S.J. (1981). *The mismeasure of man.* New York: W.W. Norton.

Gower, A.L., Cousin, M., & Borowsky, I.W. (2017). A multilevel, statewide investigation of school district anti-bullying policy quality and student bullying involvement. *Journal of School Health, 87,* 174–181.

Graber, J.A. (2004). Internalizing problems during adolescence. In R. Lerner & L. Steinberg (Eds.), *Handbook of adolescent psychology.* New York: Wiley.

Graber, J.A. (2013). Pubertal timing and the development of psychopathology in adolescence and beyond. *Hormones and Behavior, 64,* 262–269.

Graber, J.A., Brooks-Gunn, J., & Warren, M.P. (2006). Pubertal effects on adjustment in girls: Moving from demonstrating effects to identifying pathways. *Journal of Youth and Adolescence, 35,* 391–401.

Graber, J.A., & Sontag, L. (2009). Internalizing problems during adolescence. In R.M. Lerner & L. Steinberg (Eds.), *Handbook of adolescent psychology* (3rd ed.). New York: Wiley.

Graber, R., Turner, R., & Madill, A. (2016). Best friends and better coping: Facilitating psychological resilience through boys' and girls' closest friendships. *British Journal of Psychology, 107,* 338–358.

Grafenhain, M., Behne, T., Carpenter, M., & Tomasello, M. (2009). Young children's understanding of joint commitments. *Developmental Psychology, 45*(5), 1430–1443.

Graham, J., & Valdesolo, P. (2017, in press). Morality. In K. Deaux & M. Snyder (Eds.), *Oxford handbook of personality and social psychology.* New York: Oxford University Press.

Graham, J., & others (2017, in press). Centripetal and centrifugal forces in the moral circle: Competing constraints on moral learning. *Cognition.*

Graham, S. (1986, August). *Can attribution theory tell us something about motivation in blacks?* Paper presented at the meeting of the American Psychological Association, Washington, DC.

Graham, S. (1990). Motivation in Afro-Americans. In G.L. Berry & J.K. Asamen (Eds.), *Black students: Psychosocial issues and academic achievement.* Newbury Park, CA: Sage.

Graham, S. (2017). Writing research and practice. In D. Lapp & D. Fisher (Eds.), *Handbook of research on teaching the English language arts* (3rd ed.). New York: Routledge.

Graham, S., & Harris, K.R. (2016). Evidence-based practice and writing instruction. In C. MacArthur, S. Graham, & J. Fitzgerald (Eds.), *Handbook of writing research* (2nd ed.). New York: Guilford.

Graham, S., & Harris, K.R. (2017, in press). Evidence-based writing practices: A meta-analysis of existing meta-analyses. In R. Fidalgo & others (Eds.), *Studies in writing.* Leiden, Netherlands: Brill Editions.

Graham, S., & Perin, D. (2007). A meta-analysis of writing instruction for adolescent students. *Journal of Educational Psychology, 99,* 445–476.

Graham, S., & Rijalsardamm, G. (2016). Writing instruction across the world. *Reading and Writing, 29*(5).

Granat, A., & others (2017). Maternal depression and anxiety, social synchrony, and infant regulation of negative and positive emotions. *Emotion, 17,* 11–27.

Grand, J.A. (2017). Brain drain? An examination of stereotype threat effects during training on knowledge acquisition and organizational effectiveness. *Journal of Applied Psychology, 102,* 115–150.

Grant, A.M., & Gino, F. (2010). A little thanks goes a long way: Explaining why gratitude expressions motivate prosocial behavior. *Journal of Personality and Social Psychology, 98,* 946–955.

Grant-Marsney, H., Grotevant, H.D., & Sayer, A. (2015). Links between adolescents' closeness to adoptive parents and attachment style in young adulthood. *Family Relations, 64,* 221–232.

Grassman, V., & others (2017). Possible cognitive benefits of acute physical exercise in children with ADHD. *Journal of Attention Disorders, 21,* 367–371.

Graven, S. (2006). Sleep and brain development. *Clinical Perinatology, 33,* 693–706.

Gravetter, F.J., & Forzano, L.B. (2017). *Research methods for the behavioral sciences* (5th ed.). Boston: Cengage.

Gray, K., & Graham, J. (2018, in press). *The atlas of moral psychology.* New York: Guilford.

Gray, K.A., Day, N.X., Leech, S., & Richardson, G.A. (2005). Prenatal marijuana exposure: Effect on child depressive symptoms at ten years of age. *Neurotoxicology and Teratology, 27,* 439–448.

Green, J., & others (2017, in press). Randomized trial of parent-mediated intervention for infants at high risk for autism: Longitudinal outcomes to age 3 years. *Journal of Child Psychology and Psychiatry.*

Green, S.A., Hernandez, L.L., Bookheimer, S.Y., & Dapretto, M. (2017). Reduced modulation of thalamocortical connectivity during exposure to sensory stimuli in ASD. *Autism Research, 10,* 801–809.

Greene, M.F. (2009). Making small risks even smaller. *New England Journal of Medicine, 360,* 183–184.

Greenfield, P.M. (1966). On culture and conservation. In J.S. Bruner, R.P. Oliver, & P.M. Greenfield (Eds.), *Studies in cognitive growth.* New York: Wiley.

Greenfield, P.M., Suzuki, L.K., & Rothstein-Fisch, C. (2006). Cultural pathways through human development. In W. Damon & R. Lerner (Eds.), *Handbook of child psychology* (6th ed.). New York: Wiley.

Greer, F.R., Sicherer, S.H., Burks, A.W., & The Committee on Nutrition and Section on Allergy and Immunology (2008). Effects of early nutritional interventions on the development of atopic disease in infants and children: The role of maternal dietary restriction, breast feeding, timing of introduction of complementary foods, and hydrolyzed formulas. *Pediatrics, 121,* 183–191.

Gregory, R.J. (2016). *Psychological testing* (8th ed.). Upper Saddle River, NJ: Pearson.

Griesler, P.C., Hu, M.C., & Kandel, D.B. (2016). Nicotine dependence in adolescence and physical health symptoms in early adulthood. *Nicotine and Tobacco Research, 18,* 950–958.

Griffin, J.A., Freund, L.S., & McCardle, P. (Eds.) (2015). *Executive function in preschool age children.* Washington, DC: American Psychological Association.

Griffiths, S., & others (2017, in press). Sex differences in quality of life impairment associated with body dissatisfaction in adolelscents. *Journal of Adolescent Health.*

Grigorenko, E. (2000). Heritability and intelligence. In R.J. Sternberg (Ed.), *Handbook of intelligence.* New York: Cambridge University Press.

Grigorenko, E.L., & others (2016). The trilogy of G × E. Genes, environments, and their interactions: Conceptualization, operationalization, and application. In D. Cicchetti (Ed.), *Developmental psychopathology* (3rd ed.). New York: Wiley.

Grimberg, A., & Allen, D.B. (2017, in press). Growth hormone treatment for growth hormone deficiency and idiopathic short stature: New guidelines shaped by the presence and absence of evidence. *Current Opinion in Pediatrics.*

Grindal, M., & Nieri, T. (2016). The relationship between ethnic-racial socialization and adolescent substance abuse: An examination of social learning as a causal mechanism. *Journal of Ethnicity in Substance Abuse, 15,* 3–24.

Grinde, B. (2016). Evolution and well-being. In M. Pluess (Ed.), *Genetics of psychological well-being.* New York: Oxford University Press.

Groh, A.M., & others (2014). The significance of attachment security for children's social competence with peers: A meta-analytic study. *Attachment and Human Development, 16,* 103–136.

Groh, A.M., & others (2015). Mothers' electrophysiological, subjective, and observed emotional responding to infant crying: The role of secure base script knowledge. *Development and Psychopathology, 27,* 1237–1250.

Grondahl, M.L., & others (2017). Effects of women's age on embryo morphology, cleavage rate, and competence—a multicenter, cohort study. *PLoS One, 12(4),* e0172456.

Groppe, K., & Elsner, B. (2017). Executive function and weight status in children: A one-year prospective investigation. *Child Neuropsychology, 23,* 129–147.

Gross, J.J., Frederickson, B.L., & Levenson, R.W. (1994). The psychology of crying. *Psychophysiology, 31,* 460–468.

Gross, T.T., & others (2017). Long-term breastfeeding in African American mothers. *Journal of Human Lactation, 33,* 128–139.

Grossmann, K., Grossmann, K.E., Spangler, G., Suess, G., & Unzner, L. (1985). Maternal sensitivity and newborns' orientation responses as related to quality of attachment in northern Germany. In I. Bretherton & E. Waters (Eds.), *Growing points of attachment theory and research. Monographs of the Society for Research in Child Development, 50*(1–2, Serial No. 209).

Grotevant, H.D., & McDermott, J.M. (2014). Adoption: Biological and social processes linked to adaptation. *Annual Review of Psychology* (Vol. 65). Palo Alto, CA: Annual Reviews.

Grotevant, H.D., McRoy, R.G., Wrobel, G.M., & Ayers-Lopez, S. (2013). Contact between adoptive and birth families: Perspectives from the Minnesota/Texas Adoption Research Project. *Child Development Perspectives, 7,* 193–198.

Gruber, K.J., Cupito, S.H., & Dobson, C.F. (2013). Impact of doulas on healthy birth outcomes. *Journal of Perinatal Education, 22,* 49–58.

Grusec, J.E. (2017). A domains-of-socialization perspective on children's social development. In N. Budwig, E. Turiel, & P.D. Zelazo (Eds.), *New perspectives on human development.* New York: Cambridge University Press.

Grusec, J.E., Chaparro, M.P., Johnston, M., & Sherman, A. (2013). Social development and social relationships in middle childhood. In I.B. Weiner & others, *Handbook of psychology* (2nd ed., Vol. 6). New York: Wiley.

Grusec, J.E., Chaparro, M.P., Johnston, M., & Sherman, A. (2014). The development of moral behavior from a socialization perspective. In M. Killen & J.G. Smetana (Eds.), *Handbook of moral development* (2nd ed.). New York: Psychology Press.

Guevremont, A., Findlay, L., & Kohen, D. (2014). Organized extracurricular activities: Are in-school and out-of-school activities associated with different outcomes for Canadian youth? *Journal of School Health, 84,* 317–325.

Gui, D.Y., Gan, T., & Liu, C. (2016). Neural evidence for moral intuition and the temporal dynamics of interactions between emotional processes and moral cognition. *Social Neuroscience, 11,* 380–394.

Guilford, J.P. (1967). *The structure of intellect.* New York: McGraw-Hill.

Guimaraes, E.L., & Tudellia, E. (2015). Immediate effect of training at the onset of reaching in preterm infants: Randomized clinical trial. *Journal of Motor Behavior, 47,* 535–549.

Gump, B.B., & others (2009). Trajectories of maternal depression symptoms over her child's life span: Relation to adrenocortical, cardiovascular, and emotional functioning in children. *Development and Psychopathology, 21,* 207–225.

Gunderson, E.A., Ramirez, G., Beilock, S.L., & Levine, S.C. (2012). The role of parents and teachers in the development of gender-related attitudes. *Sex Roles, 66,* 153–166.

Gunn, J.K., & others (2016). Prenatal exposure to cannabis and maternal and child health outcomes: A systematic review and meta-analysis. *BMJ Open, 6*(4), e009986.

Gunnar, M.R., Fisher, P.A., & The Early Experience, Stress, and Prevention Science Network (2006). Bringing basic research on early experience and stress neurobiology to bear on preventive interventions for neglected and maltreated children. *Development and Psychopathology, 18,* 651–677.

Gunnar, M.R., Malone, S., & Fisch, R.O. (1987). The psychobiology of stress and coping in the human neonate: Studies of the adrenocortical activity in response to stress in the first week of life. In T. Field, P. McCabe, & N. Schneiderman (Eds.), *Stress and coping.* Hillsdale, NJ: Erlbaum.

Gupta, A., Thornton, J.W., & Huston, A.C. (2008). Working families should not be poor—the New Hope project. In D.R. Crane & T.B. Heaton (Eds.), *Handbook of families and poverty.* Thousand Oaks, CA: Sage.

Gur, R.C., & others (1995). Sex differences in regional cerebral glucose metabolism during a resting state. *Science, 267,* 528–531.

Gurwitch, R.H., Silovksy, J.F., Schultz, S., Kees, M., & Burlingame, S. (2001). *Reactions and guidelines for children following trauma/disaster.* Norman, OK: Department of Pediatrics, University of Oklahoma Health Science Center.

Gustafsson, J-E. (2007). Schooling and intelligence: Effects of track of study on level and profile of cognitive abilities. In P.C. Kyllonen, R.D. Roberts, & L. Stankov (Eds.), *Extending intelligence.* Mahwah, NJ: Erlbaum.

Gutierrez-Galve, L., & others (2015). Paternal depression in the postnatal period and child development: Mediators and moderators. *Pediatrics, 135,* e339–e347.

Gutman, L.M., Eccles, J.S., Peck, S., & Malanchuk, O. (2011). The influence of family relations on trajectories of cigarette and alcohol use from early to late adolescence. *Journal of Adolescence, 34*(1), 119–128.

Guttentag, C.L., & others (2014). "My Baby and Me": Effects of an early, comprehensive parenting intervention on at-risk mothers and their children. *Developmental Psychology, 50,* 1482–1496.

Guttmannova, K., & others (2012). Examining explanatory mechanisms of the effects of early alcohol use on young adult alcohol competence. *Journal of Studies of Alcohol and Drugs, 73,* 379–390.

Guyer, A.E., Silk, J.S., & Nelson, E.E. (2016). The neurobiology of the emotional adolescent: From the inside out. *Neuroscience and Neurobehavioral Reviews, 70,* 74–85.

H

Hadiwijaya, H., & others (2017, in press). On the development of harmony, turbulence, and independence in parent-adolescent relationships: A five-wave longitudinal study. *Journal of Youth and Adolescence.*

Hadland, S.E., & others (2015). Suicide attempts and childhood maltreatment among street youth: A prospective cohort study. *Pediatrics, 136,* 440–449.

Haertle, L., & others (2017). Epigenetic signatures of gestational mellitus on cord blood methylation. *Clinical Epigenetics, 9,* 28.

Hafner, J.W., & others (2017, in press). Child passenger restraint system misuse in rural versus urban children: A multisite case-control study. *Pediatric Emergency Care.*

Hagborg, J.M., Tidefors, I., & Fahlke, C. (2017). Gender differences in the association between emotional maltreatment with mental, emotional, and behavioral problems in Swedish adolescents. *Child Abuse and Neglect, 67,* 249–259.

Hagmann-von Arx, P., Lemola, S., & Grob, A. (2017, in press). Does IQ = IQ? Comparability of intelligence test scores in typically developing children. *Assessment.*

Hahn, W.K. (1987). Cerebral lateralization of function: From infancy through childhood. *Psychological Bulletin, 101,* 376–392.

Haidt, J. (2006). *The happiness hypothesis.* New York: Basic Books.

Haidt, J. (2013). *The righteous mind.* New York: Random House.

Haidt, J. (2017). *Three stories about capitalism.* New York: Pantheon.

Hair, N.L., Hanson, J.L., Wolfe, B.L., & Pollack, S.D. (2015). Association of poverty, brain development, and academic achievement. *JAMA Pediatrics, 169,* 822–829.

Hakkarainen, P., Bredikyte, M., & Safarov, I. (2017). Child development and pretend play. In T. Bruce (Ed.), *Routledge international handbook of early childhood play.* New York: Routledge.

Hakuta, K. (2001, April 5). *Key policy milestones and directions in the education of English language learners.* Paper prepared for the Rockefeller Foundation Symposium, "Leveraging change: An emerging framework for educational equity," Washington, DC.

Hakuta, K. (2005, April). *Bilingualism at the intersection of research and public policy.* Paper presented at the meeting of the Society for Research in Child Development, Atlanta.

Hakuta, K., Butler, Y.G., & Witt, D. (2001). *How long does it take English learners to attain proficiency?* Berkeley, CA: The University of California Linguistic Minority Research Institute Policy Report 2000–1.

Hakvoort, E.M., Bos, H.M.W., Van Balen, F., & Hermanns, J.M.A. (2011). Postdivorce relationships in families and children's psychosocial adjustment. *Journal of Divorce and Remarriage, 52,* 125–146.

Hale, N., Picklesimer, A.H., Billings, D.L., & Covington-Kolb, S. (2014). The impact of Centering Pregnancy group prenatal care on postpartum family planning. *American Journal of Obstetrics and Gynecology, 210,* 50, e1–e7.

Hales, D. (2018a). *An invitation to health* (10th ed.). Boston: Cengage.

Hales, D. (2018b). *Personal stress management.* Boston: Cengage.

Haley, M.H., & Austin, T.Y. (2014). *Content-based second language teaching and learning* (2nd ed.). Upper Saddle River, NJ: Pearson.

Halim, M.L. (2016). Pink princesses and strong superheroes: Gender rigidity in early childhood. *Child Development Perspectives, 10,* 155–160.

Halim, M.L., & others (2016). Children's dynamic gender identities: Cognition, context, and culture. In B. Balter & C.S. Tamis-LeMonda (Eds.), *Child psychology* (3rd ed.). New York: Routledge.

Hall, G.S. (1904). *Adolescence* (Vols. 1 & 2). Englewood Cliffs, NJ: Prentice Hall.

Hall, J.W. (2014). *Introduction to audiology today.* Upper Saddle River, NJ: Pearson.

Hall, S.S., & others (2014). Using discrete trial training to identify specific learning impairments in boys with fragile X syndrome. *Journal of Autism and Developmental Disorders, 44,* 1659–1670.

Hall, W. (2017). The effectiveness of policy recommendations for school bullying: A systematic review. *Journal of the Society for Social Work and Research, 8,* 45–69.

Hallahan, D.P., & Kauffman, J.M. (2006). *Exceptional learners* (10th ed.). Boston: Allyn & Bacon.

Hallahan, D.P., Kauffman, J.M., & Pullen, P.C. (2015). *Exceptional learners* (13th ed.). Upper Saddle River, NJ: Pearson.

Halldorsdottir, T., & Binder, E.B. (2017). Gene × environment interactions: From molecular mechanisms to behavior. *Annual Review of Psychology* (Vol. 68). Palo Alto, CA: Annual Reviews.

Halpern, C.T., & Haydon, A.A. (2012). Sexual timetables for oral-genital, vaginal, and anal intercourse: Sociodemographic comparisons in a nationally representative sample of adolescents. *American Journal of Public Health, 102,* 1221–1228.

Halpern, D. (2006). Assessing gender gaps in learning and academic achievement. In P.A. Alexander & P.H. Wynne (Eds.), *Handbook of educational psychology* (2nd ed.). Mahwah, NJ: Erlbaum.

Halpern, D.F. (2012). *Sex differences in cognitive abilities* (2nd ed.). New York: Psychology Press.

Halpern, D.F., & others (2007). The science of sex differences in science and mathematics. *Psychological Science in the Public Interest, 8,* 1–51.

Halpern, D.F., & others (2011). The pseudoscience of single-sex schooling. *Science, 333,* 1706–1717.

Hamilton, E., & Klimes-Dougan, B. (2015). Gender differences in suicide prevention responses: Implications for adolescents based on an illustrative review of the literature. *International Journal of Environmental Research and Public Health, 12,* 2359–2372.

Hamilton, J.L., & others (2014). Pubertal timing and vulnerabilities to depression in early adolescence: Differential pathways to depressive symptoms by sex. *Journal of Adolescence, 37,* 165–174.

Hamlin, J.K. (2013). Moral judgment and action in preverbal infants and toddlers: Evidence for an innate moral core. *Current Directions in Psychological Science, 22,* 186–193.

Hamlin, J.K. (2014). The origins of human morality: Complex socio-moral evaluations by preverbal infants. In J. Decety & Y. Christen (Eds.), *New frontiers in social neuroscience.* New York: Springer.

Hammond, S.I., & others (2012). The effects of parental scaffolding on preschoolers' executive function. *Developmental Psychology, 48,* 271–281.

Han, J.J., Leichtman M.D., & Wang, Q. (1998). Autobiographical memory in Korean, Chinese, and American children. *Developmental Psychology, 34,* 701–713.

Han, J.Y., & others (2015). The effects of prenatal exposure to alcohol and environmental tobacco smoke on risk for ADHD: A large population-based study. *Psychiatry Research, 225,* 164–168.

Hanc, T., & others (2017, in press). Perinatal risk factors and ADHD in children and adolescents:

A hierarchical structure of disorder predictors. *Journal of Attention Disorders.*

Hancox, R.J., Milne, B.J., & Poulton, R. (2004). Association between child and adolescent television viewing and adult health: A longitudinal birth cohort study. *Lancet, 364,* 257–262.

Handler, A., Rankin, K., Rosenberg, D., & Sinha, K. (2012). Extent of documented adherence to recommended prenatal care content: Provider site differences and effect on outcomes among low-income women. *Maternal and Child Health, 16(2),* 393–405.

Hanish, L.D., & Guerra, N.G. (2004). Aggressive victims, passive victims, and bullies: Developmental continuity or developmental change? *Merrill-Palmer Quarterly, 50,* 17–38.

Hanna-Attisha, M., & Kuehn, B.M. (2016). Pediatrician sees long road ahead for Flint after lead poisoning crisis. *JAMA, 315,* 967–969.

Hansen, M.L., Gunn, P.W., & Kaelber, D.C. (2007). Underdiagnosis of hypertension in children and adolescents. *Journal of the American Medical Association, 298,* 874–879.

Hanson, M., & others (2017). Interventions to prevent obesity before conception, during pregnancy, and postpartum. *Lancet: Diabetes and Endocrinology, 5,* 65–76.

Harackiewicz, J.M., & Knogler, M. (2017). Interest: Theory and application. In A.J. Elliott, C.S. Dweck, & D.S. Yeager (Eds.), *Handbook of competence and motivation* (2nd ed.). New York: Guilford.

Hardy, S.A., & others (2014). Moral identity as moral ideal self: Links to adolescent outcomes. *Developmental Psychology, 50,* 45–57.

Hargreaves, D.A., & Tiggemann, M. (2004). Idealized body images and adolescent body image: "Comparing" boys and girls. *Body Image, 1,* 351–361.

Hari, R., & Puce, A. (2017). *MEG-EEG primer.* New York: Oxford University Press.

Harkness, S., & Super, E.M. (1995). Culture and parenting. In M.H. Bornstein (Ed.), *Handbook of parenting* (Vol. 3). Hillsdale, NJ: Erlbaum.

Harlow, H.R. (1958). The nature of love. *American Psychologist, 13,* 673–685.

Harmon, O.R., Lambrinos, J., & Kennedy, P. (2008). Are online exams an invitation to cheat? *Journal of Economic Education, 39,* 116–125.

Harrington, B.C., Jimerson, M., Haxton, C., & Jimerson, D.C. (2015). Initial evaluation, diagnosis, and treatment of anorexia nervosa and bulimia nervosa. *American Family Physician, 9,* 46–52.

Harris, J., Golinkoff, R.M., & Hirsh-Pasek, K. (2011). Lessons from the crib for the classroom: How children really learn vocabulary. In S.B. Neuman & D.K. Dickinson (Eds.), *Handbook of early literacy research* (Vol. 3). New York: Guilford.

Harris, J.L., Hyary, M., & Schwartz, M.B. (2016). Effects of offering look-alike products as smart snacks in schools. *Childhood Obesity, 12,* 432–439.

Harris, K.R., & Graham, S. (2017, in press). Self-regulated strategy development: Theoretical bases, critical instructional elements, and future research. In R. Fidalgo, K.R. Harris, & M.

Braaksma (Eds.), *Design principles for teaching effective writing.* Leiden, The Netherlands: Brill.

Harris, K.R., Graham, S., & Adkins, M. (2015). Practice-based professional development and self-regulated strategy development for tier 2, at-risk writers in second grade. *Contemporary Educational Psychology, 40,* 5–16.

Harris, K.R., & others (2017). Self-regulated strategy development in writing. A classroom example of developing executive function and future directions. In L. Meltzer (Eds.), *Executive functioning in education* (2nd ed.). New York: Guilford.

Harris, P.L. (2006). Social cognition. In W. Damon & R. Lerner (Eds.), *Handbook of child psychology* (6th ed.). New York: Wiley.

Harrison, A.L., Shields, N., Taylor, N.F., & Frawley, H.C. (2016). Exercise improves glycemic control in women diagnosed with gestational diabetes mellitus: A systematic review. *Journal of Physiology, 62,* 188–196.

Harrison, M., Brodribb, W., & Hepworth, J. (2017, in press). A qualitative systematic review of maternal infant feeding practices in transitioning from milk to solid foods. *Maternal and Child Nutrition.*

Harrist, A.W. (1993, March). *Family interaction styles as predictors of children's competence: The role of synchrony and nonsynchrony.* Paper presented at the biennial meeting of the Society for Research in Child Development, New Orleans.

Hart, B., & Risley, T.R. (1995). *Meaningful differences in the everyday experience of young Americans.* Baltimore: Paul H. Brookes.

Hart, C.H., Yang, C., Charlesworth, R., & Burts, D.C. (2003, April). *Early childhood teachers' curriculum beliefs, classroom practices, and children's outcomes: What are the connections?* Paper presented at the biennial meeting of the Society for Research in Child Development, Tampa, FL.

Hart, C.N., Cairns, A., & Jelalian, E. (2011). Sleep and obesity in children and adolescents. *Pediatric Clinics of North America, 58,* 715–733.

Hart, D. (2005). The development of moral identity. In G. Carlo & C.P. Edwards (Eds.), *Nebraska Symposium on Motivation* (Vol. 51). Lincoln, NE: U. of Nebraska Press.

Hart, D., Goel, N., & Atkins, R. (2017, in press). Prosocial tendencies, antisocial behavior, and moral development in childhood. In A. Slater & G. Bremner (Eds.), *Introduction to developmental psychology* (3rd ed.). New York: Wiley.

Hart, D., & Karmel, M.P. (1996). Self-awareness and self-knowledge in humans, great apes, and monkeys. In A. Russon, K. Bard, & S. Parker (Eds.), *Reaching into thought.* New York: Cambridge University Press.

Hart, D., & Matsuba, M.K. (2010). Urban neighborhoods as contexts for moral identity development. In D. Narváez & D.K. Lapsley (Eds.), *Moral personality, identity, and character.* New York: Cambridge University Press.

Hart, D., Matsuba, M.K., & Atkins, R. (2008). The moral and civic effects of learning to serve. In L. Nucci & D. Narváez (Eds.), *Handbook of moral and character education.* Clifton, NJ: Psychology Press.

Hart, D., Matsuba, M.K., & Atkins, R. (2014). The moral and civic effects of learning to serve. In L. Nucci, T. Krettenauer, & D. Narváez (Eds.), *Handbook of moral and character education* (2nd ed.). New York: Routledge.

Hart, D., Richardson, C., & Wilkenfeld, B. (2011). Citizenship and civic identity. In S. Schwartz, K. Luyckx, & V. Fignoles (Eds.), *Handbook of identity theory and research.* New York: Springer.

Hart, D., & van Goethem, A. (2017). The role of civic and political participation in successful early adulthood. In L. Padilla-Walker & L. Nelson (Eds.), *Flourishing in emerging adulthood.* New York: Oxford University Press.

Hart, D., Watson, N.C., Dr, A., & Atkins, R. (2011). Prosocial tendencies, antisocial behavior, and moral development in childhood. In A. Slater & G. Bremner (Eds.), *Introduction to developmental psychology* (2nd ed.). Oxford, UK: Blackwell.

Hart, D., & others (2017). Morality and mental health. In C. Markey (Ed.), *Encyclopedia of mental health.* New York: Elsevier.

Hart, S., & Behrens, K.Y. (2013). Regulation of jealousy protest in the context of reunion following differential treatment. *Infancy, 18*(6), 1076–1110.

Hart, S., & Carrington, H. (2002). Jealousy in 6-month-old infants. *Infancy, 3,* 395–402.

Harter, S. (2006). The self. In W. Damon & R. Lerner (Eds.), *Handbook of child psychology* (6th ed.). New York: Wiley.

Harter, S. (2012). *The construction of the self* (2nd ed.). New York: Wiley.

Harter, S. (2016). I-self and me-self processes affecting developmental psychopathology and mental health. In D. Cicchetti (Ed.), *Developmental psychopathology* (3rd ed.). New York: Wiley.

Hartshorne, H., & May, M.S. (1928–1930). *Moral studies in the nature of character: Studies in deceit (Vol. 1); Studies in self-control (Vol. 2); Studies in the organization of character (Vol. 3).* New York: Macmillan.

Hartup, W.W. (1983). The peer system. In P.H. Mussen (Ed.), *Handbook of child psychology* (4th ed., Vol. 4). New York: Wiley.

Hartup, W.W. (1996). The company they keep: Friendships and their development significance. *Child Development, 67,* 1–13.

Hartup, W.W. (2009). Critical issues and theoretical viewpoints. In K.H. Rubin, W.M. Bukowski, & B. Laursen (Eds.), *Handbook of peer interactions, relationships, and groups.* New York: Guilford.

Harville, E.W., & others (2017). Multigenerational cardiometabolic risk as a predictor of birth outcomes: The Bogalusa Heart Study. *Journal of Pediatrics, 181,* 154–162.

Hasbrouck, S.L., & Pianta, R. (2016). Understanding child care quality and implications for dual language learners. In K.E. Sanders & Guerra, A.W. (Eds.), *The culture of child care.* New York: Oxford University Press.

Hasson, R.E., & others (2013). Sociocultural and socioeconomic influences on type 2 diabetes risk in overweight/obese African-American and Latino-American children and adolescents. *Journal of Obesity, 2013,* 512914.

Hausman, B.L. (2005). Risky business: Framing childbirth in hospital settings. *Journal of Medical Ethics, 26,* 23–38.

Hawk, S.T. (2017). Chinese adolescents' reports of covert parental monitoring: Comparisons with overt monitoring and links with information management. *Journal of Adolescence, 55,* 24–35.

Hawk, S.T., Becht, A., & Branje, S. (2016). "Snooping" as a distinct monitoring strategy: Comparison with overt solicitation and control. *Journal of Research on Adolescence, 26,* 443–458.

Hawkins, J.A., & Berndt, T.J. (1985, April). *Adjustment following the transition to junior high school.* Paper presented at the biennial meeting of the Society for Research in Child Development, Toronto.

Hay, W.W., & others (2017). *Current diagnosis and treatment pediatrics* (23rd ed.). New York: McGraw-Hill.

Hayashi, A., & Mazuka, R. (2017). Emergence of Japanese infants' prosodic preferences in infant-directed vocabulary. *Developmental Psychology, 53,* 28–37.

Hayatbakhsh, R., & others (2013). Early childhood predictors of early onset of smoking: A birth prospective study. *Addictive Behaviors, 38,* 2513–2519.

Haydon, A., & Halpern, G.T. (2010). Older romantic partners and depressive symptoms during adolescence. *Journal of Youth and Adolescence, 39,* 1240–1251.

Haydon, A.A., Herring, A., Prinstein, M.J., & Halpern, C.T. (2012). Beyond age at first sex: Patterns of emerging sexual behavior in adolescence and young adulthood. *Journal of Adolescent Health, 50,* 456–463.

Hazeldean, D. (2014). Being fit in pregnancy. *Practicing Midwife, 17,* 11–12.

He, M., Walle, E.A., & Campos, J.J. (2015). A cross-national investigation between infant walking and language development. *Infancy, 20,* 283–305.

Hebebrand, J., & Bulik, C.M. (2011). Critical appraisal of provisional DSM-5 criteria for anorexia nervosa and an alternative proposal. *International Journal of Eating Disorders, 44*(8), 665–678.

Heberlein, E.C., & others (2016). The comparative effects of group prenatal care on psychosocial outcomes. *Archives of Women and Mental Health, 19,* 259–269.

Hebert, J.J., & others (2017). The prospective association of organized sports participation with cardiovascular disease risk in children (the CHAMPS study-DK). *Mayo Clinic Proceedings, 92,* 57–65.

Hechtman, L., & others (2016). Functional adult outcomes 16 years after childhood diagnosis of attention-deficit/hyperactivity disorder: MTA results. *Journal of American Academcy of Child and Adolescent Psychiatry, 55,* 945–952.

Heimann, M., & others (2006). Exploring the relation between memory, gestural communication, and the emergence of language in infancy: A longitudinal study. *Infant and Child Development, 15,* 233–249.

Heinonen, M.T., & others (2015). GIMAP GTPase family genes: Potential modifiers in autoimmune diabetes, asthma, and allergy. *Journal of Immunology, 194,* 5885–5894.

Helgeson, V.S. (2017). *The psychology of gender* (5th ed.). New York: Routledge.

Hellgren, K., & others (2017, in press). The new Swedish report on shaken baby syndrome is misleading. *Acta Pediatrica.*

Henderson, J., & others (2014). Laboring women who used a birthing pool in obstetric units in Italy: Prospective observational study. *BMC Pregnancy and Childbirth, 14*(1), 17.

Henderson, V.L., & Dweck, C.S. (1990). Motivation and achievement. In S.S. Feldman & G.R. Elliott (Eds.), *At the threshold: The developing adolescent.* Cambridge, MA: Harvard University Press.

Hendricks-Munoz, K.D., & Mayers, R.M. (2014). A neonatal nurse training program in kangaroo mother care (KMC) decreased barriers to KMC utilization in the NICU. *American Journal of Perinatology, 31,* 987–992.

Hendricks-Munoz, K.D., & others (2013). Maternal and neonatal nurse perceived value of kangaroo mother care and maternal care partnership in the neonatal intensive care unit. *American Journal of Perinatology, 30*(10), 875–880.

Hendry, J. (1995). *Understanding Japanese society.* London: Routledge.

Hennessey, B. (2017). Intrinsic motivation and creativity: Have we come full circle? In R.A. Beghetto & J.C. Kaufman (Eds.), *Nurturing creativity in the classroom* (2nd ed.). New York: Cambridge University Press.

Hennessey, B.A. (2011). Intrinsic motivation and creativity: Have we come full circle? In R.A. Beghetto & J.C. Kaufman (Eds.), *Nurturing creativity in the classroom.* New York: Cambridge University Press.

Hennessey, B.A., & Amabile, T.M. (2010). Creativity. *Annual Review of Psychology* (Vol. 61). Palo Alto, CA: Annual Reviews.

Henniger, M.L. (2017). *Teaching young children* (6th ed.). Upper Saddle River, NJ: Pearson.

Henricks, T.S. (2015b). Modern theories of play. In J.E. Johnson & others (Eds.), *Handbook of the study of play.* Blue Ridge Summit, PA: Rowman & Littlefield.

Henricks, T.S. (2015a). Classical theories of play. In J.E. Johnson & others (Eds.), *Handbook of the study of play.* Blue Ridge Summit, PA: Rowman & Littlefield.

Henriksen, T.B., & others (2004). Alcohol consumption at the time of conception and spontaneous abortion. *American Journal of Epidemiology, 160,* 661–667.

Henslin, J.M. (2017). *Essentials of sociology* (12th ed.). Upper Saddle River, NJ: Pearson.

Herbers, J.E., & others (2011). Direct and indirect effects of parenting on academic functioning of young homeless children. *Early Education and Development, 22,* 77–104.

Herbers, J.E., & others (2014). Trauma, adversity, and parent-child relationships among young children experiencing homelessness. *Journal of Abnormal Child Psychology, 42,* 1167–1174.

Herbst, M.A., Mercer, B.M., Beasley, D., Meyer, R., & Carr, T. (2003). Relationship of prenatal care and perinatal morbidity in low-birth-weight infants. *American Journal of Obstetrics and Gynecology, 189,* 930–933.

Hernandez-Reif, M., Diego, M., & Field, T. (2007). Preterm infants show reduced stress behaviors and activity after 5 days of massage therapy. *Infant Behavior and Development, 30,* 557–561.

Heron, M. (2016). Deaths: Leading causes for 2013. *National Vital Statistics Reports, 65*(2), 1–95.

Herting, M.M., Colby, J.B., Sowell, E.R., & Nagel, B.J. (2014). White matter connectivity and aerobic fitness in male adolescents. *Developmental Cognitive Neuroscience, 7,* 65–75.

Herting, M.M., & Sowell, E.R. (2017). Puberty and structural brain development in humans. *Frontiers in Neuroendocrinology, 44,* 122–137.

Hetherington, E.M. (2006). The influence of conflict, marital problem solving, and parenting on children's adjustment in nondivorced, divorced, and remarried families. In A. Clarke-Stewart & J. Dunn (Eds.), *Families count.* New York: Cambridge University Press.

Hetherington, E.M., & Kelly, J. (2002). *For better or for worse: Divorce reconsidered.* New York: Norton.

Hetherington, E.M., & Stanley-Hagan, M. (2002). Parenting in divorced and remarried families. In M.H. Bornstein (Ed.), *Handbook of parenting* (2nd ed., Vol. 3). Mahwah, NJ: Erlbaum.

Heuwinkel, M.K. (1996). New ways of learning: Five new ways of teaching. *Childhood Education, 72,* 27–31.

Heward, W.L., Alber-Morgan, S., & Konrad, M. (2017). *Exceptional children* (11th ed.). Upper Saddle River, NJ: Pearson.

Hewlett, B.S. (2000). Culture, history and sex: Anthropological perspectives on father involvement. *Marriage and Family Review, 29,* 324–340.

Hewlett, B.S., & MacFarlan, S.J. (2010). Fathers' roles in hunter-gatherer and other small-scale cultures. In M.E. Lamb (Ed.), *The role of the father in child development* (5th ed.). New York: Wiley.

Heyman, G.D., Fu, G., & Lee, K. (2013). Selective skepticism: American and Chinese children's reasoning about evaluative feedback. *Developmental Psychology, 49,* 543–553.

Heyman, G.D., & Legare, C.H. (2005). Children's evaluation of sources of information about traits. *Developmental Psychology, 41,* 636–647.

Hickson, G.B., & Clayton, E.W. (2002). Parents and children's doctors. In M.H. Bornstein (Ed.), *Handbook of parenting* (Vol. 5). Mahwah, NJ: Erlbaum.

Higginbotham, H., Yokota, Y., & Anton, E.S. (2011). Strategies for analyzing neuronal progenitor development and neuronal migration in the developing cerebral cortex. *Cerebral Cortex, 21*(7), 1465–1474.

Highfield, R. (2008, April 30). Harvard's baby brain research lab. Retrieved January 24, 2009, from http://www.telegraph.co.uk/scienceandtechnology/science/sciencenews/3341166/Harvards

Hilger, K., & others (2017). Efficient hubs in the intelligent brain: Nodal efficiency of hub regions in the salience network is associated with general intelligence. *Intelligence, 60,* 10–25.

Hill, C.R., & Stafford, F.P. (1980). Parental care of children: Time diary estimate of quantity, predictability, and variety. *Journal of Human Resources, 15,* 219–239.

Hill, E.M. (2016). The role of narcissism in health-risk and health-protective behaviors. *Journal of Health Psychology, 21,* 2021–2032.

Hill, K., & Roth, T.L. (2016). Epigenetic mechanisms in the development of behavior. In D. Cicchetti (Ed.), *Developmental psychopathology* (3rd ed.). New York: Wiley.

Hillman, C.H., & others (2009). The effect of acute treadmill walking on cognitive control and academic achievement in preadolescent children. *Neuroscience, 3,* 1044–1054.

Hillman, C.H., & others (2014). Effects of the FITKids randomized controlled trial on executive control and brain function. *Pediatrics, 134,* e1063–e1071.

Hines, M. (2015). Gendered development. In R.M. Lerner (Ed.), *Handbook of child psychology and developmental science* (7th ed.). New York: Wiley.

Hirsh-Pasek, K., & Golinkoff, R.M. (2014). Early language and literacy: Six principles. In S. Gilford (Ed.), *Head Start teacher's guide.* New York: Teachers College Press.

Hirsh-Pasek, K., Golinkoff, R.M., Singer, D., & Berk, L. (2009). *A mandate for playful learning in preschool: Presenting the evidence.* New York: Oxford University Press.

Hirsh-Pasek, K., & others (2015). The contribution of early communication quality to low-income children's language success. *Psychological Science, 26,* 1071–1083.

Hjortsvang, K., & Lagattuta, K.H. (2017, in press). Emotional development. In A.E. Wentzel (Ed.), *SAGE encyclopedia of abnormal and clinical psychology.* Thousand Oaks, CA: Sage.

Hockenberry, M.J., Wilson, D., & Rodgers, C.C. (2017). *Wong's essentials of pediatric nursing* (10th ed.). Maryland Heights, MO: Mosby.

Hocutt, A.M. (1996). Effectiveness of special education: Is placement the critical factor? *Future of Children, 6*(1), 77–102.

Hodapp, R.M., Griffin, M.M., Burke, M., & Fisher, M.H. (2011). Intellectual disabilities. In R.J. Sternberg & S.B. Kaufman (Eds.), *Cambridge handbook of intelligence.* New York: Cambridge University Press.

Hoehl, S., & Striano, T. (2015). The development of brain mechanisms of joint attention. In S.D. Calkins (Ed.), *Handbook of biopsychosocial development.* New York: Guilford.

Hofer, A., & others (2007). Sex differences in brain activation patterns during processing of positively and negatively balanced emotional stimuli. *Psychological Medicine, 37,* 109–119.

Hofer, M., & Fries, S. (2016). A multiple goal perspective on academic motivation. In K. Wentzel & D. Miele (Eds.), *Handbook of motivation at school* (2nd ed.). New York: Routledge.

Hoff, E. (2014). *Language development* (5th ed.). Boston: Cengage.

Hoff, E. (2015). Language development. In M.H. Bornstein & M.E. Lamb (Eds.), *Developmental science* (7th ed.). New York: Psychology Press.

Hoff, E., Laursen, B., & Tardif, T. (2002). Socioeconomic status and parenting. In M.H. Bornstein (Ed.), *Handbook of parenting* (2nd ed.). Mahwah, NJ: Erlbaum.

Hoff, E., & Place, S. (2013). Bilingual language learners. In S.L. Odom, E. Pungello, & N. Gardner-Neblett (Eds.), *Re-visioning the beginning: Developmental and health science contributions to infant/toddler programs for children and families living in poverty.* New York: Guilford.

Hoff, E., & others (2014). Expressive vocabulary development in children from bilingual homes: A longitudinal study from two to four years. *Early Childhood Research Quarterly, 29,* 433–444.

Hoffend, C., & Sperhake, J.P. (2014). Sudden unexpected death in infancy (SUDI) in the early neonatal period: The role of bed sharing. *Forensic Science, Medicine, and Pathology, 10,* 157–162.

Hofferth, S.L., & Reid, L. (2002). Early child-bearing and children's achievement behavior over time. *Perspectives on Sexual and Reproductive Health, 34,* 41–49.

Hoffman, E., & Ewen, D. (2007). Supporting families, nurturing young children. *CLASP Policy Brief, No. 9,* 1–11.

Hoffman, K., Cooper, G., Powell, B., & Benton, C.M. (2017). *Raising a secure child.* New York: Guilford.

Hoffman, K., & others (2017). *Raising a secure child.* New York: Guilford.

Hoffman, S., & Warschburger, P. (2017). Weight, shape, and muscularity concerns in male and female adolescents: Predictors of change and influences on eating disorders. *International Journal of Eating Disorders, 50,* 139–147.

Hoffman, T. (2017). Constructive grammars. In B. Dancygier (Ed.), *Cambridge handbook of cognitive linguistics.* New York: Cambridge University Press.

Hogan, C. (2014). Socioeconomic factors affecting infant sleep-related deaths in St. Louis. *Public Health Nursing, 31,* 10–18.

Holden, G.W., Vittrup, B., & Rosen, L.H. (2011). Families, parenting, and discipline. In M.K. Underwood & L.H. Rosen (Eds.), *Social development.* New York: Guilford.

Holden, G.W., & others (2017). The emergence of "positive parenting" as a new paradigm: Theory, processes, and evidence. In D. Narváez & others (Eds.), *Contexts for young child flourishing.* New York: Oxford University Press.

Holding, P., & others (2017, in press). Can we measure cognitive constructs consistently within and across cultures? Evidence from a test battery in Bangladesh, Ghana, and Tanzania. *Applied Neuropsychology: Child.*

Hollams, E.M., de Klerk, N.H., Holt, P.G., & Sly, P.D. (2014). Persistent effects of maternal smoking during pregnancy on lung function and asthma in adolescents. *American Journal of Respiratory and Critical Care Medicine, 189,* 401–407.

Holland, J.C., & others (2014). Modifications in parent feeding practices and diet during family-based behavioral treatment improve child BMI. *Obesity, 22,* E119–E126.

Holler-Wallscheid, M.S., & others (2017). Bilateral recruitment of prefrontal cortex in working memory is associated with task demand but not with age. *Proceedings of the National Academy of Sciences U.S.A., 114,* E830–E839.

Hollich, G., Newman, R.S., & Jusczyk, P.W. (2005). Infants' use of synchronized visual information to separate streams of speech. *Child Development, 76,* 598–613.

Holmes, C.J., & Kim-Spoon, J. (2016a). Positive and negative associations between adolescents' religiousness and health behaviors via self-regulation. *Religion, Brain, and Behavior, 6,* 188–206.

Holmes, C.J., & Kim-Spoon, J. (2016b). Why are religiousness and spirituality associated with externalizing psychopathology? A literature review. *Clinical Child and Family Psychology Review, 19,* 1–20.

Holmes, C.J., Kim-Spoon, J., & Deater-Deckard, K. (2016). Linking executive function and peer problems from early childhood through middle adolescence. *Journal of Abnormal Child Psychology, 44,* 31–42.

Holmes, L.B. (2011). Human teratogens: Update 2010. *Birth Defects Research A: Clinical and Molecular Teratology, 91,* 1–7.

Holmes, R.M., Little, K.C., & Welsh, D. (2009). Dating and romantic relationships, adulthood. In D. Carr (Ed.), *Encyclopedia of the life course and human development.* Boston: Gale Cengage.

Holsen, I., Carlson Jones, D., & Skogbrott Birkeland, M. (2012). Body image satisfaction among Norwegian adolescents and young adults: A longitudinal study of interpersonal relationships and BMI. *Body Image, 9,* 201–208.

Holtz, P., & Appel, M. (2011). Internet use and video gaming predict problem behavior in early adolescence. *Journal of Adolescence, 34,* 49–58.

Holzman, L. (2016). *Vygotsky at work and play* (2nd ed.). New York: Routledge.

Hood, B.M. (1995). Gravity rules for 2- to 4-year-olds? *Cognitive Development, 10,* 577–598.

Hoogenhout, M., & Malcolm-Smith, S. (2017). Theory of mind predicts severity level in autism. *Autism, 21,* 242–252.

Hook, P.E., & Haynes, C.W. (2017). Reading and writing in child language disorders. In R. Schwartz (Eds.), *Handbook of child language disorders* (2nd ed.). New York: Routledge.

Hooper, S.R., & others (2008). Executive functions in young males with fragile X syndrome in comparison to mental age-matched controls: Baseline findings from a longitudinal study. *Neuropsychology, 22,* 36–47.

Hoover, J., & others (2018, in press). Into the wild: Building value through moral pluralism. In K. Gray & J. Graham (Eds.), *Atlas of moral psychology.* New York: Guilford.

Hopkins, B. (1991). Facilitating early motor development: An intercultural study of West Indian mothers and their infants living in Britain. In J.K. Nugent, B.M. Lester, & T.B. Brazelton (Eds.), *The cultural context of infancy, Vol. 2: Multicultural and interdisciplinary approaches to parent-infant relations.* New York: Ablex.

Hopkins, B., & Westra, T. (1990). Motor development, maternal expectations, and the role of handling. *Infant Behavior and Development, 13,* 117–122.

Horne, R.S., Franco, P., Adamson, T.M., Groswasser, J., & Kahn, A. (2002). Effects of body position on sleep and arousal characteristics in infants. *Early Human Development, 69,* 25–33.

Hoskin, J., & Herman, R. (2001). The communication, speech, and gestures of a group of hearing impaired children. *International Journal of Language and Communication Disorders, 36*(Suppl.), 206–209.

Hoskyn, M.J., Iarocci, G., & Young, A.R. (Eds.) (2017). *Executive functions in children's everyday lives.* New York: Oxford University Press.

Hospital for Sick Children & others (2010). *Infant sleep.* Toronto: Author.

Hostinar, C., Cicchetti, D., & Rogosch, F.A. (2014). Oxytocin receptor gene (OXTR) polymorphism, perceived social support, and psychological symptoms in maltreated adolescents. *Development and Psychopathology, 26,* 465–477.

Hou, Y., Kim, S.Y., & Wang, Y. (2016). Parental acculturative stressors and adolescent adjustment through interparental and parent-child relationships in Chinese American families. *Journal of Youth and Adolescence, 45,* 1466–1481.

Houde, O., & others (2011). Functional magnetic resonance imaging study of Piaget's conservation-of-number task in preschool and school-age children: A neo-Piagetian approach. *Journal of Experimental Child Psychology, 110(3),* 332–346.

House, L.D., Mueller, T., Reininger, B., Brown, K., & Markham, C.M. (2010). Character as a predictor of reproductive health outcomes for youth: A systematic review. *Journal of Adolescent Health, 46*(Suppl. 1), S59–S74.

Howard, L.H., Henderson, A.M.E., Carrazza, C., & Woodward, A.L. (2015). Infants' and young children's imitation of linguistic in group and outgroup informants. *Child Development, 86,* 259–275.

Howe, L.D., Huttly, S.R., & Abramsky, T. (2006). Risk factors for injuries in young children in four developing countries: The Young Lives Study. *Tropic Medicine and International Health, 11,* 1557–1566.

Howe, M.J.A., Davidson, J.W., Moore, D.G., & Sloboda, J.A. (1995). Are there early childhood signs of musical ability? *Psychology of Music, 23,* 162–176.

Howell, D.C. (2017). *Fundamental statistics for the behavioral sciences* (9th ed.). Boston: Cengage.

Howell, P. (2013). Screening school-aged children for risk of stuttering. *Journal of Fluency Disorders, 33,* 102–123.

Howes, C. (2009). Friendship in early childhood. In K.H. Rubin, W.M. Bukowski, & B. Laursen (Eds.), *Handbook of peer interactions, relationships, and groups.* New York: Guilford.

Howes, C. (2016). Children and child care: A theory of relationships within cultural communities. In K. Sanders & A.W. Guerra (Eds.), *The culture of child care.* New York: Oxford University Press.

Howlin, P., Magiati, I., & Charman, T. (2009). Systematic review of early intensive behavioral interventions with autism. *American Journal on Intellectual and Developmental Disabilities, 114,* 23–41.

Hsieh, M., & Stright, A.D. (2012). Adolescents' emotion regulation strategies, self-concept, and internalizing problems. *Journal of Early Adolescence, 32,* 876–901.

Hsin, A., & Xie, Y. (2014). Explaining Asian Americans' academic advantage over whites. *Proceedings of the National Academy of Sciences U.S.A., 111,* 8416–8421.

Hsu, H-C. (2004). Antecedents and consequences of separation anxiety in first-time mothers: Infant, mother, and social-contextual characteristics. *Infant Behavior & Development, 27,* 113–133.

Hu, H., & others (2007). Fetal lead exposure at each stage of pregnancy as a predictor of infant mental development. *Environmental Health Perspectives, 114,* 1730–1735.

Hua, L., & others (2016). Four-locus gene interaction between IL13, IL4, FCER1B, and ADRB2 for asthma in Chinese Han children. *Pediatric Pulmonology, 51,* 364–371.

Huang, L., & others (2017, in press). The mediating role of the placenta in the relationship between maternal exercise during pregnancy and full-term low birth weight. *Journal of Maternal-Fetal and Neonatal Medicine.*

Huang, L.N. (1989). Southeast Asian refugee children and adolescents. In J.T. Gibbs & L.N. Huang (Eds.), *Children of color.* San Francisco: Jossey-Bass.

Huang, Y., & Spelke, E. (2015). Core knowledge and the emergence of symbols: The case of maps. *Journal of Cognition and Development, 16,* 81–96.

Huang, Y.A., & others (2017). ApoE2, ApoE3, and ApoE4 differentially stimulate APP transcription and *AB* secretion. *Cell, 168,* 427–441.

Huckle, W.R. (2017). Cell- and tissue-based models for study of placental development. *Progress in Molecular Biology and Translational Science, 145,* 29–37.

Hudson, A., & Jacques, S. (2014). Put on a happy face! Inhibitory control and socioemotional knowledge predict emotion regulation in 5- to 7-year-olds. *Journal of Experimental Child Psychology, 123,* 36–52.

Hudson, N.W., Fraley, R.C., Chopik, W.J., & Hefferman, M.E. (2016). Not all attachment relationships change alike: Normative cross-sectional age trajectories in attachment to romantic partners, friends, and parents across the lifespan. *Journal of Research in Personality, 59,* 49–55.

Huebner, A.M., & Garrod, A.C. (1993). Moral reasoning among Tibetan monks: A study of Buddhist adolescents and young adults in Nepal. *Journal of Cross-Cultural Psychology, 24,* 167–185.

Huesmann, L.R., Dubow, E.F., Eron, L.D., & Boxer, P. (2006). Middle childhood family-contextual and personal factors as predictors of adult outcomes. In A.C. Huston & M.N. Ripke (Eds.), *Developmental contexts in middle childhood: Bridges to adolescence and adulthood*. New York: Cambridge University Press.

Hughes, C., & Devine, R.T. (2015). Individual differences in theory of mind: A social perspective. In R.M. Lerner (Ed.), *Handbook of child psychology and developmental science* (7th ed.). New York: Wiley.

Hughes, C., Devine, R.T., & Wang, Z. (2017, in press). Does parental mind-mindedness account for cross-cultural differences in preschoolers' theory of mind? *Child Development.*

Hughes, C., Marks, A., Ensor, R., & Lecce, S. (2010). A longitudinal study of conflict and inner state talk in children's conversations with mothers and younger siblings. *Social Development, 19,* 822–837.

Hughes, E.K., & others (2017, in press). A case series of family-based treatment for adolescents with atypical anorexia nervosa. *International Journal of Eating Disorders.*

Hughes, H.K., & others (2017). Pediatric asthma health disparities: Race, hardship, housing, and asthma in a national survey. *Academic Pediatrics, 17,* 127–134.

Huizink, A.C., & Mulder, E.J. (2006). Maternal smoking, drinking, or cannabis use during pregnancy and neurobehavioral and cognitive functioning in human offspring. *Neuroscience and Biobehavioral Research, 30,* 24–41.

Hunter, L.P. (2009). A descriptive study of "being with woman" during labor and birth. *Journal of Midwifery and Women's Health, 54,* 111–118.

Hurst, C. (2013). *Social inequality* (8th ed.). Upper Saddle River, NJ: Pearson.

Hurt, H., Brodsky, N.L., Roth, H., Malmud, F., & Giannetta, J.M. (2005). School performance of children with gestational cocaine exposure. *Neurotoxicology and Teratology, 27,* 203–211.

Hustedt, J.T., Friedman, A.H., & Barnett, W.S. (2012). Investments in early education: Resources at the federal and state levels. In R.C. Pianta (Ed.), *Handbook of early childhood education.* New York: Guilford.

Huston, A.C., & Ripke, M.N. (2006). Experiences in middle childhood and children's development: A summary and integration of research. In A.C. Huston & M.N. Ripke (Eds.), *Developmental contexts in middle childhood.* New York: Cambridge University Press.

Huston, A.C., & others (2006). Effects of a poverty intervention program last from middle childhood to adolescence. In A.C. Huston & M.N. Ripke (Eds.), *Developmental contexts of middle childhood: Bridges to adolescence and adulthood.* New York: Cambridge University Press.

Huttenlocher, J., Haight, W., Bruk, A., Seltzer, M., & Lyons, T. (1991). Early vocabulary growth: Relation to language input and gender. *Developmental Psychology, 27,* 236–248.

Huttenlocher, P.R., & Dabholkar, A.S. (1997). Regional differences in synaptogenesis in human cerebral cortex. *Journal of Comparative Neurology, 37*(2), 167–178.

Huynh, M., & others (2017, in press). Spatial social polarization and birth outcomes: Preterm birth and infant mortality—New York City, 2010–2014. *Scandinavian Journal of Public Health.*

Hwalla, N., & others (2017, in press). The prevalence of micronutrient deficiencies and inadequacies in the Middle East and approaches to interventions. *Nutrients.*

Hyde, J.S. (2007a). *Half the human experience* (7th ed.). Boston: Houghton Mifflin.

Hyde, J.S. (2007b). New directions in the study of gender similarities and differences. *Current Directions in Psychological Science, 16,* 259–263.

Hyde, J.S. (2009). The gender similarities hypothesis. *American Psychologist, 60,* 581–592.

Hyde, J.S. (2014*).* Gender similarities and differences. *Annual Review of Psychology* (Vol. 65). Palo Alto, CA: Annual Reviews.

Hyde, J.S., & DeLamater, J.D. (2017). *Human sexuality* (13th ed.). New York: McGraw-Hill.

Hyde, J.S., Lindberg, S.M., Linn, M.C., Ellis, A.B., & Williams, C.C. (2008). Gender similarities characterize math performance. *Science, 321,* 494–495.

Hysing, M., & others (2015). Sleep and school attendance in adolescence: Results from a large population-based study. *Scandinavian Journal of Public Health, 43,* 2–9.

Hysing, M., & others (2016). Sleep and academic performance in later adolescence: Results from a large population-based study. *Journal of Sleep Research, 25,* 318–324.

Hyson, M.C., Copple, C., & Jones, J. (2006). Early childhood development and education. In W. Damon & R. Lerner (Eds.), *Handbook of child psychology* (6th ed.). New York: Wiley.

I

"I Have a Dream" Foundation (2017). About us. Retrieved January 4, 2017, from www.ihad.org

Ibitoye, M., & others (2017). Early menarche: A systematic review of its effect on sexual and reproductive health in low- and middle-income families. *PLoS One, 12*(6), e0178884.

Ige, F., & Shelton, D. (2004). Reducing the risk of sudden infant death syndrome (SIDS) in African-American communities. *Journal of Pediatric Nursing, 19,* 290–292.

Ikram, U.Z., & others (2016). Perceived ethnic discrimination and depressive symptoms: The buffering effects of ethnic identity, religion, and ethnic social network. *Social Psychiatry and Psychiatric Epidemiology, 51,* 679–688.

Im, Y., Oh, W.O., & Suk, M. (2017). Risk factors for suicide ideation among adolescents: Five-year national data analysis. *Archives of Psychiatric Nursing, 31,* 282–286.

Ingul, C.B., & others (2016). Maternal obesity affects fetal myocardial function as early as in the first trimester. *Ultrasound in Obstetrics and Gynecology, 47,* 433–442.

Innella, N., & others (2016). Determinants of obesity in the Hispanic preschool population: An integrative review. *Public Health Nursing, 33,* 189–199.

Insel, P., & Roth, R. (2016). *Connect core concepts in health* (14th ed.). New York: McGraw-Hill.

International Montessori Council (2006). Larry Page and Sergey Brin, founders of Google.com, credit their Montessori education for much of their success on prime-time television. Retrieved June 24, 2006, from http://www.Montessori.org/enews/Barbara_walters.html

Ip, S., Chung, M., Raman, G., Trikaliinos, T.A., & Lau, J. (2009). A summary of the Agency for Healthcare Research and Quality's evidence report on breastfeeding in developed countries. *Breastfeeding Medicine, 4* (Suppl. 1), S17–S30.

Isgut, M., & others (2017, in press). The impact of psychological distress during pregnancy on the developing fetus: Biological mechanisms and the potential benefits of mindfulness interventions. *Journal of Perinatal Medicine.*

Ishak, S., Franchak, J.M., & Adolph, K.E. (2014). Fear of height in infants. *Current Directions in Psychological Science, 23,* 60–66.

Ismail, F.Y., Fatemi, A., & Johnston, M.V. (2017). Cerebral plasticity: Windows of opportunity for the developing brain. *European Journal of Pediatric Neurology, 21,* 23–48.

Israelashvili, M., & Romano, J. (Eds.) (2017). *Cambridge handbook of international prevention science.* New York: Cambridge.

Issel, L.M., & others (2011). A review of prenatal home-visiting effectiveness for improving birth outcomes. *Journal of Obstetric, Gynecologic, and Neonatal Nursing, 40*(2), 157–165.

Ivanenko, A., & Larson, K. (2013). Nighttime distractions: Fears, nightmares, and parasomnias. In A.R. Rolfson & H.E. Montgomery-Downs (Eds.), *Oxford handbook of infant, child, and adolescent sleep and behavior.* New York: Oxford University Press.

Iwata, S., & others (2012). Qualitative brain MRI at term and cognitive outcomes at 9 years after very preterm birth. *Pediatrics, 129,* e1138–1147.

J

Jaarsveld, S., & Lachmann, T. (2017). Intelligence and creativity in problem solving: The importance of test features in cognition research. *Frontiers in Psychology, 8,* 134.

Jackson, A., & Davis, G. (2000). *Turning points 2000.* New York: Teachers College Press.

Jackson, M.I. (2015). Early childhood WIC participation, cognitive development and academic achievement. *Social Science and Medicine, 126,* 145–153.

Jackson, S.L. (2016). *Research methods* (5th ed.). Boston: Cengage.

Jackson, S.L. (2017). *Statistics plain and simple* (4th ed.). Boston: Cengage.

Jackson, T., Jiang, C., & Chen, H. (2016). Associations between Chinese/Asian versus Western mass media influences and body image disturbances among young Chinese women. *Body Image, 17,* 175–183.

Jackson, W.M., & others (2016). Physical activity and cognitive development: A meta analysis.

Journal of Neurosurgery and Anesthesiology, 28, 373–380.

Jacob, J.I. (2009). The socioemotional effects of non-maternal childcare on children in the USA: Critical review of recent studies. *Early Child Development and Care, 179,* 559–570.

Jacobson, S.W., & others (2017, in press). Heavy prenatal alcohol exposure is related to smaller corpus callosum in newborn MRI scans. *Alcoholism: Clinical and Experimental Research.*

Jacoby, N., Overfeld, J., Brinder, E.B., & Heim, C.M. (2016). Stress neurobiology and developmental psychopathology. In D. Cicchetti (Ed.), *Developmental psychopathology* (3rd ed.). New York: Wiley.

Jaddoe, V.W., & others (2008). Active and passive smoking during pregnancy and the risks of low birth weight and preterm birth: The Generation R Study. *Pediatric and Perinatal Epidemiology, 22,* 162–171.

Jaffee, S., & Hyde, J.S. (2000). Gender differences in moral orientation: A meta-analysis. *Psychological Bulletin, 126,* 703–726.

Jaffee, S.R. (2016). Quantitative and molecular genetic studies of gene-environmental correlation. In D. Cicchetti (Ed.), *Developmental psychopathology* (3rd ed.). New York: Wiley.

Jager, S., & others (2014). Breast-feeding and maternal risk of type 2 diabetes: A prospective study and meta-analysis. *Diabetologia, 57,* 1355–1365.

Jakobsen, I.S., Larsen, K.J., & Horwood, J.L. (2017, in press). Suicide risk assessment in adolescents—C-SSRS, K20, and READ. *Crisis.*

Jakobsen, K.V., Umstead, L., & Simpson, E.A. (2016). Efficient human face detection in infancy. *Developmental Psychobiology, 58,* 129–136.

Jaleel, S., & Premachandran, P. (2016). A study on the metacognitive awareness of secondary school students. *Universal Journal of Educational Research, 4,* 165–172.

Jambon, M., & Smetana, J.G. (2017, in press). Individual differences in prototypical moral and conventional judgments and children's proactive and reactive aggression. *Child Development.*

James, W. (1890/1950). *The principles of psychology.* New York: Dover.

Janssen, I., & others (2005). Comparison of overweight and obesity prevalence in school-aged youth from 34 countries and their relationships with physical activity and dietary patterns. *Obesity Reviews, 6,* 123–132.

Janssen, J.A., & others (2017). Childhood temperament predictors of adolescent physical activity. *BMC Public Health, 17*(1), 8.

Janssens, A., & others (2017, in press). Adolescent externalizing behavior, psychological control, and rejection: Transactional links and dopaminergic moderation. *British Journal of Developmental Psychology.*

Jaramillo, N., & others (2017). Associations between sex education and contraceptive use among heterosexually active adolescent males in the United States. *Journal of Adolescent Health, 60,* 534–540.

Jardri, R., & others (2012). Assessing fetal response to maternal speech using a noninvasive functional brain imaging technique. *International Journal of Developmental Neuroscience, 30,* 159–161.

Jarosinska, D., Polanska, K., Woityniak, B., & Hanke, W. (2014). Towards estimating the burden of disease attributable to second-hand smoke exposure in Polish children. *International Journal of Occupational Medicine and Environmental Health, 27,* 38–49.

Jarquin, V.G., & others (2011). Racial disparities in community identification of autism spectrum disorders over time: Metropolitan Atlanta, Georgia, 2000–2006. *Journal of Developmental and Behavioral Pediatrics, 32,* 179–187.

Jarris, P.E., & others (2017). Group prenatal care compared with traditional prenatal care: A systematic review and meta-analysis. *Obstetrics and Gynecology, 129,* 384–385.

Jaruratanasirikul, S., & others (2017). A population-based study of Down syndrome in Southern Thailand. *World Journal of Pediatrics, 13,* 63–69.

Jasinksa, K.K., & Petitto, L-A. (2017, in press). Age of bilingual exposure is related to the contribution of phonological and semantic knowledge to successful reading development. *Child Development.*

Jelding-Dannemand, E., Malby Schoos, A.M., & Bisgaard, H. (2015). Breast-feeding does not protect against allergic sensitization in early childhood and allergy-associated disease at age 7 years. *Journal of Allergy and Clinical Immunology, 136,* 1302–1308.

Jenkins, J.M., & Astington, J.W. (1996). Cognitive factors and family structure associated with theory of mind development in young children. *Developmental Psychology, 32,* 70–78.

Jensen, A.R. (2008). Book review. *Intelligence, 36,* 96–97.

Ji, B.T., & others (1997). Paternal cigarette smoking and the risk of childhood cancer among offspring of nonsmoking mothers. *Journal of the National Cancer Institute, 89,* 235–244.

Ji, J., Negriff, S., KIim, H., & Susman, E.J. (2016). A study of cortisol reactivity and recovery among young adolescents: Heterogeneity and longitudinal stability and change. *Developmental Psychobiology, 58,* 283–302.

Jia, R., & Schoppe-Sullivan, S.J. (2011). Relations between coparenting and father involvement in families with preschool-age children. *Developmental Psychology, 47,* 106–118.

Jia, Y., & others (2017). Attachment avoidance is significantly related to attention preferences for infant faces: Evidence from eye movement data. *Frontiers in Psychology, 8,* 85.

Jiang, Y., Abiri, R., & Zhao, X. (2017). Tuning up the old brain with new tricks: Attention training via neurofeedback. *Frontiers in Aging Neuroscience, 9,* 52.

Jiang, Z., & others (2017, in press). Event-related theta oscillatory substrates for facilitation and interference effects of negative emotion on children's cognition. *International Journal of Psychophysiology.*

Jimerson, S.R. (2009). High school dropout. In D. Carr (Ed.), *Encyclopedia of the life course and human development.* Boston: Gale Cengage.

Jin, Y., Seiber, E.E., & Ferketich, A.K. (2013). Secondhand smoke and asthma: What are the effects on healthcare utilization among children? *Prevention Medicine, 57,* 125–128.

Jo, J., & Lee, Y.J. (2017, in press). Effectiveness of acupuncture in women with polycystic ovarian syndrome undergoing in vitro fertilization or intracytoplasmic sperm injection: A systematic review and meta-analysis. *Acupuncture in Medicine.*

Job, V., Walton, G.M., Bernecker, K., & Dweck, C.S. (2015). Implicit theories about willpower predict self-regulation and grades in everyday life. *Journal of Personality and Social Psychology, 108,* 637–647.

Joh, A.S., Jaswal, V.K., & Keen, R. (2011). Imagining a way out of the gravity bias: Preschoolers can visualize the solution to a spatial problem. *Child Development, 82,* 744–750.

John, R.M. (2017, in press). Imprinted genes and the regulation of placental endocrine function: Pregnancy and beyond. *Placenta.*

Johnson, A.D., Martin, A., & Brooks-Gunn, J. (2013). Child-care subsidies and school readiness in kindergarten. *Child Development, 84,* 1806–1822.

Johnson, J.A., & others (2018). *Foundations of American education* (17th ed.). Upper Saddle River, NJ: Pearson.

Johnson, J.S., & Newport, E.L. (1991). Critical period effects on universal properties of language: The status of subjacency in the acquisition of a second language. *Cognition, 39,* 215–258.

Johnson, M. (2008, April 30). Commentary in R. Highfield, Harvard's baby brain research lab. Retrieved January 24, 2008, from http://www.telegraph.co.uk/science/science-news/3341166/Harvards-baby-brain-research-lab.html

Johnson, M.D. (2017). *Human biology* (8th ed.). Upper Saddle River, NJ: Pearson.

Johnson, M.H., Gliga, T., Jones, E., & Charman, T. (2015). Annual research review: Infant development, autism, and ADHD—early pathways to emerging disorders. *Journal of Child Psychology and Psychiatry, 56,* 228–247.

Johnson, M.H., Grossmann, T., & Cohen-Kadosh, K. (2009). Mapping functional brain development: Building a social brain through interactive specialization. *Developmental Psychology, 45,* 151–159.

Johnson, M.H., Jones, E., & Gliga, T. (2015). Brain adaptation and alternative developmental trajectories. *Development and Psychopathology, 27,* 425–442.

Johnson, M.H., Senju, A., & Tomalski, P. (2015). The two-process theory of face processing: Modifications based on two decades of data from infants and adults. *Neuroscience and Biobehavioral Reviews, 50,* 169–179.

Johnson, S.B., Riis, J.L., & Noble, K.G. (2016). State of the art review: Poverty and the developing brain. *Pediatrics, 137,* e20153075.

Johnson, S.P. (2010). Perceptual completion in infancy. In S.P. Johnson (Ed.), *Neoconstructivism: The new science of cognitive development* (pp. 45–60). New York: Oxford University Press.

Johnson, S.P. (2011). A constructivist view of object perception in infancy. In L.M. Oakes, C.H. Cashon, M. Casasola, & D.H. Rakison (Eds.), *Infant perception and cognition*. New York: Oxford University Press.

Johnson, S.P. (2013). Object perception. In P.D. Zelazo (Ed.), *Handbook of developmental psychology*. New York: Oxford University Press.

Johnson, S.P., & Hannon, E.H. (2015). Perceptual development. In R.M. Lerner (Ed.), *Handbook of child psychology and developmental science* (7th ed.). New York: Wiley.

Johnson, W., & Bouchard, T.J. (2014). Genetics of intellectual and personality traits associated with creative genius: Could geniuses be cosmobian dragon kings? In D.K. Simonton (Ed.), *Wiley-Blackwell handbook of genius*. New York: Wiley.

Johnson, W., & others (2007). Genetic and environmental influences on the Verbal-Perceptual-Image Rotation (VPR) Model of the Structure of Mental Abilities in the Minnesota Study of Twins Reared Apart. *Intelligence, 35,* 542–562.

Johnson-Motoyama, M., & others (2016). Parent, teacher, and stakeholder perspectives on adolescent pregnancy prevention programming for Latino youth. *Journal of Primary Prevention, 37,* 513–525.

Johnston, C., & others (2017). Skin-to-skin care for procedural pain in infants. *Cochrane Database of Systematic Reviews, 2,* CD008435.

Johnston, L.D., O'Malley, P.M., Bachman, J.G., & Schulenberg, J.E. (2015). *Monitoring the Future national results on drug use: 2014 overview, key findings on adolescent drug use*. Ann Arbor: Institute of Social Research, University of Michigan.

Johnston, L.D., & others (2017). *Monitoring the Future national results 2017*. Ann Arbor, MI: Institute of Social Research, University of Michigan.

Jones, D., & others (2010). The impact of the Fast Track prevention trial on health services utilization by youth at risk for conduct problems. *Pediatrics, 125,* 130–136.

Jones, H.W. (2007). Iatrogenic multiple births: A 2003 checkup. *Fertility and Sterility, 87,* 453–455.

Jones, J.D., & others (2017, in press). Stability of attachment style in adolescence: An empirical test of alternative developmental processes. *Child Development*.

Jones, J.M. (1994). The African American: A duality dilemma? In W.J. Lonner & R. Malpass (Eds.), *Psychology and culture*. Needham Heights, MA: Allyn & Bacon.

Jones, L., & others (2012). Pain management for women in labor: An overview of systematic reviews. *Cochrane Database of Systematic Reviews, 3,* CD009234.

Jones, N.A. (2012). Delayed reactive cries demonstrate emotional and physiological dysregulation in newborns of depressed mothers. *Biological Psychology, 89,* 374–381.

Jones, S.C., & Magee, C.A. (2014). The role of family, friends, and peers in Australian adolescents' alcohol consumption. *Drug and Alcohol Review, 33,* 304–313.

Jonson-Reid, M., Kohl, P.L., & Drake, B. (2012). Child and adolescent outcomes of chronic child maltreatment. *Pediatrics, 129,* 839–845.

Jordan, C.H., & Zeigler-Hill, V. (2013). Secure and fragile forms of self-esteem. In V. Zeigler-Hill (Ed.), *Self-esteem*. New York: Psychology Press.

Joseph, J. (2006). *The missing gene*. New York: Algora.

Josephson Institute of Ethics (2006). *2006 Josephson Institute report card on the ethics of American youth. Part one—integrity*. Los Angeles: Josephson Institute.

Jouriles, E.N., McDonald, R., & Kouros, C.D. (2016). Interparental conflict and child adjustment. In D. Cicchetti (Ed.), *Developmental psychopathology* (3rd ed.). New York: Wiley.

Juang, L.P., & Umana-Taylor, A.J. (2012). Family conflict among Chinese- and Mexican-origin adolescents and their parents in the U.S.: An introduction. *New Directions in Child and Adolescent Development, 135,* 1–12.

Julvez, J., & others (2016). Maternal consumption of seafood in pregnancy and child neuropsychological development: A longitudinal study based on a population with high consumption levels. *American Journal of Epidemiology, 183,* 169–182.

Jung, E.Y., & others (2017). Amniotic fluid infection, cytokine levels, and mortality and adverse pulmonary, intestinal, and neurologic outcomes in infant at 32 weeks' gestation or less. *Journal of Korean Medical Science, 32,* 480–487.

Juraska, J.M., & Willing, J. (2017). Pubertal onset as a critical transition for neural development and cognition. *Brain Research, 1654*(Pt. B), 87–94.

Juster, R-P., & others (2016). Social inequalities and the road to allostatic load. In D. Cicchetti (Ed.), *Developmental psychopathology* (3rd ed.). New York: Wiley.

K

Kadir, M.S., & Yeung, A.S. (2018). Academic self-concept. In V. Zeigler-Hill & T.K. Shackelford (Eds.), *Encyclopedia of personality and individual differences*. New York: Springer.

Kagan, J. (1992). Yesterday's premises, tomorrow's promises. *Developmental Psychology, 28,* 990–997.

Kagan, J. (2000). Temperament. In A. Kazdin (Ed.), *Encyclopedia of psychology*. New York: Oxford University Press.

Kagan, J. (2002). Behavioral inhibition as a temperamental category. In R.J. Davidson, K.R. Scherer, & H.H. Goldsmith (Eds.), *Handbook of affective sciences*. New York: Oxford University Press.

Kagan, J. (2008). Fear and wariness. In M.M. Haith & J.B. Benson (Eds.), *Encyclopedia of infant and early childhood development*. Oxford, UK: Elsevier.

Kagan, J. (2010). Emotions and temperament. In M.H. Bornstein (Ed.), *Handbook of cultural developmental science*. New York: Psychology Press.

Kagan, J. (2013). Temperamental contributions to inhibited and uninhibited profiles. In P.D. Zelazo (Ed.), *Oxford handbook of developmental psychology*. New York: Oxford University Press.

Kagan, J., Kearsley, R.B., & Zelazo, P.R. (1978). *Infancy: Its place in human development*. Cambridge, MA: Harvard University Press.

Kagan, J., & Snidman, N. (1991). Infant predictors of inhibited and uninhibited behavioral profiles. *Psychological Science, 2,* 40–44.

Kahn, J.A., & others (2008). Patterns and determinants of physical activity in U.S. adolescents. *Journal of Adolescent Health, 42,* 369–377.

Kahrs, B.A., Jung, W.P., & Lochman, J.J. (2013). Motor origins of tool use. *Child Development, 84*(3), 810–816.

Kalant, H. (2004). Adverse effects of cannabis on health: An update of the literature since 1996. *Progress in Neuropsychopharmacology and Biological Psychiatry, 28,* 849–863.

Kalesan, B., & others (2017). The hidden epidemic of firearm injury: Increasing firearm injury rates during 2001–2013. *American Journal of Epidemiology, 185,* 546–553.

Kamii, C. (1985). *Young children reinvent arithmetic: Implications of Piaget's theory*. New York: Teachers College Press.

Kamii, C. (1989). *Young children continue to reinvent arithmetic*. New York: Teachers College Press.

Kamp Dush, C.M., Rhoades, G.K., Sandberg, S.E., & Schoppe-Sullivan, S. (2014). Commitment across the transition to parenthood among married and cohabiting couples. *Couple and Family Psychology, 3,* 126–136.

Kanazawa, S. (2015). Breastfeeding is positively associated with child intelligence even net of parental IQ. *Developmental Psychology, 51,* 1683–1689.

Kane, J.C., & others (2016). The impact of intergenerational cultural dissonance on alcohol use among Vietnamese and Cambodian adolescents in the Untied States. *Journal of Adolescent Health, 58,* 174–180.

Kang, E., Klein, E., Lillard, A., & Lerner, M. (2016). Predictors and moderators of spontaneous pretend play in children with and without autism spectrum disorder. *Frontiers in Pschology, 7,* 1577.

Kang, P.P., & Romo, L.F. (2011). The role of religious involvement on depression, risky behavior, and academic performance among Korean American adolescents. *Journal of Adolescence, 34*(4), 767–778.

Kang, X., & others (2017, in press). Post-mortem whole-body magnetic resonance imaging of human fetuses: A comparison of 3-T vs. 1.5-T MR imaging with classical autopsy. *European Radiology*.

Kann, L., & others (2016a, June 10). Youth Risk Behavior Surveillance—United States 2015. *MMWR, 65,* 1–174.

Kann, L., & others (2016b, August 12). Sexual identity, sex of sexual contacts, and health-related behaviors among students in grades 9–12—United States and selected sites, 2015. *MMWR Surveillance Summary, 65*(9), 1–202.

Kantrowitz, B. (1991, Summer). The good, the bad, and the difference. *Newsweek*, pp. 48–50.

Kao, T.A., & Huang, B. (2015). Bicultural straddling among immigrant adolescents: A concept analysis. *Journal of Holistic Nursing, 33,* 269–281.

Kaplan, R.M., & Saccuzzo, D.P. (2018). *Psychological testing* (9th ed.). Boston: Cengage.

Kar, B.R., Rao, S.L., & Chandramouli, B.A. (2008). Cognitive development in children with chronic energy malnutrition. *Behavioral and Brain Functions, 4,* 31.

Karasik, L.B., Tamis-LeMonda, C.S., & Adolph, K.E. (2016). Decisions on the brink: Locomotor experience affects infants' use of social information on an adjustable drop-off. *Frontiers in Psychology, 7,* 797.

Karniol, R., Grosz, E., & Schorr, I. (2003). Caring, gender-role orientation, and volunteering. *Sex Roles, 49,* 11–19.

Karoly, L.A., & Bigelow, J.H. (2005). *The economics of investing in universal preschool education in California.* Santa Monica, CA: RAND Corporation.

Karreman, A., van Tuijl, C., van Aken, M.A.G., & Dekovic, M. (2008). Parenting, coparenting, and effortful control in preschoolers. *Journal of Family Psychology, 22,* 30–40.

Kashou, N.H., & others (2017). Somatic stimulation causes frontoparietal cortical changes in neonates: A functional near-infrared spectroscopy study. *Neurophotonics, 4,* 011004.

Kastbom, A.A., & others (2015). Sexual debut before the age of 14 leads to poorer psychosocial health and risky behavior in later life. *Acta Pediatrica, 104,* 91–100.

Kato, T., & others (2016). Extremely preterm infants small for gestational age are at risk for motor impairment at 3 years corrected age. *Brain Development, 38,* 188–195.

Katsiaficas, D., Suarez-Orozco, C., Sirin, S.R., & Gupta, T. (2013). Mediators of the relationship between acculturative stress and internalizing symptoms for immigrant origin youth. *Cultural Diversity and Ethnic Minority Psychology, 19,* 27–37.

Katz, J., & others (2013). Mortality risk in preterm and small-for-gestational-age infants in low-income and middle-income countries: A pooled country analysis. *Lancet, 382,* 427–451.

Katz, L. (1999). Curriculum disputes in early childhood education. *ERIC Clearinghouse on Elementary and Early Childhood Education,* Document EDO-PS-99–13.

Katz, P.A. (1987, August). *Children and social issues.* Paper presented at the meeting of the American Psychological Association, New York.

Kauchak, D., & Eggen, P. (2017). *Introduction to teaching* (6th ed.). Upper Saddle River, NJ: Pearson.

Kauffman Early Education Exchange (2002). *Set for success: Building a strong foundation for school readiness based on the social-emotional development of young children* (Vol. 1, No. 1). Kansas City: The Ewing Marion Kauffman Foundation.

Kauffman, J.M., & Hallahan, D.P. (2005). *Special education.* Boston: Allyn & Bacon.

Kauffman, J.M., McGee, K., & Brigham, M. (2004). Enabling or disabling? Observations on changes in special education. *Phi Delta Kappan, 85,* 613–620.

Kaunhoven, R.J., & Dorjee, D. (2017). How does mindfulness modulate self-regulation in pre-adolescent children? An integrative neurocognitive review. *Neuroscience and Biobehavioral Reviews, 74*(Pt. A), 163–184.

Kaushik, G., & others (2016). Maternal exposure to carbamazepine at environmental concentrations can cross intestinal and placental barriers. *Biochemical and Biophysical Research Communications, 474,* 291–295.

Kavanaugh, R.D. (2006). Pretend play and theory of mind. In L.L. Balter & C.S. Tamis-LeMonda (Eds.), *Child psychology* (2nd ed.). New York: Psychology Press.

Kavsek, M. (2004). Predicting IQ from infant visual habituation and dishabituation: A meta-analysis. *Journal of Applied Developmental Psychology, 25,* 369–393.

Kawakita, T., & others (2016). Adverse maternal and neonatal outcomes in adolescent pregnancy. *Journal of Pediatric and Adolescent Gynecology, 29,* 130–136.

Kaye, W.H., & others (2013). Nothing tastes as good as skinny feels: The neurobiology of anorexia nervosa. *Trends in Neuroscience, 36,* 110–120.

Kaynak, O., & others (2013). Relationships among parental monitoring and sensation seeking on the development of substance use disorder among college students. *Addictive Behaviors, 38,* 1457–1463.

Kazdin, A.E. (2017). *REVEL for research design in clinical psychology* (5th ed.). Upper Saddle River, NJ: Pearson.

Keating, D.P. (1990). Adolescent thinking. In S.S. Feldman & G.R. Elliott (Eds.), *At the threshold: The developing adolescent.* Cambridge, MA: Harvard University Press.

Keating, D.P. (2004). Cognitive and brain development. In R. Lerner & L. Steinberg (Eds.), *Handbook of adolescent psychology.* New York: Wiley.

Keating, D.P. (2007). Understanding adolescent development: Implications for driving safety. *Journal of Safety Research, 38,* 147–157.

Keating, D.P. (2009). Developmental science and giftedness: An integrated life-span framework. In F.D. Horowitz, R.F. Subotnik, & D.J. Matthews (Eds.), *The development of giftedness and talent across the life span.* Washington, DC: American Psychological Association.

Keen, R. (2005). Unpublished review of J.W. Santrock, *A topical approach to life-span development,* 3rd ed. (New York: McGraw-Hill).

Keen, R. (2011). The development of problem solving in young children: A critical cognitive skill. *Annual Review of Psychology* (Vol. 63). Palo Alto, CA: Annual Reviews.

Keen, R., Lee, M-H., & Adolph, K.E. (2014). Planning and action: A developmental progression for tool use. *Ecological Psychology, 26,* 98–108.

Keller, A., Ford, L., & Meacham, J. (1978). Dimensions of self-concept in preschool children. *Developmental Psychology, 14,* 483–489.

Keller, A., & others (2016). Validating Alzheimer's disease micro RNAs using next-generation sequencing. *Alzheimer's and Dementia, 12,* 565–576.

Kelley, G.A., & Kelley, K.S. (2013). Effects of exercise in the treatment of overweight and obese children and adolescents: A systematic review and analysis. *Journal of Obesity.* doi:10.1155/2013/783103

Kellman, P.J., & Banks, M.S. (1998). Infant visual perception. In W. Damon (Ed.), *Handbook of child psychology* (5th ed., Vol. 2). New York: Wiley.

Kellogg, R. (1970). *Understanding children's art: Readings in developmental psychology today.* Del Mar, CA: CRM.

Kelly, A.B., & others (2011). The influence of parents, siblings, and peers on pre- and early-teen smoking: A multilevel model. *Drug and Alcohol Review, 30,* 381–387.

Kelly, A.B., & others (2016). Depressed mood during early to middle adolescence: A bi-national longitudinal study of the unique impact of family conflict. *Journal of Youth and Adolescence, 45,* 604–613.

Kelly, D.J., & others (2007). Cross-race preferences for same-race faces extend beyond the African versus Caucasian contrast in 3-month-old infants. *Infancy, 11,* 87–95.

Kelly, D.J., & others (2009). Development of the other-race effect in infancy: Evidence towards universality? *Journal of Experimental Child Psychology, 104,* 105–114.

Kelly, J.P., Borchert, J., & Teller, D.Y. (1997). The development of chromatic and achromatic sensitivity in infancy as tested with the sweep VEP. *Vision Research, 37,* 2057–2072.

Kelly, Y., & others (2013). Light drinking versus abstinence in pregnancy—behavioral and cognitive outcomes in 7-year-old children: A longitudinal cohort study. *BJOG, 120,* 1340–1347.

Kelmanson, I.A. (2010). Sleep disturbances in two-month-old infants sharing the bed with parent(s). *Minerva Pediatrica, 62,* 162–169.

Keltner, K.W. (2013). *Tiger babies strike back.* New York: William Morrow.

Kendler, K.S., Ohlsson, H., Sundquist, K., & Sundquist, J. (2016). The rearing environment and risk for drug abuse: A Swedish national high-risk adopted and not adopted co-sibling control study. *Psychological Medicine, 46,* 1359–1366.

Kendrick, K., Jutengren, G., & Stattin, H. (2012). The protective role of supportive friends against bullying perpetration and victimization. *Journal of Adolescence, 35*(4), 1069–1080.

Kennedy, E., & Guthrie, J.F. (2016). Nutrition assistance programs: Cause or solution to obesity. *Current Obesity Reports, 5,* 175–183.

Kennell, J.H. (2006). Randomized controlled trial of skin-to-skin contact from birth versus conventional incubator for physiological stabilization in 1200 g to 2199 g newborns. *Acta Paediatrica, 95,* 15–16.

Kenner, C., Sugrue, N.M., & Finkelman, A. (2007). How nurses around the world can make a difference. *Nursing for women's health, 11,* 468–473.

Kerig, P. (2016). Family systems from a developmental psychopathology perspective. In D. Cicchetti (Ed.), *Developmental psychopathology* (3rd ed.). New York: Wiley.

Kerns, K.A., & Brumariu, L.E. (2016). Attachment in middle childhood. In J. Cassidy & P. Shaver (Eds.), *Handbook of attachment* (3rd ed.). New York: Guilford.

Kerns, K.A., & Seibert, A.C. (2012). Finding your way through the thicket: Promising approaches to assessing attachment in middle childhood. In E. Waters & B. Vaughn (Eds.), *Measuring attachment.* New York: Guilford.

Kerns, K.A., & Seibert, A.C. (2016). Finding your way through the thicket: Promising approaches to assessing attachment in middle childhood. In E. Waters, B. Vaughn, & H. Waters (Eds.), *Measuring attachment.* New York: Guilford.

Kerns, K.A., Siener, S., & Brumariu, L.E. (2011). Mother-child relationships, family context, and child characteristics as predictors of anxiety symptoms in middle childhood. *Development and Psychopathology, 23,* 593–604.

Kerr, G., & Stirling, A. (2017). Issues of maltreatment in high-performance athlete development: Mental toughness as a threat. In J. Baker & others (Eds.), *Routledge handbook of talent identification and development in sport.* New York: Routledge.

Kerstis, B., & others (2016). Association between parental depressive symptoms and impaired bonding with the infant. *Archives of Women's Mental Health, 19,* 87–94.

Kessler, R.C., & Waters, E.E. (1988). Epidemiology of DSM-III-R major depression and minor depression among adolescents and young adults in the National Comorbidity Survey. *Depression and Anxiety, 7,* 3–14.

Kesten, J.M., & others (2015). Understanding the accuracy of parental perceptions of child physical activity: A mixed methods analysis. *Journal of Physical Activity and Health. 12,* 1529–1535.

Keunen, K., Counsell, & Benders, M.J. (2017, in press). The emergence of functional architecture during early brain development. *NeuroImage.*

Keyes, K.M., Maslowsky, J., Hamilton, A., & Schulenberg, J. (2015). The great sleep recession: Changes in sleep duration among U.S. adolescents, 1991–2012. *Pediatrics, 135,* 460–468.

Kharitonova, M., Winter, W., & Sheridan, M.A. (2015). As working memory grows: A developmental account of neural bases of working memory capacity in 5- to 8-year-old children and adults. *Journal of Cognitive Neuroscience, 27,* 1775–1788.

Khoury, J.E., & Milligan, K. (2017, in press). Comparing executive functioning in children and adolescents with fetal alcohol spectrum disorders and ADHD: A meta-analysis. *Journal of Attention Disorders.*

Khundrakpam., B.S., & others (2017, in press). Cortical thickness abnormalities in autism spectrum disorders through late childhood, adolescence, and adulthood: A large-scale MRI study. *Cerebral Cortex.*

Khurana, A., & others (2012). Early adolescent sexual debut: The mediating role of working memory, sensation seeking, and impulsivity. *Developmental Psychology, 48,* 1416–1428.

Kiblawi, Z.N., & others (2013). The effect of prenatal methamphetamine exposure on attention as assessed by continuous performance tests: Results from the Infant Development, Environment, and Lifestyle Study. *Journal of Developmental and Behavioral Pediatrics, 34,* 31–37.

Kidd, C., Piantadosi, S.T., & Aslin, R.N. (2012). The Goldilocks effect: Human infants allocate attention to visual sequences that are neither too simple nor too complex. *PLoS One, 7*(5), e36399.

Kiess, W., & others (2016). Puberty—genes, environment, and clinical issues. *Journal of Pediatric Endocrinology and Metabolism, 29,* 1229–1231.

Kilic, S., & others (2012). Environmental tobacco smoke exposure during intrauterine period promotes granulosa cell apoptosis: A prospective, randomized study. *Journal of Maternal-Fetal and Neonatal Medicine, 25*(10), 1904–1908.

Killen, M., & Dahl, A., (2018). Moral judgment: Reflective, interactive, spontaneous, challenging, and always evolving. In K. Gray & J. Graham (Eds.), *The atlas of moral psychology.* New York: Guilford.

Killen, M., & Smetana, J.G. (2015). Morality: Origins and development. In R.M. Lerner (Ed.), *Handbook of child psychology and developmental science* (7th ed.). New York: Wiley.

Kim, B.R., & others (2017). Trajectories of mothers' emotional availability: Relations with infant temperament in predicting attachment security. *Attachment and Human Development, 19,* 38–57.

Kim, H.J., Yang, J., & Lee, M.S. (2015). Changes of heart rate variability during methylphenidate treatment in attention-deficit hyperactivity disorder children: A 12-week prospective study. *Yonsei Medical Journal, 56,* 1365–1371.

Kim, K.H. (2010, May). Unpublished data. School of Education, College of William & Mary, Williamsburg, VA.

Kim, M.J., Catalano, R.F., Haggerty, K.P., & Abbott, R.D. (2011). Bullying at elementary school and problem behavior in young adulthood: A study of bullying, violence, and substance use from age 11 to age 21. *Criminal Behavior and Mental Health, 21,* 36–44.

Kim, P., Strathearn, L., & Swain, J.E. (2016). The maternal brain and its plasticity in humans. *Hormones and Behavior, 77,* 113–123.

Kim, S., & Kochanska, G. (2017, in press). Relational antecedents and social implications of the emotion of empathy: Evidence from three studies. *Emotion.*

Kim, S., Kochanska, G., Boldt, L.J., Nordling, J.K., & O'Bleness, J.J. (2014). Developmental trajectory from early responses to transgressions to future antisocial behavior: Evidence for the role of the parent-child relationship from two longitudinal studies. *Development and Psychopathology, 26,* 93–109.

Kim, S.H., & others (2017, in press). Early menarche and risk-taking behavior in Korean adolescent students. *Asia Pacific-Psychiatry.*

Kim, S.M., Han, D.H., Trksak, G.H., & Lee, Y.S. (2014). Gender differences in adolescent coping behaviors and suicidal ideation: Findings from a sample of 73,238 adolescents. *Anxiety, Stress, and Coping, 27,* 439–454.

Kim, S.Y., Wang, Y., Chen, Q., Shen, Y., & Hou, Y. (2015). Parent-child acculturation profiles as predictors of Chinese American adolescents' academic trajectories. *Journal of Youth and Adolescence, 44,* 1263–1274.

Kindermann, T.A. (2016). Peer group influences on students' academic achievement and social behavior. In K. Wentzel & G. Ramani (Eds.), *Handbook of social influences in school contexts.* New York: Psychology Press.

King, J.D., & others (2017, in press). The interpersonal-psychological theory of suicide in adolescents: A preliminary report of changes following treatment. *Suicide and Life-Threatening Behavior.*

King, K.M., & others (2017, in press). Externalizing behavior across childhood as reported by parents and teachers: A partial measurement invariance model. *Assessment.*

King, L.A. (2017). *Psychology: An appreciative experience* (4th ed.). New York: McGraw-Hill.

King, P.E., & Boyatzis, C.J. (2015). The nature and functions of religious and spiritual development in childhood and adolescence. In R.M. Lerner (Ed.), *Handbook of child psychology and developmental science* (7th ed.). New York: Oxford University Press.

King, P.E., Carr, A., & Boiter, C. (2011). Spirituality, religiosity, and youth thriving. In R.M. Lerner, J.V. Lerner, & J.B. Benson (Eds.), *Advances in child development and behavior: Positive youth development.* New York: Elsevier.

Kingdon, D., Cardoso, C., & McGrath, J.J. (2016). Research review: Executive function deficits in fetal alcohol spectrum disorders and attention-deficit/ hyperactivity disorder—a meta-analysis. *Journal of Child Psychology and Psychiatry, 57,* 116–131.

Kingo, O.S., & Krojgaard, P. (2015). Eighteen-month-olds' memory for short movies of simple shots. *Scandinavian Journal of Psychology, 56,* 151–156.

Kingsbury, A.M., & others (2017). Does having a difficult child lead to poor mental health outcomes? *Public Health, 146,* 46–55.

Kiray, H., Lindsay, S.L., Hosseinzadeh, S., & Barnett, S.C. (2016). The multifaceted role of astrocytes in regulating myelination. *Experimental Neurology, 283*(Pt. B), 541–549.

Kirbas, A., Gulerman, H.C., & Daglar, K. (2016). Pregnancy in adolescence: Is it an obstetrical risk? *Journal of Pediatric and Adolescent Gynecology, 29,* 367–371.

Kirk, S.M., & Kirk, E.P. (2016). Sixty minutes of physical activity per day included within preschool academic lessons improves early literacy. *Journal of School Health, 86,* 155–163.

Kirkham, N.Z., Wagner, J.B., Swan, K.A., & Johnson, S.P. (2012). Sound support: Intermodal information facilitates infants' perception of an occluded trajectory. *Infant Behavior and Development, 35,* 174–178.

Kirkorian, H.L., Anderson, D.R., & Keen, R. (2012). Age differences in online processing of video: An eye movement study. *Child Development, 83,* 497–507.

Kisilevsky, B.S., & others (2009). Fetal sensitivity to properties of maternal speech and language. *Infant Behavior and Development, 32,* 59–71.

Kitagawa, H., & Pringle, K.C. (2017, in press). Fetal surgery: A critical review. *Pediatric Surgery International.*

Kitsantas, P., & Gaffney, K.F. (2010). Racial/ ethnic disparities in infant mortality. *Journal of Perinatal Medicine, 38,* 87–94.

Kiuhara, S.A., Graham, S., & Hawken, L.S. (2009). Teaching writing to high school students: A national survey. *Journal of Educational Psychology, 101,* 136–160.

Klaczynski, P.A., & Narasimham, G. (1998). Development of scientific reasoning biases: Cognitive versus ego-protective explanations. *Developmental Psychology, 34,* 175–187.

Klahr, A.M., & Burt, S.A. (2014). Elucidating the etiology of individual differences in parenting: A meta-analysis of behavioral genetic research. *Psychological Bulletin, 140,* 544–586.

Klatt, J., & Enright, R. (2009). Investigating the place of forgiveness within the positive youth development paradigm. *Journal of Moral Education, 38,* 35–52.

Klaus, M., & Kennell, H.H. (1976). *Maternal-infant bonding.* St. Louis: Mosby.

Klein, A.C. (2017). *Every Student Succeeds Act.* Retrieved from http://blogs.edweek.org/edweek/ campaign-k-12/2017/03/trunp_educ. . .

Klein, M.R., & others (2017, in press). Bidirectional relations between temperament and parenting predicting preschool-age children's adjustment. *Journal of Clinical Child and Adolescent Psychology.*

Klein, S. (2012). *State of public school segregation in the United States 2007–2010.* Washington, DC: Feminist Majority Foundation.

Kliegman, R.M., Stanton, B., St. Geme, J., & Schor, N. (2016). *Nelson textbook of pediatrics* (20th ed.). New York: Elsevier.

Kliegman, R.M., & others (2017). *Nelson pediatric symptom-based diagnosis.* New York: Elsevier.

Klimstra, T.A., & others (2017). Daily dynamics of adolescent mood and identity. *Journal of Research on Adolescence, 28,* 459–473.

Klimstra, T.A., Hale, W.W., Raaijmakers, Q.A.W., Branje, S.J.T., & Meeus, W.H.H. (2010). Identity formation in adolescence: Change or stability? *Journal of Youth and Adolescence, 39,* 150–162.

Klug, J., & others (2016). Secondary school students' LLL competencies, and their relation with classroom structure and achievement. *Frontiers in Psychology, 7,* 680.

Klug, W.S., & others (2017). *Essentials of genetics* (9th ed.). Upper Saddle River, NJ: Pearson.

Knapp, K., & Morton, J.B. (2017). Executive functioning: A developmental cognitive neuroscience perspective. In M.J. Hoskyn & others (Eds.), *Executive function in children's everyday lives.* New York: Oxford University Press.

Knight, C.J. (2017). Family influences on talent development in sport. In J. Baker & others (Eds.), *Routledge handbook of talent identification and development in sport.* New York: Routledge.

Knowles, E.E., & others (2016). Genome-wide linkage on chromosome 10q26 for a dimensional scale of major depression. *Journal of Affective Disorders, 191,* 123–131.

Knox, M. (2010). On hitting children: A review of corporal punishment in the United States. *Journal of Pediatric Health Care, 24,* 103–107.

Ko, Y.L., Yang, C.L., Fang, C.L., Lee, M.Y., & Lin, P.C. (2013). Community-based postpartum exercise program. *Journal of Clinical Nursing, 22,* 2122–2131.

Kobak, R.R., & Kerig, P.K. (2015). Introduction to the special issue: Attachment-based treatments for adolescents. *Attachment and Human Development, 17,* 111–118.

Kobayashi, K., & others (2005). Fetal growth restriction associated with measles virus infection during pregnancy. *Journal of Perinatal Medicine, 31,* 67–68.

Kobayashi, S., & others (2017). Assessment and support during early labor for improving birth outcomes. *Cochrane Database of Systematic Reviews, 4,* CD011516.

Kochanska, G., & Aksan, N. (2007). Conscience in childhood: Past, present, and future. *Merrill-Palmer Quarterly, 50,* 299–310.

Kochanska, G., Aksan N., Prisco, T.R., & Adams, E.E. (2008). Mother-child and father-child mutually responsive orientation in the first two years and children's outcomes at preschool age: Mechanisms of influence. *Child Development, 79,* 30–44.

Kochanska, G., Forman, D.R., Aksan, N., & Dunbar, S.B. (2005). Pathways to conscience: Early mother-child mutually responsive orientation and children's moral emotion, conduct, and cognition. *Journal of Child Psychology and Psychiatry, 46,* 19–34.

Kochanska, G., Gross, J.N., Lin, M., & Nichols, K.E. (2002). Guilt in young children: Development, determinants, and relations with a broader set of standards. *Child Development, 73,* 461–482.

Kochanska, G., & Kim, S. (2012). Toward a new understanding of the legacy of early attachments for future antisocial trajectories: Evidence from two longitudinal studies. *Development and Psychopathology, 24*(3), 783–806.

Kochanska, G., & Kim, S. (2013). Early attachment organization with both parents and future behavior problems: From infancy to middle childhood. *Child Development, 84*(1), 283–296.

Kochanska, G., Koenig, J.L., Barry, R.A., Kim, S., & Yoon, J.E. (2010). Children's conscience during toddler and preschool years, moral self, and a competent, adaptive development trajectory. *Development Psychology, 46,* 1320–1332.

Kochendorfer, L.B., & Kerns, K.A. (2017, in press). Perceptions of parent-child attachment relationships and friendship qualities: Predictors of romantic relationship involvement and quality in adolescence. *Journal of Youth and Adolescence.*

Koeneman, O., & Zeijstra, H. (2017). *Introducing syntax.* New York: Cambridge University Press.

Koenig, L.B., McGue, M., & Iacono, W.G. (2008). Stability and change in religiousness during emerging adulthood. *Developmental Psychology, 44,* 523–543.

Koh, H. (2014). The Teen Pregnancy Prevention Program: An evidence-based public health program model. *Journal of Adolescent Health, 54*(Suppl. 1), S1–S2.

Kohan-Ghadr, H.R., & others (2016). Potential role of epigenetic mechanisms in regulation of trophoblast differentiation, migration, and invasion in the human placenta. *Cell Adhesion and Migration, 10,* 126–135.

Kohlberg, L. (1958). *The development of modes of moral thinking and choice in the years 10 to 16.* Unpublished doctoral dissertation, University of Chicago.

Kohlberg, L. (1969). Stage and sequence: The cognitive-developmental approach to socialization. In D.A. Goslin (Ed.), *Handbook of socialization theory and research.* Chicago: Rand McNally.

Kohlberg, L. (1986). A current statement of some theoretical issues. In S. Modgil & C. Modgil (Eds.), *Lawrence Kohlberg.* Philadelphia: Falmer.

Kohlhoff, J., & others (2017). Oxytocin in the postnatal period: Associations with attachment and maternal caregiving. *Comprehensive Psychiatry, 76,* 56–68.

Kok, F.M., Groen, Y., Fuermaler, A.B., & Tucha, O. (2016). Problematic peer functioning in girls with ADHD: A systematic literature review. *PLoS One, 11,* e0165118.

Kok, R., & others (2015). Normal variation in early parental sensitivity predicts child structural brain development. *Journal of the American Academy of Child and Adolescent Psychiatry, 54,* 824–831.

Kominiarek, M.A., & Chauhan, S.P. (2016). Obesity before, during, and after pregnancy: A review and comparison of five national guidelines. *American Journal of Perinatology, 33,* 433–441.

Kondolot, M., & others (2017, in press). Risk factors for overweight and obesity in children 2–6 years. *Journal of Pediatric Endocrinology and Metabolism.*

Kong, A., & others (2012). Rate of *de novo* mutations and the importance of father's age to disease risk. *Nature, 488,* 471–475.

Kopp, C.B. (2008). Self-regulatory processes. In M.M. Haith & J.B. Benson (Eds.), *Encyclopedia of infant and early childhood development.* Oxford, UK: Elsevier.

Koppelman, K.L. (2017). *Understanding human differences* (5th ed.). Upper Saddle River, NJ: Pearson.

Korat, O. (2009). The effect of maternal teaching talk on children's emergent literacy as a function of type of activity and maternal education level.

Journal of Applied Developmental Psychology, 30, 34–42.

Korja, R., & others (2017, in press). The relations between maternal prenatal anxiety or stress and the child's early negative reactivity or self-regulation: A systematic review. *Child Psychiatry and Human Development.*

Kornblum, J. (2006, March 9). How to monitor the kids? *USA Today,* 1D, p.1.

Kornienko, O., Santos, C.E., Martin, C.L., & Granger, K.L. (2016). Peer influence on gender identity development in adolescence. *Developmental Psychology, 52,* 1578–1592.

Koss, K.J., & others (2011). Understanding children's emotional processes and behavioral strategies in the context of marital conflict. *Journal of Experimental Child Psychology, 109,* 336–352.

Koss, K.J., & others (2013). Patterns of children's adrenocortical reactivity to interparental conflict and associations with child adjustment: A growth mixture modeling approach. *Developmental Psychology, 49*(2), 317–326.

Koss, K.J., & others (2014). Asymmetry in children's salivary cortisol and alpha-amylase in the context of marital conflict: Links to children's emotional security and adjustment. *Developmental Psychobiology, 56,* 836–849.

Koss-Chioino, J.D., & Vargas, L.A. (1999). *Working with Latino youth: Culture, context, and development.* New York: Jossey-Bass.

Kostelnik, M.J., Rupiper, M.L., Soderman, A.K., & Whiren, A.P. (2014). *Developmentally appropriate curriculum in action.* Upper Saddle River, NJ: Pearson.

Kothandan, S.K. (2014). School-based interventions versus family-based interventions in the treatment of childhood obesity—a systematic review. *Archives of Public Health, 72,* 3.

Kotovsky, L., & Baillargeon, R. (1994). Calibration-based reasoning about collision events in 11-month-old infants. *Cognition, 51,* 107–129.

Koumbaris, G., & others (2016). Cell-free DNA analysis of targeted genomic regions in maternal plasma for non-invasive prenatal testing of trisomy 21, trisomy 18, trisomy 13, and fetal sex. *Clinical Chemistry, 62,* 848–855.

Kouros, C.D., & El-Sheikh, M. (2017, in press). Within-family relations in objective sleep duration, quality, and schedule. *Child Development.*

Kouros, C.D., Morris, M.C., & Garber, J. (2016). Within-person changes in individual symptoms of depression predict subsequent depressive episodes in adolescents: A prospective study. *Journal of Abnormal Child Psychology, 44,* 483–494.

Kovar, S.K., Combs, C.A., Campbell, K., Napper-Owen, G., & Worrell, V.J. (2007). *Elementary classroom teachers as movement educators* (2nd ed.). New York: McGraw-Hill.

Kowalski, R.M., Giumetti, G.W., Schroeder, A.N., & Lattanner, M.R. (2014). Bullying in the digital age: A critical review and meta-analysis of cyberbullying research on youth. *Psychological Bulletin, 140,* 1073–1137.

Kozhimannil, K.B., & others (2013). Doula care, birth outcomes, and costs among Medicaid beneficiaries. *American Journal of Public Health, 103,* e113–e121.

Kozol, J. (2005). *The shame of the nation.* New York: Crown.

Krafft, C.E., & others (2014). An 8-month randomized controlled exercise trial alters brain activation during cognitive tasks in overweight children. *Obesity, 22,* 232–242.

Kramer, H.J., & Lagattuta, K.H. (2018, in press). Social categorization. In M.H. Bornstein & others (Eds.), *SAGE handbook of lifespan development.* Thousand Oaks, CA: Sage.

Kramer, L. (2006, July 10). Commentary in "How your siblings make you who you are" by J. Kluger. *Time,* pp. 46–55.

Kramer, L., & Perozynski, L. (1999). Parental beliefs about managing sibling conflict. *Developmental Psychology, 35,* 489–499.

Kramer, L., & Radey, C. (1997). Improving sibling relationships among young children: A social skills training model. *Family Relations, 46,* 237–246.

Kranz, S., & Siega-Riz, A.M. (2002). Sociodemographic determinants of added sugar intake in preschoolers 2 to 5 years old. *Journal of Pediatrics, 140,* 667–672.

Krebs, A., & others (2016). Decrease of small dense LDL and lipoprotein-associated phospholipase A_2 due to human growth hormone treatment in short children with hormone growth deficiency and small for gestational age status. *Journal of Pediatric Endocrinology and Metabolism, 29,* 203–208.

Kretch, K.S., & Adolph, K.E. (2013). No bridge too high: Infants decide whether to cross based on bridge width, not drop-off height. *Developmental Science, 16,* 336–351.

Kretch, K.S., & Adolph, K.E. (2017, in press). The organization of exploratory behaviors in infant locomotor planning. *Developmental Science.*

Kretch, K.S., Franchak, J.M., Adolph, K.E. (2014). Crawling and walking infants see the world differently. *Child Development, 85,* 1503–1516.

Kreutzer, M., Leonard, C., & Flavell, J.H. (1975). An interview study of children's knowledge about memory. *Monographs of the Society for Research in Child Development, 40*(1, Serial No. 159).

Kriemler, S., & others (2010). Effect of school-based physical activity programme (KISS) on fitness and adiposity in primary schoolchildren: Cluster randomised controlled trial. *British Medical Journal, 340.*

Krimer, L.S., & Goldman-Rakic, P.S. (2001). Prefrontal microcircuits. *Journal of Neuroscience, 21,* 3788–3796.

Kring, A.M. (2000). Gender and anger. In A.H. Fischer (Ed.), *Gender and emotion.* New York: Cambridge University Press.

Kroger, J. (2015). Identity development through adulthood: The move toward "wholeness." In K.C. McLean & M. Syed (Eds.), *Oxford handbook of identity development.* New York: Oxford University Press.

Kroger, J., Martinussen, M., & Marcia, J.E. (2010). Identity change during adolescence and young adulthood: A meta-analysis. *Journal of Adolescence, 33,* 683–698.

Krogh-Jespersen, S., Liberman, Z., & Woodward, A.L. (2015). Think fast! The relationship between goal prediction speed and social competence in infants. *Developmental Science, 18,* 815–823.

Krogh-Jespersen, S., & Woodward, A.L. (2016). Infant origins of social cognition. In L. Balter & C. Tamis-LeMonda (Eds.), *Child psychology* (3rd ed.). New York: Psychology Press.

Kroll-Desrosiers, A.R., & others (2016). Improving pregnancy outcomes through maternity care coordination: A systematic review. *Women's Health Issues, 26,* 87–99.

Kucian, K., & von Aster, M. (2015). Developmental dyscalculia. *European Journal of Pediatrics, 174,* 1–13.

Kuebli, J. (1994, March). Young children's understanding of everyday emotions. *Young Children,* pp. 36–48.

Kuhl, P.K. (1993). Infant speech perception: A window on psycholinguistic development. *International Journal of Psycholinguistics, 9,* 33–56.

Kuhl, P.K. (2000). A new view of language acquisition. *Proceedings of the National Academy of Science, 97*(22), 11850–11857.

Kuhl, P.K. (2007). Is speech learning "gated" by the social brain? *Developmental Science, 10,* 110–120.

Kuhl, P.K. (2009). Linking infant speech perception to language acquisition: Phonetic learning predicts language growth. In J. Colombo, P. McCardle, & L. Freund (Eds.), *Infant pathways to language.* Clifton, NJ: Psychology Press.

Kuhl, P.K. (2011). Social mechanisms in early language acquisition: Understanding integrated brain systems and supporting language. In J. Decety & J. Cacioppo (Eds.), *Handbook of social neuroscience.* New York: Oxford University Press.

Kuhl, P.K. (2013). Language learning and the developing brain: Cross-cultural studies unravel the effects of biology and culture. *Journal of the Acoustical Society of America 131*(4), 3207.

Kuhl, P.K. (2015). Baby talk. *Scientific American, 313,* 64–69.

Kuhn, D. (1998). Afterword to Volume 2: Cognition, perception, and language. In W. Damon (Ed.), *Handbook of child psychology* (5th ed., Vol. 2). New York: Wiley.

Kuhn, D. (1999). Metacognitive development. In L. Balter & S. Tamis-Lemonda (Eds.), *Child psychology: A handbook of contemporary issues.* Philadelphia: Psychology Press.

Kuhn, D. (2009). Adolescent thinking. In R.M. Lerner & L. Steinberg (Eds.), *Handbook of adolescent psychology* (3rd ed.). New York: Wiley.

Kuhn, D. (2011). What is scientific thinking and how does it develop? In U. Goswami (Ed.), *Wiley-Blackwell handbook of childhood cognitive development* (2nd ed.). New York: Wiley.

Kuhn, D. (2013). Reasoning. In P.D. Zelazo (Ed.), *Oxford handbook of developmental psychology.* New York: Oxford University Press.

Kuhn, D., Cheney, R., & Weinstock, M. (2000). The development of epistemological understanding. *Cognitive Development, 15,* 309–328.

Kuhn, D., & Franklin, S. (2006). The second decade: What develops (and how)? In W. Damon & R. Lerner (Eds.), *Handbook of child psychology* (6th ed.). New York: Wiley.

Kuhn, D., Schauble, L., & Garcia-Mila, M. (1992). Cross-domain development of scientific reasoning. *Cognition and Instruction, 9,* 285–327.

Kuhnert, R.L., & others (2017). Gender-differentiated effects of theory of mind, emotion understanding, and social preferences on prosocial behavior development: A longitudinal study. *Journal of Experimental Child Psychology, 154,* 13–27.

Kumar, S., & Kelly, A.S. (2017). Review of childhood obesity: From epidemiology, etiology, and comorbidities to clinical assessment and treatment. *Mayo Clinic Proceedings, 92,* 251–265.

Kuntsche, S., & Kuntsche, E. (2016). Parent-based interventions for preventing or reducing adolescent substance use: A systematic literature review. *Clinical Psychology Review, 45,* 89–101.

Kunzweiler, C. (2007). Twin individuality. *Fresh Ink: Essays from Boston College's First-Year Writing Seminar, 9*(1), 2–3.

Kuo, L.J., & Anderson, R.C. (2012). Effects of early bilingualism on learning phonological regularities in a new language. *Journal of Experimental Child Psychology, 111,* 455–467.

Kupari, M., Talola, N., Luukkaala, T., & Tihtonen, K. (2016). Does an increased cesarean section rate improve neonatal outcome in term pregnancies? *Archives of Gynecology and Obstetrics, 294,* 41–46.

Kurth, S., & others (2010). Characteristics of sleep slow waves in children and adolescents. *Sleep, 33,* 475–480.

Kvalo, S.E., & others (2017, in press). Does increased physical activity in school affect children's executive function and aerobic fitness? *Scandinavian Journal of Medicine and Science in Sports.*

Kymre, I.G. (2014). NICU nurses' ambivalent attitudes in skin-to-skin care practice. *International Journal of Qualitative Studies on Health and Well-Being, 9,* 23297.

Kyratzis, A. (2017). Children's co-construction of sentence and discourse in early childhood: Implictions for development. In N. Budwig & others (Eds.), *New perspectives on human development.* New York; Cambridge University Press.

L

Labella, M.H., Narayan, A.J., & Masten, A.S. (2016). Emotional climate in families experiencing homelessness: Associations with child affect and socioemotional adjustment in school. *Social Development, 25,* 304–321.

Laborte-Lemoyne, E., Currier, D., & Ellenberg, D. (2017). Exercise during pregnancy enhances cerebral maturation in the newborn: A randomized controlled trial. *Journal of Clinical and Experimental Neuropsychology, 39,* 347–354.

Lacelle, C., Hervert, M., Lavoie, F., Vitaro, F., & Tremblay, R.E. (2012). Sexual health in women reporting a history of child abuse. *Child Abuse and Neglect, 36,* 247–259.

Laciga, J., & Cigler, H. (2017, in press). The Flynn effect in the Czech Republic. *Intelligence.*

Ladd, G., Buhs, E., & Troop, W. (2004). School adjustment and social skills training. In P.K. Smith & C.H. Hart (Eds.), *Blackwell handbook of childhood social development.* Malden, MA: Blackwell.

Ladd, G., Ettekal, I., & Kochenderfer-Ladd, B. (2017, in press). Peer victimization trajectories from kindergarten through high school: Differential pathways for children's school engagement and achievement. *Journal of Educational Psychology.*

Ladd, H.C. (2017). No Child Left Behind: A deeply flawed federal policy. *Journal of Policy Analysis and Management, 36,* 461–469.

Ladewig, P.W., London, M.L., & Davidson, M. (2017). *Contemporary maternal-newborn nursing* (9th ed.). Upper Saddle River, NJ: Pearson.

Laflin, M.T., Wang, J., & Barry, M. (2008). A longitudinal study of adolescent transition from virgin to nonvirgin status. *Journal of Adolescent Health, 42,* 228–236.

LaFrance, M., Hecht, M.A., & Paluck, E.L. (2003). The contingent smile: A meta-analysis of sex differences in smiling. *Psychological Bulletin, 129,* 305–334.

Lagattuta, K.H. (2014a). *Children and emotion. New insights into developmental affective science.* Basel, Switzerland: Karger.

Lagattuta, K.H. (2014b). Linking past, present, and future: Children's ability to connect mental states and emotions across time. *Child Development Perspectives, 8,* 90–95.

Lahat, A., & others (2014). Early behavioral inhibition and increased error monitoring predict later social phobia symptoms in childhood. *Journal of the American Academy of Child and Adolescent Psychiatry, 53,* 447–455.

Lai, M-C., & others (2017). Imaging sex/gender and autism in the brain: Etiological implications. *Journal of Neuroscience Research, 95,* 380–397.

Lai, M-C., Lombardo, M.V., Chakrabarti, B., & Baron-Cohen, S. (2013). Subgrouping the autism "spectrum": Reflections on DSM-5. *PLoS Biology, 11*(4), e1001544.

Laible, D.J., & Thompson, R.A. (2007). Early socialization: A relationship perspective. In J.E. Grusec & P.D. Hastings (Eds.), *Handbook of socialization.* New York: Guilford.

Laible, D.J., Thompson, R.A., & Froimson, J. (2015). Early socialization: The influence of close relationships. In J.E. Grusec & P.D. Hastings (Eds.), *Handbook of socialization* (2nd ed.). New York: Guilford.

Laible, D.J., & others (2017, in press). The longitudinal associations among temperament, parenting, and Turkish children's prosocial behaviors. *Child Development.*

Lamb, M.E. (1994). Infant care practices and the application of knowledge. In C.B. Fisher & R.M. Lerner (Eds.), *Applied developmental psychology.* New York: McGraw-Hill.

Lamb, M.E. (2013). Non-parental care and emotional development. In S. Pauen & M. Bornstein (Eds.), *Early childhood development and later outcomes.* New York: Cambridge University Press.

Lamb, M.E., Bornstein, M.H., & Teti, D.M. (2002). *Development in infancy* (4th ed.). Mahwah, NJ: Erlbaum.

Lamb, M.E., & Lewis, C. (2015). The role of parent-child relationships in child development. In M.H. Bornstein & M.E. Lamb (Eds.), *Developmental science* (7th ed.). New York: Psychology Press.

Lamb, M.E., Malloy, L.C., Hershkowitz, I., & La Rooy, D. (2015). Children and the law. In R.E. Lerner (Ed.), *Handbook of child psychology and developmental science* (7th ed.). New York: Wiley.

Lamb, M.E., & Sternberg, K.J. (1992). Sociocultural perspectives in nonparental childcare. In M.E. Lamb, K.J. Sternberg, C. Hwang, & A.G. Broberg (Eds.), *Child care in context.* Hillsdale, NJ: Erlbaum.

Lambert, N.M., Fincham, F.D., & Stillman, T.F. (2012). Gratitude and depressive symptoms: The role of positive reframing and positive emotion. *Cognition and Emotion, 26,* 615–633.

Lamela, D., & Figueiredo, B. (2016). Co-parenting after marital dissolution and children's mental health: A systematic review. *Jornal de Pediatria (Rio), 92,* 331–342.

Lampard, A.M., Byrne, S.M., McLean, N., & Fursland, A. (2012). The Eating Disorder Inventory-2 perfectionism scale: Factor structure and associations with dietary restraint and weight and shape concern in eating disorders. *Eating Behaviors, 13,* 49–53.

Lampl, M. (1993). Evidence of saltatory growth in infancy. *American Journal of Human Biology, 5,* 641–652.

Lampl, M., & Johnson, M.L. (2011). Infant growth in length follows prolonged sleep and increased naps. *Sleep, 34,* 641–650.

Lampl, M., & Schoen, M. (2017, in press). How long bones grow children: Mechanistic paths to variation in human height growth. *American Journal of Human Biology.*

Lan, X., & others (2011). Investigating the links between the subcomponents of executive function and academic achievement: A cross-cultural analysis of Chinese and American preschoolers. *Journal of Experimental Child Psychology, 108,* 677–692.

Landau, B., Smith, L., & Jones, S. (1998). Object perception and object naming in early development. *Trends in Cognitive Science, 2,* 19–24.

Landor, A., Simons, L.G., Simons, R.L., Brody, G.H., & Gibbons, F.X. (2011). The role of religiosity in the relationship between parents, peers, and adolescent risky sexual behavior. *Journal of Youth and Adolescence, 40*(3), 296–309.

Landrum, A.R., Mills, C.M., & Johnston, A.M. (2013). When do children trust the expert? Benevolence information influences children's trust more than expertise. *Developmental Science, 16,* 622–638.

Landrum, A.R., Pflaum, A., & Mills, C.M. (2017, in press). Inducing knowledgeability from niceness:

Children use social features for making epistemic inferences. *Journal of Cognition and Development.*

Lane, A., Harrison, M., & Murphy, N. (2014). Screen time increases risk of overweight and obesity in active and inactive 9-year-old Irish children: A cross sectional analysis. *Journal of Physical Activity and Health, 11,* 985–991.

Lane, H. (1976). *The wild boy of Aveyron.* Cambridge, MA: Harvard University Press.

Lane, J.D., Evans, E.M., Brink, K.A., & Wellman, H.M. (2016). Developing concepts of ordinary and extraordinary communication. *Developmental Psychology, 52,* 19–30.

Langacker, R.W. (2017). Cognitive grammar. In B. Dancygier (Ed.), *Cambridge handbook of cognitive linguistics.* New York: Cambridge University Press.

Langer, E.J. (2005). *On becoming an artist.* New York: Ballantine.

Langille, D.B., Asbridge, M., Cragg, A., & Rasic, D. (2015). Associations of school connectedness with adolescent suicidality: Gender differences and the role of risk of depression. *Canadian Journal of Psychiatry, 60,* 258–267.

Lansford, J.E. (2009). Parental divorce and children's adjustment. *Perspectives on Psychological Science, 4,* 140–152.

Lansford, J.E. (2012). Divorce. In R.J.R. Levesque (Ed.), *Encyclopedia of adolescence.* New York: Springer.

Lansford, J.E. (2013). Single- and two-parent families. In J. Hattie & E. Anderman (Eds.), *International handbook of student achievement.* New York: Routledge.

Lansford, J.E., Wager, L.B., Bates, J.E., Pettit, G.S., & Dodge, K.A. (2012). Forms of spanking and children's externalizing problems. *Family Relations, 61,* 224–236.

Lansford, J.E., & others (2005). Cultural normativeness as a moderator of the link between physical discipline and children's adjustment: A comparison of China, India, Italy, Kenya, Philippines, and Thailand. *Child Development, 76,* 1234–1246.

Lansford, J.E., & others (2010). Developmental precursors of number of sexual partners from ages 16 to 22. *Journal of Research on Adolescence, 20,* 651–677.

Lansford, J.E., & others (2014). Corporal punishment, maternal warmth, and child adjustment: A longitudinal study in eight countries. *Journal of Clinical Child and Adolescent Psychology, 43,* 670–685.

Lantagne, A., & Furman, W. (2017, in press). Romantic relationship development: The interplay between age and relationship length.

Lantolf, J. (2017). Materialist dialectics in Vygotsky's methodological approach: Implications for second language education research. In C. Ratner & D. Silva (Eds.), *Vygotsky and Marx.* New York: Routledge.

LaPrade, R.F., & others (2016). AOSSM early sport specialization consensus statement. *Orthopedic Journal of Sports Medicine, 28*(4), 232596711644241.

Lapsley, D., & Hardy, S.A. (2017). Identity formation and moral development in emerging adulthood.

In L.M. Padilla-Walker & L.J. Nelson (Eds.), *Flourishing in emerging adulthood.* New York: Oxford University Press.

Lapsley, D.K., & Hill, P.L. (2010). Subjective invulnerability, optimism bias, and adjustment in emerging adulthood. *Journal of Youth and Adolescence, 39,* 847–857.

Lapsley, D.K., & Yeager, D. (2013). Moral-character education. In I.B. Weiner & others (Eds.), *Handbook of psychology* (2nd ed., Vol. 7). New York: Wiley.

Laranjo, J., Bernier, A., Meins, E., & Carlson, S.M. (2010). Early manifestations of theory of mind: The roles of maternal mind-mindedness and infant security of attachment. *Infancy, 15,* 300–323.

Larson, R.W. (2001). How U.S. children and adolescents spend their time: What it does (and doesn't) tell us about their development. *Current Directions in Psychological Science, 10,* 160–164.

Larson, R.W., & Dawes, N.P. (2015). How to cultivate adolescents' motivation: Effective strategies employed by the professional staff of American youth programs. In S. Joseph (Ed.), *Positive psychology in practice.* New York: Wiley.

Larson, R.W., & Lampman-Petraitis, C. (1989). Daily emotional states as reported by children and adolescents. *Child Development, 60,* 1250–1260.

Larson, R.W., McGovern, G., & Orson, C. (2018, in press). How adolescents develop self-motivation in complex learning environments: Processes and practices in afterschool programs. In A. Renninger & S. Hidi (Eds.), *Cambridge handbook of motivation and learning.* New York: Cambridge University Press.

Larson, R.W., Orson, C., & Bowers, J. (2017). Positive youth development: How intrinsic motivation amplifies social-emotional learning. In M. Warren & S. Donaldson (Eds.), *Scientific advances in positive psychology.* Santa Barbara, CA: Praeger.

Larson, R.W., & Richards, M.H. (1994). *Divergent realities.* New York: Basic Books.

Larson, R.W., Rickman, A.N., Gibbons, C.M., & Walker, K.C. (2009). Practitioner expertise: Creating quality within the daily tumble of events in youth settings. *New Directions in Youth Development, 2009*(121), 71–88.

Larson, R.W., Shernoff, D.J., & Bempechat, J. (2014). A new paradigm for the science and practice of engaging young people in schools: Evidence-based models to guide future innovations. In D.J. Shernoff & J. Bempechat (Eds.), *NSSE Yearbook.* New York: Columbia Teachers College Record.

Larson, R.W., & Verma, S. (1999). How children and adolescents spend time across the world: Work, play, and developmental opportunities. *Psychological Bulletin, 125,* 701–736.

Larson, R.W., & Walker, K.C. (2010). Dilemmas of practice: Challenges to program quality encountered by youth program leaders. *American Journal of Community Psychology, 45,* 338–349.

Larson, R.W., Walker, K.C., & McGovern, G. (2018, in press). Youth programs as contexts for development of moral agency. In L.A. Jensen (Ed.),

Handbook of moral development: An interdisciplinary perspective. New York: Oxford University Press.

Larson, R.W., & Wilson, S. (2004). Adolescence across place and time: Globalization and the changing pathways to adulthood. In R. Lerner & L. Steinberg (Eds.), *Handbook of adolescent psychology.* New York: Wiley.

Larzelere, R.E., & Kuhn, B.R. (2005). Comparing child outcomes of physical punishment and alternative disciplinary tactics: A meta-analysis. *Clinical Child and Family Psychology Review, 8,* 1–37.

Lau, J.Y., & Waters, A.M. (2017). Annual research review: An expanded account of information-processing mechanisms in risk for child and adolescent anxiety and depression. *Journal of Child Psychology and Psychiatry, 58,* 387–407.

Lauff, E., Ingels, S.J., & Christopher, E.M. (2014). *Educational longitudinal study of 2002 (ELS:2002): A first look at 2002 high school sophomores 10 years later.* NCES 2014-36. Washington, DC: U.S. Department of Education.

Lavender, J.M., & others (2014). Dimensions of emotion dysregulation in bulimia nervosa. *European Eating Disorders Review, 22,* 212–216.

Lazarus, J.H. (2017a, in press). Role of the Iodine Global Network in elimination of iodine deficiency. *Recent Patents on Endocrine, Metabolic, and Immune Drug Discovery.*

Lazarus, J.H. (2017b). Relevance of iodine nutrition to health in the 21st century. *Minerva Medicine, 108,* 114–115.

Le Doare, K., & Kampmann, B. (2014). Breast milk and Group B streptococcal infection: Vector of transmission or vehicle for protection? *Vaccine, 32,* 3128–3132.

Leadbeater, B.J., & Way, N. (2001). *Growing up fast.* Mahwah, NJ: Erlbaum.

Leaper, C. (2013). Gender development during childhood. In P.D. Zelazo (Ed.), *Oxford handbook of developmental psychology.* New York: Oxford University Press.

Leaper, C. (2015). Gender development from a social-cognitive perspective. In R.M. Lerner (Ed.), *Handbook of child psychology and developmental science* (7th ed.). New York: Wiley.

Leaper, C., & Farkas, T. (2015). The socialization of gender during childhood and adolescence. In J.E. Grusec & P.D. Hastings (Eds.), *Handbook of socialization* (2nd ed.). New York: Guilford.

Leaper, C., & Smith, T.E. (2004). A meta-analytic review of gender variations in children's language use: Talkativeness, affiliative speech, and assertive speech. *Developmental Psychology, 40,* 993–1027.

Leary, M.R. (2017). *REVEL for introduction to behavioral research methods* (7th ed.). Upper Saddle River, NJ: Pearson.

Lecarpentier, E., & others (2016). Computational fluid dynamic simulations of maternal circulation: Wall shear stress in the human placenta and its biological implications. *PLoS One, 11,* e0147262.

Ledesma, K. (2012). A place to call home. *Adoptive Families.* Retrieved August 8, 2012, from www.adoptivefamilies.com/articles.php?aid=2129

Lee, C.T., Tsai, M.C., Lin, C.Y., & Strong, C. (2017, in press). Longitudinal effects of self-report pubertal timing and menarchal age on adolescent psychological and behavioral outcomes in female youths from Northern Taiwan. *Pediatrics and Neonatology.*

Lee, J.M., & Howell, J.D. (2006). Tall girls: The social shaping of a medical therapy. *Archives of Pediatric and Adolescent Medicine, 160,* 1035–1059.

Lee, K., Cameron, C.A., Doucette, J., & Talwar, V. (2002). Phantoms and fabrications: Young children's detection of implausible lies. *Child Development, 73,* 1688–1702.

Lee, K., Quinn, P.C., Pascalis, O., & Slater, A. (2013). Development of face processing ability in childhood. In P.D. Zelazo (Ed.), *Oxford handbook of developmental psychology.* New York: Oxford University Press.

Lee, K.Y., & others (2011). Effects of combined radiofrequency radiation exposure on the cell cycle and its regulatory proteins. *Bioelectromagnetics, 32,* 169–178.

Lee, S., & others (2012). Effects of aerobic versus resistance exercise without caloric restriction on abdominal fat, intrahepatic lipid, and insulin sensitivity in obese adolescent boys: A randomized, controlled trial. *Diabetes, 61,* 2787–2795.

Leedy, P.D., & Ormrod, J.E. (2016). *Practical research* (11th ed.). Upper Saddle River, NJ: Pearson.

Leerkes, E.M., & others (2017a). Maternal physiological dysregulation while parenting poses risks for infant attachment disorganization and behavior problems. *Development and Psychopathology, 29,* 245–257.

Leerkes, E.M., & others (2017b). Further evidence of the limited role of candidate genes in relation to mother-infant attachment. *Attachment and Human Development, 19,* 76–105.

Leerkes, E.M., Parade, S.H., & Gudmundson, J.A. (2011). Mothers' emotional reactions to crying pose risk for subsequent attachment insecurity. *Journal of Family Psychology, 25*(5), 635–643.

Leffel, K., & Suskind, D. (2013). Parent-directed approaches to enrich the early language environments of children living in poverty. *Seminars in Speech and Language, 34,* 267–278.

Leftwich, H., & Alves, M.V. (2017). Adolescent pregnancy. *Pediatric Clinics of North America, 64,* 381–388.

Legerstee, M. (1997). Contingency effects of people and objects on subsequent cognitive functioning in 3-month-old infants. *Social Development, 6,* 307–321.

Lehr, C.A., Hanson, A., Sinclair, M.F., & Christensen, S.L. (2003). Moving beyond dropout prevention towards school completion. *School Psychology Review, 32,* 342–364.

Lehrer, R., & Schauble, L. (2006). Scientific thinking and scientific literacy. In W. Damon & R. Lerner (Eds.), *Handbook of child psychology* (6th ed.). New York: Wiley.

Leifer, A.D. (1973). *Television and the development of social behavior.* Paper presented at the meeting of the International Society for the Study of Behavioral Development, Ann Arbor, Michigan.

Lemez, S., & Rongen, F. (2017). High performance sport and athlete health. In J. Baker & others (Eds.), *Routledge handbook of talent identification and development in sport.* New York: Routledge.

Lempers, J.D., Flavell, E.R., & Flavell, J.H. (1977). The development in very young children of tacit knowledge concerning visual perception. *Genetic Psychology Monographs, 95,* 3–53.

Lems, K., Miller, L.D., & Soro, T.M. (2017). *Building literacy with English Language Learners* (2nd ed.). New York: Guilford.

Lenhart, A. (2015, April 9). *Teens, social media, and technology overview 2015.* Washington, DC: Pew Research Center.

Lenhart, A., Smith, A., Anderson, M., Duggan, M., & Perrin, A. (2015, August 6). *Teens, technology, and friendships.* Washington, DC: Pew Research Center,

Lennon, E.M., Gardner, J.M., Karmel, B.Z., & Flory, M.J. (2008). Bayley Scales of Infant Development. In M.M. Haith & J.B. Benson (Eds.), *Encyclopedia of infant and early childhood development.* Oxford, UK: Elsevier.

Lenoir, C.P., Mallet, E., & Calenda, E. (2000). Siblings of sudden infant death syndrome and near miss in about 30 families: Is there a genetic link? *Medical Hypotheses, 54,* 408–411.

Lenroot, R.K., & Giedd, J.N. (2006). Brain development in children and adolescents: Insights from anatomical magnetic resonance imaging. *Neuroscience and Biobehavioral Reviews, 30,* 718–729.

Leone, J.E., Mullin, E.M., Maurer-Starks, S.S., & Rovito, M.J. (2014). The Adolescent Body Image Satisfaction Scale (ABISS) for males: Exploratory factor analysis and implications for strength and conditioning professionals. *Journal of Strength and Conditioning Research, 28,* 2657–2668.

Lereya, S.T., Samara, M., & Wolke, D. (2013). Parenting behavior and the risk of becoming a victim and a bully/victim: A meta-analysis study. *Child Abuse and Neglect, 37*(12), 1091–1098.

Lerner, J.V., & others (2013). Positive youth development: Processes, philosophies, and programs. In I.B. Weiner & others (Eds.), *Handbook of psychology* (2nd ed., Vol. 6). New York: Wiley.

Lerner, R.M., Boyd, M., & Du, D. (2008). Adolescent development. In I.B. Weiner & C.B. Craighead (Eds.), *Encyclopedia of psychology* (4th ed.). New York: Wiley.

Lerner, R.M., Lerner, J.V., Urban, J.B., & Zaff, J. (2017, in press). Evaluating programs aimed at promoting positive youth development: A relational developmental systems-based view. *Applied Developmental Science.*

Lesaux, N.K., & Siegel, L.S. (2003). The development of reading in children who speak English as a second language. *Developmental Psychology, 39,* 1005–1019.

Leslie, S.J., Cimpian, A., Meyer, M., & Freeland, E. (2015). Expectations of brilliance underlie gender distributions across academic disciplines. *Science, 347,* 262–265.

Lester, B.M., & others (2002). The maternal lifestyle study: Effects of substance exposure during pregnancy on neurodevelopmental outcome in 1-month-old infants. *Pediatrics, 110,* 1182–1192.

Lester, B.M., & others (2011). Infant neurobehavioral development. *Seminars in Perinatology, 35,* 8–19.

Letourneau, E.J., McCart, M.R., Sheidow, A.J., & Mauro, P.M. (2017). First evaluation of contingency management intervention addressing adolescent substance use and sexual risk behaviors: Risk reduction therapy for adolescents. *Journal of Substance Abuse and Treatment, 72,* 56–65.

Leu, D.J., & Kinzer, C.K. (2017). *Phonics, phonemic awareness, and word analysis for teachers* (10th ed.). Upper Saddle River, NJ: Pearson.

Leung, J.Y., Lam, H.S., Leung, G.M., & Schooling, C.M. (2016). Gestational age, birthweight for gestational age, and childhood hospitalizations for asthma and other wheezing disorders. *Pediatric and Perinatal Epidemiology, 30,* 149–159.

Leung, R.C., & others (2016). The role of executive functions in social impairment in autism spectrum disorder. *Child Neuropsychology, 22,* 336–344.

Lever-Duffy, J., & McDonald, J. (2018). *Teaching and learning with technology* (6th ed.). Upper Saddle River, NJ: Pearson.

Levine, T.P., & others (2008). Effects of prenatal cocaine exposure on special education in school-aged children. *Pediatrics, 122,* e83–e91.

Levy, E., & others (2017). Pediatric obesity and cardiovascular disorders: Risk factors and biomarkers. *EJIFCC 28,* 8–24.

Lewanda, A.F., & others (2016). Preoperative evaluation and comprehensive risk assessment for children with Down syndrome. *Pediatric Anesthesia, 26,* 356–362.

Lewis, A.C. (2007). Looking beyond NCLB. *Phi Delta Kappan, 88,* 483–484.

Lewis, B.A., & others (2007). Prenatal cocaine and tobacco effects on children's language trajectories. *Pediatrics, 120,* e78–e85.

Lewis, G.J., Asbury, K., & Plomin, R. (2017). Externalizing problems in childhood and adolescence predict subsequent educational achievement but for different genetic and environmental reasons. *Journal of Child Psychology and Psychiatry, 58,* 292–304.

Lewis, M. (2005). Selfhood. In B. Hopkins (Ed.), *The Cambridge encyclopedia of child development.* Cambridge, UK: Cambridge University Press.

Lewis, M. (2007). Early emotional development. In A. Slater & M. Lewis (Eds.), *Introduction to infant development.* Malden, MA: Blackwell.

Lewis, M. (2010). The emergence of consciousness and its role in human development. In W.F. Overton & R.M. Lerner (Eds.), *Handbook of life-span development* (2nd ed.). New York: Wiley.

Lewis, M. (2014). *The rise of consciousness and the development of emotional life.* New York: Guilford.

Lewis, M. (2015). Emotional development and consciousness. In R.M. Lerner (Ed.), *Handbook of child psychology and developmental science* (7th ed.). New York: Wiley.

Lewis, M. (2016). Self-conscious emotions: Embarrassment, pride, shame, guilt, and hubris. In L.F. Barrett, M. Lewis, & J.M. Haviland-Jones (Eds.), *Handbook of emotion* (4th ed.). New York: Guilford.

Lewis, M., & Brooks-Gunn, J. (1979). *Social cognition and the acquisition of the self.* New York: Plenum.

Lewis, M., Feiring, C., & Rosenthal, S. (2000). Attachment over time. *Child Development, 71,* 707–720.

Lewis, R.B., Wheeler, J.J., & Carter, S.L. (2017). *Teaching students with special needs* (9th ed.). Upper Saddle River, NJ: Pearson.

Lewis, T.L., & Maurer, D. (2005). Multiple sensitive periods in human visual development: Evidence from visually deprived children. *Developmental Psychobiology, 46,* 163–183.

Lewis, T.L., & Maurer, D. (2009). Effects of early pattern deprivation on visual development. *Optometry and Vision Science, 86,* 640–646.

Lewis-Morrarty, E., & others (2015). Infant attachment security and early childhood behavioral inhibition interact to predict adolescent social anxiety symptoms. *Child Development, 86,* 598–613.

Leyton, M., & Vezina, P. (2014). Dopamine ups and downs in vulnerability to addictions: A neurodevelopmental model. *Trends in Pharmacological Sciences, 35,* 268–276.

Li, B.J., Jiang, Y.J., & Yuan, F., & Ye, H.X. (2010). Exchange transfusion of least incompatible blood for severe hemolytic disease of the newborn due to anti-Rh17. *Transfusion Medicine, 20,* 66–69.

Li, D., Karmath, H.O., & Xu, X. (2017). Candidate biomarkers in children with autism spectrum disorder: A review of MRI studies. *Neuroscience Bulletin, 33,* 219–237.

Li, D., Zhang, W., Li, X., Li, N., & Ye, B. (2012). Gratitude and suicidal ideation and suicide attempts among Chinese adolescents: Direct, mediated, and moderated effects. *Journal of Adolescence, 35,* 55–66.

Li, G., Kung, K.T., & Hines, M. (2017, in press). Childhood gender-typed behavior and adolescent sexual orientation: A longitudinal population-based study. *Developmental Psychology.*

Li, J., & others (2011). Low Apgar scores and risk of childhood attention deficit hyperactivity disorder. *Journal of Pediatrics, 158,* 775–779.

Li, J., & others (2017, in press). Heritability of children's dietary intake: A population-based study in China. *Twin Research and Human Genetics.*

Li, J.W., & others (2017, in press). The effect of acute and chronic exercise on cognitive function and academic performance in adolescents: A systematic review. *Journal of Science and Medicine in Sport.*

Li, M., & others (2017, in press). Getting to the heart of personality in early childhood: Cardiac electrophysiology and stability of temperament. *Journal of Research in Psychology.*

Li, M., & others (2017, in press). Parental expectations and child screen and academic sedentary behaviors in China. *American Journal of Preventive Medicine.*

Li, M., & others (2017, in press). Robust and rapid algorithms facilitate large-scale whole genome sequencing downstream analysis in an integrative framework. *Nucleic Acids Research.*

Li, Q., Alonge, O., & Hyder, A.A. (2016). Children and road traffic injuries: Can't the world do better? *Archives of Disease in Childhood, 101,* 1063–1070.

Li, W., Farkas, G., Duncan, G.J., Burchinal, M.R., & Vandell, D.L. (2013). Timing of high-quality child care and cognitive, language, and preacademic development. *Developmental Psychology, 49(8),* 1440–1451.

Li, Z., & others (2013). Maternal severe life events and risk of neural tube defects among rural Chinese. *Birth Defects Research A: Clinical and Molecular Teratology, 97,* 109–114.

Liang, W., & Chikritzhs, T. (2015). Age at first use of alcohol predicts the risk of heavy alcohol use in early adulthood: A longitudinal study in the United States. *International Journal on Drug Policy, 26,* 131–134.

Liang, Y.J., Xi, B., Song, A.Q., Liu, J.X., & Mi, J. (2012). Trends in general and abdominal obesity among Chinese children and adolescents, 1993–2009. *Pediatric Obesity, 7,* 355–364.

Liben, L.S. (1995). Psychology meets geography: Exploring the gender gap on the national geography bee. *Psychological Science Agenda, 8,* 8–9.

Liben, L.S. (2017). Gender development: A constructivist-ecological perspective. In N. Budwig, E. Turiel, & P.D. Zelazo (Eds.), *New perspectives on human development.* New York: Cambridge University Press.

Liben, L.S., Bigler, R.S., & Hilliard, L.J. (2014). Gender development. In E.T. Gershoff, R.S. Mistry, & D.A. Crosby (Eds.), *Societal contexts of child development.* New York: Oxford University Press.

Liberati, A., & others (2017, in press). A statistical physics perspective to understand social visual attention in autism spectrum disorder. *Perception.*

Liberman, Z., Woodward, A.L., & Kinzler, K.D. (2017, in press). The origins of social categorization. *Trends in Cognitive Science.*

Libertus, K., Grief, M.L., Needham, A.W., & Pelphrey, K. (2016). Infants' observations of tool-use events over the first year of life. *Journal of Experimental Child Psychology, 152,* 123–135.

Libertus, K., Joh, A.S., & Needham, A.W. (2016). Motor training at 3 months affects object exploration 12 months later. *Developmental Science, 19,* 1058–1066.

Libertus, K., & others (2013). Size matters: How age and reaching experiences shape infants' preferences for different sized objects. *Infant Behavior and Development, 36,* 189–198.

Lickliter, R. (2017, in press). Developmental evolution. *Wiley Interdisciplinary Reviews. Cognitive Science.*

Lickliter, R., & Honeycutt, H. (2015). Biology, development, and human systems. In R.M. Lerner (Ed.), *Handbook of child psychology and developmental science* (7th ed.). New York: Wiley.

Liddon, N., & others (2016). Withdrawal as pregnancy prevention and associated risk factors among U.S. high school students: Findings from the 2011 National Youth Behavior Risk Survey. *Contraception, 93,* 126–132.

Lie, E., & Newcombe, N. (1999). Elementary school children's explicit and implicit memory for faces of preschool classmates. *Developmental Psychology, 35,* 102–112.

Lieber, M. (2017). Assessing the mental health impact of the 2011 Great Japan earthquake, tsunami, and radiation disaster on elementary and middle school children in the Fukushima Prefecture of Japan. *PLoS One, 12(1),* e170402.

Lieberman, A.F., & Chu, A.T. (2016). Childhood exposure to interpersonal trauma. In D. Cicchetti (Ed.), *Developmental psychopathology* (3rd ed.). New York: Wiley.

Lieberman, P. (2016). The evolution of language and thought. *Journal of Anthropological Studies, 94,* 127–146.

Liebermann, J. (2017). Chapter 11: Human embryo vitrification. *Methods in Molecular Biology, 1568,* 141–159.

Liederman, J., Kantrowitz, L., & Flannery, K. (2005). Male vulnerability to reading disability is not likely to be a myth: A call for new data. *Journal of Learning Disabilities, 38,* 109–129.

Lieven, E. (2008). Language development: Overview. In M.M. Haith & J.B. Benson (Eds.), *Encyclopedia of infant and early childhood development.* Oxford, UK: Elsevier.

Likis, F.E., & others (2012). Progestogens for preterm birth prevention: A systematic review and meta-analysis. *Obstetrics and Gynecology, 120,* 897–907.

Lillard, A. (2006). Pretend play in toddlers. In C.A. Brownell & C.B. Kopp (Eds.), *Socioemotional development in the toddler years.* New York: Oxford University Press.

Lillard, A.S. (2012). Preschool children's development in classic Montessori, supplemented Montessori, and conventional programs. *Journal of School Psychology, 50,* 379–401.

Lillard, A.S., & Kavanaugh, R.D. (2014). The contribution of symbolic skills to the development of explicit theory of mind. *Child Development, 85,* 1535–1551.

Lin, C.C., & others (2013). In utero exposure to environmental lead and manganese and neurodevelopment at 2 years of age. *Environmental Research, 123,* 52–57.

Lin, L.Y., & others (2015). Effects of television exposure on developmental skills of young children. *Infant Behavior and Development, 38,* 20–26.

Lin, M., Johnson, J.E., & Johnson, K.M. (2003). *Dramatic play in Montessori kindergartens in Taiwan and Mainland China.* Unpublished manuscript, Department of Curriculum and Instruction, Pennsylvania State University, University Park, PA.

Lin, X., & others (2017). Developmental pathways to adiposity begin before birth and are influenced by genotype, prenatal development, and epigenome. *BMC Medicine, 15(1),* 50.

Lin, Y.C., & Seo, D.C. (2017). Cumulative family risks across income levels predict deterioration of children's health during childhood and adolescence. *PLoS One, 12*(5), e0177531.

Lindberg, L.D., & Maddow-Zimet, I. (2012). Consequences of sex education on teen and young adult sexual behaviors and outcomes. *Journal of Adolescent Health, 51*, 332–338.

Lindberg, S.M., Hyde, J.S., Petersen, J.L., & Linn, M.C. (2010). New trends in gender and mathematics performance: A meta-analysis. *Psychological Bulletin, 136*, 1123–1136.

Lindsay, A.C., Sussner, K.M., Kim, J., & Gortmaker, S. (2006). The role of parents in preventing childhood obesity. *The Future of Children, 16*(1), 169–186.

Lindsay, M.K., & Burnett, E. (2013). The use of narcotics and street drugs during pregnancy. *Clinical Obstetrics and Gynecology, 56*, 133–141.

Linnenbrink-Garcia, L., & Patall, E.A. (2016). Motivation. In L. Corno & E.M. Anderman (Eds.), *Handbook of educational psychology* (3rd ed.). New York: Routledge.

Linsell, L., & others (2017). Risk factor models for neurodevelopmental outcomes in children born very preterm or with very low birth weight: A systematic review of methodology and reporting. *American Journal of Epidemiology, 185*, 601–612.

Lintu, N., & others (2016). Determinants of cardiorespiratory fitness in a population sample of girls and boys 6–8 years. *Journal of Physical Activity and Health,13*, 1149–1155.

Lipowski, M., Lipowska, M., Jochimek, M., & Krokosz, D. (2016). Resilience as a factor protecting youths from risky behavior: Moderating effects of gender and sport. *European Journal of Sport Science, 16*, 246–255.

Lipschitz, J.M., Yes, S., Weinstock, L.M., & Spirito, A. (2012). Adolescent and caregiver perception of family functioning: Relation to suicide ideation and attempts. *Psychiatry Research, 200*, 400–403.

Lipsky, L.M., & others (2017). Diet quality of U.S. adolescents during the transition to adulthood: Changes and predictors. *American Journal of Clinical Nutrition, 105*, 1424–1432.

Litz, J., Snyder, W., & Pater, J. (Eds.) (2017). *Oxford handbook of developmental linguistics.* New York: Oxford University Press.

Liu, D., Wellman, H.M., Tardif, T., & Sabbagh, M.A. (2008). Theory of mind development in Chinese children: A meta-analysis of false-belief understanding across cultures and languages. *Developmental Psychology, 44*, 523–531.

Liu, J., Raine, A., Venables, P.H., & Mednick, S.A. (2004). Malnutrition at 3 years and externalizing behavior problems at age 8, 11, and 17 years. *American Journal of Psychiatry, 161*, 2005–2013.

Liu, R., Chao, M.T., Jostad-Laswell, A., & Duncan, L.G. (2017). Does CenteringPregancy group prenatal care affect the birth experience of underserved women? A mixed methods analysis. *Journal of Immigrant and Minority Health, 19*, 415–422.

Liu, X., & others (2017). Prenatal care and child growth and schooling in four low- and medium-income countries. *PLoS One, 12*, e0171299.

Liu, Y.H., Chang, M.Y., & Chen, C.H. (2010). Effects of music therapy on labor pain and anxiety in Taiwanese first-time mothers. *Journal of Clinical Nursing, 19*, 1065–1072.

Lively, W., & Bromley, D. (1973). *Person perception in childhood and adolescence.* New York: Wiley.

Livingston, G. (2014, June 5). *Growing number of dads home with the kids.* Washington, DC: Pew Research Center.

Lloyd-Fox, S., Wu, R., Richards, J.E., Elwell, C.E., & Johnson, M.H. (2015). Cortical activation to action perception is associated with action production abilities in young infants. *Cerebral Cortex, 25*, 289–297.

Lo, C.C., & others (2017). Racial/ethnic differences in emotional health: A longitudinal study of immigrants' adolescent children. *Community Mental Health Journal, 53*, 92–101.

Lo, C.K., & others (2017). Risk factors for child physical abuse and neglect among Chinese young mothers. *Child Abuse and Neglect, 67*, 193–206.

Lo, K.Y., & others (2017, in press). Association of school environment and after-school physical activity with health-related physical fitness among junior high school students. *International Journal of Environmental Research and Public Health.*

Lockhart, G., & others (2017). Prospective relations among low-income African American adolescents' maternal attachment security, self-worth, and risk behaviors. *Frontiers in Psychology, 8*, 33.

Lockl, K., & Schneider, W. (2007). Knowledge about the mind: Links between theory of mind and later metamemory. *Child Development, 78*, 147–167.

Loebel, M., & Yali, A.M. (1999, August). *Effects of positive expectancies on adjustments to pregnancy.* Paper presented at the meeting of the American Psychological Association, Boston.

Loeber, R., & Burke, J.D. (2011). Developmental pathways in juvenile externalizing and internalizing problems. *Journal of Research on Adolescence, 21*, 34–46.

Logsdon, M.C., Wisner, K., & Hanusa, B.H. (2009). Does maternal role functioning improve with antidepressant treatment in women with postpartum depression? *Journal of Women's Health, 18*, 85–90.

Loi, E.C., & others (2017). Using eye movements to assess language comprehension in toddlers born preterm and full-term. *Journal of Pediatrics, 180*, 124–129.

Loizou, E. (2017). Children's sociodramatic play typologies and teacher play involvement within the zone of proximal development. In T. Bruce (Ed.), *Routledge international handbook of early childhood play.* New York: Routledge.

Lomanowska, A.M., & others (2017). Parenting begets parenting: A neurobiological perspective on early adversity and the transmission of parenting styles across generations. *Neuroscience, 342*, 120–139.

London, M.L., & others (2017). *Maternal and child nursing care* (5th ed.). Upper Saddle River, NJ: Pearson.

Longo, G.S., Bray, B.C., & Kim-Spoon, J. (2017). Profiles of adolescent religiousness using latent profile analysis: Implications for psychopathology.

British Journal of Developmental Psychology, 35, 91–105.

Loop, L., & others (2017). One or many? Which and how many parenting variables should be targeted in interventions to reduce children's externalizing behavior? *Behavior Research and Therapy, 92*, 11–23.

Lopez, A.B., Huynh, V.W., & Fuligni, A.J. (2011). A longitudinal study of religious identity and participation during adolescence. *Child Development, 82*, 1297–1309.

Lopez-Maestro, M., & others (2017, in press). Quality of attachment in infants less than 1500g or less than 32 weeks. Related factors. *Early Human Development.*

Lord, R.G., & others (2017). Leadership in applied psychology: Three waves of theory and research. *Journal of Applied Psychology, 102*, 434–451.

Lorenz, K.Z. (1965). *Evolution and the modification of behavior.* Chicago: University of Chicago Press.

Losel, F., & Bender, D. (2011). Emotional and antisocial outcomes of bullying and victimization at school: A follow-up from childhood to adolescence. *Journal of Aggression, Conflict, and Peace Research, 3*, 89–96.

Love, J.M., Chazan-Cohen, R., Raikes, H., & Brooks-Gunn, J. (2013). What makes a difference: Early Head Start evaluation findings in a developmental context. *Monographs of the Society for Research in Child Development, 78*, 1–173.

Lovely, C., & others (2017, in press). Gene-environment interactions in development and disease. *Wiley Interdisciplinary Review of Developmental Biology.*

Low, S., & Shortt, J.W. (2017, in press). Family, peer, and pubertal determinants of dating involvement in adolescence. *Journal of Research in Adolescence.*

Lowry, R., & others (2017). Early sexual debut and associated risk behaviors among sexual minority youth. *American Journal of Preventive Medicine, 52*, 379–384.

Lowson, K., Offer, C., Watson, J., McGuire, B., & Renfrew, M.J. (2015). The economic benefits of increasing kangaroo skin-to-skin care and breastfeeding in neonatal units: Analysis of a pragmatic intervention in clinical practice. *International Journal of Breastfeeding, 10*, 11.

Lu, C., Black, M.M., & Richter, L.M. (2016). Risk of poor development in young children in low-income and middle-income countries: An estimation and analysis of the global, regional, and country level. *Lancet. Global Health, 4*(12), e916–e922.

Luders, E., & others (2004). Gender differences in cortical complexity. *Nature Neuroscience, 1*, 799–800.

Ludvigsson, J.F., & others (2017). European Academy of Pediatrics Statement: Vision zero for child deaths in traffic accidents. *European Journal of Pediatrics, 176*, 291–292.

Luecken, L.J., & others (2016). A longitudinal study of the effects of child-reported warmth on cortisol stress response 15 years after parental divorce. *Psychosomatic Medicine, 78*, 163–170.

Luiselli, J.K. (Ed.) (2014). *Children and youth with autism spectrum disorder (ASD)*. New York: Oxford University Press.

Lukowski, A.F., & Bauer, P. (2014). Long-term memory in infancy and early childhood. In P. Bauer & R. Fivush (Eds.), *Wiley-Blackwell handbook of children's memory*. New York: Wiley.

Lumpkin, A. (2014). *Introduction to physical education, exercise science, and sport studies* (9th ed.). New York: McGraw-Hill.

Lund, H.G., Reider, B.D., Whiting, A.B., & Prichard, J.R. (2010). Sleep patterns and predictors of disturbed sleep in a large population of college students. *Journal of Adolescent Health, 46,* 124–132.

Lundblad, K., Rosenberg, J., Mangurten, H., & Angst, D.B. (2017, in press). Severe iron deficiency anemia in infants and young children requiring hospital admission. *Global Pediatric Health.*

Lunenfeld, B., & others (2015). Recommendations on the diagnosis, treatment, and monitoring of hypogonadism in men. *Aging Male, 18,* 5–15.

Luo, Y., & Baillargeon, R. (2010). Toward a mentalistic account of early psychological reasoning. *Current Directions in Psychological Science, 19(5),* 301–307.

Luria, A., & Herzog, E. (1985, April). *Gender segregation across and within settings.* Paper presented at the biennial meeting of the Society for Research in Child Development, Toronto.

Lusby, C.M., & others (2017, in press). Infant EEG and temperament negative affectivity: Coherence of vulnerabilities to mothers' perinatal depression. *Development and Psychopathology.*

Lushington, K., Pamula, Y., Martin, J., & Kennedy, J.D. (2014). Developmental changes in sleep: Infancy and preschool years. In A.R. Wolfson & E. Montgomery-Downs (Eds.), *Oxford handbook of infant, child, and adolescent sleep and behavior.* New York: Oxford University Press.

Luyckx, K., & others (2017, in press). Identity processes and intrinsic and extrinsic goal pursuits: Directionality of effects in college students. *Journal of Youth and Adolescence.*

Lyon, T.D., & Flavell, J.H. (1993). Young children's understanding of forgetting over time. *Child Development, 64,* 789–800.

M

Maag, J.W. (2018). *Behavior management: From theoretical implications to practical applications* (3rd ed.). Boston: Cengage.

Maas, J. (2008, March 4). Commentary in L. Szabo, "Parents with babies need time to reset inner clock." *USA Today,* p. 4D.

MacArthur, C., Graham, S., & Fitzgerald, J. (Eds.) (2016). *Handbook of research on writing* (2nd ed.). New York: Guilford.

Maccoby, E.E. (1998). *The two sexes: Growing up apart, coming together.* Cambridge, MA: Harvard University Press.

Maccoby, E.E. (2002). Gender and group processes. *Current Directions in Psychological Science, 11,* 54–58.

Maccoby, E.E. (2007). Historical overview of socialization theory and research. In J.E. Grusec & P.D. Hastings (Eds.), *Handbook of socialization.* New York: Guilford.

Maccoby, E.E., & Martin, J.A. (1983). Socialization in the context of the family: Parent-child interaction. In P.H. Mussen (Ed.), *Handbook of child psychology* (4th ed., Vol. 4). New York: Wiley.

Macdonald, I., & Hauber, R. (2016). Educating parents on sports-related concussions. *Journal of Neuroscience Nursing, 48,* 297–302.

Macedo, D.B., & others (2016). Sexual precocity—genetic bases of central precocious puberty and autonomous gonadal activation. *Endocrine Development, 29,* 50–71.

MacFarlane, J.A. (1975). Olfaction in the development of social preferences in the human neonate. In *Parent-infant interaction.* Ciba Foundation Symposium No. 33. Amsterdam: Elsevier.

Machado, B., & others (2014). Risk factors and antecedent life events in the development of anorexia nervosa: A Portuguese case-control study. *European Eating Disorders Review, 22,* 243–251.

Machalek, D.A., & others (2017). Genetic and environmental factors in invasive cervical cancer: Design and methods of a classical twin study. *Twin Research and Human Genetics, 20,* 10–18.

Macionis, J.J. (2017). *Society* (14th ed.). Upper Saddle River, NJ: Pearson.

MacKenzie, A., Hedge, N., & Enslin, P. (2017). Sex education: Challenges and choices. *British Journal of Educational Studies, 65,* 27–44.

MacKinnon, S.P., & others (2017, in press). Cross-cultural comparisons of drinking motives in 10 countries: Data from the DRINC project. *Drug and Alcohol Review.*

Macpherson, A.K., Jones, J., Rothman, L., Macarthur, C., & Howard, A.W. (2010). Safety standards and socioeconomic disparities in school playground injuries: A retrospective cohort study. *BMC Public Health, 10,* 542.

Madden, K., & others (2016). Hypnosis for pain management during labor and childbirth. *Cochrane Database of Systematic Reviews, 5,* CD009356.

Maddison, R., & others (2016). Results from New Zealand's 2016 report card on physical activity for children and youth. *Journal of Physical Activity and Health, 13*(11, Suppl 2), S225–S230.

Magno, C. (2010). The role of metacognitive skills in developing critical thinking. *Metacognition and Learning, 5,* 137–156.

Magro-Malosso, E.R., & others (2017, in press). Exercise during pregnancy and risk of gestational hypertensive disorders: A systematic review and meta-analysis. *Acta Obstetrica and Gynecologica Scandinavia.*

Maher, H., Winston, C.N., & Ur, S. (2017). What it feels like to be me: Linking emotional intelligence, identity, and intimacy. *Journal of Adolescence, 56,* 162–165.

Mahler, M. (1979). *Separation-individuation* (Vol. 2). London: Jason Aronson.

Mahoney, J.L., Parente, M.E., & Zigler, E. (2010). After-school program engagement and in-school competence: Program quality, content, and staffing. In J. Meece & J. Eccles (Eds.), *Handbook of research on schools, schooling, and human development.* New York: Routledge.

Mahoney, J.L., & Vest, A.E. (2012). The overscheduling hypothesis revisited: Intensity of organized activity participation during adolescence and young adult outcomes. *Journal of Research on Adolescence, 22,* 409–418.

Malmberg, L.E., & others (2016, in press). The influence of mothers' and fathers' sensitivity in the first year of life on childen's cognitive outcomes at 18 and 36 months. *Child Care, Health, and Development.*

Maloy, R.W., Verock-O'Loughlin, R-E., Edwards, S.A., & Woolf, B.P. (2017). *Transforming learning with new technologies* (3rd ed.). Upper Saddle River, NJ: Pearson.

Mandara, J. (2006). The impact of family functioning on African American males' academic achievement: A review and clarification of the empirical literature. *Teachers College Record, 108,* 206–233.

Mandler, J.M. (2004). *The foundations of the mind: Origins of conceptual thought.* New York: Oxford University Press.

Mandler, J.M. (2009). Conceptual categorization. In D.H. Rakison & L.M. Oakes (Eds.), *Early category and concept development.* New York: Oxford University Press.

Mandler, J.M. (2010). Jean Mandler. Retrieved May 26, 2010, from http://www.cogsci.ucsd.edu/~jean/

Mandler, J.M., & McDonough, L. (1993). Concept formation in infancy. *Cognitive Development, 8,* 291–318.

Mangelsdorf, S.C., & Wong, M.S. (2008). Independence/dependence. In M.M. Haith & J.B. Benson (Eds.), *Encyclopedia of infant and early childhood development.* Oxford, UK: Elsevier.

Manuck, S.B., & McCaffery, J.M. (2014). Gene-environment interaction. *Annual Review of Psychology* (Vol. 65). Palo Alto, CA: Annual Reviews.

Manzanares, S., & others (2016). Accuracy of fetal sex determination on ultrasound examination in the first trimester of pregnancy. *Journal of Clinical Ultrasound, 44,* 272–277.

Manzo, K.K. (2008). Motivating students in the middle years. *Education Week, 27,* 22–25.

Maramara, L.A., He, W., & Ming, X. (2014). Pre- and perinatal risk factors for autism spectrum disorder in a New Jersey cohort. *Journal of Child Neurology, 29,* 1645–1651.

Maravilla, J.C., & others (2017, in press). Factors influencing repeated adolescent pregnancy: A review and meta-analysis. *American Journal of Obstetrics and Gynecology.*

March of Dimes (2017). *Multiple pregnancy and birth: Considering fertility treatments.* White Plains, NY: Author.

Marchman, V.A., & others (2017, in press). Caregiver talk to young Spanish-English bilinguals: Comparing direct observation and parent report measures of dual-language exposure. *Developmental Science.*

Marcia, J.E. (1980). Ego identity development. In J. Adelson (Ed.), *Handbook of adolescent psychology*. New York: Wiley.

Marcia, J.E. (1994). The empirical study of ego identity. In H.A. Bosma, T.L.G. Graafsma, H.D. Grotevant, & D.J. De Levita (Eds.), *Identity and development*. Newbury Park, CA: Sage.

Marcia, J.E. (2002). Identity and psychosocial development in adulthood. *Identity: An International Journal of Theory and Research, 2,* 7–28.

Marcoux, S., & others (2017, in press). The PETALE study: Late adverse effects and biomarkers in childhood acute lymphoblastic leukemia survivors. *Pediatric Blood & Cancer.*

Marcovitch, S., Clearfield, M.W., Swingler, M., Calkins, S.D., & Bell, M.A. (2016). Attentional predictors of 5-month-olds' performance on a looking A-not-B task. *Infant and Child Development, 25,* 233–246.

Marcovitch, S., & others (2015). A longitudinal assessment of the relation between executive function and theory of mind at 3, 4, and 5 years. *Cognitive Development, 33,* 40–55.

Mares, M-L., & Pan, Z. (2013). Effects of *Sesame Street:* A meta-analysis of children's learning in 15 countries. *Journal of Applied Developmental Psychology, 34,* 140–151.

Marie, C., & Trainor, L.J. (2013). Development of simultaneous pitch encoding: Infants show a high voice superiority effect. *Cerebral Cortex, 23*(3), 660–669.

Marjanovic-Umek, L., Fekonja-Peklaj, U., & Socan, G. (2017). Early vocabulary, parental education, and the frequency of shared reading as predictors of toddlers' vocabulary and grammar at age 2; 7: A Slovenian longitudinal CDI study. *Journal of Child Language, 44,* 457–479.

Mark, K.S., & others (2015). Knowledge, attitudes, and practice of electronic cigarette use among pregnant women. *Journal of Addiction Medicine, 9,* 266–272.

Markant, J.C., & Thomas, K.M. (2013). Postnatal brain development. In P.D. Zelazo (Ed.), *Oxford handbook of developmental psychology*. New York: Oxford University Press.

Markham, C.M., & others (2010). Connectedness as a predictor of sexual and reproductive health outcomes for youth. *Journal of Adolescent Health*(Suppl. 1), S23–S41.

Markham, K.B., Walker, H., Lynch, C.D., & Iams, J.D. (2014). Preterm birth rates in a prematurity prevention clinic after adoption of progestin prophylaxis. *Obstetrics and Gynecology, 123,* 34–39.

Marsh, H.L., & Legerstee, M. (2017, in press). Awareness of goal-directed behavior during infancy and early childhood, in human- and non-human primates. *Infant Behavior and Development.*

Marshall, S.L., Parker, P.D., Ciarrochi, J., & Heaven, P.C.L. (2014). Is self-esteem a cause or consequence of social support? A 4-year longitudinal study. *Child Development, 85,* 1275–1291.

Martin, C., Sargrad, S., & Batel, S. (2016). Making the grade: A 50-state analysis of school accountability systems. *ERIC,* ED567858.

Martin, C.L., & Cook, R. (2017, in press). Cognitive perspectives on children's toy choices and play styles. In E. Wigram & L. Dinella (Eds.), *Gender-typing of children's toys*. Washington, DC: American Psychological Association.

Martin, C.L., Fabes, R.A., & Hanish, L. (2018, in press). Differences and similarities: The dynamics of same- and other-sex peer relationships. In W. Bukowski, B. Laursen, & K. Rubin (Eds.), *Handbook of peer interactions, relationships, and groups* (2nd ed.). New York: Guilford.

Martin, C.L., & others (2013). The role of sex of peers and gender-typed activities in young children's peer affiliative networks: A longitudinal analysis of selection and influence. *Child Development, 84,* 921–937.

Martin, C.L., & others (2017). A dual identity approach for conceptualizing and measuring children's gender identity. *Child Development, 88,* 167–182.

Martin, J.A., & others (2005, September). Births: Final data for 2003. *National Vital Statistics Reports, 54,* 1–116.

Martin, J.A., & others (2017). Births: Final data for 2015. *National Vital Statistics Reports, 66,* 1–69.

Martin, J.A., Hamilton, B.E., & Osterman, M.J. (2015, September). Births in the United States, 2014. *NCHS Data Brief, 216,* 1–8.

Martin, K.B., & Messinger, D.B. (2018, in press). Smile. In M.H. Bornstein & others (Eds.), *SAGE encyclopedia of lifespan development*. Thousand Oaks, CA: Sage.

Martin, M.J., & others (2017, in press). The mediating role of cortisol reactivity and executive functioning difficulties in the pathways between childhood histories of emotional insecurity and adolescent school problems. *Development and Psychopathology.*

Martin, M.M., & others (2016). Cocaine-induced neurodevelopmental deficits and underlying mechanisms. *Birth Defects Research C. Embryo Today, 108,* 147–173.

Martin-Espinosa, N., & others (2017). Prevalence of high blood pressure and association with obesity in Spanish schoolchildren aged 4-6 years old. *PLoS One, 12*(1), e170926.

Martinez-Brockman, J.L., & others (2017). An assessment of the social cognitive predictors of exclusive breastfeeding behavior using the Health Action Process Approach. *Social Science and Medicine, 182,* 106–116.

Martz, M.E., Patrick, M.E., & Schulenberg, J.E. (2016). Alcohol mixed with energy drink use among U.S. 12th grade students: Prevalence, correlates, and associations with safe driving. *Journal of Adolescent Health, 56,* 557–563.

Marusak, H.A., & others (2017). Dynamic functional connectivity of neurocognitive networks in children. *Human Brain Mapping, 38,* 97–108.

Mary, A., & others (2016). Executive and attentional contributions to theory of mind deficit in attention deficit/hyperactivity disorder (ADHD). *Child Neuropsychology, 22,* 345–365.

Masapollo, M., Polka, L., & Menard, L. (2016). When infants talk, infants listen: Pre-babbling infants prefer listening to speech with infant vocal properties. *Developmental Science, 19,* 318–328.

Mash, E.J., & Wolfe, D.A. (2016). *Abnormal child psychology* (6th ed.). Boston: Cengage.

Mashburn, A.J., Justice, L.M., Downer, J.T., & Pianta, R.C. (2009). Peer effects on children's language achievement during pre-kindergarten. *Child Development, 80,* 686–702.

Mason, A., & others (2017). Family factors and health behavior of thin adolescent boys and girls. *Journal of Advanced Nursing, 73,* 177–189.

Masten, A.S. (2001). Ordinary magic: Resilience processes in development. *American Psychologist, 56,* 227–238.

Masten, A.S. (2006). Developmental psychopathology: Pathways to the future. *International Journal of Behavioral Development, 31,* 46–53.

Masten, A.S. (2009). Ordinary magic: Lessons from research on resilience in human development. Retrieved October 15, 2009, from http://www.cea-ace.ca/media/en/Ordinary_Magic_Summer09.pdf

Masten, A.S. (2011a). Resilience in children threatened by extreme adversity: Frameworks for research, practice, and translational synergy. *Development and Psychopathology, 23,* 493–506.

Masten, A.S. (2011b). Understanding and promoting resilience in children. *Current Opinion in Psychiatry, 24*(4), 267–273.

Masten, A.S. (2012). Faculty profile: Ann Masten. *The Institute of Child Development further developments*. Minneapolis: School of Education.

Masten, A.S. (2013). Risk and resilience in development. In P.D. Zelazo (Ed.), *Oxford handbook of developmental psychology*. New York: Oxford University Press.

Masten, A.S. (2014a). Global perspectives on resilience in children and youth. *Child Development, 85,* 6–20.

Masten, A.S. (2014b). *Ordinary magic: Resilience in development*. New York: Guilford.

Masten, A.S. (2015). Pathways to integrated resilience science. *Psychological Inquiry, 26,* 187–196.

Masten, A.S. (2016a). Resilience in the context of ambiguous loss: A commentary. *Journal of Family Theory and Review, 8,* 287–293.

Masten, A.S. (2016b). Resilience in developing systems: The promise of integrated approaches. *Journal of Developmental Psychology, 13,* 297–312.

Masten, A.S. (2017). Building a transactional science on children and youth affected by political violence and armed conflict. *Development and Psychopathology, 29,* 79–84.

Masten, A.S., & Cicchetti, D. (2016). Resilience in development. In D. Cicchetti (Ed.), *Developmental psychopathology* (3rd ed.). New York: Wiley.

Masten, A.S., Fiat, A.E., Labella, M.H., & Strack, R. (2015). Educating homeless and highly mobile students: Implications of research on risk and resilience. *School Psychology Review, 44,* 315–330.

Masten, A.S., & Kalstabakken, A.W. (2017, in press). Developmental perspectives on psychopathology in children and adolescents. In J.

Butcher (Ed.), *APA handbook of psychopathology.* Washington, DC: APA Press.

Masten, A.S., & Labella, M.H. (2016). Risk and resilience in child development. In L. Balter & C.S. Tamis-LeMonda (Eds.), *Child psychology* (2nd ed.). New York: Routledge.

Masten, A.S., Narayan, A.J., Silverman, W.K., & Osofsky, J.D. (2015). Children in war and disaster. In R.M. Lerner (Ed.), *Handbook of child psychology and developmental science* (7th ed.). New York: Wiley.

Masten, A.S., & others (2008). School success in motion: Protective factors for academic achievement in homeless and highly mobile children in Minneapolis. *Center for Urban and Regional Affairs Reporter, 38,* 3–12.

Mastin, J.D., & Vogt, P. (2017, in press). Infant engagement and early vocabulary development: A naturalistic observation study of Mozambican infants from 1:1 to 2:1. *Journal of Child Language.*

Mastronardi, C.A., & others (2016). Linkage and association analysis of ADHD endophenotypes in extended and multigenerational pedigrees from a genetic isolate. *Molecular Psychiatry, 21,* 1434–1440.

Mastropieri, M.A., & Scruggs, T.E. (2018). *Inclusive classroom* (6th ed.). Upper Saddle River, NJ: Pearson.

Masumoto, D., & Juang, L. (2017). *Culture and psychology* (6th ed.). Boston: Cengage.

Mathews, B., Lee, X., & Norman, R.E. (2016). Impact of a new mandatory reporting law on reporting and identification of child abuse: A seven-year time trend analysis. *Child Abuse and Neglect, 56,* 62–79.

Mathias, S.R., & others (2016). Recurrent major depression and right hippocampal volume: A bivariate linkage and association study. *Human Brain Mapping, 37,* 192–202.

Matlin, M.W. (2012). The *psychology of women* (7th ed.). Belmont, CA: Wadsworth.

Matlow, J.N., Jubetsky, A., Alesksa, K., Berger, H., & Koren, G. (2013). The transfer of ethyl glucuronide across the dually perfused human placenta. *Placenta, 34,* 369–373.

Matsuba, M.K., Murazyn, T., & Hart, D. (2014). Moral identity and community. In M. Killen & J.G. Smetana (Eds.), *Handbook of moral development* (2nd ed.). New York: Psychology Press.

Matsumoto, D., & Juang, L. (2017). *Culture and psychology* (6th ed.). Boston: Cengage.

Matthiessen, C. (2013). *Overweight children: Tips for parents.* Retrieved February 21, 2013, from www.webmd.com/parenting/raising-fit-kids/mood/talking-kids

Maurer, D. (2016). How the baby learns to see: Donald O. Hebb award lecture, Canadian Society for Brain, Behavior, and Cognitive Science, Ottawa, June 2015. *Canadian Journal of Experimental Science, 70,* 195–200.

Maurer, D., & Lewis, T.L. (2013). Sensitive periods in visual development. In P.D. Zelazo (Ed.), *Oxford handbook of developmental psychology.* New York: Oxford University Press.

Maurer, D., Lewis, T.L., Brent, H.P., & Levin, A.V. (1999). Rapid improvement in the acuity of infants after visual input. *Science, 286,* 108–110.

Maurer, D., Mondloch, C.J., & Leis, T.L. (2007). Effects of early visual deprivation on perceptual and cognitive development. In C. von Hofsten & K. Rosander (Eds.), *Progress in Brain Research, 164,* 87–104.

Mayer, K.D., & Zhang, L. (2009). Short- and long-term effects of cocaine abuse during pregnancy on heart development. *Therapeutic Advances in Cardiovascular Disease, 3,* 7–16.

Mayer, R.E. (2008). *Curriculum and instruction* (2nd ed.). Upper Saddle River, NJ: Prentice Hall.

Mayo Clinic (2017). Pregnancy and fish: What's safe to eat? Retrieved January 10, 2017, from http://www.mayoclinic.com/health/pregnancy-and-fish/PR00158

Mazul, M.C., Salm Ward, T.C., & Ngui, E.M. (2017). Anatomy of good prenatal care: Perspectives of low income African-American women on barriers and facilitators to prenatal care. *Journal of Racial Ethnic Health Disparities, 4,* 79–86.

Mazza, M., & others (2017, in press). The role of theory of mind on social information processing in children with autism spectrum disorders: A mediation analysis. *Journal of Autism and Developmental Disorders.*

Mazzucato, V., & Schans, D. (2011). Transnational families and the well-being of children: Conceptual and methodological challenges. *Journal of Marriage and the Family, 73,* 704–712.

Mbonye, A.K., Neema, S., & Magnussen, P. (2006). Treatment-seeking practices for malaria in pregnancy among rural women in Mukono district, Uganda. *Journal of Biosocial Science, 38,* 221–237.

Mbugua Gitau, G., & others (2009). The influence of maternal age on the outcomes of pregnancy complicated by bleeding at less than 12 weeks. *Acta Obstetrica et Gynecologica Scandinavica, 88,* 116–118.

McAdams, D.P., Josselson, R., & Lieblich, A. (2006). *Identity and story: Creating self in narrative.* Washington, DC: American Psychological Association.

McAdams, D.P., & Zapata-Gietl, C. (2015). Three strands of identity development across the human life course: Reading Erik Erikson in full. In K.C. McLean & M. Syed (Eds.), *Oxford handbook of identity development.* New York: Oxford University Press.

McAllister, S., & others (2017). Healthcare professionals' attitudes, knowledge, and self-efficacy levels regarding the use of self-hypnosis in childbirth: A prospective questionnaire survey. *Midwifery, 47,* 8–14.

McAvoy, M., & others (2016). Unmasking language lateralization in human brain intrinsic activity. *Cerebral Cortex, 26,* 1733–1746.

McBean, A.L., Kinsey, S.G., & Montgomery-Downs, H.E. (2016). Effects of a single night of postpartum sleep on childless women's daytime functioning. *Physiology and Behavior, 156,* 137–147.

McBride-Chang, C. (2004). *Children's literacy development* (Texts in Developmental Psychology Series). London: Edward Arnold/Oxford Press.

McBride-Chang, C., & others (2005). Changing models across cultures: Associations of phonological and morphological awareness to reading in Beijing, Hong Kong, Korea, and America. *Journal of Experimental Child Psychology, 92,* 140–160.

McBride-Chang, C., & others (2008). Word recognition and cognitive profiles of Chinese preschool children at risk for dyslexia through language delay or familial history of dyslexia. *Journal of Child Psychology and Psychiatry, 49,* 211–218.

McCabe, A., & others (2013). Multilingual children: Beyond myths and practices. *Social Policy Report of the Society for Research in Child Development, 27*(4).

McCabe, S.E., & others (2017). Adolescents' prescription stimulant use and adult functional outcomes: A national prospective study. *Journal of the American Academy of Child and Adolescent Psychiatry, 56,* 226–233.

McCarroll, J.E., & others (2017). Characteristics, classification, and prevention of child maltreatment fatalities. *Military Medicine, 182,* e1551–e1557.

McCartney, K. (2003, July 16). Interview with Kathleen McCartney in A. Bucuvalas, "Child care and behavior." *HGSE News,* pp. 1–4. Cambridge, MA: Harvard Graduate School of Education.

McClelland, M.M., Acock, A.C., Piccinin, A., Rhea, S.A., & Stallings, M.C. (2013). Relations between preschool attention span-persistence and age 25 educational outcomes. *Early Childhood Research Quarterly, 28,* 314–324.

McClelland, M.M., & Tominey, S.L. (2015). *Stop, act, think.* New York: Taylor & Francis.

McClelland, M.M., & others (2017, in press). Self-regulation. In N. Halfon (Ed.), *Handbook of life course health development.* New York: Springer.

McCloskey, K., & others (2017, in press). The association between higher maternal pre-pregnancy body mass index and increased birth weight, adiposity, and inflammation in the newborn. *Pediatric Obesity.*

McCormack, L.A., & others (2011). Weight-related teasing in a racially diverse sample of sixth-grade children. *Journal of the American Dietetic Association, 111,* 431–436.

McCormack, S.E., & others (2014). Effects of exercise and lifestyle modification on fitness, insulin resistance, skeletal muscle oxidative phosphorylation and intramyocellular lipid content in obese children and adolescents. *Pediatric Obesity, 9,* 281–291.

McCormick, C.B., Dimmitt, C., & Sullivan, F.R. (2013). Metacognition, learning, and instruction. In I.B. Weiner & others (Eds.), *Handbook of psychology* (2nd ed., Vol. 7). New York: Wiley.

McCoy, D.C., & Raver, C.C. (2011). Caregiver emotional expressiveness, child emotion regulation, and child behavior problems among Head Start families. *Social Development, 20,* 741–761.

McCoy, D.C., & others (2016). Differential effectiveness of Head Start in urban and rural communities. *Journal of Applied Developmental Psychology, 43,* 29–42.

McCoy, K.P., George, M.R., Cummings, E.M., & Davies, P.T. (2013). Constructive and destructive marital conflict, parenting, and children's school and social adjustment. *Social Development, 22,* 641–662.

McCulloch, S. (2016). *Highest C-section rates by country.* Retrieved April 26, 2017, from www. bellybelly.com

McDonald, J.A., Argotsinger, B., Mojarro, O., Rochar, R., & Amalya, A. (2015). First trimester initiation of prenatal care in the U.S.–Mexico border. *Medical Care, 53,* 700–707.

McElhaney, K.B., & Allen, J.P. (2012). Sociocultural perspectives on adolescent autonomy. In P.K. Kreig, M.S. Schulz, & S.T. Hauser (Eds.), *Adolescence and beyond.* New York: Oxford University Press.

McElvaney, R., Greene, S., & Hogan, D. (2014). To tell or not to tell? Factors influencing young people's informal disclosures of child sexual abuse. *Journal of Interpersonal Violence, 29,* 928–947.

McGarry, J., Kim, H., Sheng, X., Egger, M., & Baksh, L. (2009). Postpartum depression and help-seeking behavior. *Journal of Midwifery and Women's Health, 54,* 50–56.

McGarvey, C., McDonnell, M., Hamilton, K., O'Regan, M., & Matthews, T. (2006). An 8-year study of risk factors for SIDS: Bed-sharing versus non-bed-sharing. *Archives of Disease in Childhood, 91,* 318–323.

McGillion, M., & others (2017a). What paves the way to conventional language? The predictive value of babble, pointing, and socioeconomic status. *Child Development, 88,* 156–166.

McGillion, M., & others (2017b, in press). A randomized controlled trial to test the effect of promoting caregiver contingent talk on language development in infants from diverse socioeconomic status backgrounds. *Journal of Child Psychology and Psychiatary.*

McGilvray, J. (Ed.) (2017). *The Cambridge companion to Chomsky.* New York: Cambridge University Press.

McGregor, K.K. (2017). Semantics in child language disorders. In R. Schwartz (Ed.), *Handbook of child language disorders* (2nd ed.). New York: Routledge.

McHale, S.M., Updegraff, K.A., & Whiteman, S.D. (2013). Sibling relationships. In G.W. Peterson & K.R. Bush (Eds.), *Handbook of marriage and family* (3rd ed.). New York: Springer.

McKelvey, K., & Halpern-Felsher, B. (2017). Adolescent cigarette smoking perceptions and behavior: Tobacco control gains and gaps amidst the rapidly expanding tobacco products market from 2001 to 2015. *Journal of Adolescent Health, 60,* 226–228.

McKeown, M., & others (2017). *Vocabulary assessment to support instruction.* New York: Guilford.

McLaughlin, K.A., Sheridan, M.A., & Nelson, C.A. (2017, in press). Neglect as a violation of species-expectant experience: Neurodevelopmental consequences. *Biological Psychiatry.*

McLean, K.C., & Jennings, L.E. (2012). Teens telling tall tales: How maternal and peer audiences support narrative identity development. *Journal of Adolescence, 35,* 1455–1469.

McLean, K.C., Syed, M., Yoder, A., & Greenhoot, A. (2016). The role of domain content in understanding identity development processes. *Journal of Research on Adolescence, 26,* 60–75.

McLoyd, V.C., Kaplan, R., Purtell, K.M., & Huston, A.C. (2011). Assessing the effects of a work-based antipoverty program for parents on youths' future orientation and employment experiences. *Child Development, 82,* 113–132.

McLoyd, V.C., & others (2009). Poverty and social disadvantage in adolescence. In R.M. Lerner & L. Steinberg (Eds.), *Handbook of adolescent psychology* (3rd ed.). New York: Wiley.

McMahon, D.M., Liu, J., Zhang, H., Torres, M.E., & Best, R.G. (2013). Maternal obesity, folate intake, and neural tube defects in offspring. *Birth Defects A: Clinical and Molecular Teratology, 97,* 115–122.

McMahon, M., & Stryjewski, G. (2012). *Pediatrics.* New York: Elsevier.

McMurray, B. (2016). Language at three timescales: The role of real-time processes in language development and evolution. *Topics in Cognitive Science, 8,* 393–407.

McMurray, R.G., Harrell, J.S., Creighton, D., Wang, Z., & Bangdiwala, S.I. (2008). Influence of physical activity on change in weight status as children become adolescents. *International Journal of Pediatric Obesity, 3,* 69–77.

McNicholas, F., & others (2014). Medical, cognitive, and academic outcomes of very low birth weight infants at 10–14 years in Ireland. *Irish Journal of Medical Science, 183,* 525–532.

McQueen, D.V. (2017). Policy development and decision making in prevention science. In M. Israelashvili & J. Romano (Eds.), *Cambridge handbook of international prevention science.* New York: Cambridge University Press.

Meade, C.S., Kershaw, T.S., & Ickovics, J.R. (2008). The intergenerational cycle of teenage motherhood: An ecological approach. *Health Psychology, 27,* 419–429.

Medford, E., & others (2017, in press). Treatment adherence and psychological wellbeing in maternal caregivers of children with phenylketonuria (PKU). *JMD Reports.*

Meehan, W.P., & Mannix, R. (2013). A substantial proportion of life-threatening injuries are sports-related. *Pediatric Emergency Care, 29,* 624–627.

Meeus, W. (2017). Adolescent ethnic identity in social context: A commentary. *Child Development, 88,* 761–766.

Meghea, C.L., & others (2015). Statewide Medicaid enhanced prenatal care programs and infant mortality. *Pediatrics, 136,* 334–342.

Mehta, C.M., Gruen, J.R., & Zhang, H. (2017, in press). A method for integrating neuroimaging into genetic models of learning performance. *Genetic Epidemiology.*

Meins, E., Bureau, J.F., & Fernyhough, C. (2017, in press). Mother-child attachment from infancy to the preschool years: Predicting security and stability. *Child Development.*

Meins, E., & others (2013). Mind-mindedness and theory of mind: Mediating processes of language and perspectival symbolic play. *Child Development, 84,* 1777–1790.

Meisel, V., Servera, M., Garcia-Banda, G., Cardo, E., & Moreno, I. (2013). Neurofeedback and standard pharmacological intervention in ADHD: A randomized controlled trial with six-month follow-up. *Biological Psychology, 94,* 12–21.

Meldrum, R.C., & others (2017). Reassessing the relationship between general intelligence and self-control in childhood. *Intelligence, 60,* 1–9.

Melinder, A., & others (2016). The emotional child witness effect survives presentation mode. *Behavioral Sciences and the Law, 34,* 113–125.

Meltzer, L.J. (2017). Future directions in sleep and developmental psychopathology. *Journal of Clinical Child and Adolescent Psychology, 46,* 295–301.

Meltzoff, A.N. (1988). Infant imitation and memory: Nine-month-old infants in immediate and deferred tests. *Child Development, 59,* 217–225.

Meltzoff, A.N. (2004). Imitation as a mechanism of social cognition: Origins of empathy, theory of mind, and the representation of action. In U. Goswami (Ed.), *Blackwell handbook of childhood cognitive development.* Malden, MA: Blackwell.

Meltzoff, A.N. (2005). Imitation. In B. Hopkins (Ed.), *Cambridge encyclopedia of child development.* Cambridge, UK: Cambridge University Press.

Meltzoff, A.N. (2007). "Like me": A foundation for social cognition. *Developmental Science, 10,* 126–134.

Meltzoff, A.N. (2011). Social cognition and the origins of imitation, empathy, and theory of mind. In U. Goswami (Ed.), *Wiley-Blackwell handbook of childhood cognitive development* (2nd ed.). New York: Wiley.

Meltzoff, A.N., & Moore, M.K. (1999). A new foundation for cognitive development in infancy: The birth of the representational infant. In E.K. Skolnick, K. Nelson, S.A. Gelman, & P.H. Miller (Eds.), *Conceptual development.* Mahwah, NJ: Erlbaum.

Meltzoff, A.N., & Williamson, R.A. (2013). Imitation: Social, cognitive, and theoretical perspectives. In P.D. Zelazo (Ed.), *Oxford handbook of developmental psychology.* New York: Oxford University Press.

Meltzoff, A.N., Williamson, R.A., & Marshall, P.J. (2013). Developmental perspective on action science: Lessons from infant imitation and cognitive neuroscience. In W. Prinz & others (Eds.), *Action science.* Cambridge, MA: MIT Press.

Melzi, G., Schick, A.R., & Kennedy, J.L. (2011). Narrative elaboration and participation: Two dimensions of maternal elicitation style. *Child Development, 82,* 1282–1296.

Mendelson, M., & others (2016). Sleep quality, sleep duration, and physical activity in obese adolescents: Effects of exercise training. *Pediatric Obesity, 11,* 26–32.

Mendoza, M.M., & others (2017). The effects of economic and sociocultural stressors on the well-being of children of Latino immigrants living in poverty. *Cultural Diversity and Ethnic Minority Psychology, 23,* 15–26.

Menesini, E., Palladino, B.E., & Nocentini, A. (2016). Let's not fall into the trap: Online and school-based program to prevent cyberbullying among adolescents. In T. Vollink, F. DeHue, & C. McGuckin (Eds.), *Cyberbullying.* New York: Psychology

Menesini, E., & Salmivalli, C. (2017). Bullying in schools: The state of the knowledge and effective interventions. *Psychology, Health, and Medicine, 22*(Suppl. 1), S240–S253.

Meng, X., Uto, Y., & Hashiya, K. (2017). Observing third-party attentional relationships affects infants' gaze following: An eye-tracking study. *Frontiers in Psychology, 7,* 2065.

Menias, C.O., & others (2007). CT of pregnancy-related complications. *Emergency Radiology, 13,* 299–306.

Menn, L., & Stoel-Gammon, C. (2009). Phonological development: Learning sounds and sound patterns. In J. Berko Gleason (Ed.), *The development of language* (7th ed.). Boston: Allyn & Bacon.

Mennella, J.A. (2009). Taste and smell. In R.A. Shweder & others (Eds.), *The child: An encyclopedic companion.* Chicago: University of Chicago Press.

Menon, M., & others (2007). The developmental costs of high self-esteem in aggressive children. *Child Development, 78,* 1627–1639.

Menon, R., & others. (2011). Cigarette smoking induces oxidative stress and apoptosis in normal fetal membranes. *Placenta, 32*(4), 317–322.

Menyuk, P., Liebergott, J., & Schultz, M. (1995). *Early language development in full-term and premature infants.* Hillsdale, NJ: Erlbaum.

Mercer, N., Farrington, D.P., Ttofi, M.M., Keijsers, L., Branje, S., & Meeus, W. (2016). Childhood predictors and adult life success of adolescent delinquency abstainers. *Journal of Abnormal Child Psychology, 44,* 613–624.

Meredith, N.V. (1978). Research between 1960 and 1970 on the standing height of young children in different parts of the world. In H.W. Reece & L.P. Lipsitt (Eds.), *Advances in child development and behavior* (Vol. 12). New York: Academic Press.

Merewood, A., & others (2007). Breastfeeding duration rates and factors affecting continued breastfeeding among infants born at an inner-city U.S. baby-friendly hospital. *Journal of Human Lactation, 23,* 157–164.

Merianos, A.L., Dixon, C.A., & Mahabee-Gittens, E.M. (2017). Tobacco smoke exposure-related illnesses among pediatric emergency department patients. *Journal of Pediatric Health Care, 31,* 161–166.

Merrill, S.M., Steif, M.C., & Savin-Williams, R.C. (2016). LGBTQ umbrella. In A.E. Goldberg (Ed.), *SAGE encyclopedia of LGBTQ studies.* Thousand Oaks, CA: Sage.

Messiah, S.E., Miller, T.L., Lipshultz, S.E., & Bandstra, E.S. (2011). Potential latent effects of prenatal cocaine exposure on growth and the risk of cardiovascular and metabolic disease in childhood. *Progress in Pediatric Cardiology, 31,* 59–65.

Metz, E.C., & Youniss, J. (2005). Longitudinal gains in civic development through school-based required service. *Political Psychology, 26,* 413–437.

Meuwissen, A.S., & Carlson, S.M. (2015). Fathers matter: The role of father parenting in preschool children's executive function. *Journal of Experimental Child Psychology, 140,* 1–15.

Michaud, I., & others (2017). Physical activity and sedentary behavior levels in children and adolescents with type 1 diabetes using insulin pump or injection therapy—The importance of parental activity profile. *Journal of Diabetes and Its Complications, 31,* 381–386.

Middleton, R.J., & others (2017). Epigenetic silencing of the human 18 kDA translocator protein in a T cell leukemia cell line. *DNA and Cell Biology, 38,* 103–108.

Miele, D., & Scholer, A.A. (2016). Self-regulation of motivation. In K. Wentzel & D. Miele (Eds.), *Handbook of motivation at school* (2nd ed.). New York: Routledge.

Miguel-Neto, J., & others (2016). New approach to phenotypic variability and karyotype-phenotype correlation in Turner syndrome. *Journal of Pediatric Endocrinology and Metabolism, 29,* 475–479.

Milesi, G., & others (2014). Assessment of human hippocampal developmental neuroanatomy by means of ex-vivo 7T magnetic resonance imaging. *International Journal of Developmental Neuroscience, 34,* 33–41.

Miller, A.L., & others (2017). Child cortisol moderates the association between family routines and emotion regulation in low-income children. *Development and Psychopathology, 59,* 99–110.

Miller, B. (2017). *Cultural anthropology* (4th ed.). Upper Saddle River, NJ: Pearson.

Miller, B.C., Benson, B., & Galbraith, K.A. (2001). Family relationships and adolescent pregnancy risk: A research synthesis. *Developmental Review, 21,* 1–38.

Miller, C., Martin, C.L., Fabes, R., & Hanish, D. (2013). Bringing the cognitive and social together: How gender detectives and gender enforcers shape children's gender development. In M. Banaji & S. Gelman (Eds.), *Navigating the social world: A developmental perspective.* New York: Oxford University Press.

Miller, C.B. (2017). *The character gap.* New York: Oxford University Press.

Miller, C.F., Lurye, L.E., Zosuls, K.M., & Ruble, D.N. (2009). Accessibility of gender stereotype domains: Developmental and gender differences in children. *Sex Roles, 60,* 870–881.

Miller, C.R. (2013). Project Impact: Service-learning's impact on youth with disabilities. *School Social Work Journal, 37,* 52–75.

Miller, E.B., Farkas, G., & Duncan, G.J. (2016). Does Head Start differentially benefit children with risks targeted by the program's service model? *Early Childhood Research Quarterly, 34,* 1–12.

Miller, E.M., & others (2012). Theories of willpower affect sustained learning. *PLoS One, 7*(6), e38680.

Miller, J.G., & Bland, C.G. (2014). A cultural perspective on moral development. In M. Killen & J.G. Smetana (Eds.), *Handbook of moral development* (2nd ed.). New York: Psychology Press.

Miller, M.B., Janssen, T., & Jackson, K.M. (2017). The prospective association between sleep and initiation of substance use in young adolescents. *Journal of Adolescent Health, 60,* 154–160.

Miller, P.H. (2016). *Theories of developmental psychology* (6th ed.). New York: Worth.

Miller, R., Wankerl, M., Stalder, T., Kirschbaum, C., & Alexander, N. (2013). The serotonin transporter gene-linked polymorphic region (5-HTTLPR) and cortisol stress reactivity: A meta-analysis. *Molecular Psychiatry, 18,* 1018–1024.

Miller, S., Malone, P., Dodge, K.A., & Conduct Problems Prevention Research Group (2010). Developmental trajectories of boys' and girls' delinquency: Sex differences and links to later adolescent outcomes. *Journal of Abnormal Child Psychology, 38*(7), 1021–1032.

Miller, S., McCulloch, S., & Jarrold, C. (2015). The development of memory maintenance strategies: Training cumulative rehearsal and integrative imagery in children aged between 5 and 9. *Frontiers in Psychology, 6,* 524.

Miller, S.E., & Marcovitch, S. (2015). Examining executive function in the second year of life: Coherence, stability, and relations to joint attention and language. *Developmental Psychology, 51,* 101–114.

Miller, S.L., Huppi, P.S., & Mallard, C. (2016). The consequences of fetal growth restriction on brain structure and neurodevelopmental outcome. *Journal of Physiology, 594,* 807–823.

Miller, W.R. (2017, in press). Self-management behaviors of children with spina bifida. *Journal of Neuroscience Nursing.*

Miller-Graff, L.E., Cummings, E.M., & Bergman, K.N. (2016). Effects of a brief psychoeducational intervention for family conflict: Constructive conflict, emotional insecurity, and child adjustment. *Journal of Abnormal Child Psychology, 44,* 1399–1410.

Miller-Perrin, C.L., Perrin, R.D., & Kocur, J.L. (2009). Parental, physical, and psychological aggression: Psychological symptoms in young adults. *Child Abuse and Neglect, 33,* 1–11.

Mills, C.M., & Elashi, F.B. (2014). Children's skepticism: Developmental and individual differences in children's ability to detect and explain distorted claims. *Journal of Experimental Child Psychology, 124C,* 1–17.

Mills, D., & Mills, C. (2000). *Hungarian kindergarten curriculum translation.* London: Mills Production.

Mills, M.T. (2015). Narrative performance of gifted African American school-aged children from low-income backgrounds. *American Journal of Speech-Language Pathology, 24,* 36–46.

Mills-Koonce, W.R., Propper, C.B., & Barnett, M. (2012). Poor infant soothability and later insecure-ambivalent attachment: Developmental change in phenotypic markers of risk or two measures of the same construct? *Infant Behavior and Development, 35,* 215–225.

Milne, E., & others (2012). Parental prenatal smoking and risk of childhood acute lymphoblastic leukemia. *American Journal of Epidemiology, 175,* 43–53.

Milosavljevic, B., & others (2017, in press). Anxiety and attentional bias to threat in children at increased familial risk for autism spectrum disorder. *Journal of Autism and Developmental Disorders.*

Minic, P.B., & Sovtic, A.D. (2017). Exercise intolerance and exercise-induced broncho-constriction in children. *Frontiers of Bioscience, 9,* 21–32.

Minnes, S., & others (2010). The effects of prenatal cocaine exposure on problem behavior in children 4–10 years. *Neurotoxicology and Teratology, 32,* 443–451.

Minnes, S., & others (2016). Executive function in children with prenatal cocaine exposure (12–15 years). *Neurotoxicology and Teratology, 57,* 79–86.

Minsart, A.F., Buekens, P., De Spiegelaere, M., & Englert, Y. (2013). Neonatal outcomes in obese mothers: A population-based analysis. *BMC Pregnancy and Childbirth, 13,* 36.

Mischel, W. (2004). Toward an integrative science of the person. *Annual Review of Psychology* (Vol. 55). Palo Alto, CA: Annual Reviews.

Mischel, W., Cantor, N., & Feldman, S. (1996). Principles of self-regulation: The nature of will power and self-control. In E.T. Higgins & A.W. Kruglanski (Eds.), *Social psychology.* New York: Guilford.

Mischel, W., & Moore, B.S. (1980). The role of ideation in voluntary delay for symbolically presented rewards. *Cognitive Therapy and Research, 4,* 211–221.

Mischel, W., & others (2011). 'Willpower' over the life span: Decomposing self-regulation. *Social Cognitive and Affective Neuroscience, 6,* 252–256.

Mistry, J., & Dutta, R. (2015). Human development and culture: Conceptual and methodological issues. In R.M. Lerner (Ed.), *Handbook of child psychology and developmental science* (7th ed.). New York: Wiley.

Mitchell, A.B., & Stewart, J.B. (2013). The efficacy of all-male academies: Insights from critical race theory (CRT). *Sex Roles, 69,* 382–392.

Mitchell, D.M. (2017). Growth in patients with type 1 diabetes. *Current Opinion in Endocrinology, Diabetes, and Obesity, 24,* 67–72.

Mitchell, E.A., & Krous, H.F. (2015). Sudden unexpected death in infancy: A historical perspective. *Journal of Pediatrics and Child Health, 5,* 108–112.

Miyahara, R., & others (2017). Exposure to paternal tobacco smoking increased child hospitalization for lower respiratory infections but not for other diseases in Vietnam. *Scientific Reports, 7,* 45481.

Miyake, K., Chen, S., & Campos, J. (1985). Infants' temperament, mothers' mode of interaction and attachment in Japan: An interim report. In I. Bretherton & F. Waters (Eds.), Growing points of attachment theory and research, *Monographs of the Society for Research in Child Development, 50*(1–2, Serial No. 109), 276–297.

Miyake, S., & others (2017). Community midwifery initiatives in fragile and conflict-affected countries: A scoping review of approaches from recruitment to retention. *Health Policy Planning, 32,* 21–33.

Mize, K.D., & Jones, N.A. (2012). Infant physiological and behavioral responses to loss of maternal attention to a social rival. *International Journal of Psychophysiology, 83,* 16–23.

Mize, K.D., Pineda, M., Blau, A.K., Marsh, K., & Jones, N.A. (2014). Infant physiological and behavioral responses to a jealousy provoking condition. *Infancy, 19,* 1–11.

Mnyani, C.N., & others (2017, in press). Infant feeding knowledge, perceptions, and practices among women with and without HIV in Johannesburg, South Africa: A survey in healthcare facilities. *International Breastfeeding Journal.*

Modecki, K.L., Barber, B.L., & Eccles, J.S. (2014). Binge drinking trajectories across adolescence: For early maturing youth, extra-curricular activities are protective. *Journal of Adolescent Health, 54,* 61–66.

Moed, A., & others (2015). Parent-adolescent conflict as sequences of reciprocal negative emotion: Links with conflict resolution and adolescents' behavior problems. *Journal of Youth and Adolescence, 44,* 1607–1622.

Moffitt, T.E. (2012). *Childhood self-control predicts adult health, wealth, and crime.* Paper presented at the Symposium on Symptom Improvement in Well-being, Copenhagen.

Moffitt, T.E., & others (2011). A gradient of childhood self-control predicts health, wealth, and public safety. *Proceedings of the National Academy of Sciences U.S.A, 108,* 2693–2698.

Mohagheghi, A., & others (2017). A randomized trial of comparing the efficacy of two neurofeedback protocols for treatment of clinical and cognitive symptoms of ADHD: Theta suppression/beta enhancement and theta suppression/alpha enhancement. *Biomedical Research International, 2017,* 3513281.

Molina, B.S., & others (2013). Adolescence substance use in the multimodal treatment study of attention-deficit/hyperactivity disorder (ADHD) (MTA) as a function of childhood ADHD, random assignment to childhood treatments, and subsequent medication. *Journal of the American Academy of Child and Adolescent Psychiatry, 52,* 250–263.

Molina, B.S., & others (2014). Heavy alcohol use in early adulthood as a function of childhood ADHD: Developmentally specific mediation by social impairment and delinquency. *Experimental and Clinical Psychopharmacology.*

Molina, R.C., Roca, C.G., Zamorano, J.S., & Araya, E.G. (2010). Family planning and adolescent pregnancy. *Best Practices and Research: Clinical Obstetrics and Gynecology, 24,* 209–222.

Moline, H.R., & Smith, J.F. (2016). The continuing threat of syphilis in pregnancy. *Current Opinion in Obstetrics and Gynecology, 28,* 101–104.

Mollborg, P., Wennergren, G., Almqvist, P., & Alm, B. (2015). Bed sharing is more common in sudden infant death syndrome than in explained sudden unexpected deaths in infancy. *Acta Pediatrica, 104,* 777–783.

Mollborn, S. (2017). Teenage mothers today: What we know and how it matters. *Child Development Perspectives, 11,* 63–69.

Mon, E., & others (2017, in press). Fatigue, depression, maternal confidence, and maternal satisfaction during the first month postpartum: A comparison of Japanese mothers by age and parity. *International Journal of Nursing Practice.*

Monahan, K., Guyer, A., Sil, J., Fitzwater, T., & Steinberg, L. (2016). Integration of developmental neuroscience and contextual approaches to the study of adolescent psychopathology. In D. Cicchetti (Ed.), *Handbook of developmental psychology* (3rd ed.). New York: Wiley.

Monahan, K.C., & others (2016). Integration of developmental neuroscience and contextual approaches to the study of adolescent development. In D. Cicchetti (Ed.), *Developmental psychopathology* (3rd ed.). New York: Wiley.

Mond, J., & others (2011). Obesity, body satisfaction, and emotional well-being in early and late adolescence: Findings from the Project EAT Study. *Journal of Adolescent Health, 48,* 373–378.

Moninger, J. (2013). *How to talk with your child about losing weight.* Retrieved February 21, 2013, from www.parents.com/kids/teens/weight-loss/how-to-talk-to-your-child-about-losing-weight/

Monn, A.R., & others (2017). Executive function and parenting in the context of homelessness. *Journal of Family Psychology, 31,* 61–70.

Monni, G., & others (2016). How to perform transabdominal chorionic villus sampling: A practical guideline. *Journal of Maternal-Fetal and Neonatal Medicine, 29,* 1499–1505.

Montana, S. (2007). Increased risk in the elderly parturient. *Current Opinion in Obstetrics and Gynecology, 19,* 110–112.

Montemayor, R. (1982). The relationship between parent-adolescent conflict and the amount of time adolescents spend with parents, peers, and alone. *Child Development, 53,* 1512–1519.

Moon, R.Y., Hauck, F.R., & Colson, E.R. (2016). Safe infant sleep interventions: What is the evidence for successful behavior change? *Current Pediatric Reviews, 12,* 67–75.

Mooney-Leber, S.M, & Brummelte, S. (2017). Neonatal pain and reduced maternal care: Early-life stressors interacting to impact brain and behavioral development. *Neuroscience, 342,* 21–36.

Moore, D.S. (2001). *The dependent gene.* New York: W.H. Freeman.

Moore, D.S. (2013). Behavioral genetics, genetics, and epigenetics. In P.D. Zelazo (Ed.), *Oxford handbook of developmental psychology.* New York: Oxford University Press.

Moore, D.S. (2015). *The developing genome.* New York: Oxford University Press.

Moore, D.S. (2017, in press). Behavioral epigenetics. *Wiley Interdisciplinary Reviews. Systems Biology and Medicine.*

Moore, M.W., Brendel, P.C., & Fiez, J.A. (2014). Reading faces: Investigating the use of a novel face-based orthography in acquired alexia. *Brain and Language, 129C,* 7–13.

Moore, S.R., Harden, K.P., & Mendle, J. (2014). Pubertal timing and adolescent sexual behavior in girls. *Developmental Psychology, 50,* 1734–1745.

Moosmann, D.A., & Roosa, M.W. (2015). Exploring Mexican American adolescent romantic relationship profiles and adjustment. *Journal of Adolescence, 43,* 181–192.

Mooya, H., Sichimba, F., & Bakermans-Kranenburg, M. (2016). Infant-mother and infant-sibling attachment in Zambia. *Attachment and Human Development, 18,* 618–635.

Moradi, B., & others (2016). A content analysis of literature on trans people and issues: 2002–2012. *The Counseling Psychologist, 44,* 960–965.

Morasch, K.C., & Bell, M.A. (2009). Patterns of frontal and temporal brain electrical activity during declarative memory performance in 10-month-old infants. *Brain and Cognition, 71,* 215–222.

Moravcik, E., Nolte, S., & Feeney, S. (2013). *Meaningful curriculum for young children.* Upper Saddle River, NJ: Pearson.

Morgan, P.J., & others (2017, in press). Practicalities and research considerations for conducting childhood obesity prevention interventions with families. *Children.*

Moriguchi, Y., Chevalier, N., & Zelazo, P.D. (2016). Editorial: Development of executive function during childhood. *Frontiers in Psychology, 7,* 6.

Moro, M.R. (2014). Parenthood in migration: How to face vulnerability. *Culture, Medicine, and Psychiatry, 38,* 13–27.

Morosan, L., & others (2017). Emotion recognition and perspective taking: A comparison between typical and incarcerated male adolescents. *PLoS One, 12*(1), e0170646.

Morra, S., Gobbo, C., Marini, Z., & Sheese, R. (2007). *Cognitive development: Neo-Piagetian perspectives.* Mahwah, NJ: Erlbaum.

Morrill, M.I., Hawrilenko, M., & Cordova, J.V. (2016). A longitudinal examination of positive parenting following an acceptance-based couple intervention. *Journal of Family Psychology, 30,* 104–113.

Morris, A.S., & others (2017, in press). Targeting parenting in early childhood: A public health approach to improve outcomes of children living in poverty. *Child Development.*

Morrison, D.C. (Ed.) (2017). *Organizing early experience.* New York: Routledge.

Morrison, G.S. (2017). *Fundamentals of early childhood education* (8th ed.). Upper Saddle River, NJ: Pearson.

Morrison, G.S. (2018). *Early childhood education today* (14th ed.). Upper Saddle River, NJ: Pearson.

Morrison, S.C., Fife, T., & Hertlein, K.M. (2017). Mechanisms behind prolonged effects of parental divorce: A phenomenological study. *Journal of Divorce and Remarriage, 58,* 44–63.

Morrison-Beedy, D., & others (2013). Reducing sexual risk behavior in adolescent girls: Results from a randomized trial. *Journal of Adolescent Health, 52,* 314–322.

Morrissey, T.W. (2009). Multiple child-care arrangements and young children's behavioral outcomes. *Child Development, 80,* 59–76.

Morrissey-Ross, M. (2000). Lead poisoning and its elimination. *Public Health Nursing, 17,* 229–230.

Morrow, C.E., Culbertson, J.L., Accornero, V.H., Xue, L., Anthony, J.C., & Bandstra, E.S. (2006). Learning disabilities and intellectual functioning in school-aged children with prenatal cocaine exposure. *Developmental Neuropsychology, 30,* 905–931.

Morton, R.W., & others (2017, in press). STAAR: A randomized controlled trial of electronic adherence monitoring with reminder alarms and feedback to improve clinical outcomes for children with asthma. *Thorax, 72,* 347–354.

Moulson, M.C., & Nelson, C.A. (2008). Neurological development. In M.M. Haith & J.B. Benson (Eds.), *Encyclopedia of infant and early childhood development.* Oxford, UK: Elsevier.

Moura da Costa, E., & Tuleski, S.C. (2017). Social constructivist interpretation of Vygotsky. In C. Ratner & D. Silva (Eds.), *Vygotsky and Marx.* New York: Routledge.

Movahed Abtahi, M., & Kerns, K.A. (2017). Attachment and emotion regulation in middle childhood: Changes in affect and vagal tone during a social stress task. *Attachment and Human Development, 19,* 221–242.

Moyer, C., Reoyo, O.R., & May, L. (2016). The influence of prenatal exercise on offspring health. *Clinical and Medical Insights: Women's Health, 9,* 37–42.

Mparmpakas, D., & others (2013). Immune system function, stress, exercise, and nutrition profile can affect pregnancy outcome: Lessons from a Mediterranean cohort. *Experimental and Therapeutic Medicine, 5,* 411–418.

Mruk, C.J., & O'Brien, E.J. (2013). Changing self-esteem through competence and worthiness training: A positive therapy. In V. Zeigler-Hill (Ed.), *Self-esteem.* New York: Psychology Press.

Mueller, T., & others (2017). Teen pregnancy prevention: Implementation of a multicomponent, community-wide approach. *Journal of Adolescent Health, 60* (Suppl. 3), S9–S17.

Muijs, D. (2017, in press). Can schools reduce bullying? The relationship between school characteristics and the prevalence of bullying behaviors. *British Journal of Educational Psychology.*

Mukherjee, S.B. (2017, in press). Autism spectrum disorders—diagnosis and management. *Indian Journal of Pediatrics.*

Muller, C.L., Anacker, A.M., & Veenstra-VanderWeele, J. (2017). The serotonin system in autism spectrum disorder: From biomarker to animal models. *Neuroscience, 42,* 427–436.

Muller, U., Miller, M., Hutchison, S., & Ten Eycke, K. (2017). Transition to school: executive function, emergent academic skills, and early school achievement. In M.J. Hoskyns & others (Eds.), *Executive functions in children's everyday lives.* New York: Oxford University Press.

Muller, U., Zelazo, P.D., Lurye, L.E., & Lieberman, D.P. (2008). The effect of labeling on preschool children's performance in the Dimensional Change Card Sort task. *Cognitive Development, 23,* 395–408.

Muller, U., & others (2017). Transition to school: Executive function, emergent academic skills, and early school achievement. In M.J. Hoskyn & others (Eds.), *Executive functions in children's everyday lives.* New York: Oxford University Press.

Muller Mirza, N. (2016). Emotions, development, and materiality at school: A cultural-historical approach. *Integrative Psychological and Behavioral Science, 50,* 634–654.

Mullola, S., & others (2012). Gender differences in teachers' perceptions of students' temperament, educational competence, and teachability. *British Journal of Educational Psychology, 82*(Pt. 2), 185–206.

Mulvey, K.L., Hitti, A., Smetana, J.G., & Killen, M. (2016). Morality, context, and development. In L. Balter & C.S. Tamis-LeMonda (Eds.), *Child psychology: A contemporary handbook* (3rd ed.). New York: Psychology Press.

Mundy, P., & others (2007). Individual differences and the development of joint attention in infancy. *Child Development, 78,* 938–954.

Murdock, D.R., & others (2017, in press). Whole-exome sequencing for diagnosis of Turner syndrome: Towards next generation sequencing and newborn screening. *Journal of Clinical Endocrinology and Metabolism.*

Murdock, T.B., Miller, A., & Kohlhardt, J. (2004). Effects of classroom context variables on high school students' judgments of the acceptability and likelihood of cheating. *Journal of Educational Psychology, 96,* 765–777.

Murin, S., Rafii, R., & Bilello, K. (2011). Smoking and smoking cessation in pregnancy. *Clinics in Chest Medicine, 32,* 75–91.

Murnane, R.J., & Levy, F. (1996). *Teaching the new basic skills.* New York: Free Press.

Murphy, D.A., Brecht, M.L., Huang, D., & Herbeck, D.M. (2012). Trajectories of delinquency from age 14 to 23 in the National Longitudinal Survey of Youth sample. *International Journal of Adolescence and Youth, 17,* 47–62.

Murray, A. (2011). Montessori elementary philosophy reflects current motivation theories. *Montessori Life, 23,* 22–33.

Murray, A.L., & others (2017). Investigating diagnostic bias in autism spectrum conditions: An item response theory analysis of sex bias in the AQ-10. *Autism Research, 10,* 790–800.

Murray, E.A. (2007). Visual memory. *Annual Review of Neuroscience* (Vol. 29). Palo Alto, CA: Annual Reviews.

Murray, H.B., & others (2017, in press). Will I get fat? 22-year weight trajectories of individuals with eating disorders. *International Journal of Eating Disorders.*

Murray, P.G., Dattani, M.T., & Clayton, P.E. (2016). Controversies in the diagnosis and management of growth hormone deficiency in childhood and adolescence. *Archives of Disease in Childhood, 101,* 96–100.

Muthuri, S.K., & others (2016). Relationships between parental education and overweight with childhood overweight and physical activity in

9–11-year-old children: Results from a 12-country study. *PLoS One, 11*(8), e0147746.

Mutreja, R., Craig, C., & O'Boyle, M.W. (2016). Attentional network deficits in children with autism spectrum disorder. *Developmental Neurorehabilitation, 19,* 389–397.

Myers, D.G. (2010). *Psychology* (9th ed.). New York: Worth.

Myerson, J., Rank, M.R., Raines, F.Q., & Schnitzler, M.A. (1998). Race and general cognitive ability: The myth of diminishing returns in education. *Psychological Science, 9,* 139–142.

N

Naaijen, J., & others (2017). Glutamatergic and GABAergic gene sets in attention-deficit/hyperactivity disorder: Association to overlapping traits in ADHD and autism. *Translational Psychiatry, 7*(1), e999.

Nader, P.R., Bradley, R.H., Houts, R.M., McRitchie, S.L., & O'Brian, M. (2008). Moderate-to-vigorous physical activity from 9 to 15 years. *Journal of the American Medical Association, 300,* 295–305.

NAEYC (2009). *Developmentally appropriate practice in early childhood programs serving children from birth through age 8.* Washington, DC: Author.

Nagahawatte, N.T., & Goldenberg, R. (2008). Poverty, maternal health, and adverse pregnancy outcomes. *Annals of the New York Academy of Sciences, 1136,* 80–85.

Nagel, B.J., & others (2011). Altered white matter microstructure in children with attention-deficit/hyperactivity disorder. *Journal of the American Academy of Child and Adolescent Psychiatry, 50,* 283–292.

Naicker, K., Galambos, N.L., Zeng, Y., Senthilselvan, A., & Colman, I. (2013). Social, demographic, and health outcomes in the 10 years following adolescent depression. *Journal of Adolescent Health, 52,* 533–538.

Naidoo, S., Satorius, B.K., de Vines, H., & Taylor, M. (2016). Verbal bullying changes among students following an educational intervention using the integrated model for behavior change. *Journal of School Health, 86,* 813–822.

Nair, S., & others (2017, in press). Local resting state functional connectivity in autism: Site and cohort variability and the effect of eye status. *Brain Imaging and Behavior.*

Najar, B., & others (2008). Effects of psychosocial stimulation on growth and development of severely malnourished children in a nutrition unit in Bangladesh. *European Journal of Clinical Nutrition, 63*(6), 725–731.

Najjar, R., & Brooker, R.J. (2017). Delta-beta coupling is associated with paternal caregiving behaviors during preschool. *International Journal of Psychophysiology, 112,* 31–39.

Najman, J.M., & others (2009). The impact of episodic and chronic poverty on child cognitive development. *Journal of Pediatrics, 154,* 284–289.

Najman, J.M., & others (2010). Timing and chronicity of family poverty and development of unhealthy behaviors in children: A longitudinal study. *Journal of Adolescent Health, 46,* 538–544.

Nam, C.S., Li, Y., Yamaguchi, T., & Smith-Jackson, T.L. (2012). Haptic user interfaces for the visually impaired: implications for haptically enhanced science learning systems. *International Journal of Human-Computer Interaction, 28,* 784–798.

Nanni, V., Uher, R., & Danese, A. (2012). Childhood maltreatment predicts unfavorable course of illness and treatment outcome in depression: A meta-analysis. *American Journal of Psychiatry, 169,* 141–151.

Nansel, T.R., & others (2001). Bullying behaviors among U.S. youth. *Journal of the American Medical Association, 285,* 2094–2100.

Naranjo, M. (2017). The safest carseat for your child. *Consumer Reports, 82*(1), 56–58.

Narrog, H. (2017). Typology and grammaticalization. In A.Y. Aikhenvaid & R.M.W. Dixon (Eds.), *Cambridge handbook of linguistic typology.* New York: Cambridge University Press.

Narváez, D. (2006). Integrative moral education. In M. Killen & J. Smetana (Eds.), *Handbook of moral development.* Mahwah, NJ: Erlbaum.

Narváez, D. (2008). Four component model. In F.C. Power, R.J. Nuzzi, D. Narváez, D.K. Lapsley, & T.C. Hunt (Eds.), *Moral education: A handbook.* Westport, CT: Greenwood Publishing.

Narváez, D. (2010). The embodied dynamism of moral becoming. *Perspectives on Psychological Science, 5*(2), 185–186.

Narváez, D. (2010a). Building a sustaining classroom climate for purposeful ethical citizenship. In T. Lovat, R. Toomey, & N. Clement (Eds.), *International research handbook of values education and student wellbeing.* New York: Springer.

Narváez, D. (2010b). The embodied dynamism of moral becoming. *Perspectives on Psychological Science, 5*(2), 185–186.

Narváez, D. (2014). *The neurobiology and development of human morality.* New York: Norton.

Narváez, D. (2015). The neurobiology of moral sensitivity: Evolution, epigenetics, and early experience. In D. Mowrer & P. Vanderberg (Eds.), *The art of morality.* New York: Routledge.

Narváez, D. (2016). Baselines for virtue. In J. Annas, D. Narváez, & N.E. Snow (Eds.), *Developing the virtues.* New York: Oxford University Press.

Narváez, D. (2016). *Embodied morality.* New York: Palgrave Macmillan.

Narváez, D. (2017, in press). Evolution, childrearing, and compassionate morality. In P. Gilbert (Ed.), *Compassion.* New York: London.

Narváez, D. (2017b). The ontogenesis of moral becoming. In A. Fuentes & A. Visala (Eds.). *Verbs, bones, and brains.* Notre Dame, IN: University of Notre Dame Press.

Narváez, D. (2018, in press). Ethogenesis: Evolution, early experience, and moral becoming. In J. Graham & K. Gray (Eds.), *The atlas of moral psychology.* New York: Guilford Press.

Narváez, D., & Gleason, T.R. (2013). Developmental optimism. In D. Narváez & others (2013). *Evolution,* early experience, and human development. New York: Oxford University Press.

Narváez, D., & Lapsley, D. (Eds.). (2009). *Moral personality, identity, and character: An interdisciplinary future.* New York: Cambridge University Press.

NASSPE (2012). *Single-sex schools/schools with single-sex classrooms/what's the difference.* Retrieved from www.singlesexschools.org/schools-schools.com.

Nathan, G.S. (2017). Phonology. In B. Dancygier (Ed.), *Cambridge handbook of cognitive linguistics.* New York: Cambridge University Press.

National Assessment of Educational Progress (NAEP) (2012). *The nation's report card 2011.* Washington, DC: U.S. Office of Education.

National Assessment of Educational Progress (NAEP) (2016). *The nation's report card 2015.* Washington, DC: U.S. Office of Education.

National Association for Gifted Children (2017). *Frequently asked questions about gifted children.* Washington, DC: Author.

National Association for Sport and Physical Education. (2002). *Active start: A statement of physical activity guidelines for children birth to five years.* Reston, VA: National Association for Sport and Physical Education.

National Cancer Institute (2017). *Childhood cancer.* Rockville, MD: Author.

National Center for Education Statistics (2016). *The condition of education, 2015.* Washington, DC: U.S. Department of Education.

National Center for Education Statistics (2016). *School dropouts.* Washington, DC: Author.

National Center for Health Statistics (2017). *Death statistics.* Atlanta: Centers for Disease and Control.

National Center for Health Statistics (2017a). *Asthma: Data and surveillance.* Atlanta: Centers for Disease Control and Prevention.

National Center for Health Statistics (2017b). *Child safety.* Atlanta: Centers for Disease Control and Prevention.

National Center for Health Statistics (2017c). *National diabetes fact sheet.* Atlanta: Centers for Disease Control and Prevention.

National Center for Learning Disabilities (2006). *Learning disabilities.* Retrieved March 6, 2006, from http://www.ncld.org/

National Center on Shaken Baby Syndrome (2012). *Shaken baby syndrome.* Retrieved July 29, 2012, from www.dontshake.org/

National Clearinghouse on Child Abuse and Neglect (2017). *What is child abuse and neglect?* Washington, DC: U.S. Department of Health and Human Services.

National Institute for Early Education Research (2016). *Did state pre-K get back on track in 2015?* Retrieved November 29, 2016, from http://nieer/org

National Institute of Mental Health (2017). *Autism spectrum disorder.* Retrieved March 30, 2017, from www.nimh.nih.gov/health/topics/autism-spectrum-disorders-asd/index.shtml

National Institutes of Health (2008). *Clinical trial. gov.* Retrieved April 22, 2008, from http://clinicaltrials.gov/ct2/show/NCT00059293?cond 5%22Intracranial 1 Embolism%22&r.

National Research Council (2004). *Engaging schools: Fostering high school students' motivation to learn.* Washington, DC: National Academies Press.

National Sleep Foundation (2007). *Sleep in America poll 2007.* Washington, DC: Author.

National Sleep Foundation (2017). *Children's sleep habits.* Retrieved January 7, 2017, from http://www.sleepfoundation.org

National Vital Statistics Reports (2004, March 7). *Deaths: Leading causes for 2002.* Atlanta: Centers for Disease Control and Prevention.

Naughton, A.M., & others (2017, in press). Ask me! Self-reported features of adolescents experiencing neglect or emotional maltreatment: A rapid systematic review. *Child: Care, Health, and Development.*

Naumova, O.Y., & others (2016). Epigenetic patterns modulate the connection between developmental dynamics of parenting and offspring psychosocial adjustment. *Child Development, 87,* 98–110.

Ncube, C.N., & Mueller, B.A. (2017). Daughters of mothers who smoke: A population-based cohort study of maternal prenatal tobacco use and subsequent prenatal smoking in offspring. *Pediatric and Perinatal Epidemiology, 31,* 14–20.

Nearing, G.B., & others (2012). Psychosocial parental support programs and short-term clinical outcomes in extremely low-birth-weight infants. *Journal of Maternal-Fetal and Neonatal Medicine, 25(1),* 89–93.

Needham, A.W. (2016). *Learning about objects in infancy.* New York: Psychology Press.

Needham, A., Barrett, T., & Peterman, K. (2002). A pick-me-up for infants' exploratory skills: Early simulated experiences reaching for objects using "sticky mittens" enhances young infants' object exploration skills. *Infant Behavior and Development, 25,* 279–295.

Negriff, S., Susman, E.J., & Trickett, P.K. (2011). The development pathway from pubertal timing to delinquency and sexual activity from early to late adolescence. *Journal of Youth and Adolescence, 40(10),* 1343–1356.

Neiterman, E., & Fox, B. (2017). Controlling the unruly maternal body: Losing and gaining control over the body during pregnancy and the postpartum period. *Social Science & Medicine, 174,* 142–148.

Nelson, C.A. (2003). Neural development and lifelong plasticity. In R.M. Lerner, F. Jacobs, & D. Wertlieb (Eds.), *Handbook of applied developmental science* (Vol. 1). Thousand Oaks, CA: Sage.

Nelson, C.A. (2007). A developmental cognitive neuroscience approach to the study of atypical development: A model system involving infants of diabetic mothers. In D. Coch, G. Dawson, & K.W. Fischer (Eds.), *Human behavior, learning, and the developing brain.* New York: Guilford.

Nelson, C.A. (2013a). The effects of early psycho-social deprivation. In M. Woodhead & J. Oates (Eds.), *Early childhood in focus 7: Developing brains.* Great Britain: The Open University.

Nelson, C.A. (2013b). Some thoughts on the development and neural bases of face processing.
In M. Banaji & S. Gelman (Eds.), *The development of social cognition.* New York: Oxford University Press.

Nelson, C.A., Fox, N.A., & Zeanah, C.H. (2014). *Romania's abandoned children.* Cambridge, MA: Harvard University Press.

Nelson, C.A., Thomas, K.M., & Haan, M. (2006). Neural bases of cognitive development. In W. Damon & R. Lerner (Eds.), *Handbook of child psychology* (6th ed.). New York: Wiley.

Nelson, J.A., O'Brien, M., Blankson, A.N., Calkins, S.D., & Keane, S.P. (2009). Family stress and parental responses to children's negative emotions: Tests of spillover, crossover, and compensatory hypotheses. *Journal of Family Psychology, 23,* 671–679.

Nelson, J.A., & others (2012). Maternal expressive style and children's emotional development. *Infant and Child Development, 3,* 267–286.

Nelson, J.A., & others (2013). Preschool-aged children's understanding of gratitude: Relations with emotion and mental state knowledge. *British Journal of Developmental Psychology, 31,* 42–56.

Nelson, K. (1999). Levels and modes of representation: Issues for the theory of conceptual change and development. In E.K. Skolnick, K. Nelson, S.A. Gelman, & P.H. Miller (Eds.), *Conceptual development.* Mahwah, NJ: Erlbaum.

Nelson, S.E., Van Ryzin, M.J., & Dishion, T.J. (2015). Alcohol, marijuana, and tobacco use trajectories from ages 12 to 24 years: Demographic correlates and young adult substance use problems. *Development and Psychopathology, 27,* 253–277.

Nelson, S.K., Kushley, K., & Lyubomirsky, S. (2014). The pains and pleasures of parenting: When, why, and how is parenthood associated with more or less well-being? *Psychological Bulletin, 140,* 846–895.

Nemet, D. (2016). Childhood obesity, physical activity, and exercise. *Pediatric Exercise Science, 28,* 48–51.

Nesi, J., & others (2017, in press). Friends' alcohol-related social networking site activity predicts escalations in adolescent drinking: Mediation by peer norms. *Journal of Adolescent Health.*

Neuenschwander, R., & Blair, C. (2017). Zooming in on children's behavior during delay of gratification: Disentangling impulsigenic and volitional processes underlying self-regulation. *Journal of Experimental Child Psychology, 154,* 146–163.

Nevarez, M.D., & others (2010). Associations of early life risk factors with infant sleep duration. *Academic Pediatrics, 10,* 187–193.

Neville, H.J. (2006). Different profiles of plasticity within human cognition. In Y. Munakata & M.H. Johnson (Eds.), *Attention and Performance XXI: Processes of change in brain and cognitive development.* Oxford, UK: Oxford University Press.

Nevitt, S.J., Jones, A.P., & Howard, J. (2017). Hydroxyurea (hydroxcarbamide) for sickle cell disease. *Cochrane Database of Systematic Reviews, 4,* CD002202.

Newcombe, N. (2008). The development of implicit and explicit memory. In N. Cowan &
M. Courage (Eds.), *The development of memory in childhood.* Philadelphia: Psychology Press.

Newell, K., Scully, D.M., McDonald, P.V., & Baillargeon, R. (1989). Task constraints and infant grip configurations. *Developmental Psychobiology, 22,* 817–832.

Newton, E.K., & Thompson, R.A. (2010). Parents' views of early social and emotional development: More and less meets the eye. *Zero to Three, 30(4),* 10–16.

Ng, F.F., Pomerantz, E.M., & Deng C. (2014). Why are Chinese parents more psychologically controlling than American parents? "My child is my report card." *Child Development, 85,* 355–369.

Ng, F.F., Pomerantz, E.M., & Lam, S. (2013). European American and Chinese parents' beliefs about children's schoolwork. *International Journal of Behavioral Development, 37,* 387–394.

Ng, M., & others (2017). Environmental factors associated with autism spectrum disorder: A scoping review for the years 2003–2013. *Health Promotion and Chronic Disease Prevention in Canada, 37,* 1–23.

Nguyen, P.V., Hong, T.K., Nguyen, D.T., & Robert, A.R. (2016). Excessive screen viewing time by adolescents and body fatness in a developing country: Vietnam. *Asia Pacific Journal of Clinical Nutrition, 25,* 174–183.

NICHD (2017). *SIDS facts.* Retrieved January 3, 2017, from www.nichd.nih/gov/sids

NICHD Early Child Care Research Network (2001). Nonmaternal care and family factors in early development: An overview of the NICHD study of early child care. *Journal of Applied Developmental Psychology, 22,* 457–492.

NICHD Early Child Care Research Network (2002). Structure→process→outcome: Direct and indirect effects of child care quality on young children's development. *Psychological Science, 13,* 199–206.

NICHD Early Child Care Research Network (2003). Does amount of time spent in child care predict socioemotional adjustment during the transition to kindergarten? *Child Development, 74,* 976–1005.

NICHD Early Child Care Research Network (2004). Type of child care and children's development at 54 months. *Early Childhood Research Quarterly, 19,* 203–230.

NICHD Early Child Care Research Network (2005a). *Child care and development.* New York: Guilford.

NICHD Early Child Care Research Network (2005b). Duration and developmental timing of poverty and children's cognitive and social development from birth through third grade. *Child Development, 76,* 795–810.

NICHD Early Child Care Research Network (2006). Infant-mother attachment classification: Risk and protection in relation to changing maternal caregiving quality. *Developmental Psychology, 42,* 38–58.

NICHD Early Child Care Research Network (2009). Family-peer linkages: The mediational role of attentional processes. *Social Development, 18,* 875–895.

NICHD Early Child Care Research Network (2010). Testing a series of causal propositions relating time spent in child care to children's externalizing behavior. *Developmental Psychology, 46*(1), 1–17.

Nickalls, S. (2012, March 9). Why college students shouldn't online date. *The Tower*. Philadelphia: Arcadia University. Retrieved February 27, 2013, from http://tower.arcadia.edu/?p5754

Nicklas, T.A., Webber, L.S., Jonson, C.S., Srinivasan, S.R., & Berensen, G.G. (1995). Foundations for health promotion with youth: A review of observations from the Bogalusa Heart Study. *Journal of Health Education, 26,* S18–S26.

Nicklas, T.A., Yang, S.J., Baranowski, T., Zakeri, I., & Berensen, G. (2003). Eating patterns and obesity in children: The Bogalusa Heart Study. *American Journal of Preventive Medicine, 25,* 9–16.

Nicolaisen, M., & Thorsen, K. (2017). What are friends for? Friendships and loneliness over the lifespan—from 18 to 79 years. *International Journal of Aging and Human Development, 84,* 126–158.

Nielsen, S.J., Siega-Riz, A.M., & Popkin, B.M. (2002). Trends in energy intake in U.S. between 1977 and 1996: Similar shifts seen across age groups. *Obesity Research, 10,* 370–378.

Nieto, S., & Bode, P. (2018). *Affirming diversity* (7th ed.). Upper Saddle River, NJ: Pearson.

Nilsen, E.S., & Basco, S.A. (2017). Cognitive and behavioral predictors of adolescents' communicative perspective-taking and social relationships. *Journal of Adolescence, 56,* 52–63.

Nisbett, R. (2003). *The geography of thought.* New York: Free Press.

Nisbett, R.E., & others (2012). Intelligence: New findings and theoretical developments. *American Psychologist, 67,* 130–159.

Nishamura, Y., Kanakogi, Y., & Myowa-Yamakoshi, M. (2016). Infants' emotional states influence maternal behaviors during holding. *Infant Behavior and Development, 43,* 66–74.

Noddings, N. (2008). Caring and moral education. In L. Nucci & D. Narváez (Ed.), *Handbook of moral and character education.* Clifton, NJ: Psychology Press.

Nogueira, M., & others (2014). Early-age clinical and developmental features associated with substance use disorders in attention-deficit/hyperactivity disorder in adults. *Comprehensive Psychiatry, 55,* 639–649.

Noll, J.G., & others (2017). Childhood sexual abuse and early timing of puberty. *Journal of Adolescent Health, 60,* 65–71.

Nomaguchi, K., & others (2017). Clarifying the association between mother-father relationship aggression and parenting. *Journal of Marriage and the Family, 79,* 161–178.

Nora, A., & others (2017). Children show right-lateralized effects of spoken word-form learning. *PLoS One, 12*(2), e0171034.

Norman, E. (2017). Metacognition and mindfulness: The role of fringe consciousness. *Mindfulness, 8,* 95–100.

Norona, A.N., & Baker, B.L. (2017). The effects of early positive parenting and developmental delay

status on child emotion dysregulation. *Journal of Intellectual Disability Research, 61,* 130–143.

North American Montessori Teachers' Association (2016). *Montessori schools.* Retrieved January 6, 2016, from www.montessori-namta.org

Nottelmann, E.D., & others (1987). Gonadal and adrenal hormone correlates of adjustment in early adolescence. In R.M. Lerner & T.T. Foch (Eds.), *Biological-psychological interactions in early adolescence.* Hillsdale, NJ: Erlbaum.

Nouwens, S., Goren, M.A., & Verhoeven, L. (2017). How working memory relates to children's reading comprehension: The importance of domain-specificity in storage and processing. *Reading and Writing, 30,* 105–120.

Novick, G., & others (2013). Group prenatal care: Model fidelity and outcomes. *American Journal of Obstetrics and Gynecology, 209*(2), 112.e1–112.e6.

Nucci, L. (2006). Education for moral development. In M. Killen & J. Smetana (Eds.), *Handbook of moral development.* Mahwah, NJ: Erlbaum.

Nucci, L. (2014). The personal and the moral. In M. Killen & J.G. Smetana (Eds.), *Handbook of moral development* (2nd ed.). New York Psychology Press.

Nucci, L., & Narváez, D. (Eds.). (2008). *Handbook of moral and character education.* New York: Psychology Press.

Nutter, E., Meyer, S., Shaw-Battista, J., & Marowitz, A. (2014). Waterbirth: An integrative analysis of peer-reviewed literature. *Journal of Midwifery and Women's Health, 59,* 286–319.

Nyaradi, A., Li, J., Hickling, S., Foster, J., & Oddy, W.H. (2013). The role of nutrition in children's neurocognitive development, from pregnancy through childhood. *Frontiers of Human Neuroscience, 7,* 97.

O

O'Brien, M., & others (2011). Longitudinal associations between children's understanding of emotions and theory of mind. *Cognition and Emotion, 25,* 1074–1086.

O'Brien, M., & others (2014). Women's work and child care: Perspectives and prospects. In E.T. Gershoff, R.S. Mistry, & D.A. Crosby (Eds.), *Societal contexts of child development.* New York: Oxford University Press.

O'Callaghan, F.V., & others (2010). The link between sleep problems in infancy and early childhood and attention problems at 5 and 14 years: Evidence from a birth cohort study. *Early Human Development, 86,* 419–424.

O'Callaghan, M.E., & others (2013). Genetic and clinical contributions to cerebral palsy: A multiple-variable analysis. *Journal of Pediatrics and Child Health, 49,* 575–581.

O'Donnell, L., O'Donnell, C., Wardlaw, D.M., & Stueve, A. (2004). Risk and resiliency factors influencing suicidality among urban African American and Latino youth. *American Journal of Community Psychology, 33,* 37–49.

O'Hara, M., & others (2017, in press). Children neglected: Where cumulative risk theory fails. *Child Abuse and Neglect.*

O'Hara, M.W., & McCabe, F. (2013). Postpartum depression: Current status and future directions. *Annual Review of Clinical Psychology* (Vol. 9). Palo Alto, CA: Annual Reviews.

O'Kearney, R., & others (2017). Emotional abilities in children with oppositional defiance disorder (ODD): Impairments in perspective-taking and understanding mixed emotions are associated with high callous-unemotional traits. *Child Psychiatry and Human Development, 48,* 346–357.

O'Keeffe, L.M., Greene, R.A., & Kearney, P.M. (2014). The effect of moderate gestational alcohol consumption during pregnancy on speech and language outcomes in children: A systematic review. *Systematic Reviews, 3,* 1.

O'Reilly, M.F., & others (2014). Naturalistic approaches to social skills training and development. In J.K. Luiselli (Ed.), *Children and youth with autism spectrum disorder.* New York: Oxford University Press.

Oakley, M., Farr, R.H., & Scherer, D.G. (2017, in press). Same-sex parent socialization: Understanding gay and lesbian parenting practices as cultural socialization. *Journal of GLBT Family Studies.*

Obermann, M.L. (2011). Moral disengagement in self-reported and peer-nominated school bullying. *Aggressive Behavior, 37,* 133–144.

Oberwelland, E., & others (2017). Young adolescents with autism show abnormal joint attention network: A gaze contingent fMRI study. *Neuroimage.Clinical, 14,* 112–121.

Obradovic, J. (2010). Effortful control and adaptive functioning of homeless children: Variable- and person-focused analyses. *Journal of Applied Developmental Psychology, 39,* 90–102.

Obradovic, J., Yousafzai, A.K., Finch, J.E., & Rasheed, M.A. (2016). Maternal scaffolding and home stimulation: Key mediators of early intervention effects on children's cognitive development. *Developmental Psychology, 52,* 1409–1421.

Ochs, E., & Schieffelin, B. (2008). Language socialization and language acquisition. In P.A. Duff & N.H. Hornberger (Eds.), *Encyclopedia of language and education.* New York: Springer.

Offer, D., Ostrov, E., Howard, K.I., & Atkinson, R. (1988). *The teenage world: Adolescents' self-image in ten countries.* New York: Plenum.

Ogbu, J., & Stern, P. (2001). Caste status and intellectual development. In R.J. Sternberg & E.L. Grigorenko (Eds.), *Environmental effects on cognitive abilities.* Mahwah, NJ: Erlbaum.

Ogden, C.L., Carroll, M.D., Kit, B.K., & Flegal, K.M. (2014). Prevalence of childhood and adult obesity in the United States, 2011–2012. *Journal of the American Medical Association, 311,* 308–314.

Ogden, C.L., & others (2016). Trends in obesity prevalence among children and adolescents in the United States, 1988–1994 through 2013–2014. *JAMA, 315,* 2292–2299.

Ogino, T., & others (2017). Predicting the reading skill of Japanese children. *Brain and Development, 39,* 112–121.

Oh, S., & others (2017). Prevalence and correlates of alcohol and tobacco use among pregnant women in the United States: Evidence from the NSDUH 205-2014. *Preventive Medicine, 97*, 93–99.

Okun, N., & others (2014). Pregnancy outcomes after assisted human reproduction. *Journal of Obstetrics and Gynecology Canada, 36*, 64–83.

Okuzono, S., & others (2017). Spanking and subsequent behavioral problems in toddlers: A propensity score-matched prospective study in Japan. *Child Abuse and Neglect, 69*, 62–71.

Olds, D.L., & others (2004). Effects of home visits by paraprofessionals and nurses: Age 4 follow-up of a randomized trial. *Pediatrics, 114*, 1560–1568.

Olds, D.L., & others (2007). Effects of nurse home visiting on maternal and child functioning: Age 9 follow-up of a randomized trial. *Pediatrics, 120*, e832–e845.

Olds, D.L., & others (2014). Effects of home visits by paraprofessionals and by nurses on children: Follow-up of a randomized trial age 6 and 9 years. *JAMA Pediatrics, 168*, 800–806.

Olino, T.M., & others (2016). Maternal depression, parenting, and youth depressive symptoms: Mediation and moderation in short-term longitudinal study. *Journal of Clinical Child and Adolescent Psychology, 45*, 279–290.

Olson, B.H., Haider, S.J., Vangjel, L., Bolton, T.A., & Gold, J.G. (2010). A quasi-experimental evaluation of a breastfeeding support program for low-income women in Michigan. *Maternal and Child Health Journal, 14*, 86–93.

Olweus, D. (2003). Prevalence estimation of school bullying with the Olweus bully/victim questionnaire. *Aggressive Behavior, 29*(3), 239–269.

Olweus, D. (2013). School bullying: Development and some important challenges. *Annual Review of Clinical Psychology* (Vol. 9). Palo Alto, CA: Annual Reviews.

Ongley, S.F., & Malti, T. (2014). The role of moral emotions in the development of children's sharing behavior. *Developmental Psychology, 50*, 1148–1159.

Opfer, J.E., & Gelman, S.A. (2011). Development of the animate-inanimate distinction. In U. Goswami (Ed.), *Wiley-Blackwell handbook of childhood cognitive development* (2nd ed.). New York: Wiley.

Oreland, L., & others (2017, in press). Personality as an intermediate phenotype for genetic dissection of alcohol use disorder. *Journal of Neural Transmission.*

Ornstein, P., Coffman, J.L., & Grammer, J.K. (2007, April). *Teachers' memory-relevant conversations and children's memory performance.* Paper presented at the biennial meeting of the Society for Research in Child Development, Boston.

Ornstein, P.A., Coffman, J.L., Grammer, J.K., San Souci, P.P., & McCall, L.E. (2010). Linking the classroom context and the development of children's memory skills. In J. Meece & J. Eccles (Eds.), *The handbook of research on schools, schooling, and human development.* New York: Routledge.

Ornstein, P., Grammer, J., & Coffman, J. (2010). Teachers' "mnemonic style" and the development of skilled memory. In H.S. Waters & W. Schneider (Eds.), *Metacognition, strategy use, and instruction.* New York: Guilford.

Orpinas, P., McNicholas, C., & Nahapetyan, L. (2015). Gender differences in trajectories of relational aggression perpetration and victimization from middle to high school. *Aggressive Behavior, 41*, 401–412.

Orth, U. (2017, in press). The family environment in early childhood has a long-term effect on self-esteem: A longitudinal study from birth to age 27 years. *Journal of Personality and Social Psychology.*

Orth, U., Robins, R.W., Meier, L.L., Conger, R.D. (2016). Refining the vulnerability model of low self-esteem and depression: Disentangling the effects of genuine self-esteem and narcissism. *Journal of Personality and Social Psychology, 110*, 133–149.

Ortigosa, S., & others (2012). Feto-placental morphological effects of prenatal exposure to drugs of abuse. *Reproductive Toxicology, 34*, 73–79.

Ostlund, B.D., & others (2017). Shaping emotion regulation: Attunement, symptomatology, and stress recovery within mother-infant dyads. *Development and Psychopathology, 59*, 15–25.

Ota, M., & Skarabela, B. (2017, in press). Reduplication facilitates early word segmentation. *Journal of Child Language.*

Otto, H., & Keller, H. (Eds.) (2013). *Different faces of attachment.* New York: Cambridge University Press.

Owe, K.M., & others (2016). Exercise during pregnancy and risk of cesarean delivery in nulliparous women: A large population-based cohort study. *American Journal of Obstetrics and Gynecology, 215,* 791.e1–791.e13

Owens, J.A., Belon, K., & Moss, P. (2010). Impact of delaying school start time on adolescent sleep, mood, and behavior. *Archives of Pediatric and Adolescent Medicine, 164*, 608–614.

Owens, J.A., & Mindell, J. (2011). *Sleep in children and adolescents.* New York: Elsevier.

P

Pace, A., Hirsh-Pasek, K., & Golinkoff, R.M. (2016). How high-quality language environments create high-quality learning environments. In S. Jones & N. Lesaux (Eds.), *The leading edge of early childhood education.* Cambridge, MA: Harvard University Press.

Pace, A., Levine, D.F., Morini, G., Hirsh-Pasek, K., & Golinkoff, R.M. (2016). Language acquisition: From words to world and back again. In L. Balter & C.S. Tamis-LeMonda (Eds.), *Child psychology: A contemporary handbook* (3rd ed.). New York: Psychology Press.

Pace, C.S., & others (2015). Adoptive parenting and attachment: Association of the internal working models between adoptive mothers and their late-adopted children during adolescence. *Frontiers in Psychology, 6*, 1433.

Padilla-Walker, L.M., Coyne, S.M., & Collier, K.M. (2016). Longitudinal relations between parental media monitoring and adolescent aggression, prosocial behavior, and externalizing problems. *Journal of Adolescence, 46*, 86–97.

Padilla-Walker, L.M., & Nelson, L.J. (2017). Flourishing in emerging adulthood: An understudied

approach to the third decade of life. In L.M. Padilla-Walker & L. Nelson (Eds.), *Flourishing in emerging adulthood.* New York: Oxford University Press.

Pagani, L.S., Levesque-Seck, F., Archambault, I., & Janosz, M. (2017). Prospective longitudinal associations between household smoke exposure in early childhood and antisocial behavior at age 12. *Indoor Air, 27*, 622–630.

Pakpreo, P., Ryan, S., Auinger, P., & Aten, M. (2005). The association between parental lifestyle behaviors and adolescent knowledge, attitudes, intentions, and nutritional and physical activity behaviors. *Journal of Adolescent Health, 34*, 129–130.

Palermo, T.M. (2014). A brief history of child and adolescent sleep research: Key contributions in psychology. In A.R. Wolfson & E. Montgomery-Downs (Eds.), *Oxford handbook of infant, child, and adolescent sleep and behavior.* New York: Oxford University Press.

Pallini, S., & others (2014). Early child-parent attachment and peer relations: A meta-analysis of recent research. *Journal of Family Psychology, 28*, 118–123.

Paloutzian, R.F. (2000). *Invitation to the psychology of religion* (3rd ed.). Needham Heights, MA: Allyn & Bacon.

Pan, B.A. (2008). Unpublished review of J.W. Santrock's *Life-span development*, 12th ed. (New York: McGraw-Hill).

Pan, B.A., Rowe, M.L., Singer, J.D., & Snow, C.E. (2005). Maternal correlates of growth in toddler vocabulary production in low-income families. *Child Development, 76*, 763–782.

Pan, B.A., & Uccelli, P. (2009). Semantic development. In J. Berko Gleason & N. Rather (Eds.) (2009), *The development of language* (7th ed.). Boston: Allyn & Bacon.

Pan, C.Y., & others (2017, in press). Effects of physical exercise intervention on motor skills and executive functions with ADHD: A pilot study. *Journal of Attention Disorders.*

Parent, J., & others (2016). Mindfulness in parenting and coparenting. *Mindfulness, 7*, 504–513.

Paris, S.G., Yeung, A.S., Wong, H.M., & Luo, S.W. (2012). Global perspectives on education during middle childhood. In K.R. Harris & others (Eds.), *APA handbook of educational psychology.* Washington, DC: American Psychological Association.

Park, E.M., Meltzer-Brody, S., & Stickgold, R. (2013). Poor sleep maintenance and subjective sleep quality are associated with postpartum depression symptom severity. *Archives of Women's Mental Health, 16*, 539–547.

Park, M.J., Paul Mulye, T., Adams, S.H., Brindis, C.D., & Irwin, C.E., Jr. (2006). The health status of young adults in the United States. *Journal of Adolescent Health, 39*, 305–317.

Park, Y.M. (2017). Relationship between child maltreatment, suicidality, and bipolarity: A retrospective study. *Psychiatry Investigation, 14*, 136–140.

Parkay, F.W. (2016). *Becoming a teacher* (10th ed.). Upper Saddle River, NJ: Pearson.

Parke, R.D. (2013). *Future families: Diverse forms, rich possibilities.* New York: Wiley-Blackwell.

Parke, R.D. (2017). Family psychology: Past and future reflections on the field. *Journal of Family Psychology, 31,* 257–260.

Parke, R.D., & Clarke-Stewart, A. (2011). *Social development.* New York: Wiley.

Parkes, A., Sweeting, H., Young, R., & Wight, D. (2016). Does parenting help to explain socioeconomic inequalities in children's body mass index trajectories? Longitudinal analysis using the Growing Up in Scotland study. *Journal of Epidemiology and Community Health, 70,* 868–873.

Parrillo, V.N. (2014). *Strangers to these shores* (11th ed.). Upper Saddle River, NJ: Pearson.

Parrish-Morris, J., Golinkoff, R.M., & Hirsh-Pasek, K. (2013). From coo to code: A brief story of language development. In P.D. Zelazo (Ed.), *Oxford handbook of developmental psychology.* New York: Oxford University Press.

Parrott, A.C., & others (2014). MDMA and heightened cortisol: A neurohormonal perspective on the pregnancy outcomes of mothers who used 'Ecstasy' during pregnancy. *Human Psychopharmacology, 29,* 109–119.

Parsons, C.E., & others (2017). Interpreting infant emotional expressions: Parenthood has differential effects for men and women. *Quarterly Journal of Experimental Psychology, 70,* 554–564.

Pasco-Fearon, R.M., & Belsky, J. (2016). Precursors of attachment security. In J. Cassidy & P.R. Shaver (Eds.), *Handbook of attachment* (3rd ed.). New York: Guilford.

Pasco-Fearon, R.M., & others (2016). Attachment and developmental psychopathology. In D. Cicchetti (Ed.), *Developmental psychopathology* (3rd ed.). New York: Wiley.

Pasley, K., & Moorefield, B.S. (2004). Stepfamilies. In M. Coleman & L. Ganong (Eds.), *Handbook of contemporary families.* Thousand Oaks, CA: Sage.

Pate, R.R., Pfeiffer, K.A., Trost, S.G., Ziegler, P., & Dowda, M. (2004). Physical activity among children attending preschools. *Pediatrics, 114,* 1258–1263.

Pate, R.R., & others (2009). Age-related change in physical activity in adolescent girls. *Journal of Adolescent Health, 44,* 275–282.

Pate, R.R., & others (2015). Prevalence of compliance with a new physical activity guideline for preschool-aged children. *Childhood Obesity, 11,* 45–70.

Patel, N., & others (2017). Role of second-hand smoke (SH)-induced proteostasis/autophagy impairment in pediatric lung diseases. *Molecular and Cellular Pediatrics, 4*(1), 3.

Patel, R., & others (2011). European guideline for the management of genital herpes, 2010. *International Journal of STD and AIDS, 22,* 1–10.

Pathman, T., Doydum, A., & Bauer, P.J. (2013). Bringing order to life events: Memory for the temporal order of autobiographical events over an extended period in school-aged children and adults. *Journal of Experimental Child Psychology, 115,* 309–325.

Pathman, T., & St. Jacques, P.L. (2014). Locating events in personal time: Time in autobiography.

In P. Bauer & R. Fivush (Eds.), *Wiley-Blackwell handbook of children's memory.* New York: Wiley.

Patrick, M.E., & Schulenberg, J.E. (2010). Alcohol use and heavy episodic drinking prevalence among national samples of American eighth- and tenth-grade students. *Journal of Studies on Alcohol and Drugs, 71,* 41–45.

Patterson, C.J. (2013). Family lives of gay and lesbian adults. In G.W. Peterson & K.R. Bush (Eds.), *Handbook of marriage and the family* (3rd ed.). New York: Springer.

Patterson, C.J. (2014). Sexual minority youth and youth with sexual minority parents. In G.B. Melton & others (Eds.), *SAGE handbook of child research.* Thousand Oaks, CA: Sage.

Patterson, C.J., & D'Augelli, A.R. (Eds.) (2013). *The psychology of sexual orientation.* New York: Cambridge University Press.

Patterson, C.J., & Farr, R.H. (2014). Children of lesbian and gay parents: Reflections on the research-policy interface. In H.R. Schaffer & K. Durkin (Eds.), *Blackwell handbook of developmental psychology in action.* New York: Wiley.

Patterson, C.J., Farr, R.H., & Hastings, P.D. (2015). Socialization in the context of family diversity. In J.E. Grusec & P.D. Hastings (Eds.), *Handbook of socialization* (2nd ed.). New York: Guilford.

Patterson, J., & others (2018). *Essential skills in family therapy* (3rd ed.). New York: Guilford.

Patterson, K., & Wright, A.E. (1990, Winter). The speech, language, or hearing-impaired child: At-risk academically. *Childhood Education,* 91–95.

Patton, G.C., & others (2011). Overweight and obesity between adolescence and early adulthood: A 10-year prospective study. *Journal of Adolescent Health, 48*(3), 275–280.

Paul, G.R., & Pinto, S. (2017). Sleep and the cardiovascular system in children. *Sleep Medicine Clinics, 12,* 179–191.

Paulhus, D.L. (2008). Birth order. In M.M. Haith & J.B. Benson (Eds.), *Encyclopedia of infant and early childhood development.* Oxford, UK: Elsevier.

Pauliks, L.B. (2015). The effect of pregestational diabetes on fetal heart function. *Expert Review of Cardiovascular Therapy, 13,* 67–74.

Paulson, J.F., Bazemore, S.D., Goodman, J.H., & Leiferman, J.A. (2016). The course and interrelationship of maternal and paternal perinatal depression. *Archives of Women's Mental Health, 19,* 655–663.

Paus, T., & others (2008). Morphological properties of the action-observation cortical network in adolescents with low and high resistance to peer influence. *Social Neuroscience, 3*(3), 303–316.

Pavlov, I.P. (1927). In G.V. Anrep (Trans.), *Conditioned reflexes.* London: Oxford University Press.

Pawellek, I., & others (2017). Factors associated with sugar intake and sugar sources in European children from 1 to 8 years of age. *European Journal of Clinical Nutrition, 71,* 25–32.

Pawlikowska-Haddal, A. (2013). Growth hormone therapy with norditropin (somatropin) in growth

hormone deficiency. *Expert Opinion on Biological Therapy, 13,* 927–932.

Pawluski, J.L., Lonstein, J.S., & Fleming, A.S. (2017). The neurobiology of postpartum period anxiety and depression. *Trends in Neuroscience, 40,* 106–120.

Paxton, S.J., & Damiano, S.R. (2017). The development of body image and weight bias in childhood. *Advances in Child Development and Behavior, 52,* 269–298.

Payne, T.E. (2017). Morphological typology. In A.Y. Aikhenvald & R.M.W. Dixon (Eds.), *Cambridge handbook of linguistic typology.* New York: Cambridge University Press.

Pea, R., & others (2012). Media use, face-to-face communication, media multitasking, and social well-being among 8- to 12-year-old girls. *Developmental Psychology, 48,* 327–336.

Pearlman, E. (2013). Twin psychological development. Retrieved February 14, 2013, from http://christinabaglivitinglof.com/twin-pregnancy/six-twin-experts-tell-all/

Pearson, N., & others (2017). Clustering and correlates of screen time and eating behaviors among young adolescents. *BMC Public Health, 17,* 533.

Pearson, R.M., & others (2013). Maternal depression during pregnancy and the postnatal period: Risk and possible mechanisms for offspring depression at age 18 years. *JAMA Psychiatry, 70,* 1312–1319.

Peasgood, T., & others (2016). The impact of ADHD on the health and well-being of ADHD children and their siblings. *European Child and Adolescent Psychiatry, 25,* 1217–1231.

Pechorro, P., & others (2014). Age of crime onset and psychopathic traits in female juvenile delinquents. *International Journal of Offender Therapy and Comparative Criminology, 58,* 1101–1109.

Pedersen, C.B., McGrath, J., Mortensen, P.B., & Pedersen, L. (2014). The importance of the father's age to schizophrenia risk. *Molecular Psychiatry, 19,* 530–531.

Pederson, D.R., & Moran, G. (1996). Expressions of the attachment relationship outside of the Strange Situation. *Child Development, 67,* 915–927.

Peek, L., & Stough, L.M. (2010). Children with disabilities in the context of disaster: A social vulnerability perspective. *Child Development, 81,* 1260–1270.

Peets, K., Hodges, E.V., & Salmivalli, C. (2013). Forgiveness and its determinants depending on the interpersonal context of hurt. *Journal of Experimental Child Psychology, 114,* 131–145.

Pei, J., & others (2017). Intervention recommendations and subsequent access to services following clinical assessment for fetal alcohol syndrome disorders. *Research in Developmental Disabilities, 60,* 176–186.

Peitzmeier, S.M., & others (2016). Intimate partner violence perpetration among adolescent males in disadvantaged neighborhoods globally. *Journal of Adolescent Health, 59,* 696–702.

Pelayo, R., Owens, J., Mindell, J., & Sheldon, S. (2006). Bed sharing with unimpaired parents is not an important risk for sudden infant death syndrome [Letter to the editor]. *Pediatrics, 117,* 993–994.

Pelissari, D.M., & Diaz-Quijano, F.A. (2017). Household crowding as a potential mediator of socioeconomic determinants of tuberculosis incidence in Brazil. *PLoS One, 12*(4), e0176116.

Pelka, M., & Kellman, M. (2017). Understanding underrecovery, overtraining, and burnout in the developing athlete. In J. Baker & others (Eds.), *Routledge handbook of talent identification and development in sport.* New York: Routledge.

Pelton, S.I., & Leibovitz, E. (2009). Recent advances in otitis media. *Pediatric and Infectious Disease Journal, 28*(10, Suppl.), S133–S137.

Pena, J.B., Zayas, L.H., Cabrera, P., & Vega, W.A. (2012). U.S. cultural involvement and its association with suicidal behavior among youth in the Dominican Republic. *American Journal of Public Health, 102,* 664–671.

Pena, L., & others (2017). Parental style and its association with substance use in Argentinian youth. *Substance Use and Misuse, 52,* 518–526.

Penela, E.C., & others (2012). Maternal caregiving moderates the relation between temperamental fear and social behavior with peers. *Infancy, 17*(6), 715–730.

Peng, P., & Fuchs, D. (2016). A meta-analysis of working memory deficits in children with learning difficulties: Is there a difference between the verbal domain and numerical domain? *Journal of Learning Disabilities, 49,* 3–20.

Pennington, C.R., & others (2016). Twenty years of stereotype threat research: A review of psychological mediators. *PLoS One, 11*(1), e0146465.

Perales, M., & others (2016). Benefits of aerobic or resistance training during pregnancy on maternal health and perinatal outcomes: A systematic review. *Early Human Development, 94,* 43–48.

Peregoy, S.F., & Boyle, O.F. (2017). *Reading, writing, and learning ESL* (7th ed.). Upper Saddle River, NJ: Pearson.

Pereira, P.P., & others (2017). Maternal active smoking during pregnancy and low birth weight in the Americas: A systematic review and meta-analysis. *Nicotine and Tobacco Research, 19,* 497–505.

Perez, E.M., & others (2015). Massage therapy improves the development of HIV-exposed infants living in a low socioeconomic, peri-urban community of South Africa. *Infant Behavior and Development, 38,* 135–146.

Perez-Edgar, K.E., & Guyer, A.E. (2014). Behavioral inhibition: Temperament or prodrome? *Current Behavioral Neuroscience Reports, 1,* 182–190.

Perez-Escamilla, R., & Moran, V.H. (2017). The role of nutrition in integrated early child development in the 21st century: Contribution from the Maternal and Child Nutrition Journal. *Maternal and Child Nutrition, 13,* 3–6.

Perkins, S.C., Finegood, E.D., & Swain, J.E. (2013). Poverty and language development: Roles of parenting and stress. *Innovations in Clinical Neuroscience, 10,* 10–19.

Perlman, L. (2008, July 22). Am I an I or We? *Twins,* pp. 1–2.

Perone, S., Almy, B., & Zelazo, P.D. (2017). Toward an understanding of the neural basis of executive function development. In R.L. Gibb & B. Kolb (Eds.), *The neurobiology of brain and behavioral development* (2nd ed.). New York: Elsevier.

Perry, D.G., & Pauletti, R.E. (2011). Gender and adolescent development. *Journal of Research on Adolescence, 21,* 61–74.

Perry, N.B., Swingler, M.M., Calkins, S.D., & Bell, M.A. (2016). Neurophysiological correlates of attention behavior in early infancy: Implications for emotion regulation during early childhood. *Journal of Experimental Child Psychology, 142,* 245–261.

Perry, N.B., & others (2013). *Early cardiac vagal regulation predicts the trajectory of externalizing behaviors across the preschool periods.* Unpublished manuscript, University of North Carolina–Greensboro.

Perry, R.A., Daniels, L.A., Bell, L., & Magarey, A.M. (2017, in press). Facilitators and barriers to the achievement of healthy lifestyle goals: Qualitative findings from Australian parents enrolled in the PEACH child weight management program. *Journal of Nutrition Education and Behavior.*

Persky, H.R., Dane, M.C., & Jin, Y. (2003). *The nation's report card: Writing 2002.* U.S. Department of Education.

Peskin, H. (1967). Pubertal onset and ego functioning. *Journal of Abnormal Psychology, 72,* 1–15.

Petersen, A.C., & others (Eds.) (2017). *Positive youth development in global contexts of social and economic change.* New York: Routledge.

Petersen, I.T., & others (2012). Interaction between serotonin transporter polymorphism (5-HTTLPR) and stressful life events in adolescents' trajectories of anxious/depressed symptoms. *Developmental Psychology, 48*(5), 1463–1475.

Peterson, C.B., & others (2017, in press). The effects of psychotherapy treatment on outcome in bulimia nervosa: Examining indirect effects through emotion regulation, self-directed behavior, and self-discrepancy within the mediation model. *International Journal of Eating Disorders.*

Peterson, C.C. (2005). Mind and body: Concepts of human cognition, physiology and false belief in children with autism or typical development. *Journal of Autism and Developmental Disorders, 35,* 487–497.

Peterson, C.C., Wellman, H.M., & Slaughter, V. (2012). The mind behind the message: Advancing theory-of-mind scales for typically developing children and those with deafness, autism, or Asperger syndrome. *Child Development, 83,* 469–485.

Peterson, C.C., & others (2016). Peer social skills and theory of mind in children with autism, deafness, or typical development. *Developmental Psychology, 52,* 46–57.

Peterson, E.R., & others (2017, in press). Infant Behavior Questionnaire–Revised Very Short Form: A new factor structure's associations with parenting perceptions and child outcomes. *Journal of Personality Assessment.*

Petrenko, C.L. & Alto, M.E. (2017). Interventions in fetal alcohol spectrum disorders: An international perspective. *European Journal of Medical Genetics, 60,* 79–91.

Petry, N., & others (2017). The proportion of anemia associated with iron deficiency in low, medium, and high human development index countries: A systematic analysis of national surveys. *Nutrients, 49,* 43–52.

Pew Research Center (2010). *Millennials: Confident, connected, open to change.* Washington, DC: Pew Research Center.

Peyre, H., & others (2017, in press). Contributing factors and mental health outcomes of first suicide attempt during childhood and adolescence: Results from a nationally representative study. *Journal of Clinical Psychiatry.*

Peyre, H., & others (2017). Do developmental milestones at 4, 8, 12, and 24 months predict IQ at 5–6 years old? Results of the EDEN mother-child cohort. *Child Development.*

Pfeifer, C., & Bunders, M.J. (2016). Maternal HIV infection alters the immune balance in the mother and fetus: Implications for pregnancy outcome and infant health. *Current Opinion in HIV and AIDS, 11,* 138–145.

Philibert, R.A., & Beach, S.R.H. (2016). The genetic and epigenetic essentials of modern humans. In M. Pluess (Ed.), *Genetics of psychological well-being.* New York: Oxford University Press.

Phillips, D.A., & Lowenstein, A. (2011). Early care, education, and development. *Annual Review of Psychology* (Vol. 62). Palo Alto, CA: Annual Reviews.

Phinney, J.S. (2008). Bridging identities and disciplines: Advances and challenges in understanding multiple identities. In M. Azmitia, M. Syed, & K. Radmacher (Eds.), The intersections of personal and social identities. *New Directions for Child and Adolescent Development, 120,* 81–95.

Phinney, J.S., & Vedder, P. (2013). Family relationship values of adolescents and parents: Intergenerational discrepancies and adaptation. In J.W. Berry & others (Eds.), *Immigrant youth in cultural transition.* New York: Psychology Press.

Piaget, J. (1932). *The moral judgment of the child.* New York: Harcourt Brace Jovanovich.

Piaget, J. (1952). *The origins of intelligence in children* (M. Cook, Trans.). New York: International Universities Press.

Piaget, J. (1954). *The construction of reality in the child.* New York: Basic Books.

Piaget, J. (1962). *Play, dreams, and imitation.* New York: W.W. Norton.

Piaget, J., & Inhelder, B. (1969). *The child's conception of space* (F.J. Langdon & J.L. Lunger, Trans.). New York: W.W. Norton.

Piekarski, D.J., & others (2017). Does puberty mark a transition in sensitive periods for plasticity in the associative neocortex? *Brain Research, 1654*(Pt. B), 123–144.

Pike, A., & Oliver, B.R. (2017). Child behavior and sibling relationship quality: A cross-lagged analysis. *Journal of Family Psychology, 31,* 250–255.

Pinderhughes, E.E., Zhang, X., & Agerbak, S. (2015). "American" or "multiethnic"? Family ethnic identity among transracial adoptive families, ethnic-racial socialization, and children's self-perception. *New Directions in Child and Adolescent Development, 150,* 5–18.

Ping, H., & Hagopian, W. (2006). Environmental factors in the development of type 1 diabetes. *Reviews in Endocrine and Metabolic Disorders, 7,* 149–162.

Pinhas, L., & others (2017, in press). Classification of childhood onset eating disorders: A latent class analysis. *International Journal of Eating Disorders.*

Pinquart, M. (2017). Associations of parenting dimensions and styles with externalizing problems of children and adolescents: An updated meta-analysis. *Developmental Psychology, 53,* 873–932.

Pinquart, M., Feubner, C., & Ahnert, L. (2013). Meta-analytic evidence for stability of attachments from infancy to early adulthood. *Attachment and Human Development, 15,* 189–218.

Pinto, A., & others (2017, in press). Nutritional stutus in patients with phenylketonuria using glycomacropeptide as their major protein source. *European Journal of Clinical Nutrition.*

Pinto, T.M., & others (2017, in press). Maternal depression and anxiety and fetal-neonatal growth. *Journal of Pediatrics.*

Pinto Pereira, S.M., van Veldhoven, K., Li, L., & Power, C. (2016). Combined early and adult life risk factor associations for mid-life obesity in a prospective birth cohort: Assessing potential public health impact. *BMJ Open, 6*(4), e011044.

PISA (2015). *PISA 2015: Results in focus.* Paris, France: OECD.

Pitkanen, T., Lyyra, A.L., & Pulkkinen, L. (2005). Age of onset of drinking and the use of alcohol in adulthood: A follow-up study from age 8–42 for females and males. *Addiction, 100,* 652–661.

Pittman, J.F., Kerpelman, J.L., Soto, J.B., & Adler-Baeder, F.M. (2012). Attachment, identity, and intimacy: Parallels between Bowlby's and Erikson's paradigms. *Journal of Adolescence, 35,* 1485–1499.

Planalp, E.M., & others (2017). Genetic and environmental contributions to the development of positive affect in infancy. *Emotion, 17,* 412–420.

Platt, B., Kadosh, K.C., & Lau, J.Y. (2013). The role of peer rejection in adolescent depression. *Depression and Anxiety, 30,* 809–821.

Plucker, J. (2010, July 19). Commentary in P. Bronson & A. Merryman, The creativity crisis. *Newsweek,* 45–46.

Pluess, M., & Belsky, J. (2009). Differential susceptibility to rearing experience: The case of child care. *Journal of Child Psychology and Psychiatry, 50*(4), 396–404.

Pluess, M., & others (2011). Serotonin transporter polymorphism moderates effects of prenatal maternal anxiety on infant negative emotionality. *Biological Psychiatry, 69,* 520–525.

Podgurski, M.J. (2016). Theorists and techniques: Connecting education theories to Lamaze teaching techniques. *Journal of Perinatal Education, 25,* 9–17.

Podrebarac, S.K., & others (2017). Antenatal exposure to antidepressants is associated with altered brain development in very preterm-born neonates. *Neuroscience, 342,* 252–262.

Poehlmann-Tynan, J., & others (2016). A pilot study of contemplative practices with economically disadvantaged preschoolers: Children's empathic and self-regulatory behaviors. *Mindfulness, 7,* 46.

Pohlabein, H., & others (2017, in press). Further evidence for the role of pregnancy-induced hypertension and other early life influences in the development of ADHD: Results from the IDEFICS study. *European Child and Adolescent Psychiatry.*

Polan, H.J., & Hofer, M.A. (2016). Psychobiological origins of infant attachment and its role in development. In J. Cassidy & P.R. Shaver (Eds.), *Handbook of attachment* (3rd ed.). New York: Guilford.

Polka, L., & others (2017, in press). Segmenting words from fluent speech during infancy—challenges and opportunities in a bilingual context. *Developmental Science.*

Pollack, W. (1999). *Real boys.* New York: Owl Books.

Pollock, C. (2017, February 14). Study: A quarter of Texas public schools no longer teach sex ed. *Texas Tribune.* Retrieved June 27, 2017, from www.texastribune.org/2017/02/14/texas-public-schools-largely-teach-abstinence-only-sex-education-repor/

Pomerantz, E.M. (2017). *Center for Parent-Child Studies.* Retrieved May 31, 2017, from http://labs.psychology.illinois.edu/cpcs/

Pomerantz, E.M., Cheung, C.S., & Qin, L. (2012). Relatedness between children and parents: Implications for motivation. In R. Ryan (Ed.), *Oxford handbook of motivation.* New York: Oxford University Press.

Pomerantz, E.M., & Grolnick, W.S. (2017). The role of parenting in children's motivation and competence: What underlies facilitative parenting? In A.S. Elliott, C.S. Dweck, and D.S. Yeager (Eds.), *Handbook of competence and motivation* (2nd ed.). New York: Guilford.

Pomerantz, E.M., & Kempner, S.G. (2013). Mothers' daily person and process praise: Implications for children's intelligence and motivation. *Developmental Psychology, 49,* 2040–2046.

Pomerantz, E.M., Kim, E.M., & Cheung, C.S. (2012). Parents' involvement in children's learning. In K.R. Harris & others (Eds.), *APA educational psychology handbook.* Washington, DC: American Psychological Association.

Pomerantz, H., & others (2017). Pubertal timing and internalizing psychopathology: The role of relational aggression. *Journal of Child and Family Studies, 26,* 416–423.

Pong, S., & Landale, N.S. (2012). Academic achievement of legal immigrants' children: The roles of parents' pre- and post-immigration characteristics in origin-group differences. *Child Development, 83,* 1543–1559.

Pontifex, M.B., Saliba, B.J., Raine, L.B., Picchietti, D.L., & Hillman, C.H. (2013). Exercise improves behavioral, neurocognitive, and scholastic performance in children with attention-deficit/hyperactivity disorder. *Journal of Pediatrics, 162,* 543–551.

Poole, D.A., & Lindsay, D.S. (1995). Interviewing preschoolers: Effects of nonsuggestive techniques, parental coaching, and leading questions on reports of nonexperienced events. *Journal of Experimental Child Psychology, 60,* 129–154.

Popham, W.J. (2017). *Classroom assessment* (8th ed.). Upper Saddle River, NJ: Pearson.

Popoola, I., & others (2017). How does ethics institutionalization reduce academic cheating? *Journal of Education for Business, 92,* 29–35.

Porath, A.J., & Fried, P.A. (2005). Effects of prenatal cigarette and marijuana exposure on drug use among offspring. *Neurotoxicology and Teratology, 27,* 267–277.

Posada, G., & Kaloustian, G. (2010). Parent-infant interaction. In J.G. Bremner & T.D. Wachs (Eds.), *Wiley-Blackwell handbook of infant development* (2nd ed.). New York: Wiley.

Posada, G., & others (2002). Maternal caregiving and infant security in two cultures. *Developmental Psychology, 38,* 67–78.

Posner, M.I., & Rothbart, M.K. (2007). *Educating the human brain.* Washington, DC: American Psychological Association.

Posner, M.I., Rothbart, M.K., Sheese, B.E., & Voelker, P. (2014). Developing attention: Behavioral and brain mechanisms. *Advances in Neuroscience, 2014,* 405094.

Poston, L., & others (2016). Preconceptual and maternal obesity: Epidemiology and health consequences. *Lancet: Diabetes and Endocrinology, 4,* 1025–1036.

Potapova, N.V., Gartstein, M.A., & Bridgett, D.J. (2014). Paternal influences on infant temperament: Effects of father internalizing problems, parent-related stress, and temperament. *Infant Behavior and Development, 37,* 105–110.

Powers, K.E., Chavez, R.S., & Heatherton, T.F. (2016). Individual differences in response of dorsomedial prefrontal cortex predict daily social behavior. *Social Cognitive and Affective Neuroscience, 11,* 121–126.

Powers, S.K., & Dodd, S.L. (2017). *Total fitness and wellness* (7th ed.). Upper Saddle River, NJ: Pearson.

Prager, E.O., Sera, M.D., & Carlson, S.M. (2016). Executive function and magnitude skills in preschool children. *Journal of Experimental Child Psychology, 147,* 126–139.

Prameela, K.K. (2011). Breastfeeding—anti-viral potential and relevance to the influenza virus pandemic. *Medical Journal of Malaysia, 66,* 166–169.

Pratt, C., & Bryant, P.E. (1990). Young children understand that looking leads to knowing (so long as they are looking in a single barrel). *Child Development, 61,* 973–982.

Prenoveau, J.M., & others (2017). Maternal postnatal depression and anxiety and their association with child emotional negativity and behavior problems at two years. *Developmental Psychology, 53,* 50–62.

Pressler, E., Raver, C.C., Friedman-Krauss, A.H., & Roy, A. (2016). The roles of school readiness and poverty-related risk for 6th grade outcomes. *Journal of Educational and Developmental Psychology, 6,* 140–156.

Pressley, M. (2003). Psychology of literacy and literacy instruction. In I.B. Weiner (Ed.), *Handbook of psychology* (Vol. 7). New York: Wiley.

Pressley, M., Allington, R., Wharton-McDonald, R., Block, C.C., & Morrow, L.M. (2001). *Learning to read: Lessons from exemplary first grades.* New York: Guilford.

Pressley, M., & McCormick, C.B. (2007). *Child and adolescent development for educators.* New York: Guilford.

Pressley, M., Mohan, L., Fingeret, L., Reffitt, K., & Raphael-Bogaert, L.R. (2007). Writing instruction in engaging and effective elementary settings. In S. Graham, C.A. MacArthur, & J. Fitzgerald (Eds.), *Best practices in writing instruction.* New York: Guilford.

Pressley, M., Mohan, L., Raphael, L.M., & Fingeret, L. (2007). How does Bennett Woods Elementary School produce such high reading and writing achievement? *Journal of Educational Psychology, 99,* 221–240.

Pressley, M., Raphael, L., Gallagher, D., & DiBella, J. (2004). Providence-St. Mel School: How a school that works for African-American students works. *Journal of Educational Psychology, 96,* 216–235.

Pressley, M., & others (2003). *Motivating primary-grades teachers.* New York: Guilford.

Prinstein, M.J. (2007). Moderators of peer contagion: A longitudinal examination of depression socialization between adolescents and their best friends. *Journal of Clinical Child and Adolescent Psychology, 36,* 159–170.

Prinstein, M.J., & Giletta, M. (2016). Peer relations and developmental psychopathology. In D. Cicchetti (Ed.), *Developmental psychopathology* (3rd ed.). New York: Wiley.

Prinstein, M.J., Rancourt, D., Guerry, J.D., & Browne, C.B. (2009). Peer reputations and psychological adjustment. In K.H. Rubin, W.M. Bukowski, & B. Laursen (Eds.), *Handbook of peer interactions, relationships, and groups.* New York: Guilford.

Proctor, B.D., Semega, J.L., & Kollar, M.A. (2016, September 13). Income and poverty in the United States: 2015. *Report Number P60-256.* Washington, DC: U.S. Census Bureau.

Prot, S., & others (2015). Media as agents of socialization. In J.E. Grusec & P.H. Hastings (Eds.), *Handbook of socialization* (2nd Ed.). New York: Guilford.

Pruett, M.K., & others (2017). Enhancing father involvement in low-income families: A couples group approach to preventive intervention. *Child Development, 88,* 398–407.

Psychster Inc (2010) Psychology of social media. Retrieved February 21, 2013, from www.psychster.com

Puccini, D., & Liszkowski, U. (2012). 15-month-old infants fast map words but not representational gestures of multimodal labels. *Frontiers in Psychology, 3,* 101.

Pugmire, J., Sweeting, H., & Moore, L. (2017). Environmental tobacco smoke exposure among infants, children, and young people: Now is no time to relax. *Archives of Disease in Childhood, 102,* 117–118.

Puhl, R.M., & King, K.M. (2013). Weight discrimination and bullying. *Best Practice and Research: Clinical Endocrinology and Metabolism, 27,* 117–127.

Pujol, J., & others (2004). Delayed myelination in children with developmental delay detected by volumetric MRI. *NeuroImage, 22,* 897–903.

Puma, M., & others (2010). *Head Start impact study: Final report.* Washington, DC: Administration for Children & Families.

Pungello, E.P., Iruka, I.U., Dotterer, A.M., Mills-Koonce, R., & Reznick, J.S. (2009). The effects of socioeconomic status, race, and parenting on language development in early childhood. *Developmental Psychology, 45,* 544–557.

Puranik, S., Forno, E., Bush, A., & Celedon, J.C. (2017). Predicting severe asthma exacerbations in children. *American Journal of Respiratory and Critical Care Medicine, 195,* 854–859.

Putallaz, M., & others (2007). Overt and relational aggression and victimization: Multiple perspectives within the school setting. *Journal of School Psychology, 45,* 523–547.

Puzzanchera, C., & Robson, C. (2014, February). Delinquency cases in juvenile court, 2010. *Juvenile offenders and victims: National report series.* Washington, DC: U.S. Department of Justice.

Q

Qin, J.B., & others (2014). Risk factors for congenital syphilis and adverse pregnancy outcomes in offspring of women with syphilis in Shenzhen, China: A prospective nested case-control study. *Sexually Transmitted Diseases, 41,* 13–23.

Qu, Y., & Pomerantz, E.M. (2015). Divergent school trajectories in early adolescence in the United States and China: An examination of underlying mechanisms. *Journal of Youth and Adolescence, 44,* 2095–2109.

Qu, Y., & Telzer, E.H. (2017). Cultural differences and similarities in beliefs, practices, and neural mechanisms of emotion regulation. *Cultural Diversity and Ethnic Minority Psychology, 23,* 36–44.

Qu, Y., & others (2016). Conceptions of adolescence: Implications for differences in engagement in school over early adolescence in the United States and China. *Journal of Research on Adolescence, 26,* 126–141.

Quek, Y.H., & others (2017). Exploring the association between childhood and adolescent obesity and depression: A meta-analysis. *Obesity Reviews, 18,* 742–754.

Quinn, P.C. (2016). What do infants know about cats, dogs, and people? Development of a "like-people" representation for nonhuman animals. In L. Esposito & others (Eds.), *The social neuroscience of human-animal interaction.* New York: Elsevier.

Quinn, P.C., & others (2013). On the developmental origins of differential responding to social category information. In M.R. Banaji & S.A. Gelman (Eds.), *Navigating the social world: What infants, children, and other species can teach us.* New York: Oxford University Press.

Quinn, S.F. Locating play today. In T. Bruce (Ed.), *Routledge international handbook of early childhood play.* New York: Routledge.

R

Radvansky, G.A. (2017). *Human memory* (3rd ed.). New York: Elsevier.

Raffaelli, M., & Ontai, L.L. (2004). Gender socialization in Latino/a families: Results from two retrospective studies. *Sex Roles, 50,* 287–299.

Rageliené, T. (2016). Links of adolescent identity development and relationship with peers: A systematic literature review. *Journal of the Canadian Academy of Child and Adolescent Psychiatry, 25,* 97–105.

Raglan, G.B., Lannon, S.M., Jones, K.M., & Schulkin, J. (2016). Racial and ethnic disparities in preterm birth among American Indian and Alaska Native women. *Maternal and Child Health Journal, 20,* 16–24.

Rahimi-Golkhandan, S., & others (2017). A fuzzy trace theory of risk and time preferences in decision making: Integrating cognition and motivation. In J.R. Stevens (Ed.), *Impulsivity: How risk and time influence decision making.* New York: Springer.

Rahmani, E., & others (2017, in press). Genome-wide methylation data mirror ancestry information. *Epigenetics and Chromatin.*

Raikes, H., & others (2006). Mother-child bookreading in low-income families: Correlates and outcomes during the first three years of life. *Child Development, 77,* 924–953.

Raikes, H.A., & Thompson, R.A. (2009). Attachment security and parenting quality predict children's problem-solving, attributions, and loneliness with peers. *Attachment and Human Development, 10,* 319–344.

Railton, P. (2017, in press). Moral learning: Why learning? Why moral? And why now? *Cognition.*

Rajaraman, P., & others (2011). Early life exposure to diagnostic radiation and ultrasound scans and risk of childhood cancer: Case-control study. *British Medical Journal, 342,* d472.

Rajeh, A., & others (2017). Interventions in ADHD: A comparative review of stimulant medications and behavioral therapies. *Asian Journal of Psychiatry, 25,* 131–135.

Rakison, D.H., & Lawson, C.A. (2013). Categorization. In P.D. Zelazo (Ed.), *Oxford handbook of developmental psychology.* New York: Oxford University Press.

Rakoczy, H. (2012). Do infants have a theory of mind? *British Journal of Developmental Psychology, 30,* 59–74.

Rambusch, N.M. (2010). Freedom, order, and the child: Self-control and mastery of the world mark the dynamic Montessori method. *Montessori Life, 22,* 38–43.

Ramchandani, P.G., & others (2008). Depression in men in the postnatal period and later psychopathology: A population cohort study. *Journal of the American Academy of Child and Adolescent Psychiatry, 47,* 390–398.

Ramchandani, P.G., & others (2013). Do early father-infant interactions predict the onset of externalizing behaviors in young children? Findings from a longitudinal cohort study. *Journal of Child Psychology and Psychiatry, 54,* 56–64.

Ramey, C.T., & Campbell, F.A. (1984). Preventive education for high-risk children: Cognitive consequences of the Carolina Abecedarian Project. *American Journal of Mental Deficiency, 88,* 515–523.

Ramey, C.T., & Ramey, S.L. (1998). Early prevention and early experience. *American Psychologist, 53,* 109–120.

Ramey, C.T., & Ramey, S.L. (2004). Early learning and school readiness: Can early intervention make a difference? *Merrill-Palmer Quarterly, 50,* 471–491.

Ramey, C.T., Ramey, S.L., & Lanzi, R.G. (2001). Intelligence and experience. In R.J. Sternberg & E.L. Grigorenko (Eds.), *Environment effects on cognitive development.* Mahwah, NJ: Erlbaum.

Ramey, S.L. (2005). Human developmental science serving children and families: Contributions of the NICHD study of early child care. In NICHD Early Child Care Network (Eds.), *Child care and development.* New York: Guilford.

Ramey, S.L., & Ramey, C.T. (1999). *Going to school: How to help your child succeed.* New York: Goddard Press.

Ramirez-Esparza, N., Garcia-Sierra, A., & Kuhl, P.K. (2014). Look who's talking: Speech style and social context in language input to infants are linked to concurrent and future speech development. *Developmental Science, 17,* 880–891.

Ramirez-Esparza, N., Garcia-Sierra, A., & Kuhl, P.K. (2017, in press). The impact of early social interactions on later language development in Spanish-English bilingual infants. *Child Development.*

Ramsdell, H.L., Oller, D.K., Buder, E.H., Ethington, C.A., & Chorna, L. (2012). Identification of prelinguistic phonological categories. *Journal of Speech, Language, and Hearing Research, 55*(6), 1626–1639.

Rangey, P.S., & Sheth, M. (2014). Comparative effect of massage therapy versus kangaroo mother care on body weight and length of hospital stay in low birth weight preterm infants. *International Journal of Pediatrics, 2014,* 434060.

Rankin, J. (2017). *Physiology in childbearing* (4th ed.). New York: Elsevier.

Rankin, J., & others (2016). Psychological consequences of childhood obesity: Psychiatric comorbidity and prevention. *Adolescent Health, Medicine, and Therapeutics, 7,* 125–146.

Rao, S., & others (2017). Resequencing three candidate genes discovers seven potentially deleterious variants susceptibility to major depressive disorder and suicide attempts in Chinese. *Gene, 603,* 34–41.

Rapee, R.M. (2014). Preschool environment and temperament as predictors of social and nonsocial anxiety disorders in middle adolescence. *Journal of the American Academy of Child and Adolescent Psychiatry, 53,* 320–328.

Ratner, N.B. (2013). Why talk with children matters: Clinical implications of infant- and child-directed speech research. *Seminars in Speech and Language, 34,* 203–214.

Raver, C.C., & others (2011). CSRP's impact on low-income preschoolers' preacademic skills: Self-regulation as a mediating mechanism. *Child Development, 82,* 362–378.

Raver, C.C., & others (2012). Testing models of children's self-regulation within educational contexts: Implications for measurement. *Advances in Child Development and Behavior, 42,* 245–270.

Raver, C.C., & others (2013). Predicting individual differences in low-income children's executive control from early to middle childhood. *Developmental Science, 16,* 394–408.

Ray, J., & others (2017). Callous-unemotional traits predict self-reported offending in adolescent boys: The mediating role of delinquent peers and the moderating role of parenting practices. *Developmental Psychology, 53,* 319–328.

Razaz, N., & others (2016). Five-minute Apgar score as a marker for developmental vulnerability at 5 years of age. *Archives of Disease in Childhood: Fetal and Neonatal Edition, 101,* F114–F120.

Razza, R.A., Martin, A., & Brooks-Gunn, J. (2012). The implications of early attentional regulational for school success among low-income children. *Journal of Applied Developmental Psychology, 33,* 311–319.

Reader, J.M., Teti, D.M., & Cleveland, M.J. (2017, in press). Cognitions about infant sleep: Interparental differences, trajectories across the first year, and coparenting quality. *Journal of Family Psychology.*

Realini, J.P., Buzi, R.S., Smith, P.B., & Martinez, M. (2010). Evaluation of "big decisions": An abstinence-plus sexuality. *Journal of Sex and Marital Therapy, 36,* 313–326.

Reddy, R., & others (2017, in press). Impact of sleep restriction versus idealized sleep on emotional experience, reactivity, and regulation in healthy adolescents. *Journal of Sleep Research.*

Reece, E., & others (2017). Telling the tale and living well: Adolescent narrative identity, personality traits, and well-being across cultures. *Child Development 88,* 612–628.

Reed, R., Rowe, J., & Barnes, M. (2016). Midwifery practice during birth: Ritual companionship. *Women and Birth, 29,* 269–278.

Reef, S.E., & others (2011). Progress toward control of rubella and prevention of congenital rubella syndrome—worldwide, 2009. *Journal of Infectious Diseases, 204*(Suppl. 1), S24–S27.

Reese, B.M., Haydon, A.A., Herring, A.H., & Halpern, C.T. (2013). The association between sequences of sexual initiation and the likelihood of teenage pregnancy. *Journal of Adolescent Health, 52,* 228–233.

Regalado, M., Sareen, H., Inkelas, M., Wissow, L.S., & Halfon, N. (2004). Parents' discipline of young children: Results from the National Survey of Early Childhood Health. *Pediatrics, 113,* 1952–1958.

Regev, R.H., & others (2003). Excess mortality and morbidity among small-for-gestational-age premature infants: A population-based study. *Journal of Pediatrics, 143,* 186–191.

Reid, P.T., & Zalk, S.R. (2001). Academic environments: Gender and ethnicity in U.S. higher education. In J. Worell (Ed.), *Encyclopedia of women and gender.* San Diego: Academic Press.

Reiersen, A.M. (2017). Early identification of autism spectrum disorder: Is diagnosis by age 3 a reasonable goal? *Journal of the American Academy of Child and Adolescent Psychiatry, 56,* 284–285.

Reijntjes, A., & others (2013). Costs and benefits of bullying in the context of the peer group: A three-wave longitudinal analysis. *Journal of Abnormal Psychology, 41,* 1217–1219.

Reilly, D. (2012). Gender, culture, and sex-typed cognitive abilities. *PLoS One, 7*(7), e39904.

Reilly, D., & Neumann, D.L. (2013). Gender-role differences in spatial ability: A meta-analytic review. *Sex Roles, 68,* 521–535.

Reinehr, T., & others (2014). Is growth hormone treatment in children associated with weight gain? *Clinical Endocrinology, 81,* 721–726.

Reis, S.M., & Renzulli, J.S. (2014). Challenging gifted and talented learners with a continuum of research-based intervention strategies. In M.A. Bray & T.J. Kehle (Eds.), *Oxford handbook of school psychology.* New York: Oxford University Press.

Ren, H., & others (2017). Excessive homework, inadequate sleep, physical inactivity, and screen viewing time are major contributors to high pediatric obesity. *Acta Pediatrica, 106,* 120–127.

Renzulli, J. (2017). Developing creativity across all areas of the curriculum. In R.A. Beghetto & J.C. Kaufman (Eds.), *Nurturing creativity in the classroom* (2nd ed.). New York: Cambridge University Press.

Repacholi, B.M., & Gopnik, A. (1997). Early reasoning about desires: Evidence from 14- and 18-month-olds. *Developmental Psychology, 33,* 12–21.

Reproductive Endocrinology and Infertility Committee & others (2011). Advanced reproductive age and fertility. *Journal of Obstetrics and Gynecology Canada, 342,* d472.

Reville, M.C., O'Connor, L., & Frampton, I. (2016). Literature review of cognitive neuroscience and anorexia nervosa. *Current Psychiatric Reports, 18*(2), 18.

Reyna, V.F. (2004). How people make decisions that involve risk: A dual-process approach. *Current Directions in Psychological Science, 13,* 60–66.

Reyna, V.F., & Brainerd, C.J. (1995). Fuzzy-trace theory: An interim analysis. *Learning and Individual Differences, 7,* 1–75.

Reyna, V.F., & Mills, B.A. (2014). Theoretically motivated interventions for reducing sexual risk taking in adolescence: A randomized controlled experiment applying fuzzy-trace theory. *Journal of Experimental Psychology: General, 143,* 1627–1648.

Reyna, V.F., & Rivers, S.E. (2008). Current theories of risk and rational decision making. *Developmental Review, 28,* 1–11.

Reyna, V.F., Wilhelms, E.A., McCormick, M.J., & Weldon, R.B. (2015). Development of risky decision making: Fuzzy-trace theory and neurobiological perspectives. *Child Development Perspectives, 9,* 122–127.

Reyna, V.F., & others (2011). Neurobiological and memory models of risky decision making in adolescents versus young adults. *Journal of Experimental Psychology: Learning, Memory, and Cognition, 37,* 1125–1142.

Reynolds, G.D., & Romano, A.C. (2016). The development of attention systems and memory in infancy. *Frontiers in Systems Neuroscience, 10,* 15.

Rhodes, M., & Brandone, A.C. (2014). Three-year olds' theories of mind in actions and words. *Frontiers in Psychology, 5,* 263.

Rhodes, M., Hetherington, C., Brink, K., & Wellman, H.M. (2015). Infants' use of social partnerships to predict behavior. *Developmental Science, 18,* 909–916.

Riano-Galan, I., & others (2017, in press). Proatherogenic lipid profile in early childhood: Association with weight status at 4 years and parental obesity. *Journal of Pediatrics.*

Ribeiro, C.D., & others (2017). Development skills of children born premature with low and very low birth weight. *CoDAS, 29,* e20160058.

Rice, F., & others (2017). Antecedents of new-onset major depressive disorder in children and adolescents at high familial risk. *JAMA Psychiatry, 74,* 153–160.

Richards, J.E. (2009). Attention to the brain in infancy. In S. Johnson (Ed.), *Neuroconstructivism: The new science of cognitive development.* New York: Oxford University Press.

Richards, J.E. (2010). Infant attention, arousal, and the brain. In L.M. Oakes, C.H. Cashon, M. Casasola, & D.H. Rakison (Eds.), *Infant perception and cognition.* New York: Oxford University Press.

Richards, J.E. (2011). Infant attention, arousal, and the brain. In L. Oakes & others (Eds.), *Infant perception and cognition.* New York: Oxford University Press.

Richards, J.E. (2013). Cortical sources of ERP in the prosaccade and antisaccade task using realistic source models. *Frontiers in Systems Neuroscience, 7,* 27.

Richards, J.E., Boswell, C., Stevens, M., & Vendemia, J.M. (2015). Evaluating methods for constructing average high-density electrode positions. *Brain Topography, 28,* 70–86.

Richards, J.E., Reynolds, G.D., & Courage, M.I. (2010). The neural bases of infant attention. *Current Directions in Psychological Science, 19,* 41–46.

Richards, T., & others (2017, in press). Event-related potentials in children with and without learning disabilities during a sentence judgment task. *Developmental Neuropsychology.*

Richardson, G.A., Goldschmidt, L., & Larkby, C. (2008). Effects of prenatal cocaine exposure on growth: A longitudinal analysis. *Pediatrics, 120,* e1017–e1027.

Richardson, G.A., Goldschmidt, L., Leech, S., & Willford, J. (2011). Prenatal cocaine exposure: Effects on mother- and teacher-rated behavior problems and growth in school-aged children. *Neurotoxicology and Teratology, 33,* 69–77.

Richardson, G.A., Ryan, C., Willford, J., Day, N.L., & Goldschmidt, L. (2002). Prenatal alcohol and marijuana exposure: Effects on neuropsychological outcomes at 10 years. *Neurotoxicology and Teratology, 24,* 309–320.

Richardson, M.A., & others (2016). Psychological distress among school-aged children with and without intrauterine cocaine exposure: Perinatal versus contextual effects. *Journal of Abnormal Child Psychology, 44,* 547–560.

Rideout, V. (2011). *Zero to eight: Children's media use in America.* San Francisco: Commonsense Media.

Rideout, V.J., Foehr, U.G., & Roberts, D.F. (2010). *Generation M²: Media in the lives of 8- to 18-year-olds.* Menlo Park, CA: Kaiser Family Foundation.

Rieger, S., Gollner, R., Trautwein, U., & Roberts, B.W. (2016). Low self-esteem prospectively predicts depression in the transition to young adulthood: A replication of Orth, Robins, & Roberts (2008). *Journal of Personality and Social Psychology, 110,* e16–e22.

Ries, S.K., Dronkers, N.F., & Knight, R.T. (2016). Choosing words: Left hemisphere, right hemisphere, or both? Perspective on the lateralization of word retrieval. *Annals of the New York Academy of Sciences, 1369,* 111–131.

Riggins, T. (2012). Building blocks of recollection. In S. Ghetti & P.J. Bauer (Eds.), *Origins of recollection.* New York: Oxford University Press.

Righi, G., & others (2014). Infants' experience-dependent processing of male and female faces: Insights from eye tracking and event-related potentials. *Developmental Cognitive Neuroscience, 8,* 144–152.

Riley, M., & Bluhm, B. (2012). High blood pressure in children and adolescents. *American Family Physician, 85,* 693–700.

Rimfeld, K., & others (2017, in press). Phenotypic and genetic evidence for a unifactorial structure of spatial abilities. *Proceedings of the National Academy of Sciences USA.*

Rink, B.D., & Norton, M.E. (2016). Screening for fetal aneuploidy. *Seminars in Perinatology, 40,* 35–43.

Riva Crugnola, C., Ierardi, E., Gazzotti, S., & Albizzati, A. (2014). Motherhood in adolescent mothers: Maternal attachment, mother-infant styles of interaction, and emotion regulation at three months. *Infant Behavior and Development, 37,* 44–56.

Rivas-Drake, D., & others (2017). Ethnic-racial identity and friendships in early adolescence. *Child Development, 88,* 710–724.

Rizzo, M.S. (1999, May 8). Genetic counseling combines science with a human touch. *Kansas City Star,* p. 3.

Roberts, D.F., Henriksen, L., & Foehr, U.G. (2004). Adolescents and the media. In R. Lerner & L. Steinberg (Eds.), *Handbook of adolescent psychology* (2nd ed.). New York: Wiley.

Roblyer, M.D. (2016). *Integrating education technology into teaching* (7th ed.). Upper Saddle River, NJ: Pearson.

Robson, S. (2017). Creativity and play. In T. Bruce & others (Eds.), *Routledge international handbook of early childhood play.* New York: Routledge.

Rocca, M.S., & others (2016). The Klinefelter syndrome is associated with high recurrence of copy number variations on the X chromosome with a potential role in the clinical phenotype. *Andrology, 4,* 328–334.

Rochlen, A.B., McKelley, R.A., Suizzo, M.A., & Scaringi, V. (2008). Predictors of relationship satisfaction, psychological well-being, and life-satisfaction among stay-at-home fathers. *Psychology of Men and Masculinity, 9,* 17–28.

Rode, S.S., Chang, P., Fisch, R.O., & Sroufe, L.A. (1981). Attachment patterns of infants separated at birth. *Developmental Psychology, 17,* 188–191.

Rodgers, C. (2013). Why kangaroo care should be standard for all newborns. *Journal of Midwifery and Women's Health, 58,* 249–252.

Rodriguez, E.T., & others (2009). The formative role of home literacy experiences across the first three years of life in children from low-income families. *Journal of Applied Developmental Psychology, 30,* 677–694.

Roeser, R.W., & Eccles. J.S. (2015). Mindfulness and compassion in human development: Introduction to the special section. *Developmental Psychology, 51,* 1–6.

Roeser, R.W., & Zelazo, P.D. (2012). Contemplative science, education and child development. *Child Development Perspectives, 6,* 143–145.

Roeser, R.W., & others (2014). Contemplative education. In L. Nucci & others (Eds.), *Handbook of moral and character education.* New York: Routledge.

Rogers, M.L., & others (2016). Maternal emotion socialization differentially predicts third-grade children's emotion regulation and liability. *Emotion, 16,* 280–291.

Roggman, L.A., & others (2016). Home visit quality variations in two Early Head Start programs in relation to parenting and child vocabulary outcomes. *Infant Mental Health Journal, 37,* 193–207.

Rognum, I.J., & others (2014). Serotonin metabolites in the cerebrospinal fluid in sudden infant death syndrome. *Journal of Neuropathology and Experimental Neurology, 73,* 115–122.

Roisman, G.I., & Cicchetti, D. (2018, in press). Attachment in the context of atypical caregiving: Harnessing insights from developmental psychopathology. *Development and Psychopathology.*

Roisman, G.I., & others (2017, in press). Strategic considerations in the search for transactional processes. *Development and Psychopathology.*

Rolfes, S.R., Pinna, K., & Whitney, E. (2018). *Understanding normal and clinical nutrition* (11th ed.). Boston: Cengage.

Rolland, B., & others (2016). Pharmacotherapy for alcohol dependence: The 2015 recommendations of the French Alcohol Society, issued in partnership with the European Federation of Addiction Societies. *CNS Neuroscience and Therapeutics, 22,* 25–37.

Romero, L.M., & others (2017). Efforts to increase implementation of evidence-based clinical practices to improve adolescent-friendly reproductive health services. *Journal of Adolescent Health, 60*(Suppl. 3), S30–S37.

Rommel, A.S., & others (2015). Is physical activity causally associated with symptoms of attention-deficit/hyperactivity disorder? *Journal of the American Academy of Child and Adolescent Psychiatry, 54,* 565–570.

Romo, D.L., & others (2017, in press). Social media use and its association with sexual risk and parental monitoring among a primarily Hispanic adolescent population. *Journal of Pediatric and Adolescent Gynecology.*

Romo, L.F., Mireles-Rios, R., & Lopez-Tello, G. (2014). Latina mothers' and daughters' expectations for autonomy at age 15 (La Quinceañera). *Journal of Adolescent Research, 29*(2), 279–294.

Roopnarine, J.L., & Metindogan, A. (2006). Early childhood education research in cross-national perspective. In B. Spodek & O.N. Saracho (Eds.), *Handbook of research on the education of young children.* Mahwah, NJ: Erlbaum.

Roos, L.E., & others (2017). Validation of autonomic and endocrine reactivity to a laboratory stressor in young children. *Psychoneuroimmunology, 77,* 51–55.

Rose, A.J., Carlson, W., & Waller, E.M. (2007). Prospective associations of co-rumination with friendship and emotional adjustment: Considering the socioemotional trade-offs of co-rumination. *Developmental Psychology, 43,* 1019–1031.

Rose, S.A., Feldman, J.F., & Jankowski, J.J. (2015). Pathways from toddler information processing to adolescent lexical proficiency. *Child Development, 86,* 1935–1947.

Rose, S.A., Feldman, J.F., Jankowski, J.J., & Van Rossem, R. (2012). Information processing from infancy to 11 years: Continuities and prediction of IQ. *Intelligence, 40,* 445–457.

Rose, S.A., Feldman, J.F., & Wallace, I.F. (1992). Infant information processing in relation to six-year cognitive outcomes. *Child Development, 63,* 1126–1141.

Roseberry, S., Hirsh-Pasek, K., & Golinkoff, R. (2014). Skype me! Socially contingent interactions help toddlers learn language. *Child Development, 85,* 956–970.

Roseberry, S., Hirsh-Pasek, K., Parish-Morris, J., & Golinkoff, R. (2009). Live action: Can young children learn verbs from video? *Child Development, 80,* 1360–1375.

Rosenberg, M.D., & others (2016). A neuromarker of sustained attention from whole-brain functional connectivity. *Nature Neuroscience, 19,* 165–171.

Rosenblith, J.F. (1992). *In the beginning* (2nd ed.). Newbury Park, CA: Sage.

Rosenblum, G.D., & Lewis, M. (2003). Emotional development in adolescence. In G. Adams & M. Berzonsky (Eds.), *Blackwell handbook of adolescence.* Malden, MA: Blackwell.

Rosengard, C. (2009). Confronting the intendedness of adolescent rapid repeat pregnancy. *Journal of Adolescent Health, 44,* 5–6.

Rosenstein, D., & Oster, H. (1988). Differential facial responses to four basic tastes in newborns. *Child Development, 59,* 1555–1568.

Rosenstrom, T., & others (2017, in press). Genetic and environmental structure of DSM-IV criteria for antisocial personality disorder. *Behavior Genetics.*

Ross, J. (2017). You and me: Investigating the role of self-evaluative emotion in preschool prosociality. *Journal of Experimental Child Psychology, 155,* 67–83.

Ross, J.L., Lee, P.A., Gut, R., & Gemak, J. (2015). Attaining genetic height potential: Analysis of height outcomes from the ANSWER program in children treated with growth hormone over 5 years. *Growth Hormone & IGF Research, 25,* 286–293.

Ross, J.L., & others (2012). Behavioral and social phenotypes in boys with 47, XYY syndrome or 47, XXY Klinefelter syndrome. *Pediatrics, 129,* 769–778.

Rossiter, M.D., & others (2015). Breast, formula, and combination feeding in relation to childhood obesity in Nova Scotia, Canada. *Maternal and Child Health Journal, 19,* 2048–2056.

Rote, W.M., & Smetana, J.G. (2016). Beliefs about parents' right to know: Domain distinctions and associations with change in concealment. *Journal of Research on Adolescence, 26,* 334–344.

Roth, B., & others (2015). Intelligence and school grades: A meta-analysis. *Intelligence, 53,* 118–137.

Roth, J.L., Brooks-Gunn, J., Murray, L., & Foster, W. (1998). Promoting healthy adolescents: Synthesis of youth development program evaluations. *Journal of Research on Adolescence, 8,* 423–459.

Roth, W.M. (2016). The primacy of the social and sociogenesis. *Integrative Psychological and Behavioral Science, 50,* 122–141.

Rothbart, M.K. (2004). Temperament and the pursuit of an integrated developmental psychology. *Merrill-Palmer Quarterly, 50,* 492–505.

Rothbart, M.K. (2011). *Becoming who we are.* New York: Guilford.

Rothbart, M.K., & Bates, J.E. (2006). Temperament. In W. Damon & R. Lerner (Eds.), *Handbook of child psychology* (6th ed.). New York: Wiley.

Rothbart, M.K., & Gartstein, M.A. (2008). Temperament. In M.M. Haith & J.B. Benson (Eds.), *Encyclopedia of infant and early childhood development.* Oxford, UK: Elsevier.

Rothbart, M.K., & Posner, M. (2015). The developing brain in a multitasking world. *Developmental Review, 35,* 42–63.

Rothbaum, F., & Trommsdorff, G. (2007). Do roots and wings complement or oppose one another?: The socialization of relatedness and autonomy in cultural context. In J.E. Grusec & P.D. Hastings (Eds.), *Handbook of socialization.* New York: Guilford.

Rothbaum, F., Weisz, J., Pott, M., Miyake, K., & Morelli, G. (2000). Attachment and culture: Security in the United States and Japan. *American Psychologist, 55,* 1093–1104.

Rothman, R. (2016). Accountability for what matters. *State Education Standard, 16,* 10–13.

Rousssotte, F.F., & others (2011). Abnormal brain activation during working memory in children with prenatal exposure to drugs of abuse: The effects of methamphetamine, alcohol, and polydrug exposure. *NeuroImage, 54,* 3067–3075.

Rovee-Collier, C. (1987). Learning and memory in children. In J.D. Osofsky (Ed.), *Handbook of infant development* (2nd ed.). New York: Wiley.

Rovee-Collier, C. (2004). Infant learning and memory. In U. Goswami (Ed.), *Blackwell handbook of childhood cognitive development.* Malden, MA: Blackwell.

Rovee-Collier, C. (2008). The development of infant memory. In N. Cowan & M. Courage (Eds.), *The development of memory in infancy and childhood.* Philadelphia: Psychology Press.

Rovee-Collier, C., & Barr, R. (2010). Infant learning and memory. In J.G. Bremner & T.D. Wachs (Eds.), *Wiley-Blackwell handbook of infant development* (2nd ed.). New York: Wiley.

Rovee-Collier, C., & Cuevas, K. (2009). The development of infant memory. In M.L. Courage & N. Cowan (Eds.), *The development of memory in infancy and childhood.* New York: Psychology Press.

Rowe, M., Ramani, G., & Pomerantz, E.M. (2016). Parental involvement and children's motivation and achievement: A domain-specific perspective. In K. Wentzel & D. Miel (Eds.), *Handbook of motivation at school* (2nd ed.). New York: Routledge.

Rowe, M.L., & Goldin-Meadow, S. (2009). Differences in early gesture explain SES disparities in child vocabulary size at school entry. *Science, 323,* 951–953.

Rozenblat, V. & others (2017). A systematic review and secondary data analysis of the interactions between the serotonin transporter 5-HTTLPR polymorphism and environmental and psychological factors in eating disorders. *Journal of Psychiatric Research, 84,* 62–72.

Rubens, D., & Sarnat, H.B. (2013). Sudden infant death syndome: An update and new perspectives of etiology. *Handbook of Clinical Neurology, 112,* 867–874.

Rubin, D.H., Krasilnikoff, P.A., Leventhal, J.M., Weile, B., & Berget, A. (1986, August 23). Effect of passive smoking on birth weight. *The Lancet,* 415–417.

Rubin, K.H., & Barstead, M. (2018, in press). Social withdrawal and solitude. In M.H. Bornstein & others (Eds.), *SAGE handbook of lifespan development.* Thousand Oaks, CA: Sage.

Rubin, K.H., Bukowski, W.M., & Bowker, J. (2015). Children in peer groups. In R.E. Lerner (Ed.), *Handbook of child psychology and developmental science* (7th ed.). New York: Wiley.

Rubin, K.H., Bukowski, W.M., & Parker, J.G. (2006). Peer interactions, relationships, and groups.

In W. Damon & R. Lerner (Eds.), *Handbook of child psychology* (6th ed.). New York: Wiley.

Rubin, K.H., & others (2016). Peer relationships. In M.H. Bornstein & M.E. Lamb (Eds.), *Developmental science* (7th ed.). New York: Psychology Press.

Rubio-Codina, M., & others (2016). Concurrent validity and feasibility of short tests currently used to measure early childhood development in large-scale studies. *PLoS One, 11*(8), e0160962.

Rubio-Fernandez, P. (2017). Why are bilinguals better than monolinguals at false-belief tasks? *Psychonomic Bulletin and Review, 24,* 987–998.

Ruble, D. (1983). The development of social comparison processes and their role in achievement-related self-socialization. In E. Higgins, D. Ruble, & W. Hartup (Eds.), *Social cognitive development: A social-cultural perspective.* New York: Cambridge University Press.

Ruck, M.D., Peterson-Badali, M., & Freeman, M. (Eds.). (2017). *Handbook of children's rights.* New York: Routledge.

Rudolph, K.D., Troop-Gordon, W., Lambert, S.F., & Natsuaki, M.N. (2014). Long-term consequences of pubertal timing for youth depression: Identifying personal and contextual pathways of risk. *Development and Psychopathology, 26,* 1423–1444.

Rueda, M.R., Posner, M.I., & Rothbart, M.K. (2005). The development of executive attention: Contributions to the emergence of self-regulation. *Developmental Neuropsychology, 28,* 573–594.

Rumberger, R.W. (1995). Dropping out of middle school: A multilevel analysis of students and schools. *American Education Research Journal, 3,* 583–625.

Russell, P.J., Hertz, P.E., & McMillan, B. (2017). *Biology* (4th ed.). Boston: Cengage.

Russell, S.T., Crockett, L.J., & Chao, R.K. (2010). *Asian American parenting and parent-adolescent relationships.* New York: Springer.

Rutman, L., & others (2016). Standardized asthma admission criteria reduce length of stay in a pediatric emergency department. *Academic Emergency Medicine, 23,* 289–296.

Rutter, M., & Schopler, E. (1987). Autism and pervasive developmental disorders: Concepts and diagnostic issues. *Journal of Autism and Pervasive Developmental Disorders, 17,* 159–186.

Ryan, R.M., & Deci, E.I. (2001). When rewards compete with nature. In C. Sansone & J.M. Harackiewicz (Eds.), *Intrinsic and extrinsic motivation.* San Diego: Academic Press.

Ryan, R.M., & Deci, E.L. (2016). Facilitating and hindering motivation, learning, and well-being in schools: Research and observations from self-determination theory. In K.R. Wentzel & D.B. Miele (Eds.), *Handbook of motivation at school* (2nd ed.). New York: Routledge.

Ryan, R.M., & Moller, A.C. (2017). Competence as central, but not sufficient, for high-quality motivation: A self-determination theory perspective. In A.J. Elliott, C.S. Dweck, & D.S. Yeager (Eds.), *Handbook of competence and motivation* (2nd ed.). New York: Guilford.

S

Saarni, C., Campos, J., Camras, L.A., & Witherington, D. (2006). Emotional development. In W. Damon & R. Lerner (Eds.), *Handbook of child psychology* (6th ed.). New York: Wiley.

Sabbagh, M.A., Xu, F., Carlson, S.M., Moses, L.J., & Lee, K. (2006). The development of executive functioning and theory of mind: A comparison of Chinese and U.S. preschoolers. *Psychological Science, 17,* 74–81.

Sackett, P.R., Borneman, M.J., & Connelly, B.S. (2009). Responses to issues raised about validity, bias, and fairness in high-stakes testing. *American Psychologist, 64,* 285–287.

Sackett, P.R., & others (2017, in press). Individual differences and their measurement: A review of 100 years of research. *Journal of Applied Psychology.*

Sacrey, L.A., Germani, T., Bryson, S.E., & Zwaigenbaum, L. (2014). Reaching and grasping in autism spectrum disorder: A review of recent literature. *Frontiers in Neurology, 5,* 6.

Sadeh, A. (2008). Sleep. In M.M. Haith & J.B. Benson (Eds.), *Encyclopedia of infant and early childhood development.* Oxford, UK: Elsevier.

Sadeh, A., & others (2015). Infant sleep predicts attention regulation and behavior problems at 3–4 years of age. *Developmental Neuropsychology, 40,* 122–137.

Sadker, D.M., & Zittleman, K. (2016). *Teachers, schools, and society* (4th ed.). New York: McGraw-Hill.

Sadker, M.P., & Sadker, D.M. (2005). *Teachers, schools, and society* (7th ed.). New York: McGraw-Hill.

Sadovsky, A.D., & others (2016). LBW and IUGR temporal trend in 4 population-based cohorts: The role of economic inequality. *BMC Pediatrics, 16,* 115.

Saez de Urabain, I.R., Nuthmann, A., Johnson, M.H., & Smith, T.J. (2017). Disentangling the mechanisms underlying infant fixation durations in scene perception: A computational account. *Vision Research, 134,* 43–59.

Sajber, D., & others (2016). Alcohol drinking among Kosovar adolescents: An examination of gender-specific sociodemographic, sport, and family factors associated with harmful drinking. *Substance Use and Misuse, 51,* 533–539.

Sala, G., & Gobet, F. (2017, in press). Working memory training in typically developing children: A meta-analysis of the available evidence. *Developmental Psychology.*

Salam, R.A., & others (2016). Improving adolescent sexual and reproductive health: A systematic review of potential interventions. *Journal of Adolescent Health, 59,* S11–S28.

Salama, R.H., & others (2013). Clinical and biochemical effects of environmental tobacco smoking on pregnancy outcome. *Indian Journal of Clinical Biochemistry, 28,* 368–373.

Salkind, N.J. (2017). *Exploring research* (9th ed.). Upper Saddle River, NJ: Pearson.

Salley, B., & Colombo, J. (2016). Conceptualizing social attention in developmental research. *Social Development, 25,* 687–703.

Salley, B., & others (2016). Infants' early visual attention and social engagement as developmental precursors to joint attention. *Developmental Psychology, 52,* 1721–1731.

Salmivalli, C., & Peets, K. (2009). Bullies, victims, and bully-victim relationships in middle childhood and adolescence. In K.H. Rubin, W.M. Bukowski, & B. Laursen (Eds.), *Handbook of peer interactions, relationships, and groups.* New York: Guilford.

Salzwedel, A.P., & others (2016). Thalamocortical functional connectivity and behavioral disruptions in neonates with prenatal cocaine exposure. *Neurotoxicology and Teratology, 56,* 16–25.

Samek, D.R., & others (2017). Antisocial peer affiliation and externalizing disorders: Evidence for gene × environment × development interaction. *Development and Psychopathology, 29,* 155–172.

Sameroff, A.J. (2009). The transactional model. In A.J. Sameroff (Ed.), *The transactional model of development: How children and contexts shape each other.* Washington, DC: American Psychological Association.

Sampath, A., Maduro, G., & Schillinger, J.A. (2017, in press). Infant deaths due to herpes simplex virus, congenital syphilis, and HIV in New York City. *Pediatrics.*

Sanders, K.E., & Guerra, A.W. (Eds.) (2016). *The culture of child care.* New York: Oxford University Press.

Sanem, J.R., & others (2015). Association between alcohol-impaired driving enforcement related strategies and alcohol-impaired driving. *Accident Analysis and Prevention, 78,* 104–109.

Sangganjanavanich, V.F. (2016). Trans identities, psychological perspectives. In *Wiley Blackwell encyclopedia of gender and sexuality studies.* New York: Wiley.

Sankupellay, M., & others (2011). Characteristics of sleep EEG power spectra in healthy infants in the first two years of life. *Clinical Neurophysiology, 122,* 236–243.

Sann, C., & Streri, A. (2007). Perception of object shape and texture in human newborns: Evidence from cross-modal tasks. *Developmental Science, 10,* 399–410.

Sanson, A., & Rothbart, M.K. (1995). Child temperament and parenting. In M.H. Bornstein (Ed.), *Handbook of parenting* (Vol. 4). Hillsdale, NJ: Erlbaum.

Santangeli, L., Satter, N., & Huda, S.S. (2015). Impact of maternal obesity on perinatal and child outcomes. *Best Practices and Research. Clinical Obstetrics and Gynecology, 29,* 438–448.

Santiago, A., Aoki, C., & Sullivan, R.M. (2017). From attachment to independence: Stress hormone control of ecologically relevant emergence of infants' responses to threat. *Current Opinion in Behavioral Science, 14,* 78–85.

Santos, C.E., Komienko, O., & Rivas-Drake, D. (2017). Peer influences on ethnic-racial identity development: A multi-site investigation. *Child Development, 88,* 725–742.

Santos, L.M., & others (2016). Prevention of neural tube defects by fortification of flour with folic acid:

A population-based retrospective study in Brazil. *Bulletin of the World Health Organization, 94,* 22–29.

Santrock, J.W., Sitterle, K.A., & Warshak, R.A. (1988). Parent-child relationships in stepfather families. In P. Bronstein & C.P. Cowan (Eds.), *Fatherhood today: Men's changing roles in the family.* New York: Wiley.

Sarchiapone, M., & others (2014). Hours of sleep in adolescents and its association with anxiety, emotional concerns, and suicidal ideation. *Sleep Medicine, 15,* 248–254.

Saroglou, V. (2013). Religion, spirituality, and altruism. In K.I. Pargament, J. Exline, & J. Jones (Eds.), *Handbook of psychology, religion, and spirituality.* Washington, DC: American Psychological Association.

Sarquella-Brugada, G., & others (2016). Sudden infant death syndrome caused by cardiac arrhythmias: Only a matter of genes encoding ion channels? *International Journal of Legal Medicine, 130,* 415–420.

Sasayama, D., Washizuka, S., & Honda, H. (2016). Effective treatment of nightmares and sleepwalking with Ramelteon. *Journal of Child and Adolescent Psychopharmacology, 26,* 948.

Sauber-Schatz, E.K., & others (2014). Vital signs: Restraint use and motor vehicle occupant death rates among children aged 0–12—United States, 2002–2011. *MMWR Morbidity and Mortality Weekly Reports, 63*(5), 113–118.

Saunders, N.R., & others (2017). Risk of firearm injuries among children and youth of immigrant families. *Canadian Medical Association Journal, 189,* E452–E458.

Savin-Williams, R.C. (2016). *Becoming who I am: Young men on being gay.* Cambridge, MA: Harvard University Press.

Savin-Williams, R.C. (2017). *Mostly straight: Sexual fluidity among men.* Cambridge, MA: Harvard University Press.

Savin-Williams, R.C. (2018, in press). Developmental trajectories and milestones of sexual-minority youth. In J. Gilbert & S. Lamb (Eds.), *Cambridge handbook of sexuality.* New York: Cambridge University Press.

Saxena, M., Srivastava, N., & Banerjee, M. (2017, in press). Cytokine gene variants as predictors of type 2 diabetes. *Current Diabetes Review.*

Scaife, J.C., & others (2017). Reduced resting-state functional connectivity in current and recovered restrictive anorexia nervosa. *Frontiers in Psychology, 8,* 30.

Scales, P.C., Benson, P.L., & Roehlkepartain, E.C. (2011). Adolescent thriving: The role of sparks, relationships, and empowerment. *Journal of Youth and Adolescence, 40*(3), 263–277.

Scarlett, W.G., & Warren, A.E.A. (2010). Religious and spiritual development across the life span: A behavioral and social science perspective. In M.E. Lamb, A.M. Freund, & R.M. Lerner (Eds.), *Handbook of life-span development.* New York: Wiley.

Scarr, S. (1993). Biological and cultural diversity: The legacy of Darwin for development. *Child Development, 64,* 1333–1353.

Scelfo, J. (2015, February 3). A university recognizes a third gender: neutral. *New York Times.* Retrieved December 20, 2016, from www. newyorktimes.com/2015/02/08/education/edlife/a-university-re...

Schaefer, F., & others (2017). Cardiovascular phenotypes in children with CKD: The 4C study. *Clinical Journal of the American Society of Nephrology, 12,* 19–28.

Schaffer, H.R. (1996). *Social development.* Cambridge, MA: Blackwell.

Schaie, K.W. (2013). *Developmental influences on adult intellectual development.* New York: Oxford University Press.

Schaie, K.W. (2016). Theoretical perspectives for the psychology of aging in a lifespan context. In K.W. Schaie & S.L. Willis (Eds.), *Handbook of the psychology of aging* (8th ed.). New York: Elsevier.

Schalkwijk, F., & others (2016). The conscience as a regulatory function: Empathy, shame, pride, guilt, and moral orientation in delinquent adolescents. *International Journal of Offender Therapy and Comparative Criminology, 60,* 675–693.

Scharf, R.J. (2016). School readiness. *Pediatrics in Review, 37,* 501–503.

Scheinost, D., & others (2017). Does prenatal stress alter the development connectome? *Pediatric Research, 81,* 214–226.

Scher, A., & Harel, J. (2008). Separation and stranger anxiety. In M.M. Haith & J.B. Benson (Eds.), *Encyclopedia of infant and early childhood development.* Oxford, UK: Elsevier.

Schick, U.M., & others (2016). Genome-wide association study of platelet count identifies ancestry-specific loci in Hispanic/Latino Americans. *American Journal of Human Genetics, 98,* 229–242.

Schieffelin, B. (2005). *The give and take of everyday life.* Tucson, AZ: Fenestra.

Schieve, L.A., & others (2016). Population impact of preterm birth and low birth weight on developmental disabilities in U.S. children. *Annals of Epidemiology, 26,* 267–274.

Schiff, R., Nuri Ben-Shushan, Y., & Ben-Artzi, E. (2017). Metacognitive strategies: A foundation for early word spelling and reading in kindergarteners with SLI. *Journal of Learning Disabilities, 50,* 143–157.

Schiff, W.J. (2016). *Nutrition for healthy living* (4th ed.). New York: McGraw-Hill.

Schiff, W.J. (2017). *Nutrition essentials* (5th ed.). New York: McGraw-Hill.

Schittny, J.C. (2017, in press). Development of the lung. *Cell & Tissue Research.*

Schlam, T.R., Wilson, N.L., Shoda, Y., Mischel, W., & Ayduk, O. (2013). Preschoolers' delay of gratification predicts their body mass 30 years later. *Journal of Pediatrics, 162,* 90–93.

Schlegel, M. (2000). All work and play. *Monitor on Psychology, 31*(11), 50–51.

Schmidt, J.A., Shumow, L., & Kackar, H. (2007). Adolescents' participation in service activities and its impact on academic, behavioral, and civic outcomes. *Journal of Youth and Adolescence, 36,* 127–140.

Schmidt, U. (2003). Aetiology of eating disorders in the 21st century: New answers to old questions. *European Child and Adolescent Psychiatry, 12* (Suppl. 1), 1130–1137.

Schmitt, D.P., & Pilcher, J.J. (2004). Evaluating evidence of psychological adaptation: How do we know one when we see one? *Psychological Science, 15,* 643–649.

Schmitt, S.A., & others (2017, in press). Examining the relations between executive function, math, and literacy during the transition to kindergarten: A multi-analytic approach. *Journal of Educational Psychology.*

Schneider, B. (2016). *Childhood friendship and peer relations.* New York: Routledge.

Schneider, W. (2011). Memory development in childhood. In U. Goswami (Ed.), *Wiley-Blackwell handbook of childhood cognitive development.* New York: Wiley.

Schoffstall, C.L., & Cohen, R. (2011). Cyber aggression: The relation between online offenders and offline social competence. *Social Development, 20*(3), 587–604.

Schonert-Reichl, K.A., & others (2015). Enhancing cognitive and socio-emotional development through a simple-to-administer mindfulness-based school program for elementary school children: A randomized controlled trial. *Developmental Psychology, 51,* 52–56.

Schoon, I., Jones, E., Cheng, H., & Maughan, B. (2012). Family hardship, family instability, and cognitive development. *Journal of Epidemiology and Community Health, 66*(8), 716–722.

Schrag, S.G., & Dixon, R.L. (1985). Occupational exposure associated with male reproductive dysfunction. *Annual Review of Pharmacology and Toxicology, 25,* 467–592.

Schreiber, L.R. (1990). *The parents' guide to kids' sports.* Boston: Little, Brown.

Schulenberg, J.E., & Zarrett, N.R. (2006). Mental health during emerging adulthood: Continuity and discontinuity in courses, causes, and functions. In J.J. Arnett & J.L. Tanner (Eds.), *Emerging adults in America.* Washington, DC. American Psychological Association.

Schultz, M.L., Kostic, M., & Kharasch, S. (2017, in press). A case of toxic breast-feeding? *Pediatric Emergency Care.*

Schumacher, M., Zubaran, C., & White, G. (2008). Bringing birth-related paternal depression to the fore. *Women and Birth, 21,* 65–70.

Schunk, D.H. (2016). *Learning theories: An educational perspective* (7th ed.). Upper Saddle River, NJ: Prentice Hall.

Schunk, D.H., & Greene, J.A. (Eds.) (2018). *Handbook of self-regulation of learning and performance* (2nd ed.). New York: Routledge.

Schutten, D., Stokes, K.A., & Arnell, K.M. (2017). I want to media multitask and I want to do it now: Individual differences in media multitasking predict delay of gratification and system-1 thinking. *Cognitive Research Principles and Implications, 2*(1), 8.

Schutze, U. (2017). *Language learning and the brain.* New York: Cambridge University Press.

Schwalbe, C.S., Gearing, R.E., MacKenzie, M.J., Brewer, K.B., & Ibrahim, R. (2012). A meta-analysis of experimental studies of diversion programs for juvenile offenders. *Clinical Psychology Review, 32,* 26–33.

Schwartz, D., & others (2014, in press). Peer victimization during middle childhood as a lead indicator of internalizing problems and diagnostic outcomes in late adolescence. *Journal of Clinical Child and Adolescent Psychology.*

Schwartz, S.J., & others (2015). The identity of acculturation and multiculturalism: Situation acculturation in context. In V. Benet-Martinez & Y.Y. Hong (Eds.), *Oxford handbook of multicultural identity.* New York: Oxford University Press.

Schwartz, S.J., Zamboanga, B.L., Meca, A., & Ritchie, R.A. (2012). Identity around the world: An overview. *New Directions in Child and Adolescent Development, 138,* 1–18.

Schweinhart, L.J., & others (2005). *Lifetime effects: The High/Scope Petty Preschool study through age 40.* Ypsilanti, MI: High/Scope Press.

Sciberras, E., & others (2017, in press). Prenatal risk factors and the etiology of ADHD of existing evidence. *Current Psychiatry Reports.*

Scott, R.M., & Baillargeon, R. (2017). Early false-belief understanding. *Trends in Cognitive Science, 21,* 237–249.

Scott-Goodwin, A.C., Puerto, M., & Moreno, I. (2016). Toxic effects of prenatal exposure to alcohol, tobacco, and other drugs. *Reproductive Toxicology, 61,* 120–130.

Scourfield, J., Van den Bree, M., Martin, N., & McGuffin, P. (2004). Conduct problems in children and adolescents: A twin study. *Archives of General Psychiatry, 61,* 489–496.

Scupin, R., & DeCorse, C.R. (2017). *Anthropology* (8th ed.). Upper Saddle River, NJ: Pearson.

Search Institute (2010). *Teens' relationships.* Minneapolis: Search Institute.

Sedgh, G., & others (2015). Adolescent pregnancy, birth, and abortion rates across countries: Levels and recent trends. *Journal of Adolescent Health, 56,* 223–230.

Segal, N.L. (2016). The 2016 Satellite Meeting of the International Society of Twin Studies: An overview/tribute to Irving I. Gottesman/research. *Twin Research and Human Genetics, 19,* 588–593.

Selemon, L.D. (2016). Frontal lobe synaptic plasticity in development and disease: Modulation by the dopamine D1 receptor. *Current Pharmaceutical Design, 20,* 5194–5201.

Selman, R.L. (1980). *The growth of interpersonal understanding.* New York: Academic Press.

Semenov, A.D., & Zelazo, P.D. (2017). The development of hot and cool executive function: A foundation for learning and a framework for early childhood education. In L. Meltzer & J. Dunstan-Brewer (Eds.), *Executive function in education* (2nd ed.). New York: Guilford.

Sen, B. (2010). The relationship between frequency of family dinner and adolescent problem behaviors after adjusting for other characteristics. *Journal of Adolescence, 33,* 187–196.

Sengpiel, V., & others (2013). Maternal caffeine intake during pregnancy is associated with birth weight but not gestational length: Results from a large prospective observational cohort study. *BMC Medicine, 11,* 42.

Senin-Calderon, C., & others (2017). Body image and adolescence: A behavioral impairment model. *Psychiatry Research, 248,* 121–126.

Senju, A., & others (2016). Early social experience affects the development of eye gaze processing. *Current Biology, 25,* 3086–3091.

Senko, C. (2016). Achievement goal theory: A story of early promises, eventual discords, and future possibilities. In K. Wentzel & D. Miele (Eds.), *Handbook of motivation at school* (2nd ed.). New York: Routledge.

Senter, L., Sackoff, J., Landi, K., & Boyd, L. (2010). Studying sudden and unexpected deaths in a time of changing death certification and investigation practices: Evaluating sleep-related risk factors for infant death in New York City. *Maternal and Child Health, 15*(2), 242–248.

Seo, J.H., Kim, J.H., Yang, K.I., & Hong, S.B. (2017, in press). Late use of electronic media and its association with sleep, depression, and suicidality among Korean adolescents. *Sleep Medicine.*

Seo, Y.S., Lee, J., & Ahn, H.Y. (2016). Effects of kangaroo care on neonatal pain in South Korea. *Journal of Tropical Pediatrics, 62,* 246–249.

Serrano-Villar, M., Huang, K.Y., & Calzada, E.J. (2017, in press). Social support, parenting, and social emotional development in young Mexican American and Dominican American children. *Child Psychiatry and Human Development.*

Sethna, V., Murray, L., & Ramchandani, P.G. (2012). Depressed fathers' speech to their 3-month-old infants: A study of cognitive and mentalizing features in paternal speech. *Psychological Medicine, 42*(11), 2361–2371.

Sethna, V., & others (2017, in press). Father-child interactions at 3 months and 24 months: Contributions to children's cognitive development at 24 months. *Infant Mental Health Journal.*

Shago, M. (2017). Chromosome preparation for acute lymphoblastic leukemia. *Methods in Molecular Biology, 1541,* 19–31.

Shah, M.K., & Austin, K.R. (2014). Do home visiting services received during pregnancy improve birth outcomes? Findings from Virginia PRAMS 2007–2008. *Public Health Nursing, 31,* 405–413.

Shah, R., & others (2012). Prenatal methamphetamine exposure and short-term maternal and infant medical outcomes. *American Journal of Perinatology, 29*(5), 391–400.

Shalitin, S., & Kiess, W. (2017, in press). Putative effects of obesity on linear growth and puberty. *Hormone Research in Pediatrics.*

Shang, L., & others (2015). Screen time is associated with dietary intake in overweight Canadian children. *Preventive Medicine Reports, 2,* 265–269.

Shankaran, S., & others (2010). Prenatal cocaine exposure and BMI and blood pressure at 9 years of age. *Journal of Hypertension, 28,* 1166–1175.

Shapiro, A.F., & Gottman, J.M. (2005). Effects on marriage of a psycho-education intervention with couples undergoing the transition to parenthood: Evaluation at 1-year post-intervention. *Journal of Family Communication, 5,* 1–24.

Shapiro, D.N., & Stewart, A.J. (2012). Dyadic support in stepfamilies: Buffering against depressive symptoms among more and less experienced stepparents. *Journal of Family Psychology, 26,* 833–838.

Sharma, N., Classen, J., & Cohen, L.G. (2013). Neural plasticity and its contribution to functional recovery. *Handbook of Clinical Psychology, 110,* 3–12.

Shatz, M., & Gelman, R. (1973). The development of communication skills: Modifications in the speech of young children as a function of the listener. *Monographs of the Society for Research in Child Development, 38* (Serial No. 152).

Shaw, P., & others (2007). Attention-deficit/hyperactivity disorder is characterized by a delay in cortical maturation. *Proceedings of the National Academy of Sciences USA, 104,* 19649–19654.

Shaywitz, S.E., Gruen, J.R., & Shaywitz, B.A. (2007). Management of dyslexia, its rationale, and underlying neurobiology. *Pediatric Clinics of North America, 54,* 609–623.

Shaywitz, S.E., Morris, R., & Shaywitz, B.A. (2008). The education of dyslexic children from childhood to young adulthood. *Annual Review of Psychology* (Vol. 59). Palo Alto, CA: Annual Reviews.

Shaywitz, S.E., & Shaywitz, B.B. (2017). Dyslexia. In R. Schwartz (Ed.), *Handbook of child language disorders* (2nd ed.). New York: Routledge.

Shebloski, B., Conger, K.J., & Widaman, K.F. (2005). Reciprocal links among differential parenting, perceived partiality, and self-worth: A three-wave longitudinal study. *Journal of Family Psychology, 19,* 633–642.

Sheeder, J., & Weber Yorga, K. (2017). Group prenatal care compared with traditional prenatal care: A systematic review and meta-analysis. *Obstetrics and Gynecology, 129,* 383–384.

Sheehan, M.J., & Watson, M.W. (2008). Reciprocal influences between maternal discipline and techniques and aggression in children and adolescents. *Aggressive Behavior, 34,* 245–255.

Sheftall, A.H., Mathias, C.W., Furr, R.M., & Dougherty, D.M. (2013). Adolescent attachment security, family functioning, and suicide attempts. *Attachment and Human Development, 15,* 368–383.

Sheldrick, R.C., Maye, M.P., & Carter, A.S. (2017). Age at first identification of autism spectrum disorder: An analysis of two U.S. surveys. *Journal of the American Academy of Child and Adolescent Psychiatry, 56,* 313–320.

Shen, J., & others (2017, in press). Genome-wide two-locus interaction analysis identifies multiple epistatic SNP pairs that confer risk of prostate cancer: A cross-population study. *International Journal of Cancer.*

Shenhav, A., & Greene, J.D. (2014). Integrative moral judgment: Dissociating the roles of the amygdala and the ventromedial prefrontal cortex. *Journal of Neuroscience, 34,* 4741–4749.

Shenk, D. (2017, in press). What is the Flynn effect, and how does it change our understanding of IQ? *Wiley Interdisciplinary Reviews. Cognitive Science.*

Shenoda, B.B. (2017, in press). An overview of the mechanisms of abnormal GABAeric interneuronal cortical migration associated with prenatal ethanol exposure. *Neurochemical Research.*

Shetgiri, R., Lin, H., Avila, R.M., & Flores, G. (2012). Parental characteristics associated with bullying perpetration in U.S. children aged 10 to 17 years. *American Journal of Public Health, 102,* 2280–2286.

Sheu, Y., Chen, L.H., & Hedegaard, H. (2016). Sports- and recreation-related injury episodes in the United States, 2011–2014. *National Health Statistics Reports,* Nov., 1–12.

Shi, L., & Stevens, G.D. (2005). Disparities in access to care and satisfaction among U.S. children: The roles of race/ethnicity and poverty status. *Public Health Report, 120,* 431–441.

Shiba, N., & others (2016). Whole-exome sequencing reveals the spectrum of genetic mutations and the clonal evolution patterns in pediatric acute myeloid leukemia. *British Journal of Hematology, 175,* 476–489.

Shimony-Kanat, S., & Benbenishty, J. (2017, in press). Age, ethnicity, and socioeconomic factors impacting infant and toddler fall-related trauma. *Pediatric Emerging Care.*

Shiner, R.L., & DeYoung, C.G. (2013). The structure of temperament and personality: A developmental approach. In P.D. Zelazo (Ed.), *Oxford handbook of developmental psychology.* New York: Oxford University Press.

Shiner, S., Many, A., & Maslovitz, S. (2016). Questioning the role of pituitary oxytocin in parturition: Spontaneous onset of labor in women with panhypopituitarism—a case series. *European Journal of Obstetrics and Gynecology and Reproductive Medicine, 197,* 83–85.

Shiva, F., Nasiri, M., Sadeghi, B., & Padyab, M. (2004). Effects of passive smoking on common respiratory symptoms in young children. *Acta Paediatrica, 92,* 1394–1397.

Shivers, E., & Farago, F. (2016). Where the children are: Exploring quality, community, and support for family, friend, and neighbor care. In K.E. Sanders & Guerra, A.W. (Eds.), *The culture of child care.* New York: Oxford University Press.

Shneidman, L., & Woodward, A.L. (2016). Are child-directed interactions the cradle of social learning? *Psychological Bulletin, 142,* 1–17.

Shneidman, O., Gweon, H., Schultz, L., & Woodward, A.L. (2016). Learning from others and spontaneous exploration: A cross-cultural investigation. *Child Development, 87,* 1221–1232.

Showell, N.N., & others (2013). A systematic review of home-based childhood obesity prevention studies. *Pediatrics, 132,* e193–e200.

Shulman, E., Harden, K., Chein, J., & Steinberg, L. (2016a). The development of impulse control and sensation-seeking in adolescence: Independent and interdependent processes? *Journal of Research on Adolescence, 26,* 37–44.

Shulman, E., & Steinberg, L. (2015). Human development and the juvenile justice system. In K. Heilbrun (Ed.), *Handbook of psychology and juvenile justice.* Washington, DC: APA Books.

Shulman, E., & others (2016b). The dual systems model: Review, reappraisal, and reaffirmation. *Developmental Cognitive Neuroscience, 17,* 103–117.

Shuman, V., & Scherer, K. (2014). Concepts and structure of emotions. In R. Pekrun & L. Linnenbrink-Garcia (Eds.), *International handbook of emotions in education.* New York: Routledge.

Sibley, M.H., & others (2012). Diagnosing ADHD in adolescence. *Journal of Consulting and Clinical Psychology, 80,* 139–150.

Siegel, D.H. (2013). Open adoption: Adoptive parents' reactions two decades later. *Social Work, 58,* 43–52.

Siegel, L.S. (2003). Learning disabilities In I.B. Weiner (Ed.), *Handbook of psychology* (Vol. VI). New York: Wiley.

Siegel, R.S., & Brandon, A.R. (2014). Adolescents, pregnancy, and mental health. *Journal of Pediatric and Adolescent Gynecology, 27,* 138–150.

Siegler, R.S. (2006). Microgenetic analysis of learning. In W. Damon & R. Lerner (Eds.), *Handbook of child psychology* (6th ed.). New York: Wiley.

Siegler, R.S. (2013). From theory to application and back: Following in the giant footsteps of David Klahr. In S.M. Carver & J. Shrager (Ed.), *The journey from child to scientist.* Thousand Oaks, CA: Sage.

Siegler, R.S. (2016a). Continuity and change in the field of cognitive development and in the perspective of one cognitive developmentalist. *Child Development Perspectives, 10,* 128–133.

Siegler, R.S. (2016b). How does change occur? In R. Sternberg, S. Fiske, & D. Foss (Eds.), *Scientists make a difference: One hundred eminent behavioral and brain scientists talk about their most important contributions.* Cambridge, UK: Cambridge University Press.

Siegler, R.S. (2017). Foreword: Build it and they will come. In D.G. Geary & others (Eds.), *Acquisition of complex arithmetic skills and higher order mathematics concepts.* New York: Academic Press.

Siegler, R.S., & Braithwaite, D.W. (2017). Numerical development. *Annual Review of Psychology* (Vol. 68). Palo Alto, CA: Annual Reviews.

Siegler, R.S., & Mu, Y. (2008). Chinese children excel on novel mathematics problems even before elementary school. *Psychological Science, 19,* 759–763.

Siegler, R.S., & others (2015). The Center for Improving Learning of Fractions: A progress report. In S. Chinn (Ed.), *The international handbook for dyscalculia and mathematical difficulties.* New York: Guilford.

Siener, S., & Kerns, K.A. (2012). Emotion regulation and depressive symptoms in preadolescence. *Child Psychiatry and Human Development, 43,* 414–430.

Silber, S. (2017). Chapter 13: Human ovarian tissue vitrification. *Methods in Molecular Biology, 1568,* 177–194.

Silva, C. (2005, October 31). When teen dynamo talks, city listens. *Boston Globe,* pp. B1, B4.

Silva, K., Chein, J., & Steinberg, L. (2016). Adolescents in peer groups make more prudent decisions when a slightly older adult is present. *Psychological Science, 27*(3), 322–330.

Silverman, M.E., & others (2017). The risk factors for postpartum depression: A population-based study. *Depression and Anxiety, 34,* 178–187.

Silvers, J.A., & others (2017, in press). The transition from childhood to adolescence is marked by a general decrease in amygdala reactivity and an affect-specific ventral-to-dorsal shift in medial prefrontal recruitment. *Developmental Cognitive Neuroscience.*

Sim, Z.L., & Xu, F. (2017). Learning higher-order generalizations through free play: Evidence from 2- and 3-year-old children. *Developmental Psychology, 53,* 642–651.

Simkin, P., & Bolding, A. (2004). Update on nonpharmacological approaches to relieve labor pain and prevent suffering. *Journal of Midwifery and Women's Health, 49,* 489–504.

Simmons, D. (2011). Diabetes and obesity in pregnancy. *Best Practice and Research, Clinical Obstetrics and Gynecology, 25,* 25–36.

Simmons, E.S., Lanter, E., & Lyons, M. (2014). Supporting mainstream educational success. In F.R. Volkmer & others (Eds.), *Handbook of autism and pervasive developmental disorders.* New York: Wiley.

Simmons, R.G., & Blyth, D.A. (1987). *Moving into adolescence.* Hawthorne, NY: Aldine.

Simon, E.J. (2017). *Biology* (2nd ed.). Upper Saddle River, NJ: Pearson.

Simon, E.J., Dickey, J.L., Reece, J.B., & Hogan, K.A. (2016). *Campbell essential biology* (5th ed.). Upper Saddle River, NJ: Pearson.

Simons, L.G., & others (2016). Mechanisms that link parenting practices to adolescents' risky sexual behavior: A test of six competing theories. *Journal of Youth and Adolescence, 45,* 255–270.

Simos, P.G., & others (2007). Altering the brain circuits for reading through intervention: A magnetic source imaging study. *Neuropsychology, 21,* 485–496.

Simpkins, S.D., Fredricks, J.A., Davis-Kean, P.E., & Eccles, J.S. (2006). Healthy mind, healthy habits: The influence of activity involvement in middle childhood. In A.C. Huston & M.N. Ripke (Eds.), *Developmental contexts in middle childhood.* New York: Cambridge University Press.

Simpson, H.B., & others (2013). Treatment of obsessive-compulsive disorder complicated by comorbid eating disorders. *Cognitive Behavior Therapy, 42*(1), 64–76.

Simpson, J., & Belsky, J. (2016). Attachment theory within a modern evolutionary framework. In J. Cassidy & P. Shaver (Eds.), *Handbook of attachment theory and research* (3rd ed.). New York: Guilford.

Singarajah, A., & others (2017). Infant attention to same- and other-race faces. *Cognition, 159,* 76–84.

Singer, D., Golinkoff, R.M., & Hirsh-Pasek, K. (Eds.) (2006). *Play = learning: How play motivates and enhances children's cognitive and social-emotional growth.* New York: Oxford University Press.

Singh, L., & others (2017, in press). Novel word learning in bilingual and monolingual infants: Evidence for a bilingual advantage. *Child Development.*

Singh, N.N., & others (2016). Effects of Samatha meditation on active academic engagement and math performance of students with attention-deficit/hyperactivity disorder. *Mindfulness, 7,* 68–75.

Singh, S., Darroch, J.E., Vlasoff, M., & Nadeau, J. (2004). *Adding it up: The benefits of investing in sexual and reproductive health care.* New York: The Alan Guttmacher Institute.

Singh, S., Wulf, D., Samara, R., & Cuca, Y.P. (2000). Gender differences in the timing of first intercourse: Data from 14 countries. *International Family Planning Perspectives, 26,* 21–28, 43.

Sirard, J.R., & others (2013). Physical activity and screen time in adolescents and their friends. *American Journal of Preventive Medicine, 44,* 48–55.

Siren, P.M. (2017). SIDS-CDF hypothesis revisited: Cause vs. contributing factors. *Frontiers in Neuroscience, 7,* 244.

Siu, A.M., Shek, D.T., & Law, B. (2012). Prosocial norms as a positive youth development construct: A conceptual review. *Scientific World Journal, 2012,* 832026.

Sivell, S., & others (2008). How risk is perceived, constructed, and interpreted by clients in clinical genetics, and the effects on decision making: A review. *Journal of Genetic Counseling, 17,* 30–63.

Skiba, M.T., Sternberg, R.J., & Grigorenko, E.L. (2017). Roads not taken, new roads to take. In R.A. Beghetto & J.C. Kaufman (Eds.), *Nurturing creativity in the classroom* (2nd ed.). New York: Cambridge University Press.

Skinner, B.F. (1938). *The behavior of organisms: An experimental analysis.* New York: Appleton-Century-Crofts.

Skinner, B.F. (1957). *Verbal behavior.* New York: Appleton-Century-Crofts.

Skinner, O.D., & McHale, S.M. (2016). Parent-adolescent conflict in African American families. *Journal of Youth and Adolescence, 45,* 2080–2093.

Slater, A.M., Bremner, J.G., Johnson, S.P., & Hayes, R. (2011). The role of perceptual processes in infant addition/subtraction events. In L.M. Oakes, C.H. Cashon, M. Casasola, & D.H. Rakison (Eds.), *Early perceptual and cognitive development.* New York: Oxford University Press.

Slater, A., Field, T., & Hernandez-Reif, M. (2007). The development of the senses. In A. Slater & M. Lewis (Eds.), *Introduction to infant development* (2nd ed.). New York: Oxford University Press.

Slater, A., Morison, V., & Somers, M. (1988). Orientation discrimination and cortical function in the human newborn. *Perception, 17,* 597–602.

Slater, A., & others (2010). Visual perception. In J.G. Bremner & T.D. Wachs (Eds.), *Wiley-Blackwell handbook of infant development* (2nd ed.). New York: Wiley.

Slaughter, V., & others (2014). Meta-analysis of theory of mind and peer popularity in the preschool and early school years. *Child Development, 86,* 1159–1174.

Sleet, D.A., & Mercy, J.A. (2003). Promotion of safety, security, and well-being. In M.H. Bornstein, L. Davidson, C.L.M. Keyes, & K.A. Moore (Eds.), *Well-being.* Mahwah, NJ: Erlbaum.

Slobin, D. (1972, July). Children and language: They learn the same way around the world. *Psychology Today,* 71–76.

Slomkowski, C., Rende, R., Conger, K.J., Simons, R.L., & Conger, R.D. (2001). Sisters, brothers, and delinquency: Social influence during early and middle adolescence. *Child Development, 72,* 271–283.

Smaldino, S.E., Lowther, D.L., Russell, J.W., & Mims, C. (2015). *Instructional technology and media for learning* (11th ed.). Upper Saddle River, NJ: Pearson.

Smetana, J.G. (2011a). *Adolescents, families, and social development: How adolescents construct their worlds.* New York: Wiley-Blackwell.

Smetana, J.G. (2011b). Adolescents' social reasoning and relationships with parents: Conflicts and coordinations within and across domains. In E. Amsel & J. Smetana (Eds.), *Adolescent vulnerabilities and opportunities: Constructivist and developmental perspectives.* New York: Cambridge University Press.

Smetana, J.G. (2013). Moral development: The social domain theory view. In P.D. Zelazo (Ed.), *Handbook of developmental psychology.* New York: Oxford University Press.

Smetana, J.G., Robinson, J., & Rote, W.M. (2015). Socialization in adolescence. In J.E. Grusec & P.D. Hastings (Eds.), *Handbook of socialization* (2nd ed.). New York: Guilford.

Smetana, J.G., Wong, M., Ball, C., & Yau, J. (2014). American and Chinese children's evaluations of personal domain events and resistance to parental authority. *Child Development, 85,* 626–642.

Smith, C.A., Armour, M., & Ee, C. (2016). Complementary therapies and medicines and reproductive medicine. *Seminars in Reproductive Medicine, 34,* 67–73.

Smith, C.L., Diaz, A., Day, K.L., & Bell, M.A. (2016). Infant frontal electroencephalogram asymmetry and negative emotional reactivity as predictors of toddlerhood effortful control. *Journal of Experimental Child Psychology, 142,* 262–273.

Smith, E.R., & others (2017). Barriers and enablers of health system adoption of kangaroo care: A systematic review of caregiver perspectives. *BMC Pediatrics, 17*(1), 35.

Smith, J., & Ross, H. (2007). Training parents to mediate sibling disputes affects children's negotiation and conflict understanding. *Child Development, 78,* 790–805.

Smith, L.B. (1999). Do infants possess innate knowledge structures? The con side. *Developmental Science, 2,* 133–144.

Smith, L.E., & Howard, K.S. (2008). Continuity of paternal social support and depressive symptoms among new mothers. *Journal of Family Psychology, 22,* 763–773.

Smith, L.M., & others (2008). The infant development, environment, and lifestyle study: Effects of prenatal methamphetamine exposure, polydrug exposure, and poverty on intrauterine growth. *Pediatrics, 118,* 1149–1156.

Smith, R.A., & Davis, S.F. (2016). *The psychologist as detective* (7th ed.). Upper Saddle River, NJ: Prentice Hall.

Smith, R.L., Rose, A.J., & Schwartz-Mette, R.A. (2010). Relational and overt aggression in childhood and adolescence: Clarifying mean-level gender differences and associations with peer acceptance. *Social Development, 19,* 243–269.

Smith, R.P. (2017). *Netter's obstetrics and gynecology* (3rd ed.). New York: Elsevier.

Smithbattle, L. (2007). Legacies of advantage and disadvantage: The case of teen mothers. *Public Health Nursing, 24,* 409–420.

Smitsman, A.W., & Corbetta, D. (2010). Action in infancy—perspectives, concepts, and challenges. In J.G. Bremner & T.D. Wachs (Eds.), *Wiley-Blackwell handbook of infant development* (2nd ed.). New York: Wiley.

Smokowksi, P.R., Bacallao, M.L., Cotter, K.L., & Evans, C.B. (2015). The effects of positive and negative parenting practices on adolescent mental health outcomes in a multicultural sample of rural youth. *Child Psychiatry and Human Development, 46,* 333–345.

Smokowski, P.R., & others (2017). Family dynamics and aggressive behavior in Latino adolescents. *Cultural Diversity and Ethnic Minority Psychology, 23,* 81–90.

Smoreda, Z., & Licoppe, C. (2000). Gender-specific use of the domestic telephone. *Social Psychology Quarterly, 63,* 238–252.

Snarey, J. (1987, June). A question of morality. *Psychology Today,* pp. 6–8.

Snow, C.E. (2010). Commentary in E. Galinsky, *Meaning in the making.* New York: Harperstudio.

Snow, C.E., & Beals, D.E. (2006, Spring). Mealtime talk that supports literacy development. *New Directions for Child and Adolescent Development, 111,* 51–66.

Snow, C.E., & Kang, J.Y. (2006). Becoming bilingual, biliterate, and bicultural. In W. Damon & R. Lerner (Eds.), *Handbook of child psychology* (6th ed.). New York: Wiley.

Snow, C.E., Burns, M.S., & Griffin, P. (1998). *Preventing reading difficulties in young children.* Washington, DC: National Academy Press.

Snyder, K.A., & Torrence, C.M. (2008). Habituation and novelty. In M.M. Haith & J.B. Benson (Eds.), *Encyclopedia of infant and early childhood development.* Oxford, UK: Elsevier.

Snyder, W. (2017). Compound word formation. In J. Lidz, W. Snyder, & J. Pater (Eds.), *Oxford* *handbook of developmental linguistics.* New York: Oxford University Press.

Society for Adolescent Health and Medicine (2017). Improving knowledge about, access to, and utilization of long-acting reversible contraception among adolescents and young adults. *Journal of Adolescent Health, 60,* 472–474.

Sodian, B., & others (2016). Understanding of goals, beliefs, and desires predicts morally relevant theory of mind: A longitudinal investigation. *Child Development, 87,* 1221–1232.

Sokol, R.L., Qin, B., & Poti, J.M. (2017). Parenting styles and body mass index: A systematic review of prospective studies among children. *Obesity Reviews, 18,* 281–292.

Sokolowski, M., Wasserman, J., & Wasserman, D. (2016). Polygenic associations of neurodevelopmental genes in suicide attempt. *Molecular Psychiatry, 21,* 1381–1390.

Soller, B. (2014). Caught in a bad romance: Adolescent romantic relationships and mental health. *Journal of Health and Social Behavior, 55,* 56–72.

Solomon, D., Watson, P., Schapes, E., Battistich, V., & Solomon, J. (1990). Cooperative learning as part of a comprehensive program designed to promote prosocial development. In S. Sharan (Ed.), *Cooperative learning.* New York: Praeger.

Solomon-Krakus, S., & others (2017). Body image self-discrepancy and depressive symptoms among early adolescents. *Journal of Adolescent Health, 60,* 38–43.

Solovieva, Y., & Quintanar, L. (2017). Play with social roles as a method for psychological development in young children. In T. Bruce & others (Eds.), *Routledge international handbook of early childhood play.* New York: Routledge.

Somerville, L.H. (2016). Emotional development in adolescence. In L.F. Barrett, M. Lewis, & J.M. Haveland-Jones (Eds.), *Handbook of emotions* (4th ed.). New York: Guilford.

Sommer, T.E., Sabol, T.J., Chase-Lansdale, P.L., & Brooks-Gunn, J. (2016). Two-generation education programs for parents and children. In S. Jones & N. Lesaux (Eds.), *The leading edge of early childhood education.* Cambridge, MA: Harvard Education Press.

Son, W.M., & others (2017, in press). Combined exercise training reduces blood pressure, arterial stiffness, and insulin resistance in obese prehypertensive adolescent girls. *Clinical and Experimental Hypertension.*

Song, P., & others (2017, in press). Prevalence and correlates of metabolic syndrome in Chinese children: The China Health and Nutrition Survey. *Nutrients.*

Sontag, L.M., Graber, J., Brooks-Gunn, J., & Warren, M.P. (2008). Coping with social stress: Implications for psychopathology in young adolescent girls. *Journal of Abnormal Child Psychology, 36,* 1159–1174.

Sophian, C. (1985). Perseveration and infants' search: A comparison of two- and three-location tasks. *Developmental Psychology, 21,* 187–194.

Sorbye, I.K., Wanigaratne, S., & Urgula, M.L. (2016). Variations in gestational length and preterm delivery by race, ethnicity, and migration. *Best Practices in Research. Clinical Obstetrics and Gynecology, 32,* 60–68.

Sorensen, L.C., Dodge, K.A., & Conduct Problems Prevention Research Group (2016). How does the Fast Track intervention prevent adverse outcomes in young adulthood? *Child Development, 87,* 429–445.

Sorof, J.M., Lai, D., Turner, J., Poffenberger, T., & Portman, R.J. (2004). Overweight, ethnicity, and the prevalence of hypertension in school-aged children. *Pediatrics, 113,* 475–482.

Sorte, J., Daeschel, I., & Amador, C. (2017). *Nutrition, health, and safety for young children* (3rd ed.). Upper Saddle River, NJ: Pearson.

Souza, B.G., & others (2017). Parental awareness and perception for correct use of child restraint systems and airbags in Brazil. *Traffic Injury Prevention, 18,* 171–174.

Sowell, E.R., & others (2004). Longitudinal mapping of cortical thickness and brain growth in children. *Journal of Neuroscience, 24,* 8223–8231.

Spandel, V. (2009). *Creating young writers* (3rd ed.). Boston: Allyn & Bacon.

Spangler, G., Johann, M., Ronai, Z., & Zimmermann, P. (2009). Genetic and environmental influence on attachment disorganization. *Journal of Child Psychology and Psychiatry, 50,* 952–961.

Spelke, E.S. (1979). Perceiving bimodally specified events in infancy. *Developmental Psychology, 5,* 626–636.

Spelke, E.S. (1991). Physical knowledge in infancy. Reflections on Piaget's theory. In S. Carey & R. Gelman (Eds.), *The epigenesis of mind: Essays on biology and cognition.* Hillsdale, NJ: Erlbaum.

Spelke, E.S. (2000). Core knowledge. *American Psychologist, 55,* 1233–1243.

Spelke, E.S. (2003). Developing knowledge of space: Core systems and new combinations. In S.M. Kosslyn & A. Galaburda (Eds.), *Languages of the brain.* Cambridge, MA: Harvard University Press.

Spelke, E.S. (2011). Natural number and natural geometry. In E. Brannon & S. Dehaene (Eds.), *Space, time, and number in the brain.* New York: Oxford University Press.

Spelke, E.S. (2013). Developmental sources of social divisions. *Neurosciences and the human person: New perspectives on human activities.* Unpublished manuscript, Department of Psychology, Harvard University, Cambridge, MA.

Spelke, E.S. (2016a). Core knowledge and conceptual change: A perspective on social cognition. In D. Barner & A.S. Baron (Eds.), *Core knowledge and conceptual change.* New York: Oxford University Press.

Spelke, E.S. (2016b). Cognitive abilities of infants. In R.J. Sternberg, S.T. Fiske, & J. Foss (Eds.), *Scientists making a difference.* New York: Cambridge University Press.

Spelke, E.S., & Hespos, S.J. (2001). Continuity, competence, and the object concept. In E. Dupoux (Ed.), *Language, brain, and behavior.* Cambridge, MA: Bradford/MIT Press.

Spelke, E.S., & Owsley, C.J. (1979). Intermodal exploration and knowledge in infancy. *Infant Behavior and Development, 2,* 13–28.

Spelke, E.S., Bernier, E.P., & Snedeker, J. (2013). Core social cognition. In M.R. Banaji & S.A. Gelman (Eds.), *Navigating the social world: What infants, children, and other species can teach us.* New York: Oxford University Press.

Spelke, E.S., Breinlinger, K., Macomber, J., & Jacobson, K. (1992). Origins of knowledge. *Psychological Review, 99,* 605–632.

Spence, J.T., & Helmreich, R. (1978). *Masculinity and femininity: Their psychological dimensions.* Austin: University of Texas Press.

Spencer, M.B., & Swanson, D.P. (2016). Vulnerability and resilience in African American youth. In D. Cicchetti (Ed.), *Developmental psychopathology* (3rd ed.). New York: Wiley.

Spencer, S., & others (2017). Contribution of spoken language and socio-economic background to adolescents' educational achievement at age 16 years. *International Journal of Language and Communication Disorders, 52,* 184–196.

Spencer, S.J., Logel, C., & Davies, P.G. (2016). Stereotype threat. *Annual Review of Psychology* (Vol. 67). Palo Alto, CA: Annual Reviews.

Spiegler, M.D. (2016). *Contemporary behavior therapy* (6th ed.). Boston: Cengage.

Spilman, S.K., Neppl, T.K., Donnellan, M.B., Schofield, T.J., & Conger, R.D. (2013). Incorporating religiosity into a developmental model of positive family functioning across generations. *Developmental Psychology, 49*(4), 762–774.

Spindel, E.R., & McEvoy, C.T. (2016). The role of nicotine in the effects of maternal smoking during pregnancy and lung development and childhood respiratory disease. Implications for dangers of E-cigarettes. *American Journal of Respiratory and Critical Care Medicine, 193,* 486–494.

Spittle, A.J., & others (2017). Neurobehavior at term-equivalent age and neurodevelopmental outcomes at 2 years in infants born moderate-to-late preterm. *Developmental Medicine and Child Neurology, 59,* 207–215.

Springelkamp, H., & others (2017, in press). New insights into the genetics of primary open-angle glaucoma based on a meta-analysis of intraocular pressure and optic disc characteristics. *Human Molecular Genetics.*

Sreetharan, S., & others (2017, in press). Ionizing radiation exposure during pregnancy: Effects on postnatal development and life. *Radiation Research.*

Sroufe, L.A. (2016). The place of attachment in development. In J. Cassidy & P.R. Shaver (Eds.), *Handbook of attachment* (3rd ed.). New York: Guilford.

Sroufe, L.A., Coffino, B., & Carlson, E.A. (2010). Conceptualizing the role of early experience: Lessons from the Minnesota longitudinal study. *Developmental Review, 30,* 36–51.

Sroufe, L.A., Egeland, B., Carlson, E., & Collins, W.A. (2005). The place of early attachment in developmental context. In K.E. Grossman,

K. Krossman, & E. Waters (Eds.), *The power of longitudinal attachment research: From infancy and childhood to adulthood.* New York: Guilford.

Stadelmann, S., & others (2017). Self-esteem in 8- to 14-year-old children with psychiatric disorders: Disorder- and gender-specific effects. *Child Psychiatry and Human Development, 48,* 40–52.

Stamatakis, E., & others (2013). Type-specific screen time associations with cardiovascular risk markers in children. *American Journal of Preventive Medicine, 44,* 481–488.

Stancil, S.L., & others (2017, in press). Contraceptive provision to adolescent females prescribed teratogenic medicines. *Pediatrics.*

Stanford University Medical Center (2017). *Growth hormone deficiency.* Palo Alto, CA: Author.

Stangor, C. (2015). *Research methods for the behavioral sciences* (5th ed.). Boston: Cengage.

Staples, A.D., Bates, J.E., & Petersen, I.T. (2015). Bedtime routines in early childhood: Prevalence, consistency, and associations with nighttime sleep. *Monographs of the Society for Research in Child Development, 80,* 141–159.

Starr, C., Evers, C., & Starr, L. (2018). *Biology* (10th ed.). Boston: Cengage.

Staszewski, J. (Ed.) (2013). *Expertise and skill acquisition: The impact of William C. Chase.* New York: Taylor & Francis.

Steca, P., Bassi, M., Caprara, G.V., & Fave, A.D. (2011). Parents' self-efficacy beliefs and their children's psychosocial adaptation during adolescence. *Journal of Youth and Adolescence, 40,* 320–331.

Steckler, C.M., & Hamlin, J.K. (2016). Theories of moral development. In H. Miller (Ed.), *Encyclopedia of theory in psychology.* Thousand Oaks, CA: Sage.

Steele, C.M., & Aronson, J.A. (2004). Stereotype threat does not live by Steele and Aronson (1995) alone. *American Psychologist, 59,* 47–48.

Steiger, A.E., Allemand, M., Robins, R.W., & Fend, H.A. (2014). Low and decreasing self-esteem during adolescence predict adult depression two decades later. *Journal of Personality and Social Psychology, 106,* 325–338.

Stein, M., & others (2018). *Direct instruction mathematics* (5th ed.). Upper Saddle River, NJ: Pearson.

Stein, M.T. (2004). ADHD: The diagnostic process from different perspectives. *Journal of Developmental and Behavioral Pediatrics, 25*(Suppl. 5), S54–S58.

Steinberg, L. (2011). Adolescent risk-taking: A social neuroscience perspective. In E. Amsel & J. Smetana (Eds.), *Adolescent vulnerabilities and opportunities: Constructivist developmental perspectives.* New York: Cambridge University Press.

Steinberg, L. (2014). *Age of opportunity.* Boston: Houghton Mifflin Harcourt.

Steinberg, L. (2016). Commentary on the special issue on the adolescent brain: Redefining adolescence. *Neuroscience and Biobehavioral Reviews, 70,* 343–346.

Steinberg, L., & Collins, W.A. (2011). Psychosocial development and behavior. In M. Fisher, E. Alderman, R. Kreipe, & W. Rosenfeld (Eds.), *Textbook of adolescent health care.* Elk Grove, IL: American Academy of Pediatrics.

Steinberg, L., & others (2017, in press). Around the world, adolescence is a time of heightened sensation-seeking and immature self-regulation. *Developmental Science.*

Steinberg, S.J., & Davila, J. (2008). Romantic functioning and depressive symptoms among early adolescent girls: The moderating role of parental emotional availability. *Journal of Clinical Child and Adolescent Psychology, 37,* 350–362.

Steiner, J.E. (1979). Human facial expressions in response to taste and smell stimulation. In H. Reese & L. Lipsitt (Eds.), *Advances in child development* (Vol. 13). New York: Academic Press.

Stenberg, G. (2017). Does contingency in adults' responding influence 12-month-old infants' social referencing? *Infant Behavior and Development, 46,* 67–79.

Stephens, J.M. (2008). Cheating. In N.J. Salkind (Ed.), *Encyclopedia of educational psychology.* Thousand Oaks, CA: Sage.

Steric, M., & others (2015). The outcome and course of pregnancies complicated with fetal neural tube defects. *Clinical and Experimental Obstetrics and Gynecology, 42,* 57–61.

Stern, D.N., Beebe, B., Jaffe, J., & Bennett, S.L. (1977). The infant's stimulus world during social interaction: A study of caregiver behaviors with particular reference to repetition and timing. In H.R. Schaffer (Ed.), *Studies in mother-infant interaction.* London: Academic Press.

Sternberg, R.J. (1986). *Intelligence applied.* San Diego: Harcourt Brace Jovanovich.

Sternberg, R.J. (2004). Individual differences in cognitive development. In U. Goswami (Ed.), *Blackwell handbook of childhood cognitive development.* Malden, MA: Blackwell.

Sternberg, R.J. (2010). Componential models of creativity. In M. Runco & S. Spritzker (Eds.), *Encyclopedia of creativity.* New York: Elsevier.

Sternberg, R.J. (2011). Individual differences in cognitive development. In U. Goswami (Ed.), *Blackwell handbook of childhood cognitive development.* Malden, MA: Blackwell.

Sternberg, R.J. (2012). Human intelligence. In V.S. Ramachandran (Ed.), *Encyclopedia of human behavior* (2nd ed.). New York: Elsevier.

Sternberg, R.J. (2013). Contemporary theories of intelligence. In I.B. Weiner & others (Eds.), *Handbook of psychology* (2nd ed.), Vol. 7. New York: Wiley.

Sternberg, R.J. (2014a). Building wisdom and character. In S. Lynn (Ed.), *Health, happiness, and well-being.* Thousand Oaks, CA: Sage.

Sternberg, R.J. (2014b). Teaching about the nature of intelligence. *Intelligence, 42,* 176–179.

Sternberg, R.J. (2015). Successful intelligence: A new model for testing intelligence beyond IQ tests. *European Journal of Education and Psychology, 8,* 76–84.

Sternberg, R.J. (2016a). What does it mean to be intelligent? In R.J. Sternberg & others (Eds.), *Scientists making a difference.* New York: Cambridge University Press.

Sternberg, R.J. (2016b). Theories of intelligence. In S. Pfeiffer (Ed.), *APA handbook of giftedness and talent.* Washington, DC: American Psychological Association.

Sternberg, R.J. (2016c). Wisdom. In S.J. Lopez (Ed.), *Encyclopedia of positive psychology* (2nd ed.). New York: Wiley.

Sternberg, R.J. (2017a). Intelligence and competence in theory and practice. In A.J. Elliot & C.S. Dweck (Eds.), *Handbook of competence and motivation* (2nd ed.). New York: Guilford.

Sternberg, R.J. (2017b). IQ testing. In S. Ayers & others (Eds.), *Cambridge handbook of psychology, health, and medicine* (3rd ed.). New York: Cambridge University Press.

Sternberg, R.J. (2017c, in press). 21 ideas: A 42-year search to understand the nature of giftedness. *Roeper Review.*

Sternberg, R.J. (2017d, in press). ACCEL: A new model for identifying the gifted. *Roeper Review.*

Sternberg, R.J. (2018a, in press). Successful theory in theory, research, and practice. In R.J. Sternberg (Ed.), *The nature of intelligence.* New York: Cambridge University Press.

Sternberg, R.J. (2018b, in press). The triangle of intelligence. In R.J. Sternberg & J.C. Kaufman (Eds.), *The nature of human creativity.* New York: Cambridge University Press.

Sternberg, R.J. (2018c, in press). Triarchic theory of intelligence. In B. Frey (Eds.), *SAGE encyclopedia of educational research, measurement, and evaluation.* Thousand Oaks, CA: Sage.

Sternberg, R.J. (2018d, in press). The triarchic theory of successful intelligence. In D.P. Flanagan & P.L. Harrison (Eds.), *Contemporary intellectual assessment* (4th ed.). New York: Guilford Press.

Sternberg, R.J. (2018e, in press). Wisdom. In S.J. Lopez (Ed.), *Encyclopedia of positive psychology* (2nd ed.). New York: Wiley.

Sternberg, R.J. (2018f, in press). Types of generalization: Introduction to the special section. *Perspectives on Psychological Science.*

Sternberg, R.J. (2018g, in press). The psychology of creativity. In S. Nalbantian & P.M. Matthews (Eds.), *Secrets of creativity.* New York: Oxford University Press.

Sternberg, R.J. (2018h, in press). The triangle of creativity. In R.J. Sternberg & J.C. Kaufman (Eds.), *The nature of human creativity.* New York: Cambridge University Press.

Sternberg, R.J., & Bridges, S.L. (2014). Varieties of genius. In D.K. Simonton (Ed.), *Wiley-Blackwell handbook of genius.* New York: Wiley.

Sternberg, R.J., & Hagen, E. (2018, in press). Wisdom. In M.H. Bornstein & others (Eds.), *SAGE encyclopedia of lifespan development.* Thousand Oaks, CA: Sage.

Sternberg, R.J., & Kaufman, J.C. (2018a, in press). Theories and conceptions of giftedness. In S. Pfeiffer (Ed.), *Handbook of giftedness in children* (2nd ed.). New York: Springer.

Sternberg, R.J., & Kaufman, J.C. (2018b, in press). Societal forces that erode creativity. *Teachers College Record.*

Sternberg, R.J., & Sternberg, K. (2017). *Cognitive psychology* (7th ed.). Boston: Cengage.

Stevens, E.A., Walker, M.A., & Vaughn, S. (2017, in press). The effects of reading fluency interventions on the reading fluency and reading comprehension performance of elementary students with learning disabilities: A synthesis of research from 2001 to 2014. *Journal of Learning Disabilities.*

Stevenson, H.W. (1995). Mathematics achievement of American students: First in the world by the year 2000? In C.A. Nelson (Ed.), *Basic and applied perspectives on learning, cognition, and development.* Minneapolis: University of Minnesota Press.

Stevenson, H.W. (2000). Middle childhood: Education and schooling. In A. Kazdin (Ed.), *Encyclopedia of psychology.* Washington, DC, & New York: American Psychological Association and Oxford University Press.

Stevenson, H.W., & others (1990). Contexts of achievement. *Monographs of the Society for Research in Child Development, 55*(Serial No. 221).

Stevenson, H.W., Hofer, B.K., & Randel, B. (1999). *Middle childhood: Education and schooling.* Unpublished manuscript, Department of Psychology, University of Michigan, Ann Arbor.

Stevenson, H.W., Lee, S., & Stigler, J.W. (1986). Mathematics achievement of Chinese, Japanese, and American children. *Science, 231,* 693–699.

Stewart, J.G., & others (2017, in press). Cognitive control deficits differentiate adolescent suicide ideators from attempters. *Journal of Clinical Psychology.*

Stewart, J.G., & others (2017, in press). Peer victimization and suicidal thoughts and behaviors in depressed adolescents. *Journal of Abnormal Child Psychology.*

Stice, E., & others (2017). Risk factors that predict future onset of each DSM-5 eating disorder: Predictive specificity in high-risk adolescent females. *Journal of Abnormal Psychology, 126,* 38–51.

Stifter, C., & Dollar, J. (2016). Temperament and developmental psychopathology. In D. Cicchetti (Ed.), *Developmental psychopathology* (3rd ed.). New York: Wiley.

Stiggins, R. (2008). *Introduction to student-involved assessment for learning* (5th ed.). Upper Saddle River. NJ: Prentice Hall.

Stilwell, D. (2016). Helping couples fulfill the "highest of life's goals": Mate selection, marriage counseling, and genetic counseling in the United States. *Journal of Genetic Counseling, 25,* 157–165.

Stipek, D. (2005, February 16). Commentary in *USA Today,* p. 1D.

Stipek, D.J. (2002). *Motivation to learn* (4th ed.). Boston: Allyn & Bacon.

Stockwell, S. (2017, in press). Benefits of kangaroo care for premature babies continue into young adulthood. *American Journal of Nursing.*

Stoel-Gammon, C., & Sosa, A.V. (2010). Phonological development. In E. Hoff & M. Shatz (Eds.), *Blackwell handbook of language development* (2nd ed.). New York: Wiley.

Stracciolini, A., & others (2013). Pediatric sports injuries: An age comparison of children versus adolescents. *American Journal of Sports Medicine, 41,* 1922–1929.

Straker, L.M., & Howie, E.K. (2016). Young children's screen time: It is time to consider healthy bodies as well as healthy minds. *Journal of Developmental and Behavioral Pediatrics, 37,* 265.

Strassberg. D.S., Cann, D., & Velarde, V. (2017, in press). Sexting by high school students. *Archives of Sexual Behavior.*

Strathearn, L. (2007). Exploring the neurobiology of attachment. In L.C. Mayes, P. Fonagy, & M. Target (Eds.), *Developmental science and psychoanalysis.* London: Karnac Press.

Streib, H. (1999). Off-road religion? A narrative approach to fundamentalist and occult orientations of adolescents. *Journal of Adolescence, 22,* 255–267.

Streit, C., & others (2017, in press). Family relationships and prosocial behavior in U.S. Mexican youth: The mediating effect of cultural processes. *Journal of Family Issues.*

Strenze, T. (2007). Intelligence and socioeconomic success: A meta-analytic review of longitudinal research. *Intelligence, 35,* 401–426.

Striegel-Moore, R.H., & Bulik, C.M. (2007). Risk factors for eating disorders. *American Psychologist, 62,* 181–198.

Stright, A.D., Herr, M.Y., & Neitzel, C. (2009). Maternal scaffolding of children's problem solving and children's adjustment in kindergarten: Hmong families in the United States. *Journal of Educational Psychology, 101,* 207–218.

Stringer, M., Ratcliffe, S.J., Evans, E.C., & Brown, L.P. (2005). The cost of prenatal care attendance and pregnancy outcomes in low-income working women. *Journal of Obstetrical, Gynecologic, and Neonatal Nursing, 34,* 551–560.

Strohmeier, D., & Noam, G.G. (2012). Bullying in schools: What is the problem and how can educators solve it? *New Directions in Youth Development, 133,* 7–13.

Strong, D.R., & others (2017, in press). Pre-adolescent receptivity to tobacco marketing and its relationship to acquiring friends who smoke and cigarette smoking initiation. *Annals of Behavioral Medicine.*

Stroobant, N., Buijus, D., & Vingerhoets, G. (2009). Variation in brain lateralization during various language tasks: A functional transcranial Doppler study. *Behavioral Brain Research, 199,* 190–196.

Stuebe, A.M., & Schwarz, E.G. (2010). The risks and benefits of infant feeding practices for women and their children. *Journal of Perinatology, 30,* 155–162.

Stumper, A., & others (2017). Parents' behavioral inhibition moderates association between preschoolers' BI with risk for age 9 anxiety disorders. *Journal of Affective Disorders, 210,* 35–42.

Suarez, L., & others (2011). Maternal smoking, passive tobacco smoke, and neural tube defects. *Birth Defects Research A: Clinical and Molecular Teratology, 91,* 29–33.

Sue, D., Sue, D.W., & Sue, D.M. (2017). *Essentials of understanding abnormal psychology* (3rd ed.). Boston: Cengage.

Sugden, N.A., & Moulson, M.C. (2017). Hey baby, what's "up"? One- and 3-month-olds experience faces primarily upright but non-upright faces offer the best views. *Quarterly Journal of Experimental Psychology, 70,* 959–969.

Sugisaki, K. (2017). On the acquisition of prepositions and particles. In J. Lidz, W. Snyder, & J. Pater (Eds.), *Oxford handbook of developmental linguistics.* New York: Oxford University Press.

Sugita, Y. (2004). Experience in early infancy is indispensable for color perception. *Current Biology, 14,* 1267–1271.

Suh, S., & others (2017). Cross-cultural relevance of the interpersonal theory of suicide across Korean and U.S. undergraduate students. *Psychiatry Research, 251,* 244–252.

Sullivan, H.S. (1953). *The interpersonal theory of psychiatry.* New York: W.W. Norton.

Sullivan, K., & Sullivan, A. (1980). Adolescent-parent separation. *Developmental Psychology, 16,* 93–99.

Sullivan, R., & Wilson, D. (2018). Neurobiology of infant attachment. *Annual Review of Psychology* (Vol. 69). Palo Alto, CA: Annual Reviews.

Sumontha, J., Farr, R.H., & Patterson, C.J. (2016). Social support and coparenting among lesbian, gay, and heterosexual adoptive parents. *Journal of Family Psychology, 30,* 987–996.

Sun, R., & others (2016). Congenital heart disease: Causes, diagnosis, symptoms, and treatment. *Cellular Biochemistry and Biophysics, 13,* e34399.

Sun, S.S., & others (2008). Childhood obesity predicts adult metabolic syndrome: The Fels Longitudinal Study. *Journal of Pediatrics, 152,* 191–200.

Sun, Y., Tao, F., Hao, J., & Wan, Y. (2010). The mediating effects of stress and coping on depression among adolescents in China. *Journal of Child and Adolescent Psychiatric Nursing, 23,* 173–180.

Sun, Y., & others (2012). National estimates of the pubertal milestones among urban and rural Chinese girls. *Journal of Adolescent Health, 51,* 279–284.

Sunderam, S., & others (2017). Assisted reproduction technology surveillance—United States 2014. *MMWR Surveillance Summaries, 66*(6), 1–24.

Sundstrom Poromaa, I., & others (2017). Sex differences in depression during pregnancy and the postpartum period. *Journal of Neuroscience Research, 95,* 719–730.

Super, C.M., & Harkness, S. (2010). Culture in infancy. In J.G. Bremner & T.D. Wachs (Eds.), *Wiley-Blackwell handbook of infant development* (2nd ed.). New York: Wiley.

Susman, E.J., & Dorn, L.D. (2013). Puberty: Its role in development. In I.B. Weiner & others (Eds.), *Handbook of psychology* (2nd ed., Vol. 6). New York: Wiley.

Sutin, A.R., Robinson, E., Daly, M., & Terracciarno, A. (2016). Parent-reported bullying and child weight gain between 6 and 15. *Child Obesity, 12,* 482–487.

Sutphin, G.L., & Korstanje, R. (2016). Longevity as a complex genetic trait. In M.R. Kaeberlein & G.M. Martin (Eds.), *Handbook of the biology of aging* (8th ed.). New York: Elsevier.

Swaab, D.F., Chung, W.C., Kruijver, F.P., Hofman, M.A., & Ishunina, T.A. (2001). Structural and functional sex differences in the human hypothalamus. *Hormones and Behavior, 40,* 93–98.

Swamy, G.K., Ostbye, T., & Skjaerven, R. (2008). Association of preterm birth with long-term survival, reproduction, and next-generation preterm birth. *Journal of the American Medical Association, 299,* 1429–1436.

Swanson, H.L. (1999). What develops in working memory? A life-span perspective. *Developmental Psychology, 35,* 986–1000.

Swanson, H.L. (2016). Cognition and cognitive disabilities. In L. Corno & E.M. Anderman (Eds.), *Handbook of educational psychology* (3rd ed.). New York: Routledge.

Swanson, H.L. (2017). Verbal and visual-spatial working memory: What develops over a life span? *Developmental Psychology, 53,* 971–995.

Swartzendruber, A., Sales, J.M., Rose, E.S., & DiClemente, R.J. (2016). Alcohol use problems and sexual risk among young adult African American mothers. *AIDS Behavior, 20*(Suppl. 1), S74–S83.

Sweeting, H.N. (2008). Gendered dimensions of obesity in childhood and adolescence. *Nutrition Journal, 7,* 1.

Swing, E.L., Gentile, D.A., Anderson, C.A., & Walsh, D.A. (2010). Television and video game exposure and the development of attention problems. *Pediatrics, 126,* 214–221.

Swingler, M.M., & others (2017). Maternal behavior predicts infant neurophysiological and behavioral attention processes in the first year. *Developmental Psychology, 53,* 13–37.

Swingley, D. (2017). The infant's developmental path in phonological acquisition. *British Journal of Psychology, 108,* 28–30.

Sykes, C.J. (1995). *Dumbing down our kids: Why America's children feel good about themselves but can't read, write, or add.* New York: St. Martin's Press.

Szwedo, D.E., Hessel, E.T., & Allen, J.P. (2017). Supportive romantic relationships as predictors of resilience against early adolescent maternal negativity. *Journal of Youth and Adolescence, 46,* 454–465.

Szyf, M., & Pluess, M. (2016). Epigenetics and well-being: Optimal adaptation to the environment. In M. Pluess (Ed.), *Genetics of psychological well-being.* New York: Oxford University Press.

T

Taddio, A. (2008). Circumcision. In M.M. Haith & J.B. Benson (Eds.), *Encyclopedia of infant and early childhood development.* Oxford, UK: Elsevier.

Taggart, J., Eisen, S., & Lillard, A.S. (2018, in press). Pretense. In M.H. Bornstein & others (Eds.), *The SAGE encyclopedia of lifespan development.* Thousand Oaks, CA: SAGE.

Taige, N.M., Neal, C., Glover, V., and the Early Stress, Translational Research and Prevention

Science Network: Fetal and Neonatal Experience on Child and Adolescent Mental Health (2007). Antenatal maternal stress and long-term effects on neurodevelopment: How and why? *Journal of Child Psychology and Psychiatry, 48,* 245–261.

Talib, M.A., & Abdollahi, A. (2017). Spirituality moderates hopelessness, depression, and suicidal behavior among Malaysian adolescents. *Journal of Religion and Health, 56,* 784–795.

Tamis-LeMonda, C.S., Kuchirko, Y., & Song, L. (2014). Why is infant language learning facilitated by parental responsiveness? *Current Directions in Psychological Science, 23,* 121–126.

Tan, B.W., Pooley, J.A., & Speelman, C.P. (2016). A meta-analytic review of the efficacy of physical exercise interventions on cognition in individuals with autism spectrum disorder and ADHD. *Journal of Autism and Developmental Disorders, 46,* 3126–3143.

Tan, P.Z., Armstrong, L.M., & Cole, P.M. (2013). Relations between temperament and anger regulation over early childhood. *Social Development, 22,* 755–772.

Tan, T., Mahoney, E., Jackson, A., & Rice, J. (2017). East meets West: Adopted Chinese girls' nighttime sleep problems and adoptive parents' self-judgment about parenting. *Behavioral Sleep Medicine, 15,* 242–255.

Tanaka, C., & others (2017). Association between objectively evaluated physical activity and sedentary behavior and screen time in primary school children. *BMC Research Notes, 10*(1), 175.

Tang, S., Davis-Kean, P.E., Chen, M., & Sexton, H.R. (2016). Adolescent pregnancy's intergenerational effects: Does an adolescent mother's education have consequences for children's achievement? *Journal of Research on Adolescence, 26,* 180–193.

Tang, S., McLoyd, V.C., & Hallman, S.K. (2016). Racial socialization, racial identity, and academic attitudes among African American adolescents: Examining the moderating influence of parent-adolescent communication. *Journal of Youth and Adolescence, 45,* 1141–1155.

Tannen, D. (1990). *You just don't understand!* New York: Ballantine.

Tanrikulu, M.A., Agirbasli, M., & Berenson, G. (2017). Primordial prevention of cardiometabolic risk in childhood. *Advances in Experimental Medicine and Biology, 956,* 489–496.

Tarokh, L., Carskadon, M.A., & Achermann, P. (2010). Developmental changes in brain connectivity assessed using the sleep EEG. *Neuroscience, 17*(2), 622–634.

Tartaglia, N.R., & others (2017). Autism spectrum disorder in males with sex chromosome aneuploidy: XXY/Klinefelter syndrome, XYY, and XXYY. *Journal of Developmental and Behavioral Pediatrics, 38,* 197–207.

Taylor, A.W., & others (2017, in press). Estimated perinatal infection among infants born in the United States, 2002–2013. *JAMA Pediatrics.*

Taylor, C., & others (2016). Examining ways that a mindfulness-based intervention reduces stress in

public school teachers: A mixed-methods study. *Mindfulness, 7,* 115–129.

Taylor, C.A., Manganello, J.A., Lee, S.J., & Rice, J.C. (2010). Mothers' spanking of 3-year-old children and subsequent risk of children's aggressive behavior. *Pediatrics, 125,* e1057–e1065.

Taylor, C.A., & others (2017). Traumatic brain injury-related emergency department visits, hospitalizations, and deaths—United States, 2007 and 2013. *MMWR Surveillance Summaries, 55*(9), 1–16.

Taylor, F.M.A., Ko, R., & Pan, M. (1999). Prenatal and reproductive health care. In E.J. Kramer, S.L. Ivey, & Y.W. Ying (Eds.), *Immigrant women's health.* San Francisco: Jossey-Bass.

Taylor, H., & others (2016). Neonatal outcomes of waterbirth: A systematic review and meta-analysis. *Archives of Disease in Childhood: Fetal and Neonatal Edition, 101,* F357–F365.

Taylor, J.R. (2017). Lexical semantics. In B. Dancygier (Ed.), *Cambridge handbook of cognitive linguistics.* New York: Cambridge University Press.

Taylor, R., & others (2016). A simple screen performed at school entry can predict academic under-achievement at age seven in children born very preterm. *Journal of Pediatric and Child Health, 52,* 759–764.

Taylor, R.D., & Lopez, E.I. (2005). Family management practice, school achievement, and problem behavior in African American adolescents: Mediating processes. *Applied Developmental Psychology, 26,* 39–49.

Tchamo, M.E., Prista, A., & Leandro, C.G. (2016). Low birth weight, very low birth weight, and extremely low birth weight in African children aged between 0 and 5 years old: A systematic review. *Journal of the Developmental Origins of Health and Disease, 7,* 408–415.

te Velde, S.J., & others (2012). Energy balance-related behaviors associated with overweight and obesity in preschool children: A systematic review of prospective studies. *Obesity Reviews, 13*(Suppl. 1), S56–S74.

Tee, L.M., Kan, E.Y., Cheung, J.C., & Leung, W.C. (2016). Magnetic resonance imaging of the fetal brain. *Hong Kong Medical Journal, 6,* 328466.

Teenage Research Unlimited (2004, November 10). *Diversity in word and deed: Most teens claim multicultural friends.* Northbrook, IL: Teenage Research Unlimited.

Temple, C.A., & others (2018). *All children read: Teaching for literacy* (5th ed.). Upper Saddle River, NJ: Pearson.

Templeton, J.L., & Eccles, J.S. (2005). The relation between spiritual development and identity processes. In E. Roehlkepartain, P.E. King, L. Wagener, & P.L. Benson (Eds.), *The handbook of spirituality in childhood and adolescence.* Thousand Oaks, CA: Sage.

ten Hoope-Bender, P., & others (2016, in press). Midwifery 2030: A woman's pathway to health. What does this mean? *Midwifery.*

Ten Hoor, G.A., & others (2016). A new direction in psychology and health: Resistance exercise training for obese children and adolescents. *Psychology & Health, 31,* 1–8.

Tenenbaum, H., & May, D. (2014). Gender in parent-child relationships. In P. Leman & H. Tenenbaum (Eds.), *Gender and development.* New York: Psychology Press.

Tenenbaum, H.R., Callahan, M., Alba-Speyer, C., & Sandoval, L. (2002). Parent-child science conversations in Mexican-descent families: Educational background, activity, and past experience as moderators. *Hispanic Journal of Behavioral Sciences, 24,* 225–248.

Terman, L. (1925). *Genetic studies of genius. Vol. 1: Mental and physical traits of a thousand gifted children.* Stanford, CA: Stanford University Press.

Terry-McElrath, Y.M., O'Malley, P.M., & Johnston, L.D. (2011). Exercise and substance use among American youth, 1991–2009. *American Journal of Preventive Medicine, 40,* 530–540.

Teti, D. (2001). Retrospect and prospect in the psychological study of sibling relationships. In J.P. McHale & W.S. Grolnick (Eds.), *Retrospect and prospect in the psychological study of families.* Mahwah, NJ: Erlbaum.

Tevendale, H.D., & others (2017). Practical approaches to evaluating progress and outcomes in community-wide teen pregnancy prevention initiatives. *Journal of Adolescent Health, 60*(Suppl. 3), S63–S68.

Thabet, A.A., Ibraheem, A.N., Shivram, R., Winter, E.A., & Vostanis, P. (2009). Parenting support and PTSD in children of a war zone. *International Journal of Social Psychiatry, 55,* 225–227.

Thagard, P. (2014). Artistic genius and creative cognition. In D.K. Simonton (Ed.), *Wiley-Blackwell handbook of genius.* New York: Wiley.

Thanh, N.X., & Jonsson, E. (2016). Life expectancy of people with fetal alcohol syndrome. *Journal of Population Therapeutics and Clinical Pharmacology, 23,* e53–e59.

Tharp, R.G. (1994). Intergroup differences among Native Americans in socialization and child cognition: An ethnogenetic analysis. In P.M. Greenfield & R. Cocking (Eds.), *Cross-cultural roots of minority child development.* Mahwah, NJ: Erlbaum.

Tharp, R.G., & Gallimore, R. (1988). *Rousing minds to life: Teaching, learning, and schooling in social context.* New York: Cambridge University Press.

The, N.S., & others (2010). Association of adolescent obesity with risk of severe obesity in adulthood. *Journal of the American Psychological Association, 304,* 2042–2047.

Thelen, E. (2000). Perception and motor development. In A. Kazdin (Ed.), *Encyclopedia of psychology.* Washington, DC, & New York: American Psychological Association and Oxford University Press.

Thelen, E., & Smith, L.B. (1998). Dynamic systems theory. In W. Damon (Ed.), *Handbook of child psychology* (5th ed., Vol. 1). New York: Wiley.

Thelen, E., & Smith, L.B. (2006). Dynamic development of action and thought. In W. Damon &

R. Lerner (Eds.), *Handbook of child psychology* (6th ed.). New York: Wiley.

Thelen, E., & others (1993). The transition to reaching: Mapping intention and intrinsic dynamics. *Child Development, 64,* 1058–1098.

Thoma, S.J., & Bebeau, M. (2008). *Moral judgment competency is declining over time: Evidence from 20 years of defining issues test data.* Paper presented at the meeting of the American Educational Research meeting, New York, NY.

Thomas, A., & Chess, S. (1991). Temperament in adolescence and its functional significance. In R.M. Lerner, A.C. Petersen, & J. Brooks-Gunn (Eds.), *Encyclopedia of adolescence* (Vol. 2). New York: Garland.

Thomas, J.C., & others (2017). Developmental origins of infant emotion regulation: Mediation by temperamental negativity and moderation by maternal sensitivity. *Developmental Psychology, 53,* 611–628.

Thomas, J.R., & Hognas, R.S. (2015). The effect of parental divorce on the health of adult children. *Longitudinal and Life Course Studies, 6,* 279–302.

Thomas, K.A., & Spieker, S. (2016). Sleep, depression, and fatigue in late postpartum. *MCN: American Journal of Maternal and Child Nursing, 41,* 104–109.

Thomas, K.J. (2016). Adoption, foreign-born status, and children's progress in school. *Journal of Marriage and Family, 78,* 75–90.

Thomas, M.S.C., & Johnson, M.H. (2008). New advances in understanding sensitive periods in brain development. *Current Directions in Psychological Science, 17,* 1–5.

Thompson, A.E., & Voyer, D. (2014). Sex differences in the ability to recognize non-verbal displays of emotion: A meta-analysis. *Cognition and Emotion, 28,* 1164–1195.

Thompson, D.R., & others (2007). Childhood overweight and cardiovascular disease risk factors: The National Heart, Lung, and Blood Institute Growth and Health Study. *Journal of Pediatrics, 150,* 18–25.

Thompson, J., Manore, M., & Vaughan, L. (2017). *Science of nutrition* (4th ed.). Upper Saddle River, NJ: Pearson.

Thompson, M.P., & Swartout, K. (2017, in press). Epidemiology of suicide attempts among youth transitioning to adulthood. *Journal of Youth and Adolescence.*

Thompson, P.M., & others (2000). Growth patterns in the developing brain detected by using continuum mechanical tensor maps. *Nature, 404,* 190–193.

Thompson, R., & Murachver, T. (2001). Predicting gender from electronic discourse. *British Journal of Social Psychology, 40,* 193–201.

Thompson, R., & others (2012). Suicidal ideation in adolescence: Examining the role of recent adverse experiences. *Journal of Adolescence, 35,* 175–186.

Thompson, R., & others (2017). Is the use of physical discipline associated with aggressive behaviors in children? *Academic Pediatrics, 17,* 34–44.

Thompson, R., & others (2017, in press). Relationships between language input and letter output

modes in writing notes and summaries for students in grades 4 to 9 with persisting writing disabilities. *Assistive Technology Journal.*

Thompson, R.A. (2006). The development of the person. In W. Damon & R. Lerner (Eds.), *Handbook of child psychology* (6th ed.). New York: Wiley.

Thompson, R.A. (2012). Whither the preoperational child? Toward a life-span moral development theory. *Child Development, 6,* 423–429.

Thompson, R.A. (2013). Attachment and its development: Precis and prospect. In P. Zelazo (Ed.), *Oxford handbook of developmental psychology.* New York: Oxford University Press.

Thompson, R.A. (2015). Relationships, regulation, and development. In R.M. Lerner (Ed.), *Handbook of child psychology* (7th ed.). New York: Wiley.

Thompson, R.A. (2016). Early attachment and later development: New questions. In J. Cassidy & P.R. Shaver (Eds.), *Handbook of attachment* (3rd ed.). New York: Guilford.

Thompson, R.A., & Goodvin, R. (2016). Social support and developmental psychopathology. In D. Cicchetti (Ed.), *Developmental psychopathology* (3rd ed.). New York: Wiley.

Thompson, R.A., Meyer, S., & McGinley, M. (2006). Understanding values in relationships: The development of conscience. In M. Killen & J. Smetana (Eds.), *Handbook of moral development.* Mahwah, NJ: Erlbaum.

Thompson, R.A., & Newton, E.K. (2010). Emotion in early conscience. In W. Arsenio & E. Lemerise (Eds.), *Emotions, aggression, and morality: Bridging development and psychopathology* (pp. 6–32), Washington, DC: American Psychological Association.

Thompson, R.A., & Newton, E.K. (2013). Baby altruists? Examining the complexity of prosocial motivation in young children. *Infancy, 18,* 120–133.

Thompson, R.A., Winer, A.C., & Goodvin, R. (2014). The individual child: Temperament, emotion, self, and personality. In M.H. Bornstein & M.E. Lamb (Eds.), *Developmental science* (6th ed.). New York: Psychology Press.

Thornburg, K.L., & others (2016). Biological features of placental programming. *Placenta, 48*(Suppl. 1), S47–S55.

Thornton, J.D., Deb, A., Murray, P.J., & Kelly, K.M. (2017). Seat belt safety: Typologies of protective health and safety behaviors for mothers in West Virginia. *Maternal and Child Health Journal, 21,* 326–334.

Thornton, R. (2016). Acquisition of questions. In J. Lidz, W. Snyder, & J. Pater (Eds.), *Oxford handbook of developmental linguistics.* New York: Oxford University Press.

Thurman, A.J., & others (2017, in press). Language skills of males and Fragile X syndrome or nonsyndromic autism spectrum disorder. *Journal of Autism and Developmental Disorders.*

Tiggemann, M., & Slater, A. (2017). Facebook and body image concern in adolescent girls: A prospective study. *International Journal of Eating Disorders.*

Tikotzky, L., & Shaashua, L. (2012). Infant sleep and early parental sleep-related cognitions predict sleep in pre-school children. *Sleep Medicine, 13,* 185–192.

Tilton-Weaver, L.C., Burk, W.J., Kerr, M., & Stattin, H. (2013). Can parental monitoring and peer management reduce the selection or influence of delinquent peers? Testing the question using a dynamic social network approach. *Developmental Psychology, 49,* 2057–2070.

TIMMS (2015). *TIMMS 2015 and TIMMS advanced 2015 international results.* Chestnut Hill, MA: TIMMS.

Tincoff, R., & Jusczyk, P.W. (2012). Six-month-olds comprehend words that refer to parts of the body. *Infancy, 17,* 432–444.

Tinloy, J., & others (2014). Exercise during pregnancy and risk of late preterm birth, cesarean delivery, and hospitalizations. *Women's Health Issues, 24,* e99–e104.

Tinsley, B.J. (2003). *How children learn to be healthy.* New York: Cambridge University Press.

Tobin, J.J., Wu, D.Y.H., & Davidson, D.H. (1989). *Preschool in three cultures.* New Haven, CT: Yale University Press.

Tolani, N., & Brooks-Gunn, J. (2008). Family support, international trends. In M.M. Haith & J.B. Benson (Eds.), *Encyclopedia of infant and early childhood development.* Oxford, UK: Elsevier.

Tomasello, M. (2003). *Constructing a language: A usage-based theory of language acquisition.* Harvard University Press.

Tomasello, M. (2006). Acquiring linguistic constructions. In W. Damon & R. Lerner (Eds.), *Handbook of child psychology* (6th ed.). New York: Wiley.

Tomasello, M. (2011). Language development. In U. Goswami (Ed.), *Wiley-Blackwell handbook of childhood cognitive development* (2nd ed.). New York: Wiley.

Tomasello, M. (2014). *A natural history of human thinking.* Cambridge, MA: Harvard University Press.

Tomasello, M., & Hamann, K. (2012). Collaboration in young children. *Quarterly Journal of Experimental Psychology, 65,* 1–12.

Tomasello, M., & Vaish, A. (2013). Origins of human cooperation and morality. *Annual Review of Psychology* (Vol. 64). Palo Alto, CA: Annual Reviews.

Tomassay, G.S., Dershowitz, L.B., & Arlotta, P. (2016). Diversity matters: A revised guide to myelination. *Trends in Cellular Biology, 26,* 135–147.

Tomlinson, M., & others (2016). Improving early childhood care and development, HIV-testing, treatment and support, and nutrition in Mokhotlong, Lesotho: Study protocol for a cluster randomized controlled trial. *Trials, 17*(1), 538.

Tompkins, G.E. (2016). *Language arts* (9th ed.). Upper Saddle River, NJ: Pearson.

Tompkins, G.E. (2017). *REVEL for literacy in the 21st century* (7th ed.). Upper Saddle River, NJ: Pearson.

Tompkins, V., & others (2017). Child language and parent discipline mediate the relation between family income and false belief understanding. *Journal of Experimental Psychology, 158,* 1–18.

Tomporowski, P.D. (2016). Exercise and cognition. *Pediatric Exercise Science, 28,* 23–27.

Tong, X., Deacon, S.H., & Cain, K. (2014). Morphological and syntactic awareness in poor comprehenders: Another piece of the puzzle. *Journal of Learning Disabilities, 47,* 22–33.

Top, N., Liew, J., & Luo, W. (2017). Family and school influences on youths' behavioral and academic outcomes: Cross-level interactions between parental monitoring and character development curriculum. *Journal of Genetic Psychology, 178,* 108–118.

Toplak, M.E., West, R.F., & Stanovich, K.E. (2017). The assessment of executive functions in attention deficit/hyperactivity disorder (ADHD): Performance-based measures versus ratings of behavior. In M.J. Hoskyns & others (Eds.), *Executive functions in children's everyday lives.* New York: Oxford University Press.

Torstveit, L., Sutterlin, S., & Lugo, R.G. (2016). Empathy, guilt proneness, and gender: Relative contributions to prosocial behavior. *European Journal of Psychology, 12,* 260–275.

Tough, S.C., & others (2002). Delayed childbearing and its impact on population rate changes in lower birth weight, multiple birth, and preterm delivery. *Pediatrics, 109,* 399–403.

Trainor, L.J., & He, C. (2013). Auditory and musical development. In P.D. Zelazo (Ed.), *Handbook of developmental psychology.* New York: Oxford University Press.

Traisrisilp, K., & Tongsong, T. (2015). Pregnancy outcomes of mothers with very advanced age (40 years and more). *Journal of the Medical Association of Thailand, 98,* 117–122.

Trehub, S.E., Schneider, B.A., Thorpe, I.A., & Judge, P. (1991). Observational measures of auditory sensitivity in early infancy. *Developmental Psychology, 27,* 40–49.

Treiman, R., & others (2014). Statistical learning, letter reversals, and reading. *Scientific Studies of Reading, 8,* 383–394.

Tremblay, M.S., & others (2012). Canadian sedentary behavior guidelines for the early years (0–4 years). *Applied Physiology, Nutrition, and Metabolism, 37,* 370–380.

Trimble, J.E. (1988, August). *The enculturation of contemporary psychology.* Paper presented at the meeting of the American Psychological Association, New Orleans.

Trinkner, R., Cohn, E.S., Rebellon, C.J., & Van Gundy, K. (2012). Don't trust anyone over 30: Parental legitimacy as a mediator between parenting style and changes in delinquent behavior over time. *Journal of Adolescence, 35,* 119–132.

Troia, G., Graham, S., & Harris, K.R. (2017, in press). Writing and students with language and learning disabilities. In J.M. Kauffman & others (Eds.), *Handbook of special education* (2nd ed.). New York: Routledge.

Troop-Gordon, W. (2017). Peer victimization in adolescence: The nature, progression, and consequences of being bullied within a developmental context. *Journal of Adolescence, 55,* 116–128.

Troppe, P., & others (2017). Implementation of Title I and Title II-A program initiatives. Results from 2013–2014. NCEE 2017-4014. *ERIC,* ED572281.

Trotman, G., & others (2015). The effect of CenteringPregnancy versus traditional prenatal care models on improved adolescent health behaviors in the prenatal period. *Journal of Pediatric and Adolescent Gynecology, 28,* 395–401.

Truglio, R.T., & Kotler, J.A. (2014). Language, literacy, and media: What's the word on *Sesame Street?* In E.T. Gershoff, R.S. Mistry, & D.A. Crosby (Eds.), *Societal contexts of child development.* New York: Oxford University Press.

Truzzi, A., & others (2017). Serotonin transporter gene polymorphisms and early parent-infant interactions are related to adult male heart rate responses to female crying. *Frontiers in Physiology, 8,* 111.

Trzaskowski, M., Yang, J., Visscher, P.M., & Plomin, R. (2014). DNA evidence for strong genetic stability and increasing heritability of intelligence from age 7 to 12. *Molecular Psychiatry, 19,* 380–384.

Tsal, Y., Shalev, L., & Mevorach, C. (2005). The diversity of attention deficits in ADHD. *Journal of Learning Disabilities, 38,* 142–157.

Tsang, T.W., & others (2016). Prenatal alcohol exposure, FASD, and child behavior: A meta-analysis. *Pediatrics, 137,* e20152542.

Tso, W., & others (2016). Sleep duration and school readiness of Chinese preschool children. *Journal of Pediatrics, 169,* 266–271.

Tsubomi, H., & Watanabe, K. (2017). Development of visual working memory and distractor resistance in relation to academic performance. *Journal of Experimental Psychology, 154,* 98–112.

Ttofi, M.M., Farrington, D.P., Losel, F., & Loeber, R. (2011). The predictive efficiency of school bullying versus later offending: A systematic/meta-analytic review of longitudinal studies. *Criminal Behavior and Mental Health, 21,* 80–89.

Tucker, C.J., & others (2015). Proactive and reactive sibling aggression and adjustment in adolescence. *Journal of Interpersonal Violence, 30,* 965–987.

Tucker, J.S., Ellickson, P.L., & Klein, M.S. (2003). Predictors of the transition to regular smoking during adolescence and young adulthood. *Journal of Adolescent Health, 32,* 314–324.

Tung, R., & Ouimette, M. (2007). *Strong results, high demand: A four-year study of Boston's pilot high schools.* Boston: Center for Collaborative Education.

Turecki, G., & Meaney, M.J. (2016). Effects of the social environment and stress on glucocorticoid receptor gene methylation: A systematic review. *Biological Psychiatry, 79,* 87–96.

Turiel, E. (2014). Morality: Epistemology, development, and social judgments. In M. Killen & J.G. Smetana (Eds.), *Handbook of moral development* (2nd ed.). New York: Psychology Press.

Turiel, E. (2015). Moral development. In R.M. Lerner (Ed.), *Handbook of child psychology and developmental science* (7th ed.). New York: Wiley.

Turiel, E., & Gingo, M. (2017). Development in the moral domain: Coordination and the need to consider other domains of social reasoning. In N. Budwig, E. Turiel, & P.D. Zelazo (Eds.), *New perspectives on human development*. New York: Cambridge University Press.

Turnbull, A., Rutherford-Turnbull, H., Wehmeyer, M.L., & Shogren, K.A. (2016). *Exceptional lives* (8th ed.). Upper Saddle River, NJ: Pearson.

Turner, S., & others (2017, in press). The relationship between childhood sexual abuse and mental health outcomes among males: Results from a nationally representative United States sample. *Child Abuse and Neglect.*

Tweed, E.J., & others (2016). Five-minute Apgar scores and educational outcomes: Retrospective cohort study of 751,369 children. *Archives of Disease in Child, Fetal, and Neonatal Medicine, 101,* F121–F126.

Tylka, T.L., Lumeng, J.C., & Eneli, I.U. (2015). Maternal intuitive eating as a moderator of the association between concern about child weight and restrictive child feeding. *Appetite, 95,* 158–165.

Tyrell, F.A., & others (2016). Family influences on Mexican American adolescents' romantic relationships: Moderation by gender and culture. *Journal of Research on Adolescence, 26,* 142–158.

U

U.S. Census Bureau (2016). *People.* Washington, DC: Author.

U.S. Department of Energy (2001). *The human genome project.* Washington, DC: U.S. Department of Energy.

U.S. Department of Health and Human Services (2015). *Child maltreatment 2013.* Washington, DC: Author.

U.S. Food and Drug Administration (FDA) (2017). *Fish: What pregnant women and parents should know.* Retrieved April 24, 2017, from www.fda.gov/Food/FoodbornIllnessContaminants/Metals/uc...

U.S. Office of Education (2000). *To assure a free and appropriate public education of all children with disabilities.* Washington, DC: U.S. Office of Education.

Uba, L. (1992). Cultural barriers to health care for Southeast Asian refugees. *Public Health Reports, 107,* 544–549.

Ueno, M., & others (2011). The organization of wariness of heights in experienced crawlers. *Infancy, 17,* 376–392.

Umana-Taylor, A.J., & Douglass, S. (2017). Developing an ethnic-racial identity intervention from a developmental perspective: Process, content, and implementation of the Identity Project. In N.J. Cabrera & B. Leyendecker (Eds.), *Handbook on positive development of minority children and youth.* New York: Springer.

Umana-Taylor, A.J., & Updegraff, K.A. (2013). Latino families in the United States. In G.W. Patterson & K.R. Bush (Eds.), *Handbook of marriage and the family* (3rd ed.). New York: Springer.

Umana-Taylor, A.J., & others (2013). U.S. Latinas/os' ethnic identity: Context, methodological approaches, and considerations across the lifespan. *Counseling Psychologist, 42,* 170–200.

Underwood, M.K. (2011). Aggression. In M.K. Underwood & L.H. Rosen (Eds.), *Social development.* New York: Wiley.

Ungar, M. (2015). Practitioner review: Diagnosing childhood resilience: A systematic diagnosis of adaption in diverse social ecologies. *Journal of Child Psychology and Psychiatry, 56,* 4–17.

UNICEF (2004). *The state of the world's children, 2004.* Geneva, Switzerland: Author.

UNICEF (2007). *The state of the world's children, 2007.* Geneva, Switzerland: Author.

UNICEF (2012). *The state of the world's children, 2012.* Geneva, Switzerland: Author.

UNICEF (2014). *The state of the world's children, 2014.* Geneva, Switzerland: Author.

UNICEF (2017). *The state of the world's children, 2017.* Geneva, Switzerland: Author.

UNICEF (2018, in press). *The state of the world's children, 2018.* Geneva, Switzerland: Author.

Urdan, T. (2012). Factors affecting the motivation and achievement of immigrant students. In K.R. Harris, S. Graham, & T. Urdan (Eds.), *APA educational psychology handbook.* Washington, DC: American Psychological Association.

Usher, E.L., & Schunk, D.H. (2018). Social cognitive perspective of self-regulation. In D.H. Schunk & J.A. Greene (Eds.), *Handbook of self-regulation of learning and performance* (2nd ed.). New York: Routledge.

V

Vahratian, A., Siega-Riz, A.M., Savitz, D.A., & Thorp, J.M. (2004). Multivitamin use and risk of preterm birth. *American Journal Epidemiology, 160,* 886–892.

Valente, T.W., & others (2013). A comparison of peer influence measures as predictors of smoking among predominately Hispanic/Latino high school adolescents. *Journal of Adolescent Health, 52,* 358–364.

Valentino, K., & others (2014). Mother-child reminiscing and autobiographical memory specificity among preschool-age children. *Developmental Psychology, 50,* 1197–1207.

Valenzuela, C.F., Morton, R.A., Diaz, M.R., & Topper, L. (2012). Does moderate drinking harm the fetal brain? Insights from animal models. *Trends in Neuroscience, 35,* 284–292.

Vallotton, C., & others (2017). Parenting supports for early vocabulary development: Specific effects of sensitivity and stimulation through infancy. *Infancy, 22,* 78–107.

Van Beveren, T.T. (2011, January). Personal conversation. Richardson, TX: Department of Psychology, University of Texas at Dallas.

Van Bussel, I.P., & others (2016). Differences in genome-wide gene expression response in peripheral blood mononuclear cells between young and old men upon caloric restriction. *Genes & Nutrition, 11,* 13.

Van de Vandervoort, J., & Hamlin, J.K. (2016). Evidence for intuitive morality: Preverbal infants make sociomoral evaluations. *Child Development Perspectives, 10,* 143–148.

Van de Vandervoort, J., & Hamlin, J.K. (2018). The infantile roots of sociomoral evaluations. In K. Gray & J. Graham (Eds.), *The atlas of moral psychology.* New York: Guilford.

van de Weijer-Bergsma, E., Formsa, A.R., de Bruin, E., & Bogels, S.M. (2012). The effectiveness of mindfulness training on behavioral problems and attentional functioning in adolescents with ADHD. *Journal of Child and Family Studies, 21,* 775–787.

van den Boom, D.C. (1989). Neonatal irritability and the development of attachment. In G.A. Kohnstamm, J.E. Bates, & M.K. Rothbart (Eds.), *Temperament in childhood.* New York: Wiley.

van den Bos, W., & Hertwig, R. (2017). Adolescents display distinctive tolerance to ambiguity and to uncertainty during risky decision making. *Scientific Reports, 7,* 40962.

van den Dries, L., Juffer, F., van IJzendoorn, M.H., & Bakermans-Kranenburg, M.J. (2010). Infants' physical and cognitive development after international adoption from foster care or institutions in China. *Journal of Developmental and Behavioral Pediatrics, 31,* 144–150.

van der Hulst, H. (2017). Phonological typology. In A.Y. Aikhenvald & R.M.W. Dixon (Eds.), *Cambridge handbook of linguistic typology.* New York: Cambridge University Press.

van der Stel, M., & Veenman, M.V.J. (2010). Development of metacognitive skillfulness: A longitudinal study. *Learning and Individual Differences, 20,* 220–224.

Van Doren, J., & others (2017). Theta/beta neurofeedback in children with ADHD: Feasibility of a short-term setting and plasticity effects. *International Journal of Psychophysiology, 112,* 80–88.

van Geel, M., Vedder, P., & Tanilon, J. (2014). Relationship between peer victimization, cyberbullying, and suicide in children and adolescents: A meta-analysis. *JAMA Pediatrics, 168,* 435–442.

van Goethem, A.A.J., & others (2012). The role of adolescents' morality and identity in volunteering. Age and gender differences in the process model. *Journal of Adolescence, 35,* 509–520.

Van Hecke, V., & others (2012). Infant responding to joint attention, executive processes, and self-regulation in preschool children. *Infant Development and Behavior, 35,* 303–311.

van Hout, A. (2017). Lexical and grammatical aspect. In J. Lidz, W. Snyder, & J. Peter (Eds.), *Oxford handbook of developmental linguistics.* New York: Oxford University Press.

van IJzendoorn, M.H., & Kroonenberg, P.M. (1988). Cross-cultural patterns of attachment: A meta-analysis of the Strange Situation. *Child Development, 59,* 147–156.

van IJzendoorn, M.H., & Sagi-Schwartz, A. (2009). Cross-cultural patterns of attachment: Universal and contextual dimensions. In J. Cassidy & P.R. Shaver (Eds.), *Handbook of attachment* (2nd ed.). New York: Guilford.

Van Lieshout, M., & others (2017). Neurocognitive predictors of ADHD outcome: A 6-year follow-up study. *Journal of Abnormal Child Psychology, 45,* 261–272.

Van Lissa, C.J., & others (2015). Divergence between adolescent and parent perceptions of conflict in relationship to adolescent empathy development. *Journal of Youth and Adolescence, 44,* 48–51.

van Oosten, J.M., & Vandenbosch, L. (2017). Sexy online self-presentation on social network sites and the willingness to engage in sexting: A comparison of gender and age. *Journal of Adolescence, 54,* 42–50.

Van Ryzin, M.J., Carlson, E.A., & Sroufe, L.A. (2011). Attachment discontinuity in a high-risk sample. *Attachment and Human Development, 13,* 381–401.

Vandehey, M., Diekhoff, G., & LaBeff, E. (2007). College cheating: A 20-year follow-up and the addition of an honor code. *Journal of College Development, 48,* 468–480.

Vandell, D.L., & others (2010). Do effects of early childcare extend to age 15 years? From the NICHD Study of Early Child Care and Youth Development. *Child Development, 81,* 737–756.

Vanderwert, R.E., Zeanah, C.H., Fox, N.A., & Nelson, C.A. (2016). Normalization of EEG activity among previously institutionalized children placed in foster care: A 12-year follow-up of the Bucharest Early Intervention Project, *17,* 68–75.

Vanitallie, T.B. (2017, in press). Alzheimer's disease: Innate immunity gone awry? *Metabolism.*

Varcin, K.J., & others (2016). Visual evoked potentials as a readout of cortical function in infants with tuberous sclerosis complex. *Journal of Child Neurology, 31,* 195–202.

Vardavas, C.I., & others (2016). The independent role of prenatal and postnatal exposure to active and passive smoking on the development of early wheeze in children. *European Respiratory Journal, 48,* 115–124.

Varga, N.L., & others (2018, in press). Knowledge. In M.H. Bornstein & others (Eds.), *SAGE encyclopedia of lifespan development.* Thousand Oaks, CA: Sage.

Varner, M.W., & others (2014). Association between stillbirth and illicit drug use and smoking during pregnancy. *Obstetrics and Gynecology, 123,* 113–125.

Vaughan, C.A., & Halpern, C.T. (2010). Gender differences in depressive symptoms during adolescence: The contributions of weight-related concerns and behaviors. *Journal of Research on Adolescence, 20,* 389–419.

Vaughan, O.R., & others (2017). Regulation of placental amino acid transport and fetal growth. *Progress in Molecular Biology and Translational Science, 145,* 217–251.

Vaughn, B.E., & Bost, K.K. (2016). Attachment and temperament as intersecting developmental products and interacting developmental contexts throughout infancy and childhood. In J. Cassidy & P.R. Shaver (Eds.), *Handbook of attachment* (3rd ed.). New York: Guilford.

Vaughn, B.E., Elmore-Staton, L., Shin, N., & el-Sheikh, M. (2015). Sleep as a support for social competence, peer relations, and cognitive functioning in preschool children. *Behavioral Sleep Medicine, 13,* 92–106.

Vaughn, M.G., Beaver, K.M., Wexler, J., DeLisi, M., & Roberts, G.J. (2010). The effect of school dropout on verbal ability in adulthood: A propensity score matching approach. *Journal of Youth and Adolescence, 40*(2), 197–206.

Vazsonyi, A.T., & Huang, L. (2010). Where self-control comes from: On the development of self-control and its relationship to deviance over time. *Developmental Psychology, 46,* 245–257.

Veldman, S.L., Palmer, K.K., Okely, A.D., & Robinson, L.E. (2017). Promoting ball skills in preschool-age girls. *Journal of Science and Medicine in Sport, 20,* 50–54.

Velez, C.E., Wolchik, S.A., Tein, J.Y., & Sandler, I. (2011). Protecting children from the consequences of divorce: A longitudinal study of the effects of parenting on children's coping responses. *Child Development, 82,* 244–257.

Vella, S.A., Cliff, D.P., Magee, C.A., & Okely, A.D. (2014). Sports participation and parent-reported health-related quality of life in children: Longitudinal associations. *Journal of Pediatrics, 164,* 1469–1474.

Veness, C., Prior, M., Eadie, P., Bavin, E., & Reilly, S. (2014). Predicting autism diagnosis by 7 years of age using parent report of infant social communication skills. *Journal of Pediatrics and Child Health, 50,* 693–700.

Venetsanou, F., & Kambas, A. (2017). Can motor proficiency in preschool age affect physical activity in adolescence? *Pediatric Exercise Science, 49,* 254–259.

Venners, S.A., & others (2004). Paternal smoking and pregnancy loss: A prospective study using a biomarker of pregnancy. *American Journal of Epidemiology, 159,* 993–1001.

Vergara-Castaneda, A., & others (2010). Overweight, obesity, high blood pressure, and lifestyle factors among Mexican children and their parents. *Environmental Health and Preventive Medicine, 15,* 358–366.

Verhagen, J., & Leseman, P. (2016). How do verbal short-term memory and working memory relate to the acquisition of vocabulary and grammar? A comparison between first and second language learners. *Journal of Experimental Child Psychology, 141,* 65–82.

Verhoef, M., van den Eijnden, R.J., Koning, I.M., & Vollebergh, W.A. (2014). Age at menarche and adolescent alcohol use. *Journal of Youth and Adolescence, 43*(8), 1333–1345.

Verloigne, M., & others (2016). Variation in population levels of sedentary time in European children and adolescents according to cross-European studies: A systematic literature review within DEDIPAC. *International Journal of Behavioral Nutrition and Physical Activity, 13,* 69.

Vernberg, E.M. (1990). Psychological adjustment and experience with peers during early adolescence: Reciprocal, incidental, or unidirectional relationships? *Journal of Abnormal Child Psychology, 18,* 187–198.

Vernini, J.M., & others (2016). Maternal and fetal outcomes in pregnancies complicated by overweight and obesity. *Reproductive Health, 13,* 100.

Vetter, N.C., & others (2013). Ongoing development of social cognition in adolescence. *Child Neuropsychology, 19,* 615–629.

Vidal, S., & others (2017). Maltreatment, family environment, and social risk factors: Determinants of the child welfare to juvenile justice transition among maltreated children and adolescents. *Child Abuse and Neglect, 63,* 7–18.

Vieira, J.M., Matias, M., Ferreira, T., Lopez, F.G., & Matos, P.M. (2016). Parents' work-family experiences and children's problem behaviors: The mediating role of parent-child relationship. *Journal of Family Psychology, 39,* 419–430.

Vignoles, V.L., & others (2016). Beyond the 'east-west' dichotomy: Global variation in cultural models of selfhood. *Journal of Experimental Psychology: General, 145,* 966–1000.

Villamor, E., & Jansen, E.C. (2016). Nutritional determinants of the timing of puberty. *Annual Review of Public Health, 37,* 33–46.

Villanueva, C.M., & Buriel, R. (2010). Speaking on behalf of others: A qualitative study of the perceptions and feelings of adolescent Latina language brokers. *Journal of Social Issues, 66,* 197–210.

Villeda, S. (2017). Brain and aging. *Annual Review of Neuroscience* (Vol. 40). Palo Alto, CA: Annual Reviews.

Villegas, R., & others (2008). Duration of breast-feeding and the incidence of type 2 diabetes mellitus in the Shanghai Women's Health Study. *Diabetologia, 51*(2), 258–266.

Villodas, M.T., Litrownik, A.J., Newton, R.R., & Davis, I.P. (2016). Long-term placement trajectories of children who were maltreated and entered the child welfare system at an early age: Consequences for physical and behavioral well-being. *Journal of Pediatric Psychology, 41,* 46–54.

Vinik, J., Almas, A., & Grusec, J. (2011). Mothers' knowledge of what distresses and comforts their children predicts children's coping, empathy, and prosocial behavior. Parenting: *Science and Practice, 11,* 56–71.

Viswanathan, M., & others (2017). Folic acid supplementation: An evidence review for the U.S. Preventive Services Task Force. Rockville, MD: U.S. Preventive Services.

Vittrup, B., Holden, G.W., & Buck, M. (2006). Attitudes predict the use of physical punishment: A prospective study of the emergence of disciplinary practices. *Pediatrics, 117,* 2055–2064.

Vo, P., & others (2017). Individual factors, neighborhood social context, and asthma at age 5 years. *Journal of Asthma, 54,* 265–272.

Voelker, D.K., Reel, J.J., & Greenleaf, C. (2015). Weight status and body image perceptions in adolescents: Current perspectives. *Adolescent Health, Medicine, and Therapeutics, 6,* 149–158.

Vogels, T.P. (2017). Inhibitory plasticity. *Annual Review of Neuroscience* (Vol. 40). Palo Alto, CA: Annual Reviews.

Voigt, R.G., & others (2017, in press). Academic achievement in adults with a history of attention-deficit/hyperactivity disorder: A population-based prospective study. *Journal of Developmental and Behavioral Pediatrics.*

Volkmar, F.R., Riechow, B., Westphal, A., & Mandell, D.S. (2014). Autism and autism spectrum diagnostic concepts. In F.R. Volkmar & others (Eds.), *Handbook of autism and pervasive developmental disorders.* New York: Wiley.

Volkow, N.D., Compton, W.M., & Wargo, E.M. (2017). The risks of marijuana use during pregnancy. *JAMA, 317,* 129–130.

Vollink, T., Dehue, F., & McGuckin, C. (Eds.) (2016). *Cyberbullying.* New York: Psychology Press.

Volpe, E.M., Hardie, T.L., Cerulli, C., Sommers, M.S., & Morrison-Beedy, D. (2013). What's age got to do with it? Partner age difference, power, intimate partner violence, and sexual risk in urban adolescents. *Journal of Interpersonal Violence, 28,* 2068–2087.

von dem Hagen, E.A., & Bright, N. (2017). High autistic trait individuals do not modulate gaze behavior in response to social presence but look away more when actively engaged in an interaction. *Autism Research, 10,* 359–368.

von Hippel, C., Kalokerinos, E.K., & Zacher, H. (2017). Stereotype threat and perceptions of family-friendly policies among female employees. *Frontiers in Psychology, 7,* 2043.

Von Hofsten, C. (2008). Motor and physical development manual. In M.M. Haith & J.B. Benson (Eds.), *Encyclopedia of infant and early childhood development.* Oxford, UK: Elsevier.

Vonk, J.M., & others (2004). Childhood factors associated with asthma remission after 1-year follow up. *Thorax, 59,* 925–929.

Vorona, R.D., & others (2014). Adolescent crash rates and school start times in two Central Virginia counties, 2009–2011: A follow-up study to a Southeastern Virginia study, 2007–2008. *Journal of Clinical Sleep Medicine, 10,* 1169–1177.

Votavova, H., & others (2012). Deregulation of gene expression induced by environmental tobacco smoke exposure in pregnancy. *Nicotine and Tobacco Research, 14*(9), 1073–1082.

Vreeman, R.C., & Carroll, A.E. (2007). A systematic review of school-based interventions to prevent bullying. *Archives of Pediatric and Adolescent Medicine, 161,* 78–88.

Vu, J.A. (2016). The fourth 'R': Relationships, shifting from risk to resilience. In K.E. Sanders & Guerra, A.W. (Eds.), *The culture of child care.* New York: Oxford University Press.

Vukelich, C., Christie, J., Enz, B.J., & Roskos, K.A. (2016). *Helping children learn language and literacy* (4th ed.). Upper Saddle River, NJ: Pearson.

Vurpillot, E. (1968). The development of scanning strategies and their relation to visual differentiation. *Journal of Experimental Child Psychology, 6,* 632–650.

Vygotsky, L.S. (1962). *Thought and language.* Cambridge, MA: MIT Press.

Vysniauske, R., Verburgh, L., Oosteriaan, J., & Molendijk, M.L. (2017, in press). The effects of physical exercise on functional outcomes in the treatment of ADHD. *Journal of Attention Disorders.*

W

Wachs, T.D. (2000). *Necessary but not sufficient.* Washington, DC: American Psychological Association.

Wachs, T.D., & Bates, J.E. (2011). Temperament. In J.G. Bremner & T.D. Wachs (Eds.), *Wiley-Blackwell handbook of infant development* (2nd ed.). New York: Wiley.

Wadsworth, M.E., & others (2016) Poverty and the development of psychopathology. In D. Cicchetti (Ed.), *Developmental psychopathology* (3rd ed.). New York: Wiley.

Wagner, D.A. (2018). *Human development and international development.* New York: Routledge.

Wagner, N.J., Camerota, M., & Propper, C. (2017, in press). Prevalence and perceptions of electronic cigarette use during pregnancy. *Maternal and Child Health Journal.*

Waldenstrom, U., Cnattingius, S., Norman, M., & Schytt, E. (2015). Advanced maternal age and stillbirth risk in nulliparous and parous women. *Obstetrics and Gynecology, 126,* 355–362.

Waldenstrom, U., & others (2014). Adverse pregnancy outcomes related to advanced maternal age compared with smoking and being overweight. *Obstetrics and Gynecology, 123,* 104–112.

Waldman, Z., & Cleary, M. (2017). Hearing loss. In R. Schwartz (Ed.), *Handbook of child language disorders* (2nd ed.). New York: Routledge.

Waldner, L.S., McGorry, S.Y., & Widener, M.C. (2012). E-service learning: The evolution of service learning to engage a growing online student population. *Journal of Higher Education Outreach and Engagement, 16,* 123–150.

Walker, L. (1982). The sequentiality of Kohlberg's stages of moral development. *Child Development, 53,* 1130–1136.

Walker, L.J. (2002). In W. Damon (Ed.), *Bringing in a new era of character education.* Stanford, CA: Hoover Press.

Walker, L.J. (2004). Progress and prospects in the psychology of moral development. *Merrill-Palmer Quarterly, 50,* 546–557.

Walker, L.J. (2013a). Moral personality, motivation, and identity. In M. Killen & J.G. Smetana (Eds.), *Handbook of moral development* (2nd Ed.). New York: Taylor & Frances.

Walker, L.J. (2013b). Moral motivation through the perspective of exemplarity. In K. Heinrichs, F.K. Oser, & T. Lovat (Eds.), *Handbook of moral motivation.* Rotterman, Netherlands: Sense Publishers.

Walker, L.J. (2014a). Moral personality, motivation, and identity. In M. Killen & J.G. Smetana (Eds.), *Handbook of moral development* (2nd ed.). New York: Taylor & Francis.

Walker, L.J. (2014b). Prosocial exemplarity in adolescence and adulthood. In L. Padilla-Walker & G. Carlo (Eds.), *Prosocial behavior.* New York: Oxford University Press.

Walker, L.J. (2016). The moral character of heroes. In S.T. Allison & others (Eds.), *Handbook of heroism and heroic leadership.* New York: Routledge.

Wallace, M.E., & others (2016). Preterm birth in the context of increasing income inequality. *Maternal and Child Health Journal, 20,* 164–171.

Walle, E.A. (2016). Infant social development across the transition from crawling to walking. *Frontiers in Psychology, 7,* 960.

Waller, E.M., & Rose, A.J. (2010). Adjustment trade-offs of co-rumination in mother-adolescent relationships. *Journal of Adolescence, 33,* 487–497.

Wallerstein, J.S. (2008). Divorce. In M.M. Haith & J.B. Benson (Eds.), *Encyclopedia of infant and early childhood development.* Oxford, UK: Elsevier.

Walsh, B.A., DeFlorio, L., & Burnham, M. (Eds.) (2017). *Introduction to human development and family studies.* New York: Routledge.

Walsh, L.V. (2006). Beliefs and rituals in traditional birth attendant practice in Guatemala. *Journal of Transcultural Nursing, 17,* 148–154.

Walsh, P., & others (2014). Using a pacifier to decrease sudden infant death syndrome: An emergency department educational intervention. *PeerJ, 2,* e309.

Walton, E., & others (2017). Epigenetic profiling of ADHD symptoms trajectories: A prospective, methylome-wide study. *Molecular Psychiatry, 22,* 250–256.

Wang, B., & others (2014). The impact of youth, family, peer, and neighborhood risk factors on developmental trajectories of risk involvement from early through middle adolescence. *Social Science Medicine, 106C,* 43–52.

Wang, B., & others (2016a). The influence of sensation-seeking and parental and peer influences in early adolescence on risk involvement through middle adolescence: A structural equation modeling analysis. *Youth and Society, 48,* 220–241.

Wang, C., & others (2016b). Coevolution of adolescent friendship networks and smoking and drinking behaviors with consideration of parental influence. *Psychology of Addictive Behaviors, 30,* 312–324.

Wang, C., & others (2017). Longitudinal relationships between bullying and moral disengagement among adolescents. *Journal of Youth and Adolescence, 46,* 1304–1317.

Wang, G.S. (2017). Pediatric concerns due to expanded cannabis use: Unintended consequences of legalization. *Journal of Medical Toxicology, 13,* 99–105.

Wang, H., Lin, S.L., Leung, G.M., & Schooling, C.M. (2017, in press). Age at onset of puberty and adolescent depression: "Children of 1997" birth cohort. *Pediatrics.*

Wang, H.J., & others (2016). Association of common variants identified by recent genome-wide association studies with obesity in Chinese children: A case-control study. *17*(1), 7.

Wang, J., Nansel, T.R., & Iannotti, R.J. (2011). Cyber and traditional bullying: Differential association with depression. *Journal of Adolescent Health, 48*(4), 415–417.

Wang, J., & others (2017). Sex differences in the effects of prenatal lead exposure on birth outcomes. *Environmental Pollution, 225,* 193–200.

Wang, L., & Palacios, E.L. (2017, in press). The social and spatial patterning of life stress among immigrants in Canada. *Journal of Immigrant and Minority Health.*

Wang, M.T., Ye, F., & Degol, J.L. (2017, in press). Who chooses STEM careers? Using a relative cognitive strength and interest model to predict careers in science, technology, engineering, and mathematics. *Journal of Youth and Adolescence.*

Wang, S., & others (2017). Early and late state processing abnormalities in autism spectrum disorders: An ERP study. *PLoS One, 12*(5), e0178542.

Wang, T., & others (2017). Polygenic risk for five psychiatric disorders and cross-disorder and disorder-specific neural connectivity in two independent populations. *Neuroimage Clinics, 14,* 441–449.

Wang, W.Y., & others (2017). Impacts of CD33 genetic variations on the atrophy rates of hippocampus and parahippocampal gyrus in normal aging and mild cognitive impairment. *Molecular Neurobiology, 54,* 1111–1118.

Ward, D.S., & others (2017). Strength of obesity prevention interventions in early care and education settings: A systematic review. *Preventive Medicine, 95*(Suppl. 1), S37–S52.

Wardlaw, G., Smith, A., & Collene, A. (2018). *Wardlaw's contemporary nutrition* (5th ed.). New York: McGraw-Hill.

Warren, S.F., & others (2017). The longitudinal effects of parenting on adaptive behavior in children with fragile X syndrome. *Journal of Autism and Developmental Disorders, 47,* 768–784.

Warrick, P. (1992, March 1). The fantastic voyage of Tanner Roberts. *Los Angeles Times,* pp. E1, E11, E12.

Warshak, R.A. (2008, January). Personal communication. Department of Psychology, University of Texas at Dallas, Richardson.

Warshak, R.A. (2014). Social science and parenting plans for young children: A consensus report. *Psychology, Public Policy, and the Law, 20,* 46–67.

Wasserberg, M.J. (2014). Stereotype threat effects on African American children in an urban elementary school. *Journal of Experimental Education, 82,* 502–517.

Wataganara, T., & others (2016). Fetal magnetic resonance imaging and ultrasound. *Journal of Perinatal Medicine, 44,* 533–542.

Watamura, S.E., Phillips, D.A., Morrissey, T.W., McCartney, K., & Bub, K. (2011). Double jeopardy: Poorer socio-emotional outcomes for children in the NICHD SECCYD who experience home and child-care environments that confer risk. *Child Development, 82,* 48–65.

Watanabe, E., Lee, J.S., Mori, K., & Kawakubo, K. (2016). Clustering patterns of obesity-related multiple lifestyle behaviors and their associations with overweight and family environments: A cross-sectional study in Japanese preschool children. *BMJ Open, 6* (11), e012773.

Waterman, A.S. (1985). Identity in the context of adolescent psychology. In A.S. Waterman (Ed.), *Identity in adolescence: Processes and contents.* San Francisco: Jossey-Bass.

Waterman, A.S. (1999). Identity, the identity statuses, and identity status development: A contemporary statement. *Developmental Review, 19,* 591–621.

Waters, S.F., West, T.V., & Mendes, W.B. (2014). Stress contagion: Physiological covariation between mothers and infants. *Psychological Science, 25,* 934–942.

Waters, T.E., Ruiz, S.K., & Roisman, G.I. (2017). Origins of secure base script knowledge and the developmental construction of attachment representations. *Child Development, 88,* 198–209.

Watson, G.L., Arcona, A.P., Antonuccio, D.O., & Healy, D. (2014). Shooting the messenger: The case of ADHD. *Journal of Contemporary Psychotherapy, 44,* 43–52.

Watson, J.B. (1928). *Psychological care of infant and child.* New York: W.W. Norton.

Watson, J.B., & Rayner, R. (1920). Conditioned emotional reactions. *Journal of Experimental Psychology, 3,* 1–14.

Waxman, S. (2013). Building a better bridge. In M. Banaji, S. Gelman, & S. Lehr (Eds.), *Navigating the social world: The early years.* New York: Oxford University Press.

Waxman, S., & others (2013). Are nouns learned before verbs? Infants provide insight into a longstanding debate. *Child Development Perspectives, 7,* 155–159.

Weatherhead, D., & White, K.S. (2017). Read my lips: Visual speech influences word processing by infants. *Cognition, 160,* 103–109.

Webb, L.D., & Metha, A. (2017). *Foundations of American education* (8th ed.). Upper Saddle River, NJ: Pearson.

Webber, T.A., & others (2017). Neural outcome processing of peer-influenced risk-taking behavior in late adolescence: Preliminary evidence for gene x environment interactions. *Experimental and Clinical Psychopharmacology, 25,* 31–40.

Weber, D., Dekhtyar, S., & Herlitz, A. (2017). The Flynn effect in Europe—effects of sex and region. *Intelligence, 60,* 39–45.

Weber, M.A., Risdon, R.S., Ashworth, M.T., Malone, M.T., & Sebire, N.J. (2012). Autopsy findings of co-sleeping-associated sudden unexpected death in infancy: Relationship between pathological features and asphyxial mode of death. *Journal of Pediatric and Child Health, 48,* 335–341.

Webster, N.S., & Worrell, F.C. (2008). Academically-talented adolescents' attitudes toward service in the community. *Gifted Child Quarterly, 52,* 170–179.

Weersing, V.R., & others (2016). Prevention of depression in at-risk adolescents: Predictors and moderators of acute effects. *Journal of the American Academy of Child and Adolescent Psychiatry, 55,* 219–226.

Weersing, V.R., & others (2017). Evidence base update of psychosocial treatments for child and adolescent depression. *Journal of Clinical Child and Adolescent Psychology, 46,* 11–43.

Weikart, D.P. (1993). [Long-term positive effects in the Perry Preschool Head Start Program.] Unpublished data. HighScope Foundation, Ypsilanti, MI.

Weiler, L.M., & Taussig, H.N. (2017, in press). The moderating effect of risk exposure on an efficacious intervention for maltreated children. *Journal of Clinical Child and Adolescent Psychology.*

Weinraub, M., & others (2012). Patterns of developmental change in infants' nighttime sleep awakenings from 6 through 36 months of age. *Developmental Psychology, 48,* 1511–1528.

Weinstein, N., Deci, E.L., & Ryan, R.M. (2012). Motivational determinants of integrating positive and negative past identities. *Journal of Personality and Social Psychology, 100,* 527–544.

Weisleder, A., & Fernald, A. (2013). Talking to children matters: Early language experience strengthens processing and builds vocabulary. *Psychological Science, 24,* 2143–2152.

Weisman, O., Zagoory-Sharon, O., & Feldman, R. (2014). Oxtocin administration, salivary testosterone, and father-infant social behavior. *Progress in Neuro-Psychopharmacology and Biological Psychiatry, 49,* 47–52.

Weisner, T.S., & Duncan, G.J. (2014). The world isn't linear or additive or decontextualized: Pluralism and mixed methods in understanding the effects of antipoverty programs on children and parenting. In E.T. Gershoff, R.S. Mistry, & D.A. Crosby (Eds.), *The societal contexts of child development.* New York: Oxford University Press.

Weiss, L.A., & others (2008). Association between microdeletion and microduplication at 16p11.2 and autism. *New England Journal of Medicine, 358,* 667–675.

Weissenberger, S., & others (2017). ADHD, lifestyles, and comorbidities: A call for an holistic perspective—from medical to societal intervening factors. *Frontiers in Psychology, 8,* 454.

Weisstanner, C., & others (2017). Fetal MRI at 3T—ready for routine use? *British Journal of Radiology, 90,* 20160362.

Wekerle, C., & others (2009). The contribution of childhood emotional abuse to teen dating violence among child protective services–involved youth. *Child Abuse and Neglect, 33*(1), 45–58.

Wellman, H.M. (2011). Developing a theory of mind. In U. Goswami (Ed.), *Wiley-Blackwell handbook of childhood cognitive development* (2nd ed.). Wiley.

Wellman, H.M. (2015). *Making minds.* New York: Oxford University Press.

Wellman, H.M., Cross, D., & Watson, J. (2001). Meta-analysis of theory-of-mind development: The truth about false belief. *Child Development, 72,* 655–684.

Wellman, H.M., & Woolley, J.D. (1990). From simple desires to ordinary beliefs: The early development of everyday psychology. *Cognition, 35,* 245–275.

Wells, E.M., & others (2011). Body burdens of mercury, lead, selenium, and copper among Baltimore newborns. *Environmental Research, 111*(3), 411–417.

Wendelken, C., Gerrer, E., Whitaker, K.J., & Bunge, S.A. (2016). Fronto-parietal network reconfiguration supports the development of reasoning ability. *Cerebral Cortex, 26,* 2178–2190.

Wennergren, G., & others (2015). Updated Swedish advice on reducing the risk of sudden infant death syndrome. *Acta Pediatrica, 104,* 444–448.

Wentzel, K.R., & Asher, S.R. (1995). The academic lives of neglected, rejected, popular, and controversial children. *Child Development, 66,* 754–763.

Wentzel, K.R., Barry, C.M., & Caldwell, K.A. (2004). Friendships in middle school: Influences on motivation and school adjustment. *Journal of Educational Psychology, 96,* 195–203.

Wentzel, K.R., & Miele, D.B. (Eds.) (2016). *Handbook of motivation at school* (2nd ed.). New York: Routledge.

Wentzel, K.R., & Munecks, K. (2016). Peer influence on students' motivation, academic achievement, and social behavior. In K.R. Wentzel & G. Ramani (Eds.), *Handbook of social influences in school contexts.* New York: Routledge.

Wentzel, K.R., & Ramani, G. (2016). *Social influences on social-emotional, motivational, and cognitive outcomes in school contexts.* New York: Taylor & Francis.

Werker, J.F., & Gervain, J. (2013). Speech perception in infancy: A foundation of language acquisition. In P.D. Zelazo (Ed.), *Handbook of developmental psychology.* New York: Oxford University Press.

Werker, J.F., & Tees, R.C. (2005). Speech perception as a window for understanding plasticity and commitment in language systems of the brain. *Developmental Psychobiology, 46,* 233–251.

Wermelinger, S., Gampe, A., & Daum, M.M. (2017). Bilingual toddlers have advanced abilities to repair communication failure. *Journal of Experimental Child Psychology, 155,* 84–94.

Werner, N.E., & others (2014). Maternal social coaching quality interrupts the development of relational aggression during early childhood. *Social Development, 23,* 470–486.

Wesseling, P.B., Christmann, C.A., & Lachmann, T. (2017). Shared book reading promotes not only language development, but also grapheme awareness in German kindergarten children. *Frontiers in Psychology, 8,* 364.

Westermann, G. (2016). Experience-dependent brain development as a key to understanding the language system. *Topics in Cognitive Science, 8,* 446–458.

Westermann, G., Thomas, M.S.C., & Karmiloff-Smith, A. (2011). Neuroconstructivism. In U. Goswami (Ed.), *Wiley-Blackwell handbook of childhood cognitive development* (2nd ed.). New York: Wiley.

Westmoreland, P., Krantz, M.J., & Mehler, P.S. (2016). Medical complications of anorexia nervosa and bulimia. *American Journal of Medicine, 129,* 30–37.

Weyandt, L.L., & others (2017). Neuropsychological functioning in college students with and without ADHD. *Neuropsychology, 31,* 160–172.

Whaley, S.E., Jiang, L., Gomez, J., & Jenks, E. (2011). Literacy promotion for families participating in the Women, Infants, and Children program. *Pediatrics, 127,* 454–461.

Wheeden, A., & others (1993). Massage effects on cocaine-exposed preterm neonates. *Journal of Developmental and Behavioral Pediatrics, 14,* 318–322.

White, B.A., & Kistner, J.A. (2011). Biased self-perceptions, peer rejection, and aggression in children. *Journal of Abnormal Child Psychology, 39,* 645–656.

White, R.E., & Carlson, S.M. (2016). What would Batman do? Self-distancing improves executive function in young children. *Developmental Science, 19,* 419–426.

White, R.E., & others (2017, in press). The "Batman effect": Improving perseverance in young children. *Child Development.*

White, R.M., & others (2017, in press). Ethnic socialization in neighborhood contexts: Implications for ethnic attitude and identity development among Mexican-origin adolescents. *Child Development.*

Whiten, A. (2017). Social learning and culture in child and chimpanzee. *Annual Review of Psychology* (Vol. 68). Palo Alto, CA: Annual Reviews.

Widman, L., Choukas-Bradley, S., Helms, S.W., & Prinstein, M.J. (2016). Adolescent susceptibility to peer influence in sexual situations. *Journal of Adolescent Health, 58,* 323–329.

Widom, C.S., Czaja, S.J., & DuMont, K.A. (2015). Intergenerational transmission of child abuse and neglect: Real or detection bias? *Science, 347,* 1480–1485.

Wiesen, S.E., Watkins, R.M., & Needham, A.W. (2016). Active motor training has long-term effects on infants' object exploration. *Frontiers in Psychology, 7,* 599.

Wigfield, A., & Asher, S.R. (1994). Social and motivational influences on reading. In P.D. Pearson & others (Eds.), *Handbook of reading research.* New York: Longman.

Wigfield, A., Eccles, J.S., Fredricks, J., Simplins, S., Roeser, R., & Schiefele, U. (2015). Development of achievement motivation and engagement. In R.M. Lerner (Ed.), *Handbook of child psychology and developmental science* (7th ed.). New York: Wiley.

Wigfield, A., Tonks, S.M., & Klauda, S.L. (2016) Expectancy-value theory. In K.R. Wentzel & D.B. Miele (Eds.), *Handbook of motivation at school.* New York: Routledge.

Wigfield, A., & others (2015). Development of achievement motivation and engagement. In R.M. Lerner (Ed.), *Handbook of child psychology and developmental science* (7th ed.). New York: Wiley.

Wigginton, B., Gartner, C., & Rowlands, I.J. (2017). Is it safe to vape? Analyzing online forums discussing E-cigarette use during pregnancy. *Women's Health Issues, 27,* 93–99.

Wilce, J.M. (2017). *Culture and communication.* New York: Cambridge University Press.

Wilcox, S., & Occhino, C. (2017). Signed languages. In B. Dancygier (Ed.), *Cambridge handbook of cognitive linguistics.* New York: Cambridge University Press.

Willey, J., Sherwood, L., & Woolverton, C. (2017). *Prescott's microbiology* (10th ed.). New York: McGraw-Hill.

Williams, A.M., & others (2016). Breastfeeding and complementary feeding practices among HIV-exposed infants in coastal Tanzania. *Journal of Human Lactation, 32,* 112–122.

Williams, C.M., & others (2017). Kentucky health access nurturing development services home visiting program improves maternal and child health. *Maternal and Child Health Journal, 21,* 1166–1174.

Williams, D., & Happe, F. (2010). Representing intentions in self and others: Studies of autism and typical development. *Developmental Science, 13,* 307–319.

Williams, J.H., & Ross, L. (2007). Consequences of prenatal toxin exposure for mental health in children and adolescents: A systematic review. *European Child and Adolescent Psychiatry, 16,* 243–253.

Williams, K.M., Nathanson, C., & Paulhus, D.L. (2010). Identifying and profiling academic cheaters: Their personality, cognitive ability, and motivation. *Journal of Experimental Psychology: Applied, 16,* 293–307.

Williams, S.R., & others (2016). Shared genetic susceptibility of vascular-related biomarkers with ischemic and recurrent stroke. *Neurology, 86,* 351–359.

Williamson, R.A., Donohue, M.R., & Tully, E.C. (2013). Learning how to help others: Two-year-olds' social learning of a prosocial act. *Journal of Experimental Child Psychology, 114,* 543–550.

Willoughby, M.T., Gottfredson, N.C., & Stifter, C.A. (2016). Observed temperament from ages 6 to 36 months predicts parent- and teacher-reported attention deficit/hyperactivity disorder symptoms in first grade. *Development and Psychopathology, 29,* 107–120.

Willoughby, M.T., & others (2017, in press). Developmental delays in executive function from 3 to 5 years of age predict kindergarten academic readiness. *Journal of Learning Disabilities.* doi:10.1177/0022219415619754

Wilson, B.J. (2008). Media and children's aggression, fear, and altruism. *Future of Children, 18*(1), 87–118.

Wilson, S.F., & others (2017). Doulas for surgical management of miscarriage and abortion: A randomized controlled trial. *American Journal of Obstetrics and Gynecology, 216,* e1–e44.

Winne, P.H. (2018). Cognition and metacognition within self-regulated learning. In D.H. Schunk & J.A. Greene (Eds.), *Handbook of self-regulation of learning and performance* (2nd ed.). New York: Cambridge University Press.

Winner, E. (1986, August). Where pelicans kiss seals. *Psychology Today,* pp. 24–35.

Winner, E. (1996). *Gifted children: Myths and realities.* New York: Basic Books.

Winner, E. (2000). The origins and ends of giftedness. *American Psychologist, 55,* 159–169.

Winner, E. (2006). Development in the arts. In W. Damon & R. Lerner (Eds.), *Handbook of child psychology* (6th ed.). New York: Wiley.

Winner, E. (2009). Toward broadening our understanding of giftedness: The spatial domain. In F.D. Horowitz, R.F. Subotnik, & D.J. Matthews (Eds.), *The development of giftedness and talent across the life span.* Washington, DC: American Psychological Association.

Winner, E. (2014). Child prodigies and adult genius: A weak link. In D.K. Simonton (Ed.), *Wiley-Blackwell handbook of genius.* New York: Wiley.

Winsler, A., Carlton, M.P., & Barry, M.J. (2000). Age-related changes in preschool children's systematic use of private speech in a natural setting. *Journal of Child Language, 27,* 665–687.

Witherington, D.C., Campos, J.J., Harriger, J.A., Bryan, C., & Margett, T.E. (2010). Emotion and its development in infancy. In J.G. Bremner & T.D. Wachs (Eds.), *Wiley-Blackwell handbook of infant development* (2nd ed.). New York: Wiley.

Witkow, M.R., Rickert, N.P., & Cullen, L.E. (2017). Daily school context of adolescents' single best friendship and adjustment. *Journal of Genetic Psychology, 178,* 119–132.

Witt, N., Coynor, S., Edwards, C., & Bradshaw, H. (2016). A guide to pain assessment and management in the neonate. *Current Emergency and Hospital Medicine Reports, 4,* 1–10.

Wojcicki, J.M. (2017). Time to consider moving beyond exclusive breastfeeding in Southern Africa. *Children, 4,* 1.

Wolke, D., Lee, K., & Guy, A. (2017, in press). Cyberbullying: A storm in a teacup? *European Child and Adolescent Psychiatry.*

Wolke, D., & Lereya, S.T. (2015). Long-term effects of bullying. *Archives of Disease in Childhood, 100,* 879–885.

Women's Sports Foundation (2001). *The 10 commandments for parents and coaches in youth sports.* Eisenhower Park, NY: Women's Sports Foundation.

Wong, M., & others (2017, in press). Use of time and adolescent health-related quality of life/wellbeing: A scoping review. *Acta Pediatrica.*

Wood, D., Kaplan, R., & McLoyd, V.C. (2007). Gender differences in educational expectations of urban, low-income African American youth: The role of parents and schools. *Journal of Youth and Adolescence, 36,* 417–427.

Woodward, A.L., & Markman, E.M. (1998). Early word learning. In D. Kuhn & R.S. Siegler (Eds.), *Handbook of child psychology* (5th ed., Vol. 2). New York: Wiley.

Woodward, A., Markman, E., & Fitzsimmons, C. (1994). Rapid word learning in 13- and 18-month-olds. *Developmental Psychology, 30,* 553–556.

World Health Organization (2000, February 2). Adolescent health behavior in 28 countries. Geneva, Switzerland: World Health Organization.

World Health Organization (2017). *Micronutrients.* Retrieved May 1, 2017, from www.who.int/nutrition/micronutrients/en/

World Health Organization (2017). *Quality of care in contraceptive information and services, based on human rights standards: A checklist for health care providers.* Geneva, Switzerland: Author.

Wu, R., & Scerif, G. (2018, in press). Attention. In M.H. Bornstein & others (Eds.), *SAGE encyclopedia of lifespan development.* Thousand Oaks, CA: Sage.

Wu, X., & others (2017 in press). Finding gastric cancer related genes and clinical biomarkers for detection based gene-gene interaction network. *Mathematical Biosciences.*

Wu, Z.M., & others (2017). White matter microstructural alterations in children with ADHD: Categorical and dimensional perspectives. *Neuropsychopharmacology, 42,* 572–580.

Wuest, D.A., & Fisette, J.L. (2015). *Foundations of physical education, exercise science, and sport* (18th ed.). New York: McGraw-Hill.

Wyciszkiewicz, A., Pawlak, M.A., & Krawlec, K. (2017). Cerebral volume in children with attention-deficit/hyperactivity disorder (ADHD): Replication study. *Journal of Child Neurology, 32,* 215–221.

X

Xaverius, P., Alman, C., Holtz, L., & Yarber, L. (2016). Risk factors associated with very low birth weight in a large urban area, stratified by adequacy of prenatal care. *Maternal Child Health Journal, 20,* 623–629.

Xia, N. (2010). *Family factors and student outcomes.* Unpublished doctoral dissertation, RAND Corporation, Pardee RAND Graduate School, Pittsburgh.

Xie, C., & others (2017). Exercise and dietary program-induced weight reduction is associated with cognitive function in obese adolescents: A longitudinal study. *PeerJ, 5,* e3286.

Xie, Q., & Young, M.E. (1999). Integrated child development in rural China. *Education: The World Bank.* Washington, DC: The World Bank.

Xie, W., & Richards, J.E. (2016). Effects of interstimulus intervals on behavioral, heart rate, and event-related potential indices of infant engagement and sustained attention. *Psychophysiology, 53,* 1128–1142.

Xie, W., & Richards, J.E. (2017). The relation between infant covert orienting, sustained attention, and brain activity. *Brain Topography, 30,* 198–219.

Xu, H., Wen, L.M., Hardy, L.L., & Rissel, C. (2016). Associations of outdoor play and screen time with nocturnal sleep duration and pattern among young children. *Acta Pediatrica, 105,* 297–303.

Xu, J., & others (2016). DNA methylation levels of imprinted and nonimprinted genes DMRs associated with defective human spermatozoa. *Andrologia, 48,* 939–947.

Xu, L., & others (2011). Parental overweight/obesity, social factors, and child overweight/obesity at 7 years of age. *Pediatric International, 53*(6), 826–831.

Xue, F., Holzman, C., Rahbar, M.H., Trosko, K., & Fischer, L. (2007). Maternal fish consumption, mercury levels, and risk of preterm delivery. *Environmental Health Perspectives, 115,* 42–47.

Y

Yamaoka, Y., Fujiwara, T., & Tamiya, N. (2016). Association between maternal postpartum depression and unintentional injury among 4-month-old infants in Japan. *Maternal and Child Health Journal, 20,* 326–336.

Yang, B., Ren, B.X., & Tang, F.R. (2017). Prenatal irradiation-induced brain neuropathy and cognitive impairment. *Brain Development, 39,* 10–22.

Yanof, J.A. (2013). Play technique in psychodynamic psychotherapy. *Child and Adolescent Psychiatric Clinics of North America, 22,* 261–282.

Yap, M.B., & others (2017, in press). Modifiable parenting factors associated with adolescent alcohol misuse: A systematic review and meta-analysis of longitudinal studies. *Addiction.*

Yasnitsky, A., & Van der Veer, R. (Eds.) (2016). *Revisionist revolution in Vygotsky studies.* New York: Psychology Press.

Yawn, B.P., & John-Sowah, J. (2015). Management of sickle-cell disease: Recommendations from the 2014 expert panel report. *American Family Physician, 92,* 1069–1076.

Yazejian, N., & others (2017, in press). Child and parenting outcomes after 1 year of Educare. *Child Development.*

Yazigi, A., & others (2017). Fetal and neonatal abnormalities due to congenital rubella syndrome: A review of the literature. *Journal of Maternal-Fetal and Neonatal Medicine, 30,* 274–278.

Yen, C.F., & others (2014). Association between school bullying levels/types and mental health problems among Taiwanese adolescents. *Comprehensive Psychiatry, 55,* 405–413.

Yeo, S., Crandell, J.L., & Jones-Vessey, K. (2016). Adequacy of prenatal care and gestational weight gain. *Journal of Women's Health, 25,* 117–123.

Yeon, S., Bae, H.S., & Joshi, M. (2017, in press). Cross-language transfer of metalinguistic skills: Evidence from spelling English words by Korean students in grades 4, 5, and 6. *Dyslexia.*

Yi, X., & others (2017, in press). Interaction among COX-2, P2Y1, and GPIIIa gene variants is associated with aspirin resistance and early neurological deterioration in Chinese stroke patients. *BMC Neurology.*

Yilmaz, D., & others (2017). Screening 5- and 6-year-old children starting primary school for development and language. *Turkish Journal of Pediatrics, 58,* 136–144.

Yin, R.K. (2012). Case study methods. In H. Cooper (Ed.), *APA handbook of research methods in psychology.* Washington, DC: American Psychological Association.

Yonker, J.E., Schnabelrauch, C.A., & DeHaan, L.G. (2012). The relationship between spirituality and religiosity on psychological outcomes in adolescents and emerging adults: A meta-analytic review. *Journal of Adolescence, 35,* 299–314.

Yoon, E., & others (2017). East Asian adolescents' ethnic identity and cultural integration: A qualitative investigation. *Journal of Counseling Psychology, 64,* 65–79.

Yoshikawa, H., & others (2016). Money, time, and peers in antipoverty programs for low-income families. In C.S. Tamis-LeMonda & L. Balter (Eds), *Child psychology: A handbook of contemporary issues.* New York: Taylor & Francis.

Yoshikawa, H., & others (2017, in press). New directions in developmentally informed intervention research for vulnerable populations. *Child Development*.

You, W., & others (2016). Robust preprocessing for stimulus-based functional MRI of the moving fetus. *Journal of Medical Imaging, 3,* 026001.

Young, K.T. (1990). American conceptions of infant development from 1955 to 1984: What the experts are telling parents. *Child Development, 61,* 17–28.

Youniss, J., McLellan, J.A., & Yates, M. (1999). Religion, community service, and identity in American youth. *Journal of Adolescence, 22,* 243–253.

Yow, W.Q., & others (2017, in press). A bilingual advantage in 54-month-olds' use of referential cues in fast mapping. *Developmental Science*.

YRBSS (2016). *Youth Risk Surveillance System.* Atlanta: Centers for Disease Control and Prevention.

Yu, C., & Smith, L.B. (2016). The social origins of sustained attention in one-year-old humans. *Current Biology, 26,* 1235–1240.

Yu, C., & Smith, L.B. (2017, in press). Hand-eye coordination predicts joint attention. *Child Development*.

Yu, J., Cheah, C.S., & Calvin, G. (2016). Acculturation, psychological adjustment, and parenting styles of Chinese immigrant mothers in the United States. *Cultural Diversity and Ethnic Minority Psychology, 22,* 504–516.

Yu, J., Wu, Y., & Yang, P. (2016). High glucose-induced oxidative stress represses sirtuin deacetylase expression and increases histone acetylation leading to neural tube defects. *Journal of Neurochemistry, 137,* 371–383.

Yu, R., Branje, S., Keijsers, L., Koot, H.M., & Meeus, W. (2013). Pals, problems, and personality: The moderating role of personality in the longitudinal association between adolescents' and best friends' delinquency. *Journal of Personality, 81,* 499–509.

Yu, S., & Hu, G. (2017). Can higher-proficiency L2 learners benefit from working with lower-proficiency partners in peer feedback? *Teaching in Higher Education, 22,* 178–192.

Yuan, A.S.V. (2010). Body perceptions, weight control behavior, and changes in adolescents' psychological well-being over time: A longitudinal examination of gender. *Journal of Youth and Adolescence, 39,* 927–939.

Yuan, B., & others (2017). Autism-related protein MeCP2 regulates FGF13 expression and emotional behaviors. *Journal of Genetics and Genomics, 44,* 63–66.

Yudkin, D., Hayward, B., Aladjem, M.I., Kumari, D., & Usdin, K. (2014). Chromosome fragility and the abnormal replication of the FMR1 locus in fragile X syndrome. *Human Molecular Genetics, 23,* 2940–2952.

Yun, K., & others (2014). Effects of maternal-child home visitation on pregnancy spacing for first-time Latina mothers. *American Journal of Public Health, 104* (Suppl. 1), S152–S158.

Z

Zabaneh, D., & others (2017). Fine mapping genetic associations between the HLA region and extremely high intelligence. *Scientific Reports, 7,* 41182.

Zaca, C., & Borini, A. (2017). Chapter 8: Human oocytes slow-rate freezing: Methodology. *Methods in Molecular Biology, 1568,* 105–117.

Zachrisson, H.D., Lekhal, R., Dearing, E., & Toppelberg, C.O. (2013). Little evidence that time in child care causes externalizing problems during early childhood in Norway. *Child Development, 84,* 1152–1170.

Zalewski, B.M., & others (2017). Nutrition of infants and young children (one to three years) and its effect on later health: A systematic review of current recommendations (EarlyNutrition project). *Critical Reviews in Food Science and Nutrition, 57,* 489–500.

Zamuner, T., Fais, L., & Werker, J.F. (2014). Infants track words in early word-object associations. *Developmental Science, 17,* 481–491.

Zandoná, M.R., & others (2017). Validation of obesity susceptibility loci identified by genome-wide association studies in early childhood in South Brazilian children. *Pediatric Obesity*.

Zannas, A.S., & others (2012). Stressful life events, perceived stress, and 12-month course of geriatric depression: Direct effects and moderation by the 5-HTTLPR and COMT Val158Met polymorphisms. *Stress, 15*(4), 425–434.

Zarate-Garza, P.P., & others (2017). How well do we understand the long-term health implications of childhood bullying? *Harvard Review of Psychiatry, 25,* 89–95.

Zelazo, P.D. (2013). Developmental psychology: A new synthesis. In P.D. Zelazo (Ed.), *Oxford handbook of developmental psychology.* New York: Oxford University Press.

Zelazo, P.D., & Lyons, K.E. (2012). The potential benefits of mindfulness training in early childhood: A developmental social cognitive neuroscience perspective. *Child Development Perspectives, 6,* 154–160.

Zhang, L.-F., & Sternberg, R.J. (2012). Learning in cross-cultural perspective. In T. Husen & T.N. Postlethwaite (Eds.), *International encyclopedia of education* (3rd ed.). New York: Elsevier.

Zelazo, P.D., & Muller, U. (2011). Executive function in typical and atypical children. In U. Goswami (Ed.), *Wiley-Blackwell handbook of childhood cognitive development* (2nd ed.). New York: Wiley.

Zeller, M.H., Reiter-Purtill, J., & Ramey, C. (2008). Negative peer perceptions of obese children in the classroom environment. *Obesity, 16,* 755–762.

Zentall, S.S. (2006). *ADHD and education.* Upper Saddle River, NJ: Prentice Hall.

Zeskind, P.S. (2007). Impact of the cry of the infant at risk on psychosocial development. In R.E. Tremblay, R. deV. Peters, M. Boivin, & R.G. Barr (Eds.), *Encyclopedia on early childhood development.* Montreal: Centre of Excellence for Early Childhood Development. Retrieved November 24, 2008, from http://www.child-encyclopedia.com/en-ca/list-of-topics.html

Zhai, F., Raver, C.C., & Jones, S. (2012). Quality of subsequent schools and impacts of early interventions: Evidence from a randomized controlled trial in Head Start settings. *Children and Youth Services Review, 34,* 946–954.

Zhai, L., & others (2015). Association of obesity with onset of puberty and sex hormones in Chinese girls: A 4-year longitudinal study. *PLoS One, 10*(8), e134656.

Zhang, D., & others (2017). Is maternal smoking during pregnancy associated with an increased risk of congenital heart defects among offspring? A systematic review and meta-analysis of observational studies. *Journal of Maternal-Fetal and Neonatal Medicine, 30,* 645–657.

Zhang, H., & others (2017). Prolactin, a potential mediator of reduced social interactive behavior in newborn infants following maternal perinatal depressive symptoms. *Journal of Affective Disorders, 215,* 274–280.

Zhang, J., & others (2017, in press). Sleep patterns and mental health correlates in U.S. adolescents. *Journal of Pediatrics*.

Zhang, T., & others (2016). Temporal relationship between childhood body mass index and insulin and its impact on adult hypertension: The Bogalusa Heart Study. *Hypertension, 68,* 818–823.

Zhang, W., & others (2017, in press). Reconsidering parenting in Chinese culture: Subtypes, stability, and change of maternal parenting style during early adolescence. *Journal of Youth and Adolescence*.

Zhang, Y., & others (2017). Cross-cultural consistency and diversity in intrinsic functional organization of Broca's region. *NeuroImage, 150,* 177–190.

Zhang, Y.X., Wang, Z.X., Zhao, J.S., & Chu, Z.H. (2016). The current prevalence and regional disparities in general and central obesity among children and adolescents in Shandong, China. *International Journal of Cardiology, 227,* 89–93.

Zheng, Y., & others (2017). Capturing parenting as a multidimensional and dynamic construct with a person-oriented approach. *Prevention Science, 18,* 281–291.

Zhou, Q. (2013). Commentary in S. Smith, Children of "tiger parents" develop more aggression and depression, research shows. Retrieved July 20, 2013, from http://www.cbsnews.com/news/children-of-tiger-parents-develop-more-aggression-and-depression-research-shows/

Zhou, Q., & others (2013). Asset and protective factors for Asian American children's mental health adjustment. *Child Development Perspectives, 6,* 312–319.

Zhu, H. (2016). Forkhead box transcription factors in embryonic heart development and congenital heart disease. *Life Sciences, 144,* 194–201.

Zielinski, D.S. (2009). Child maltreatment and adult socioeconomic well-being. *Child Abuse and Neglect, 33,* 666–678.

Zielinski, R.E., Brody, M.G., & Low, L.K. (2016). The value of the maternity care team in the promotion of physiologic birth. *Journal of Obstetric, Gynecological, and Neonatal Nursing, 45,* 275–284.

Ziermans, T., & others (2017, in press). Formal thought disorder and executive functioning in children and adolescents with autism spectrum disorder: Old leads and new avenues. *Journal of Autism and Developmental Disorders.*

Zigler, E., Gilliam, W.S., & Jones, S.M. (2006). *A vision for universal preschool education.* New York: Cambridge University Press.

Zigler, E.F., & Styfco, S.J. (1994). Head Start: Criticisms in a constructive context. *American Psychologist, 49,* 127–132.

Zigler, E.F., & Styfco, S.J. (2010). *The hidden history of Head Start.* New York: Oxford University Press.

Zimmerman, B.J., Schunk, D.H., & DiBenedetto, M.K. (2017). Role of self-efficacy and related beliefs in self-regulation of learning and performance. In A.J. Elliott, C.S. Dweck, & D.S. Yeager (Eds.). *Handbook of competence and motivation* (2nd ed.). New York: Guilford.

Zimmerman, F.J., Christakis, D.A., & Meltzoff, A.N. (2007). Association between media viewing and language development in children under age 2 years. *Journal of Pediatrics, 151,* 364–368.

Zinn, M.B., & Wells, B. (2000). Diversity within Latino families: New lessons for family social science. In D.M. Demo, K.R. Allen, & M.A. Fine (Eds.), *Handbook of family diversity.* New York: Oxford University Press.

Ziol-Guest, K.M. (2009). Child custody and support. In D. Carr (Ed.), *Encyclopedia of the life course and human development.* Boston: Cengage.

Zirpoli, T.J. (2016). *Behavior management* (7th ed.). Upper Saddle River, NJ: Pearson.

Zoller, D., & others (2017). Home exercise training in children and adolescents with pulmonary arterial hypertension: A pilot study. *Pediatric Cardiology, 38,* 191–198.

Zosh, J., & others (2017). Putting the education back in education apps: How content and context interact to promote learning. In R. Barr & D. Linebarger (Eds.), *Media exposure during infancy and early childhood.* New York: Springer.

Zosh, J.M., Hirsh-Pasek, K., & Golinkoff, R. (2015). Guided play. In D.L. Couchenour & K. Chrisman (Eds.), *Encyclopedia of contemporary early childhood education.* Thousand Oaks, CA: Sage.

Zosuls, K., & others (2016). Developmental changes in the link between gender typicality and peer victimization and exclusion. *Sex Roles, 75,* 243–256.

Zucker, K.J., Lawrence, A.A., & Kreukels, B.P. (2016). Gender dysphoria in adults. *Annual Review of Psychology, 12,* 217–247.

Zucker, R.A., Hicks, B.M., & Heitzeg, M.M. (2016). Alcohol use and the alcohol use disorders over the life course. In D. Cicchetti (Ed.), *Developmental psychopathology* (3rd ed.). New York: Wiley.

name index

Buhs, E., 402
Buhs, E. S., 401
Buijus, D., 125
Buitelaar, J., 330
Bukowski, R., 93, 108
Bukowski, W. M., 303, 304, 400–402, 500
Bulik, C. M., 442, 443
Bullard, J., 229, 230
Bullock, M., 199
Bumpus, M. F., 483
Bunders, M. J., 75
Bunn, J., 53
Buratti, S., 351
Burchinal, M., 212
Bureau, J. F., 279, 483
Burger, S., 83
Burgers, D. E., 401
Burgette, J. M., 268
Buriel, R., 302
Burke, J. D., 497
Burkhart, J. M., 355
Burnett, E., 91
Burnette, J., 337
Burnham, D., 149
Burnham, M. (Ed.), 6
Burnham, M. M., 129
Burns, L., 91
Burns, M. S., 180
Burt, K. B., 420
Burt, S. A., 65
Bush, K. R., 291
Bushnell, E. W., 150
Bushnell, I. W. R., 146
Buss, D. M., 48, 286
Buss, K. A., 195
Bussey, K., 287
Bustos, N., 323
Busuito, A., 200
Butler, Y. G., 367
Butte, N. F., 233
Butts, B., 52
Byard, R. W., 129
Byers, B. E., 48
Byne, W., 481
Byrd-Bredbenner, C., 319
Byrne, J. L., 235
Byrne, R. W., 176
Byrnes, J. P., 249

C

Cabeza, R., 12, 29
Cabrera, N. J., 211
Cacioppo, J. T., 490
Cai, M., 484
Cain, K., 363
Cain, M. A., 90
Cain, M. S., 495
Caino, S., 123
Cairncross, M., 332
Cairns, A., 232
Caldwell, B. A., 231
Caldwell, K. A., 405
Calenda, E., 129
Calkins, S. D., 123, 189, 192, 196, 281, 385, 480
Callaghan, T., 246

Callaway, L. K., 94
Callina, K., 419
Caltran, G., 191
Calvert, S. L., 308, 495
Calvin, G., 296
Calvo-Garcia, M. A., 59
Calzada, E. J., 289
Camacho, A. V., 83
Camacho, D. E., 466
Cameron, C. M., 133
Cameron, J., 369
Camerota, M., 89
Campaert, K., 402
Campbell, B., 355
Campbell, F. A., 357
Campbell, L., 355, 434
Campione-Barr, N., 296
Campos, J. J., 139, 191, 193, 201, 204
Canfield, R. L., 92, 239
Canivez, G. L., 354
Cann, D., 427
Cano, M. A., 7, 301
Canterino, J. C., 94
Cantone, E., 404
Cantor, N., 257
Capaldi, D. M., 488, 489
Carbajal-Valenzuela, C. C., 201
Carbia, C., 452
Card, N. A., 394
Cardoso, C., 88
Carlin, R. E., 129, 130
Carling, S. J., 131
Carlo, G., 7, 67, 290, 391, 392, 460
Carlson, E. A., 205
Carlson, N. S., 103
Carlson, S. M., 257, 258, 317
Carlson, W., 500
Carlson Jones, D., 424
Carlton, M. P., 250
Carnegie Council on Adolescent Development, 465
Carpendale, J. I., 162, 164, 260
Carpendale, J. I. M., 199, 402
Carpenter, M., 180
Carr, R., 443
Carrell, S. E., 461
Carrington, H., 190
Carroll, A. E., 404
Carroll, L., 475
Carskadon, M. A., 438
Carson, V., 308
Carter, A. S., 334
Carter, S. L., 330, 333, 335
Carter, T., 437
Cartwright, R., 128
Caruthers, A. S., 304
Carvalho Bos, S., 231
Carver, L. J., 167
Case, R., 344
CASEL, 385
Casey, B. J., 224, 425, 426, 454
Casey, E. C., 346
Cash, J. E., 474, 475

Casper, D. M., 394
Caspers, K. M., 67
Caspi, A., 67
Cassidy, A. R., 257, 348, 452
Cassidy, J., 15, 203, 205, 206
Cassina, M., 86
Castellvi, P., 500
Castillo, M., 443
Castle, J., 61
Catani, C., 386
Caton-Lemos, L., 113
Catts, H., 177
Cauffman, B. E., 441
Cauffman, E., 497
Causadias, J. M., 189
Cavanagh, S., 467
Cavanagh, S. E., 425
Cazzato, V., 443
Ceci, S. J., 255, 256, 356
Cecil, C. A., 331
Center for Science in the Public Interest, 233
Centers for Disease Control and Prevention, 60, 131, 222, 322, 330, 331, 334, 335, 430, 431, 435
Cercignani, M., 125, 224
Cerrillo-Urbina, A. J., 332
Chaco, A., 181
Chae, S., 211
Chae, S. Y., 83
Challacombe, F. L., 203
Chan, C. H., 429, 502
Chandler, M. J., 260
Chandramouli, B. A., 133
Chandra-Mouli, V., 83
Chang, E. C., 501
Chang, H. Y., 94
Chang, M. W., 134
Chang, M. Y., 105
Chang, Y., 368
Chang, Y. K., 332
Chao, G., 420
Chao, R. K., 291
Chaplin, J. E., 223
Chaplin, T. M., 395
Chapman, L., 112
Charlet, J., 86
Charman, T., 335
Charpak, N., 110
Chase-Lansdale, P. L., 10, 408
Chasnoff, I. J., 91
Chassin, L., 441
Chatterton, Z., 52
Chattin-McNichols, J., 267
Chaturvedi, S., 234
Chaudry, A., 7, 301, 302, 408, 494
Chauhan, S. P., 79
Chavarria, M. C., 425
Chavez, R. S., 261
Cheah, C. S., 296
Chein, J., 455
Chemtob, C. M., 386
Chen, C., 373
Chen, C. H., 105
Chen, D., 401
Chen, F. R., 425

Chen, H., 492
Chen, J., 425, 499
Chen, L. H., 320
Chen, L. W., 88
Chen, M., 478
Chen, P. J., 81
Chen, R., 208
Chen, S., 204
Chen, S. W., 451
Chen, W., 326
Chen, X., 7, 196, 287
Chen, X. K., 109
Cheney, R., 260
Cheng, C. A., 93
Cheng, S., 308
Cheong, J. I., 425
Cherlin, A. J., 399
Cheron, C., 320
Chess, S., 193, 194, 196, 197
Cheung, C. S., 373
Cheung, H. Y, Wu, J., 460, 461
Cheung, R. Y. M., 208
Chevalier, N., 255, 257, 348, 452, 453
Cheyney, M., 105
Chi, M. T., 347
Chikritzhs, T., 440
Childers, J. B., 263
Child Trends, 429
Chin, K. J., 103
Chin, M., 478
Chin, M. Y., 481
Chinn, P. C., 7, 301, 372, 408, 494
Chiocca, E. M., 291
Chiou, W. B., 451
Cho, E. S., 110
Cho, M., 51, 53
Choi, Y. J., 199
Chomsky, N., 178
Chong, C. M., 486
Chou, C. C., 332
Choudhary, M., 110
Choukas-Bradley, S., 405, 429, 441, 487
Chow, C. M., 405
Christ, S. L., 500
Christakis, D. A., 308
Christen, M., 390
Christensen, D. L., 261, 334
Christensen, L. F., 102
Christensen, S., 483
Christmann, C. A., 181
Christopher, E. M., 466
Chu, A. T., 386
Chua, A., 374
Chuang, S. S., 397
Chyka, D. L., 457
Cicchetti, D., 6, 8, 14, 15, 32, 67, 190, 204–206, 292–295, 385, 386, 420, 502
Cigler, H., 357
Cillessen, A. H. N., 304
Cisneros, A. A., 271
Cisneros-Cohernour, E. J., 271
Clara, M., 249–251, 344
Clark, B., 362
Clark, C. D., 304

Clark, D. A., 482
Clark, E. V., 173, 175, 179, 262, 263, 363
Clark, M. S., 500
Clarke-Stewart, A. K., 211–213, 291, 297, 299, 398
Claro, S., 370
Classen, J., 127
Clauss, J. A., 195, 196
Claxton, L. J., 257
Clay, R., 114
Clayton, E. W., 238
Clayton, P. E., 223
Clearfield, M. W., 163
Cleary, M., 333
Cleveland, M. J., 292
Clifton, R. K., 141, 150
Cloud, J., 362
Cloy, J. A., 500
Cnattingius, S., 79
Coan, J. A., 206
Coard, S., 36
Cochet, H., 176
Coffino, B., 205
Coffman, J. L., 348
CogMed, 348
Cohen, A. O., 224, 425, 426, 454
Cohen, G. L., 487
Cohen, J., 82
Cohen, L. G., 127
Cohen, R., 403
Coie, J., 401
Coker, T. R., 308
Colby, A., 389
Colby, S. L., 7
Cole, D. A., 500
Cole, P. M., 190, 195, 281, 282, 385
Cole, W. G., 135, 136
Coleman, M., 399
Coleman-Phox, K., 130
Colemenares, F., 48
Colen, C. G., 132
Coleridge, S. T., 74
Coles, C. D., 88
Coley, R. L., 302
Collene, A., 133, 232, 234
Collier, K. M., 496
Collins, C. E., 323
Collins, D., 458
Collins, M., 342, 343
Collins, W. A., 400, 468, 483, 488, 490
Colombo, B., 95
Colombo, J., 165, 166, 361
Colonnesi, C., 176
Colson, E. R., 129
Colunga, E., 225
Comalli, D. M., 136
Comer, J., 410
Committee for Children, 385
Committee on the Rights of the Child, 291
Common Core State Standards Initiative, 407
Commoner, B., 51

Dunkel Schetter, C., 94
Dunn, E. C., 295
Dunn, J., 295, 296
Dunsmore, J. C., 282
Dunson, D. B., 95
Dupere, V., 468
Durham, R., 112
du Roscoat, E., 501
Durrant, J. E., 7, 292, 294
Durston, S., 317, 453
Dursun, A., 91
Dutta, R., 301
Dweck, C. S., 342, 369, 370
Dworkin, S. L., 428

E

Eagan, K., 457
Eagly, A. H., 287, 394
Eaton, D. K., 428–430
Eaton, W. O., 139
Eccles, J. S., 349, 398, 462, 465, 466
Echevarria, J. J., 36, 367
Ecker, C., 335
Eckstein, K. C., 233
Edel, M. A., 332
Edelman, M. W., 10, 39
Edmiston, B., 305
Ednick, M., 129
Edwards, M. L., 103
Edwardson, C. L., 320
Ee, C., 105
Egeland, B., 294, 468
Eggen, P., 406
Eggum, N. D., 283, 395
Ehehalt, S., 325
Eijkemans, M., 326
Eilertsen, T., 356
Einstein, A., 16
Einziger, T., 195
Eisen, S., 305, 306
Eisenberg, N., 281, 283, 285, 383, 391–393, 395, 396, 457, 459
Eisharkawy, H., 103
Eisler, I., 443
Ekema-Agbaw, M. L., 459
Eklund, K., 360
Elashi, F. B., 279, 280, 382
Elkind, D., 248, 344, 384, 450, 451
Ellenberg, D., 81
Ellickson, P. L., 440
Elliot, A. J., 371
Ellis, B. J., 48, 424
Ellison, A., 166
El-Sheikh, M., 231, 298
Elsner, B., 257, 348
Eltonsy, S., 88
eMarketeer.com, 496
Emberson, L. L., 124
Emerson, R. W., 174, 418
Emery, R. E., 299
Emmer, E. T., 368
Emond, A., 237
Endendijk, J. J., 287
Eneli, I. U., 233

Enfield, A., 458
Engels, A. C., 59
English, G. W., 10
Englund, M. M., 468
Ennett, S. T., 441
Enright, R., 459
Enright, R. D., 459
Ensembl Human, 51
Enslin, P., 434
Ensor, R., 281
Ephron, D., 234
Erickson, S. J., 209
Ericsson, K. A., 346
Erikson, E. H., 18–20, 27, 29, 198, 199, 202, 278, 304, 380, 384, 462, 475–477, 479
Erikson, J., 18
Eriksson, U. J., 92
Erkut, S., 434
Erlich, K. B., 207
Erskine, H. E., 331
Erzinger, A. G., 188, 211
Escalante, Y., 319
Espie, J., 443
Espinosa, A., 479
Esposito, G., 193, 206
Estes, K. G., 176
Estrada, E., 353
Ethier, K. A., 429
Ettekal, I., 402
Etzel, R., 238
Evans, C. E., 325
Evans, G. W., 10, 301, 302
Evans, S. Z., 487, 498
Evans-Lacko, S., 403
Evereklian, M., 110
Evers, C., 14, 48, 53
Everson, C., 105
Evertson, C. M., 368
Ewen, D., 268
Ezkurdia, L., 51

F

Fabes, R. A., 287, 393
Fabiano, G. A., 331
Fabricius, W. V., 299
Fagan, J. F., 172
Fagot, B. I., 288
Fahlke, C., 294
Fairclough, S. J., 323
Fais, L., 176
Faja, S., 257, 317
Falbo, T., 296
Fantz, R. L., 144, 146
Farago, F., 212
Farkas, G., 268
Farkas, T., 287
Farr, R. H., 61, 62, 300, 301
Fasano, R. M., 91
Fasig, L., 198
Fatemi, A., 127, 128
Fatima, M., 94
Faucher, M. A., 102
Faye, P. M., 110
Fazio, L. K., 22
Fear, N. T., 95

Fearon, R. P., 205
Feeney, S., 229, 266, 269
Fein, G. G., 305
Feiring, C., 205
Fekonja-Peklaj, U., 181
Feldman, J. F., 172, 255
Feldman, R., 206, 207
Feldman, S., 257, 427
Feldman, S. S., 429, 483
Feldstein Ewing, S. W., 502
Feleszko, W., 325
Fenning, R. M., 282
Fenson, L., 177
Fergus, T. A., 351, 456
Ferguson, C. J., 292
Fergusson, D. M., 132, 298
Ferketich, A. K., 325
Fernald, A., 180, 181
Fernandez-Jaen, A., 331
Fernandez-Ruiz, J., 228
Fernyhough, C., 250, 279, 483
Ferriby, M., 209
Fertig, A. R., 109
Feubner, C., 205
Fidalgo, R., 365
Field, A. E., 441
Field, T., 111, 147, 163
Field, T. M., 80, 81, 90, 105, 110, 111, 114
Fife, P. J., 394
Fife, T., 298
Figueiredo, B., 299
Filho, R. C., 443
Fillo, J., 209
Finch, K. H., 124
Fincham, F. D., 459
Findlay, L., 465
Fine, A., 497, 498
Fine, M., 399
Finegood, E. D., 180, 281, 383
Finger, B., 204
Fingeret, L., 352
Fingerman, K. L., 12, 15
Finke, E. H., 30, 145
Finkelman, A., 84
Finnane, J. M., 319
Fischer, N., 465
Fischhoff, B., 451
Fisette, J. L., 235, 236, 319
Fisher, D., 364
Fisher, K. R., 250
Fisher, P. A., 294
Fitzgerald, A., 437
Fitzgerald, J. (Ed.), 365
Fitzgerald, L. M., 351, 456
Fitzgerald, N., 437
Fitzsimmons, C., 263
Fivush, R., 256
Fivush, R. (Ed.), 167, 256, 347
Flam, K. K., 299
Flanagan, J. C., 114
Flanagan, K. S., 459
Flannery, D. J., 404
Flannery, K., 328
Flannery, M., 368
Flavell, E. R., 259, 260
Flavell, J. H., 259, 260, 351, 352

Fleischmann, 479
Fleming, A. S., 113, 207
Flensborg-Madsen, T., 140
Fletcher, P., 263
Fletcher, S., 233
Fletcher-Watson, S., 30, 145, 261
Flicek, P., 51
Flint, M. S., 52
Flipsen, P., 332
Flores, G., 238
Flouri, E., 383
Flynn, J. R., 356, 357
Foehr, U. G., 308, 495, 496
Foley, J. T., 235
Follari, L., 266
Fonseca-Machado Mde, O., 95
Fontaine, R. G., 401
Ford, D. Y., 360, 362
Ford, L., 279
Forster, D. A., 91
Forzano, L. B., 30, 32
Foster, B. A., 235
Fourneret, P., 450
Fouts, H. N., 295
Fox, B., 112
Fox, E., 364
Fox, M. K., 131, 233
Fox, N. A., 124, 127, 189
Fraiberg, S., 136
Fraley, R. C., 206
Frampton, I., 442
France, A., 406
Franchak, J. M., 143, 145
Francis, J., 477
Francis, J. K. R., 430
Franco, P., 129
Franklin, A., 146
Franklin, S., 452
Fraser, G., 477
Frawley, J., 105
Frederick II, 175
Frederickson, B. L., 395
Frederikse, M., 394
Freedman, D. G., 14
Freedman, D. S., 326
Freeman, M., 9, 419
Freeman, S., 53
French, D. C., 463
Frenkel, T. I., 189
Freud, S., 17, 18, 20, 23, 27, 202, 283, 287, 304
Freund, L. S., 281
Frey, N., 364
Frick, J., 200
Fried, P. A., 90
Friedman, A. H., 268
Friedman, H. S., 360
Friedman, J., 65
Friedman, N. P., 258
Friedman, S. L., 214
Friedrichs, A., 352
Friend, M., 328
Fries, S., 371
Frizelle, P., 263
Froh, J. J., 459
Froimson, J., 200, 292
Fu, G., 382

Fu, R., 196
Fuchs, D., 346
Fuchs, L. S., 346
Fuhs, M. W., 257
Fujiki, M., 264
Fujiwara, T., 114
Fukushima, A., 51
Fuligni, A. J., 437, 462, 466, 485, 493, 494
Fulkerson, J. A., 436
Fung, H., 25
Funk, C. M., 128
Furman, L., 110
Furman, W., 488–490
Furstenberg, F. F., 399
Furth, H. G., 343

G

Gadsby, S., 441
Gaffney, K. F., 129
Gaias, L. M., 196
Gaillard, A., 113
Gaither, S. E., 146
Galambos, N. L., 395, 438
Galbally, M., 207
Galbraith, K. A., 429
Galdiolo, S., 292
Galea, L. A., 114
Galinsky, E., 182, 265, 279, 300, 383, 418, 452–454
Gallagher, B., 365
Galland, B. C., 128
Gallant, S. N., 349
Galler, J. R., 133
Galliano, D., 79
Galliher, R. V., 475
Gallimore, R., 251
Gallo, E. F., 330
Galloway, J. C., 123
Gallup, G. W., 461
Gallup Poll, 436
Galvan, A., 425, 454
Gampe, A., 366
Gan, T., 390
Gandhi, M., 29
Ganea, N., 124
Ganguli, M., 12
Ganong, L., 399
Gao, W., 126
Garandeau, C. F., 404
Garber, J., 499, 500
Garcia, Y., 268, 269
Garcia Bengoechea, E., 320
Garcia Coll, C., 494
Garcia-Hermoso, A., 319
Garcia-Mila, M., 350
Garcia-Sierra, A., 181
Gardner, H., 351, 354–356, 359
Gardner, M., 10, 408, 455, 466
Gardner, P., 420
Gardosi, J., 93
Gareau, S., 84
Garfield, C. F., 331
Gariepy, G., 437
Garrison, M. M., 308
Gartner, C., 89

Gartstein, M. A., 193, 194, 195, 196, 254
Garvey, C., 305
Gaskins, S., 301
Gasser, L., 404
Gates, G. J., 300
Gates, W., 361, 362
Gattamorta, K. A., 484
Gauvain, M., 22, 26, 250, 251, 450
Gawlik, S., 114
Gaylord, N., 457
Gebremariam, M. K., 307
Gee, C. L., 279
Gelfand, J., 432
Geller, E. S., 459
Gelman, R., 249, 264, 343
Gelman, S. A., 169, 247, 263, 450
Gendle, M. H., 239
Genesee, F., 366, 367
Gennetian, L. A., 10
Gentile, D. A., 308
George Dalmida, S., 463
Gerenser, J., 334
German, T. P., 260
Gernhardt, A., 204
Gershoff, E., 268
Gershoff, E. T., 7, 291, 292, 397, 408
Gerson, S. A., 144
Gerst, E. H., 346, 452
Gervain, J., 176
Gesell, A. L., 135, 151, 171
Gestwicki, C., 266, 267, 269
Geva, R., 130
Gewirtz, J., 193
Ghasemi, M., 105
Ghazarian, S. R., 497
Ghetti, S., 255
Ghosh, S., 94
Gialamas, A., 213
Gibbons, J., 366
Gibbs, J. C., 389, 390
Gibson, E. J., 143, 147, 150, 151, 163, 228
Gibson, J. J., 143, 150, 151
Giedd, J. N., 224, 393
Gilbert, G., 365
Giles, E. D., 52
Giletta, M., 303, 402, 403, 405, 441, 487
Gillen-O'Neel, C., 437
Gilligan, C., 391, 393
Gilstrap, L. L., 356
Gingo, M., 389, 392
Gino, F., 459
Giofre, D., 353
Girling, A., 107
Girls Inc, 434
Giuntella, O., 35, 301
Gleason, T., 289
Gleason, T. R., 390, 459
Gliga, T., 124, 164
Gnambs, T., 451
Goad, H., 262
Gobet, F., 346
Gockley, A. A., 94

Godding, V., 89
Goddings, A-L., 425, 454
Godfrey, K. M., 52
Godwin, J., 503
Goel, N., 457
Goffin, S. G., 267
Gogtay, N., 126
Goh, S. N., 307
Goksan, S., 149
Gold, A. L., 331
Gold, M. A., 430, 463
Goldberg, E., 128
Goldberg, S. K., 428
Goldberg, W., 329
Goldberg, W. A., 297
Goldenberg, R., 109
Goldenberg, R. L., 83, 108
Goldfield, G. S., 322, 436
Golding, J., 93
Goldin-Meadow, S., 176
Goldman-Rakic, P. S., 225
Goldschmidt, L., 91
Goldsmith, H. H., 195
Goldstein, M. H., 179
Goldston, D. B., 501
Goleman, D., 221
Golinkoff, R., 179, 305
Golinkoff, R. M., 176, 179–182, 263, 306, 363
Gollnick, D. M., 7, 301, 372, 408, 494
Golomb, C., 229, 230
Golombok, S., 61, 286, 300, 301
Gomez, R. L., 164
Gomez, S. H., 170, 294
Gomez-Bruton, A., 319
Gomez-Moya, R., 228
Gonçalves, L. F., 59
Goncu, A., 251
Gonzales, E., 478, 479
Gonzales, N. A., 7, 9, 10, 301, 418, 494
Gonzales, R., 479
Gonzalez, A., 207
Gonzalez-Echavarri, C., 87
González-Ruiz, K., 436
Good, C., 370
Good, M., 462
Goodenough, J., 50
Goodkind, S., 397
Goodman, E., 61
Goodman, J. C., 263
Goodnough, L. T., 91
Goodvin, R., 189, 190, 195, 197, 199, 279, 281, 385, 395
Goodyer, I. M., 500
Gopnik, A., 169, 259
Gordon, A. M., 266, 269
Gordon, I., 207
Gorely, T., 320
Gorroochum, P., 231
Gorukanti, A., 440
Gosselin, J., 399
Goswami, U. C., 174
Gotlieb, R., 351
Gottfredson, N. C., 195

Gottlieb, A., 10
Gottlieb, G., 52, 66
Gottman, J. M., 209, 281, 282, 405
Gouin, K., 89
Gould, J. F., 126
Gould, S. J., 49
Gower, A. L., 404
Goyet, L., 124
Graber, J. A., 291, 423, 425, 441, 498
Graber, R., 487
Grafenhain, M., 280
Graf Estes, K., 366
Graham, J., 283, 389, 390
Graham, S., 365, 372, 466
Grammer, J. K., 348
Granat, A., 190
Grand, J. A., 358
Grant, A. M., 459
Grant-Marsney, H. A., 62
Grassman, V., 332
Graven, S., 128
Graves, C. R., 89
Gravetter, F. J., 30, 32
Gray, D. L., 368
Gray, K., 283, 389, 390
Green, F. L., 260
Green, J., 61, 182
Green, K. M., 432
Green, S. A., 335
Greene, J. A. (Ed.), 383, 384
Greene, J. D., 390
Greene, M. F., 104
Greene, R. A., 88
Greene, S., 482
Greenfield, P. M., 344, 358
Greenleaf, C., 424
Greenough, W., 68
Greenwald, A. G., 394
Greer, F. R., 131
Greer, K. B., 296
Gregory, R. J., 29
Griesler, P. C., 435
Griffin, J. A., 281
Griffin, P., 180
Griffiths, S., 424
Grigorenko, E., 356
Grigorenko, E. L., 30, 67, 358
Grimberg, A., 222, 223
Grimbal, M., 479
Grinde, B., 48
Grob, A., 355
Grogan-Kaylor, A., 292
Groh, A. M., 193, 205
Grolnick, W. S., 373, 374
Grondahl, M. L., 33
Groppe, K., 257, 348
Gross, J. J., 395
Gross, T. T., 134
Grossmann, K., 204, 206
Grosz, E., 480
Grotevant, H. D., 61, 62, 478
Gruber, K. J., 103
Gruen, J. R., 329
Grusec, J., 282
Grusec, J. E., 289, 292, 391, 398

Guay, F., 26
Gudmundson, J. A., 193
Guerra, A. W. (Ed.), 213
Guerra, N. G., 402
Guevremont, A., 465
Gui, D. Y., 390
Guilford, J. P., 349
Guimaraes, E. L., 141
Gulerman, H. C., 109
Gump, B. B., 114
Gunderson, E. A., 394
Gunn, J. K., 90
Gunn, P. W., 325
Gunnar, M. R., 149, 207, 294
Gupta, A., 409
Gur, R. C., 394
Gustafsson, J-E., 356
Guthrie, J. F., 134
Gutierrez-Galve, L., 114
Gutman, L. M., 441
Guttentag, C. L., 433
Guttmannova, K., 440
Gutzwiller, E., 390
Guy, A., 403
Guyer, A. E., 194, 480

H

Hadani, H., 258
Haden, C. A., 256
Hadiwijaya, H., 483
Hadland, S. E., 501
Haertle, L., 92
Hafner, J. W., 326
Hagborg, J. M., 294
Hagekull, B., 196
Hagen, E., 355
Hagmann-von Arx, P., 355
Hagopian, W., 131
Hahn, W. K., 125
Haidt, J., 390
Hair, N. L., 225
Hakkarainen, P., 305
Hakuta, K., 367
Hakvoort, E. M., 399
Hale, N., 83
Hales, D., 6, 435
Haley, M. H., 367
Halim, M. L., 288, 393
Hall, G. S., 418, 479, 484
Hall, J. W., 333
Hall, S. S., 56
Hall, W., 402, 404, 418
Hallahan, D. P., 329, 333, 335, 336
Halldorsdottir, T., 67
Halliwell, J. O., 394
Hallman, S. K., 478, 479
Halpern, C. T., 428, 429, 500
Halpern, D., 393
Halpern, D. F., 394, 396, 397
Halpern, G. T., 489
Halpern-Felsher, B., 440
Hamann, K., 280
Hamilton, B. E., 432
Hamilton, E., 500
Hamilton, J. L., 425
Hamlin, J. K., 162–164

Hammond, R., 498, 499
Hammond, S. I., 162, 164, 258
Han, J. J., 348
Han, J. Y., 89
Han, W-J., 297
Hanc, T., 107
Hancox, R. J., 320
Handler, A., 83
Handler, A. S., 134
Handren, L. M., 482
Hanish, L., 287
Hanish, L. D., 402
Hanna-Attisha, M., 239
Hannon, E. H., 143, 147, 150, 151, 163
Hansen, M. L., 325
Hanson, M., 93
Hanusa, B. H., 113
Happe, F., 261
Harackiewicz, J. M., 368
Harden, K. P., 425
Hardy, S. A., 391, 420
Harel, J., 192
Hargreaves, D. A., 441
Hari, R., 123
Harkness, S., 140, 206
Harlow, H. R., 202
Harmon, O. R., 461
Harrington, B. C., 443
Harris, J., 176, 263
Harris, J. L., 323
Harris, K. R., 365
Harris, P. L., 229, 258
Harrison, A. L., 81
Harrison, M., 130, 322
Harrist, A. W., 209
Hart, B., 180, 356
Hart, C. H., 268
Hart, C. N., 232
Hart, D., 198, 391, 457, 458
Hart, S., 190
Harter, S., 260, 278–280, 381, 382, 384
Hartshorne, H., 285, 461
Hartup, W. W., 304, 401, 405
Harville, E. W., 326
Harwood, L. J., 132
Hasbrouck, S. L., 212
Hashiya, K., 30, 145
Hasson, R. E., 325
Hastings, P. D., 300
Hattenschwiler, N., 347, 348
Hauber, A., 320
Hauck, F. R., 129
Hausman, B. L., 102
Hawk, S. T., 483
Hawken, L. S., 365
Hawkins, J. A., 464
Hawrilenko, M., 296
Hay, W. W., 222
Hayashi, A., 180
Hayatbakhsh, R., 239
Haydon, A., 489
Haydon, A. A., 428, 429
Haynes, C. W., 329
Hazeldean, D., 81
He, C., 148, 149
He, M., 139

Landrum, A. R., 279
Lane, A., 322
Lane, H., 173
Lane, J. D., 258
Langacker, R. W., 174
Langer, E. J., 349
Langille, D. B., 501
Lansford, J. E., 292, 298, 299, 430
Lantagne, A., 488
Lanter, E., 335
Lantolf, J., 250
Lanzi, R. G., 357
LaPrade, R. F., 320
Lapsley, D., 391, 420
Lapsley, D. K., 451, 459
Laranjo, J., 261
Larkina, M., 167, 168, 254, 256, 347, 348
Larsen, K. J., 501
Larson, K., 232
Larson, R. W., 9, 301, 480, 485, 487, 491–493
Larzelere, R. E., 292
Lathrop, A. L., 143, 146
Lau, J. Y., 401, 453
Lauff, E., 466
Laursen, B., 302, 303, 500
Lavender, J. M., 443
Law, B., 460
Lawley, G., 457
Lawrence, A. A., 481
Lawson, C. A., 169
Lazarus, J. H., 133
Leadbeater, B. J., 433
Leandro, C. G., 109
Leaper, C., 287, 288, 395, 397
Leary, M. R., 28, 30
Leboeuf-Yde, C., 320
Leboyer, F., 103
Lecarpentier, E., 75
Ledesma, K., 62
Le Doare, K., 131
Lee, C. T., 424
Lee, J., 149
Lee, J. M., 223
Lee, K., 143, 146, 279, 348, 349, 382, 403
Lee, K. Y., 52
Lee, M. S., 29
Lee, M-H., 141
Lee, R. M., 189
Lee, S., 373, 436
Lee, S. J., 7, 292
Lee, X., 294
Lee, Y. J., 105
Leedy, P. D., 27
Leerkes, E. M., 190, 193, 203, 206
Leffel, K., 180
Leftwich, H., 432
Legare, C. H., 382
Legerstee, M., 200, 201
Lehr, C. A., 468
Lehrer, R., 350
Leibovitz, E., 131
Leichtman M. D., 348
Leifer, A. D., 308

Leinbach, M. D., 288
Lemez, S., 320
Lemola, S., 355
Lempers, J. D., 259
Lems, K., 174
Lenhart, A., 496
Lennon, E. M., 172
Lenoir, C. P., 129
Lenroot, R. K., 224
Leonard, C., 352
Leonard, J., 494
Leonard, L. B., 174
Leonardo da Vinci, 11
Leone, J. E., 424
Leong, D. J., 252, 349
Lereya, S. T., 403
Lerner, J. V., 462
Lerner, R. M., 419, 426
Lesaux, N. K., 367
Le Scanff, C., 320
Leseman, P., 346
Leslie, S. J., 358
Lester, B. M., 89, 107
Lester, L., 403
Letourneau, E. J., 429
Leu, D. J., 364
Leung, J. Y., 109, 261
Levenson, R. W., 395
Leventhal, T., 408, 497
Leventon, S. J., 225
Lever-Duffy, J., 13, 307, 495, 496
Levine, T. P., 89
Levy, E., 322
Levy, F., 466
Lewanda, A. F., 55
Lewis, A. C., 407
Lewis, B. A., 89
Lewis, C., 199, 200, 205, 211, 212, 402
Lewis, G. J., 334
Lewis, J., 46
Lewis, M., 190, 198, 205, 280, 479, 480
Lewis, R. B., 330, 333, 335
Lewis, T. L., 150, 151
Lewis-Morrarty, E., 205
Lew-Williams, C., 176
Leyton, M., 426
Li, B. J., 91
Li, D., 301, 335, 459
Li, D-K., 130
Li, G., 286
Li, J., 64, 107
Li, J. W., 437
Li, M., 51, 124, 307
Li, Q., 237
Li, W., 214
Li, Z., 78
Liang, W., 440
Liang, Y. J., 322
Liao, C. Y., 322
Liao, D. C., 451
Liben, L. S., 211, 286–288, 391, 394, 397
Liberati, A., 145
Liberman, Z., 201
Libertus, K., 141

Lickliter, R., 48, 66, 68
Licoppe, C., 395
Liddon, N., 502
Lie, E., 168
Lieber, M., 386
Liebergott, J., 176
Lieberman, A. F., 386
Lieberman, P., 178
Liebermann, J., 60
Lieblich, A., 476
Liederman, J., 328
Liekweg, K., 308
Lieven, E., 177
Liew, J., 482
Lifter, K., 177
Likis, F. E., 108
Lillard, A., 306
Lillard, A. S., 246, 260, 267, 305, 306
Lin, C. C., 92
Lin, L. Y., 179
Lin, M., 271
Lin, X., 86
Lin, Y. C., 238
Lindberg, L. D., 434
Lindberg, S. M., 394
Lindholm-Leary, K., 366, 367
Lindsay, A. C., 323
Lindsay, D. S., 256
Lindsay, M. K., 91
Linnenbrink-Garcia, L., 369
Linsell, L., 109
Lintu, N., 235, 319
Lionetti, F., 61
Lipowski, M., 430
Lipschitz, J. M., 501
Lipsky, L. M., 436
Liszkowski, U., 263
Little, K. C., 490
Litz, J., 262
Liu, C., 7, 287, 390
Liu, D., 259
Liu, J., 235
Liu, R., 83
Liu, X., 82
Liu, Y. H., 105
Lively, A., 409
Lively, V., 381
Livingston, G., 211
Lloyd-Fox, S., 124
Lo, C. C., 36, 419, 494
Lo, C. K., 293
Lo, K. Y., 320
LoBue, V., 147
Lochman, J. J., 141
Lockhart, G., 6, 68, 484
Lockl, K., 258
Loebel, M., 95
Loeber, R., 497
Logel, C., 358
Logsdon, M. C., 113
Lohaus, A., 172
Lohr, M. J., 488
Loi, E. C., 30, 145
Loizou, E., 305
Lomanowska, A. M., 210, 225
London, M. L., 103, 104, 106, 109, 123, 134

Longfellow, H. W., 5, 450
Longo, G. S., 462
Longo, M. R., 147
Lonstein, J. S., 113
Loomans, D., 1
Loop, L., 281
Lopez, A. B., 462
Lopez, E. I., 398
Lopez, K., 334
Lopez, L., 347
Lopez-Maestro, M., 203
Lopez-Tello, G., 483
Lord, R. G., 287
Lorenz, K. Z., 24, 27, 115
Losel, F., 403
Love, J. M., 268, 356
Love, V., 91
Lovely, C., 54
Low, L. K., 103
Low, S., 482, 489
Lowe, N. K., 103
Lowenstein, A., 268
Lowry, R., 429
Lowson, K., 110
Lu, C., 240
Lu, T., 500
Lucas-Thompson, R., 297
Ludden, A. B., 441
Luders, E., 393
Ludvigsson, J. F., 237
Luecken, L. J., 299
Lugo, R. G., 284
Luiselli, J. K. (Ed.), 261
Lukowski, A. F., 167, 168, 352
Lumeng, J. C., 233
Lumpkin, A., 320
Lund, H. G., 438
Lundblad, K., 235
Lunenfeld, B., 55
Luo, W., 482
Luo, Y., 162, 199
Luria, A., 287
Lusby, C. M., 29, 124, 189
Lushington, K., 128
Lust, K., 94
Lutkenhaus, P., 199
Luyckx, K., 368, 475
Lyon, T. D., 352
Lyons, K. E., 349
Lyons, M., 335
Lyubomirsky, S., 289
Lyyra, A. L., 440

M

Ma, Y. -Y., 362
Maag, J. W., 23
Maas, J., 112
Macari, S., 170
Macarthur, C., 114
MacArthur, C., 365
MacCallum, F., 61
Maccoby, E. E., 288, 290, 291
Macdonald, I., 320
Macedo, D. B., 424
MacFarlan, S. J., 211
MacFarlane, J. A., 149

Machado, B., 443
Machalek, D. A., 64
Macionis, J. J., 497
MacKenzie, A., 434
MacKinnon, S. P., 492
Macpherson, A. K., 237
Madden, K., 105
Maddison, R., 226
Maddow-Zimet, I., 434
Madill, A., 487
Maduro, G., 92
Magee, C. A., 487
Maggs, J. L., 438
Magiati, I., 335
Magno, C., 456
Magnuson, K., 7, 9, 10, 372, 408, 418
Magnussen, P., 84
Magro-Malosso, E. R., 81
Mahabee-Gittens, E. M., 239
Maher, H., 475, 476
Mahler, M., 199
Mahoney, A., 463
Mahoney, J. L., 465, 466
Malby Schoos, A. M., 131
Malcolm-Smith, S., 261
Mallard, C., 78
Mallet, E., 129
Malmberg, L. E., 211
Malmstrom, F. V., 461
Malone, J. C., 394
Maloy, R. W., 13, 307, 308, 495, 496
Malti, T., 283
Mandara, J., 399
Mandler, J. M., 167–170
Mangelsdorf, S. C., 199
Mannix, R., 320
Manore, M., 322
Manuck, S. B., 67
Many, A., 103
Manzanares, S., 60
Manzo, K. K., 465
Mao, A. R., 331
Maramara, L. A., 109
Maravilla, J. C., 432
Marchetti, D., 89
Marchman, V. A., 174, 179, 180, 182
March of Dimes, 60
Marcia, J. E., 476–477
Marcoux, S., 324
Marcovitch, S., 163, 167, 260
Mares, M-L., 308
Margraf, J., 330
Marie, C., 149
Marjanovic-Umek, L., 181
Mark, K. S., 89
Markant, J. C., 426
Markham, C. M., 430
Markham, K. B., 108
Markman, E., 263
Markman, E. M., 177
Marsh, H. L., 201
Marshall, P. J., 168
Marshall, S. L., 383
Martin, A., 254, 270
Martin, C., 406

Martin, C. L., 286–288
Martin, J. A., 83, 102, 104–105, 108, 109, 290, 432
Martin, K. B., 192
Martin, M. J., 189, 298
Martin, M. M., 90
Martin-Espinosa, N., 322
Martinez-Brockman, J. L., 134
Martz, M. E., 440
Marusak, H. A., 225
Marwaha, R., 232
Marx, G., 234
Mary, A., 331
Masapollo, M., 175
Mash, C., 151
Mash, E. J., 331, 334
Mashburn, A. J., 264
Maslovitz, S., 103
Mason, A., 437
Masten, A. S., 8, 68, 205, 349, 386, 420
Master, A., 370
Mastergeorge, A. M., 268, 269
Mastin, J. D., 167
Mastronardi, C. A., 51
Mastropieri, M. A., 336
Masumoto, D., 7, 301
Mathews, B., 294
Mathias, S. R., 51
Matlin, M. W., 288, 395
Matlow, J. N., 75
Matsuba, M. K., 391, 457
Matthiessen, C., 324
Mattock, K., 149
Maurer, D., 150, 151
May, D., 287
May, L., 81
May, M. S., 285, 461
Maye, M. P., 334
Mayer, K. D., 90
Mayer, R. E., 365
Mayers, R. M., 110
Mayo, A. M., 320
Mayo Clinic, 93
Mazuka, R., 180
Mazul, M. C., 82
Mazza, M., 261
Mazzucato, V., 301
Mbonye, A. K., 84
Mbugua Gitau, G., 94
McAdams, D. P., 476, 477
McAllister, S., 105
McAvoy, M., 125
McBean, A. L., 112
McBride-Chang, C., 265
McCabe, A., 367
McCabe, F., 113, 114
McCabe, S. E., 331
McCaffery, J. M., 67
McCardle, P. (Eds.), 281
McCarroll, J. E., 294
McCartney, K., 213
McClelland, A., 410
McClelland, M. M., 254, 256–258, 383
McCloskey, K., 79
McCormack, L. A., 323

McCormack, S. E., 325
McCormick, C. B., 351, 352, 364, 365
McCourt, S. N., 503
McCoy, D. C., 268, 281, 282
McCoy, K. P., 298
McCulloch, S., 105, 347
McCutchen, J. A., 459
McDermott, J. M., 61, 62
McDonald, J., 13, 307, 495, 496
McDonald, J. A., 82
McDonald, R., 298
McDonough, L., 169
McElhaney, K. B., 483
McElvaney, R., 482
McEvoy, C. T., 89
McGarry, J., 113
McGarvey, C., 130
McGee, K., 336
McGillion, M., 176, 179, 180, 182
McGilvray, J. (Ed.), 178
McGinley, M., 285
McGorry, S. Y., 458
McGovern, G., 493
McGrath, J. J., 88
McGregor, K. K., 263
McGuckin, C. (Ed.), 403
McGue, M., 461
McGuire, B. A., 50
McHale, M., 483
McHale, S. M., 295, 395, 484
McKelvey, K., 440
McKenna, K. Y. A., 490
McKenzie, B. E., 146, 147
McKeown, M., 174
McLaughlin, K. A., 124, 126–127
McLean, K. C., 475, 476, 478
McLellan, J. A., 462
McLeod, G. F., 298
McLeod, S., 326, 327
McIntyre, H. D., 94
McLoyd, V. C., 372, 409, 466, 467, 478, 479
McIsaac, C., 488, 489
McMahon, D. M., 78
McMahon, M., 222
McMillan, B., 48, 57
McMurray, B., 178
McMurray, R. G., 437
McNicholas, C., 394
McNicholas, F., 109
McQueen, D. V., 9, 10, 419
Meacham, J., 279
Meade, C. S., 432
Meaney, M. J., 52
Medford, E., 56
Meehan, W. P., 320
Meeus, W., 458, 475, 479
Meghea, C. L., 84
Mehler, P. S., 442
Mehta, C. M., 329
Meidenbauer, K. L., 280
Meins, E., 261, 279, 483
Meisel, V., 332
Meldrum, R. C., 356

Melhuish, E., 214
Melinder, A., 255
Mellor, D., 435
Melnyk, L., 255
Meltzer, L. J., 437
Meltzer-Brody, S., 113
Meltzoff, A. N., 166–169, 180, 308, 394
Melzi, G., 209–210
Menard, L., 175
Mendelson, M., 437
Mendes, W. B., 191
Mendle, J., 425
Mendoza, M. M., 9
Menesini, E., 402, 404
Menesini, E, Palladino, B. E., 404
Meng, X., 30, 145
Menias, C. O., 91
Menn, L., 144
Mennella, J. A., 149
Menon, M., 383
Menon, R., 75, 90
Menyuk, P., 176
Mercer, N., 498
Mercy, J. A., 237
Meredith, N. V., 222
Merewood, A., 132
Merianos, A. L., 239
Merilees, C. E., 298
Merrill, S. M., 427
Merz, E-M., 399
Messiah, S. E., 90
Messinger, D. B., 192
Metha, A., 406
Metindogan, A., 271
Metz, E. C., 458
Meuwissen, A. S., 258
Mevorach, C., 330
Meyer, S., 285
Mezzacappa, E., 383
Michaud, I., 437
Michaud, P. A., 83
Mickelson, K. D., 209
Middleton, R. J., 86
Miele, D., 368
Miele, D. B. (Ed.), 369, 396
Miga, E. M., 484
Miguel-Neto, J., 56
Milesi, G., 59
Miller, A., 461
Miller, A. L., 189
Miller, B., 492
Miller, B. C., 429
Miller, C., 10, 288
Miller, C. B., 460
Miller, C. F., 393
Miller, C. J., 332
Miller, C. R., 457–458
Miller, D. D., 112
Miller, E. B., 268
Miller, E. M., 370
Miller, J. G., 390
Miller, L. D., 174
Miller, L. M., 298
Miller, M., 237
Miller, M. B., 438

Miller, P. H., 450
Miller, R., 67
Miller, S., 347, 503
Miller, S. E., 167
Miller, S. L., 78
Miller, W. R., 78
Miller-Graff, L. E., 298
Miller-Perrin, C. L., 295
Milligan, K., 88
Mills, B. A., 455
Mills, C., 254
Mills, C. M., 279, 280, 382
Mills, D., 254
Mills, K., 425, 454
Mills, M. T., 362
Mills-Koonce, W. R., 193
Milne, B. J., 320
Milne, E., 95
Milosavljevic, B., 124
Mindell, J., 231, 232
Miner, J. L., 212, 213
Minero, L. P., 481
Ming, X., 109
Minic, P. B., 326
Minnes, S., 89
Minsart, A. F., 93
Mireles-Rios, R., 483
Mirpuri, S., 478
Mischel, W., 257, 285
Mistry, J., 301
Mistry, R. S., 397
Mitchell, A. B., 397
Mitchell, D. M., 325
Mitchell, D. W., 166
Mitchell, E. A., 130
Mitchell, W., 213
Miyahara, R., 238
Miyake, A., 204
Miyake, S., 102
Mize, K. D., 190, 195
Mnyani, C. N., 121, 132
Modecki, K. L., 466
Modrek, A., 231
Moed, A., 484
Moffitt, T. E., 257, 453
Mohagheghi, A., 331
Mohan, L., 352
Molina, B. S., 331
Molina, R. C., 433
Moline, H. R., 92
Mollborg, P., 130
Mollborn, S., 433
Moller, A. C., 368
Mon, E., 112
Monahan, K., 425, 426
Monahan, K. C., 125, 453
Mond, J., 441
Mondal, A. C., 94
Moninger, J., 324
Monn, A. R., 257, 349
Monni, G., 59
Montana, S., 94
Montemayor, R., 484
Montessori, M., 267
Montgomery-Downs, H. E., 112
Moodley, D., 121
Moon, R. Y., 129, 130

Mooney-Leber, S. M., 110
Moore, B. S., 257
Moore, D. S., 15, 30, 51–54, 57, 66–68, 128, 210
Moore, G. A., 200
Moore, L., 238
Moore, M. K., 168
Moore, S. R., 425
Moorefield, B. S., 399
Moosmann, D. A., 489
Mooya, H., 204, 206
Moradi, B., 481
Moran, G., 204
Moran, V. H., 130
Morasch, K. C., 168
Moravcik, E., 229, 266, 269
Moreno, I., 90
Moreno, R. P., 271
Morgan, P. J., 323
Moriguchi, Y., 257, 348, 452
Morison, V., 144, 145
Morley, C., 222
Moro, M. R., 302
Morosan, L., 382
Morra, S., 344
Morrill, M. I., 296
Morris, A. S., 357, 459
Morris, D., 44
Morris, M. C., 499
Morris, P. A., 25, 26
Morris, R., 329
Morris, R. G., 402
Morrison, D. C., 15
Morrison, G. S., 7, 227, 245, 266, 267, 269, 305, 344, 357
Morrison, S. C., 298
Morrison-Beedy, D., 430
Morrissey, T. W., 213
Morrissey-Ross, M., 238
Morrow, C. E., 89
Mortensen, E. L., 140
Morton, J. B., 256, 348, 452
Morton, R. W., 325
Moses, L. J., 257
Moss, P., 438
Mother Teresa, 11
Moulson, M. C., 143, 200, 225
Mounts, E. L., 57
Moura da Costa, E., 249
Movahed Abtahi, M., 385
Moyer, C., 81
Mparmpakas, D., 94
Mruk, C. J., 384
Mu, Y., 373
Mueller, B. A., 89
Mueller, C. E., 369
Mueller, M. P., 344
Mueller, T., 433
Muijs, D., 402, 404
Mukherjee, S. B., 261
Mulder, E. J., 90
Muller, C. L., 51
Muller, U., 256–258, 348
Muller Mirza, N., 251
Mullola, S., 396
Mulvey, K. L., 392

Rothman, E. F., 425
Rothman, R., 407
Rothstein-Fisch, C., 358
Rousseau, J. -J., 158, 219
Rousssotte, F. F., 90
Rovee-Collier, C., 144, 165, 167
Rowe, J., 102
Rowe, M., 398
Rowe, M. L., 176
Rowlands, I. J., 89
Royer, C. E., 255, 256
Rozenblat, V., 67
Rubeling, H., 204
Rubens, D., 129
Rubin, D. H., 95
Rubin, K. H., 14, 303, 304, 400–402, 405, 486, 487
Rubin, K. H. (Ed.), 303
Rubio-Codina, M., 228
Rubio-Fernandez, P., 366
Ruble, D., 381
Ruck, M. D., 9, 419
Rudolph, K. D., 425
Rueda, M. R., 254
Ruiz, S. K., 484
Rumberger, R. W., 468
Russell, L., 399
Russell, P. J., 48, 57
Russell, S. T., 291
Rutman, L., 325
Rutter, M., 335
Ryan, R. M., 368

S

Saarni, C., 386
Saavedra, J. M., 319
Sabbagh, M., 256, 348, 452
Sabbagh, M. A., 258, 260
Saccuzzo, D. P., 29
Sackett, P. R., 353, 359
Sacrey, L. A., 141
Sadeh, A., 128, 130
Sadeh (Ed.), 231
Sadker, D. M., 396, 407
Sadker, M. P., 396
Sadovsky, A. D., 238
Saez de Urabain, I. R., 124, 164
Safarov, I., 305
Safford, P., 410
Safranek, S., 88
Sagi-Schwartz, A., 206
Sajber, D., 482
Sala, G., 346
Salam, R. A., 430
Salama, R. H., 89
Salapatek, P., 150
Salkind, N. J., 27
Salley, B., 165, 166
Salmivalli, C., 402–404, 459
Salmon, J., 227
Salm Ward, T. C., 82
Salzwedel, A. P., 89
Samara, M., 403
Samek, D. R., 67
Sameroff, A. J., 209

Sampath, A., 92
Sanborn, M., 239
Sanders, K. E., 213
Sanem, J. R., 440
Sanford, D., 114
Sangganjanavanich, V. F., 481
Sankupellay, M., 128
Sann, C., 150
Sanson, A., 197
Santangeli, L., 93
Santelli, J., 428
Santiago, A., 189
Santos, C. E., 479
Santos, L. M., 78
Santos, M. J. D., 459
Santrock, A., 170
Santrock, J. W., 170, 399
Sapirstein, M., 484
Sarchiapone, M., 437
Sargrad, S., 406
Sarnat, H. B., 129
Saroglou, V., 462
Sarquella-Brugada, G., 129
Sasayama, D., 232
Sauber-Schatz, E. K., 326
Saunders, N. R., 237
Savage, J. S., 487
Savendahl, L., 423
Savin-Williams, R. C., 427, 428, 489
Saxena, M., 55
Sayer, A., 62
Scaife, J. C., 443
Scales, P. C., 418
Scarlett, W. G., 462
Scarr, S., 65, 66
Scelfo, J., 481
Scerif, G., 165, 253
Schaefer, F., 325
Schaffer, H. R., 203
Schaie, K. W., 12, 25, 33
Schalkwijk, F., 390
Schans, D., 301
Scharf, R. J., 270
Scharrer, E., 308
Schauble, L., 350
Scheinost, D., 331
Scher, A., 192
Scherer, D. G., 300
Scherer, K., 189
Schick, A. R., 209–210
Schick, U. M., 51
Schieffelin, B., 182
Schieve, L. A., 109
Schiff, R., 363, 364, 441
Schiff, W. J., 130, 131, 133, 321, 435
Schillinger, J. A., 92
Schittny, J. C., 75
Schlam, T. R., 257
Schlegel, M., 258
Schmidt, J. A., 458
Schmidt, L. A., 196
Schmidt, U., 443
Schmitt, D. P., 48
Schmitt, S. A., 257
Schnabelrauch, C. A., 462
Schneider, B., 303, 405

Schneider, S., 330
Schneider, W., 255, 258, 347, 352
Schoen, M., 123
Schoffstall, C. L., 403
Scholer, A. A., 368
Schonert-Reichl, K. A., 349
Schoon, I., 302
Schopler, E., 335
Schoppe-Sullivan, S. J., 292
Schorr, I., 480
Schrag, S. G., 91
Schreiber, L. R., 321
Schubiger, M. N., 355
Schuler, M. S., 498
Schulenberg, J. E., 440, 441, 497, 498
Schuler, M. S., 498
Schultz, M., 176
Schultz, M. L., 132
Schumacher, M., 115
Schunk, D. H., 369, 371, 372, 383, 384
Schutten, D., 495
Schutze, U., 178
Schwab, C., 329
Schwalbe, C. S., 498
Schwartz, D., 403
Schwartz, S. J., 477–479
Schwartz-Mette, R. A., 395
Schwarz, E. G., 132
Schweinhart, L. J., 269, 503
Sciberras, E., 51
Scott, R. M., 259
Scott-Goodwin, A. C., 90
Scourfield, J., 64
Scruggs, T. E., 336
Scupin, R., 492
Search Institute, 417, 419
Sedgh, G., 431
Segal, N. L., 64
Seiber, E. E., 325
Seibert, A. C., 385
Selemon, L. D., 126
Selman, R. L., 382
Semega, J. L., 9
Semenov, A. D., 257
Sen, B., 441
Sengpiel, V., 88
Senin-Calderon, C., 424, 441
Senju, A., 124
Senko, C., 371
Senter, L., 129, 130
Seo, D. C., 238
Seo, J. H., 437
Seo, Y. S., 149
Sepanski Whipple, S., 301
Sera, M. D., 257
Serrano-Villar, M., 289
Sethna, V., 188, 211
Shaashua, L., 128
Shago, M., 324
Shah, M., 149
Shah, M. K., 84
Shah, R., 90
Shakespeare, W., 101
Shakespeare-Pellington, S., 435
Shalev, L., 330
Shalitin, S., 422

Shang, L., 320
Shankaran, S., 89
Shannon, F. T., 132
Shapiro, A. F., 209
Shapiro, D. N., 399
Sharland, M., 92
Sharma, N., 127
Shatz, M., 264
Shaw, G. B., 289
Shaw, P., 331
Shaywitz, B. A., 329
Shaywitz, B. B., 329
Shaywitz, S. E., 329
Shebloski, B., 296
Sheeder, J., 81
Sheehan, M. J., 292
Sheftall, A. H., 484
Shek, D. T., 460
Sheldrick, R. C., 334
Shelton, D., 129
Shen, J., 51
Shen, Y-L., 430
Shenhav, A., 390
Shenk, D., 357
Shenoda, B. B., 128
Sheridan, M. A., 124, 126–127, 346
Shernoff, D. J., 492
Sherwood, L., 53
Shetgiri, R., 402
Sheth, M., 110
Sheu, Y., 320
Shi, L., 238
Shiba, N., 324
Shimony-Kanat, S., 134
Shiner, R. L., 196
Shiner, S., 103
Shiva, F., 239
Shivers, E., 212
Shneidman, L., 201
Short, D. J., 36, 367
Shortt, J. W., 482
Showell, N. N., 319
Shulman, E., 426, 455, 497
Shuman, V., 189
Shumow, L., 458
Sibley, M. H., 330
Sica, L. S., 479
Sichimba, F., 204, 206
Siega-Riz, A. M., 233, 234
Siegel, D. H., 62
Siegel, L. S., 329, 367
Siegel, R. S., 432
Siegler, R. S., 22, 253, 352, 373
Siener, S., 385
Silber, S., 60
Silk, J. S., 480
Silva, C., 474, 475
Silva, K., 455
Silverman, M. E., 113
Silvers, J. A., 12, 206
Sim, Z. L., 305
Simcock, G., 170
Simion, F., 191
Simkin, P., 105
Simmons, D., 79
Simmons, E. S., 335

Simmons, R. G., 425
Simon, E. J., 48, 53, 54
Simon, T., 353
Simons, L. G., 429, 487, 498
Simons, R. L., 487, 498
Simos, P. G., 330
Simpkins, S. D., 398
Simpson, E. A., 143, 145, 200
Simpson, H. B., 442
Simpson, J., 197
Simpson, L. L., 94
Sims, C. E., 225
Sims, D. A., 112
Singarajah, A., 143, 200
Singer, D., 306
Singh, L., 366
Singh, N. N., 349
Singh, S., 428, 431
Sirard, J. R., 437
Siren, P. M., 129
Sitterle, K. A., 399
Siu, A. M., 460
Sivell, S., 57
Skarabela, B., 176
Skiba, M. T., 351
Skinner, B. F., 23, 24, 27, 165, 178
Skinner, O. D., 484
Skjaerven, R., 109
Skogbrott Birkeland, M., 424
Slater, A., 144, 145, 147, 163, 443
Slater, A. M., 146, 150, 151
Slaughter, V., 261
Sleet, D. A., 237
Slobin, D., 177
Slomkowski, C., 498
Smaldino, S. E., 496
Smetana, J. G., 392, 482
Smith, A., 133, 232, 234
Smith, C. A., 105
Smith, C. L., 124, 383
Smith, E. R., 110
Smith, J., 295
Smith, J. F., 92
Smith, L., 169
Smith, L. B., 135, 138, 151, 163, 165, 166, 201
Smith, L. E., 114–115
Smith, L. M., 90
Smith, R. A., 16
Smith, R. L., 395
Smith, R. P., 104
Smith, S. S., 425
Smith, T. E., 395
Smith, T. J., 124
Smithbattle, L., 94
Smitsman, A. W., 141
Smokowski, P. R., 478, 484, 500
Smoreda, Z., 395
Snarey, J., 390
Snedeker, J., 163, 450
Snidman, N., 15
Snow, C. E., 180, 265, 367
Snow, N. (Ed.), 283
Snyder, K. A., 166
Snyder, W., 262, 263, 430

Socan, G., 181
Society for Adolescent Health and Medicine, 430
Sodian, B., 201, 258
Sokol, R. L., 290
Sokolowski, M., 51
Soller, B., 489
Solomon, D., 461
Solomon-Krakus, S., 424
Solovieva, Y., 306
Somers, M., 144, 145
Somerville, L. H., 425, 452
Sommer, T. E., 9, 10, 408
Son, W. M., 437
Song, L., 179
Song, P., 322
Sonny, A., 103
Sontag, L., 498
Sontag, L. M., 423
Sophian, C., 162
Sorbye, I. K., 108
Sorensen, L. C., 503
Soro, T. M., 174
Sorof, J. M., 325
Sorte, J., 232, 233, 235, 237, 238, 319, 322
Sosa, A. V., 262
Souza, B. G., 327
Sovtic, A. D., 326
Sowell, E. R., 317, 422
Spalding, J. L., 313
Spandel, V., 365
Spangler, G., 206
Speelman, C. P., 332
Spelke, E., 163
Spelke, E. S., 150, 162–164, 450
Spence, C., 228
Spence, J. T., 480
Spence, M. J., 148
Spencer, D., 281
Spencer, M. B., 7, 419, 494
Spencer, S., 372
Spencer, S. J., 358
Sperhake, J. P., 129
Spiegler, M. D., 23
Spieker, S., 112
Spilman, S. K., 463
Spindel, E. R., 89
Spinrad, T. L., 281, 283, 285, 383, 391, 392, 396, 459
Spinrad, T. R., 283, 395
Spinrad, T. L., 393
Spittle, A. J., 107
Springelkamp, H., 51
Springer, J., 46
Springer, M. G., 407
Spuhl, S. T., 250
Sreetharan, S., 91
Srivastav, S., 94
Srivastava, N., 55
Sroufe, L. A., 204–206, 294
St. Jacques, P. L., 256, 347
Stadelmann, S., 383
Stafford, F. P., 398

Stamatakis, E., 325
Stancil, S. L., 87
Stanford University Medical Center, 223
Stangor, C., 28, 31
Stanley-Hagan, M., 297, 298
Stanovich, K. E., 331
Staples, A. D., 231
Starr, C., 14, 48, 53
Starr, L., 14, 48, 53
Staszewski, J. (Ed.), 347
Stattin, H., 402
Steca, P., 371
Steckler, C. M., 163
Steele, C. M., 358
Steffen, V. J., 394
Steif, M. C., 427
Steiger, A. E., 383
Stein, M., 329
Stein, M. T., 330
Steinbeck, K. S., 423
Steinberg, L., 206, 224, 225, 290, 425, 426, 453–455, 483, 488, 490, 497
Steinberg, S. J., 500
Steiner, J. E., 149
Stenberg, G., 201
Stephens, J. M., 460, 461
Steric, M., 78
Stern, D. N., 209
Stern, P., 358
Stern, W., 353
Sternberg, K., 349
Sternberg, K. J., 15
Sternberg, R. J., 349–351, 354–362
Stevens, E. A., 364
Stevens, G. D., 238
Stevenson, H. W., 373
Stewart, A. J., 399
Stewart, J. B., 397
Stewart, J. E., 415
Stewart, J. G., 452, 453, 500, 501
Stice, E., 443
Stickgold, R., 113
Stifter, C., 193, 289
Stifter, C. A., 195
Stiggins, R., 407
Stigler, J. W., 373
Stillman, T. F., 459
Stilwell, D., 57
Stipek, D., 383
Stipek, D. J., 371
Stirling, A., 320
Stockwell, S., 110
Stoel-Gammon, C., 144, 262
Stokes, K. A., 495
Stone, M., 465
Stough, L. M., 386
Stovall-McClough, K. C., 295
Stracciolini, A., 320
Straker, L. M., 307
Strassberg, D. S., 427
Strathearn, L., 207
Streib, H., 463
Streit, C., 392
Strenze, T., 355

Streri, A., 150
Striano, T., 201
Striegel-Moore, R. H., 443
Stright, A. D., 210, 480
Stringer, M., 83
Strohmeier, D., 404
Strong, D. R., 440, 441
Stroobant, N., 125
Stryjewski, G., 222
Stuebe, A. M., 132
Stumper, A., 196
Sturge-Apple, M. L., 298
Styfco, S. J., 268
Suarez, L., 78
Sue, D. M., 494
Sue, D. W., 494
Sugden, N. A., 143, 200
Sugisaki, K., 263
Sugita, Y., 146
Sugrue, N. M., 84
Suh, S., 301
Suh, Y., 51, 53
Suk, M., 501
Sullivan, A., 484
Sullivan, F. R., 351, 364, 365
Sullivan, H. S., 486
Sullivan, K., 484
Sullivan, M. W., 144
Sullivan, R., 12, 123, 206, 207
Sullivan, R. M., 189
Sumontha, J., 300
Sun, R., 60
Sun, S. S., 322
Sun, Y., 424, 499
Sunderam, S., 60
Sundstrom Poromaa, I., 114
Super, C. M., 140
Super, E. M., 206
Suskind, D., 180
Susman, E. J., 422–425
Sutin, A. R., 403
Sutphin, G. L., 50
Sutterlin, S., 284
Suzuki, L. K., 358
Swaab, D. F., 394
Swain, J. E., 180, 207
Swamy, G. K., 109
Swanson, D. P., 7, 419, 494
Swanson, H. L., 346, 452, 453
Swartout, K., 501
Swartzendruber, A., 502
Sweeting, H., 238
Sweeting, H. N., 322
Swing, E. L., 253
Swingler, M. M., 200
Swingley, D., 174
Syed, M., 475
Sykes, C. J., 383
Szwedo, D. E., 489
Szyf, M., 66

T

Taddio, A., 149
Taggart, J., 305, 306
Taige, N. M., 94
Talib, M. A., 462
Tamayo, S., 367

Tamis-LeMonda, C., 135, 138, 140, 179, 397
Tamiya, N., 114
Tampi, R. R., 232
Tan, B. W., 332
Tan, C. C., 405
Tan, J., 15, 484
Tan, P. Z., 190, 195
Tan, T., 63
Tanaka, C., 320
Tang, F. R., 91
Tang, S., 433, 478, 479
Tanilon, J., 501
Tannen, D., 395
Tanrikulu, M. A., 322–323, 326
Tardif, T., 302
Tarokh, L., 438
Tartaglia, N. R., 56
Tasker, F., 61, 300, 301
Taussig, H. N., 295
Taylor, A. W., 92
Taylor, C., 349
Taylor, C. A., 237, 292
Taylor, F. M. A., 85
Taylor, H., 105
Taylor, J. R., 174
Taylor, R., 329
Taylor, R. D., 398
Tchamo, M. E., 109
Tee, L. M., 59
Teenage Research Unlimited, 13
Tees, R. C., 366
Tehrani, H. G., 105
Teller, D. Y., 146
Telzer, E. H., 189, 190
Temich, P., 103
Temple, C. A., 264, 329, 364, 406
Templeton, J. L., 462
Tenenbaum, H., 287
Tenenbaum, H. R., 28
ten Hoope-Bender, P., 102
Ten Hoor, G. A., 437
Te'o, M., 490
Terman, L., 360, 362
Terry-McElrath, Y. M., 437
Teti, D., 296
Teti, D. M., 158, 292
te Velde, S. J., 235, 307
Tevendale, H. D., 431, 432
Thabet, A. A., 386
Thagard, P., 361
Thanh, N. X., 88
Tharp, R. G., 251
The, N. S., 435
Theis, D., 465
Thelen, E., 123, 135, 136, 138, 151
Thoma, S. J., 390, 459
Thomas, A., 193, 194, 196, 197
Thomas, C. A., 91
Thomas, D., 222, 306
Thomas, H., 172
Thomas, J. C., 192
Thomas, J. R., 299

Thomas, K. A., 112
Thomas, K. J., 62
Thomas, K. M., 426
Thomas, M. S. C., 5, 128, 366
Thompson, A. E., 395
Thompson, D. R., 322
Thompson, J., 322
Thompson, M. P., 501
Thompson, P. M., 126, 224
Thompson, R., 83, 210, 329, 395, 501
Thompson, R. A., 189–191, 193, 195–197, 199–201, 203, 205, 206, 210, 278–281, 283, 285, 292, 383, 385, 391, 395, 480, 483
Thonneau, F., 95
Thornburg, K. L., 75
Thornton, J. D., 327
Thornton, J. W., 409
Thornton, R., 263
Thorsen, K., 67
Thurman, A. J., 56
Tidefors, I., 294
Tiggemann, M., 441, 443
Tikotzky, L., 128
Tilton-Weaver, L. C., 304
TIMMS, 372
Tincoff, R., 177
Tinloy, J., 81
Tinsley, B. J., 238
Tobin, J. J., 271
Tolani, N., 212
Tomalski, P., 124
Tomany-Korman, S. C., 238
Tomasello, M., 167, 177, 180, 263, 280
Tomassay, G. S., 125
Tomblin, J. B., 177
Tominey, S. L., 256
Tomlinson, M., 240
Tompkins, G. E., 264, 265, 364, 365
Tompkins, V., 259
Tomporowski, P. D., 320
Tong, X., 363
Tongsong, T., 94
Tonks, S. M., 372, 464
Top, N., 482
Toplak, M. E., 331
Torrence, C. M., 166
Torstveit, L., 284
Toth, S. L., 32, 292–295
Tottenham, N., 425, 454
Tough, S. C., 94
Trainor, L. J., 148, 149
Traisrisilp, K., 94
Traustadottir, T., 52
Trehub, S. E., 148
Treiman, R., 364
Tremblay, M. S., 307
Trickett, P. K., 424, 425
Trimble, J. E., 35
Trinh, K.-H., 448
Trinkner, R., 498
Troia, G., 365
Trommsdorff, G., 190

Tronick, E., 107
Troop, W., 402
Troop-Gordon, W., 402, 403
Troppe, P., 408
Trotman, G., 84
Troutman, A. C., 335
Truglio, R. T., 308
Truzzi, A., 67
Trzaskowski, M., 356
Trzesniewski, K. H., 370
Tsal, Y., 330
Tsang, T. W., 88
Tso, W., 232
Tsubomi, H., 346, 452
Ttofi, M. M., 403
Tucker, C. J., 498
Tucker, J. S., 440
Tudellia, E., 141
Tuleski, S. C., 249
Tully, E. C., 285
Tung, R., 467
Turecki, G., 52
Turiel, E., 288, 389, 392
Turnbull, A., 328, 336
Turner, R., 429, 487
Turner, S., 501
Twain, M., 140, 483
Tweed, E. J., 107
Tylka, T. L., 233
Tyrell, F. A., 489

U

U. S. Census Bureau, 448
U. S. Department of Energy, 51
U. S. Department of Health and
    Human Services, 293
U. S. Food and Drug
    Administration (FDA),
    88, 93
U. S. Office of Education, 337
Uba, L., 85
Uccelli, P., 180, 363
Udry, J. R., 487
Ueno, M., 148
Uher, R., 295
Umana-Taylor, A. J., 35, 36,
    291, 301, 302, 408, 419,
    479, 484, 485
Umstead, L., 143, 145, 200
Underwood, M. K., 394
Ungar, M., 386
UNICEF, 9, 92, 121, 132,
    133, 235, 240, 397,
    430, 492
Updegraff, K. A., 291, 295
Ur, S., 475, 476
Urbina, S., 358
Urdan, T., 479
Urgula, M. L., 108
Usher, E. L., 383
Uto, Y., 30, 145

V

Vahratian, A., 80
Vaish, A., 180
Valdesolo, P., 390

Valente,T. W., 440
Valentino, K., 256
Valentino, K. V., 298
Valenzuela, C. F., 88
Valiente, C., 281, 283,
    285, 383
Vallotton, C., 179, 182
Vallotton, C. D., 268, 269
Van Beveren, T. T., 106, 171
Van Bussel, I. P., 52
Vandehey, M., 461
Vandell, D. L., 214
van den Boom, D. C., 197
van den Bos, W., 454
Vandenbosch, L., 427
van den Dries, L., 61
van der Hulst, H., 173
van der Stel, M., 456
Van der Veer, R. (Ed.),
    249, 251
Vanderwert, R. E., 124
Van de Vandervoort, J.,
    162–164
van de Weijer-Bergsma, E., 332
Van Doren, J., 331
van Dulmen, M., 400
van Geel, M., 501
van Goethem, A., 458
van Goethem, A. A. J., 458
Van Hecke, V., 167
van Hout, A., 263
van IJzendoorn, M. H., 67,
    197, 204, 206, 210
Vanitallie, T. B., 51
Van Lieshout, M., 331
Van Lissa, C. J., 485
van Oosten, J. M., 427
Van Ryzin, M. J., 205,
    304, 441
van Schaik, C. P., 355
Varcin, K. J., 124
Vardavas, C. I., 89
Varga, N. L., 346
Vargas, L. A., 6
Varner, M. W., 89, 91
Vaughan, C. A., 500
Vaughan, L., 322
Vaughan, O. R., 75
Vaughn, B. E., 206, 232
Vaughn, M. G., 468
Vaughn, S., 364
Vazsonyi, A. T., 383
Vedder, P., 479, 501
Veenman, M. V. J., 456
Veenstra-VanderWeele, J., 51
Velarde, V., 427
Veldman, S. L., 227
Velez, C. E., 299
Vella, S. A., 320
Veness, C., 166
Venetsanou, F., 228
Venners, S. A., 95
Vergara-Castaneda, A., 322
Verhagen, J., 346
Verhoef, M., 425
Verhoeven, L., 346
Verkuylen, 479
Verloigne, M., 492

Verma, S., 485, 493
Vernberg, E. M., 500
Vernini, J. M., 79
Vest, A. E., 466
Vetter, N. C., 402
Vezina, P., 426
Vidal, S., 497
Vieira, J. M., 297
Vignoles, V. L., 7, 492
Villamor, E., 424
Villanueva, C. M., 302
Villeda, S., 127
Villegas, R., 131
Villodas, M. T., 293
Viner-Brown, S., 134
Vingerhoets, G., 125
Vinik, J., 282
Virgil, 370
Viswanathan, M., 78, 93
Vittrup, B., 210, 211
Vo, P., 239
Voelker, D. K., 424
Vogels, T. P., 127
Vogt, M. J., 36, 367
Vogt, P., 167
Voigt, R. G., 331
Volkmar, F. R., 334
Volkow, N. D., 90
Vollink, T., 403
Volpe, E. M., 430
Volpe, S., 435
von Aster, M., 329
von dem Hagen, E. A., 261
von Hippel, C., 358
Von Hofsten, C., 135
Vonk, J. M., 326
Vorona, R. D., 438
Votavova, H., 89
Votruba-Drzal, E., 7, 9, 10,
    372, 408, 418
Voyer, D., 395
Vreeman, R. C., 404
Vu, J. A., 213
Vukelich, C., 264
Vurpillot, E., 254
Vygotsky, L. S., 20–22, 26,
    27, 209, 246, 249–253,
    266, 305, 344
Vysniauske, R., 332

W

Wachs, H., 343
Wachs, T. D., 196, 197
Wadsworth, M. E., 9, 302,
    357, 408
Wagner, D. A., 450
Wagner, N. J., 89
Wahlsten, D., 66
Waldenstrom, U., 94
Waldfogel, J., 297
Waldman, Z., 333
Waldner, L. S., 458
Walk, R. D., 147
Walker, A., 4, 8
Walker, K. C., 493
Walker, L. J., 389, 391, 459
Walker, M. A., 364

Wallace, I. F., 172
Wallace, M. E., 109
Walle, E. A., 139, 176
Waller, E. M., 499, 500
Wallerstein, J. S., 298
Walsh, B. A., 6
Walsh, L. V., 84
Walsh, P., 129
Walters, B., 267
Walton, E., 330, 331
Wang, B., 441, 482
Wang, C., 402, 487
Wang, G. S., 91
Wang, H., 423–425
Wang, H. J., 51
Wang, J., 92, 430, 500
Wang, L., 301
Wang, M. T., 453
Wang, Q., 348
Wang, S., 261, 335
Wang, W. Y., 57
Wang, Y., 485
Wang, Z., 261
Wanigaratne, S., 108
Wanstrom, L., 356
Ward, D. S., 234
Wardlaw, G., 133, 232, 234
Wargo, E. M., 90
Warner, C. D., 392
Warner, L., 433
Warren, A. E. A., 462
Warren, M. P., 423, 425
Warren, S. F., 56, 182
Warrick, P., 100
Warschburger, P., 424
Warshak, R. A., 63,
    299, 399
Washington, G., 11
Washizuka, S., 232
Wasserberg, M. J., 358
Wasserman, D., 51
Wasserman, J., 51
Wataganara, T., 59
Watamura, S. E., 214
Watanabe, E., 323
Watanabe, K., 346, 452
Waterman, A. S., 477
Waters, A. M., 453
Waters, E. E., 498
Waters, S. F., 191
Waters, T. E., 484
Watkins, M. W., 354
Watkins, R. M., 142
Watson, G. L., 330
Watson, J., 259
Watson, J. B., 23, 193
Watson, M. W., 292
Watson, W., 344
Waxman, S., 173, 177, 264
Way, N., 433
Weatherhead, D., 143, 200
Webb, L. D., 406
Webber, T. A., 426
Weber, D., 356, 357
Weber, M. A., 129
Weber Yorga, K., 81
Webster, N. S., 457
Wechsler, D., 353

Weersing, V. R., 334, 498
Weikart, D. P., 269,
    502–503
Weiler, L. M., 295
Weinraub, M., 128
Weinstein, N., 368
Weinstock, M., 260
Weiselberg, E., 443
Weisleder, A., 180, 181
Weisman, O., 207
Weisner, T. S., 409
Weiss, L. A., 335
Weissenberger, S., 89
Weisstanner, C., 59
Wekerle, C., 294
Wellman, H. M., 258–261, 279
Wells, A., 114
Wells, B., 291
Wells, E. M., 93
Wells, M. G., 384
Welsh, D., 490
Wendelken, C., 317, 384
Wennergren, G., 131
Wentzel, K. R., 369, 396, 400,
    401, 405, 486
Wenzel, A., 94
Werker, J. F., 176, 366
Wermelinger, S., 366
Werner, N. E., 304
Wesseling, P. B., 181
West, J. E., 461
West, M. J., 179
West, R. F., 331
West, T. V., 191
Westermann, G., 128
Westmoreland, P., 442
Westra, T., 140
Weyandt, L. L., 331
Whaley, S. E., 134
Wheeden, A., 111
Wheeler, J. J., 330, 333, 335
Wheeler, K., 172
Whipple, N., 258
White, B. A., 402
White, G., 115
White, K. S., 143, 200
White, N., 296
White, R. E., 257, 258
White, R. M., 479
Whiteman, S. D., 295
Whiteman, V., 90
Whitney, E., 6, 130, 133
Widaman, K. F., 296
Widener, M. C., 458
Widman, L., 430, 487
Widom, C. S., 294, 295
Wiesen, S. E., 142
Wiesner, G., 320
Wigfield, A., 371, 372,
    396, 464
Wigginton, B., 89
Wilce, J. M., 175, 179
Wilcox, S., 173
Wilkenfeld, B., 391
Wilkinson, K. M., 30, 145
Willey, J., 53
Willford, J., 91
Williams, A. M., 121, 132

subject index

bottle feeding, 131
Bradley Method, 104
brain
  cognitive development and, 225
  early experiences and, 126–127
  gender and, 394
  infant-mother attachment and, 207
  neuroconstructivist view of, 127–128
  neuronal changes in, 224
  structural changes in, 224–225
brain development
  in adolescence, 425–426
  in early childhood, 223–225
  in infancy, 123–128, 168
  in middle and late childhood, 316–317
  prenatal, 78
brainstorming, 350, 351
Brazelton Neonatal Behavioral Assessment Scale (NBAS), 107, 171
breast cancer, 132
breast feeding
  benefits of, 131
  bottle feeding vs., 131–132
  cultural diversity and, 121
  HIV/AIDS and, 92
  trends in, 131
breech position, 105
Bringing Home Baby project, 209
Broca's area, 178
Bronfenbrenner's ecological theory, 26
bulimia nervosa, 443
bullying
  cyberbullying, 403
  explanation of, 402
  outcomes of, 403
  perspective taking and moral motivation and, 404
  social contests as influence on, 402–403
  victims of, 402–404
bullying interventions, 403

C

caffeine, 88
cancer
  breast feeding and incidence of, 132
  in children, 324–325
cardiovascular disease, 325
career counselors, 42
careers, 40–43. See also child development careers
caregivers/caregiving
  attachment to, 202–207
  child maltreatment by, 293–295
  eating behavior and, 233

emotional expressiveness of, 282
  fathers as, 188
  of infants, 130
  moral development and, 283
care perspective, 391
case studies, 29
cataracts, 150
causality, 162
CenteringPregnancy program, 83–84
centration, 248–249
cephalographic pattern, 122
cerebral cortex, 124, 125, 317
cerebral palsy, 333
cesarean delivery, 104–105
character education, 460–461
cheating, 460–461
childbirth
  bonding following, 115
  cesarean, 104–105
  emotional and psychological adjustments following, 113–116
  medication for, 103
  natural, 103–104
  physical adjustments following, 112–113
  prepared, 104
  setting and attendants for, 102–103
  stages of, 101–102
child care
  international policies for, 212
  overview of, 212
  parental leave and, 212
  research on, 214
  safety issues and, 238
  variations in, 212, 213
child development, importance of studying, 5
child development careers. See also specific careers
  clinical and counseling, 41–42
  dealing with education and research, 40–41
  dealing with families and relationships, 43
  medical, nursing, and physical development, 42–43
child development theories. See also specific theories
  behavioral and social cognitive, 23–24
  cognitive, 20–23
  eclectic theoretical orientation to, 26
  ecological, 25–26
  ethological, 24–25
  overview of, 17
  psychoanalytic, 17–20
child-directed speech, 180–181
childhood amnesia, 168
child life specialists, 43

child maltreatment, 293–295
child neglect, 293–294
children. See also adolescents/adolescence; early childhood; infants/infancy; middle and late childhood
  adopted, 61–63
  depression in, 114
  in divorced families, 297–299, 399
  gender development and, 8
  health and well-being of, 5–6
  media use by, 495–496
  parenting practices and, 6–7
  quality of education for, 7
  resilience in, 8–10
  social policy and, 8–10
  sociocultural contexts and diversity of, 7–8
children with disabilities
  attention deficit hyperactivity disorder, 330–332
  autism spectrum disorders, 334–335
  educational issues related to, 335–336
  emotional and behavioral disorders, 334
  intellectual disabilities, 359–360
  learning disabilities, 328–330
  overview of, 328
  physical disorders, 333–334
  sensory disorders, 332–333
  speech disorders, 332
child welfare workers, 43
China
  education in, 467
  onset of puberty in, 424
  overweight children in, 322
chorionic villus sampling (CVS), 59
chromosomal abnormalities, sex-linked, 54–56
chromosomes
  explanation of, 50
  male and female, 52–53, 286
chronosystem, 25–26
cigarette smoking. See tobacco use
classical conditioning theory, 23
clinical psychologists, 42
cliques, 487
cocaine, prenatal exposure to, 89–90
cocaine-related infertility, 95
Code of Ethics (American Psychological Association), 33

cognition, stages of development and, 159
cognitive control, 453–454
cognitive development
  adoption and, 62
  brain and, 225
  exercise and, 320
  gender and, 394
  in infancy, 171
  malnutrition and, 235
  sleep and, 130, 231
  working memory and, 346–347
cognitive developmental neuroscience, 426
cognitive flexibility, 453–454
cognitive processes
  explanation of, 11
  in infancy, 158–159
cognitive reappraisal strategy, 480
cognitive theories. See also Piaget's theory; Vygotsky's theory; specific theories
  evaluation of, 22–23
  information-processing approach to, 22
  overview of, 20
cognitive therapy, for postpartum depression, 113–114
cohort effects, 12–14
college/university professors, 40, 41
color vision, 146
commitment
  explanation of, 477
  understanding, 280
Common Core State Standards Initiative, 407
communication
  about divorce, 300
  gender differences in, 395
  online, 490–491
  between parents and adolescents, 482–483
computers. See technology
conception, 74
concepts, 169–170
concrete operational stage
  applied to education, 345
  evaluation of, 344
  explanation of, 21, 343–344, 449
confidentiality, in research, 33
connectedness, 478
conscience, 283
conservation, 248–249
constructivist approach, 344–345, 406
context, 7. See also sociocultural contexts
continuity-discontinuity issue, 14–15
contraceptive use, 430
control groups, 32
controversial children, 401

conventional reasoning, 388
convergent thinking, 349–350
cooing, 176
coordination of secondary circular reactions substage, 160–161
coparenting, 292
coping
  in infancy, 192–193
  with traumatic events, 386–387
core knowledge approach, 163–164
corporal punishment. See punishment
corpus callosum, 425
correlational research, 30–31, 383
correlation coefficient, 31
counseling psychologists, 42
crawling, 136, 138
creative intelligence, 354
creative thinking
  explanation of, 349–350
  strategies to increase, 351
creativity, encouragement of, 221
crisis, 476–477
critical thinking, 349, 455–456
cross-cultural studies, 7. See also culture/cultural diversity
cross-sectional approach to research, 32
crowds, 488
crying
  explanation of, 176
  parent responses to, 193
  types of, 191–192
cultural bias, 35–36
cultural-familial intellectual disability, 360
cultural mediators, 410
culture/cultural diversity. See also ethnicity/ethnic groups
  achievement and, 372–374
  adolescent pregnancy and, 433
  adolescent suicide and, 501
  adoption and, 62
  among adolescents, 491–496
  attachment and, 205–206
  attention and, 254
  autobiographical memory and, 347–348
  breast feeding vs. bottle feeding and, 121
  childbirth and, 102
  child care and, 212
  early childhood education and, 270, 271
  emotional expression and, 190
  exercise and, 436–437
  explanation of, 7

gender roles and, 397
health and, 237
identity development and, 478–479
immigration and, 493–494
intelligence and, 358
language development and, 177
low birth weight infants and, 109
moral reasoning and, 390
motor development and, 140
parent-adolescent conflict and, 485
parenting and, 301–302
pregnancy and, 84, 85
punishment and, 291
secondary schools and, 467
sexual activity and, 427
shared sleeping and, 129
socioeconomic status and, 408, 494
temperament and, 196
culture-fair tests, 358
curriculum, in early childhood education, 269
cyberbullying, 403
cystic fibrosis, 57

D

danger invulnerability, 451
dating/romantic relationships
    adjustment in, 489–490
    heterosexual relationships and, 488–489
    identity and, 478
    online, 490–491
    in sexual minority youth, 489
death
    in adolescence, 438–439
    of children, 237, 240
    in infancy, 129–130, 132
debriefing, 33
deception, in research, 33–34
decision making, in adolescence, 454–455
deferred imitation, 169
Denver Developmental Screening Test II, 228
dependent variables, 31–32
depression
    in adolescents, 498–501
    maternal, 128, 432, 499–500
    peer rejection and, 401
    postpartum, 113–115
    treatment for, 500
    in withdrawn children, 303
depth perception, 147–148
descriptive research, 30
design stage, in artistic expression, 230
development, 5
    evolutionary psychology and, 48–49
    genetic foundations of, 50–58

key processes in, 11–12
periods of, 12, 13
developmental cascade model, 205
developmental cognitive neuroscience, 11
developmentally appropriate practice (DAP), 267–268
developmental quotient (DQ), 172
developmental social neuroscience, 12, 206–207
diabetes, 57, 68, 92, 132, 325
diarrhea, 240
diet. See also eating behavior; nutrition
    in early childhood, 232
    in middle and late childhood, 319
    overweight and, 322, 323
    during pregnancy, 79–80, 93–94
dietary fats, 233–234
Differential susceptibility model, 197
difficult child, 193, 197
digitally mediated communication, 496
direct instruction approach, 406
disabilities. See children with disabilities
discipline, 210–211, 398. See also punishment
discontinuity, 14–15
disease
    cultural beliefs about, 85
    in middle and late childhood, 324–326
    overweight and, 322–323
    during pregnancy, 92
dishabituation
    explanation of, 143–145
    in infancy, 166
divergent thinking, 350
diversity. See culture/cultural diversity
divorce
    communicating with children about, 300
    effects on children, 297–299, 399
    remarriage and, 399
    statistics related to, 297–298
DNA (deoxyribonucleic acid), 50–53, 57, 67. See also genes; genetics
domain-specific giftedness, 361–362
domain theory of moral development, 392
dominant-recessive genes principle, 53–54
dose-response effects, 386
doulas, 103
Down syndrome, 55, 94
dropout rate. See school dropout rate

drug counselors, 42
drugs. See also substance use/ abuse
    during childbirth, 103
    for postpartum depression, 113
    during prenatal period, 75, 87–88
    psychoactive, 89–91
dual-language learning, 366, 367
dual-process model, 455
dynamic systems theory, 135–136
dyscalculia, 329
dysgraphia, 329
dyslexia, 329

E

early bloomers, 489
early childhood. See also children
    adopted children and, 63
    artistic expression in, 221, 229–230
    brain development in, 223–225
    cognitive changes in, 246–261
    egocentrism in, 246–247, 280, 285
    emotional development in, 280–282
    explanation of, 12
    health, safety and illness in, 237–240
    illness and injuries in, 237–240
    information processing in, 253–261
    moral development in, 283–285
    motor skills in, 226–228
    nutrition in, 232–235
    peer relations in, 303–304
    perceptual development in, 228–229
    physical activity in, 235–236
    physical growth in, 222–223
    preoperational stage in, 246–249
    prosocial behavior in, 392–393
    self-understanding in, 278–279
    sleep in, 231–232
    understanding others in, 279–280
early childhood education. See also education
    child-centered kindergarten and, 266
    for children who are disadvantaged, 268–269
    controversies in, 269

developmentally appropriate practice in, 267–268
    in Japan and developing countries, 270
    Montessori approach to, 267
early childhood educators, 41
Early Head Start, 268–269
early-later experience issue, 14–15
easy child, 193
eating behavior. See also diet; nutrition
    in adolescents, 441–443
    in early childhood, 232
    in infancy, 130–131
eclectic theoretical orientation, 26
ecological theory, 25–26
ecological view, of perception, 143
ectoderm, 74, 75
education. See also achievement; early childhood education; high schools; junior high schools; schools
    accountability in, 406–407
    character, 460–461
    of children from low-income backgrounds, 408
    of children who are gifted, 362
    of children with disabilities, 335–336
    constructivist approach to, 406
    developmentally appropriate, 267–268
    direct instruction approach to, 406
    early childhood, 266–271
    effect on intelligence, 357
    ethnicity and, 408–410
    moral, 460–461
    Piaget's theory applied to, 344–345
    poverty and, 268–269, 408
    quality of, 7
    service learning, 457–458
    sex, 434
    single-sex, 396–397
    socioeconomic status and, 303, 408
educationally blind, 333
educational psychologists, 41
Education for all Handicapped Children Act (Public Law 94-142), 335
effortful control, 194–195, 453
egocentrism
    in adolescence, 450–451
    in early childhood, 246–247, 280, 285
    explanation of, 246
ego ideal, 283

eight frames of mind (Gardner), 355
elaboration, as memory strategy, 347
electroencephalogram (EEG), 123
elementary school teachers, 40
embryonic period, 74–76
emerging adulthood, 419–421, 477–478. See also adolescents/adolescence
emotional abuse, 294
emotional and behavioral disorders, 334
emotional development
    in adolescence, 479–480
    in early childhood, 280–282
    in infancy, 191–193
    in middle and late childhood, 385–387
emotional expression
    cultural diversity and, 190
    in early childhood, 280–281
    in infancy, 191–192
emotional regulation
    caregivers and, 282
    in early childhood, 282
    gender differences in, 394–395
    in infancy, 192–193
    peer relations and, 282
emotion-coaching parents, 281–282
emotion-dismissing parents, 281–282
emotions. See also temperament
    biological and environmental influences on, 189–190
    explanation of, 189
    moral development and, 283–285
    in postpartum period, 113
    during pregnancy, 94–95
    primary, 190
    self-conscious, 190, 280
    understanding, 280
empiricists, 150, 151
endoderm, 74, 75
energy needs, 232–233
English language learners, 366, 367
environmental hazards
    lead exposure and, 238, 239
    prenatal exposure to, 91–92
    tobacco smoke as, 238–239
environmental influences. See also nature-nurture issue
    brain activity and, 126–127
    on emotions, 189–190
    on intelligence, 356–358
    on language development, 178–181
    on onset of puberty, 424

overweight children and, 322

epigenetic view, 66–68

equilibration, 159

Erikson's psychosocial theory
explanation of, 18–19
identity development and, 462–463, 476
infant development and, 202
life-span stages in, 278, 384
strategies based on, 19

estradiol, 422–423

ethical issues, related to research, 33–34

ethnic bias, 35–36, 409–410

ethnic gloss, 35–36

ethnic identity, 479

ethnicity/ethnic groups. See also culture/cultural diversity
achievement and, 372
adolescent pregnancy and, 432
education and, 408–410
exercise and, 436–437
explanation of, 7–8
health and, 238
immigration and, 494
parenting and, 301–302
school dropout rate and, 468
in schools, 408–410
sexual activity and, 429
socioeconomic status and, 408, 494
special education programs and, 337

ethological theory, 24–25

ethology, 24

evocative genotype-environment correlations, 65–66

evolutionary developmental psychology, 48–49

evolutionary psychology
evaluation of, 49
explanation of, 48–49
gender and, 286–287

exceptional children teachers, 40–41

executive attention, 253, 254

executive function
in adolescence, 452
explanation of, 256–258, 348
in middle and late childhood, 348–349
school readiness and, 257
theory of mind and, 260

exercise. See also physical activity
ADHD and, 332
in adolescence, 436–437
in early childhood, 235–236
in middle and late childhood, 319–320
for overweight children, 323

in postpartum period, 113, 114
during pregnancy, 80–81
weight and, 436–437

exosystem, 25

expanding, 181

experimental groups, 32

experimental research, 31–32

expertise, memory and, 347

extracurricular activities, 465–466

extraversion/surgency, 194

extrinsic motivation, 368

eye tracking, 30, 145

F

faces, perception of, 143, 146

face-to-face play, 200

Fagan test, 172

false beliefs, 259

false-belief tasks, 259

families/family influences. See also fathers; mothers; parents/parenting
as constellation of subsystems, 208
cultural diversity and, 492
delinquency and, 498
educating children from low-income, 268–269
effect of birth order in, 296
identity development and, 478
managing and guiding infant behavior in, 210–211
moral development and, 390–391
mothers and fathers as caregivers in, 211–212
reciprocal socialization and, 209
sibling relationships in, 295–296
socioeconomic status and, 302–303
transition to parenthood and, 208–209

family and consumer science educators, 41

Family Matters program, 442

family processes, divorce and, 299

family trends
children in divorced families, 297–299, 399
cross-cultural studies on, 301–302
ethnicity and, 301–302
gay and lesbian parents, 300–301
overview of, 297–298
socioeconomic status and, 302–303
stepfamilies, 399
working parents, 297

fast mapping, 263

Fast Track, 503

fathers. See also caregivers/caregiving; families/family influences; parents/parenting
as caregivers, 188, 211–212
gender development and, 287
postpartum depression in, 115

fear, 192

females. See also gender/gender differences
brain structure in, 393–394
cognitive development in, 394
communication and, 395
early and late maturation in, 425
emotional regulation in, 394–395
moral reasoning and, 391
onset of puberty in, 422, 424
overweight, 322
sexual activity and, 429
sexual maturation in, 422
socioemotional development and, 394–397

fertilization, 52–53, 74

fetal alcohol spectrum disorders (FASD), 88

fetal MRI, 59

fetal period, 76

fetal sex determination, 60

fetus. See also pregnancy; prenatal development; prenatal development hazards
development of, 74–78
diagnostic tests for, 58–60
hazards to, 86–95
senses in, 148
transition from newborn from, 106

fine motor skills
in early childhood, 228
explanation of, 141
in infancy, 141–142
in middle and late childhood, 318

firearm access, 237

first habits and primary circular reaction substage, 160

fish, mercury in, 93

5-HTTLPR gene, 67, 206

fluency disorders, 332

food. See diet; nutrition

forebrain, 124

forgiveness, 459

formal operational stage, 21, 449–450

foster care, 62. See also adopted children

fragile X syndrome, 55, 56

fraternal twins, 64

Freudian theory
attachment in, 202
ego ideal and, 283
gender development and, 287
overview of, 17–18

friends/friendship. See also peer relations
in adolescence, 486–487, 500
in early childhood, 304
functions of, 405
intimacy in, 405
in middle and late childhood, 405

frontal lobe, 124, 224–225

fuzzy trace theory, 347

fuzzy-trace theory dual-process model, 455

G

gastrointestinal infections, 131

gays
as parents, 300–301
romantic relationships among adolescent, 489

gender bias
in research, 35
in school settings, 395–396

gender/gender differences. See also females; males
in academic achievement, 395–396
autism spectrum disorders and, 334, 335
in autonomy-granting in adolescence, 483
biological influences on, 286–287
bullying and, 402
in cognitive development, 394
cognitive influences on, 288
in communication, 395
in context, 397
cultural diversity and, 492
in depression, 498–499
early and late maturation and, 424–425
evolutionary psychology view of, 286–287
explanation of, 8, 9
learning disabilities and, 329, 396
moral development and, 391
overweight children and, 322
in physical development, 393–394
puberty onset and, 422, 424
school dropout rate and, 468
in sexual activity, 428–429
social influences and, 287–288

socioemotional development and, 394–397

gender identity, 286

gender roles, 286

gender schema theory, 288

gender stereotypes, 393

gender typing, 286

gene × environment (G × E) interaction, 67

gene-linked abnormalities, 56–57

generativity vs. stagnation stage, 19

genes
collaborative action of, 50–52
dominant-recessive principle and, 53–54
explanation of, 50
mitosis, meiosis, and fertilization and, 52–53
polygenic inheritance and, 54–55
sex-linked, 54
sources of variability of, 53

genetic abnormalities
chromosomal, 55–56
dealing with, 57
gene-linked, 56–57

genetic counselors, 43, 57

genetic imprinting, 54

genetics. See also nature-nurture issue
behavior, 64–65
collaborative gene and, 50–52
genes and chromosomes and, 52–53
intelligence, effect on, 356
principles of, 53–55

genital herpes, 92

genome-wide association method, 51

genotype, 53

germinal period, 74

gestational diabetes, 92

gestures, in infancy, 176

giftedness
characteristics of, 360
developmental changes and domain-specific, 361–362
education of children with, 362
explanation of, 360
nature-nurture issue and, 360–361

Girls, Inc., 434

goal-directed behavior, 200–201

goal setting, 371

gonadotropins, 422

gonads, 286, 422, 423

goodness of fit, 196–197

grammar, in middle and late childhood, 363

grasping, 141

kindergarten,
    child-centered, 266
kindergarten teachers, 41
Klinefelter syndrome, 55–56
knowledge, memory and, 347
Kohlberg's theory of moral
    development
    background of, 387
    criticisms of, 389–392
    social conventional
        approach vs., 392
    stages in, 387–389, 459
kwashiorkor, 133

L

labeling, 181
labor, 102–103. *See also*
    childbirth
laboratory, 28
Lamaze method, 104
language
    explanation of, 173
    rule systems of, 174–175
    thought and, 250
language acquisition device
    (LAD), 178
language development
    behavioral view of,
        179–180
    biological influences on,
        177–178, 181–182
    in early childhood, 262–265
    environmental influences
        on, 178–181
    in infancy, 175–178
    interactionist view of,
        181–182
    literacy and, 264–265
    in middle and late
        childhood, 363–367
    phonology and morphology
        understanding and,
        175–176, 262–263
    pragmatics advances and,
        174, 175, 264
    syntax and semantics
        changes and, 174, 175,
        263–264
    theory of mind and, 260
    in toddlers, 180,
        181–182, 262
    working memory and,
        346–347
late bloomers, 489
late childhood. *See*
    adolescents/
    adolescence; children;
    middle and late
    childhood
lateralization, 124
Latinos. *See also* ethnicity/
    ethnic groups
    adolescent pregnancy
        and, 432
    as ethnic group, 7
    gifted programs and, 362
    overweight, 322

parental authority and, 483
poverty among, 9
school dropout rates
    among, 468
school segregation and,
    408–409
in single-parent families, 301
lead exposure, 238, 239
learning disabilities
    causes and intervention
        strategies for, 329–330
    characteristics and
        identification of,
        328–329
    explanation of, 328, 329
    gender and, 329, 396
    reading, writing and math
        difficulties and, 329
least restrictive environment
    (LRE), 336
lesbians
    as parents, 300–301
    romantic relationships
        among adolescent, 489
limbic system, 426
linkage analysis, 51
literacy, 264–265
locomotion, 138, 139,
    200–201
longitudinal approach to
    research, 32–33
long-term memory, 255, 346
low birth weight infants
    adolescent mothers
        and, 432
    explanation of, 108
    incidence and causes of,
        108, 109
    issues affecting, 108–111
low vision, 333

M

macrosystem, 25
magnetoencephalography
    (MEG), 123, 124
males. *See also* gender/gender
    differences
    aggression in, 394
    brain structure in,
        393–394
    as bullies, 402
    cognitive development
        in, 394
    communication and, 395
    early and late maturation
        in, 424
    emotional regulation in,
        394–395
    onset of puberty in, 422, 424
    sexual activity and, 429
    sexual maturation in, 422
    socioemotional
        development and, 394–
        397
malnutrition. *See also*
    nutrition
    in infancy, 132–133

low-income families
    and, 235
MAMA cycles, 477
manual approaches, 333
marasmus, 133
marijuana, prenatal exposure
    to, 90–91
marital conflict, effect on
    children, 297–299
marriage and family
    therapists, 43
massage therapy
    during labor, 105
    for preterm infants,
        110, 111
mastery motivation, 369
maternal blood screening, 60
mathematical intelligence, 355
mathematics
    gender and, 394
    learning disabilities
        and, 329
media multitasking, 495
media/screen time. *See also*
    technology
    adolescents and, 495–496
    trends in use of, 13,
        307–308
    young children and,
        307–308
medications. *See* drugs
meiosis, 52
melatonin, 438
memory
    autobiographical, 256,
        347–348
    in early childhood,
        254–256
    explicit, 167
    false, 255–256
    fuzzy trace theory and, 347
    implicit, 167
    in infancy, 167–168
    knowledge and expertise
        and, 347
    long-term, 255
    metamemory, 351–352
    in middle and late
        childhood, 346–348
    short-term, 255
    strategies to improve,
        347, 348
    working, 346–347, 349
menarche, 422, 423
mental age (MA), 353
mesoderm, 74, 75
mesosystem, 25
metacognition
    in adolescence, 456
    explanation of, 350–351
    in middle and late
        childhood, 351–352
    writing and, 364–365
metalinguistic awareness, 363
metamemory, 351–352
methamphetamine, 90
microgenetic method, 22
microsystem, 25

middle and late childhood.
    See also children
    accidents and injuries in,
        326–327
    adopted children and, 63
    asthma in, 325–326
    attachment in, 385
    attention deficit
        hyperactivity disorder
        in, 330–332
    autism spectrum disorders
        in, 334–335
    brain development in,
        316–317
    cancer in, 324–325
    cardiovascular disease
        in, 325
    concrete operational
        thought in, 343–344
    coping with stress in,
        386–387
    diabetes in, 325
    educational issues in,
        335–337
    emotional and behavioral
        disorders in, 334
    emotional development in,
        385–387
    exercise in, 319–320
    explanation of, 12
    gender issues in, 392–397
    intelligence in, 353–362
    language development in,
        363–367
    learning disabilities in,
        328–330
    memory in, 346–348
    moral development in,
        387–393
    motor development in, 318
    nutrition in, 319
    overweight children in,
        321–324
    peer relations in, 400–402
    physical activity in,
        319–321
    physical disorders in,
        333–334
    physical growth in, 316
    self-esteem and self-
        concept in, 382–383
    self in, 381–384
    self-regulation in, 383
    self-understanding in,
        381–382
    sensory disorders in,
        332–333
    skeletal and muscular
        systems in, 316
    social cognition in, 402
    speech disorders in, 332
    sports in, 320
    understanding others
        in, 382
middle schools, 464–466
midwives, 102
Millennials, 12, 13
mindfulness, 332, 349

mindset, 369–370
Minnesota Family Investment
    Program (MFIP), 10
mitosis, 52
Montessori approach, 267
moral behavior, 285, 389–390
moral character, 391
moral development
    in adolescence, 459–461
    domain theory of, 392
    explanation of, 283
    families and, 390–391
    gender and care perspective
        on, 391
    Kohlberg's theory of,
        387–390
    moral behavior and, 285
    moral feelings and,
        283–284
    moral reasoning and,
        284–285
    parenting and, 285
    prosocial behavior and,
        392–393, 459–460
moral education
    character education and,
        460–461
    cheating and, 460–461
    hidden curriculum and, 460
    integrative approach
        to, 461
moral exemplars, 391
moral feelings, 283–284
moral identity, 391
moral motivation, 404
moral personality, 391
moral reasoning
    culture and, 390
    explanation of, 284–285
moral thought, moral
    behavior and, 389–390
Moro reflex, 136, 137
morpheme, 174
morphology, 174, 175,
    262–263
mothers. *See also* caregivers/
    caregiving; families/
    family influences;
    parents/parenting
    adolescent, 431–433
    as caregivers, 211–212
    depression in, 113–115
    gender development
        and, 287
motivation, 368, 369
motor development
    cultural variations in, 140
    dynamic systems view of,
        135–136
    in early childhood, 226–228
    fine motor skills and,
        141–142
    gross motor skills and,
        138–139
    in infancy, 135–142
    in middle and late
        childhood, 318
    reflexes and, 136–137

motor vehicle accidents, 237, 438–439

multiple-intelligences theories, 354–355

multitasking, media, 495–496

musical intelligence, 355

music therapy, 105

mutual expectations, relationships and interpersonal conformity stage, 388

myelination, 125, 126, 224, 316–318

myelin sheath, 125

N

Native Americans, school dropout rate among, 468

nativists, 150

natural childbirth, 103–104

naturalistic intelligence, 355

naturalistic observation, 28

natural selection, 47–48

nature-nurture issue. *See also* heredity-environment interaction
  evaluation of, 15
  explanation of, 14
  giftedness and, 360–361
  infant development and, 163–164
  intelligence and, 358
  perceptual development and, 151

negative affectivity, 194

neglected children, 401

neglectful parenting, 290

Neonatal Intensive Care Unit Network Neurobehavioral Scale (NNNS), 107

neonatal nurses, 43

neonates. *See* newborns

neo-Piagetians, 344

neural tube, 78

neural tube defects, 78

neuroconstructivist view, 127–128

Neurofeedback, 332

neurogenesis, 78

neurons
  development of, 125, 224
  explanation of, 78
  function of, 224

newborns. *See also* infants/infancy
  assessment of, 106–107
  attention in, 165
  bonding with, 115
  brain activity in, 125
  intermodal perception in, 150–151
  perception in, 144–145
  physical growth in, 123
  preterm and small for date, 108–109
  reflexes in, 136–137

sensory development in, 148–149

sleep in, 128–130

transition from fetus to, 106

New Hope program, 409

next-generation sequencing, 51

nicotine, 88–89, 440. *See also* tobacco use

nightmares, 232

night terrors, 232

No Child Left Behind (NCLB) Act, 335, 362, 396–397, 406–407

noninvasive prenatal diagnosis (NIPD), 60

nonshared environmental experiences, 66, 67

normal curve, 354

normal distribution, 353, 354

nurse-midwifes, 43

nurture. *See* nature-nurture issue

nutrition. *See also* diet; eating behavior
  in adolescence, 435–436
  in early childhood, 232–235
  in infancy, 130–133
  in low-income families, 235
  in middle and late childhood, 319
  during pregnancy, 79–80, 93–94

O

obesity. *See also* overweight children
  in adolescence, 435–436
  breast vs. bottle feeding and, 131
  during pregnancy, 79–80, 93
  risk factors for, 322

object permanence, 161–162

observation, as data collection method, 27–28

observational learning, 24

obstetricians/gynecologists, 42

occipital lobes, 124

operant conditioning theory, 23, 165

operations, in preoperational stage, 246

oral approaches, 333

organic intellectual disability, 359

organization, Piaget and, 159

organogenesis, 75–76

orienting/investigative process, 166

orienting response, 144–145

orthopedic impairments, 333

otitis media, breast feeding and, 131

ovarian cancer, 132

overextension, 177

overweight children. *See also* obesity
  in adolescence, 435–436, 500
  breast vs. bottle feeding and, 131
  in children, 232, 233–234
  in infancy, 130
  in middle and late childhood, 321–324
  during pregnancy, 79–80
  risk associated with, 322–323, 325
  statistics related to, 234–235, 322
  treatment for, 323

Oxytocin, 103

P

pain, in infancy, 149

pain cry, 192

palmer grasp, 141

parental leave, 212, 213

parenting styles
  authoritarian, 289–290, 498
  authoritative, 290, 498
  in context, 290–291
  indulgent, 290
  neglectful, 290

parents/parenting. *See also* caregivers/caregiving; families/family influences; fathers; mothers
  of adopted children, 63
  bullying and, 402–403
  child development and, 6–7
  child maltreatment by, 293–295
  conflict between adolescents and, 484–485
  coparenting, 292
  culture/cultural diversity and, 301–302
  discipline and, 210–211, 398
  emotional development and, 281–282
  ethnic minority, 301–302
  executive functioning and, 257–258
  facilitation of achievement by, 371, 398–399
  feeding styles, 233
  gay and lesbian, 300–301
  as health-conscious role models, 441
  influence of, 256
  language development and, 178, 179, 181
  literacy promotion by, 265
  as managers, 210–211, 398–399
  in middle and late childhood years, 398–399
  moral development and, 285
  overweight children and, 323, 324

peer relations and, 304

relationship between adolescents and, 482–483

religious beliefs and, 463

remarried, 399

role in substance use prevention, 440–441

socialization between children and, 209

temperament and, 197

transition to, 208–209

working, 297

parietal lobes, 124

passive genotype-environment correlations, 65, 66

paternal factors, in prenatal development, 95

pediatricians, 42

pediatric nurses, 43

peer relations. *See also* friends/friendship
  in adolescence, 478, 486–491
  adolescent depression and, 500
  aggression and, 304
  bullying and, 403
  cliques and, 487
  crowds and, 488
  cultural diversity and, 492
  dating and romantic, 488–491
  delinquency and, 498
  in early childhood, 303–304
  emotional regulation and, 282
  gender development and, 287–288
  in high school, 468
  in infancy, 200
  in middle and late childhood, 400–402
  moral reasoning and, 284
  parent-child relations and, 304
  pressure and conformity in, 487
  sexual risk taking and, 430
  social cognition and, 402
  substance use/abuse and, 440, 441

peers, as teachers, 251

peer status, 400–401

perception
  depth, 147–148
  ecological view of, 143
  explanation of, 143
  intermodal, 150–151
  of occluded objects, 147
  visual, 143–148

perceptual categorization, 169

perceptual constancy, 146–147

perceptual development. *See also* sensory development
  in early childhood, 228–229

ecological view of, 143

in infancy, 143–148, 163, 228–229

nature vs. nurture and, 151

perceptual-motor coupling, 151

perceptual narrowing, 146

performance orientation, 369

personal fable, 451

personality
  birth order and, 296
  cheating and, 461
  independence and, 199
  sense of self and, 198–199
  temperament and, 196
  trust and, 198

perspective taking, 279, 283, 382, 404

phenotype, 53

phenylketonuria (PKU), 56, 57

phonics approach, 364

phonology, 174, 262–263

physical abuse, 293

physical activity. *See also* exercise
  in early childhood, 235–236
  in middle and late childhood, 319–320
  in postpartum period, 113, 114
  during pregnancy, 80–81
  sports as, 320

physical development
  in adolescence, 422
  in early childhood, 222–223
  gender differences in, 393–394
  in infancy, 122–123
  in middle and late childhood, 316
  patterns of, 122–123
  prenatal, 74–78

physical disorders, 333–334

physical education classes, 320

physiological measures, 29–30

Piaget's theory
  applied to education, 344–345
  concrete operational stage in, 21, 343–345
  evaluation of, 162–164, 344, 450
  explanation of, 20–21, 158
  formal operational stage in, 21, 449–450
  moral development and, 284
  overview of, 20
  perceptual development and, 150
  preoperational stage in, 246–249
  processes of development in, 158–159
  sensorimotor stage in, 159–164

Vygotsky's theory compared to, 253
pincer grip, 141
pituitary gland, 422, 423
placement stage, in artistic expression, 230
placenta, 75, 76
play
  face-to-face, 200
  functions of, 304–305
  screen media and, 307–308
  trends in, 306
  types of, 305–306
playgrounds, 237
pneumonia, 240
pointing, 176
polygenic inheritance, 54–55
popular children, 401
positive youth development (PYD), 419
postconventional reasoning, 388–389
postpartum depression
  in fathers, 115
  in mothers, 113–115
postpartum period
  bonding during, 115
  emotional and psychological adjustments during, 113–115
  exercise in, 113, 114
  explanation of, 112
  physical adjustments during, 112–113
posture, 138
poverty
  achievement and, 408, 468
  bullying and, 402
  early intervention programs and, 357–358
  education and, 268–269, 408
  health risks and, 238, 240
  intellectual stimulation and, 357
  language development and, 180
  nutrition and, 232–235
  prenatal care and, 82
  sexual risk factors and, 429–430
  social policy and, 8–10
  stress and, 10
practical intelligence, 354–355
practice play, 305
pragmatics, 174, 175, 264, 363
precocity, 360
preconventional reasoning, 387–388
prefrontal cortex, 126, 225, 317
pregnancy. See also prenatal development
  adolescent, 431–433
  conception and, 74
  cultural beliefs about, 84, 85

diagnostic tests during, 58–60
diet and nutrition during, 79–80, 93–94
exercise during, 80–81
exposure to environmental hazards during, 91–92
maternal age and, 94
maternal diseases during, 92
medication use during, 75, 87–88
prenatal care during, 81–84
psychoactive drug use during, 89–91
trimesters of, 77
weight during, 79–80, 93
prenatal care, 81–84
prenatal development
  of brain, 78
  embryonic period of, 74–76
  explanation of, 12, 74
  exposure to tobacco during, 88–89, 95
  fetal period of, 76–77
  germinal period of, 74
  trimesters of, 77
prenatal development hazards
  emotional states and stress as, 94–95
  environmental hazards as, 91–92
  general principles related to, 86–87
  incompatible blood type as, 91
  maternal age as, 94
  maternal diet and nutrition as, 93–94
  maternal diseases as, 92
  paternal factors as, 95
  prescription and nonprescription drugs as, 87–88
  psychoactive drugs as, 89–91
prenatal diagnostic tests, 58–60
prenatal period, 12
prenatal programs, 83
preoperational stage
  centration and limits of, 248–249
  explanation of, 20–21, 246, 343
  intuitive thought substage of, 247–248
  symbolic function substage of, 246–247
preoperational thought, 246
prepared childbirth, 104
preschool programs
  Project Head Start, 268–269
  views regarding universal, 271
preschool teachers, 41

pretense/symbolic play, 305–306
preterm infants
  explanation of, 108
  issues affecting, 108–111
  methods to nurture, 110–111
primary circular reactions, 160
primary emotions, 190
professional journals, 34
Project Head Start, 268–269
prosocial behavior
  in adolescence, 459–460
  explanation of, 392–393
  television and, 308
proximodistal pattern, 123
psychiatrists, 42
psychoactive drugs, during pregnancy, 89–91
psychoanalytic theories
  Erikson's psychosocial, 18–19
  evaluation of, 19–20
  explanation of, 17–18
  Freud's, 17–18
  of gender, 287
psychological invulnerability, 451
psychology, evolutionary, 48–49
psychosocial moratorium, 476, 477
psychosocial theory. See Erikson's psychosocial theory
puberty. See also adolescents/adolescence
  body image and, 424
  early and late maturation in, 424–425
  explanation of, 421–422
  growth spurt in, 422
  hormonal changes in, 422–423
  psychological dimensions of, 424–425
  timing and variations in, 423–424
Public Law 94-142, 335
punishment
  outcomes of, 291–292
  overview of, 291, 398
  socioeconomic status and, 302
  of toddlers, 210–211

R

radiation, 91
rapport talk, 395
readiness. See school readiness
reading
  gender differences in, 394
  learning disabilities and, 329
  in middle and late childhood, 364

reasoning
  conventional, 388
  hypothetical-deductive, 450
  moral, 284–285, 390
  postconventional, 388–389
  preconventional, 387–388
  social conventional, 392
recasting, 179
reciprocal socialization, 209, 291
reflexes, 136–137
reflexive smile, 192
Reggio Emilia approach, 245, 266
rejected children, 401–402
relational aggression, 394
religion
  cognitive changes and, 462
  developmental changes and, 462
  Erikson's theory and identity and, 462–463
  explanation of, 461
  parenting and, 463
  role of, 462
  sexual behavior and, 428
religiousness, 461, 463
remarried parents, 399
REM sleep, 128
report talk, 395
research
  bias in, 35–36
  correlational, 30–31, 383
  data collection methods for, 26–30
  descriptive, 30
  ethical issues related to, 33–34
  experimental, 31–32
  journal publication of, 34
  scientific method in, 16–17
  time span of, 32
researchers, 40
resilience, 8–10
respiratory tract infections, 131
Rh factor, 91
risk taking
  fuzzy-trace theory dual-process model, 455
  sexual, 429–433
  stress level and, 455
  substance use and, 454–455
Ritalin, 331
rite of passage, 492–493
romantic relationships. See dating/romantic relationships
rooting reflex, 136
Rubella, 92

S

safety, 238. See also accidents
scaffolding, 209–210, 250
schema theory, 288
schemes, 158
school counselors, role of, 42

school dropout rate
  adolescent pregnancy and, 432
  causes of, 468
  ethnicity and, 468
  gender and, 468
  pregnancy and, 468
  strategies to reduce, 468–469
school psychologists, 41
school readiness
  attention and, 254
  executive function and, 257
  requirements for, 270
schools. See also achievement; education
  accountability of, 406–407
  ethnic groups in, 408–409
  extracurricular activities in, 465–466
  function of, 405
  gender bias in, 395–396
  healthy foods in, 323, 326
  high schools, 466–467
  middle or junior high, 464–466
  moral education in, 460–461
  physical education programs in, 320
  segregation in, 408–409
  service learning programs in, 457–458
  special education services in, 335–336
scientific method, 16–17. See also research
scientific thinking, 350
scribbles, 229
secondary circular reactions, 160
secondary schools. See high schools
second-language learning, 366, 367
securely attached babies, 204
self
  in early childhood, 278–279
  in middle and late childhood, 381–384
  sense of, 198–199
self-concept, 382–383
self-conscious emotions, 190, 280
self-control, 498
self-efficacy, 370, 454
self-esteem
  explanation of, 382
  methods to increase, 384
  variations in, 382–383
self-regulation, 167, 371, 383
self-understanding
  in early childhood, 278–279
  in middle and late childhood, 381–382
semantics, 174, 175
sensation, 142

sensorimotor play, 305
sensorimotor stage
   A-not-B error and, 162–163
   evaluation of, 162–164
   explanation of, 20, 159
   object permanence in, 161–162
   substages of, 159–161
sensory development
   hearing and, 148–149
   in infancy, 148–149
   smell and, 149
   taste and, 149
   touch and pain and, 149
   visual perception and, 143–148
sensory disorders, 332–333
separation protest, 192
seriation, 344
service learning, 457–458
sex education programs, 434
sex-linked chromosomal abnormalities, 55–56
sex-linked genes, 54
sexual abuse, 294
sexual activity
   adolescent pregnancy and, 431–433
   eating disorders and, 441
   risk taking and, 429–433
   timing and trends in, 428–429
sexual identity, in adolescence, 427–428
sexually transmitted infections (STIs)
   explanation of, 430–431
   during pregnancy, 92
sexual maturation, 422
shaken baby syndrome, 123
shape constancy, 147
shape stage, in artistic expression, 230
shared environmental experiences, 66, 67
shared sleeping, 129
short-term memory, 255
siblings
   birth order of, 296
   delinquency and, 498
   relationships between, 295–296
   theory of mind tasks and, 261
sickle-cell anemia, 56, 57
simple reflexes, 160
single-sex education, 396–397
size constancy, 146
Sleep in America Survey, 112
sleep/sleep problems
   in adolescence, 437–438
   in early childhood, 231–232
   function of, 231–232
   in infancy, 128–130
   in postpartum period, 112–113
   REM, 128
   shared, 129

slow-to-warm-up child, 193
small for date infants, 108–109
smell, sense of, 149
smiling, 192
smoking. See tobacco use
social cognition
   explanation of, 402
   in middle and late childhood, 402
   peer relations and, 402
social cognitive theory
   evaluation of, 24
   explanation of, 23
   of gender, 287
   overview of, 23
social constructivist approach, 251
social contract or utility and individual rights stage, 388
social conventional reasoning, 392
social developmental neuroscience, 426
socialization, reciprocal, 209
social orientation, in infancy, 200
social play, 306
social policy
   effects of, 8–10
   explanation of, 8–9, 418
   strength-based approach to, 419
social referencing, 201
social relationships, achievement and, 371–372
social role theory, 287
social smile, 192
social systems morality, 388
social workers, 42
sociocultural cognitive theory. See Vygotsky's theory
sociocultural contexts. See also culture/cultural diversity; ethnicity/ ethnic groups
   child development and, 7–8
   dating and, 489
   explanation of, 7
socioeconomic status (SES). See also poverty
   children in divorced families and, 299
   delinquency and, 498
   ethnicity and, 408, 494
   explanation of, 8
   families and, 302–303
   immigrants and, 494
   language development and, 180
   sexual risk factors and, 429–430
socioemotional development. See also specific age groups
   child care and, 212–215
   family and, 208–212
   gender and, 394–397

socioemotional processes, 11–12
sociometric status, 400–401
somnambulism, 232
sound recognition, 175
spatial intelligence, 355
speech disorders, 332
speech therapists, 43
spina bifida, 57, 78
spirituality, 461, 463. See also religion; religiousness
sports, 320
standardized tests, 29
Stanford-Binet test, 353, 354
stepfamilies, 399
stereotype threat, 358
still-face paradigm, 200
stoicism, 85
stranger anxiety, 192
Strange Situation, 204
strategies, to improve information processing, 347, 348
stress
   ability to cope with, 386–387
   ethnicity and, 301–302
   poverty and, 10
   during pregnancy, 94–95
   risk taking and, 455
substance use/abuse
   educational achievement and, 441
   parental role in preventing, 440–441
   peer relations and, 440, 441
   during pregnancy, 89–91
   trends in, 439–440
sucking, 144
sucking reflex, 136
sudden infant death syndrome (SIDS), 129–130, 132
sugar consumption, 233–234
suicide/suicidal ideation, in adolescence, 439, 500–501
surveys, as data collection method, 28–29
sustained attention, 369
symbolic function substage, 246–247
synapses, 224, 225
syntax, 174, 175, 263–264
syphilis, 92

T

task persistence, 369
taste, sense of, 149
Tay-Sachs disease, 57
teachers
   expectations of, 372
   gender bias and, 395–396
teaching. See education; schools
teaching strategies, based on Vygotsky's theory, 250–251

technology
   media use and screen time and, 307–308
   online dating and, 490–491
   for students with disabilities, 334
   trends in use of, 13
Teen Outreach Program (TOP), 434
Teen Pregnancy Prevention (TPP), 434
telegraphic speech, 178
television, 308
temperament
   biological influences on, 195–196
   classification of, 193–195
   developmental connections to, 195–196
   developmental contexts of, 196
   explanation of, 193
   goodness of fit and, 196–197
   parenting and, 197
temporal lobes, 124
teratogens. See also prenatal development hazards
   explanation of, 86
   exposure to, 86
   medications as, 86–87
   psychoactive drugs as, 89–91
tertiary circular reactions, novelty, and curiosity substage, 161
testosterone, 422
theories, 16, 17
theory of mind
   autism and, 261
   developmental changes and, 258–260
   explanation of, 258, 280
   individual differences and, 260–261
thinking
   convergent, 349–350
   creative, 349–351
   critical, 349
   divergent, 350
   executive function and, 348–349
   as information processing, 22
   language and, 250
   in middle and late childhood, 348–350
   preoperational, 246
   scientific, 350
Thousand Genomes Project, 51
thyroid gland, 423
Tiger moms, 373–374
time out, 292
time span of research, 32
tobacco use
   among adolescents, 440
   exposure to, 238–239
   family programs to reduce, 442
   during pregnancy, 88–89, 95

toddlers. See also early childhood; infants/ infancy
   development of independence in, 199
   discipline of, 210–211
   language development in, 180, 181–182, 262
   theory of mind and, 258–259
Tools of the Mind curriculum, 252
tool use, in infancy, 141
top-dog phenomenon, 464
touch, in newborns, 149
training parents, 291
transitivity, 344
traumatic events, coping with, 386–387
triarchic theory of intelligence, 354–355
trimesters, 77
trophoblast, 74
trust vs. mistrust stage, 18, 198
Turner syndrome, 55, 56
twins, 53, 64–65
twin studies, 64–65
Type 1 diabetes, 325. See also diabetes
Type 2 diabetes, 325. See also diabetes

U

ultrasound sonography, 59
umbilical cord, 75, 76
underextension, 177
universal ethical principles, 388–389
Urban Prep Academy for Young Men, 397

V

values, 457–458
verbal aggression, 394
victimization, bullying and, 402–403
vigilance, 253–254
violence. See aggression
visual acuity, 143, 146
visual impairments, 332–333
visual perception, in infancy, 143–148
visual preference method, 143, 144
visuospatial skills, 394
vocabulary development, in middle and late childhood, 363
vocalizations, infant, 176
voice disorders, 332
Vygotsky's theory
   evaluation of, 251, 253
   explanation of, 21–22, 249
   language and thought in, 250

Piaget's theory compared
to, 253
scaffolding in, 250
teaching strategies based
on, 250–251
Tools of the Mind
curriculum and, 252
zone of proximal
development in,
249–250